ISBN 978-0-428-09544-4
PIBN 11244846

1 MONTH OF
FREE
READING

at

www.ForgottenBooks.com

By purchasing this book you are eligible for one month membership to ForgottenBooks.com, giving you unlimited access to our entire collection of over 1,000,000 titles via our web site and mobile apps.

To claim your free month visit:
www.forgottenbooks.com/free1244846

English
Français
Deutsche
Italiano
Español
Português

www.forgottenbooks.com

Mythology Photography **Fiction**
Fishing Christianity **Art** Cooking
Essays Buddhism Freemasonry
Medicine **Biology** Music **Ancient**
Egypt Evolution Carpentry Physics
Dance Geology **Mathematics** Fitness
Shakespeare **Folklore** Yoga Marketing
Confidence Immortality Biographies
Poetry **Psychology** Witchcraft
Electronics Chemistry History **Law**
Accounting **Philosophy** Anthropology
Alchemy Drama Quantum Mechanics
Atheism Sexual Health **Ancient History**
Entrepreneurship Languages Sport
Paleontology Needlework Islam
Metaphysics Investment Archaeology
Parenting Statistics Criminology
Motivational

4/6

INQUIRY INTO OCCUPATION AND ADMINISTRATION OF HAITI AND SANTO DOMINGO

251..
336

HEARING

BEFORE A

SELECT COMMITTEE ON

HAITI AND SANTO DOMINGO

UNITED STATES SENATE

SIXTY-SEVENTH CONGRESS

FIRST SESSION

PURSUANT TO

S. RES. 112

AUTHORIZING A SPECIAL COMMITTEE TO INQUIRE
INTO THE OCCUPATION AND ADMINISTRATION OF
THE TERRITORIES OF THE REPUBLIC OF HAITI
AND THE DOMINICAN REPUBLIC

PART 1

AUGUST 5, 1921

Printed for the use of the Select Committee
on Haiti and Santo Domingo

WASHINGTON
GOVERNMENT PRINTING OFFICE
1921

SELECT COMMITTEE ON HAITI AND SANTO DOMINGO.

MEDILL McCORMICK, Illinois, *Chairman*.

PHILANDER C. KNOX, Pennsylvania. ATLEE POMERENE, Ohio.
TASKER L. ODDIE, Nevada. WILLIAM H. KING, Utah.

ELISHA HANSON, *Clerk*.

2

INQUIRY INTO OCCUPATION AND ADMINISTRATION OF HAITI AND SANTO DOMINGO.

FRIDAY, AUGUST 5, 1921.

UNITED STATES SENATE,
SELECT COMMITTEE ON HAITI AND SANTO DOMINGO,
Washington, D. C.

The committee met at 10.30 o'clock a. m., in the committee room, Capitol, Senator Medill McCormick presiding.

Present: Senators McCormick (chairman), Oddie, and King.

Also present: Mr. Ernest Angell, representing the Haiti-Santo Domingo Independence Society, the National Association for the Advancement of Colored People, and the Union Patriotique d'Haiti; Mr. Stenio Vincent, representing Union Patriotique d'Haiti; Mr. O. G. Villard, representing Haiti-Santo Domingo Independence Society; Mr. Horace G. Knowles, representing the Patriotic League of the Dominican Republic, and the deposed Dominican Government; Maj. Edwin N. McClellan, United States Marine Corps, as custodian of certain reports and correspondence taken from Navy and Marine Corps files, bearing on Republic of Haiti; Capt. C. S. Freeman, United States Navy, as custodian of certain correspondence and documents bearing on the situation in the Dominican Republic.

The CHAIRMAN. The committee will come to order. If it meets the judgment of the members of the committee, we might begin by receiving the memorial which was brought to our notice at the last meeting, and any other matter which Capt. Angell has to present.

STATEMENT OF MR. ERNEST ANGELL, 50 PINE STREET, NEW YORK, N. Y., REPRESENTING THE HAITI-SANTO DOMINGO INDEPENDENCE SOCIETY, THE NATIONAL ASSOCIATION FOR THE ADVANCEMENT OF COLORED PEOPLE, AND THE UNION PATRIOTIQUE D'HAITI.

The CHAIRMAN. Capt. Angell, will you tell the committee what memorials and other matter you have to submit?

Mr. ANGELL. We have here copies of the so-called Haitian Memoir, and I am going to ask the indulgence of the committee to permit Mr. Vincent to present that memorial, since he was instrumental in its preparation and holds a high position in the unofficial representation of his country. Mr. Stenio Vincent is the former minister of justice and interior, and minister to The Hague. He was president of the Haitian Senate at the time of its dissolution by the United States armed forces.

The CHAIRMAN. You may proceed, Mr. Vincent.

STATEMENT OF MR. STENIO VINCENT, NEW YORK, N. Y., REPRESENTING THE UNION PATRIOTIQUE D'HAITI, FORMERLY MINISTER OF JUSTICE AND INTERIOR, MINISTER TO THE HAGUE, AND PRESIDENT OF THE SENATE, REPUBLIC OF HAITI.

Mr. VINCENT. Mr. Chairman and Senators, in the name of the Union Patriotique d'Haiti, which, with its branches in all the cities and villages of Haiti, has at least 20,000 members, I have the honor of presenting to the Senate commission of inquiry into the occupation and administration of Haiti and Santo Domingo by American forces a copy of the memoir which has already been presented to the Senate Committee on Foreign Affairs.

3

This memoir relates the conditions and circumstances in which the treaty of September 16, 1915, was imposed upon the Haitian people, the violent means used to achieve this result, and the consequent position of the Haitian Government, which has, in fact, lost the characteristics of a real Government.

Despite the violence with which it was imposed, this treaty has not been carried out. As regards the relations of the Haitian Government to the treaty officials, there is nothing to be added to the forceful declarations made by President Dartiguenave, which have already been made public and when the memoir reproduces.

From the point of view of international law it is plain that the Wilson Government had no right to order an invasion of Haitian territory and to take possession of that small and friendly country. President Wilson himself, at almost the same time, proclaimed that "all the Governments of the Americas are, as far as we are concerned, upon a footing of perfect equality and unquestioned independence," and that "no nation should seek to extend its policy over any other nation or people, but that every people should be left free to determine its own policy, its own way of development, unhindered, unthreatened, unafraid, the little along with the great and powerful."

The only avowed pretext for intervention I find in the Annual Report of the Secretary of the Navy for 1920. The Secretary wrote as follows:

"The crisis in Haitian affairs demanded immediate and energetic action on the part of the Navy to protect American and foreign lives and property and to restore order throughout that distressed country."

But the fact is that while tragic events occurred in Port-au-Prince on July 27, 1915, resulting in the overthrow and death of President Vilbrun Guillaume Sam, throughout this affair the life of not a single American citizen or foreigner was taken or jeopardized. No property was destroyed. And although there was for the moment no Government, there was no burning or killing or robbing. Quiet was promptly restored and a committee of public safety assumed responsibility for order until a new Government should be elected. It must be borne in mind that there is not a single instance of an American or, indeed, of any foreigner having been killed or molested in Haiti prior to the American occupation.

The truth is that the Wilson administration took advantage of the political adventures of a weak and defenseless nation and forced upon it an intervention which, through the agency of the American minister in Haiti in December, 1914, of the Fort Smith mission in March, 1915, and of the Paul Fuller, jr., mission in May, 1915, had been long in preparation.

It is sometimes alleged—most curious of all—that the Haitian people invited the United States to straighten out its affairs. The facts are these: Toward the end of 1914 the new Haitian Government was notified that the American Government was disposed to recognize the newly elected Haitian President, M. Davilmar Theodore, as soon as a Haitian commission should sign at Washington a "satisfactory protocol" on the model of the American-Dominican convention of 1907. On December 15, 1914, the Haitian Government, through its secretary of foreign affairs, replied:

"The Government of the Republic of Haiti would consider itself lacking in its duty to the United States and to itself if it allowed the least doubt to exist of its irrevocable intention not to accept any control of the administration of Haitian affairs by a foreign power.

The Haitian people never asked American intervention. The conditions of the American occupation, as described in the Haitian memoir, have not been such as to cause the Haitian people to change their minds. They ask, as that memoir states:

First. Immediate abolition of martial law and of the courts-martial.

Second. Immediate reorganization of the Haitian police and military forces and withdrawal within a short period of the United States military occupation.

Third. Abrogation of the convention of 1915.

Fourth. Convocation within a short period of a constituent assembly, with all the guaranties of electoral liberty.

In concluding this statement I beg leave to draw the most earnest attention of the committee to the existence of martial law in Haiti, a fact which, unless measures are taken to obviate the consequences, may seriously obstruct the investigation. The entire Haitian people rejoiced to hear of the formation of this committee; it firmly believes that the task of justice and of truth is at last to be accomplished. But if it is to participate freely, it is important that every guaranty be given Haitian citizens. I hope that this committee will arrange with the Government to do away with the serious inconvenience which would result were martial law to continue during the period of an inquiry into the abuses committed under the shelter of that law.

Senator KING. Mr. Chairman, I presume that at a later date these gentlemen, as well as others who may submit documents, will be available for cross-examination, if the committee desires?

The CHAIRMAN. I understand, Capt. Angell, that it is your purpose to-day to file such memorials as you have prepared, and after the committee has had an opportunity to examine them to be prepared to submit to us a list of witnesses whom you would like to have called?

Mr. ANGELL. That is our intention, Senator.

We have here copies of the so-called Haitian memoir to which Mr. Vincent has referred in his statement. We intend to file with the committee now several copies, which will be at the disposition of the committee.

(The memoir referred to is here printed in full, as follows:)

[The Nation, New York, Wednesday, May 25, 1921.]

MEMOIR ON THE POLITICAL, ECONOMIC, AND FINANCIAL CONDITIONS EXISTING IN THE REPUBLIC OF HAITI UNDER THE AMERICAN OCCUPATION BY THE DELEGATES TO THE UNITED STATES OF THE UNION PATRIOTIQUE D'HAÏTI.[1]

I.

BEFORE MILITARY INTERVENTION.

The fact that Mr. Wilson's Government, in its military intervention in Haiti, acted under the influence of certain big financial interests will be shown in the following account:

The National Bank of Haiti, founded in 1881 with French capital and intrusted from the start with the administration of the Haitian treasury, disappeared in 1910 and was replaced by a financial institution known as the National Bank of the Republic of Haiti.

Like the old one the new bank was intrusted, under certain conditions and for the duration of its contract, with the administration of the treasury of the Haitian Government. But a part of the capital stock had been subscribed by the National City Bank of New York, which became for the first time interested in the financial affairs of Haiti.

It was from this time on that financial control of Haiti began to be talked of, and the National Bank of the Republic of Haiti immediately adopted a new attitude with regard to the Haitian Government, never ceasing to create difficulties for it.

On June 21, 1914, President Oreste Zamor left Port au Prince to check a revolutionary movement which had broken out in the North Province. During his absence the National Bank of the Republic of Haiti, giving as a pretext the moratorium decreed in France, the diminution of receipt as a result of the European war, and the insurrection in the North, stopped the execution of a budget convention between it and the Haitian Government, which was drawn up with the object of assuring, until September 30, 1914, the monthly and regular payment of public expenses. In order to live up to its obligations, the Government had to submit to the demands of the National Bank of the Republic of Haiti. It authorized the latter to dispose of an amount of $200,000 drawn from the funds applied to the redemption of paper money, and under this condition the bank resumed the regular administration.

Because of increasing difficulties with the bank, and lack of effective means for checking the revolutionary movement, President Oreste Zamor had to abandon the struggle. He refused the offer that was made to him of help from the United States to keep himself in power, not wishing to compromise the independence of the country, and resigned on October 29, 1914.

Meanwhile an active propaganda was being carried on, spreading the rumor that the President had agreed to sign a treaty with the United States. This rumor persisting, on October 26 Senator Lhérisson demanded an explanation on this subject from the state secretary of foreign affairs, at the senate tribune. The latter denied the existence of any negotiations with the United States, and the senate unanimously passed the following resolution, which fully expressed the sentiment of the country:

---

[1] This memoir was presented to the Department of State and to the Senate Foreign Relations Committee on May 9.

"The senate, after hearing the denial of the state secretary of foreign affairs of the existence of negotiations between the national administration and the Government of the United States, declares its satisfaction with his explanations, condemns any kind of a treaty, and passes the order of the day."

On November 7, 1914, Senator Davilmar Theodore was elected President of the Republic in place of Oreste Zamor. From the very start he was confronted by the same difficulties with the bank. Moreover, the United States Goverament made as a condition for the recognition of the new administration of Haiti the sending of a commission to Washington for the purpose of signing "satisfactory protocols" relating to various questions, notably a convention for the control of the Haitian customhouses with the United States, modeled after the Dominican-American convention.

On November 27 Senator Lhérisson asked to interpellate the state secretary of foreign affairs with regard to negotiations said to have been agreed upon between the Governments of Haiti and the United States. On December 3, through explanations presented to the senate tribune by Monsieur J. Justin, state secretary of foreign affairs, it was learned that Mr. Bailly-Blanchard. envoy extraordinary and minister plenipotentiary of the United States at Port au Prince, had made proposals to the Haitian Government relative to a convention for the control of the Haitian customhouses. M. Justin was hooted by the audience, and even threatened, so strong was the national sentiment against anything which might interfere with the independence and sovereignty of the country.

On December 10, 1914, Hon. A. Bailly-Blanchard, American minister, had presented to the Haitian Government a project for a convent on in 10 articles. (See Appendix No. 1.)   The United States asked in this project for the control of the administration of the Haitian customhouses, and asked the Haitian Government to agree not to modify the custom duties in such a way as to reduce the revenues, etc., without the consent of the President of the United States.

The Haitian Government, considering that the signature of such a convention would have the effect of placing the country under a protectorate, and dreading the discontent of a people particularly jealous of its independence, notified Mr. Bailly-Blanchard on December 15 of its regret that it could not accept the agreement, in spite of its friendly sentiments for the United States. On the 19th the American minister replied that his Government would not insist upon the question of the treaty.

Two days previous to this communication from Mr. Bailly-Blanchard, in order to force the Haitian Government to accept the control of the customhouses by systematically depriving it of financial resources, American marines carried off the strong boxes of the National Bank of the Republic of Haiti in broad daylight and took on board the gunboat *Machias* a sum of $500,000 belonging to the Republic of Haiti and destined to be used for the redemption of paper money. In his notes of December 19 and 26, the state secretary of foreign affairs asked him in vain for explanations from the United States Legation regarding this military kidnapping of the funds of the Haitian treasury. This amount is still in the United States, where it was transported and deposited in a New York bank.

In March, 1915, similar measures for procuring control of the Haitian customs began again. This time an American commission landed at Port au Prince, composed of Messrs. Ford and Smith. Mr. Vilbrun Guillaume Sam had just been elected President of the Republic by the National Assembly. On March 15 the commission got in touch with M. Duvivier, state secretary of foreign affairs. After the usual compliments, Mr. Ford, president of the commission, began to communicate to M. Duvivier the object of his mission. It soon appeared to the Haitian minister that the commission had no full powers to negotiate. Mr. Ford readily admitted this; he declared, however, that he was the personal friend of President Wilson and seeme l to indicate that he was authorized to speak in the name of the President of the United States. M. Duvivier having shown him the objection to receiving communications from agents without due authorization the negotiations were broken off and the commission returned to the United States.

Scarcely two months later, during the first two weeks of May, 1915, Mr. Paul Fuller, jr., arrived at Port au Prince with the official title of special agent of the United States and envoy extraordinary and minister plenipotentiary to the Government of Haiti. He was received on the 21st by the President of the Republic, to whom he explained the object of his mission. Mr. Fuller was heard with all the attention to which his official standing and the Government that he represented entitled him. He was asked to submit his proposals to the Haitian Government in writing. On the following day, the 22d, he addressed to the state secretary of foreign affairs a project of a treaty in four articles. (See Appendix No. 2.) The preamble of the project contained the following statements:

"Whereas it is the mutual desire of the high contracting parties that there shall exist between an American minister plenipotentiary—hereafter to be appointed—and the President of Haiti such an intimate and confidential relationship as will enable the American minister plenipotentiary to advise as to such matters as affect the honest and efficient administration of the Government, the President of Haiti agreeing that he will follow the advice so given to the extent of requiring honesty and efficiency in officials and of removing those found to be dishonest and inefficient; the President of the United States and the President of the Republic of Haiti have resolved to enter into a convention for that purpose."

By the terms of the project presented by Mr. Paul Fuller, jr., the United States agrees to protect the Republic of Haiti against any attack by any foreign power, using for this purpose its military and naval forces. The United States also agrees to aid the Haitian Government to put down any internal troubles, and to give it effective support by the use of American military and naval forces within the necessary limits. Moreover, the President of Haiti must agree not to grant any rights, privileges, or facilities of any kind with regard to St. Nicholas Mole—not to concede, sell, rent, or otherwise give up, directly or indirectly through the Government of Haiti, the occupation or use of St. Nicholas Mole to any foreign Government or to any national or nationals of a foreign Government.

This project was examined in the most friendly way, and on June 2 the state secretary of foreign affairs, M. Duvivier, presented a counterproject to the American envoy as a basis of negotiations. Regarding the question of St. Nicholas Mole the Haitian Government accepted unreservedly the draft proposed by Mr. Paul Fuller. On the other hand, he asked that the first article of the project should read as follows:

"The Government of the United States agrees to lend its aid to the Republic of Haiti for the conservation of its independence. With this object it promises to intervene in order to prevent any intrusion by any foreign power in the affairs of Haiti and to repulse any act of aggression against the country. It will use for this purpose such forces of its Army and of its Navy as are necessary."

The Haitian counterproject also admitted the principle of a cooperation of American forces to check internal troubles, but stipulated that these forces, after cooperating with the Haitian troops in the reestablishment of order, should be promptly withdrawn from the territory of the Republic on demand of the constitutional authorities.

The Haitian Government asked, moreover, that the United States Government should promise to favor the entrance of American capital into the country and to aid in the improvement of Haitian finances in such a way as to bring about the unification of the public debt and an effective monetary reform. (See Appendix No. 3.)

On June 3, in acknowledging the receipt of the counterproject of the 2d to the state secretary of foreign affairs, Mr. Paul Fuller proposed, in turn, certain modifications of the Haitian text. In a note dated the 4th the state secretary of foreign affairs notified the American envoy of the acceptance of some of the modifications proposed and the rejection of others. On the 5th Mr. Paul Fuller acknowledged the receipt of this note without expressing any opinion on its contents.

The discussion had reached this point when it was learned that the American envoy had suddenly left for the United States. The negotiations were not resumed.

II.

LANDING OF AMERICAN TROOPS IN HAITI.

Treaty of September 16, 1915.—On July 27, 1915, an attack was directed during the night against the President's palace by a revolutionary group—a group which militantly represented amid other antagonisms the overwhelming sentiment against any policies which tended or seemed to tend to the compromising of Haitian independence. On the next day President Vilbrun Guillaume Sam, wounded in the struggle, abandoned the palace and took refuge in the legation of the French Republic.

On the morning of the same day the rumor spread through the town that some political prisoners had been summarily executed in the prisons of Port au Prince during the attack on the national palace. This terrible and deplorable news was only too true. A great cry of grief arose from all classes of the people and soon changed into indignation and anger. Agitation was increasing. On July 28 the relatives of the victims, mostly young people, carried away by grief, invaded the French Legation, seized the ex-President, who was thrown into the street and killed. At the time when these confused scenes occurred there was for the moment no government nor any kind of an organization capable of preventing them. Yet there was no burning or robbing, and no one except the ex-President and the ex-governor of Port au Prince, who were held responsible for the execution of the political prisoners, met death through this tragic incident.

After this act of reprisal, quiet was promptly restored, and a committee of public safety assumed responsibility for order.

Meanwhile, on July 28, the American cruiser *George Washington*, bearing the flag of Rear Admiral W. B. Caperton, anchored in the harbor of Port au Prince. No notice was taken of it, because it was generally believed that the presence of this vessel had no other object than that of protecting foreign interests if necessary, since Europe was at that time plunged in war.

On July 29, the population awoke to learn that the territory of Haiti was invaded by American forces that had landed at the extreme south of the city the night before. Hundreds and soon thousands of American marines occupied the town and disarmed the surprised Haitians, who were completely bowled over by the terrible events of the last two days—and so the American forces did not meet with any resistance from the population. Two weeks passed, during which the landed forces succeeded in getting control of Port au Prince and its immediate vicinity. Meanwhile other American troops had occupied the city of Cape Haitien, in the northern part of the country. On August 12, 1915, after numerous conferences between leading members of the Haitien Chamber and Senate with the American naval authorities, at the United States Legation and elsewhere, a presidential election was held by permission of the occupation, and M. Dartiguenave, president of the senate, was elected, the majority of the members of the two houses agreeing to support him. It was made clear that the choice of M. Dartiguenave was essentially agreeable to the American occupation. He was therefore elected for a term of seven years in accordance with the Haitian constitution then in force.

Two days after the establishment of the new government, Mr. Robert Beale Davis, jr., American chargé d'affaires, in the name of his Government, presented to President Dartiguenave a project for a treaty. (See Appendix No. 4.) This project was accompanied by a memorandum, in which the President was informed "that the State Department at Washington expected that the Haitian National Assembly, warranting the sincerity and the interest of the Haitians, would immediately pass a resolution authorizing the President of Haiti to accept the proposed treaty without modification." Since this request indicated a certain ignorance of Haitian constitutional practice, as regards the negotiation of treaties, the Government hastened to call Mr. Davis's attention to the article of the constitution relating to this subject and showed him that the President of Haiti did not need special authority of the chambers to negotiate and sign treaties with a foreign power.

The American chargé d'affaires, after examining the constitutional text, readily acknowledged it and withdrew. Imagine the surprise of the Government on receiving the next day a threatening note signed by the chargé d'affaires, insisting that the resolution indicated in the memorandum should be passed by the Haitian Chambers, and setting in the form of an ultimatum a time limit within which that resolution must be passed.

To this demand the Haitian Government replied, through the state secretary of foreign affairs, M. Pauléus Sannon, that it was guided by the most friendly disposition and was ready to negotiate a treaty with the United States, but that rather than accept without modification the project presented it would prefer to resign as a body.

By the occupation of its territory the Government, which had been deprived of even its police power and which had none of the essential attributes of authority, was in reality without independence, without liberty of action. Its existence and its working depended upon the invading American forces, equipped with all modern armaments and now occupying the country.

While the negotiations were being continued laboriously as a result of the determination of the American representative not to accept any modifications in the project of the treaty, Rear Admiral W. B. Caperton, commander in chief of the expeditionary force of the United States, seized the customhouses of Port de Paix, Cap, and St. Marc on August 24, driving out the Haitian officials. And in spite of the repeated official protestations of the Government to the American legation all the customhouses of the Republic were successively occupied and thus came under the control of the officers of the United States Navy. On September 1, 1915, President Dartiguenave solemnly protested in a proclamation against this long series of violations of law, which had just resulted in the occupation of the customhouse of Port au Prince. On the 3d Rear Admiral W. B. Caperton issued a proclamation in which he declared that he had assumed control of the Government and that the town of Port au Prince (the seat of the Government) and its vicinity were under martial law. (See Appendix No. 5.)

In face of the impossibility of getting certain modifications of the project accepted two members of President Dartiguenave's cabinet, the state secretary of foreign affairs, and the state secretary of public works handed in their resignations on September 8, 1915.

The treaty was signed on the 16th of the same month by M. Louis Borno, the new state secretary of foreign affairs, and Mr. Robert Beale Davis, jr., American chargé d'affaires at Port au Prince.

In reality the Government had been from the beginning to end oppressed by a series of violent acts. Apart from the occupation of its territory, the customhouses, which were the chief object of the treaty, had been seized manu militari, and the funds belonging to the Haitian treasury and deposited in the National Bank of the Haitian Republic had been transferred to the account of Rear Admiral W. B. Caperton by his orders.

The convention, after being ratified by the President of the Republic, was sanctioned by the Chamber of Deputies on October 6, 1915, and by the Senate on November 11, 1915.

EXECUTION OF THE TREATY.

1. *Modus vivendi of November 29, 1915.*—The convention of September 16. 1915, having been negotiated and ratified by the Haitian Government and sanctioned by the Haitian Chambers under the conditions and circumstances set forth above, there was some hope that its execution would soon bring about the return to a situation which would naturally be cleared up by the rules of cooperation and collaboration established between the two Governments by this diplomatic instrument and by the fulfillment of the obligations entered into by the American Government toward the Haitian people.

The Haitian Government, after the landing of the American troops, was actually nothing more than a purely nominal government. It had neither the power to enforce its authority nor finances. The American military authorities had taken possession of the customhouses, had invaded the territory of the nation, and, by the establishment of martial courts, had practically suppressed the Haitian administration of justice. The protests of the Government against these acts of interference in internal politics had remained a dead letter. And it was precisely " to put an end to these difficulties and to obtain the liberation of the territory that was formally promised " that it had to " yield." [1] Consequently pending the sanction of the treaty by the American Senate and the exchange of ratifications the Haitian Government had to accept the arrangement proposed by the American Government itself for the provisional execution of the convention of September 16, 1915.[2] A modus vivendi was signed at Port au Prince on November 29, 1915. It stipulated that "the convention signed on September 16, 1915, between the Haitian Republic and the United States and ratified by the Chamber of Deputies of Haiti on October 6, 1915, and by the Senate of Haiti November 11, 1915, would provisionally go into full effect and would remain in force until the vote of the American Senate was taken regarding the convention, leaving the methods of application of the treaty to be decided at Washington between the Department of State and the Haitian commission named for the purpose." (See Appendix No. 6.)

---

[1] See Exposé Général de la Situation de la République d'Haïti, année 1917, pp. 5–6.
[2] Ibid.

At the same time that this modus vivendi was signed it was understood between the two high contracting parties that—

1. The municipal administrations actually in the hands of the American occupation should be returned to the Haitian Government after a special agreement for each case.

2. The customs administration should be settled by an understanding between the state secretary of finance and the receiver general relative to the elements of control of customs operations to be furnished to the Haitian Government and its participation in the appointment of employees according to the terms of the convention.[3]   ·

1-A. *Municipal administrations.*—The modus vivendi dealing with this subject was not carried out in any particular. The municipal administrations were not restored to the Haitian authority, in spite of the formal promise which had been made to this effect. As it had been understood that a special agreement would be made for each case, the Haitian Government, in a memorandum dated December 20, 1915, asked the legation of the United States to begin as soon as possible the restoration of those of Port au Prince. (See Appendix No. 7.) This memorandum, in indicating the procedure which it would be convenient to adopt under the circumstances, added:

" This restoration necessarily involves expenses, and the means of meeting them are a necessary part of this restoration. But as these expenses have actually been paid to the American occupation by Admiral Caperton out of the funds of the Public Treasury their future payment to the Haitian authority would not be a new expense.

" Consequently the Haitian Government considers that in cases where the details of the agreement will bring expense to the Haitian administration the means for meeting them will be furnished from the funds of the Public Treasury."[4]

On January 3, 1916, Mr. A. Bailly-Blanchard, the American minister, in referring to his note of November 29, 1915, and to the Haitian memorandum of December 20, 1915, relative to the restoration of the municipal administrations to the Haitian Government, informed M. Louis Borno, state secretary of foreign affairs, that Rear Admiral Caperton, United States Navy, commanding the forces of the United States in Haiti and in Haitian waters, had received instructions to suspend action in the affair for the time being until the employees provided for in the treaty and the modus vivendi should be named and ready to take office.[5]

Thus, in spite of the modus vivendi of November 29, 1915, proposed by the Government of the United States (which provided for the complete execution of the convention of September 16, 1915, pending the vote o fthe American Senate), the Haitian Government was always confronted by the state of affairs previous to the convention. And the Haitian Government, through the state secretary of foreign affairs, stated to the American minister at Port au Prince that " such a situation could not last any longer without creating between the two Governments a very serious equivocation which would not be pleasant for either party."[6]

2-A. *Customs officials and employees.*—Since the constitution of the Haitian Republic states clearly that the President of Haiti alone appoints and recalls public officials, article 2 of the treaty of 1915 could only mean a modification of that constitution when it states that the agents of control designated by it, namely, the receiver general, the financial adviser, and the assistants and employees of their offices—offices of collection and offices of payment—may be Americans and subject to nomination by the President of the United States. It was, clear, therefore, that the other officials and employees of the public administration of Haiti, and particularly of the customs administration, must be Haitians and appointed exclusively by the President of Haiti. This interpretation was self-evident. In addition to the correspondence exchanged at the time of the signing of the modus vivendi of November 29, 1915—correspondence in which the American Legation determined the following point:

³ Correspondence between M. Bailly-Blanchard, American minister to Port au Prince, and M. Louis Borno, state secretary of foreign affairs. See Exposé Général de la Situation de la République d'Haïti, année 1917, p. 14.
⁴ Ibid.
⁵ See communication of the American Legation, Report of M. Louis Borno, state secretary of foreign affairs, to the President of Haiti. vol. 1, pp. 219, 220, 221.
⁶ See Report of M. Louis Borno, state secretary of foreign affairs, to the President of Haiti, vol. 1, p. 221.

"(2) The customs administration will be settled by an understanding between the state secretary of finance and the receiver general relative to the elements of control of customs operations to be furnished to the Haitian Government, and its participation in the appo.ntment of employees according to the terms of the treaty"—the interpretations referred to in the law of sanction for the said treaty, dated November 11, 1915, which had been officially transmitted to the Government at Washington before the sanction of this same treaty by the American Senate and the exchange of ratifications, contain the following explanation with regard to article 2:

"B. The customs personnel is Haitian, appointed exclusively and directly by the President of Haiti. The ' assistants and employees ' designated in article 2 are assistants of the receiver; they do not make up the customs personnel. They are assigned to the customs by the receiver's office and control the customs operations."

Moreover, in a communication of September 16, 1915, addressed to Mr. R. B. Davis, chargé d'affaires ad interim of the United States of America at Port au Prince, the state secretary of foreign affairs, M. Louis Borno, recalled in the following terms the specifications relating to this subject, which he had fixed at a conference held the day before at the department of foreign affairs:

"With the sincere desire of avoiding from now on any misunderstanding upon certain important points, I have drawn your attention to the following: ' * * * (3) By the words "collect," "receive," and "apply," in article 2, first paragraph, etc., the Government understands that what has been fixed by those words is a service of collectorship (collect, receive) and of payment (apply).' (See art. 5.) The receiver general and the assistants and employees to be appointed by the President of Haiti upon the nomination of the President of the United States form a service of collection of all customs duties, a separate department from the customs administration as such, which latter consists in the storing, verification, and taxation of merchandise according to the tariff. Consequently, the Haitian employees of this customs service will depend upon the exclusive appointment of the President of Haiti."

Nevertheless, on this point also the modus vivendi remained a dead letter.

AFTER THE EXCHANGE OF RATIFICATIONS.

The formality of the exchange of ratifications of the treaty of September 16, 1915, was carried out at Washington, D. C., on May 3, 1916. The régime of military administration established by the American occupation nearly a year before had now become definitely incompatible with the terms of the convention which established the rights and duties of the high contracting parties. The question was, then, to keep the two Governments henceforth within the limits of the rules contained in the convention. In the departments of public administration which were not touched upon by the convention of 1915 it goes without saying that exclusively American action could not rightly be imposed upon the Haitian Government, however disposed it might be to accept a certain cooperation. But the legitimate and judicial claims of the Haitian Government met with no success. When the treaty became a fact, it had no more effect in relieving the situation than the modus vivendi. The municipal administrations still remained in the hands of the American military authorities.

In reference to the public works which the occupation had taken over in the month of June, 1916, without any agreement with the Haitian Government, or even the slightest warning to the minister concerned, the Haitian Government protested to the American legation and declared that it declined all responsibility for any expenses against the Haitian State which might be incurred by the occupation, whether for the public works or for any other cause not justified by the convention;[1] whereupon a letter on this subject from Col. Littleton W. T. Waller, addressed to the American minister, was sent to the Haitian Government, from which we quote the following paragraph:

"3. If, as stated by the minister of foreign affairs, the treaty has been in operation since May 3, 1916, I know nothing of it; I must receive my information through proper military channels before I can relax the established rules under which we have been operating."[2]

---

[1] See letter of June 28, 1916, Louis Borno, Report to the President of Haiti, etc., vol. 1, p. 227.

[2] Letter of June 30, 1916, from the commander of the expeditionary force. See Borno, Report to the President of Haiti, etc., vol. 1, p. 231.

Thus it is clear that the occupation, up to the end of 1917, carried on all public works, without any control by the Haitian Government over the nature of the works, the manner of carrying them out, their expediency, or even the amount spent on these works.[9] Twice, meanwhile, on January 3, 1916, and July 14, 1916, Mr. Bailly-Blanchard, the American minister, officially declared that the occupation would continue to operate the public works only until the officials designated in the treaty should be appointed and ready to exercise their duties. Now, since in the month of September, 1916, Mr. E. G. Oberlin, United States Navy, had been named engineer for the department of public works, he had immediately informed the said department that he was ready to enter completely into the execution of his duties as specified in article 13 of the treaty of September 16, 1915, and into the regulations of the bureau of engineering.

Mr. Oberlin, after passing several months at the department of public works without being able to accomplish anything, was recalled early in 1917 and replaced immediately by Mr. E. R. Gayler, United States Navy. Nothing had changed, that is to say, the agents of the occupation had continued to operate the public works without any participation by the department of public works.[10]

And the Haitian Government was justified in drawing the following conclusions in said Exposé Général de la Situation, etc., 1917, in the chapter on foreign relations, and in the section dealing with the difficulties just described:

" It can be said, then, that the treaty of September 16 has not been carried out, and that this violation of the engagements entered into is due to the agents of the American Government." [11]

When the first officials of the treaty arrived at Port au Prince in July, 1916, and entered upon their duties, the question of appointments to the customs of the Republic which had come up at the signing of the modus vivendi and which had not yet been solved promptly arose again.

Mr. Addison T. Ruan, financial adviser, and Mr. Maumus, receiver general, claimed that these appointments were subject to the nomination of the President of the United States. The Haitian Government maintained that they depended upon the exclusive designation of the President of the Republic of Haiti. In spite of everything, the opinion of Mr. Ruan and Mr. Maumus was indorsed by the Department of State; whence it would have resulted, by adhering to the text which was the object of the controversy, that the most insignificant employee in any customhouse in Haiti whatsoever must be nominated by the President of the United States and appointed by the President of Haiti. " In fact," said the state secretary of foreign affairs of Haiti in a communication of March 26, 1916, to Mr. Bailly-Blanchard, American minister at Port au Prince, " neither has the President of the United States ever presented such proposals, nor has the President of Haiti until now been responsible for the appointment of any of the Haitians actually employed in the customs administration or in the office of the receiver general. These citizens have been appointed in these two administrations by the military occupation, without any participation by the President of Haiti." And on this occasion the state secretary of foreign affairs of Haiti drew the attention of the United States legation to a most serious and unjust act, namely, the introduction into Haitian public administrations by the American occupation of various persons of foreign nationality other than American, much to the prejudice of our compatriots.

The point of view of the State Department on this question of appointment of Haitian officials in the customhouses of the Republic was accepted only under the express reserve of recourse to arbitration by virtue of the arbitration treaty between Haiti and the United States of January 7, 1909.[12]

Far from stopping at these encroachments, which already constituted so many violations of the treaty, far from consenting to the restoration of the municipal administrations just mentioned, the constant and willful tendency of the American military authorities in Haiti has been, on the contrary, to extend more and more the powers, either of the gendarmerie or the occupation itself, which was by the terms of the treaty purely temporary and provisional, adding to them by assigning still other public functions. The serious difficulties created at Port au Prince with regard to the postal and telegraph administrations show clearly the nature of the procedure adopted to set the treaty aside and to absorb in the most unjustifiable manner what was left of the national administration.

---

[9] See Exposé Général de la Situation de la République d'Haiti, année 1917, p. 90.
[10] Ibid., pp. 90, 91, and 92.
[11] Ibid., p. 16.
[12] See communication of Mar. 26, 1917. Borno. Report to the President of Haiti, etc., pp. 216, 217.

On February 8, 1916, the State Department and the Haitian commission sent to Washington in December, 1915, at the proposal of the United States Government, had settled the terms of an agreement relative to the gendarmerie of Haiti. The signing of this agreement had been postponed at the request of the American State Department until the sanction of the treaty by the American Senate and the congressional vote of a special act to permit United States officers to serve in the Haitian administration. When this sanction had been given and the special act had been voted, the State Department, instead of signing the agreement that had been drawn up and decided upon, proposed a new one to the Haitian Legation at Washington, which had just been invested with the full powers of the Haitian commission recalled toward the beginning of June, 1916. The new project, transmitted to the Haitian Government by M. Solon Ménos, Haitian minister at Washington, contained an article 2, drawn up as follows:

"* * * The medical officers necessary for the sanitary measures provided in article 13 of the treaty, the operation, management, and maintenance of the telegraphs, telephones, the lighthouse service, and the postal service shall be directed and controlled by the commandant of the gendarmerie."

This meant the turning over of the whole civil administrat on to an organization whose exclusively military and policing character had been determined in the treaty of September 16, 1915. The Haitian Government decided not to accept this article. In the course of a conference held on August 3, 1916, at the United States legation between Mr. G. Scholle, American chargé d'affaires, Col. Waller, commandant of the expeditionary corps, and Maj. Smedley D. Butler, commandant of the gendarmerie of Haiti, on one hand, and M. Edmond Héraux, secretary of state for finance, and M. Louis Borno, secretary of state for foreign affairs, on the other, the American chargé d'affaires produced a text which he declared was that of the State Department and which differed considerably from the official text transmitted to the Haitian Government by M. Solon Ménos, Haitian minister at Washington. This new text read as follows:

"Article 2. The department of public health and public works, as prescribed by article 13 of the treaty, the operation, the management, and maintenance of telegraphs, telephone, the light house service, and the postal service shall be directed and controlled by the commandant of the gendarmerie."

Mr. Gustave Scholle declared that if within 24 hours the Haitian Government did not take official steps for placing under the control of the Haitian gendarmerie the services indicated by this article 2, the United States legation would telegraph to the State Department not to sign the agreement on hand. And Col. Waller added that if in 24 hours this step was not taken, he would telegraph to Washington that the Haitian Government was insincere and unstable. M. Louis Borno asked Mr. Scholle to communicate to him in writing the statement which he had just made. Mr. Scholle would not consent.

The situation was not improved and the pressure became more and more violent. In informing the Haitian minister at Washington of the verbal ultimatum which the Haitian Government had received, M. Louis Borno, secretary of state for foreign affairs, said, in a cablegram of August 5, 1916:

"* * * Inform immediately the Secretary of State of this state of coercion. Say that the Haitian Government has decided to refuse all military demands contrary to the convention. Do not fail to make clear and defend our government's position. Meanwhile we are replying to the legation that since negotiations are being carried on at Washington, you are deciding the question with the State Department. Keep me constantly informed of your activities and of results. Situation serious, demands speed and energy. Our government stands firm and does not intend to yield to the new demands of the occupation, which are supported by the American legation."

Finally an agreement was reached, signed August 24, 1916, at Washington, by the terms of which " the operation, management, and maintenance of the telegraphs and telephones in the Republic' of Haiti shall be under the control and direction of the engineer or engineers to be nominated by the President of the United States and authorized for that purpose by the Government of Haiti in accordance with article 13 of the treaty of September 16, 1915."

This agreement added to the convention by increasing the powers and authority of the engineer or engineers designated by article 13.

Instead of simply keeping to the régime fixed by the treaty, the Haitian Government was constantly obliged by the American officials to take unjustified initiatives. It was forced to accept the placing of American superintendents in charge of the postal service and of the ministry of public education, with salaries equal to and in some cases even higher than those of the state secretaries.

At the municipal councils it was obliged to appoint so-called council officers who had, actually, the exclusive administration of the communes and absolute control of municipal affairs, including revenues and expenses. This state of affairs, not provided for in the treaty, gave rise to regrettable conflicts. When a council officer (American) was confronted by an administrator of finances and provisional prefect (Haitian official) wishing to investigate the accounts of the commune, as the law obliges him to do, it always ended either with the forced silence of the Haitian official or with all kinds of difficulties which he had to face simply because he was trying to do his duty. In this connection we particularly desire to call attention to the case of M. Auguste Magloire, administrator of finances and provisional prefect of the district of Port au Prince, and therefore appointed by law to verify the accounts of the communes in his section. This high official, with no reason that could ever be found, was one day brutally arrested and imprisoned by the American military occupation. After 21 days of detention he was released without ever having undergone any examination. He was again arrested, shortly after, and made to understand that his difficulties would be over as soon as he should resign as administrator of finances and provisional prefect of the district of Port au Prince. In fact, he sent in his resignation to the President of Haiti and immediately was released. Since then he has not been disturbed. It seems to have been too attentive an examination of the accounts of the council officers for certain communes of the district of Port au Prince that caused all his troubles. We think that it would be interesting, in an investigation, to determine this point and others with similar implications.

The treaty of September, 1915, in addition to the military officials of the gendarmerie, provides for (1) a fincial adviser; (2) a receiver general of customs, his assistants and employees; (3) one or more engineers of public works; (4) one or more engineers for public hygiene.

The rights and duties of these officials are clearly determined by the treaty or by special agreements or regulations which determine the departments of public administration in which they must cooperate with the Haitian Government. Consequently, all other departments of the public administration should have remained under the exclusive control of the Haitian Government. But actually there is not a branch of public service in Haiti which has not had to submit, at one time or another, to illegal interference, often brutal, either by the gendarmerie laying down the law to the Government or by the military occupation, the absolute master of the situation.

Even the Haitian department of justice has not escaped serious traces of their domination. In fact, in the "Exposé Général de la Situation de la République d'Haïti, 1917," p. 15, a chapter is found which presents the case as follows:

"The encroachments of American agents have been felt also in the department of justice. In spite of all the protests of the department of foreign affairs to the American Legation, these encroachments have not ceased. Great harm has been caused both to the persons under jurisdiction and to the dignity of the magistracy itself, whose decisions usually encounter obstacles on the part of the agents from Washington. It is most necessary that such a state of things cease at once."

By the terms of article 10 of the treaty of September 16, 1915, the gendarmerie was created for the sake of preserving internal peace, security of individual rights, and complete observance of the said treaty.

The maintenance of peace, which had been disturbed too often in recent times, was one of the essential objects of American intervention, and it was to obtain this that provision was made for an effective rural and urban gendarmerie composed of Haitians, but organized and directed by American officers. How has the Haitian gendarmerie, commanded by American officers, who themselves never acted except under orders of the American occupation, how has this public force understood and carried out the object of article 10 of the treaty? The answer to this is the whole history of American intervention in Haiti.

Internal peace could not be preserved because the permanent and brutal violation of individual rights of Haitian citizens was a perpetual provocation to revolt, because the terrible military despotism which has ruled in Haiti for the last six years has not created and could not create for the Haitian people that security which it was hoped the application of the treaty would bring about. Among other things, it is sufficient to call attention here to the system of corvée, that is to say, forced unpaid labor on public roads, imposed for military purposes upon the Haitian peasant. This will give some idea of why the gendarmerie, aided and encouraged by the American occupation, instead of assuring respect for individual rights, caused the revolt known as the revolt of the Cacos, for the repression of which so many useless atrocities were committed by the marines in our unhappy country. This gendarmerie, in spite of the aid of the marines of the occupation and the use of the most modern armament (machine guns, military planes, armored cars, etc.), was never able, by purely military methods, to contend with these undisciplined and unarmed bands known as Cacos. Therefore it is ineffective. And if it is ineffective it is because, in spite of the repeated warnings of the Government, the personnel which composes it was not chosen as it should have been. In fact, it contains men "wanted" by the Haitian courts for criminal acts (robberies, murders, etc.). Examination of the archives of the ministries of the interior and of justice of Haiti will throw light on this subject.

The same article 10 of the treaty of September 16, 1915, provides that "the American officers of the gendarmerie will be replaced by Haitians when the latter, after an examination by a committee chosen by the superior officer in charge of the Haitian gendarmerie, are judged capable of carrying out their duties effectively." This provision naturally implied the establishment of an officers' training school. But this officers' training school has never been established. It could not be, for two reasons:

1. As a general rule, the American officers of the gendarmerie are privates (in the American Marine Corps) who have been made officers in Haiti, and who have had nothing but a most elementary education, which naturally renders them incapable of any military training.

2. For this officers' school a special recruitment would have to be made, since the rank and file of the gendarmerie, as it is, is composed chiefly of illiterates. After the voting of the treaty, a certain number of young Haitians, expecting the early establishment of an officers' training school, enrolled themselves as students. But the American military authorities, knowing well that the former American privates who had become officers in Haiti could not be converted into military instructors, put off, under one pretext or another, the cooperation that was offered them.

And this provision of the treaty, too, remained a dead letter. If the urban gendarmerie is ineffective, the rural gendarmerie does not exist at all, despite article 10 of the treaty. After the arrival of the American occupation an old constabulary which had been serviceable and could easily have been improved and adapted to new conditions was abolished. It was not replaced by any kind of an organization, and so far the rural gendarmerie has not been established. The insecurity in the country is such as to discourage the peasants, causing them to leave the country where they were born and spent their entire lives and to emigrate in large numbers to Cuba.

Here is the way with the customary reserve characteristic of official documents and their euphemisms dictated by policy, in which the Haitian department of the interior expresses its judgment of the gendarmerie:

"It renders to the country, if not all the services that might be expected of it, at least those which its organization, still incomplete, permits it. * * * [13] One of the greatest concerns of the department is to assure complete and absolute security in the country. It is working there tenaciously, and hopes shortly, with the active aid of the gendarmerie, to be rewarded for its efforts and to accomplish its aim.[15] "

The President of the Republic of Haiti, in an interview with correspondents of American newspapers (New York Tribune, Chicago Tribune, etc.) at Port-au-Prince in November, 1920, expressed a more precise and more categorical criticism than that of the department of the interior: "The rural police," he said, "which was abolished after the occupation, has not been reorganized as provided by article 10 of the convention and article 118 of the constitution. The robberies and insecurity in the country discourage the peasants in their work; they emigrate in crowds to Cuba."[16]

Official documents of Haiti clearly confirm that the treaty of September 16, 1915, has never been carried out by the American Government.

[13] Exposé Général de la Situation de la République d'Haiti, année, 1917, p. 76.
[15] Exposé Général de la Situation de la République d'Haiti, 1917, p. 62.
[16] See L'Essor, Port au Prince, Nov. 24, 1920.

On January 13, 1916, more than a month after the modus vivendi of November 29, 1915, signed between the two Governments for the provisional execution of the treaty, M. Louis Borno, state secretary for foreign affairs, wrote to Mr. Bailly-Blanchard, American minister at Port-au-Prince:

"We are continually confronted with proceedings antedating the convention. * * * The rule which the two high parties sanctioned by their signatures is the only one which ought to be applied. The Haitian Government must, then, require the fullest application actually possible.[17]

By the exchange of ratifications which took place at Washington on May 3, 1916, the treaty had gone fully into force. On June 5, 1916, the State secretary for foreign affairs, in a communication to M. Solon Ménos, Haitian minister at Washington, protested against the continuation of conditions which the treaty should have ended. Asking that a copy of his communication be submitted to Mr. Lansing, the Haitian secretary of foreign affairs stated, among other things:

"Is it possible to permit the administration of the Haitian customs and of the Haitian national treasury to be carried on any longer without any control by the Haitian Government? What is the amount of the customs revenues? Just what are all the expenses that are being incurred? What are the funds at the disposal of the treasury? The Government, in spite of its repeated demands, is unable to say. Up to the present the occupation has not, for nearly a year, supplied any report or any accounts. The Government has not the slightest doubt regarding the absolute honesty of the American officers; this honesty is above all question. What it wants to have established is the abnormal and disagreeable position of a Government which is refused information concerning its own affairs, and even refused any knowledge of circumstances or control of the situation. * * *"[18]

On June 29, 1916, in another communication to M. Solon Ménos, minister to Washington, the state secretary for foreign affairs expressed himself as follows:

"* * * You can not do too much to keep the State Department on guard against the usurping tendencies of the occupation. Do not spare any effort to make the American Government understand that the Dartiguenave Government, which signed the convention, must necessarily be firmly bound to the success of its work; that it is, therefore, strictly interested in supplying the greatest and frankest cooperation to the intervention, but within the limits of the convention as faithfully interpreted. If it acted otherwise, if, now that this convention has been proclaimed by President Wilson and is in full force, the Haitian Government permitted its clauses not to be observed in the spirit which dictated them; that is to say, a spirit respectful of our rights as a free State, if the military occupation can be permitted to invade all Haitian public services, public works, and others—in violation of the clauses of the convention which provide for the appointment of special agents, engineers, and others—what would happen? The Haitian people, humiliated by this contempt for solemn promises, would have nothing but hatred and repulsion for American intervention. The Haitian Government which would accept such a situation would find itself generally discredited, to say nothing of the fact that it would assume terrible responsibilities in the eyes of its country.

"Keep in mind these ideas, Mr. Minister. They suffice for you to know what solutions the Government will accept in the negotiations which are confided to you.

"Most especially I draw your attention to the necessity for putting an end to martial law. As long as there were any threats of revolutionary trouble, unimportant as they might be, the Government said nothing about its existence. But it is undeniably certain that nothing really serious and of a general character could be attempted now against the public peace. Therefore this martial law which weighs upon the country has become utterly useless. Demand its abolition with insistence. * * *"[19]

In a communication of June 28, 1916, the Haitian secretary of state for foreign affairs, stated to Mr. Bailly-Blanchard, American minister, at Port au Prince:

"* * * However strong may be our desire always to maintain perfect harmony with the American authorities, a natural duty, higher than anything

[17] Communication of Jan. 13, 1916. Report to the President of Haiti, by Louis Borno, secretary for foreign affairs, vol. 1, p. 222.
[18] Communication of June 5, 1916   Ibid., vol. 1, p. 225.
[19] Communication of June 24, 1916, Louis Borno, Report to the President of Haiti, vol. 1, pp. 200–201.

... binds up—the duty of scrupulously watching out for the observance of the ... of the solemn convention which binds our two countries and which has ... in effect since the 3d of last March.

"The Haitian Government would betray its duty if, by its silence, it sanc-... the formal violations of this convention which have just been de-..., etc." [20]

As for the civil administrations which, against the will of the Haitian Gov-...ment and contrary to the modus vivendi of November 29, 1915, still remained ... the hands of the occupation, the state secretary of foreign affairs, in a commu-...ion of July 17, 1916, made the following remark to Mr. Gustave Scholle, ...gé d'affaires ad interim of the United States of America:

" * * * Such an abnormal situation can not be indefinitely permitted. ... the exchange of ratifications definitely did put the treaty into force, the ...tian Government, as well as the Government of the United States, was ...d to adjust everything as soon as possible to the rules of the new régime, ...mly sanctioned and proclaimed by the public authorities of the two ...tries. The occupation should have from that time on restrained its ...ities and confined itself within the limitations of its military functions. * * * But contrary to that, etc." [21]

According to the Haitian constitution (art. 80) the executive power must ...it annually to the two legislative chambers within a week of the opening ... the regular session a sort of general report covering everything of a political ... administrative nature that has been done during the past year. This ...al document is known as "Exposé Général de la Situation de la Republique ...iti." Following are the comments found therein with regard to the non-...cution of the convention of September 16, 1915:

"* * * It can be said that the convention of September 16, 1915, has ...t been carried out to date, and that this breach of promises is due to the ...ts of the American Government. * * *" [22]

"* I deeply regret to state that the various matters which formed the subject ... the last exposé regarding the convention of 1915 are still unchanged. The ... differences still exist, and I should only repeat myself by relating them ... your excellency.

"I confine myself to giving you assurance that the department will continue ... activities, convinced of our right and confident of the triumph of all that ... just and fair." [23]

"* * * My department is obliged to repeat what the Exposés of 1917 ... 1918 stated with regard to the application of the convention of 1915. ... only has it been impossible to solve the matters brought up after the ...cation of the convention, but, moreover, the vote of the budget of 1918–19 ... rise to such difficulties between the Government and the financial adviser, ... was supported by the chief of the military occupation at this time, Col. ... Russell, that the department of foreign affairs was obliged to address ...te to the State Department at Washington [24] to protest against the pro-...re which certain American officials considered themselves entitled to adopt ...rd us.

"To this note the Secretary of State at Washington, Mr. Robert Lansing. ...ed a few days later, saying to the Haitian Government that, 'in view of the ... serious implication of the general accusation against American officials in ... contained in the above-mentioned note, the Government of the United ...s desires the Government of Haiti to make a more precise and more detailed ...ration regarding the questions raised in the note of November 20, 1918.' [25]

"To satisfy this entirely just demand of the Secretary of State the depart-... of foreign affairs collected in a memorandum all the facts pertaining to ... matters of which the Haitian Government had complained in its note of ...mber 20 and sent it to our legation at Washington, with instruction for ... submission to the Department of State. It was submitted on February 14 ... by our chargé d'affaires ad interim in Washington." [26]

Communication of June 28, 1916. Ibid., pp. 227–228.
Communication of July 17, 1916. Louis Borno, Report to the President of Haiti, ... pp. 233–234.
Ibid., p. 15.
Ibid., p. 7.
See Appendix No. 8.
See Appendix No. 9.
See Exposé Général de la Situation de la République d'Haiti, 1919, pp. 14, 15.

In November, 1920, it was the President of the Haitian Republic himself who, in a striking declaration made to the correspondents of American newspapers who had followed in Haiti the naval court of inquiry presided over by Admiral Mayo, formulated the grievances of the Haitian Government with regard to the nonexecution of the convention of September 16, 1915.

After recalling the aims of American intervention in Haiti, such as they were indicated in the preamble of the treaty of September 16, 1915; that is to say, (a) maintenance of public peace, and (b) establishment of the finance on a sound basis and the economic development of Haiti, M. Dartiguenave made ponits indicated subsequently. (1) As to the matter of general peace, he had hoped that the commission of inquiry presided over by Admiral Mayo would try to find out how the Americans charged with maintaining this peace understood and accomplished their mission. M. Dartiguenave had granted his interview to the American journalist while the naval court of inquiry was being held at Port au Prince, and he had doubtless been unwilling, in communicating his opinions as chief of the Haitian Government, to appear to exercise any influence on the work of this court. He received no report either from the gendarmerie, of which he was legally commander in chief, or from the occupation. This is what he said on this subject:

" * * * Article 103 of the Constitution, in the third paragraph, provides that a law shall establish in the communes and provinces [Haitian] civil officials who are to represent directly the executive power. It is impossible for the Haitian Government to have these civil officials, because the American minister and the financial adviser have refused the appropriations, however small, for salaries for these positions, in consequence of which the executive power has no special agent to report to him—the gendarmerie making no reports on general conditions in the country, except to the chief of the occupation.

"If a paid official reports to the executive power, his salary is cut off if indeed he is not arrested and tried by court-martial, whether he be judge, a Government commissioner, or a mayor [magistrat communal], and this happens in contravention of the law and articles 101 and 102 of the constitution."

Regarding the aid which the Government of the United States had solemnly promised to the Haitian people for the improvement of their finances, their economic development, and the prosperity of the Republic, the declarations of the President of Haiti are as follows:

" * * * No effective aid has been brought to Haiti for the development of its agricultural and industrial resources, and no constructive measure has been proposed, for the purpose of placing its finances on a really solid basis.

" By the terms of article 2, paragraph 2, of the convention, the President of Haiti appoints, upon the nomination of the President of the United States, a financial adviser who will be an official attached to the ministry of finance. The adviser is, then, a Haitian official paid $10,000 (American gold) annually by the Haitian public treasury. But in reality the financial adviser is not responsible to the Haitian Government. On the contrary his actions indicate his purpose to subject it to his will.

" Numerous facts show the omnipotence which the financial adviser arrogates to himself. Nothing more strikingly illustrates this than the confiscation by the financial adviser, with the support of the American minister, of the salaries of the President of the Republic, the State secretaries, and the members of the legislative council, because the Government had refused to insert in the contract of the National Bank of Haiti (which is controlled by the National City Bank of New York), a clause prohibiting the importation into Haiti of foreign gold coins, which the financial adviser wanted to upon them. He also prevented the voting of the budget, contrary to the vision of the Haitian constitution.

"Article 2 of the convention says: ' The financial adviser shall draw adequate system of public accounting.' We are still waiting for this new tem which was to simplify the accounts of the State. Instead of introducing such a system, the financial adviser demanded the abolition of an old institution, the audit office (chambre des comptes), In spite of all the of the Government to reestablish this indispensable organization, the adviser persistently refused to have it done. Consequently there is no the Haitian people to control its finances, which are entirely in the hands American officials of the treaty.

"Article 2 of the convention says also: ' The financial adviser shall increase the revenues.' The financial adviser has so far proposed n the Government to bring this about. The only attempt he has made in this direction was the project for the creation of internal taxes, which he presented in 1918 and which he wanted the Government to pass within 24 hours. The project was so crude and so badly drawn up that the Government had to refuse this demand and prepare a counterproject better adapted to the customs and financial resources of the Hawaiian nation.

"It is about 20 months since this counterproject was returned to the financial adviser for further consideration; we have heard nothing more of it.

"Article 2 of the convention says further: 'The financial adviser shall inquire into the validity of the debts of the Republic, shall keep the two Governments informed regarding all future debts, shall recommend improved methods of collecting and applying the revenues, and shall make such recommendations to the state secretary for finances as are judged necessary for the well-being and prosperity of the Republic. * * *.'

"No inquiry into the validity of our debts has been made.

"No improved method of collecting the revenues has been recommended.

"No recommendation for the well-being and prosperity of the Republic has yet been made to the Haitian Government.

"The duties of the financial adviser, as defined in article 2 of the convention, doubtless require a man of great financial experience. This essential consideration does not seem to have had any weight in the choice of the financial adviser. This is proved by the unfortunate transaction which he put through for the Republic last year, in the face of directly contrary instructions of the Haitian Government. Three million American dollars were to be converted into francs for Haiti's best interests." He converted them in October, 1919, at a time when the value of the franc was lowering rapidly, the exchange being 9 and a fraction francs for a dollar. Shortly afterwards the dollar was worth 17 francs. This transaction involved the Haitian people in a loss of several millions of francs.

"Faced with this inertia on the part of the financial adviser, the Haitian Government is augmenting its efforts. It is studying various measures and preparing projects which it considers more likely to meet the numerous needs of progress of the Haitian people. All its measures, all its projects encounter the opposition either of the financial adviser or of the American minister, who very often rejects them without examination and without condescending to say why.

"Now we come to the strangest phase of the situation from the point of view of the Haitian Government. Not only have American officials done nothing that could have been done for the intellectual development and economic prosperity of the country, but they oppose the Government's work in this direction. Numerous projects for laws dealing with the finances, agriculture, public education, administrative and rural organization meet with either the direct opposition of the American officials or lie unanswered in the archives of the American Legation.

"Particular resistance is made to projects dealing with the education of the people, such as for the preparation of teachers for primary education, industrial and agricultural schools, secondary or higher education, and for the construction of school buildings.

"The Government does not pretend to believe that the projects which it prepares are perfect, but since they approximate the vital needs of the country the American officials ought to take the trouble to examine them, and if they find that they are imperfect or bad, should propose modifications or substitute other projects which could be discussed with the common desire to arrive at a satisfactory solution. In this way alone can a 'cordial cooperation' be obtained, and only in this way ought it to be understood.

"Is it understood in this way? Never.

"When the financial adviser proposes a measure he understands that this measure is to be adopted without any examination by the Government.

"When the Government does the proposing, the proposal is rejected without examination or modifications are made which it must accept without discussion.

"And it is always in the name of the Government of the United States that the American minister imposes upon the Haitian people the least worthy demands of the American officials, who are paid with Haitian money. And if the Government refuses to yield the worst humiliations are inflicted upon it.

" For a payment of interest on the debt of France, then due.

"The excuse usually made in support of the rejection of Government projects is the following: 'There is no money.'

"Of course there is always enough money for American uses.

"Here are two striking examples:

"Two cases of plague in New Orleans are reported. The financial adviser, who was in Washington at this time, authorizes the appointment of two 'rat catchers'—not for New Orleans, where the plague was discovered but for Port-au-Prince, which was never troubled with this disease. He fixes their monthly salary at $250 each, quite without any word to the Government, regardless of any law or budget appropriation.

"But at the same time the financial adviser refused appropriations for three associate professors from the University of France, who were offered to the Haitian Government by the French Government for the Lycée of Port-au-Prince.

"Article 7 of the convention is drawn up as follows:

"All amounts collected by and in keeping of the receiver general shall be used (1) for the payment of the salaries and allowances of the receiver general, his assistants, and employees for the expenses of the collector's office, which, shall include the salary of the financial adviser, salaries to be determined by a previous agreement; (2) for the interest and amortization of the public debt of Haiti; (3) for the maintenance of the police referred to in article 10, and the balance for the current expenses of the Haitian Government.

"This article establishes the order in which the expenses of the Republic of Haiti should be met by means of the custom duties collected from the customhouses by the receiver general.

"The expenses of the Government come last of all, and include (1) salaries of public officials other than those indicated in the first part of the article; (2) expenses of the public works and hygiene administrations; (3) expenses for material, office furniture, etc.

"It will be noticed that the expenses that come second are those relating to the Haitian public debt, interest, and amortization. If these disbursements were known, the amount due the Government for its current expenses would also be established, and the Government would be free to dispose of it. But this has never been done, and for the following reason:

"To hold the Government in curb, to be able whenever it resists an unjustified demand to exert a pressure which will oblige it to yield, it must be kept completely dependent upon the financial adviser and the receiver general, so far as finances are concerned.

"If it is a question of a new expense considered necessary by the Government, which the American authorities do not wish to grant, the answer is: 'There is no money—the reserve funds must go toward the payment of the public debt.'

"Very often this same reply is made for regular expenses provided for in the budget.

"In addition to the custom duties, there are other budget resources which the convention has left to the free disposal of the Government for its legal expenses. The financial adviser, supported by the American minister and the military authorities who on this occasion resorted to martial law, demanded that these funds be turned over to him.

"In this way the Government is entirely at the mercy of the caprices and of the arbitrary will of the financial adviser.

"The State Department, absorbed, doubtless, in more important questions of foreign policy or ill informed by its official agents, is deaf to our protests, or simply upholds the position of the American authorities.

"We have been reproached by certain American newspapers on the ground that Haiti did not pay its debts before the occupation. This is entirely false. In spite of all its financial difficulties, Haiti has always lived up to her agreements. The administration of the public debt was not suspended until after the occupation; it was resumed at the beginning of this year, and just at this time the Government is insisting with the greatest energy on the payment of the internal debt.

"Each year the American minister and the financial adviser reject the project of the Haitian Government for the application of the second paragraph of article 116 of the constitution, which reads: 'The examination and liquidation of the accounts of the general administration and of everything accountable to the public treasury shall be carried on according to the method established by law.'

"The examination and liquidation of accounts, according to Haitian law, was carried on by an institution of long standing, called the Chambre des Comptes.

"In conformity with article 2 of the convention, the Haitian Government is vainly demanding the adequate system of public accounting that the financial adviser is supposed to draw up in order to replace the audit office.

"All of article 2 of the convention is a dead letter. The financial adviser ignores it. He pays no attention to the urgent and necessary credits of the Haitian Government established by law; he spends at will, regardless of any law, obliging the Government to ratify his acts.

"To sum up, the Haitian Government is under humiliating subjection through lack of cooperation. Its efforts to collaborate in good faith are fruitless—they are scorned and rejected. There does not seem to exist between the two Governments a reciprocal contract that the two parties must respect." [2]

This conclusion of the important declaration of the President of Haiti regarding the total failure of the American Government to execute the convention of September 16, 1915, is the point of view of the entire Haitian people.

HAITIAN FINANCES—THE FINANCIAL AID PROMISED BY THE UNITED STATES.

Haiti has always lived up loyally to her financial agreements. One of the reasons given for American intervention is the breaking of these agreements. As those of many other countries, Haitian finances have passed through critical periods, but the leaders of the country have always been able to find the necessary solution to the problems that confronted them.

For a long time Haiti has borne the weight of a heavy debt which has hindered her economic development.

By a royal decree King Charles X of France in return for 150,000,000 francs as indemnity for the losses incurred by the former colonists and payable in five equal installments granted to Haiti on April 17, 1825, an independence which the Haitians had conquered at the price of hard and bloody sacrifices. In the continual expectation of the offensive return of the French and weary of maintaining the country for more than 20 years in a state of war, the Government of President Boyer accepted the arrangement of the King of France which stipulated these painful conditions.

By means of a loan of 24,000,000 francs, issued at Paris at the rate of 80 per cent and bearing 6 per cent interest, to which was added 6,000,000 francs paid in specie by the Haitian treasury, the first installment of the indemnity was paid.

But owing to the energetic protests of the Haitian people and the refusal of the French Government to reduce this heavy indemnity, the Haitian Government suspended the payment of the four other installments of the indemnity with the clear intention, however, of paying the annuities (interest and principal) of the loan. After long and delicate negotiations the Government of Louis Philippe consented on February 12, 1838, to recognize the independence of Haiti by treaty. At the same time a financial convention was signed reducing the balance of the indemnity from 120,000,000 fran. ; to 60,000,000.

The loan of 24,000,000 francs and the indemnity were k;tiiwn as "the double French debt." It was entirely paid off in 1893, after 58 yeane

Soon after the first payments of the 30,000,000 francs the aitian Government found itself handicapped in meeting its most urgent budg sulexpenses. In 1826 it had to resort to paper money. The burdens imposed u the country were too heavy; this was the beginning of all its troubles. Tl(thquation was barely able to recover from the losses incurred by the wars of illeito Domingo," the war with the English, the struggle of the French againsila(Toussaint-Louverture, and the war of independence, which started in 1802 itté ended with the surrender of Rochambeau at Cap Haitien in November, 18(.ssu.The plantation had disappeared, the towns and villages had been near onll destroyed—nearly a hundred thousand Haitians had lost their live   n the pitiless struggle for liberty. Sugar and indigo, the chief exports of tnoneland, had n) markets in France, and there was not enough capital to ~omive the sugg.' With Courageously the Haitian people undertook and intensive other forn s of cultivation, and in this way coffee, cotton, and cocoa became ge principal products of the land. In spite of so many misfortunes the countcon;continually made sacrifices to live loyally up to its agreements. Thus next n, (r the balance of the loan of 1875 will be paid off if the expected conditions,le p fulfilled.

---

* L'Essor, Port au Prince Nov. 24, 1920.
*Former name of Haiti under the French rule.

This loan, originally of 21,000,000 francs, consisting of bonds of 300 franc denomination bearing interest at 5 per cent was to carry out the agreements with France (French double debt) and to pay certain internal debts.

In 1922 the balance due will be:

	Francs.
Capital	2, 513, 760
Interest	179. 778
Total	2, 693, 538

In the month of April, 1896, on the account of the Republic of Haiti, a loan was floated at Paris amounting to 50,000,000 francs, nominal value, represented by 100,000 shares of 500 francs, at 6 per cent a year, payable in 37 years. The balance of this loan now outstanding, represented by 59,349 shares, is 29,674,500 francs. Its complete amortization will take place in 1932.

The loan of 1910 was authorized by a law of October 21, 1910. It was to redeem the old internal debt and to provide for the final redemption of the paper money. It was actually issued on February 17, 1911, but it bears the date of the year when the act was voted. Of its face of 65,000,000 francs— 130,000 shares of 500 francs—only 47,000,000 francs were turned over to the Government by the banking syndicate and deposited in the National Bank of the Republic of Haiti. This loan bears interest at 5 per cent a year, and is payable in 50 years. The amortization must take place either by means of purchases at the Bourse de Paris while the shares are below par, or by means of draft by lot, at their nominal value, when they have reached par. Interest is payable semiannually by coupons of 12 francs 50, due May 15 and November 15 of each year.

The present status of this loan is as follows:

In circulation, 123,153 shares of 500 francs; that is, 61,576,500 francs.

The status of the triple foreign debt of Haiti was therefore on July 28, 1915,[21] as follows:

Loan of 1875.—The coupons due on July 1, 1915, had been paid and the work of amortization had been carried out.

Loan of 1896.—The interest on the coupons due June 30, 1915, had been paid. The amortization drafts for December, 1914, had been suspended, because of the world-wide situation created by the European war. It was no more than a delay. The necessary provisions had already been made for amortization.

Loan of 1910.—On this loan, the interest had been paid and the amortization carried out on May 15, 1915.

From the time of the landing of American troops on July 28, 1915, the military occupation suspended payment of the foreign debt of the Republic which the Haitian Government had been able to carry on until then to the satisfaction of its creditors. But not even the signing and execution of the treaty of September 16, 1915, was to put an end to this state of affairs, which was so injurious to the credit of the country. This decision was even more incomprehensible when the special funds for the payment of the interest and amortization of this debt as had accumulated and were remaining unproductive in the vaults of the National Bank of the Republic of Haiti. It was not until last year (1920) that the interest due was finally paid, upon the repeated demands of the bondholders, almost all foreigners, and upheld by their respective Governments. As for the internal debt, except for a partial payment made in April, 1916, no payment of interest has been made up to now, in spite of the demands of the bondholders. Their voices were not heard for the simple reason that they were nearly all Haitians.

In a report of March 20, 1917, the consul general of the United States at Port au Prince said on this subject: " It is unfortunate for commerce that the internal debt has not been adjusted, nor the interest paid, this default having resulted in reducing sales very materially for 1917. Most of the bonds are held by the people, who have been expecting the interest to be paid as formerly, thereby to defray their living expenses. The failure to do this has embarrassed them financially and will tend to diminish the sale of imported goods." [22]

Thus the principal object of the treaty, which was to place Haitian finances on a solid basis, has not been fulfilled, nor has the financial aid which was promised the United States been effectively given. In fact, up to the present time, the monetary circulation of Haiti is still paper money, and instead of substituting metal money for it the financial adviser has fixed the Haitian gourde at one-fifth of the American dollar, to the detriment of all those who receive it in payment for their work.[25] A further resulting injustice is involved in the fact that, in conformity with the budget of the Haitian Republic, certain officials are paid in American gold and others are paid in Haitian money, no calculation being made in favor of these latter, in consideration of the depreciation of this money in relation to the American dollar. Naturally, all the officials from the United States are in the first category.

As another proof that no financial aid has been given to Haiti since the signing of the treaty, it is sufficient to bear in mind that since the year 1917, acting upon the suggestions of the financial adviser, the Government has been trying to float a loan of several million dollars in the United States, and that its efforts have been unsuccessful, in spite of the fact that the American Government realizes the urgent necessity of this loan for the improvement of Haitian finances.

In a report of October 14, 1920, addressed to the Secretary of the Navy, Rear Admiral Knapp stated as to this projected loan:

"To place the finances on a firm bases in accordance with modern ideas a loan is necessary * * * and such a loan was the early confident anticipation, not only of the Haitian Government but of the American Government when the treaty was concluded. Constant efforts have since been made to obtain it and great disappointment is felt that its flotation has so far proved impossible."[26]

The internal debt is at present $2,278,886.20. Up to January 31, 1921, interest due amounted to $705,366.25. There is needed for the monthly payment of interest on this debt only $12,514.93.

Floating debt.—There is a floating debt which reaches an approximate figure of $4,420,920. It should be submitted to careful examination, so that it may be reduced and be restored to its real amount. Those who are interested are waiting in vain for this to be carried out.

SUPPRESSION OF THE HAITIAN LEGISLATURE.

Immediately after the ratification by the Haitian chambers of the convention of September 16, 1915, the provisions of which were not consistent with the constitution in force, the question arose in governmental circles of a constitutional revision. Legally this revision could be carried out only by the Chamber of Deputies and the Senate, meeting as the National Assembly. Instead of following this procedure, which was established by the constitution, the Government preferred to resort to a coup d'état.

Under pressure of the American occupation President Dartiguenave, on April 5, 1916, issued an unconstitutional decree dissolving the Senate. The same decree transformed the Chamber of Deputies in a constituent assembly for revising the constitution. Another decree created a Council of State to be appointed by the President of the Republic.

All these measures were illegal and undemocratic. They substituted dictatorship for constitutional government.

On April 7 the deputies and senators protested against them, since the constitution in force did not grant the President of the Republic the right of dissolution. But the legislative building was closed, and gendarmes were placed there to keep out the representatives of the people. The latter turned to the courts, and on April 15 the civil court of Port au Prince issued two judicial decrees authorizing the deputies and senators to open the gates of the legislative building.

The two eminent jurists, MM. Luxembourg Cauvin and Edmond Lespinasse, who had obtained the decrees, went to Col. Littleton W. Waller, commanding the United States expeditionary forces in Haiti, to make sure there would be no obstacle to the execution of the decisions of the Haitian judicial authorities. Without hesitation the colonel replied that such a step would be considered as a provocation to the American occupation. It was the occupation, then, that forbade the entrance of the legal representatives of the Haitian people into their legislative building.

---

[25] The value of the Haitian gourde is $1.
[26] Annual Report of the Secretary of the Navy, 1920, pp. 230–231.

But, still wishing to carry out their constitutional mandate, the deputies and senators assembled in houses rented at their own expense. On April 17 and 18, 1916, they elected their committees, and on the 27th they opened the third session of the twenty-eighth legislature in the regular way. The president of the Senate. M. Paul Laraque, received the following letter from Col. Littleton W. Waller:

HEADQUARTERS UNITED STATES EXPEDITIONARY FORCE,
Port au Prince, Haiti, April 27, 1916.

MY DEAR MR. LARAQUE: Replying to your verbal request for a meeting to-day, I have the honor to inform you that this can not be granted except under conditions of the proposals of yesterday, accepted in writing, with the clear understanding that the general revision of the constitution is understood and agreed upon between us.

1. The National Assembly constituent has constituent powers only, and upon completion of their labors in revision of the constitution can not resume legislative powers.

2. If the Senate declines to act in conjunction with the deputies, it remains dissolved.

3. The acceptance of this agreement to be given in writing.

Hoping for an amicable settlement of this and other vexed questions.
With expressions of esteem and regard,
Sincerely, yours,

LITTLETON W. WALLER.

Port au Prince, April 27, 1916. Agreed and subscribed to this date. President of the Senate.

Answer:

PORT AU PRINCE, *April 28, 1916.*

Col. LITTLETON W. WALLER,
Chief of the United States Expeditionary Forces in Haiti.

DEAR SIR: In reply to your letter of the 27th instant, containing proposals regarding an amicable arrangement of the present crisis, I have the honor to inform you that these proposals surprised and pained me, and are, I am convinced, only the result of a misunderstanding.

The chambers are, in fact, most desirous of amicably solving the present situation, for which they are not responsible. Although they have the law and all public opinion on their side, their spirit is most conciliatory.

But they could not, under any condition, sanction any unconstitutional measure, or even less, act illegally themselves.

On the other hand, the members of the present cabinet trample upon the most elementary principles of our parliamentary rule, a rule which, while placing the person of the President above all controversy, makes the cabinet responsible to the chambers, and by these acts of aggression give rise to reports which are injurious to the national representative body. Such procedure can not aid in bringing about an amicable solution of the crisis.

The Government of the United States had let it be understood that it would uphold in Haiti the constitutional government of the country and would have its laws observed.

The attempt to abolish the senate is a flagrant violation of the constitution, and constitutes consequently a revolutionary act, just as much as the decree of the revolutionary committee of August, 1915.

It is a question of finding out if the Government and the people of the United States are now upholding this revolutionary act.

Like you, I am always hoping that it will be possible to arrive at a satisfactory solution, since the senate is prepared to accept any proposal compatible with its dignity and with respect for the laws.

Accept, Colonel, expressions of my highest esteem.

PAUL LARAQUE,
President of the Senate.

On May 2, 1916, Rear Admiral Caperton had the following notice published in the columns of the Matin and the Nouvelliste:

[Decree of Apr. 5.]

"Rear Admiral Caperton stated that after having tried for the last three weeks in the most friendly way, with the aid of certain neutral Haitian patriots, to reach an understanding in the conflict of the Haitian Government.

It is impossible to find a basis of understanding that could be accepted by the two parties to the controversy.

" Consequently, in view of the impossibility of reconciling the Government and the opposition, in spite of the conciliatory offers made by the Government to the opposition, he has advised the officers of the chamber and the senate which had been dissolved by the decree of April 5, 1916, that his full duty of maintaining peace and order in Haiti rendered it necessary for him to uphold the decree of the constituted and recognized Government of Haiti."

The Haitian chambers protested against this intervention. On May 5, the senators were assembling in their provisional quarters when an American officer brutally ordered them to leave the place, threatening violent measures to force them to go. At the suggestion of M. Paul Laraque, president of the senate, they met at his house, where they drew up a formal account of the incident. (See Appendix No. 10.)

On the next day, May 6, the president of the senate and the president of the chamber were summoned by Col. Waller. He told them that if they persisted in assembling they would expose themselves to violent expulsion.

A few days before, on April 20, Le Constitutionnel, a paper edited by Deputy Léon Louhis, had been suppressed by Capt. Alexander Williams, provost marshal. The Government, supported by the American occupation, had the last word.

By a decree dated June 23, 1916, President Dartiguenave convoked the Chamber of Deputies as constituent assembly for August 14; but the deputies abstained and refused to accept an unconstitutional mandate.

Discontent was spreading among all classes in the nation, deprived as they were of their legal representatives.

On August 29, Col. Waller published the following declaration:

" Since the mission of occupation in Haiti is essentially a mission of pacification, work, and progress, it is recalled that no political agitation will be tolerated which tends to provoke manifestations against the express declaration of Admiral Caperton regarding the decree of April 5, 1916, and to compromise, contrary to the terms and spirit of the convention, the stability of the Government of President Dartiguenave, which is the free expression of the vote of the National Assembly."

As the authority of the Chamber of Deputies expired on January 10, 1917, there had to be new elections.

On September 22, 1916, the President of the Republic published a decree modifying the electoral law and certain articles of the constitution relative to the legislative power. He reduced the number of deputies to 36 and of senators to 15; he fixed the date of the elections for January 15 and 16, 1917; and this time he accepted the reunion of the two branches of the legislative body in the National Assembly for the revision of the constitution.

The elections took place on January 15, 1917. The new chambers assembled in April. On April 7, M. Louis Borno, secretary of state for foreign affairs, received a communication from Mr. Bailly-Blanchard, American minister. The latter informed him that after a careful examination of the project for the constitution the State Department had several suggestions which it considered obligatory and which could be submitted to the study and examination of M. Dartiguenave's Government before any definite action was taken in this respect by the legislative body. He stated at the same time that the suggestions mentioned would be sent by cable. On April 11, the American minister sent them to the secretary of state for foreign affairs. (See Appendix No. 11.)

On the 24th the secretary of state for the interior, in his turn, sent them to the committee for constitutional reform appointed by the new National Assembly to draw up a project for the constitution. The committee had just started its work and had not made any report. It was justly astonished at such suggestions, and on April 30 the secretary of state for the interior declared that the project for the constitution in question was a work of the council of state.

And the council of state, an unconstitutional body, had no authority to present a project for the constitution.

On June 8 the committee laid before the National Assembly the constitutional project which it had just drawn up and the discussion began. Since the first days of the meeting of the chambers rumors of dissolution had been circulating. No one wanted to believe them, especially since the elections had been supervised and controlled by American officers. Ten days after the elections, on January 25, an American squadron, commanded by Admiral Mayo, anchored in the Bay of Port au Prince. The next day, January 26, Admiral Mayo, in return for the dinner that was given in his honor, gave a luncheon to M. Sudre Dartiguenave on board the *Pennsylvania*, in the course of which the latter received from Admiral Caperton, commander of the Pacific division, a radiogram as follows:

"I congratulate you, you and the Republic of Haiti, upon the successful outcome of the recent elections, and wish the country continuous prosperity. With my best personal wishes for you and all my friends."

The same day, during a visit to the President of the Republic, Mr. Franklin D. Roosevelt, who was also on a cruise, made a speech in which he spoke of the interest of the United States for the sovereign people of Haiti.

Thus there was no reason to expect a new attempt against the legislative chambers. The Haitian Parliament wishes, it is true, to give the country a liberal constitution, and not an undemocratic work which would sanction the despotism of the Government and martial law.

Early on June 19 the legislative building was invaded by police under command of American officers. Without showing any agitation the deputies and senators took their seats and resumed the discussion of the project of the constitution. The vote was still being taken when M. André Chevallier, general secretary of the gendarmerie, came to tell the President of the National Assembly, M. Sténio Vincent, that the chief of the gendarmerie demanded to see him. Senator Vincent replied that since he was in session he regretted that he could not leave for the moment. M. Chevallier repeated the communication a second and a third time, and received the same reply. In the meantime, the gendarmerie closed the entrance of the legislative building, preventing both the public and the members of the National Assembly from going out. Seeing the impatience that was shown around him, M. Vincent made inquiries to determine the cause of this strange action. Just then Brig. Gen. Smedley D. Butler burst into the hall, followed by American officers armed with their revolvers, and handed M. Vincent a paper, declaring that it was the decree of the President of Haiti who proclaimed the dissolution of the legislative body. Senator Vincent refused to read it. He returned to his chair, and addressed the National Assembly, declaring that he would not read this act, which was brought, not by a regular agent of the executive power, but by the chief of the gendarmerie entirely outside of his powers. In the face of the resolute attitude of the deputies and senators, who refused to act upon such a document, the gendarmerie decided to open the gates of the legislative building. The same day the editors of all the newspapers were summoned to the gendarmerie where they received a written order to publish nothing whatever concerning the dissolution of the chambers.

The next day, Gen. Butler had the archives of the two chambers searched, and removed the reports on the constitution just voted.

On June 19, 1918, one year after the second dissolution of the Haitian Parliament, President Dartiguenave promulgated another constitution, voted by a so-called plebiscite. Those who presided over this plebiscite were American officers. They employed force and threats to make the citizens vote.

Read this announcement, published by the Courier Haitien of November 8, 1920:

REPUBLIC OF HAITI,
Port de Paix, June 11, 1918.

In accordance with the decree of his excellency, the President of the Republic, published in the Monitor of May 8, last, all the citizens of the commune of Port de Paix are asked to be present to-morrow at the Hotel Communal to vote on the new constitution published in the Monitor of the same date.

Any abstention from such a solemn occasion will be considered an unpatriotic act.

Maintenance of order will be assured by the gendarmerie, and the ballots will be distributed by a member of the administration of finances opposite the voting offices.

The polls will be open from 7 o'clock in the morning till 5 o'clock in the evening.

HERMAN H. HANNEKEN,
Lt. O. d'Haiti.

E. LESCOT,
Government Commissioner, Northwest District.

There was only one kind of ballot, bearing the word "Yes." For purposes of deception some ballots were distributed with the word "No," but they went to certain paid confederates, in order to give the impression that the number of opponents was insignificant. Spies kept watch over the ballot boxes. Certain officials who, be ng obliged to vote, had turned in a negative vote, were dismissed from office. (See Appendix No. 12.)

The plebiscite is not one of the Haitian constitutional traditions. The constitution of 1889 indicated the procedure to be followed in case of revision of the constitution. But the prescribed procedure was not carried out. What actually happened was that one so-called constitution was substituted for another, and, to give it some appearance of verity, the plebiscite vote was invented.

THE NAVAL COURT OF INQUIRY IN HAITI.

When Mr. Daniels, United States Secretary of the Navy, in order to calm the emotion aroused in America by the terrible revelations of the press regarding the acts of the American occupation in Haiti, announced that he had instituted a naval court of inqu'ry to throw light on this subject, the public might have believed that it was to be genuine, although, according to certain newspapers, it was to be merely a case of "whitewash." In fact, the high officials of the Navy Department who composed this court might well inspire confidence. They were Admiral Henry T. Mayo, Rear Admiral James H. Oliver, Maj. Gen. Wendell C. Neville, of the Marine Corps, and Maj. Jesse F. Dyer, as judge advocate. The Haitians were the first to believe that a work of truth and justice was at last going to be carried out.

Th's naval court of inquiry arr.ved at Port au Prince on November 8, 1920.

On the 9th it got in touch with the Haitian Government, and on the same day informed the Haitian public of the names of its members and of the nature of its mission.

"It had come," it said, "to investigate the way in which the forces of the occupation had carried out the'r duty, in order to furnish the Secretary of the Navy with complete information on this subject." The terms of this declaration seemed to imply a very broad mission, and the Haitians who were prepared to testify before the naval court of inquiry were anxious to know how it was going to proceed. But not a single rule was ever established for the inquiry and no form of procedure was indicated. The court never made known where it would hold its sessions, on what days they would take place, whether they would be public, whether the court itself would call in witnesses, whether the people who were acquainted with the whole thing or who were victims of acts at the hands of the forces of occupation could go and testify freely before the court, or what guarant'es of safety it offered to Haitian citizens who wished to prove charges of criminal acts against officers who still had military authority, knowing well the cruelty of martial law in the country for the past five years. (See Appendix No. 13.)

November 11, the second anniversary of the World War armistice, was a holiday, and when no newspapers appeared it was generally thought that an announcement from the court of inquiry would inform the public the next day how it was going to proceed.

On November 12, instead of the expected note, people were astonished to read in a Port au Prince paper, the Nouvelliste, of the testimony of President Dartiguenave before the court:

"From a visit by Mr. Wilbur Forrest, correspondent of the New York Tribune [says the Nouvelliste], we learn the news that the court of inquiry was to hold its first session on November 11, at 10 o'clock in the morning, at the Dessalines Barracks and that his excellency M. Sudre Dartiguenave was to testify."

No one knew anything about it. Now, it happened, according to the Nouvelliste, that after this testimony Maj. Dyer, judge advocate, announced "that there were no other witnesses for the present," and the session was adjourned. Did this mean witnesses summoned by the court, or else persons who had decided on their own initiative to go and testify? No one knew. In any case, how could anyone else have gone to witness on that day when it had not been announced anywhere that the court of inquiry would hold its first meeting at the Dessalines Barracks on November 11 at 10 o'clock in the morning, or that such persons could go to testify? But when the Nouvelliste asked the judge advocate for his opinion on this subject Maj. Jesse F. Dyer replied:

"So far I have no precise facts; everyone speaks of rumors, and I am looking for evidence. I am leaving for the northern towns, and hope to find this evidence; and if no one comes with statements here in Port au Prince in all probab'ity the other sessions of the court will not be held here, but at the Cape, where we shall go to hear the witnesses we can find in the interior towns."

So, after hearing but a single witness, Maj. Dyer already had concluded that there were no precise facts and merely rumors, and announced that he was leaving for the north of the island, where he hoped to find evidence.

Nevertheless, as soon as the Haitians learned that the court of inquiry was in session, and where it was being held, from all parts of the country the demand came to be heard.

From the following account of the work (?) of the court it will be seen that all Haitians who had anything to say regarding the numerous cases of murder, brutality, robbery, rape, arson, etc.—that is, Haitians who wished to convince the court of inquiry of "the way in which the forces of the occupation had carr ed out their duty in Haiti"—were systemat.cally excluded. Many of them have published in the press of Haiti the letters which they sent to the court demanding to be heard.

On November 17 the court heard Col. Hooker, of the Haitian gendarmerie, Mr. Harry Lifchitz, Mr. Daggett, Col. Little, Lieut. Lang, and a Haitian gendarme named Adolphe Burgot.

Col. Hooker spoke chiefly of the attack of Port au Prince by the "Cacos" on January 15, 1920, declaring that all the victims of this unlucky day—that is 66 Haitians—were assailants (?).

Mr. Harry Lifchitz accused Lieut. Haski Koff of having killed a gendarme at Cayes with a revolver, Lieut. Barrett of having killed a Haitian civilian at Aquin, and ended his testimony by exposing the case of a woman who was beaten to death at Saint-Louis-du-Sud.

Col. Little accused a naval pharmacist, Mr. Thompson, of having murdered a judge at Las Cahobas.

The other witnesses testified on the case of Lieut. Lang, accused of having killed three prisoners with his own hand at Hinche, making them go out of the prison one at a time, firing a revolver shot in the back of each one.

On November 18 there was another investigation of Lieut. Lang's case. The court heard Mr. Grant, gendarmes Adolphe Burgot and Meratus. The two latter confirmed the charges brought against Lieut. Lang.

On November 19 gendarmes Carmelus Monfiston, Petit Daubrave, Eugene Jean, and Carlus Absolu testified against Lieut. Lang regarding the affair of the murder of the prisoners at Hinche. Gendarme Petit Daubrave accused Lang of having killed, to his knowledge, five prisoners, detailing all the circumstances of these crimes. Mr. Daggett, who was hesitant during the first investigation, reappeared on the scene and stated that Lang had killed some prisoners. Théomène Rouchon, former gendarme at Milot, declared that Lang had killed the prisoner Teka with a machine gun under a mango tree.

On November 20 the court held a short session and heard the testimony of Gendarme Siméon Gabeau regarding the terrible circumstances of the assassination of the notary Jean Garnier, a peaceful citizen of Maissade, by Lieut. Williams.

Lang asked to present a memorandum on his case, which he obtained, and the court went into secret sessions.

On November 22 the court continued Lieut. Lang's case. Then it heard Col. Hooker, of the Haitian gendarmerie, who spoke in favor of Haski Koff, lieutenant at Cayes, and Dr. Louis Gille, who testified in his turn in favor of Barrett, lieutenant at Aquin.

In the sessions of November 29 and 31 the court devoted its time to new testimony regarding the murder of the notary Jean Garnier, of Maissade.

And this was all. This naval court, which had been talked of in the United States, probably at the suggestion of Mr. Daniels, as the greatest naval commission formed since the one charged with inquiring into the conditions of the naval battle of Santiago de Cuba, this naval court of inquiry in reality inquired only into the charges brought against Lieuts. Lang and Williams. Up till the last minute people thought it was going to Cap-Haiten and various other towns in the north of the island to continue the investigation, especially since Maj. Jesse F. Dyer had publicly declared so. Moreover, during the first two weeks of November Admiral Knapp had gone to Cap-Haitien and called the people to the Union Club, asking them to expose their grievances against the occupation without fear of reprisals. At this meeting the principal personages of the town of Cap-Haitien spoke: M. W. Leconte, former state secretary of the interior, spoke of the murderous régime in the prisons. M. Adhémar Auguste, former mayor of the town, pointed out that the horrible system of the corvée was the only cause of the uprising of the "Cacos." M. L. Duvivier told of the slaughter of Haitiens in the streets of Cap-Haitien during the night of Christmas, 1919. M. Charles Zamor exposed great wrongs done by certain officers of the gendarmerie, and M. Dacosta, a merchant, denounced the abuses at the Cap-Haitien customhouse. Other people tried to make their complaints heard. But Admiral Knapp announced that he himself had no authority to carry on the investigation; that he had merely come to prepare the way for the court of inquiry; and that all those who had complaints to make would soon have the opportunity of being heard before this court.

Judge Advocate Maj. Jesse F. Dyer and Admiral Knapp had, then, both announced, some days apart, the intention of the court of inquiry to go to Cap-Haitien to continue the investigation. And yet the court did not go. Why? Mr. Daniels and the members of the naval court of inquiry alone can explain this mystery.

Meanwhile, by November 26, the Haitian public found out, in an indirect way, that this investigation, announced with such flourish in the United States, was nothing more than a joke, unworthy of the American administration which had sent it, and unacceptable to the great American people who demanded truth and justice, and who, we are convinced, will want the truth to be known and justice to triumph at any price. In fact, in the course of interviews which took place between the editors of the Courier Haitien and the American correspondents at Port au Prince it was alleged by one of them that the powers of the naval court of inquiry were so limited that they did not, in reality, permit it to make any investigation. The Haitian people had no authoritative information on the subject.

Nevertheless, when, on November 30, in the evening, the *Niagara* left the waters of Port au Prince, bearing with it the naval court of inquiry, the news of its departure caused general surprise and profound indignation. To calm the Haitians they were given to understand, by notices adroitly slipped into the newspapers, that the *Niagara* was going to coal at Guantanamo and that from there the naval court of inquiry was going to Cap-Haitien.

On December 2 a group of Port au Prince citizens, feeling that the comedy had gone too far and that it was unworthy to play with a whole people in this way, sent a cablegram to the Secretary of the Navy informing him that the naval court of inquiry had left without having fulfilled its duty, that a number of complainants had not been heard, etc. Mr. Daniels hastened to reply, by the following communication, published in the Courier Haitien:

Citizens of Port au Prince:[*]

Referring to your communication relative to the naval court, I have directed Vice Admiral Knapp to carry on any investigation considered necessary concerning the United States marines; and all the cases that you may wish to have submitted to him.

SECRETARY OF THE NAVY.

WASHINGTON, *December 2, 1920.*

Vain hopes! Admiral Knapp did even much less than the naval court of inquiry, in that he did nothing, absolutely nothing at all; he never informed the Haitian people of the new mission which had been confided to him, he never heard a single witness, and he continued to enjoy his winter quarters in peace in the harbor of Port au Prince.

The behavior of the naval court of inquiry in Haiti which we have just set forth was even more surprising because the mandate of this court had been established by Mr. Josephus Daniels, Secretary of the Navy, as follows:

[Precept of the court of inquiry.]

" DEPARTMENT OF THE NAVY,
" *Washington, October 16, 1920.*

"To: Rear Admiral Henry T. Mayo, United States Navy.
"Subject: Court of inquiry to inquire into the alleged indiscriminate killing of Haitians and unjustifiable acts by members of the United States naval service, including those detailed to duty with the gendarmerie d'Haiti against the persons and property of Haitians since the American occupation, July 28, 1915.

"1. A court of inquiry, consisting of yourself as president, and of Rear Admiral James H. Oliver, United States Navy, and Maj. Gen. W. C. Neville,

[*] Message retranslated from the French.

United States Marine Corps, as additional members, and of Maj. Jesse F. Dyer, United States Marine Corps, as judge advocate, is hereby ordered to convene at the Navy Department, Washington, D. C., Friday, October 22, 1920, or as soon thereafter as practicable, and thereafter at such places as may be deemed necessary to inquire into the question of the conduct of the personnel of the United States Naval Service in Haiti since the marines were landed in that country on July 28, 1915, with the view to determining whether any unjustifiable homicide has been committed by any of such personnel, whether any other unjustifiable acts of oppression or violence have been perpetrated against any of the citizens of Haiti or any unjustifiable damage or destruction of their property has occurred." [25]

According to the mandate of the naval court of inquiry, it was to make a report on its findings and the degree of responsibility attached to each act, and on all persons immediately or indirectly responsible for such unjustifiable acts.

And no report of this court has been published. The "Annual Report of the Secretary of the Navy for 1920" contains all the reports on Haitian affairs except the report of the naval court of inquiry. Would it not be a good idea to publish this report in the interest of truth and justice?

The naval court of inquiry did not reply to the letters, often confirmed by follow-up letters, which were addressed to it by those who wanted to be heard. Certain complainants were obliged to resort to the press to make known the wrongs of which they or their relatives were victims.

The Haitian people feel that if the naval court of inquiry has not fulfilled in Haiti the broad mandate conferred upon it by Mr. Josephus Daniels, it is because it was faced with charges of such a horrible nature that it thought best to pass them over in silence. And this is why the tactics of the Navy Department have been and still are to consider the "incident" as closed. This can not be. The voice of truth and justice can not be stilled. The Haitian people await with confidence an honest, impartial, and thorough investigation.

In Haiti numberless abominable crimes have been committed. To give some idea of their horror we cite only a few cases made public through the press which the naval court did not feel the need to investigate.

1. Hanging of M. Cicéron Lacroix, execution of Léon Moricet, Téca, and other persons in October and November, 1918, by Lieut. Lang, acts denounced to the naval court of inquiry by M. Philocles Lacroix in his letter of October 20, 1920.

2. Execution of the Péralte brothers by Lieut. Wallace at Mirebalais in December, 1918. Here are the names of those shot: Philoxène Péralte, Emmanuel Péralte, Péralte, jr., and Léosthène Péralte.

3. Execution by the marines of Joseph Marseille and his two sons, Michel and Estima Marseille, of Princivil Mesadieux, Baye section, district of Mirebalais; assassination by the marines of Guerrier Josaphat and one of his children, aged 14, in his own house, acts denounced by M. Louis Charles, sr., December 8, 1920.

4. Arrest by an American officer, and mysterious disappearance of M. Charrite Fleuristone, former school inspector at Chappelle district of St. Marc. He was arrested in the first part of 1919, at the same time as MM. Jean Baptiste and Clément Clerjeune.

5. At Marin, district of Mirebalais, in December, 1919, assassination and mutilation of Joseph Duclerc, a respectable old man of 60, by marines and gendarmes. After the crime they burned his cottage.

6. At the same time and in the same section the same group fired on a school-teacher and wounded her in the mouth. She managed to escape. The marines and gendarmes burned her house as well as everything that went with it. They were accompanied by an American officer, a lieutenant, whose name can be established by an investigation.

7. Near Marin, at Collier, district of Mirebalais, the same band cut the head off a blind man named Néis 25 years old, and did the same thing to a child who was with him, named Jules Louisville.

8. At Marin, at the same time, another group of gendarmes and marines assaulted Mathieu Cadet, aged 35, in his house, shooting him. Although wounded in the shoulder, he was able to escape his assailants through a concealed door. His house was robbed and burned. The gendarme Joanis took off a mule belonging to Mathieu.

9. In January, 1919, at Noailles some marines and gendarmes coming from Beaurepos killed Jean Luc, an invalid. Torn from his house, firearms were emptied into his body. His house was robbed and burned.

10. On the same day the same band of marines and gendarmes surprised Esca Estinfil in his house at Caye-Beau with his young sons. They shot all three, father and children. Then they robbed his house and burned it. Esca was a great planter, and had a large quantity of coffee stored, and a good sum of money ready for commercial transactions.

11. On January 25, 1919, at "Savane Longue," near Marin, a group of marines and gendarmes coming from Terre-Rouge, district of Mirebalais, killed Hon. Auré Bayard, who was ill in bed. They pulled him from his bed, and shot him through and through. The house was robbed and burned. Then they forced Mme. Auré Bayard, by striking her with the butt ends of their rifles, to take the things that they had just stolen and carry them along with them. It was not until the next day that the poor woman could render her last services to her husband.

12. On January 30 some marines and gendarmes, led by spies named Néis (des Orangers) and Auré Fleury (du Carrefour grand-mât), killed a pregnant woman in a place called Thomaus. The cottage was robbed.

13. In December, 1919, some marines and gendarmes coming from Saut d'Eau or Mirebalais arrived at the second section of the Crochus, district of Mirebalais, and shot, at Beauvoir, Saint-Félix Geffard, who lived with his two little daughters aged 8 and 12 years. The terrified children managed to escape the shots of the assassins.

14. On the same day, at Beuuvoir, the same band robbed the cottage of Tinhomme Saint-Félix, then shot him and burned his corpse.

15. On the same day, at Beauvoir, the same band killed a respectable old man named Saintime Vernet. His cottage was robbed. Then the band burned the little village of Beauvoir.

16. No attention was paid to a denunciation by M. Paul Bayard, sent to the naval court of inquiry in a letter dated November 26, relative to the crimes enumerated below, committed by the Haitian sergeant of the gendarmerie, Maurice Lafontant, by the American captains, O'Neil and Verdier, and by the American lieutenant, Rogers, at Montagne, Goanau and Serin neighborhood, district of Jacmel (a section where there have never been any of the so-called "Cacos") : (1) Thirty-eight houses burned ; (2) assassination of Michael Jean François, age 74 years—his house was burned ; (3) Paul Bayrd, wounded by two bullets, one in his thigh and the other in his abdomen—his house was burned ; (4) assassination of Enélien Ladouceur ; (5) Francisque Gabriel, wounded by one bullet in the thigh.

17. Bodily tortures were inflicted by the American captain of gendarmerie, Fitzgerald Brown, upon M. Polydor St. Pierre, clerk of the St. Marc police court, in the prison of that town. He was arrested on January 3, 1919, on a false charge of theft, and was imprisoned for six months. Brown administered the "water cure" to him and burned his body with a red-hot iron ; to say nothing of the beatings and other tortures which he inflicted upon him. St. Pierre vainly begged a hearing from the naval court of inquiry.

18. Executions by night at St. Marc during the first months of 1919 in the localities known as "Grosses Roches" and "Gros-Morne" by Capt. Fitzgerald Brown.

19. Hanging of Fabre Yoyo from a mango tree on March 13, 1919, at Pivert, on property belonging to the Orius Paultre family of St. Marc ; execution on this same property this same day of two young boys of 14 and 15 years, Nicolas Yoyo and Salnave Charlot, by Capt. Fitzgerald Brown.

20. Among the crimes perpetrated in the region of Hinche, Maissade, from 1916 to 1919, by Lieuts. Lang and Williams, acts little known, and denounced by M. Méresse Wooley, former mayor of Hinche, on December 10, 1920, in the Courier Haitien, are the following: (1) M. Onexil hanged and burned alive in his house at Lauhaudiagne ; (2) execution of Madame Eucharice Cadichon at Mamon ; (3) execution of Madame Romain Brigade at l'Herr'itte, near Maissade ; (4) execution of Madame Prevoit with a baby of a few months at "Savane-à-Lingue" on her own property.

21. Madame Garnier, widow of the notary who was killed by Lieut. W' 'ms at Maissade, told Judge Advocate Dyer privately, on November 27, 1 m a of the shooting of Madame Lumenesse, mother of eight children, by Lieutation il-'ring

liams of the Haitian gendarmerie. Madame Garnier's declaration was published in the Courier Haitien of December 18, 1920.

22. Execution of Gen. Saül Péralte, near the Canary, by Gendarme Lamartine Toussaint, assisted by the American Lieut. Vernon, and ordered by the American Capt. Verdier, published in the Courier Haitien.

23. Arrest of Cadéus Bellegarde and cruelty inflicted upon him by the American Lieut. Dukela on December 2, 1919, at Saut-d'Eau, district of Mirebalais. According to a complaint made before a Haitian court, on December 8, 1920, and published in the Courier Haitien of February 9, 1921, Cadéus Bellegarde accused Lieut. Dukela of having burned 10 of his houses and stolen all of his property, including 12 horses, 3 mules, 70 oxen, etc.

24. In a letter published February 22, 1921, in the Courier Haitien, dated at Belladere, January 31, 1921, M. Casimir, jr., gives the following list of Haitians executed at Belladere by certain officers and soldiers of the Marine Corps: Gabriel Morette, Saint-For Jean-Baptiste, Frésirus Dufresin, Elie Ladomate, Bristoul Michel, Achille Vincent, Lorme Lorendou, Petika Casian, Normelus Saint-Charles, Adou Domingue, Aritus Domingue, Erisma Barau, Ehelusma Barau, Ocean Noisette, Surprilus Vilette, Saint-Pierre Infine, Monexa Chitry, Salomon Suprien, Fleury Pierre, a small daughter of M. Raymond Dominique, Lami Pinal, Lhérisson Pinal, Marcelus Joseph and his son, Georges Ledou, Francisque Contrairie, Princy Lachapelle, Céus Grandin, Jocelin, jr., Saint-Uma Pierre, Elie Morette, Stiven Calixte, Barjon Charles, Dumorne Vincent, jr., Juste Glodin, Donil Cyriaque. M. Casimir, jr., gave also the names of 48 proprietors whose houses and fields had been burned by certain officers and soldiers of the Marine Corps in the commune of Belladere.

25. In a petition addressed on December 16, 1920, to M. Barnave Dartiguenave, state secretary of the interior for Haiti, by the members of the League for the Public Good, at Cap-Haitien, whose president is Pastor Auguste Albert of the Baptist Church, which petition was published in the Courier Haitien on February 26, 1921, we notice the following facts:

(a) In the prisons of Cap-Haitien, during the years 1918, 1919, and 1920, more than 4,000 prisoners died.

(b) At Chabert, an American camp, 5,475 prisoners died during these three years, the average being five deaths a day.

(c) At Cap-Haitien, in 1919, eight corpses of prisoners a day were thrown into the pits.

(d) The mortality rate is just as high in the prisons of Port-au-Prince and Gonaives.

(e) At Cap-Haitien, out of 500 prisoners, the average mortality is four a day, i. e., 24 per cent per month, or only 1 per cent less a quarter of this whole number.

(f) Before American occupation and the seizure of the prisons by the American officers the number of prisoners in the Cap-Haitien prison did not exceed, on an average, 40 a year.

(g) At this time the mortality rarely reached the number of four prisoners a year.

The ghastly mortality in the prisons together with confirmation by survivors reveals a record of atrocities, of brutality, and cruelty which defies description. It is a record for which it would be difficult to find a parallel.

CONCLUSION.

The Haitian Republic was the second nation of the New World—second only to the United States—to conquer its national independence. We have our own history, our own traditions, customs, and national spirit, our own institutions, laws, and social and political organization, our own culture, our own literature (French language), and our own religion. For 111 years the little Haitian nation has managed its own affairs; for 111 years it has made the necessary effort for its material, intellectual, and moral development as well as any other nation—better than any other nation, because it has been from the start absolutely alone in its difficult task, without any aid from the outside, bearing with it along the harsh road of civilization the glorious misery of its beginning. And when, one fine day, under the merest pretext, without any possible explanation or justification on the grounds of violation of any American right or interest, American forces landed on our national territory and actually : bo *sh* the vereignty and independence of the Haitian Republic.

We have just given an account of the chief aspects of the American military occupation in our country since July 28, 1915.

It is the most terrible régime of military autocracy which has ever been carried on in the name of the great American democracy.

The Haitian people, during these past five years, has passed through such sacrifices, tortures, destructions, humiliations, and misery as have never before been known in the course of its unhappy history.

The American Government, in spite of the attitude of wisdom, moderation, and even submission which it has always found in dealing with the Haitian Government, has never lived up to any of the agreements which it had solemnly entered into with regard to the Haitian people.

The Haitian people is entitled to reparations for the wrongs and injuries committed against it.

The great American people can only honor themselves and rise in universal esteem by hastening the restoration of justice—of all the justice due a weak and friendly nation which the agents of its Government have systematically abused.

Reparations are due for the human lives that have been taken and for the property that has been destroyed or abstracted. An impartial investigation will provide the necessary statements and supply the basis for the estimates to be determined.

The present political aspirations of the Haitian nation have been formulated by the Union Patriotique, a comprehensive national association which, through its numerous branches throughout the country and in all levels of society, includes virtually all the Haitian people. The undersigned have been sent to the United States by this association to make the will of the country clearly known.

The Haitian people are filled with peaceful sentiments, but there is no doubt that they intend to recover definitely the administration of their own affairs and to resume under their own responsibility the entire life of the country, with full sovereignty and independence. They will never rest until they have obtained them.

The salient aspirations of the Haitian people are summarized as follows:

1. Immediate abolition of martial law and courts-martial.

2. Immediate reorganization of the Haitian police and military forces, and withdrawal within a short period of the United States military occupation.

3. Abrogation of the convention of 1915.

4. Convocation within a short period of a constituent assembly, with all the guaranties of electoral liberty.

But the Haitian people desire too strongly the friendship of the great American people, and are too anxious for their own material, intellectual, and moral development not to wish and bespeak for themselves the impartial and altruistic aid of the United States Government. They have urgent needs, vital to the development of the natural resources of the country and essential to the full expansion of its agricultural, industrial, and commercial activity. The satisfying of these needs is absolutely necessary for the continued progress of the Haitian community.

Nothing would serve better to bring about the speedy reestablishment of normal relations between the two countries than the friendly aid of the United States Government in the economic prosperity and social progress of the Haitian Republic.

H. PAULÉUS SANNON.
STÉNIO VINCENT.
PERCEVAL THOBY.

———

[Outline of a draft of a convention between the United States and the Republic of Haiti.]

APPENDIX No. 1.

LEGATION OF THE UNITED STATES OF AMERICA,
Port au Prince, Haiti, December 10, 1914.

PREAMBLE.

The United States and the Republic of Haiti, desiring to confirm and strengthen the amity existing between them by the most cordial cooperation in making for their common advantage, and the Republic of Haiti desiring to remedy the present unsatisfactory condition of its revenues and finances, to check the loss of much of its revenues due in part to internal disturbances, to provide against injudicious increase of its public debt, to inaugurate a comprehensive system of public accounts and audits, to make adequate provision to meet its exterior debts, to maintain the tranquillity of the Republic, to carry out plans for the economic development and prosperity of the Republic and its people, to strengthen its credit, and generally to fix and maintain its finances upon a firm and stable basis, and the United States being in full sympathy with all of these aims and objects and desiring to contribute in all proper ways to their accomplishment:

The United States and the Republic of Haiti, having resolved to conclude a convention with these objects in view, have appointed for that purpose plenipotentiaries, on the part of the United States and on the part of the Republic of Haiti, who having exhibited to each other their respective powers which are seen to be full in good and true form, have agreed as follows:

1. The President of the United States shall appoint a general receiver, who, with such assistants and employees as the President of the United States may appoint or authorize, shall collect, receive, and apply all customs duties on imports and exports accruing at the several customhouses and ports of entry of the Republic of Haiti; and if he shall deem it necessary and expedient, or if the Haitian Government shall request, the President of the United States shall designate a financial adviser to the Republic of Haiti, who shall devise an adequate system of public accounting, aid in increasnig the revenues and adjusting them to the expenses, inquire into the validity of the debts of the Republic, enlighten both Governments with reference to all eventual debts, recommend improved methods of collecting and applying the revenues, and generally exercise the functions of a comptroller of accounts.

2. The Government of the Republic of Haiti will provide by law or appropriate decrees for the payment of all customs duties to the general receiver, and will extend to the receivership all needful aid and full protecton in its execution of the powers conferred and duties imposed herein; and the United States on its part will extend like aid and protection.

3. Upon the appointment of the general receiver, the Government of the Republic of Haiti in cooperation with the general receiver shall collect, classify, arrange, and make full statement of all the debts of the Republic, the amounts, character, maturity, and condition thereof, the interest accruing, and the sinking fund requisite to their final discharge.

4. All sums collected and received by the general receiver shall be applied by him first, to the payment of the salaries and allowances of the general receiver, his assistants and employees, and expenses of the receivership, including the salary and expenses of the financial adviser, if one shall be appointed; second, to the interest and sinking fund of the public debt of the Republic of Haiti; and, third, the remainder to the Haitian Government for purposes of current expenses.

In making these applications the general receiver will proceed to pay salaries and allowances monthly and expenses as they arise, and on the first of each calendar month will set aside in a separate fund the quantum of the collections and receipts of the previous month found to be a fair contribution to the ultimate sum required to meet interest and provide the sinking funds.

5. The expenses of the receivership, including salaries and allowances of the general receiver, his assistants and employees, shall not exceed five per cent of the collections and receipts from custom duties, unless by agreement of the two Governments.

6. The general receiver shall make monthly reports of all collections, receipts, and disbursements to the appropriate officer of the Republic of Haiti and to the Department of State of the United States, which reports shall be open to inspection and verification at all times by the appropriate authorities of each of the said Governments.

7. The Republic of Haiti shall not increase its public debt except by previous agreement with the President of the United States and shall not contract any debt or assume any financial obligation unless the ordinary revenues of the Republic available for that purpose after defraying the expenses of the Government shall be adequate to pay the interest and provide a sinking fund for the final discharge of such debt.

8. The Republic of Haiti will not, without the assent of the President of the United States, modify the customs duties in a manner to reduce the revenues therefrom; and in order that the revenues of the Republic may be adequate to

meet the public debt and the expenses of the Government, to preserve tranquillity, and to promote material prosperity, the Republic of Haiti will cooperate with the financial adviser, if one is appointed, in his recommendations for improvement in the methods of collecting and disbursing the revenues and for new sources of needed income.

9. The United States shall have authority to prevent any and all interferences with the receipt, collection, or free course of the customs, or, with the free exercise of any of the powers conferred or duties imposed herein upon the receivership or with the attainment of any of the objects comprehended in this convention.

10. This agreement shall continue in force for a period of ———— years from and after its ratification by the contracting parties in accordance with their respective laws.

APPENDIX NO. 2.

Whereas the President of the United States of America and the President of the Republic of Haiti are animated by the desire to strengthen the bonds of friendship between the two countries; and

Whereas the high contracting parties realize the mutual advantages which would lie in more intimate commercial and financial relations; and

Whereas the President of the Republic of Haiti has expressed his sincere desire and firm intention to guarantee the honest and efficient administration of a government in Haiti according to the constitution and laws of that Republic, government which will give expression to the will of the people of Haiti, protect their rights and interests, and respect international obligations; and

Whereas it is the mutual desire of the high contracting parties that there shall exist between the American minister plenipotentiary—hereafter to be appointed—and the President of Haiti such an intimate and confidential relationship as will enable the American minister plenipotentiary to advise as to such matters as affect the honest and efficient administration of the Government, the President of Haiti agreeing that he will follow the advice so given to the extent of requiring honesty and efficiency in officials and of removing those found to be dishonest and inefficient;

The President of the United States of America and the President of the Republic of Haiti have resolved to enter into a convention for that purpose and have appointed their respective plenipotentiaries, to wit:

The President of the United States of America, the Hon. Paul Fuller, jr., United States commissioner with the rank of envoy extraordinary and minister plenipotentiary;

The President of the Republic of Haiti, the Hon. Ulrick Duvivier, secretary of state for foreign relations;

Who, after exchange of their full powers, found to be in good and due form, have, in consideration of and in compensation for the respective concession and engagements made by each to the other as herein recited, agreed, and do hereby agree, as follows, to wit:

1. The Government of the United States of America will protect the Republic of Haiti from outside attack and from the aggression of any foreign power, and to that end will employ such forces of the Army and Navy of the United States as may be necessary.

2. The Government of the United States of America will aid the Government of Haiti to suppress insurrection from within and will give effective support by the employment of the armed forces of the United States Army and Navy to the extent needed.

3. The President of the Republic of Haiti covenants that no rights, privileges, or facilities of any description whatsoever will be granted, sold, leased, or otherwise accorded directly or indirectly by the Government of Haiti concerning the occupation or use of the Mole Saint-Nicholas to any foreign Government or to a national or the nationals of any other foreign Government.

4. The President of the Republic of Haiti covenants that within six months from the signing of this convention the Government will enter into an arbitration agreement for the settlement of such claims as American citizens or other foreigners may have against the Government of Haiti, such arbitration agreement to provide for the equal treatment of all foreigners to the end that the

people of Haiti may have the benefit of competition between the nat'onals of all countries.

The present convention shall be ratified by the appropriate authorities of the respective countries, and the ratification shall be exchanged at Port au Prince, Haiti, as soon as may be after the —— day of ——, 1915.

In witness whereof we, the respective plenipotentiaries, have signed the same in duplicate in English and in French and have affixed our respective seals at Port au Princ, Haiti, this —— day of May, in the year 1915.

[To the convention project presented by Mr. Fuller.]

APPENDIX No. 3.

COUNTERPROJECT.

The President of the United States of America and the President of the Republic of Haiti desiring to strengthen the bonds of friendship which exist between the two countries;

The high contracting parties being convinced of the advantages they would obtain through closer commercial and financial relations, considering that the introduction of capital into Haiti would be sufficiently profitable, and that it would be assured of all the necessary guaranties, and is recognized as indispensable to the economic development of Haiti;

The President of the Republic of Haiti, constitutionally elected, who has shown by the acts already accomplished by his Government his sincere desire to assure the country through complete and faithful execution of the laws of a wise, regular, and honorable administration, capable of assuring as much protection as possible to legitimate interests, both national and foreign;

The President of the United States of America, with views in harmony with those of the Government of the Haitian Republic, and disposed to lend it all the assistance and aid necessary to the conservation of its independence, and to permit its free development;

The President of the United States of America and the President of the Republic of Haiti have resolved to conclude with these aims a convention, and have named for their respective plenipotentiaries:

The President of the United States of America, the Hon. Paul Fuller, special envoy of the United States, ranking as envoy extraordinary and minister plenipotentiary;

The President of the Republic of Haiti, Hon. Ulrick Duvivier, state secretary of foreign affairs;

Who, after exchange of their full respective powers, found in good and due form, have accepted and hereby accept what follows:

1. The Government of the United States of America agrees to lend its aid to the Republic of Haiti for the conservation of its independence.

With this object it binds itself to intervene to prevent any intrusion of any foreign power in the affairs of Haiti and to repulse any act of aggression attempted against this country.

It shall employ for this purpose such forces of the Army and Navy of the United States as are necessary.

' 2. The Government of the United States shall facilitate the entrance into Haiti of sufficient capital to assure the full economic development of this country, to improve within a very short period its financial situation, especially to bring about the unification of its debt in such a way as to reduce the customs guaranties which are affected by it at present, and to carry out an effective monetary reform.

In order to grant to capital all desirable guaranties, the Government of Haiti agrees to employ in the customhouses, as well as in collectors' offices and others, only Haitian officials whose morality and capability are well known.

The lenders may be consulted regarding the choice of the higher customs officials.

The Haitian Government shall also assure protection to capital and to all foreign interests in general by the organization of a rural horse guard, instructed according to the most modern methods.

Meanwhile it may, if necessary, resort to the aid of the American Government in order to check disorders and serious troubles which might compromise foreign interests.

The American forces which would, if the case should come up, cooperate with Haitian troops for the reestablishment of order, must be withdrawn from Haitian territory at the first demand of the constitutional authorities.

3. The President of the Republic of Haiti agrees not to grant any rights, privileges, or facilities whatsoever on the St. Nicholas mole, nor to concede, sell, rent, or otherwise permit, directly or indirectly, the occupation or use of the St. Nicholas mole to any Government, to any national or nationals of any Government.

4. The President of the Republic of Haiti agrees, within six months of the ratification of the present convention, to sign a convention of arbitration with the powers concerned for the settlement of pending diplomatic claims, which convention of arbitration shall recognize equal treatment to all claimants; that is to say, that no privilege for the profit of any of them shall be recognized.

The present convention shall be ratified by the competent authorities in the two countries, and the exchange of ratifications shall be made at Port-au-Prince as soon as possible after the ———. Presented on June 2, 1915.

———

[Texte Proposé par la Légation des Etats-Unis d'Amérique Aout 1915.]

APPENDIX No. 4.[37]

MEMORANDUM.

Eu vue de l'attitude amicale montrée par le Gouvernement haïtien, le Chargé d'Affaires par interim des Etats-Unis a reçu instruction de rédiger et de soumettre officieusement au Président de la République d'Haïti, sans délai, le projet de traité ci-joint de l'informer que le Département d'Etat à Washington croit que l'Assemblée Nationale haïtienne, garante de la sincérité et de l'intérêt des haïtiens, voudra voter immédiatement une résolution autorisant le Président d'Haïti à accepter *sans modification*, le traité suivant:

[Projet de Convention entre les Etats-Unis et la République d'Haïti.]

PREAMBLE.

Les Etats-Unis et la République d'Haïti, désireux d'affermir et de fortifier l'amitié existant entre eux par une plus cordiale coopération à des mesures pour leur avantage commun, et la République d'Haïti désirant rémédier à la situation de ses finances qui n'est pas satisfaisante, empêcher la perte de beaucoup de ses revenus, due en partie aux troubles intérieurs, prendre des dispositions contre l'augmentation peu judicieuse de sa dette publique, inaugurer un système compréhensible pour l'examen et la tenue de la comptabilité publique, faire provision suffisante pour le service de ses dettes extérieures, maintenir la tranquillité de la République, exécuter des projets pour le développement économique et la prospérité de la République et du peuple haïtiens, consolider son crédit et en général asseoir et maintenir ses finances sur une base solide et stable, les Etats-Unis sympath'sant entièrement avec toutes ces vues et ces objets, et désireux de contr.buer à leur réalisation par tous les moyens convenables;

Les Etats-Unis et la Républ'que d'Haïti, ayant résolu de conclure une convention ayant ces objets en vue, ont nommé à cet effet comme Plénipotentiares, les Etats-Unis, Mr. ———, et Haïti ———, Mr. ———, lesquels s'étant mutuellement communiqué leurs pleins pouvoirs respectifs trouvés en bonne et due forme, ont convenu ce qui suit:

1. Le Président des Etats-Unis nommera un receveur général, qui, avec tels aides et employés que le Président des Etats-Unis pourra nommer ou autoriser, recouvrera, recevra et appliquera tous les droits de douane tant à l'importation qu'à l'exportation provenant des diverses douanes et ports d'entrée de la République d'Haïti. Le Président des Etats-Unis désignera à la République d'Haïti un conseiller financier qui élaborera un système adéquat de comptabilité publique, a'dera à l'augmentation des revenus et à leur ajustement aux dépenses, enquêtera sur la validité des dettes de la République, éclairera les deux Gouvernements relativement à toutes dettes éventuelles, recommandera

———

[37] This is a translation into French, published at Port au Prince of the original Englis' text, which is not now available.

des méthodes perfectionnées d'encaisser et d'appliquer les revenus, et en général exercera les fonctions d'un contrôleur.

2. Le Gouvernement de la République d'Haïti pourvoiera par une loi ou par un décret approprié, à ce que le paiement de tous les droits de douane soit fait au receveur général, et il accordera au bureau de la recette et au conseiller financier toute l'aide et la protection nécessaires à l'exécution des pouvoirs qui lui sont conférés et à l'accomplissement des devoirs qui lui sont imposés par les présents; les Etats-Unis, de leur côté, accorderont la même aide et la même protection.

3. A la nomination du conseiller financier, le Gouvernement de la République d'Haïti, avec la coopération du conseiller financier, collationnera, classera, arrangera et fera un relevé complet de toutes les dettes de la République, de leur montant, caractère, échéance et condition, intérêts y afférents, et amortissement nécessaire à leur complet paiement.

4. Toutes les valeurs recouvrées et encaissées par le receveur général seront appliquées: premièrement au paiement des appointements et allocations du receveur général, de ses auxiliaires et employés, et les dépenses du bureau de la recette comprendront les appointements et les dépenses du conseiller financier; deuxièmement, à l'intérêt et à l'amortissement de la dette publique de la République d'Haïti; troisièmement à l'entretien de la police visée à l'article huit et alors le reste, au Gouvernement haïtien pour les dépenses courantes.

En faisant ces applications, le receveur général procédera au paiement des appointements et allocations mensuelles et des dépenses telles qu'elles se présentent, et au premier de chaque mois, il mettra à un compte spécial le montant des recouvrements et recettes du mois précédent.

5. Les dépenses du bureau de la recette, y compris les appointements et allocations du receveur général, de ses auxiliaires et employés, ne devront pas dépasser cinq pour cent des recouvrements et recettes provenant des droits de douane, à moins d'une convention entre les deux Gouvernements.

6. Le receveur général fera un rapport mensuel au fonctionnaire haïtien comobligation financière à moins que, les dépenses du Gouvernement défrayées, les recettes et les dépenses; ces rapports seront soumis à l'inspection et à la vérification des autorités compétentes de chacun des dits Gouvernements.

La République d'Haïti ne devra pas augmenter sa dette ni assumer aucune obligation financière à moins que, les dépenses du Gouvernement défrayées, les revenus de la République disponibles à cette fin, soient suffisants pour payer les intérêts et pourvoir à un amortissement pour l'extinction complète d'une telle dette.

7. La République d'Haïti, sans l'assentiment du Président des Etats-Unis, ne modifiera pas les droits de douane d'une façon qui en réduise les revenus, et afin que les revenus de la République soient suffisants pour faire face à la dette publique et aux dépenses du Gouvernement, pour préserver la tranquillité et promouvoir la prospérité matérielle, la République d'Haïti coopérera avec le conseiller financier suivant ses recommandations relatives à l'amélioration des méthodes de recouvrer, de dépenser les revenus, et à la création des sources nouvelles de revenus qui feront besoin.

8. Le Gouvernement haïtien, en vue de la préservation de la paix intérieure, de la sécurité des droits individuels et de la complète observance des dispositions de ce traité, s'engage à créer sans délai une police efficace, composée d'haïtiens. Cette police sera organisée par des américains qui en seront les officiers, désignés par le Gouvernement des Etats-Unis et que le Gouvernement haïtien nommera et revêtira de l'autorité voulue et nécessaire, et soutiendra dans l'exercice de leurs fonctions. La police ici prévue aura, sous la direction du Gouvernement haïtien, la surveillance et le contrôle des armes et munitions, des articles militaires et du commerce qui s'en fait dans tout le pays. Les stipulations de cet article sont nécessaires pour prévenir les luttes des factions et les désordres.

9. Le Gouvernement d'Haïti convient de ne céder aucune partie du territoire de la République d'Haïti par vente, bail ou autrement, ni conférer juridiction sur tel territoire à aucune Puissance ou Gouvernement étrangers, excepté aux Etats-Unis, ni signer avec aucune autre puissance, ni autres puissances, aucun traité ni contrat qui diminuera ou tendra à diminuer l'indépendance d'Haïti.

10. Le Gouvernement haïtien convient de signer avec les Etats-Unis un protocole pour le règlement, par arbitrage ou autrement, de toutes les réclamations pécuniaires pendantes entre les corporations, compagnies, citoyens ou sujets étrangers et Haïti.

11. La République d'Haïti désirant activer le développement de ses ressources naturelles, convient d'entreprendre et d'exécuter telles mesures qui, dans

l'opinion du Gouvernement des Etats-Unis, peuvent être nécessaires au point de vue de l'hygiène et de l'avancement de la République d'Haïti, sous la surveillance et la direction d'un ou plusieurs ingénieurs qui seront désignés par le Président des Etats-Unis, nommés et autorisés à cette fin par le Gouvernement d'Haïti.

12. Les Etats-Unis auront autorité pour empêcher toute ingérence dans l'accomplissement d'un point (object) quelconque compris dans cette convention; ils auront aussi bien le droit d'intervenir pour la préservation de l'indépendance haïtienne et pour le maintien d'un Gouvernement capable de protéger la vie, la propriété et la liberté individuelle.

13. Le présent traité sera approuvé et ratifié par les hautes parties contractantes conformément à leurs lois respectives, et la ratification sera échangée dans la ville de Washington aussitôt que possible.

14. Le présent traité restera en force et vigueur pendant une durée de dix années à partir du jour de l'échange des ratifications, et en outre pour une autre période de dix années à la demande d'une des parties.

En foi dequoi les Plénipotentiaires ont signé la présente convention en double et y ont apposé leurs sceaux.

APPENDIX No. 5.

PROCLAMATION.

To the people of Port au Prince, Haiti:

Information having been received from the most reliable sources that the present Government of Haiti is confronted with the conditions which they are unable to control, although loyally attempting to discharge the duties of their respective offices; and these facts having created a condition which requires the adoption of different measures than those heretofore applied; and in order to afford the inhabitants of Port au Prince and other territory hereinafter described, the privileges of the Government, exercising all the functions necessary for the establishment and maintenance of the fundamental rights of man: I hereby, under my authority as commanding officer of the forces of the United States of America in Haiti and Haitien waters, proclaim that marshal law exists in the city of Port au Prince and the immediate territory now occupied by the forces under my command.

I further proclaim in accordance with the law of nations and the usages, customs, and functions of my own and other Governments, that I am invested with the power and responsibilty of government in all its functions and branches throughout the territory above described and the proper administration of such Government my martial law will be provided for in regulations to be issued from time to time, as required, by the commanding officer of the forces of the United States of America in Haiti and Haitien waters.

The martial law herein proclaimed, and the things in that respect so ordered, will not be deemed or taken to interfere with the proceedings of the constitutional Government and Congress of Haiti, or with the administration of justice in the courts of law existing therein: which do not affect the military operations or the authorities of the Government of the United States of America.

All the municipal and other civil employees are, therefore, requested to continue in their present vocations without change; and the military authorities will not interfere in the functions of the civil administration and the courts, except in so far as relates to persons violating military orders or regulations, or otherwise interfering with the exercise of military authority. All peaceful citizens can confidently pursue their usual occupations, feeling that they will be protected in their personal rights and property, as well as in their proper social relations.

The commanding officer of the United States Expeditionary Force, Col. Littleton W. T. Waller, United States Marine Corps, is empowered to issue the necessary regulations and appoint the necessary officers to make this material law effective.

Done at the city of Port au Prince, Haiti, this 3d day of September, A. D. 1915.

W. B. CAPERTON,
Rear Admiral, United States Navy,
Commanding the Forces of the United States of America
in Haiti and Haitian Waters.

APPENDIX No. 6.

MODUS VIVENDI.

Considering that, pending the exchange of ratifications of the treaty of September 16, 1915, it is essential that a provisional arrangement be entered into between the two Governments with a view to guarantee the working of the administrative services, the repression of disorder, and the maintenance of public peace:

The following Modus Vivendi has been agreed upon between the Haitian Government and the Government of the United States of America, represented respectively by Louis Borno, secretary of state for foreign affairs, and Arthur Bailly-Blanchard, envoy extraordinary and minister plenipotentiary.

The treaty signed September 16, 1915, between the Republic of Haiti and the United States and ratified by the Haitian Chamber of Deputies on October 6, 1915, and by the Haitian Senate on November 11, 1915, shall go provisionally into full force and effect from this date and shall be operated thereunder until the Senate of the United States has acted upon the treaty, under reserve of the details of the operation of the treaty to be arranged at Washington between the Department of State and the Haitian commission appointed for that purpose.

Signed and sealed in duplicate, in the English and French languages, at Port au Prince, Haiti, the 29th day of November, 1915, by the aforesaid representatives on behalf of their respective Governments.

LOUIS BORNO.
A. BAILLY-BLANCHARD.

APPENDIX No. 7.

MEMORANDUM.

REPUBLIC OF HAITI,
STATE SECRETARY OF FOREIGN AFFAIRS,
Port au Prince, December 20, 1915.

The Haitian Government is ready to receive from the Occupation the municipal administrations which it has taken over.

As it was understood that a special agreement would be made for each case the Government asks to resume as soon as possible the administration of the public services of Port au Prince, the water works, and the municipal services. With this object the United States Legation is informed that the water works will be taken by Mr. Thomas Price, engineer, and the municipal administrations by a commission whose members will be named later. The United States Legation will kindly inform the department of foreign affairs of the American officer who will be in charge of returning the administrations to the agents of the Haitian Government, that he is to make out with them all inventories, accounts of works needed, reparations, etc., in short, to carry out the details of the agreement.

When the municipal services of Port au Prince are returned to Haitian control the same procedure shall be applied to the other communes; that is, the department of foreign affairs and the United States Legation, respectively, shall indicate one or more agents to make out the inventories or accounts of works, reparations, etc., to be carried on under Haitian control, and the agreement for each case shall be sent to the legation and to the department of foreign affairs.

As for the funds needed to carry on the administrations, for reparations, works, etc., the Haitian Government expects Admiral Caperton to supply them to the Haitian agents designated for these works.

In fact, the revenues of the Government are collected by the occupation; it has at its disposal only the amounts paid it by Admiral Caperton and which are devoted to the necessities of governmental existence. They are not sufficient to cover, among other things, the expenses of the various waterworks and municipalities, expenses which are now paid directly by the American authorities.

The return of these services was the object of a formal agreement established by the Appendix of the Modus Vivendi. This return necessarily involves expenses, and the means of meeting them are a necessary part of this return. Moreover, these expenses are now paid to the American occupation by Admiral Caperton out of the funds of the public Treasury; in paying them to the Haitian authorities henceforth, it shall not be considered a new expense.

Consequently, the Haitian Government considers that when the details of the agreement charge expenses against the Haitian administration, the means of meeting them shall be furnished to the latter out of the funds of the public treasury.

Immediate action on the part of the American authorities, in accordance with the present memorandum, would be highly appreciated by the Haitian Government.

APPENDIX No. 8.

HAITIAN LEGATION,
Washington, November 15, 1918.

In the name of the Government, go without delay, personally, and transmit, in writing, the following note to the Secretary of State, personally: "Just at the time when Your Excellency is addressing the Haitian Government as the Government of a free and independent nation, just at the time when, thanks to the power of the United States, the sacred principles of law, justice, and respect for small nations are triumphant in the world, the Haitian nation is prey to the distressing and unjust tyranny of American officials who, contrary to the treaty, are trying to impose upon the Republic of Haiti budget laws and taxes, without examining anything with us, without recognizing the right of the Haitian Government even to rectify evident errors, material and others, made in their projects. The Haitian people are very sincerely determined to bring about, with the aid of the American Government, all the reforms which progress demands, but by means of the very cordial cooperation stipulated in the treaty, of cooperation arising from examinations in common and not at all by means of imperative injunctions, announced without respect for national dignity, and sometimes inspired by sentiments of a personal nature, in which the superior interests of the two countries are not considered. Also, the Haitian Government is convinced that the State Department, which is incompletely informed regarding the actual situation in Haiti, will take careful measures for the legitimate satisfaction of the Haitian nation, which has full confidence in the noble impartiality of the honorable chief of the State Department and the illustrious chief of the Government of the United States."

APPENDIX No. 9.

Le Secrétaire d'Etat présente ses compliments au Chargé d'Affaires ad interim de la République d'Haïti et a l'honneur d'accuser réception de sa Note datée du 20 Novembre, 1918, par lequelle, selon les instructions expresses de son Gouvernement, le Chargé d'Affaires a fait connaître certaines plaintes contre les actes des fonctionnaries américains, en contravention avec le traité de 1915, entre le Gouvernement des Etats-Unis et le Gouvernement d'Haïti, et dans la quelle le Gouvernement haïtien a exprimé sa conviction que le Département d'Etat jugera à propos de prendre des measures pour donner satisfaction aux désirs légitimes de la nation haïtienne.

En addition aux accusations générales du Gouvernement haïtien touchant "les vexations et la tyrannie injuste des fonctionnaires américains" en Haïti, le Département d'Etat note que le Gouvernement haïtien est de l'opinion que le Gouvernement des Etats-Unis n'est pas complètement renseigné au sujet de la vraie situation en Haïti. Comme suite à ces affirmations et en vue de la très sérieuse portée de l'accusation générale contre les fonctionnaires américains en Haïti que la note plus haut mentionnée contient, le Gouvernement des Etats-Unis désire que le Gouvernement d'Haïti fasse une déclaration plus précise et plus détaillée en ce qui regarde les questions exposées dans la note du 20 Novembre, 1918.

ROBERT LANSING.

Département d'Etat.
Washington, 30 Novembre, 1918.

APPENDIX No. 10.

PROTEST.

We, undersigned Senators, assembled in a hall on the corner of Peuple and Dantes Destouches Streets, formerly Pavée Street, temporarily taken over for our legislative work, because of the closing of the National Building for the past month by order of executive power, to prevent us from working there.

APPENDIX No. 6.

MODUS VIVENDI.

Considering that, pending the exchange of ratifications of the treaty of September 16, 1915, it is essential that a provisional arrangement be entered into between the two Governments with a view to guarantee the working of the administrative services, the repression of disorder, and the maintenance of public peace:

The following Modus Vivendi has been agreed upon between the Haitian Government and the Government of the United States of America, represented respectively by Louis Borno, secretary of state for foreign affairs, and Arthur Bailly-Blanchard, envoy extraordinary and minister plenipotentiary.

The treaty signed September 16, 1915, between the Republic of Haiti and the United States and ratified by the Haitian Chamber of Deputies on October 6, 1915, and by the Haitian Senate on November 11, 1915, shall go provisionally into full force and effect from this date and shall be operated thereunder until the Senate of the United States has acted upon the treaty, under reserve of the details of the operation of the treaty to be arranged at Washington between the Department of State and the Haitian commission appointed for that purpose.

Signed and sealed in duplicate, in the English and French languages, at Port au Prince, Haiti, the 29th day of November, 1915, by the aforesaid representatives on behalf of their respective Governments.

LOUIS BORNO.
A. BAILLY-BLANCHARD.

APPENDIX No. 7.

MEMORANDUM

...otre Excellence préalable- ...ion que dans les quelques prochains ...xpédiées par cable.

Veuillez ...tre, les assurances de ma haute con- ...idération.

A. BAILLY-BLANCHARD,
Ministre Américain.

LÉGATION DES ETATS-UNIS D'AMÉRIQUE,
Port au Prince, Haiti, 11 Avril, 1917.

S. E. MONSIEUR LOUIS BORNO,
Secrétaire d'Etat des Relations Extérieures.

MONSIEUR LE MINISTRE: Me référant à ma note du 7 Avril relative à certaines suggestions touchant le projet de la Nouvelle Constitution haïtienne et à mon avis que la Légation serait en possession des suggestions en question dans quelques jours, j'ai l'honneur de dire que mon Gouvernement m'a chargé de porter à l'attention du Gouvernement de Votre Excellence son désir de voir les changements suivants dans le dit projet:

Art. 4. Les étrangers jouiront de toutes les protect ons accordées aux haïtiens sans exception.

Art. 5. La condition de cinq années de résidence serait écartée. L'intention de faire le commerce et de résider serait ajoutée à la liste des entreprises pour lesquelles la propriété immobilière peut être acquise. L'exception concernant l'intervention diplomatique serait écartée.

Art. 96. Les Secrétaires d'Etat ne recevraient aucun frais de représentation en plus de leurs indemnités.

Art. 97 à 104 inclus: Le Conseil d'Etat n'est pas nécessaire, étant donnée l'existence du Corps Législatif, et les dépenses y afférentes ne sont pas justifiées: à omettre tout ce qui s'y réfère des articles 81, 94 et autres.

Art 121. Des dispositions seraient prévues pour la poursuite des juges en Cassation et des juges d'appel de la même façon que pour celle des Secrétaires d'Etat.

Art. 131. Serait lu: L'examen et la liquidation des comptes de l'Administration générale et de tous autres offices comptables envers le Trésor Public seront déterminés par la loi.

Les articles 132, 133 et 134 seraient écartés.

Art. 140. Les étrangers jouiraient de toute protection accordée aux haïtiens, sans exception, et en outre, il ne serait pas refusé le droit de réclamer des indemnités pour les torts ou pertes éprouvés.

ᵃ This is a translation into French of the original English text, which is not now available.

Consequently, the Haitian Government considers that when the details of the agreement charge expenses against the Haitian administration, the means of meeting them shall be furnished to the latter out of the funds of the public treasury.

Immediate action on the part of the American authorities, in accordance with the present memorandum, would be highly appreciated by the Haitian Government.

APPENDIX No. 8.

HAITIAN LEGATION,
Washington, November 15, 1918.

In the name of the Government, go without delay, personally, and transmit, in writing, the following note to the Secretary of State, personally: "Just at the time when Your Excellency is addressing the Haitian Government as the Government of a free and independent nation, just at the time when, thanks to the power of the United States, the sacred principles of law, justice, and respect for small nations are triumphant in the world, the Haitian nation is prey to the distressing and unjust tyranny of American officials who, contrary to the treaty, are trying to impose upon the Republic of Haiti budget laws and taxes, without examining anything with us, without recognizing the right of the Haitian Government even to rectify evident errors, material and others, made in their projects. The Haitian people are very sincerely determined to bring about, with the aid of the American Government, all the reforms which progress demands, but by means of the very cordial cooperation stipulated in 'ino) vtriwoay aou sign.arising from examinations in common and not at all terrorized and helpless to resistons, announced without respect for national mitted, as most of them were brosentiments of a personal nature, in which closely watched." [39]   ~ountries are not considered. Also, the ——he State Department, wh'·' 'ltuation in 'l· ' '

APPENDIX No....

In a memorandum dated January 25, 1919, addressed by the Haitian secretary of foreign affairs to the State Department at Washington, in reply to Mr. Robert Lansing's note of November 30, 1918, we quote the following passage:

"When the Haitian newspaper Le Nouvelliste announced on November 22, 1918, in most cautious terms and in a tentative way, the recall of the financial adviser, even ending its notice with praise for President Wilson, the owner of the paper, M. Chauvet, was arrested by the agents of the occupation, imprisoned, sentenced by court-martial to a fine of $800, and forced to suspend his paper for three months."

For the enlightenment of all, we reproduce the article from Le Nouvelliste:

MR. RUAN RECALLED.

"It appears that Mr. A. T. Ruan has been relieved of his duties as financial adviser as a result of difficulties with our Government. The recall of Mr. Ruan affirms the sentiments of right and justice proclaimed by President Wilson and which, as the eminent statesman has often repeated, must be the compass which guides the relations between all nations, great and small." [40]

"This time also the mere announcement of this change, although it is made without comment, is sufficient to indicate the nature of the unjust and distressing tyranny practiced by American officials in Haiti toward the Haitian people." [41]

In a communication dated April 5, 1919, Mr. Charles Moravia, Haitian minister to Washington, recalled this serious incident to the State Department, directing attention to " * * * the excessive severity of these provost courts ordering punishments out of all proportion t. the crime committed." As an example he cited the Chauvet case mentioned in the memorandum of the Haitian Government, dated February 25, 1919, and presented to the State Department on February 14 of the same year. And he added, "there are many others." [42]

---

[39] Pastor Evans of the Protestant Church of St. Mark (Haiti), in the New York Herald, Oct. 25, 1920.
[40] Italics ours.
[41] See Haitian Blue Book, 1921, p. 48.
[42] Ibid., p. 172.

In reply to the communication of the Haitian minister, Mr. Robert Lansing, Secretary of State, said, in reference to the Chauvet case, in his communication of October 10, 1919:

" You refer to the ' excessive severity ' of the gendarmerie or provost courts and cite as an instance thereof the case of Chauvet. In regard to this case, it may be stated that the sentence is considered as in all ways a proper punishment of the offense committed." [43]

Union Patriotique d'Haïti.

The Union Patriotique d'Haïti is a nonpartisan organization founded at Port au Prince, November 17, 1920, to crystallize the national aspirations of the Haitians for the return of their independence, maintained, until the American invasion, for 111 years. Every one of the 27 districts which constitute the Republic of Haiti is represented, and the Union has virtually the unanimous support of the entire Haitian people.

LIST OF MEMBERS OF THE BOARD OF DIRECTORS.

Chairman.—M. Georges Sylvain, lawyer, former envoy extraordinary and minister plenipotentiary of Haiti in France and at the Holy See, and officer of the Legion of Honor.

General Secretary.—M. Perceval Thoby, former chargé d'affaires of the Haitian Legation at Washington, and former chief of division of the department of foreign affairs, former inspector general of the consular service.

Treasurer.—M. Moravia Morpeau, lawyer, manufacturer, and former senator.

Archivist.—M. Ch. Rosemond, notary.

Members of the board.—MM. H. Baussan, lawyer, planter, former president of the senate; D. Bourand, merchant, former secretary of the interior; F. L. Cauvin, lawyer, former secretary of the interior and of justice; D. Jeannot, lawyer, former secretary of the interior and of justice; Lespinasse, lawyer, former envoy extraordinary and minister plenipotentiary of Haiti in France, former secretary of foreign affairs, of finance, and of justice; L. Liautaud, lawyer; Price Mars, professor, former envoy extraordinary and minister plenipotentiary of Haiti in France; Léon Nau, lawyer, former dean of the civil court of Port-au-Prince; Pauléus Sannon, publicist, former envoy extraordinary and minister plenipotentiary of Haiti to the United States, former secretary of foreign affairs; Ls. Ed. Pouget, manufacturer, former senator, former chargé d'affaires of Haiti at Berlin, decorated with the black eagle; Sténio Vincent, former secretary of the interior and of justice, former president of the senate, former resident minister of Hiati in Holland.

Advisory Council.—MM. G. Boco, planter, former secretary of agriculture and public works; Victor Cauvin, lawyer; F. Colcou, physician, president of the medical board; V. Delbeau, teacher, former secretary of the Haitian Legation at Washington; Arthur Holly, physician; Abel N. Léger, lawyer, former secretary of the Haitian legation at Paris; Clément Lespinasse, planter and manufacturer; Alexander Lilavois, former head of accounts in the department of finance and publicist; A. Rigal, lawyer, former district governor; P. Salomon, head doctor of the St. François de Sales Hospital, former dean of the Medical School, former secretary of public education; F. Viard, merchant, former secretary of the Haitian legation at London; Constant Vieux, planter, coeditor of the Courier Haitien, former secretary of the interior; Is. Vieux, lawyer, former government commissioner at the civil court of Port-au-Prince; S. Pradel, lawyer, former secretary of the interior and of justice; H. Dorsainville, lawyer, editor of L'Essor; Hyson, physician, managing editor Le Matin; F. Diambois, lawyer, editor of La Renaissance; Fréd. Duvignaud, lawyer, coeditor of the Nouvelliste; Jérémie, planter, former secretary of public education, of justice, and of the interior; J. C. Dorsainvil, physician, chief of division of the department of public education; A. Pierre Paul, merchant, former deputy; Pierre Eugène de Lespinasse, lawyer; Fleury Lavelanet, manufacturer, former communal councillor; Fiorvil Nau, planter; Jules Canal, manufacturer, former deputy; St. Martin B. Canal, planter, former deputy; R. Brouard, merchant; Raymond Carrié, lawyer; H. Laventure, teacher; Edmond Roumain, pharmacist

[43] See Haitian Blue Book, 1921, p. 175.

and chemist, former senator; Paul Laroque, lawyer, former judge of the court of cassation, former president of the senate; T. Laleau, president of bar of Port-au-Prince, former secretary of justice; H. Brisson, president of the chamber of commerce, former president of the commerce court at Port-au-Prince; V. Gervais, lawyer, former chargé d'affaires of Haiti in Cuba; Florian Alfred, former chief of the communal administration; F. B. César, manufacturer; Vil Lubin, planter; René E. Auguste, planter, former deputy.

Mr. ANGELL. I have here a brief statement in the nature of an outline not of specific charges but an outline of charges which have been made and have been laid, and a suggested scope of the inquiry for the committee, offered with the idea that we will supplement that within a very short time by a list of specific witnesses whom we think it will be absolutely necessary for the committee to call, in order that it may arrive at the facts underlying the occupation.

That is all, gentlemen, that we have.

The CHAIRMAN. The committee had better receive your outline and incorporate it in the record. It will not be necessary for you to read it, I think. It will be available to the members of the committee and the press when filed with the committee.

(The statement referred to is here printed in full as follows:)

On behalf of the Haiti-Santo Domingo Independence Society and the Union Patriotique d'Haiti and the National Association for the Advancement of Colored People:

We respectfully protest to the Senate Committee of Inquiry into Conditions in Haiti and Santo Domingo against the present occupation of the Republics of Haiti and San Domingo by the armed forces of the United States and demand their withdrawal and the restoration of the two Republics to their complete and absolute independence in accordance with their previously existing constitution as soon as effective native civilian governments can be erected.

We make this demand in the name of justice, liberty, and the sacred right, upheld by the outcome of the World War to a separate existence and complete freedom of every small nation and in accordance with our historic American traditions.

We declare that the pulling down by violence of these Republics was without adequate reason, was unwarranted in American or international law, uncalled for by the then existing political conditions, and in direct violation of the fourteenth peace point of the United States as enunciated by President Woodrow Wilson, the guaranteeing " of political independence and territorial integrity to great and small States alike."

We declare that the American occupation of these lands has to date been destructive and without fundamental constructive value; that no foundation has been laid for the permanent rebuilding of these governments; that the physical improvements made, such as the building of roads and the sanitation of cities have been achieved at an indefensible cost—in Haiti at the price of a forced enslavement under the Corvée, which the American conscience would never have permitted to exist had it not been veiled by an impenetrable naval censorship.

We declare that American domination of Haiti and Santo Domingo has been accompanied by individual wrongs and military excesses accentuated by the difference in language, race, and traditions, and that it has afforded completest proof of the truth of Alabama Lincoln's immortal saying that " No man is good enough to govern any other man without that other man's consent."

We declare that the constitution and treaty forced upon the Haitian people and the military régime imposed upon the Dominican people without even the sanction of a constitution or treaty are unworthy of the genius and the generosity of the American people and tend to the establishment of perpetual protectorates involving the domination of the development of those republics by an alien government at Washington.

We declare that the efforts of the State Department to compel the Dominicans to sign a treaty ratifying and approving every official act of this Government to be utterly unworthy of any righteously minded country; we affirm the right of these people to complete redress for any injuries committed by the military government.

We declare that the acts of this Government in Haiti and Santo Domingo since July 29, 1915, have injured our relations with the Central American and

South American Republics, threaten seriously to affect our trade with those countries, and have gravely intensified the distrust of the United States by the smaller American nations.

A. REPUBLIC OF HAITI.

The memoir presented to the Senate Foreign Relations Committee on May 9, 1921, by the delegation of the Union Patriotique d'Haiti contains serious and documented charges against American administration in that Republic, which require most searching investigation. These charges attack the motive of the intervention, the manner of the intervention, the imposition of a treaty upon Hai't', the subsequent repeated violations of the modus vivendi imposed by American forces upon Haiti, the failure of the American régime to pay interest in Haitian debts which have never before been defaulted, the suppression of the Haitian legislature by armed American officers, the régime of martial law and censorship, the failure of the Mayo court of inquiry to call Haitian witnesses or hear the Haitian complaints. The memoir also lists 25 cases of "atrocities" alleged to have been committed by the American forces with names and dates.

B. DOMINICAN REPUBLIC.

As to the Dominican Republic, we know of no single comprehensive report or memoir similar to the Haitian memoir which summarizes adequately the various charges brought against the principle and the method of the armed United States seizure and continued occupation of the country. We respectfully suggest, however, that the following summary of important matters might provide a working basis of inquiry. Charges have been made of such serious nature as to warrant and demand a thorough probe by this committee of all of these topics.

1. Conditions in the Dominican Republic, an independent sovereignty, and status of that Government vis-à-vis the United States prior to 1916: trade, commerce, and industry; political stability and internal order; the public debt; treaties; convention of 1907; receivership of customs; agreement of 1912.

2. Landing of United States armed forces, May, 1916; seizure of customs, etc.; pretext and character of this violation of neutrality of an independent sovereign nation.

3. Extension of United States military rule, supplanting and superseding Dominican Government; immediate establishment of censorship; executive order No. 1 removing secretaries of war and interior, declaring ineligibility of Dominicans to hold these offices, and vesting these offices in Col. J. H. Pendleton, United States Marine Corps; further executive orders replacing other ministers by officers of the United States Marine Corps; executive order No. 12, suspending elections; executive order No. 18, January 2, 1917, suspending Dominican Congress, expelling Senators and deputies from office and stopping the salaries; attempted negotiation of new treaty; charge that official salaries of President and others was made conditional on its acceptance; their refusal and exile; assumption of executive, administrative, legislative, and judicial power by United States military forces; "pacification"; total Dominican and total American losses; the Macoris campaign.

4. Methods and procedure of United States military government: (a) censorship decree of December, 1918; of December 28, 1919; executive order No. 385 (Jan. 15, 1920) "abolishing" censorship but proscribing articles "hostile to the military government, its policy, or its civil and military officers"; system of provost courts and martial law; prosecutions under these decrees. (b) alleged military excesses; Archbishop Nouel's charges; later instances alleged; imprisonment for political offenses. (c) Alleged administrative abuses and laxity. (d) Encouragement of immigration of cheap West Indian labor. (e) Increase of public debt; reduction of customs dues. (f) Neglected reports and recommendations of consulting commission of Dominicans, appointed by Admiral Snowden.

5. Alleged advantages and benefits of the military occupation:
(a) Schools. (b) Roads. (c) Land law. (d) Measures, if any, to encourage trade and industry.

6. Effect in Central and South America of military occupation:
(a) Publicity given imprisonment of Fabio Fiallo. (b) Dominican mission which preceded Secretary Colby's visit to South America. (c) Effect upon trade.

7. Proposals of the United States for withdrawal of forces and termination of military occupation; proclamations of December, 1920, and June, 1921; proposed ratification of all of the acts of the military government, validation of loan, etc.

CONCLUSION.

This preliminary statement is submitted as an outline of charges and as suggesting the scope of inquiry. We desire respectfully to reserve the right to alter, amend, or supplement this statement.

Upon the termination of the hearings of the committee we shall request the privilege of submitting briefs upon the evidence adduced. We propose, with the consent of the committee, also to submit constructive proposals for the setting up of native governments in these two Republics and the transfer to native governments of the governmental functions now exercised by the United States military forces by such means as shall enable the American Nation to be of the utmost friendly assistance to these neighboring peoples in the free and unfettered exercise of their sovereign independence.

Respectfully submitted.

> HAITI-SANTO DOMINGO INDEPENDENCE SOCIETY,
> By OSWALD GARRISON VILLARD.
> NATIONAL ASSOCIATION FOR THE ADVANCEMENT
> OF COLORED PEOPLE,
> By JAMES WELDON JOHNSON, *Secretary.*
> UNION PATRIOTIQUE D'HAITI,
> By STENIO VINCENT.
> ERNEST ANGELL, *Counsel.*

Mr. ANGELL. That, gentlemen, is a general statement of the position which we assume. The brief which, with your permission, I shall file to day, refers, as to the Republic of Haiti, to the memoir introduced by Mr. Vincent, as a summary statement of charges which have been made, and which we are convinced your committee should investigate impartially and thoroughly, to the end that all the facts may be brought out.

As to the Dominican Republic, we call attention in this brief to the fact that there is, as far as we know, no comprehensive report similar to the Haitian memoir, which adequately summarizes the various and collective charges which have been made against the military seizure and occupation of the Dominican Republic and its country. In this brief, therefore, we outline the principal topics under which charges have been made, and which we respectfully suggest the committee should investigate, and we shall be prepared, at your convenience, gentlemen, to offer testimony, documentary and by witnesses, upon the principal topics set out in the Haitian memoir and in our suggested outline of matters regarding the Dominican Republic.

In order to be able to do that, it is obvious that we must ask the committee respectfully to subpoena witnesses. Many witnesses naturally will not appear voluntarily, merely at our request. That happens in every law case and in every disputed investigation. People are unwilling to come unless they are directed to appear. When they are directed to appear, then they come and testify to all they know.

Senator KING. Are all the witnesses you have in mind in the United States?

Mr. ANGELL. Not at all, Senator. There are many in Haiti and Santo Domingo. It would not be our suggestion, of course, that the witnesses now in those countries should be brought up here, but, rather, that they should appear before the committee when, as I understand, the committee or a subcommittee of the committee goes there. We shall be prepared in a very short time to submit to the committee a list of the witnesses whom we believe it is absolutely indispensable to call in order to arrive at the facts. That is our sole aim here, to assist the committee in so far as we can to arrive at the facts.

Senator KING. When would you produce the witnesses in the United States before the committee? Will they need to be subpoenaed?

Mr. ANGELL. Oh, yes; some of them will need to be subpoenaed.

Senator KING. How many are there in the United States.

Mr. ANGELL. We have a tentative list of witnesses which comprises about 20 or 25, I think. That will undoubtedly have to be supplemented, and some of those names that we have on the tentative list we will cross off, but we are convinced, Senator, that the only way we can arrive at the facts here is, for instance, to request your committee to call before it a number of the naval and marine officers who have occupied important positions in the administration of the American occupation there. Obviously these gentlemen are not going to come at our mere request. I say, obviously. I take it for granted they would not. They would require at least a suggestion from the committee to appear. Other officers of the Government may turn up; former officers who might have to be requested to appear here in order that we may find out, for example, why the United States went down there and occupied those two countries.

Senator KING. When will you be ready to submit to the chairman a list of the names of the witnesses in the United States whose examination will be necessary to elucidate the facts in the case?

Mr. ANGELL. Certainly within a week, possibly within a very much shorter time, if the committee absolutely needs it.

The CHAIRMAN. I think a week will be time enough.

Senator KING. Well, Mr. Chairman, I, of course, feel like we ought to subpœna any witnesses who refuse to come upon notification, after we shall have been satisfied that their testimony is necessary. I think the captain should submit a list, and then he and his associates tell us the materiality and pertinency of their testimony, and if the committee believes their testimony pertinent, we ought to subpœna them if they refuse to come.

The CHAIRMAN. Is there anything further, Captain?

Mr. ANGELL. I think not, Senator. We hoped the committee would to-day give us some indication of when you propose to begin the actual hearings, both here and in Haiti and Santo Domingo, if the committee proposes to go down there, so that we can, of course, prepare accordingly.

The CHAIRMAN. Until we have examined the memorials and statements filed to-day, I do not believe we could fix the course of the hearings, or, indeed, until the list of names of those whom you intend to have called as witnesses has been filed. These hearings do not follow a set program. We go forward as fast as we can. Unhappily, we have other duties to occupy us.

Mr. ANGELL. Coming back to what we were discussing a moment ago, that is the question of the witnesses, you asked me to submit a list of the witnesses, indicating the probable materiality of their evidence, and, if I understood Senator King correctly, whether or not they would come voluntarily at our request. For example, as one name that occurs to me right away, we shall want to request the presence here of Gen. Barnett for examination. I understand he is on the Pacific coast. If we write to him and say, "Will you come?" obviously he could not leave his assigned duties and would not come on.

The CHAIRMAN. If you have nothing further to offer, Capt. Angell, we will now hear Mr. Knowles.

STATEMENT OF MR. HORACE G. KNOWLES, REPRESENTING THE PATRIOTIC LEAGUE OF THE DOMINICAN REPUBLIC AND THE DEPOSED DOMINICAN GOVERNMENT.

Mr. KNOWLES. Mr. Chairman and gentlemen: I represent the Patriotic League of the Dominican Republic, and the deposed Dominican Government.

Senator KING. The latter consists of whom?

Mr. KNOWLES. The President and chief remnants or remains of that Government which exists to-day.

Senator KING. You do not represent Haiti?

Mr. KNOWLES. No. Owing to the absence of Dr. Henriquez from the city, who arrived only this morning, an hour or so ago, we have not been able to prepare on the part of the Dominican Republic any form of memorandum or statement. That will be done, however, in the shortest possible time.

I would like to inquire, in order that these two cases may not overlap or may not be treated as exactly similar, because the conditions and the actions of our Government in each of those countries were entirely separate and distinct from what they were in the other, whether, as a matter of procedure and policy, the committee would not prefer to take up the one and go forward with it, and then take up the other.

The CHAIRMAN. Perhaps after you have filed the memorial on behalf of your clients the committee can decide whether to proceed with the investigation into the Haitian occupation first or the Dominican occupation. We have nothing before us at this time. When can we expect a copy of your memorial?

Mr. KNOWLES. When will the committee have another session?

The CHAIRMAN. I was going to ask the consent of the committee that the Chair might receive that memorial and distribute it in advance of the next meeting of the committee.

Senator KING. Surely.

The CHAIRMAN. May we have that some time within the week?

Mr. KNOWLES. Yes, indeed.

The CHAIRMAN. Then I can receive it, and it can be incorporated in this record, with the unanimous consent of the committee, and distributed to the members for their information.

Mr. KNOWLES. I think we can present that to you, Mr. Chairman, either Tuesday or Wednesday, at the latest.

Senator KING. I think it is very wise that we, so far as possible, keep the two cases apart, and yet I can conceive that there may be witnesses who are here from a distance who may be required to testify on both cases. In that event I would, of course, feel that we ought to hear the testimony distinct on one case. on Santo Domingo, and then move over and take their testimony on the Haitian case, so as not to be compelled to overlap.

Mr. KNOWLES. That is practical, Senator.

(Mr. Knowles subsequently submitted to the chairman the following statement on behalf of the Republic of Santo Domingo:)

To the chairman and members of the Special Committee of the United States Senate to investigate the occupation by and administration of the United States in the Dominican Republic.

GENTLEMEN: The undersigned, Horace G. Knowles, adviser and assistant of the Dominican National Commission in the United States, respectfully represents to your honorable committee, that since 1844 the Dominican Republic has been a sovereign nation, and its people free and independent, and in no less degree than the United States, Great Britain, France, the Argentine, Chile, or Peru, and it has been so recognized by all the nations of the earth. Since its independence and until the invasion and armed occupation by the United States, which began May 15, 1916, and has continued uninterruptedly since that date, it has been accorded an unconditional place in the family of nations, and with many of them, including the United States, it maintained diplomatic relations of the pleasantest character, and with them it negotiated treaties of friendship and commerce. It is a member of The Hague International Court of Arbitration, and it would have taken an active part in the late World War, alongside the United States, of course, and probably would have joined the League of Nations, had it not been deprived of its sovereignty, liberty, and right of free and independent action.

In 1916 when the Dominican Republic was at peace with the world, while it was a party to two existing treaties with the United States, and in direct violation to one of them, and without the Dominican Republic having violated in any way the other; against the sovereign rights of the Dominican Nation; contrary to the everywhere recognized principles of international law; breaking the pledges contained in the United States' own interpretation of the Monroe doctrine; disregarding both the letter and spirit of a resolution proposed by the United States at the second peace conference of The Hague, and then and there adopted and being in full force since then and until now; contrary to.the unquestionable meaning of No. 14 of the famous Wilson's "Fourteen Points"; and in violation of the Constitution of the United States; President Wilson, without the slightest attempt to appeal to or use diplomatic means, ordered a part of the United States Navy to go secretly, and without giving any notice whatever to the Dominican Government, to Santo Domingo and to land there its troops, to seize the Government, and proceed to subjugate the people. Obedient to such instructions, partly in the handwriting of President Wilson, and signed by him, without in any way either consulting or informing Congress, without a declaration of war, an illegal, unprovoked, unjustified, and totally unwarranted act of war was committed against the Dominican Republic and its people. and for more than five years the United States Government has maintained a state of war in that country.

Stealthily American battleships entered the roadstead of Santo Domingo City, and under cover of a score or more of long-range, big-caliber guns the American admiral, with a large force of marines, landed on Dominican territory. That was a paramount act of war. A little later the said admiral presented to the

Dominican President, Francisco Henriquez y Carvajal, who had been duly elected and formally inaugurated, a ready-made treaty, an exact duplicate of the one that had just been, by guns and bayonets, forced upon the helpless Haitian Government and people, and which treaty destroyed completely their sovereignty. took from them their liberty and independence, and put the country under the absolute control of the United States Government. The Dominican President, mindful of the sovereign rights of his nation and of his oath of office, his promise to uphold the constitution and laws of his country and to defend it in every necessary and possible way, informed the admiral of the reasons why he could and would not accept such a treaty. It might be argued that the Dominican Republic would be better off under the control of the United States; and so might Brazil, the Argentine, Chile, and Peru, and even England and France. That was the object and argument, which is the corner stone of imperialism, that the Germans had in mind in 1914. The Dominicans were a sovereign people, no less so than the Brazilians, Argentinians, Chileans, Peruvians, the English, and French, and people of the United States, and they, as would the others under the same circumstances, wanted to remain free and independent, and it was their right to do so. That country was theirs as much as this country is ours, and so long as they respected their treaty obligations and in no way molested foreigners or their interests they had and have the right to do what they please in and with it. That has ever been the American policy, and never was it better expressed than by President Wilson.

President Henriquez refused to accept the demands of the American admiral, whereupon the admiral, acting, of course, under orders from Washington, proceeded to use pressure and force. One of his first acts was to issue a proclamation of occupation, and in which he announced himself as the military governor of the Dominican Republic. The proclamation gave two alleged reasons for the armed intervention and occupation, the first of which was a violation of the treaty of 1907, which allegation was, has been, and is stoutly denied by the Dominicans: and the second was to quell disorders and disturbances in the country. At the time the proclamation was issued and for several months prior thereto there were no disorders and absolute peace reigned throughout the country. Disorders, when occasionally they did occur, were of a purely political character, confined to the natives, and never even in a single instance did they involve foreigners or in any way affect the liberty, property, or person of Americans or other foreigners. Never has an American or other foreigner been attacked or killed or his property injured or imperiled in that country. Never in the history of the country has there been a disturbance comparable to the one that occurred recently at Tulsa, a short time ago at Springfield and Boston, and that occur with increasing frequency in Chicago, New York, and all the larger American cities. In that country lynchings, burnings at the stake. and tar and feathering, now pastimes in some parts of the United States, are unknown and never practiced. Life and property are more secure in any part of that country than they are to-day or to-night in Central Park or on Broadway. New York, and the total lawlessness for a year throughout the Republic is less than that which is recorded in any one of the five largest cities of the United States in 24 hours.

In accordance with the plan of the said proclamation the President and his ministers of state were forced out of office; the Government treasury was seized; the national congress was dismissed; elections were prohibited; thousands of marines were spread over the country and with unlimited authority over the natives: public meetings were not permitted; a censorship of tongue, pen, press, mail, and telegraph of the severest k'nd was establ shed: a reign of intense terror was inaugurated: destructive bombs were dropped from airplanes upon towns and hamlets; every home was searched for arms, weapons, and implements; homes were burned; natives were killed: tortures and cruelties committed: and "Butcher" Weyler's horr.ble concentration camps were established, and his brutal methods that did so much to bring about our war with Spain were imitated. Repressions and oppressions followed in succession. When protests were made the protestants were fined heavily and also imprisoned, and when resistance or defense attempted bullets and bayonets were used. Criticism of the acts of the military government were not permitted, nor the use of any patriotic expressions allowed, and those who violated the order were severely punished by fines and imprisonment. Hundreds of capable native Government employees were dismissed and their families distressed in order to make jobs for incompetent men sent from the States, and to whom much larger salaries were paid than to the natives, and the Dominicans compelled to pay all their traveling and incidental expenses. The Dominican people have been "taxed without representation" and the money so raised expended recklessly and without in any way consulting them. Their foreign indebtedness has been greatly increased against their protests and in violation of the treaty of 1907.

For five years this policy of suppression, repression, oppression, and maladministration has continued. In the country protests were neither listened to nor permitted. The practically deposed President came to Washington with his protest and the appeal of the Dominican people. He asked President Wilson and Secretary of State Lansing for the courtesy of an audience, and not even the courtesy of a reply to his formal but polite requests was shown.

That evidence may be produced before your honorable committee to substantiate the foregoing statements the Dominican people charge against the United States Government as follows:

1. That there was no legal ground for the invasion and armed occupation by the United States Government of the Dominican Republic.

2. That such invasion was in direct violation of (1) the Constitution of the United States; (2) existing treaties with the United States; (3) a resolution proposed by the United States and adopted by the third conference of The Hague Tribunal; (4) international law; (5) the object and purpose of the Monroe doctrine as defined by the United States Government; and (6) of the fourteenth of the "fourteen points" of President Wilson.

3. That excesses, abuses, cruelties, and murders were committed by the marines, the people terrorized and their homes burned.

4. That the orders issued and enforced by the military Government were unreasonable, cruel, and totally un-American.

5. That private rights were invaded, and bersonal and corporate property injured, damaged, or destroyed by the military Government or its agents, and great losses incurred because of them and their orders.

6. That the administration of the military Government has been incompetent, wasteful, and extravagant.

The Dominican people are profoundly impressed and deeply gratified by the action of the United States Senate in coming to their rescue, and that it has ordered a full, fair, and honest investigation of all of the conditions antecedent to the occupation of the Dominican Republic and the acts of administration of that country during the occupation by the United States Government.

With an abiding faith in the American people and in those fundamental principles of personal liberty, "consent of the governed," respect for the rights of foreign nations, large or small, and inherent justice to all, that have made them into such a large and magnificent nation, the Dominicans will appear before your committee with all the proofs and evidence they can produce to enable you to ascertain the truth, the rights and wrongs of the subject matter so solemnly confided to you to investigate and report to the Senate your conscientious findings and recommendations.

HORACE G. KNOWLES.

WASHINGTON, *August 12, 1921.*

[Memorandum presented to the committee of the Senate of the United States, named to investigate the Military Occupation in Santó Domingo, by Dr. Henríquez y Carvajal, Washington, D. C., Aug. 12, 1921.]

On November 29, 1916, acting under instructions issued by the President of the United States, a captain in the United States Navy proclaimed himself military governor of the Dominican Republica, and declared that country in a state of military occupation by the forces under his command. Shortly afterward, through personal decrees termed "Executive Orders," the aforesaid naval officer ejected from office the duly appointed officials of the Dominican executive, dissolved the national congress, forbade the holding of any elections, and arrogated to himself all the powers which the Dominican constitution invests in the executive, legislative, and judicial branches of the Government. Justification for that astounding action was based on the theory that an existing treaty, the Dominican-American Convention, concluded in 1907, with the object of insuring a regular settlement of the external debt of the Dominican Republic, empowered the Government of the United States to wrest from the Dominican people their sovereignty, and to install an appointee of the American Government over their institutions, with the same power as comes from martial law during a state of war. Acting on this theory, "under the authority of the Government of the United States," according to the proclamation of occupation, the military governor subsequently declared himself, in his own words, "supreme legislator, supreme judge, and supreme executor"; established a regimè of military force and courts-martial; set up a rigid censorship of a public and private opinion; reformed existing civil, criminal, and administrative laws; levied public taxes, and increased the public debt, and generally assumed the position of an rresponsble dictator over the population of a nation friendly to the United States, which had committed no act of aggression against that nation or her citizens, nor had been guilty, or even accused, of any breach of international law, and against which a state of war had not been declared.

The undersigned, duly elected President of the Dominican Republic, has never ceased to protest against the illegal suppression of Dominican independence and against the harsh ordeal of military dictatorship to which his people have been subjected ever since this unwarranted and illegal intervention took place.

Now that there is in the United States a new administration, pledged by the campaign declarations of its Chief Executive to right the wrongs done by the Wilson administration in the Dominican Republic, and it being bel.eved that the policy of the present administration toward the weaker nations of the American Continent will revert to the honorable and traditional standards of justice set by the founders of this great Republic, the Dominican people, through the medium of their rightful President, invite the urgent attention to this international affair, affecting so vitally the happiness and the l:berty of the Dominican people and the honor and good name of the American Nation.

The reasons asserted by President Wilson for the intervention and occupation, as set forth in the proclamat on of occupation issued by Capt. H. S. Knapp. recite that the Dominican Republic had violated article 3 of the Dominican-American convent:on by having increased its public debt w:thout the consent of the Government of the United States. The proclamation reads, in part:

"Whereas a treaty was concluded between the United States of America and the Republic of Santo Domingo on February 8, 1907, article 3 of wh:ch reads: 'Until the Dom'nican Republic has paid the whole amount of the bonds of the debt its public debt shall not be increased except by previous agreement between the Dom nican Government and the United States. * * *'

"Whereas the Government of Santo Domingo has v:olated said article 3 on more than one occasion; and

"Whereas the Government of Santo Domingo has from time to time explained such violation by the necessity of incurring expense incident to the repress'on of revolution; and

"Whereas the United States Government, with great forbearance and with a friendly des:re to enable Santo Domingo to maintain domestic tranquillity and observe the terms of the aforesaid treaty, has urged upon the Government of Santo Domingo certain necessary measures which that Government has been unwilling or unable to adopt: and

"Whereas in consequence domestic tranquillity has been disturbed and is not now established, nor is the future observance of the treaty by the Government of Santo Domingo assured; and

"Whereas the Government of the United States is determined that the time has come to take measures to insure the observance of the provisions of the aforesaid treaty by the Republic of Santo Dom'ngo and to mainta:n domestic tranquillity in the said Republic of Santo Domingo necessary thereto:

"Now, therefore, I, H. S. Knapp, captain, United States Navy, commanding the cruiser force of the United States Atlantic Fleet and the armed forces of the Un'ted States stationed in various places within the territory of the Domin'can Republic, acting under the authority and by the direction of the Government of the United States, declare and announce to all concerned that the Republic of Santo Domingo is hereby placed in a state of military occupat on by the forces under my command and is made subject to military government and to the exercise of military law applicable to such occupat:on."

The "necessary measures" as expressed in the proclamation of occupation wh ch the Government of the United States "had urged upon the Government of Santo Domingo," and which the latter had "been unwilling or unable to adopt,' were embodied in a proposed protocol of a treaty similar to the one which the Republic of Haiti had been compelled to accept under threat of military occupation, called for the control of the Dominican treasury and the Dominican Army and police and every instrument of public author:ty by officials appointed by the President of the United States. Said officials were to be pa'd by the Dominican Republic, yet held to no responsibility for their acts before the laws or the authorities of the Dominican Republic; and inasmuch as they were not subject either to the laws of the United States, they were to enjoy an unprecedented immunity and exercise an unlimited and irresponsible power over the Dominican people. It is clear that such appointees would contravene Dominican sovereignty, and the exercise of their dictatorial powers would mean the end of free government in the Dominican Republic and the erection of an irresponsible, dangerous, and despotic dictatorship over the Dominican people.

On December 4, 1916, the Dominican minister in Washington, acting under instructions received from the deposed Dominican Government, filed a protest at the State Department and before the Latin-American legations against the proceedings carried out in Santo Domingo and the resulting attack on Dominican sovereignty. The protest was based on the following general premises, forming the statement of the case from the Dominican standpoint:

1. Far from having violated Article III of the Dominican-American convention, that covenant had been most faithfully obsered in all its clauses and purposes by the Dominican Government, and, whereas the service of the 1908 loan was being met even in excess of the minimum sums provided in the treaty, no public debt increasing the liabilities assumed by the United States in connection therewith had been created.

2. The Dominican Government denied that the Government of the United States had any right to intervene in the internal affairs of the Dominican Republic, excepting as provided in the convention to lend their protection, in case of necessity, to the officials in charge of the customs collections, which case had not occurred and was not in any way at issue. Nevertheless, the Dominican Government was willing to offer to the Government of the United States every substantial pledge in connection with their purpose to bring about the establishment of public order in a permanent way, and to provide for an improved national financial system. But, great and sincere as their desire was to satisfy the Government of the United States in this respect, and to insure for the Dominican people the benefits of political and financial reorganization, they could not be brought to accept measures involving a loss of national sovereignty, and the forfeiture of the liberty and the safety of the Dominican people, such as would result if they would agree to the treaty proposed by the American Government.

3. In the face of the accomplished fact of the military occupation and the violent suppression of Dominican sovereignty, the Dominican Republic made a formal protest to the American Government.

It can be said that the kernal of the whole matter is to be found in the refusal of the Dominican Government to accede to and sign a protocol of a protectorate, exactly similar to the one imposed on the Republic of Haiti, which the Government of the United States had been trying to force upon the Dominican Republic since November, 1915, providing for the control of the Dominican army and police by officials appointed by the President of the United States, tantamount to the forfeiture of Dominican independence and the suppression of free government in the Dominican Republic. The Dominican-American convention is a clearly framed covenant, entered into for clearly defined purposes. It is held by the President of the Dominican Republic that no interpretation of its clauses, however strained, could rightfully justify such a demand nor supply a legal basis for intervention and military occupation in any case.

In order to ascertain the scope of the provisions contained in Article III of the Dominican-American convention, it is necessary to recall the circumstances which brought about its creation, and to examine the aims of the parties thereto at the time of its conclusion. They may be summarized as follows:

Prior to the year 1905 the Dominican Republic had incurred in a foreign debt, arising principally out of loans contracted with creditors of different nationalities. Owing to lack of development and ensuing scarcity of revenue, the service of these foreign obligations was frequently interrupted. Attempts at consolidation brought no relief, until, in 1905, enormous arrears in unpaid principal and interest had accumulated.

In 1907 the Dominican Republic, desirous of sparing the United States a possible cause of embarrassment in connection with the maintenance of the Monroe doctrine, and at the same time, to give its foreign creditors full confidence in the solvency of the Dominican Government and its ability to pay the principal and interest of its national indebtedness, entered into a treaty with the United States, after a provisional agreement between the Executives of both nations had been in effect for two years.

The outstanding features of this covenant were:

(a) The consolidation of the external debt of the Republic;

(b) The issue of $20,000,000 bonds of the Dominican Republic, applicable to the cancellation of the public debt;

(c) The guaranty offered by the United States Government covering his bond issue;

(d) The supervision, by the United States Government, of the customs collections of the Dominican Republic, which were liened in the transaction;

(e) The allocation of a certain proportion of the customs receipts, collected by a receiver general, appointed by the President of the United States, for the service of the loan, as provided in the convention;

(f) The delivery by the general receiver to the Dominican Government of any surplus revenues, after the provisions relating to the service of the loan had been complied with, and the receivership expenses had been covered;

(g) The obligation, entered into by the Dominican Republic, not to increase its public debt, except by previous agreement with the Government of the United States, until the bond issue should be totally paid off.

The avowed motives of the military occupation rest on the interpretation of the clauses dealing with the features embodied in paragraphs (g) and (f), reading in their essential parts:

" On the first day of each calendar month the sum of $100,000 shall be paid by the receiver to the fiscal agent of the loan, and the remaining collection of the preceding month shall be paid over to the Dominican Government, or applied to the sinking fund for the purchase or redemption of bonds, as the Dominican Government may direct."   (Art. I.)

" Until the Dominican Republic has paid the whole amount of the bonds of the debt, its public debt shall not be increased except by previous agreement between the Dominican Government and the United States."   (Art. III.)

The purposes of the clause contained in Article III, to the effect that the Dominican Republic should not increase its public debt without the consent of the Government of the United States, was as must be clear; first, to prevent any impairment of the security covering the liabilities assumed by the United States through the treaty, the customs collections. Any increase in the public debt of the creditor—the Dominican Republic—might originate claims affecting her principal asset, the customs collections, on which the guarantor—the United States—held a lien; second, to prevent the Dominican Republic, while engaged in the gradual cancellation of the existing foreign indebtedness, to what then appeared to be the limit of her financial ability, from incurring in indiscriminate borrowing, which might result in a potential menace to the Monroe doctrine.

The provisions were being faithfully complied with by the Dominican Republic as follows:

(a) The sums provided in the convention to the ends specified in Article I were being collected without hindrance or opposition by the general receiver, and applied by him as directed in the treaty; and cancellation of the loan was proceeding more rapidly than contemplated by the covenant.

The following excerpts from the report of the general receiver for the year 1919 will show how the situation stood in this respect:

Statement of sinking fund, Dominican Republic, $20,000,000, customs administration loan as of Dec. 31, 1919.

RECEIPTS.

From general receiver of customs, account calendar year—

1908	$331, 757. 53
1909	200, 000. 00
1910	260, 820. 90
1911	394, 092. 24
1912	482, 772. 25
1913	782, 908. 34
1914	207, 666. 01
1915	593, 588. 13
1916	664, 644. 47
1917	1, 295, 042. 73
1918	788, 668. 51
1919	846, 961. 59
From interest allowed by fiscal agent	165, 623. 46
From interest received on bonds purchased	1, 294, 491. 83
Total	8, 309, 037. 90

For $7,784,950 customs administrations bonds purchased, par
value _____ $7,784,950.00
Less discount _____ 341,851.14

                                                                7,443,098.86
Cash balance (several items) _____ 865,989.13

    Total _____ 8,309,087.99
Total of assets in sinking fund _____ 8,813,075.59

The above figures demonstrate that when intervention took place the Dominican Republic was fulfilling the financial obligations of the convention in excess of the minimum stipulated; and that the sinking fund, with the exception of the year 1914—owing then to commercial paralyzation resulting from the outbreak of the World War—kept steadily increasing.

(b) The Dominican Republic had not contracted any new public debt, increasing the liabilities assumed by the United States through the convention or impairing the security—the customs collections—pledged to the service of the loan.

As provided in Article I of the convention, the general receiver paid over to the Dominican Government the surplus outstanding of every month's collection after all the charges and expenses provided for the service of the loan had been met. There is no provision in the treaty determining the application of these sums, and so far as the Government of the United States is concerned in connection with the duties and liabilities assumed through the treaty, whatever application the Dominion Government saw fit to make of these funds would be legally and practically inconsequential, as long as their application in no way interferred with the duties of the general receiver and the service of the loan, and as long as new obligations, increasing the liabilities assumed by the United States through the Dominican-American convention, were not contracted.

The surplus thus received by the Dominican Government was generally applied to current budget expenses. During different periods in the years 1912–1916 the Dominican Government was forced to suspend payment on the regular national budget in order to provide for the expenses incidental to the existence of political disturbances. These conditions, however, in no way interfered with the service of the loan or the customs collections, which were being collected and applied by the general receiver, as specified in the convention. But salaries and other internal public items thus went partially unpaid, and a floating indebtedness, arising out of these arrears, principally on services rendered by Dominican citizens to the Dominican Government, was formed.

The Government of the United States on several occasions remonstrated with the Dominican Government over the creation of these internal credits, alleging that same were a "public debt" and that the Republic was thereby violating article 3 of the convention.

The Dominican Government held that the internal floating indebtedness was not a "public debt," whether legally or in the sense carried by the aim and words of the convention, and that the spirit and the letter of the treaty in the provision contained in article 3 directed the restriction therein included to apply to a regular public debt, increasing the liabilities assumed by the United States through the treaty or impairing the securities tendered in the same by the Dominican Republic.

It would seem that but little doubt can be entertained regarding the status of the internal floating indebtedness and the inadequacy of its being considered a public debt from a legal point of view. All authors agree that a public debt must bear a distinctive condition, the fact of its having been legally contracted or accepted by the State. A public debt is a contract debt, while the indebtedness incurred by the Dominican Government toward its own citizens was an occasional liability resulting from force majeure, which prevented the executive from making effective all the appropriations provided in the budget.

Regarding the point, still more important, perhaps, and more pertinent to the purpose and object of the convention, as to whether the existence of these internal credits increased in any way the liabilities assumed by the United States through that covenant, it seems absolutely impossible to argue successfully any such contention. How could these internal obligations, due in their immense majority to Dominican citizens, constitute a menace to the Monroe doctrine, which the convention was designed to safeguard in its integrity, or impair in any way the guarantee offered by the United States to cover the bond issue? They had not been and could not possibly become a cause for action by a foreign Government. Their creation and existence had not interfered and could not possibly interfere with the proper management and application of the customs collections as provided in the treaty by the receiver general.

The situation on its face does not seem to have justified the allegation made by the United States Government to the effect that the Dominican Republic had violated article 3 of the convention. But even had that claim been established, there is nothing in convention, nothing in international law, and it would seem, from the viewpoint of the Monroe doctrine, nothing in the fundamental policy of the United States to justify the violent action taken by the American Government of invading the Dominican Republic, overthrowing the constitutional Government, and suppressing its sovereignty as a sanction for an alleged violation of a treaty clause and for the refusal of the Dominican Government to subscribe to an unconstitutional protocol surrendering the sovereignty of the nation, the liberty of the people, and the principle of free government into the hands of appointees of the American Government.

How far the recent policy of the United States Government in the Dominican Republic has strayed from the true aims of the convention and from the principles and purposes pleading the American Government to conclude that treaty may be judged on examination of the following excerpt from President Roosevelt's address to the Senate on the subject in 1905, when he submitted the provisional protocol preceding the treaty:

" It can not be too often and too emphatically asserted that the United States has not the slightest desire for territorial aggrandizement at the expense of any of its southern neighbors and will not treat the Monroe doctrine as an excuse for such aggrandizement on its part.

"We do not propose to take any part of Santo Domingo or exercise any other control over the island save what is necessary to its financial rehabilitation in connection with the collection of revenue, part of which will be turned over to the Government to meet the necessary expense of running it, and part of which will be distributed pro rata among the creditors of the Republic upon a basis of absolute equity."

The mechanism provided in the treaty for the regular and unhampered collection of the customs duties by the general receiver and their proper application was designed to work adequately—as it actually and effectually did, under all circumstances. Had the United States Government considered, at the time the treaty was drafted, that military control of the Dominican Republic might become necessary to insure the attainment of the object pursued—the settlement of the foreign debt of the Dominican Republic—they would certainly not have consented to assume the liabilities and responsibilities devolving upon the United States through the covenant without securing by adequate provision the right to that action. As a matter of fact, at the time the convention was being drafted the Government of the United States had the opportunity to satisfy itself that possible revolutionary disturbances would not interfere with the management of customs collections by the general receiver as long as the officials in charge of the collections received due protection in the discharge of their duties, as was provided in the convention. This conviction was the result of experience, for during the initial period of the "modus vivendi" the supervision of customs collections and their application to a provisional fund by American officials was carried out under a state of widespread revolution. It is difficult to conceive that, with such an experience to build upon, the United States Government should have neglected to obtain by provision the necessary liberty of action, had the sound, evident object of the treaty been other than to insure a regular settlement of the Dominican external debt, or had that Government foreseen—as they could not fail to have foreseen if the case could really present itself—that revolutionary disturbances might interfere with the proper observance of the treaty. On the contrary, and as a result of their experience, the treaty was made revolution proof through the placing of the customs collections under the absolute control of the American general receiver, and the granting to that official and to his subordinates of due protection by both Governments.

The consequences of the violent and unwarranted action adopted by the Government of the United States in the Dominican Republic appear now in the form of a dismal legal situation. The constituted authorities of the Republic were deposed, and the military government, whose authority originates in the laws of war, has governed with dictatorial powers a people who were in no sense at war with the United States, and against whom no legal state of war existed. In the exercise of this singular authority the military government has overstepped even the broadest interpretation of the powers vested in such a government by the laws of war, inasmuch as it has assumed to act for the Dominican Republic in the performance of actions which only the people of that Republic, in the exercise of their sovereignty, and through their legal representatives, have the capacity to perform. Among the actions thus performed it is only necessary to cite the appointment of certain diplomatic envoys and the contraction of public debts. Outside of this special phase, and always assuming to act in the name of the Dominican Republic, the military government has promulgated and enforced taxation and legislation without the slightest representation of the people, without their consent, and in many instances indirect opposition to their expressed wishes.

The substance of the whole situation is that of an illegal government, arising out of an illegal intervention—as the present President of the United States characterized the Dominican occupation—suppressing the lawful Government of the Dominican Republic, and has been promulgating constitutional legislation, in the name of the Dominican Republic, for a period of nearly five years. That such proceedings should have been carried out under the authority of the people of the United States, the pioneers and champions of free government and liberty in the continent and throughout the world, adds only to the amazement of the case.

The illegal status of the military administration in the Dominican Republic is so evident as to necessitate no elaborate discussion. The late administration, a few months before its end was made aware of it, and undertook to get out of the trouble it had placed itself in.

The plan prescribed by the last administration on 23d of December, 1920, for the prompt withdrawal of the American forces, which had occupied the territory of the Dominican Republic, was repudiated by the majority of the Dominican people in view of the conditions which were to be carried out before the retirement of the American forces and the restoration of the Dominican Government, and this notwithstanding the positive declaration that the time had arrived when the American Government should divest itself of the responsibilities assumed in the Republic. That plan was followed by another announced by the present administration and published by Rear Admiral Robison in Santo Domingo on the 14th day of June last. This new plan indicates a period of eight months for the definite withdrawal of the American forces and the restoration of a national Dominican Government; it constitutes the military governor the provisional Dominican executive, giving him the authority to promulgate an electoral law, to convene the people to the elections, to name diplomats who will receive his instructions, to join with the American Government in a treaty of evacuation, according to which the Dominican Republic will obligate itself (a) to ratify the acts of the military government; (b) to agree to a loan of $2,500,000 to be applied by the military government to complete certain public improvements; (c) to agree to a further guaranty to protect the payment of the public debt in case the customs revenues are not sufficient; and (d) to intrust the command and organization of the public Dominican forces to American officials, who would form a military mission, would receive compensation from the Dominican Government, be under the authority of the Dominican President, but would be named by the President of the United States.

This last plan has aroused a unanimous and formidable protest among the Dominican people, who absolutely repudiate it, for they understand such plan is in conflict with the inherent rights of their sovereignty and independence.

Without touching on any legal premises, I must distinctly point out that the demand to have the Dominican people consent to a control and command of its armed forces by American officers would in fact create a fundamental obstacle to the success of those aims of friendly assistance which, it is assumed, the Government of the United States has toward the people of the Dominican Republic.

This is not a proposition whose acceptance might depend on a more or less accurate comprehension on the part of the Dominican people of the friendly purposes by which it is inspired. There underlies a question most vital to the Dominican people, who long ago formed their opinions and intentions in regard to this matter that so much concerns their national life, present and future. It need only be recalled that it was precisely because of this that in 1916 they chose to incur—temporarily they were told it would be—the painful trial of military occupation and military Government rather than submit to the demand first made by the American Government upon the Dominican Government and people.

This same proposition, for the control of the armed forces of the Dominican Republic by American officers, "appointed by the President of the Dominican Republic," but "on designation or recommendation of the President of the United States," is textually the basis of the treaty proposed by President Wilson's administration to the Dominican Government in a note sent through the United States Legation in Santo Domingo on November 19, 1915, and later sought by that same administration to be forced by military occupation upon the Dominican Government; and it was this very intervention that the present Chief Executive of the United States charged as "illegal," when outlining before the American electorate his contemplated governmental policies.

The proposition was rejected by President Jimenez's administration in 1915. It was again rejected by my own administration in 1916, in the face of the most ruthless financial and military coercion, said rejection being the cause of proclamation of military government in the Dominican Republic. The people at that time manifested in an unmistakable manner that they preferred to suffer the consequences of that or any other act of force of the Government of the United States rather than voluntarily divest themselves of their sovereignty, surrendering by a treaty forced upon them the control and command of their armed forces to foreign officers. This predicament of the Dominican people in this respect has not undergone the slightest change or alteration throughout the five years of military occupation, and is the same to-day. If there is any change, it is that the harshness, incompetency, and costliness of the American military government have only strengthened their determination and confirmed them in their apprehension of the ills that would surely result from such an arrangement as Washington proposed and tried to force upon us.

The refusal of the Dominican Government, the President, his ministers of state, and the national congress to accept the proposition was inspired by unchallengeable motives of fidelity to the sacred trust committed to them and a firm desire to uphold and protect the constitution of their country. Had either the Jimenez administration in 1915, or my own in 1916, yielded to the demand of the Government of the United States, their officials would have been protected and kept in power by the Government of the United States through the contemplated arrangement, but they would have become justly and properly objects of execration by the Dominican people.

The motives, therefore, standing behind this steadfast and honest conduct on the part of the officials of two different and distinct Dominican administrations, and which were so loyally approved by the people even in the face of untold hardships and suffering caused by the military occupation of their territory, should, it seems to me, command serious consideration from all men inspired by the love of justice and patriotism. The opposition of the Dominican people, to the Government or rule the United States sought and endeavored to impose upon them, was based upon two grounds: First, on an inherent love of liberty and independence such as inspired your forefathers to rebel against the British; and second, a well-grounded fear of countless irremediable ills they would be compelled to suffer as a consequence of the irresponsible power which such an arrangement would place in the hands of foreign officers destined to rule over them.

Such an apprehension, events have shown, was fully justified. The officers called to exercise these extraordinary powers would be really placed above every law and every effective control, other than the distant, indirect, and totally inadequate control which might be exercised over them by the Government of the United States. Possessing themselves or controlling every material agency of authority, they could easily force the legal agencies to conform entirely to their will, however arbitrary. The government of the Republic would soon become a sad tool of their caprice; the national institutions would function under their dictation, and the people would have no legal or material recourse open against this condition of vassalage, while their Government would either remain impotent to protect them against any excesses of such foreign officers, or, if perchance it would fall into weak or unworthy hands, it might accept any kind of tyranny in order to perpetuate themselves in power descending even to abuse of the laws and a prostitution of the public suffrage.

It is a universally admitted social axiom that no irresponsible agency of government can remain in existence without degenerating by natural gravitation into effective tyranny.   The proposition in question would simply resolve itself in fact, if not in statute, in the perpetuation of an irresponsible military régime in Santo Domingo. Should any doubt as to the propriety of the foregoing assertion arise, such doubt might be dispelled by an impartial ponderation of the excesses committed by the subaltern military authorities of occupation in Santo Domingo, committed while these subaltern officers were responsible for their conduct, not before a native government, helpless to repress them, but before their own senior officers, who were honestly bent on having the laws and all personal and property rights respected.   These excesses have been witnessed and commented upon by impartial Americans, and recognized by the authorities of the occupation in a general order of Rear Admiral H. S. Knapp, and in an official statement published by order of Admiral Snowden on January 9, 1920, in which it was specifically stated that " some subaltern military authorities had exceeded themselves to cruelty in their measures of repression."   Such excesses are fatally inherent to a military régime and to the exercise of military supremacy in public administration.   I hope I will not incur an indiscretion by recalling in this connection the condition of the Southern States of the Union when, at the termination of the Civil War, they were subjected to military governments; and these were administered, it is admitted, by general officers of national birth and unimpeachable character.   No possible excellence of personal conditions can compensate or offset the blemishes and wrongs of a régime of force.   A régime of absolute control of the armed forces of the Dominican Republic by American officers, whatever its external characteristics, will inevitably degenerate into a régime of force.

I can not bring myself to believe that the Dominican people merit in any way such harsh and severe treatment, whatever be the friendly motives inspiring such a policy on the part of the United States Government.   Such a policy, furthermore, could not claim any other basis than the right of conquest, which the repeated pronouncements of the United States Government and its international policy, recently expressed by President Harding and Secretary Hughes, seem to conflict in every way.   The fears expressed in regard to the future security of American life and property in the Dominican Republic can not, to my knowledge, be substantiated in one single instance of attack upon such persons or property, or any other foreigners, prior to the intervention.

The Dominican people, however, are willing and able to tender the most effective guaranties, not only in regard to the security of foreign life and property upon a cessation of the military occupation, but also in regard to a permanent suppression of political disturbances and the maintenance of public peace.   I feel inclined to believe that an unbiased consideration of the suggestions I am about to submit will convince of the feasibility of harmonizing the interest of the United States Government by obtaining sufficent guaranties for the maintenance of public peace in Santo Domingo and in such a way as will not conflict with the just aspirations of the Dominican people for the preservation of their liberty and national dignity.

Summarizing our views on the basis of the foregoing considerations, we may reduce them to the following propositions:

1. The restoration of national government in the Dominican Republic should be carried out in such a way as to in no way impair or restrict the sovereignty of the Dominican people.

2. To this end the total evacuation of Dominican territory by the American naval forces, now exercising control through a military government, should be carr.ed out as soon as said national government is duly constituted.

3. Concurrent upon the precedent conditions, the Dominican people should be accorded full opportunity to freely reorganize their administration in accordance with their own constitution and their own laws, and within the unhampered exercise of their sovereignty.

CONCLUSION.

(A) The Dominican Republic has always been, is, and desires to be a free and independent nation that has always been governed by its own laws since it was constituted on February 27, 1844, a sovereign State and assumed its position internationally.

(B) The Dominican Republic has been and is recognized by the nations of the world as a sovereign nation, self-governing and sufficient unto itself to comply with its duties as a sovereign State. The recognition has been recorded many times in treaties of peace, amity, and commerce entered into not only with the United States but also with the principal countries of the world. In consequence of such recognition the Dominican Republic has figured equally with the other nations, great and small, as an integral part with its voice and vote in international congresses, such as the Second Peace Congress at The Hague in 1907 and the Pan American Congresses called on different dates at distinct points in the Americas on the initiative of the Government of the United States or some of the Latin American Republics.

(C) The Dominican Republic has never subscribed with any nation any agreement which would restrict its capacity as sovereign State, nor established to its prejudice any kind of subordination of its political organization or own administration. The convention with the United States in 1907 alone demonstrates the sincere desire of the Dominican Republic to pay its debts, and the unlimited confidence which it had and maintains in the good faith and loyal friendship of the United States. That convention granted to the United States the authority to control the Dominican customs service, with the specific and exclusive object that each month there would be separated from the customs collections a fixed sum to insure the payment of interest and amortization of the public debt. During the 14 years under the convention the service of the Dominican debt has never failed to be met with absolute promptness, and more, by virtue of contingent receipts which might be and in effect have been increased year by year, the debt has been liquidated to such an extent that notwithstanding additional increases authorized by the American Government, it will be entirely liquidated, according to the calculations made and published by American officials, 33 years before the date of maturity stipulated.

(D) In no clause of that convention is the United States given the authority to undertake any kind of intervention, much less an armed one, in Dominican territory.

(E) The convention of 1907 does not accord any authority to the United States to intervene in any manner in the Dominican Republic, and though on the supposition that it might have been granted in the case of the failure of payment of the debt, nevertheless, in no way would such intervention be explained when the payments, as the annual reports of the general receiver show, has never failed to be regular, authentic, and publicly known.

(F) Neither does the convention of 1907 nor any other treaty made by the Dominican Republic accord to the Government of the United States or to the Government of any other nation the authority to intervene in the domestic affairs of the Republic on account of political disturbances. The real cause of these disturbances constitute a subject for deep study and concern for Dominicans, who for many years have sought as a remedy for this evil a new and modern political and administrative organization which would suppress political bossism and put an end to abuses of unscrupulous public officials and would permit the establishment of a popular, responsible government of, by, and for the people, capable of maintaining a broad program of peace, progress, and greater liberty.

(G) The friendly influence of the Government of the United States can be very beneficial to the Dominican people. It should not aspire to anything more than to be useful in the development both commercial and industrial and economic and political. But a system of subjection sanctioned by the American Government to accomplish these ends would only produce lamentable consequences. Instinctively the Dominican people have rejected it, because it constituted a threat against their national life. After having compared demonstrated acts, Dominicans are justified conscientiously in continuing to repudiate it.

(H) Finally, the situation created in Santo Domingo after five years of military occupation, with the destruction of the civil government by virtue of a foreign military government which has acted without the consent of the people, is anomalous, illogical, unjustifiable, and indefensible.

It is urged that an end be put to it, leaving the Dominican people alone and free to reconstruct their system of government and to continue managing it with their own laws, in their capacity of being free, sovereign, and independent.

STATEMENTS OF CAPT. C. S. FREEMAN, UNITED STATES NAVY, NAVY DEPARTMENT, WASHINGTON, D. C., AND MAJ. EDWIN N. McCLELLAN, UNITED STATES MARINE CORPS, HEADQUARTERS UNITED STATES MARINE CORPS.

The CHAIRMAN. Capt. Freeman, you have a statement, I think, prepared at the request of the Secretary?

Capt. FREEMAN. Yes, sir; the Navy Department has prepared two separate statements, one on the Dominican Republic and the other on Haiti. They have been prepared in different offices of the department, and approach the subject in different ways. The Navy Department has had a very short time to make up a statement for the committee, and consequently it was thought best by the Assistant Secretary—the Secretary being absent from the city—to send down the officers who have been mainly responsible for making up these statements.

I have a memorandum prepared on the Dominican Republic, and Maj. McClellan has a somewhat different document prepared on the Haitian Republic. We are here simply to submit these; and if the committee requires any information in the shape of facts in regard to the Dominican Republic or Haiti we are prepared to answer in regard to them, but we do not represent the department as to its policy.

Senator KING. Mr. Chairman, may I inquire of Maj. McClellan whether he prepared that statement in the light of this memoir?

Maj. McCLELLAN. This statement was prepared at the direction of the Secretary of the Navy, to include all the possible facts, from the date of the original occupation of the Republic of Haiti in 1915 until the present time. It is just a copy of documents and reports. In other words, it is not a compilation of opinions or anything like that. It has nothing to do with any memorials or anything else. It is purely an open, frank statement, as far as possible, from the records of the Navy Department.

Senator KING. Then you might want to supplement that after an examination of the charges preferred in the memoir? I do not use the word "charges" in any offensive way, but the charges which may be preferred by the Dominican Government.

Maj. McCLELLAN. I should say that the Secretary of the Navy would direct a representative to prepare a reply, or to cross-examine and carry on every investigation necessary which is disclosed by the memorial.

Senator KING. You would not feel, then, like withholding what you have this morning until——

Maj. McCLELLAN (interposing). No, sir; it is for the benefit of the committee in arriving at their conclusions on the facts.

The CHAIRMAN. Is there no summary of the occupation, no preface to the——

Maj. McCLELLAN. This is contained in chronological order, Senator. As a matter of fact, it gives a brief history of the Republic of Haiti right from the beginning down to 1921. Everything is chronologically arranged. If the committee desires, the Navy Department would be very glad to prepare a brief summary, but, in view of the fact that this material was prepared in practically two days, you can well see that one would not have the time to put the essential points in any digest or any summary.

The CHAIRMAN. I suggest that since two different officers in the department have prepared these records in two days, that they be prepared to file with the committee next week such supplementary matter as in their judgment would be useful to the committee; in the case of one, perhaps, a summary statement; and, in the case of the other, perhaps, some additional documentary matter.

Senator KING. I was going to suggest that that seems to me to be an immense volume, much of which is wholly irrelevant and immaterial.

Maj. McCLELLAN. It is all very relevant, so far as any investigation is concerned. It shows the events, as well as the cause or reasons, historically, as well as the expedients, at the time of the occupation in 1915. It is not an argument, but merely the facts.

Senator KING. Then if you had further time, you would not abridge that?

Maj. McCLELLAN. Not at all; I would merely supplement it with an index for the benefit of the committee, as well as certain documents.

The CHAIRMAN. You have, of course, a copy of that in the department?

Maj. McCLELLAN. I have copies, except of the last 20 pages. I wrote it so hurriedly this morning that I could not finish it.

The CHAIRMAN. Will you take that with you for your convenience, and return it to us with your index and summary, if that suits the other members of the committee?

Senator KING. I think that is a good suggestion.

(The matter referred to is here printed in full, as follows:)

HEADQUARTERS UNITED STATES MARINE CORPS,
Washington, August 15, 1921.

Memorandum for Senator McCormick.
Subject: Memorandum on the Republic of Haiti.
Inclosure: 1.

1. In accordance with instructions received from the Assistant Secretary of the Navy, there is transmitted herewith a short and concise report on the Republic of Haiti, in place of the original and more voluminous report which was delivered to you by Maj. McClellan on August 5, 1921.

JOHN A. LEJEUNE,
Major General, Commandant.

[Memorandum on the Republic of Haiti prepared for Senate committee appointed to inquire into the occupation and administration of the Republic of Haiti and the Dominican Republic by the forces of the United States.]

EARLY HISTORY OF THE REPUBLIC OF HAITI.

The west one-third of the island of Haiti forms the Republic of Haiti while the east two-thirds comes within the boundaries of the Dominican Republic.

Haiti was discovered by Columbus, who landed on the Mole St. Nicholas December 6, 1492. Slaves were imported into Haiti by the Spaniards as early as 1512, and their descendants now reside in the Republic of Haiti. The treaty of 1697 divided the island, the western part to France and the eastern part to Spain. The treaty of 1777 fixed the boundaries between the two divisions. The national convention of 1791 conferred upon the free mulattoes all the privileges of French citizens. The decree conferring these rights being revoked, the mulattoes, joined by the plantation slaves, broke out in insurrection, and turmoil lasted for several years. A French commission proclaimed the abolition of slavery in 1793. In 1795 France acquired title to the entire island.

Toussaint l'Ouverture brought order out of the chaos that had existed since 1791 and then published, subject to the approval of France, a form of constitutional government under which he was to govern for life. This step aroused the suspicions of Bonaparte, who sent Gen. Le Clerc with 25,000 troops to thwart the ambitions of Toussaint. Le Clerc reestablished slavery. After a long struggle Le Clerc proposed terms, and Toussaint, induced by the most solemn guaranties on the part of the French, laid down his arms. He was sent to France, where, in 1803, he died in prison. This treatment of Toussaint caused the Haitians to believe themselves betrayed by the French, and they renewed the struggle under the leadership of Dessalines. The French withdrew from Haiti in 1803.

On January 1, 1804, occurred the declaration of Haitian independence and the restoration of the original name of Haiti. Since this date, a period of over 117 years, Haiti has maintained her independence without break, and this has caused the Haitians to be imbued with the most intense of national spirit. Dessalines was made ruler for life and later proclaimed himself Emperor. He was assassinated in 1806. Between 1806 and 1810 there was civil war between the followers of Christophe and Petion, and during this period the Spaniards reestablished themselves on the eastern part of the island. In 1818 Gen. Boyer succeeded Petion as ruler in the south, and after Christophe's death in 1820 reunited Haiti under one government. The entire island in 1822 again came under one ruler when Boyer reconquered the east from the Spaniards, the name Republic of Haiti being adopted. Boyer was driven into exile in 1848. In the next year the eastern part of the island established itself as the Dominican Republic, and, except for a period of about four years, starting with 1861, when Spain reasserted her authority, has remained independent.

Then followed Herard for the first five months of 1844; Guerrier, who was driven out of office and then died; Pierrot, who was overthrown in February, 1846; Riche, who died suddenly in February, 1847; Soulonque, who was at first President, then Emperor, abdicating under pressure in January, 1859;

Geffrard, who served from 1859 to 1867 and who instituted and developed public instruction; Salnave, who was executed by his countrymen in 1870; Saget, who served out his full term of four years and peacefully retired.

Dominque fled in 1876; Canal resigned; Salomon was overthrown in 1888; Legitime was forced into exile in 1889; Hyppolite fell from his horse and died in 1896; Simon Sam fled in 1902 as a rioting mob threatened his life; Nord Alexis fled in 1908; Antoine Simon fled in 1911; Leconte was blown up with his palace in 1912; Auguste died of a slow and vicious sickness, probably poison, in 1913; Michel Oreste fled into exile in January, 1914; Oreste Zamor ruled for only a brief period, February to October, 1914, his being a revolutionary government, retrograde and ephemeral; Theodore was overthrown in January, 1915; Vilbrun Guillaume Sam was murdered in 1915; and finally we have the present President, Philippe Sudre Dartiguenave, elected in August, 1915.

Thus there have been 2 Emperors, 1 King (Christophe), and 24 Presidents who rose and fell during the history of Haiti.

THE UNITED STATES CALLED UPON FREQUENTLY.

From the days of the American Revolution to the present the United States has been compelled to keep a watchful eye upon the incidents in Haiti, and a casual reading of the fates of the above-named rulers and the many reports on file in the Navy Department will indicate that naval vessels visited that island in the interest of the Haitians themselves, Americans, and other foreigners many times.

Without searching the records earlier than 1857 we find that the United States was called upon to send naval vessels to Haitian waters in the interest of law and order, for the annual report of the Secretary of the Navy for that year shows that the *Cyane* visited Cape Haitien for the relief of an American vessel and two American seamen seized upon suspicion by order of the Haitian Government, and the Secretary's report for 1859 discloses that the *Brooklyn* proceeded to Port au Prince and Aux Cayes to protect United States interests from suffering by the revolution then prevailing in Haiti.

The Secretary's report shows that naval vessels visited Haiti in 1866 because "revolutionary movements and civil disturbances" threatened "to place in jeopardy the lives and property of American residents." In the next year the Secretary reported that naval vessels had visited Haiti, a country "afflicted with perpetual discontent and revolution." Then follows visits in 1868, 1869, 1876, 1888, 1889, 1892, 1902, 1903, 1904, 1905, 1906, 1907, 1908, 1909, 1911, 1912, and 1913. In these years the trouble and disturbances in Haiti was of such a serious nature that the Secretary of the Navy felt called upon to comment upon the fact that warships had been sent there. No doubt there were many times during this period that interior disturbances affected foreign interests without the restraining hands of the United States.

CHRONIC CONDITIONS RECUR IN 1914—FOUR NATIONS LAND.

The U. S. S. *South Carolina* arrived at Port au Prince January 28, 1914, and found conditions so threatening to foreign residents and interests that it became urgently necessary to land the entire marine guard, in company with forces from the *Lancaster* (British), *Conde* (French), and *Bremen* (German). The marines of the *South Carolina* returned on board ship on the 9th of February. Returning to Port au Prince on March 8, 1914, because of political disturbances, the *South Carolina* found it imperatively necessary to remain in that port until April 14, 1914, while the U. S. S. *Montana* was also stationed at Port au Prince from January 25 to February 13, 1914.

The U. S. S. *Washington* arrived at Cape Haitien on June 29, 1914, for the purpose of protecting American and other foreign interests and remained there until July 8, 1914, when relieved by the U. S. S. *South Carolina*. Other naval vessels serving in Haitian waters during the political disturbances of 1914 were the U. S. S. *New Jersey*, U. S. S. *Georgia*, U. S. S. *Tacoma*, U. S. S. *Petrel*, U. S. S. *Nashville*, U. S. S. *Wheeling*, and the U. S. S. *Hancock*, carrying the Fifth Regiment of Marines.

The political situation in Haiti in 1914 was so uncertain that it occupied considerable time of the State Department.

Early in 1915 the political situation in Haiti was such that the State Department became apprehensive for the safety of American and other foreign interests therein, the American consul at Cape Haitien requesting that a warship be sent there. In compliance with this request the U. S. S. *Washington* arrived at Cape Haitien an January 23, 1915, for the purpose of investigating political conditions, and left on the 25th for Port au Prince. It was during this month that Theodore was overthrown as President, and in March was succeeded by the most unfortunate Vilbrun Guillaume Sam. Shortly after the overthrow of Theodore, on February 2, the Secretary of State authorized the Secretary of the Navy to land marines and bluejackets to aid the American minister to Haiti, if such action became necessary; but as events turned out no forces were landed at this time, and Sam entered office as president.

During June, 1915, the French warship *Descartes* proceeded to Cape Haitien, as the French consular agent at that port was fearful for the safety of French residents and interests, and upon the arrival of the *Descartes* a landing party was sent ashore from that vessel. This force was withdrawn on the 24th.

The U. S. S. *Washington*, with Rear Admiral Caperton, arrived at Cape Haitien July 1, 1915, and on the 3d established a field radio station ashore, and on the 9th landed marines from the U. S. S. *Washington* and bluejackets from the *Eagle*.

On July 27, 1915, a revolution broke out in Port au Prince that resulted in the execution by the Haitians of a large number of political prisoners and the death of the President of Haiti, Sam, at the hands of a mob that violated the French Legation, in which Sam had taken asylum. Rear Admiral Caperton reported in part: "Dominican Legation violated Tuesday; Gen. Oscar, chief of arrondissement force, removed and killed. At about 10.30 a. m. this morning French Legation invaded by a mob of about 60 Haitians, better class; President Guillaume forcibly removed from upstairs room and killed at legation gate and body cut in pieces and paraded about town. No government or authority in city."

Upon the first report Rear Admiral Caperton, in the *Washington*, sailed from Cape Haitien for Port au Prince, leaving the *Eagle* to attend to affairs at the cape.

Upon arriving at Port au Prince at 11.50 a. m., July 28, Rear Admiral Caperton immediately assumed control of the situation. Under orders of the Navy Department, and in cooperation with the Department of State, Rear Admiral Caperton, on the afternoon of July 28, 1915, landed a provisional regiment of two battalions, composed of marines and bluejackets, under command of Capt. George Van Orden, United States Marine Corps, and occupied Port au Prince. No resistance was encountered except some sniping at the marines, which fire was returned, resulting in 2 Haitians being killed and 10 wounded.

The U. S. S. *Eagle* landed 20 men at Cape Haitien at the request of the French consul on the 28th. The *Descartes* landed a small French force at Port au Prince on August 2, 1915.

At the request of Rear Admiral Caperton an additional regiment of marines was sent to Haiti, arriving at Port au Prince on August 4, 1915. The U. S. S. *Tennessee* arrived at Port au Prince on August 15, 1915, with another regiment and Col. Littleton W. T. Waller, United States Marine Corps, who was placed in command of all troops ashore in Haiti.

Pursuant to instructions received from the Navy Department on August 7, 1915, Rear Admiral Caperton on August 10 issued the following proclamation to the Haitian people:

"I am directed by the United States Government to assure the Haitian people that the United States has no object in view except to insure, establish, and help to maintain Haitian independence and the establishment of a stable and firm government by the Haitian people.

"Every assistance will be given to the Haitian people in their attempt to secure these ends. It is the intention to retain United States forces in Haiti only so long as will be necessary for this purpose."

This proclamation was also published at St. Marc, Haiti, on August 10, 1915, and on August 18 Rear Admiral Caperton requested the American consul at Port au Prince to direct the several consular representatives of the United States in Haiti to give out the above proclamation in their districts.

PROCEDURE ADOPTED TO ASSIST HAITI.

On August 10, 1915, the Secretary of State advised the American minister in Haiti concerning the procedure which he should adopt for the purpose of assisting the Haitian National Assembly to elect a president of the Republic, viz: First. That Congress understand that the Government of the United States intends to uphold it but that it can not recognize action which does not establish in charge of Haitian affairs those whose abilities and dispositions give assurance of putting an end to factional disorder. Second. In order that no misunderstandings can possibly occur after election it should be made perfectly clear to candidates, as soon as possible, and in advance of their election, that the United States expects to be intrusted with the practical control of the customs and such financial control over the affairs of the Republic of Haiti as the United States may deem necessary for efficient administration. Further, that the Government of the United States considers it its duty to support a constitutional government. It means to assist in the establishment of such a government and to support it as long as necessity may require. It has no design upon the political or territorial integrity of Haiti. On the contrary what has been done, as well as what will be done, is conceived in an effort to aid the people of Haiti in establishing a stable Government and maintaining domestic peace throughout the Republic.

DARTIGUENAVE ELECTED PRESIDENT.

Election day, August 12, 1915, passed without disorder and Dartiguenave was elected president, votes for president being cast by congress as follows: Dartiguenave, 94; Cauvin, 14; Thezan, 4; Bobo, 3; 1 blank. Dartiguenave was declared elected amidst enthusiasm and immediately took the oath of office. Following his election he spoke, stating that he had never been chief of any faction, band, or group, and that he would govern solely for the benefit of Haiti, according to the constitution and the laws; he later expressed appreciation for American forces, which, he stated, had made possible an election free from intimidation.

REINFORCEMENTS SENT TO HAITI.

Rear Admiral Caperton, on August 19, 1915, requested that an additional regiment of marines of not less than two battalions of four companies each of infantry and an Artillery battalion with five additional officers for staff positions, together with eight medical officers and hospital corpsmen and other equipment, be sent to Haiti and that upon receipt of said reinforcements he stated he would occupy the seaport towns in accordance with departmental instructions relative to occupation of customhouses. In compliance with this request the U. S. S. Tennessee on August 31 arrived in Port au Prince and landed Headquarters Artillery Battalion and the First and Ninth Companies, and then proceeded to Cape Haitien, where the Thirteenth Company landed on September 3. This battalion had an enlisted strength of 318 men, armed with twelve 2-inch landing guns and two 4.7-inch heavy field guns, and sailed from the United States August 26.

THE CUSTOMS TAKEN OVER.

The Navy Department cooperating with the State Department, on August 19, 1915, directed Rear Admiral Caperton to assume charge of the customhouses at Jacmel, Aux Cayes, Jeremie, Miragoane, Petit Goave, Port au Prince, St. Marc. Gonaives, Port de Paix, Cape Haitien, funds collected to be use for organization and maintenance of an efficient constabulary, for conducting such temporary public works as will afford immediate relief through employment for starving populace and discharged soldiers, and finally for supporting Dartiguenave government.

On August 30, 1915, Rear Admiral Caperton informed the Secretary of the Navy that he had organized customs service for the seacoast of Haiti with Paymaster Charles Morris as administrator of customs, Navy pay and line officers being appointed as collectors of customs and captains of ports for the different ports and that he could not occupy Aux Cayes and Jacmel until the arrival of the U. S. S. *Sacramento* and requested that the arrival of that vessel be expedited. On August 31, Rear Admiral Caperton informed the Secretary of the Navy that "unless otherwise directed will occupy and begin administering customhouse at Port au Prince at 10 a. m., September 2." The customhouse at Port au Prince was taken over by the United States naval force on September 2, the Haitian Government having been advised in the premises and the following notice was published in the newspapers and otherwise:

" NOTICE.

"For the protection of the Haitian Government and people and for better safe guarding their interests, under the direction of the Government of the United States of America, I have assumed control of the maritime customs service of Haiti.

"The receipts from these customs will be collected by officers of the United States Navy and will be applied to improving the condition of the Haitian people and to the support of the Haitian Government. Funds not so expended will be held in trust for the time being for the people of Haiti by the Government of the United States."

THE TREATY.

As a result of the negotiations which had been carried on over a considerable period of time between the American chargé d'affaires and representatives of the Republic of Haiti, a treaty of mutual amity for the purpose of remedying the financial conditions and assisting the economic development and tranquility of Haiti was signed at Port au Prince, September 16, 1915, subsequently ratified by both the contracting parties, and proclaimed in the United States, May 3, 1916. The United States Government recognized the government of Dartiguenave of Haiti on September 17, fired the necessary salute, and Rear Admiral Caperton, accompanied by his staff, called on the President of the Republic of Haiti, his call being returned by the President of Haiti and his cabinet on September 18.

In the following proclamation the President of the United States proclaimed this treaty on May 3, 1916:

"Whereas a treaty between the United States of America and the Republic of Haiti having for its objects the strengthening of the amity existing between the two countries, the remedying of the present condition of the revenues and finances of Haiti, the maintenance of the tranquility of that Republic, and the carrying out of plans for its economic development and prosperity was concluded and signed by their respective plenipotentiaries at Port au Prince on the 16th day of September, 1915, the original of which treaty, being in the English and French languages, is word for word as follows."

The preamble reads in part as follows:

"The United States and the Republic of Haiti desiring to confirm and strengthen the amity existing between them by the most cordial cooperation in measures for their common advantage;

"And the Republic of Haiti desiring to remedy the present condition of its revenues and finances, to maintain the tranquility of the Republic, to carry out plans for the economic development and prosperity of the Republic and its people;

"And the United States being in full sympathy with all of these aims and objects and desiring to contribute in all proper ways to their accomplishment" ; etc.

Article II of this treaty provides for the nomination by the President of the United States and appointment by the President of the Republic of Haiti of a general receiver to supervise customs, and of a financial adviser. Article X provides for the establishment of the Gendarmerie d'Haiti, to be organized and officered by Americans, nominated by the President of the United States and appointed by the President of Haiti. Article XIV provides that should the necessity occur the United States "will lend an efficient aid for the preservation of Haitian independence and the maintenance of a government adequate for the protection of life, property, and individual liberty," and furthermore that the United States and the Republic of Haiti " shall have authority to take such steps as may be necessary to insure the complete attainment of any of the objects comprehended " in the treaty.

This treaty shall remain in " full force and virtue for the term of 10 years," and " further for another term of 10 years if, for specific reasons represented by either of the high contracting parties, the purpose " of the treaty has not been fully accomplished.   Over five years of this period has expired.

MARTIAL LAW.

On August 30, 1915, Rear Admiral Caperton informed the Secretary of the Navy and the Commander in Chief as follows:

" On account increasing uneasiness Port au Prince, present Government confronted with conditions apparently unable to control, propagation by newspapers and public men of inflammatory propaganda against Government and American occupation, disloyalty to present Government of some Government officials, and in order to better support the present Government I will tomorrow, September 3, proclaim martial law in Port au Prince, Haiti.   This action in accordance with American chargé d'affaires."   Rear Admiral Caperton further announced, on the same date, that he had been requested by the President of Haiti to establish martial law.   Pursuant to the above information, Rear Admiral Caperton formally issued the proclamation of martial law on September 3. 1915, at Port au Prince, Haiti:

" PROCLAMATION.

" Information having been received from the most reliable sources that the present Government of Haiti is confronted with conditions which they are unable to control, although loyally attempting to discharge the duties of their respective offices; and these facts having created a condition which requires the adoption of different measures than those heretofore applied; and in order to afford the inhabitants of Port au Prince and other territory hereinafter described the privileges of the Government, exercising all the functions necessary for the establishment and maintenance of the fundamental rights of man, I hereby, under my authority as commanding officer of the forces of the United States of America in Haiti and Haitian waters, proclaim that martial law exists in the city of Port au Prince and the immediate territory now occupied by the forces under my command.

" I further proclaim, in accordance with the law of nations and the usages, customs, and functions of my own and other Governments, that I am invested with the power and responsibility of government in all its functions and branches throughout the territory above described, and the proper administration of such government by martial law will be provided for in regulations to be issued from time to time as required by the commanding officer of the forces of the United States of America in Haiti and Haitian waters.

" The martial law herein proclaimed, and the things in that respect so ordered, will not be deemed or taken to interfere with the proceedings of the constitutional Government and Congress of Haiti, or with the administration of justice in the courts of law existing therein, which do not affect the military operations or the authorities of the Government of the United States of America.

" All the municipal and other civil employees are, therefore, requested to continue in their present vocations without change; and the military authorities will not interfere in the functions of the civil administration and the courts, except in so far as relates to persons violating military orders or regulatons, or otherwise interfering with the exercise of military authority.   All peaceful citizens can confidently pursue their usual occupations, feeling that they will be protected in their personal rights and property, as well as in their proper social relations.

" The commanding officer of the United States expeditionary force, Col. Littleton W. T. Waller, United States Marine Corps, is empowered to issue the necessary regulations and appoint the necessary officers to make this martial law effective.

" Done at the city of Port au Prince, Haiti, this 3d day of September, A. D. 1915."

The commanding officers who had taken over the various coast towns in the adjoining territory of Haiti were informed by Rear Admiral Caperton on September 21 that his proclamation of September 3, relative to martial law, applied to all the territory within their jurisdiction, and appointed the provost marshal and the provost judge for each said town and territory immediately surrounding.

On September 4, 1916, the chargé d'affaires, Port au Prince, reported to the Secretary of State that all civil officials provided for by the treaty have now taken their offices, and requested information as to turning over all Federal civil administration at present conducted by President's orders to the Haitian Government, in reply to which the Secretary of State announced that the time had not yet arrived for the withdrawal of the naval forces in Haiti and the termination of martial law, and that it was the desire of the department that the present status be continued until such time as the gendarmerie has proven itself loyal and efficient in all emergencies and the internal peace of Haiti is thereby definitely assured.

On September 22, 1920, the Judge Advocate General of the Navy rendered a legal opinion with reference to the status of the marines in Haiti, which is partially quoted below:

" The military forces of the United States have not displaced the civil government of Haiti and established a military government of the United States in that country, but are engaged pursuant to law in lending efficient aid to the Republic of Haiti in preserving a republican form of government and suppressing domestic violence. By treaty between the United States and Haiti, signed September 16, 1915, duly ratified by both Governments and proclaimed May 3, 1916 (39 Stat., 1654), one object of which, as stated in the preamble, was ' to maintain the tranquility of the Republic [of Haiti],' it was provided (Art. XIV) that—

" ' The high contracting parties shall have authority to take such steps as may be necessary to insure the complete attainment of any of the objects comprehended in this treaty, and should the necessity occur the United States will lend an efficient aid for the preservation of Haitian independence and the maintenance of a government adequate for the protection of life, property, and individual liberty.'

" Pursuant to the above treaty and upon recommendation of the State Department expressly reciting the desirability ' that every effort should be made to put the provisions thereof in operation with the least delay,' Congress enacted a law which was approved by the President of the United States on June 12, 1916 (39 Stat., 223), and which provided in part—

" 'That the President of the United States be, and he is hereby, authorized, in his discretion, to detail to assist the Republic of Haiti such officers and enlisted men of the United States Navy and the United States Marine Corps as may be mutually agreed upon by him and the President of the Republic of Haiti.'

" Thereafter, on June 12, 1918, the Republic of Haiti adopted a new constitution, article 127 of which provided that—

" ' The present constitution and all the treaties actually in force or to be concluded hereafter and all the laws decreed in accordance with this constitution or with these treaties shall constitute the law of the country, and their relative superiority shall be determined by the order in which they are here mentioned.'

" The treaty of 1916 above quoted was in force on the date of the Haitian constitution, it having been expressly provided in said treaty (Art. XVI) that ' the present treaty shall remain in full force and virtue for the term of 10 years, to be counted from the day of exchange of ratifications, and, further, for another term of 10 years if, for specific reasons presented by either of the high contracting parties, the purpose of this treaty has not been fully accomplished.' Accordingly, the said treaty of 1916 was by explicit provision of the Haitian constitution of 1918 declared to be ' the law of the country '; that is, the law of Haiti, just as under the United States Constitution (Art. VI) the said treaty of May 3, 1916, and the act of Congress of June 12, 1916, enacted pursuant to said treaty, are declared to be ' the supreme law of the land '; that is, the law of the United States.

" In other words, the United States has guaranteed to the Haitian Republic that it will lend efficient aid in preserving government and tranquillity in that country, just as it has given a similar guaranty to the States of this Union; and Congress has given discretion to the President of the United States to detail land and naval forces to enforce this guaranty in both cases upon mutual agreement between the President of the United States and the Government requiring such assistance.

"The marine brigade is now in Haiti by authority of law for the purposes of maintaining the recognized Government of that Republic and preserving tranquillity, occupying in this respect a status substantially identical with that which would exist should Federal troops be sent into a State of this Union upon the request of the recognized government of that State for the same purpose.

"Our military forces operating in Haiti, pursuant to the treaty and the act of Congress above cited, by mutual agreement between this Government and the Republic of Haiti, for the purpose of suppressing armed uprisings and maintaining the constitutional Government which has been recognized by the President of the United States, have the same powers and duties as the military forces of Haiti in the administration of martial law in that country and in the resort to the laws and usages of war, for the existing conditions of local disturbance constitute, in the language of the Supreme Court, 'a state of war'—not a state of war between the United States and Haiti, but domestic war which the United States, in the fulfillment of its treaty obligations, is bound to assist the Government of Haiti to suppress.

"That martial law in Haiti was originally established by the head of our military forces in that country upon the request of the Haitian President is shown by the official records of this department; and indirect reference to this fact is also to be found in the opening paragraph of the proclamation of martial law.

"That the martial law thus established was not intended to displace the constitutional Government of Haiti, but was in support of that Government, is expressly disclosed by the following further paragraph of the aforesaid proclamation:

"'The martial law herein proclaimed, and the things in that respect so ordered, will not be deemed or taken to interfere with the proceedings of the constitutional Government and congress of Haiti, or with the administration of justice in the courts of law existing therein, which do not affect the military operations or the authorities of the Government of the United States of America.'

"The above-quoted proclamation was issued on September 3, 1915. The martial law thus established has been continued ever since, with the consent of the Government of Haiti, as shown by the numerous instances in which the President of that Republic has decorated members of our military forces and extended to them his most cordial expressions of appreciation for their services to his country; also, the new Haitian constitution expressly provides (Title VII) that 'all the acts of the Government of the United States during its military occupation of Haiti are ratified and validated.' Our operations in Haiti have also been conducted with the express sanction of Congress since the act of June, 1916, above cited, which placed entirely in the discretion of the President of the United States the detail of such military forces of the Navy and Marine Corps to assist the Republic of Haiti 'as may be mutually agreed upon by him and the President of the Republic of Haiti.'

"Such being the status of our military forces in Haiti, engaged in administering martial law in support of the constitutional government, in a country in which a state of domestic war exists, there can be no question that the military commander of such forces is authorized to take any steps necessary and sanctioned by the laws and customs of war to meet the exigencies of the situation. Military commissions and provost courts are recognized instrumentalities of martial law. Recourse to such exceptional military courts is justified whenever the civil courts are closed, or when necessary for the trial of offenses against the military forces or violations of regulations required to make martial law effective. Otherwise, in the language of the Supreme Court above quoted, 'martial law and the military array of the Government would be mere parade, and rather encourage attack than repel it.' In the proclamation hereinbefore quoted, it was stated that upon this point that 'the military authorities will not interfere in the functions of the civil administration and the courts except in so far as relates to persons violating military orders or regulations, or otherwise interfering with the exercise of military authority.' This department's records show that the territory under martial law has been extended to include parts of Haiti not specifically embraced in the original proclamation;

It does not, however, appear that the jurisdiction of military courts has been enlarged so as to embrace offenses not described in that proclamation, and therefore the trial of such other offenses must properly be left to the civil courts."

THE SO-CALLED CENSORSHIP.

The following order was promulgated throughout the Republic of Haiti on September 3, 1915:

"The freedom of the press will not be interfered with, but license will not be tolerated. The publishing of false or incendiary propaganda against the Government of the United States or the Government of Haiti, or the publishing of any false, indecent, or obscene propaganda, letters signed or unsigned, or matter which tends to disturb the public peace will be dealt with by the military courts. The writers of such articles and the publishers thereof will be held responsible for such utterances and will be subject to fine or imprisonment, or both, as may be determined."

This ban was modified inferentially recently and with unfortunate results.

A paraphrase of a dispatch from the brigade commander dated January 9, 1921, to the Major General Commandant follows:

"Rush. 8608. President of Haiti sent me to-day the following letter:

"'DEAR MONSIEUR LE COLONEL: Certain newspapers, relying upon an impunity which until now has been assured them, for some time past have been insulting the officers of the gendarmerie and the Government, spreading the most insidious propaganda and causing uneasiness among the people.

"'If we persist in viewing with indifference this state of affairs which I qualify as intolerable, I foresee that the military officials must expect to witness acts of a still more regrettable nature.

"'I therefore address myself to you, to whom is intrusted the maintaining of public security and peace, asking you to take all measures that are demanded by the circumstances.

"'In case you judge it is necessary to have them, the Government holds at your disposition other facts, apart from the above.

"'Accept, Dear Monsieur le Colonel, the assurance of my sentiments of cordial consideration.

"'DARTIGUENAVE.'

"Have replied, acknowledging receipt of letter and stating that I have taken the subject matter under consideration. Prompt instructions requested.

"JOHN H. RUSSELL."

The following letter dated January 18, 1921, was written by the brigade commander to the Chief of Naval Operations, Navy Department, via the Major General Commandant:

"1. In paragraphs 11 and 12 of the above reference, copy attached hereto, it was pointed out that the Haitian politicians had found a veritable gold mine in the situation that had been created for them during the summer months.

"2. Since the writing of the above report the political conditions in Haiti have gradually been growing worse. There have been several causes that have contributed to this end. Among them may be named the following:

"(1) The scurrilous and insulting articles that daily appear in the press defaming the Haitian Government, the occupation, and the gendarmerie.

"(2) So-called patriotic meeting and assemblies where unbridled tongues give forth vilifying words against the Haitian Government, the occupation, and the gendarmerie.

"(3) The lack of any attempt on the part of the Haitian Government to put a stop to such abuses and the knowledge that the military occupation will not interfere.

"(4) The knowledge of the people that the Haitian courts would not support the Haitian Government in any attempt to check abuses.

"(5) The general dislike of the black man for the white.

"(6) The prevalent belief that the occupation will soon be withdrawn and Haiti left to her own devices.

"(7) The support of certain so-called patriotic societies by persons or organizations in the United States.

"(8) The present poor economic condition of the country which has led to many unemployed.

"(9) And last, but far from least, the intense rivalry among the politicians for the next presidency. The candidates are lining up and seeking by every means to promote their own interests.

"3. The result of all this turmoil and license is bound to affect the military situation. Tranquillity continues to reign throughout the entire country, but rumors regarding contemplated disturbances are daily becoming more numerous. It is true that when run down nothing is found, but it is my opinion, founded on a knowledge of the Haitian and an absolute knowledge of the military situation in Haiti that, unless steps are shortly taken to curb the license now being permitted, local disturbances will occur and eventually the tranquillity of the country will be again disrupted.

"4. From a military point of view the situation can be kept well in hand with the troops at my command, but life and property can be destroyed and a general condition of unrest created that will again necessitate active and forceful measures which, in my opinion, could well be avoided.

"5. It is my opinion that the Haitian Government should be forced to openly admit its inability to restrain the press and protect itself, the occupation and the gendarmerie, from its insulting and scurrilous remarks due to the inefficiency and inadequacy of the judiciary system of Haiti. Such admission has already been made but not openly. If so made it would throw the onus of such work on the military occupation, which could put in operation laws similar to those now existing in the Dominican Republic relating to the press, freedom of speech, etc.

"6. I have deemed it my duty to make the above report, as I am firmly of the belief that some action toward the bridling of the press should be undertaken, and I desire, as a matter of self-protection, to present this opinion in order that if such a condition is allowed to continue unabated and disturbances occur the military occupation will not be held responsible therefor."

On January 28, 1921, Rear Admiral Snowden, United States Navy, military governor of Santo Domingo and military representative of the United States in Haiti, placed the following indorsement on the above letter:

"1. A copy of the above-mentioned report has just come into the hands of the undersigned.

"2. I approve and support in the strongest terms the letter and advice of the brigade commander in Haiti and believe that the situation is critical as regards the near future.

"3. The conditions are such as can not be permitted to continue and is impossible of control under the present policy of free and unlimited license as to libel, defamation, and malicious propaganda.

"4. I can not too strongly urge the defense of the military forces from malicious libel and propaganda by laws or orders permitting free speech but not license.

"5. It is a fact that the present policy of license regarding propaganda, etc., here and in Haiti will before long no doubt use the power of the military forces to control the situation at the expense of many lives on both sides, but measures should be at once taken to curb these attacks upon the military forces, in order that a critical condition may not be brought about."

The Secretary of the Navy wrote as follows to the Secretary of State on February 15, 1921:

Referring to my letter of February 7, 1921 (P. D. 238–6), in which I inclosed copies of two confidential reports from the brigade commander of the United States marine brigade in Haiti, I have the honor to transmit herewith a copy of a report from the military governor of Santo Domingo, who is also the military representative of the United States in Haiti, in which he submits his comment on the brigade commander's report of January 18, 1921, which was one of the reports submitted in my letter, above cited.

Particular attention is invited to the closing sentence of the governor's letter, in which he states as follows:

"I have no doubt of the power of the military forces to control the situation at the expense of many lives on both sides, but measures should be at once taken to curb these attacks upon the military forces in order that a critical condition may not be brought about."

In the following dispatch to the commandant of the Marine Corps, date May 17, 1921, the brigade commander requested authority to bring to trial certain persons:

"Special rush 8617 for Opnav Haitian press continues to publish scurrilous and insulting articles daily. These articles are untruthful, incendiary in character, and seriously tend to disturb the peace in Port au Prince, creating a condition of grave danger between the gendarmerie and marines and natives. The Haitian Government should be forced to protect the officers and men of the gendarmerie and occupation, or the occupation should be allowed to protect itself. The gendarmerie begin to feel that they are not being supported. It is generally known, and has been stated by the President, that Haitian courts will not convict such cases, as trial must be by jury, and the juries are with the people whose passions have been aroused by unbridled press. Believe that threat of trial or only one case would be sufficient to restore to normal conditions. Earnestly recommend that I be authorized to try by provost court those concerned in the publishing of falsehoods or articles against the gendarmerie and occupation. Request early reply. 1640."

The following dispatch, dated May 24, 1921, was sent by the Secretary of the Navy to the brigade commander:

" 8624. The proclamation of martial law as proclaimed on September 3, 1915, and ratified by Haitian constitution reserved from the jurisdiction of civil courts of Haiti those things which affect the military operations or the authorities of the Government of the United States of America. Agitation against United States officials who are aiding and supporting constitutional Government tending to undermine their authority and coupled with political agitation looking to destruction of the constitutional government will lead to revolution and anarchy with consequent destruction of life and property and prolonged misery for Haitian people. Not only in self-defense of American forces but in self-defense of Haitian Government and people such measures must be taken as will suppress such agitation and prevent return of violent disorders. From the information before you, you will determine what action under martial law the crisis demands and act accordingly, keeping in mind the idea of action only in self-defense of your command and Haitian Government, and employing processes of martial law only where your conservative judgment admits the situation demands its exercise, and then restricting penalties to serve the purposes of prevention rather than punishment. In respect to those who attack the Haitian President and Government direct rather than through the American forces, it would be advisable to have the Haitian President request you or direct the chief of gendarmerie to proceed against them through the agencies of martial law which is maintained for and in behalf of the constitutional Government of Haiti. You would thereby have on record a statement of what the Haitian state construes the crisis demands in the way of prevention in order to preclude the engineering of domestic disorder and attempts to overthrow the constitutional government by violence. In trials before military commissions or provost courts the charge should cite the offense against the military forces or the violation of a regulation adopted to make martial law effective. Should there be insufficient regulations to cover the existing situation such should be promulgated. In the absence of appropriate regulations on which to base a trial, those who, from the information before you, you have reasonable grounds to believe are concerned in unlawful opposition and the encouragement of domestic violence may be arrested and held in confinement until the exigency has passed and the constituted authorities are able to execute the laws, 1645, Sec. Nav."

In carrying out the above instructions the brigade commander on May 26, 1921, published the following proclamation:

HEADQUARTERS FIRST PROVISIONAL BRIGADE,
UNITED STATES MARINE CORPS,
Port au Prince, Republic of Haiti, May 26, 1921.

To all inhabitants:

The United States forces in Haiti are engaged in aiding and supporting the constitutional Government of Haiti and are your friends.

By their efforts and those of the gendarmerie of Haiti peace and tranquillity have been established throughout your land, permitting you to cultivate your gardens, conduct your business, and earn an honest living.

The only agitation that is being carried on in all Haiti is that undertaken by a few newspapers in the large cities and by a few persons in so-called political speeches.

This agitation, however, is a menace to the condition of law and order that has been given to you, and consequently it becomes necessary to issue the following order under the powers and authority of martial law.

ORDER.

While the freedom of the press and speeches are practically unrestricted, articles or speeches that are of an incendiary nature or reflect adversely upon the forces in Haiti or tend to stir up an agitation against the United States officials who are aiding and supporting the constitutional Government of Haiti, or articles or speeches at the President or the Haitian Government are prohibited. Any offender against this order will be brought to trial before a military tribunal.

JOHN H. RUSSELL,
Colonel, United States Marine Corps, Commanding First Brigade,
United States Marines, and United States Forces in Haiti.

On the date the above proclamation was published the President of the Republic of Haiti wrote a letter to the brigade commander reading in part as follows:

"I have this day received your proclamation dated May 26, 1921. It has my full and entire approval, and I desire that it be given its full and entire effect.

"Pray accept dear M. le Colonel the renewed expression of my best sentiments.

" DARTIGUENAVE."

On June 24, 1921, the following memorandum was prepared for the Secretary of the Navy and the major general commandant:

MEMORANDUM.

"1. For some time past the American authorities in Haiti did not concern themselves with the character of articles published in the Haitian newspapers. A very small percentage of the population in Haiti is able to read, and as the circulation of the Haitian newspaper seldom exceeds a few hundred it was considered that such newspapers would not exercise much influence outside of a few large towns, and they did not exercise much influence until recently.

2. "Partly as a reflection of race disturbances and agitation in the United States, partly as a reflection of the late political campaign in the United States, but principally owing to the characteristic which many Haitian writers have of working themselves into a passion with little or no propocation, freedom of the press was construed to be unlimited license to attack not only the Government of Haiti and the American occupation, but also the personal and private character of any American or any Haitian official.

"3. Continued and unrestrained abuse of officers and men had a tendency to destroy any friendly relationship between the marines and the native population, and the attacks gradually assumed more and more the nature of propaganda toward a new revolution against the constitutional government of Haiti and threatened to recall the condition of anarchy which had recently been suppressed.

"4. A copy of the dispatch from the brigade commander in Haiti quoting from an article published in a Haitian newspaper, a copy of the order prohibiting incendiary articles from being published in Haiti, and a copy of the department's dispatch to the brigade commander authorizing such action are attached hereto.

"5. In interpreting the order the usual rules of interpretation should be followed and the order should be considered as a whole. Considered in such wise, it is apparent that it is intended not to prohibit constructive criticism or the advocation of policies different from those advocated by the Government of Hati, or to otherwise interfere with freedom of speech and press, but simply to prevent the publication of articles or speeches which are in the nature of propaganda calculated and intended to bring on a new revolution and a condition of anarchy which, as stated in the Secretary's dispatch, will inevitably lead to destruction of life and property and prolonged misery for the Haitian people.

"6. So far as attacks on individuals are concerned, no action is intended to suppress these unless they are slanderous or libelous. Charges made against Americans, whether presented privately or publicly, are always properly investigated, and no attempt to suppress such charges is contemplated, except in those cases where they are inspired by a desire to create disorder and are based on nothing but an evil imagination.

"7. In our own country we are not without examples, and recent ones, of unfortunate riotings and killings having resulted from a failure of the proper authorities to prevent the cultivation of criminal mob violence. It is the desire to avoid such violence in Haiti that led to the department's action in respect to those in Haiti who attempt to stir up the evil and the ignorant to violence. There is inclosed a quotation from a letter from the President of Haiti to the brigade commander fully approving the action taken. It was largely upon the President's urgent representation that the proclamation was issued.

"8. In addition to the above-mentioned inclosures there is also attached an excerpt from a Haitian newspaper article which refers particularly to ex-President Wilson."

The dispatch of the brigade commander referred to in the above memorandum follows:

"8627. Reference your 8625-1415, Courier Haitien published article April 16 on departure of Col. Hooker, in part as follows: 'Man proposes, God disposes. He did not think that he would leave Haiti so soon. He did not think that he would go without having executed his infamous project against us.

"'PAR. 2. We wish you bon voyage, Col. Hooker. As to the money that you have taken from Haiti, as to the fortune that you have amassed in the country in violation of our poor peasants, the brave Cacos, you will not enjoy it yourself, and for all the wrong that you have done to a good, peaceful, and hardworking people for the sole purpose of enriching yourself at its expense, your children will pay to the fourth generation for this.

"'PAR. 4. Col. Hooker, the shades of Pierre Pinede, of Saj Peralte, and of such others that you have sent to their forefathers rejoice at your departure and curse you.

"'PAR. 5. With pockets full of gold, depart happily, but remember that there is an eminent justice that sooner or later will make you pay for all the suffering that you have made the Haitian people endure.

"'PAR. 6. The curses of the widows, the orphans, and the bereaved fiancees of your innumerable victims accompany you, Col. Hooker.'

"PAR. 7. Jolibois Fils editor sent paper to Hooker marked, 'Copy of paper with compliments.' Some days afterwards Hooker entered Cinema and spoke to Chevallier. Jolibois was talking with Chevallier at the time and saluted Hooker. Hooker told him he did not mind attacks on or criticism of his official acts, but that he had protected him, and that a personal attack was the act of a pig. Hooker then went to a theater and nothing further occurred. Long account of incident published in paper by Jolbois, together with letter and cable sent. Summon ordering brigade inspector immediately investigated. Jolibois' manner and demeanor as taken by Hooker, Jolibois in no way threatens at any time during evening.

"PAR. 8. Officers and men of brigade and gendarmes were sent the Haitien daily. Call Marine Corps veritable Huns. Presence of marine alone permits such insulting attacks, for under Haitian régime the editor would have been imprisoned and papers would have been stopped. Pinede died natural death from consumption and smallpox. Hooker not in Haiti when Saul Peralte was killed.

"PAR. 9. In above attack Jolibois is evidently trying to stir up people against occupation. Notice how he speaks of brave Cacos. Papers distributed and are read to people by agents in interior. 1745."

The newspaper article referred to in the foregoing memorandum that villifies ex-President Wilson reads as follows:

[Extract from article appearing in Les Annales Capoises, Cape Haitien, Republic of Haiti, under date of Mar. 4, 1921.]

"To-day in the history of Haiti the 4th of March is the beginning of a new era. Mr. Harding, the defender of our cause and advocate of our rights, had entered the White House as President of the United States in place of Mr. Woodrow Wilson, the man of baneful prejudices, who conspired against the existence of our country with the complicity of a group of business men in America, such as Messrs. Farnham & Co. May he retire to private life followed by the maledictions of Haitian people and may he be perpetually tormented by remorse, that canker of a guilty conscience, have a sad and taciturn ending, continually gnashing his teeth, a prey to horrible hallucinations and believing himself to be always pursued by the invisible specters of those of us who have died martyrs to the cause of liberty. Like Cain may he never find a resting place upon the face of this earth and may he on his death bed eat 'Les Excrements De Son

se,' like the man who no longer has faith in the divine mercy. This is the
[..]e that I wish for him and which will without failure come to him, for there
[..]sts that Heavenly justice which never forgives the crimes that have been
committed against an entire nation."

LARGE FORCE REQUIRED.

Rear Admiral Caperton on March 13, 1916, reported that the total shore
forces in Haiti amounted to not more than 1,700 enlisted men, and stated that
it was not considered practicable to maintain military control of the country
with a smaller force.

On March 11, 1916, the Secretary of the Navy sent Rear Admiral Caperton
the following dispatch paraphrased as follows: " Relinquish no part of military
control which you are now exercising in Haiti, nor without receipt of further
instructions put end to martial law as now in force."

POLICY OF UNITED STATES.

During December, 1916, the Secretary of the Navy in a dispatch to Capt.
Knapp outlined the attitude of the United States Government toward the
Government of Haiti as follows:

" *   *   *   the United States policy has been to support President Dartiguenave so long as his conduct conforms to correct principles and to the agreements between Haiti and the United States. Any attempt to overthrow
President Dartiguenave will not be countenanced, nor will any legislative action
annulling any decree of the President during the time when no legislative body
was in session be permitted. On the other hand, the United States will consider such action to be the beginning of revolution and disorder in the Republic. *   *   *"

THE ELECTIONS.

The general elections in Haiti were held on January 16 and 17, 1917, without
any marked disorder. Considerable repeating and other frauds were attempted,
but generally without success. Arrangements for the election were apparently
thoroughly successful and the action of the occupation widely appreciated.

On April 21, 1917, the cabinet and national assembly met in apparently the
best of feeling with no friction present. In a speech Vincent, who presided,
stated that Haitian peace was due to the United States, and with her assistance
much progress would result. Following adjournment the entire cabinet called
on the commander of the first provisional brigade and assured him that they
desired America's continued assistance and wished to cooperate.

The present situation with regard to elections in Haiti is summed up in the
following extracts from a report by the brigade commander dated April 4,
1921, reading as follows:

"In a study of the political situation in Haiti it must be ever borne in
mind that the Haitian politician represents but an infinitesimal part of the
population of Haiti."

"The possibility of an election being held next January [1922] for Haitian
deputies and senators and the election of a president by the assembly in the
following April has served to complicate an already involved political situation.

"Numerous candidates for the presidency have already announced themselves. In fact, the time is apparently propitious for the Haitian politician
and any Haitian, born of a Haitian father, who has engaged in politics, has
any following and some money to spend in advancing his cause may be considered to be in the field for the highest honors.

"The one outstanding fact that is apparent through the midst of political
talk, which has now reached the boiling point, is the intense hatred of all
Haitian politicians for the existing Government. To their minds the Government must be changed, they care not how, in order to make room for
some one else to fill the presidential chair, and consequently they are united
against the Government.

"Recently an educated Haitian in northern Haiti, who advocated the withdrawal of the occupation, was asked whether if the occupation withdrew he
would support the Government, the constitution, and the laws of Haiti. He
replied that if the occupation withdrew that, of course, the existing Government must fall at once. When asked if another president was installed who

was not to his liking he would support him or endeavor to overthrow his Government, he could conceive of only the latter alternative.

"The question that is heard on all sides is, 'Will the elections for the assembly be held next January?' At present it is impossible to answer, as the Haitian Government has given no definite reply to this question, which has been asked many times.

"The question that one naturally asks is, Does the law require the holding of the elections for the National Assembly in January next? The constitution of Haiti states that the election must be held on the 10th of January in an even year. The year shall be set by the President of the Republic in a decree issued at least three months before the meeting of the primary assemblies. In other words, the elections will be held when the President believes that the condition of the country is such as to permit of it. The question of holding the election, therefore, lies entirely with the President, but next year a new President must be elected, or rather the time of office of the present incumbent expires, and if there is no assembly who will elect the President? The Conseil d'Etat was empowered by the constitution to act, for legislative purposes, in the place of the assembly. This Council of State is, however, but a creature of the President, as all its members are appointed by him and it is reasonable to expect that if so empowered it would reelect him. Has it the power to elect a President? It is my understanding that the Department of State has already stated that the functions of this body must be confined to legislative acts, and under such an interpretation it would unquestionably not have the power. On the other hand, from my talks with Haitian Government takes the view that the acts of the Conseil d'Etat can not be confined to legislative acts only, but that it has as broad powers as those of the National Assembly.

"If, on the other hand, the claim is upheld that the Conseil d'Etat has not the power to assume electoral functions, and, furthermore, the President fails to hold the elections in January for senators and deputies, how, then, can a President be elected, and under such conditions would the present incumbent be justified in remaining.

"These are all questions that here in Haiti are uppermost in the minds of those closely allied to Haitian affairs, and at the present time it is difficult to see how any of them can be settled without causing much discontent and feeling among the Haitian politicians, of whom many are already sinking their small fortunes in promoting their candidacies. It must be further remembered that the Haitian politician has heretofore run the country—he has controlled the mass. The Union Patriotique has among its members many candidates for the Presidency, but if no election is held all these men will unite in a common cause, and then we have a more or less organized body united against the Haitian Government and against our efforts here if we support that Government in its action.

"In addition, in the coast towns the newspapers are maintaining their antioccupation and anti-Government attitude, and are almost daily publishing insulting and vitriolic articles.

WAR DECLARED ON GERMANY.

On May 3 the Haitian cabinet decided to send the National Assembly a message recommending that war be declared on Germany. Much confusion resulted. On May 5 the National Assembly received the President's message recommending the declaration of war. This caused an attack on the cabinet but the cabinet was sustained. On May 12 the brigade commander reported to the State Department that the Haitian cabinet had decided to break diplomatic relations with Germany and to hand the chargé d'affaires his passport. War against Germany was eventually declared by Haiti on July 13, 1918.

VISITS OF PRESIDENT INTO COUNTRY.

On December 11, 1917, an automobile was driven for the first time over the road from Gonaives to Cape Haitien. This was the first wheeled vehicle that had traveled this road in 112 years. Having received a report concerning this the Major General Commandant addressed the brigade commander as follows: "My sincere congratulations to all who have been instrumental in doing this great work."

On January 3, 1913, the President of the Republic of Haiti with his party left Port au Prince in an automobile at 4 a. m. and arrived at Cape Haitien at

7.50 p. m., making stops at Arcahaie, St. Marc, Dessalines, Gonaives, Ennery, Plaisance, and Limbe. On January 9, the presidential party left Cape Haitien and returned to Port au Prince. The towns passed through were all decorated and great enthusiasm was shown, clearly demonstrating the contentment and happiness of the people. This was the first time in the history of the country that a President of Haiti had been able to visit the northern cities of Haiti without a protecting army at his back.

In a speech to Haitian people on April 15, 1920, the President of the Republic stated that he, the President, had five years ago signed a convention with the United States, that he was a Haitian and loved his country, and that he would sign such a convention five times over if need be to clear up the brigandage in Haiti. He further told them what a great and powerful country the United States was, and that the white officers and men now giving them protection and allowing them to pursue their work were men of the highest honor and integrity, who were devoted to the interest of their country and were working for the good of Haiti, and that it was necessary that the Haitians assist them in every way. His remarks were well received and in the opinion of the brigade commander had an excellent effect. This speech by the President was made during a tour in which he made an extended trip through northern Haiti delivering addresses in many of the larger cities. The president was received enthusiastically everywhere along the route and newspaper men who accompanied the party declared in their papers that pacification was restored. The President made excellent speeches and was greatly pleased at the results of the trip.

THE CONSTITUTION.

It having been agreed that the new constitution for Haiti as amended by order of the State Department should be submitted to the Haitian people for their vote on June 12, 1918, arrangements were made by Col. Russell for taking care of any disturbances that might arise. In his report Col. Russell stated that the voting polls were opened at 7 a. m. and closed at 5 p. m. At Port au Prince all stores were closed, and although crowds were around the voting booths they were most orderly. Reports from all over the Republic soon indicated that the new constitution would be adopted by a large majority vote and that no disorders would occur. In his report the next day, June 13, 1917, Col. Russell reported that the constitution had been adopted by an overwhelming majority, up to the present time returns showed 69,337 affirmative votes and 335 negatives. No disorders during the day.

Shortly after the adoption of the constitution the President of Haiti stated that he intended to call only such men to his assistance (in his cabinet) as he knew to be capable, honorable, and disposed to assist him in the work of reconstruction of the country.

THE CONVENTION WITH CACO CHIEFS.

Col. Waller on October 1, 1915, met the hostile Caco chief at Quartier Morin and an agreement was drawn up, signed by both sides, providing in part that the Cacos would disarm immediately and turn in all arms and ammunitions to the United States forces and return to their homes and not interfere with railroads, telegraph, telephone, commerce, agriculture, or other industries of the country, etc. After the signing of this convention there ensued a period during which conditions were very unsettled in northern Haiti. The Caco forces were scattered over a territory of approximately 2,000 to 2,500 square miles, roughly, within the territory included between St. Marc, Gonaives, Port de Paix, Cape Haitien, Fort Liberte, Hinche, Ennery, the principal centers of their activities being Gonaives, Quartier Morin, Le Trou, Fort Liberte district, and Grand Riviere; the district along the border from Ouanaminth to Carice was held by troops of the former Government. It was understood that the disarming of the soldiers would take place at the same time as the disarming of the Cacos by their chief in the same district. The Cacos, however, proved to be very insincere in their attitude on disarming, which resulted in several operations of some importance during the month of October, 1915, chief of which was the attack by the American forces on Fort Dipitie and operations incident thereto, which resulted in a considerable number of casualties of the Cacos. On October 27, Col. Waller left Port au Prince for Cape Haitien to conduct the necessary operations to subdue the Cacos. Arriving at Cape Haitien the plans for the operations were somewhat accelerated by the continued attacks on the marines at Bajon and the sniping at patrols between Grand Riviere and Bajon. During November, 1915, these operations were carried out and Fort Riviere the stronghold of the Cacos was captured November 17.

"CACO" DEFINED.

In a report to the commander of the cruiser squadron, Col. Waller gave the following definition of a "Caco": "It must be explained that the Cacos have been the controlling elements in all revolutions. They were purchased by first one candidate and then another. Finishing a contract with one man, they, having put him in power, would immediately sell their services to the next aspirant to unseat the first."

UNNECESSARY FORCE PROHIBITED.

On November 20 the Secretary of the Navy informed Rear Admiral Caperton that the department was strongly impressed with the number of Haitians killed and felt that a severe lesson had been taught the Cacos and believed that a proper control could be maintained to preserve order and protect innocent without further offensive operations. In reply Rear Admiral Caperton informed the Secretary of the Navy that all operations except protective patrolling had been suspended and that directions had been given that every effort should be to prevent loss of life on both sides, that the expeditionary force is maintaining military control of the ports of entry of Haiti and undertaking such other operations as necessary to preserve peace and order in the territory contiguous thereto.

MODUS VIVENDI EMBODYING TERMS OF TREATY.

On November 11, 1915, the treaty was ratified by the Haitian Senate after much delay, and on November 29 a modus vivendi embodying the exact terms of the treaty was signed by plenipotentiaries of the United States and Haiti to establish some method of procedure while awaiting exchange of ratifications. The modus vivendi, however, was not carried out by the United States at this time owing to constitutional restrictions in the matter of appointing officers as officials without congressional action.

THE GENDARMERIE.

The American minister in Haiti on January 10 informed Rear Admiral Caperton that the State Department on January 8, 1916, had advised him concerning the organization of the gendarmerie; that it had been agreed between the State Department and the Haitian commission that "members of the gendarmerie shall form the personal guard of the President of Haiti and the gendarmerie shall be the sole police and military force of the country," thereby abolishing the palace guard as unnecessary.

On October 15, 1915, the Secretary of the Navy decided as follows:

"Article I, section 9, clause 8, of the Constitution of the United States prohibits any person holding any office of profit or trust under the United States from holding or accepting any office, present, or emolument, or title from any foreign State, unless Congress shall consent thereto. While officers of the United States on duty in Haiti could not without the consent of Congress hold office, receive emolument, etc., under the Haitian Government, they are not prohibited by the Constitution or any law of the United States 'from rendering a friendly service' to that State, such as assisting to organize a gendarmerie. (See Op. 13, Atty. Gen., 537, 538.) However, at the present date there is no authority whereby such officers could become officers in such a force by appointment from the Government of Haiti."

On June 12, 1916, an act to authorize and empower officers and enlisted men of the Navy and Marine Corps to serve under the Government of the Republic of Haiti was enacted, as follows:

"*Be it enacted by the Senate and House of Representatives of the United States of America in Congress assembled,* That the President of the United States be, and he is hereby, uthorized, in his discretion, to detail to assist the Republic of Haiti such officers and enlisted men of the United States Navy and the United States Marine Corps as may be mutually agreed upon by him and the President of the Republic of Haiti: *Provided,* That the officers and enlisted men so detailed be, and they are hereby, authorized to accept from the Government of Haiti the said employment with compensation and emoluments from the said Government of Haiti, subject to the approval of the President of the United States.

"SEC. 2. That to insure the continuance of this work during such time as may be desirable, the President may have the power of substitution in the case of the termination of the detail of any officer or enlisted man, for any cause: *Provided,* That during the continuance of such details the officers and enlisted men shall continue to receive the pay and allowances of their ranks or ratings in the Navy or Marine Corps.

"SEC. 3. That the following increase in the United States Marine Corps be, and the same is hereby authorized: Two majors, 12 captains, 18 first lieutenants, 2 assistant quartermasters with the rank of captain, 1 assistant paymaster with the rank of captain, 5 quartermaster sergeants, 5 first sergeants, 5 gunnery sergeants, and 11 sergeants.

"SEC. 4. That the following increase in the United States Navy be, and the same is hereby, authorized: One surgeon, 2 passed assistant surgeons, 5 hospital stewards, and 10 hospital apprentices, first class.

"SEC. 5. That officers and enlisted men of the Navy and Marine Corps detailed for duty to assist the Republic of Haiti shall be entitled to the same credit for such service, for longevity, retirement, foreign service, pay, and for all other purposes, that they would receive if they were serving with the Navy or with the Marine Corps."

Marine and naval officers were immediately appointed by the President of the Republic of Haiti after nomination by the President of the United States to officer and administer the Gendarmerie d'Haiti.

From October 13, 1915, to February 1, 1916, the gendarmerie acted in accordance with instructions issued by the expeditionary commander. On February 1, 1916, the following proclamation was issued changing those duties from purely police to include both military and police and absolutely supplanted the old régime:

" PROCLAMATION.

"Whereas the President of Haiti and his cabinet have decreed that on this date the commandants of communes and the chiefs of sections are abolished, and also that all military and police duties of the commandants of arrondisements are taken away, it is hereby ordered that, from this date, all the military and police duties heretofore performed by those officers be performed by the Gendarmerie d'Haiti supported by the expeditionary forces under my command."

Pursuant to this order, the gendarmes then in service were transferred to all parts of Haiti, both in the large and small towns, appropriate increase made in strength, and the gendarmerie took up its duties under the following instructions issued by the expeditionary commander regarding its functions:

1. Preservation of order.
2. Protection of individual rights.
3. Protection of property.
4. Supervision of arms.
5. Prevention of smuggling.
6. Protect and report on conditions of highways and bridges. When so ordered by the commandant of the gendarmerie, the genedarmes will require, according to law, the proper inhabitants to alter or repair public highways and bridges, and will supervise this work. At the request of the mayor of the commune they may, when ordered by the proper officer of the gendarmerie, undertake this work.
7. Protect and report on conditions of the telegraph and telephone service. When ordered by a commissioned officer of the gendarmerie, will have the authority to censor all messages and to take charge of any station or office when necessary for the good of the public.
8. Report on and supervise the use of the public lands according to law.
9. Protect and report on conditions of public buildings.
10. Collection of vital statistics, including the census, when ordered.
11. Report on and protect public irrigation works.
12. Enforce sanitary orders and regulations.
13. Report on and enforce regulations preventing spread of animal diseases.
14. Report on and enforce regulations preventing spread of epidemics.

15. Plenary control in time of great disorder following war, rebellion, earthquakes, typhoons, etc.
16. Control of prisons.
17. Issuance of permits for travel within the Republic.
18. Agricultural reports.
19. Require all weights and measures to conform to legal standards.
20. Enforce harbor and docking regulations.

These duties have since been modified as follows:

On August 24, 1916, in an agreement between the United States and Haiti the maintenance and operation of the telegraph and telephone lines were put under the engineer of Haiti.

On January 4, 1917, the Secretary of the Interior issued an order that permits for travel within the Republic were no longer necessary.

On May 31, 1919, the building, upkeep, and repair of roads were turned over to the direct supervision of the engineer of Haiti.

With these exceptions the duties and functions of the gendarmerie are at present as outlined above.

On August 24, 1916, the gendarmerie agreement (protocol to treaty) was ratified by the United States, and on the same date the commandant of the Marine Corps directed that the officers and enlisted men then serving be transferred out of the marine brigade and into the gendarmerie.

The difficulties with which the gendarmerie had to cope in the early days were almost multitudinous. The conditions, both urban and rural, the results of over a hundred years' custom, were suddenly changed, and these changes were manifestly not agreeable to the old officials replaced by this new organization.

On July 5, 1916, the municipal and rural police were abolished and the entire policing of Haiti placed in the hands of the gendarmerie. This had to be done, as each commune had its own "private" police which extended into the sections of the commune and through custom and law degenerated to such an extent that the chief of section had the authority to require any citizen to arrest any other and countenanced arrests of which he had no previous knowledge.

The gendarme as a soldier has done excellent work not only under their white officers but under their native noncommissioned officers as well. On many occasions they have met and defeated greatly superior forces. From the date of their organization the native gendarme has on no occasion deserted his white officer.

The gendarmerie has direct charge of all the prisons and prisoners of Haiti. During the past year the number of prisoners had increased, due to captures made in the field. At each district headquarters there is a main prison. Each district and post have a "lockup."

The following is a list of district prisons, with a tabulation of prisoners on hand, June 30, 1920, and the number confined and released during the month of June, 1920:

Districts.	On hand June 30.	Confined during month.	Released during month.
Port au Prince	451	100	147
Petionville	175	279	198
Petit Goave	289	267	281
Jacmel	113	155	139
Aux Cayes	171	111	100
Jeremie	126	74	49
Mirebalais	190	85	54
St. Marc	173	254	218
Gonaives	387	327	292
Cape (civil)	491	263	181
Cape (district)	20	80	90
Port de Paix	132	113	129
La Trou	34	18	15
Port Chabert	305	80	52
Grand Riviere	97	116	72
Ouanaminthe	116	275	243
Hinche	147	130	95
Circa La Source	54	76	30
Total	3,471	2,743	2,381

NOTE.—This table is practically the average number per month during the past year.

At the larger prisons, Port au Prince and Cape Haitien, the prisoners are taught a trade, and when their product is marketable they are given a percentage on their work. The money derived in this manner is given to them on release or may be allotted by them to their families if the term of confinement is for a long period. All the gendarme uniforms and the clothing for prisoners are manufactured by prison labor. A garden is required for prisons for the betterment of the gendarme and prison rations. At Post Chabert, neaar Cape Haitien, a prison farm is in operation, giving healthy, open-air work to over 300 prisoners. The idea of this farm is in addition to aiding the ration in cost, to experiment as to the methods of cultivation, mostly in native products, and to give the benefit of better methods to the Haitian general public, letting them graphically see the results. Gardens are also in operation at all posts.

Telegraph and telephone lines all over Haiti were put in working order and kept up by the gendarmerie, assisted by the occupation until turned over to the engineer. Since that time side lines necessary for official work were put in by the gendarmerie connecting Circa la Source, Hinche, Thomonde, Thomassique, Port de Paix, Valliere, etc., with the outer world. With the exception of the last two places the material was specially ordered from the United States and paid for by the gendarmerie. These lines are still kept up by the gendarmerie and held until such time as civil operators can be found to enter these localities and take over. Lately the engineer has supplied necessary repair material when needed.

With the exception of the larger seacoast towns the gendarmerie cooperating with the sanitary engineer of Haiti has supervision of the sanitary service practically over the whole island. Every gendarme post has a dispensary or small hospital where, in the absence of the sanitary service, inhabitants receive treatment free of charge.

Gendarmerie schools have been opened at all posts. This has been a godsend to the enlisted man and is greatly appreciated by them. Reading, writing, and simple figuring is as much as has been attempted so far.

The medaille militaire (Haitian medal of honor) was awarded to the following officers and men of the Constabulary Detachment. This medal is awarded for conspicuous conduct in the field:

Lieut. Col. F. M. Wise.	First Lieut. J. W. Knighton.
Lieut. Col. R. S. Hooker.	Second Lieut. H. H. Hanneken.
Maj. J. J. Meade.	Sergt. Joseph O. Vanhorn.
Maj. W. N. Hill.	Corpl. Archie M. Ackroyd.
Maj. W. W. Buckley.	Corpl. Clair S. Christian.
Maj. A. A. Vandegrift.	Corpl. Roger E. Kirchhoff.
Corpl. Eugene S. Jones.	Corpl. Manuel E. Perry.
Corpl. William R. Button.	Corpl. Lewis B. Puller.
Corpl. E. S. Winfrey.	Pvt. 1st Class M. F. Brown.
Corpl. H. R. Wood.	
Lieut. Commander J. S. Helm, M. C., U. S. N.	

One hundred and five Haitien members of the gendarmerie received the medaille militaire. These presentations were made at Port au Prince and Cape Haitien by the president of Haiti wth appropriate ceremonies. Congressional medals of honor were awarded to Second Lieut. H. H. Hanneken and Corpl. William R. Button for the successful attack on the *Charlemagne M. Peralte.*

The present organization of the gendarmerie is as follows:

Chief	1
Assistant chief	1
Directors, line	3
Director, quartermaster, paymaster	1
Director, medical	1
Inspectors, line	10
Inspectors, quartermaster	2
Inspectors, medical	2
Captains	18
Captain, inspector, Coast Guard	1
First lieutenants, line	23
First lieutenants, medical	3
Second lieutenants, line	39

Second lieutenants, medical_____ 6
Second lieutenants, machine gun_____ 10
First lieutenants, Coast Guard_____ 3
First sergeants_____ 19
Sergeants _____ 112
Corporals_____ 262
Field musicians_____ 40
Privates _____ 2,100

The pay of the enlisted personnel is as follows:

	Per month.
First sergeants	$25.00
Sergeants	20.00
Corporals	15.00
Field musicians	10.00
Privates	10.00

In addition to the above each gendarme is allowed 15 cents a day for rations. Clothing is furnished as needed, and with the exception of a few articles, such as belts, shoes, etc., is manufactured in prisons. The term of enlistment for the gendarmes is three years. The gendarmes are armed with the Springfield rifle loaned by the Marine Corps.

Without going into detail the gendarmerie is a complete military unit, modeled after our own organizations, having its own transport, medical, quartermaster, and commissary services, post exchanges, etc.

Since the formation of the Gendarmerie d'Haiti, the following-named officers of the Marine Corps have been chiefs of that organization: Maj. Smedley D. Butler, until May 1, 1918, when he was succeeded by Maj. Alexander S. Williams, who served as chief until relieved by Lieut. Col. Frederic M. Wise on July 19, 1919. Lieut. Col. Wise was relieved by Lieut. Col. Douglas C. McDougal on April 15, 1921.

CORVEE.

Soon after the American occupation of Haiti it was realized that good roads between the principal towns were a military necessity, for, due to the chaotic conditions prevailing in Haiti as a result of the almost incessant revolutions, there were no roads in Haiti outside of the towns and cities, and communication between these points by land was almost impossible. The main trunk road from Port au Prince to Cape Haitien was impassable for wheeled traffic and required from two to three weeks to make the journey by animal.

By the word " corvee " is meant a system of enforced labor on roads. In Haiti such a system has formed a part of the law for many years, but prior to the American occupation it had not been enforced for some time. By the corvee system, men living in a district were required to work on the main road or artery in that district a certain number of days during each year. The Haitian Government was without funds to employ labor for road work or, in fact, for any public work. It was heavily in debt to the extent of some $31,000,000, and the United States was trying to rehabilitate it. Naturally the first act of the United States was to enforce law and order and obtain peace throughout the land, and in order to accomplish this good roads were essential.

By authority of the President of Haiti, the law (Code Rural, sec. 3, Ch. V. arts. 52 to 65) requiring the inhabitants to do a certain amount of work on the roads was enforced. This was known as the corvee.

The gendarmie of Haiti, which was formed soon after the American occupation, acting for the Haitian Government, put into effect this old corvee law. Under this law the road to Cape Haitien was begun in October, 1917, and finished about December 31, 1917. When this road was completed the system continued, and although legal gradually fell from favor. The " membres agricol " and " magistrats communeaux," the Haitian officials who kept the lists of workmen and made out working details, saw a valuable source of income and took advantage of it. Persons who did not wish to work could buy immunity, and the consequence was that to a great extent the same man, those who could not pay, were chosen for work over and over again. An attempt to remedy this was made by the issuance of certificates to the workmen signed by the local gendarmie officer, made upon the completion of each man's work. It was rumored that these certificates were destroyed by the Haitian officials unless bribes were forthcoming, but it was difficult to obtain proof on account of their hold over the people. This, coupled with the fact that in some cases laborers were held overtime and worked out of their immediate localities, was the reason the corvee system became obnoxious to the people. The corvee was discontinued on October 1, 1918, and forbidden in any form, but unfortunately through a mis-interpretation of this order the corvee continued in the Maissade-Hinche dis-trict for a while after this date. In order to make absolutely certain that this discontinuance was complete the following proclamation was published on August 22, 1919:

"Citizens of Haiti:

" The time has come to put a stop to further bloodshed. It has been necessary to use stern measures to repress the disorders in the north, and with the recent arrival of military engines we can use even sterner methods, but I hope, with your help, to be able to abandon such means. I ask your assistance, and I ask you to have faith in the good intentions which the President and people of the United States of America entertain toward your country.

"The corvee has been done away with entirely. Work on the roads is en-tirely voluntary and will be paid for daily. The workmen will be free to come and go when it pleases them; they shall be paid for the hours they work. Any injustices committed by native or American officials should be reported to American military officials, and justice will be done and the offender punished.

" It is the desire of the American people to establish security and prosperity in this country. It can not be done while the bandits burn and pillage. All good inhabitants should give the greatest assistance to officers and men of the occupation in suppressing the bandits. All natives who have been forced to join these thieves and bandits masquerading under the name of cacos, if they desire to resume their peaceful farming, have but to report to the American military officials, assure them of their peaceful intent and future loyalty, and a full pardon and all possible protection will be granted. This protection is im-possible if the country people continue to support the bandits calling themselves cacos.

" I personally promise you that the United States Government only desires to give to the citizens of Haiti security and prosperity and the enjoyment of liberty, equality, and fraternity."

The following quotation from report of Rear Admiral H. S. Knapp, dated October 14, 1920, to the Secretary of the Navy, gives valuable information con-cerning this subject:

" 55. One of the matters undertaken by the gendarmerie was the opening up of roads for wheel traffic. Under its auspices a road over 250 miles long was opened up from a point west of Port au Prince to Cape Haitien in the north, and, indeed, to Ouanaminthe in the northeast, on the Dominican border. This was a great achievement for the progress of Haiti, whose roads capable of tak-ing wheel traffic had therefore been a negligible quantity. The road was built across the mountains for a considerable portion of its length and, in view of the fact that the gendarmerie is not by its organization provided with engi-neering talent, the achievement is all the more remarkable. In addition, other roads were built by the gendarmerie into the interior. The criticism of these roads has been made that they were built for military purposes. That they serve a military use is perfectly plain; but the critics, if they will take pains to inform themselves of the orders when the roads were built, will find that the stress laid on their building was to open up the country for the benefit of the inhabitants. The President of Haiti in public speeches has expressed high ap-preciation of the value of the roads constructed by the gendarmerie.

" 56. These roads were built under what has come to be described as the 'corvee system of labor.' The Rural Code of Haiti contains a law relating to the maintenance and repairs of public highways, of which a copy has already been sent to the department in another communication. This law provides in article 54 that—

" ' Public highways and communications will be maintained and repaired by the inhabitants, in rotation, in each section through which these roads pass and each time repairs are necessary.'

" Similar laws exist in the United States, but the word ' corvee ' is not used in their connection. Article 53 of the same law provides that—

" ' Highways, public and private roads are placed under the supervision of the authorities and agents of the rural police.'

" Other articles provide for the calling out of the necessary labor to main-tain and repair the roads. The gendarmerie, after its organization, replaced the rural police mentioned in this law, which went into effect January 1, 1865, and still remains upon the statute books. In applying the so-called corvee system the gendarmerie was acting under an existing law, and did so under an order of the President of Haiti.

" 57. As at first applied, the inhabitants of the sections through which the road passed offered no objections, but quite the reverse, and the general senti-ment was very favorable to the construction of the road, which in places was not new work but consisted of discovering and mending the old roads which existed at the time of the French in Haiti before independence, but which had become overgrown and in places entirely lost. The through road to the north was hailed on all sides as a signal mark of progress. As time went on, how-ever, an abuse crept in; the inhabitants of other sections than those through which the road passed were forced to work on the roads. This undoubtedly created grave discontent, which was reflected in the attitude of the people. I find no authority in the Rural Code for taking the inhabitants from one sec-tion and making them work in another section, but I am convinced from what I have heard that this was done. The laborers worked under the supervision of the gendarmerie and hence were under military control. When not author-ized by the Rural Code this was unjustified by law, and the whole practice, even legally administered, was a drawback to the development of the gendar-merie itself in its true function as the police agency of the country. The ranking officers of the gendarmerie at that time are not now in Haiti, and what has just been said must in justification to them be qualified by the state-ment that I have not been able since being here to ask any presentation of the case from their point of view. I am only able to state my conclusions, as far as I can reach them, from such investigations as I have made since my arrival in Haiti.

" 58. At the instigation of the senior officer of the occupation in Haiti, the President, on October 1, 1918, directed the discontinuance of the use of the corvee system on the roads of the Republic, and the commanding officer of the gendarmerie issued an order in compliance with those instructions. Even then, however, the employment of corvee labor did not cease everywhere. The order of discontinuance did not mention, in at least one instance, a road where corvee labor was then employed, and the local commanding officer took the legalistic point of view that his section was not included under the terms of the order. However legally created, the effect was unfortunate. As soon as the fact did become definitely known in Port au Prince that the order was not being obeyed steps were at once taken to stop all corvee work. In one or two instances it did not cease then. For this the local officers in immediate charge, and especially the department commander of the north, in whose juris-diction this disobedience of orders occurred, are responsible and blameworthy. The corvee is now nonexistent in any form. The law, however, has not been repealed, and it still may legally be put into operation by the Haitian Govern-ment. I personally believe the law to be a good one if legally administered.

" 59. The roads that were built by corvee labor are invaluable to the progress of the country. Had they been built in strict accord with the law, a very praise-worthy achievement would have resulted, with no reproach of illegality, or even of overstepping the law, which reproach now seems to attach to a public work of such high value in itself."

GEN. LEJEUNE INSPECTS AND IS SATISFIED.

On October 4, 1920, Major General Commandant John A. Lejeune concluded a report to the Secretary of the Navy with this paragraph:

" During my tour of inspection in Haiti I found the marines to be in a highly efficient condition. Their health, except for some cases of malaria, was excellent. Their discipline was superb and their morale high. As I inspected the detach-ments located at isolated points far in the interior of Haiti, I was filled with admiration of their fine appearance and efficient condition. My heart was filled with pride to see these splendid men giving to their country and the Republic of Haiti such intelligent, zealous, efficient, and courageous service. I feel that the American people have every right to be proud of their representatives who are now wearing the uniform of the Marine Corps in Haiti."

THE MAYO COURT OF INQUIRY.

The Secretary of the Navy, under date of October 16, 1920, convened a court of inquiry, consisting of Rear Admiral Henry T. Mayo, as president, Rear Ad-miral James H. Oliver, and Maj. Gen. Wendell C. Neville, as additional members, and Maj. Jesse F. Dyer, as judge advocate, to inquire into the alleged indiscriminate killings of Haitians and other unjustifiable acts by members of the United States naval service, including those detailed to duty with the Gendarmerie d'Haiti, against the persons and property of Haitians since the American occupation, July 28, 1915. The inquiry was completed on October 19, 1920, and the findings of the court follow :

FINDING OF FACTS.

1. The court finds that two unjustifiable homicides have been committed, one each, by two of the personnel of the United States naval service which has served in Haiti since July 28, 1915, and that 16 other serious acts of violence have been perpetrated against citizens of Haiti during the same period by individuals of such personnel.

2. The court finds further that these offenses were all isolated acts of individuals and that in every case the responsible party was duly brought to trial before a general court-martial, convicted, and sentenced.

3. The court has found no evidence of the commission of any other unjustifiable homicides or other serious unjustifiable acts of oppression or of violence against any of the citizens of Haiti or unjustifiable damage or destruction of their property caused by any of the personnel in question.

In view of the fact that the only unjustifiable acts found by the court to have been committed are those wherein disciplinary action has already been taken and where no further proceedings could be had in the matter, the court has not deemed it necessary to report further upon the question of responsibility.

CONCLUSIONS.

Referring to paragraph 2 of the precept, it is the conclusion of the court that there have been no proper grounds for the statement that "practically indiscriminate killing of natives has been going on for some time" as alleged in the letter from Brig. Gen. George Barnett, United States Marine Corps, to Col. John H. Russell, United States Marine Corps.

Referring to the amendment of the precept calling for the conclusions of the court as to the general conduct of the personnel of the naval service in Haiti since July 28, 1915, the court does not consider that the small number of isolated crimes, or offenses that have been committed by a few individuals of the service during the period in question are entitled to any considerable weight in forming a conclusion as to the general conduct of such personnel. It was inevitable that some offenses would be committed. However, considering the conditions of service in Haiti, it is remarkable that the offenses were so few in number and that they all may be chargeable to the ordinary defects of human character, such defects as result in the commission of similar offenses in the United States and elsewhere in the best regulated communities.

The general conduct of our troops of occupation can be fairly judged by the results of that occupation.

Now, for the first time in more than a hundred years, tranquillity and security of life and property may be said to prevail in Haiti.

The Haitian people themselves welcomed the coming of our men and are unwilling to have them depart.

The establishment and maintenance of tranquil conditions and then of security of life and property all over the Republic of Haiti has been an arduous and dangerous and thankless task. That task our marines have performed with fidelity and great gallantry.

The court can not refrain from recording its opinion of much, and that the most serious part, of the reflections which have been made upon the officers who have served in Haiti.

The outstanding characteristic of those officers, from the brigade commander down, has been their sympathetic attitude toward every step that would lead to a betterment of the country and to improvement in the physical, mental, and moral conditions of the population.

With slender resources and inadequate administrative authority, they have accomplished much, where anything more than suppression of organized insurrection seem impossible.

The above remarks apply with particular force to those officers and enlisted men of the Marine Corps who have been serving as officers of the gendarmerie of Haiti.

After a careful study of the matters in issue, based not only upon the evidence in the record, but also upon other original and reliable sources of information, and the court's own observations while in Haiti, the court regards the charges which have been published as ill considered, regrettable, and thoroughly unwarranted reflections on a portion of the United States Marine Corps, which has performed difficult, dangerous, and delicate duty in Haiti in a manner which, instead of calling for adverse criticism, is entitled to the highest commendation.

The record of the proceedings of this twenty-first day of the inquiry was read and approved, and the court having finished the inquiry, then at 11 o'clock a. m. adjourned to await the action of the convening authority.

LITERACY AND EDUCATION IN HAITI.

Illiteracy in the Republic of Haiti has been conservatively estimated to be at from 95 to 98 per cent. On December 3, 1920, Major General Commandant John A. Lejeune, signed the following indorsement to the Secretary of the Navy, the subject of the indorsement reading "Carrying out the terms of the treaty between the United States of America and the Republic of Haiti by organizing and administering an educational system (including primary) for the Republic of Haiti":

" 1. This correspondence is forwarded with the strongest approval and expressing the opinion that it will not be until the United States seriously assumes the duty of educating the Haitians and pursuing such duty to a satisfactory conclusion that the pacification and occupation of the Republic of Haiti, which has been so successfully accomplished, will bear fruit; and further, that the law of the United States, and the treaty proclaimed May 3, 1916, will not only permit but requires the performance of this duty.

" 2. Under the provisions of the act of June 12 1916 (39 Stat., 223), the President of the United States is authorized in his discretion, to detail to assist the Republic of Haiti such officers and enlisted men of the Navy and Marine Corps as may be mutually agreed upon by him and the President of the Republic of Haiti, and personnel so appointed are authorized by this act to accept such employment with compensation and emoluments from the Republic of Haiti, subject to the approval of the President of the United States.

" 3 The above-mentioned law was enacted solely for the purpose of carrying into effect the terms of the treaty between the United States and the Republic of Haiti proclaimed May 3, 1916, and while up to the present date its provisions have been exerted mainly for the carrying out of Articles X and XIII of the treaty concerning the gendarmerie and engineers, it is in no way restricted in its operation to those purposes, and it contains adequate authorization for the purpose of detailing personnel of the Navy and Marine Corps to initiate, organize, and administer a system of education for the Republic of Haiti.

" 4. While the subject of education is not expressly mentioned in the treaty, as is the Gendarmerie d'Haiti, sanitation, etc.. nevertheless important provisions of the treaty can not be carried out unless the United States and the Republic of Haiti, by protocol or separate agreement based on certain general provisions of the treaty, agree to have education (including primary) in the Republic of Haiti administered in a manner similar to that prescribed in Article X of the treaty for the preservation of domestic peace by the gendarmerie. While such action might be based upon moral grounds or upon the expedient of following a path necessary to the rehabilitation of Haiti, it is believed that the treaty contains sufficient and adequate authority upon which to proceed. Surely such an injection of assistance by the United States into the internal affairs of Haiti should be less criticizable than that in matters pertaining to the armed forces of the Republic through which sovereignty is usually maintained.

" 5. In effect, the treaty was negotiated and ratified by both States for the purpose of assisting in the ' economic development and prosperity ' of the Republic of Haiti (preamble), for the ' efficient development of its agricultural, mineral, and commercial resources and in the establishment of the finances of Haiti on a firm and solid basis ' (Art. I), to ' promote material prosperity ' (Art. IX) for the ' development of its natural resources ' (Art. XIII), and for the ' sanitation and public improvement of the Republic ' (Art. XIII). None of these can be accomplished unless the education of the Haitian people, beginning at the bottom, is made possible by the assistance, contemplated by the treaty, by the United States.

"6. Particular attention is invited to Article XIV providing that the United States of America and the Republic of Haiti shall have authority to take such steps as may be necessary to assure the 'complete attainment of any of the objects comprehended in this treaty,' and also to the words of the preamble reading that 'the United States being in full sympathy with all of these aims and objects and desirous to contribute in all proper ways to their accomplishment.'

"7. Without considering what might have been avoided by the inclusion of an article in the treaty providing for performance of this serious duty, or that the United States might have anticipated a failure on the part of the Haitian Government to efficiently and satisfactorily perform this duty of education, the fact confronts the United States at this time that the duty has been unperformed and also that it is highly improbable that unless the United States does assist. the Republic of Haiti will never evolve to such a self-sustaining status that the United States would be justified in withdrawing. An occupation of a foreign country, though best-intentioned, is doomed to failure if it begins and ends in a military phase.

"8. At the present time the effort of American officials, including Marine Corps and Navy personnel, have been limited to moral suasion and to influencing the Haitian officials and Haitian public opinion toward administering an efficient system of education, and these efforts, limited as they are, have failed.

"9. It might be remarked that the treaty was not negotiated primarily for the purpose of permitting the United States to conduct indefinitely those activities included within the treaty phrase of 'aims and objects,' but rather for the education of the Haitian people and thus enabling the Republic of Haiti to become a self-sustaining and 'going' State. The act of taking over certain functions of the Government was a mere incident in the course of events contemplated by the treaty, the final of which being that of turning back a practically perfect governmental machine to a people educated and capable of administering and maintaining it level with an efficient standard.

"10. The United States may install the most excellent road system, it may establish the most efficient Gendarmerie to maintain domestic peace and police, it may place sanitation upon a healthful basis, it may assist in the economic development and prosperity, and may arrange the finances satisfactorily, but if the Haitian people themselves are not elevated by education to the plane on which the people of an average modern State dwell, no positive and enduring benefit will have been conferred upon them, and the occupation will have been in vain, unless they have been educated to the degree that they are able to conduct their own affairs unaided by an occupying force.

"11. In conclusion, the recommendation of the brigade commander, approved by Rear Admiral Knapp, is approved, that a protocol or separate agreement be arranged with the Republic of Haiti, providing for the administration of educational matters, including primary education, in a manner similar to that outlined in Article X for the Gendarmerie."

The Secretary of the Navy in forwarding the above to the Secretary of State placed on it the following indorsement:

"This correspondence is forwarded with the strongest approval of the Navy Department. The opinion of the Major General Commandant, 'It will not be until the United States seriously assumes the duty of educating the Haitians and pursuing such duty to a satisfactory conclusion that the pacification and occupation of the Republic of Haiti, which has been so successfully accomplished, will bear fruit,' is concurred in.

"The Navy Department will be pleased to assist in such manner as may be possible and practicable in establishing and administering an efficient educational system for the Republic of Haiti with the object of enabling that Republic to reach such a self-sustaining status as will justify the United States in withdrawing its military forces therefrom."

TWO INTERESTING LETTERS.

The Secretary of the Navy and the Major General Commandant of the Marine Corps frequently receive letters praising the work of the naval service in the Republic of Haiti. The following replies by Gen. Lejeune to two of these letters, dated November 15 and 19, 1920, respectively, are of interest:

"I was particularly interested in your statement, which I believe is a correct conclusion, that the few irregular acts on the part of marines toward the Haitians were the acts of individuals and not a part of the policy established by those in positions of responsibility, and that the responsible officers have always been deeply chagrined by the occasional failures of their subordinates to carry out not only their definite orders and instructions but the principles to which all civilized peoples are devoted.

"As far as the participation of the Marine Corps in these affairs is concerned, it not only must but is satisfied to stand on its record, even though such record has been marred by the occasional unauthorized acts of individuals, and there is not the slightest desire to evade responsibility for any incident. Every general rule of normal human conduct has an occasgional variation, and the general rule of a successful administration of Haitian affairs, from the Marine Corps point of view, has I am sure been proved by the exception. Unfortunately, the almost consistent success of the marines' good work has been smothered by the publicity accorded the exceptions.

"Your reference to the illiteracy of the Haitian people, which you estimate is from 95 to 98 per cent, is quite pertinent, and I believe that it will not be until the United States seriously assumes the duty of educating them and pursues such duty to a successful conclusion that the pacification of the Republic of Haiti, which has been so successfully accomplished, will bear fruit.

"Upon my recent visit to both of these countries, I found the military situation and general condition to be excellent in so far as the Marine Corps was responsible, and your words and those of many others who have been kind enough to express themselves to me would indicate that the general American public will in the end undoubtedly take this viewpoint and accord to their fellow Americans, who have so unselfishly taken up this work, a degree of praise and vindication which will compensate them for the unmerited criticism caused by the delinquencies of a few individuals."

"Those parts of your letters which refer to sanitation, and its improvement under the occupation, to the roads bu'lt, to the political condition of Haiti, and to the improvement in Haitian finances proved very interesting to me. I was particularly interested in that part of your letter which outlined the duties of the United States to be: First, 'to put down rebellion, obtain all arms and ammunition, and to restore order in the country'; second, 'to provide sanitation'; third, 'to form a government for the Haitians which would be stable and secure'; fourth, 'to ascertain, adjudge, and liquidate the debts'; fifth, 'teach the Haitians how to govern themselves'; and sixth, 'turn the Government over to the Haitians for their own governing when the Haitians were capable of self-government.'

"I am sure that the great majority of Americans will agree with your conclusions that the purpose is evident that the United States desires to give to Haiti a permanent, stable and safe government, and in the meantime and while working out its destiny to educate the Haitian so that he may take over the management of that government when he is able to do so."

SECRETARY DENBY VISITI HAITI.

The Secretary of the Navy on March 27, 1921, arrived in Port au Prince, and on the same day, in company with the American minister, called on the President of the Republic of Haiti. The Secretary afterwards inspected the marines' and gendarmes' posts in Haiti and crossed the border into the Dominican Republic on March 30, 1921. Secretary Denby, upon his return to the United States, expressed high praise of the marines' work in Haiti.

OFFICERS IN COMMAND.

Rear Admiral W. B. Caperton, commander cruiser force, was senior naval officer present from July 28, 1915, to July 19, 1916, when he was relieved by Rear Admiral C. F. Pond, who in turn was relieved by Rear Admiral H. S. Knapp on November 22, 1916.

Since March 31, 1917, these naval officers have held the designation of military governor of Santo Domingo and military representative of the United States in Haiti. When the revolution broke out in the Dominican Republic in May, 1916, Rear Admiral Caperton proceeded to the city of Santo Domingo and assumed control of the situation. From that date on he and his successors resided in that city and despite the above-mentioned title could, if necessity, exercise but little direct control over Haitian affairs.

Rear Admiral Thomas Snowden on February 25, 1919, relieved Rear Admiral Knapp, and remained in command until relieved by Rear Admiral S. S. Robison, June 2, 1921.

The following-named officers of the Marine Corps have been in command of the First Provisional Brigade, United States Marine Corps, ashore in the Republic of Haiti, since the formation of that brigade: Col. Littleton W. T. Waller, until November 22, 1916, when he was relieved by Col. Eli K. Cole. Col. Cole was relieved by Col. John H. Russell on November 28, 1917. Brig. Gen. Albertus W. Catlin on December 7, 1918, relieved Col. Russell and was succeeded on July 15, 1919, by Lieut. Col. Louis McC. Little. Lieut. Col. Little was relieved on October 1, 1919, by Col. John H. Russell, who is at present in command. Since May, 1916, these officers have virtually been in control of naval affairs in the Republic of Haiti, in view of the demands made upon the time of above-mentioned naval officers by Dominican affairs.

This memorandum practically contains no reference to military operations. Such is unnecessary, except to state that the marines successfully carried out the major mission assigned to them by the Navy Department that acted in accordance with the requests of the Department of State. This major mission was the military one of pacification and the maintenance of peace and order in the Republic of Haiti.

In addition to having so thoroughly completed their military mission, the marines have done everything legally within their power to assist the Haitian people and their Government. It would take many pages to adequately describe the constructive measures they have carried out. Handicapped by a total absence of any express control over education, judiciary, agricultural, etc., systems, they have done what they could through informal and persuasive methods. The gendarmerie is a monument to the military, administrative, and executive efficiency of the marines. They pay all the Haitian civil employees coming under their jurisdiction and there is yet to be any malfeasance in such duty. They have built roads, administer the telegraph and telephone systems, assist in agricultural matters, hold schools for the gendarmes, and so on. The contrast between the ordinary natives and the native gendarme is so marked that any observing American is thrilled with pride in viewing the superior condition, both physically and mentally, of the latter. When it is realized that the mission of the marines in Haiti is first the pacification and maintenance of order and the constitutional government, the success achieved by him in these matters beyond the military is remarkable and encourages those interested in Haiti to believe in the ultimate success of the occupation.

INVESTIGATION BY SENATE COMMITTEE.

Three Haitian delegates (H. Pauléus Sannon, Sténio Vincent, and Perceval Thoby) who visited Washington on May 9, 1921, with the purpose of presenting memorials to President Harding, the State Department, and Congress, demanding the withdrawal of the United States military forces, the immediate abolition of martial law and courts based on it, abrogation of the convention of 1915, and the convocation of a constituent assembly, issued a copy of the memorial on May 8, 1921, in which were repeated such charges against our military forces as caused an investigation to be made by the Navy Department through the medium of the Mayo court of inquiry in 1920. On May 9, 1921, Secretary of the Navy Denby stated that the Navy Department welcomed any investigation that Congress might care to make. "The Marine Corps did a splendid work there as humanely as it was possible to do it," Secretary Denby is quoted as saying, "and the Naval Establishment has functioned in Haiti in a manner seldom equalled by military occupation anywhere." When he visited Haiti recently on a tour of inspection he saw evidence on every hand, Mr. Denby said, to convince him that the continued presence of American marines on the island was desirable.

The first meeting of the Senate committee, of which Senator Medill McCormick is chairman, was held on August 5, 1921.

THIS MEMORANDUM IS BUT A SYNOPSIS.

The foregoing is but a brief and synoptical summary of the events occurring in the Republic of Haiti. In order to ascertain any desired details, the annual reports of the Secretary of the Navy, reports of the Major General Commandant, particularly those of Gens. Lejeune and Barnett, the various reports of Rear Admiral H. S. Knapp, and the files, records, and archives of the Navy Department and Marine Corps should be consulted.

Capt. FREEMAN. This matter I have is with regard to the Dominican Republic.

The CHAIRMAN. Will you leave that with us?

Capt. FREEMAN. Yes, sir.

The CHAIRMAN. Any additional matter that you care to present next week we will be glad to have.

Senator KING. Do you mean to say that is the case of the Navy with respect to the Dominican Republic?

Capt. FREEMAN. I do not mean, Mr. Senator, that it is a case, because we are not making a case. It is a statement of the facts. It is simply an attempt to state the facts in relation to the occupation and administration of the Dominican Republic.

The CHAIRMAN. Let me suggest that I do not conceive that the committee ought to address itself to the consideration of a case. This inquiry is pretty broad in its scope.

Senator KING. I used the word "case" as a sort of generic term. The presentation of the facts as they consider them to be is what I meant.

Capt. FREEMAN. That is what it is intended to be—a summary of the facts in regard to the occupation and subsequent administration of the Dominican Republic to date.

Senator KING. Upon reading the presentation by Mr. Knowles and those whom he represents would it necessitate a revision and a review or a supplementing of this document? If so, it occurs to me, if you have got to file another, that you better keep this until you can bring it down to date. Of course I am only saying that in the interest of saving the expense of printing. We do not want to print two statements.

The CHAIRMAN. I think we want their statements independently of one another in the first instance. We will receive your statement if there is no objection.

(The matter referred to is here printed in full, as follows:)

OFFICIAL DOCUMENTS AND CORRESPONDENCE ON DOMINICAN REPUBLIC.

There are in print available for distribution the following volumes treating in part or in whole of the Dominican Republic:

Annual reports of the Secretary of the Navy, 1916, 1917, 1918, 1919, 1920. Attention is especially invited to Appendix D of the Report of 1920.

Santo Domingo; Its Past and Its Present Condition. Prepared by members of the military government of Santo Domingo.

Report on Economic and Financial Conditions of the Dominican Republic. Lieut. Commander Arthur H. Mayo, Supply Corps, United States Navy.

Report of Department of State of Finance and Commerce of the Dominican Republic, 1916–1919, with Estimates for 1920. Lieut. Commander Arthur H. Mayo, Supply Corps, United States Navy.

In addition there are available in the files of the Navy Department:

Seven bound volumes of correspondence covering Santo Domigan affairs during the years 1905, 1906, 1911.

Collections of executive orders issued by the military governor of Santo Domingo.

Quarterly reports of the military governor of Santo Domingo.

Records of military commissions and other military courts held in the Dominican Republic.

Special reports and general correspondence relating to the Dominican Republic.

— —

[Memorandum on Dominican Republic prepared for Senate committee appointed to inquire into the occupation and administration of the territories of the Republic of Haiti and the Dominican Republic by the forces of the United States.]

NAVY DEPARTMENT,
OFFICE OF NAVAL OPERATIONS,
Washington, August 5, 1921.

The Dominican Republic, occupying the eastern two-thirds of the island of Haiti, was proclaimed on February 27, 1844, and the present flag of the Republic was raised. This inception of the present Republic represented a successful revolt against the then Haitian (black) ruler of the Spanish-speaking survivors of a series of wars and uprisings extending over the beginning of the nineteenth century. A constitution, modeled after our own, was promulgated in November, 1844, and the commanding general of the Dominican army was elected president. He resigned in August, 1848, in the face of a threatened revolution and two successive presidents were in power during the next 18 months. The third president of the Republic was the first to serve a full term of office. Following his administration, revolution succeeded revolution in seemingly endless sequence. These civil quarrels of the Dominicans, interspersed with wars with Haiti, brought about an occupation of the Republic by Spanish troops from 1861 to 1865. When the Spanish troops were withdrawn, following a two years' revolt against their rule, and it is to be noted that the Dominican people actually fought against the Spanish occupation, after bearing with it from March, 1861, to August, 1868, the revolutionary struggles for political power continued and have marked the history of the country up until its occupation by United States forces.

The steps leading up to the present occupation by United States forces may be traced back to 1904. The culmination of more than a half century of revolutions was a hopeless piling up of the public debt and ultimately, in 1904, the default of the entire interest on this debt. Negotiations were entered into which resulted in arrangements being made to liquidate the debts owed the United States by pledging the customhouse receipts of some of the larger ports as security. On October 20, 1904, an American agent was, by agreement with the Dominican Government, placed in charge of the customhouse at Puerto Plata.

Foreign nations, noting the success of this plan, began to exert pressure with a view to securing the payment of their debts through control of certain customhouses pledged to them. Foreign intervention becoming imminent, the Dominican Government applied to the United States for assistance, and, in February, 1905, the protocol of an agreement between the United States and the Dominican Republic was approved, providing for the collection of the Dominican customs revenues under the direction of the United States, and the segregation of a specified portion toward the ultimate payment of the debt. This agreement went into effect on April 1, 1905, and continued as the modus vivendi until superseded by a new fiscal treaty agreed upon by the United States and the Dominican Congress, and taking effect on August 1, 1907. The provisions of this fiscal treaty still apply and require that the customs revenues of the Republic be collected by a general receiver of Dominican customs, appointed by the President of the United States, and that a portion of the income be set aside by him for the service of the bond issues made by the Dominican Government for the defrayment of the public debt.

Although the political leaders could no longer count on captured customhouses to give them an immediate financial return on their revolutionary activities, revolutions nevertheless continued. This unsettled condition of the country necessitated the maintenance of a considerable naval force in Dominican waters, in order that our assistant collectors of customs might not be at the mercy of irresponsible mobs or bands of irregular troops. During 1905 an average of 11 vessels, mostly of the gunboat and cruiser type, was continuously maintained in Dominican waters throughout the 12 months of the year. This force was a source of considerable expense and constant concern to the Navy Department. The number of vessels decreased in subsequent years, as the country gradually accepted the idea of American customs receivers in its ports, but the repeated revolutions and disturbances continued to give concern, and our naval vessels in Dominican waters were a familiar sight until after the establishment of the occupation. Now, visits of strictly military units are very rare, naval communication with the Republic being largely confined to transports and cargo vessels.

While it may be admitted that conditions improved somewhat in the Dominican Republic after 1905, it may be well to indicate the almost continuous condition of turmoil and agitation, which existed even after the prize of office yielded less financial return than when all of the revenues of the Republic were at the disposition of the Government. As a result of a revolution, Gen. Carles F. Morales became President on June 19, 1904. It was during his administration that the collection of Dominican customs by American agents began. Naturally, the "outs" strongly opposed this method of assuring the payment of the public debt, and the agitation against Morales finally reached such a violent stage that he fled the country to save his life. He returned ultimately, and resigned on January 12, 1906, the vice president, Gen. Ramon Caceres, assuming the presidency. Caceres completed his term of office and was reelected on July 1, 1908.

There followed various uprisings of political malcontents and a border clash with Haiti also occurred. Then on November 19, 1911, Caceres was assassinated by political conspirators, and Senator Eladio Victoria was designated provisional president by the National Assembly (both houses of the Dominican Congress). On February 27, 1912, he was duly elected constitutional president, but the method of his election was contested by opposing factions, and uprising began throughout the country. When it became evident that the Government could not control the situation, the United States Government offered its good offices. As a result of joint negotiations, the Dominican Congress convened, accepted the resignation of Victoria, and designated Monseigeur Adolfo A. Nouel, archbishop of Santo Domingo, as President. The archbishop appears to have recognized the hopeless state of the Government, due to the inability of the professional politicians to accept anything except personal success in the shape of appointments and patronage. He therefore resigned and left for Europe. He has since returned and continues his labors as a public-spirited citizen.

The Dominican Congress filled the vacancy caused by the resignation of the archbishop by designating Gen. Jose Bordas Valdez provisional president. He assumed office on April 14, 1913, with a view to serving out a one-year term. His assumption of office was the signal for another revolution. Again a United States commission came to Santo Domingo. The agreement then arrived at provided for the resignation of Bordas, and the Dominican Congress designated Dr. Ramon Baez, son of a former president, as provisional president on August 27, 1914. The agreement also provided for the general election of a constitutional president, and the popular elections which followed resulted in the reelection of a former president, Juan Isidro Jimenez.

Through this series of uprisings and revolutions we come to the situation that confronted the United States during that delicate period when, with a World War gathering headway, the usual international checks and balances were all awry. The Dominican Congress needed money. The customs receipts were in the hands of the United States. The internal revenues were undependable and might, and very generally did, fall into the hands of a local political chief at any time. The granting of an increasing number of foreign concessions, therefore represented an easy means of acquiring quickly the needed ready money to finance the mushroom governments. German and British influence possessed considerable strength in the country, the former doubtless preponderant. The Dominican Republic would prove a military base of importance for commerce destroyers if it could be involved in the European struggle. The whole influence of our country was being thrown on the side of preserving neutrality and preventing a spread of the European quarrel to the Western Hemisphere.

Fortunately the election of Jimenez, who took office on December 5, 1914, was followed by a brief period of comparative calm in the Dominican Republic. The elements of disorganization were present, however, awaiting favorable opportunity for expression. In April, 1916, Gen. Desiderio Arias, secretary of war, executed a coup d'etat, deposed Jimenez, and seized the executive power. At this point the United States Government intervened and with the consent of the rightful though deposed President, Jimenez, landed naval forces on May 5, 1916, and pacified Santo Domingo City, the capital. Jimenez then resigned, and the council of ministers assumed control of affairs.

During June, 1916, United States naval and marine forces were landed at various points in the country with a view to putting an end to the rebellion still being actively fostered under the leadership of Gen. Arias. A short and decisive campaign of about two weeks was conducted by the marines under the command of Col. Joseph H. Pendleton in the north of the island, which resulted in the quelling of organized opposition and the occupation of the principal north coast ports. Thereafter the important interior points of the country were occupied without serious difficulty, and peace was restored, except for the operation of bandit bands.

Meanwhile the Dominican Congress convened, following the resignation of President Jimenez, and designated as provisional president Dr. Federico Henriquez y Carvajal to serve for a period of six months. It is to be observed that the Dominican constitution of 1908, which is still in force, did not provide for a vice president, the motive doubtless being to avoid the temptation afforded to the incumbent of that office to do away with his chief and establish himself in power. The Dominican d͟ ⸲ovides, however, that the Congress shall designate by law the per⸲⸲ ⸲⸲c office of the presidency in case of the incapacity, resignation, removal, or death of the President, and the secretaries of state (council of ministers) are obliged to convoke the Congress for this specific purpose immediately when the vacancy exists.

Our international relations were now rapidly approaching a critical stage. It was highly desirable to have peaceful conditions close to our own boundaries, and the United States Government therefore stipulated that a new treaty be drawn with the new Dominican Government guaranteeing the maintenance of law and order and further assuring the payment of Dominican financial obligations. This treaty was in reality the price of recognition, and Dr. Henriquez refused to accede to the terms. Thereupon the United States authorities refused to pay over any of the revenues of the Republic. There being no surplus in the treasury, Government salaries ceased throughout the Republic. This deadlock continued from early August, 1916, until late November of the same year, when, all efforts to induce the Dominican authorities to conduct their Government in a manner conducive to the maintenance of internal peace and to the satisfactory conduct of foreign relations having proved of no avail, the United States Government on November 29, 1916, proclaimed a state of military occupation of the Dominican Republic by the naval and marine forces of the United States and made the Republic subject to military government. The proclamation of occupation, prepared in its essentials in the city of Washington, was issued by Capt. H. S. Knapp, United States Navy, commander cruiser force, United States Atlantic Fleet, and over his signature, and was in the following words:

"PROCLAMATION OF OCCUPATION.

" Whereas a treaty was concluded between the United States of America and the Republic of Santo Domingo on February 8, 1907, Article III of which reads:

"'Until the Dominican Republic has paid the whole amount of the bonds of the debt its public debt shall not be increased except by previous agreement between the Dominican Government and the United States. A like agreement shall be necessary to modify the import duties, it being an indispensable condition for the modification of such duties that the Dominican Executive demonstrate, and that the President of the United States recognize, that, on the basis of exportations and importations to the like amount and the like character during two years preceding that in which it is desired to make such modification, the total net customs receipts would at such altered rates of duties have been for each of such two years in excess of the sum of $2,000,000 United States gold'; and

" Whereas the Government of Santo Domingo has violated the said Article III on more than one occasion; and

" Whereas the Government of Santo Domingo has from time to time explained such violation by the necessity of incurring expense incident to the repression of revolution; and

" Whereas the United States Government, with great forbearance and with a friendly desire to enable Santo Domingo to maintain domestic tranquillity and observe the terms of the aforesaid treaty, has urged upon the Government of Santo Domingo certain necessary measures which that Government has been unwilling or unable to adopt; and

" Whereas in consequence domestic tranquillity has been disturbed and is not now established, nor is the future observance of the treaty by the Government of Santo Domingo assured; and

" Whereas the Government of the United States is determined that the time has come to take measures to insure the observance of the provisions of the aforesaid treaty by the Republic of Santo Domingo and to maintain the domestic tranquillity in the said Republic of Santo Domingo necessary thereto:

"Now, therefore, I. H. S. Knapp, captain, United States Navy, commanding the cruiser force of the United States Atlantic Fleet, and the armed forces of the United States stationed in various places within the territory of the Republic of Santo Domingo, acting under the authority and by direction of the Government of the United States, declare and announce to all concerned that the Republic of Santo Domingo is hereby placed in a state of military occupation by the forces under my command, and is made subject to military government and to the exercise of military law applicable to such occupation.

"This military occupation is undertaken with no immediate or ulterior object of destroying the sovereignty of the Republic of Santo Domingo, but, on the contrary, is designed to give aid to that country in returning to a condition of internal order that will enable it to observe the terms of the treaty aforesaid, and the obligations resting upon it as one of the family of nations.

"Dominican statutes, therefore, will continue in effect in so far as they do not conflict with the objects of the occupation or necessary regulations established thereunder, and their lawful administration will continue in the hands of such duly authorized Dominican officials as may be necessary, all under the oversight and control of the United States forces exercising military Government.

"The ordinary administration of justice, both in civil and criminal matters, through the regularly constituted Dominican courts will not be interfered with by the military government herein established; but cases to which a member of the United States forces in occupation is a party, or in which are involved contempt or defiance of the authority of the military government, will be tried by tribunals set up by the military government.

"All revenue accruing to the Dominican Government, including revenues hitherto accrued and unpaid, whether from custom duties under the terms of the treaty concluded on February 8, 1907, the receivership established by which remains in effect, or from internal revenue, shall be paid to the military government herein established which will, in trust for the Republic of Santo Domingo, hold such revenue and will make all the proper legal disbursements therefrom necessary for the administration of the Dominican Government, and for the purposes of the occupation.

"I call upon the citizens of, and residents, and sojourners in Santo Domingo, to cooperate with the forces of the United States in occupation to the end that the purposes thereof may promptly be attained, and that the country may be restored to domestic order and tranquillity, and to the prosperity that can be attained only under such conditions.

"The forces of the United States in occupation will act in accordance with military law governing their conduct, with due respect for the personal and property rights of citizens of and residents and sojourners in Santo Domingo, upholding Dominican laws, in so far as they do not conflict with the purposes for which the occupation is undertaken.

"H. W. KNAPP,
"Captain, United States Navy,
"Commander Cruiser Force, United States Atlantic Fleet.
"U. S. S. 'OLYMPIA,' FLAGSHIP,
"SANTO DOMINGO CITY, DOMINICAN REPUBLIC,
"November 29, 1916."

22. The military government established under Capt. (later Rear Admiral) Knapp as the first military governor of Santo Domingo has continued in force throughout the Dominican Republic ever since. It suffered, however, an unexpected evolution almost at its inception because of the refusal of the leading Dominican authorities to function with but under it, as called for in the terms of the proclamation. The situation which developed is perhaps best expressed in the words of the military governor as follows:

"After the issuance of the proclamation of military government, I waited for some days to see if the members of the provisional government would in any way cooperate with the military government in carrying on the ordinary administration of affairs. The hope that I had in this direction proved to be unfounded, and I was assured by persons most familiar with conditions here that I could expect no assistance of the kind. I established the offices of the military government in the Government palace. Upon taking possession, it was found that the President and all of the members of the cabinet had come to their offices after the proclamation of military government, had cleaned out their desks, and had not since appeared in the Government palace. It was an evident case of desertion. Under the circumstances, as the affairs of government had to go on under intelligent administration, I placed the several departments of the Dominican Government in charge of officers under my command.

"This action was forced upon me by the attitude of the members of the Dominican Government. It did not appear possible to get Dominicans of the proper caliber who would accept these high administrative offices, for they were afraid of the criticism that they would receive from their own people.

I could not force Dominicans into office, but I was able to direct officers under my command to assume these duties. The action taken prevented the utter disorganization of governmental administration. There were, moreover, some particular reasons why it was necessary to have some of the cabinet offices promptly filled. It was desirable to begin as soon as possible public works, which had been interrupted by the state of turmoil that had existed, and by the arrangements under the treaty of 1907 the necessary funds required the signature of Dominican officials before they could be withdrawn from the Guaranty Trust Co., of New York, which is the depositary of the Dominican loan.

"The result has been most fortunate. Unforeseen as the action taken was to me when I came to Santo Domingo, looking back, I now consider that it has helped enormously in the progress of the objects for which the occupation was undertaken. The American officers have been administering their departments with a high degree of intelligence and zeal, and, of course, with integrity and freedom from affiliations here that have never been questioned in them, but could not have been counted upon with Dominican officials. Had Dominicans remained in office, I should have had to have their actions constantly observed in any event; but the advantage of having officers actually administering, instead of observing and checking the administration of others, has been evident. Not only is this true from the point of view of the military government but it is true also from the point of view of many disinterested Dominicans. I have myself been asked, almost begged, by Dominicans not to disturb the existing order of things for a long period; not to think of putting Dominicans in these offices, but to continue the administration of affairs through the American officers, whose work is giving such great satisfaction to all disinterested people and whose presence in the responsible Dominican offices is resented only by the class which has brought the Dominican Government to the low plane which has made it a reproach. I can not claim any prevision leading up to my action, but I regard that action, taken by force of circumstances, as the most fortunate thing that could have happened.

"The sessions of the Dominican Congress, by the constitution in effect, begin on the 27th of February, which is the day celebrated as the anniversary of independence. The sessions last for 90 days, and may be prolonged for 60 days more. Every two years the terms expire of one-half of the deputies and one-third of the senators. Upon the advent of military government there were calls for election which had been issued by the late provisional government to fill these vacancies. The holding of elections at that time was out of the question in the minds of all persons whom I consulted, including Dominicans themselves. I therefore issued executive order No. 12 on the 26th of December, 1916, after I had had sufficient time to familiarize myself with conditions and to receive reports from the marine officers in the more distant parts of the country, none of whom believed in the elections being held. The executive order met the approval of all who wished well to Santo Domingo.

"In view of the fact that a quorum of the Congress did not exist, owing to the constitutional termination of the services of certain of the senators and representatives, and to the fact that elections were forbidden in the interests of the general pacification of the country, the existence of Congress became of no value to the country; on the contrary, it was represented to me, and I concurred in the conclusion, that it would be unwise to leave the country with the anticipation of an early filling of the congressional vacancies with the subsequent elections that should be held. I, therefore, on January 2, suspended the Congress and likewise suspended from office senators and deputies whose terms had not expired. Like the order suspending elections, that suspending the Congress met with almost universal approbation, as a measure that would go far to removing disturbing political agitation.

"For some time before the advent of military government, there had been sitting in Santo Domingo a special constituent assembly under the auspices of the provisional government, which the United States had refused to recognize. This constituent assembly finished its work on the very day that military government was proclaimed, and shortly thereafter the new constitution appeared in print. I refused to recognize it and the calls for election that were issued in accordance with its provisions. The proposed constitution is a dead letter, except for such value as it may have when a recognized constitutional assembly shall meet in the future."

With the failure of Dominicans of sufficient education to cooperate with the military government, the administration of the Dominican Republic and the destinies of the Dominican people passed entirely into the hands of the United States Government. The situation was without precedent. To withdraw meant anarchy. To remain meant the acceptance of undivided responsibility for the functioning of a nation which, basically the United States recognized as a sovereign power. Some working doctrine was essential upon which to base our conduct of affairs. It was found in the thought that the military Government administers the government of the Dominican Republic in trust for the Dominican people, in whom, in the words of article 13 of the Dominican constitution, "sovereignty is vested solely."

If the small political class, constituting perhaps about 5 per cent of the population, and the remaining persons of some degree of education, constituting at most another 5 per cent, would not or could not unite to contribute to the military Government that small measure of cooperation which would serve automatically to shorten the occupation and restore the absolute and unqualified sovereignty of the Dominican State, then it behooved the military Government to produce out of the people of the Republic a personnel who could be entrusted with the lawful and just administration of a modern civilized sovereign power in the family of nations.

With this end in view and in the hope meanwhile that actual contact with honest administration might produce enlightenment and a desire to assist in the minds of that small percentage of the population, qualified mentally, if not morally, to conduct affairs of state, the military Government proceeded to establish complete peace throughout the Republic, and began an intensive system of public instruction, public works, and honest control of finance.

The government of the Republic is administered by the military Government in accordance with Dominican laws, except as it has been found necessary to modify or supplement them by executive orders. The general policy of administration is set by the Department of State of the United States, acting through the Navy Department. The general policy being outlined by the Department of State, the Navy Department indicates this policy to the military governor who applies it in his administration of affairs. The Navy Department does not interfere with the details of administration, leaving all such matters to the determination and initiative of the military governor. Through his quarterly reports and special correspondence to the Navy Department, together with a consideration of his executive orders, copies of which he submits for information upon issue, the Department is enabled to determine whether the policy outlined by the Department of State is being carried out by the military governor. Major questions are referred to the Navy Department by the military governor for consideration, and, as such questions usually involve matters of policy, the opinion of the Department of State is sought. Occasionally situations develop in which a change of policy appears warranted. At such times, a more or less considerable interchange of correspondence occurs, followed by a return to normal conditions, when the intercourse between the military governor and the Navy Department is confined to routine reports on accomplished facts. In this manner, the closest cooperation and coordination exists between the Navy Department and the military governor, without the Navy Department being an administrative agency and with the military governor left with a free hand under the guidance of policy dictated by the Department of State. This method of carrying on the military government in its relations with the United States Government has produced excellent results, and the occasional lapses from it that have produced slight confusion at times have proved its efficacy as an established practice.

INITIAL ESTABLISHMENT OF PEACE.

Owing to the custom of jail deliveries upon the outbreak of every revolution, the country was overrun with criminals of all classes, many of them of the most brutal kind. To this custom is attributable the system of brigandage in the Dominican Republic, which continuously worked against the improved conditions in the country, the so-called bandits robbing and murdering their own people while avoiding the military authorities. Under the military government this banditry has been practically wiped out, although there exist still certain vagabonds or highway robbers in the eastern section of the country. The military forces occupied the country with garrisons in certain cities and outposts, with a system of patrols to insure the maintenance of peace and to protect inhabitants against the attacks of ne'er-do-wells. Under this system the country is receiving the blessings of peace and is progressing as never before in its history. Fully 95 per cent of the people avail themselves of the peaceful opportunity to pursue their callings, the remainder being revolutionary and obstructive politicians incapable of any fruitful work.

Upon the remains of the old Guardia Republicana has been erected an efficient constabulary, which is intended to police the entire Republic and to be the only military force in the country upon the turning over of the Government to its own representatives. This organization has been vastly improved and is still undergoing an evolution to perfect it and to make it an object of pride to all law-abiding citizens. It is the purpose to have this constabulary cover the entire Republic and to absorb all police functions. At present a large number of its officers are United States citizens, selected from the Marine Corps and elsewhere, but it is hoped to bring the force to such a high state of efficiency that Dominicans of good families will be glad to be identified with it.

INTERIOR ADMINISTRATION.

Before the occupation by the United States, the laws of the Dominican Republic provided for a division of the country into 12 Provinces, for each of which there was a governor appointed by the executive power. Communication by road between the various sections of the country and the capitals of the Provinces was practically nonexistent. This condition fostered the growth of an undue power on the part of the governors of the Provinces, who exercised within their respective jurisdictions practically complete control over the public forces, the police, and other governmental agencies.

The weakness of the central government, combined with the lack of proper means of communication, frequently resulted in defiance of the authority of the central government by the provisional governors and the consequent illegal abuse of power.

The military government has succeeded in reducing the power of these semi-independent governors to the status of proper civil governors with limited governmental functions. The governors now, instead of being oppressors of people of their Provinces, as was so frequently the case under the old régime, are able assistants of the military governor through their efforts for the education of the people, and they are exerting much influence toward good government generally.

The communes into which the Provinces are divided are governed locally by the ayuntamientos, or boards of aldermen, which formerly were elected, but since the occupation have been appointed by the military governor. The former system permitted of many abuses and much misgovernment, particularly through lack of accountability to any authority higher than their own.

Great improvement has been made in municipal administration through laws issued by the military Government. One of these laws constitutes a commission form of local government through the reduction in the number of members of the aldermanic boards, a change which has produced much greater efficiency in the conduct of municipal business.

Vexatious local taxes have been abolished and the financial affairs of the municipalities have been put upon a sound basis, while the control of the central government by means of an auditing system has removed many of the old opportunities for defalcations and misappropriations of funds. Certain handicaps have been encountered because of the lack of suitable personnel among the Dominicans to carry on the local governments, but the contrast for the better is marked between the old careless and inefficient and frequently dishonest local governments and the present Ayuntamientos, which endeavor to act for the good of their communes.

FINANCES.

When the United States intervened in the governmental affairs of the Dominican Republic there were six months' salaries of all government officials unpaid. Supply bills of the various departments of the governments had not been settled for long periods. The employees of the Government and merchants were demanding the payment of their just claims. A floating indebtedness consisting of claims of all descriptions had been created to the amount of approximately $15,000,000 in direct disregard of the terms of the American-Dominican convention of 1907. The cash balance of the Government was nonexistent, since the Government account with the depository was overdrawn in the amount of $14,234.68.

62269—21—PT 1——7

Instances were found where officials who had certified their right to salaries had not been within 30 miles of their work or office and had never occupied the positions designated, except in name. Pay rolls with a dozen or more names were found that had been receipted in the handwriting of one individual, and it was also found to be the custom with the heads of some offices to obtain the salaries of all of the employees of their office and to pay the employees such part of their salaries as was deemed fit, the head of the office retaining the balance for his own use. Other pay rolls were found pledged by the head of the office to local speculators who had purchased them for trivial amounts and were loudly demanding payment. The whole fiscal system was found to be honeycombed with graft. The vast majority of officers were dishonest and the records were found to have been deliberately falsified in hundreds of cases. Officials charged with the collection of internal revenue, with disbursing funds, and with the receipt and custody of supplies were receiving ridiculously low salaries, and graft had become so much a part of the system that practically all officials took toll of the funds passing through their hands, or accepted bribes, turning their backs to permit others to commit similar breaches of their trust.

The military government had organized the collection of the internal revenues of the country, and under honest and efficient management the collections have increased from an average of $700,000 prior to the occupation to about $4,000,000 annually. The cost of collection of internal revenues had dropped from 14 per cent in 1915 to about 5 per cent. In order to adjudicate the multitude of claims presented to the Government there was appointed in 1917 a Dominican claims commission, which continued in session for about three years. A total of 9,088 claims were filed, amounting to $19,960,513.48. Awards were made by the commission on 6,287 of these claims, to the amount of $4,292,342.52.

Many taxes existed, especially communal taxes, which bore unfairly upon the poor and acted as a drag to business in general. The military Government has eliminated the majority of these taxes and has established a tax on property, which has been successfully administered.

A tariff commission was appointed to make a study of the tariff and make recommendations for a downward reduction. The consent of the United States Government was secured to this revision of the tariff and a new tariff was placed in effect on January 1, 1920. Under this new tariff, transportation media, agricultural machinery and tools, industrial machinery, building material, and, in general, articles necessary for the development of the Republic have been placed upon the free list. The rates of duty have been greatly reduced on articles of necessity where the reductions would assist in lowering the cost of living. This tariff revision resulted in an increase in importations, which, although entering the country at reduced rates, have resulted in record customs collections due to the increase in the volume of importations.

Criticism has been made from time to time of the fact that it has been found necessary to borrow money and thus nominally increase the bonded indebtedness in the face of the increased prosperity of the Republic known generally to exist. This condition is brought about by the terms of the various loan agreements. If the Dominican Government, in the person of the military governor, could slow up the redemption of bonds, this course would certainly be followed. The money paid against the defrayment of the Dominican national debt, as represented by its bond issues, is obligatory under the loan terms. As a matter of fact the Dominican Republic, under the military government, is a victim of overprosperity. In general the loan agreements provide for the payment of a fixed sum annually plus a percentage of the amount by which the customs revenues of any year exceed another fixed sum. It is apparent from this general statement that increased prosperity represented by increased amounts from the customs revenue does not and can not redound to the immediate advantage of the Dominican Government. In other words, surplus customs revenues go, in the main, to the retirement of bond issues before they are due rather than to apply to expenditures wholly justifiable for the good of the people and the country, and warranted by the revenue returns. Needless to say, this condition of affairs is only temporary under existing conditions. It is at present evident that the $20,000,000 customs administration loan made in 1908 will be paid off by 1925, instead of 1958; that is, 33 years before it is due. The $4,000,000 bond issue of 1918 will be paid off about the end of the next calendar year, instead of in 1938; that is, about 16 years before it is due.

The recent $2,500,000 short-term bond issue will be paid by June 1, 1925. The short term and consequently high rate of this last bond issue results from the basic stipulation that its life be limited by the duration of the term of the present receivei. 1,,) general of customs, which expires with the final payment of the $20,000,000 loan of 1908.

At the present writing the Dominican Republic, in common with other West Indian governments, is suffering from the decided slump in the sugar, coffee, and cacao markets. This set-back can be only temporary in character, and is due to trade conditions over which the military government of the Dominican Republic has no control.

The diligent conserving of public funds has permitted more than three and a half million dollars to be assigned from the surplus for appropriations for the building of roads, schools, public buildings, and port improvements. Every effort is being bent to the completion of suitable roads which will open much-needed communication between all parts of the Republic and permit of the development of the interior.

The customhouses, wharves, and other properties of the State were found to be in a deplorable condition. These properties have now been placed in good condition. Wharves have been extended and warehouse facilities increased at practically all the ports. This work is still being continued.

The military government has been obliged to contend against a standard of honesty in the Republic, which, in so far as Government funds were concerned, was decidedly low. It is only by continual watchfulness, constant supervision, and frequent and efficient inspection that considerable losses in Government funds can be avoided even now. Some small losses have been suffered, but the general graft, dishonesty, and inefficiency with which the former treasury organization was honeycombed have been almost wholly eliminated.

ROADS AND OTHER PUBLIC WORKS.

The military government is carrying on an extensive road-building program with the intention of connecting all the roads of the Republic. These roads will at the same time open up and facilitate the development of large areas of very fertile country. Previous to 1916 there were only about 65 kilometers of good roads in the entire Dominican Republic. Since November, 1916, there have been constructed more than 150 kilometers of new macadam roads, 7 large steel bridges, 8 large concrete bridges, and many wooden bridges. In addition there have been more than 150 kilometers of second and 300 kilometers of third-class roads constructed in various parts of the country. Five large concrete bridges are being constructed and will be finished before the withdrawal of the occupation. The most ambitious as well, as the most important road now under construction, is a highway of about 290 kilometers, extending from Santo Domingo city on the south coast to the cities of La Vega, Santiago, and Monte Cristi on the north coast. This road will shorten travel time between Santo Domingo city and New York by four days, the time involved in the steamer trip around the eastern end of the island. Another important road, which will be finished before the withdrawal of the occupation, is that from Santo Domingo city to San Pedro de Macoris, connecting the two most important ports on the south coast. This road is 70 kilometers long.

The military government has constructed a new customhouse at Santo Domingo city, and has plans for the improvement of the present wharf and dredging of the channel. The same kind of work has been carried on at San Pedro de Macoris, where two new reinforced concrete piers are nearing completion. At Puerto Plata, on the north coast, a modern reinforced concrete pier was completed a short time ago. A modern water supply system has been installed in the town of Azua, near Santo Domingo city, and plans are under way for an excellent water system in the capital city itself.

Along the coast the lighthouse service has been improved and maintained and new burners installed everywhere. A lighthouse tender has been purchased and placed in service. The former Government-owned dredge has been docked, repaired, and maintained in operation. A new dredge, the *Yaque*, has been purchased and is in use.

Repairs and alterations have been made to numerous Government buildings which were in very poor condition. These buildings have been made serviceable and sanitary improvements installed.

Two steel radio towers 150 feet high have been erected at Santo Domingo City and a radio station has been placed in operation. Many new school buildings are under way, and provision has been made for the expenditure of about $150,000 more to complete construction.

In place of the paralyzed condition of the mail and telegraph service, due to disorders existent when the military occupation took over the administration of affairs, the post-office and telephone system has been unified and placed under civil service. Twice as much business has been handled as formerly and such important changes made in the systems that the time required for the delivery of mail across the island has been reduced to 4 days instead of 10 to 14 days. A trunk telephone line from Santo Domingo City to the northern coast has been undertaken. City telephone systems have been established in Santo Domingo City, Le Vega, Santiago de los Caballeros, La Romana, San Francisco de Macoris, San Pedro de Macoris, Monte Cristi, and Puerto Plata. A topographical survey of the Dominican Republic is being made and will be well advanced before it will be necessary to discontinue it due to the prospective withdrawal. This topographical survey has been accompanied by the making of a land survey for the purpose of properly delineating and marking the boundaries of land under various owners.

On account of the richness of the Dominican Republic in minerals it has been found necessary to promulgate orders to stop exploitation of the mineral wealth, which was not being carried on in good faith, and a new mining law has been promulgated covering mining concessions. A law for the conservation and distribution of water in arid and semiarid regions has been promulgated and is in operation.

It has been the endeavor of the military government to build up and improve all means of communication between the various sections of the country, to improve the numerous ports, and to maintain and better the conditions of navigation aids, to modernize all construction, and to open the interior of the Republic to a higher civilization..

AGRICULTURE.

Before June, 1917, nothing had been done in the Dominican Republic along the line of modern agriculture education. Since then educational work has been instituted and has expanded and improved considerably, until at present there are between 30 and 40 instructors in various sections of the country.

In order to focus this work and provide the necessary places for experiments with various crops, an agricultural experimental station has been established near Santo Domingo City, with a ground area of about 150 acres. The following structures have been placed in operation: Barn, bangalow, silo, dipping tank, and propagation house. A veterinarian and an animal husbandryman have been employed to improve conditions of the stock. Pure-bred poultry, horses, cattle, and hogs have been imported. At the same location there has been constructed an agricultural college, with a view of educating one Dominican from each Province yearly, in order to fit them for agricultural instructors and managers of agricultural enterprises. Two agricultural experimental substations have been established. Orchards of American fruit trees have been planted and appear to be doing well. Demonstration plots are being worked on various farms, with a view to showing by practical physical demonstration the best agricultural methods.

A forestry law has been promulgated with a view to protecting the soil from erosion and thus conserve the forests and the natural beauty of the country. Laws have been established prohibiting the importation of coconut seeds in order to protect the Republic from the introduction of the destructive bud rot disease present in the other Antilles. A similar law has been issued covering the importation of cotton seeds. The Agricultural Review, a Government publication, is published monthly. It contains information of value to agricultural interests and has a free circulation of about 3,000.

JUSTICE AND PRISONS.

During the military occupation of Santo Domingo there has not been one case of corruption of a judge, nor has any venal act upon the part of a judge been reported. Many reforms have been made in the judicial organization with a view to expediting the trial of offenders.

Ramshackle and unsanitary prisons have been repaired or rebuilt and new ones constructed. A modern penitentiary is now in course of construction which will accommodate 500 prisoners. Two correctional schools for boys of tender age have been established. In these two schools manual training is taught and the inmates are trained in carpentering, tailoring, and shoemaking.

At the time of the occupation only civil marriages were recognized by law, and the judges, who had a monopoly of the business, charged such high fees for marriages that many of the poorer classes could ill afford to have the ceremony performed. Executive orders issued by the military government have corrected this evil, and hundreds and perhaps thousand of persons who have openly lived as husband and wife without ever enjoying a civil ceremony have now taken advantage of the inexpensive cost of marriage and have thereby in many cases legitimatized their children.

PUBLIC INSTRUCTION.

Before the reforms initiated under the military Government, public education in the Dominican Republic was very ineffective. There was great confusion in regard to the law on the subject, and for several years practically no school law was recognized. Primary education was for the most part confined to schools with one or two teachers in the most important towns. There were no rural schools. Town schools deserved the name only when they were in the hands of private teachers. The usual salaries of teachers in primary schools ranged from $8 to $9 a month, and, under favorable conditions, were not paid more than eight or nine months in the year. There were no more than 18,000 pupils in all schools, although statistics of these times are neither constant nor reliable.

One of the first acts of the military Government was to form a commission of prominent Dominicans to report upon conditions then existing regarding education, and to formulate recommendation looking to their improvement and the establishment of a system of education that would best serve the interests of the people of the Republic.

This commission sat for almost a year, and prepared and recommended the following draft of laws:

1. Law on compulsory school attendance.
2. Law for the direction of public schools.
3. General studies law.
4. University law.
5. Law on theological seminary.
6. Organic law on public education.
7. Law of school revenues.

The first six laws were promulgated with very slight modification by the military Government and now constitute the school code of the country.

There were until recently about 1,500 teachers of all classes in actual service. It has been temporarily necessary to consolidate certain of the schools and the duties of certain of the teachers, on account of the decrease in internal revenues due to unfavorable economic conditions which have prevailed more or less throughout the West Indies. This situation will undoubtedly be of comparatively short duration, although it has been made the subject of unfavorable criticism of the military Government. It may be pertinent to remark at this point on the peculiarly vexatious character of such unfavorable criticism. The statement is made that schools have been closed by direction of the military Government. This statement is wholly true. It is added that the military Government is depriving the children of the Dominican Republic of their right to an elementary education. In so far as the temporary closing of certain schools is concerned, this statement is also true. The presentation of these two isolated facts, however, wholly ignores the increase of school attendance during the military occupation and the vast improvement in school conditions.

The rural school-teachers draw a salary of from $55 to $75 a month, as against salaries of $8 to $15 before the reform. Graded school-teachers draw salaries of from $60 to $100 a month, as against salaries of from $20 to $40 before the reform. Summer schools are provided for the teachers and certificates are required for all teachers. The capacity of the teaching force has been one of the surprises of the development of the schools.

The school attendance has increased from about 18,000 to more than 100,000 in all schools. The increase in the school population is not due to the compulsory attendance alone. It is a consequence of the more efficient school work of the teachers, as well as of the greater attraction in the schools for the pupils and a better social condition resulting from the occupation.

Before the reform, schools were invariably located in dirty, miserable quarters. A school usually consisted of a room of small size with two or

three board benches for the pupils and a broken chair for the teacher. At present the schools are working in the best houses of every town, and schools are now neat, pleasant places, although it has been necessary to maintain the schools very largely in rented buildings until the program of construction of schoolhouses has been completed.

There is a recognized drawback to this otherwise favorable review of the school situation. Although efforts are made to employ competent teachers and certificates of qualification are required of them, there is a lack of thorough school inspection and an absence of definite information as to the actual progress of the pupils as a whole under the opportunities afforded them. With time, this drawback would undoubtedly disappear, under the present administration of affairs.

SANITARY AND PUBLIC HEALTH CONDITIONS.

Upon the establishment of the military government, sanitary and public health activities in the Dominican Republic were almost entirely lacking. A sanitary law was in existence, but little or no attention was paid to it. Cities and towns were dirty, elementary sanitation was neglected, and the few hospitals in the country were in a sadly neglected state and totally inadequate. There was no real attempt toward disease control.

A new sanitary law has been promulgated, creating a national department of sanitation and beneficence. This law centralizes the administration of sanitation and public health matters and the practice of medical professions under the control of a secretary of state for sanitation and beneficence and places this department on a level with the other departments of the Government. The secretary is assisted by a national public-health council, an advisory body of representative Dominicans.

The country is divided into sanitary districts, each district being in charge of a district sanitary officer immediately responsible to the secretary. Dominicans are appointed to all positions of responsibility under the department of sanitation and beneficence wherever practicable.

A national leper colony and leprosarium is being completed. Inadequate charity hospitals and orphanages have been reorganized under the general direction of the department of sanitation. Existing hospitals are being enlarged, and plans for several new hospitals are being completed. A series of small dispensaries for the treatment of the poor throughout the country is a feature of the sanitary administration.

Under the military government, there has been established an adequate national sanitary organization for the administration of sanitary and public health affairs, including municipal sanitation, hospitalization, quarantine, the practice of the medical profession, the sale of drugs, national and municipal charity work so far as the public health is concerned, the compilation of vital statistics, and the control of disease. The training of personnel under this organization is going forward, with a view to making secure the future sanitation and public health of the country as a whole.

GENERAL COMMENT.

It has been pointed out that, following a long period of turmoil in the Dominican Republic, during which the United States repeatedly offered its good offices with a view to straightening out affairs and preventing foreign intervention, the United States Government directed the occupation of the country and its administration under military government by forces under the immediate supervision of the Navy Department. The Navy was assigned the task of carrying on in the Dominican Republic under policy outlined by the United States Government and has continued to do so until the present time, when an endeavor is being made to accomplish a withdrawal of the military government in accordance with the terms of a proclamation issued on June 14, 1921, in the following terms:

" PROCLAMATION.

" Whereas, by proclamation of the military governor of Santo Domingo, dated December 23, 1920, it was announced to the people of the Dominican Republic that the Government of the United States desired to inaugurate the simple processes of its rapid withdrawal from the responsibilities assumed in connection with Dominican affairs; and

"Whereas, it is necessary that a duly constituted government of the Dominican Republic exist before the withdrawal of the United States may be effective, in order that the functions of Government may be resumed by it in an orderly manner.

"Now, therefore, I, Samuel S. Robinson, rear admiral, United States Navy, military governor of Santo Domingo, acting under the authority and by direction of the Government of the United States, declare and announce to all concerned that the Government of the United States proposes to withdraw its military forces from the Dominican Republic in accordance with the steps set forth herein. It is the desire of the Government of the United States to assure itself before its withdrawal is accomplished that the independence and territorial integrity of the Dominican Republic, the maintenance of public order, and the security of life and property, will be adequately safeguarded, and to turn over the administration of the Dominican Republic to a responsible Dominican Government duly established in accordance with the existing constitution and laws. To this end, it calls upon the Dominican people to lend to it their helpful cooperation with the hope that the withdrawal of the United States may be completed, if such cooperation is given, in the manner hereinafter provided, within a period of eight months.

"The executive power vested by the Dominican constitution in the President of the Republic will be exercised by the military governor of Santo Domingo until a duly elected and proclaimed president of the Republic shall have taken office and until a convention of evacuation shall have been signed by the President and confirmed by the Dominican Congress.

"Within one month from the date of this proclamation the military governor will convene the primary assemblies to assemble 30 days after the date of the decree of convocation in conformity with articles 82 and 83 of the constitution. These assemblies shall proceed to elect the electors as prescribed by article 84 of the constitution. In order that these elections may be held without disorder and in order that the will of the Dominican people may be freely expressed, these elections will be held under the supervision of the authorities designated by the military governor.

"The electoral college thus elected by the primary assemblies shall, in accordance with article 85 of the constitution, proceed to elect senators, deputies, and alternates for the latter, and to prepare lists for the justices of the supreme court of justice, of the appellate courts, and the tribunals and courts of the first instance, as prescribed by article 85 of the constitution. The military governor, performing the functions of chief executive, will then appoint, in accordance with article 53 of the constitution, certain Dominican citizens as representatives of the Republic to negotiate a convention of evacuation. In order that the enjoyment of individual rights may be insured, and in order that the peace and prosperity of the Republic may be conserved, the said convention of evacuation shall contain the following provisions:

"1. Ratification of all of the acts of the military government.

"2. Validation of the final loan of $2,500,000, which is the minimum loan required in order to complete the public works which are now in actual course of construction and which can be completed during the period required for the withdrawal of the military occupation, and which are deemed essential to the success of the new Government of the Republic and to the well-being of the Dominican people.

"3. Extension of the duties of the general receiver of Dominican customs, appointed under the convention of 1907, to the said loan.

"4. Extension of the powers of the general receiver of Dominican customs to the collection and disbursement of such portion of the internal revenue of the Republic as may prove to be necessary should the custom revenue at any time be insufficient to meet the service of the foreign debt of the Republic.

"5. The obligations on the part of the Dominican Government, in order to preserve peace, to afford adequate protection to life and property, and to secure the discharging of all obligations of the Dominican Republic, to maintain an efficient Guardia Nacional, urban and rural, composed of native Dominicans. To this end it shall also be agreed in said convention that the President of the Dominican Republic shall at once request the President of the United States to send a military mission to the Dominican Republic charged with the duty of securing the competent organization of such Guardia Nacional, the Guardia Nacional to be officered by such Dominican officers as may be competent to undertake such service conditions, and for such time as may be found necessary to effect the efficient organization with American officers appointed by the President of the Dominican Republic upon nomination of the President of the United States. The expenses of said mission will be paid by the Dominican Republic, and the said mission will be invested by the Executive of the Dominion Republic with proper and adequate authority to accomplish the purpose above stated.

"The military governor will thereupon convene the Dominican Congress in extraordinary session to confirm the convention of evacuation referred to above. The military governor will then assemble the electoral college for the purpose of electing a President of the Dominican Republic in accordance with article 85 of the constitution, and simultaneously officials other than the Senators and deputies elected at the first convocation of the electoral college will be installed in office. The Dominican President so elected will then take office in accordance with article 51 of the constitution upon this ratification of the convention of evacuation, at the same time signing the convention of evacuation as confirmed by the Dominican congress. Assuming that through the cooperation of the people of the Dominican Republic a condition of peace and good order obtains, the military governor will transfer to the duly elected President of the Republic all of his authority and the military Government will cease, and thereupon the forces of the United States will be at once withdrawn.

"The further assistance of the advisory commission appointed under the proclamation of December 23, 1920, being no longer required, it is hereby dissolved, with the expression of the grateful appreciation of the Government of the United States for the self-sacrificing service of the patriotic citizens of the Dominican Republic of whom it has been composed.

"S. S. ROBISON,
"*Rear Admiral, United States Navy,*
"*Military Governor of Santo Domingo.*
"SANTO DOMINGO, DOMINICAN REPUBLIC.
"*June 14, 1921.*"

(Whereupon the committee adjourned, subject to the call of the chairman.)

INQUIRY INTO OCCUPATION AND ADMINISTRATION OF HAITI AND SANTO DOMINGO

HEARINGS

BEFORE A

SELECT COMMITTEE ON
HAITI AND SANTO DOMINGO
UNITED STATES SENATE

SIXTY-SEVENTH CONGRESS
FIRST SESSION

PURSUANT TO

S. RES. 112

AUTHORIZING A SPECIAL COMMITTEE TO INQUIRE INTO THE OCCUPATION AND ADMINISTRATION OF THE TERRITORIES OF THE REPUBLIC OF HAITI AND THE DOMINICAN REPUBLIC

PART 2

October 4 to November 16, 1921.

Printed for the use of the Select Committee
on Haiti and Santo Domingo

WASHINGTON
GOVERNMENT PRINTING OFFICE
1921

SELECT COMMITTEE ON HAITI AND SANTO DOMINGO.

MEDILL McCORMICK, Illinois, *Chairman*.

ATLEE POMERENE, Ohio.
TASKER L. ODDIE, Nevada.   WILLIAM H. KING, Utah.

ELISHA HANSON, *Clerk*.

II

INQUIRY INTO OCCUPATION AND ADMINISTRATION OF HAITI AND SANTO DOMINGO.

TUESDAY, OCTOBER 4, 1921.

UNITED STATES SENATE,
SELECT COMMITTEE ON HAITI AND SANTO DOMINGO,
Washington, D. C.

The committee met pursuant to adjournment at 10.30 o'clock a. m., in the committee room, Capitol, Senator Medill McCormick presiding.

Present: Senators McCormick (chairman), Oddie, and Pomerene.

Also present: Mr. Ernest Angell, representing the Haiti-Santo Domingo Independence Society, the National Association for the Advancement of Colored People, and the Union Patriotique D'Haiti; Mr. Horace G. Knowles, representing the Patriotic League of the Dominican Republic and the deposed Dominican Government; and Mr. Roger L. Farnham, representing the National City Bank of New York City.

STATEMENT OF MR. ROGER L. FARNHAM, VICE PRESIDENT NATIONAL CITY BANK, NEW YORK, N. Y.

The CHAIRMAN. Mr. Farnham, will you please give your full name?

Mr. FARNHAM. Roger L. Farnham.

The CHAIRMAN. Give your connection with the National City Bank and your business.

Mr. FARNHAM. Vice president National City Bank, New York.

The CHAIRMAN. And your business interests are those of the Bank in Haiti?

Mr. FARNHAM. Yes.

The CHAIRMAN. You may go to any length you choose on that subject.

Mr. FARNHAM. As to the position of the bank, you mean?

The CHAIRMAN. How does it come that the bank is interested in Haiti, or the National Bank of Haiti, and to what extent is it interested?

Mr. FARNHAM. In 1910 the old National Bank of Haiti was reorganized in connection with a new Government loan taken by some French bankers.

Senator POMERENE. Was that a private bank?

Mr. FARNHAM. Yes; that was a private bank, which had had a contract to act as treasury of the Haitian Government. But due to some internal difficulties and bad management, the bank had practically failed, and it was reorganized with strong group of French bankers behind it, and in connection with that reorganization a new contract was made between the Haitian Government and the bank, under which contract the bank was to make certain annual loans to the Government, for purposes of the budget, and it also was to act as the treasury of the Government, receiving all revenues—not collecting any, but receiving them—and paying out all disbursements for account of the Government.

Senator POMERENE. That was prior to 1910?

Mr. FARNHAM. No; I am reciting the subject of the 1910 contract.

Also under that contract the bank was to be the bank of issue of the currency of the country.

For some reason, Senator Knox, who was then Secretary of State here, intervened in the matter, and objected to the contract as it originally was drawn, saying that it was very onerous to the Haitian people, and also he felt that some American banking interests ought to be represented. He did not favor the preponderance of French interests, and at his request several bankers from New York visited Washington and discussed the matter with him. The result was that the National City Bank of New York, Messrs. Speyer & Co., Hallgarten & Co., and Ladenburg Thalmann & Co. each became subscribers to 2,000 shares of the capital stock of the company, which is a French organization operating under a French charter.

The capital stock was 40,000 shares. Out of that the National City Bank acquired 2,000 shares, and the other interests, respectively, 2,000 shares each. Those shares represented 125 francs paid in, the par value being 500 francs. At the same time the German bank, Berliner Handel Gelselschaf, acquired 2,000 shares.

The changes which Senator Knox, then Secretary of State, brought about in the original contract, were qu te to the benefit of the Haitians. From that time on the bank has been conducted as a French institution, with, I think, three Americans on the board of directors, but the practical management of the bank was from Paris. The American directors had practically little to do. The bank has its principal office in Port au Prince, and nine branches or agencies throughout the country.

That situation continued until the time of the American intervention in Haiti in 1915 or perhaps a short time before that, when, because of the World War, the French people were so taken up with matters at home that they asked the American directors to assume the management of the affairs of the bank, and from that time on the active management has been from New York rather than from Paris, although the board was continued in Paris and was consulted from time to time.

Shortly after the European war broke out Secretary of State Bryan, in several interviews, suggested the advisability of the American interests acquiring the French shares in the bank, and making it an American bank. That suggestion was repeated from time to time, and after some extended conferences, I think in 1917, just before the United States entered the war, the National City Bank purchased the stock held by the other three American parties, Hallgarten, Speyer, and Ladenburg Thalmann, so that that gave the National City Bank about 8,000 shares of stock in the bank, out of 40,000 shares.

Senator POMERENE. At 500 francs per share?

Mr. FARNHAM. Yes; par value, of which 125 francs had been paid in. The stock of the bank never was issued, never has been issued. An inscription was made on the books of the bank in Paris, stating the fact of the subscription, and each participant was issued a certificate.

Senator POMERENE. Well, your subscribers were without the evidence——

Mr. FARNHAM. Except in the form of a certificate.

About a year and a half ago, after several suggestions from the State Department, negotiations were entered into, with the result that the National City Bank purchased all the assets of the French institution.

Senator POMERENE. Including the German interests?

Mr. FARNHAM. All, yes, all of the assets. Under the circumstances, Senator, it was rather difficult to buy the stock. At a shareholders' meeting held in Par's, where all the shareholders were represented—and there were about 6,000 shareholders of the bank altogether—it was voted to accept the offer of th National City Bank, which was $1,400,000.

Senator POMERENE. Let me understand that. Do I understand you to say all the shareholders? Does that include the German shareholders who were there?

Mr. FARNHAM. Yes; all shares of the German bank had been seized by the French Government, and the French Government acted in that matter.

The CHAIRMAN. Who was Secretary of State at that time?

Mr. FARNHAM. At the time we made the offer for the assets?

The CHAIRMAN. Yes.

Mr. FARNHAM. I think Mr. Lansing. The bank paid $1,400,000, the understanding being that the assets would be transferred to a new company which the National City Bank would create; the French company would be discontinued, the charter surrendered, and the money would be distributed to the shareholders. That has not been carried out because it has been impossible to obtain from the Haitian council of state its approval for the transfer of the contract between the Haitian Government and the French bank to the new organization. The Haitians agreed to do it. Their minister and representatives went over the matter here in Washington at the State Department and signed their assent to the transfer, requesting that the new corporation, if we could see our way to do it, should be a Haitian corporation rather than an American one, and we complied, and drew up an organization in Haiti, under the same title as now exists, the Banque Nationale Republique d'Haiti, but up to now it has been impossible to get the approval of that Government to the transfer of the contract, and so we are continuing the bank under the actual ownership of the National City Bank, but under the French charter, and with the French officials and directors remaining as they have been. Mr. Polson, the vice president of the Banque Un'on Parisien, is president and I am vice president. The board is equally divided between French and Americans. That is the only interest the National City Bank has in Haiti, and all that it ever has had.

Senator POMERENE. You are continuing your operations down there just as heretofore.

Mr. FARNHAM. We are continuing operations as a bank; yes, sir. We have carried out the obligations of the contract; from time to time we have made advances to the Haitian Government, so that the obligations of the Government to the bank amount to-day to $1,733,154. I forget the exact cents.

Senator POMERENE. What are your assets?

Mr. FARNHAM. That we hold a note of the Haitian Government for, which is at the approval of the State Department here, and bears the signature of the American financial adviser. That note is due and payable on the 31st of December of this year. It was made two years ago.

Senator POMERENE. What are the total assets of the bank?

Mr. FARNHAM. Of the Haiti Bank?

Senator POMERENE. Yes.

Mr. FARNHAM. We have just had an examination made. They are approximately a million and a half, with the note of the Haitian Government.

Senator POMERENE. In addition to that?

Mr. FARNHAM. No; including that.

The CHAIRMAN. Perhaps I might ask here, in order that the information might be in the record, what other banking institution is there in Haiti, and how many branches has it?

Mr. FARNHAM. The Royal Bank of Canada, a British bank, is there. It has an office in Port au Prince, one at Aux Cayas, and one at Cape Haitien.

The CHAIRMAN. What relation, if any, is there between the National City Bank, its stockholders, and the railways built under the so-called McDonald concess ons?

Mr. FARNHAM. The National City Bank did not have and never has had any interest in that railroad except a loan of $500,000 made to the contracting company building the railroad, the bank receiving as collateral for that loan, $870,000 and some odd, of the bonds of the railroad company. That is the only interest the National City Bank has ever had in the railroad. The railroad was financed by a syndicate gotten up by W. R. Grace & Co., and the control of the capital stock of the railroad is with that syndicate. In that syndicate—the Grace Syndicate, so-called—one of its subscribers is the Ethelburga Syndicate, an English institution which owns 50 per cent of the capital stock of the railroad, so that the ownership of the railroad is divided equally between the English interests and a group of Americans. I think there are 12 in the American group. The stock never was issued to the public. It has always been held by the group.

The CHAIRMAN. That was one of those English interests which makes a business of investing in the enterprises and utilities of undeveloped countries, I take it?

Mr. FARNHAM. Yes.

The CHAIRMAN. Will you indicate where this railroad is on the map?

Mr. FARNHAM. The railroad runs from Port au Prince, following practically that red line out to the shore there, and from here out to that point, St. Marc. It runs from Gonaives to a place called Ennery; and from Cape Haitien to a place called Bahon. It is in three sections. The original plan was to bring it way down here into this country [indicating on map], and so on below the Artibonite River, until it got to St. Marc, but that is practically an impossible proposition on account of the mountains. It can be brought over the mountains here at Bahon, and come in through here, and the engineers have been trying to find some way to get across this range of mountains here.

Senator POMERENE. This is all Greek to me. You say there are three sections. Are they not connected?

Mr. FARNHAM. No; not at all. They were built at the same time. One section was started here and another section here. [Indicating on map.]

Senator POMERENE. Now, you say here and here. Will you indicate it for the record?

Mr. FARNHAM. From Cape Haitien to Bahon. From Cape Haitien, on the north, it goes south to a point called Bahon 37 kilometers; and from Gonaives, on the west coast—that is another section—inland and eastward 33 kilometers to Ennery; and from St. Marc, also on the west coast, south to Port au Prince 102 kilometers.

Senator POMERENE. What are the several industrial activities which suggested the building of these roads in those particular sections or localities?

Mr. FARNHAM. In the Gonaives-Ennery section of the road the idea was to reach some coal deposits inland. The coal was thought to be valuable. It is not, because it is nothing but lignite and of a rather poor quality at that. The remainder of the line, from Cape Haitien to Bahon and from Port au Prince to St. Marc, are the two ends, if you please, of what was laid out to be a through line from the north to the south. They pass through a country which could produce sugar cane in large quantities, bananas, and cotton. There is no cultivation in Haiti, as we understand the term.

Senator POMERENE. Are the climatic and soil conditions there such as to make it a reasonable competitor of Cuba?

Mr. FARNHAM. Well, in a small way. The climatic and soil conditions are quite all right for sugar, cotton, coffee, and cocoa. There is an abundance of labor, after it is educated. The area susceptible of that sort of cultivation, of course, is somewhat limited compared to Cuba. It is generally thought by those who have investigated the situation that sugar can be made in Haiti as cheaply as in Cuba after the natives have been taught how to handle the cultivation of the cane. The same applies to cotton, cocoa, and coffee. At the present time the cotton and coffee grows practically wild. It was brought there in the days of the French, but for the last 100 years it has just taken care of itself. It propagates itself; there is no cultivation. There are no plantations. The only cultivation that you see as you go through the country is here and there small garden patches, which are cultivated by the women, of beans, sweet potatoes, and yams. There is no cultivation of bananas, no cultivation of cotton; and the sugar cane which you see growing practically all over the country in the fertile parts, the valleys and plains, is a propagation of what was put there by the French. The country is susceptible of a good deal of development, but it will require capital, and it will require some time to educate the Haitian to become a good laborer.

In recent years a number of Haitians—several thousand—have been taken over to Cuba during the sugar season to work in the fields. They are fair laborers. They can not match up with the Jamaican in the fields nor with the Spanish Gallego. If you sit on your horse in the cane fields in the cane season, as I have done, and watch two Gallegos working together and two Jamaican Negroes and two Haitians, you will see the piles of cane cut by the two Gallegos and the two Jamaicans grow almost twice as fast as the pile cut and thrown by the Haitians. They seem to lack the muscular strength. I know that in the construction of this railroad in Haiti, where we had them as laborers, the American foremen, who had previously been on railroad construction in Mexico and all up and down South America and in the United States, told me—and I saw myself, too—that they reckoned four Haitians were necessary to do the work of one good Irish track hand.

The CHAIRMAN. Let me ask, Mr. Farnham, is that possibly——

Mr. FARNHAM. They were very weak, and they had no food.

The CHAIRMAN (continuing). A matter of nourishment?

Mr. FARNHAM. Nourishment almost entirely, and ignorance in handling matters of that sort.

Senator POMERENE. Naturally, they have the physical strength, have they?

Mr. FARNHAM. Generally speaking, I should say no. The women are all strong, big, husky persons. The majority of the men are rather light and small, underfed. They seem to lack the physique.

Senator POMERENE. How do you account for the difference between the sexes?

Mr. FARNHAM. I do not know, but it is observable as soon as you go among the people, particularly in the country. The men are rather light in weight, and they do not seem to have the stamina. They can not stand up under hard work?

Senator ODDIE. Is there anything in the climate?

Mr. FARNHAM. I think the climate has something to do with it, but still in Santo Domingo, which has practically the same climate, or in Panama, which has even a worse climate to work in than Haiti, the Negroes there work satisfactorily.

Senator POMERENE. That statement surprises me very much. I am not disputing it at all. Do you mean to say that the women are actually or simply relatively stronger than the men?

Mr. FARNHAM. On the whole, I think they are actually stronger. The women perform the labor in the gardens; they do all the marketing; they think nothing of tramping 50 miles to market, carrying on their heads almost unbelievable loads. You will see a woman driving two or three burros, and she will be carrying on top of her own head more than any one of the burros. They will walk all night, many of them very fast. They will walk as fast as a good horse will walk and carry that heavy load over the island. They come into the market place at Port au Prince two or three times a week, particularly on Saturday, probably 5,000 or 6,000 women, who have come in from all directions. You will see some at the other principal towns like Cape Haitien and St. Marc. Fifty per cent of them have carried on their own heads what they bring to market.

Senator POMERENE. In doing this work in the construction of the railroads, is that done by the women or the men?

Mr. FARNHAM. The men. The women would not work at that. You can not get a woman to work cutting cane, but they will pick coffee and cotton, they will work in the garden, they will cultivate their garden stuff. I think if you should see a group of women and a group of men you would immediately notice the difference in their physique, their whole set-up.

The CHAIRMAN. Mr. Farnham, I think the committee would be interested to have your impression of political and economic conditions preceding the occupation, and the incidents of the occupation, and all events and conditions subsequent to the occupation.

Mr. FARNHAM. Well, I would like to preface what I would say by the statement that what I know of this country is gained by trips on horseback through the interior. I have made in Haiti seven trips on horseback, one of 33 days and one of 30 days and five of a fortnight each. I have made two in Santo Domingo, one of 34 days and another of 17 days, on the trail. I went with a party through Santo Domingo, and usually there have been two or three men with me on the trips through Haiti, and we have gone very well equipped, because we had saddle horses brought there from Wyoming and American pack mules. We had two horses apiece, so that we rode one in the morning and one in the afternoon, which permitted of pretty fast riding. In that way we have covered all of Santo Domingo and all of Haiti, except these two arms. That portion I have not been in. I have sailed around the coast of the arms, but I have not traveled over them. But I have been over practically all the rest of Haiti and Santo Domingo on horseback, and it is from these trips that I have been able to observe conditions.

My first trip was made in June, 1911, in Haiti. In 1913 I made the first trip through Santo Domingo and in 1918 the second. At that time—I am speaking now of 1911—and from then until the American occupation in Haiti, it was almost a condition——

Senator POMERENE. What was the date of the American occupation in Haiti?

Mr. FARNHAM. July, 1915. The country was in a state of almost continuous revolution, one man trying to succeed the other as President and so get control of the treasury.

Senator POMERENE. You are speaking of Haiti, not of Santo Domingo?

Mr. FARNHAM. Haiti. In that time I think there were seven Presidents.

The CHAIRMAN. In four years—from 1911 to 1915?

Mr. FARNHAM. Yes. Simon was President in 1911, and went out on the 1st of August that year, and so on. There were seven Presidents up to the time of the American occupation in July, 1915. During that period, in riding through the country one saw very few men. They were either in the Government army or in the revolutionary army, or hiding out in the hills to escape both. The majority of them were engaged in the latter occupation, keeping out there with their families. The cultivation, such as it was, by the women was considerably limited, and between either the revolutionary army or the Government army a great many small villages were destroyed, the houses burnt up, the people killed, and every sort of an outrage which you may imagine going with a movement of that sort.

It was under those conditions that they attempted to construct the Haiti railroad, but revolutionary conditions became so bad in 1913 that the management suspended the construction of it, and in 1914 they had to suspend operation of the sections which had been completed, and no trains were operated for nearly a year—until after the American troops landed there. Then, at the request of the commanding officers, the road was put in some operation, with an occasional train, which gradually increased until conditons permitted the normal daily operation of trains.

The Governments which followed each other were revolutionary Governments, each one getting the country into debt more deeply. I think that was the situation which the Americans found when they arrived there, following the killing of the last President, Sam.

As to Santo Domingo, the conditions there, you should understand, are quite different from Haiti.

The CHAIRMAN. Let me submit this to the members of the committee: It seems to me that we had better confine the witnesses to one subject. If we attempt to consider the conditions and the problems in both countries simultaneously, I think we shall be in great difficulties. Will you just address yourself, therefore, Mr. Farnham, to the question of Haiti?

Mr. FARNHAM. I think that is all I can say about that. The business of the country was in control of the Germans, 90 per cent of it.

The CHAIRMAN. The commerce?

Mr. FARNHAM. The commerce of the country, both the import and export business. The German ships controlled the shipping. No other vessels went there, with the exception of an occasional ship from France, of the French Transatlantic Line. They had a vessel which called there about once a month, sometimes once in two months, but outside of that the traffic was in the control of the Hamburg-American Line, and the German merchants worked in conjunction with that line. They profited considerably through the revolutions. They loaned money to the would-be presidents to finance their revolutionary movements at what resulted in a profitable rate of remuneration to them.

In 1917, when we went into the war, Haiti declared war also on Germany, and the Germans were forced to leave the island. Their property was conscripted by the Haitian Government and placed in liquidation. Some two months ago that ban was lifted and practically all the Germans are back in Haiti, they have resumed their old business, and the property and funds which were taken from them then are now being returned to them, their buildings, lands, stores, together with some $2,000,000 cash, which was realized from the sale of certain goods taken from their stores.

There are two or three half-German, half-Haitian houses in the country, one English house, and in the last two or three years two or three American individuals have opened up business there, but they are small.

The country has been served during the war by the Panama Steamship Line, which passes practically by the door, going back and forth to the canal—the diversion in and out is rather small—and that has rendered a weekly service which has been very necessary to the country for both passengers and mail, freight, and merchandise. An effort, I understand, is being made to discontinue that service. I think it is very desirable——

Senator POMERENE. An effort by whom?

Mr. FARNHAM. I do not know. I understand the Shipping Board have some control over it. A petition is now being circulated for everyone interested to sign to have the Panama steamship service to Haiti retained. Personally, I think it should be. I think it is very desirable to have an American steamship line going into that country?

Senator POMERENE. Has the German service been continued there, or renewed again?

Mr. FARNHAM. No; not yet. I understand it is to be. I was informed a week ago by one of the former employees of the Hamburg-American Line that it is now attempting to resume their service from New York to Haiti and through the Caribbean.

The CHAIRMAN. Did not the Hamburg-American Line, in a sense, dominate that entire island trade?

Mr. FARNHAM. Yes; before the war they did. They practically made the rates for the whole Caribbean, for all the American lines and all other lines.

The CHAIRMAN. With headquarters at St. Thomas?

Mr. FARNHAM. They had a big coaling station there; yes; but they served Venezuela, Panama, Jamaica, and Haiti. They laid out a certain district, which they monopolized to themselves and fixed rates.

Senator POMERENE. You have spoken of the National City Bank's interest there, and of the Canadian bank. Did the Germans have any banking interests there?

Mr. FARNHAM. No, sir. Quite a number of German houses were private banks themselves. They practically did their own banking business. Very few of the Germans did business with any outside bank. They shipped their goods by the German line, and their mail was handled in the same way, and their drafts went out in the same way. The only thing they did with the National Bank of Haiti prior to the American intervention was to obtain from the bank from time to time as they wanted them the necessary paper gourde, which was the money of the country, of the denomination of 20 cents, nominal value, and then when the crop season would be over they would change these gourdes back to dollars. The gourde is a paper bill about the size of our dollar bill, in denominations of ones, twos, tens, and twenties.

Senator ODDIE. You mentioned some influence that is being brought to bear to have the Panama steamship service discontinued.

Mr. FARNHAM. Yes.

Senator ODDIE. I would like to know a little more about that.

Mr. FARNHAM. Senator, I can not tell you very much about it myself. Two or three times it has been reported that the Panama steamship service was to be withdrawn from Haiti and to be substituted by the Royal Mail Steam Packet Co. For some years that company has maintained a service through the Carribean, particularly to Jamaica and some of the eastward islands, but more recently they have operated ships from Nova Scotia to Haiti and to Santo Domingo. That service seemed to come about after the establishment in Haiti of the Royal Bank of Canada. I do not know if this is true, but it has been reported to us by our representatives in the island that the English bank offered loans to Haitian merchants on condition that they would buy Canadian goods rather than American goods. It is a fact that the ships from Nova Scotia brought out fish, cotton goods, and supplies of that sort which are used in Haiti, and would take away coffee, cocoa, and logwood. Whether they intend to put on a regular service in the event the Panama service is withdrawn I do not know, but a week ago I was advised by a former employee of the Hamburg-American Line that they soon expected to resume their service to Haiti.

Senator ODDIE. Who is pressing to bring about the withdrawal of the Panama ships?

Mr. FARNHAM. I could not tell you, Senator.

Senator ODDIE. I wondered what interest was dominant in that effort.

Mr. FARNHAM. I do not know. That service is a very good one. It is regular, and I think the rates probably are more favorable to the Haitians than previously the country has enjoyed.

Senator POMERENE. You have spoken of the interest of the National City Bank. What other substantial interests are there in Haiti?

Mr. FARNHAM. There are two only. A group of Americans organized a company about three years ago to undertake to develop a plain located about here [indicating on map] in cotton, and they put into cultivation, I think, some 2,500 or 3,000 acres. Instead of using the Haitian cotton, which is a long staple and very tough sort of cotton, and which the island originally grew, they brought seed from the United States. Whether that was responsible for what happened I do not know, but the whole thing was a failure. The cotton did not grow. It would grow that high [indicating] and then proceed to die. They sprayed it, they did everything, but they could not cultivate it.

Alongside of it they had a small tract of Haitian cotton which grew. I think they gathered about 100 bales from that, but their 2,500 acres of cotton raised from the imported seed, I think, died, and they have practically abandoned for the time being their plants there. I understand they invested altogether nearly $1,000,000. They acquired a very large tract of land, and they brought tractors and breaking-up plows; they brought a great deal of machinery into Haiti. For the time being they are doing nothing.

There was another company formed, in which the Germans, who originally controlled the entire property, participated. That was called the Haitian-American Sugar Co. That was organized by some Americans, in conjunction with certain Germans in Port au Prince. That company acquired the stock of the electric light company of Port au Prince; also a small, narrow-gauge railroad running from Port au Prince out to this lake, about 30 miles; also a tramway in the city, the wharf at Port au Prince, and they were also to build, and did build, a sugar mill about a mile and half from Port au Prince. They have there a very fine mill. I think it has a capacity of about 200,000 sacks of sugar.

They undertook to get sugar cane from the plains of Cul-de-Sac, which 100 or more years ago under French management was a very productive territory for sugar. They had some difficulties with the natives, and were unable to get a sufficient supply of cane, and their affairs went badly and did not work out. About nine months ago the company went into the hands of receivers, and about eight weeks ago the property was sold at a receiver's sale in New York, and it was bought in by several banks that had loaned money to the enterprise and were interested. I believe they contemplate reorganization when conditions get a little better.

Senator POMERENE. What is the total of the American investment in Haiti?

Mr. FARNHAM. It is rather hard to answer, Senator. As to the bank. I have told you. As to the railroad, the so-called Grace syndicate paid in practically all of its underwriting obligations, $2,225,000. The cotton enterprise at the north involved about $1,000,000. What was put into the Haitian-American operation by Americans I do not know. They claimed to have assets altogether of about $12,000,000, but I rather doubt that.

The CHAIRMAN. What did they sell for at the receiver's sale?

Mr. FARNHAM. $650,000; but that was a mere nominal figure. It was bought in by the banks, with the understanding on the part of the court which appointed the receiver that a reorganization would be effected and that all subscribers to the original company would be given an opportunity to participate.

Senator POMERENE. What did the German interests amount to, in your judgment?

Mr. FARNHAM. In invested capital I should say a relatively small amount, representing investments only in buildings at the different ports and in lighters and a wharf. The Germans built this wharf at Port au Prince. I think that cost them about $275,000. Perhaps in the railroad, the tramway, and the electric light company they had invested $1,000,000.

The CHAIRMAN. They were primarily merchants and middlemen?

Mr. FARNHAM. They were merchants and middlemen. You see, before the American occupation, and before the treaty and the new constitution of Haiti, foreigners could not own any land. That was prohibited. Some of the Germans married Haitian women in order to get land, but the amount of land they acquired was relatively small, and was of no importance. They bought the products of the country and exported them, and they imported cotton goods, eatables, etc. They did their own banking business. They speculated in gourdes, and they made considerable profit out of financing revolutions. They were not landowners, in the proper sense of the word. Through a marriage or some association with a Haitian woman they would own a few houses in one town or another.

Senator POMERENE. They were rather exploiters?

Mr. FARNHAM. Yes.

Senator POMERENE. What have you to say about the British and the amount of their interests there?

Mr. FARNHAM. Nil.

Senator POMERENE. And the Canadians?

Mr. FARNHAM. Nil.

The CHAIRMAN. Outside of the bank.

Mr. FARNHAM. Yes; outside of the Canadian bank. The American-Foreign Banking Corporation opened a bank there and carried it on for a year and a half, but that is closed and discontinued.

Senator ODDIE. Who were the Americans interested with the Haitians in the Haitian-American Corporation?

Mr. FARNHAM. I could not tell you, Senator. A private banking house in Chicago, by the name of Breed, Elliott & Harrison, and some others, were interested in it, and I think the preferred stock of the company was sold generally to the public, more in the Middle States, I think in Illinois and Indiana, than in the East. I think the bulk of the preferred stock of that corporation was sold in those States.

Senator POMERENE. Who was it that first took the initiative which led up to our sending our marines into Haiti?

Mr. FARNHAM. I think we went in there primarily because the French had already stepped in and taken possession. When we went in there the French had sent a warship and troops and had landed at Cape Haitien, on account of the revolutionary conditions, and were in possession, administering the affairs of the city.

The CHAIRMAN. I think the Navy Department has covered that.

Mr. FARNHAM. And on account of that situation we sent Admiral Caperton out there. He displaced the French occupation. Later they landed their troops at Port au Prince at the same time we did, and those troops remained there until a treaty was negotiated six months later.

Senator POMERENE. How many troops have we down there now?

Mr. FARNHAM. I could not tell you.

The CHAIRMAN. That is all in the record. We should like very much to have Mr. Farnham give us his impressions of the occupation and its administration of the country.

Mr. FARNHAM. My impressions on that, Senator, will have to be confined to just what I saw there.

The CHAIRMAN. The occupation has continued now nearly six years. There was a period of what we might call pacification, and there was later a period— I think you might designate it——

Mr. FARNHAM. I would like to mention that before the American occupation there were no roads in Ha'ti; there was only one way of going about, and that was by horseback, anywhere and everywhere. There were a few automobiles that had been introduce'l 'nto Port au Prince, but they could not go outside of the town. All travel was either on foot or on horse all over the country. The idea of this railroad was to effect some means of communication between the north and south. Before the roads were built travel was very tiresome and tedious. You had to go over mountains, swim rivers, and it was a very difficult tr'p, particularly in the rainy season, when it was almost impossible to get through.

After the American occupation, and the country had become qu'eted down, there was some discussion by Government officials at this en'l about road building and improvement, but there was no policy, and there was nothing except talk. In the meanwhile the marines started in and built a road so that it was possible to go from Port au Prince through St. Marc to Gonaives, and overland to Cape Haitien easily in 12 hours. It was a wonderful road, beautifully done.

Senator POMERENE. How is that done; by what means of locomotion?

Mr. FARNHAM. Automobile.

Senator POMERENE. What is the distance?

Mr. FARNHAM. Well, that road, I would say, is about 140 miles.

Senator POMERENE. Was that done by the Americans, at their expense, or was it charged to the Hait'en Government?

Mr. FARNHAM. That was done under the d'rection of the marines, with their own engineers, and by Haitian labor.

Senator POMERENE. Who paid the labor?

Mr. FARNHAM. That labor was handled under a law of Haiti which provides that all men can be conscr'pted for three days at a time to work upon the roads, and it was under that law that the actual labor was performed. The marine engineers laid out the lines, and did all of the engineering work. It was supervise'l by marines. The labor was by Haitians.

Senator POMERENE. Then the only cash outlay would be for overhead expenses, substantially?

Mr. FARNHAM. I was told—whether it 's true or not I have no means of knowing—that the entire cash outlay for that road was something under $250,000, covering the outlay for powder and dynamite, for in some places they had to blast, and for the material necessary to make some small bridges. I am inclined to think that is perhaps true.

Senator POMERENE. It costs $250,000 to build about 5 miles of road in the United States.

Mr. FARNHAM. Any person who had traveled the country before and subsequently went over that road and saw the sort of road that was built could have nothing but commendation for the mar'nes. It was a great piece of work.

The CHAIRMAN. Have they built other roads?

Mr. FARNHAM. Yes; they have made other roads there, but I am calling this the main road through to the north. They have built something like 100 m les of other roads in different parts of the island, and very good roads. I might ad l that they are wide enough for two automobiles to pass, and they are over the mountains some 4,000 feet above the sea and down again.

Senator POMERENE. Am I to infer from your statement that while they had this law for conscr'pting labor for road building they had never operated under it until the marines took hold of it?

Mr. FARNHAM. No; the Haitians had built no roads. There were no roads, only trails; that is all, bridle paths.

Senator ODDIE. How many miles is the main road?

Mr. FARNHAM. I think about 140. I may be in error, but that is approximately the distance.

Senator ODDIE. In figuring the cost of that road, labor——

Mr. FARNHAM (interposing). The labor was paid nothing. The officers adopted generally the plan which was adopted in the construction of railroads. They fed the men—gave them meals such as they probably never before had had. From my observation in many places it was difficult to drive the men away from the work. They were taken for three days and then told to get out. A large percentage said they wanted to stay in the camp and work. There have been statements made that men were abused and shot, and that may be true—I do not know—but I was up and down that trail quite a bit during the construction at infrequent periods, and I saw nothing of that.

Senator POMERENE. Did you hear of it while you were there?

Mr. FARNHAM. Only in one case. I heard they had a gang of prisoners in one spot that were pretty bad, and that they had had to shoot two or three of them that tried to run away. I rode into one place one afternoon, and I did see some men that were marked off as prisoners. I saw men with handcuffs tucked in their belts working away with the rest. The thing that attracted my attention was the handcuffs hanging to the belts. I think the marines had a very difficult time when they first went in there; there is no doubt about it. The Haitians had all sorts of rifles, good, bad, and indifferent. They were out in the woods. They were bossed by various military chiefs who did not want to lose their positions.

Senator POMERENE. Haitian chiefs?

Mr. FARNHAM. Haitians entirely—in the Haitian Army. And so in the early part of the invasion there was a good deal of sniping and bushwhacking on the part of the natives. Before the American occupation there was never any danger to a white man who traveled in the country. I have been through while the revolutions were on, and a white man was not molested. If he kept out of the mess himself and minded his own business he was perfectly safe.

Senator POMERENE. The white men felt perfectly free to travel across the country?

Mr. FARNHAM. Yes. There were not many white men in the country. Before the American occupation I doubt if there were 75 white men in the whole country—straight whites. There were some mulattoes; but, including the Germans, I doubt if there were over 75 white men in the entire country of Haiti. After the American occupation many of the Haitians seemed to turn against the whites, and all white men looked alike.

Senator POMERENE. After the occupation?

Mr. FARNHAM. Yes, sir.

Senator POMERENE. To what do you attribute that?

Mr. FARNHAM. I think that the natives were aroused by the talk of the chiefs and the military generals to believe that the whites were going to make slaves of them again. That was the usual cry; and that the Haitians would have to resist the marines if they wanted to get rid of them, otherwise they would be made slaves. That is the fear that is uppermost in the minds of all Haitians, as ignorant as they are.

Senator POMERENE. What portion of those people can read and write?

Mr. FARNHAM. I doubt if out of the two and a half million there are 50,000 that can read or write. They speak an unknown patois; I do not know what it is. I remember that on one of my trips through the island I had an Englishman with me who had lived for many years in South Africa, in the Congo country, and spoke Kaffir. He tried it on the natives, and all of the old people seemed to understand it, and could talk with him, and he had never been in Haiti before. He noticed many peculiarities of the people, which he said were the same as those of some tribes on the West Coast of Africa. The Haitians, as you probably know, were brought from Africa to Haiti. As late as 1800 they were bringing them in as slaves.

Senator POMERENE. Who?

Mr. FARNHAM. The French, who occupied the island and controlled it in those days. It was the French who developed the coffee, sugar, and indigo industry in Haiti. They had large plantations there, and Haiti produced in those days great quantities of sugar, but in the revolution of 1804 those were all destroyed.

Senator POMERENE. Are the literate and the educated class pure blacks?

Mr. FARNHAM. Of the educated class the majority of them are. A few of the mulattoes are well educated. There are perhaps 250 or 300 men in the whole island who have had a very superior education abroad. They are very highly educated, members of the French bar, some of the English bar, some educated at Oxford, and others at educational institutions in France. They have lived abroad and have acquired the polish of the Europen; they are very well read in literature; they are pretty good diplomats, very cunning, and a considerable number of them are absolutely untrustworthy; I mean they do not stick to what they agree to.

Senator POMERENE. Are they leaders in these revolutionary movements?

Mr. FARNHAM. They are leaders. The country, up to the time of the American occupation, had been at the mercy of that small coterie of intellectuals who had kept themselves in power by means of revolutions, and who had controlled the finances of the country and profited out of the revenues. The bank, which is the treasury of the government, was compelled, of course, to honor the order of the secretary of the treasury, whoever he might be, nor could we question payments directed by him, although we might realize that they were not really payments which should be made. The arrangement, of course, left the treasury at the mercy of the politicians. They did observe their foreign obligations; they always met the interest on the outstanding bonds in France; they usually took care of their budget, until 1912, when they began to run behind and spent money faster than they were taking it in. Their income in normal times should be between $6,000,000 and $7,000,000 gold, United States money, just from their customs. There was and is no other income, no method of taxation.

Land titles are without value. In the city of Port au Prince, Cape Hatien, and one or two of the other important points, I think the titles to city property are good, generally speaking, but when you get out in the open country, outside of these cities, there are no points of survey. There evidently has been no survey of the island in 100 years. It is difficult to locate land, as described by the property owners. People will offer for sale land which they claim to own. If you ask if they have a deed, they will say " yes," but when they hand it to you it is usually a letter from some general who has taken their horse or pigs or other valuables, and in substance it says, " You can live where you are as long as you want." That is a literal translation of the paper they call a deed.

The CHAIRMAN. That is from the general d'arrondissement?

Mr. FARNHAM. Yes, sir.

The CHAIRMAN. Mr. Farnham, I wish you would speak of the work of pacification and the policy of development of the occupation.

Mr. FARNHAM. I never knew of any policy, Senator. I think that is the trouble with Haiti.

The CHAIRMAN. When the work of pacification was complete—and that was about when, in your judgment?

Mr. FARNHAM. In 1918 Haiti was as quiet as a churchyard—practically disarmed.

The CHAIRMAN. We had been there three years?

Mr. FARNHAM. And the relations, as far as I could observe, between the occupation and the natives were very good. The people who were educated, one and all, were awaiting the announcement of some plan of development—something which would bring about the construction of roads or bring in American capital to develop the sugar industry or cotton industry under the occupation. No plan seemed to be forthcoming. The men who were in charge of the military occupation all were awaiting it, and they did not know what to do. Many of them had programs which they worked out themselves, or thought out, but they were powerless to put them into effect. I think it was due almost entirely to our failure at that time—and when I say our failure I mean the failure of the United States Government—to present some well-defined plan for the development of that country that led to the renewal of revolutionary conditions. The war came on; they could not export their commodities; there were no ships; they had no money; the best people were really hungry, and they were hard put to it to get enough to eat—people who were theretofore well to do—and they appealed to the American officials for something, but the American officials could do nothing.

The CHAIRMAN. What form did the appeal take, if you know? Was there any formal memorial?

Mr. FARNHAM. No; I do not know of anything of that sort, but I know that individuals and groups did go to the financial adviser at that time, Mr. Ruan, I believe, and to the American minister and others, asking that something be done to give employment to the people of the country—something which would take the place of the ordinary exports and the funds derived therefrom which had stopped. I was informed that representations repeatedly were made to Washington of the whole situation, with the request that some plan of development be given them. Personally I called on the Secretary of State at Washington two or three times and suggested that something of that sort should be done and done rather promptly. It was not done, and the fallen Haitian military leaders began to talk to the ignorant countrymen——

The CHAIRMAN. We were pursuing a policy of watchful waiting?

Mr. FARNHAM. Yes. They led the countryman to believe, and rightly, that he was much worse off than before the American occupation; that the occupation had, not brought any benefits to him, except perhaps the death of some of his relatives in the early days, and out of that grew conditions which were worse than prevailed when we first went in. Now, the country is again quiet and again disarmed, and we have conditions to-day in Haiti practically the same as they were in 1918, peaceful, the people being ready for some comprehensive plan of development. I think before that can be carried out some change will have to be brought about in the Government position. There is a dual government under the treaty which it seems to me makes impossible any progress there. Nothing can be done by the United States officials.

The CHAIRMAN. There is no central, responsible authority to be found?

Mr. FARNHAM. No. The representatives of the United States, the financial adviser, the military commanders, and the American minister can do nothing without the consent of the Haitians, which they do not get, and the Haitians on their part can do nothing without the approval of the financial adviser, and it is a deadlock, and has been so so ever since the treaty was put into effect. I do not believe the American officials are to blame for the failure to do something.

The CHAIRMAN. Now, if you would care to do so, will you fix responsibility for the failure to develop and to apply a policy in Haiti?

Mr. FARNHAM. I would not to do that, Senator; I do not think I can. I can only say that no policy was forthcoming.

The CHAIRMAN. Was it in Washington or Port au Prince?

Mr. FARNHAM. I think it was in Washington. Port au Prince had to wait on instructions from Washington. I think that the officers at that time in command—and they were all strangers to me; I never met any of them until I met them in Haiti, men like Gen. Butler and Gen. Cole, who were then in command of the military, and some of the engineers—I think they went just as far as they dared go to do something in the way of progress and development. I think, in building these roads, they acted on their own initiative. I never understood that instuctions about that came from Washington. They wanted to have the people occupied at something. Gen. Cole approached the officials of the railroad company to see whether a resumption could be had of the construction of the railroad, but that was impossible, due to the financial situation.

Senator ODDIE. Is there any trouble or lack of unity among the Haitians; that is, in regard to supporting their President?

Mr. FARNHAM. In doing what?

Senator ODDIE. In supporting their President.

Mr. FARNHAM. I think there are the usual political difficulties that there are in every country.

Senator ODDIE. Nothing serious now?

Mr. FARNHAM. No. Of course, each man thinks he ought to be president and would give a good administration. It is the usual political situation.

Mr. ODDIE. Well, the present President, then, is as strong as any man could be there?

Mr. FARNHAM. I think so, under the circumstances. I do not see what any man could do more than this man has done. There has been for the last year a well-defined position on the part of the President and the members of his cabinet and the leading politicians against the American occupation. I think they were aroused to that by the writings and talk of certain people who thought the Haitians were being abused and that the Americans had no business to be in Haiti. Of course, that would be a popular topic with the Haitian politicians, because if the Americans got out they would at once come in control of the funds of the country again; but I feel confident that if the Americans do leave, there would be no development of the country by the Haitians. It would be left just where it was before we went there. The people are not sufficiently educated yet to take up, of their own initiative, any development.

They have not the money and they have yet to learn agriculture, as we understand it, and the politicians have no interest in doing that sort of thing.
(Whereupon, at 12 o'clock noon, a recess was taken until 3 o'clock p. m.)

AFTER RECESS.

The committee reassembled at 3 o'clock p. m., pursuant to the taking of recess, Senator McCormick (chairman) presiding.

The CHAIRMAN. You were saying, when the hearing was suspended, Mr. Farnham, that the Haitians knew nothing of agriculture, as we understand it. Has anything been done under the occupation to teach them?

Mr. FARNHAM. Not that I know of. I know of nothing that has been definitely undertaken in Haiti since the occupation commenced to develop with the natives the agricultural resources of the island or to seriously develop schools or educational methods. The only schools that I know of in the island are those maintained (and existing before the occupation) by the Jesuit priests, the French priests in the island. At some points they have schools, and they are undertaking to teach the Haitian children. They receive a very small amount of money annually from the Haitian Government, which they apply to purchasing books and materials for those schools—an exceedingly small amount.

The CHAIRMAN. Is anything being done to encourage the Haitians to work? Is he any more secure in the possession of his property or his savings than he was before?

Mr. FARNHAM. Well, he is not now liable to have what he has taken away from him, as under the old rule. Before the American occupation there was a military government in vogue throughout the island. The generals were divided into the generals d'arondissement and the generals de la place. In their respective districts they were all powerful. They controlled the people as absolutely as if they were czars. The majority of the people did not know who was president and had no interest in it. They were interested more particularly in who might be, under some revolution, the general de la place or the general d'arondissement, and how much that general might take away from them of their property. In traveling through the country it was necessary to have a pass, which you presented when you arrived at each place where there was a body of troops.

The CHAIRMAN. Was that true for the Haitian citizen as well as the foreigner?

Mr. FARNHAM. All Haitians had to get a pass to travel. You had to present your pass to the officer at that place, tell him whence you had come, and about how long you would stay, and where you were going. In the majority of cases the officer was unable to read your passport. Frequently they would hold it upside down and pretend to read it and hand it back to you, but if you gave them a little compensation that was all that was necessary. Those generals controlled practically everything in their districts when the construction of the railroad was commenced. During the first year it was quite customary, when the men who worked for the construction company received their pay, for the general of that vicinity to be on hand with troops and seize those men as soon as they were paid, put them in jail and take their money away from them, and on Monday they would bring them back to work, all tied together with ropes, and deliver them here. We appealed to the President to break that practice up, because it was difficult to get men. After they had been robbed in that way two or three times they would not work, and we were all the time having to obtain new men. But the appeals to the President at Port au Prince were without avail. It was some time before the practice was given up, and then it was very largely due to the activities of the people in charge of the construction work.

The market women, in passing these places of residence of the commander in the country districts, usually had to give up some of their coffee and some of their cotton as a toll, and frequently, after selling their produce in the town, they would have what they purchased in part taken away from them when they went out. I have frequently seen one woman driving a whole lot of burros on the return trip, while the other women of the party were making a detour through the woods with what they had purchased, in order to avoid the military posts.

In Port au Prince, up to 1915, if you wanted to go out after 6 o'clock at night and wanted to take dinner with a fr'end, for example, you had to get a pass to go from your house to his. You were stopped at every street corner by the military. That was so in every town of the island. There were military guards posted at the corners always all night. That custom persisted up to the time of the American occupation.

The CHAIRMAN. Now, let us go back a little, Mr. Farnham. In what sense did Senator Knox secure the modification of the terms of the bank contract in favor of th eHaitians?

Mr. FARNHAM. As I was not present at that time, but was in Europe, I can simply state what I was informed. The terms of the loan were rather excessive in favor of the bankers. My understanding is that Senator Knox caused a modification of the terms, so that the bonds brought to the Haitians a larger return. Also I think he succeeded in having reduced the charges which the contract provided the bank should make for the service rendered to the Haitian Government. I was informed by some of my associates who took part in the conferences that he caused modifications to be conceded by the French bankers which were very considerable to the advantage of the Haitian Government.

The CHAIRMAN. I want to turn for a moment again to the question of the corveé, to learn if you have anything to say with regard to the policy which I think subsequently was attempted by the department of taking men away from the neighborhood in which they lived, and to what extent that practice created trouble.

Mr. FARNHAM. I can not answer that from personal knowledge, Senator. It is only hearsay. I was told that the practice had obtained to some extent, and that men from the south were carried to the north, and vice versa, but that is a matter of hearsay only.

The CHAIRMAN. Do you know anything about the charge that the men working under the corveé, when they attempted to escape, were shot?

Mr. FARNHAM. That is a matter of hearsay; I do not know of my own knowledge. At the times when I was in Haiti, when I was along that road I saw none of that. I would say, however, in that connection that my observations of the work were during the régime of Gen. Butler. The people in our employ in Haiti have informed me that after he left the island to go to France in the war a good deal happened under his successor that did not occur under his administration.

The CHAIRMAN. Who was his successor?

Mr. FARNHAM. A naval officer.

The CHAIRMAN. Williams?

Mr. FARNHAM. William, yes; I do not know what his rank was. I think he was a marine officer; I am not sure. I could not tell you about him. As I recall, his name was Williams.

The CHAIRMAN. It has been reported that under Alexander Williams there were abuses in the administration of the corveé which did not obtain under Butler.

Mr. FARNHAM. That was the report that came to me from our employees in the office.

The CHAIRMAN. Were they specific abuses?

Mr. FARNHAM. No; the shifting of men from one part of the island to another, the abuse of some of the men by the minor officers in immediate charge of them, and I have heard that some of them, trying to get away, were shot; but, as I say, that is not a matter of my personal, direct knowledge.

The CHAIRMAN. In your judgment, were the roads, and especially the principal highway, of commercial as well as military value?

Mr. FARNHAM. That they built?

The CHAIRMAN. Yes.

Mr. FARNHAM. Yes, indeed; they facilitated very greatly the travel between the north and the south, which theretofore was confined to the few people who could make it on horseback and by the rather infrequent passage of steamers around the coast.

The CHAIRMAN. Do the peasants avail themselves of these roads in great numbers?

Mr. FARNHAM. I have always found it so when I have been on the road—market women traveling to market and coming back, and quite a number of people on foot traveling from one point to another in the interior of the country. One road in particular I think has been of very great advantage to the people in the interior; that is the road from Port au Prince across the plains of Cul-de-Sac, over the mountains to a place called Mirebalais, which was almost inaccessible before that road was built. People had to come down the Artibonite River to St. Marc, and then down the coast to Port au Prince, rather than make that journey across there.

The CHAIRMAN. The road, of course, was built out of Haitian funds?

Mr. FARNHAM. That is my understanding; such expenses as were incurred.

The CHAIRMAN. What were the circumstances under which Secretary Bryan suggested that Americans acquire the French shares in the bank; did that suggestion come directly to the National City Bank?

Mr. FARNHAM. Yes; because—well, it came, in the first instance, to Mr. Werhane, who at that time was vice president of the bank, and myself, in a conference which we had one day with Secretary Bryan, in which he expressed the view that it would be rather advantageous to the country if the banking interests of the island were American rather than French, and asked why we did not undertake to acquire control of the bank. There was some discussion of the suggestion, and from time to time thereafter the matter was brought up in conferences which we had with the Secretary on Haitian matters in general. The idea seemed to be to eliminate, so far as possible, European influences in the island.

The CHAIRMAN. As I remember it, you testified that $1,400,000 was paid for the assets of the bank remaining in the hands of foreign owners?

Mr. FARNHAM. No, sir; if you will pardon me; we paid $1,400,000 for all the assets of the bank, that purchase price to be distributed to the shareholders.

The CHAIRMAN. What were those assets?

Mr. FARNHAM. The assets were all the property of the bank, including the real estate. The bank owned its building in Port au Prince, and at two or three other places in the island.

The CHAIRMAN. That included the Government note?

Mr. FARNHAM. It included the value of the Government contract.

The CHAIRMAN. No; I meant the sum due the bank from the Government of Haiti, which is now maturing in December?

Mr. FARNHAM. No; the $1,400,000 included all assets, including the money in bank, receivables, the property of the bank, loans outstanding, which were considered good, reserves in Paris, and the reserve in New York. The bank has very few deposits.

The CHAIRMAN. Did they at that time include the sum due the bank from the Government of Haiti?

Mr. FARNHAM. Yes. I think, perhaps, I may have answered wrongly to your question before. I had it in mind during the recess when Senator Pomerene spoke of it. The amount due the Government was included in the assets.

The CHAIRMAN. I am just trying to make clear to myself the probable value of the assets for which you paid that sum.

Mr. FARNHAM. Well, I think I answered that this morning, $1,500,000. We paid practically what the bank was worth, Senator.

The CHAIRMAN. Well, the bank was worth $1,500,000, and the note of the Government of Haiti amounted to $1,000,000?

Mr. FARNHAM. To-day its assets are worth $1,500,000.

The CHAIRMAN. You do not include among the assets that note, then, which amounts to $1,500,000?

Mr. FARNHAM. Yes; including that, and then deducting the liabilities of the bank, we will get a net worth of $1,500,000. We had to assume practically all the liabilities of the bank in purchasing it. You see, the bank is owing now, and has to pay—in fact, is paying out, $2,000,000, which it holds for the account of the Germans in Haiti. We had also to pay the cost of creating the new currency of the bank, as provided under the contract.

The CHAIRMAN. When was the interest payment on the foreign debt suspended, in 1914 or 1915?

Mr. FARNHAM. In 1914, on the interest. They defaulted on the payment of the amortization, I think, about 1911.

The CHAIRMAN. On the amortization?

Mr. FARNHAM. Yes, sir; the sinking-fund charges on one of the issues. You see, there are three loans outstanding, the last one being a loan of 1910.

The CHAIRMAN. Did they begin to default on the interest before the occupation?

Mr. FARNHAM. They were actually in default. The bank loaned them the money to complete that payment in 1914.

The CHAIRMAN. They were in arrears?

Mr. FARNHAM. They were in arrears. They had not the money themselves.

The CHAIRMAN. Has any of the interest on the debt been paid since the occupation?

Mr. FARNHAM. Yes, sir; under Mr. McIlhenny, who has applied some of the income to the payment of the interest. I think, if I recall right, it was brought up to the 1st of January last. I know we transferred and converted into francs $3,000,000 United States money, which was sent to Paris and applied to the payment of the interest and arrears, and I think some other sums also were transferred for that purpose.

The CHAIRMAN. What about the payment of the interest on the internal debt?

Mr. FARNHAM. I do not believe that has been taken care of.

The CHAIRMAN. When was the default on that begun?

Mr. FARNHAM. I am inclined to think that on some of that internal debt, on some of those bonds the default took place in 1913 on the first issue, and subsequently on the other issues.

The CHAIRMAN. The Government had ceased payment of the internal debt before the occupation, then?

Mr. FARNHAM. That is my recollection, sir.

The CHAIRMAN. Do you care to say anything of the capacity and qualifications of the Americans in Haiti, whether in the diplomatic service or the office of the financial adviser or the collector?

Mr. FARNHAM. I do not think it is my province to make any criticisms. Those officers whom I met in Haiti in those capacities were all strangers to me. I knew none of them until I met them in the positions they held. My feeling, speaking of them as a group, is that they did the best they could, in view of the conditions with which they were confronted under the treaty, in the absence of any definite policy to be pursued. They always seemed to me to be drifting and waiting for some plan to be presented to them, along which they should proceed. Their hands practically were tied because of the necessity of obtaining the approval or consent of the Haitian administration to everything they proposed to be done.

The CHAIRMAN. In connection with the recalcitrancy of the Haitian Government, is there anything you can tell the committee about the dissolution of the Haitian Senate?

Mr. FARNHAM. I could not. I was not there when it occurred, and all I know is hearsay statements by people who were there. I think the situation was told fully in the newspapers at the time.

The CHAIRMAN. As you remember those newspaper accounts, were they substantially accurate?

Mr. FARNHAM. Well, generally speaking, I think they were correct. There were some extravagances in them.

The CHAIRMAN. If I understood you correctly this afternoon, in your judgement there has been no policy established here in Washington?

Mr. FARNHAM. So far as I ever heard of.

The CHAIRMAN. And nothing has been done for the economic rehabilitation of the country?

Mr. FARNHAM. Not that I know of.

The CHAIRMAN. Or the establishment of schools generally?

Mr. FARNHAM. No, sir.

The CHAIRMAN. Nor for the development of agriculture?

Mr. FARNHAM. Not that I know of. I would say that Gen. Cole—I think it is General, or Col. Cole—who was first in command, and subsequently Col. Russell, now in command of the marines, and Mr. McIlhenny all had projects of that sort. My understanding is that they sent them to Washington as suggestions for which they would like to have had approval so that they could proceed to carry such ideas out, but, to the best of my knowledge, no approval was forthcoming, and certainly nothing has ever been done there.

The CHAIRMAN. The Government has done nothing to develop the capacity of the Haitien people for self-government, locally or generally?

Mr. FARNHAM. Not so far as I know.

The CHAIRMAN. I wonder if you would not be willing to send to the committee from New York any suggestions which you might care to make for a constructive economic and political policy in Haiti?

Mr. FARNHAM. Well, I would be glad to do so.

The CHAIRMAN. I would like you to think over that.

We were talking this morning of the railroad, which is now in the hands of a receiver, is it not?

Mr. FARNHAM. Yes.

The CHAIRMAN. And you are the receiver of the railroad?

Mr. FARNHAM. Yes, sir.

The CHAIRMAN. Are you the president of the railroad, too, Mr. Farnham?

Mr. FARNHAM. I was president of the railroad company; yes, sir. I took that in order to look after the interests of the bank in respect of the loan made to the construction company.

The CHAIRMAN. Were you originally the president of the railroad?

Mr. FARNHAM. No, sir.

The CHAIRMAN. It was only when the financial situation became hazardous?

Mr. FARNHAM. I think at the commencement of 1913, if I recall rightly, I was made president of the railroad.

The CHAIRMAN. Was it in financial difficulties then, as far back as then?

Mr. FARNHAM. Yes, sir; it had been experiencing a good deal of trouble in the construction. The Haitian Government had refused to deliver the definitive bonds on such portion of the work as had been completed. The money provided by the bonds had been exhausted, and the syndicate had been called upon to furnish money through the underwriting which had been undertaken. My position in respect of the railroad is one of a representative character, in so far as being president and director is concerned. I have no personal interest in it. I have no personal investment in Haiti of any kind, in anything, and never have had.

The CHAIRMAN. Is the contract between the Haitien Government and original concessionaire available?

Mr. FARNHAM. Well, you mean the present railroad? The original railroad was commenced, I think, away back in 1905, and——

The CHAIRMAN. You were speaking of the bonds which the——

Mr. FARNHAM. Well, yes; that contract I have in New York.

The CHAIRMAN. Could you send us a copy of that?

Mr. FARNHAM. Yes, sir.

The CHAIRMAN. What was the security which the bank had for this advance to the construction company?

Mr. FARNHAM. The definitive bonds of the railroad company, bearing the guaranty of the Republic of Haiti to pay the interest and sinking-fund charges whenever this railroad was unable to earn the same.

The CHAIRMAN. How much in bonds was the Haitian Government obliged to put up as security for that credit?

Mr FARNHAM. The construction company deposited bonds of the value of $878,000, I think. I can give you the exact figure later, Senator.

The CHAIRMAN. For a loan of half a million?

Mr. FARNHAM. Yes, sir.

The CHAIRMAN. And is half a million the sum they advanced?

Mr. FARNHAM. Yes, sir.

The CHAIRMAN. Is the Government in default now on those bonds, or on the interest on those bonds?

Mr. FARNHAM. Yes, sir. They paid two coupons, and after that they were in default.

The CHAIRMAN. In this connection, who is Mr. Lind?

Mr. FARNHAM. He was a telegraph lineman employed by the construction company at the time they were erecting the telephone and telegraph line of the railroad company. Subsequently, he did general work for the construction company, and at the time the construction work and operation of the railroad was suspended he was maintained there, after the forces were dismissed, as a sort of watchman, with headquarters at St. Marc. He was for the time being in charge of the property of the construction company. He was there at the time the American occupation occurred and had general charge of the property at the time the resumption of the railroad service took place. He continued, I do not know how long, Senator, a few months, and then it was advisable to make a change, and he went out of the employ of the company.

The CHAIRMAN. At the time he left the employ of the company what work was he engaged in doing for the company?

Mr. FARNHAM. He was engaged, in general, in looking after the operation of the trains. He was not a railroad man at all, but we could not get anyone to go there at that time to do that work.

The CHAIRMAN. What was he a sort of operating superintendent?

Mr. FARNHAM. Yes; without that title. It seemed advisable to make a change in his position at the time it was done.

The CHAIRMAN. I do not want to press for the reasons for his dismissal.

Mr. FARNHAM. Well, I think the high officials of the American occupation felt that a change in the management would be desirable. I think there was a lack of cooperation. Mr. Lind and the resident manager in Cape Hait'en, the northern sect'on, Mr. Woolard, both received very explicit instruct'ons when the American occupat'on commenced to cooperate in every way and to afford all facilities for the officers and the troops, and to put themselves practically at the disposal of the officials of the occupat'on, and to not haggle over any point at all but to do what was wanted, and if there was a difference of opinion it would be dealt with later on. Mr. Woolard was able to observe those 'nstructions very fully, but Mr. Lind did not seem to be able to comprehend them. It was a matter of temperament, I think, more than anything else.

The CHAIRMAN. I want before we adjourn to touch aga'n upon the circumstances of the landing of the marines. You 'ndicated this morning that the landing of Aner'can naval forces had been precip'tated by the landing of French forces first, prior to the landing of our forces?

Mr. FARNHAM. Yes; the French had landed at Cape Haitien. A revolution was on in the north.

The CHAIRMAN. What occasion had they to land? Were they French nationals or French interests?

Mr. FARNHAM. There have always been, s'nce I have known the country anyway, more French people and more French capital engaged in commercial pursuits in Haiti at and around Cape Haitien than in any other part of the island. There are probably, too, fewer Germans there than at other points 'n the island, and it was, I think, largely on account of that predom'nance of French interests and because the revolution at that moment was prevail'ng in that vicinity. Cape Haitien, that the French landed at that place. They landed a force of men, and practically took possession of the whole s'tuation, with the result that peace was restored, the revolutionists were driven out to the country, and things were going along in normal fashion in Cape Haitien.

The CHAIRMAN. Prior to the landing of any American force?

Mr. FARNHAM. Yes s!r.

The CHAIRMAN. Did American forces land them at Cape Haitien, or only at Port au Prince later on?

Mr. FARNHAM. No; Admiral Caperton was sent to Cape Haitien, and he outranked the French capta'n or the French officer, whoever it might be, and the French withdrew on board their ship, which, my understanding, did not go away; they s'mply took their men on board ship.

Te CHAIRMAN. After the American forces had landed?

Mr. FARNHAM. Yes, sir.

The CHAIRMAN. Did the French land at Port au Prince later?

Mr. FARNHAM. Yes, sir. My understanding of that is that they landed there before the Americans. I was not present at that time in Haiti, so I am giving you the reports made to me by our railroad and bank people who were there.

The CHAIRMAN. Since we have discussed the landing at that time, can you throw any light upon the landing of the marines from the *Machias* at Port au Prince on December 17, 1914—that would be prior to the occupation—and their remo al of a sum of money from the bank vaults in Port au Prince to New York?

Mr. FARNHAM. Yes, sir. We had in the vaults of the bank at that time a considerable amount of gold. There had been repeated demands upon the part of the Haitian Government for further loans from the bank, which demands had been refused, and there were threats by the various officials of the Haitian Government that they would raid the bank and take that money. Those rumors or threats had reached Mr. Bryan—how I do not know—who was then Secretary of State, and he requested some of us to come to Washington and discuss the matter with him. Mr. Werhane, the then vice president of the Haiti Bank, and myself came here, and after a long discussion of the whole situation it was arranged that at least half a million dollars should be brought to New York.

The CHAIRMAN. Out of how much?

Mr. FARNHAM. I think we had then about a million dollars there. We had to retain some in the island. We had thought some of transferring it to Jamaica ourselves, but there was no way of getting it over there at that time.

The CHAIRMAN. Was that the gold reserve of the gourde circulation?

Mr. FARNHAM. Yes, sir; it was a part of that.

The CHAIRMAN. Now, under the terms of the contract with the bank, was that gold reserve the property of the bank or of the Government?

Mr. FARNHAM. It was held by the bank in trust for that particular purpose. The money had been derived from the sale of the bonds issued by the Haitian Government in the loan of 1910, to the specific amount of $2,000,000, or 10,000,000 francs, which was set aside under the contract for the purpose of retiring the old paper money under a law of retirement to be enacted by the Haitian Congress. Such a law was not enacted promptly. In fact, I think it was about 1913 when it was passed, and the bank was instructed to commence the retirement of the old paper gourdes, and for that purpose, if I recall rightly, of the $2,000,000 we sent $1,000,000 in gold to Haiti.

The CHAIRMAN. The bonds had been sold in New York?

Mr. FARNHAM. No; in France. No issue had ever been brought out in New York, but all in France. The retirement had proceeded for only a very small amount when a new government came in power, and they stopped the retreat, as it was called.

The CHAIRMAN. The retreat of the money?

Mr. FARNHAM. Yes; and the subsequent Government ordered it commenced again, and then countermanded its order, and it was in those times when the demands were made upon the bank for further loans, and we refused those after a consultation with the State Department here.

The reason the money was brought from Haiti to New York in a warship was because it was impossible to obtain insurance upon it in the small ships of the Dutch Line which were then operating. It was after presenting that situation to the Secretary of State that it was arranged that the *Machias*, I think it was, should bring the money to New York. It was brought up and placed on deposit in New York and held there for the account of the retreat, in which it subsequently was employed. The Haitian officials did carry out their threat finally to raid the bank. The then minister of state, I think it was, the minister of foreign affairs, led a detachment of troops one day to the bank and they broke in. The man in charge managed to close the door of the large vault, but the soldiers obtained $62,000 in gold from the cash drawers and went away with that.

The CHAIRMAN. What was the attitude of the resident director of the bank, whose name was Desrue?

Mr. FARNHAM. Well, Mr. Desrue had been employed in the bank for quite awhile. What do you mean by his attitude?

The CHAIRMAN. Well, I see in a report by M. Louis Borno that he attributes to Mr. Desrue the information that the removal of the Treasury to New York was unnecessary.

Mr. FARNHAM. Well, Mr. Desrue, I do not imagine, knew anything about it until he received instructions to deliver the money to the officers of the ship.

The CHAIRMAN. What was his function in the bank there?

Mr. FARNHAM. He was at that time acting manager of the bank. He was in charge of the affairs of the bank at that time.

The CHAIRMAN. Did he remain there in charge for long afterwards?

Mr. FARNHAM. No; he was succeeded by a new manager whom we obtained, a Mr. Scarpa. Mr. Desrue is now acting assistant manager of the bank. He is still in the employ of the bank.

The CHAIRMAN. Subsequently, the bank, acting through Monsieur Casenave and yourself, under date of the 10th of July, 1916, made what agreement relative to the reserve?

Mr. FARNHAM. That was an agreement which was arrived at after about a year's discussion here, participated in by the officials of the Haitian Government, who were sent here for that purpose, in an endeavor to reach a new and final agreement covering the retreat of the old money, the issue of new bills for the bank, and an adjustment as to the amount which had been so far retired, and how much of the money had been used for that purpose. There were some other considerations also.

The CHAIRMAN. You made that agreement?

Mr. FARNHAM. Yes, sir; that was entered into.

The CHAIRMAN. Has it been carried out?

Mr. FARNHAM. Yes, sir.

The CHAIRMAN. Has the money been retired and the new issue made?

Mr. FARNHAM. Practically all of it; yes, sir. There is a relatively small amount of the old money remaining outstanding.

The CHAIRMAN. You agreed at the same time to return the sum carried to New York?

Mr. FARNHAM. It has been done, together with all the accrued interest thereon during the time it was up here, a part of the time 2½ per cent, a part of the time 3 per cent.

The CHAIRMAN. Now, I think before we conclude we ought to try to clear up the charges which are made in Haiti relative to a monopoly of the import and export of gold, and perhaps foreign exchange. Can you throw some light on that, Mr. Farnham?

Mr. FARNHAM. Well, I personally did not take part in those negotiations concerning the matter you refer to. That was attended to by Mr. Allen, at that time one of the vice presidents of the City Bank, and who for three years had been manager of the bank in Haiti. I think there has always prevailed a misunderstanding about that. The paragraph which the Haitian Government objected to in the monetary reform agreement, as it was called, was not intended to give the bank any monopoly of the sort described. The bank never has had that monopoly, except in so far as you would find it in the fact that it was the only bank in Haiti until the advent of the American-Foreign Banking Corporation, and subsequently the Royal Bank of Canada. Nothing had operated during the life of the bank to prevent the German merchants from bringing in gold if they wanted to or shipping gold out, and they did. You could have brought gold into the country, or I could or anybody. Some dealt with the bank and others brought in and shipped out their own currency.

In this connection—and, if you please, I am giving my own understanding, because at the time I did not participate in the matter—Mr. McElhenny and some of the other officials who were then representing this Government in Haiti felt that it would be advisable to have some sort of a control of the amount—not control, but a means of knowing, if you please, the movement of any considerable amount of gold in or out, and in that connection Mr. Allen prepared a paragraph, which was inserted in the agreement and which we subsequently modified. In its changed form it was referred to the State Department, and I know quite a number of those merchants and others who had misunderstood the original paragraph and opposed it in its then form did give their approval to the amended form. Under the modified form any other banks could have brought in gold, and they could have shipped it out. The Haiti Bank would have purchased bills on responsible banks in New York at the prevailing rate of exchange plus the ordinary commission of the bank, which was what it had always done. or what the Royal Bank of Canada would do, or what the American-Foreign Banking Corporation would do.

The CHAIRMAN. Mr. Farnham, Mr. Allen is now in New York?

Mr. FARNHAM. Yes, sir. He resigned from the National City Bank last November, I think, to become the president of the American-Foreign Banking Corporation, where he now is.

The CHAIRMAN. What are his initials?

Mr. FARNHAM. John H.

The CHAIRMAN. Is there anything else you have to say to the committee?

Mr. FARNHAM. I think not.

I would, however, like to answer one question you asked me concerning the future of Haiti. I believe that Haiti can be made exceedingly productive in certain lines—sugar, coffee, cotton, and tobacco. I think that the Haitian can be taught to become a good and efficient laborer. If let alone by the military chiefs, he is as peaceful as a child, and as harmless. In fact, to-day they are nothing but grown-up children, ignorant of all agricultural methods, and they know nothing of machinery. They must be taught. I think that if a policy could be put into effect in Haiti, which would give the people, the younger people particularly, the children, opportunities for education; establish for some years a direct and complete control over the finances of the country, handled under a budget, I think it would be but a few years before Haiti would be able to take care of all her obligations out of her revenues, and have a surplus left, and I think it would become, considering its relative size, as prosperous a country as Cuba has proven to be.

The CHAIRMAN. At various times in the past you made suggestions to the State Department for the development of a policy. Were those specific? Were they formal, written suggestions, or only in the course——

Mr. FARNHAM. No; they were made, on two or three occasions, at the request of the President, through Mr. Bryan. They went to Mr. Bryan at his own request.

The CHAIRMAN. In writing?

Mr. FARNHAM. Yes, sir. I do not know whether they are in the department, or whether they were passed on to President Wilson, but on two occasions I was requested to prepare a paper of that sort.

Senator ODDIE. What are the sanitary conditions in Haiti?

Mr. FARNHAM. Now, in Port au Prince and in the principal towns they are fair. The buildings and houses lack sanitary appliances, as we understand them, almost completely, but the streets in Port au Prince, the principal streets, have been paved.

The CHAIRMAN. Is that true of St. Marc and Cape Haitien, too?

Mr. FARNHAM. Yes, sir; the streets of Port au Prince have been paved, some of them, and some of the principal streets of St. Marc and Cape Haitien and Aulx Cayas have been macadamized, and all are swept and kept quite clean under the supervision of the military.

Senator ODDIE. Have the conditions along that line been improved since the American occupation?

Mr. FARNHAM. There was not any such thing before. The only thing which existed before anywhere was in Port au Prince, where about a year, I think, before the American occupation some contractors had undertaken the pavement of some of the streets in Port au Prince. That work was suspended at the time of the American occupation and resumed some months later under the supervision of Army or Navy engineers, and a considerable amount of work has been done there. The noticeable change, however, is in the small towns, which were very filthy, and with nothing at all approaching sanitation. Now, the atmosphere is different and the streets are clean.

Senator ODDIE. What has been done since the American occupation in regard to the public health?

Mr. FARNHAM. Beyond the measures I have just described, I know of nothing particularly. I do not know just what could be done. The people live all over the country. They live in little shacks which are pretty dirty. The people themselves, the Haitian country people, are very clean. They spend a considerable portion of their time in the rivers and streams washing themselves as well as their clothes.

Senator ODDIE. I mean in regard to combating disease.

Mr. FARNHAM. I think very little. Until this smallpox outbreak of a year ago, it has been quite some years since there has been any epidemic in the island. Last time it was yellow fever. I think that was 12 or 14 years ago. The United States marines have charge of the sanitation there, and they employ Haitians in cleaning up the streets and keeping them clean.

(The witness was thereupon excused.)

(Mr. Angell thereupon presented the following list of witnesses, whom he suggested to the committee should be called during the course of its hearings:)

Admiral W. B. Caperton United States-Navy.

Hon. Josephus Daniels, Raleigh, N. C.

Hon. Robert Lansing. Washington, D. C.

H. R. Pilkington, P. W. Chapman & Co., third floor, 115 Broadway, New York City.

E. J. Lind, 3604 Broadway, apartment 4, New York City, telephone Audubon 3574.

H. R. Tippenhauer, 723 Seventh Avenue, New York City.

Max Zuckerman, 110 Crawford Street, care of E. Levy, Roxbury, Mass.

C. A. Burrows, 253 Belgrade Avenue, Roslindale, Mass.

James W. Johnson, 70 Fifth Avenue, New York City.

Herbert J. Seligman, care of James W. Johnson, 70 Fifth Avenue, New York City.

Rev. L. Ton Evans, First Baptist Church, Port Matilda, Pa.

Gen. George Barnett, United States Marine Corps, headquarters Department of the Pacific, San Francisco, Calif.

Gen. Smedley Butler, United States Marine Corps, Quantico, Va.

Rear Admiral Knapp, United States Navy.

Col. Littleton W. Waller, United States Marine Corps.

Roger L. Farnham, vice president National City Bank, New York City.

John A. McIlhenny, financial adviser Haitian Government, care of State Department, Washington, D. C.

Bainbridge Colby, 1315 F Street, American National Bank Building, Washington, D. C.; 32 Nassau Street. New York City.

John H. Allen, president American-Foreign Banking Corporation, New York N. Y.

(Whereupon the committee adjourned until 10.30 o'clock a. m. Wednesday October 5, 1921.)

INQUIRY INTO OCCUPATION AND ADMINISTRATION OF HAITI AND SANTO DOMINGO.

WEDNESDAY, OCTOBER 5, 1921.

UNITED STATES SENATE,
SELECT COMMITTEE ON HAITI AND SANTO DOMINGO,
Washington, D. C.

The committee met at 10.30 o'clock a. m. pursuant to adjournment, Senator Medill McCormick (chairman) presiding.

Present: Senators McCormick, Oddie, King, and Pomerene.

Also present: Mr. Ernest Angell, representing the Haiti-Santo Domingo Independence Society, etc.

Mr. ANGELL. I request the privilege of the committee of being allowed to put questions directly to witnesses called before the committee. In making this request, I do so because I feel that it is probable that as to many of the witnesses it is only in this manner that the essential facts can be brought out, because I have made a detailed study of the situation, and in many cases have had long and detailed interviews with the witnesses; know what they will have to say before the committee, and, without any reflection whatever upon the committee, in many of these instances the members of the committee have not had the opportunity to talk with the witnesses beforehand, and can have only the most general idea as to what the witnesses will testify, so I therefore request that privilege.

Senator POMERENE. In whose behalf do you appear?

Mr. ANGELL. I appear on behalf of the Haiti-Santo Domingo Independence Society, the Union Patriotique d'Haiti, and the National Association for the Advancement of Colored People. I appeared at the first hearing, and have been at all the hearings, in fact, and submitted on behalf of these organizations the Haitian Memoir, and an outline statement of the joint position assumed by these several groups.

The CHAIRMAN. I suggest that the committee consider Capt. Angell's request at a later time and make its decision.

Senator POMERENE. Yes.

(The following papers are copies of memorandum, sworn affidavits, and letters to President Harding, ex-President Woodrow Wilson, ex-President Theodore Roosevelt, Senator Hitchcock (then chairman of Foreign Relations Committee), and letters subsequently written the Hon. Josephus Daniels, Secretary of the United States Navy, by Hon. T. Ch. Moravia, consul general of the Republic of Haiti at Washington, D. C., with replies of Second Assistant Secretary A. A. Adee, of State Department, in behalf of then President Wilson, from Secretary Daniels, etc., showing the strenuous and persistent efforts made through official channels of Government of late administration for over two years so as to right the wrongs of same in the black Republic of Haiti, and earnest appeals made for interviews and the appointment of a commission to carefully investigate the conduct of American forces in Haiti and by the Republic's first official spokesman the Rev. L. Ton Evans until at last brought Haiti's sad and scandalous conditions, with the approval of the late Theodore Roosevelt, to President Harding and the national Republican council at Washington, D. C., with the result of present Senate committee (commission) appointed by President to investigate the occupation and administrations of the territories of the Republics of Haiti and Santo Domingo by the forces of the United States.)

127

CHESTNUT AVENUE, KINGSTON, PA., *October 1, 1918.*

Hon. WOODROW WILSON,
  President of United States.

DEAR PRESIDENT: May I respectfully request a brief interview re Haiti affairs, that I hope will lead to the appointment of a commission to thoroughly investigate conditions there?

The present situation is very bad, and I have faithfully pledged to the leaders of this little nation, irrespective of creed or politics, that I will not merely see you but assured them the moment matters are placed before our Pres'dent a commiss'on will be granted to go carefully into these serious and grave Haitian affairs.

I have just forwarded a memorandum addressed to you, sir, to the care of my friend Dr. T. Jesse Jones, of the Government Bureau of Education, and containing brief sketch of self, with relation to Haiti grievances complained of, with recommendations.

The names of Dr. Moton, Dr Dillard, Dr. Brink, Hon. Geo. Foster Peabody, Father Curran, Dr. Jesse Jones, and Admiral Caperton, or men of such high type are suggested as members of this commiss'on, not merely to make a careful and thorough investigation of present wrong but from the evidence produced at the inquiry, so as to formulate a simple and satisfactory plan for the future development of this Negro republic along the lines of treaty, and in light of " war ideals."

Having come directly to the States, and mainly for this purpose, I shall profoundly appreciate such an interview at this time, and, if agreeable, bring Dr. Jesse Jones, and Dr. Brown (president of my own missionary board) with me whenever convenient for you to see us next week or at least before my return to Haiti this month.

I am most anxious for the sake of our President and our Government that everything shall be satisfactorily adjusted and real constructive work of developing Haiti shall as soon as possible be proceeded with on treaty lines, as understood and explained by our President.

I have purposely· refrained from making any public references to these serious and sad conditions in the Black Republic in preaching or public addresses, and thus far have kept from Negro convention, and for same shall not attend forthcoming race congress (though invited) at Washington this month; for the iteration of the cruel and brutal scenes, as I have personally witnessed them, will immediately " fire " not only an audience of Negroes but white Baptists of both North and South and Protestants of America generally, which at this critical period we are anxious to avoid, sincerely believing (as I have repeatedly assured the leaders and Haitians) will be immediately and effectively remedied the moment matters are brought to your personal attention and grounds furnished to justify such action on your part.

As I am leaving for Baptist conventions in North Carolina, where wife and self shall speak on conditions of Negro womanhood in Haiti, and where we expect to meet Dr. Brown, a reply addressed to him there will reach me Saturday or Monday. Praying God to spare your valuable life, etc., and for Christ and Haiti.

NOTE.—As requested, Mr. Tumulty replied in behalf of President, that my letter was handed over to Mr. Lansing to be dealt with, directing me to direct all further communications re Haiti to Secretary of State. All further efforts both with Lansing and Tumulty in behalf of poor Haiti proved of no avail.—L. T. E.

NATIONAL TRAINING SCHOOL, LINCOLN HEIGHTS,
  Washington, D. C., October 18, 1918.

Hon. GILBERT M. HITCHCOCK,
  Chairman of Senate Committee on Foreign Relations.

DEAR SIR: While appreciating the brief interview given me on Wednesday re serious conditions in Haiti, and demanding urgent attention of the Government, I wish to state that the following morning Mr. Stabler, an Assistant Secretary at the State office and in charge of Haiti affairs, and after my presistent appeal (and even threat of bringing matters before Senate and Congress) at last fixed Monday morning, 11 o'clock, to go carefully with me into these matters.

As I understand that this very official it was who made complaint to my missionary board, absolutely misunderstood my position, and therefore grossly misrepresented my attitude to these Negroes, demand'ng of them my being recalled from the black Republic on account of my Christian activities (without defining those activities) has now granted me the opportunity sought (though positively refused me by the Negro committee of the Lott Carey Mission Board), you will understand I am sure under these circumstances the reasonableness of your excusing my placing these facts before you, with evidence substantiating same, for consideration of yourself and Senate Foreign Relations Committee until after this interview (official) with above Secretary Stabler.

Should he and the State Department fail to attend at once to this urgent matter, and call the special attention of the President to same, then it will be my duty as an American citizen, not to say a Christian m'ssionary, to come to the Senate Committee on Foreign Relations, through you as cha:rman, with a v.ew of having this special comm'ssion immediately appointed, and see that the recent treaty made by our own Government is scrupulously carried out, and that in the light of our present " war ideals " proclaimed at this moment throughout the whole civilized world.

Our civilized, humane, democratic United States Government, with a Christian President, and at a moment we ourselves are champion'ng the sanctity of treaties and liberties and rights of small nations in Europe and As'a must itself be absolutely freed from the very insinuation, not to say the open charge now made in Haiti and by Haitians all over the.r Republ:c, of actual insincer:ty and a desire and attempt to repud:ate our solemn treaty obligations at this time in the black Republic.

I have myself personally and persistently maintained that all mistakes, blunders, if not something worse (crimes and treachery on the part of officers of marine both in Haiti, backed by some in Washington), which have caused the strong reversion of feeling in Haiti's present attitude toward our President, Government, and everything American, and which are back of these insinuations and charges are without the knowledge of President or responsible United States Government, and, furthermore, the moment these are directly and officially brought before them the whole business will receive immediate attention and everything adjusted.

Thanking you for interview and interest, I have the honor to remain, sincerely yours, and for Christ and Haiti.

[Prepared at request of Senator Hitchcock, chairman of Committee on Foreign Relations, of the Government; and also Mr. Stabler, of the Latin-American section of the State Department, to latter of whom it was submitted Monday morning, October 21, 1918, for presentation through Secretary Lansing to the President.]

MEMORANDUM TO THE HON. WOODROW WILSON, PRESIDENT OF THE UNITED STATES, RE PRESENT SITUATION IN HAITI, SHOWING SOME OF THE CAUSES OF DISCONTENT; WITH RECOMMENDATIONS AND REQUEST FOR A COMMISSION TO CAREFULLY INVESTIGATE THE MATTERS COMPLAINED OF AND FURTHER FORMULATE A SIMPLE PLAN FOR THE DEVELOPMENT OF THE BLACK REPUBLIC ALONG TREATY LINES, IN THE LIGHT OF WAR IDEALS OF OUR GOVERNMENT, PARTICULARLY AS SET FORTH BY THE PRESIDENT HIMSELF AT WASHINGTON'S TOMB THE 4TH OF JULY LAST AND SINCE.

PREAMBLE.

Though as an American citizen and a Christian missionary, naturally moved with sympathy for Haiti and its over 2,000,000 Negroes at this time of suffering and distress, and looking to the United States for redress of their grievances; and while assuring you of the genuine gratitude, shared by every loyal and patriotic Haitian, both educated and uneducated alike, that Admiral Caperton landed his American marines at Port au Prince, thus rescuing their politically torn and revolutionary bleeding Republic from the iron grasp and selfish greed of Germans, who for years had financially and murderously exploited them by aid of Berlin money and ammunition; and expressing our deep appreciation of the splendid work already done in Haiti by our "American occupation," and under exceptional (European) war conditions, the Lott Carey Missionary Foreign Baptist Board and myself, as its missionary and superintendent in Haiti, are at the present moment, and just when our Christian President and civilized, humane, and democratic United States Government are championing the " sanctity of treaties," liberties, and rights of small nations, still more anxious, if possible, we shall ourselves be perfectly free from every suspicion, not to say insincerity, and charges of a desire to "repudiate" even our own treaty obligations either in Haiti or any other part of the world.

I have therefore respectfully but resolutely maintained that whatever mistakes, blunders, or, indeed, something worse, committed by officers, gendarmes (native police), and other representatives we have in Haiti, causing the reversion of feeling throughout the whole black Republic against our President, our Government, and everything American, which is positively the case; such mistakes, blunders, etc., have been actually committed without the knowledge, therefore without the sanction or authority, of either our President or responsible United States Government; and, indeed, moreover, I added, that when such are properly brought to the direct attention of our Government at Washington a fair and thorough investigation will be at once made and matters adjusted, for in the expressed language of the treaty itself—

"The United States, as well as the Republic of Haiti, desire to conform and strengthen the amity existing between them by the most cordial cooperation in measures for their common advantages, to maintain tranquillity of the Republic to carry out plans for the economic development and prosperity of the Republic and its people."

· As showing my own position, relation to, and interest in Haiti, the following brief statement regarding myself may be necessary:

BIOGRAPHICAL SKETCH.

Born and educated in Wales; graduated in 1887 from Haverfordwest Baptist Seminary, specializing in theology, philosophy, and political economy, as well as securing the London scholarship.

I was ordained the same year at the new and growing Barry Dock as a missionary-pastor, and where I also soon became the organizing secretary of the Barry and District Gospel Temperance Council, embracing the religious-social as well as temperance activities; in fact, of all the evangelical churches and friendly societies of that section.

This brought me into personal touch and active association with Christian leaders and social reformers of Britain, many of whom, such as Hon. Donald Maclean, chairman of committees in the British House of Commons; Hon. D. Lloyd-George, prime minister and secretary of war of Great Britain (both of whom I have been privileged to instruct in fights against booze); together with the late Sir Sam T. Evans, president-judge of Britain's prize war court. I count as personal friends.

The latter also defended me before Lord Mercy, of *Titanic* and *Lusitania* fame, in a libel case, which drew considerable attention at the time, and when plaintiff pleaded guilty to prostituting his public position, misappropriating public funds, and had to quit all civic and public offices and leave the town. (Lord Mercy commended the valuable service rendered by the writer to the community through exposing dishonesty in high public offices.)

In 1891 my Barry church allowed me to travel in the East, visiting Egypt, Palestine, Asia Minor, Turkey, etc.; and in 1892 I accepted the position of general missionary of the Jamaica Missionary Board in Haiti, but in two years, owing to serious illness of wife, returned to Wales and settled again at Barry Dock.

Early in 1902 resigned to accept First Baptist Church, Edwardsville, Pa., when among other letters of commendation was one from Mr. Lloyd George. Believing in a republican form of government, I took out citizen papers while in Pennsylvania, but in 1908, after resigning this charge, and speaking throughout the churches of Wales on Haiti and its people, as well as here in the States, I returned as field secretary to the Black Republic.

While in Jamaica in 1910, in behalf of Haiti, and after personally investigating the religious and social as well as economic conditions there and seeing the abject state of East Indians (coolies), called contract laborers by white planters (and corporations), but better known as "scabs" in this country; and how Jamaica was being depleted of its own Negro sons of the soil, who (through this species of slavery) were forced in thousands to Cuba, Panama, and States for work or starve in their island home, I took up the matter with the British Government and through the parliamentary secretary of the Labor Party in the House of Commons.

With the aid of the Anti-Slavery Society (London), and after circularizing 300 Welsh, Irish, Scotch, as well as English members of the British Parliament, including Prime Minister Asquith, George, and others of the cabinet, as well as the King, and setting forth some very startling facts, substantiated by official figures (colonial) and documentary evidence, the Government (in spite of the so-called findings and recommendations of their recent royal commission to perpetuate the unjust, immoral, and cruel system in the West Indies) by an "act in council" very soon compelled the governors of Jamaica and Trinidad, etc., to pass at once legislation curbing those (British and American) white planters and fruit growers who insisted on having cheap coolie labor.

The Labor Party further got the Government to prohibit the exploitation of their East Indian British subjects as serfs and slaves. (Sir Lewis Harcourt, Britain's Secretary for their Colonies, wrote thanking me in Haiti for furnishing his Government with these facts.)

In 1911 I not only represented Haiti at and took public part in the World's Baptist Alliance in Philadelphia but was privileged that same year to bring a petition to the States from Haiti signed by late President Leconté, Hon. J. E. Leger (for years representing Haiti in Washington and at Berlin), with nearly 3,000 leading Haitians, such as senators and ex-senators, deputies and ex-deputies, judges of all the courts, inspectors, generals, Haitian employers of labor, etc., earnestly praying Messrs. Rockefeller, Carnegie, and others of our American philanthropists to establish in Haiti a "national industrial college" on Christian basis, such for instance as Hampton and Tuskegee.

This was deposited for some time here in Washington at the Carnegie Endowment for International Peace (through victory) Bureau, under the care of Drs. Scott and North.

President Simon and his Government at the time, who heartily supported this "noble project," as they called it, promised 300 acres of land for this purpose; also practically all the civic councils in the Republic passed resolutions and officially wrote thanking me for my deep interest in Haiti and their people and expressing sincere hope that my mission to the States in their behalf would be crowned with success. (Dr. Furniss, our United States minister at Port au Prince, and our American Consul Livingston at the Cape, enthusiastically indorsed the petition and gave highest commendations.)

While pleading with our Negroes of the South during 1912 to come to the aid of their own race in the black Republic, the present Lott Carey Foreign Baptist Board heartily responded, and to their credit it decided to undertake the evangelization of this field, and for this purpose sent their president, Dr. C. S. Brown, and Dr. A. M. Moore to visit the Republic. The white Baptists of the States contemplate to cooperate with our board after the war.

In November of last year Mrs. Evans and myself again left the States to labor as superintendents, etc., under our Lott Carey Board in Haiti.

SPECIAL GRIEVANCES.

Having appealed repeatedly to our Government for aid and protection to Haiti and its people, and as representative of Haiti's Presidents more than once during the Roosevelt, Taft, and the present administration, I therefore not only rejoiced we had at last come to the rescue of these quiet, kind-hearted, and helpless people from Teutonic tyranny, but I was determined to assist our "American occupation" as far as possible (and proper for missionaries) in our work.

Though however delighted at the generous terms of the "treaty" which from the commencement I understood in the light of the official declarations of our President. I have during the last seven or eight months in Haiti been disappointed and saddened by what I have been an eyewitness of, apart altogether from the evidence of others, as to the deliberate and ruthless violations of the "treaty," both in spirit and letter, to wit:

1. The forcing of a new constitution upon the people, under military pressure of armed gendarmes (native police) of the American occupation, on the 12th day of June last, and so as to change the land clause in favor of the white and foreigner, and accomplishing this by methods which would be declared in the States and all civilized countries as both illegal and fraudulent.

The intelligent Haitians connected with the Government, or American occupation, who in fear and trembling were compelled to vote, be dismissed, or imprisoned if they refused, very aptly described these humiliating proceedings as "thrusting a dagger into the very heart of their own Negro Republic."

2. The closing on two separate occasions of Senate and Chamber of Deputies at Port au Prince and turning out by military force (gendarmes) under the occupation of the Haiti people's only representative bodies; then locking the

Senate and Chamber doors against them, exactly as the late Czar did with the Russian people's Duma; and while friendly to our United States Government and favorable to our American occupation merely, it is said, because they protested against and opposed (as illegal and unconstitutional) to change what they felt to be the vital clause in their constitution, namely, the withholding of land from the white foreigner and American speculator.

Haitian judges who declared this to be illegal are said were either driven out of office or imprisoned, or both, and in spite that under the old Haitian constitution foreigners (white and colored) could hold real estate in Haiti on same terms as in District of Columbia—that is, by becoming Haitian citizens. See "Haiti, Her History and Her Detractors," by the late Hon. J. N. Leger, Haitian minister for years in Washington.

3. The taking through force and much brutality, leading frequently to murders by ignorant, immoral, and drunken "armed gendarmes" in the employment of our "occupation" of innocent men and women; even members and native preachers from their simple homes, small habitations, at their work, and going to their business, as well as on the way to divine worship—cruelly roping them tightly together and marching same as African slave gangs to prison, etc.

The writer and others were eyewitnesses of this Sunday morning of last June, and present at the occupation doctor's treatment of the wounds caused through such brutal handling, unhealed for many weeks and months, after which the white American doctor said was very frequently the case.

It is only fair to state, however, that owing to the terrible amount of liquor and taffia drinking among white and native officers and gendarmes of the "occupation," Col. Russell (to whose attention I had called a few specific cases) has lately and as a protective measure issued a proclamation prohibiting under heavy penalty the sale of such to their men in uniform. This prohibition should now be made to extend to the whole Republic, and applied to both white and black.

4. The arresting of natives in large numbers (again by force) at their homes, on their small farms, and making them work on new roads miles away under "armed gendarmes," and for merely a gourde (20 American cents) a week, and without food, as affirmed by the natives and corroborated by the gendarmes.

The reason given is twofold—the failure of our United States Government to make the necessary "loans" to enable the "occupation" to pay a proper wage, and an illegal construction placed by American representatives on an old law (or custom) called corvee; requiring natives (farmers) to give so many days a year to repair roads opposite their own habitations.

OTHER REASONS GENERALLY ALLEGED.

These serious frictions and cruel treatment of natives which excite the passions, leading to resentment and murder, are said also to be the result of the frequent changes made by the United States Government as to their officers in Haiti since Admiral Caperton and his marines landed in the Republic three years ago; and that in and for most of such appointments subsequently made the Roman Catholic Church, through the Pope's special delegate at Port au Prince, and the American capitalists now in Haiti, are largely responsible.

Entangling alliances of such character and diverse interests can neither strengthen the position and add to the power and efficiency of our American occupation (whose influence and official authority in Haiti should certainly be paramount), nor can they inspire the confidence of either the Haitian Government or its people, in fact, in the pure and impartial administration of affairs, our own President and Government stand for, and we have officially pledged to give Haiti after years of exploitation by European filibusterers and unscrupulous and dishonest speculators.

The influence of the Pope's white delegate and the white priests on Haiti's black Presidents, cabinets, etc., has always been something akin to that of Rasputin, the monk, on the late Czar and Czarina, plus the corporations which have invaded the Black Republic, and one of which boasts of unlimited capital, with stockholders close to the United States Government, and therefore has the right of way in the Black Republic.

This one claims in Haiti to supply the United States Government with oil for their airplane fleet, etc., and its representative in our Republic, writing to the "Pan-American Magazine" last year, admits "that soldier and sailor in

Haiti and Santo Domingo switch from soldier to anything from blacksmith to superior court judge," and in another number of the same magazine he peremptorily demanded " that article 6 of the Haitian constitution, which specifies that no foreigner (which is entirely false, as shown already by the late Hon. J. N. Leger) may own land, must be repealed."

RECOMMENDATIONS SINCERELY URGED.

After a very careful observation, frequent consultations with Presidents and leaders, both educated and uneducated, Catholics and Protestants alike, white and black, including officers of our American occupation, and those even next to President Dartiguenave at this moment—and especially since Haiti, l ke every other country, must in the main, educationally, industrially—as well as religiously, be gradually developed by its own trained Negro sons and daughters under sympathetic, experienced, and efficient American leadership—I have no hes tation therefore in suggesting the following to the earnest consideration of our President and Government :

(a) That in the spiritual interests of the Protestant and Catholic churches, and indispensable to honest and efficient administration, both should be officially and financially separated from the Haitian Government exactly as in the United States.

At present the Protestant churches receive a small subvention (appropriation) to aid their missionaries and pastors' salaries of something like $4,000 annually ; while the Catholic Church, altogether and including maintenance of the Roman Catholic College to train white priests for Haiti in France, draws probably $150,000 to $200,000 yearly from the coffers of the bankrupt Black Republic (now through the hands of the United States general receiver), though the constitution of the Haitian Republic strictly stipulates that all churches, whether Protestant or Catholic, in Haiti are equally free. The old concordat is defunct several years ago, and the Pope, a foreign potentate, and as such has no right to make any contract with the Haitian Government, nor vice versa. (See Art. XI, on p. 8 of treaty.)

Articles VIII and IX, on pages 6 and 7 of treaty, not only make no provision whatever for the financing of either Protestant preachers or Catholic priests, nuns, etc., but emphatically prohibits the diversion by the American general receiver in Haiti, and appointed by our United States Government, of any portion of the revenues collected by him for any such purpose, and more especially in the financial condition the Haitian Government is in at the present moment. (See above articles of treaty.)

(b) The United States Government shall itself, or jointly with Rockefeller, Carnegie, and other such known foundations, and in accord with the prayer of petition referred to deposited at Carnegie Endowment for International Peace Bureau, establish in Haiti a " National Industrial School," with such a man as Dr. Moton or Dr. T. Jesse Jones at the head, and under a joint board of Americans and Haitians appointed by our President, and for the training of the Negro manhood and womanhood for educational, industrial, and even religious leadership in their own Republic.

(c) That our Government shall also see that when Haiti's new public instruction scheme is introduced, free, compulsory, and under present changed conditions—English made equally as essential with French and the Bible, or such selections thereof as agreeable to both Protestant and Catholic—is read daily, the above industrial college shall become incorporated as an important and basic part of Haiti's educational equipment.

(d) That small native ownership of land shall be created by the United States Government and " loans " made on simplest terms, and through a special department of above " industrial school " conferences and exhibitions shall be annually planned at convenient centers to encourage and teach the small farmer to cultivate his habitation along scientific lines and to the best advantage.

(e) As contemplated by the treaty between the United States and Haiti, "the material, agricultural, and industrial," as well as the educational development of the Black Republic shall be initiated by, financed through, and supervised under the United States Government, and neither delegated to individuals or corporations who may have officials of the United States or the Haitian Governments financially interested therein. (See treaty, Art. Q, and p. 4.)

(*f*) Now that Haiti has declared war, Germans interned, our United States Government shall grant us our full share of all necessaries by way of food at the lowest price; make generous "loans" to enable our occupation to proceed with its constructive program, and give all their Haitian laborers not less than a gourde and a half (30 American cents) a day. All forced labor (except in case of prisoners and known criminals) to be at once abolished among these quiet and peace-loving people. (Maintenance "by the United States" of a government in Haiti adequate for the protection of life, property, and individual liberty. See treaty, Art. XIV, p. 9.)

(*g*) Consistent with the sacred principle of "religious liberty" and in the interest of sane Christian efforts and efficient missionary work among the Negroes of Haiti, all tendencies to multiply sects should be discouraged, and the evangelical churches now in the Republic be encouraged to (voluntarily) cooperate or even unite where this can be done in the interest or gospel truth and New Testament life and conduct.

(*h*) Finally, and with a view of speedily adjusting matters in Haiti, convincing the people of the sincerity and absolute "good faith" of our President and Government, I respectfully but strongly recommend that a commission be appointed with authority to hear evidence, protect witnesses, whether civilians or employees of the Haitian Government or our own occupation, and also composed of gentlemen who will make a fair and thorough investigation into present conditions, but will further be able to formulate a satisfactory plan for the future development of the black republic along treaty lines, and in present light of "war ideals" as expressed by both our President and Secretary of State. (This commission is especially demanded by the Haitian people.)

To this end I, therefore, suggest the following names: Hon. Maj. Foster Peabody, Massachusetts; Dr. T. Jesse Jones, Educational Bureau, New York; Hon. G. Moton, Tuskegee, Ala.; Dr. J. Dilliard, Virginia; Dr. Gilbert N. Brink; Dr. Gambrell, Texas; Father Curran, Pennsylvania; and Admiral Caperton, of the United States Government, who first landed marines in Haiti.

Our President and Government, as well as any commission of such able, experienced, and highly qualified persons commanding the implicit confidence of both our Government and the American people, can rely not only that the Lott Carey Baptist Foreign Board and myself, as its representative in Haiti, but all the Protestant and Haitian Catholic leaders alike throughout the Republic will render every assistance possible so as to adjust matters amicably and satisfactorily, maintaining, for instance, our American ideals, present influence and power among the civilized nations of the world, and at the same time developing long-neglected Haiti and its people into a model Negro Republic, and cementing them as mentioned in the treaty in the closest bonds of amity and brotherhood to us as an United States sister Republic. I have the honor to remain,

Sincerely and loyally, yours, and for Christ and Haiti,

L. TON EVANS.

(A civilian possessed with expert knowledge of the Republic and bearing about the same relation to Secretary of State as Col. House does to the President, should prove an invaluable aid to the state office in handling the Haitian problem.)

DISTRICT OF COLUMBIA, *to wit;*

On this 30th day of October, 1918, before me, the subscriber, a notary public in and for the District aforesaid, personally appeared Rev. L. Ton Evans, an American citizen, residing at St. Mark, Haiti, being superintendent of missions, and made oath in due form of law that facts stated herein with exception of those under section 2, in the memorandum submitted to President in re of grievances of Haiti, are true to the best of my knowledge and belief; and those under section 2 of the same will be attested to before a commission asked to be created by the President, and under the United States Government's protection and by leading persons in Haiti.

L. TON EVANS.

Subcribed and sworn to before me.
[SEAL.]
CHARLES S. CUNEY,
Notary Public, District of Columbia.

My commission expires June 13, 1923.

PEACE THROUGH VICTORY.

CARNEGIE ENDOWMENT FOR INTERNATIONAL PEACE,
No. 2 Jackson Place, Washington, D. C., October 18, 1918.

This is to certify that in the fall of 1912 the (Rev.) Dr. L. Ton Evans, general missionary and educational superintendent of the Baptist Mission in Haiti, left in my hands a petition signed by some 3,000 leading and influential citizens of that island, praying for the establishment in Haiti of a " national normal and industrial college," similar to Tuskegee and Hampton, on a Christian basis.

This remarkable petition remained in the hands of the endowment for some months, and after consideration by the executive committee of the endowment was returned to Dr. Evans, who, unfortunately, lost it while traveling in the city in company with Dr. T. Jesse Jones (commissioner of education).

S. N. S. NORTH.
Assistant Secretary.

A number of copies of the above was ordered to be printed by the executive committee of the " National Race Congress " at its Wednesday meeting, October 23, so as to further inform itself with a view to taking some definite action in bringing this important matter before the President and our Government for the protection of their own people in Haiti.

DEPARTMENT OF STATE,
Washington, November 2, 1918.

Dr. L. TON EVANS,
226 Chestnut Street, Kingston, Pa.

SIR: The department has received your memorandum upon conditions in Haiti, presented on October 21, addressed to the President of the United States, and wishes to inform you that it is receiving the serious consideration of this department as well as of the various other branches of the Government concerned.

The department will be pleased to communicate with you at a later date after the careful study of the matters contained in your memorandum is terminate l.

I am, sir, your obedient servant, for the Secretary of State.

ALVEY A. ADEE.
Second Assistant Secretary.

[Copy of letter to Hon. Hitchcock, chairman of Foreign Relations Committee, pleading through him for an interview with President Wilson, and presentation of petition (memorandum) urging the appointment of a commission re Haiti affairs.]

SENATE OFFICE OF FOREIGN RELATIONS.
November 2, 1918.

DEAR CHAIRMAN HITCHCOCK: Accompanying this note is the memorandum promised at our previous interview, and setting forth the serious conditions in Haiti.

Yesterday, while again at the State Department, I handed a copy of same to private secretary of Mr. Lansing; he assured me it would be given the Secretary of State the same evening. It was also given Mr. Tumulty, for presentation without fail this morning to the President, and promised to be informed to-day as to whether an interview would be allowed in reference to appointment of commission for investigation of affairs in the Black Republic.

As you have undoubtedly seen the statement made through the Associated Press by ex-President Theodore Roosevelt, to the effect that the Haiti Republic as such is nonexistent to-day, which is true in substance and in fact. I must respectfully urge your immediate attention to this important matter.

I am anxious, if possible, to prevent this from becoming a political party affair, and so can not believe that either our President or our responsible United States Government actually know the real facts, which by military or political officialism have been persistently withheld from President Wilson and Government, though I sent a registered letter last June direct from Port au Prince, Haiti, to President at the White House, setting forth these things. (Also another registered letter was forwarded by same mail to ex-President Theodore Roosevelt at Oyster Bay.)

62269—21—PT 2——3

Can you therefore at once and before Monday secure this interview and get our President to prom'se to consider the matter and appointment of said commission to thoroughly and carefully go into Haitian affairs, and—

1. With such promise of commission, to invest same with power to call witnesses, pay necessary expenses of same, and give these our United States Government adequate protection.

2. Give immediate notification of appointment of commission both in French and English, in the Monitor (Haiti Government's official daily) and all other Haitian papers.

3. Finally, that some such person of the legal status of ex-Justice Charles Hughes be counsel or chairman of same, so as to guarantee that every phase of and matter referred to shall be impartially and thoroughly gone into, and so that our President and responsible Government shall be cleared from every suspic on of insincerity, and especially the serious charge (in Haiti) of a desire on their part to repudiate in the Black Republic the sacred obligations of their own solemn treaty, made and ratified by the United States and Haiti Governments, through their representatives, May, 1916.

Sincerely yours,   L. Ton Evans,
                                    General Superintendent of Haiti Baptist Mission.

NOTE.—Though subsequently waited upon Senator Hitchcock, at his Senate chambers, accompanied by a strong delegation of white and colored ministers, representing northern and southern wh.te Baptists; National and Lott Carey, colored Baptist conventions, chairman of Race Congress, Colored Methodist Church, with chairman of Washington Baptists, etc., pleading for this commission, we failed to move the Senator.

SENATE FOREIGN RELATIONS,
Washington, D. C., November 2, 1918.

Hon. THEODORE ROOSEVELT,
    Ex-President of the United States.

DEAR COLONEL: Am writing to heartily thank you for your reply sent after me here, and to my letter sent from Port au Prince (Haiti) to Oyster Bay, setting forth the terrible conditions in poor Haiti consequent of the foolish and criminal blunders of the American occupation.

Your own statement this week, issued through the Associated Press, namely, that Haiti, under the United States treaty, has completely lost her Negro Republic as such, and such an exposure by you, as the black man's real friend, will bring joy and hope to thousands in Haiti who will read this.

As I anticipated in my letter to you from Port au Prince (immediately after my interview with Col. Russell and earnest pleading with him not to rape poor Haiti's constitution the following week, but to indefinitely postpone the fake voting and allow me to cable President Wilson at once send a committee of investigation here, which reason I gave for inclosing a copy of my communication to President Wilson), the latter was intercepted by either military officialism and profiteering politicians of the occupation in Haiti or certain members of the administration who determinedly and wickedly withhold the sad conditions in the Black Republic.

As seen in inclosed copy of letter to Senator Hitchcock, it's now up to President Wilson and the administration. If they refuse to appoint the commission and immediately and efficiently act in the matter, then I will see Senator Lodge and insist on bringing it before Foreign Relations Committee and Congress and the great American public.

Sincerely thanking you for your interest, for Christ and Haiti.

                                                                L. Ton Evans.

[Reply and indorsement of suggestion to bring before Senator Lodge and Senate if chairman of Foreign Relations declines finally to act and President refuses to appoint, the demanded commission of investigation.]

THE KANSAS CITY STAR,
OFFICE OF THEODORE ROOSEVELT.
347 Madison Avenue, November 23, 1918.

L. Ton Evans,
    New Howard House, 600 Pennsylvania Avenue, Washington, D. C.

MY DEAR MR. EVANS: I thank you for your letter. After what you have already done, the suggestion you yourself make is certainly as good as anything I can offer. In fact, in the face of the conditions which exist and you have described, I do not really know what else to suggest.

Faithfully, yours,

T. ROOSEVELT.

WYOMING, PA., *March 27, 1920.*

Hon. SECRETARY DANIELS,

United States Navy, District of Columbia.

DEAR SECRETARY: Inclosed memorandum and sworn affidavit submitted through Latin America, and State Departments, and Senator Hitchcock to President Wilson, October, 1918, with present folder will show the serious and criminal conditions now in vogue in Haiti consequent chiefly to blundering, brutal, savage, and murderous methods adopted most unfortunately by our American occupation, nullifying and directly repudiating both in spirit and letter the sacred treaty made between great and powerful United States Government, on one hand, and small, weak, and helpless Black Republic on the other.

Though Second Assistant Secretary Adee, of State Department, in the name of President acknowledged receipt of this memorandum, etc., with its earnest prayer for the immediate appointment of a special commission to thoroughly investigate matters, and the Government solemnly assured me in Secretary Adee's letter that prompt measures were actually then being taken by all departments interested in Haiti affairs, and conditions " were at the moment under serious consideration " that were set forth in said memorandum; and further, that the United States Government would notify me officially of the result of their investigations.

Over 17 months have elapsed since above assurance, with not a word from the Government.

In the meantime, however, conditions have been allowed to grow rapidly worse, as stated in the " folder," and these suffering, oppressed, enraged, and terror-stricken people, as evidenced even by riots between marines and gendarmes, not to say the more frequent and daring raids by so-called bandits, or Caco, daily growing in strength and numbers as well, and having the sympathy more and more of the moderate, intelligent, and educated and better class of Haitians, who have lost respect for and confidence in our American occupation on this account.

With our influence, therefore, on the wane, and our prestige and power all but gone, and our motive and integrity as a democratic, civilized, not to say a Christian nation (and as pointed out in memorandum) suspected and impugned (in 1918), it is no wonder that the staff correspondent of the New York World, who, visiting Haiti a little over a month ago, should state:

" It should be remembered that there are many highly educated and substantial citizens of Port au Prince (and he might add in other towns and cities of the Republic) who are no more Cacos than Henry Cabot Lodge is a Hudson duster, who none the less desire a complete change of administration and the ending of the present occupation." (See Literary Digest, Mar. 27, 1920, p. 52.)

So, under this brutal, bolshevistic American régime, and owing to this criminal neglect and willful refusal of said departments at Washington to officially and effectively function after acknowledging receipt of direct and definite information re conditions, and the responsible United States Government's official assurance, they were then (October, 1918) actually dealing with the situation; it was not surprising that consequently the white drinking portion of our American officials complained of and their gendarmes should become more daring and defiant in their barbaric treatment of the poor natives, and even more cruel and inhuman toward the whites (both American and European).

Therefore, with these conditions in Haiti, under the complete political and military domination and control of the United States Government marines, and in spite of the emphatic terms of the treaty, drawn up and ratified in Washington by our President Wilson and United States Senate, in May of 1916, guaranteeing the integrity of the Negro Republic as such, and ample protection to individual liberty, etc.; on my own return to Haiti in December of 1918 (two months after the official assurance was given me by the State Department, and on which assurance I relied), it was not at all surprising to have my private study immediately and ruthlessly invaded by armed native police without notice or warrant at the imperative and imperious command of one of these white marine officers of the American occupation.

After arrest I was paraded under heavy armed Negro guard through the public streets, cursed and threatened with being shot, etc., by enraged, apparently intoxicated white American marine officers, then driven to prison; when I was thoroughly searched and photo of my wife and two boys, photo of President Wilson, with Mr. Adee, of the State Department's official letter (and assuring me of the United States Government's investigation into cruel, barbaric, and murderous conduct in Haiti, etc.), were all with other articles—money, testament, glasses, etc.—all taken away, thence thrust into a dark, small cell, and strictly confined behind a thick door, the heavy bar drawn with a thud behind me, and a constant armed guard kept day and night, and no member or any other person dare visit or see me.

Within this strictly confined and guarded old French small cell, narrow, and with hard, bare floor, without stool nor chair, half starved and literally gasping for air in a close tropical climate, I thus spent 13 longest and darkest days and nights of my life, amid the yells and groans of about 180 half-clad Negro men and women, and some babes, prisoners, beaten, bruised, and at times battered or starved to death by native officials commanded by a stern, drunken marine officer of the occupation, often away a whole day, with no food provided for prisoners, most of whom were marched like slaves every morning under armed guard to do corvee work some miles away.

Every moment amid this hideous surroundings and expecting myself to be pounced upon and beaten to death or violently dragged forth from my small, dark dungeon before a "firing squad" like the British nurse, Edith Cavell, by the Huns at Brussels (for these poor Negro armed officers dared not disobey the white marine captain at the risk of their lives, when enraged like a madman under the influence of liquor).

After being here 11 days in this condition, physically tortured and mentally agonizing, the St. Marc, Negro high court, feeling that such barbarity disgraced and scandalized Haiti, for never did the Haiti Government arrest or imprison even native Christian ministers, not to say white missionaries and American citizens, so the high Negro court commanded bringing the prisoner at once for trial.

I was informed by the Negro judge advocate, the natives unknown to myself (Catholics and Protestants) had employed to defend me at this court, afterwards that every charge completely broke down, the high court declaring the arrest and imprisonment illegal and unwarrantable; demanded my immediate liberty, with ample protection; further decreeing that I be paid substantial damage in lieu of sufferings caused and torture and agony endured.

Wherefore, Mr. Secretary, and as I understand you to be the officer in supreme command and directly responsible to the Government for affairs in Haiti, I respectfully request an interview in reference—

1. Question of indemnity decreed by judgment of Negro high court of St. Marc for illegal imprisonment, etc., by white marine officer of the United States after notification and warning.

2. The matter of appointment of special commission, as demanded by the memorandum presented, and composed of such competent statesmen as therein suggested, with Hon. Charles Hughes or some one of equal status as chairman, to thoroughly investigate Haiti affairs and formulate a simple plan to develop Haiti according to treaty.

Though pressed to bring this matter before Senate in 1919, and again on landing in New York from Haiti, April of last year, I have persisted so far in believing in the sincerity of the present Government, in spite of constant insinuations and bitter criticisms of the administration, but at last must respectfully insist on approaching the President, through you, re my own illegal imprisonment and the appointment at once of a commission.

In my patient effort to see the President before resorting to the Senate or appealing to the American public, I have had the indorsement of Haiti's educated and intelligent leaders; native and white missionaries of the Black Republic; the Hon. T. Ch. Moravia, present minister of the Haiti Government at Washington; and even the late ex-President Roosevelt wrote me not long before his death that I try every possible means to reach President Wilson direct before bringing this matter before either Senate or Congress and the American people, stating, "I can not think of any better plan and more honorable than the very one you pursue," though previous to this Roosevelt, this real friend of Haiti, whose untimely death, much lamented in the Black Republic, issued through the Associated Press, as seen in the Washington Post of October 23, 1918, "That the Haiti-Negro Republic under the Democratic administration, and in spite of their treaty to the contrary, had become nonexistent," which is perfectly true in substance and in fact.

To save, therefore, more cruel sufferings and prevent further ruthless brutality and wanton bloodshed by either white or colored, the restoration of order, and establishment of peace and good will, which alone can bring prosperity and plenty to Haiti, actually restore the lost influence, prestige, and, if possible, confidence and power in and of the United States and the American Nation as humane and a civilized people, if not the greatest civilizing and Christianizing nation in the world to-day.

Hence I pray that this final attempt will prove successful, amid other pressing duties, to interview the President and lead even yet to a satisfactory solution of the two questions mentioned.

In case we are, however, denied and finally driven to the Senate, and a special Senate committee or commission be appointed, then an exhaustive inquiry will be held, when not only Col. Russell, Brig. Gen. Catlin, Gen. Williams, of the Haiti Gendarmerie, the two American corporations, with certain administration officials here at Washington, will be summoned and carefully examined with a view at last to right poor Haiti's wrongs and remove the stain and disgrace now upon our own flag.

Thus Haiti in all probability will help finally settle both the fate of the present treaty with Europe as well as the fate also of the Democratic administration, if I trow not, at the forthcoming general election, and by the American people themselves. To avoid this I sincerely hope you and the President will grant this interview.

Yours, for Christ and Haiti.

L. Ton Evans.

————

THE SECRETARY OF THE NAVY,
Washington, May 1, 1920.

Mr. L. Ton Evans,
Wyoming, Pa.

My Dear Mr. Evans: I have received your letter and will be pleased to see you at such time as you may suggest. The Navy Department has been very much interested in the work in Haiti and is doing all it can to secure the best possible conditions.

Very truly, yours,

Josephus Daniels.

————

THE SECRETARY OF THE NAVY,
Washington, September 1, 1920.

Mr. L. Ton Evans,
Wyoming, Pa.

My Dear Mr. Evans: I am in receipt of your favor of August 27, and write to say that I am having a study made of the situation in Haiti, and when this is received I will let you hear from me.

Sincerely, yours,

Josephus Daniels.

This letter of August 27 expressed the missionary's plan to come at once to Washington for the interview as per Secretary of Navy's letter of May 1, 1920, that conditions in Haiti were growing worse, and that delay meant not only oppression and brutality but more murder of innocent Haitiens. Since his May reply the Navy Secretary hurriedly dispatched Gen. John A. Lejeune to Haiti to inquire and immediately report up to date. Mr. Daniels, according to promise, sent copy of Lejeune's report to writer, but put off the personal interview.—L. T. E.

The report of Gen. Lejeune was officially forwarded to Mr. Ton Evans, and is as follows:

HEADQUARTERS UNITED STATES MARINE CORPS,
Washington, October 4, 1920.

From: The Major General Commandant.
To: The Secretary of the Navy.
Subject: Report of the military situation in Haiti during the period July 1, 1920, to date and report of my inspection of the First Brigade, United States Marines, stationed in the Republic of Haiti.

1. Pursuant to your verbal instructions, I am submitting for your information and consideration a report covering the period that I have held the office of

Major General Commandant United States Marine Corps, concerning the conditions affecting the military situation in Haiti.

2. The area of Haiti is approximately 10,000 square miles. The country is very mountainous. Between the great mountain ranges lie densely populated river valleys of extraordinary fertility. Haiti is, therefore, exceptionally well adapted for the activities of bandit bands. In fact, throughout the history of Haiti banditry has been prevalent, the bands being recruited from released or escaped criminals and from the class of men who prefer to live by robbing the industrious, peaceful people in the valleys rather than by earning their bread by their own labor. Banditry has been one of the greatest evils which the Haitian people have had to contend with, not only because of the actual injury done the people by the depredations of the bandits but also for the reason that the bandit bands have formed the nuclei of the so-called revolutionary armies which have so frequently devastated Haiti and drenched its soil in blood. The mission of the marines stationed in Haiti is the suppression of banditry and the maintenance of peace and tranquillity.

3. All reports received at headquarters United States Marine Corps since I have been on duty as Major General Commandant have indicated that the bandit situation was steadily improving, and that conditions from the Marine Corps point of view were very satisfactory. However, in order that I might be fully informed in regard to Marine Corps affairs, it was deemed advisable for me to visit Haiti and make a personal inspection of the marines on duty there. I accordingly proceeded to Haiti early in the month of September in company with Brig. Gen. Smedley D. Butler, who assisted me in my inspection.

4. The marines in Haiti are commanded by Col. John H. Russell, an able, just, and humane officer. I found, during my inspection, that not only had he handled the bandit situation in a masterly manner, but that he had issued the most comprehensive instructions requiring a kindly treatment of the inhabitants by our own men, and that his subordinate officers were enforcing his instructions in a loyal and conscientious manner.

DIARY OF EVENTS.

September 4, 1920.—6.15 p. m., arrived at Port au Prince, Haiti, and immediately disembarked.

September 5, 1920.—9 a. m., conferred with brigade commander and members of his staff at brigade headquarters. 11 a. m., received all officers stationed in Port au Prince. In the afternoon, conferred with the financial adviser to the Government of Haiti and other officials of the Marine Corps concerning conditions in Haiti.

September 6, 1920.—Forenoon, reviewed and inspected the battalion of the Haitien gendarmerie stationed in Port au Prince; inspected the battalion of marines also stationed in Port au Prince, the marine barracks, the barracks of the gendarmerie of Haiti, the gendarmerie headquarters, the national penitentiary of Haiti, the Marine Corps depot of supplies, radio station, aviation station, and the naval field hospital. Called on the American minister.

12 noon, called officially on the President of Haiti, and was received by him and his entire cabinet. The President made an address in which he eulogized the work of the marines and of the gendarmerie in Haiti, and expressed his gratitude to the Marine Corps for having maintained peace and tranquillity in the Republic of Haiti. I replied to the address. The President then decorated Brig. Gen. Butler with the Medaille Militaire of Haiti on account of his distinguished service to Haiti in organizing, equipping, training, and commanding the gendarmerie.

Afternoon, the American minister returned my call and I conferred with him and the officers of the first brigade of marines and the gendarmerie concerning conditions in Haiti.

September 7, 1920.—6 a. m., left Port au Prince and proceeded by automobile to Mirebalais and Las Cahobas, at which places I inspected the Marine Corps garrisons and camps and the detachments of gendarmes and their barracks.

At both places we were received by large delegations of Haitien citizens headed by the local officials, who made addresses expressing their great appreciation of the splendid work done by the marines in maintaining peace and good order, thereby permitting the industrious and peaceful people of Haiti to cultivate their farms and conduct their business without molestation. I replied to each of these addresses, and greeted personally each member of the delegations.

6.15 p. m., returned to Port au Prince.

September 8, 1920.—Continued conferences with officers, the financial advisor, the American minister, and with Haitien citizens.

September 9, 1920.—5 a. m., left Port au Prince by automobile for San Michel via St. Marc, Gonaives, and Ennery: inspected all gendarme posts at towns en route. 6.30 p. m., arrived at San Michel.

September 10, 1920.—7 a. m., left San Michel for Maissade and Hinche. I was received at each place by large delegations of Haitian citizens headed by local officials and French priests. Inspected Marine Corps and gendarme posts at Maissade and Hinche and the small detachments of marines en route. The delegations of citizens above referred to expressed their appreciation of the good work that was being done by the Marine Corps and the Haitian gendarmerie in maintaining peace and good order. 5.30 p. m., returned to San Michel. 7 to 10 p. m., conducted investigation of affairs in Haiti, conferring with former officers of the gendarmerie.

September 11, 1920.—7.30 a. m., inspected marine detachment and camp at San Michel. 11 a. m., left San Michel for Cape Haitien via Ennery, Plaisance, and Limbe, inspecting gendarmes and the gendarm posts en route. At 4 p. m., arrived at Cape Haitien.

September 12, 1920.—9 a. m., inspected marine detachment, camp, depot of supplies, radio station, naval field hospital, detachment of gendarmes, their barracks, and the Haitian prison. 11.30 a. m., received a delegation of prominent citizens of Cape Haitien and conferred with them concerning the condition in that section.

Afternoon, received all Marine Corps officers stationed at Cape Haitien.

September 13, 1920.—4 a. m., left Cape Haitien for Ouanaminthe via Quartier Morin, Limonade, and Le Trou. Inspected all detachments of gendarmes en route, the prison farms at Poste Chaubert, and the marine and gendarme detachments at Ouanaminthe.

At 10 a. m., having completed my inspection of the First Brigade United States Marines, we left Haiti, crossed the Massacre River (boundary between Haiti and Santo Domingo), and began the inspection of the Second Brigade United States Marines and the Guardia Nacional of Santo Domingo.

DISTRIBUTION OF FIRST BRIGADE.

The force of marines in Haiti, consisting of about 1,350 men, is organized into a brigade of two small regiments, the Second and Eighth. The Eighth Regiment is stationed in southern Haiti and the Second Regiment in the north. One battalion of the Eighth Regiment is quartered in Port au Prince, the headquarters of the regiment is near Mirebalais, and the remainder of the regiment is camped at Mirebalais and Las Cahobas, with small posts along the road to Port au Prince. The headquarters and one battalion of the Second Regiment are located at Cape Haitien and the remainder of the regiment is stationed at San Michel, Hinche, and Maissade, with small detachments at Thomonde, Ouanaminthe, and at points along the roads from Hinche and Maissade to Cape Haitien. Brigade headquarters and the aviation squadron are located at Port au Prince.

For tactical purposes the forces of both regiments in the interior of Haiti are commanded by the commanding officer of the Eighth Regiment. This arrangement is necessary in order to secure coordination in putting down bandit bands. The Second Regiment is commanded by Col. Randolph C. Berkeley and the Eighth Regiment by Lieut. Col. Louis McC. Little. Naval field hospitals are located at Port au Prince and Cape Haitien.

SUPPLY.

The troops in the field are supplied by means of railroads, motor trucks, and pack trains, motor trucks being utilized wherever the roads are passable, and pack trains over trails. In spite of great difficulties, due to almost impassable roads, high mountain ranges, and rivers swollen by tropical rains, the troops are well supplied.

I found the rations and other supplies to be up to the standard. There were no complaints, except at Hinche, where there was a temporary scarcity of fresh beef in the country.

THE MILITARY SITUATION.

I found the military situation to be in excellent condition and a state of peace and tranquillity prevailing throughout Haiti. We traveled through the country without a guard and found no evidences of hostility on the part of the natives.

The marines and gendarmes stationed in the interior of Haiti send out visiting patrols in command of officers. The patrols visit all sections of the country, not only to prevent banditry but also in order to assure the natives that they will be protected from depredations by bandits. This has had a very beneficial effect, and throughout Haiti we found the natives busily at work cultivating their farms and carrying their produce to market.

There are now no large bandit bands in existence, the only menace to security being a number of small bands who hide in the mountains and live by stealing. These bands are being gradually dispersed. One of the most encouraging circumstances connected with the bandit situation is the fact that many former bandits have voluntarily quit the mountains and gone to work.

A short while ago a small patrol of gendarmes engaged in a skirmish with one of these bands and dispersed it, and Louisnord, the last important bandit leader in Haiti, was killed.

Until banditry has been completely stamped out, however, it is essential for the welfare of Haiti that the present disposition of Marine Corps forces in the interior should not be changed.

RELATIONS BETWEEN THE MARINE CORPS AND THE CIVIL POPULATION OF HAITI.

In my inspection of marines I conferred with large numbers of Haitian officials, including the President and his cabinet, with Haitians not holding any official positions, and with French priests. I found that there existed throughout Haiti a strong sentiment of gratitude to the marines for the work that they were doing for the welfare of the industrious, peaceful, and law-abiding Haitian people, and that, on the whole, very friendly feelings existed on the part of the inhabitants toward the marines. There have been, of course, some cases of ill feeling between individuals. For instance, while I was in Port au Prince two marines, while walking along a city street at night, were severely stabbed from behind by Haitians, who succeeded in making good their escape, and I found in the guardhouse there several marines who had been tried by court martial for engaging in brawls with Haitians. Affairs of this kind are, of course, very regrettable, but are, nevertheless, unavoidable, and are liable to occur at any place at home or abroad where troops are stationed.

The French priest at Hinche, with whom I had a long conference, stated that he had been stationed there for 13 years, and that conditions at Hinche, which had been a center of bandit activity, were better than they had ever been during his ministry in Haiti, and that the officers and marines now stationed there were doing all in their power to cultivate good feeling and to gain the confidence of the Haitian people.

In visiting the various posts I invariably made inquiry concerning the relations between the marines and the population, and found at each place that the commanding officer, acting under the instructions of Col. John H. Russell, the brigade commander, was insistent that the men under his command should treat the inhabitants in a just and kindly manner. It was easy to see by the manner and actions of the thousands of people we met in the towns and on the roads in the interior that a very kind and friendly feeling exists toward persons wearing the uniform of the United States Marine Corps.

GENDARMERIE D'HAITI.

The Gendarmerie d'Haiti is a force of 2,500 Haitians, officered chiefly by commissioned officers and enlisted men of the Marine Corps. This force is the sole police and military force authorized by Haitian laws. It polices the towns and country districts, and is therefore a combination of municipal police and rural constabulary. It also has charge of all Haitian prisons and jails. I made careful inspection of the detachments of gendarmes, their barracks, and Haitian prisons, and at all places visited found the Gendarmerie d'Haiti, which is now highly commanded by Lieut. Col. Frederic M. Wise, to be in a highly efficient condition. It was most gratifying to see the soldierly bearing, neatness, and efficient performance of duty on the part of the gendarmes; also the immaculate cleanliness of their barracks and the prisons of which they are in charge. The condition of the national penitentiary at Port au Prince and the prison at Cape Haitien is especially deserving of the highest commendation. The officers and men of the Marine Corps, who command the gendarmerie, informed me that there had not been a single case of disloyalty to their officers on the part of any member of the gendarmerie since this organization had been established, and that they felt perfect confidence in the courage and loyalty of the Haitians serving in its ranks.

DISCIPLINE, CONDUCT, HEALTH, AND MORALE OF MARINE CORPS FORCES.

During my tour of inspection in Haiti I found the marines to be in a highly efficient condition. Their health, except for some cases of malaria, was excellent. Their discipline was superb and their morale high. As I inspected the detachments located at isolated points far in the interior of Haiti, I was filled with admiration of their fine appearance and efficient condition. My heart was filled with pride to see these splendid men giving to their country and to the Republic of Haiti such intelligent, zealous, efficient, and courageous service. I feel that the American people have every right to be proud of their representatives who are now wearing the uniform of the Marine Corps in Haiti.

JOHN A. LEJEUNE.

_____

SAYS HAITIANS APPROVE OUR ACTION.

MY DEAR SECRETARY DANIELS: When about to mail you my letter to-day I came across in this morning's New York Times what purports to be a reply to Senator Harding, as to conditions and cruelties in Haiti, etc.

After a careful reading of quotations from official statements or report of Gen. John A. Lejeune's hurried visit made after my first letter to you in March, I find they fail to touch the vital points.

Nevertheless if a report of the administration's own official, specially appointed by yourself (since, if not directly through my own letter to the Navy Department six months ago) as the new directing head of the Marine Corps since June 30, 1920, in Haiti, and as having so recently assumed official duties, can be relied upon, I am certainly glad to learn that at last our officials (whatever may be the attitude of the gendarmerie) are beginning not only to understand the Haitians, but the actual meaning of their own mission and that of the United States Government's real purpose in the Black Republic.

I candidly state that had I not been anxious from the commencement (three years ago) to keep entirely out of party politics in missionary and Haitian matters, that I still, in spite of the strong criticism and severe condemnation of President, Secretary of the Navy, etc., firmly believed that you both sincerely wished to right all the past and present wrongs committed under this administration in poor Haiti, I would certainly, after reading this morning's statement, have immediately wired a most startling reply through the Associated Press and at once directed my steps to Marion and the headquarters of the Republican Party, disappointingly convinced that further efforts on the part of Haiti and myself were utterly futile and a mere waste of time.

If therefore Secretary Daniels means to have this interview at once, and he and our President are prepared to act, as suggested in my previous letter and present appeal herein attached, will you then please send prompt reply by letter or wire?

I still remain, sincerely, yours, etc.

L. TON EVANS.

BWTHYN, WYOMING COUNTY, PA., October 6, 1920.

_____

BWTHYN, WYOMING COUNTY, PA., October 2, 1920.

Hon. JOSEPHUS DANIELS,
Secretary of the Navy, Washington, D. C.

MY DEAR SECRETARY: After what has just transpired through the public press from Marion, as well as from Washington, I must respectfully insist on the promised official interview with you (and the President) not later than this coming week, and as stated in letter of March 27 last in reference to—

1. A substantial reparation from the United States Government as decreed by judgment of Saint Marc high court (Haiti) in January of 1918 (an

abstract official copy of which is in my possession) and as previously stated consequent of my illegal arrest and imprisonment with malicious intent causing such physical torture, mental agony, moral and financial damages; from which I have suffered since, as borne out by the four medical certificates forwarded to my annuity board, of the Baptist Union of Great Britain and Ireland, in London, and which board has recognized my claim (as member thereof) in lieu of services rendered as Baptist missionary in and cruel treatment endured on the foreign mission field of Haiti, under my own American flag; and while strictly confined, deprived of nourishment, etc., for 13 days and 12 nights in a small, narrow dungeon, momentarily expecting (like the Negro prisoners) to be either set upon and clubbed to death, or violently dragged out before a firing squad like Edith Cavell, the British nurse, only in my case at the stern command of an American white officer, in collusion and conspiracy with other drinking and drunken officials of my own United States Government, and representatives of our President Wilson, under what can be termed the mad, savage, and murderous régime pursued by the American occupation in the black republic.

It should be pointed out that previous to this, a proclamation of Secretary Daniels (of the United States Navy) faithfully signed, and publicly and officially issued, both in English and French, by Col. John H. Russell, United States Marine Corps, commanding United States forces ashore in Haiti, had been scattered throughout the republic, supposed to be observed and strictly enforced in the interest of the morale of our own boys; all officials, including general officers and members of gendarmerie (native armed police) for decency as well as essential to official discipline, the military authority and the moral efficiency of our United States Government's American occupation service in Haiti; but forsooth this was spurned, and flouted by many if not most officials members of Marine Corps, and especially (if not following example of their superior officers) the gendarmes.

Seeing therefore that the Haiti rum (if not the Haiti brand of Romanism) demoralized, stupefied, and brutalized the supposed better educated and superiorly civilized white American soldier and civilian exactly (only worse through tropical heat, and other climatic conditions to which the whites were unaccustomed) the same as they did their less fortunate Negro brethern, I respectfully, and most earnestly pleaded with Col. Russel at the time of the issuance of this proclamation (owing to the degrading, and constant fatal effects of alcohol upon white and black in our midst) to apply its operation to all throughout the Haiti Republic, and forbid the manufacture, and importation, as well as the sale of liquors of all kinds.

Above proclamation reads as follows:

"The sale of intoxicants to persons of military and naval forces of the United States in uniform is forbidden throughout the Republic of Haiti, from and after July 20, 1918. A violation of this order will be considered inimical to the interests of the United States, and the offender will be liable to trial before a United States military tribunal.

"Done at Port au Prince, Republic of Haiti, this 16th day of July, 1918."

This official interview (or confidential if preferred) is immediately now requested, furthermore—

2. For the purpose of a guarantee from our own President of the appointment at once by him of a special commission of some such Chr'stian statesmen, negro educational experts, military, legal, and religious representatives as Hon. James H. Dillard, Virginia; Maj. Moton, principal of Tuskegee, Ala.; Dr. J. B. Gambrell, president of southern Baptists, whose convention of 3,000,000 members decided to evangelize Haiti through breakdown of small, inefficient, and incompetent negro committee (Texas); Hon. George Peabody, philanthropist, New York; Dr. Gilbert N. Brink, education secretary of Latin America, Philadelphia, Pa.; Dr. Thomas Jesse Jones, author of standard work on the training institutions for colored and negro industrial schools, officially indorsed by United States Government, Washington, D. C.; Rev. J. J. Curran, well-known Roman Catholic social and temperance reformer, Pennsylvan'a; Dr. Robert E. Speer, president of Latin-American cooperative missionary committee, New York; Admiral Caperton, United States Government's officer of present administration, who first landed the marines in Haiti, July, 1915; with, as chairman and legal adviser of same, Charles E. Hughes, ex-Justice of the United States Supreme Court; and so as to carefully and thoroughly investigate Haitian affairs and formulate a simple plan whereby to develop the negro republic and its people according to the treaty made and s'gned by President Woodrow Wil-

son's representative on the one part and representative of the Haitian Republic on the other in Washington, D. C., May, 1916.

This is exactly as requested by Haiti, as far as this little nation has been permitted to express itself through me as its representative, and demanded in that memorandum presented the President through Mr. Tumulty and Mr. Robert Lansing through his confidential clerk, two years ago, and expressly prepared in a typewritten and printed form setting forth the grievances of Haiti, with recommendations, at request of Senator Hitchcock and one Stabler, secretary of the Latin-American section of the State Department, in charge of Haitian affairs, as well as the request of the executive committee of the American negro race congress at its duly convened meeting in the city of Washington, D. C., October 23, 1918.

The above secretary of the Latin-American section of the State Department, however, thought it a part of his Government official duties and as a diplomat in special charge of Haitian affairs, and while Mrs. Evans and myself were absent on the Haiti mission field, with no knowledge of what was going on nor any opportunity to defend ourselves, to enter with others into collusion with negro members of our Haiti committee in North Carolina, Richmond, and Baltimore, it seems, not only to deliberately and falsely misrepresent us and our work in Haiti, but to take further mean advantage of our morally weak and intellectually incompetent negro brethren of above missionary committee by secret intrigue and political, if not also by financial, influence to abruptly, without the knowledge or consent of the Lott Carey Colored Baptist Convention or its general foreign missionary board, and without absolutely any chance of investigation, to cut off our small, irregularly paid salaries at the moment I was pining on the hard, bare floor of an old French negro slave prison cell in a tropical country, literally gasping for a breath of air.

On learning that my typewritten copy of memorandum and petition in behalf of Haiti, in spite of urgency and the personal promise of secretary of Latin-American section, etc., to present it immediately to the Secretary of State and for the President, still remained in his own office or pigeonholed 12 days after, I at once handed another and a printed copy of memorandum, including a duly sworn affidavit to facts contained therein, through Mr. Tumulty at the White House for President, with another printed copy, etc., on same day through his confidential clerk to Mr. Lansing at the State Department, and also furnished several copies to Senator Hitchcock, for members of Senate Foreign Relations Committee, of which he was chairman, on the day I interviewed him at the foreign Senate chambers, with a delegation of some 12 Christian ministers (white and colored) and representing national negro Baptist conventions, Lott Carey negro convention; colored Methodists; white Baptists (North and South), Baptist ministers and Baptist associations (white) of District of Columbia, federal council of the Churches of Christ in America, as well as the president of the negro race congress, pleading with him to arrange an interview with the President.

The Hon. A. A. Adee, on November 2, 1918, wrote acklowledging receipt of memorandum directed to President, as stated in previous letters, and in which he officially informed me that the grave conditions set forth therein "were actually at that moment" (of his writing) "receiving the most serious consideration of the Department of State, as well as all the other branches of the Government directly concerned in Haiti."

He further assured me that the department would communicate with me at a later date, "after the careful study of the matters contained in memorandum." Though now two years have passed not a single word has been received from either Mr. Tumulty or Second Assistant Secretary of State as to the result of the Government's own so-called private and official investigation, if indeed such an "investigation" was ever seriously contemplated, not to say undertaken.

Hence this deliberate and criminal neglect in a matter of vital and urgent importance in a close island of the Caribbean Sea, and touching our honor as a Nation, and directly affecting the life and death of thousands of helpless Negroes, pointed out at the time in memorandum, and this flat refusal of President to appoint commission to thoroughly investigate, or the responsible departments of the administration themselves to take action after giving an official assurance to do so, thus allowing things to take their own course and drift from bad to worse is directly responsible not simply for the continuance of those drunken and brutal white and colored officials of the "American occupation," referred to in the said memorandum, in their immoral and barbaric conduct unchecked.

But this deliberate and criminal neglect is responsible for their encouragement, and their growing more daring and defiant in their brutality and savagery, with consequently more murders among whites as well as blacks, and at last culminating in the infamous "official conspiracy" of illegally invading a private study, without summons, arresting, street parading under armed guard, imprisoning, inhumanly treating with malicious and murderous intent of a white civilian American citizen and a Protestant and Baptist missionary.

Such indeed was the disgrace and scandal at this high-handed, arbitrary, brutal attack of "American occupation" officials, unheard of and unknown before in the history of the Negro Republic, even in the bloodiest revolutionary period, and such the moral shock, profound indignation, and bitter resentment of the natives that the Negro high court of St. Marc felt compelled, for humanity's sake, to at last interfere, call a session extraordinare, and demand (though in so doing they risked their jobs, and even their own lives, the "occupation" officials being supreme) that the white American officers bring the United States citizen and Baptist missionary at once from his confined cell so as to be legally tried, with the result stated, that on examination every trumpery charge completely broke down, the officers of the "American occupation" implicated commanded to immediately set free the missionary, and what remained of the little raped and robbed Negro Republic called upon to protect him and his Christian work, the court adding that for the grave injustice done and cruel suffering inflicted the Haiti law decreed that on demand a substantial indemnity be paid.

I have sincerely believed and stoutly maintained, Mr. Secretary, for close on three years, as you may see from the memorandum in your possession—

(1) That our President and administration at Washington would welcome real facts and correct and true statement as to exact conditions in poor Haiti; that you would not hesitate to move for an impartial investigation, as I told Senator Hitchcock when pleading with him to see the President more than two years ago, by a competent commission, and that the very moment such unjustifiable blunders, wrongs, crimes, political frauds, military atrocities, slamming of senate and chamber's doors in face of people's representatives, as late Czar to his sorrow did with the Russian people's duma, not indeed to mention the further infamous rape of the Negro constitution and putting up of a figurehead and a puppet Negro president by the responsible "American occupation" as a bluff and blind, but immediately seen through and resented as an insult by rank and file, as well as intelligent and educated Haitians, were proven and shown beyond a doubt to have been the real causes of the complete reversion of feeling toward the "American occupation," hatred for the United States Government, and actual contempt for our American flag you would have instantly acted.

Is it not sad indeed to have to state that after nearly five years of the "American occupation" operations in Haiti, under our Democratic administration, the people of the little black republic sincerely and firmly believe that the real mission of the United States Government and the American people there is to reestablish slavery in their midst once more; abrogate and annul the work of Toussaint Loverture (their Washington and Lincoln), just exactly as in the nineteenth century Napoleon, then the terror, tyrant, and bloody Kaiser of Europe, which France, treacherously tried, but ignominiously failed, after a waste of millions of dollars, and a loss of 40,000 of their proud, profligate soldiers, who were as much killed by the negroes' rum, the negroes' yellow fever, as by the negroes' sword, and which apparently Almighty God had summoned as powerful allies to assist these despised, and inferiorly equipped blacks, in their gallant, righteous, and then successful struggles for personal liberty and national independence over 100 years ago; and just as Americans under George Washington a few years before had successfully fought to break away from the conservative oppression and the Tory tyranny of old England and its then proud and Prussian King.

(2) It was my own firm belief furthermore, based upon President Wilson's own address at Washington's tomb July 4, 1918, a careful study of his fourteen points, and his courageous and unflinching stand against Germany and central powers; with the principles he and our Representatives in Congress enunciated and declared, echoed by the whole American Nation, on our entering into, as well as throughout the World War, which, by the way, with his photo from Philadelphia Ledger, with Washington on one side, and immortal Lincoln on the other, I had prominently hanging up in my study down in Haiti, not to mention his present attitude on the European treaty and League of Nations, to

which the whole Democratic Party is committed and morally our whole American people, in fact, and in some form or another—

That the President and administration would therefore seize on the first possible opportunity " to indignantly repudiate " all such acts, not merely in his own behalf and the Government, but in behalf of the whole American people, and immediately proceed in a statesmanlike manner to carry out the recommendations of said commission, appointed by himself, and in this black republic, closely bound to us by a sacred treaty—he would without hesitation *apply these very principles*, he rightly insisted that Germany and all Europe, and indeed the world, should be made to adopt by he himself establishing at the close of the war a civil occupation in Haiti, through at once reopening of senate and chamber of deputies, and by also the complete restoration of the raped constitution.

Moreover, that he would in the spirit, and according to the wording of the generous treaty, have initiated with indorsement (after due explanation) by the Haitian senate and chambers, such industrial, economical, fiscal, and educational reforms as would at once win the implicit confidence of the natives, and absolutely convince these Negroes, whom we must not forget have been persistently and systematically deceived, betrayed, exploited, and plundered for the last 100 years by Europeans, and so-called white friends, under religious, commercial, and phinalthropic pleas, and pretenses, consisting of priests, politicians, profiteers, if not a few Protestants, unfortunately, but invariably somewhere back of their revolutions, for which Negroes themselves are blamed.

And that our United States Government would show as stipulated in our sacred covenant, that we are in Haiti first, last, and all, the time to protect the negro republic as much indeed from the horde of American land grabbers, white and colored, as from German, French, Dutch, or even British and Irish unscrupulous and dishonest speculators, thus proving beyond the shadow of a doubt to Haiti, America, and the whole world—*that our mission in the small black republic is none other than humane and benevolent, as a great civilizing, if not Christianizing, Nation to honorably carry out the terms of our generous and honestly meant treaty.*

If, however, I am seriously mistaken in my estimate of our President and absolute sincerity of his administration, and that after two years of persistent denial, shown by the silence of Hitchcock, Tumulty, and Adee, the Navy Department, in complete charge of Marines in Haiti, as well as gendarmerie, and through you as Secretary, will further delay or decline to listen to present and final appeal in behalf of Haiti, and now also for myself, then as a duty to myself and family, and more especially to these nearly 3,000,000 Negroes, who, with their leaders, are absolutely gagged while their country is pillaged, their constitution raped, and people butchered by hyphenated Americans who as officials feign represent our own Government and liberty-loving nation, who believe in a square deal, I shall now have to comply with the personal advice of my illustrious friend and sincere friend of Haiti, the late ex-President Theodore Roosevelt, revered and never more lamented in the black republic than at this moment of their dire distress, and given me in his last letter from his New York office in Madison Avenue November 2, 1918, on the eve of my own last and never to be forgotten visit from the States to my old missionary field of Haiti. This advice was, that after failing in my efforts with President Wilson and his administration, whose duty was to right their own Democratic wrongs in Haiti, then to immediately approach the Republican Party, who with such leaders as Root, Hughes, Taft, Lodge, Knox, Johnson, and, say, Harding, would not fail me and the Negroes of Haiti the moment they were given the opportunity.

Should I now therefore, be compelled to direct my Haiti appeal to Marion I shall no doubt be welcomed by Senator Harding, Republican nominee for the presidency, and also the Republican leaders if it were only as an eyewitness of the heartless, criminal, and scandalous rape committed upon this small, helpless Negro Republic by her big neighbor and wealthy, strong sister Republic of the United States, officially bound by a sacred treaty, signed and ratified in Washington during this World War May, 1916, and in which treaty the present administration solemnly pledged, if necessary, to use the United States powerful fleet and whole Army of Uncle Sam to jealously protect and safely defend her against all nations, etc.

They will be also glad to greet me as the only one American citizen doing missionary work there, and privileged on the spot, and therefore before the rape was committed, to strongly protest in my own behalf, and even in behalf of British and French white protestant Christian missionaries of Haiti, not to mention the broken-hearted ex-senators, ex-deputies, weeping judges of "American occupation," with ex-judges, lawyers, doctors, Negro preachers, and natives in general, and with whom I came in contact everywhere throughout the whole Republic as a missionary superintendent.

All my endeavors to reach the President at Washington and so as to save us as Americans from this great humiliation and prevent us from being called a Government of hypocrites and termed a Nation of traitors, classed, indeed, with Germany and her now ex-Kaiser in that nefarious rape of Belgium, another small country, and under so-called military necessity, viewing their own treaty as a mere "scrap of paper," were all at that time, as they have been since intercepted, before the censorship was applied to Haiti, and purposely and most deliberately and determinedly frustrated by either incompetent or profiteering officials, or both, in Haiti and at Washington, with the sad conditions and disgrace herein described as the logical and inevitable result, and as truthfully set forth by Senator Harding in his Marion address.

As being the oldest white missionary, as well as then the only American citizen laboring in the black Republic, and who for years had used his influence with our United States Government and in behalf of Haiti presidents, and the Republic's leaders during Roosevelt's, Taft's, and the present administration, and visited Mr. Adee at our State Department more than once so as to beseech Uncle Sam to come to Haiti's rescue and act the part of a big brother, as the late President Theodore Roosevelt and Gen. Wood, under the Republican administration, for instance, did in Cuba. I therefore felt not only proud of the 1916 treaty, but had unflinching faith in the integrity of our President Woodrow Wilson, and sincerity of our responsible Democratic administration this treaty would be lived up to. Hence, the first intimation, followed by an announcement in the Monitor, Haiti's official paper, that the "American occupation" proposed to radically change the constitution of the Negro Republic personally startled me and of course caused a moral shock throughout Haiti and declared as illegal, immoral, and dishonest everywhere.

At first I thought it a foolish, though senseless, hoax, but when assured by intelligent, excited, and half-frenzied natives of its truth, then I declared that any such document proposing to take negro lands and give to whites, etc., must have been inspired at some German headquarters in New York or Chicago, and by hyphenated Americans with Berlin money at the back of it. It was decidedly, I thought, the work of persons jealous of our "American occupation," who were determined not merely to kill our (then) American growing influence in the black republic, but, in fact, intriguing with the enemy (the United States had by this time joined Britain and the Allies in the war), the overthrow of President Wilson, and the downfall of his administration.

I immediately, therefore, as a loyal American, left St. Marc, our home in Haiti, for Port-au-Prince, from where on the 5th of June, 1918, and having been first officially denied the opportunity of cabling the White House, Washington, I sent a registered letter to President Wilson, explaining the consternation in Haiti, respectfully demanding postponement of so-called "voting" on new constitution, with an appointment by him of a committee to at once investigate matters so as to avoid this public and national scandal, but this registered letter was intercepted by the President's own private secretary, or at the State Department.

Anticipating this, however, from reliable information to hand, as to relations between officials in Haiti and at Washington, with certain financial projects in the island, I sent also another registered letter the very same day to ex-President Theodore Roosevelt at Oyster Bay. N. Y., inclosing therein a copy of that written our President, with my special reason for adopting this unusual course. The latter was safely received at Sagamore Bay, and a courteous reply duly arrived.

Definite information conveyed in this, with additional evidence supplied, though it failed to move Senator Hitchcock, etc., enabled ex-President Roosevelt in his criticism of the 14 points, etc., to emphatically declare through the Associated Press, as appeared in Washington papers October 23, 1918—

"That the Negro Republic of Haiti was nonexistent under the Democratic administration, in spite of their treaty." and which the Government at Washington dared not then nor since his death to deny.

All these letters and copies of other communications in Haiti and with Government I have in my possession, including photograph of President, my wife, and two little lads, with Hon. Adee's official acknowledgment of memorandum, and assurance of the Government's investigation, "serious consideration" of sad conditions in Haiti, etc., which were on me when arrested, paraded through public streets, under armed guard, but taken from me in prison when searched, and thrown into my cell at the stern command of United States' white captain of the "occupation."

I have also the photograph of the negro judge advocate, the poor natives unknown to myself had engaged to assist in my defense at the aforesaid high court, but whom like the rest was too terrified to attempt to visit my strictly confined cell for fear of being shot.

I have, in addition to these, a photograph of myself surrounded by native Christians, which was taken in the far interior, and four days after my release and with my prison-grown beard. I was en route for the cape (extreme north) driven midnight of same day the high court set me free (and by same white captain, under threats of using military force, and in a small boat), to the open Caribbean Sea, for another trial, with probable imprisonment before me, if not this time certain death.

When the capital of the north, Cape Haiti, was at last reached, having been warned never to preach in that section, threatened to be shot by a white, excited, and intoxicated American officer who, ignoring and sneering at Secretary Lansing's official letter, and another of an American captain of that section, wildly raved like a maniac, and before the terrorized native Christians, who accompanied me to his American headquarters, openly cursed God, Christianity, declaring Christian ministers and missionaries to be imposters and hypocrites. I found that the "malicious conspiracy" of our American official drunken-crowd had suddenly collapsed.

This poor Negro judge, forced, like others, by the officials, assured me and my witnesses there was absolutely no legal charge brought against me, and that he had just been communicated with to drop everything. My own presence with British, French (white), and native witnesses, and the St. Marc's high court judgment must have evidently filled the conspirators with consternation, confusion, and fear, if not shame.

Unless this reproach upon the honesty, veracity, not to say honor, of our American people, which I sincerely sought to prevent, but through American officialism absolutely so far failed, is now immediately and irrevocably eradicated and w'ped out forever, such treacherous conduct can not fail to recoil upon our whole nation, as, for instance, the betrayal of those negroes of the Congo Free State, Africa, recently was revisited upon Belgium; and even the capture and banishment of Napoleon to St. Helena by the British swiftly and inevitably followed his own treacherous treatment of Toussaint, "the Moses of Haiti and Savior of the Blacks," for in the inspiring words of this great African chief and noble as well as gallant general, to Brunet, his French captor (as he bound him in chains on transferring him from the frigate Creole to the French man-of-war, the Heros, off Cape Haiti, the beginning of last century, to be sent to his cruel and shameful torture and death in the south of France), Loverture said:

"You may indeed to-day cut down the tree of the negro's liberty and independence, but the roots are so deep and profound that the trunk will soon sprout and grow again in Haiti."

In closing this statement and further reiteration of present sad conditions, and making my last appeal in spite of the startling published admission and most damaging confession of your late Assistant Secretary of the Navy, Hon. Franklin Roosevelt (cause of my suspicion June 5, 1918, and justifying my own writing to ex-President Theodore Roosevelt, as well as President Wilson), and further, the fact that our President and the administration's present term of office and exercise of power are about to expire, to be followed, possibly by a Republican Government, I still confidently believe that if the President and yourself will only respond to poor Haiti's cry, immediately act and seriously and courageously undertake to right the Republic's wrongs along such lines as set forth herein and as pointed out two years ago in the memorandum presented, not only law and order will be at once established, but real peace and absolute confidence will also follow throughout Haiti; yes, including the mountain fastnesses where the supposed Cacos are said to dwell, etc.

This would not fail to secure for President, yourself, and administration (and our whole American Nation) the undying gratitude of these misunderstood and maligned but kind-hearted negroes, and even the sincere admiration of the whole civilized and Christian world.

Allow me to add that as a pioneer missionary with over 25 years of unique experience in Haiti: with an intimate acquaintance of these negroes of every religious creed and political persuasion throughout the Republic (which I have again and again traveled through by day and by night, even in times of revolutions, without either a revolver or a knife) and as an American citizen and missionary lecturer on " Haiti's past, present, and future," given thousands of times in churches, ministers' conferences, colleges, associations, and conventions in States (North and South), England, Wales Jamaica, Cuba, thus internationally known among Baptists and leading evangelicals, to finally beseech you to heed Haiti's imperative demand for justice at the hands of the United States.

I have sincerely desired and earnestly prayed you might give me the opportunity, pleasure, and delight, not only to defend, but applaud, from Maine to the Pacific and from Dakotas to Gulf, as well as in other lands (from pulpit and press), President Wilson and his administration's sound, constructive, if not regenerative work and creation in fact of a peaceful, prosperous, and model negro republic in land of Loverture, superstitious, priest-ridden, illiterate, distracted, politically exploited, revolutionary torn, financial and morally bankrupt only a few years ago, thus showing the world the potential future of the whole Negro race.

Yes; if, by your present prompt action I am indeed now permitted, it will be a pleasure in describing Haiti as the unfortunate man referred to by Christ in the parable, waylaid, robbed, and bleeding from every pore, between Jerusalem and Jericho, to express also my joy, that while others passed by on the other side, in the Providence of a merciful God who created of one blood all nations, it was our own wealthy, strong, and powerful United States Government and great American Nation under Christian leadership of courageous and competent statesman. President Wilson, which came along and played the rôle of good Samaritan.

Whether my prayer will be answered, and desire gratified now, and Haiti's bleeding wounds shall be healed, or this waylaid black republic shall be further plundered and butchered, is, therefore, now up to you and President, sir.

Sincerely, yours, for Christ, Haiti, and humanity,

L. Ton Evans.

THE SECRETARY OF THE NAVY,
Washington, October 18, 1920.

MY DEAR SIR: In the absence of Secretary Daniels, I wish to acknowledge receipt of your letter of October 5. Upon the Secretary's return to the city I will bring the matter to his attention.

Very truly, yours,

EDWARD E. BRITTON, *Private Secretary.*

Mr. L. Ton Evans,
Biethyn, Wyoming, Pa.

STATEMENT OF REV. L. TON EVANS, WYOMING, PA. (AND LATE OF HAITI).

The CHAIRMAN. Mr. Evans, will you give your name and address?

Mr. EVANS. My name is L. Ton Evans.

The CHAIRMAN. Your address?

Mr. EVANS. Since returning from Haiti my residence is at Wyoming, Pa.

The CHAIRMAN. Your purpose of vocation in Haiti?

Mr. EVANS. I have been pioneer missionary and field secretary of the Baptists of the United States.

The CHAIRMAN. In Haiti?

Mr. EVANS. Yes; in Haiti, and for, altogether, 28 years either in Haiti or speaking and pleading in behalf of Haiti and the Haitian people throughout the United States and in England and Wales.

The CHAIRMAN. Were you in Haiti during the years immediately preceding the occupation?

Mr. EVANS. Yes; many years before.

The CHAIRMAN. During the years immediately preceding the occupation?

Mr. EVANS. I left at the beginning of 1912, and again returned with my family in 1917.

The CHAIRMAN. And from 1917 until when were you in Haiti?

Mr. EVANS. From 1917 to April of 1919, when I returned to the States.

The CHAIRMAN. Then your knowledge of conditions prior to the occupation terminated in 1912, or three years before the occupation took place?

Mr. EVANS. Personally, yes; but early in 1912 I had a long private interview with the late President Leconte at the palace in Port au Prince, and brought several requests from him to our State Department here at Washington, but the department failed to act.

The CHAIRMAN. Let us go back to the period prior to your departure in 1912. How long were you in the Republic of Haiti consecutively before you left in 1912?

Mr. EVANS. I was there from 1908, though I made a short visit to Jamaica and officially as delegate to Baptist World Alliance in Philadelphia in the meantime.

The CHAIRMAN. Until the year 1912?

Mr. EVANS. Until 1912; but as superintendent missionary I frequently visited the States and other countries, churches, and societies, returning again to Jacmel, in the southeast, where I resided, though as field secrtary and superintendent my work took me all over the Republic.

The CHAIRMAN. How many missionaries were under your direction as superintendent, or how many missions, let me say?

Mr. EVANS. Well, altogether, we had over 1,000 members at that time in something like 16 churches, 12 mission stations with 8 missionaries and 20 native preachers or assistants, and in addition 15 or more teachers in our day schools.

The CHAIRMAN. How many American missionaries were under your supervision in Haiti?

Mr. EVANS. Eight. I was the only American citizen, however, among all Protestant ministers at that time in Haiti. Several of these native missionaries and one white French citizen were educated here in the States.

Haiti Baptist Mission (operated by both Lott Cary Foreign Board and the Jamaica Baptist Missionary Society)—Statistics re churches, missions, pastors, native preachers, members, baptisms, with Sunday and evangelical day schools, offerings, etc., for year ending June, 1918.

[By L. Ton Evans, general superintendent.]

Church	Mission	Pastor	Native preachers	Sunday school teachers	Baptisms	Converts taught	Candidates	Died	Members	Sunday School scholars	New missions	Marriages	Total offerings	Haitian gourdes	Day schools	Church buildings	Wattled buildings	Homes and huts
Cape Haiti		C. Jean Jacques	4	3	3	14			40	59	1	1	47	235	1	1		†1
Dondon		V. Eustach		3					52	77	1		41	205		1	1	
Fort Liberty		C. Jean Jacques	2	3	3	35	2			32	1				2	1		†1
Grand Riviere		Elie Mark		3		15	1			100					1	1		
Du Nord Zebing				3			30	2	682	34	1	40	540	2,000	1	*1	1	
Jacmel (Tabernacle)		N. P. Lherisson	15	3	95	2,000		3		40						1	1	
	Bethlehem			1						45						1		
	Carmel			2						50						1		
	Jericho			2						39						1		
	Moriah			3						35						*1		
	Olivière			1						38						1		
	Bainet			2						37						1		
	Bethesda			2						24								
	Central			3						28						*1		
	Bethel			1						22								
	Gebeon			2						32								†1
Massade		Dumay Alexis	1	2	2	27			12	36			9	45		1	1	†1
Pignon			1	1	9	4			20	37		3	15	75				
Port au Prince (Capital)		L. Hypolite	1	2		3	2		25	24		2	10	50	1		*1	
Port de Paix (Mission)		J. Thomas	1	1		2		1	9	28	1	2	214	1,070	1	1		†1
St. Marc (Ebenezer)		L. Ton Evans	5	3	17	65	x	3	58	22		1	10	50	1		1	†1
St. Michel (Isle Gonave)		V. Eustache	2	1	9	27	12		14	32					1	*1		
Pisgah				2						36					1			
St. Raphael (Habitation Baille)		Dumay Alexis	2	1		6	6	4	33	15		2	45	225	1	1		†1
Bethania				5					5	20								†1
St. Louis (Mission)			1	4	2	12	4		35	26	2	2	155	775	1	1	1	†1
Trou (Du Nord)		Elie Mark	4			7	1			8		1				1		†1
	San Busan					7	2			51								†1
	Caracol					4												
	Lunette																	
Total (12 churches, 18 missions, 2 pastors).			**39**	**51**	**141**	**2,228**	**66**	**14**	**986**	**918**	**6**	**49**	**1,126**	**5,630**	**12**	**15**	**6**	**9**

"The 15 church buildings are of stone, or in Spanish walls, comfortable, and free of debt, but the two marked * not finished. St. Marc, the largest Protestant church on island, has $200 debt, with $200 more added in purchasing a valuable lot adjoining for parsonage and woman's training school. This, with $100 to complete church (now 25 years in building), makes total indebtedness $500, or 2,500 gourdes.

"The 6 wattling-built and covered with brush roof have sides covered with mud, whitewashed within and without, constructed by the voluntary labor of the people of the immediate section, anxious for a place of worship and the preaching of the evangel in their midst. They are in all country places, and mark the first stage of the cause, and as such serve their purpose well; they are replaced by substantial churches as the mission progresses, and funds come in.

"Of the 9 with mark † 7 are merely wattled-made houses ,or huts, small and inconvenient, and simply meant for temporary use, and as yet really preaching stations.

"Since the burning down of our substantial and comfortable churches at the important towns of Portdepaix and Cape Haiti, with a population of 7,000 and 30,000 or more, respectively, the few believers now in the former worship at the native preacher's own home, while the latter hold divine worship and their preaching service in a house whose rent is paid for by the Haiti Government.

"To command the respect of all classes of Haitians, and Government representatives and other Americans coming here just Baptists must have substantial churches and comfortable Christian homes in the cities and towns along the coast. These and a parsonage are essential for a missionary so as to be independent and devote himself whole-heartedly to aggressive evangelism, and making it absolutely unnecessary to compromise the board, denomination, as well as church and himself, by accepting Government aid of any kind."

Senator POMERENE. Black were they?

The CHAIRMAN. Were they native Haitians?

Mr. EVANS. Native Haitians; yes.

The CHAIRMAN. Negro citizens of the Republic?

Mr. EVANS. Yes; of the Republic, but educated some of them at the Baptist Theological Seminary, Newton Center, Mass.—New England.

The CHAIRMAN. Will you tell the committee, in your own way, briefly, your estimate of the Government of Haiti during the years from 1908 to 1912; the condition of public order, the security of the Haitian citizen in his person and in his property. The administration of justice and, in short, the various aspects of the Haitian Government state?

Mr. EVANS. I am sorry to say that conditions were far from satisfactory. In fact there were periodical political disturbances, which at times culminated in bloody fights, and followed by devastation of the country, discouraging the people, all but crushing their native aspirations, and hope of ever becoming fit to take their place among surrounding nations. It is but fair to add, however, that I found the people of Haiti, a simple, innocent, peace-loving, if not the most kind-hearted I ever met with. During all the years spent there, and I frequently traveled night and day all over the country, even the most outlandish, alone and without a guide, and never carried any weapon, even during the exciting periods of revolutions. Once only did the natives make an attempt to attack me, and then it was through my own aggressiveness in penetrating into the mysteries of devil worship—voodooism and the demon dance; the voodoo priest, known as papa-loi, who actually led in what appeared to be a ferocious attack, has been long converted, and many of his followers, while the papa-loi has been one of our faithful assistant preachers in that section for years.

Back of these revolutions to my own knowledge, and commonly known throughout Haiti, has always been the white man, and the white man's money, and among whom have been at times British, American, French, and other European, but chief among these the last 20 years has been a strong German element, I regret to say. I brought these conditions, with main causes of the political disturbances, during 1902, by means of a letter before President Theodore Roosevelt—which I shall put in the record—and came to Washington again during President Taft's and the beginning of President Wilson's administrations, specially pointing out this fact, and urging our Government to come to Haiti, and Haitians' defense.

Merchants throughout Haiti, the majority of whom are Germans, have been all along acting either as consuls, or vice consuls of their European Government, hence are in Haiti unfortunately in this dual capacity. These are really the invisible but potent political forces back of the Haitian revolutions.

HAITIAN CIVIL WAR.

MOUNT VERNON, EDWARDSVILLE, PA., *August 20, 1902.*

President ROOSEVELT.

SIR: I beg very respectfully to call your special attention to a matter from political and humanitarian point of view is of urgent importance, viz: The present revolutionary war that is now being waged in north and south Haiti, and causing such misery and suffering not to mention cruel bloodshed by assassination and murder.

The barbaric methods adopted to establish certain political parties in power and which are such frequent occurrence both in Haiti and Santo Domingo, and among peoples of the same race, religion, and language are not by any means initiated by the masses, but are simply the work of a few greedy office seekers who subordinate and sacrifice the public welfare to their own personal and sordid interests.

For many years past these revolutionary movements, bring disaster and desolation to the country in general and people in particular, mentally and morally, by denying necessary security for life and property, thwarting personal enterprise and legitimate developments along commercial lines, thus completely crushing national aspirations to rise in the march of progress and civilization, although as a race they have now been politically free for more than 100 years.

These constant upheavals, fraught with so much ruin and loss of life, and which the island seems utterly unable to resist, are the work as already stated of a few natives, mostly refuges, residing in Jamaica and France, and aided by European and American money lenders, who financially support and otherwise fomented them. Ammunition for such purpose is smuggled in from above two places, where these plots are planned and hatched by Europeans, especially Germans.

While rejoicing at your Government's prompt action in dispatching a gunboat to aid American citizens in the north (Cape Haitian), yet from high political as well as humanitarian reasons, may I strongly urge upon you also the advisability of extending the same protection at least for life to the defenseless natives themselves here, and in other cities along the coast, where they are left at the mercy of these unscrupulous, unprincipled avaricious and murderous mauraders whose one desire is to get a firm grip hold of the small Republic's purse strings so as to enrich themselves and few following at the expense of robbing the whole community, and keeping the country in abject poverty.

Should you be able to offer this protection and to safeguard the island from this policy of rapine and plunder long persued by dishonest political exploiters, I can assure you, sir, that hundreds of thousands of the sons of Ham throughout that region would feel forever grateful to the United States, look at such benevolent interposition as nothing less than a godsend, the dawn of long looked and much prayed for day of deliverance and the inauguration at last of a new era; after many years in a state of political and moral subjugation, worse, if possible, than that of slavery in olden days.

In advising and urging this immediate interference I am by no means insensible to the delicate nature of the task, and certainly some of the apparent risks which such a procedure involves.

Yet is it not immoral, cruel, yes criminal, that poor Haiti, like the man of old who fell among thieves on the highway to Jericho, robbed, wounded, and bleeding from every pore, should be severely left alone in her blood to pine and die, simply for fear of being misunderstood or of arousing the suspicion and jealousy of some other nation? Such risks are certainly more imaginary than real.

If this great commonwealth that without a single moment's delay rushed to the aid of Fort De France recently, showed its practical sympathy with and gave its generous help to the sorrow-stricken inhabitants of Martinique and St. Vincent, were again, and in this case, to play the part of the Good Samaritan, and with or without the cooperation of England act as guarantors or guarantor for order and good government, and see that the laws governing elections, as stipulated by the Constitution, were rigidly enforced, you would further merit the unstinted praise and unbounded admiration of the civilized world.

It is quite patent to all that those who now pretend to rule Haiti are politically as well as morally utterly unfit; and that the sad and heart-rending state of affairs in that island constitutes a serious menace to the best interests of England and the States, which, if continued, must reflect discreditably upon these two great powers so immediately concerned in the Carribean Sea.

The practice of appointing storekeepers and merchants who do business with the natives, and who so often benefit financially by these internal troubles as official and semiofficial representatives of foreign Governments, is neither calculated to inspire confidence in the inhabitants nor likely to add to official efficiency in the discharge of their duties to their respective governments.

The cost of supervising the island, as suggested, if thought practical, might be easily borne by Haiti itself, seeing the advantages derived from such a course. The expenses would be more than saved by disbanding the present army (for should the States safeguard the shores from invasions by foreign powers and political filibusters) so that the men can go home to cultivate their grounds and otherwise develop their country—a small number only retained merely to police the interior and preserve law and order in cities along the coasts.

In addition to the immense benefits bestowed upon these Republics, such as placing the race in a position to work out its political and social salvation, this great Commonwealth would once more demonstrate to the world at large her position in the forefront of governments, which seeks to use her great power and mighty influence not to add territorial possessions and increase her wealth, but for something higher and nobler, viz, to protect the weak against the strong, to establish law and order where now chaos and terror reign supreme, to encourage honest industry, to further national progress, yea, to develop and advance the truest and best form of civilization.

An expression of sympathy with above object and appeal, and especially of hearty willingness, with or without the cooperation of England, to take immediate steps in this matter so as to save further suffering and prevent bloodshed, will be esteemed a great favor.

In behalf of hundreds of thousands of neglected and downtrodden negroes of Haiti.

Yours, very sincerely,

L. TON EVANS,
Field Secretary and Baptist Pioneer Missionary in Haiti.

Mr. EVANS. While dealing with this phase of the question in fixing responsibility I should point to the committee, how intelligent, educated Haitians, and there are quite a number of smart and bright persons among the better class, with a touch of French politeness and some refinement after years of training in the schools, colleges, and universities of Paris, return to their island home with changed ideas and altogether different, and in many respects higher aspirations. Their education and classical training in Europe makes them dissatisfied with conditions in Haiti, and properly so.

The CHAIRMAN. Now, if you will not go too far afield, Mr. Evans, what is the bearing of the education of these Haitians on the machinations of the foreigners when incited to revolution?

Mr. EVANS. The direct bearing of it is this, that being discontented with conditions in Haiti, and moved with a strong desire and newly enkindled patriotism as the result of their training in Paris and contact with Europeans, and having nothing special to do in poor Haiti they become an easy prey to foreigners, and the white man with political intentions and profiteering desires, to be used and exploited by them under the pretence that an overthrow of the president and change of government will result, and, indeed, is inevitable to the bettering of conditions and development of the Black Republic.

Senator POMERENE. Do I understand you to mean that they become the prey of these foreign elements?

Mr. EVANS. Exactly so, through their dissatisfaction with Haiti's very low and backward condition, and often a burning love for their country, with desire for the betterment of Haiti, mostly inexperienced, unsuspecting the white foreigner's motive, and that they merely meant to exploit them and their country and get a firm grip of the Republic's purse strings—customs.

Senator POMERENE. I take it that your thought is that these foreigners are there for the purpose of exploiting rather than for the improvement of the country?

Mr. EVANS. I would not like to put it in that way in reference to all foreigners. There might have been other motives at first, but seeing a fine opportunity for exploitation among these good natured, innocent, impoverished, yet unskilled, though somewhat educated people, these foreigners, and especially Germans, have been eager to take full advantage of it, also opposing by every means and actually stultifying Haiti's efforts to disentangle itself from Germans, and their intrigues when discovered, so as to ally itself with the United States and seek our Government's closer friendship and good will and practical encouragement and protection to develop their own rich resources, being geographically their closest neighbor, in fact.

The CHAIRMAN. Mr. Evans, are these foreigners who foment revolutions accustomed to make monetary advances to revolutionary generals at usurious rates?

Mr. EVANS. Yes, sir; most decidedly.

The CHAIRMAN. Selling arms?

Mr. EVANS. That is so.

The CHAIRMAN. In short, they have a direct profit in inciting revolutions?

Mr. EVANS. Absolutely so, and in constantly fomenting political disturbances. For instance, in August of 1911, when returning from the World's Baptist Alliance, which I attended as Haiti's representative, and took part and held that year at Philadelphia, a German banker from Haiti sat next me at the table on the boat. In conversing about the recent revolutions of 1910 and 1911, which I had seen and gone through, and describing to him the terrible conditions, sufferings, and bloodshed, this German banker answered, though not himself in Haiti, that he actually knew more about them than I did. Boastingly he added: "I financed them from Berlin, as well as the previous revolutions, and furnished ammunition, and have been staying in Germany several years arranging these matters." Remembering the devastation and murder of my friend the Rev. George Angus, a British subject and missionary from Jamaica, through stray shots of revolutionists fomented and financed from Berlin, I jumped to my feet, denounced his cowardly, cruel, and murderous German mission, adding, he should have been made to face the Haitian cannon, and first to smell his own German powder from the barrel of the Haitian gun. I felt ashamed of his mean, despicable, and, indeed, devilish acts, then hiding himself and his crowd, while the poor, helpless, and deluded Haitians, forsooth, bore the whole blame and were called "assassins" and "cutthroats."

There is also jealousy and a growing hatred against the United States increasing interest and influence in Haiti and the Caribbean Sea, which interest and influence are always recognized and backed up by England, to the bitter chagrin of Germans and their supporters in Haiti the last decade.

The CHAIRMAN. Mr. Evans, I do not think we need to go so far afield.

Mr. EVANS. But is it not too bad that these Negroes should be made to bear the whole blame and painted everywhere as brutes and savages, if not a nation of cannibals, through the cowardly and greedy exploitation of the white man and his money?

The CHAIRMAN. Well, Mr. Evans, we want all the facts rather than opinion. During those four years preceding your departure in 1912 what was the condition of the Haitian peasant, his relation to the general de la place and the general d'arondissement; did he get justice in the courts?

Mr. EVANS. I believe they did. I heard very little complaint. Whenever I had an occasion to go to court the Haitian judge showed ability and impartiality. Officials of the court and other Government departments, in spite of occasional delays, were invariably polite. Being privileged as a Christian missionary and an American citizen, I was given a free pass, hence I was never bothered with ordinary officials about "permits" to travel, and of which they were somewhat strict on account of the said revolutions. I put in the record a copy of one of these free permits, signed by the secretary of the interior and member of Haitian cabinet.

[Liberte.   Egalite.   Fraternite.]

REPUBLIQUE D'HAITI.

PORT AU PRINCE le 23 Décembre, 1911, an 10 8me De l'Indépendance.

LE SECRÉTAIRE D'ETAT,
          au Département de l'Intérieur:

Accorde, par les présentes, permis au Révérend I. Ton Evans, Secrétaire Général de la Mission Baptiste pour Haiti de voyage Librement vaus toute l'éntendue de la République.

Les autorité civile et militaires sout invitées à lui prétes aide et protection au besoin.

Fait à Port au Prince le 23 Décembre, 1911, an 10 8° de l'Indépendance.

Emigista à le Secrétaire d'Etat de l'Intérieur et de lut Police Générale, le 23 Décembre, 1911, an 10 8° de l'Indépendence, an No. 461.

LE CHEF DE DIVISION.

The CHAIRMAN. Tell us the lot of the peasant. What is his relation to the general d'arondissement and general-da-la-place? Is he free to go where he will? Are his taxes justly levied, and so on?

Mr. EVANS. Taxes? There are not many taxable things in Haiti.

The CHAIRMAN. Yes.

Mr. EVANS. There are not many articles taxed in Haiti. Imports are the chief source of revenue. These financial arrangements of the Government did not come within my purview. As I have said, the political conditions obligated them to be strict as to permits for traveling within or for leaving the Republic. Though discouraged by revolutions to raise crops, I found the peasants often thrifty, and certain sections of the Republic showed labor and skill with some good crops. As a whole, however, and considering the richness of the soil, instability of government, and no market, Haiti is in a very backward condition industrially. To prevent revolutions and encourage the cultivation of this rich land, I came again and again to our State Department at Washington urging our Government to protect Haiti and act the big brother to this weak and defenceless little nation.

For this reason the petition signed by nearly 3,000 Haitians, including Presidents Simon and Laconte and all leading Haitians of the Republic, was gotten up and presented to secretary of Carnegie's international peace bureau and of the Rockefeller Foundation praying for a normal and industrial college for Haiti and on Christian basis like Tuskegee. A copy of this will be placed in record.

The granting of large concessions by way of plantations and the land for railroads to the American contractor Macdonald by President Simon was an honest endeavor to open up the country for industrial cultivation of the land on a large scale by Haitians and for Haiti's benefit, but under leadership of the white man with modern implements.

This was defeated through the German propaganda in starting a revolution and the overthrow of President Simon and his government in 1911. The Germans persisted that Simon had "sold Haiti to the United States."

Senator POMERENE. Who was this railroad contractor?

Mr. EVANS. Mr. Macdonald, of New York. It was freely said in Haiti that in addition to subsequently fomenting and financing this revolution which finally ousted President Simon, a sum of not less than $350,000 of German money was actually spent in bribing senate or house members or both, at Port au Prince so as not to ratify the said contracts. In his heroic endeavor to put down this rebellion and emphatically contradicting the Germans' propaganda, I saw the aged President in actual tears and all but broken hearted, as he told me if the United States Government had come to his aid the Government and so the railroad and plantations would have been saved, if not thousands of Haitian lives.

Senator POMERENE. As I understood you, you used the expression "sold to the United States." What did you mean by that?

Mr. EVANS. That the Haiti Republic had been handed over to the United States Government and people for a consideration, and that President Simon had betrayed the Haitians.

Senator POMERENE. That the President did?

Mr. EVANS. Yes; that Antoine Simon, the then President of the black Republic, had done it. This, of course, was revolution propaganda of the German element—to arouse the natives to rebel against and overthrow their President—and it succeeded, whereas he had done the best possible thing under the circumstances to open up industries, and, as he said, to secure labor, with fair pay to the natives. These contracts and land to Macdonald were to revert to the Haitian Government after a number of years.

Senator POMERENE. I think I misunderstood you at first. You mean they said he had sold Haiti; is that it?

Mr. EVANS. Yes; it was a willful misrepresentation of the actual truth by these German propagandists, playing on the sentiment of these quiet, ignorant people, who have a burning passion, however, for their own Negro republic.

The CHAIRMAN. You started to tell a while ago of a message which President Leconte gave you. What message was that?

Mr. EVANS. It was that if he was to have a stable Government, and be continued in the executive office to carry out the urgent reforms he had actually commenced, and those he contemplated, "he must have the close friendship, practical help, protection, and encouragement of the United States Government, whose interests were paramount in Haiti and Central America."

Cincinnatus Leconte had spent some years at Washington as Haiti's chief consul, could speak English fluently, and, in my opinion, was the best educated and cultured Haitian, with a practical turn of mind, that ever sat in the presidential palace at Port au Prince.

I put in a quotation in the record, from one of my circulars, written June of 1912, and referring to Leconte's election as President and consequent bright prospects at last for Haiti politically, educationally, and religiously:

THE RADICAL CHANGE IN THE HAITI GOVERNMENT.

"America and the outside world, and even 90 per cent of the Haitians themselves, are at present ignorant as to the magnitude of the change, in fact, transformation, which has recently taken place with the coming in of the new Government, and that in the most unexpected and providential manner. The second revolution of last year was started by the savage Caicos, or snake worshippers and devil devotees near the Dominican frontier in the north and out-of-the-way part of the Republic. In reality it was a case of Satan casting out Satan.

"President Leconte and his ministry represent the intelligence and energy of the country. There is to be found to-day in palace and cabinet not only a high type of civilization but an atmosphere of refinement, which, if wisely and firmly directed, backed up by a fearless policy and sympathetic and efficient support of our United States Government, and the blessing of God, must ere long effect a beneficent change throughout the country, long neglected, with its nearly 3,000,000 poverty-stricken but withal kind-hearted people.

"It is really Haiti's first civil government. The next few years, therefore, are fraught with tremendous consequences to this land.

"Yes; the psychological moment has come, and which many have looked hopefully and anxiously forward to, and some of us even fervently prayed God for the last 10, 15, and 20 years. There must now be no time lost in coming to our help and rescue; for the uplift of Haiti means actually the lifting up of the whole Negro race. For reasons partly geographical, political, and especially providential, the true character and capacity of the African for self-government, etc., will be judged by what the black man is really in his own independent Republic of Haiti."

Senator POMERENE. Without going into details, and the chairman objects to opinions rather than facts, and I do not care to pursue that further, but you stated that this German banker in Haiti told you that he financed the revolution?

Mr. EVANS. Yes, sir; I did.

Senator POMERENE. Have you any other evidential facts which would support your conclusion that he or other Germans were financing that revolution?

Mr. EVANS. It was common knowledge in 1910 or 1911, perhaps both, that something like $350,000 of German money had been spent to prevent the confirmation or ratification of the Macdonalds contracts and land concessions. Ex-President Simon, who still lives in Haiti and can be called before this committee, was in consequence compelled to threaten the use of force so as to bring the senate or house together for the purpose of ratification.

Senator POMERENE. You regard him as entirely loyal to Haiti's ambitions, etc.?

Mr. EVANS. I believe so; many—in fact all the Presidents who seek to bring in reforms are powerless because of the German influence in the past.

Senator POMERENE. Is that true of President Leconte?

Mr. EVANS. Indeed, even more so than in President Simon's case, because he was better educated, had filled important offices, and knew the United States and American people, if not also Germany and Germans, better than any President before or after him at Port au Prince.

Senator POMERENE. Were any of these Presidents that they have had down there since your own acquaintance with Haiti under the domination or control of these German propagandists?

Mr. EVANS. I would like to explain here, so that the committee may really understand the difficulty and impossibility for any Haitian President alone and unaided by the United States, England, or France to withstand the powerful, ruthless, and murderous German propaganda at Port-au-Prince and Cape Haitien in the past. Leconte at one time was absolutely dominated by these Germans, and was put up by them for the Presidency, and made a strong candidate, and was all but elected several years ago. He was again their candidate in 1911 against Simon, but, having at last seen through the German intrigue, refused to head the revolution and become candidate, and only reluctantly consented at the last moment, seeing the serious peril to himself of blank refusal, being under, no doubt, special obligation to this controlling and financing German power.

During our interview at the presidental palace, alone, discussing, in view of the backward condition of the country, his—Leconte—responsibility as Haiti's newly elected President, how we in the United States, with Britain, looked for a real change in the conduct of Haiti affairs, and, indeed, that the time had arrived, unless we saw a decided improvement—the United States Government had for years felt a grave responsibility re Haiti and could not put off much longer the demand for a stable Government with, indeed, a higher civilization and a more humane conduct of political and public affairs—we would be compelled to act. I assured him, however, that there was absolutely no truth, as I had assured Simon and Haiti's responsible leaders, in the statements made by Germans and others, namely, "That we coveted an acre of Haitian territory," which, if we did, we could have had the two Republics, in fact, 20 years ago with Britain and France's unanimous consent and hearty benediction, but this was not American policy.

He believed implicitly what I said, expressed his strong desire and determination to proceed with improvements, but stated he would be helpless against the influence mentioned, and then his last wish was that I immediately return to Washington to urge the Government to assist and stand behind him.

The CHAIRMAN. Is this President Leconte to whom you refer, or is it Simon?

Mr. EVANS. I am now referring to the late President Leconte. At his special request, I came to Washington and had an interview with Second Assistant State Secretary Adee, but nothing was done, I deeply regret to say.

The CHAIRMAN. What year was this?

Mr. EVANS. The beginning of 1912. In requesting that a capable person be at once sent to Haiti in an unofficial capacity, altogether apart from our American minister or United States consul in the black Republic, yet close to the Secretary of State and United States President, and one that would have a freer access to Haiti's President than any diplomat, Mr. Adee termed what I suggested as new diplomacy and expressed a doubt as to whether the black President would really be willing to receive such. I replied that President Leconte had expressed a very similar doubt as to the United States President and our State Department, adding that unfortunately we forgot that white as well as colored were not free from suspicion. Though no one was sent from Washington, Leconte started to reform—made voodoo dances and orgies illegal; reduced the army to one-third or one-half; and raised the type standard; built the present fine barracks occupied now by our marines at Port-au-Prince. As anticipated, he was assassinated with others, and palace blown up. The leaders in Haiti have but one opinion as to how it was done. In 1912, not long after that, I left for Washington.

The CHAIRMAN. Now, Mr. Evans, after your departure in 1912 you did not return again until 1917. Tell us of your impressions as to conditions in Haiti on your arrival in 1917 and give us any facts regarding the occupation which you think might be useful to the committee.

Mr. EVANS. Before answering this question, may I briefly explain?

The CHAIRMAN. Certainly.

Mr. EVANS. Between 1912 and 1917, though away from Haiti, I was in constant correspondence with the churches and our missionary brethren there without any censor, which, however, I have had since my coming from Haiti in 1919 to date, and in my position as honorary field secretary. Thus, for instance, I was kept in close touch with affairs in Haiti by this means and what appeared in our American press. For instance, finding that our Government had landed the marines in Haiti, and preparing a treaty with the Negro Republic, I wrote to President Wilson, inclosing a number of my references—one from Right Hon. David Lloyd-George—offering to resign my church at Lansford, Pa., and as an American citizen and Christian missionary with long experience for the purpose of rendering assistance to our Government by explaining to leading Haitians the meaning of apparent "invasion" so as to avoid serious misunderstanding, bloody conflicts, if not open rebellion, and prove equally helpful to officers of American marines as to the Haitians themselves. A copy of this letter is handed here for the record and is as follows:

[Copy of letter to President Woodrow Wilson, United States.]

LANSFORD, PA., *September 1, 1915.*

Hon. WOODROW WILSON,
President of the United States.

DEAR PRESIDENT: I propose next week to visit Washington, D. C., so as to see the two native young women I brought a few years ago from Haiti, and who have just graduated at the National Missionary Training School for Colored Young Women on Lincoln Heights, D. C.

I am very anxious to have the honor of a brief interview on this occasion in reference to Haiti, either Monday, Wednesday, Thursday, or Friday of next week, and at a time most convenient to the President, especially seeing that the present is the most momentous period in the history of the black Republic (since the discovery of the island by Columbus) and the people, under the generalship of the brave, noble, and immortal Touissant L'Overture (Haiti's Lincoln and George Washington in one), secured for them both emancipation from slavery and political independence from France and Napoleon.

Hundreds of thousands of Haitians, if not indeed the rank and file of the whole Republic, when the high motives and benevolent intentions of our United States Government and the true meaning of the present step become clearly and thoroughly understood, will sincerely thank God and the present administration, through you, sir, for establishing a protectorate, thus actually at last coming to Haiti's rescue and saving her from cruel and savage bloodshed, etc., perpetrated by a few selfish, professional, and corrupted politicians exploited by certain Europeans and "hyphenated" Americans residing in Haiti, and ostensibly German bankers, merchants, etc., but filled with wicked jealousy and bitter hatred (unfortunately) against our Government, and the natural and inevitable growing influence of this Christian and humane nation in the Caribbean Sea and throughout Central America, if not, indeed, the whole civilized world at the present moment.

Inclosed [1] will show the President my own present and past relation to the black Republic and its people, as well as the "raison d'etre" in ask'ng for the honor of a short interview at this important juncture.

For Christ and Haiti,
Yours, sincerely,

L. TON EVANS,
Honorary Foreign Secretary, etc., to Haiti Missionary Council.

P. S.—Though a native of Wales, and claim among my personal friends and associates in social, moral, and religious work there the Right Hon. David Lloyd-George, M. P., Sir Sam. T. Evans, president-judge of Great Britain's war prize court, etc., yet I am a full-fledged American citizen, without either an "if" or a "hyphen."

Mr. Tumulty replied in behalf of the President, requested me to write fully, rather than have an interview with Mr. Wilson at that time, and which I immediately did, though it amounted to nothing. In fact, my candid opinion is that neither my first nor second letter went further than Secretary Tumulty.

With the committee's permission, I shall read a page of my report sent from Haiti in 1918 to my missionary committee in the States, showing, on landing and looking around both my surprise and deep appreciation of some of the good work of our American marines.

The CHAIRMAN. I wonder if you might not give that to the stenographer for incorporation in the record.

Mr. EVANS. Yes.

The CHAIRMAN. It will be unnecessary to read it. Just give it to him, if you will?

Mr. EVANS. May I read a few paragraphs before I hand it over for the record?

The CHAIRMAN. Yes.

[1] These meant references as to character and work in Haiti, etc.

(Mr. Evans thereupon read certain portions of report referred to, which is here printed, as follows:)

HAITI BAPTIST MISSION REPORT FOR 1918.

After an enjoyable voyage from New York, and in spite of war, submarines, etc., we landed safely in Haiti Thanksgiving Day, November 29, last year, and were welcomed back by all the churches and friends, and none more heartily than by late Judge Orius and family (whom we mourn and miss). Letters and wires of welcome also came from pastors and friends from all over the Republic.

POLITICAL AND SANITARY REFORMS, WITH PEACE AT LAST.

The first thing which struck me as soon as we landed and looked around was the complete change wrought through the coming of our American occupation.

The general appearance in this little filthy town and all towns and cities in Haiti, though from nestling between the hills and shaded by the broad banana leaves and stately palm and coconut trees have a beautiful tropical appearance from aboard of steamers, away at sea, are on closer acquaintance proverbially dirty, yet since our marines have been here things have greatly improved by way of well-swept roads, free of decayed vegetation and mosquito-breeding stagnant pools, etc.

What, however, surprised and pleased me most was the order and quiet, with pleasant and placid faces of natives, instead of suppressed feelings, anxious fears, and sad countenances, with exciting looks; the running here and there; then the sound of doors and shutters (there are no glass windows in Haiti) suddenly banged and bolted, followed by shots and bullets, no one seemed to know from where, in fact; then cries and wild shrieks of women and small children rending the midday as well as the midnight air—I well remember in old revolutionary days. As the result, such a calm and growing confidence among the natives themselves as the result of the occupation compels me to thank God, and I am sure tens of thousands of others here all over the Republic, do so in silent gratitude, both to the Almighty as well as the United States Government, that at last (at the earnest bidding of the British consul general and French minister in Haiti) Admiral Caperton landed our American marines that day at Port-au-Prince, and thus rescue poor, politically and revolutionary torn and bleeding Haiti from the selfish and sordid greed and iron grasp of Germans, who financially and murderously exploited this country and people for many years with Berlin money and ammunition.

Great, indeed, as above reforms have been, I saw actual transformation in prisons and hospitals (called hospices by the Catholics), and so your superintendent will quote from his recent letter to chief of hygiene department of the occupation:

"Mrs. Evans and myself take quite an interest in our little St. Marc Hospital, as we do in our local calabash (prison), and often go around the sick of the one and conduct religious services on Sunday afternoons in the other.

"We can not but notice the contrast between things to-day and years ago due to your efficient work.

"This is particularly true of the Jacmel prison and hospital which on my recent tour south as superintendent I had the privilege of visiting in company with our marine captain and doctor.

"These reforms alone, in interest of health and humanity, proved what a godsend has been the friendly intervention of our Government (so far) along these lines in Haiti.

"May I respectfully ask whether you contemplate changing the name of hospice into city or general hospital, so as to make them equally as accessible, pleasant, and agreeable to Protestants and Catholics alike, and seeing they are maintained by the Government, aided by local and general public?"

Sickly Protestants could not be persuaded to go to the hospice. There was a fundamental objection which I desired to remove, if possible, now that the United States Government operated them.

Senator POMERENE. This was a report made by you to whom?

Mr. EVANS. To my Negro missionary committee in the States, and show them some of the blessings brought to Haiti through our friendly intervention as an United States Government, and for all of which there was then a profound feeling of gratitude.

Senator POMERENE. Do you discuss the following conditions there, do you, and the revolutionary conditions?

Mr. EVANS. No; but there seemed to be such misunderstanding, if not misrepresentations, in the States, and even a bitter feeling among American Negro Baptists, absolutely ignorant of real conditions in Haiti, through the German fomented and financial revolutions—to any kind of United States intervention, that I felt it my duty as an American and a friend of Haiti, as well as a Christian missionary, and by way of an introduction to my first annual report, to correct these misunderstandings and, if possible, remove certain prejudices which colored as well as white folks sometimes are afflicted with.

My criticism of the United States Government and the Democratic administration is not that they intervened in Haiti when they landed marines under Admiral Caperton, neither to the treaty our Government negotiated and signed with the Haitian Republic, which guaranteed the Negro republic's integrity, protection, the liberties of the Haitians, and undertook to develop Haiti educationally and industrially by constitutional means and civilized and humane methods. My criticism and personal protest has been that the United States Government, either through its responsible departments at Washington or the American occupation in Haiti, or both, and under the late administration, closed the Haiti Senate and House of Representatives through United States armed force, and as if this was not sufficient, again by threats, military force, and "fraud," "raped" the Haiti constitution in absolute violation of said treaty, and, as stated in my memorandum presented to President Wilson, in direct repudiation of our own treaty obligations.

This latter and most fraudulent act clinched the nail in the coffin of our American reputation and influence in the Black Republic and with the Haitian people, as well as aroused and embittered the feeling of intelligent and loyal Negroes, and even white Americans, throughout the country against the occupation.

According to Haiti's request, as expressed through Laconte and others and the generous terms of our treaty, we assumed a friendly mandate and under-took to act the big brother.

Senator POMERENE. That is, they wanted us to be the guardian angel; is that it?

Mr. EVANS. No; something more than mere protection of life and liberty, important as that is. They expected, and as stipulated in our treaty, that they should have the full benefit of the United States money, the best American brains, as well as that of our experience in civilized government, if not in a steady and strong Christian statesmanship; but our conduct in Haiti, as described, has largely verified German predictions concerning us, namely:

"The moment the American Government puts its foot down in Haiti, whether under the plea of having land at Mole St. Nicholas for a coaling station or the pretense of an invasion by its marines at Port-au-Prince, to save ruthless murder during a revolution, and in spite of any treaty they may negotiate, their one purpose is to conquer Haiti, take away the island, and bring them all back to slavery."

Haitians have no means of judging motives, only by methods, and the real purpose of the United States Government and the American people these 90 or 95 per cent illiterate Negroes of Haiti—judging by the slamming of their senate and chamber's doors, the putting out by military force their Haitian leaders, the rape of their constitution, and roping and driving of their fathers, husbands, and brothers to prisons and marched about as slaves, and beaten down and shot without due process of law—absolutely believed to be exactly what the Germans and others had told them. We can not help being judged by our official representatives whom we send to the Black Republic and elsewhere.

To correct this impression and expose and refute the base falsehoods as to American policy, I have for years carried an old copy of the New York Outlook with me all over Haiti, containing an article by late ex-President Theodore Roosevelt, beloved and now mourned in Haiti, on the United States policy, explaining it in English, French, and patois, and pointed to the Cuban Republic in verification of Mr. Roosevelt's reassuring message to Haiti and Latin America.

The following declaration of ex-President Wilson to Congress on our entrance into the World War on the side of the Allies I had also hanging in a prominent place in my study, and read and explained repeatedly to leading Haitians who bitterly complained, and even wept, saying, "We have lost our Republic missionary," when I counseled them to be patient and wait until we brought the facts before the responsible United States Government and they were known to the great American people. It is as follows:

"WE HAVE NO SELFISH ENDS TO SERVE, WE DESIRE NO CONQUEST, NO DOMINION.

"We are, let me say again, the sincere friends of the German people, and shall desire nothing so much as the early reestablishment of intimate relations of mutual advantage between us, however hard it may be for them for the time being to believe that this is spoken from our hearts.

"We have borne with their present Government through all these bitter months, because of their friendship, that friendship exercising a patience and forbearance which would otherwise have been impossible. We shall happily still have an opportunity to prove that friendship in our daily attitude and action toward the millions of men and women of German birth, and native sympathy, who live among us and share our life, and we shall be proud to prove toward all who are in fact loyal to their neighbors and to the Government in the hour of test.

"It is a distressing thing and an oppressive duty, gentlemen of the Congress, which I have performed in thus addressing you. There are it may be many months of fiery trial and sacrifice ahead of us. It is a fearful thing to lead this great, peaceful people into war—into the most terrible and disastrous of all wars—civilization itself seeming to be in the balance.

"But the right is more precious than peace, and we shall fight for the things which we have always carried nearest our hearts—for democracy, for the right of those who submit to authority to have a voice in their own government, for the rights and liberties of small nations, for a universal dominion of right by such a concert of free peoples as shall bring peace and safety to all nations and make the world itself at last free." (United States Congress on Apr. 2, 1917.)

From my reading and study of the treaty we entered Haiti solemnly pledged to help place her and her people eventually on such a civilized basis as to enable her to enter the circle of surrounding civilized and progressive nations, and nothing should be permitted to cause us to deviate from this purpose and play into the hands of Haiti's foes if not also the enemies of the United States.

The CHAIRMAN. Mr. Evans, I do not believe the committee can go so far afield. We have got to hold to the facts you observed there, and not to the expression of opinion or the history of your efforts in defense of the United States.

Mr. EVANS. The purpose of our Government going to Haiti is one thing while the violation of the treaty and the conduct of the American marines and gendarmes in the island is another. These should not be confused, so I felt justified in explaining this in the report to my missionary board.

The CHAIRMAN. I understand this part of your report to your board has been given for the record. Now, let us come back to what you saw on your return to the island.

Senator POMERENE. At what time?

The CHAIRMAN. In 1917 and thereafter. For example, if you care to speak of the amendment to the constitution; the dissolution of the Parliament or the corvee, any one of them, the committee will be glad to hear you.

Mr. EVANS. I will say that the corvee business was brought to my attention not long after I returned. It was an old custom in Haiti, but never I think a law. It is customary in backward countries for farmers, or those who have their small habitations or small holdings in Haiti, once or twice a year to devote two or three days or so to help repair roads opposite their own farms.

The occupation in Haiti, however, intentionally or ignorantly put a new and altogether an erroneous meaning to it by actually turning it into an instrument for oppressing and torturing the Haitian people, and exciting their passions, and apparently some times for no other purpose than to provide them with an excuse to beat, if not shoot them down. Excitable gendarmes in the United States marines' employ and often, under influence of liquor, when arresting, roping, then drving along roads, and mountains as gangs of African slaves rather than as citizens of the Haiti Republic, whom the great American Government by a sacred treaty, had officially pledged to protect, were very often roughly and brutally handled, for no native could be expected to voluntarily submit to such humiliation. From what I have seen and heard I verily believe that more have met their deaths through the corvee thus illegally practiced, willfully or ignorantly, by marines and gendarmes and acquiesced in by those in supreme command and at Washington than were killed in open conflict with Cacos, if it was not indeed the chief cause and mainstay of Cacoism.

Senator KING. Who did this?

Mr. EVANS. The American occupation.

Senator KING. Who?

Mr. EVANS. There was a captain or lieutenant at every town or village throughout Haiti in official charge of these gendarmes (Negro soldiers), armed and chosen by these white marines of the American occupation. Many of these marines, and probably most of the gendarmes, were fond of drink. The latter under official orders of the marines would catch, arrest, and rope the natives and drive them to prison, and from prison to work on the roads, and under such conditions often cruelly deal with them.

The last Sunday of June, 1918, going on Sunday afternoon from Gros Morne's service toward Jacmel, in the far southeastern part of the Republic, I met several gangs, altoghter perhaps 60 or 80 or more, and in charge of gendarme officials who rode along side and well armed. On inquiry from the gendarme officers, I was informed that these were paid 1 gourde or, in American money, 20 cents a week; without any food. It is therefore to imagine how such ill-paid, ill-fed native driven to work like these, many miles away from homes and families as there were, become uneasy, irritated, and even revolt, which invariably means death.

The CHAIRMAN. Will you give specific instances of ill treatment that you saw yourself?

Mr. EVANS. I have repeatedly seen ill treatment. Both in and outside of St. Marc, perhaps 2 or 3 miles on the way to Gonaive, I have seen in the gangs at work men, for merely turning the head and without the slightest provocation as far as I could see struck until actually stunned. Prisoners from St. Marc working around the gendarme barracks, almost opposite where we lived, I have seen on week days and on Sunday unmercifully striking the poor native, and I have walked on and intervened at times on my way to church with my family.

The CHAIRMAN. Struck by whom?

Mr. EVANS. By gendarmes, and at times a boss, the marine officer, would appoint as overseer over the natives, who would be a robust Negro.

The CHAIRMAN. Who dealt the blow, a marine or a gendarme?

Mr. EVANS. By the gendarme or the native boss. The marine officer himself would seldom be seen with the corvee gangs. The marine captain or lieutenant would generally be at his headquarters. The marine chief at this time in St. Marc would be either Capt. Kenny or Capt. Brown. They would have several of these gangs in two, three, or more places along the roads, in special charge of armed gendarmes.

The CHAIRMAN. The man who dealt the blow was a member of the Haitian gendarmerie organized by the marines; is that right?

Mr. EVANS. Yes; exactly so. He would be under him and receive his orders from him as chief of the occupation for that district.

Senator POMERENE. But a black?

Mr. EVANS. Yes; they would be natives.

Senator POMERENE. You do not mean to say that our marines used violence?

Mr. EVANS. Yes; though I myself never actually saw this. Of course I would not expect our marines and white officers of the American occupation to use any violence in my presence or that of any other Christian missionary. They give the orders and see they are carried out. They supervise, receive reports, and are responsible. It is quite possible that gendarmes at times, unless deterred from utter fear of being shot, do certain things on their own initiative.

Senator KING. Mr. Evans, we will devote our attention to fixing the responsibility, and if you will limit yourself to that and answer the questions we will get along.

Mr. EVANS. I have already stated that marines are seldom with corvee gangs, and would not personally if they were guilty of violence in the presence of a missionary. They mostly are at headquarters and give orders. I am anxious to assist the committee to ascertain real facts.

Senator POMERENE. You said these workmen would get 20 cents a week in American money?

Mr. EVANS. No; but that the natives received an equivalent to our 20 cents in value. They would be paid in Haitian money, which would be then 1 gourde.

Senator POMERENE. Paid by whom?

Mr. EVANS. By the United States general receiver, through the American occupation's marine officers.

Senator POMERENE. Well, I know, but did that money come from the Haiti Government, or from the United States forces?

Mr. EVANS. I understand that all moneys in Haiti come through the hands of the United States general receiver, who pays everybody through the occupation, or the American marine officers, and even the Catholic archbishop, bishops, priests, etc.

Senator POMERENE. Well, it was stated here yesterday that most of these men were called in for a few days, and stayed voluntarily because of the good food they got.

Mr. EVANS. That is absolutely wrong, speaking generally. This might be so with a very few who act as bosses, or overseers under the gendarmes on the roads, or in gaol, but false as to the majority of corvee men and roped gangs referred to.

Senator POMERENE. Let me ask you a further question, because we do not want any misunderstanding as to the facts. Is the committee to understand that the money which was paid these men for their work was money raised by the Haitian Government by taxation?

Mr. EVANS. I can only reply that I understand that every dollar in Haiti, whether American loans, imports, or local taxes, come directly through the hands of America's general receiver.

Senator POMERENE. But they were Haitian funds, were they, raised by the Haitian taxpayers or by the Haitian importers?

Mr. EVANS. I do not think this is so. Referring to the food question, I saw while in the prison at St. Marc these men, working under the corvee, lined up in front of my cell and driven out about 6 o'clock in the morning, often with nothing but a little coffee, marched under armed guard to work miles away, then brought back to prison, carefully searched, and compelled to wait from about 4 until nearly 6 without being fed; a few times when the captain was said to have gone drinking, with keys, if not money, there was not a scrap for any.

The CHAIRMAN. Was this at St. Marc?

Mr. EVANS. Yes; at St. Marc. I have seen these men here struck with such force by the gendarme officer, and for the merest trifle, until they would fall like logs. Many for want of food fainting and at times falling their full length on the hard floor of the prison yard. Whether once members of the corvee gang or not I can not say, but I have actually seen dead bodies covered with vermin exposed and naked for days—one would be obliged to pass, with men and women, and some of latter with babies—lying around.

Senator POMERENE. Let me ask you, because I want to get the facts just as they are, and I have no interest in this matter at all. You speak of these men being struck, and you said they were struck by Haitian gendarmes.

Mr. EVANS. Yes.

Senator POMERENE. Are we to understand that this method of discipline was encouraged or fostered or directed by the American marines, or was that a general method of attempting to enforce discipline?

Mr. EVANS. Certainly, I am sorry to say. It was owing to the low type of gendarmes so often employed by the marines, and again through the want of proper discipline, if not in some cases the immoral and drunken habits, inexperience, and ignorance of the native language by the American captain or lieutenant in charge, though probably there are improvements since the various inquiries recently made and publicity and exposure through the press.

Senator POMERENE. Well, can we infer from what you say that the marines, or the American occupation, has been in any wise responsible for this condition?

Mr. EVANS. Positively. There has been a sad neglect, even recklessness, in the choice of these gendarmes by marine officers, in view of the great authority and power of "life and death" given them in various sections of Haiti; and again there has been a criminal laxity on the part of the general and chief of gendarmerie d'Haiti at Port au Prince and his subordinate officer at Cape Haitien in not demanding regular reports of all activities and strictly supervising same. Where there has been care taken, proper discipline exercised by an intelligent, experienced, right-living marine officer, there has been no trouble with gendarmes and no friction between these native officers and the people. Whisky (taffia) and women have been large factors in the demoralization of many marines, but most so of the type of gendarmes these marines employed.

Senator POMERENE. Mr. Evans, we all agree that such a condition ought not to exist, but suppose the marines were withdrawn now; if the Haitian gendarmes were using these brutal methods with our marines there, what likely would happen if there were no marines there in the way of treatment of these workmen?

Mr. EVANS. I think my statement at the opening and in my memorandum to President Wilson in October, 1918, and how I came to Washington urging our own United States Government to assume a friendly mandate over Haiti and act the big brother is a proof that I am not in agreement with some of the witnesses from Haiti and some of our own American people, that our marine should be taken out and our Government be prepared to withdraw from the Black Republic. This would be an admission of failure to carry out our treaty and a certainty that it would not be to the real interest of Haiti itself for years to come. My firm belief is, now that there is no danger with Germany, and as one of the results of this Senate committee inquiry the American marines should be reduced to about 220 and their personnel of a higher type and, with all other departments, a civil occupation replace the military, through which the marines and a higher type and best natives as gendarmes function under its strict supervision.

Senator POMERENE. Mr. Evans, that does not directly answer my question. I am trying to get your idea as to what would happen.

Mr. EVANS. I do not exactly know——

Senator POMERENE. In the treatment of these men——

Mr. EVANS. I can only express an opinion——

Senator POMERENE. By the Haitian gendarmes, in the event that our people were not there.

Mr. EVANS. I can only express an opinion; and my opinion is this: That under responsible Haitian authority, who would exercise fairly good judgment in the choice of their gendarmes, supervise their conduct, and speak their language, that it could not, indeed, be much worse than what I have seen in some cases under many American marines.

Senator POMERENE. Now, let me ask you another question. How many instances of this brutal treatment have you seen?

Mr. EVANS. In the discharge of my work as superintendent missionary and visiting our mission church on Gros Morne and on the way to Jacmel and southeast of the Republic in company with our native pastor and other assistant preachers Sunday morning the last of June, 1918, I saw, for instance, women decently dressed on their way to the Baptist mission church (the only Protestant church near by in that section) actually stopped at the headquarters of the native gendarmes. Immediately after and going the opposite way, saw two groups of natives, and including native members and native preachers who had been caught, roped tightly and cruelly together, and driven like slaves toward the same calabash. Then I saw our native missionary turning back, and, galloping toward me, shouting, "Missionary, missionary, come quickly."

I at once hastened to see what was the matter, that he and others were so excited, and at once liberated the women, who came along to church. When told by the native (excited, if not intoxicated) corporal they had committed no crime and there was no charge brought against them, I demanded they should be freed and permitted to come back with us to the House of God. This he sternly refused to do and forcibly drove them along like cattle. Where they were put and what became of them, I do not know.

From the common talk of these mountain people, and what I witnessed, I believe that many are caught, arrested, and roped thus on Sunday, as well as during the week, not merely for the "corvee," but for the sake of graft and extortion of money, when some would be let free again on payment of 2 or 3 gourdes.

As soon as we reached Jacmel, about perhaps 40 miles or so away, I paid a visit of inspection to see the prison and hospital, with our American occupation's chief officer and white doctor (of the occupation), I was startled to see two or more prisoners with their arms like jelly or raw beef and being treated by our American doctor.

As he was putting the salve on their arms, while I stood watching him, and the captain by my side, and unable to understand what this meant, and forgetting what I saw the previous Sunday on Gros Morne, I turned around and said, "Why, Captain, have you some kind of an epidemic here in Jacmel?" "Oh,

no," answered the captain, "it is the roping business connected with the corvee." While walking with the said doctor to see the new hospital, I asked, "How often do these cases occur such as you treated just now at the prison?" "They constantly occur," replied American marine doctor, adding, " I am heartily ashamed of them. It is a disgrace to the United States, and to us all as American people." Such was the appreciation of these poor, suffering natives, and the comfort and ease ministered by this sympathetic, humane, medical officer, that they were ready to drop on their knees and actually kiss the feet
· of the doctor.

I mentioned to the marine captain of gendarmes at Jacmel what Rev. Nosirel Lherisson, the native missionary, and myself witnessed the previous Sunday on going to our mission church on Gros Morne.

Senator KING. Who was the captain?

Mr. EVANS. It was something like Capt. Williams, or Williamson, if I remember well. A well-built officer, genial, and, I should take, a high type of a marine officer, and well spoken of by the Baptist native pastor and others. The captain voluntarily informed me, though a nominal Catholic in the States, he regularly attended the Protestant church, and much enjoyed the preaching of this native Haitian, whom he praised as a good man, doing excellent Christian and educational work in that town and section, only somewhat hampered for lack of proper means adding that he became so interested in his efforts that he had written requesting the Government to present its unused plot of land for Rev. Lherisson to build and enlarge his boys' school.

In reply to my question, " Gros Morne is in the Leogane district, and not that of Jacmel, so you should see Lieut. Kulp, who when he gets the facts will no doubt take steps to remedy the matter." I thanked him for this information and after a few more days busily inspecting our rural public schools for the native children in the far interior many miles from Jacmel, I returned to Port Au Prince, on my way back to St. Marc.

Meantime, however, Sunday came, while still at Jacmel (first Sunday of July, 1918), when as an ex-pastor and missionary I presided with this native whom I had ordained some 25 years before. As the result of the faithful work done, and growth of church, and missions all around, something like 700 and even more attend the communion service the first Lord's day each month. These come the Saturday for Saturday evening conference, 20, 30, 40, and even from 50 miles away, report converts, candidates for baptism, sickness, death, or any misconduct among members, which are all carefully attended to before they partake of the sacred rite of Lord's Supper the following Sunday.

The native pastor pointed out the fewness of the men present, less than one-half the usual number, and when I asked the reason why, " Oh, the ' corvee ' of our American marines," was the answer, as he shook his head. " Missionary," he added, " it grieves me to see the present condition of my country under the ' occupation.' " These men, husbands, fathers, and brothers are mortally afraid to leave their little homes, even on Sundays, to attend their church. For if seen, they are in peril of being caught, arrested, roped, roughly handled, and driven as described like slaves to prison, to work many miles from home, and for two and three weeks and more without their families knowing anything about them, whether dead or living.

I saw a number of letters written on old scraps of paper in the native patois, asking their pastor to excuse them, and telling him their distress and why compelled to hide from the gendarmes as if they were ravaging wolves or a pack of blood-thirsty bloodhounds haunting every hill and valley, chosen by and in the employ and officered by American marines of my own United States Government, solemnly pledged by treaty to protect the liberty, limb, and life of the natives of Haiti.

I insert in the record a copy of one of these notes to the Jacmel missionary pastor, penned, no doubt, with a trembling hand and in native-made ink by this Negro assistant preacher, and so faint that it can not all be deciphered, hence can only quote a part, expressing sadness of being thus deprived of the means of grace and begging dear pastor to pray that this reign of terror and death may soon come to an end:

" LA VALLEE DE JACMEL.

"Le cher Pasteur P. N. LHERISSON.

" MON CHER PASTEUR: Je vous prie votre bonte si'l y'apossibble en vous de me faire trouve un permi entre les mains les autorites. Car je trouve des miserables legars le travo," etc. ; here it becomes too indistinct to continue.

While in Haiti I expect the committee's permission to call Pastor Lherisson, with some of these native preachers, as well as those from Gros Morne, to testify in reference to the groups roped and driven as slaves, and providing this committee asks our President to issue a proclamation, to be inserted, in English and French, in the Monitor and all other Haitian papers in Haiti, inviting the natives to testify freely before this committee investigating affairs in the Black Republic, and guaranteeing ample protection of the United States Government to same, with heavy penalty for intimidation and threatened reprisals, whether made by American occupation corporation or priests of the Roman Catholic Church (in pay of American marines).

The CHAIRMAN. Give us what other matters you may have to put in the record. Is there anything more you would like to say?

Mr. EVANS. Yes; I wish to add that crossing rivers and high mountains (Gros Morne), and as directed by the marine captain of Jacmel, I came to the little town of Leogane, on the plain, to see Lieut. Kulp, and stayed that evening and partook of this genial marine's hospitality. On being informed of the brutal conduct of his Gros Morne gendarmes, and names of our witnesses, he faithfully promised to immediately attend to this serious matter.

I am prepared, however, to show this committee that Gen. Alexander Williams, chief of the whole gendarmie of Haiti (and said marine officer Kulp's superior in command), deliberately interfered and prevented the lieutenant of the Leogane district from discharging his official duty of investigating these brutal and criminal charges brought against the Gros Morne gendarmes, who with others should be demanded to appear before you gentlemen.

Not finding Gen. Williams at the headquarters of Gendarmerie d'Haiti in Port-au-Prince after my leaving Leogane next day, I returned by train home to St. Marc, after my missionary tour of inspection of church, missions, and schools throughout the southeast section of Haiti and, owing to a proposed conference in reference to a national normal and industrial college I was arranging to be held at the Haiti bureau of public instruction, with our American superintendent of public instruction, the Haitian inspector, to which we invited Col. Russell (in supreme command of United States marines, etc.), Gen. Williams, Dr. Maclean, Dr. Laroche (Haiti National Council), Dr. Livingstone (United States consul), Cape Haiti, etc., and my planning to leave with wife and children on a visit to see my missionary committee in the States, as well as seek an interview with President Wilson and Secretary Lansing at Washington, I wrote the following letter to Gen. Williams:

ST. MARC, HAITI, *July 17, 1918.*

Gen. WILLIAMS,
    Chief of the Gendarmerie d'Haiti.

DEAR GENERAL: I have already called the special attention of your Lieut. Kulp, of Leogane, to what must be termed not only an undue interference with the rights of the Haitian people, and especially the quiet and orderly members of our Baptist Mission Church on Gros Morne, while on their way to public worship and to particularly attend holy communion service, but the inhuman and brutal if not savage conduct of his gendarmes (in the Gros Morne section), as witnessed by myself, our missionary pastor, Rev. Nosirel Lherisson (Jacmel), and many others on the Sunday morning of June 30, ultimo.

For fear, therefore, that Lieut. Kulp has not been able to see to this matter, and act in a definite way with a view to at least the dismissal of these gendarmes as totally unfit to serve "our occupation" in any capacity really, and whose conduct actually and naturally filled the Haitians generally with fear and dread, and righteously inflamed them and engendered hatred against the gendarmes themselves, and moreover against our American occupation throughout Haiti and even indeed against our United States Government and President, which must not be permitted to go on.

What I personally saw this early morning, not only the stopping of two brethren and two quietly and decently dressed native sisters at the headquarters of the gendarmes' corporal, while going to the house of God, but the catching, arresting, and roping in a cruel manner, if not barbaric, groups of men, who were made to march like a pack of slaves, brigands, or murderers (among whom were some of our native preachers), and whose arms I have found afterwards (and under treatment of our own white medical men of the occupation) a whole mass of jelly, etc., which reminded me of brutal slavery with savage treatment practiced by unfortunate Belgium a few years ago in Africa.

And this, forsooth, though we are in Haiti, and where to-day these people are supposed to be under the civilized, humane, if not Christian Government of the United States and the protection of our American flag.

It is generally believed and openly said by the inhabitants of Gros Morne and Jacmel sections that many of these drinking and lowest type of gendarmes of our occupation continually arrest, rope brutally, and treat these poor innocent people for the sake of dishonestly extorting money from them, who when they pay 2 or 3 gourds may be set free.

I made a careful inquiry on Gros Morne this Sunday morning (June 30) and, so as to make sure as to whether the so-called prisoners had committed any crime or there were serious charges of wrongdoing brought against them, and being assured by the native corporal there was absolutely nothing, I dismounted from my horse and demanded they should be set free and allowed to accompany me and Lherisson to our mission church that morning. This was peremptorily refused by this excited and apparently intoxicated corporal, though his fellow gendarme tried to persuade him to do so.

For this reason, therefore, may I ask you to see if Lieut. Kulp has been able to take any action, and if not will you call his attention to it and dismiss them, especially the corporal (right away) as irresponsible savages, unworthy and unfit for their important positions.

*   *   *   *   *   *

It is believed and stated that the gendarmes of the sections mentioned are heavy taffia drinkers (native liquor), most immoral, ruffians, etc.. From their conduct that day, and more especially that of the corporal (Desselus), his wild gestures, excitement, etc., from influence of alcohol or other evil spirits, I am personally confirmed of the truth of all they say.

On my return to the States (if possible within a few weeks) in order to report the religious, moral, and social conditions to my missionary Baptist boards, practically representing 3,000,000 Negroes, morally backed by 5,000,000 more white Baptists of the North and South land of the United States, and particularly interested in our Haiti mission just now, I shall therefore be indeed glad to be assured by you as chief of our gendarmerie that Lieut. Kulp, on whom I called last week, and who faithfully promised, has acted, and that these men have been dismissed even as unworthy of such important positions and authority under our marines.

As chief of gendarmerie over Haiti (knowing of the sufferings caused by gendarmes through drink and abuse of power), I shall be glad if you impress upon these gendarmes through your marine officers that on no account they should deliberately inflame these poor people and prejudice them against our occupation, and at this time create hatred and wrath toward our United States Government.

No doubt our (American) folks there celebrated the Fourth in a manner worthy of our noble traditions and the flag, which to-day flies over our brave boys fighting at this moment in the trenches of Europe with British, French, etc., for the sanctity of treaties, liberties, and rights of small nations like Belgium, Servia, and even this little Black Republic of Haiti.

Yours, very sincerely,

L. TON EVANS,
Baptist Missionary Superintendent.

Returning to Haiti on the 18th or 19th of December, 1918, after said visit to the United States and Washington, when I presented the memorandum to President Wilson, Secretary of State Lansing, and Chairman Hitchcock, of the Senate Foreign Relations Committee, setting forth conditions in Haiti, and praying for a special commission of inquiry, and found my Negro missionary committee intimidated if not threatened by certain officials of State Department, in collusion with Marine officers in Haiti, who intercepted if not confiscated my private and official letters, demanding, it seems, my immediate recall on account of my Christian and educational activities in behalf of these poor Haitians, I called that very day at our American occupation's headquarters to pay my respects to Brig. Gen. Catlin, who had succeeded Col. John H. Russell as the United States Government's chief in supreme command of all marine and land forces in the Black Republic, giving him a copy of said memorandum, showing him Hon. A. A. Adee's official reply in behalf of the President and Secretary of State, assuring me after the strict investigation the Government was supposed to be then carrying on (through Gen. Catlin, Gen. Williams,

Maj. Welles, etc.) in the Black Republic, Mr. Adee would immediately further communicate with me.

At the close of this interview with Chief Catlin, a very amiable gentleman, who thanked me for calling, and information and explanation given, he informed me that Gen. Williams (who was seated with Brig. Gen. Catlin when I entered the office that morning) wished to see me at gendarmerie headquarters before I left for St. Marc.

The following letters to Gen. Williams and Brig. Gen. Catlin refers to that interview, the Gros Mourne scandal, and Gen. Williams's special interest and activities through Haitian courts to uphold and vindicate a drunken American Marine officer who had been disciplined by Col. Russell and in the interest of military discipline and United States occupation efficiency in Haiti.

BUREAU OF THE SUPERINTENDENT OF PUBLIC INSTRUCTION,
Port au Prince, Haiti, December 20, 1918.

Gen. WILLIAMS,
Chief of Gendarmerie d'Haiti.

DEAR SIR: Referring to yesterday's conversation (at your request to me, through Brig. Gen. Catlin), I herein inclose quotation from letter I wrote Judge Obas, Cape Haiti, on July 19:

" I received mandate requesting me to appear to be questioned about something purported to have been uttered by me about somebody. I shall be glad for definite information as to person and specific (exact) nature of complaint or alleged remarks.

"As United States citizen, and general secretary of American Baptists in Haiti, I am entitled to this definite information from you and your court. I must say, however, that as I plan to leave with my wife and family if possible on the Panama boat the end of this month on official business with my board and interview our President at Washington, it will be impossible for me to be at the cape the time you mention."

(Here is reference to propose Dillard's conference with superintendent of public instruction, etc.)

"After this definite information requested has been received, I may arrange what steps to take, and when I return, sometime in October this year, when you can expect me at the cape."

(The Cape Haiti and court are in the north under direct control of Maj. Welles, marine officer next in command to Gen. Williams, under whom the drunken marine disciplined by the colonel was still employed by the occupation, and which major is officially held for insubordination and directly responsible for the wholesale murders in the north and perpetuation of corvee, etc.)

Having therefore learned for the first time through you yesterday, and not as requested in July from Judge Obas, in my letter, that the supposed complainant is the late occupation's marine officer at St. Raphael, and seeing (as already stated to you at your office) that Col. John H. Russell, supreme commander of United States Marine Corps and land forces ashore in Haiti, has left for the States, my own judgment is that in the absence of said Col. Russell this matter can not be properly and legally entered into at the present time.

Again, inasmuch as Col. Russell and myself alone were present at this personal and private official interview, and therefore the only two persons who can testify as to what exactly passed and was thereat said, entirely in the interest of the United States service in Haiti, as well as in the interest of the moral welfare of the said officer of St. Raphael, himself, for which the colonel thanked me, and with all respect for you and Judge Obas (Cape), it is still my further and firm judgment that this matter does not come within the jurisdiction of our Haitian court.

Of course, if you yourself (personally and officially) wish to insist on forcing the said judge to take up the matter in spite of the facts pointed out, then, and under protest, I shall go cheerfully and submit to attending the court, but in order to arrange for my witnesses from St. Raphael, Dondon, Grande Riviere, Trou, and may be from the Cape, and so as to prove beyond a doubt that at a given date, etc., said officer was under the influence of liquor, and further justify an American citizen and a Christian missionary laboring in Haiti for the social, moral, and religious welfare of both white and native, together with the course I felt it my duty to take in my personal and private interview with the supreme head of our American occupation in Haiti at the time, and with a view to save both our United States service as well as the said marine officer himself, if possible (thus vindicating Col. Russell's action and subsequent sending forth the proclamation prohibiting all liquors to be sold marines and gendarmes of the United States Government), hence must ask Judge Obas and the court to grant reasonable time, with name and definite complaint given in meantime, say until the middle of February, if not the last week of that month (being expected the arrival of Dr. Dillard by any boat).

I am responsible only for what transpired between me and the colonel, for which service he thanked me. Though as a Christian missionary I advised moral suasion, I know not the military method Col. Russell (who naturally knew more about his marine officers, and may be their drinking habits than anyone else) felt compelled to take in this particular case or the military discipline he imposed. It would be presumption on the part of a Christian missionary therefore to criticize him.

This drinking habit among marines and gendarmes is well known in Haiti, and so increased as to jeopardize in fact the work of the occupation and become such a menace to the United States service in Haiti that Col. Russell himself on the 16th day of July, 1918 (exactly three days after my writing Judge Obas), felt it necessary as officer in supreme command of all marines and land forces operating in the black Republic to issue a proclamation absolutely forbidding the sale of intoxicants to all men in uniform, under a very heavy penalty.

On seeing this proclamation, I wrote to immediately thank the colonel, and praying in the interest of all he would extend the same to include both white and native civilians throughout Haiti.

Under these significant and serious circumstances, therefore, I can hardly believe that such an important officer of our United States Government, as the chief of the whole gendarmerie of Haiti, through personal forcing and display of official activities of such matter as upholding and actually vindicating the drinking and drunken habits of a marine officer under you and Maj. Welles of the Cape, thus permitting yourself to go on record as sympathizing with those whose conduct is termed by said proclamation as directly inimical to the interests of the United States, thus in so doing contradict, oppose, and condemn Col. Russell's discipline, and officially do what you can to defeat the efforts of four superior officers and in supreme command, as well as Secretary Daniels of the United States Navy, to save the morale of the boys and secure military efficiency of the American occupation.

You have no doubt received word from Mr. Stabler (Latin American department of our Government) as to presentation of recent petition (of which inclosed memorandum is copy). I may add that the State Department has replied not only of receipt of same but that the United States Government, through a department interested in Haiti, are seriously considering matters set forth therein. An official request may soon be made for leading Haitians to visit Washington, therefore, and previous to appointment of commission.

Dr. Dillard of the Rockefeller Foundation is expected in January or beginning of February to survey Haiti and confer with Haitian leaders and our Government officers refounding of an industrial school, such as referred to in memorandum.

I deeply regret the attitude you thought fit to assume yesterday toward the very serious affair on Gros Morne last June, brought to your attention and marine officer Kulp. When informed that my presence is required at Cape, and as American citizen will claim the presence at court of our United States consul, Dr. Livingston, to whom I have an official letter from Secretary of State Robert Lansing, etc.

Yours,

L. TON EVANS.

A copy of above, with following explanatory note, was also sent Brig. Gen. Catlin:

BUREAU OF SUPERINTENDENT OF PUBLIC INSTRUCTION,
Port au Prince, Haiti, December 20, 1918.

Gen. CATLIN,
Chief of the American Occupation in Haiti.

DEAR GENERAL: As officer in supreme command of our United States Marines and military forces and successor of Col. John H. Russell, I feel that I ought to send you inclosed copy of my letter to Gen. Alexander E. Williams, whose attitude, of course, and language as an officer of our occupation when I called Thursday at your request entirely took me by surprise.

I naturally put this down to some grave misunderstanding on his part as to my own standing, and long and close relation with Haiti, our responsible United States Government, as well as to our own occupation, but it is most unfortunate that this should happen in a person holding such responsible and honorable a function.

The inclosed letter makes reference to your worthy predecessor, Col. Russell, and explains itself, and again calls attention to the arresting and roping of our native members, etc., on morning of last Sunday, June, this year. I respectfully called the attention of Lieut. Kulp and the general to this. Unless inquired into and given the satisfaction demanded, it may have to be investigated by another committee or commission and when witnesses shall have a chance to testify.

I sincerely thank you for the interview Thursday morning and information, and earnestly hope that such a gallant officer, who has seen distinguished service at the front and helped in bringing about the glorious victory for sanctity of treaties, liberties, and rights of small nations like Haiti, etc., will be spared many years to serve our flag with same ability and unswerving loyalty in the trying climate of this black republic.

For Christ, Haiti, and humanity.

L. Ton Evans.

PROCLAMATION ISSUED BY COL. JOHN H. RUSSELL.

The sale of intoxicants to persons of military and naval forces of the United States in uniform is forbidden throughout the Republic of Haiti, from and after July 20, 1918. A violation of this order will be considered inimical to the interests of the United States, and the offenders will be liable to trial before a United States military tribunal.

Done at Port au Prince, Republic of Haiti, this 16th day of July, 1918.

JOHN H. RUSSELL,
Colonel, United States Marine Corps,
Commanding United States Forces ashore in Haiti.

Senator POMERENE. Is he in charge of the marines there?

Mr. EVANS. No; Gen. Alexander Williams was the chief of the whole gendarmerie of Haiti (the native armed police), seeing the great authority and power placed in the hands of the gendarmes all over the Republic, this was really one of the very most responsible positions in Haiti, hence he is rightly blamed for the low, drunken, and ferocious type of gendarmes under his Marine officers all over Haiti, and for the lack of discipline, brutality, resulting in the killings, both of prisoners and Cacos in the calabash (jail) and in the bush. Such officers as Maj. Welles (Cape), Capt. Brown (St. Marc), Capt. Kenny (Massade), Lieut. Haug (St. Raphael), etc., were under him, if not appointed by him, and chief of the American occupation would in most cases be obliged to act through this Gen. Williams in the event of punishing drunken marine officers.

Senator POMERENE. Let me ask you just one question. You can answer it generally, I think. You said you have been there for many years.

Mr. EVANS. Yes.

Senator POMERENE. Twenty-eight years, did you say?

Mr. EVANS. Altogether; laboring in and for Haiti.

Senator POMERENE. And, of course, you were there for many years before the American marines entered?

Mr. EVANS. Exactly so.

Senator POMERENE. And you had the opportunity of observing the treatment of the Haitians by their Haitian officers, superiors, etc.?

Mr. EVANS. Yes, sir.

Senator POMERENE. Just as you had the opportunity of observing their treatment since 1917 in the way that you have described here. Now, were these people treated more cruelly while we were there than they were before or is there any difference in their treatment? What have you to say, comparatively?

Mr. EVANS. I readily admit that a certain type of Haitians, unless sometimes watched and cautioned, when elevated to certain position, maybe love of authority, and in many cases overzeal and devotion for his white employer, suffers somewhat from a swollen head, and overrides his duty and goes beyond his authority, and especially this is done when they think it pleases the white man.

This is a special reason for a higher type of Marine officers, sober, intelligent, sympathetic, yet firm, strong in moral fiber, with knowledge of men and faith in the black race, and his ability and readiness to respond when treated "with a little of the milk of human kindness." During all the years spent in Haiti, and with all my traveling and mingling with these folks, I have seen little of real barbarity and cruelty among them and have never seen women actually fighting or two men stripped and pounding one another. There has often been yelling and wild demonstrations and terrible threats.

Marines have told me through Haiti that when properly treated and firm discipline exercised, and they come to understand the language of the natives and, moreover, show them a little of the higher educational and Christian civilization of the United States, and true American homes—there is seldom if ever a friction. We need more of our Marine officers—generals and colonels—sent to Haiti, imbued with a true missionary spirit and a real Christian optimism .

Senator POMERENE. Well, am I right in drawing this inference from your statement here, that your thought is that the American marines should stay there and control the situation, but they should have men in control who would use more humane methods in controlling these men; is that your idea?

Mr. EVANS. No; not exactly. It is that our United States Government should stay in Haiti, but not the marines as such. My demand is for a civil occupation composed of some of the most intelligent, broadminded, experienced jurists and Christian statesmen we have in the United States, in cooperation with and supervision of the Haiti Government, can freely function; and something like 200 of high type marines, and a gendarmerie composed of the most intelligent, cleanest, and best Haitians, subject to the civil authority, will suffice for protection.

Senator POMERENE. Well, I used the expression "United States marines" inadvertently; I meant really the United States Government or its representatives. Is that your idea?

Mr. EVANS. Emphatically so. For instance, President Laconte and President Simmon (who immediately preceded him), and for reasons already given this committee the latter and his government were ruthlessly overthrown; and the former, after only being in office a year, with brightest prospects and just started most important reforms, when behold he is fatally struck down by the hidden hand assassin (soon after my own return in 1912), as well as such intelligent, educated natives, if not Christian statesmen, as Gen. Firmin (who wrote a French life of late President Theodore Roosevelt, much admired and greatly mourned in Haiti); ex-Senator Dutreville Lamour, ex-attorney general of the Republic; Voltaire Dommond; ex-deputy Dr. Nerva Ghouse, Hon. J. N. Leger, for years in Haiti legation at Washington (author of Haiti, Her History, Her Traducers), as well as leaders, if not rank and file, of Haiti to-day, sick and tired and even heartily ashamed of these political disturbances and devastating revolutions, moreover have for years sincerely felt (because of these insidious and powerful influences and political and profiteering intrigues invariably operating through the financial and officially allied (with the Haiti Government) Roman Catholic Church and her European French-speaking priests as agency and shield) that their only hope was in a close alliance and real union with the United States, and that their political, industrial, educational, as well indeed as their spiritual, salvation can only be realized through their strong government's protection and their generous Christian philanthropists' practical support and efficient leadership for many years to come.

This conviction was universally and most sincerely and enthusiastically expressed in their following prayer and petition to the Rockefeller, Carnegie, and other believers in and lovers of the race in America early in the year 1911, and reads thus in French:

NÉCESSITÉ URGENTE D'UN COLLEGE NORMAL ET INDUSTRIAL A HAITI. APPEL DIRECT DES PRINCIPAUX HAITIANS, AUX PHILANTHROPES, AUX AMIS DE LA RACE NOIRE, ET A TOUS CEUX QUI, EN AMERIQUE, CROIENT A SON DEVELOPPEMENT INTELLECTUEL, MORAL, ET INDUSTRIEL.

Nous soussignes, natifs d'Haiti, sans distinction de croyances religieuses ou de partis politiques, en vue de considerations patriotiques les plus elevees et dans le but d'assurer l'avancement moral et religieux ainsi le progress industrils et sociaux de notre chere patrie.   .

Par ces presentes nous invitons et sollicitons respectueusement les amis sinceres et genereux de l'instruction et de notre race, tels que l'honorable J. D. Rockefeller, l'honorable Andrew Carnegie et autres—soit separement ou conjointement—d'etablir dans cette ile un college normale et industriel dans le genre de l'institut de Tuskegee aux Etats-Unis, preside par le distingue ami et membre de la race—Dr. Booker T. Washington.

Nous sommes convaincus que si Haiti, doit s'elever parmi les Republiques du Nouveau-Monde et remplir dignement sa destinee, ce sera par le moyen et a l'aide de nobles institutions telles que le college normal, et industriel ou sera donnee a nous jeunes et intelligents compatriotes une education saine, pratique effective que leur permettra de remplir avec distinction les plus hautes fonctions que confere le droit de citoyen de cette Republique.

Ce sera nonseulement un des plus puissanys facteurs dans le developpement de la race-le garanti d'une paix durable, et d'une prosperite permanente mais comme nous le souhaitons ardemment, ce sera aussi la mise en pratique autant que la theorie, la realisation du haut ideal de l'immortel emancipateur Touissant l'Ouverture, le George Washington de la Republique noir.

Nous, donnons l'assurance formelle aux donateurs ci-dessus designs ainsi qu'a tous ceux repondront au coeu des petitionnaires en etendant leur bienfaisance a Haiti, qui ce serait grand honneur pour notre gouvernement (1 Pouvoirs publics) d'avoir le privilege d'accorder une portion de terrain concenable, au centre de l'ile, pour l'etablissment du college, comme une preuve de mon appreciation des efforts, faits pour l'education des fils et des filles d'Haiti.

L'etablissement d'une telle institution dans notre pays placera notre petite mais heroique nation dans une eternelle obligation envers ses bienfaiteurs et nous attachera beaucoup plus par les liens de sympathie et de bonne volonte a notre soeur-la granted republique etoilee.

Cette petition en faveur de notre pays, dont nous voulons servir le hauts interets, est fait par l'intermediare du Rev. L. Ton Evans, missionaire evangelique des Etats-Unis, actuellement au milieu de nous, qui pendant des annees, a montre un reel et profound interet dans le developpement et le progres de la republique et qui a beaucoup voyage sur terre et sur mer plaidant en faveur de la cause religieuse de ce Oays parmi plusieurs nation.

18 Janvier, 1911, et 108 eme de l'independance Cap-Haitien, Haiti.

The English rendering of above petition and prayer of nearly 3,000 Haitians, or practically the leaders of the whole little black republic (as one voice) for presentation to trustees of Rockefeller and Carnegie Foundations and Bureau of International Peace, in New York, and at Washington by the United States Baptist missionary in 1911.

TRANSLATION.

Haiti's urgent need of a normal and industrial college. A national and direct appeal by native leaders to America's philanthropists and friends of the Negro, and believers in his intellectual, moral, as well as industrial development.

We, the undersigned natives of Haiti, irrespective of religious creeds and political parties, and simply from the highest patriotic considerations and in the interest of the mental, moral, and religious improvement of our countrymen and the industrial and social progress of our beloved island home, hereby invite and respectfully solicit the generous and sincere friends of education and the Negro race, such as Hon. John D. Rockefeller and Hon. Andrew Carnegie and others, either separately or jointly, to establish in our land a normal and industrial school something on the line of Tuskegee Institute in the United States, presided over by our distinguished friend and member of the same race, Dr. Booker T. Washington.

If Haiti is to rise among the Republics of the West and to fulfill in a worthy manner, each and all of us whose names are below are convinced that this can only be achieved through such noble institutions as a normal and industrial school which shall give a sound, practical, and efficient training of head and hands, as well as of heart, to our most promising young men and women so as to prepare them for the noble and responsible functions of civil and Christian citizenship in this Republic.

This will prove a most potent agency in the development of our race and materially help in securing a lasting peace, which must precede prosperity.

which we most devoutly desire at this moment,[1] and thus enable us some day to fulfill in practice and by deeds the splendid theories and noble and inspiring ideals of Haiti's immortal emancipator, Touissant L'overture, the George Washington of the Black Republic.

We furthermore assure the generous donors herein named, or whosoever shall respond to this sincere prayer of the petitioners and extend their benefactions to Haiti, that our Government will deem it the greatest honor to be privileged to make an adequate grant of suitable land in the most central part of the island for the express purpose of such an industrial school and as a practical proof of our profound appreciation of the efforts of Americans and true friends of our race for the uplift of our own sons and daughters.

The establishment of such an institution in Haiti will place this small, a once heroic little nation, under a lasting obligation to the benefactors, actually link us together in a close bond of unity, sympathy, and good will to our rich, strong, big sister Republic of America more than anything else could.

This sincere request and the petition of practically our whole little nation, which we seek to serve in various capacities, is made through and brought to the United States in our behalf by our friend the Rev. L. Ton Evans, Evangelical Baptist missionary of the United States, laboring here in our midst, and who for years has shown deep and profound interest in the welfare of our Republic and people and has traveled much over sea and land pleading the religious and educational claims of this country in different lands and among different surrounding Christian nations.

The original and copper plate like petition was written (French) at Dondon in extreme north by a young native craving for education. It was started at the cape, and following official letter, with official seal, and written and signed in behalf of council by the mayor of that little town of Saint Raphael (all three in the so-called north Haiti-Cacos district), and a specimen of such official indorsement from practically all the towns and mayors through Haiti, expressing delight at the step taken, and sincerely praying for the success of the noble project and safety of missionary voyage and speedy return to them:

Liberte, Egalite, fraternite. Republique d'Haiti.
Saint-Raphael, le 8 Avril. 1911 an 108me de l'Independance. No. 69 Saint Pierre Milien Jn. Francois. (Magistrat Communal de cette commune.)

Rev. L. Ton Evans,
Missionaire Evangelique des Etats-Unis, en Ville.

Monsieur le Missionaire: Votre petition que j'ai lue avec beaucoup d'attention, et que j'ai fait lire par tous mes administres, a produit un reel effet sur l'esprit des uns et des autres se sont empresses de la signer avec moi.

L'idee de fonder une ecole normale, industrielle a l'instant de l'institution de Booker Washington en Haiti, est de plus louables etant donne que cette institution fera un bien immense au triple developpement—moral, industriel et intellectuel d'Haiti, et de la race noire.

Combien cher missionaire serious-nous heureux si cette idee pourrait etre applandie par le Rockerfeller, et Carnegie philanthropes qui aiment tant le race noire.

A ces deux grands hommes, nous vous prions de presenter nos respectheuse hommages.

Puisse dieu benir vos efforts et faire reussir votre vaste et philanthropique project.

Puisse dieu vous accompagner dans votre route et vous ramener en bien aux Etats-Unis. Bon voyage cher missionaire, et recevez je vous en prie.

Mes respectueuses salutations,

LeMagistrat Communal,
S. P. M. Jn. Francois.

Note.—Strange this man to-day, if alive, was termed a rabid so-called Cacos, brutally treated by marines and cast without trial into Cape Prison.

Letters of hearty indorsement from American minister, United States consul, and white European employee of Haitian native labor in the Black Republic five years before American occupation, etc.:

---

[1] At the time this petition was written, carried around all over the Republic, mostly on horseback, wading through rivers, and mud saddle deep, climbing rocky mountains, and descending deep ravines (a most daring adventure), while poor Haiti was plunged into the bloody revolution (through Germans) of 1910 and 1911.

AMERICAN LEGATION,
Port au Prince, Haiti, April 28, 1911.

Rev. L. TON EVANS,
General Missionary in Haiti.

MY DEAR REV. EVANS: I am indeed very pleased to learn that you as an American Baptist missionary are endeavoring to establish a normal and industrial college, a long felt want I can assure you, in Haiti.

I have carefully looked over all your documents and am agreeably surprised to note the apparent interest so generally, if not enthusiastically, manifested toward your plan by leading Haitian officials. I sincerely trust your laudable efforts will succeed.

Yours, truly,

H. W. FURNISS,
American Minister.

——

AMERICAN CONSULAR SERVICE,
Cape Hatian, Haiti, May 6, 1911.

The undersigned has great pleasure in heartily commending the work now being undertaken by Pastor L. Ton Evans for the establishment of an industrial school in the Republic of Haiti. There is probably no place in the world where such an establishment would be of greater utility or where it ought to produce greater results.

The extraordinary energy and indefatigability of Mr. Ton Evans, as well as his good faith and philanthropic abnegation, eminently qualify him to take the lead in such an enterprise.

C. M. WASHINGTON,
American Consul.

——

COMPAGNIE HAITIENNE,
Port de Paix, Haiti, February 13, 1911.

Rev. L. TON EVANS,
General Secretary of Haiti Missions, Port de Paix.

DEAR MR. TON EVANS: As directors of the Compagnie Hatienne and employer of a large number of Haitians on our railroad and in the log-wood business since many years, allow me to express my very deep interest in the proposed normal and industrial college you seek to establish in the island.

From my intimate knowledge of this country, I believe that the scheme that you propose is a most excellent one, and can not but produce the best possible results in the social and industrial development of both country and people.

Such an institution will further help materially to change the present political and unsatisfactory social conditions and insure real permanent peace and good will throughout Haiti.

I therefore most sincerely, Mr. Evans, wish you every success in this laudable effort of yours in the uplift of Haiti.

Yours, very truly,

J. ABROG.

A Haitian graduate of a theological seminary at Newton, Mass, who attended Baptist World Alliance at Philadelphia, Pa., in 1911, with his superintendent missionary, and interviewed at the time by a Pennsylvania paper, referred as follows to the benefits of an industrial school, effects of such on revolutions and cacoism, and eagerness of native young people for training, and in reply to " What do you know about Superintendent Ton Evans in Haiti, and how do the natives look upon his proposal of a normal and industrial school?" said:

" We look at him as Haiti's best friend, and no man ever was more highly esteemed and enjoyed the confidence of the people than Missionary Evans; in fact, we look at his coming as God's answer to our prayers. The moment we heard of his project of a normal and industrial school to teach my countrymen the value and dignity of honest labor, and divert the Haitian mind away from revolutions and politics to the cultivation of their rich soil, we at once fell in love with the idea, and though in the midst of a terrible revolution I and a few others inspired by his undaunted courage and incessant efforts associated ourselves with him and gave him what support we could.

" Yes, I am certain that a large number of the best young men and women all over the Republic now eager for an education and practical training such as given at an institution of this kind would immediately enter. In addition to the benefit to us in the way of training for useful vocations in life, developing our industries, a gift of such an institution by the United States Government, or the Messrs. Rockefeller and Carnegie trustees, would be a standing reminder to us of your Christian generosity and practical good will and cement Haiti forever to the United States Government and people, and for these reasons all Haiti is praying for brother Ton Evans' success in this undertaking."

This pastor and professor who has taught young men successfully for years at the Cape is one of those whose appropriations has been withheld by the American occupation nearly three years ago.

[Pittsburgh Dispatch Apr. 1, 1913.]

HAITIANS ASK SCHOOL FROM FUND.

REV. L. TON EVANS PRESENTS PETITION TO CARNEGIE ENDOWMENT FOR PEACE—HIS GRAPHIC RECITAL—SPENT YEARS AMONG DEVIL WORSHIPPERS AND BELIEVES IN THEIR FUTURE.

Rev. L. Ton Evans, pastor of the Welsh Baptist Church in Chatham Street, has just returned from Washington, D. C., where he presented to the Carnegie Endowment for International Peace a petition signed by 3,000 natives of the Black Republic of Haiti, urging the great advantages which would accrue by founding at Port au Prince a normal and industrial college, modeled somewhat after the famous Booker T. Washington Institute at Tuskegee, Ala.

The money involved in realizing such a project is about $3,000,000, and the direct result announced by its promoters would be the stoppage of the interminable series of revolutions by diverting the native mind from the military system of government and intrigue into industrial grooves. It is argued that Haiti is the richest field for development of the republican ideas in the world. Though occupying only one-half as much of the island as Dominica, its population is twice as great. The natives own their own soil, have most fertile fields for sugar and cotton production, and the fiscal affairs and State debt are solely demoralized by chronic grafting of military officials taught in a long, persistnet military system, and for which German propaganda, aided by other influences, were largely and directly responsible.

BELIEVES IN HIS PLAN.

Comparatively a modicum of Pittsburgh people know of the notably energetic work of Rev. Mr. L. Ton Evans here in recent months since his return from Haiti, though he is known internationally among Baptist organizations. His absorbing enthusiasm, his nervous and unflagging recital of the situation there, his thorough conviction of the feasibility of his plan and his elucidation of it by speech and tireless gesture, hold the listener like the ancient mariner did the wedding guest, but with no tale of the Flying Dutchman and the albatross. He is now 50 years old, born in Barry, Wales. His folk were rich brewery people, but he gave up his large patrimony to become a Baptist missionary. He first went to Haiti as a field secretary 18 years ago. Then he came to Wilkes-Barre and was pastor of a Welsh church at Edwardsville near by. There six years ago the Negro Baptist Missionary Society found him and sent him back to Haiti.

Seldom is one encountered more ebullient with his theme and scheme. In his sacred calling he is a promoter unrivaled, but his facts and experiences leave no suggestion of doubt. At Washington he saw Alvu A. Adee, the real diplomat of the State Department, and outlined to him this plan of transforming Haiti from a Republic of turmoil into a stable government. When nearly the whole of Port-au-Prince en mass turned out to pay honor to the highest official of the United States Government—next only to their President—his official speech and encouraging words, with his special visit, removed much of the deep-seated prejudice against Americans, the result of the United States traducers and this Government's seeming aloofness from these people. He has fears of President Wilson changing for the worse the attitude toward the American Republics to the south. He asserts that the system of conducting Dominican finances has been a great success and something like it should be proposed to the Haitian officials, but not with any notion of coercion or territorial aggrandizement.

Talking on this latter branch in his rapid-fire style, he unfolded his other striking thought of this Government sending some civilian to Haiti to remain for a time and to convince the authorities and the people that the United States has no ulterior aims against it, that the concessionaires, who obtain franchises there and stir up trouble, are not the American Government. Rev. Mr. Evans belongs to that amiable class who would fight for peace. During the many years he labored all over Haiti he learned the perversion of the national destiny by the military control. He alluded to the expenditure of thousands of dollars by the natives to give Secretary Knox only a two days' entertainment and vouched for the vast benefit accomplished by that brief visit some months ago.

It was through this so-called purchase, but really a gift, said the ex-Haiti missionary, that the United States previously with only 800,000 square miles of territory, without an outlet to the Pacific Slope, and Pacific Ocean, soon emerged from comparative obscurity right into the forefront of the nations of the world, or, in the words of our own United States Minister, Livingstone, at Paris, immediately after closing this astonishing deal (the black man of Haiti compelled Napoleon to make for fear Britain might sweep down through Canada and immediately annex it) written to President Thomas Jefferson : " From this day the United States becomes a first-class power, and this without the flash of a gun and the clashing of swords. There will be no tears and sorrow, but ages of happiness to countless human beings."

The donation, therefore, of this normal and industrial school to Haiti by the great wealthy American Government as a recognition of what Toussant L'overture in the providence of God did to more than double our map by one stroke of the pen is urged by Rev. Evans as a matter of honor and debt of gratitude at this time to poor Haiti.

He says the Haitians are the kindest people in the world. About 10 per cent have some book education, largely in the classics through the French language. But " education," as its derivation implies, is the bringing out from a man the useless and inserting the practical. Nearly all the people are illiterate. They speak a French patois. The State religion is Catholic, but the utmost freedom is permitted to other sects. But underneath the outward pretensions of Christianity or some faith higher than savagery is the proneness to devil worship. Therein lay his own chief physical danger, for the natives were imbued with superstitions and often could be incited to waylay him in his journeys.

He told many instances where only his self-reliance saved him from harm. But all this wild dancing and sacrificing, even of a little child to appease an angry devil god, is now giving way to the longing of the people for the substance of the Christian faith. Teaching the gospel was the dire necessity in Haiti. They called h'm " negre blanc," the black white man, and revered him and gave him a bodyguard of pompously uniformed generals. The vineyard is ready for cultivation.

Rev. Mr. Evans some years ago took back with him to Wales a Haiti native girl and had her with him as he talked about the Haiti missionary field. He finds the United States more sympathetic and its people fuller of push. This girl and another one he has now in a school in Washington City being educated for missionaries. Her name is Christine Francois, and she is a cousin of a former Pres'dent.

As Rev. Mr. Evans chatted at his home, 3202 Craft Place, yesterday, with a volume and velocity that astonished for its not ending in fatigue, he mentioned the historical fact of the debt owed by the United States to Haiti. It was the defeat of Napoleon by Toussaint L'Overture and his black forces at the end of the eighteenth century and their securing escape from further slavery that compelled the emperor to sell to Thomas Jefferson the 1,200,000 square miles he held in the United States for about 2 cents an acre (4).

In his native land Mr. Evans knew well Lloyd-George, the British chancellor of the exchequer, and like him he has always been an insurgent. He insists that if the Haitians could be made to believe that the United States is actually without designs upon them, and is willing to aid wherever it can, revolutions would stop and peace and prosperity succeed the constant internecine slaughter. He knew the recent Presidents well, and said that La Conte was a splendid character, but too highly cultured to become a leader of the people. He objects to any use of the "big stick," but he does not want this Government to absolutely withdraw all its guardian interests. The president of the Carnegie Endowment is Senator Elihu Root, who himself has visited the tropical Americas and is a noted advocate of more amicable relations with them.

JOURNEYING THROUGH HAITI.

It is intensely interesting to hear Rev. Mr. Evans describe his journeys all through the interior of Haiti on horseback, eight relays having been used. His native band of missionary assistants are proving successful in the work of evangelization. On one Sunday afternoon he had the privilege of carrying out all the instruments, such as tom-toms, troughs in which the soup is served to the demon god, rattles, and other voodoo utensils, and reducing the pile to ashes, and later he assisted in tearing down the altar or houndfort of the devil god. Once he held services near where a devil dance was progressing, with the natives foaming at the mouth from the liquor they distil from the sugar cane. The papaloi or priest of the voodoo cult brandished a big stick, but the rest realized that all their incantations were without avail on the Christians. The signers to the petition are among the best citizens of the Republic—senators, judges, etc.

After 10 years of interviews and a busy correspondence on the subject of a national, normal, and industrial school, the sincere prayer of Haiti has not been answered, otherwise probably our Government would not have entered the Black Republic, and many thousands of Haitian lives saved. There are indications, however, that even the blood of these Negroes has not been shed in vain, and that soon through the present competent Senate committee investigation either the United States Government itself, or aided by the Rockefeller and Carnegie Foundations will come to the rescue. The following letters will show sympathy and will be of interest:

CARNEGIE FOUNDATION,
FOR THE ADVANCEMENT OF TEACHING,
New York City, August 28, 1911.

MY DEAR MR. EVANS: I acknowledge the interesting letter of August 26, with its copies of your petition, as well as letters of Messrs. Abegg, Furniss, and Livingstone, I shall be glad to see that your letter is brought to the attention of President Pritchett when he returns to the city. I shall be glad to see also, that your letter to Mr. Carnegie is sent to his secretary.

I return herewith your letter of introduction from Dr. MacArthur, president of the World's Baptist Alliance, and suggest that it would be helpful for you to communicate your plans also, if not already done so, to the General Education Board, 17 Battery Place, New York City. This is one of Mr. Rockefeller's foundations which has given such aid as you hope for.

Very truly, yours,

CLYDE DAVIES. *Secretary.*

L. TON EVANS, Esq.,
Edwardsville, Pa.

[The constitutional convention of the State of New York, Albany, 1915.]

CLINTON, N. Y., *September 27, 1915.*

DEAR SIR: I have to acknowledge the receipt of your letter of September 1, addressed to me as president of the Carnegie Endowment of Peace, in reference to the establishment of a national normal and industrial school in Haiti, and I have been glad to lay it before the executive committee of the endowment for consideration at its next meeting. I would suggest that you correspond with Dr. James Brown Scott, secretary of the endowment, 2 Jackson Place, Washington, D. C., regarding the petition which you wish to present in this connection.

Very truly, yours,

ELIHU ROOT.

Rev. L. TON EVANS,
First Baptist Church, Lansford, Pa.

Senator KING. Was the situation when the American troops went there such, in your opinion, as to justify our intervention?

Mr. EVANS. Certainly; as I have before stated. But to wait for this blood conflict and regrettable revolution, and the manner the situation was handled by those at Port au Prince, and State and Navy Departments at Washington, by a stealthy landing of American marines during the cover of night below the city, etc., made it appear more like the invasion of Haiti (to most Haitians) by a foreign and alien power, looking for a mere excuse for annexing their island, than a friendly intervention. It was a deplorable blunder in diplomacy, and in my opinion and on this very account justified the bitter resentment shown, and in spite of Admiral Caperton's disavowal of any other intention but to " protect Americans, Europeans, and even the lives, and property of Haitians "—the criminal additional blunders if not more than blunders, as will be shown to this investigating committee, before we are through, of slam- ming their Senate and Chamber doors in the Haitians' face, raping their con- stitution, and resurrecting the corvee, with oppressive if not murderous inten- tions—by the American occupation, officially backed up by Washington, intensi- fied this bitterness, and at last convinced the Haitians, that what Admiral Caperton said—and possibly he sincerely meant—was a mere cloak to dominate Haiti, crush their national spirit, if not lead them back to slavery.

To avoid all this, I specially wrote offering my services to President Wilson in Haiti, and as much for our American Chief's guidance as for the pacifica- tion and securing the confidence and hearty cooperation of the Haitian people with our Government's real purpose in the Black Republic, to protect life and otherwise help Haiti.

Senator KING. For the preservation of life and for protection of property?

Mr. EVANS. Yes. But the methods adopted then and subsequently, almost, indeed, ever since, have been most incompatible with this motive of preserving life and protecting property and liberties of the people, which made me offer to give up my church to go back immediately to Haiti, knowing the seriousness of the situation.

Senator KING. I wish you would not make explanations, but answer my questions. I want to get through as soon as I can, and get the facts. As I recall, there was revolution, assassination and bloodshed, which was quite extensive in the island at the time we intervened?

Mr. EVANS. I am as anxious as the Senator is to get through, but I take it that this committee is appointed to thoroughly investigate not only facts as to entering Haiti and present conditions under American administration but with a view of better understanding these, what actually led up to them even though it does take a little time, and to suggest a real remedy. Yes; I have seen in the American press the description of the deplorable and heartrending conditions you mention when we intervened.

Senator KING. But when you returned you verified that?

Mr. EVANS. Yes. The British consul general as well as several other trust- worthy officials and Haitians told me the whole sad story, which then when I read the account in papers here, and ever since in my opinion amply justified our intervention. My criticism is, that we did not go to the rescue of Haiti 20 years ago, assume a friendly mandate and act the big brother to defend this Republic and help these people irrespective of any apparent offense given Germany and other minor European countries at the time; and in which act of befriending Haiti, and the Haitian people (as I wrote President Roosevelt in 1902), Great Britain, and France would have gladly supported us, as their consul generals after serious consultation at this time and in view of the sad affair referred to especially urged the United States to send their admiral and marines at once to Port au Prince, which at last they did, and for which I thanked God.

Senator KING. Have the marines, since they have been in power, made im- provements in the island in the way of sanitary improvements, the building of roads, etc.?

Mr. EVANS. I have made special reference to this important phase of their work in my missionary report and shown my profound appreciation of the cleaning up so much needed, and did this with a view of removing, as stated, the prejudice against our American occupation among colored brethren and others in the southland and on my own missionary committee, for instance.

Senator KING. Did you ever see any of the marines themselves do any of these acts of brutality of which you have been speaking, or were these acts committed by the blacks who were in charge of the corvee system?

Mr. EVANS. You mean personally committed by the white marine?

Senator KING. Yes.

Mr. EVANS. I think I have answered this question before to Senator Pomerene. It is not likely that marine officers will actually beat or kill a native in the presence of an American, and a Christian missionary like myself, more than the average gendarme would. The marines who officer these gendarmes give the orders, which probably most of them receive from Maj. Welles (in north) or the major at Port au Prince, and these two from the chief of the Haiti gendarmerie, Gen. Williams at headquarters, who is directly responsible not to the Haiti President but to Col. John H. Russell, who is the United States Government's chief of Navy marine and land forces operating in Haiti and the official head of the American occupation.

I have repeatedly seen marines and officers drinking and drunk at Port au Prince, Cape, and St. Marc; have heard them boastfully speak of their killing, or, as they termed it, bagging cacos on shooting expeditions to the north; have seen in prison (day I left) a Haitian carried and laid on his stomach with his back one mass of jelly, attended by a native doctor's assistant and another, who informed me that it was done by the United States marine captain in another drunken craze of his. I have heard two marine officers of the United States Government, apparently intoxicated, and in the presence of Christian natives and others in a mad rage, cursing religion, preachers, and missionaries, and damning myself for my efforts in giving the Gospel, seeking to educate and morally and industrially uplift "damned niggers of Haiti," with their fists clinched, and again aiming to take their revolvers and shoot me, stating they opened and intercepted my letters and taking an oath they would crush me, and then hurried me off to prison.

A St. Marc captain was court-martialed while I was there for kicking and brutally treating (it was alleged) his British Negro housekeeper, while another captain at St. Marc was alleged while I was there to have taken three Haitians from prison and without due process of law made them cut their graves and then had them shot, the bodies rolling into these holes. The people were horror-stricken. A member (in mourning) at our church in the Cape informed me (confirmed by pastor and others) that her two brothers, by order of Maj. Welles in command, after being tortured by water cure in prison, were taken out at night and without process of law also made to dig their own graves and shot into them, and neither this sister nor her aged Christian mother were informed as to spot. I hardly, however, believe all said about either marines or gendarmes and the diabolical butchering of natives attributed to them, and sincerely believed all over Haiti, by those driven almost hysterical by methods and brutality of marines and gendarmes of the occupation itself very largely.

Senator KING. I asked you if you had ever seen any marines commit any of these acts of brutality as to which you have just testified.

Mr. EVANS. Yes; those that I have here specifically mentioned, and the others personally informed can be verified by credible witnesses in Haiti. Marine officers as a rule give the orders; gendarmes have to obey their commands.

Senator KING. When I was in Haiti over a year ago I talked with a good many men that were working on the road—natives—and they told me that they sought employment because they got better wages working for the Government on the roads than they did from the natives, and they got better wages, low as they were, than they ever got before.

Mr. EVANS. This was more than a year after I had left, and through my own efforts, writing Secretary Daniels, of the United States Navy, and that of others as to the corvee curse, relaxing conditions of labor, if not advancing pay especially around Port-au-Prince, where Senators, Congressmen, and American leaders dropped in on way to and from Panama—what you say may be true; but certainly it was not so in 1918 and beginning of 1919. I quite understand that the impoverished natives were not able to compete with the United States Government either in amount of labor or in pay.

Natives would work for food rather than starve. All bread, etc., was in the hands of American occupation and their Marines, and woefully mismanaged with us at St. Marc, and probably somewhat similar in other parts, unless they were fortunate to have sympathetic, businesslike, efficient Marine officers who knew how to properly distribute American flour so as to keep the folks contented rather than leave it spoil at the customs. We ourselves went months without seeing a morsel of bread, without knowing conditions of World War, and no efforts whatever at informing the Haitians through Washington or any other United States Government publicity bureau, as I complained at Washington's headquarters. The people of St. Marc, if not the masses through Haiti, thought this withholding of breadstuff and other vital articles of food, no ships coming in from Germany and other European countries, was a part of the United States program to subject, if not to crush, Haitians; hence laid all the blame on the American occupation.

Senator KING. What was the fact as to whether they got better wages from the Government than in private employment?

Mr. EVANS. My reply to the previous question largely answers this. The relaxing of conditions of labor on roads at Port-au-Prince, possibly a little better pay in 1920; and the fact that German merchants who formerly had control of Haiti business had been interned, with piles of logwood lying about the wharves everywhere in Haiti, hence scarcely any employment for natives, would partly account for this.

Senator KING. Is it a fact that they did get better wages than they did in private employment?

Mr. EVANS. No; it was simply 20 cents (American money) a week, and without food, as the gendarmé officers and others informed me at Jacmel in June of 1918, and around St. Marc that year and beginning of 1919, it was absolutely false unless a distinction was made in favor of Port-au-Prince and for reason stated.

The CHAIRMAN. Mr. Evans, distinguish in your replies between the period of the corvee, which terminated in 1918, I think, and the period which followed after abolishment of the corvee, when the laborers on the roads were paid.

Mr. EVANS. If the following special recommendation of mine in the memorandum which I presented President Wilson and Secretary Lansing in October of 1918, was carried out and explained and emphasized on my return to Port au Prince to Brig. Gen. Catlin, December of that year, and a copy of which I handed each of you this morning (see p. 4, and sec. —):

" Now that Haiti has declared war, the Germans at last interned, our United States Government shall grant us our full share of all necessaries by way of food at the lowest price; make generous loans to enable our occupation to proceed with its constructive program, and give all Haitian laborers not less than a gourde and a half (30 American cents) a day. All forced (corvee) except in case of prisoners and known criminals to be at once abolished among the quiet and peace-loving people, was faithfully carried out by our United States Government through brigadier general during 1919 (not 1918), when Senator King visited Port au Prince. Very likely what you say is true, and what you relate is the fact; and if so, I am glad the memorandum helped to at last abolish forced, in fact slave, labor of our Government at this time, at least around Port au Prince and further increase wage.

" I understand, however, from Gen. Barnett's report to Secretary of the Navy Daniels that it was through his own imperative command to Brig. Gen. Catlin that he abolished the corvee October of 1919, or 5 months after I left Haiti and 12 months (nearly) after specifically pointing out to the United States Government at Washington, and to Gen. Catlin at Port au Prince, Haiti, this grave injustice. And that even then throughout the whole of the north under Maj. Welles, as in some other sections, it was defiantly persisted in and Haitians promiscuously killed as the result of these revolutionary methods and insubordinate conduct of Marine officers of the United States Government filling some of the most responsible positions under the American occupation in Haiti. I beg to insert the following in record in reference to Cacoism and conduct of Maj. Welles and his marines:

CORROBORATION OF MEMORANDUM STATEMENTS TO THE UNITED STATES GOVERNMENT AND SENATE COMMITTEE ON FOREIGN RELATIONS DIRECT FROM HAITI, AND SHOWING CAUSE OF CACOISM THROUGHOUT THE NORTH.

Further evidence re the tearing of treaty, the rein of terror, and bloody bolshevism by white United States officers and their armed native police (gendarmes) under them in Haiti at this moment, which has made our United States Government a by-word and disgraced the Stars and Stripes in the Black Republic, now aroused with indignation and writhing under present cruel régime.

A Baptist missionary, with 25 years' experience in Haiti, French citizen and white, writing from the northern section of the Republic recently to General Superintendent L. Ton Evans, and after referring to appalling spiritual need of the people, the lack of laborers, and financial support, adding:

"I most highly estimate your persistent labor and incessant toil and pain in behalf of Haiti and real love for these oppressed people and greatly admire your faith and sincerely pray for your success at this time in this supreme effort of yours to get white Baptists to take hold of this important field.

"As you are now in the United States pleading with the Government at Washington to appoint a commission to make a thorough investigation into the internal affairs of Haiti and cause of present unrest, disturbances, and murders here, it may add to your already strong testimony and as further proof of the absolute necessity of such commission that you be informed that since you left for the States months ago bands of Cacos have appeared again at Hinche and throughout that section, armed with Mauser guns (they say) and making terrible trouble in that part of the island. This new and native uprising it is emphatically stated is directly due to the bad administration and cruelty of American marine officers.

"Though I can not personally prove it (as eyewitness), yet judging by the general situation (and as no one knows better than yourself) I certainly believe that this is the real reason back of these present troubles. Some say that this movement is a part of the German intrigues against the United States. This may be true to some extent, but the real truth is that if the American officers themselves, with those immediately under them, adopted a different method, showed more wisdom and humanity in their administrative policy, and endeavored to conciliate the Haitians and gain the love and confidence of these Negroes so as to make them feel that the United States is their protector and the "American occupation" with its officers are their true friends, the Haitians themselves would never turn against and oppose them, even if our Negroes in Haiti were supplied with all the money and all the guns that Germans could furnish them.

"You can use this argument not only for the appointment of the proposed commission, but for a complete change of the present régime in Haiti (that is the establishment of a civil occupation), but do not give my name. There is absolutely no fear on my part, but it is somewhat difficult to personally and positively prove some of these things. We can not, however, count on the Haitian people themselves (unless amply protected by United States Government) to declare the truth as regard, the great injustice and cruel sufferings they have to endure under the American occupation, for fear and dread on their part that the moment they do so they will have to suffer even more prosecutions, imprisonment, hard labor, if not something worse, as soon as the Senate committee is gone and these officers of the occupation remain in Haiti."

"This is perfectly true, for when the commission (even) of investigation is gone the American officers in Haiti will immediately persecute, illtreat, and brutally abuse all those who have dared to testify or denounce them. My own case is precisely the same as theirs. Apart from all this our missionaries, as well as our work here, will be looked upon—that is, Protestants and protestantism or evangelicalism—as the American occupation's worst enemies. We shall be compelled as the result to endure greater sufferings and oppressions than ever, and every possible obstacle will be placed in our way by American officers. The Roman Catholic Church and her priests (now financially sustained and supported through the American occupation, therefore its servants and slaves) will be more in favor than ever with them.

"However, as you yourself are a true American citizen, white and with many years of experience in Haiti, and expert knowledge of its people before as well as after the coming of the American occupation, you have more liberty and a better right both to speak and to act than any of us here, and who are already looked upon with strong suspicion, if not indeed counted as enemies, and simply for the reason that we preach the Gospel, and of course show disapproval of every injustice and tyranny, and even condemn the spirit and often unbearable prejudice that some white people (especially from America) persistently show toward these natives. I really believe that this terrible prejudice and abominable hatred of certain unconverted, dominating, if not intemperate and immoral, Americans have a great deal to do with the actual bad situation throughout Haiti. In writing thus to you, dear brother Evans, and supporting your plea at Washington by furnishing present information as to moral, social, and political reformation absolutely needed in this neglected and suffering Black Republic, you must not therefore think that I am quite converted to your opinion that the political, educational, and industrial and economic reforms your own President and Unite1 States Government may br'ng about in Haiti, and according to that splendid treaty you attached so much importance to and feel so proud of, can really regenerate Haiti and its people apart from the Gospel of the blessed God, and through His word which we both believe and preach, etc."

This white and experienced brother, laboring_29 years solidly in north Haiti and the center of so-called cacoism, will testify if called at the Cape.

Senator KING. Then the evils of which you speak were confined within a few months, or confined to a limited period?

Mr. EVANS. I had two years and five months of the corvee, which was practiced all over Haiti, causing serious frictions, indescribable brutality everywhere, and arousing a strong feeling and bitter hatred against the occupation, marines, and United States throughout the whole Republic; until this unbridled passion and unchecked recklessness and ruthlessness of our marine officers filled Haitian prisons, and the shooting of prisoners dragged out of their cells at night, without pretence of trial, and killing of cacos by the thousands could no longer be smothered, and official reports held back and absolutely suppressed and falsified—the marine scandal in Haiti and the atrocities perpetrated under and by the American occupation in the Black Republic was exposed and shocked the whole Nation, if not the civilized world.

The CHAIRMAN. It is set down in the report of the Navy Department that in violation of the orders of the commanding officer the corvee in the remoter parts of Haiti was continued. I think, therefore, before we conclude this morning, we ought to ask Mr. Evans about the framing of the new constitution and the objections to it. I think that will be interesting.

Mr. EVANS. May I hand the following for the record from the report to my missionary committee of Negroes in North Carolina who had, like American officials at Washington and of the occupation in Haiti, become deflected from their original plan and purpose and had· become more interested officially, if not financially, in the sugar corporation (which has grabbed something like 200,000 acres of the best land of the Haitians) than in the salvation of souls and education of their own Negro people, and therefore never read it, placing instead an elaborated and illustrated American sugar corporation "prospectus" on the table, while pushing aside the official report of their mission, account of work done under exceptional difficulties, and paying no heed to the crying spiritual needs of oppressed, imprisoned, and murdered natives. The part of the report dealing with the new constitution is as follows:

ANNUAL REPORT SUBMITTED TO LOTT CAREY HAITI MISSIONARY COMMITTEE AT WASHINGTON, D. C., FOR YEAR 1918.

[By L. Ton Evans, Baptist missionary superintendent of the Lott Carey Convention, St. Marc, Haiti.

SUDDEN CHANGE AND REVERSION OF NATIVE FEELING IN HAITI, AND REASON WHY.

Through the feeling of gratitude to God, our President, and United States Government and American people for restoration of complete order and establishment of real peace throughout the whole Republic, great sanitary and other special improvements, was both genuine and general and shared by all classes alike, including the most loyal and patriotic Haitians, who naturally love their own little country and flag as we Americans love the Stars and Stripes.

It was indeed a pity, yea worse, a political calamity if not a moral tragedy, that just at the moment when our leaders and people here were recovering from the shock of an apparent invasion by American armed marines under the cover of night, and beginning to seriously question the truth of German merchants, filibusterers, and exploiters, whom through various channels have for years persisted in poisoning these natives and Negro mind against the United States and everything American. That Uncle Sam's desire for Mole St. Nicholas was only a guise, for the purpose of a foothold on Haitian soil, to annex the Republic with its rich land and lead them back eventually to slavery with its horrors, in spite of their heroic struggles and bloody sacrifices under the immortal L'overture for their freedom and independence some 115 years ago.

To our astonishment and consternation, however, and with the suddeness of an earthquake violent jolt, or as if a German airplane passing over Haiti had actually dropped a bomb from the clear blue sky right down upon a vast but hidden powder magazine at Port au Prince, not merely changing, but completely reversing and actually revolutionizing everything over night as it were.

Behold, one great but subdued cry from one end of the Republic to the other, even the most remote—American deceit! American treachery!!—the occupation is going to forcibly change our constitution so as to give our richest and best lands to American corporations and white wealthy profiteers, and force us again as slaves to work, exactly as we were warned by our German friends, they would do the moment they put their feet on Haitian territory.

Personally finding out therefore what your superintendent at first thought a stupendous blunder in diplomacy by an amateur politician, or a raw inexperienced official around the State and Latin-American departments, or some one close to the President at Washington, totally ignorant of the sacredness of treaty obligations and the seriousness of meddling with a nation's constitution, was but a clever scheme and deeply-laid plot of certain newly-formed corporations of the United States, boasting of unlimited wealth, with stockholders within the administration who had followed the American occupation to the Black Republic in the twentieth century, much like the Spaniards and pirates came in the wake of Columbus in the fifteenth; and unless their grab for land and greed for gold is speedily checked, it will result in same barbarous and disastrous end, when poor colored Carib Indians were robbed and perished at the hands of stronger white Europeans.

On thus seeing our treaty, pledging protection to the Negro Republic, people's liberties, and rights, undertaking to agriculturally, minerally, if not educationally cultivate the soil and develop the Negroes, for Negroes, and by Negroes—ruthlessly ignored and openly repudiated, and that hundreds of thousands of acres of the best lands were already taken or being negotiated by two of these corporations by the aid of, if not through the American occupation, caused this bitter reversion and serious opposition to, and anger against, and hatred toward, the United States.

And more especially that this betrayal of Haiti and cruel rape of their constitution as now proposed, coming so soon after American Marines had disarmed Haiti soldiers, disbanded their army and the Republic's senate and house of representatives had been slammed in their face, as the Russian Duma was by the late Czar, against the Russians, and that these politically and financially bankrupt Negroes felt utterly helpless, daring not to openly discuss these vital matters, much less to publicly protest for fear of imprisonment as suspects, or being instantly shot as rebels against authority and enemies of the United States.

Your superintendent therefore felt it his personal and imperative duty as an American citizen and a Christian missionary and representative of the millions of white and colored Baptists of the United States, to step into the breach, and under these conditions and as mediator, to at once hasten to Port au Prince so as to have a quiet talk and special interview with Col. Russell, the able and genial military chief of our occupation.

Failing to obtain an American official English copy of the proposed new constitution, with change of the vital clauses re land, etc., from either our American legation, or the colonel at the occupation headquarters, I respectfully suggested to the military chief (who pleaded ignorance as to its origin) and asserted that I had certain knowledge as to the real interests back of the present propaganda, and averred that neither President Wilson, at Washington, nor our Negro President Dartiguenave of Haiti, had absolutely anything to do with this new constitution movement;[1] and after pointing out the very serious change already come over Haiti, and arousing, and embittering of the Haitians, how the mere announcement of the intention of the occupation to force this, had stirred the wrath of this little nation, I earnestly appealed, therefore, to the colonel (rather than seemingly put coals on already kindled fire) to postpone the so-called voting until we could send to, and hear from President Wilson.

---

[1] President Dartiguenave of Haiti, practically elected by the United States President, and paid through the hands of the United States' general-receiver in Haiti his salary, was made forcibly and under his own name the instrument for proclaiming the said fake election and the issuing of the French copy of the new constitution for publication in Le Moniteur Wednesday, May 8, 1918, and since transpired rewritten at the office of the United States Navy Department, Washington, D. C., and a fact that must have been within the personal knowledge of both Col. Russell and United States Minister Blanchard, who were conniving together by this method to deceive the Haitians, blind the American people, and to shield the United States Navy officials and those back of them.

This, Col. Russell said, either he could or would not do, wherefore your superintendent asked permission for him to cable directly to Washington, to defer indefinitely the fake voting and ask that a small commission to investigate be at once sent as I had possession of facts the United States Government and United States people should, and would know.

When the colonel declined also this, stating he would proceed with the election, so called, the following week, and, as announced by President Dartiguenave, I expressed profound regret to him that it should be thus made to appear to these Haitians that our American occupation—whose mission in Haiti was plainly set forth in the treaty to tranquilize the natives, strengthen the amity existing with a view to create implicit confidence between Haiti and the United States and not to stir up opposition and strife—was, after all, an instrument of American financial interests now operating in the Black Republic. The colonel and marines were determined to serve these financial interests at the expense of ignoring, openly and ruthlessly violating the United States Government's solemn and sacred covenant obligations to these Negroes, hence taking a mean advantage of their utter helplessness in the hands of the American occupation.

Under these peculiar and most painful and treacherous conditions it became my imperative duty, as a Christian missionary and an American with more than 25 years' experience in and working for the moral, social, and industrial as well as religious welfare of Haiti, and one who had endeavored to champion their individual and national liberties and legitimate rights when attacked by Europeans and Germans, hence now to protect and defend them from being robbed and exploited by the American occupation and under our own Stars and Stripes, solemnly pledged by treaty to protect the integrity of the Negro Republic and defend the rights and liberties of every Haitian.

As a true American, therefore, who scorns official treachery and military fraud upon a black and helpless little nation, your superintendent, in taking leave of the colonel and chief of our United States marines at Port au Prince, respectfully assured him that this whole matter would be brought directly before President Wilson, in spite of obstructing and profiteering officialism, and that probably both of them would meet face to face at Washington or before a commission of investigation when this proposed voting on the so-called new constitution would be declared a military farce and a political fraud.

In taking this stand, I added, if absolutely necessary, I would bring Haiti's case before the nearly 8,000,000 white and colored Baptists of the United States, the Federal Council of the Churches of Christ in America, the Federation of Labor, and, finally, to the great American people so as to remove forever this foul blot from off the folds of our hitherto stainless flag.

Your superintendent, however, assured the chief of occupation that he would strictly refrain from any kind of agitation in the Black Republic; that he would personally submit to the colonel there and, moreover, use his efforts and influence and that of their native preachers and Christians, to loyally, as far as possible and proper for missionaries to do so, to maintain law and order and add to the authority and efficiency of American occupation in their faithful attempt to discharge their duty to the United States Government and to the Haitian people according to the spirit and letter of the signed treaty.

The day of so-called voting (sic) arrived, and passed off quietly enough on the 12th of June, 1918; and when thousands, of course, throughout the Republic (considered, nevertheless, but a very small fraction of the real voting power of Haiti), and nearly all of whom were in the official and financial pay, and in some way or another employed by the American occupation, and weekly receiving their salaries or wages through the hands of the United States official receiver in Haiti.

This is true from Haiti's present figurehead Negro President, ex-President Legitime, chairman and members of national council (and illegal and unconstitutional substitute of the American occupation, created so as to usurp the functions of the Negro Republic's senate and chambers), judges, magistrates, commissaires (mayors), clerks of customs, post-office servants, gendarmes, school inspectors and teachers, employees of castor-seed, sugar, and railroad corporations, etc., employed around courts and prisons, to the remotest man who received pay and was under control of American armed marines in Haiti, with one exception; that is, the European Roman Catholic archbishop, bishops, priests, freres, and nuns in Haiti and professors and faculty of the Haiti Roman Catholic college for training of white European priests; and, though on poor bankrupt Haiti pay roll through American general receiver, directly against the stipulation of the treaty, were rounded up, carefully watched, and presumably cast at least one ballot.

The processions of voters (sic) few literate, with 95 per cent illiterates, and employees of corporations in whose sole interest the occupation was acting that day, resembled funerals as to their silence and solemnity if not in their mournful character, all over the Republic, and as they passed along like sheep, with broken hearts, into Haiti's courts of justice—but transformed that day through the whole country and by the American occupation into slaughter-houses for to slay both the Negro constitution and the treaty of President Wilson and the United States Government.

Each voter (sic) was watched with an eagle eye, and guarded by the poor native gendarme (Negro police) who were everywhere in evidence, and specially officered by American marines of the occupation for this special occasion, and consisted of American generals, colonels, majors, captains, and lieutenants, not to mention American-paid Catholic archbishops, bishops, priests, and other civilians, who were around and presence and influence requisitioned, for no risk must be taken.

As there possibly might still linger in the mind of a poor black Haitian gendarme, though trampled and all but crushed, a spark of true patriotism, which, at the remembrance of the immortal Touissant L'Overture, might chance kindle into a burning flame and cause another conflagration. Thus, each court had a special white marine officer in supreme command, but for the sake of perfecting the farce, there were Haitian dummies sitting handing out the slips at the box which received it, and a dummy Haiti commissaire sat alongside of the American marine officer.

On entering the court a small white paper, stamped with police administration, bearing date June 11, 1918, and with the French word oui (yes), was placed in the trembling hands of the native, who was signed (no word spoken) as to slip or anything else, to the box directly under and in front of white American marine and dummy native assistant, who sat on a dais.

The bundle of pink slips with the French non (no), curious enough and most significantly showing the fraudulent nature of this whole scandalous business, remained on the other side of the table tied together, the poor native in charge, as well as so-called voters, knowing these packets were meant for mere show; for even if cut lose their terror-stricken brother Haitians dared not refuse the oui (yes) and ask for the non (no) at the risk of being imprisoned and shot as an enemy of the occupation and foe of the United States Government.

Thus, terrorized and helpless to resist, these people sorrowfully were made to slavishly and tremblingly submit, as brought in from small country villages and mountain sides, guarded and closely watched every step and turn by armed native gendarmes, under strict supervision of marine officers.

This comedy, or rather rape and indeed tragedy, is best described by the intelligent, heartbroken natives (nearly all of whom except those mentioned abstained in face of being blacklisted, imprisonment, etc.), as follows:

"We were compelled to-day by the United States Government to take a dagger, then forced by the military occupation to plunge it into the very heart of our own Negro Republic; and so that, like Pilate of old, they might wash their hands and say hereafter that Haitians themselves actually did the slaughtering."

Hence, June 12, 1918, will be remembered in Haitian history as the day their Negro Republic was not merely raped (as President Harding described it) but indeed assassinated and buried through the heartless betrayal of the United States Government, under the Democratic administration, with its Christian President, Woodrow Wilson, to the everlasting humiliation and shame of every American, and accomplished by a method surpassing the most cowardly, deceptive, and diabolic conceived and practiced by the worst Hun in the World War.

In spite of the disarming of the Haitian soldiers, the disbanding of the Negro army, the closing of their Senate and House of Representatives twice, and which are at this moment under lock and key (and what no other little nation would have slavishly submitted to and tolerated on the part of our own United States Government), these Haitians patiently endured this national humiliation, in face of the treaty, with a flickering hope that such would soon end, there would be a turn in the tide, and a change for the better until April of 1918.

And until the rumor suddenly was heard, that rapidly spread like wildfire, the occupation is actually going, by the same American military force, to rob

Haiti of her constitution, so as to give our lands to foreigners, speculators, and corporations of the United States! Hence the sudden change and the bitter reversion of feeling which followed, as described in my report to missionary committee, which I expected to take prompt action at Washington with President Wilson and State Department, until I found they also had been caught and captured by Haiti corporations and made even an attempt to exploit their missionary superintendents also.

I felt the disappointment and humiliation all the more in having, as stated, done all in my power to foster a friendly feeling toward the United States for over 20 years; urged our Government in Roosevelt, Taft, and beginning of Wilson's administrations to assume a friendly mandate over Haiti and act the big brother toward these people; and therefore, being personally and partly responsible for the fact of our Government's coming to Haiti, though not responsible for the time nor the manner of the seeming invasion of the Black Republic by the armed American military marines.

I therefore feel convinced that this committee, in its thorough investigation into Haiti affairs, as I urged upon the so-called "Haitian navy court" in my letter to Hon. Josephus Daniels, anxious to get the whole truth, make an investigation into the following to get back of marine scandal and occupation failures—

1. Into the nature and extent of the alliance between marine officers of the United States at Washington, as well as in Haiti, with American corporations which followed the "occupation" to the Black Republic and the European special delegate of the Pope (a foreign potentate who dictates the appointments of Haiti ministers in Jamaica, Washington, etc.) sent to Haiti during the present American occupation; with the archbishop, bishops, priests, friars, nuns, etc., of Roman Catholic Church, and all of whom are paid their salaries like officers and members of American marines and the native gendarmes—only they, like marines, receive theirs in American gold, and not like Haitians, in gourdes—from American loans to the little Black Republic and directly through the hands of the United States, financial receiver; and

2. Further, must determine what influence and power such alliance with corporations and close relation of the Catholic Church with the Haiti so-called Government and the American occupation of the United States Government as now existed—from the time we entered—in the Black Republic of Haiti has been responsible for the appointments of American marine officers to and removals from Haiti—under guise of promotions, etc.—under the present occupation; for the demoralization (through constant interference, etc.) of the United States marines from their usual high standard of military discipline and moral efficiency; and for the deflection also of the administration at Washington or officers of the Navy Department, as well as the American occupation on the island, from the high purpose of the United States Government's special mission in Haiti, according to specific terms of our treaty, to apparently serve financial interests and sectarian ends by withholding all appropriations from Protestant day schools, change of constitution, etc.

As I wrote to my Negro missionary committee (in that report) I here emphasize "That unless (rape of constitution already described) this torpedoing by an American submarine of a small and friendly Negro Republic craft (it solemnly undertook to protect, succor, and help) unexpectedly, in Haitian waters, and without warning, and absolutely without provocation, for it had neither gun forehead or aft for either defensive or offensive purposes (having been previously and forcibly dismantled) and the United States President and Government immediately 'disavow' and 'repudiate' such action, and declare same as piratical and the work of irresponsible hyphenated Americans, restore the constitution (with senate and chambers) thus remove the blotch from the folds or our American flag, then in words of the Hon. D. Lloyd George, British Prime Minister, at the great Queen's Hall, London, and had Britain and the whole British Empire not gone immediately to the defense of Belgium and honestly and honorably filled their treaty obligations with that small nation, so in the case of Haiti, disgrace and dishonor will cling to our United States Government and the great American people down the everlasting ages.

A man named Davies, chief of one of the American corporations, swaggering a great deal in Haiti and with our occupation demanded this change of the Haiti constitution, and had already written articles in the National Geographical Magazine and other journals months before declaring (in the interest of his corporation, etc.) that Haiti's ancient constitution must be rewritten, and more especially the clause re lands.

Furthermore, in an interview I had with him at the Cape April, 1918 (during my tour among the native churches), when he seemed to unfold his plans, adding that his corporation had unlimited capital, his own salary more than that of President Wilson, with stockholders if not directors from within the United States Government, thus the occupation was practically at his and his corporation's command; that they had the right of way in Haiti; and that he was then contemplating taking over the mail from the Haitian Government, etc. This was said in presence of an educated native missionary.

Hence the announcement in the Moneteur, Haiti so-called government, but really official paper of the American occupation, and under the name of Haiti president, at once brought to my mind the Cape Haiti interview and the financial interests behind the American occupation, and working through either or both the Navy and State Departments of the United States Government at Washington, compelling Col. John H. Russell to change the Haiti constitution and rob it of its vital and protecting proviso, and so arouse and further embitter the feelings of Haitians whom he describes in his report to Gen. George Barnett, major general commandant United States Marine Corps, at Washington, "Are a very hysterical people; like children, they believe every rumor and completely lose their heads, and in consequence are very hard to quiet."

Senator POMERENE. Who is this Davies?

Mr. EVANS. He professes to be the financial head, if not also the brains, of an American corporation which has already secured—aided by Haitian courts in the hands and under complete domination of American marines—many thousands of acres of the choicest lands in Haiti, mainly for the purpose and advertised all over the Republic of raising castor seed and supplying the United States Government's airplane fleet with oil, etc.

The CHAIRMAN. I heard that he resigned the presidency of the corporation to become a Congressman.

Mr. EVANS. I submit for record a digest of my notes made of interview with this H. P. Davies, and brief quotations from his articles, which I hope will prove as illuminating to the Senate committee of inquiry as they were to me as to himself and corporation's intentions in Haiti, which he affirmed with a view only to make money, irrespective of the treaty or welfare of the Haitians, and disclaimed emphatically that neither himself or his corporation had the least idea of any philanthropic purpose such as to assist in educating industrially or otherwise the Haitians. This Davies, if in Congress, and in this country, or Haiti, should be summoned to appear before this committee.

(Notes of interview with H. P. Davies, official head of castorseed corporation in Haiti, with certain quotations cited re constitution, and comments of editors on United States treaty with Haiti.)

The reading of articles written by Davies, with the interview Saturday afternoon, April 20, 1918, taken with me to my apartments and ponder fills me with dismay as regarding Haiti and the future of these poor Negroes, in spite of the splendid treaty, if the American occupation in the Black Republic, and even the Latin America, Navy or State Department, are to be exploited by this and other corporations. I felt determined to watch the future developments, not merely for sake of Haiti and Haitians, but chiefly the integrity and honor of the United States Government and that of the whole American people, and our honesty and veracity in just going into the World War with the Allies, because of the Kaiser's tearing of the treaty with little Belgium. I shall spare no effort, I said, to prevent the repetition of Germany's crime against Belgium by the United States Government and people (through these unscrupulous corporations and with the aid of United States Marine officers) against weak, bankrupt Haiti, whom we are pledged before the world and God by a sacred covenant to protect and assist.

Therefore, in a letter of April 27, that year, when writing my board on conditions, spiritual degradation, illiteracy, friction, and cruelty often culminating in deaths, I referred to impending attack upon the constitution, urging my board—jointly with northern and southern Baptist leaders— to immediately see President to absolutely prevent this disgrace and shame. I wrote:

"We have sad cases of immorality and drunkenness here among members and even officers of Marine Corps. Through lack of restrictions, either as to vice or intoxicants, the demoralization and even the fatal effects of alcohol in this tropical climate in Haiti, worse among whites than blacks, is somewhat appalling. Why is it you make no efforts there to secure for our marines a Y. M. C. A. branch and give me the necessary authorization to do Christian, social, and temperance work among them?"

Again: "Many marines feel that everything is so quiet in Haiti, and they are tired of walking about doing nothing but carry the gun all day long unless they start a scrap among themselves—and so leave to go to France. These marines should be exchanged every six months. It's cruel to keep these young, raw lads, some two and three years in this tropical climate and with such appalling temptations and degrading surrounding influences."

Further, "Though we have some excellent officers and others, and good work has been done on the roads, sanitation, etc., that are much appreciated, they are sadly hampered here by the lack of "loans" and the perverting influence of the Roman Catholic Church fastened to the Haiti Government, and, of course, our occupation, making honesty, not to say efficiency, impossible. These, with a wealthy corporation boasting of stockholders within the Government department at Washington and controlling influence over our occupation—heckling, deflecting methods—and motives, must eventually, if not doing so now, actually defeat our very purpose as United States Government in Haiti."

Says H. P. D., the official head of the castorseed corporation, in utterance defiance of the plain English of the treaty:

"This article 6 of the constitution of Haiti, which specifies that no foreigner may own lands, must be repealed or amended." Yet he admits that this article was introduced when Haiti gained its independence, and continues through the years to be the one definite thing in the constitution which appealed to every Haitian, and, above all, was understood by all the people.

As showing the complete domination of courts, judges, magistrates, etc., but specially meant as compliment to young, inexperienced, often raw American marines, and their gendarmes, H. P. D. writes in March number of Pan American Magazine (1917):

"It is fortunate for Haiti and Santo Domingo and for the United States also that the solution of these problems, or at least the practical administration (sic) of the affairs of both of the island's Republics, has been placed in the hands of our overworked and little appreciated Marine Corps. Soldier and sailor, too," does not begin to express it. I have seen marines in Haiti and Santo Domingo switching from soldier to anything—from a blacksmith to a superior court judge, etc.

Fearing that your superintendent had taken a too rosy view of the treaty and interpreted its language too generously, and that it did not actually mean that the United States Government, after all, were by its good offices aid the Haitian Government in the proper and efficient development of its (Haiti) agricultural, mineral, and commercial resources, and in the establishment of the finances of Haiti on a firm and solid basis for the sake of Haiti and Haiti people; but through American corporations with persons like H. P. D. at the head, with United States Government officers as directors and stockholders, and absolutely in the financial interests of white Americans, were in the minds of both President Wilson and United States Senate, as well as Haitian Government, while negotiating and ratifying and signing above treaty. Hence I quote what two of the leading Americans, in two of the first-class American magazines, and neither Christian missionaries or corporations promotionists say at the very time the treaty was made:

The New York Outlook for March 15, 1916, thus comments on treaty between United States and Haiti, as follows:

"The treaty as a whole represents the furthest extreme (in liberality and generosity) which we have yet gone in—the big brother attitude, with regard to the small neighboring Latin-American nations.

"Of course, the success of financial and constabulary arrangements in Haiti will largely depend upon the character of the men our Government will choose to fill the various offices."

The Washington, D. C., National Geographical Magazine for August, 1916, said thus about the treaty:

"By this treaty the United States practically underwrites a loan of sufficient amount to settle all the legitimate debts of the country and to finance the beginning of its developments—opening up its mines, putting its agriculture on a solid basis, and otherwise preparing to make it a region of plenty that nature has equipped it to be.

"This new departure probably will insure peace, quiet, honest administration, and, if it does, Haiti (not American corporations) certainly will go forward as few small countries ever have."

This is why, Mr. Chairman and members of the committee, I asked Col. Russell to postpone said so-called voting, allow me to cable President Wilson and ask for a commission to investigate matters, as I felt he ought to know what was going on both in Haiti and around him at Washington; that the Senate and the American people should also know.

Mr. ANGELL. Just to explain possibly to you gentlemen who have not read the record here—I heard Senator King say he had not read it—merely by way of explanation, which I think will give a little light on what Mr. Ton Evans is saying, the old constitution, which is in the record here—I am not testifying or adding anything—the old constitution had a prohibition clause in it against the ownership of land by any alien. Only Haitian citizens (colored or white) could own land. Exactly, for instance, the same as here in the District of Columbia, where United States citizens alone are entitled.

The new constitution, so called, however, as stated in the memorandum to this committee by the Navy Department, and appearing on page 7 of the record, part L of these hearings, the new constitution, which was amended by order • of the State Department, provided specifically in Article V that the right to own real estate (lands) be open to any person, corporation, citizens or not of Haiti. That is what the new constitution is about.

Mr. EVANS. So I submitted respectfully to the colonel, adding how deeply I regretted his refusal to postpone this so-called voting and allow me to cable the White House. In all military matters, I added, I took off my hat to him as chief of the occupation, but in constitutional matters, question of honest and honorable observance of treaty, and our moral and legal obligations as a Government, and our great American people, to live up to the spirit and letter of that sacred covenant; or the right of military occupation, to tamper with and tear up a constitution, as they were tearing up the treaty—with my education, knowledge, and experience I respectfully declined to submit to any military or other governmental authority.

I therefore took leave of the colonel, saying we should meet before a committee or commission either in Washington or Haiti, when not only the influence and power deflecting the motives of our American occupation, but actually defeat the great purpose of their coming and staying in Haiti, would be found out: Haiti Senate, Chambers, and constitution restored to them; and this part of the American marines' work and methods condemned.

On leaving the headquarters of the American occupation I turned into an office on the way to station ere boarding my train to St. Marc, and convinced that all this H. P. Davies had told me concerning our United States Government and the American occupation in Haiti was only too true, and sent a registered letter to President Woodrow Wilson, setting forth the facts, with another reg'stered letter to Ex-President Theodore Roosevelt, with a copy of my letter to President, and reason why it was inclosed to Oyster Bay.

As expected, the former was intercepted by Mr. Tumulty, or in either of Navy or State Departments. Ex-President Roosevelt replied, and sent me other letters.

The so-called voting took place June 12, 1918, precisely as announced. I have already described at length from missionary report, inserted herein.

Senator POMERENE. June, 1920?

Mr. EVANS. No, Senator; June 12, 1918, and 8 or 10 days after my visit to Port au Prince and Col. Russell.

Senator POMERENE. Who was conducting that election?

Mr. EVANS. The American occupation, though they endeavored to make it appear that the Haitian Government, which, of course, is absolutely false.

Senator POMERENE. You mean by that these marines?

Mr. EVANS. Yes; American marine officers and members of the United States Marine Corps, the Haitian officers of the occupation, for there is absolutely no Haitian Government, acted as dummies and a mere cover; you could see their spirit crushed, and sat silent and mummy-like alongside of marine, who was supreme.

Senator POMERENE. Do I understand from your statement that these native citizens were intimidated so that they would not vote against the adoption of the new section of the constitution? Is that the fact?

Mr. EVANS. Yes; most emphatically so. They were terror-stricken, or, as Col. Russell himself admits in his report to Gen. Barnett, referred to, " They were scared by rumors, and become almost hysterical with fear " of imprisonment, of being clubbed to death, or shot down by gendarmes and marines, besides the proclamation of the American occupation—through the Negro President of Haiti—announcing the so-called voting, the following notices were put up at booths, or in Haiti at the courts of justice (sic) and signed by American marine officers—who have power over life and death in the Black Republic that no American in the United States can possibly realize—and read, as the specimen below:

INTIMIDATION AND THREAT.

REPUBLIC OF HAITI,
PORT-DE-PAIX, *June 11, 1918.*

In accordance with the decree of His Excellency, the President of the Republic, published in the Monitor of May 8 last, all the citizens of this commune of Port-de-Paix are asked to be present to-morrow at the Hotel Communal to vote on the new constitution, published in the Monitor of the same date. Any abstention from such a solemn occasion will be considered an unpatriotic—that is, anti-American occupation—act. Maintenance of order will be assured by the gendarmerie (under chief, Gen. Williams, American marine officer), and the ballots will be distributed by a member of the administration of finances (an American marine officer) opposite the voting offices, etc.

HERMAN H. HANNEKIN,
Lieutenant gendarmerie d'Haïti, American marine officer.
E. LESCOT,
Government Commissaire, Northwest.

At St. Marc and other places, and if after voting and in celebration of death of the old Haiti constitution safeguarding their Republic hitherto, were allowed to indulge in all the voodoo dances and orgies they wished that night by order of the occupation and American marines, as an inducement to vote, etc.

All the pink slips with non (no) as stated in my report were tied up, and only the white slips with oui (yes) were loose and handled on the table before each of those that were driven in, and one of each given to the committee without a word spoken by either the Haitian so-called voter (sic) without looking at the word (even though nearly all were too illiterate to know what it was) and stood for if he did look, walked directly in fear and dread toward the box he was pointed to and disappeared through the back door, glad the painful performance was over.

On my return from the court at St. Marc, and met by my wife, who asked how things were, I replied, "God forbid that I should ever witness anything of this kind again. Until this shame and disgrace is wiped off by our United States Government we shall never be able to put out our Stars and Stripes again in Haiti."

Senator POMERENE. How many polling places were there?

Mr. EVANS. I believe there was a polling place at every little town and village throughout the Republic.

Senator POMERENE. Where was the polling place that you are describing now?

Mr. EVANS. St. Marc, where I was stationed.

Senator POMERENE. Was there just one polling place in the city?

Mr. EVANS. That was the only polling place in St. Marc, which was a town of 5,000 or 6,000 people, with some 12,000 to 15,000 or more within a radius of 10 or 12 miles perhaps.

Senator POMERENE. Do you know what the condition was at the other polling places?

Mr. EVANS. I did not make it my special business to go outside of St. Marc to see, for if I did this would have been construed as antipatriotic, or rebellion against constituted authority and possibly meant death. I felt my own life almost safer in Haiti before the occupation came than with a certain class of unscrupulous, drunken, brutal, American marines who seemed half crazy. I made inquiries, however, from others in various towns I visited as superintendent missionary, and from what information I received from most reliable sources—the conditions were exactly like at St. Marc, including the voodoo dances and immoral orgies, if not much drinking.

Senator POMERENE. Well, in a general way?

Mr. EVANS. Generally speaking from information given me, yes; the conditions were alike everywhere, but evidence on this and other points will be forthcoming in Haiti.

Senator POMERENE. What was the vote at St. Marc; what was the result there?

Mr. EVANS. There was no means of knowing. The natives felt no interest whatever, as it was known from the announcement by the occupation (through Dartigenauve), that whatever the American marines did no one dared to oppose or even question. All slips were taken to Port Au Prince, and published there. It was looked upon as a mere farce, and lowered the prestige of the United States among Haitians, who seriously think, and even Europeans, and indeed Americans, who felt that the American occupation had gone the limit, and made itself a laughing-stock, and looked contemptible. No votes were reckoned to my knowledge at either town, but all taken in charge of American marines to Port Au Prince.

Senator POMERENE. No, no; when the votes were counted what was the result of the election at that place?

Mr. EVANS. All were taken to Port Au Prince, and published there, but whether they gave numbers supposed to be cast at each town, I know not, and like others cared little, as I became disgusted, and felt disgraced that such was possible in the name of the United States, and by anyone who called himself an American!

Senator KING. Sixty-three thousand for, and two hundred or three hundred against in all the island——

Mr. EVANS. You mean the Republic, Senator. They might have published the vote as 1,000,000 as 63,000 there is no one to contradict or to explain for the American marines managed the whole business. I do not believe that any pink slips were put in by Haitians, and that out of shame certain marines cast in a couple of hundreds. This is the belief in Haiti.

I denounced it then, and denounce it more still to-day, as the greatest mockery I ever saw in my life, and never thought we had Americans and marine officers that could sink so low before these gendarmes, and poor Haitians, whose respect, implicit confidence, and highest admiration should be the aim of every military officer and true American who despises anything like hypocrisy, and scorns deceit and fraud.

Senator POMERENE. What part did these educated Haitians take in this election?

Mr. EVANS. The great majority, apart from those who happened as stated—to be officially and financially connected with the occupation, so-called Haiti Government, sugar, and castor-seed corporations, schools, courts, prisons, customs, railroads, etc., abstained and kept clear of the voting place, though in so doing they ran the risk of being blacklisted, run into prison on slightest suspicion, or provocation, etc.

Had they gone, they would have asked for the pink slip with non, which would have decided their lot with the occupation. It was a hard and trying situation, but many were heroic enough to stand the test, whatever has been the consequences since.

If the occupation and American marines were in the employ of Germany and receiving their pay from Berlin, they could never have gone about wrecking the reputation, and ruining the character, and destroying the growing influence of the United States Governmet, more successfully than by the blundering, brutal, fraudulent, and even murderous conduct of marines and gendarmes for the lack of moral discipline, knowledge of human nature, common sense, and true American patriotism of the Washington, Lincoln, and Roosevelt type.

Senator POMERENE. Under the Haitian law, how many voters would there be in the Republic?

Mr. EVANS. No one can say positively, for there never perhaps has been a real census. Its mere guess work.

Senator POMERENE. What portion of the votes was cast?

Mr. EVANS. You say about 63,000?

Senator KING. 69,000.

Mr. EVANS. The people of Haiti, small as that number is, believe not the published figures, though seeing how many the occupation had gathered by sending their gendarmes around, and the fact of their being dominated by fear, and loss of little pay they had, and positions held—it may be near the truth.

Senator POMERENE. We will assume it is so. What portion is embraced in the 69,000?

Mr. EVANS. Of the total population?

Senator POMERENE. No; of the voters?

Mr. EVANS. The real population of Haiti, is put down as 2,500,000.

The CHAIRMAN. You can figure the adult males.

Senator POMERENE. Probably one in five?

The CHAIRMAN. Two and a half million, roughly.

Senator POMERENE. There ought to be in the neighborhood of 400,000 or 500,000 votes then.

Mr. EVANS. I should say something more like 400,000.

Senator POMERENE. That is, if males alone voted.

Senator KING. Most of the people reside out in the hills and in the brush, do they not?

Mr. EVANS. Yes; most of the people are living in the country; and only way you can have any idea, is on Saturday their market day, when you feel astonished at their number filing in from brush, and narrow lanes bent if possible on reaching the market as early as they can, and when business is over about 1 or 2 o'clock latest, unless in the very busy cotton or coffee seasons—they quietly hasten back to their husbands, children, and homes, so that the market places are all cleared again in the early afternoons.

Senator KING. I was told when I was there that three-fourths of the population lived out of the cities.

Mr. EVANS. Yes, that is true; at least three-fourths.

Senator POMERENE. How was this amendment proposed? What was the modus operandi down there? Is it proposed by joint resolution of the Congress, similar to ours?

Mr. EVANS. Yes; precisely, so I understand, and from the time their constitution was first adopted; but their senate and chambers had been abolished by the American occupation and members forced out and doors locked by armed American marines, and as a substitute for the Haitian Congress the same American occupation created—illegally, of course—what is called a national council, which, with the Haitian President, functions at the dictation and direction of the American occupation, through the marines. This is why the Haitian courts and Haitian people—quite apart from the fraudulent methhods adopted re voting, intimidation and military force—declare the so-called new constitution as both illegal and unconstitutional; but most all of judges of said courts were dismissed, if not some imprisoned, for daring to invalidate any procedure of American marines, whose knowledge, however, of either law, constitution, or treaty in Haiti, if not also respect, has been of a somewhat negligible quantity and fundamentally lacking.

Senator POMERENE. But was there at that time?

Mr. EVANS. No; not at this time, nor some two years before. Their parliament was closed in April of 1916, whereas the American occupation's first official notification or decree—through their Haiti President—announcing the new constitution dates May, 1918. On page 25 of the record of hearing before select committee on Haiti, etc., part 1, this paragraph appears, showing the vigorous protest made by the Haitian Chambers against this annihilation process, as follows:

"The Haitian Chambers protested against this intervention. On May 5, the Senators were assembling in their provisional quarters when an American (marine) officer, brutally ordered them to leave the place, threatening violent measures to force them to go. At the suggestion of M. Paul Laraque, the President of the Haitian Senate, they met at his house, where they drew up a formal account of the incident." (See Appendix No. 10.)

Senator POMERENE. How was this amendment proposed, by what functionary?

Mr. EVANS. It was done by the same functionary, that does everything in Haiti, the American occupation, through the marines, but with Haiti President acting—under force—as medium to blind and bluff the Haitian people, and deceive the responsible United States Government, and people.

H. P. Davies, official head of castor-seed corporation in Haiti, boasts to be a functionary acting behind the American occupation, and last October a responsible official of the United States Navy Department at Washington publicly boasted that he was the functionary who changed the Haiti constitution, so there must be a conspiracy of many functionaries concerned in the proposing, and illegal, unconstitutional forcing of the new constitution as well as back of the mock voting.

Haitian intelligent and educated leaders and business men all over the Republic saw through all this, and deplored and despised such procedure.

Senator KING. Was there just one article involved in the amendment to the constitution?

Mr. EVANS. While there were minor modifications or adjustments necessary to meet new conditions, which the Haitians themselves would gradually and in a regular and constitutional way have made with little patience, and if the American military showed less intolerance and bounce, the main and vital article which the American occupation and other corporation functionaries in

Haiti and at Washington (acting together), was that concerning the land, which to the Haitians was the very heart and life of their constitution.

These are the exact words of H. P. Davies, official head of the castor seed Haiti corporation, in his magazine article he gave me to read and study at Cape Haiti in April of 1918, and as showing his emphatic (and that of his corporation) policy in the Black Republic when demanding this change:

"This article 6 of the constitution of Haiti, which specifies that no foreigner (that is, colored or white person unless a Haitian citizen) may own lands, must be repealed or amended."

Though admitting the vital importance of this one article and the very heart and life of their constitution as follows, he persists in above demand:

"That this article was introduced when Haiti gained its independence and continues through the years to be the one definite thing in the constitution which appealed to every Haitian and above all was understood by all the people."

Senator KING. If you will just answer without explanation we will get along better. I asked you if that was the only point involved in the election.

Mr. EVANS. I have already answered that no doubt there were minor points which could have been adjusted through the Haitian Senate and Chambers, regularly and constitutionally, but that it was the land part of the new constitution which aroused, embittered, and actually transformed the somewhat friendly feeling into that of opposition, anger, and hatred against us.

Senator KING. What was done?

Mr. EVANS. As I have already replied to Senator Pomerene and stated before, the question of land was the vital point demanded by H. P. Davies and his corporation, and according to his imperative demand, and that of the castor-seed corporation, and as Davies predicted to me would be the case two months previously at his bureau in Cape Haiti, the "occupation," on advice from Washington and through the Haiti President, announced that a new constitution would be submitted to the vote of the Haitian people, on June 12, 1918, and in which proposed new constitution this objectionable article, re lands, would be changed to suit of course this castor-seed if not also the Haiti Sugar Corporation, and said voting would be arranged, conducted, and guarded under strict supervision of the armed American Marines and their gendarmes.

Senator KING. You say that this article originated in the Navy Department?

Mr. EVANS. I say it originated with Davies and his corporation, and if what he claimed that there were directors and stockholders (in his corporation) members of the United States Government and administration and within the Navy Department at Washington, then Col. Russell received his instructions from the Navy Department, for these are the words of Assistant Secretary Franklin Roosevelt, of the United States Navy, which finally settles not only the complicity but official origin of the new constitution with the complete change—in fact, total elimination—of the old constitution's land clause (Art. VI):

"You know, I have had something to do with the running of a couple of little republics. The facts are that I wrote Haiti's constitution myself, and if I do say it I think it is a very good constitution."

This remarkable statement was wired all over the United States and caused astonishment and amazement among millions of Americans, but cleared up at last the mystery to me, and in Haiti, as to whom were directly and officially responsible for this betrayal of confidence and perpetration of such a crime against this little helpless nation—this admission must have been known to members of this committee.

Senator KING. Have any advantages been taken of this provision in the new constitution by Americans to acquire lands?

Mr. EVANS. Yes; and in my judgment a very unfair, unjust, if not mean, advantage. The castor-seed corporation, with its claim of abundant wealth and financial relations with members of the United States Government at Washington, through directors and stockholders, and by contract to furnish oil to the United States Government's airplane fleet, would have the right of way to the largest and best of the soil throughout the Republic, and probably amount to a considerable area of this Republic.

The Haiti sugar corporation, 1918, to which my own secretary of my Haiti Negro missionary committee transferred his interest and affections, now, I hear, in the hands of the receiver, and boosting this corporation in Lott Carey Missionary Herald for September, under his own name, and for Negro speculators of North Carolina, etc., says:

"This corporation has 130,000 acres of excellent sugar land in the plains of Leogain, which is said to be the richest land on the continent with a soil of 12 ft. depth, besides a 20,000-acre tract of 15 miles north of Port au Prince.

"*Cheap labor.*—While Cuba is paying for labor $2 a day, and more at present, Haitian laborers are only paid 20 cents a day, and in that is included a raise of over 50 per cent over what was accustomed to be given labor formerly, etc."

This negro speculator and booster forgot to add that living had gone up 150 per cent since American occupation.

These are the two main corporations, and it is stated that these lands are got through the special aid of the American occupation, who control the Haitian courts and judges, etc.

Senator KING. Were no Americans holding land in Haiti prior to this constitutional amendment?

Mr. EVANS. There might have been a few Americans, just as there were many foreigners holding individual properties, and even land for their own purpose, but no corporations or American on large scale to my knowledge, and it would be somewhat futile for an individual or native Negroes to compete in Haiti, at least during the last administration, if what Davies alleged is true, that these had United States Government officials as directors and stockholders.

I should have added that under the old constitution and previous to our American occupation there was no difficulty whatever for individuals settling in Haiti to own property. The Haiti Government, whose constitution stipulates that Protestant churches are equally free with Roman Catholic there, have always been only too glad to grant land for schools or colleges to American evangelical and missionary societies to educate and, morally and religiously, develop the Haitian people, as the following from President Leconte, whom I visited at the palace, to his secretary of state, whom I wished to talk with concerning land for Bible training and industrial seminary and school, in anticipation of the coming of secretary of Baptist Home Mission Board, and so for the same purpose the map of the island was given:

"*Le President de la Republique d'Haiti, au Hon. J. N. Leger, mon cher Secretaire d'Etat.*

"J'introduis volontiers aupres de vous le Rev. L. Ton Evans, Secretaire General de la Mission Baptiste Evangelique pour Haiti, qui desire prendre contact avec vous et vous entretenir de choses qui concernant sa Mission et son voyage dans le Pays.
* Sincere compliments,

"Cтus. Leconte.

"PALAIS NATIONAL, *22 Xbre. 1911.*
"Au Sre. d'Etat de Rel. Exterieurs."

"*Le President de la Republique d'Haiti au Secretaire de la Instruction Publique d'Haiti.*

"Envole au Reverend Ton Evans, la carte de l'ile d' Haiti, avec l'expression de ses meilleurs voeux pour le plein succes de ses nobles projects et ses souhaits de bon voyage.
"Le 29, Decembre. 1911.

"Cтus. Leconte."

Both in his own handwriting, and a few months before he was ruthlessly assassinated because he refused to be exploited and turn over the customs to German and other white speculators and political profiteers.

Senator KING. You have answered that they did; were they Americans?

Mr. EVANS. Yes; some most probably were, though I came, chiefly years ago and through the southern and southeastern part of the Republic, in contact with English, French, Dutch, and German Europeans. There was no outside corporation, to my knowledge.

Senator POMERENE. Let me ask you another question, Mr. Evans, a preliminary question. When were you last in Haiti?

Mr. EVANS. I left there in April of 1919.

Senator POMERENE. And you have not been there since?

Mr. EVANS. No.

Senator POMERENE. Suppose the question arose and was presented to the Haitians as to whether or not we should continue our occupation down there temporarily, until their Government could be completely organized and put upon a substantial footing, what would be the result of such a vote, in your judgment?

Mr. KING. Were the Germans, French, and other nationalities other than the Haitians owning land in Haiti prior to this amendment?

Mr. EVANS. Yes; small holdings for their own family purposes.

Mr. KING. But there were holdings?

Mr. EVANS. Oh, yes.

The CHAIRMAN. Let me ask Mr. Evans were these holdings in their own names? Did they have title in their own names?

Mr. EVANS. No. I understand that many merchants and others would live with native women, perhaps of education and maybe secretly married, and through whom the property would be held.

The CHAIRMAN. That was quite a common practice, was it not, among the merchants other than Americans who were down there?

Mr. EVANS. Yes; unfortunately, when this was done without a legal marriage. I do not know, however, a single case of an American living with a Haitian or colored woman, with the exception of some of the captains and lieutenants of American marines, in the gendarmerie, and most of who in these cases were English-speaking negro women from surrounding islands living in Haiti and able to assist the white American with the native through the French pato's, which something like 90 or probably 95 per cent of Haitians speak.

Some of our American marine officers in the gendarmerie live in the Roman Catholic presbytery with the priests and assist him in Roman Catholic Church matters, thus by such alliances giving the idea, which is generally believed among the illiterate inhabitants outside of the many thousand professing Protestants and Protestant adherants, that the United States Government, President, and people are Roman Catholics.

Mr. ANGELL. At this point may I introduce into the record the articles of the two constitutions covering the holding of land, that will give, so far as the record is concerned, at least a basis for Mr. Evans's testimony. I will give the stenographer the original French text of Article VI of the constitution of 1889, which was in force until this constitution was brought forward for adoption, the translation of which is as follows. The original French text is as follows:

"Nul, s'il n'est haitien, ne peut etre proprietaire de b'en fonciers en Haiti. a quelque titre que ce soit, ni acquerux aucun immeuble."

"No person who is not a Haitian can be proprietor or can own an interest in real estate in Haiti, by whatsoever title, nor acqu're any real estate."

Article V of the new, changed constitution of 1918, concerning which Mr. Evans has just been testifying and told this committee its origination through a certain Mr. H. P. Davies and the United States Navy Department at Washington, reads in translation as follows:

"The right to own real estate is granted to a foreigner res'ding in Haiti and to companies (corporations) organized by foreigners for the needs of their dwellings, of their agricultural, conmercial, and industrial enterprises, and of education. This right shall cease at the end of the period of six years after the foreigner shall have ceased to reside in the country, or shall have ceased to conduct the operations of such companies " (corporations).

The original French text of above changed article reads:

"Le droit de propriete immobiliere est accorde a l'etranger resident en Haiti, et aux soc'etes formes par des etrangers pour les besoins de leurs demeures, de leurs entreprises agricoles, commerciales, industrielles, ou d'enseignment.

"Ce droit prendra fin dans une per'ode de cinq annees apres que l'tranger aura cesse de resider dans le pays ou qu'auront cesse les operations de ces compagnies."

Mr. EVANS. At present disappointed, with b'tter feelings due not only to being robbed of their senate, their chambers, and especially what is dearest to them in the'r constitution, and resentment of their betrayal, the brutality and murders due to the mistaken and cruel working of the corvee, the overwhelming majority would, in my opinion just now, be for the United States to clear right out, which I would profoundly deplore, not simply for the sake of Haiti; it would be a humiliating confess'on on our part of failure to carry out our solemn treaty obligations, which is a most serious matter for the United States at the present moment, about to enter into conference with the civilized nations of the world, negotiate treaties, etc. We must not think of shirking our duties to Haiti and the Hait'an people, and can not thus humiliate ourselves before the world.

If this Senate committee results in some cleaning out among our American marines in Haiti, change the military into a civil occupation, give reasonable guaranties that the treaty will be honestly and honorably carried out directly by the United States Government through competent, broad-minded, educated, and even Christian statesmen of this country, possessed with faith in the Negro and imbued somewhat with a true missionary spirit, and all this carefully explained to the Haitians, the whole of Haiti would demand us to stay.

Senator POMERENE. Well, am I to infer now that your belief is that the present state of the Haitian mind is that we should get out?

Mr. EVANS. Yes. The Haitians in many respects are children, easily led and easily aroused and driven into almost hysterics with fear and terror. I fear that many Haitian leaders, as well as the mass of the Negro inhabitants, look at the cruel and criminal, if not insane, blunders of the American occupation. Officials at the Navy, if not the State Department at Washington, as to senate, chambers, and constitution, not to mention the brutalities and murders by drunken, half crazy marines and gendarmes, which some, ignorant of the situation in Haiti and the real character of the Haitian, seek to defend and a few un-American persons go so far as to justify, are looked upon not as the doings of individuals, members of corporations, and conspiring and profiteering officials but as the fixed policy of the responsible United States Government and American people who never meant from the beginning to live up to their own treaty.

Hence, if the result of this careful and thorough investigation will mean not merely an honest confession of our criminal blunder at a time we were so absorbed in the World War, and the indignant repudiation in the name of the United States Government, and the great American people, of all these blunders, brutalities, and killings, and a readiness on our part to make an adequate reparation to Haiti, we would be allowed, if not requested, to remain to finish the job we undertook, and once more lift our heads.

Senator POMERENE. Suppose we were out of there now.

Mr. EVANS. It would be an admission of incompetency and absolute failure on our part as a Government before Haiti and the world, and can not for that reason, if nothing else, be supposed for a moment.

Senator POMERENE. Suppose that we were to leave the island now and other foreign influences were eliminated entirely, what would be the result to the people of the island?

Mr. EVANS. In my firm opinion based on a careful study of and years of experience with white and colored, both in Haiti and elsewhere, and my knowledge of psychology of the white and black man, Haitians would gradually go back to their former position under the dominating and domineering influence of European merchants, politicians, and Roman Catholic priests, who they are utterly incapable at present to resist. If these were entirely eliminated and the Haitians left alone, with merely efficient Bible training schools for native preachers and teachers, and an industrial school similar to Tuskegee and on a Christian basis, I believe it would soon develop into an ideal Negro republic, and astonish America and the world.

Senator POMERENE. Assume that we were to withdraw entirely and that no other foreign nation was to step in there, what would be the result to the people from the standpoint of law and order and a civic government? In other words, could they maintain law and order down there and a proper civic government?

Mr. EVANS. Seeing that Haiti has already had over 100 years of an independent, free Republic, often seriously interrupted, it is true, by political disturbances and even bloody revolutions, in the main fomented and financed by white men; that during the last decade quite a number of young Haitians have had sound, practical education here in the States, and having among themselves many experienced, intellectually, morally, and even spiritually strong Protestant and a few Catholic leaders, their prospects would be brighter than ever from the standpoint of law, order, and civic government.

If the United States, however, protected the island from foreign invasion and political filibustering of white and colored, supervised Haiti elections and finances, and aid in the establishment of normal and industrial college, Haiti without fail would gradually but surely work out her own redemption, and quietly take her place among civilized, progressive, peaceful nations. Still, my firm belief is that we should remain in Haiti for some years to render her such aid as specified or, better, to carry out our treaty, through a civil occupation.

Senator POMERENE. What do you mean by years to come—3 or 4 years or 40 or 50 years?

Mr. EVANS. Ten or 25 years, under efficient and sympathetic American protection and leadership, but not a day longer than we can help it under present military occupation after what has transpired.

It may help to make clearer to the committee if I again briefly quote from that 1918 missionary report. It is the following:

"The invasion of the Black Republic by certain American capitalists was naturally to be expected, much like the Spanish pirates and French slave traders followed in the wake of Columbus five centuries before, but unless Uncle Sam bestirs himself, wakes up, and strictly carries out his treaty and pledge to preserve Haiti's integrity, the Haitians' liberties, etc., the result to-day will prove as disastrous to the Negroes of the black Republic as to the Carib Indians, in those far-off days when piracy and buccaneering were rife in Hispaniola.

"Whatsoever a president, government, or nation soweth, that also they will reap in the just providence of God, and the timely warning should be heeded by the United States. In his Social Aspects of Foreign Missions, Dr. Faunce, of Brown University, says:

"'Already incalculable harm has been done by the sudden influx of the white man and forcing of his ideas among the weaker peoples. In Haiti, for instance, the entire native population (about 1,000,000) died out within 40 years because of the ruthlessness and brutality of Spanish misgovernment. The atrocities wrought by the white in the Kongo, driving the black to produce rubber, are still fresh in our minds, as it should be to-day to the Belgians. Africa has been robbed for centuries, of its treasures, flesh, and blood, to satisfy European and American greed.'"

While European and German politicians and profiteers exploited the Haitian Government and customs, they were wiser than to meddle with senate and chambers of the people or attempt such a stupid and mad thing as the rape of Haiti's constitution, for instance.

Senator POMERENE. Is Gen. Williams in control there now?

Mr. EVANS. No; I think he has left at last.

Senator POMERENE. Who has succeeded him?

Mr. EVANS. I do not know; this has been since my return to the States.

The CHAIRMAN. Col. Russell.

Senator POMERENE. Col. Russell?

Mr. EVANS. Excuse me; Gen. Alexander Williams was the general over the gendarmerie of Haiti (native armed police), and under Col. John H. Russell. Col. Russell is head of the American occupation and chief in supreme command of American marines and the gendarmerie of the republic. It is important to have the two departments quite distinct in mind.

Senator POMERENE. He is there by our appointment, Senator McCormick? Who is there representing this Government?

Mr. ANGELL. Yes; he is at the head of all, as Mr. Evans said.

Mr. EVANS. There must be no confusion between the marine and the gendarme; they belong to different departments under the American occupation. The marines are about 800, perhaps, in number, most of whom are stationed at Port au Prince, with about one-fourth at Cape Haiti. Very little if any disorder or brutality are alleged against these, with the exception of a scrap now and again with the gendarmes at Port au Prince. In fact, the marines have bitterly complained they had hardly anything to do, as everything was so quiet.

The gendarmes, or armed native police, are scattered in companies all over the republic, and each company has either a white captain or white lieutenants as officer in sole charge, who also are called American marine officers.

Most of the charges of brutality and killings, both in all prisons as well as under corvee, and the so-called Cacos, are against these marine officers over the gendarmes and their gendarmes, chosen and commanded by them, all of whom were under Gen. Williams. Like the confusion between Navy and State Departments at Washington, there has been friction and confusion and a great deal of jealousy between these two departments and the two sets of marine officers, and through lack of definite policy they often overlapped, consequently had an injurious effect upon moral as well as military discipline, and seriously at times handicapped the work of the occupation.

The CHAIRMAN. Before you leave, Mr. Evans, let me ask in reference to your allusion to the papa-loi at the beginning of your testimony: in your judgment is voodoo'sm general in Haiti?

Mr. Evans. It is noth'ng like what it used to be, for instance, when I landed at Jacmel in the south, some 28 years ago. This reform, if not revolutionary change, is due chiefly, within a radius of 40 or 50 miles around Jacmel as well as in sections throughout the northeast, to faithful work of the native Christian missionary, the native small schools, and the sincerity and consistency of the daily life and conduct of the native Christians and converts (croyans) themselves.

President Leconte during his short tenure of the presidential office adopted some strict measures and made the voodoo dances, orgies, and sacrifices illegal; hence helped to put down most. Some of our better-class American marine officers of gendarmes have also informed me of using their influence in same direction.

Twenty-nine, twenty-five, and twenty years ago, and even fifteen, one could not travel 2 or 3 miles without hearing the tomtom, but of late years, and especially is this so in the Gros Morne section and Jacmel, one can travel days together without hearing a sound, nor see the effect of taffia. To me the gospel and educational work have produced if not a very high intellectual type certainly a high moral and spiritual character among these once voodoo debauched, low, superstitious Romanists and witchcraft devotees, gamblers, and cock fighters, and the remarkable stories they have to tell, evidenced by their honest and clean lives has been cheering and inspiring.

I have had the joy of burning tomtoms and the whole paraphernalia used by papa and mama lois after conversion, and Lherisson, our excellent native missionary at Jacmel, has again and again brought donkey loads of demon-worshiped implements to be publicly burned in town amid great rejoicings of the Christian believers and to the confusion, if not consternation, of priests, who unfortunately neither teach nor believe in real regenerating power of the Christian religion.

Senator Pomerene. Are you go:ng back there as a missionary again?

Mr. Evans. Possibly I may; for after 20 years of correspondence, interviews, pleadings, and praying our northern Baptist convention home mission society through its religious-education department has just decided to enter Haiti so as to establish in the most central position in the republic a Bible and theological seminary, with an industrial department to efficiently train native preachers and Christian workers right on the Haitian soil, and I may be requested, perhaps, to accompany the secretary on his survey tour about the time this committee goes to Haiti.

The committee may be interested to have inserted here in the record, and as showing the native's eagerness for education and further religious equipment and assistance by a powerful missionary organization in North America to enable them to devote their time and energy entirely to preach the Gospel and give Christian teaching to fellow Haitians, a copy of the petition I brought to New York in 1909 to above home mission society; that is, two years before I had the honor of bearing the petition and earnest prayer of nearly 3,000 Haitians, including President Simon and President Leconte (who followed him), to Messrs. Rockefeller and Carnegie, re the national normal and industrial college. This petition reads as follows:

Haiti Evangelical Baptist Mission, a cry from Macedonia, or prayer of native brethren of the black Republic:

We, the present missionaries and native assistant preachers, express our great joy at the interest which is being created in this dark and needy island and evangelization of our own superstitious country, steeped in Romanism, witchcraft, and voodooism (demon worship), through the efforts of our friend and brother, L. Ton Evans, who left his church in Pennsylvania to serve Christ and help us to give the Gospel and religious education to the black republic. Having no support from any missionary board or society, we are compelled to engage ourselves in some kind of secular occupations to struggle along, and which takes most of our time and energies to the hindrance of Gospel and educational work, and so as to carry the evangel into dark sections all around us clamoring for the light and word of truth.

For the sake of reaching these hundreds of thousands of perishing souls, the social and moral uplift of our dear country, and for Christ, we therefore most earnestly appeal to the American Home Mission Society, through our beloved brother, Ton Evans, field secretary, to undertake this mission field, so near your American shores, and yet so far away from your American civilization and your Christian privileges.

We are fully convinced that our brother's desire to establish in Haiti, in connection with a Christian mission and Bible school and seminary for training native preachers, there should be also a normal and industrial school, patterned after Tuskegee, which would prove a blessing in the mental, moral, and manual emancipation of our young people, and give solidity and permanency to the mission.

LUCIUS HYPOLITE,
Port au Prince.
P. NOSIREL LHERISSON,
Jacomel.
METELLUS MENARD,
St. Raphael.
C. JEAN-JACQUES,
Cape Haiti.
AMBROSE MARS,
St. Raphael.
T. V. EUSTACHE,
Dondon.
ELIE MARK,
Trou.
DUMAY PIERRE ALEXIS,
Milot.
DUTREVILLE LAMOUR,
Trou.
NERVA GHOUSSE,
Jacmel.
ORIOUS PAULTRE,
St. Marc.
SAMUEL BLACK,
St. Marc.
ALCIUS JOLICOEUR,
Jacmel.
HERNE GUYOT,
Port de Paix.
JOACHIM EDOUARD,
Grande Riviere.
ELIE PHELIX CADET,
Dondon.
OSIRIS LAMOUR,
Trou.

Senator POMERENE. Who has succeeded you there?

Mr. EVANS. There is no white man in my place. A good colored brother from the Southland, without any experience in Haiti, or knowledge of either the French nor patois I understand, is acting for the same colored missionary committee. The Negroes of Haiti and native government have more confidence in the stability, courage, and efficient leadership of the white man than in their own race. Besides a colored brother whether from the States, Haiti, or surrounding British Islands, feels somewhat handicapped in working alongside of a European white priest, or in reaching Americans whether from the North or South.

For this reason, when specially appealed to years ago by a delegation of clergymen of the United States Episcopal Church as to their appointment at Port au Prince of a successor to my old friend, the late Negro Bishop Holly, I advised them to send a sympathetic, broad-minded, white clergyman or bishop, which they did. Haitians are peculiar people, kind and even affectionate, whose confidence and esteem are easy to win by sober, moral, sympathetic, unprejudiced Christian white men, whose leadership they will follow and implicitly trust.

The CHAIRMAN. We can not go into these philosophic considerations of the Haitian character, interesting as it is, at this time.

Mr. EVANS. At the request of Senator Hitchcock, then chairman of Foreign Relations Committee, and Secretary Stabler, of the Latin American department in charge of Haiti affairs of the United States Government. I was asked in 1918 to state grievances of Haiti and my recommendations, and among those given on pages 3 and 4 of memorandum and a copy of which I have given members of this committee, is this as first and most vital before there can be

any effective and constructive work done by either the Haiti Government, or a
United States military or civil occupation in the black Republic:

After a very careful observation. frequent consultations with Presidents
and leaders both educated and uneducated, Catholics and Protestants alike,
white and black, including officers of our American occupation, and those next
to President Dartiguenave at this moment, I have no hesitation in stating that
essential to the spiritual interests of the Protestant and Roman Catholic Churches
and their work in Haiti, and indispensable to honest and efficient and also
stable government in the black Republic, there must be an absolute, that is,
an official and financial separation, between them and both the Haiti Negro
government, as well as any American occupation there, exactly for instance as
we have it in the United States.

The CHAIRMAN. How is that the responsibility of the American Government?
Mr. EVANS. How does it come?
The CHAIRMAN. How is that the responsibility of the American Government?
Mr. EVANS. In this way. The Government of the United States, in the
preamble of the treaty made with backward, and bankrupt Haiti, and one of the
very main reasons for our intervention with these people, states: " The United
States and the Republic of Haiti, desiring to confirm the amity (not enmity)
existing between them, by the most cordial cooperation (not domination) in
measures for their common advantage; and the Republic of Haiti desiring to
remedy the present conditions of its revenues and finances, to maintain the
tranquillity of the Republic, to carry out plans for the economic development
and prosperity of the Republic and its people."

That is, we have solemnly undertaken to place Haiti finances on a solid
basis, and to give an honest, and efficient administration to the black republic
and thus deliver them from dishonest politicians of their own, and the horde
of white profiteering foreigners who have been fattening upon them, diverting
Haiti Government revenues essential to the working of the Republic, spread of
education, among the illiterate inhabitants, and other progressive reforms.

My point is, that while Haiti Government, and United States Marine officers
pay annually something like $100,000 if not altogether about $150,000 (it is
impossible to find out the correct amount) from Haiti internal or customs
revenues, and (before the occupation) Haitian officers, but since Marine officers
of the United States, become paymasters of archbishop. bishops, priests, nuns,
etc., of the Roman Catholic Church, not to mention pay additional amount
toward the maintenance of the palace of this foreign potentate (prince of
another professing sovereign) their presbyteries, and churches' upkeep, it
becomes absolutely impossible for these United States Marine officers to loyally
serve either our Government, or the best interests of Haiti and thus carry
out the main purpose of our going to the black republic as explicitly and
most emphatically specified at the beginning of the treaty.

Again—

1. The old Haitian concordat, made between the cabinet (not the Haitians)
and the vatican at Rome is something entirely outside of the Haiti constitution.

2. This concordat, made about 1860, was for 50 years; has expired therefore for several years and never renewed. Hence if it had any apparent
legality in the past it has none to-day.

3. The Haiti Government and framers of the Haiti constitution, never anticipating such an unholy alliance as that of religion with the State, very emphatically, however. and in case such might be attempted, provide against
such, in stipulating that all churches are equally free in Haiti, and this still
remains unchanged. Therefore, an officially and financially State religion.
such as the Roman Catholic, is (in the black Republic) incompatible, irrecon-
cilable with, and alien to the spirit of, and illegal with the Haiti constitution.

4. Moreover, and in the present financial condition of Haiti and the inability
of either the native government, or the American occupation, after functioning
six years on the island to make any provision for the education of Haiti's
children but withhold appropriations from excellent Protestant schools within
the Republic on the ground of lack of money, demands that this alliance at once
cease.

Furthermore, Article V of treaty says:

"All sums collected by the general receiver (of United States Government)
shall be applied—

" First. To the payment of the salaries and allowances of the general receiver,
his assistants and employees. and expenses of the receivership, including the

salary and expenses of the financial advisor, which salaries will be determined by previous agreement.

"Second. To the interest and sinking fund of Haiti; and

"Third. To the maintenance of the constabulary (gendarmerie) referred to in Article X, and then—

"Last. The remainder to the Haitian Government for purposes of current expenses."

I therefore respectfully submit that this committee is authorized and expected in its present investigation to find out the causes which have contributed to the present failure of American forces in their operations in Haiti in the light of the treaty, and why no effort has been made to encourage education by way of inaugurating a system of public instruction.

The CHAIRMAN. Well, Mr. Evans, that has nothing to do with the occupation

Senator POMERENE. Let me ask one other question. Are women as a class down there stronger and more vigorous than the men?

Mr. EVANS. Probably many if not most are. The home life, generally speaking, excepting that of the educated Haitians and the Christian natives in the interior as well as towns, have little or no home attractions but their little children and husband for a woman. This being so, women and young girls, of course, work out on their habitations (little holdings) and they mainly carry the stuff to market. They are the buyers and sellers, and seem to be naturally gifted that way from early childhood.

Senator POMERENE. That does not exactly answer my question. I am speaking of them physically now.

Mr. EVANS. Of course, physiscal exercise in the open fresh air would naturally make them look and feel healthy. They are the children of nature and enjoy freedom in dress and their habits of life, which are most primitive, and as the result of this, generally speaking, they appear to be healthier and stronger in most cases, and even more active.

Senator POMERENE. Then you agree with the statement that was made here yesterday, that the women are more vigorous physically and healthier than the men are, and have more physical strength?

Mr. EVANS. Yes. Probably in most cases they are, though we have seen in Haiti, smart, vigorous men of a very fine physique.

Senator POMERENE. How about the men? Are they, as a class weaker than the women?

Mr. EVANS. The men do as a rule the heaviest work on their little holdings and watch the home and children, while the women are attending to selling and buying for the family.

There is not so much to encourage the men either in towns or country. They often talk politics—that is, about government affairs, and feel interest and long for changes for the better. I mean the better educated and thinking portion. Many resort to gambling, such as cockfighting and card playing more I fancy for the sport, diversion, and excitement in them than really for the sake of cheating, or anything like robbery, or taking mean advantage of one another. The cockfighting and the gambling like voodooism and witchcraft are gradually disappearing and dying out as the Gospel and education are quietly spreading, though no country has ever been more neglected and criminally ignored than Haiti and its people by the Protestant and evangalical missionary, and Christian education boards and societies of Europe and the United States.

Haiti, has never had any real contact with the United States until now though so near. There has been no opening for markets, and encouragement for small cultivators.

Senator KING. The fact is that without outside capital and outside influence there Haiti would soon revert to a condition of almost barbarism, would it not?

Mr. EVANS. No; I could not say that. I have seen more real barbarism and brutality, and read more of stabbing, lynching, and murder in Great Britain and the United States than I have ever seen or known in Haiti. And also of drunkenness, than among the natives of the Black Republic with all their capital and education and culture.

With American Christian education and industrial teaching and sympathetic and efficient leadership Haiti, in my opinion would soon advance, and ere long create its own capital. There are thrifty people there, kind hearted and most generous natures you can find anywhere among colored or white.

White employees of Haitian laborers in various parts of Haiti have spoken to me very highly of their thriftiness and reliability when kindly treated.

Many of our own American marines have testified to me to the same effect the moment they changed their harsh and brutal methods, came to really understand the natives, treat them humanely, and trust them they acted differently and became reliable and devoted to their work and officers.

Senator KING. Well I went out into the island and I saw little shacks and perhaps a quarter of an acre—well I will not say cultivated, but with wild fruit growing, and a woman gathering it and putting it in baskets and carrying it 20, 30, or 40 miles on her head to the town, and selling for a very inconsiderable sum, and her husband or man she is living with would take the small earnings, or part of them, and engage in cockfights and spend most of his time in idleness and indolence.

Mr. EVANS. There has been a great deal of cockfighting, and even petty gambling with other undesirable things in Haiti in the past as stated, but I blame the Protestant and Evangelical churches of America, and the United States Government for this, and hold them responsible for withholding from these Negroes all the Christian, educational, and civilizing means we have ourselves enjoyed for over 100 years, and which have made us the Nation and people we are to-day.

The CHAIRMAN. The Committee will recess until 2.30, when we may sit for a little while, and let Mr. Evans conclude.

(Mr. Angell thereupon offered for the record the following conventions and agreements between the United States, and the Republic of Haiti) :

CONVENTION BETWEEN THE UNITED STATES AND THE REPUBLIC OF HAITI.

PREAMBLE.

The United States and the Republic of Haiti, desiring to confirm and strengthen the amity existing between them by the most cordial cooperation in measures for their common advantage, and the Republic of Haiti desiring to remedy the present condition of its revenues and finances, to maintain the tranquility of the Republic, to carry out plans for the economic development and prosperity of the Republic and its people, and the United States being in full sympathy with all of these aims and objects and desiring to contribute in all proper ways to their accomplishment ;

The United States and the Republic of Haiti have resolved to conclude a convention with these objects in view, and have appointed for that purpose plenipotentiaries :

The President of the Republic of Haiti, Mr. Louis Borno, secretary of state of foreign affairs and public instruction ;

The President of the United States, Mr. Robert Beale Davis, jr., chargé d'affaires of the United States of America ;

Who, having exhibited to each other their respective powers, which are seen to be full in good and true form, have agreed as follows :

ARTICLE I.

The Government of the United States will, by its good offices, air the Haitian Government in the proper and efficient development of its agricultural, mineral, and commercial resources, and in the establishment of the finances of Haiti on a firm and solid basis.

ARTICLE II.

The President of Haiti shall appoint, upon nomination by the President of the United States, a general receiver, and such aids and employees as may be necessary, who shall collect, receive, and apply all customs duties on imports and exports accruing at the several customhouses and ports of entry of the Republic of Haiti.

The President of Haiti shall appoint, upon nomination by the President of the United States, financial adviser, who shall be an officer attached to the ministry of finance, to give effect to whose proposals and labors the minister will lend efficient aid. The financial adviser shall devise an adequate system of public accounting, aid in increasing the revenues and adjusting them to the expenses, inquire into the validity of the debts of the Republic, enlighten both Governments with reference to all eventual debts, recommend improved methods of collecting and applying the revenues, and make such other recommendations to the minister of finance as may be deemed necessary for the welfare and prosperity of Haiti.

ARTICLE III.

The Government of the Republic of Haiti will provide by law or appropriate decrees for the payment of all customs duties to the general receiver, and will extend to the receivership and to the financial adviser all needed aid and full protection in the execution of the powers conferred and duties imposed herein; and the United States on its part will extend like aid and protection.

ARTICLE IV.

Upon the appointment of the financial adviser, the Government of the Republic of Haiti, in cooperation with the financial adviser, shall collate, classify, arrange, and make full statement of all the debts of the Republic, the amounts, character, maturity and condition thereof, and the interest accruing, and the sinking-fund requisite to their final discharge.

ARTICLE V.

All sums collected and received by the general receiver shall be applied, first, to the payment of the salaries and allowances of the general receiver, his assistants, and employees, and expenses of the receivership, including the salary and expenses of the financial adviser, which salaries will be determined by previous agreement; second, to the interest and sinking fund of the public debt of the Republic of Haiti; and, third, to the maintenance of the constabulary referred to in Article X, and then the remainder to the Haitian Government for the purposes of current expenses.

In making these applications the general receiver will proceed to pay salaries and allowances monthly and expenses as they arise, and on the first of each calendar month will set aside in a separate fund the quantum of the collection and receipts of the previous month.

ARTICLE VI.

The expenses of the receivership, including salaries and allowance of the general receiver, his assistants, and employees, and the salary and expenses of the financial adviser, shall not exceed five per centum of the collection and receipts from customs duties, unless by agreement by the two Governments.

ARTICLE VII.

The general receiver shall make monthly reports of all collections, receipts, and disbursements to the appropriate officers of the Republic of Haiti and to the Department of State of the United States, which reports shall be open to inspection and verification at all times by the appropriate authorities of each of the said Governments.

ARTICLE VIII.

The Republic of Haiti shall not increase its public debt except by previous agreement with the President of the United States, and shall not contract any debt or assume any financial obligation unless the ordinary revenues of the Republic available for that purpose, after defraying the expenses of the Government, shall be adequate to pay the interest and provide a sinking fund for the final discharge of such debt.

ARTICLE IX.

The Republic of Haiti will not, without a previous agreement with the President of the United States, modify the customs duties in a manner to reduce the revenues therefrom; and in order that the revenues of the Republic may be adequate to meet the public debt and the expenses of the Government, to preserve tranquillity and to promote material prosperity, the Republic of Haiti will cooperate with the Financial Adviser in his recommendations for improvement in the methods of collecting and disbursing the revenues and for new sources of needed income.

ARTICLE X.

The Haitian Government obligates itself, for the preservation of domestic peace, the security of individual rights, and the full observance of the provisions of this treaty, to create without delay an efficient constabulary, urban and rural, composed of native Haitians. This constabulary shall be organized and officered by Americans appointed by the President of Haiti, upon nomination by the President of the United States. The Haitian Government shall clothe these officers with the proper and necessary authority and uphold them in the performance of their functions. These officers will be replaced by Haitians as they, by examination conducted under direction of a board to be selected by the senior American officer of this constabulary, in the presence of a representative of the Haitian Government, are found to be qualified to assume such duties. The constabulary herein provided for, shall, under the direction of the Haitian Government, have supervision and control of arms and ammunition, military supplies and traffic therein, throughout the country. The high contracting parties agree that the stipulations in this article are necessary to prevent factional strife and disturbances.

ARTICLE XI.

The Government of Haiti agrees not to surrender any of the territory of the Republic of Haiti by sale, lease or otherwise, or jurisdiction over such territory, to any foreign Government or power, nor to enter into any treaty or contract with any foreign power or powers that will impair or tend to impair the independence of Haiti.

ARTICLE XII.

The Haitian Government agrees to execute with the United States a protocol for the settlement, by arbitration or otherwise, of all pending pecuniary claims of foreign corporations, companies, citizens, or subjects against Haiti.

ARTICLE XIII.

The Republic of Haiti, being desirous to further the development of its natural resources, agrees to undertake and execute such measures as, in the opinion of the high contracting parties, may be necessary for the sanitation and public improvement of the Republic, under the supervision and direction of an engineer or engineers, to be appointed by the President of Haiti upon nomination of the President of the United States, and authorized for that purpose by the Government of Haiti.

ARTICLE XIV.

The high contracting parties shall have authority to take such steps as may be necessary to insure the complete attainment of any of the objects comprehended in this treaty; and, should the necessity occur, the United States will lend an efficient aid for the preservation of Haitian independence and the maintenance of a government adequate for the protection of life, property, and individual liberty.

ARTICLE XV.

The present treaty shall be approved and ratified by the high contracting parties in conformity with their respective laws, and the ratification thereof shall be exchanged in the city of Washington as soon as may be possible.

ARTICLE XVI.

The present treaty shall remain in full force and virtue for the term of ten years, to be counted from the day of exchange of ratifications, and further for another term of ten years if, for specific reasons presented by either of the high contracting parties, the purpose of this treaty has not been fully accomplished.

In faith whereof, the respective plenipotentiaries have signed the present convention in duplicate, in the English and French languages, and have hereunto affixed their seals.

Done at Port-au-Prince (Haiti) the sixteenth day of September, in the year of our Lord one thousand nine hundred and fifteen.

ROBERT BEALE DAVIS, Jr.,
Charge d'Affaires of the United States.
LOUIS BORNO,
Secretaire d'Etat des Relations Exterieures
et de l'Instruction Publique.

AGREEMENT REGARDING TELEGRAPHS AND TELEPHONES.

The undersigned, duly authorized thereto by their respective Governments, have this day agreed:

I. That the operation, management, and maintenance of the telegraphs and telephones in the Republic of Haiti shall be under the control and direction of the engineer or engineers to be appointed by the President of Haiti upon nomination by the President of the United States and authorized for that purpose by the Government of Haiti in accordance with Article XIII of the treaty of September 16, 1915.

II. That in order that officers of the gendarmerie shall be better able to fulfill their duties under the treaty, the unrestricted service of the telegraphs and telephones is hereby assured to them, and in order to provide for the prompt transmission of messages of the gendarmerie the officers thereof will afford all necessary protection to the lines.

In witness whereof the undersigned have hereunto signed their names and affixed their seals in duplicate.

Done at Washington, D. C., this twenty-fourth day of August, nineteen hundred and sixteen.

ROBERT LANSING.
SOLON MENOS.

(Whereupon, at 1 o'clock p. m., a recess was taken until 2.30 o'clock p. m.)

AFTER RECESS.

The committee reassembled at 2.30 o'clock p. m., pursuant to the taking of recess, Senator Oddie presiding.

Senator ODDIE. To begin with, Mr. Evans, I would like to ask you what was done by the American occupation to foster education and self-government?

Mr. EVANS. I have seen nothing done to foster education but rather to discourage it. Some of the schools have been actually closed up. The appropriations given to all the Protestant schools (some of a very high grade and commended by the Haiti Government before the American occupation came) have been stopped by our American occupation, and consequently some had to close up altogether.

It was reported while I was at St. Marc that the American marines were so hostile to the Haitians, so afraid to see any improvement and signs of mental and moral development in the natives tending to qualify them for anything like self-government, that they also closed some of the Government day schools, and attempted to abolish the Haitian College and medical school at Port au Prince, which they would have done but for the strong protest of President Dartiguenave at the time.

When arrested without any warrant and marched under a heavy armed guard through the streets of St. Marc to the gendarmerie of Haiti headquarters, the heinous charge against me, spluttered out amid vile oaths of a wild, intoxicated if not half-crazy American marine officer, Capt. Brown, who alternately aimed to lay hold of his revolver to shoot me in the presence of the Negro armed police under him, was that I sought by my preaching and efforts to establish in Haiti, among these damned niggers a normal and industrial school so as to Christianize and mentally and morally develop these low damned niggers, whom I labored for and loved.

I had precisely the same experience, with closed fists, wild gestures, oaths, threats of being shot, command never to preach in his section and through north Haiti by the intoxicated American marine, Lieut. Haug, who raved like a maniac in front of me, and before native Christians at the St. Michel headquarters of the Haiti gendarmerie, and an officer whom Gen. Williams had reinstated into official position under himself, and Maj. Welles, after being severely disciplined for drunkenness and misconduct by Col. Russell.

President Dartiguenave thus bitterly complains against the American occupation to the correspondents of the New York Tribune and Chicago Tribune, who visited Haiti last November, and so that they might publish the fact in the United States:

"The strangest phase of the situation, from the Haiti Government's viewpoint, is not only have the American officials done nothing for the intellectual improvement and economic development of people and prosperity of the country, but they actually opposed the little the Haiti Government tries to do in this direction. They resist every project we make to deal with the education of our people, etc."

I wish, with consent of committee, to put in the record just here a copy of certain correspondence between myself and Dr. Maclean, the chief of the bureau de l'ingenieur charge du service d'hygiene of the United States Government, in which I referred to a conference on the question of education, and had invited him, Col. Russell, etc., with President Dartiguenave to meet with me at the bureau of public instruction, at Port au Prince, which appeared to have profoundly offended him, and shows the exact attitude unfortunately taken by the American occupation in this fundamental development and regeneration of Haiti; also shows why the failure of the United States Government, through the present American occupation (and type of leading American marine officials there, out of all sympathy with the terms of the treaty), to fulfill its noble mission in the Black Republic, and its 2,500,000 Negro people, and objected to my Christian and educational "activities," and, with the aid of Washington officials, tried to have the little board to recall me, and failing this got them to stop my small salary. The two letters follow, with Dr. Maclean's reply:

ST. MARC, HAITI, WEST INDIES, *July 20, 1918.*

Dr. MACLEAN,
  Chief of Hygiene Department of American Occupation, Haiti.

DEAR DR. MACLEAN: Mrs. Evans and myself take quite an interest in our little St. Marc Hospital, as we do in our local prison, and often go the rounds of the poor and sick patients in the one and visit and conduct services in the other.

We can not but notice the transformation that has already taken place and the striking contrast between things now and a few years ago at our prisons. This is still more so, if possible, at our hospitals, due, of course, to the efficiency of the expert chief of our occupation's hygiene department.

During my recent visit as general superintendent of the Haiti field to Jacmel and the south, with all of which I was most intimately acquainted years ago, and on visiting both prison and beautifully situated new hospital there with our captain and local doctor of occupation I noticed the change and contrast were most marked.

These reforms alone in the interest of health and humanity, altogether apart from other drastic changes, not to mention what we further contemplate (now that Haiti at last has declared " war "), prove what a godsend our Government, through the " occupation," has already been to this little Black Republic.

May I ask whether you contemplate changing the name of all the hospitals, hitherto termed hospices (almshouses, but more of pest houses in the past), into the more modern city and general hospital, and so as to make them equally accessible and agreeable to both Protestant and Catholic alike, especially seeing, of course, that they are now entirely maintained by our Government occupation, aided by gifts of the local general public.

If you are not already planning this, I would respectfully suggest that a separate apartment somewhere near the hospital (for the present) be arranged for the mentally affected, now left roaming about the towns, sleeping out at nights, and in company—both men and women—together under porches, etc. These unfortunates and wrecks of poor Negro humanity, whether men or women, should be cared for, and under such restrictions as not to be permitted to propagate their kind.

Have you at present, either connected with our hospitals or directly with the Government at Port au Prince, some system of outdoor relief for the aged and genuinely but respectable poor, and so as to give 1½ to 2 gourdes a week to such when perfectly satisfied with the worthiness of the case?

I am planning before going to the States at end of present month or very early next, to visit my missionary boards with a view to cooperative and much larger mission work, to have a brief conference there at Port au Prince with Haiti minister, superintendent of public instruction, etc., in reference to the proposed national and normal industrial college for Haiti, and founded on broad Christian basis (interdenominational), exactly like Hampton and Tuskegee, for instance, with us in the States.

I have already suggested to Mr. Burgeois, United States Government superintendent of our Haiti public instruction, that we should invite Col. Russell, Gen. Williams—if not president—and members of the national council, when I shall give in rough outline as to what has been already attempted in this direction when I bore a petition seven years ago to Washington, signed by nearly 8,000 of the leading Haitians; and the first name inscribed on this unique document praying for such a noble institution and urgent necessity, as they termed it, was my old friend—broad minded, if not somewhat cultured and afterwards the late President Cincinnatus Leconté.

While calling on leading educationalists, as well as at our Government's Latin American department, at Washington last October, before my return to Haiti, I was given to understand that if this petition is now presented to our Government and has the hearty and cordial support of our United States official representatives here at the present time—as, for instance, my first petition of nearly 8,000 had the enthusiastic support of Dr. Furniss and Dr. Livingstone, United States minister and consul in Haiti during 1911—this project would go right through, and that either jointly or separately, but backed by our United States Government, our great Christian philanthropists, educationalists, and friends of the Negro in America will finance it.

I shall therefore be very glad to have you with us, if possible, as soon as Mr. Burgeois is ready to arrange this.

Very sincerely, yours, and for Christ and Haiti,

L. Ton Evans.

REPUBLIQUE D'HAITI,
BUREAU DE L'INGENIEUR CHARGE DU SERVICE D'HYGIENE.
Port au Prince, July 25, 1918.

Rev. L. Ton Evans,
St. Marc, Haiti.

SIR: Referring to your letter of July 20, I regret that from my observations of your activities during the past few months I do not feel it advisable to confer with you on any matter whatsoever.

Very truly, yours,

N. M. Lean.
Sanitary Engineer of Haiti.

[Urgent needs. From the missions of the North American Baptist Convention for September, 1917: "Regarding Haiti (Central America), after careful investigation by Drs. Barnes and Brink (field secretary and superintendent of education of the A. B. H. M. S.). the conclusion is if Haiti is to be entered at present (by way of cooperation with Lott Carey Foreign Board) the best thing for the Home Mission Society to do is to establish a school for the special training of native ministers and other Christian leaders, and to foster in connection with it a model church. The project calls for $75,000 outlay and $10,000 a year upkeep.]

ST. MARC, HAITI, WEST INDIES, July 27, 1918.

Dr. McLEAN,
Service D'Hygiene, Port au Prince.

DEAR SIR: Yours of the 25th ultimo to hand, and reference to alleged but undefined "activities" of mine, I presume as Christian minister and missionary in this Republic, preventing you from conference, as suggested in my letter of the 20th ultimo, which, of course, I regret.

In spite of my deep and profound respect and genuine admiration for Dr. McLean and the noble profession he has the honor to represent, as well as for the "opinion and judgment" of such, and holding high office under our own Government in Haiti, it has not yet occurred to me, however, as a Christian minister and missionary, with over 30 years' experience and more than 25 of these in very close touch with Haiti, its leaders of all shades of religious and political creeds, that I should in Haiti, more than in the States, really consult the medical or the military profession as such as to nature, limitations, or extent of my own "activities" in Haiti for God, country, and humanity.

While stating this, I am willing, yes, anxious, and feel it my duty as far as possible, and even use my personal influence with our Christian workers (white and native) at all times to honor and heartily support, both military and medical, as well as all other departmental, authorities in the faithful discharge of governmental functions, and carrying out in spirit and letter of the " splendid treaty " entered into by our President and United States Government with the Government and people (Negroes) of Haiti.

This " treaty," as I regretfully and respectfully informed Col. Russell (for whom I have very great respect), was grossly infringed in the matter of the " so-called voting on the new constitution," but, as stated to our colonel and as Christian minister as well as a true American, I assured him that I would take no step whatever in Haiti as regards this matter, but defer my action until I reached the States, and even there bring the whole affair, first of all, to the President's personal notice.

I stand, of course, unalterably by this " treaty " and am sure our President does, and that our Government will strictly abide by that " sacred document " as constantly emphasized by President Wilson, and which princ'ples alone justified us in entering the " war " and in continuing in it until the " sanctity of treaty " such as that between Germany and Belgium, or the States and Haiti is recognized by every civilized government, and the liberties and rights of small as well as big nations are equally safeguarded, and furthermore that everything of the nature of " secret plotting, political scheming," etc., shall be utterly abolished and a new diplomacy, open and frank and aboveboard, is adopted by nations.

The only sense and spirit therefore of the " treaty " between the States and Haiti as well as between other nations must be understood, must be interpreted and carried out as to the liberties and rights of the Negro people of Haiti as well as the liberties and rights of other nations—safeguarded in the light and along the line given and laid down in the last and final address made by President Woodrow Wilson on July Fourth (last month) at the tomb of Washington, and neither military, medical, or diplomatic representative of the President and Government in Haiti or elsewhere have any official right to give a different interpretation.

As a good American it may do no harm to mention the points of our President's latest address here, and for fear Dr. McLean has had no time to read this memorable speech, they are as follows:

" These are the ends for which the associated peoples of the world are fighting and which must be conceded them before there can be peace:

"(a) The destruction of every arbitrary power anywhere that can separately and secretly * * * disturb the peace, etc.

"(b) The settlement of every question, whether territory, sovereignty of economic arrangement of political relationship upon the basis of free acceptance of that settlement by the people immediately concerned (after due explanation and without intimidation, etc.) and not upon the basis of the material interest or advantage of any other nation or people (nor group of speculators, etc.).

"(c) The consent of all nations to be governed in their conduct toward each other by the same principles of honor and of respect for the common laws of civilized society, etc., to the end that all promises and covenants may be sacredly observed, no private plots or conspiracies hatched, no selfish injuries wrought with impunity, etc.

"(d) These great objects can be put into a single sentence: What we seek is the reign of law based upon the consent of the governed and sustained by the organized opinion," etc.

As the missionary and Christian minister is supposed to practice what he himself preaches, surely a doctor should not at all object to take his own medicine more than our own President Wilson.

Inasmuch as I have the honor of representing in Haiti something like a little over 3,000,000 colored American Baptists, and practically the 5,000,000 white Baptists of the States, who morally back the above, and expected to soon financially cooperate in our Haiti mission work, these matters will be naturally discussed by them, and action taken to bring the matter direct to the President himself for adjustment, etc., and not to any official either at the White House or of the Government.

As being yourself therefore, an official representative of our United States Government and its chief of the Haiti hygiene service, and though we may differ greatly as to the interpretation of the said " treaty " as it affects Haiti or, indeed, as to the " nature and extent of the activities of a Christian minister and a Baptist missionary representing as I do the colored Baptists of the States, etc., in Haiti, and that you may not see your way to be present at a conference to support, as stated, a national and normal college for Haiti on

Christian but interdenominational basis exactly like Hampton and Tuskegee, with us in the States for instance "—for the real uplift of Haiti and its sons and daughters, and by way of training their young Negro manhood and Negro womanhood for future religious, educational, industrial, commercial as well as judicial and civic leadership—in their own black republic, I can hardly believe that for these reasons you would decline to give me the information sought in that letter addressed you the 20th ultimo, re hospitals and our Haiti poor, and to the following effect:

"(1) If you are not already planning it, I respectfully suggest to you that a separate apartment (possibly for the present) somewhere near the hospital be arranged for the mentally affected, now left roaming about our towns, sleeping out at nights, at times in company with men under porches, etc., and so that these unfortunates and wrecks of poor Negro humanity, whether men or women, should be so restricted as not to be able to propagate their kind."

Please furnish me with information on this point, or if it does not come directly under your own department kindly let me know where to write.

"(2) Have you at present, either connected with the hospital or directly with the Government itself at Port au Prince, any real system of out-door relief for the aged and genuine but respectable poor, and so as to give one or one and a half to two gourdes per week to such, and when perfectly satisfied of the need and worthiness of the recipient?"

Again may I ask you, as chief of our Haiti hospitals, for copy of the provision made (if any) for these aged and really poor, or should they come under some other department. Please let me know where I may write.

(3) Furthermore, we have a woman and her child, of about 9, from Isle Gonave, here since Saturday. She is a member of our mission there and came to be medically examined at our hospital at St. Marc. I gave her a note, but she returned without being examined, saying the local doctor wished to see me.

I went with her to see Dr. Audin yesterday, and he explained that being from Isle of Gonave she would belong to communal Port au Prince. The doctor thought a permit from the magistrate here would be sufficient so to arrange for reimbursing St. Marc and that she might be received, and so that the doctor may examine her this morning.

However, she was up but returned again, saying Dr. Audin could not act. Inasmuch as the native sister is not only suffering but also much discouraged, and now that she is here it would be somewhat cruel for to send her back in the boat in the same condition about Saturday or Sunday to Isle Gonave, and then after several days of further waiting and suspense take another small boat and spend probably a day and night in that sailing for Port au Prince.

Under these circumstances will you kindly send word to Dr. Audin advising him to proceed with examination, and if he thinks it necessary to have her for a week or so at the hospital, and that you will see there about the communal reimbursement.

In this case we shall be glad to look after the young child and feed her, etc.

As there is so much ignorance, and indeed prejudice re hospice, and which will take time to remove, please send me any rules you may have in French or English dealing with admission of sick and aged.

It was this I had in mind when suggesting in my letter of 20th ultimo the change of names from hospices to that of city or general hospitals, as with us in the States, and so as to remove the fears re Christian and Catholic creeds, etc.

Let me again assure you, sir, that knowing, as the board and myself do, the great and gigantic task our President and United States Government have undertaken in Haiti, which has been so long criminally neglected, and whose over 2,000,000 Negro people have been for years exploited by the stronger race, white, and financial fillibusters and unscrupulous, if not mean and murderous, politicians for personal power and selfish greed, and the many and often serious difficulties which indeed confront our "American occupation" in carrying out its work of not only political, economical, educational, industrial, and sanitary reformation but actual regeneration, it is the sincere wish of the board, as well as myself, not merely to work in perfect harmony but by every possible and legitimate means to loyally support our Government and our "occupation" in the discharge of their onerous duties to Haiti, the United States, and to civilization and humanity, and if we can make it all the easier for them.

There always has been and, there will always continue, the closest relation between the spiritual, religious, and moral with the political, educational, and industrial, not to say social, life of the people in Haiti as in the States or any other country, and neither our Haitian Government and "American occupation," though acting separately and apart—and should be officially and financially perfectly free from each other for benefit and real efficiency of both—can possibly ignore the Christian church and ministers and missionaries and their specific work, more than the latter, indeed, can the former, without misunderstandings, frictions, and serious weakening and injury on both sides.

Though we thus labor in two different departments—in fact, different realms even—there is absolutely no reason why we should not be actuated in the honest, faithful service rendered to God, country, and humanity by the same high Christian motives and inspired by the same ennobling and soul-lifting ideals.

I still remain, yours, very sincerely, for Christ and Haiti,

L. Ton Evans.

Dr. McLean never replied, and the poor, sickly native woman was obliged to wait several days for an open boat, then discouraged, and almost brokenhearted and in great pain to return to her small island home on Ile Gonave, and probably was never able to proceed again by boat to Port au Prince. Dr. Audin, a clever native doctor, dared not, without special permit from Dr. McLean, either take this sick woman to the hospice, maintained by occupation with Roman Catholic sisters in charge, and where there was plenty of room; neither to personally examine her, as he privately told me, at the risk of his job, if not his life. This is the arbitrary way those poor, suffering Negroes are dealt with.—L. T. E.

In contrast with the attitude shown by the American occupation who are fundamentally opposed to the treaty of the United States Government and our real mission in Haiti, namely, as put by the chairman—to foster education and self-government—I shall place a few letters which passed between me and the natives themselves in reference to intellectual improvement, moral, and civic, as well as religious development, with a view to Haitian self-government, which Dr. Maclean and so many of the leading American marine officers fear and dread or, in the words of the Haitian President, discourage and determined by every means to resist:

HAITI NATIONAL COUNCIL, PORT AU PRINCE, HAITI,
December 31, 1918.

M. L. Ton Evans,
General Superintendent Baptist Mission, St. Marc.

DEAR SIR: I am favored with your letter of the 21st instant and thank you very much for the information you give me about your endeavoring to get Haiti rid of all her superstitions by true Christian basis and efficient civilized means.

I should really feel greatly honored to meet with M. Dr. James H. Dillard, of the Rockefeller Foundation of Learning in the United States, on his visiting in Haiti, and to personally present him to the Haitian leaders and our President, who are only too glad and ready to help him in all his inquiries about this kindhearted people.

As I intend to go to Cape Haiti through St. Marc next month, I will not fail to call on you.

Believe me to remain, yours, sincerely, and for Christ and Haiti.

Dr. LAROCHE.

(This letter reached St. Marc when I was pining for breath of air on the hard floor of the narrow, dark cell of the old St. Marc slave prison amid yells and groans of poor native prisoners cruelly beaten and brutally pounded, and myself expecting every moment at the command of the American marine captain of gendarmes to be dragged before a "firing squad" like the British Edith Cavell. Hence did not see Laroche nor his letter until on in the following New Year.)

My own communication sent my old friend a few days before was penned thus:

BAPTIST STUDY, ST. MARC, HAITI,
December 21, 1918.

Hon. Dr. LAROCHE,
Ex-Senator of the Haiti Republic and
Member of National Council, Port au Prince.

DEAR DOCTOR: Seeing the very deep and profound interest you and my friends, late President Leconte, Hon. Leger, Hon. Johnny Laroche, with other leading

Haitians, irrespective of politics and creed, showed in signing that petition eight years ago and addressed to Messrs. Rockefeller and Carnegie, etc., in States, friends of education and believers in the development of the race, and the promise of land by the Government for such a noble project as the normal and industrial school, you will be sure to rejoice in reading inclosed memorandum to President Wilson and find on bottom of page 4 that the petition was presented to trustees of Carnegie International Peace Endowment.

Matters are maturing very fast, and either next month or February Dr. James H. Dillard (whose name you will see with that of Maj. Moton, in the memorandum), representative of the Rockefeller Foundation General Education Board, New York, will visit Haiti.

I am planning a special conference with our American, as well as, of course, our Haiti leaders here, and Haiti President.

I am still of opinion but more convinced than ever that this institution is vital in the social, moral, industrial, as well as intellectual, regeneration of Haiti and its people.

Yours, for Christ and Haiti,

L. Ton Evans.

(From the scores of other letters to, and from Legation De La Republique D'Haiti, Washington, D. C.; Dr. Francois Delacour, Port au Prince; Dr. Booker T. Washington, Dr. T. Jesse Jones (Slater Foundation) Government Bureau at Washington; Dr. James H. Dillard, James Brown Scott, Esq., Secretary of Carnegie Endowment for International Peace, Washington; and from ex-Senator Elihu Root, president of same, all along the same line, and showing efforts and appreciation re native education, and Christianization will be inserted for record and perusal of this committee at close of present testimony.)

Senator KING. Is that [closing of schools] because of a lack of revenue.

Mr. EVANS. That is their excuse. They can not get any money from Washington, they blame it entirely to the United States Government, yet strange to say they have the money, about $100,000 or more a year—probably $150,000—to pay salaries of European dignitaries of the Roman Catholic Church, college (for white priests in France), annually for this illegal, anti-constitutional, and anti-treaty confiscation as well as misappropriation of Haitian funds.

Senator KING. Are these supported by the State?

Mr. EVANS. Absolutely either by the customs, or the United States Government loans, supposed to be given for the improvement and development of Haiti, and not for the fostering and boosting of any sect in Haiti, and thus directly placing that sect (Roman Catholic religion, with its archbishop, bishops, priests, etc.) in position of financial, political, and religious authority, and power over all the other protesant and evangelical Christian bodies, and their educational colleges and schools (for the benefit of Haitians) as seen in present withholding of all appropriations from protestant schools, and closing of same, while Roman Catholic are receiving theirs and thus keeping them open thereby.

Article XVII of the Haiti constitution plainly and emphatically says:

"All forms of worship are equally free. Every one has the right to profess his religion and freely perform his worship, provided he does not disturb the public order."

Yet the Roman Catholic Church is financially and officially tied to the State, and protestants as those on Gros Morne, the last Sunday of June, 1918, are arrested on the way to Baptist mission church, roped and driven like slaves by gendarmes of the American occupation, whose infringement, and brutal violation of article 17 of the constitution, is upheld by Lieut. Kulp (Leogane) and Gen. Alexander Williams, chief of Haiti gendarmerie, and with the official cognizance of Brig. Gen. Catlin, official head of the United States Government.

Senator KING. Under the jurisdiction of the State?

Mr. EVANS. Exactly; under the direct jurisdiction of the State, as everything in Haiti is completely so, and every dollar handled by our American official receiver.

Senator KING. What I mean is this, that in some places the Catholics maintain their own parochial schools, which are supported by the priests of the church and by the church itself.

Mr. EVANS. This is not so in Haiti for the last 60 years, unfortunately for the Haiti Government funds and Haiti Government's stability and efficiency. If the Roman Catholic schools and the Roman Catholic church in Haiti, like the Protestant and Evangelical churches in the black Republic and throughout the United States, maintained their own schools and paid the salaries of their archbishop, bishops, and priests there would be no objection and no injustice.

Our strong objection and protest is to the financial and official alliance with, and therefore inevitable official recognition by the Haiti and United States Governments, and arising from which is the greatest injustice done to the other churches, that are independent of State, and claim equality of treatment, which has shown by the withholding of school appropriations from Protestants while allowing for Catholic schools and maintenance of Roman Catholic church, and whose expensive régime is unfair and unjust and in contravention to both constitution and our American treaty with Haiti.

Dr. Burgeois, the United States Government superintendent of public instruction in Haiti, very kindly furnished me with an official list of Protestant colleges and schools from which appropriations were withheld, which he said then was a preparatory step to their introduction of a scheme of public instruction, popular and compulsory, and free for the whole Republic.

This was more than three years ago and must have been resisted by the American occupation, and one of the things referred to by Dartiguenave, the President, in his complaints last year to the New York correspondents.

Senator ODDIE. I would like to ask you if there was an act of censorship of mail and telegraph during your stay there from 1917 to 1919?

Mr. EVANS. Yes.

Senator ODDIE. Was there an active censorship?

Mr. EVANS. I should say so; very active; extremely so, as, for instance, on my letters to and from the States, and which were admitted by a marine captain, were opened, if not confiscated, in some cases, and we really thought that certain checks by way of my small salary from the missionary board, unduly delayed through the European war, were actually stolen.

Senator ODDIE. Was that controlled by the United States Marines?

Mr. EVANS. The American occupation, through the United States Government marine—who did not appear to be accountable to anybody—were in complete control and dominated everything.

Senator ODDIE. Did the Haitian Government have anything to do with that?

Mr. EVANS. No; nothing whatsoever. Dartiguenave is merely looked upon by the Haitian people as a figurehead, just as he is by the American marines, and he knows himself—completely stripped of every authority and the object of Haitian pity.

Haiti members of the so-called Haitian Government then, who in every case and department, such as post office, telegraph, etc., have an American marine officer over them, and who explicitly obey their American marine masters, and are compelled to ignore their own Haitian President, in spite of treaty which refers to cooperation of the Haiti Government, etc.

The Haiti Government is powerless and does not exist as such. The United States Postmaster General assures me, also the State and Latin America Departments and Assistant Secretary Roosevelt, of the Navy Department, that on this side there is absolutely no censorship on letters that go to and come from Haiti, and still it goes on.

I have even sent letters with copies of Postmaster General and Assistant Secretary of Navy down to Haiti and asked the recipients to show same to the post-office authorities at Port au Prince; St. Marc, Cape, and Jacmel. Such, however, is their fear and dread of American marines that they would not dare to do even this. Their confidence in our occupation is completely gone, and they feel they must slavishly submit or face something worse.

Senator KING. Was it during the war that they had the censorship?

Mr. EVANS. Yes; I believe around November or December, 1917, it commenced. The American marine officer came on board the same ship as we did from New York, November of 1917, to take charge of the censorship at Panama, and I believe he informed me that this was to cover Haiti as well.

Dealing further with the question of education, with your permission, I would like to place copies of additional correspondence, showing some further efforts to provide for Haiti and develop these people, kept under so long.

Senator ODDIE. Yes; if there is no objection, that will be all right, Mr. Evans. You can hand those to the stenographer afterwards.

(The correspondence referred to is here printed in full, and covering some years, as follows:)

FIRST BAPTIST CHURCH,
Lansford, Pa., September 1, 1915.

Senator ELIHU ROOT,
President of Carnegie Endowment for International Peace.

(Petition of over 2,500,000 officials, political leaders, citizens, etc., of the Black Republic, earnestly praying for a national normal and industrial college to be established on Christian basis in the new protectorate.)

DEAR SENATOR: Knowing as I do of your personal and profound interest in securing among all nations the blessed boon of peace long before you became the honored official head of the Carnegie endowment, etc., I therefore at this momentous crisis in the history of poor Haiti, torn for years by cruel and barbaric revolutions and internecine wars, and now that the long-looked and earnestly prayed for auspicious day has dawned and an American protectorate (for that is what is meant) actually established in Haiti, and so as to assist the present American occupation of our United States Government in gaining the real confidence and implicit faith of the rank and file of the Haitians throughout the whole Republic (and at the very outset) as to the purity of our motives and benevolent intentions as an American Government in taking such a step, and which is essential to real and permanent peace, I respectfully ask you just now to receive a petition intrusted to me and containing close on to 3,000 names of the most distinguished leaders, irrespective of politics and religious creeds, praying for the establishment in their Republic of a long-felt need, that of a national normal and industrial college, and on Christian basis, like our Hampton and Tuskegee.

I have had the honor of personally initiating this idea after, however, consulting and interrogating a large number of the ablest, best, and most influential Haitians, and after years of study and close observation as to Haiti's real needs.

For many weeks and even months of hard traveling on horseback during revolutionary periods throughout the interior, as well as towns and cities along the coast to carefully explain this idea at the extreme peril to life and limb, as I presented (with assistance of a few most courageous Haitians) the matter and with petition in hand approached President Simon in the midst of the great excitment of a bloody revolution and surrounded with some 8,000 or 10,000 of his Government troops at Cape Haiti, and generals and others trembling at what might happen at any moment as he sought to crush the rebellion caused directly by German money and German propaganda against the United States, etc.

I visited him subsequently at his palace, senate chambers, superior and all other courts, and civic councils of Republic, schools, plantations, and rice fields, and everywhere found the heartiest welcome and enthusiasm, as the object was elaborately and patiently explained in French and patois.

In showing how it would work to divert the thought and energies of the youths of the Republic away from politics and revolutions and militarism into the practical, profitable, and peaceful pursuits of life in Haiti, such as thrift, cultivation of the soil, etc., show to them the real dignity of labor, the tears would freely flow down their swarthy faces and hope for them and their country's future could be seen brightening and glistening in their countenances.

In addition to these thousands of names I have official letters of nearly every civic council throughout Haiti, where the petition was presented and discussed with profoundest interest, indeed breaking out into shouts of joy as they resolved to officially support it, ordering their commissaire or mayor to draw up a letter, attach his own name, and officially seal it and send me.

May I therefore be permitted to present this petition personally so as to be able to answer questions or explain any matter connected with this request and prayer, practically of a whole little nation, sick and tired of revolutions and bloody internal wars, but with no power to resist against the white and profiteering politicians and filibusters whose interest has been to keep Haiti in one great turmoil all the years, etc.

Should your peace endowment come to Haiti's help at this epochal stage in the Republic's history and grant this industrial school which will be backed by the Haiti Government, which has promised some 200 acres of land for such school purpose, it will most effectively in cooperation with the United States Government's occupation work and activities mean the real regeneration of

Haiti in a few years, the establishment of peace, without which there can be no progress, etc.

In behalf of Christ and Haiti.

Respectfully and sincerely, yours,

L. Ton Evans.

CARNEGIE ENDOWMENT FOR INTERNATIONAL PEACE,
Washington, D. C., November 1, 1915.

Rev. L. Ton Evans,
First Baptist Church, Lansford, Pa.

DEAR SIR: I am in receipt of your letter of the 28th ultimo, with reference to your petition for assistance from the endowment in the establishment of a national normal and industrial college in Haiti.

In reply, I regret to inform you that it will not be possible to comply with your request for a personal hearing before the executive commitee upon your petition. My own time is so taken up during the next few weeks that I shall be unable to grant you a personal interview. If you care to call, however, one of the assistant secretaries of the endowment will be glad to see you and what you may have to say will be presented in proper form to the executive committee when it considers your petition.

In accordance with your request, I am returning the original of Mr. Root's letter to you of September 27.

I am, very truly, yours,

JAMES BROWN SCOTT, *Secretary.*

HAITI BAPTIST MISSION,
JACMEL, D'HAITI.
West Indies, February 2, 1912.

DEAR DR. BOOKER T. WASHINGTON: In view of your important conference this year at Tuskegee, and the deep and profound interest you have shown in your people, as evinced in the noble and extensive and successful efforts, in spite of ignorance, prejudice, and opposition in the past, to educate industrially, morally, yea, and religiously members of the race, thus giving an object lesson to the whole world of what the African can and will do if only helped and encouraged along the right lines, is it not really possible for your institute, either alone or in conjunction with Hampton, to arrange to send a commissioner, each with the indorsement of your trustees, and so as to visit Haiti, present a joint official report, and furnish reliable data that will enable you to proceed to the establishment for the Black Republic a similar institute to that of Tuskegee and Hampton, and if you think proper, a kind of extension branch?

I have in my possession a petition, signed by over 2,500 of the leading Haitians, from my friend His Excellency Cincinnattus Leconté (president), Hon. Jonny Laroché (minister of public works), Hon. Legèr (minister of foreign affairs), etc., and including senators, deputies, judges, generals, etc., of all political parties, and religious creeds, earnestly praying for this and pledging every encouragement from the Government, even to the granting of land for this purpose.

Though the said petition is directed through me to Messrs. the Hon. J. D. Rockefeller and Andrew Carnegie, and other true friends of the Negro race, it contains a reference to Tuskegee and mentions your own name, which, by the way, is most highly honored here, not only by the leading Haitians without exception, but to my great astonishment by small cultivators and even laborers throughout the 28 cities, towns, and villages it was my privilege to visit along the coast and in the far interior of Haiti during last year, and the most exciting time perhaps we have had.

America has no idea, neither, in fact, over 90 per cent of our own Haitian people themselves, as to the magnitude of the present change, yea, the real transformation which has recently taken place by the incoming of the new Government, and that in a most unexpected way. It represents the real intelligence and energy of the Republic. There is to be found in palace and cabinet to-day not only a high type of civilization, but in fact an atmosphere of refinement, which if now wisely directed and strongly backed up by the sympathetic but real support of our own United States Government, and with the blessing of God, must soon effect a most beneficient change also throughout this long neglected country, with its nearly 3,000,000 priest-ridden, poverty-stricken, yet most kind and interesting people.

It is really the first civic government Haiti has ever had. The next few years are the most momentous in the history of this country of Toussaint L'Overture. Yes; the psychological moment has at last come, and which some of us have looked forward to and earnestly prayed for the last 10, 15, and 20 years.

Will you not, therefore, now act in this matter and come to our help and the rescue of Haiti, which means, in fact, the real uplift of the whole Negro race? For the character and capacity of the African is, after all, to be mainly judged not by the members of the race in the States, much less by those on the Dark Continent, but by what the black man is in his own Republic of Haiti.

You may (a) accept this petition from me and personally present it to Mr. Rockefeller or Mr. Carnegie, or both, or (b) you may arrange for a special interview and accompany and introduce me and personally support my plea in behalf of this small, brave, but much misunderstood nation, or (c) even as suggested first of all—appointing commissioners.

I have credentials from Dr. Robert S. MacArthur, president of the Baptist World's Alliance; Dr. Ferris, minister of our United States Government at Port au Prince; Dr. Livingstone, United States consul at Cape Haiti, etc. In case you can arrange an interview, then I would suggest also with us that we ask the principal of Hampton, Dr. C. E. Morris, Arkansas, and Dr. B. D. Gray, corresponding secretary of Southern Baptist Home Mission Board. The latter is planning to visit us so as to take up the whole island as their mission field.

I ought to state that already I have been in correspondence with Mr. Starr Murphy and Dr. Buttrick, of the Rockefeller Foundation, and the Government Educational Bureau at Washington, D. C. Also I have written to Dr. Pritchett and have had a long and interesting interview with the esteemed secretary of the Carnegie Foundation, etc., New York. While all deeply sympathized with poor Haiti's need and special claims upon America's help now that our interrelation was becoming much closer every year, yet not one of these foundations as at present constituted enabled them to consider objects outside of the States, however worthy these might really be, and more especially anything in the nature of an industrial school. We must have in Haiti, first of all, an efficient normal and industrial college, though no doubt if Haiti will now advance as we hope and sincerely believe before very long, no doubt, the Republic would require also a fully equipped university for the efficient training in the higher branches of the sciences, etc., on the same basis as we have in the States.

Please send me seven catalogues of your school, as parents are constantly inquiring about your school. Do you teach French?

For Christ and Haiti.

Yours, very fraternally,

L. Ton Evans.

———

THE TUSKEGEE NORMAL AND INDUSTRIAL INSTITUTE,
Tuskegee Institute, Alabama, May 24, 1909.

Rev. L. Ton Evans,
    Edwardsville, Pa.

Dear Sir: This is to acknowledge receipt of your letter in regard to the young girl's admission to this institution. The inclosed circular gives information as to the terms upon which students are accepted here.

If the young girl to whom you refer can meet the requirements in full for admission to the day school, we shall be glad to admit her to that department. Students admitted to the day school are required to be fully 14 years of age, able-bodied, strong, healthy, well grown for their age, and able to at least pass the entrance examination for the B preparatory class.

The charge for board is $8.50 per month, but students are given an opportunity to work out a portion of this amount. The entrance fee to be paid in cash is $8. This fee is to be paid once each year at the time of entering.

Should the young girl decide to enter here in August, it will be all right for her to do so. Please have her bring letters of recommendation as to her moral character from well-known persons in your community.

Please advise if we may expect her to enter.

Yours, truly,

BOOKER T. WASHINGTON,
    - - *Principal.*

(Referring to one of the Haiti girls the missionary brought to the United States, who, with boys longing for education and anxious to come to America and learn English, he also placed in American Christian schools to be trained for service in Haiti.)

 AMERICAN BAPTIST PUBLICATION SOCIETY,
Philadelphia, March 14, 1921.

Rev. L. TON EVANS,
First Baptist Church, Brisbin, Pa.

DEAR BROTHER EVANS: Answering your inquiry concerning Haiti, it has been my understanding that the home mission delegation to the West Indies are to include Haiti in their itinerary. I think I am right in this because in the earlier preparations I was invited to be a member of this delegation, and was told at the time that one of the main objects of the trip was to investigate especially conditions in Haiti, with a view to seeing whether or not northern Baptists ought to undertake work there, if funds for the same could be provided. I have not heard of any change in the original plan.

Very sincerely, yours,

GILBERT N. BRINK.
General Secretary.

BWTHYN, WYOMING, PA.,
October 3, 1921.

Dr. HOVEY,
Superintendent of Education, American Baptist Home Mission.
New York.

DEAR DR. HOVEY: This is intended, through you, the education superintendent, as an introduction for Secretary Detweiller, of the Home Missions Latin America department, to Revs. Elie Mark, Nosirel Lherisson, Lucius Hypolite, Dr. Hector Paultre, who, with all the other brethren and churches of Haiti, will heartily rejoice and feel greatly heartened at your coming to them at this time and, after our years of hopeful waiting and earnest praying, to make the official survey of the Haiti field, and with the purpose of establishing a Bible and industrial missionary school and with the view of laying a strong and broad foundation for the successful development of the Baptist mission throughout Haiti, and probably the whole island, providing Brother Deitweiller's report is favorable and our mission society thinks fit.

I can certainly bespeak for the Baptist mission's Latin America secretary a most cordial and real Haitian welcome, not only from our Baptist brethren and own churches, but also from my old friends, the Revs. Turnbull, pastor and principal of College Bird, Port au Prince; De Feu, superintendent of the London Wesleyan Mission, Cape Haiti; and churches and pastors of other denominations, as well as from leaders of the Haiti Government and people.

Am heartily delighted with dear Brother Detweiller's impending visit, and both Mrs. Evans and myself shall pray for the success of his mission and his safe return with a report of the inspiring type—of that of Caleb and Joshua, of the tribe of Judah—urging our home mission committee " To go up at once and possess it."

With a bon voyage and God bless you, the brethren and churches of Haiti, and our affectionate regards to late Judge Orius Paultre's family, whole church at St. Marc, and missions on Isle Gonave.

Fraternally and for Christ and Haiti.

L. TON EVANS.

Please make inquiries of Dr. Hector as to the safety of our packed books and things left at St. Marc.

THE AMERICAN BAPTIST HOME MISSION SOCIETY.
New York, October 4, 1921.

Rev. L. TON EVANS,
Wyoming, Pa.

DEAR BROTHER: Your letter of October 3, with inclosures, concerning Haiti have been received. I am passing them at once to Dr. Hovey, superintendent of Baptist religious education, with the suggestion that he return them to you after they have served his purpose.

I trust that you and yours are well these days and that great spiritual blessings will come to Haiti. With all best wishes,

Cordially, yours, .

C. L. WHITE, *Executive Secretary.*

—————

KINGSTON, PA., *April 17, 1919.*

Mr. S. G. INMAN,

Executive Secretary of Latin American Committee on Cooperation.

DEAR BROTHER INMAN: In reply to Mr. Colton's letter to me in Haiti, notifying me that your had been officially appointed to visit the island, and more especially after our personal interview on the occasion he visited Wilkes-Barre, allow me not only to express my great pleasure that the Latin America committee has at last shown its deep interest in the black republic but ask when you really propose to run down?

I thought of running in before you go, now that I have returned, with at the present moment uncertainty of our being able to go back, solemnly as I have pledged to Protestant Christians, Baptists, etc., as well as Haiti leaders irrespective of politics and religious creeds, never, if possible, after so many years of labor in behalf of religious, educational, and social, and industrial regeneration; and moral development of the republic and its 2,000,000 Negroes, to desert them at the present moment, and very important epoch in Haiti's history.

I have already spoken to and written leading Christian brethren there as to your coming, and fully expected to have the pleasure of seeing you before I left and accompany you around; however, if possible, would like to see you personally before you go, even should I not be able to see my way to come down with you at this time.

Am going to Washington early next week, and may arrange to come from there about Friday, or early following week to New York, so, if this will do, please write me care of Dr. Jesse Jones, United States Education Bureau, District of Columbia.

With sincere and fraternal regards, heartily yours.

L. TON EVANS.

—————

DECEMBER 21, 1918.

Dr. and Hon. LIVINGSTON,

United States Consul, Cape Haitien.

MY DEAR DR. LIVINGSTON : I have never forgotten the real and valuable assistance Dr. Furniss, Port au Prince; late President Laconte; Dr. Holly; and, of course, our pastor, Condillac Jean Jacques rendered me in regard to that wonderful petition praying for the industrial college like Hampton and Tuskegee for Haiti, and signed by nearly 3,000 leading Haitians, irrespective of religious creeds and the so-called politics of certain classes.

You will be glad, yea, you and Dr. Holly and Pastor Condillac indeed delighted, to learn that after over eight years of incessant toil and amid mountains of difficulties it looks now as if that unanimous and earnest prayer of little and poor and almost crushed Haiti is about to be answered.

This coming month, or not later than February, my friend Dr. James H. Dillard, the direct representative of the great Rockefeller Foundation, general education board, 61 Broadway, will visit Haiti, where I hope to have a conference at Port au Prince both with our United States as well as our Haitian leaders, and shall try and see he goes to the Cape as well as the South.

I have just returned last Sunday on the *Panama,* and this Thursday morning paid my respects to Gen. Catlin, our new chief of American occupation, who is not only a gallant officer but, I believe, a Christian statesman, that will prove a credit to the old flag. Did you know that I was an intimate friend of the Right Hon. D. Lloyd-George, whom our President has gone to meet and greet in France and London? Ex-President Roosevelt is also interested in this industrial college and my efforts just now.

With sincere regards to you, Holly, Jacques, and friends there, for Christ, Haiti, and humanity.

L. TON EVANS.

ADOPTION OF MISSIONARY FOR HAITI.

Whereas the Women's Home and Foreign Mission Convention of North Carolina, assembled at White Rock Baptist Church, Durham, last year, expressed an earnest desire in their report to employ a missionary of their own on the foreign field; and

Whereas our newly appointed field secretary and superintendent of Baptist missions in Haiti, the Rev. L. Ton Evans, has brought before our convention this year at Goldsboro the appalling need as well as the bright prospects of our new Haiti mission field generally, and especially the need and prospects among our own sisters of the black Republic; and

Whereas Mrs. L. Ton Evans has been already in the employ of the Women's American Baptist Home Mission Society, shown a profound interest in, and done efficient and valuable work for our own young women at the National Missionary Training School, at Washington, D. C., where Miss Alice Alexis and Miss Christine Frances, brought from Haiti by Dr. Evans, with others from Africa, etc., were trained; and also

Whereas our white sisters of the Welsh and Wyoming Associations of the northeast Pennsylvania have manifested their deep and practical interest in the evangelization of Haiti, as well as their personal interest in Mrs. L. Ton Evans and her life and work while in their midst: Be it, therefore, unanimously

Resolved by the Women's Home and Foreign Mission Convention of North Carolina and auxiliary of the Lott Carey Baptist Convention, in session at Goldsboro, N. C., October 3–7, 1917, That we set apart the sum of $300 a year for the employment of Mrs. Evans, and that we further appeal to our white sisters of the above Welsh and Wyoming Baptist Associations to donate a similar amount of $300 annually, making a total of $600, all of which shall be paid by us through the Women's American Baptist Home Mission for our sister, Mrs. L. Ton Evans, with a view of her becoming the founder and principal of a Bible and industrial missionary training school for the young women of Haiti and leader in missionary and educational efforts generally for the uplift of our long-neglected womanhood of the black Republic.

MRS. P. G. SHEPHERD,
President.
MRS. B. H. BRANDON,
Secretary.

At the official women's board meeting above it was passed that Mrs. P. G. Shepherd, president of the North Carolina Women's Home and Foreign Missions, be delegated to attend in behalf of this convention and as a member of the Lott Carey Foreign Board the missionary "send off" which the sisters of the Welsh and Wyoming Associations may plan for Mrs. L. Ton Evans before leaving this country with her husband for Haiti.

LEGATION DE LA REPUBLIQUE D'HAITI,
Washington, D. C., April 29, 1919.

Pastor L. TON EVANS, *Kingston, Pa.*

MY DEAR PASTOR TON EVANS: I was very glad to receive your letter of yesterday, in which you inform me of your present and continued effort not only to secure for Haiti the establishment of an industrial school, such as Tuskegee, on real Christian basis, but your special plea just now with the southern Baptist brethren of the United States, to undertake the evangelizing of my own dear people.

I profoundly appreciate your self-sacrificing work and the deep interest you have shown in my country the last 25 years; that I have the privilege of knowing you, and sincerely thank you for the splendid encouragement and support you have rendered Haitian missionaries and brought some over to educate in these States.

Your deep interest and untiring activities in the religious, moral and social development of our Republic have won the entire sympathy and implicit confidence of the Haitian people.

With the personal knowledge you have of my country and dear people, and should the Southern Baptist Board enter the Haiti field and thus support your efforts, I am sure that with the blessing of God you must succeed in this great enterprise of saving Haiti.

I sincerely hope, and earnestly pray therefor, that you will find in the United States Christian brethren and educational and philanthropic friends who, with the cooperation of our own best and ablest people in Haiti, will firmly stand by and support your splendid and noble work of developing my own backward country at the present moment.

My best wishes will always accompany you.

I am, my dear pastor,

Yours, very truly,

T. CH. MORAVIA.

———

HAITI FOR CHRIST.

"In order to make good the words of the Prophet Esaiah * * * the people who were dwelling in darkness have seen a brilliant light, and on those who were dwelling in the region of the shadows of death, on them light has dawned." (Math. iv., 14–16.)

"We wait for light, but behold obscurity; for brightness, but walk in darkness." (Isaiah lix, 9–10.)

History in brief.—Hispaeniola, or little Spain, as it was termed in the fifteenth century, is an island next in size to Cuba. It has two Republics, known to-day as Haiti and Santo Domingo, and where the French and Spanish patois are spoken, respectively. The total population is estimated a little over 2,000,000, i. e., some 250,000 more than the whole principality of Wales, including Monmouthshire.

Haiti was discovered by Columbus December, 1492, during his first voyage west, hence is known before America. The aborigines (Indians) were destroyed by French and Spanish pirates and exploiters who followed from Europe. To repeople the island and enrich the white settlers recourse was taken to the traffic in human flesh in vogue among the British and other civilized nations. For this purpose many thousands of Negroes—men, women, and children—were stolen, dragged from their homes in Africa, chained together as beasts of burden, and carried over high seas, in small, stifling sailing vessels. Such as escaped being beaten to death and cast overboard as food for fish—a sweet and welcome relief, no doubt—and those who survived the brutal treatment meted to them, were conveyed to Haiti and other islands as slaves.

The cruel and barbarous conduct of the slave owners, after a long period of untold suffering, brought upon them at last its own punishment, for the Negroes, failing to endure the insults, injury, and injustice any longer, engaged in a fierce and bloody war, under the leadership of Toussaint L'ouverture, thus avenging the wrongs of the past and ridding themselves forever of slavery. To achieve this, however, 80,000 blacks and whites were killed by the sword and yellow fever. Among the slain were 20,000 soldiers, the flower of the French Army, sent by Napoleon to aid the slave owners, defend and perpetuate slavery, and even at a time he himself was fighting for greater liberty to the white man of Europe!

The brave and God-given leader and noble emancipator of his race, who could neither be beaten nor bribed by the offer of a kingdom and a crown, was subsequently and treacherously allured on board a French man-of-war and taken to France, where he died in a felon's cell.

> "Sleep calmly in thy dungeon tomb
> Beneath Besancon's alien sky,
> Dark Haitien! for the time shall come
> Even now is nigh—
>
> When everywhere thy name shall be
> Redeemed from color's infamy;
> And men shall learn to speak of thee
> As one of earth's great spirits born."

Appalling condition of the people.—The Carib Indians, and first inhabitants of these islands, were polygamists and idolaters. The Negroes brought with them from Africa, as one would naturally expect, all the superstition, fetichism, and vice characteristic of the Dark Continent. Had the newly freed Haitiens only been permitted on the proclamation of freedom to retain their George Washington, in the person of Toussaint L'ouverture—as Americans, for instance, were on the declaration of their independence about 20 years prior to this, and so as to mold the policy of the new Republic and direct the government he had been instrumental in founding—Haiti undoubtedly to-day would have been a model Republic, worthy of America or England, instead of a poor, superstitious, degraded, and devil-worshipping country; it is unpitied and sometimes even sneered at by those with centuries of civilization to their back. In 1860 the Government ignorantly and mistakenly signed a concordat with the Vatican. recognizing Romanism as the island religion. By so doing they signed their own death warrant, for the brand of Romanism in this island, as very properly described by the Rev. J. G. Greenhough, M. A.—an expresident of the Baptist Union of Great Britain—simply means "the most superstitious and degraded form, well nigh as dense as the darkness of heathenism." This, therefore, with vaudooism—devil worship—the real religion of 95 per cent of the islanders, has enslaved them mentally and morally, checked the national aspiration, and literally crushed the spirit of the race, and this, forsooth, after securing for themselves political freedom 50 years earlier at such a tremendous sacrifice.

Though Haiti—called the Queen Island—is richest as regards soil and minerals in the Caribbean Sea, the people themselves—materially and socially— are in a most wretched and deplorable state. Destitution is seen everywhere. In connection with the vaudoo worship, to which they are summoned by the sound of tom-tom from hill and vale, bush and grove, the devil devotees work themselves into a frenzy, very much like devil possession. During these ceremonies, which are most immoral and revolting, fowls are killed, and even at times the blood and lives of innocent children offered, to slake the thirst and pacify the anger of the demon god, whom they in their ignorance have been taught for centuries to fear and dread. That such should be the case at the dawn of the twentieth century is almost incredible, particularly so in a large island like Haiti, and situated as it is between Jamaica and Porto Rico, which belong to England and America, the wealthiest and most humane, not to say Christian, countries of the world!

Baptist beginnings.—Early in the last century Haiti became a safe rendezvous to members of the race suffering from surrounding islands. As George Leisle and Moses Baker—two American Negroes—were the first Baptist missionaries in Jamaica 12 years previous to the English Baptist Missionary Society being formed, so colored brethren from the States—probably runaway slaves like Onesimus of old, referred to by Paul—were also the Protestant pioneers of Haiti 25 years later. The Rev. Monroe and Rev. Hill—latter an African Methodist Episcopal, afterwards baptized—are the first regular preachers—colored— of whom we have any certainty. This was prior to the year 1885. The first white brother to come from America was the Rev. W. Mead Jones, of Welsh descent, and a Baptist, who is supposed to have labored here under the Anti-Slavery Society of those days. Owing to his changed views he was recalled about 1846, when another by the name of Judd took his place. The latter again left Port au Prince in a short time for Samana, San Domingo, where it is said he soon died. The first missioner, however, to work among the Haitians proper was the Rev. E. J. Frances, who came to the island from Lucea, Jamaica; the others confined their services chiefly to the English-speaking colored people who came to the island. It was through the special pleading of the immortal William Knibb that Frances was sent by the English Baptist Society to labor in Haiti. This brother, with one Flanders, Miss Harris, and Miss Clark, landed in Jacmel Christmas, 1845. Though the missionaries at once settled down, rapidly acquired the language, and gave special promise of excellent work to be done—the leader unfortunately was struck down in a few months—for before the end of July, following year, Frances succumbed to the dread malaria fever. On account of the frequent revolutions, constant change of governments, with the consequent hardships, destruction of property and life, etc., all this entailed, missionary efforts became very protracted, and with the exception of Rev. W. H. Webley—who labored alone for years—brethren continually retired after short intervals, which told disastrously against the mission. Seeing Jamaica's proximity to Haiti, the very flourishing financial condition of the Baptist churches there at one time, as evidenced not only by their having become self-supporting but also the pleasing fact that they raised £3,000 a year for the purpose of evangelization in their own islands as well as for work outside, the committee in London thought it advisable to transfer this field to the above missionary board, though for years after they continued their interest and made certain contributions. Jamaica—for several years—has been obliged to give up this, as well as other important fields in which they were engaged simply for the lack of funds. Through the failure of the sugar industry, as well as the blind and blundering policy persisted in by succeeding British Governments in allowing and assisting thousands of East Indians—coolies—to the British colonies of the west in the shape of indentured labor—by the way, a species of slavery—the island suffers great financial depression. The latter is not only driving away from Jamaica and their island home in search of the means of livelihood a very large number of the more thrifty, but lowers the morals of the people, discourages the natives, and impoverishes, if not indeed paralyzes, the churches in their laudable efforts to uplift the Negro. Such injustice and hardship as these Negroes suffer would not be tolerated in England or America.

Bright outlook.—During the last few years, and practically since the termination of the war between America and Spain, great changes have taken place. Haiti, in addition to its close proximity to Porto Rico, is also now on the great highway to Panama. The fact of the United States warships plowing Haitian waters, and policing the island as it were, is a guaranty there shall be no filibustering from without, neither any serious rising from within, allowed again as in the past, and which have proved so destructive. This will give stability to the Republics and enable the Governments to encourage industry and commerce. A new railroad (first in Haiti) is just now being constructed, pointing to great developments in the future. There is to-day a better understanding between Haiti and America than perhaps ever before, with a growing suspicion, if not dislike to Romanism, among the more intelligent and thoughtful people, and which recent events in France is almost certain to emphasize. The outlook, therefore, has never been brighter and more promising than at present.

Proposed plans.—As soon as the native missionaries on the field can be provided for, and one or two well-qualified workers (if possible) added to them, who shall devote the whole of their time and energy to work the mission centers, the few poor scattered Christians are gathered together again and organized for regular public worship, etc., we will immediately start a normal and industrial school. A people like the Haitians, free, owning their own soil, born in a country whose climatic conditions are enervating, and where nature herself is so rich and bountiful, if not indeed extravagant, yet degraded by slavery and sunk in depravity, are not likely to be permanently benefited, unless given a full-orbed gospel, dealing with the whole of the man.

The black man of Haiti must therefore be gradually led to see the dignity of labor and believe in his own capacity and skill. While the direct aim of the mission is the regeneration of the heart, that of the normal and industrial school will be to train the hand and head of the Negro. The latter we expect to be associated with Tuskegee, Ala., United States of America, of which Dr. Booker T. Washington is president. In 1902 this great American educator writes: "We have students at our institute I could heartily recommend to you as soon as you are ready, not only as efficient for the work intended but possessing in an eminent degree, also, the missionary spirit." The proposed school will be interdenominational, open to suitable young Negroes (male and female) all over the island, and supported by friends of the Negro both in America and England, and apart from the funds of the mission board.

Why the urgent need for help?—(*a*) Because the national convention foreign mission board now, undertaking to evangelize Haiti, though the largest (2,280,000) organized body of Negro Christians in the world, is certainly also the poorest as regards money. When freed by Lincoln's proclamation January 1, 1863, the Negroes of America numbered 4,500,000; to-day they are nearly 10,000,000, who live mainly in the black belt, and one-fourth of which belong to our national convention. Though only 44 years since emerged from slavery, with its degrading effects, when thrown penniless upon the world, and in spite of discouragements, such as poverty, prejudice, and oppression, their progress during this period has been phenomenal. With the Christlike sympathy, and the generous help of the American Baptist Home Mission Society and their own personal sacrifice and self-denial, they have built schools, colleges, and maintain over 12,000 pastors half of whom were born in slavery, when it was a crime to be able to read the Bible! They also operate missions in West, South, and East Central Africa, British West Indies, and South America, which tax their scanty funds to the utmost limit. Yet, for reasons given already, they have decided to add Haiti as a special department to their work.

(*b*) Because that by giving the Gospel to Haiti, and establishing the institute (so as to help them to help themselves), we are furthering the highest type of civilization, teaching America and the world that the African, under favorable conditions, is quite capable of self-government, thus securing that respect and justice due to the race.

(c) Because the present is most opportune, as already pointed out in reference to future developments, etc. If the mission is well founded, and strenuous efforts put forth the next four or five years, the field will be practically occupied by one important section of the Evangelical Christian Church, which means greater efficiency, a great saving in energy and money, with other advantages enjoyed on a mission field, where there is no denominational and sectarian overlapping.

(d) Because money contributed to and labor bestowed on evangelization and education of the Negro is an excellent investment and bound to pay, securing, as they do, the highest results for man and God.

Dr. H. L. Morehouse, the respected secretary of American Baptist Home Missions Society and a shrewd student of missions, recently wrote to the Standard:

"Our expenditure of $4,000,000 as a society among the colored in the States during these 40 years has been one of the best investments in the world. Many, indeed, are yet degraded; but are not many white even in the old centers of Anglo-Saxon civilization? The Hebrews got out of Egypt in one day, but it took more than 40 years to get Egypt out of them. Who expects the Negro to overtake the Caucasian with a start of a thousand years? But they are coming on. Out of the depths up from slavery to noble Christian manhood and womanhood many have risen. In 26 years of service for the society I have seen poor, coarse Negro boys and girls develop into cultured, able, influential characters, consecrated to the service of Christ."

DEPARTMENT OF THE INTERIOR,
BUREAU OF EDUCATION,
Washington, July 31, 1917.

Dr. L. TON EVANS,
23 West Bertch Street, Lansford, Pa.

DEAR DR. EVANS: I was very glad to receive your letter of July 3 and to know that you are still working for Haiti. I hope that your ambitions and desires will be realized in this respect. As you know, I am much interested in the problems of that island. Thus far, however, I have not succeeded in convincing the trustees of the Phelps-Stokes fund that the conditions of the gift permit them to appropriate money for Haiti. In view of this I fear that the fund will not now be able to give you the assistance which you desire. There may be other sources of revenue that we can influence. When your plans are made I shall be glad to know of them. I have heard of the good work of Mrs. Evans through Miss Burroughs. I know that Mrs. Evans is fully equipped to work in Haiti.

I fear that I shall not be in the city during the first week in September. I shall be here on the 30th and 31st of August and will be glad to see you the last week of that month. On the days mentioned above the bureau is to hold an important conference on Negro education. This is a small deliberative meeting, to which few people are invited. Should you be in the city we would be pleased to have you there. You will be glad to know that our report is done. I shall order a copy sent to you if it has not already reached you.

With regard to passports to Haiti, I am quite certain that you would have comparatively little difficulty in obtaining the permission of the State Department to leave the country.

With very kind regards, I am.

Very sincerely, yours,

THOMAS JESSE JONES, *Specialist.*

ST. MARC, WEST INDIES,
March 5, 1919.

DEAR FRIEND DELACOUR: Am sending a note to say that I am hoping to visit Port au Prince soon on my way again to the States, and shall be greatly obliged if you can manage as one of the patriotic sons of Haiti, who by every moral, constitutional, educational, and even Christian means seek to gradually raise Haiti and people to a higher standard of thinking and living, and so some day to fulfill the destiny God has intended for your race in Haiti, as of course He has intended for us as a white nation in the States, as well as all other nationalities in fact; I shall therefore be indeed glad for you to see Pouget, Sincereg, Meyer, and two or three other real patriots with high and pure motives like yourself, so as to meet me.

I had the privilege when at Washington the last fall to have a special Haitian committee (to watch the interest of the natives here) formed in connection with the national race congress executive.

Of course, there is much connected with our colored brethren in the States at the present stage, and often inspired by ignorance, prejudice, etc., which you and those mentioned and others in Haiti would be as stoutly opposed to as myself, and felt sad and wrong to encourage here, and absolutely detrimental to all that is best in the development of the Negro people.

There are great leaders, however, such as late Dr. Booker T. Washington (my friend), present Maj. Moton (whose name you see in memorandum), that the leaders in Haiti must become acquainted with, if real, steady, mental, moral, and material progress is to be made here, that must prove a permanent success. There must, if possible, be no gerry building upon superstitions, ignorance, prejudice, etc., and education must not be confind to the head, but be of a real practical nature, etc.

As I have promised our chief of occupation (Gen. Catlin) not to give any copies away again of memorandum (at present), please keep the one you had previously to yourself. If more convenient, we can meet at your place or at Bolos. My boat may be sure to leave about end of next week. Believe me to remain your sincere friend, and for Christ, Haiti, and humanity,

—— ——.

ST. MARC, HAITI, WEST INDIES,
February 10, 1919.

THOMAS A. VILMENAY, ESQ.,
Directeur de L'informateur Haitien, Port au Prince.

MY DEAR FRIEND VILMENAY: Inasmuch that during my personal interview with our Gen. Catlin, chief of our American occupation, both the marine and the gendarmerie in Haiti, I pledged my word of honor on the next day, Thursday morning, after seeing you on the way from the depot, and as there might be a misunderstanding in some quarters, if not some advantage taken by certain natives, who may be bitterly opposed to our American Government's procedure through our occupation, owing to statements made at Washington and vouched for by myself and now officially being investigated here, I promised not to distribute another copy of this "memorandum," and containing serious charge I and others are prepared to prove before the commission sought and fully expected to be appointed by our own responsible United States Government in its own interest, and that, of course, of Haiti and its people; I have now to specially request you not to use the copy I gave you on the day previous (Wednesday) and either at the station or on my way to my hotel, when I accidentally met you.

Am sure you will comply with my personal request, and that you, as well as those friends of mine, including Dr. Laroche, Dr. Francois Delacour, minister of instruction, Dr. Holly, Revs. Turnbull, Mark, De Feu, Lherisson, Jacques, and American Consul Livingston, American Vice Consul Vital, etc., so deeply interested in the social, educational, industrial, and shall I also add the spiritual regeneration of long neglected and politically and financially exploited Haiti, and your over 2,000,000 suffering and oppressed people, and in the providence of God and through our own Government and other American religious, educational, and philanthropic agencies, essential to the uplift of every nation (be it black or white), are as anxious as myself not to place absolutely the least obstacle in the way of our "American occupation," but in every way possible add to their influence and authority, and, if possible, moral power and efficiency to carry out the intention of the American Government in Haiti through present instruments and as set forth in the excellent treaty (convention) between the two countries.

I hardly believe, however, there would be any objection from the genial new chief of our occupation if you referred to the proposed industrial college, which must take a prominent place and prove a most important, if not indispensable, factor in any future scheme of developing the black republic.

as set forth, indeed, in my "memorandum," and recommendations to our President, and through him our United States Government, who, the moment it is directly brought before him, and whether or not actually supported by officialism and certain grades of politicians, will positively go through.

The fact of the names of Maj. Moton, president of Tuskegee, Dr. Thomas Jesse Jones, and Dr. James H. Dillard, of the Jeanes, and the Rockefeller Foundation, of general education boards, of the United States, mentioned and suggested as members of that commission, is a guaranty in itself, of course, to any person who really knows President Wilson, ex-President Taft, late lamented ex-President Theodore Roosevelt, and our Government, and great American Christian leaders, that all this will—as soon as matters can be arranged properly—is already an accomplished fact.

I state this so as to encourage you to "patience, real faith, in American Government, perseverance in all that is good and uplifting, and hope in the meantime, as well as support for the present instrumentalities as pioneers, of court, and essential under present conditions, and for which undoubtedly every intelligent and thoroughly patriotic Haitian must thank God, imperfect as they are, but which will in the natural development of things and time goes on be gradually changed and so adapted as to produce the changes mentioned and outlined in the "memorandum."

Probably you and others who widely read and take such deep interest in the struggles and grand victory just achieved in Europe for liberty and right, and in which our own American Government has so distinguished itself, and our soldiers, both white and colored, have, shoulder to shoulder, so valiantly fought under that courageous and indomitable Christian, Gen. Pershing, who, like President Wilson, Lloyd-George, Secretary of our Navy Daniels, etc., is an enemy of liquor and alcohol, and to-day, because of his high and noble character is loved all over the States, and would by acclamation be made our next Pres'dent if he but consented, know also that Maj. Moton and Dr. Jesse Jones, my personal friend, have been to France and, with our President, looking after the interest of our colored American soldiers there, and even some of our Hait an young men in American colleges who volunteered to the front, such as the son of Dr. Ghousse, our Baptist deacon, and local native preacher at Jacmel, etc.

You may call attention in your paper to this and the fact that Dr. Dillard, wh.te, but real friend of race, both in States and here, pledged me again and again, and the day I left him at the Rockefeller headquarters of the general education board, in Broadway, New York, to visit Haiti, either January or th's very month, so as to investigate conditions, looking to the establishment of what was called in 1911 by Cincinnatus Leconté, Legèr, and even the then President Simon (when I took that petition around Haiti), "the noble project" of an industrial college, founded on Christian basis, like Hampton and Tuskegee here among us in Haiti.

Your paper will certainly serve a most useful purpose in informing, therefore, and thus preparing gradually our leaders in Haiti for this and showing how indispensable, with all that our own American Government can do through occupation, etc., that the Haitians themselves must not only be converted and educated but become actual tillers of their own rich soil and learn to look at honest labor not as a species of slavery and something forced and degrading, but elevating and, indeed, divine—essential, too, in their development—if ever you are to become free, independent, and a progressive people in the true sense of these terms.

If you saw account of my lecture along these lines at the cape two weeks ago, you may copy same in L'informateur, and I shall send some news occasionally from our Government educational and labor department bureaus which are sent me here to St. Marc.

With Christian regards, best wishes for new year, believe me to remain

　　Yours, and for Christ and Haiti,

　　　　　　　　　　　　　　　　　　　　L. Ton Evans.

AN URGENT APPEAL IN BEHALF OF HAITI, WEST INDIES.

"So then faith cometh by hearing and hearing the word of God "—and how shall they hear without a preacher? (Romans x, 14, 17.)

"But I can see though dimly through the mystery, His hand above."

Haiti, the black republic, as it is called, has on the whole island some 2,000,000 inhabitants, all of whom are Africans. Although a brave people as proved by the manner in which their forefathers fought and won their freedom from slavery more than 100 years ago, under that noble Negro chieftain, Toussaint Louverture, yet to-day they are in the most pitiable condition materially, politically, and morally.

Since 1860 the recognized island religion is. the lowest type of Roman.sm, though the people generally, if not entirely, are blind devotees of Voodooism, who, in addition to immoral orgies, frenzical dances, and other disgusting and revolting practices connected with devil worship, at times sacrifice human life. even the blood of innocent babes, to slake the thirst of their demon god, whom they have been taught for centuries, both in Africa and Haiti, by the papa lois (witch doctor) to fear and dread.

At the dawn of this twentieth century, and though in close proximity to American shores—for Haiti lies between Cuba and Porto Rico. on the present direct route to our Panama Canal, and within a few hurs' run of Jamaica—it is almost incredible that there should be at th's moment an island five times the size of the latter and with over three times its population in such a benighted and deplorable state and without any organized efforts whatever by our great missionary societies to evangelize its heathen.

The National Negro Baptist Convention, however, before whom the writer was invited to plead the cause of poor Haiti at Birmingham, Ala., September, 1902 (where nearly 4,000 dusky delegates attended from distances varying 500. 1,000, 1,500, and even 2,000 miles away), have now faithfully undertaken to enter this region in 1904, providing some of the Lord's stewards are willing to aid them financially, as their funds are altogether inadequate for the m'ssion board's work in other foreign fields now operated.

Therefore, should a fund of $200,000 be placed to the credit of the foreign board, the interest on the same would put at least eight brethen immediately on the island. The appointment also of an energetic agent to visit the churches here, as well as superintend the field, could in a few years through the careful and diligent development of native resources, augmented by outside subscriptions, double the above annual income. This amount under the supervision of the national foreign board would be entirely devoted to the direct evangelization of Haiti along Bible lines.

The object of thus presenting these facts is to enlist sympathy and prayer, as well as raise the above amount required, to enable the national convention to commence operations without further delay among the neglected poverty-stricken. priest-ridden, and devil-worship.ng people of this otherwise queen island of the Caribbean Sea, that at last it may be said of them as the divinely illuminated seer said of the land of Zebulun and Nephthalim, viz: " The people which sat in darkness saw great light, and to them wh ch sat in the region and shadow of death light is sprung up." (Matthew iv. 16.)

> " Heaven's gate is closed to him who comes alone :
> Save thou a soul and it shall save thine own."

For Christ and Haiti,
Yours, sincerely,

L. Ton Evans.

First Baptist Church.
Edwardsdale, Pa.

Foreign Mission of National Baptist Convention,
Louisville, Ky., September 2, 1903.

Dear Brother Ton Evans: As I see now our brethren would be exceedingly glad to have you, if possible, to take up work for Haiti. At our annual meeting in Philadelphia the matter comes before the full board, and I am sure that they will approve of it. The following is part of the board's report for the year. I have been handicapped this year with poor help, which has hampered me in much I hoped to do.

Pray for us, and visit the convention if you can. Thanks for the pledge.
Yours, in His Name,

L. G. Jordon,
Corresponding Secretary.

Taken from the annual report of Brother L. G. Jordan, D. D., to National Baptist Convention, September 18, 1903, and representing 2,100,000 Baptists:

" Haiti, almost a next door neighbor, needs our immediate attention, but the want of money hinders us from sending missionaries there.

" We recommend, should we find friends of the Master, who will aid, to commence work there in 1904.

" We highly commend the earnest efforts of Rev. L. Ton Evans, of Edwardsdale, Pa. (late of Wales and ex-missioner from Haiti), in behalf of that needy field, and pray that he might find a way to go there again as a missionary and labor among the people who lay so heavily upon his heart, and otherwise assist us as a board to take up the work there without unnecessary delay."

The appalling and urgent need of Haiti is also personally and strongly indorsed by Revs. S. MacArthur, D. D., Calvary Baptist Church, New York : George E. Henderson, M. A.; Phillip Williams (ex-president and secretary, respectively, of Jamaica Baptist Union, West Indies) ; Dr. Booker T. Washington, the great Negro educator; and F. B. Meyer, B. A. (London) ; Prof. T. Witton Davies, B. A., Ph. D., Baptist and University Colleges, North Wales; together with John Cory, Esq., J. P., D. L.; ex-Alderman R. Cory, J. P.; and Daniel Thomas, Esq., Christian philanthropists in South Wales, who have already promised conditional and generous support to this much needed missionary enterprise.

Dr. Booker T. Washington has kindly offered to train at his excellent Normal and Industrial Institute, Tuskegee, Ala., some of the most promising Haitian youths; and Rev. Dr. Bullinger, secretary of the Trinitarian Bible Society (London), will donate uncorrupted and pure translations of Scriptures, both in French and Spanish, which will be a valuable help to the mission.

Rev. Russell H. Conwell, D. D., president of Temple College, Philadelphia, who, through his private secretary, September 16, 1903, wrote :

Rev. L. Ton Evans,
    Edwardsville, Pa.

Dear Sir : Russell H. Conwell received your letter of 14th instant, and wishes me to say that he has confidence in you, and would like to be of some use to such a missionary work as that you propose to do in Haiti. While he desires to help the cause, yet regrets he has no time nor thought to give to such an enterprise now, as he is so crowded with duties which he could not omit.

———

[By the London (England) committee of the Baptist Missionary Society, showing extensive efforts in 1906 and 1907 of the pioneer missionary in behalf of Haiti's religious and educational uplift.]

RECOGNITION OF THE NEW HAITIAN MISSION.

To the Baptist churches and friends of the Negro:

We, whose names are attached hereunto, rejoice to state that the committee of our Baptist Missionary Society meeting in London January 16, 1907 (presided over by the late Charles Williams, Accrington), and after due consideration of the petition and purpose of the foreign board of the American Negro Baptists, the great importance of Haiti as a field, the wretched condition of its superstitious and devil-worshiping inhabitants, unanimously decided to recognize the much-needed mission and express its hearty smypathy with, as well as extend its moral support, to the praiseworthy efforts now made to evangelize the benighted people of this island. (Both brethren, Charles Williams and the late J. Jenkyn Brown, congratulated us on the support given to Haiti. These two veterans very deeply sympathized with our mission.)

In addition to the special claims of the field itself set before the committee by the general secretary and superintendent of the work in Haiti, supported by the strong plea of members of the society in Wales, the committee in London also takes cognizance of the sympathy and interest of the churches of the principality (Welsh and English) in this mission of their colored brethren, and which sympathy and interest found expression in resolutions forwarded by churches and associations to the Rev. C. E. Wilson, B. A., secretary of the B. M. S., as well as Rev. W. Morris, D. D., F. R. G. S., chairman of the new missionary council for Wales.

Our society rejoices that the foreign board of the National Baptist Convention of America has undertaken to operate a mission in this sadly neglected island, and further expresses its pleasure that our Negro brethren in the United States have been so fortunate as to secure such an earnest, energetic, and self-sacrificing brother as Rev. L. Ton Evans, late of Wales and Edwardsdale, Pa., U. S. A., to represent them in this important Christian enterprise.

As some churches have already been informed, the English Baptist Missionary Society has authorized its secretaries in London to receive collections and subscriptions from churches and others in Wales and elsewhere (given specially for Haiti) and forward the same to them.

Thus every sum contributed, whether by collection or subscription, will be acknowledge and shall appear in the Welsh and English annual reports of the Baptist Missionary Society, as those now given to the Zenana work.

We sincerely hope, therefore, that all the churches and friends of the once-enslaved race and despised Negroes of America anxious to give the pure gospel and carry on a mission along strictly evangelical and scriptual lines among the millions who worship the demon god in the Black Republic will appreciate and take advantage of this arrangement made and send their collections and subscriptions to the Mission House in London, marked " for Haiti."

We strongly believe and very heartily indorse also the proposal to establish a normal and industrial institute on the island concurrent with, though separate from, the mission itself, and so as to train the head and hand of the Negro with a view to the cultivation of the rich soil and development of his country, as well as to produce enlightened native Christians and furnish capable school-teachers and efficient helpers for the missionaries from among the dark-skinned race.

We further think that the fact of the Negro Baptist foreign mission board of America (through our brother and fellow countryman, the Rev. L. Ton Evans) granting us control over the money raised for the mission is not only in harmony with our democratic policy as Baptists, can not but give great and general satisfaction to all, and should, indeed, prove a strong incentive to churches and friends to help and support the new undertaking in Haiti, West Indies.

May this new missionary effort be especially blessed of the Lord.
Expect great things from God.
Attempt great things for God.

> W. Morris, Treorchy (Chairman of the Missionary Council of Wales) ; H. Cernyw Williams, Corwen ; Charles Davies, Cardiff ; J. A. Morris, Aberystwyth ; J. W. Maurice, Dinas Cross (President of Baptist Union of Wales), Members of the Committee of the Baptist Missionary Society.

Signed also by the following secretaries of associations which have already adopted resolutions supporting the mission :

	Members.
W. Rhys Jones, East Glam. Association	27, 896
W. G. Davies, Glam. and Carm. (Eng.) Association	20, 463
W. Trevor Jones, Carm. and Card. Association	19, 835
D. C. Davies, West Glam. Association	19, 442
T. E. Gravell, Pem. Association	12, 378
Edwin Jones, D., Fl., and Meirion Association	9, 152
D. Hopkins, Anglesea Association	2, 861
Total membership	112, 027

If the above membership was divided, young men and women appointed in each church to collect 1 penny per month (an average of 1 shilling per year), more than £5,000 annually could be realized for Haiti and that without interfering at all with local efforts for the church and worthy objects at present supported. This sum would enable us as a Baptist denomination to take over at once the whole island of Haiti.

We request every church to inform the secretary of its association of the amount collected for Haiti, so that it may appear in the annual report of the association.

"The earth is the Lord's, and the fulness thereof."

Among which 120 churches of Wales which have been visited up to date, and that have promised to collect in aid of our mission, are the following:

Noddfa (Treorchy) ; Zion (Llanelly) ; Bethesda and Hill Park (H. West) ; Pembroke and Bethany (Pembroke Dock) ; Bethania (Cardigan) ; Nebo (Ystrad) ; St. Dogmells, Whitland, Bethel, and Hebron (Holyhead) ; Jerusalem (Llwynypia) ; Calvaria (Aberdare) ; Amlwch, Bangor, Zion, and Tabernacle (Cefnmawr) ; Hebron (Ton, Ystrad) ; Tabernacle (Pontypridd) ; Hebron, etc. (Dowlais) ; Bethel, Moriah, etc. (Llanelly) ; Carnarvon, Pembrey, Bethania (Cwmbach) ; Blaenffos, Llwynhendy, Aberdare (Eng.) ; Nebo (Ebbw Vale) ; etc.

Received already either in subscriptions or promises to be given annually in support of the mission.

	£.	s.		£.	s.
Mr. Richard Cory, J. P.	50	0	Dr. Ivor Davies	1	1
Libanus, Treherbert (Dr. Harries)	20	0	Dr. Lewis Lewis	1	0
			Mr. Richards (Pentre)	1	0
Trecynon, Aberdare (Rev. W. .Cynog Williams)	20	0	Mr. W. C. Short	1	0
			Mr. Thos. Williams	1	0
Bethlehem, Pwll (Rev. Richard Owen)	10	0	Mr. B. Rees, J. P.	1	0
			Mrs. Cynog Williams	1	0
A friend of Christ and the Negro	10	0	Rev. Cynog Williams	1	0
			Rev. W. Rhys Jones	1	0
Mr. Sydney Rees	5	0	Rev. E. W. Davies (Ton)	1	0
Mrs. D. Rees	5	0	Rev. J. R. Evans	1	0
Mr. W .Warren Kinsey (for family of 5)	5	0	Rev. W. Trevor Jones	1	0
			Rev. Rowe Williams	1	0
Mr. and Mrs. Jenkins	3	0	Rev. Tallesyn Williams	1	0
Ald. W. H. David	2	2	Rev. W. R. Lewis	1	0
Mrs. C. Edmunds	2	0	Rev. O. D. Campbell, M. A.	1	0
Mrs. D. Francis	2	0	Rev. J. J. Richards	1	0
Mr. Thomas Evans	2	0	Rev. Morgan Jones, B. A.	1	0
Mr. Williams (Ton Ystrad)	2	0	Prof. T. Witton Davies, B. A., Ph. D.	1	0
Mrs. Lewis (Hengoed)	1	10			

L. T. E.

APRIL 20, 1907.

Senator KING. Mr. Evans, during the war there were a number of Germans in Haiti, were there not, and at the outbreak of the war?

Mr. EVANS. Quite a number.

Senator KING. And some were interned during the war?

Mr. EVANS. Quite so.

Senator KING. And some deported from the island?

Mr. EVANS. Yes; I suggested that all this should have been done, just at the time we as a Government entered the war, being that we had this treaty with Haiti, and responsible for protecting Haiti, and feeding these people.

Senator KING. If there was a censorship during the war, it grew out of the occupation of the island?

Mr. EVANS. Yes; but the Germans were allowed full sway for a long time, and the Haiti people and ourselves suffered in consequence.

Senator KING. By the Germans?

Mr. EVANS. No doubt.

Senator KING. And Europeans belonging to the Central Powers?

Mr. EVANS. Yes, sir; there was a strong feeling here among not only Germans, but the priests and whole European Catholics, practically with the Central Powers and against the Allies and United States.

Senator KING. It was a real military necessity?

Mr. EVANS. Yes; essentially so, but it was not explained as it should have been to the Haitians, and it should have resulted in a greater benefit than it really was by way of distribution of food, etc., after we declared war.

I complained at Washington for lack of suitable publicity literature explaining the whole situation, and how it affected Haiti, and work of our occupation, but nothing really was done; it was of course all Europe.

Senator KING. The Germans did have control of the wharves and the harbors and banks?

Mr. EVANS. Yes; they were the leading merchants and exporters of coffee, logwood, cotton, etc., and had a regular system through their native agents of getting around, and they had studied the Haitian characteristics, and spoke the French and patois, having been there so many years, had great influence over the island, and with all other Europeans in Haiti, including the priests. They abused Haitian confidence, of course, in political propaganda to exploit the customs.

Senator KING. And they therefore had the business activities practically of the whole island?

Mr. EVANS. Yes; and I fear that our occupation and United States have failed to really understand this, if not most of our American Marine officers had been entirely off their guard, and even ignored it by their close associations with them in drinking, and other social relations.

Senator KING. And Haiti was used as a sort of base for the dissemination of German propaganda in the Caribbean Sea, and in the South American Republics and Central American Republics?

Mr. EVANS. Undoubtedly during the beginning of the war, and for many years before in anti-British and anti-American propagandas.

Senator KING. So it was necessary that there should be some sort of censorship after we were in control, and during the war?

Mr. EVANS. Yes; it was justified, but I am a great believer in publicity propaganda, setting forth the situation, and explaining to these people, who had just come under our control, and we were pledged to protect and assist, and to forearm them against misrepresentations and falsehood spread by interested politicians.

Senator KING. Was there any oppression used in the authority exercised by the officials in——

Mr. EVANS. With regard to the Germans; no, not to my knowledge.

Senator KING. With regard to the censorship?

Mr. EVANS. With the exception of what I referred to my own letters in Haiti and here since my return, my impression is that they were too lax, before Haiti declared war and for some time after, as in allowing Germans too much freedom, knowing the unfortunate bitter feelings that the United States had entered the war on the side of the Allies, and I fear that several of the American marines were not so favorable either, thinking we had really gone in for Great Britain's sake more than anything else.

Senator KING. Do you make any complaint, then, because of the censorship?

Mr. EVANS. None whatsoever in war time and when there are enemies around; but American marines ought to have a little judgment to differentiate a loyal and true-hearted American, for instance, from a German, an Austrian, or a Turk, say.

Senator KING. But now, do you make any complaint of the fact of there being a censorship, or is your complaint merely they were too lax?

Mr. EVANS. I thought my position was quite clear. During the war and the situation obtained in Haiti, with so many Germans, I believe it tended to be somewhat lax, but to-day to use the censorship on Haitians and American loyal citizens to prevent conditions in Haiti reaching the responsible United States Government, and people whose honor and national character are at stake, is absolutely wrong and most unjustifiable. They do this, as I understand, without any authority whatever to-day from our Government, and an inquiry should be made why it is not stopped in Haiti?

Senator KING. Do you mean to say if I should write a letter to any person in Haiti it should be censored?

Mr. EVANS. No; I do not believe they would be quite so daring with a Senator of the United States after what has happened. They discriminate against individuals. It is most difficult somehow to convey a correct idea of conditions in Haiti and the conduct of the occupation, at least very many of the marines and the docile, slavish fear of Haitians under present régime there.

Senator Hitchcock (then chairman of Foreign Relations) three years ago in this room could not believe my statements re the occupation, closing up Senate and Chambers, then this " rape of the constitution," and refused to approach the President to appoint such as this committee to make inquiry ; so the scandal came out through their own Navy officer which the United States Secretary of the Navy felt bound to send to Haiti, on account of officials withholding or falsifying reports, etc.

When Senator Hitchcock expressed surprise that there was no other witness or evidence but that of my own, I replied that others were in the pay of the occupation in some way or other and dared not come or speak.

He would not allow Government protection to Haitian witnesses and have half a dozen, including Haiti President, to come here before the Foreign Relations Senate Committee. In fact he did not wish to know. It is a sad condition to crush a little nation and totally forfeit its confidence.

Senator KING. When I was there, more than a year ago, I found no evidence of a censorship, but the people were communicating as they pleased; at least their mails were received regularly, and there was not the slightest effort, so far as I would see, to intercept, censor, or scrutinize communications.

Mr. EVANS. This might be so, as possibly some change has taken place; for instance, all my periodicals are returned from Haiti the last two years and more, but not a single letter has come through. The real reason why, I suppose, will have to wait and the mystery will some day be cleared up.

Senator KING. I have received letters from Haiti, and I have not seen the slightest evidence of any censorship?

Mr. EVANS. As stated, this might be so, and things somewhat improved since the scandal was made known and so many investigations as to the conduct of these marines referred to and the flashlight thrown on them at last.

Senator KING. You are speaking in reference to conditions when you were there?

Mr. EVANS. No; I had in mind chiefly since my return and long since the war is ended.

Senator KING. Do you charge that letters written by you to people in Haiti have not been delivered or have been opened prior to delivery?

Mr. EVANS. Yes; I am of opinion that they have not been delivered; possibly they have also been opened; several of these were to missionaries and one to a United States consul, whom I recently heard has been fired by the occupation or may be through Maj. Wells, who has escaped from Haiti, or by his friend Gen. Williams, once chief of Haiti gendarmerie.

Senator KING. The Haitians are the postmasters there, are they not?

Mr. EVANS. Yes; and with whom I was always on the best of terms, as well as all other leading officials of the Haiti Government. They have in every department, however, an American marine officer over them, and they fear that anything should be done which he is not heartily in accord with; and at times, though he may not know it, in their overcautiousness (at times) fail to do their plain duty. This might be so in my case, as they all know my own attitude toward education and the reverse attitude of the occupation.

Mr. ANGELL. There is a special agreement covering that to have the general direction in the hands of our United States nominee.

Mr. EVANS. For instance, just to give you some idea of the nervous conditions of the people, through outburst of abuse of authority, if not kaiserism, a local editor had a paragraph merely stating that a high officer of the occupation had been relieved or recalled. He had his paper immediately confiscated and he himself put in prison.

Senator ODDIE. That fact is in the record?

Mr. EVANS. This is to scare and terrorize these poor people, who are already scared and terrified enough. An able Haitian and a strong intellectual native while I was at Port au Prince was scheduled as chief consul for Kingston, Jamaica, but something he had said or done was construed to be unfavorable to the Roman Catholic régime in Haiti, and his nomination was at once canceled.

Senator KING. It seems that the local priests, apparently, were the cause of his undoing?

Mr. EVANS. Exactly. The Roman Catholic Church in Haiti and its white European priests—I have never seen a colored or native priest there—as Protestants have native preachers, are the cause of undoing everything in Haiti looking forward to the mental, moral, and industrial development of Haitians and equip them for self-government of a progressive and prosperous nature. They have to be intellectual slaves. The devious ways the Roman Catholic influence and power works in Haiti is not easily discovered, but they have a perfect machinery, which works smoothly but effectively, from the nuns and priests up to bishop, archbishop, if not the late Cardinal Gibbons and the White House, through late private secretary, who are, it is said in Haiti, responsible for most of changes in occupation's efficient officers.

Senator KING. You mean by that, as I understand you, that able Americans who had gone there for service were recalled because of opposition lodged by the priests against them to the American officials or Haitian officials in Haiti?

Mr. EVANS. Yes; or charges sent from here—made by priests or bishops or special Pope's delegate, who has been some years at Port au Prince—to Washington, and that through Tumulty the State or Navy Department word would arrive he must clear out, however efficient as American marine officer he might be, simply at the caprice and dictation of the Roman Catholic apostolique—so-called church. Lack of whole-hearted sympathy with the Catholic régime in Haiti and an unwillingness to subordinate the interest of Haitians, the occupation, and that of the United States Government by an able, efficient, experienced, and true and patriotic American would suffice to remove that marine officer.

Senator KING. Your real criticism there is that the Catholic Church in Haiti interferes with the duties of persons who were sent to Haiti from the United States?

Mr. EVANS. Precisely so; deflects and demoralizes the personnel of the American occupation of the United States Government, some of whose ablest, bravest, best military equipped and most experienced and efficient in the country, as well as in the Navy Department service, to-day are Protestants.

Quite an erroneous idea has been spread abroad, which, without any investigation, was taken for granted as correct by the late administration and largely accounts for their subordinating really the interest of the occupation's mission in Haiti to the Roman Catholic régime—it is that all Haitians are Roman Catholics.

Rear Admiral H. S. Knapp, in his official report to Secretary Daniels from Port au Prince October 11, 1920, under "Haiti—Reports and inquiries regarding conditions and the conduct of marines" (Appendix C, p. 223), and in section 8, and under Article XVII of the Constitution, where it says "all forms of worship are equally free," etc., at last, and very properly, courageously, and completely explodes this myth, as follows:

"There is a considerable number of priests (including the bishop at the Cape and archbishop at Port au Prince) in the aggregate, and practically all French (white) scattered all through the country, and there are several sisterhoods of the Roman Catholic Church represented in Haiti engaged in its work.

"It is doubtful, however, if the real unmixed doctrines of the Roman Catholic Church are held by any but a very negligible minority; with most of the population the practice of the Roman Catholic faith is more or less mixed; with that of the religions brought from the jungles of Africa Voodooism is prevalent, and the farther one goes from the coast into the interior the more openly is Voodooism practiced. Consecrated wafers of the Roman Catholic Church are mixed with the blood of sacrifices by Voodoo priests at the Voodoo rites."

According to this something like $1,000,000 of American money has been misappropriated to financially sustain during the last six years a church of a very negligible minority and a semibarbarous institution (more or less mixed with Voodooism).

Senator KING. And that the work of the occupation responded to the desires of the local priests or to the Roman Catholic Church in Haiti?

Mr. EVANS. I would use a stronger word than respond; it actually deviated the occupation and American marine officers from their mission in the Black Republic, and even subordinated the interests of the United States Government—which was to carry out their treaty—to the Roman Catholic Church and her sectarian interest. I know it is a delicate matter, but it has to be plainly and courageously faced; and this unholy alliance and American corporations, no more than German propagandas, must be permitted to interfere with, much less to defeat—as they have so far done—our purpose in Haiti. The honesty and honor of the United States Government and the American people are at stake not only before Latin American Republics but before the whole civilized world, and so our influence and integrity in negotiating treaties through or independent of the League of Nations.

Senator KING. Does not that indicate that the desire seemed to be to have officials there whose administration would be in harmony with the wishes of the great majority of the people?

Mr. EVANS. The motive of avoiding unnecessary friction, and especially inflicting injury on any religious body is most commendable, and applies, according to the Constitution, to the Protestant and Evangelical churches equally as to the Roman Catholic Church. As Admiral Knapp states in his report, the Roman Catholic Church in Haiti has no right to claim the majority of the population. It is the church, as he says, a negligible minority, but owing to its financial and official alliance with Haiti and the United States Governments it is more in evidence.

Senator KING. The great majority of the people are Catholics, are they not?

Mr. EVANS. According to the report given Secretary Daniels of the United States Navy 12 months ago they are not, and this has been my position right along. The Roman Catholic Church in Haiti is a bastard production of voodooism, witchcraft, and other African heathenish cults, with a gloss of Roman Catholicism—just as described by the American marine officer.

And again, these white priests of Europe who smoke and drink their wines, etc., have little in common with Haitians and do not understand nor sympathize with a republican form of government and equal rights for all Christian churches.

On my first arrival in Jacmel, southern Haiti, in 1893, I was attacked by a European white priest for holding a gospel service in the open air, and received a warrant—both my assistant, Nosirel Lherison, and myself—to appear the following Wednesday morning at the chief court, presided over by a real and fine Haitian, a nominal Catholic.

The judge said, "The priest has failed to turn up; and if he did, he can do nothing to interfere with you. Continue to preach," he said; "this is a Republic, and the constitution gives equal rights to all churches," and he offered the Haitian soldiers to protect me in the street or elsewhere and made arrangements that I should visit the old prison every Sunday and any other time, etc.

Senator KING. Your criticism is that the priests, then, did not always represent the will of the majority of the people?

Mr. EVANS. Yes; they are actually opposed to the intellectual if not moral, industrial, and especially the Christian development of Haitians, and would not be surprised that they are not back of this occupation's resistance to education in general of Haitian children and young people.

Senator KING. And that the priests of the Catholic Church have interfered with the legitimate and proper plans of the occupation?

Mr. EVANS. Exactly so, only instead of saying priests (with whom as individuals I have no quarrel and they have as much right to preach and teach, if they believe the Roman Catholic dogmas, as Protestants and Evangelicals), I will put it the Roman Catholic Apostolique Church, so called, and their leaders in the interest of this Roman Catholic Church have interfered with the legitimate and proper plans of the occupation.

American marine officers themselves have again told me how they are detailed off to wait on bishop and assist archbishop with their Government machines, and many, with the great majority of the thinking Haitians all over the Republic, would hail the breaking of this alliance.

And this done expressly for the spiritual good of both Protestant as well as the Catholic Church and an honest and efficient Haiti and United States Governments' (latter through occupation) administration in the black republic.

Church and State have their distinct missions, and they can best carry out these distinct missions by being entirely separate, and not the one entering the others' realm and infringing upon the rights of one another, such as the American marine paying and acting the Catholic priest and the Catholic priest assuming the function of an American marine officer. You thoroughly understand what I mean.

Senator KING. I exactly comprehend your meaning.

Mr. EVANS. With your consent, I insert here for record an official letter of the Haiti Government, which means as stated the occupation and really the United States Government, and how it seeks to calm the fears of the distinguished delegate of the Pope recognized in Haiti by both the Haitian Government and the American marine officers not as a mere religious head but a prince representing in Haiti an independent and foreign sovereign, but expenses and salary in Haiti paid by Admiral Caperton (and afterwards by the American occupation) as to the continuance of financing the great Roman Catholic régime in Haiti, which intelligent Haitians in increasing numbers oppose, stating the concordat has long expired. My copy is in French and taken from the L'essor for July 6, 1918, and is as follows:

LA RELIGION CATHOLIQUE EN HAITI.

Nos lectures liront avec plaisir la lettere ci-dessus qui est un soulagement a la foi catholique du pays:

REPUBLIQUE D'HAITI,
Port au Prince, le 31 Mai, 1918.

SECRETAIRE DES RELATIONS EXTERIEURS.

MONSEIGNEUR: J'ai eu l'honneur de recevoir la lettre du 20 de ce mois par laquelle, etant donne que la religion catholique est celle de la majorite du peuple Haitien et qu'elle a toujours eu en consequence une place privilige dans le pays.

Votre excellence me demande de lui permettre de rassurer le Saint-Siege en precisant que l'Art. 17 de la nouvelle Constitution ne porte aucune atteinte a la satuation acquise a l'Eglise catholique apostolique et romaine.

Je me suis empresse de soumettre cette important question au Conseil des Secretaires d'Etat qui c'est la consideree avec l'interest legitime qui s'y attache.

Et c'est ainsi que je suis infiniment heureux de pouvoir respondre a votre excellence que l'Art. 22 de la Constitution est identique a l'Art. 22 de la Constitution de 1880 et que tous les privileges accordes a l'Eglise catholique par le concordat demeurent maintenus. Conformement al'Art. 127 du project de Constitution publie au Moniteur du 8 Mai courrant qui prevot que les Traites en vigeur constituent la Loi du Pays.

E. DUPUY.

A Son Exc. MONSEIGNEUR CHERUBINI,
Internonce Apostolique Port au Prince.

Having at my request sent me an official list of all the schools belonging to Protestants, whose names and total amount of appropriations hitherto given by the old Haitian Government—but now stopped by the American occupation—I further requested an official list from the Government's minister of religion of the Protestant churches that received Government financial help to pay their missionaries, and the amount given each. These names and amounts were given as herein shown, and following is my letter of thanks, with a kind request for a full and complete list of total or itemized grants, and actual cost to pay salaries and maintain the Roman Catholique Apostolique régime in Haiti.

To this request no answer came, and this broad-minded Catholic, but real American, superintendent of public instruction, who had prepared a scheme for public instruction in the black Republic over two years ago and anxious to launch it, has recently been fired by either the Catholic Church direct or by the American occupation at the bidding of that church.

The letter and lists follow:

ST. MARC, HAITI, WEST INDIES, *July 20, 1918.*

Hon. Mr. BURGEOIS,
Superintendent de l'Instruction Publique,
Port au Prince.

GOVERNMENT SUBVENTIÓN.

MY DEAR SUPT. BURGEOIS: Many thanks for the official statement as to the Protestant subventions given monthly by the Haiti Government; and also the official list of subventions again given to the Roman Catholic schools in your communication safely received this week.

May I ask again through you, the minister of cult, to be kind enough to give me an official list of the monthly or yearly salaries given the archbishop, bishops, vicar generals, priests, etc., and all other minor officers of the Roman Catholic Church in Haiti, with the extra subventions monthly or yearly given out of the Republic's funds to maintain these Roman Catholic chapels, archbishop's palace, and the presbyteries of said Roman Catholic priests?

Also include, if possible, in this list what is given to all freres and soeurs teaching in Haiti at their Roman Catholic schools, as well as those engaged in the various Government hospices through this Republic, and other useful information you may add to this and coming under above heading.

It is very much better that I should have a correct and, if possible, a complete list both of the Protestant and Roman Catholic subventions than one should be left merely to guess on such important matters, and this can only be got officially from you.

Is it possible to find through you and the minister of cult whether the actual and original concordat was meant for 50 years, and when did it really start? I shall be exceedingly grateful for this reliable and official information, to what you have so kindly furnished me with already, and for which I heartily thank you.

Should there be a boat leaving for New York from Port au Prince at end of this month or beginning of August, we are hoping to leave for States, so perhaps you could call, jointly with our Haiti minister of public instruction, and at a short time the conference suggested.

If agreeable to you, I would very much like to have also present, say, Col. Russell, Dr. Maclean, Gen. Williams, with the President and ex-President Legitime, if not the members of the national council itself, with our American minister; and if you thought fit, and seeing their deep interest in Haiti, the British consul general and the French minister, though if better, in your judgment, these can furnish their indorsements by way of a separate letter.

At this informal gathering I shall briefly give an outline of this "noble project," as they termed it through Haiti seven years ago, and what steps have already been taken in the matter. I shall allude to the petition bearing nearly 3,000 names of all leading Haitians, irrespective of religious creeds and party politics. I had the privilege of presenting at the Carnegie Bureau of International Peace, in Washington, and which had inscribed upon it as the first the name of my old friend—distinguished, able, cultured, and progressive (afterwards)—the late President Leconte, who was also the real friend of our own American Government.

I believe that I mentioned to you, and as showing the widespread desire and enthusiasm at the time referred to, official letters in my possession from the civic councils, St. Marc, Gonaives, Port de Paix, Grande Riviere, Trou, Fort Liberte, Dondon, St. Michael, Enery, Cape Haiti, etc., sincerely thanking me personally for getting this up and carrying through the Republic, wishing the success of my mission in their behalf in the States, and sincerely praying that the great Christian and educationist philanthropists of the States, such as Rockefeller and Carnegie, for instance, to provide this blessed boon and grant this urgent necessity, a national normal and industrial school for the uplift of Haiti and its sons and daughters and by way of training their young Negro manhood and Negro womanhood for future religious, educational, industrial, commercial, as well as judicial and civic leadership in their own Black Republic. Republic.

Our representatives at the Latin-American department of our Government and other educationists at Washington last October, and just before my return to Haiti thought that if this petition was now presented, and through our Government it would most likely go right through, as it would be in harmony with the spirit, and, indeed, letter, of our generous treaty; thus enable it to be carried out with greater effect by our United States Government, and through its occupation and the Haitian administration, though the financial end might be furnished by our generous American philanthropists, backed by our own Government.

While we shall be glad, of course, of suggestions at this proposed conference, it will be wise not to enter into matters of detail until the proposed national and normal industrial school has been sanctioned and indorsed at Washington.

I am sincerely hoping, however, that this normal and industrial school will be made fit into the new scheme of public instruction for the long-neglected children of Haiti you intend soon to launch; that in time it will provide practical and efficient teachers for same, as well as professors in agriculture for the United States Government to develop scientific cultivation of our rich soil through small Negro farmers and native cultivators, and therefore for this reason will suggest when the time comes that trustees and managing council be leading American citizens in the States (representing white and colored), who will work in close conjunction with, or, if not, through, our American occupation and as an essential part of Haiti's public-school instruction system.

I wrote our Pastor Lherisson at Jacmel concerning that Government land so urgently needed for a high-class school for boys.

With sincere regards to you and your colleague, and for Christ and Haiti.

L. Ton Evans.

République d'Haiti,
Bureau du Superintendant de l'Instruction Publique,
Port au Prince, 13 juillet, 1918.

Monsieur L. Ton Evans,
    Saint Marc.

Monsieur le Pasteur: Vous trouverez sous ce couvert la liste générale des subventions que le Département de l'Instruction Publique paye mensuellement. Recevez, Monsieur le Pasteur, l'assurance de ma parfaite considération.

M. Laurent.
Le Superintendant de l'Instruction Publique.

Subvention.

	Gourdes.
1. Ecoles des Sciences appliquées	1.200 or 150
2. Ecole de commerce	100
3. Madame Vve Paret	257
4. Mme. Torchon	200
5. Orphelina de la Madeleine	100
	1.857 or 150

Circonscription du Cap Haitien:

1. Ecole presbytérale de Milot	70
2. Ecole presbytérale de Quartier Morin	70
3. Ecole presbytérale Plaine du Nord	70
4. Ecole presbytérale Acul du Nord	100
	560

Circonscription Grande Riv. du Nord:

1. Ecole presbytérale de Ranquitte	50
2. Ecole presbytérale de Dondon	100
	150

Circonscription de Limbe Pla'sance:

1. Ecole presbytérale de Limbé	150
2. Ecole presbytérale de Plaisance	100
	250

Circonscription de Trou, ecole presbytérale du Trou	50
Circonscription de Valliere, ecole presbytérale de Vallièrè	50
Circonscription de Hinche, ecole presbytérale de Hinche	100
Circonscription de Dessalines, ecole presbytérale de la Petite Rivière	50
	3.067 or 150

REPUBLIC D'HAITI,
BUREAU DU SUPERINTENDANT DE L'INSTRUCTION PUBLIQUE,
Port au Prince, 3 juillet, 1918.

LE SUPERINTENDANT DE L'INSTRUCTION PUBLIQUE.

M. le Rev. Pasteur L. TON EVANS,
Superintendant de la Mission Baptiste, en Haiti.

CHER M. EVANS: Selon votre demand. je vous transmets sous ce couvert, la liste des Subventions accordees par le Gouvernement aux divere Cultes, etabls dans le Pays.

Cordialement,

L. J. BURGEOIS,
Supt. de l'Instruction Publique.

Liste des Subventions accordees par le Gouvernement aux divers cultes Protestants (Protestant religions) etablis dans le pays.

Savoir:

Eglise Orthodoxe Catholique G. Apostolique d'Haiti	192.50
(This is Episcopalians.)	
Baptistes de la Republique	187.50
Eglise Baptiste du Dondon	50.00
Eglise Baptiste du Cap	40.00
(This includes every Baptist church in Haiti, and rent of room where Baptists of Cape worship since church burnt down.—Paster Jaques.)	
Wesleyannes, de la Republique	120.00
Wesleyannes, Independeante	50.00
Wesleyan Methodists of England and the Port au Prince Church, which has broken away and become independent.)	

Savoir—Continued.

St. Paul-- 100.00

(Native Episcopal, whose pastor is clerk at American consulate.)

Societe Biblique et des Livres, Religieuse d'Haiti------------------ 150.00

(This is native Bible and religious books society of Haiti.)

   Certifie Sincere,

H. GAMBOUR,
Le Comptable des Cultes.

PORT AU PRINCE, *le 2 juillet, 1918.*

NOTE.—Not being able to ascertain from the native pastors and others the exact sum each received from the Government, which has been a curse on the whole to Baptist churches and natives, not to say vitally opposed to N. T. and Baptist teaching, I made an appeal to the Government direct for official information and courteously received above response.

I also applied for official information as to the total subventions paid by our American occupation to archbishops, bishops, priests, nuns, freres, seurs, and the total monthly or annually, to maintain the whole Catholic Church and the Haiti College in France for training of white Catholic priests, etc. This, of course, was never furnished me.

While the estimate is that from $100,000 to $125,000 a year from the bankrupt Haiti Republic actually paid the latter (R. C.) something like $4,000 to $5,000 a year was paid to Protestant churches and to aid Protestant schools. Latter schools have been cut off for years from list of subventions, and several thus closed by the American occupation.

(L. TON EVANS.)

Senator ODDIE. Now, I want to ask you this: In your opinion, will the evidence that is asked by this committee be offered freely by the Haitians in Haiti; and if not, why?

Mr. EVANS. No. This committee will in the present temperament of Haitians, I may say terror-stricken and almost hysteric mental condition, without confidence of any kind in the American people, through the fundamental misunderstanding of them by and the cruel conduct of the American occupation, I very sincerely believe will find itself much like the Navy court did, and, as beforehand predicted to Maj. Dyer, it would be by myself at our interview here in Washington. He thought he knew better.

The occupation is still there, and with the priests, their paid agents, and gendarmes they will know every native that attempts to give testimony, who they will probably intimidate, though this is not needed; they fear and dread, and are almost horrified at the thought of being pounced upon by way of reprisal the moment the Senate committee has left the island, and will have no court to appeal to nor a single soul to protect them, hence they will be mum.

If account of present proceedings of the committee could have been published in English and French at present in Haitian papers, this would be some kind of preparation and something to calm their minds and win their confidence, otherwise I fear that you will be sadly disappointed unless the President comes and talks to the committee as he talked, for instance, to those New York correspondents. This might encourage others, possibly.

It is a sad condition, and I feel almost heartbroken for them, for when I arrived there in 1917, and before the rape of constitution, and the actual resurrection, enforcement, with barbaric roping connected and developed with the corvee, they seemed so happy and free.

I seriously advise the committee right away to request our President to send a proclamation to be published in French and English in the Monitor and all the papers and in all the public places in every town and village in Haiti, inviting the citizens and others who have reliable evidence to testify before the present Senate committee or commission now making an exhaustive inquiry into conduct of United States forces in Haiti, assuring them of ample protection of the United States Government and the severe punishment to any members of occupation, priest, or members of corporations, etc., who would attempt to intimidate by threats, reprisals, or any other method.

State the places the commission of the United States Government will meet, approximate date of sittings. As a proof of the real and genuine desire on the part of our Government to calm all fears and create implicit confidence of the people, so as to secure their cooperation, our President should, more.

over, command that all political suspects and prisoners against whom no crime has been proved by proper process of law be liberated the day of the arrival of the commission at Port au Prince.

This proclamation, with protection, is essential, and the liberation of all such prisoners as mentioned would have an immense moral and most favorable effect.

In a sense they must be treated as children and somewhat humored.

Senator KING. When a number of Senators were there over a year ago some of us went around quite freely among the people—at least I did. I was in Port au Prince and in the region outside.

Mr. EVANS. Was that in March or April of 1919?

Senator KING. No; in 1920. Just a year ago, or a little more, and the people talked freely to me, and I am sure they did to other Senators likewise— lawyers, judges, professional men, and the people on the streets women that were coming in carrying produce on their heads.

I talked, perhaps, with 200 in the island during the two or three days that I was there. I found no one that hesitated to speak, no one that seemed to feel the slightest strictures in explaining their views, and many of them expressed a qualified sat sfaction with the conditions.

The principal objection seemed to be that there was a divided authority. They could not tell which of the three chief officials was the one having authority, and that led to confusion, but, generally speaking, there was very little criticism made by those with whom I spoke about the conditions there prevailing.

I talked with perhaps 100, and those with whom I talked were poor people, men and women on the streets. Some were working as stevedores and some coming down from the hills. They talked perfectly free about the revolution, the cacos, as you call them, and there was some criticism, I remember, about the gendarmes, not very great; but the point I am trying to make is that no one seemed to be under the slighest feeling of terror at all.

At least I did not perceive this anywhere among the classes of people, on the street or out in the hills. Nowhere was there the slightest evidence of their being repressed or existing under a state of terror. I do not know what the conditions were when you were there.

Mr. EVANS. Were these inquiries going on about the time you were there; that is, during the administration of Secretary Daniels?

Senator KING. No.

Mr. EVANS. That would be near that time.

Senator KING. That was in April and May, 1920.

Mr. EVANS. There was something going on by way of investigations—either by Gens. Lejune or Barnett; some of these were around there?

Senator KING. No; that was afterwards.

Mr. EVANS. Well, these investigations produced some moral effect, as some of our American marine officers like Maj. Wells, for instance, cleared out, and may be others. I was in communication at this time with Secretary Daniels, and he informed me of Lejune and others he sent down to bring him the latest. He it was (just before this) who sent Barnett to Port au Prince, and things were beginning to change somewhat as they saw the red light.

Gen. Williams is another who left, is he not?

Senator KING. I do not know.

Mr. EVANS. I believe he left months before your visit. I came up by a Panama boat in April of 1919. Several Senators and Congressman came up from Panama and came out at Port au Prince and witnessed a riot between the marines and gendarmes—if not saw one or two killed. I met one of the Senators here this morning—Ashurst.

There has been great strain through jealousy between these two bodies which led to confusion and lack of discipline.

Is it possible that this committee will immediately consider and act soon on the proclamation, etc.?

Senator ODDIE. They will consider that. We will take that up.

Mr. EVANS. I wish to impress the importance of such a step on the committee so that you may not be handicapped in Haiti.

Senator ODDIE. As soon as it is before them again, they will consider it.

I want to ask you what factors, in your opinion, contributed to the renewed activities in 1919 of the cacos?

Mr. EVANS. In 1919 and at the end of 1918 when I was there I saw a great deal of the corvee work and its effect. On landing in December of 1918 at

Port au Prince, as seen in this record, I called on Brig. Gen. Catlin, who gave a strict command that the corvee must be stopped, I understand, but it was still in existence at St. Marc and other places in the Artibonite and around Port au Prince, and south as well as all through the northern section.

After receiving official assurance from State Department at Washington that the corvee curse and other cruel and sad conditions were being investigated and seriously considered by all the departments interested at Washington. I made it my business not only to go and pay my respects to Brig. Gen. Catlin, the new chief of American occupation, as soon as I arrived at Port au Prince, but inquired from him personally whether he had heard from Mr. Lansing, and was there anything being actually done?

I gave him, in addition to the typewritten copy of it received from either State or Navy Department, the printed memorandum, and went over together carefully re corvee, and the insidious influences at work interfering with and deflecting it was alleged the occupation and its purpose in Haiti. This was in December, 1916. If he gave orders in October to stop the corvee, then his orders were not carried out, and to my knowledge, and after bringing it to his direct attention, he permitted Gen. Williams, chief of gendarmerie, to prevent Lieut. Kulp from investigating the brutal and barbarous conduct of his gendarmes on Gros Morne.

Gen. Barnett, in October, 1919, writing Col. Russell, who succeeded Gen. Catlin, after expressing himself as shocked at conditions of brutality and promiscuous murder by gendarmes and marines, added:

" I can not too strongly urge you the necessity of going personally and thoroughly into these matters and see to it that nothing is allowed to remain of the corvee system; let it be known throughout Haiti; it will not be tolerated hereafter."

There should be no need of this urge and imperative command from either Barnett or Knapp or Lejeune if these chiefs did their duty, and from this it's evident that the corvee existed other than in the north, and no honest effort was made to actually stop it or ameliorate the brutal sufferings of the poor natives under it.

Cacoism was mainly the product of the corvee, and the sufferings of the natives became more acute, and the marines and gendarmes conduct more brutal and barbarous and murderous in their defiance of law, and with the sad neglect and criminal laxity of American occupation, and gendarmerie chiefs, cacoism increased threefold and tenfold, and the serious attack made on Port au Prince, though, it was not a revolution, nor even a rebellion, but a kind of reprisal, and the natural protest against the inhumanity, if not insanity, of American marines and their methods.

From a document sent me from Haiti, the headquarters of this supposed cacoism, and by a Christian missionary whose valuable services, appreciated by Gen. Cole, was scouted by the notorious Maj. Wells, which I am placing at your service in the record, I quote here a paragraph or so to dispel the misleading statements about these people:

" Some say that this revival and powerful renewal of cacoism is a German intrigue against the United States. There may be a semblance of truth in it. but the real fact (and no one knows better than yourself) that this new native uprising is directly due to the terribly bad administration.

" If different methods were adopted, more wisdom and humanity less colored, prejudice and hatred by some of the American marines toward the Haitians. and a conciliatory spirit shown, they would so gain these Negroes' confidence and loyalty and love that all the money of Berlin and guns manufactured in Germany, if furnished them, would never turn these natives against our American marines and the United States Government."

This French citizen, and missionary for over 28 years in this section, is one of my witnesses to testify before this committee if I can get to Haiti, and the President's proclamation is made as requested.

Senator KING. Were you there when the cacos came into Port au Prince and attacked the sugar factory and others?

Mr. EVANS. Do you remember that date?

Senator KING. No; I do not.

Mr. ANGELL. There was an earlier one, in October, 1919.

Mr. EVANS. That was after I left.

Senator KING. I am referring to the one in 1920, when they came in perhaps a thousand strong, and created a great state of terror, and they were repulsed by the Marines and the gendarmes, and several score of the cacos killed. You were not there then?

Mr. EVANS. No; but I have seen the account. It was the accumulation of the bad feeling created through these oppressions and cruelties of Marine and gendarmes of the occupation, I trow not. If what a white American and contractor working on this sugar plant told me boastingly at the Port au Prince general post office, of his brutality toward those who worked under him, and killed one or two, and through the occupation the whole thing was squashed, though deploring these uprisings and attacks, I am not surprised therefore at them. It is cause and effect.

Senator KING. I am familiar with the history there, given by both classes, and your knowledge would be perhaps no greater than mine, unless you read more about it.

Mr. EVANS. My knowledge of Haiti and the Haitian people is not the result merely of reading, but years of my life in living and carefully observing them before our occupation came, and since.

The petty jealousies existing between Marines and the gendarmes and their Marine officers, the dual control as you put it, and confusion and military demoralization in consequence, and the cruel way Haitians are handled account largely for these. I have heard Marines repeatedly say things are so quiet, unless they have a scrap among themselves, or gendarmes or so-called cacos, they would resign and go back to the States, or ask to be transferred to France, where there was something doing.

Senator KING. I was told by a number of Haitians, some of them holding good positions, that the revolution in 1920, if that was the date, was very serious, and was the culmination not of the evils of which you speak, but resulted from the activity of a number of revolutionary leaders who had been in the bush for years, and had been disturbing factors, and participated in rebellions long before the occupation, and that they took part in the assassination or revolution which resulted in assassination of one or more Presidents, driving from power of one or more Presidents; and that their avowed purpose was to assassinate all whites, particularly Americans, and to put the government back in control of these revolutionary Negroes. That was told me by Haitians.

Mr. EVANS. I would not be at all surprised if this were true, and that even Germans would take advantage of the bitter resentment of Haitians at the way they have been treated, and the strong reversion of feeling produced against the occupation and Americans, as I have repeatedly said. It was frequently reported when I was in Haiti that Germany was winning in the war, and that it was merely a matter of a short time before they came to Haiti and cleared out all of the American marines. Those with the Central Powers (and officials of the Roman Catholic Church were) and Pope with Germany and Austria spread these stories, and I saw little or nothing to convince them otherwise.

Senator KING. Is it not a fact that there had been revolutionary movements for 100 years, which would result in the frequent deposition from authority of the Presidents, or the Chief Executives of the island, and that there were incipient revolutions in all parts of the island going on at all times?

Mr. EVANS. As I mentioned this morning, this was partly due to the dissatisfaction of educated Haitians with island conditions, readiness to be therefore used or helped by white man's influence and money to try and better the state of affairs. In the States and in Britain, where people are educated and enlightened, bad conditions are as a rule blamed on the Government, and a change is sought only with us is done by elections. Haitian agitators, however, are all unfortunately termed revolutionists, and in a sense every reformer, of course, is.

Senator KING. There have been nearly 100 Presidents there, have there not?

Mr. EVANS. I forget exactly how many, but this is somewhat exaggerated, I think.

Senator KING. In a limited number of years?

Mr. EVANS. Yes; this is true.

Senator KING. And they would be driven from power by revolution?

Mr. EVANS. Yes; being without money, and failing to secure the friendly aid of the United States, they would be too weak to resist the powerful influence of white filibusters and German money?

Senator KING. And a number have been killed?

Mr. EVANS. President Simon was driven from office and President Laconte killed, because we as an United States Government failed though requested to come to their assistance, and their Government's aid against these insidious and powerful invisible agencies working against every attempt at reforms, and progress in the black Republic.

During last 100 years we have had many elections, and some able and well-meaning Presidents have been hurled out of the executive office and many changes brought about.

Senator KING. I am speaking about conditions in Haiti. Is it not a fact that there are revolutions for 100 years almost constantly, if not in all the island, in parts of the island, and incipient revolts and movements which sought the overthrow of one political party which had triumphed, in the interests of another political party?

Mr. EVANS. Yes; perfectly true, but more or less and chiefly owing to the influences I have already mentioned and repeated. There are thoughtful, smart, and energetic people among the Haitians. Political parties even here all the year round are preparing and agitating whether their parties are in power or not.

Senator KING. Is it not a fact that when Americans came there there were incipient revolutions in many parts of the island, and that they were continued?

Mr. EVANS. Yes; that is a fact, but my impression is that these revolutions were confined to the north, and Port au Prince, or south. There is a rivalry between north and south of the Republic of Haiti, just as there is here in America, between the northern and southern States, not always beneficial. Haiti has had before now a President at Port au Prince for the south, and the north had Christoph as their king, for instance.

Senator KING. So that even when, as you said this morning, as I understood you, the Americans came, and were welcomed by a large number down there——

Mr. EVANS. Yes; this is quite so, and if they had continued their peaceful purpose of pacifying, instead of arousing the feeling, causing bitterness, and hatred through the corvee, change of constitution, etc., they would have been still welcomed by practically every Haitian.

Senator KING. Yes; by the majority; there were a large number that were opposing——

Mr. EVANS. Quite a number who misunderstood our intentions, and the manner we landed our marines; yes.

Senator KING. The occupation; or would have opposed the control by any respectable majority of the Haitian people themselves?

· Mr. EVANS. There is a difference in being controlled by a foreign nation and by a majority party of your own. As emphasized this morning which these questions indicate that you have forgotten some of my replies, these minorities you refer to, as well as Haitians in general have for years been poisoned against America and Americans and told by German and other European propagandas to beware of us; that all we wanted was a foothold, to take away their rich island and reduce them to the position of forced laborers and actual slaves; and when we entered some were honestly doubting our intentions, but to-day the majority have been convinced that the Germans were about right.

Senator KING. What I am trying to develop, if it be a fact, is, has there been in that country for many years an element that should not be satisfied with any kind of government, even the best government, that their own people could give them?

Mr. EVANS. I hardly like to say that, and if it is true as you mean it, we have the same situation in the States and other countries. Human nature whether white or black, is very much alike in these things. Haitians have a deal of energy and much time also on their hands, and there has been unfortunately not much under any government in Haiti that can satisfy reformers and intellectual and Christian progressive people among this black little nation.

Senator KING. Have there been revolutions there?

Mr. EVANS. Certainly there have.

Senator KING. And a great many men deposed from executive authority?

Mr. EVANS. They term almost everything in Haiti a revolution, if it means political activity.

Senator KING. Answer the question. Have there not been a large number of executives deposed?

Mr. EVANS. Yes.

Senator KING. And some killed?

Mr. EVANS. And some few killed.

Senator KING. You would not call the government which they have——

Mr. EVANS. A few I think, and two or so, the last 10 or 12 years.

Senator KING. In the past 50 years?

Mr. EVANS. Yes; there have been others killed I believe during the last 50 years.

Senator KING. You would not call the government which they had in Haiti for the 50 years preceding the American occupation a stable government, would you?

Mr. EVANS. Certainly not, and I have been trying to point out the reasons why. Because of this I have been for 20 years urging upon our Government at Washington to assume a friendly mandate and act the big brother toward these Haitians so as to assist them in laying down a firm foundation for a permanent government, and intellectually and industrially help to train and develop them so as to enable them to understand the secret of a stable, peaceful, and progressive government in Haiti, but which the occupation has failed to do, though an essential part of their mission in the Republic, according to the treaty.

Senator KING. There have been fewer revolutions, and there has been less banditry and outlawry since the American occupation than before, have there not?

Mr. EVANS. There have been no revolutions, but I have heard more about banditry and outlawry in Haiti since our American occupation, as well as cacoism, than I ever heard of before during nearly 25 years, but of course the stealing and banditry connected with those periodical revolutions referred to. If the natives of Haiti had their arms, and the Haiti Government her army, there would have been a revolution to-day, I fear, that would have made it impossible to close their senate and chambers and change their constitution.

Senator KING. What were the revolutions before this that resulted in the murder of President Sam?

Mr. EVANS. Those were the periodical revolutionists, which have simply the overturning of the government in view. If the President, however, uses very ruthless means to put down the revolutionists, and in desperation instead of quitting and yielding the government resorts to wholesale executions, as I understand Sam did, then a certain element goes raving mad and swear vengeance, etc., which happens in backward countries and among illiterate and quick-tempered people.

Senator KING. These cacos were revolutionists, were they not?

Mr. EVANS. No, not in the sense it is used in Haiti; they would be called bandits, and those in North Haiti, and referred to by you as attacking Port au Prince, would be these augmented in very large numbers by those driven into desperation by the corvee cruelties and brutalities and probably had escaped from the gendarmes while working on roads, etc.

Senator KING. What would you call those who have deposed the multitude of executives who have been deposed?

Mr. EVANS. The north is proverbially known as the starting place of revolutitons; some believe those at the Cape and in the northern section are stronger men intellectually, but certainly they are apparently more active and energetic. I believe, however, that an important reason is that it is more accessible to the Dominican Republic and can be easily reached, should something happen, within a few hours' ride on horseback. It has been easier to land ammunition here and more inaccessible for the Government to get up from Port au Prince. There would as a rule be certain cacos that would join and follow the revolutionary forces on their forward march on Port au Prince, and as these rebels had to be fed they would be useful in doing some looting very likely. They would be the general inhabitants, with Haiti politicians at the head, and invariably financed by whites.

Senator KING. I want to know what the fact is as to the revolutionary conditions in the island before the American occupation, for the 50 or 75 years preceding the Americans going there?

Mr. EVANS. There have been many revolutions during the nearly 30 years I have known Haiti, and some of the oldest people have told me about the real horrors of revolutions back 50, 60, and 80 years ago. Unfortunately, there have always been white men on the lookout to foment and exploit small, weak nations, unless these are merged in or cared for, protected, and otherwise receive the benefit of the leadership of a stronger, wealthier, and more developed.

The revolution which lead up to our landing in Haiti would probably be more or less typical, with its bloodshedding and devastating consequences, as those in years gone by.

Senator KING. Well, 50 or 75 years ago there could be no German influences?

Mr. EVANS. This has been true for the last 25 years, and other nations, such as England and France, have had their filibusters and political pirates as well.

Senator KING. Without attempting to determine the cause, there have been frequent revolutions there?

Mr. EVANS. Yes; very many.

Senator KING. And public peace and order constantly disturbed?

Mr. EVANS. Yes; most seriously; and formerly there would be a small colony of Haitian exiles at Kingston, Jamaica, who were induced by whites, and with money and ammunition and small ships, to go back, land at night, and start a political upheaval. There was another class who really sought to go in for a better government, but unaided, too weak. So I have often looked upon these as the birth pangs of this small nation, which seeks not only an independent existence but even a larger life of greater and larger usefulness, but too weak without special assistance and protection.

Senator KING. I am not attempting to excuse, palliate, or condemn. I am trying to find out what the fact is. I do not want the impression to go out from your testimony, unless you so want it, that whatever trouble has occurred in the island in the shape of revolution or disorder has occurred since the Americans went there.

The fact is, as I understand, that there have been trouble and revolutions for many years.

Mr. EVANS. Yes; this fact is well known in America and through all Europe.

Senator KING. Inherent—I was about to say indigenous—to the island and the people?

Mr. EVANS. Yes; under present and past peculiar conditions, and all the best. intellectual people have been long sick and tired of it, as shown by the enthusiasm in reference to a normal and industrial school and the efforts of President Simon re concessions of railroads and banana plantations, etc.

Senator KING. And the Germans before and after the outbreak of the war fomented strife?

Mr. EVANS. Quite so.

Senator KING. And used the island as a base for German propaganda?

Mr. EVANS. Yes; they were for many years entrenched through business, banks, etc., in and throughout Haiti.

Senator ODDIE. I just want to ask you what the cacos had to do with the adoption of the new constitution?

Mr. EVANS. The cacos?

Senator ODDIE. Yes; do you think they had any influence or anything to do with it?

Mr. EVANS. There was not much talk about the cacos previous to June of 1918. and. for instance, when I traveled through the north in April I found little or no evidence of their existence, which I attribute to the wise and humane methods of Maj. Cole, who sought counsel with our French missionary and used him as an intermediary more than once. but which when suggested to Maj. Wells in January of 1919, when they had so increased in number and power, he tabooed with a sneer and took as an offense, saying he could handle them without aid of a missionary or Gen. Catlin and his marines.

The arousing of the Haitians and creation of bitterness and hatred toward the occupation and Americans confirmed, I should think. whatever cacos there were in the north at this time; that the destruction of their Negro constitution, so as to give away lands all over Haiti to the white foreigners, confirmed them in their previous belief/that Americans were taking away their country from them, and therefore they were justified in their strong opposition. It must also have added large numbers to them. as well as create other bands of cacos around the outskirts of Port au Prince.

Senator ODDIE. What have the cacos had to do with this corvee system?

Mr. EVANS. Well, while the cacos have had absolutely nothing to do with the corvee system, but stoutly oppose it and denounce the occupation and Americans, the corvee system has much to do with cacoism. The forced and slavish labor on the roads, and catching, roping, brutal treatment, and killing of those who tried to escape, not merely doubled, trebled, and multiplied many folds the number and strength of the cacos by way of recruits, but it was, in my opinon. the clenching nail and proof positive at last not simply that Americans took all their lands but had come there to bring them all back to slavery with all its horrors.

Senator ODDIE. Now, I want to ask you another question with regard to the character of the gendarmes who were chosen by the marines?

Mr. EVANS. The gendarmes are chosen by the marine officers, I understand. Where the marine officer is strict, firm, yet sympathetic, as a rule he has a higher type of a gendarme, with better behavior, and quite humane because of the better type of American marine officer. Where, however, the marine officer is a drunkard, immoral, prejudiced against the colored, and curses and brutal, his gendarmes chosen are inferior and copy their white American captain or lieutenant, and probably goes beyond him, especially when he finds that this pleases his superior white officer.

Many of our American marine officers have confessed to me that when they came first to Haiti, inexperienced, somewhat prejudiced, ignorant of the language (obliged to use any kind of interpreter), they often misunderstood them, wrongly abused these men.

With better knowledge of the language and the Haiti Negro's characteristic things changed, with excellent results.

If care was taken, and chief of occupation see that not only their marine officers of the gendarmes were of the highest American type, and should hold him strictly responsible for the character and accountable for the conduct of his gendarmes, all this scandal—and providing the corvee was merely used in its true sense, and workmen were paid 25 or 30 American cents a day—this scandal would never have occurred.

Senator KING. The trouble is that when you are asked to explain one matter you also explain another about our occupation.

May I ask you a question right here? I was told by Haitians and by Americans and other foreign residents there that whereas Haitians are kindhearted, there was a callousness with regard to brutal treatment that would seem to be quite inconsistent with their other sympathetic characteristics; that they were quite brutal in their treatment of each other and did not seem to appreciate that fact; and that they are brutal to their animals, brutal in their treatment of chickens, their domestic animals, and seemed to have no sensitiveness when the question of personal suffering of animals was involved. What is the fact about that, very briefly?

Mr. EVANS. This is true in many cases, and arising from the lack of training and moral development, and being deprived of the civilizing and Christianizing influences we have, and criminally neglected by us as Americans and Christians to give these Haitians. They are not responsible for this. The Negro fiery nature and intensity of feeling would have much to do also with this.

I hardly like to think what Americans and America would be like if Christian and civilizing influences of church, schools, and in the homes were withdrawn. This what you wish to imply, in my judgment, shows what care should be taken in choosing the natives by competent marine officers, and after the spec'al training they should have for these important positions of authority they are placed in.

Senator KING. I agree with you, but I am now trying to get the characteristics of the people.

Mr. EVANS. There is a great deal of truth about that, but, as stated, if a certain type of men are given any position of authority without explaining the meaning and responsibility of such, they will abuse their trust and soon lapse. Sometimes white persons do this. They are, on the other hand, not only kind, generous, sympathetic, but scrupulously honest, generally speaking, and would put us often in so-called Christian lands to shame. Seeing how these folks are misrepresented if not villfied, the following from the New York Times for October 15, 1920, is interesting, and may modify somewhat certain views as to Haitian Cacos and bandits:

AMERICANS IN HAITI.

To the New York Times.

SIR: About eight years ago I was in Haiti on a riding trip in the interior of the island. I recall how the French priests, who were our hosts, all testified to the honesty and peacefulness of the people, and I recall in particular the words of one of the priests, who said that you could drive a donkey laden with gold from one end of the island to the other in perfect safety.

It would be interesting to learn why so many bandits have developed in Haiti since the American occupation. Is it possible that the term bandit has become confused with the term nationalist?

ELSIE CLEWS PARSONS,
Harrison, N. Y.

Senator KING. This was given me as an explanation for the alleged brutal treatment of other Haitians by some of the gendarmes. They said they did not regard it as brutal treatment to strike some one; they did not think that was anything serious at all.

Mr. EVANS. The day before I called on our American marine officer at Petite Riviere, who stated (and by the way lived in the Roman Catholic presbytery with the European priest) that the day before his gendarme had shot a prisoner. The prisoner had merely attempted to strike the gendarme because of his brutal handling of him.

This shows the poor native who receives the blow is not insensitive to the brutal treatment he gets. Prisoners and corvee workers all over Haiti have thus been shot on showing resentment to the cruel way they are dealt with, whose number during the last five years would run up into thousands and more than double Gen. Barnett's figures.

Senator KING. To illustrate what I mean, I remember seeing a number of animals being brought in, those little burros heavily laden with wood, and one of them, as it was approaching Port au Prince, fell from exhaustion because of the burden it carried——

Mr. EVANS. Yes; I have seen many of them.

Senator KING. There were several in the caravan, and as I remember, a man and a woman came up, and instead of lifting the load they beat the poor animal and the interpreter, and they were very much annoyed and continued the beating of the poor animal; and the interpreter insisted that they remove the load and permit the animal to rise, and very reluctantly they did it, and he explained that the Haitians were very brutal to animals and, indeed, to each other. They seemed to be insensible to suffering and to the infliction of pain, either upon each other or upon animals.

Mr. EVANS. Well, their moral sensibility has not been developed. Some of these finer senses take a long time to develop. What you saw I have seen also, but they were somewhat rare cases, I am glad to say. It is the other side of their nature I have most frequently witnessed. These donkeys, and especially mules, are somewhat tricky and often go down quietly, load, mother, and child, in a stream or river, and but with little weight. I have had this experience myself, in both water and mud.

Roads in Haiti have been wretched and impassable, and it is cruel to have to drive donkeys heavily loaded over them. The whole country, as well as people, are in a very backward condition in spite of some very excellent traits mentioned. It is a field with splendid opportunity for Christian statesmen, as well as teachers and missionaries.

Senator ODDIE. Were you in St. Marc's prison in 1918?

Mr. EVANS. Yes; I spent the closing days of year 1918 and the opening days of 1919 in the slave cell of St. Marc's old prison, strictly confined, and no person, not even members or officers of church, daring to come and see me.

Senator ODDIE. Did you see any acts of cruelty and ill treatment in there?

Mr. EVANS. Yes; while night after night, as well as during the day, and actually gasping for a breath of air, and expecting every moment at the command of the white, intoxicated, and raging, cursing American marine to be dragged out like others before a "firing squad," I could hear the yelling and groaning of native prisoners, as well as their being cruelly beaten and pounded by gendarmes. Many a time these yells and groans would suddenly cease, and then a scuffle, whispering, and the sound like if they were carrying out a dead body or bodies.

Through the small cross-barred window of my dark cell I could see 100 or more lined up about 6 in the morning to have coffee, at times without a morsel to eat, and without the least provocation struck a terrible blow with almost anything the gendarme might have in his hand, until the prisoner was stunned. I have seen them fall like logs in the prison yard from pure exhaustion, starved, and the lack of nourishment.

After the coffee and under armed guard of gendarmes I have seen them marched for corvee work on roads several miles from the town of St. Marc. Between 2 and 3 I have seen them brought back to prison, roughly searched, and whatever they had taken from them; whether these had any pay for corvee work I don't exactly know, though I think not.

Often they would have to wait two and three hours without a bite. A few occasions there were no food at all, the American captain having gone away with the keys or drinking.

I saw again and passed by under armed guard of the gendarmes dead body, if not bodies, in the farthest yard perfectly nude and covered with vermin, and where men and women prisoners and corvee workers stood and sat around. I saw women prisoners have their heads held under spigots by gendarmes and otherwise tortured. And the day I was taken out under gendarme guard, after being tried by Negro high court, and said American marine officer immediately commanded to liberate me, my imprisonment condemned as illegal and court decreed substantial indemnity, etc., for torture and agony suffered, a man just brought in and laid on his stomach attended to by the native assistant local doctor and another. This Haitian had his back beaten into a kind of jelly and insensible, and, on asking how it happened, was told that this American, Capt. Brown, in another of his drunken rages had pounded this man.

While staying at St. Marc, at the home of the family of the late Judge Orius Paultre, heard on credible testimony that two or three prisoners had been taken out by night, driven at the command of the American captain a mile or so from town, forced to make their own graves, and shot into them. This, with my own imprisonment, marched several times under guard through streets, almost drove natives into hysterics.

My last Sunday at St. Marc in the end of March or beginning of April of 1919, and coming from church service, saw great excitement and persons running to hide in their shacks, closing doors and shutters—as in revolutionary days—and trembling in fear, and was told that the gendarmes had just killed two natives. I returned toward our church and saw a dead body almost nude carried on a sack by four others, and swayed from one side to the other, limbs hanging over, the most gruesome sight I ever witnessed, with an armed gendarme riding along by their side.

This method was adopted, I felt, to drive the already terror-stricken natives perfectly and purposely crazy.

Senator ODDIE. Is that captain a marine?

Mr. EVANS. Yes; all captains and lieutenants over gendarmes are American marine officers.

Senator ODDIE. A captain of our marines?

Mr. EVANS. Yes; he was Capt. Fizgerald Brown in full and complete charge of the St. Marc gendarmes; the one conspiring with Gen. Williams, Port au 'Prince; Maj. Wells, captain, and lieutenant Hang (St. Michel) had me arrested and imprisoned, etc.

Senator ODDIE. Do you know of any other cases where the marine officers actually committed any cruelty?

Mr. EVANS. Yes; this Capt. Brown's own lieutenant boasted in the train between St. Marc and Port au Prince around February or March of 1919, to me and other white folks and some natives, that he had just come back from hunting Cacos in the north, and had bagged several, and that as soon as he returned from Port au Prince—I believe he said—he was going back to bag some more. He talked of killing Cacos as if shooting game and without any apparent compunction of conscience.

When left together I seriously talked to him of a humane method of dealing with these supposed Cacos, which he admitted to be the right, and he believed to be the more efficient, way. He admitted that he was sick and disgusted with the way things were in Haiti and was quitting to go back to the farm in the Middle States, and would be done forever with this kind of life.

This lieutenant sat in court during the hearing of my case before the Negro high court, and that same evening he quietly came to the door of my cell. "Cheer up, that captain is an 'insane fool," or words to that effect; "you will be free," he said.

At Cape Haiti in January of 1918 one of our members, in deep mourning, with her aged mother, informed me of her two brothers dragged out from the Cape prison at night, after cruel torture, and somewhere had to dig their own graves and shot at the command of American marine officers—Maj. Wells or his subordinate. Their father was for years a deacon and local preacher with us at the Cape.

As showing absolute ignoring of and defiance to Haiti court by the American marine officers, this captain (Brown) on being ordered by court to set me immediately at liberty and give me adequate protection to life and mission work with threats of violence and military force, compelled me to go at midnight—that same evening I came out from my cell—to go alone in an open boat to sea on the way to Gonaives and north to face another court there, under the notorious Maj. Wells, for another trial, when the St. Marc high court declared emphatically there was absolutely no case, and so-called mandates of Judge Obas issued at the instigation of Maj. Wells and other American marine officers—sent to St. Marc were not valid (illegal).

Senator ODDIE. Alone?

Mr. EVANS. Yes; only the Negro judge advocate employed by St. Marc Haitians to defend me, without my knowing, at the high court came with me for company during the sea voyage, and intending to come all the way to the Cape.

Senator ODDIE. How many miles?

Mr. EVANS. Over 100 miles, probably, altogether, through the interior; and after a sleepless voyage we both landed the following afternoon at Gonaives. To my astonishment, if not amazement, as soon as Gonaives was reached the judge refused to come a step farther and accompany me through the interior and by land.

The wild and weird stories we heard here about how American marine officers and their gendarmes were cutting out the tongues of natives, taking their eyes from their sockets, cutting their throats, etc., this educated and intelligent judge not only got excited but became hysterical, and with tears he and other leading Christian natives of Gonaives begged of me not to venture; that I would be a dead man: He therefore went back to St. Marc, leaving me alone to face the north and what now seemed positive death in the most barbaric and butchery method, according to what these natives honestly believed.

On reaching St. Michael on Sunday morning our native members failed to recognize me with a prison-grown beard. When I explained they wept. I was invited to the gendarmerie headquarters here, when denounced by the apparently intoxicated American marine officer (Lieut. Hange) whom 18 months before Col. Russell had disciplined for drunkenness and other unworthy conduct, but whom Gen. Williams and Maj. Wells had reinstated.

With the wildest gestures, clinched fists, and terrible oaths this foreign-born American officer denounced me, walking and raving like a maniac, now with fists up to my face, then turning around to grasp his revolver to shoot me, cursed God and religion and all missionaries, and warned me at the peril of imprisonment, if not death, to preach in the north, and all this in spite of the official letter of Mr. Lansing and the note I bore from Capt. Gibbon, our American marine officer and chief of the St. Michel lieutenant, stationed at Gonaives, a gentleman and a young, educated and efficient American officer.

When at last, amid all the threats, I reached the cape and got my witnesses who would testify to the drunkenness of the lieutenant, whom Col. Russell in the interest of military morale and marine efficiency in Haiti had disciplined, I found that on learning of the action of St. Marc high (Negro) court, and that I had reached the cape with my witnesses, the conspiracy of these American marine officers alleged of drunkenness and other conduct subversive to the occupation and United States mission and work in Haiti suddenly collapsed.

Maj. Wells was indignant that I refused to allow them to withdraw, and insisted upon the Negro court therefore to receive my testimony, which it did, and signed by myself under oath and witnessed by Rev. De Feu (white) and superintendent of the London Wesleyan Missionary Society (British subject), and also Rev. Elie Marc, Baptist Missionary (white) and French subject.

This judge admitted there was no case, and that he was forced to this action by American marine officers, as the judge of St. Marc petty court was compelled to condemn me at the instance of Capt. Brown.

Senator ODDIE. Did any of the United States marines at any time tell you of the killings of natives?

Mr. EVANS. The lieutenant of St. Marc and the lieutenant of Petite Riviere already referred to. It was, however, common knowledge and spoken generally among the natives as well as the whites throughout the whole Republic.

Capt. Kenny, stationed at St. Marc for some time, and at one time had a terrible reputation for brutality and the killing of natives, appeared to me at St. Marc to have reformed and greatly changed for the better. He pleaded his inexperience, his lack of really knowing the true Haitian character as reasons and excuses, but admitted his error, and now praised the natives as reliable and honorable if properly handled and trusted. Before he had, like many more, to depend upon interpreters, and all these were aliens from outside of Haiti, with a great deal of jealousy toward Haitians.

Though a Roman Catholic in the States, he showed great appreciation of our mission work at St. Marc and voluntarily gave me the following official permit, permitting Mrs. Evans and myself to regularly conduct services at the prison, with some 170 or 200 present and the greatest decorum.

The gendarme officers also showed a growing and intelligent interest and asked many questions as to the Bible and teaching. This was only a few months before Brown was made captain and succeeded Kenny as chief American marine officer in charge of St. Marc company and my own arrest, etc.

CREDENTIALS BORNE FROM WASHINGTON AND TAKEN FROM L. TON EVANS BY CAPT. BROWN.

DEPARTMENT OF STATE,
Washington, October 8, 1917.

The honorable PHILALANDER C. KNOX,
United States Senate.

SIR: I have received your letter of October 3, 1917, requesting a letter of introduction for Rev. L. Ton Evans, of Lansford, Pa., to the diplomatic and consular officers of the United States of America in Haiti.

I shall have pleasure in complying with your request after Rev. Mr. Evans has obtained a passport, for which purpose I inclose blank forms of application and a copy of the passport rules. In transmitting his application for a passport to the department, Rev. Mr. Evans should refer to this letter. I have the honor to be, sir,

Your obedient servant,

ROBERT LANSING.

———

DEPARTMENT OF STATE,
Washington, October 22, 1917.

To the diplomatic and consular officers of the United States of America in Haiti.

GENTLEMEN: At the instance of Hon. Philander C. Knox, a Senator of the United States from the State of Pennsylvania, I take pleasure in introducing to you Rev. Lewis Ton Evans, of Lansford, Pa., who is about to proceed to Haiti as general superintendent of the Baptist missions.

I cordially bespeak for Rev. Mr. Evans such courtesies and assistance which you may be able to render, consistently with your official duties.

I am, gentlemen, your obedient servant,

ROBERT LANSING.

———

COPY OF FEW REFERENCES QUOTED.

1. Right Hon. David Lloyd-George, British prime minister, written at the British House of Commons on my leaving Wales for the United States March, 1902, and an ex-president of the Baptist Union of Wales:

MY DEAR TON EVANS: I only wish I could comply with request to be at your farewell reception, but am trying to keep down my meetings, to reserve all my time and strength for the House of Commons. Here where the real battle will be for the next six months. (This was against Tory Government's sectarian education bill, which was utterly defeated as far as Wales is concerned under his masterly leadership and daring championship.)

With kind regards to yourself and friend Williams.

Yours, sincerely,

D. LLOYD-GEORGE.

P. S.—If any letter from me would be of use in the United States or Canada shall indeed be only too glad to give it you.

Rev. L. TON EVANS,
Barry, South Wales.

2. Dr. Robert S. MacArthur, president of World's Baptist Alliance and late of Calvary, New York:

This is to say that Rev. L. Ton Evans, of the Haiti Baptist Mission, is well known to me. He is a man of wide experience and varied ability and noble character. He is doing unique work in the black Republic, and no other man has ever reached the men there with whom he is in helpful touch. He deserves the unstinted support of all lovers of humanity and disciples of the Christian religion.

Truly, yours,

R. S. MACARTHUR.

3. Dr. Prestridge, editor of Baptist World (Ky.) and American secretary of Baptist World Alliance, writing from Louisville, Ky., in 1909, urging this field on southern Baptists:

This morning our Louisville pastors' conference heard with deep interest (at Theological Seminary) Rev. L. Ton Evans, field secretary of Haiti mission, and unanimously passed resolution urging southern Baptists to take up work in this close island. Brother Ton Evans is now at dinner with me, and I am touched by his thrilling stories regarding his work. Though a Welshman from Wales, he is a true American, full of life and on fire for the Christian faith. He will write to you.

Yours,

J. N. PRESTRIDGE.

4. Dr. Cynonfardd Edwards, pastor of largest Welsh and Congregational Church in United States, and internationally known and most highly esteemed on both sides of Atlantic:

I have known Rev. L. Ton Evans for more than 18 years while in Haiti, and as pastor of First Baptist Church of Edwardsville, and some years my nearest neighbor. He is a born missionary, and wherever he may be, whether in pagan land or in Christian country he will find work to do for his Master. He has been a most faithful servant of the Lord in this whole community, and leaves behind him evidences of an active and consecrated life. He is the keenest, bravest, and most consecrated Christian advocate of temperance reform I have ever seen in this State. He has had a very wide experience and has proved himself equal to every emergency.

Sincerely, yours,

T. C. EDWARDS.

3. From Dr. F. B. Meyer, secretary of National Federation of Free Churches' Council, Christ Church, Westminster, and ex-president of Baptist Union of Great Britain and Ireland:

LONDON, *January 19, 1921.*

DEAR MR. EVANS: I have read your letter and reviewed the accompanying private documents with profound interest and sympathy in all that you have suffered. I am glad to see that the new Government is likely to appoint a special commission to go thoroughly into the whole matter, and with such a President as Mr. Harding you can almost certainly reckon on a fair hearing. No one is more suited than yourself to conduct the case for the natives of Haiti.

Cordially, yours,

F. B. MEYER.

4. Hon. T. Ch. Moravia, legation de la Republique d'Haiti at Washington, D. C., under date April 28, 1919, wrote:

I am very glad of your letter and to find you still continue your laudable efforts to secure for Haiti an educational institution and industrial school like Tuskegee on Christian basis and your present endeavor to have the great Baptist denomination here to undertake the evangelization of my people.

We profoundly appreciate your interest in and sacrifice for our country the last 25 years that I have been personally privileged to know you, and the splendid encouragement and support you have rendered Haitian missionaries and the way you have brought some of our young people and placed here in American schools to be taught.

These years of deep interest and untiring activities for the religious, moral, and industrial development of our Republic have won for you, dear pastor, the entire sympathy, implicit confidence, and hearty good will of all our Haitian people.

With such intimate knowledge as you have of my country and our people's confidence and good will, should American Baptists enter the Haiti field and support your efforts you must succeed with God's help in saving Haiti. My best wishes will ever accompany you.

I am, dear pastor,

Yours, very truly,

T. CH. MORAVIA.

5. Dr. Reynold Morgan, major in United States Army, who distinguished himself in France with Canadians, then under Gen. Pershing and his own flag, once associated in Christian and temperance work in Pennsylvania and done some clerical work for Haiti mission:

How can I express to you my admiration for the determined stand which you have taken in the defense of the poor defenseless Negroes of Haiti? The spirit of sacrifice which you have manifested in working out this great problem commands the deepest respect of all true Americans.

The fruits of your great efforts will become manifested throughout the Black Republic, and future generations will give you the credit and praise which apparently is lacking now while this work of yours is in progress.

Do drop in and see me at any time you are this way and can spare a few minutes, for I always treasure you in my memory as a great pioneer who has had to cut his way through the great wilderness alone and as one who has had to blaze the trail where 'ere long multitudes will follow.

With best wishes, as ever,
Your friend and pupil,

DAVID REYNOLDS MORGAN, M. D.,
Major of United States Army Reserves.

OFFICE OF THE ATTORNEY GENERAL,
Washington, D. C., August 2, 1919.

Rev. L. TON EVANS,
   226 Chestnut Avenue, Kingston, Pa.
MY DEAR SIR: I have your letter of July 13. The matters complained of will be looked into so far as this department is able to do so.

Very truly, yours,

A. MITCHELL PALMER.

The matters complained of were "illegal arrest, and imprisonment with mental and physical torture in a small, dark, narrow slave cell of a Christian missionary, and a white American citizen, and an official credential from Secretary of State Robert Lansing (at request of Senator Philander Knox, the ex-Secretary of State, from Pennsylvania), with request to know the moral and legal responsibility of the United States Government for the criminal actions of the marine officers and the American occupation, who were direct parties to the same? No word was ever received from Mr. Mitchell Palmer. L. T. E.

ST. MARC, HAITI, WEST INDIES, *January 22, 1919.*

Senator PHILANDER KNOX,
   United States Senate, Washington, D. C.
DEAR SENATOR: You will be surprised, perhaps astonished, to learn that through a Capt. B. (marine officer), of our American occupation, and in spite of being and American citizen, ordained minister of the Gospel and general superintendent of the colored Baptists of the States, morally supported by about 5,000,000 white Baptists of America, and though bearing an official letter of Secretary Lansing (given at your own request), I was recently and without any warning or warrant arrested in my own study; marched under armed native (Negro) gendarme heavy guard through the public streets, searched, stripped of all articles, then cast into a small, dark prison cell, where I was closely confined for 13 days and 12 nights, etc., causing untold physical suffering, through hard bare floor, lack of food, and the mental strain and terrible suspense night and day through fear of being at any moment pounced upon and beaten to death, or dragged before a "firing squad" as done in many of the cases at St. Marc, and elsewhere in Haiti, by command of American marine officers.

After first three days, and again marched through public streets of the city, exposed to a strong tropical sun (my shade having been roughly torn from me by the excited black corporal), and as a criminal, robber, or murderer I was brought to the two tribunals, questioned, thence marched back under same armed Negro guard (gendarmes) to my small, almost lightless, airless, death cell, with Negro prisoners and criminals all around, yelling and groaning through flogging often the whole night long and often during the day. A Negro armed guard was stationed before my barred door.

But for the smuggling into the cell, by the Negro guard of a native straw mat, and other Catholic and Protestants of casava and other native food at times, and at risk of their own lives, my lot would have been intolerable, with the result I would have like others (I saw) weakened, fainted, and dropped dead in my close confinement struggling for a breath of air, etc.

The following week I was again marched through the public streets under armed guard, this time to the chief tribunal of justice, while the natives in the street fled in fear into their houses and shanties; trembled and wept to see their American missionary friend weak and wan with haggard appearance, and by this, a prison-grown beard passing, followed by the American occupation's armed guard, where the white United States marine captain had been commanded by the high negro court to bring the prisoner for trial at an "extraordinary session."

No sooner seated than a Negro member of the church, and moved by the white pale face and apparent frail body of her pastor, and her missionary followed him through the streets with tearful eyes and at the risk of life into the tribunal, with hot coffee, milk, and sugar so as to refresh and strengthen him, which met with the strong approval of most present, and so affected the judge that he smiled with a nod for the missionary to help himself.

Another expression of the natives' sympathy with prisoner and reversion of feeling and hatred against the occupation's tyranny was, that without my knowledge, they had engaged a Negro judge advocate to help and plead for me, but whom dared not visit my strictly watched and closely confined cell, as nearly all are terror stricken, as set forth in the memorandum presented Mr. Lansing and our President last October; and copies of which I supplied Chairman Hitchcock with for members of Foreign Relations Committee of the United States Senate last November and before I left Washington.

It was shown, of course, that there was no case; that it was mere persecution, possibly enough of a conspiracy of white American marine officers in Haiti given to drink, encouraged and partly inspired in the States; may be, at the back of all a determined and malicious attempt to drive me from the island or crush and murder me, thus bringing all my missionary, Christian, educational, and temperance work to an abrupt end. The exposure of such purpose and adoption of such methods curb and crush my missionary efforts for the spiritual, moral, and industrial development of Haiti and Haitians at this court produced a most favorable effect with exactly the contrary feeling against the poor, armed Negro corporal and white United States superior marine officer, who at first wore a pompous appearance, but somewhat dejected at the abrupt adjournment of the court proceedings.

In my address I first asked the court for an official copy of the court proceedings and verdict for my United States Government, which request was immediately granted, then went on to describe the exact nature of my activities in behalf of Haiti and Haitian people during the last 25 years. The eloquent plea of the judge advocate which followed, "praising my self-sacrificing efforts in and for the Black Republic and the Haitians, stating that Haiti constitution gave equal liberty to Protestants as to Catholics, which priests from Europe, and some marine officers from the United States, seem to be either ignorant of, or to ignore, and that President Wilson was a Protestant and a temperance reformer like the missionary, and supported war prohibition measures with present government; hence it could not be a crime in Haiti to-day, even under an American occupation, to be either a Protestant or a temperance reformer, for which a Haitian, much more an American citizen and a Christian miss'onary, should be arrested in his own private study without a warrant, denounced, and cursed, after being publicly paraded through the streets of St. Marc under heavy armed guard, then at the bidding of an American marine officer of the United States Government cast into a dark, narrow cell, so strictly confined that not one of his members dared see him, robbed of all liberty, food, and air, and light, with his own life in jeopardy every moment of the 13 days and 12 nights he remained there p'ning on the bare floor."

This caused almost a sensation, and the court abruptly adjourned until the next morning, wh:ch they did (I understand) and declared the whole procedure of the American occupation's captain illegal, demanded immediate freedom of missionary with ample reparation.

Though this was Wednesday morning, it was not until Thursday evening, and under armed Negro gendarme, that I was again paraded once more through the streets to the bureau of the American occupation, and there told (first time) by the marine captain that I was free and given back the articles, photos, and papers, including Mr. Adee's official acknowledgment of my memorandum by Pres'dent Wilson, and our United States Government's assurance that the sad conditions, then directly brought to their attention "were actually at that moment being seriously considered," etc.—taken from me, on being searched, Saturday afternoon, December 28, 1918—just before I was thrust into my slave cell and death dungeon, and the strong iron bar banged heavily behind me at the stern command of my own United States Government's white marine captain!

On seeing the judge advocate that evening I was informed of the judgment of the high court in my favor against the United States marine officer and all those who acted or conspired with him, declaring arrest and imprisonment illegal and unwarrantable, that I am entitled to substantial indemnity calling for immediate release, and commanding the Haiti Government to give me personally, as well as mission work engaged in, ample protection.

That very night, however, and in spite of my pleading for one night's rest, and in utter defiance of the high court's decree, I was driven under threat of military force by this same American marine officer in a small open boat to the wide Caribbean Sea, en route for Gonaives and north to face another court (where other parties to the official marine conspiracy operated), and on a supposed "mandate" the high court of St. Marc had emphatically declared the day before to be invalid, and so forth.

En route through the interior of the north to the cape, another white American marine officer (recently disciplined by Col. John H. Russell for drunkenness, etc., but reinstated as lieutenant in another town and over an important section), with whom I found the St. Marc captain and others in collusion, dared me to preach, cursed missionaries, denounced Christianity, and in his rage, and apparently intoxicated, and before a number of our Christian natives, and irrespective of my showing him Mr. Lansing's letter and a note from his superior marine captain (which letter and note he could not read), again and again raved like a madman and attempting to reach his revolver to shoot me, so under these serious and sad conditions inflaming the minds of the poor natives, and causing them to hate the United States and everything American, obstacles may be possibly placed in my way to return to Pennsylvania and Kingston, where my dear family live.

Hence, I shall profoundly appreciate your own personal service as our Senator from my home State, as well as an ex-Attorney General of the United States Government, with or without the cooperation of Senator Lodge and others in securing immediately, not only my own safe return unmolested, but also Government authorization and protection to bring three or four leading and responsible Haitians with me, whose presence may be essential to me in the States and at Washington.

Though incredible and almost unthinkable, I still maintain (though the late ex-President Roosevelt, the great friend of Haiti and much lamented throughout the Black Republic, strongly believes to the contrary, with others throughout the United States) that somehow the real and vital facts concerning conditions in Haiti, and brutal and murderous treatment of natives, etc., are studiously, persistently, and criminally withheld by somebody, or somebodies, from Secretary Daniels, Secretary Lansing, and our President, who repeatedly denounce secret, ancient, and defunct diplomacy.

As demanded in my memorandum presented to the President, nothing but the appointment of a special commission—by Mr. Wilson on his immediate return from Europe and through the influence of the Senate—will convince Haiti of the sincerity, veracity, and honor of the United States, and restore absolute confidence in our Government and American people's humane, benevolent, and even indeed Christian purpose according to our treaty.

Am sincerely trusting this will reach you safely through our "censor" and that you can act at once, and if possible by cable.

Fraternally and loyally to Government, country, and flag, and still for Christ, Haiti, and humanity.

L. Ton Evans.

Mrs. Ton Evans's mental distress and souls agony in the States can at this time be best judged from the following quotations from certain letters which managed to elude the censor and reach his friends, etc.:

"Had I known that my dear husband was in prison I could have done something to demand his release. Oh, that awful thought! Yes; awful that he, one of the truest and most self-sacrificing friends of Haiti, who has given his all for the black Republic and its suffering people, should be so cruelly and brutally treated. Really I feel I can never again say the word Haiti without a sharp pain, like a dagger piercing through my heart.

"Do tell me, what led to his imprisonment? How is he now, and where at this moment? What became of the impending second trial in the north? He has not received one letter from me since he has left, and I have written him every week since he left the States. Shameful conduct! What are the villains trying to do to my dear husband and the faithful and tender father of my two darling little boys (Adoniram Judson and William Carey in the photograph taken from him in prison)?

"Won't you tell him (if you dare visit and talk to him, and if he is alive) that I have written him regularly? He must know I can never, no never, forget him. Had I known about his case, I fear nothing would have kept me from coming right on. Oh, what I could have spared him, had I known immediately—of agony and anguish to him, for I would have gone to the very limit of the law of our United States to obtain his instant release.

"I shall myself go at once to Washington unless a word is received immediately. Am sure our President and responsible officials in the Government do not know the barbarity and treachery carried on in Haiti! What can we expect, however, from the low and degraded character of many of our white American officers, gendarmes, and corrupt type of representatives of our own country there. Tell dear madam and sisters and all the dear ones there that I beg them to join in prayer for my dear one's life and liberty. Oh, it is dreadful to bear all this! God alone can lift this terrible burden from my heart, and, indeed, from your own hearts as well.

"I feel I can never tell my two boys about this horrible and dreadful treatment of their dear papa in Haiti, and at the hands of white marine officers of my own American Government and under our own Stars and Stripes down in the black Republic!

"If you can possibly see my dear husband, tell him not to worry about us here in Pennsylvania, but let him know that it will certainly be the very happiest moment of our lives when he is safe back with us here again. I can not think for a moment the Lord would have him to suffer this cruelty. No; I am claiming still his promise—

"The angel of the Lord encampeth round about them that fear Him and delivereth them." (Psalms 34, 8.)

Let us, therefore, pray, pray, pray, for the Lord can as miraculously deliver His children to-day from prison as he did Paul.

Again, writing two days later, in answer to a note which had been smuggled so as to reach her home at Kingston, Pa., and thus elude the strict censorship, Mrs. Evans says:

"-DEAR HUSBAND: It seems years, indeed, have passed in the last three months. So much has happened and events have crowded that I can not imagine where I am and what I really am. When your letter of January 9 came I could no longer withhold my grief from Martha, my sister, for it seemed that my heart would really break. Oh, how dreadful to think, Dear Papa, that you were made to suffer such humiliation and barbarity at the very hands of your own so-called American countrymen. Then to think you were alone, strictly confined, and receiving no mail from me, and I have written every week since you left us.

"The grace of God alone kept you from desperation and death. Sometimes I really wish we had been there with you in Haiti at the time, and to again fear that the two little lads and myself could never have stood it. I feel sure it would have killed us all. But when I think we were so comfortable here in the States at that time, and you, Dear Papa, at the St. Marc, little dark dungeon, being physically and mentally tortured and all but starved—the tears even now force themselves into a convulsive cry."

The missionary's smuggled note in English and Welsh of January 9, 1919, which by a circuitous route at last safely reached Kingston, Pa., was scribbled hastily and tremblingly about midnight of the day the high Negro court commanded his immediate release, and the Haiti Government's protection of his life and mission work, but which the white captain of the United States marines, still and immediately in defiance of the high Negro court, and under threat of military force, compelled to take—at midnight—a small open boat and thrust out to the Caribbean open sea, en route for Gonaives, and through the far interior to face another court in the north, and on so-called charges declared by St. Marc court as illegal, etc.

Judge Advocate Stucco, engaged without the missionary's knowledge by the natives to defend him at the St. Marc high court, accompanied the missionary on that lonely voyage, but on reaching Gonaives the afternoon of next day and hearing the wild and weird stories of the natives after landing—as to the "indiscriminate killing" and pulling out of eyes, of tongues, and cutting of throats of Haitians by white marine American officers and their gendarmes throughout that section of the interior and north—this educated, intelligent, and one of Haiti's leading attorneys, absolutely convinced of the truth of what he heard, became not only excited but at the thought of being butchered and murdered by American marine officers and the gendarmerie at their bidding, became actually frenzied, refused to come a step further, and ere he deserted me to my own murderous fate to return to the little boat and back to his wife and family at St. Marc, this judge advocate and others with tearful eyes implored me also to return with him and not attempt the journey through the interior to the north.

IN RE ARREST AND IMPRISONMENT OF REV. L. TON EVANS, GENERAL SUPERINTENDENT OF BAPTIST MISSION, ST. MARC, HAITI.

Rev. L. Ton Evans was illegally arrested without warrant in his own private study at St. Marc, Haiti, on Saturday afternoon, December 28, 1918, paraded under Negro armed police through the public streets of the town, and confined in a small and narrow prison cell for 13 days and 12 nights, not only so as to rob him of all personal liberty and public rights as an ordained minister and missionary in Haiti as well as an American citizen, but further with malicious intent to do him physical harm, repudiate, crush, if not murder, as repeatedly told him, and threatened by one Capt. Brown, and a demand for heavy damages.

1. The arrest was made on Saturday, December 28, 1918, at his private study in the home of Mme. Orius Paultre and family (widow of Judge Orius Paultre), at St. Marc, Haiti, and while he was engaged at the time in the discharge of his duties as missionary and pastor, preparing on the typewriter special envelopes for his church and mission stations.

2. The request of the missionary on thus being suddenly arrested by the gendarme (armed native police) to show his authority by way of warrant or mandate and stating the cause or causes of such strange procedure on the part of Capt. Fitzgerald Brown, the white American officer, was not only peremptorialy denied but afterwards construed by above captain as constituting a case of open rebellion against public authority on the part of the Baptist missionary in question.

3. That while on the way and under arrest and proceeding to the headquarters of Capt. Brown, American officer in Haiti, another request of the missionary—upon whom it now dawned he might be taken to prison—namely, to allow him to give the key of the private study, which had been locked—and so as to get the envelopes for distribution on Sunday to the officers of the church, whose door we passed, and so as to return it to Mme. Orius, was also furiously denied and further construed by Capt. Brown as a criminal attempt to escape from the hands of public authority. The same gendarme, who appeared very excited and as if under the influence of Taffia, had amid the protests of the other native soldiers or police violently taken the umbrella or shade from the missionary, and thus exposed him to the burning tropical sun.

4. Having arrived at the headquarters of this white American captain under armed native police, these two charges were excitedly read to him by above white officer, who seemed under the influence of liquor, then the missionary was cursed and damned on account of his devotion to Haiti and his efforts to spiritually, educationally, morally, and industrously develop its 2,000,000 Negroes. Capt. Brown vowed he would degrade him lower than the lowest "nigger"; that as a minister and missionary he, captain, would have him repudiated and utterly crushed, and pointing repeatedly to his revolver excitedly added, "You ought to be shot." The missionary was dumbfounded, for this officer had a few months before acted toward him entirely the reverse.

5. After the missionary was sent under same armed guard to prison, where he was searched and everything taken from him, such as official letters from the United States State Department re official investigation conducted by the United States Government into alleged misconduct cruelties, and other crimes on part of certain officers and gendarmes in Haiti. A photograph of the missionary's wife and two little boys, as well as that of President Wilson—in States—all of which were on the missionary when arrested, were taken from him, and he was cast into prison.

6. Immediately after this search was through the missionary was cast into a small, narrow cell, almost lightless and airless, the small door banged and iron bar drawn with tremendous force as if to say, there he is safe and shall never be able to preach and help these people any more. An armed Negro was kept

marching day and night before the door. Thus for 13 days and 12 nights the missionary laid on the bare floor of cement surrounded by some 160 Negro prisoners with their yells and groans day and night when set upon on least provocation and half killed and sometimes actually murdered by certain groups of Negro officers, and in fear every moment the light flashed upon his glassless window he heard the tramp of the feet of the armed gendarme, or the sudden drawing back of the iron bar of his prison cell door, that they had come to take him before the "firing squad," like the British nurse, Edith Cavell, for instance, was taken by the Germans.

7. On Tuesday the missionary was led through the public streets, under Negro guard, to court of justice (Negro) and then to the court of public prosecutor, both of which being under the influence and dominion of American occupation, and dreaded white officers of the gendarme in Haiti. He was condemned under the two aforesaid charges preferred against him by the white captain, and in spite of his own evidence to the contrary. The missionary was afterwards taken back to his cell, where he would have starved but for the bread and fruit brought to him stealthily by the Negro prison officers (and brought by Negro Catholics and Protestants) when the American white captain was not to be seen about.

8. On the following Tuesday, January 7, 1919, pale, haggard looking, and with a prison-grown beard, Missionary L. Ton Evans was again paraded through the streets to the high court (Negro), where he was to be tried at a special and extraordinary session, the case having created not only such a deep interest, but caused a profound sensation. This court went carefully into the two preferred charges of rebellion and attempt to escape, which, after all, were only an occasion or pretense for this captain and other white American officers in Haiti, who were in some cases Catholics and rum drinkers and brutal, conspiring maliciously to destroy the Christian influence and great religious and moral usefulness of the Baptist missionary, and to absolutely crush him in spite of the Haiti constitution granting the same equal freedom and protection to Protestants as to Catholics; and that a very strict prohibition had been proclaimed throughout the Haiti Republic, printed in all the papers in both French and English and posted at every hotel and liquor store, signed by Col. Russell, in supreme command of all American forces in Haiti (both marines and gendarmerie), and as direct representative of the United States Navy, Secretary Daniels, prohibiting under very heavy penalty (though not at present enforced much) the sale of liquor to any officer or gendarme in uniform, etc.

9. After a very careful examination of witnesses and a thorough investigation into all charges, and the so-called mandate from the court in the north, and alleged defamation of a white officer seen drunk on duty, the conspiracy of certain officers on this account, and owing to the fact that Col. Russell felt compelled as the officer in supreme command to exercise rigid discipline, and in violation to the spirit and letter of the prohibition order of other superior officers in the interest of American occupation, efficiency, and necessary to secure respect and influence from United States Government in Haiti, the high court in question made therefore the following declaration in their judgment:

(a) There was absolutely no case. All charges had failed against missionary.

(b) That the arrest was without mandate was both illegal and unwarranted.

(c) That the missionary must be at once liberated and given the full protection of the Republic in life and labor there; and

(d) Further, he was entitled on demand to the most substantial damages.

The missionary has been suffering ever since his confinement, lying on floor, and mental agony he has gone through with when exposed to bodily harm every day and night, and taken before a firing squad by a Negro gendarme at command of white American Government officer in Haiti.

BWTHYN, WYOMING, PA., *October 16, 1920.*

DEAR SENATOR HARDING: Accept sincere thanks for self and nearly 3,000,000 helpless Negroes of Haiti (who, sad to say, have been worst exploited and even brutally butchered under our "American occupation," especially the last three or more years, than ever in time of German filibusters, etc.) for your correct description, only far too mild.

For over two years I have placed information with President and Secretary of State and Senator Hitchcock, but officials have either withheld facts or President, Secretary of State, etc., have proved blind, adamant, if not idiotic, and States and Nation disgraced, exactly as stated in yesterday's Ledger editorial.

I am now suing United States Government, under our President Wilson, for indemnity for false imprisonment, etc., decreed against United States and their officials in Haiti by the high Negro court of St. Marc (Haiti), who felt it a disgrace and scandal upon the Haiti Negro Republic that a white American citizen and Christian missionary should be pining in a French old slave cell, etc., and demanded the white officials of United States of America to at once bring him out for a legal trial, etc.

I wrote Secretary Daniels in March and again last week, and unless immediate settlement is made and commission appointed, then am coming to Marion, and will publish letters, with full, complete account of the "infamous rape," etc., you referred to, which, if true that it emanated from Hon. Frank Roosevelt, it has blighted his prospects for any responsible office under our American Nation, least of all the Vice Presidency.

Am leaving for Washington, D. C., this afternoon. Your letter may find me at New Howard Hotel, Sixth and Pennsylvania Avenue.

Please not make this known until I see what Secretary Daniels does on this their last opportunity. Mine is the case of the American Edith Cavell, the British nurse, rescued from the jaws of death under God by the Negro high court of Haiti, etc.

Sincerely, yours,

———— ————.

I was advised by late, illustrious friend, ex-President Theodore Roosevelt (November, 1918), to come to you and Republican Party immediately I failed with President Wilson, etc., in adjusting Haiti's wrongs.

————

BWTHYN, WYOMING, PA., *November 9, 1920.*

Hon. WARREN G. HARDING,
 President-Elect of the United States.

DEAR PRESIDENT-ELECT: Heartiest congratulations, with the millions more loyal Americans for the unheard of victory in the annals of this great Republic. May God specially succor, physically and spiritually sustain and signally bless you during your term of office, as Chief Executive of this mighty Nation.

Now, that the present administration after years of incompetency and criminal neglect and heartless betrayal of Haiti as well as the honor of this Nation—through your own clarion call—has awakened to the seriousness of the present situation in the Black Republic, and have appointed a Navy court, can not you from Texas again demand that I should be asked to accompany this court, with my attorney, not merely so as to prove the cases I definitely charged the administration's officers to have committed, and those mentioned in inclosed copy of letter to Judge Advocate Dyer, October 30—but also to assist—in my capacity of missionary superintendent, etc., among them for something like 28 years—to ass'st the natives, to place their grievances, produce evidence, etc., through the judge advocate to the court.

The natives are entitled to this assistance and protection, otherwise I fear through their exploitation, their brutal treatment, rape of their constitution, murder of thousands by United States marines, and their gendarme officers, etc., resulting in suspicion, fear, and hatred they will not feel free to come forward while the administration's side will be cared for.

If this can not possibly be done, then rather than the Haitians, should be led to think that this Navy court, and present limited and of necessity onesided inquiry, is genuine, not to say either satisfactory to the United States Government and American people, I respectfully urge, that you—

1. Make an immediate statement to this effect, that a congressional commission is at once contemplated, and a thorough and complete investigation will be made.

2. That notification of this shall be sent to, and at once be published in English and French in the Monitor and other Haiti papers.

3. That an opportunity to every Haitian, from the President down, to the poorest Protestants and Catholics alike, and of all shades of politics to testify and that the United States Government will provide an able attorney, assisted by myself, so as to enable them to gather reliable evidence all over the Republic, and place same in proper order before the congressional commission.

4. That every witness shall be protected, and necessary expense which may be incurred on account of distance to where the commission will sit will be given and paid by the United States.

5. Also, every Hait'an confined in the prisons of the Republic on mere suspicion shall, on the coming of the said commission, be allowed his and her freedom. Am sure this will be profoundly appreciated at the present moment, and as coming from the United States President elect, in fact, it will thrill them with a new confidence and hope for themselves and the future of their Negro Republic and actually look upon the recent election here as providential and, indeed, yourself as the savior raised of God at this time to deliver them and country.

Am sending the inclosed copy of letters to Major Dyer and Secretary Daniels to Senator Lodge, and am sure he (latter) would fall in with something along the lines I am here suggesting. It will be a master stroke as far as poor Haiti is concerned.

Your letter to us as ministers re the enforcement of the constitution and the benefits of temperance to our American homes, etc., was most timely, and thoroughly satisfied the most ardent temperance and Christian reformers, male and female, throughout the commonwealth, hence most heartily welcomed by all of us as your supporters and admirers.

It is s'gnificant that the President of the greatest and most civilized and Christian Republic in the world, as well as the prime minister of the greatest, most democratic, and progressive Christian empire, should be both strong and loyal Christians and Baptists at this time in history, and so as to lead in'the reconstruction not only of America and Britain but of the world, and under God the speedy healing of humanity's wounds.

Should you go to Panama from Texas, I sincerely trust you can arrange to call, either in going down or on return voyage, in Haiti. Am sure you would receive, in spite of all, a royal welcome from these misunderstood and misrepresented but kind-hearted people. In such case, if not there with the navy court, I would certainly like to join the party and act as guide, etc.

With best wishes, and hoping you can even bring influence to bear on present administration so as to secure through the present court most important evidence, and by my presence with an attorney prevent tampering for party and political purposes with some of the leading Haitians.

Fraternally and most heartily, yours, for Christ, Haiti, and humanity,

---

MISSIONARY ON ISLAND PROTESTED TO WILSON AND LANSING IN 1918—PROMISES—
NO ACTION.

AMERICAN MARINES AND OFFICIALS TREAT NATIVES LIKE DOGS—PREACHER PUT IN JAIL—HIS APPEAL TO AUTHORITIES TO END CRUELTY MEETS WITH DRASTIC REPRISAL.

[Special dispatch to the New York Herald.]

NEW YORK HERALD BUREAU,
Washington, D. C., October 24.

For almost two years the Wilson administration deliberately has suppressed full and accurate information of deplorable conditions brought about in the Republic of Haiti by the American occupation.

The evidence shows clearly that the slaughter of 3,250 natives by the Marine Corps in the last two years, which was admitted officially only after Senator Harding laid bare the Haitian scandal, is due chiefly to the strong anti-American feeling engendered in the island republic by the methods of the American occupation, which has destroyed any vestige of independence there.

These conditions are described by an eye witness who is now in Washington ready and eager to give his testimony, already long in possession of the State and Navy Departments, to the naval court of inquiry named by Secretary of the Navy Daniels after the attention of the court was brought to the situation in the little Black Republic by Senator Harding.

This man 's the Rev. Dr. L. Ton Evans, a Welshman by birth, with letters of recommendation from David Lloyd-George and from prominent Americans, including the late Theodore Roosevelt. He is a naturalized American who for 25 years had been engaged in Baptist missionary work in Haiti.

FIRST REPORT MADE IN 1918.

The New York Herald correspondent has in his possession documents which prove that Dr. Evans first brought this deplorable state of affairs in Haiti to the attention of the State Department in the fall of 1918, more than three years after the American marines were landed there. Other documents show he repeatedly has called the attention of the Navy Department and other branches of the Government to conditions there. Absolutely nothing has been done, so far as can be learned, to better these conditions, and a specific request made by Dr. Evans for an unbiased nonmilitary and nonpolitical commission to inquire into the Haitian wrongs under American occupation was ignored after repeated informal " promises " to do something about it.

Statements from Secretary Daniels and others representing the administration that they acted as soon as any irregularities in Haiti or any complaints were brought to their attention are disproved. Dr. Evans came to this country from Haiti in 1918 to bring to the attention of President Wilson and the Government authorities at Washington this state of affairs in the island Republic. He could not believe these conditions would be permitted to continue if once they were told to the responsible Government officials in Washington.

LETTER FROM STATE DEPARTMENT.

The following is a letter showing that he laid the facts before the State Department at that time:

WASHINGTON, November 2, 1918.

Dr. L. TON EVANS,
226 Chestnut Street, Kingston, Pa.

SIR: The department has received your memorandum upon conditions in Haiti presented on October 21, addressed to the President of the United States, and wishes to inform you that it is receiving the serious consideration of this department as well as of the various other branches of the Government concerned.

The department will be pleased to communicate with you at a later date after the careful study of the matter contained in your memorandum is terminated.

I am, sir, your obedient servant, for the Secretary of State,

ALVEY A. ADEE,
Second Assistant Secretary.

Everything indicates that the " careful study " given to the matters mentioned in Dr. Evans's memorandum consisted of pushing it into some already overfull pigeonhole or old letter file and forgetting all about it, if, indeed, it was not thrown into a State Department waste basket which is cleaned out by the janitor every evening.

This memorandum mentioned by Assistant Secretary Adee's letter of November 2, 1918, was handed in person by Dr. Evans to an official of the State Department, a Mr. Stabler, then in charge of the Latin-American section of the State Department and especially detailed to handle Haitian affairs. The facts were at the same time laid before Senator Hitchcock of Nebraska, then chairman of the Senate Committee on Foreign Relations.

Since that time Dr. Evans has endeavored repeatedly, but without success, to get this Government to recognize the situation in Haiti. He has several times notified Secretary Daniels, his last letter being dated as late as October 5, 1920.

Dr. Evans insists that a mere naval board of inquiry never will be able to get the facts before the American people. He said to-day that the American military representatives—the marines and the so-called gendarmes—officered in many instances by renegade white men from the States, have so overawed the natives that they can not be made to tell the truth; that they are afraid of their lives of uttering a word in criticism of their white superiors or of any of the black native policemen in the pay of the white officers.

As evidence of this state of affairs he told about his own arrest on trumped-up charges as the result of a conspiracy formulated by a white captain of gendarmes, against whom he had made a personal protest in the private office of Col. Russell, who was in supreme command of the marines, because of the bad example this captain was setting the natives in a certain village by his mode of living. When the case was brought before the high court it was at once dismissed for want of even a scintilla of evidence, and the officer who made the arrest and kept Dr. Evans in a vile native jail for thirteen days with the

Negroes, was informed abruptly there was no authority in the first place for the arrest of Dr. Evans. Nevertheless on his release he again was compelled by the same officer under threat of rearrest to go in an open boat at night a long distance to another point on the island to face again the same charges which again turned out to be groundless in every particular.

It is the first belief of the native population, as the result of the American occupation s.nce July 28, 1915, that the United States is trying to reestablish the system of slavery which their forefathers knew. Dr. Evans believes it is high time the American people were fully informed of what is being done by their Government in Haiti in order that this helpless little Black Republic have the sort of civilizing and humanizing it deserves.

Dr. Evans says the amazing number of indiscriminate killings of natives to which the Marine Corps officials have confessed and which is the subject of the present investigation is but a small part of the case.

More important than anything else, in his opinion, is the terrible blow being given to American prestige not only in Haiti but elsewhere in the Latin-American countries, to which stories of the American military methods are getting abroad, despite every effort on the part of the military overlords to keep everything unfavorable to their régime from reaching unfriendly channels.

DOCUMENTS REVEAL SCANDAL.

The New York Herald is able to present herewith extracts of the documents in the possession of various departments laying bare the whole Haitian affair and which will be brought to the attention of the Daniels inquiry board and elucidated by Dr. Evans himself. Dr. Evans is waiting in Washington for this purpose and is willing and anxious to appear before this committee or any other that may be named and to go with the committee to Haiti. He expects to have counsel to assist him in presenting the case in an orderly manner.

Dr. Evans, in a memorandum subm.tted to the State Department, after consultation with Senator Hitchcock and which bears the date of October 21, 1918, makes it clear there is no animus behind his charges.

At the beginning of this memorandum Dr. Evans assures the President and State Department of the "genuine gratitude shared by every loyal and patriotic Haitian native, both educated and uneducated alike, because Admiral Caperton landed his American marines at Port au Prince, thus rescuing them from the iron grasp and selfish greed of Germans, who for years have financially and murderously exploited them by aid of Berlin money and ammunition."

SUMMARY OF THE CHARGES.

Here briefly is a summary of the charges quoted verbatim from Dr. Evans's memorandum of October 21, 1918, as submitted to the State Department. In order to make his statement more impressive these charges were embodied in an affidavit sworn to by Dr. Evans before a notary in Washington, a copy of which is in the possession of the New York Herald correspondent:

"1. The forcing of a new constitution upon the people under military pressure of armed gendarmes (native police) of the American occupation on the 12th day of June last, so as to put in a clause in favor of the white man and foreigner, and accomplish ng this by methods which have been declared in the United States and all civilized countries to be both illegal and fraudulent. The intelligent Haitians connected with the Government of American occupation, who, in fear and trembling, were compelled to vote or be dismissed or imprisoned if they refused, very aptly described these humiliating processes as 'thrusting a dagger at the very heart of our own Negro Republic.'

"2. The closing on two separate occasions of the senate and chamber of deputies at Port au Prince; the turning out by military forces under the American occupation of the Haitian people's only representative bodies and the locking of the doors again them, just as the late Czar did with the Russian people's Duma, and while these officials were openly friendly to the United States and favorable to our American occupation, merely, it is said, because they protested and opposed as illegal and unconstitutional a change of what they felt to be the vital clause of their constitution—namely, the clause which withholds the ownership of land from the white foreigner and the speculator. Haitian judges who declared this to be illegal are said to have been either driven out of office or imprisoned or both, in spite of the fact that under the old Haitian constitution foreigners, white or colored, could hold real estate in Haiti by becoming citizens of Haiti.

"3. The taking through force and with much brutality by ignorant, immoral, and drunken gendarmes in the employment of the American occupation of innocent men and women, even native preachers and members of their churches, from their s mple small habitations or from their work and cruelly roping them tightly together and marching them as African slave gangs to prison. The writer and others were eyewitnesses on a Sunday morning in June last to the treatment of the wounds of prisoners who had undergone this experience by the occupation doctor—wounds which had gone unhealed for many weeks and months. The white American doctors said these cases were very frequent.

"4. The arresting of natives in large numbers in their homes and on the small farms and making them work on new roads under armed gendarmes for merely a gourde (20 American cents) a week, without furnishing them with food."

ALL PROTESTS ARE IGNORED.

Failing to move the State Department, Dr. Evans finally turned his attention to the Navy Department and to Secretary Daniels, the official in control of the United States marines who have been acting jointly with the State Department in the American occupation. He wrote to Mr. Daniels on March 27, 1920, calling attention to the fact that he had apprised the State Department in the fall of 1918 of what was going on in Haiti without anything being done about it. He said more than seventeen months before he had suggested to Mr. Adee the appo'ntment of an unbiased commission to inquire into the situation and was informed by letter that the department was "seriously considering the grave conditions set forth" in his memorandum. In the same letter he told Secretary Daniels that Mr. Adee had promised to let him know the result of his investigation, but had never done so.

The New York Herald correspondent quotes the following extracts from this remarkable letter from Dr. Evans to Mr. Daniels on March 27 last:

"Over 17 months have elapsed since the receipt of the above assurance from Mr. Adee, with not a word from our United States Government.

"In the meantime, however, conditions have been allowed to grow rapidly worse among these suffering, oppressed, enraged, and terror-stricken people, as evidenced even by the riots between the marines and gendarmes, not to say the more frequent and daring raids by the so-called bandits, or cacos, who are daily growing in strength and numbers and who are at the same time gaining the real sympathy of more and more of the moderate, intelligent, educated, and better class of Haitians, who have lost respect for our American occupation.

"With our influence, therefore, on the wane and our prestige and power all but gone and our motives and integrity as a democratic, civilized, not to say Christian, Nation suspected and impugned, it is no wonder that a staff correspondent of the New York World, who visited Haiti a little over a month ago, should state:

"'It should be remembered that there are many educated and substantial citizens of Port au Prince who are no more cacos than Henry Cabot Lodge is a feather duster, who none the less desire a complete change of administration and the ending of the present occupation.'"

Since the letter of March 27 Dr. Evans has had other correspondence with Secretary Daniels on the subject of Haiti, and up to the last few days he apparently continued to have faith that a proper inquiry would be made and the conditions improved. He sent Mr. Daniels, under date of October 5, 1920, an exhaustive résumé of the whole matter.

LEJEUNE'S INQUIRY BELITTLED.

In his letter Dr. Evans said:

"After a careful reading of the quotation from the official statement or report of Gen. John A. Lejeune's hurried visit to Haiti, after my letter to you of March, I find they fail even to touch the vital points. I candidly state that if I had not been anxious from the commencement, three years ago, to keep entirely out of party politics in missionary and Haitian matters, and if I had not, in spite of the strong criticism and the severe condemnation of the President and the Secretary of the Navy, still firmly believed that you both sincerely wished to right all the past and present wrongs of this administration in poor Haiti, I would certainly, after reading this morning's statement, have immediately given a startling reply to the Associated Press and at once directed my steps to Marion and the headquarters of the Republican Party, disappointedly convinced that further efforts on the part of Haiti and myself were utterly futile and a mere waste of time."

The New York Herald correspondent has before him a complete copy of the detailed and painstaking statement of Haitian conditions brought up to date and mailed to Secretary Daniels on October 5, 1920, by Dr. Evans. It contains upward of 6,000 words. It will be undoubtedly placed in evidence before Mr. Daniels's naval board, and if any attempt is made to suppress it there it will be brought to light before a congressional investigation committee.

In the meantime the New York Herald presents herewith some of the more startling passages from it:

" Is it not sad, indeed, to have to state that after nearly five years of American occupation in Haiti and under our Democratic administration people of the little black Republic sincerely and firmly believe that the real mission of the United States Government and the American people there is to reestablish slavery in their midst once more; to abrogate and annul the work of Toussaint l'Overture (who is their Washington representative) just exactly as in the nineteenth century Napoleon tried to be the tyrant of France and in recent years the German Kaiser attempted to be the ruler of the world? "

Dr. Evans then described how he hastened to write to President Wilson and to his personal friend, ex-President Roosevelt, from Haiti in June, 1918, explaining the terrible blow to American prestige in Haiti and throughout Latin America that was resulting from the actions of the American marines. It was as the result of this letter that ex-President Roosevelt stated in Washington in October of the same year in his criticism of Wilson's 14 points that " the Negro Republic of Haiti is nonexistent under the Democratic administration in spite of their treaty."

Dr. Evans here tells an almost unbelievable story, which he is prepared to substantiate in every particular, of how he was arrested on a trumped-up charge by a drunken white captain of gendarmes employed under direction of the Marine Corps, paraded through the streets, and openly insulted by this white officer. So far as he is able to learn, although he was refused a statement of the charges against him, the basis of the whole conspiracy was a determination to punish him for pleading in his capacity as white missionary for the natives and against certain methods and the immoral and drunken behavior of Americans connected with the occupation.

He was confined in a filthy native jail and forced to bathe naked with native male and female prisoners by orders of this white captain. He said the Negro judges and other officials whom he knew personally were eager to help him, but were prevented under threats of death. He was accused by this white officer with resisting arrest when he asked for a copy of the charges or an official summons or any other official authority for the action.

CHARGED WITH ATTEMPT TO ESCAPE.

When he asked permission to give to a native the key to a building which he used in his missionary work a charge of attempting to escape was placed against him by the same white officer. He was finally released by a Negro court and immediately taken by force by the same white captain to Cape Haitien, in the extreme north, by night in a small boat in the open Caribbean Sea for another trial.

Dr. Evans said he was released on the statement of the court that there were no charges against him.

The so-called voting by the people of Haiti on the constitution prepared in advance for them and rammed down their throats by the Wilson administration is ridiculed by Dr. Evans. He thus describes it to Secretary Daniels:

" The procession of voters (!) resembled funerals in their silence, solemnity, and mournful character as these people passed along like sheep into courts of justice (?), which were turned that day all through the country into Haitian slaughterhouses. Each was especially guarded by the gendarmerie. For the sake of giving a little color to the affair and thus perfecting the farce a native commissaire, or dummy officer, sat in the chair by the side of the white officer.

" When entering the court a small white paper stamped with the words ' Police administration ' and bearing date, June 11, 1918, and also the French word ' oui ' (yes) was placed in the trembling hand of the native, who then was motioned—no word being spoken or question being asked—to the box in front of the white American officer in supreme charge, with a native dummy assistant at his side. A bundle of pink papers bearing the French word 'non' (no) curiously and significantly remained tied together on the table. Thus terrorized and helpless to resist, these people sorrowfully and slavishly submitted, as most of them were brought in from small villages guarded and closely watched."

FRESH REVELATIONS ON HAITI PROMISED.

G. O. P. WILL FORESTALL MOVES TO DELAY EXPOSURES UNTIL AFTER ELECTION—REBELLION AGGRAVATED—AMERICAN-MADE CONSTITUTION FORCED DOWN THROATS AT POINT OF BAYONET.

[Special dispatch to the New York Herald.]

NEW YORK HERALD BUREAU,
Washington, D. C., October 25.

Desperate efforts of high officials of the Wilson administration to smother every move to expose true conditions in Haiti under the American occupation to-day seem doomed to failure. Even their immediate efforts to postpone until after election day the storm which is sure to follow an unbiased investigation are likely to come to naught.

The naval board of inquiry headed by Rear Admiral Mayo, which was appointed hurriedly by Secretary Daniels, after Senator Harding first directed the attention of the country to results of the American occupation of Haiti, is showing a surprising want of alacrity in proceeding with the investigation—which may or may not be particularly significant, in view of the fact that election day is only a week off.

But Republican leaders have evidence in their possession which widens the scope of the inquiry far beyond the narrow limits to which Secretary Daniels may desire to hold it. The special province of the Naval Board, by the terms of the Daniels order creating it, is an investigation of the killing by the United States marines of 3,250 natives during the last two years, already admitted by the high officials of the Marine Corps. Terrible as this is in itself, it appears to be only an incident in the forthcoming exposure of the manner in which the Wilson administration has destroyed the independence of this nation while professing to be its best friend and the protector of small and oppressed nations everywhere.

The Republican national committee to-day employed a lawyer who will assist the Rev Dr. L. Ton Evans, who was shown in the New York Herald's dispatches yesterday to have tried for nearly two years to induce the Government to make an inquiry by an unbiased nonmilitary board of these deplorable conditions now brought to light. It is the purpose of Dr. Evans and the Republican committee to prevent any further suppression of the facts by Secretary Daniels or any other board which the present administration may create in its efforts to meet the charges of Senator Harding.

RECORD SHOWS RULE OF FORCE.

It became evident to-day that the acts of the Wilson administration in Haiti, which have turned the original cordiality of the natives toward the Americans into hatred or fear, are in a large measure, if not wholly, responsible for a condition of affairs which may permit the Navy Department after five years of ineffectual "pacification" to offer some semblance of justification for the killing of the natives in such large numbers.

In other words, it now comes to light that the "indiscriminate killing" of natives, now admitted by high officials of the Wilson administration, was merely incidental to and the inevitable result of the following acts of the American forces in Haiti during the occupation:

1. The forcing down the throats of the unwilling natives of a constitution prepared in advance in this country by the Wilson administration and taken to the island Republic.

2. The almost unbelievable methods adopted by the marine officers in charge there to make it appear that the natives had by their own ballots indorsed this American-prepared constitution, which the natives did not want, because it

specifically killed the clause in their own constitution against foreign specu-lators purchasing lands from the ignorant natives.

3. The actual voting on the new constitution with American officers sitting at each ballot box with the bundles on the table in front of them. one bundle containing ballots marked " Yes " and the other containing ballots marked " No." The officials handed only ballots marked " Yes " to the ignorant natives, the bundles marked " No " remaining unopened on the table.

4. The cruel and inhuman treatment of natives in prisons presided over by white officers.

5. The imprisonment of Dr. L. Ton Evans, a white American missionary, who had preached to the natives for 25 years, by white officers, on trumped-up charges. Dr. Evans had merely sought to protest in an orderly fashion against the action of other white American officers in command of gendarmes, because these officers were setting a bad example to the natives, by openly drunken and immoral habits, in various towns and villages throughout the island.

6. The actual expulsion by the American marines of the Senate and House of Deputies because they objected to the " rape " of their Government and con stitution by the Wilson administration, which professed to represent the most civilized country on the globe, headed by the author of the doctrine of " self-determination," and the locking of the doors of the House of Parliament on two occasions by American officers when the native senators and representatives sought to return and exercise their constitutional functions.

CONSTITUTION WRITTEN IN UNITED STATES.

In the article published in the New York Herald this morning a comparatively brief portion of the suppressed evidence which Dr. Evans in the last two years has laid before the State and Navy Departments was printed.

It now seems that the so-called constitution that the Wilson admin'stration foisted on the terrorized natives in a manner by which they sought to make it appear that the Haitians wanted it—when the native efforts at that time, as well as now, showed that they did not want it—was actually written in Washington, probably by Franklin D. Roosevelt, then Assistant Secretary of the Navy and now vice-presidential candidate for the Democratic Party.

Critics of these inhuman and un-American methods of the Wilson adminis-tration in Haiti are prepared to produce eyewitnesses to this destruction of Haitian independence. They have not the slightest hesitation in issuing through the New York Herald a challenge to Franklin D. Roosevelt, who was second in authority of the Navy Department at the time these political crimes were committed, to deny that this constitution was prepared in Washington and that there was every intention on the part of the Navy Department that the natives of Haiti must be " induced " to adopt it. In fact, there is evidence in the possession of the Republican national committee to show that Mr. Roosevelt has openly boasted that he wrote it himself.

THE HAITIAN KILLINGS.

SENATOR M'CORMICK SAYS THERE WILL BE A REAL INVESTIGATION.

To the New York Herald:

I have just seen in your issue of Monday the Washington dispatch upon Haiti. It will not meet the needs of justice or satisfy the American people to have no other inquiry than that now being conducted by a board of officers appointed by the Secretary of the Navy and subject to his orders and to those of the President, who, with the Secretary, of course, is ultimately responsible for whatever may have been done in Haiti.

A committee of Congress must review all the charges made and all the evi-dence to be submitted to the board of inquiry, as it must hear any further charges and any new evidence which may be adduced after it shall be possible to provide for the appointment of the congressional committee.

MEDILL McCORMICK.

CLEVELAND, OHIO, *October 26.*

[Issued from advance copy to President-elect, Warren G. Harding, national Republican publicity committee, Chairman Henry Cabot Lodge, of Senate Foreign Relations, as well as Members of the United States Congress.]

THE PROBING OF THE HAITI SCANDAL AND AN EARNEST PLEA FOR A NONPARTISAN INVESTIGATION BY THE NEWLY APPOINTED NAVY COURT OF THE PRESENT ADMINISTRATION.

The Rev. L. Ton Evans is of the opinion that the official number given out by Gen. Barnett as shot by American marines and their gendarmes in the open does not cover more than about one-half actually killed by the American occupation through unjustifiable violence, brutality, and murder under the corvee slave labor (as applied by American occupation) and taken out from their prison cells and shot in the dead silence of the night at Port au Prince, St. Marc, Cape Haitien, and all over the Republic, as natives, if given a chance and with proper United States Government protection, are only too eager to testify.

CENTRAL UNION MISSION,
Washington, D. C., October 30, 1920.

Maj. JESSE DYER, U. S. M. C.,
  Judge Advocate Court of Inquiry
    Investigating American Occupation in Haiti,
      Navy Department, Washington, D. C.

DEAR SIR: I am astonished and concerned to learn from an article in the Washington Post of yesterday, the 29th instant, of a statement attributed to you—that you contemplated calling me as a witness before the court of inquiry, but that I had no personal knowledge of the incidents referred to, but had agreed to furnish a list of persons in Haiti who had supplied me with information, and that you had said these persons would be examined.

The statement that I have no personal knowledge of unjustifiable acts of oppression or of violence perpetrated against citizens of Haiti or unjustifiable damage or destruction to their property by marines is, of course, wholly untrue.

I assume you readily recall that in the several interviews I have hitherto had with you I explicitly stated I was prepared to testify from personal knowledge to a number of unjustifiable acts of oppression, violence, and assaults to citizens of Haiti, as well as damage and destruction to their property by gendarmes under the direct command of United States marines during the American occupation.

I explained that inasmuch as a number of necessary native witnesses, both white and colored, to corroborate my testimony were known in some instances to me by their Christian names and others only in the localities in which they lived, that my testimony should be taken in Haiti, where these crimes and atrocities occurred.

In order that there may be no possible ground of misunderstanding now, I offer, if called as a witness to testify in Haiti, to establish from my own personal knowledge the following specific acts:

1. That in Jacmel during the last week of June and the first week of July, 1918, while in my capacity of a Baptist missionary and superintendent inspecting missions and schools in that section, I saw a number of natives whose arms had been injured and the flesh reduced to jelly as the result of having been roped together and marched as slaves to prisons and for work on the outlying roads. I saw these natives being attended by a white doctor of the occupation forces, name unknown, but who I can identify if still in the service, who stated to me that he was constantly called upon to render treatment of this kind to these poor, abused natives, and that their condition was an outrage and a shame.

2. That I found during my stay at Jacmel that one-half (or so) of the male members of our Baptist Church were absent from holy communion and in hiding throughout the mountain districts in fear and terror of the cruelties of the gendarmes, who arrested and imprisoned natives, subjecting them to the grossest cruelty. I am prepared to produce as witnesses before the court the pastor of the church in that district and two or more of the officers of that church.

3. At Gros Morne, District of Leogane, on the last Sunday of June, 1918, while on my way to hold service at the Baptist mission in company with the local native pastor, I saw men and women stopped by gendarmes and turned back from attending their place of divine worship. At this time I further saw two bands of some 8 or 10 natives roped tightly together and marched like slave gangs, among whom I recognized members of our mission and our native preachers.

I inquired from the corporal in charge what crime these men had committed, and he answered nothing, but that he was determined to rope them together and take them away. I later appealed to the white lieutenant of the United States marines, over the gendarmes for that section, and demanded that an inquiry be made, the natives be at once released, and the black corporal dismissed. The lieutenant promised to make the investigation, but never did so. I will produce if given an opportunity, the pastor of this m ssion, with several officers of the church, to corroborate this statement.

4. During my imprisonment at St. Marc prison, in the Artibonite section, between December 28, 1918, and January 9, 1919, I saw the grossest brutality and cruelty practiced upon native prisoners and women.

I saw them repeatedly set upon and beaten in the jail yard and cells by gendarmes, whose captain and lieutenant were members of the Marine Corps. I have seen a number of them beaten into insensibility, felled like logs to the hard floor; others lying dead in the jail yard, occupied by prisoners, and where the bodies remained two and three days, naked and covered with flies and creeping vermin. I frequently heard in my own cell, night after night, the cries and groans of native prisoners who were constantly beaten and atrociously abused.

5. During my imprisonment I also saw each morning probably 100, more or less, ill treated and compelled, under armed gendarmes, to march to their work several miles away, often without food other than a little coffee, there to labor under supposed corvee system.

These men would be returned in the afternoon, searched and roughly treated, and made to wait hours in some cases before the first bite of food be furnished them. I have seen on many occasions as the result of this a number of these prisoners fall to the ground from sheer weakness and exhaustion. If given the opportunity, I will produce a number of native prisoners (if still alive) to corroborate these statements.

6. On January 9, 1919, the day I was discharged from prison and while waiting to be released, at stern command of negro high court, I saw a native carried into the cell in a condition of insensibility, and whose back had been beaten into a jelly. He was attended by a native assistant doctor of the American occupation, who stated that this man had been beaten by the white captain during one of his drunken rages. If given an opportunity, I will produce this native doctor (if not shot) and several native witnesses who saw the man in the condition described.

7. That if afforded an opportunity, I will testify also to indignities and brutal treatment accorded me during my imprisonment—and by this captain of the United States marines. I would have starved to death but for the fragments of food smuggled into my cell by prisoners and natives on the outside.

8. While I was at St. Marc, about March, 1919, an old native was either murdered or burned to death, with hut destroyed, in Mme. Orius's habitation. Three natives alleged to be implicated in the crime were arrested and imprisoned. Several nights later these three men were taken out of prison in the night, being first compelled to dig their graves, then were shot by the gendarmes in the presence of their white captain, and their dead bodies fell into the holes they themselves had made. I did not witness the murders myself, as they took place in the dead of night, and everybody in a state of fear and tremble, but I was staying at the home of Mme. Orius and children and saw the excitement and horror produced among the family and in town, and heard details and saw the graves.

9. On or about the second Sunday of April, 1919, and while on my way home from church at noon, I heard commotion and cries in St. Marc streets that the gendarmes (of the United States marines) had shot two men. Immediately returning toward the church, I saw a dead man, naked, carried along through the public streets on a sack by four natives, with an armed gendarme riding by their side. The body was rolling from side to side, and was the most gruesome sight I ever witnessed. The purpose of thus carrying this uncovered dead body was to further terrify the people, who were already hiding in fear and dread of their lives.

10. That at St. Raphael, about April, 1918, while as superintendent on a visit among our Baptist churches of North Haiti, I found the white lieutenant of gendarmes in charge of American occupation at that point, a United States marine in a shocking, drunken condition, and was told many stories by the Christian natives and others throughout the village of his intemperate and scandalous conduct. I am prepared to give name of the lieutenant, and if

given an opportunity will produce witnesses, both white and native, to corroborate my statements.

11. In January of 1919, at Cape Haitien (in extreme north of Republic) I personally witnessed a number of marines in broad daylight engaged in open orgies with low colored women in the streets. I saw them enter huts for immoral purposes. Later, after services held in the churches of the cape, several of the members of the Marine Corps have confessed again and again concerning the terrible amount of drinking going on, and awful temptations by way of immorality they us American boys had to contend with in Haiti.

12. That during the American occupation I have witnessed at Port au Prince and other points in the Republic drunkenness and dissipation on the part of our United States Marines. If given an opportunity I will corroborate this statement with witnesses, both white and colored.

In this connection I suggest that the court summon Dr. Samuel Inman, executive secretary of the missionary cooperative committee of Latin America, at New York. Dr. Inman visited Haiti last year in behalf of both his own committee as well as the Union Home Missions' Council of North America (New York), at my own invitation, and for the express purpose of a careful survey with a view of the establishment of religious and educational work in the black republic. He has therefore personal knowledge of the very low moral standard of many of our marines, and as stated in more detail in his able and informing article on the present situation in Haiti in this month's number of the Journal of International Relations, published in New York.

I am returning to-night to my home at Wyoming, Pa., where a telegram or letter will reach me, and shall hold myself in readiness to respond to your summons to appear in Haiti and testify before the court to the foregoing facts.

I assume, of course, that due arrangements for my transportation to Haiti and return will be arranged by you, and that upon arrival there full authority and protection will be given me so as to locate and produce the witnesses to corroborate my testimony.

Awaiting your further advices,

Yours, very truly,

L. Ton Evans.

————

Wyoming, Pa., *November 2, 1920.*

Hon. Josephus Daniels,
Secretary of the Navy, Washington, D. C.

Dear Secretary Daniels: An investigation into Haiti affairs such as you desire, so that the people of the United States may know as well as yourself as Secretary of the Navy the whole truth concerning the Haitian activities of the Marine Corps—that is, everything, the good and bad brought out, the responsibility fixed, and the whole thing cleaned up once for all—is utterly impossible by the present Navy court you have just appointed, though headed by such an able and experienced officer as Admiral Mayo, unless a careful, searching, as well as judicial inquiry is made by the said court into the following fundamental and direct causes of the present situation in Haiti, resulting in unjustifiable acts of oppression, violence, assaults, and killing of Haitian citizens:

1. The closing of senate and chambers (parliament) of the people under the armed forces of the American marine occupation.

2. The change, or what is known as the rape, of the Haiti constitution by the American occupation, and methods and force used by the United States Marines to compel the natives to adopt the new constitution, which gives away their land to foreigners and American corporations.

3. Adoption and working of the so-called corvee slave labor by American marines, and through their gendarmes, whereby, in spite of treaty, citizens of Haiti were deprived of their rights, robbed of their liberties, oppressed, assaulted and murdered, with the inevitable result that the Negroes of Haiti generally were inflamed, fierce anger engendered, and bitter hatred against the occupation of the United States Government, finding expression, now that their parliament and constitution are gone, in open fighting and defiant rebellion against what they firmly believe to be the determined and treacherous effort of the American people, through the United States occupation in Haiti, to bring them all back to slavery, with all its horrors.

4. As other material and direct factors in the absolute failure after five years of the American Government, through its marine occupation, to pacify

Haiti, establish peace and good will, not to say secure the natives' confidence and cooperation, anticipated by the treaty between America and Haiti in the economical, industrial, and social development of the black republic and its people, the present Navy court should have the right and authority to make a thorough and searching investigation into the nature and extent of the alliance between marine officers of the United States, at Washington as well as in Haiti, with American corporations which followed the " occupation " to the black republic, and the European special delegate of the Pope (a foreign potentate) sent to Haiti during the present American occupation, with the European archbishop, bishops, priests, freres, and nuns, etc., of the Roman Catholic Church in Haiti and all of whom are paid their salaries like officers and members of the American marines and the native gendarmes from the United States Government, money, loans, etc., to the little bankrupt black republic, and directly through the hands of the United States financial adviser.

5. In such thorough and searching investigation the Navy court should have the right and authority to determine what influence and power such alliance with corporations and close relation of the Catholic Church with the Haiti so-called government and the American occupation of the United States Government, as now exists in the Republic of Haiti, has been responsible for the appointments of American marine officers to and removals from Haiti under the present occupation; for the demoralization of the United States marines from their usual high standard of military discipline and moral efficiency; and for the deflection also of the administration at Washington, or officers of the Navy Department, as well as the American occupation on the island, from the high purpose of the United States Government's special mission in Haiti, according to the terms of the sacred treaty, to apparently serve financial interests and sectarian ends.

In requesting that you should reemphasize the importance of making the present investigation thorough and searching, and to authorize the Navy court to include the foregoing fundamental causes of the present sad situation of Haiti affairs, I hereby quote from the statement and the earnest plea of my personal friend, Dr. Francois Delancour (Port au Prince) in Current History for the month of December, 1919, :

"All intelligent Haitians know that American statesmen and leaders of opinion are not aware of what is happening in Haiti. The American Nation is too great and too good to tolerate such infractions of political morality. Haiti, which in July, 1918, entered the confraternity of the allied nations by declaring war on Germany, is with the approval of the American officials (occupation) in a state of anarchy, anarchy of legislation, anarchy of administration, with no parliament (senate and chamber) to discuss the living interests of the people, with no freedom of thought, of speech, of action. Deprived of justice and legality, also undermined by disorganization of labor and by pauperism, that the Haitians are driven out to Cuba to look for work in large numbers, or remain to starve."

The inclosed letter to Judge Advocate Dyer, of the Navy court you have just appointed to investigate affairs in Haiti, will show that as the person who two years ago prepared by way of a memorandum and sworn affidavit and made definite charges against the American occupation, etc. I have offered if called as a witness to personaly testify in Haiti, and so as to establish from my own personal knowledge such specific acts as related therein through him to the court.

As I have had no reply from Maj. Dyer, I hasten to repeat my offer to you as Secretary of the United States Navy, responsible for the creation of this board and, of course, to the Government and American people for affairs in Haiti, namely, to hold myself in readiness to respond to your summons and the above Navy court to appear in Haiti and testify to the facts as stated in the letter to Maj. Dyer, judge advocate of said Navy court.

As assumed in that letter, you will see to arrangements for my transportation, authority, and protection given both to myself and witnesses in Haiti, and any necessary expense the witnesses may have to incur for attending the court in various sections of the Republic, so as to corroborate my testimony.

Very sincerely, yours,

L. TON EVANS.

THE SECRETARY OF THE NAVY,
Washington, November 4, 1920.

MY DEAR MR. EVANS: I have your recent letter concerning Haiti. I thank you very much for it, and the same has been given to the court investigating Haiti matters.

Sincerely, yours,

JOSEPHUS DANIELS.

———

DOCTEUR HECTOR PAULTRE,
St. Marc, Haiti, 25 novembre, 1918.

MR. L. TON EVANS, *Kingston, Pa.*

MON BON PASTEUR: Votre lettre du 25 octobre m'est bien parvenue.

Le frere Hippolyte n'a pu venipartage le Loupe du Lciycier avec nous scion l'entente qu'il a eu avec vous. Il m' a écrit le 5 septembre pour m'annoncer qu il etait couffrant.

Nous avons depuis le mois passé une école primaire de jeunes filles avec le personnel suivants. Directrice: Mme. Hector Poultre; professeurs: Mme. Hector Paultre, Cécile Paultre et Mathilde Gresseare; surveillante: Mme. David Guillot. Nous avons maintenant 30 étéves mais nous espérons en avoir beaucoup plus a l'aveni. Nous faisons tous nos efforts pour ouvri sans trop tarde une école primaire de govçons.

Pour la muison que vous habitiez, j'oi eu de nombreuses difficultés avec Mr. Murat Monfils qui a même cu recours au Yeige de Paix. Aussi j'ai été obligé de prenotre la liberté de la remettre le 20 septembre en transportant vos effets chez ma mere et ecux de Mr. Cambell chez moi. Le garde done à vos ordret votre bon de $45. Des votre arrivé eci je voles cherchcrai une maison.

Les freres de da Gonave vout bien y'ai été une seconde fois à la Grande Laline ou j'ai eu l'avantage de faire une petite prédiction.

Cous ici vous remercient de vos bonnes salutations et implorent pour vous et les votres les secours du Crés Haut.

Votre brebis fidéla.

HECTOR PAULTRE.

———

ST. RAPHAEL, *June 8, 1911.*

Rev. L. TON EVANS,
Field Secretary of Haiti Baptist Mission.

DEAR BROTHER TON EVANS: I am profoundly glad that you have brought to the attention of the pastor, deacons, and church of St. Raphael last Sunday the matter of the entire consecration to Christian work of our Sister Christine Jean Francais, and that under God, in addition to what you have already done for us, can see your way to take her with you to the United States and to place her in the same mission college as Alice Pierre, our Haitian daughter, whom you took just three years ago from our midst, and to study so as to serve the same Master. As I have employed Christine some years as my assistant professor in our small Government school for girls here, and, as you know, I can bear testimony to her deep interest and faithfulness in her work and her especial qualifications as a teacher, even when she was staunch, if not bigoted, Romanist. However, now since her conversation to the Protestant faith and her public baptism by you in Banaha River in October of 1910 her active service in our church and Sunday school, as well as the part she takes in our open-air gospel work, her deep sincerity, quiet, steady, consistent, and loyal Christian life, in spite of persistent persecution of the priest and even or her own mother. I can further add to the above testimony that in my opinion Christine is specially called of God to work in Haiti, and with the training such as you propose to give her at the national Negro Baptist college for girls in the United States she will prove herself, if life and health are given her, a most efficient and devoted Christian when among her own people and sex in this morally and spiritually neglected and destitute country.

May God richly bless you, my beloved, for your splendid efforts in behalf of my countrymen.

Your sister in Christ,

ELIZA MENARD.

(Wife of Pastor M. Menard, directress of Government school for children at St. Raphael; age 80 years.)

HAITI BAPTIST MISSION—APPALLING NEED OF 3,000,000 PERISHING SOULS FOR THE GOSPEL.

A MISSIONARY PIONEER AND HIS EFFORTS COMMENDED TO CHRISTIANS OF BRITAIN AND AMERICA BY ONE OF JAMAICA'S BEST-KNOWN PASTOR EVANGELISTS AND SCHOLARS—YEARS OF MISSIONARY ZEAL AND DEVOTION UNDIMMED AND UNDIMINISHED—ENCOURAGED TO PROCEED "ISAIAH-LIKE ALONE TO A WORK GOD HAS CALLED HIM."

"Go ye into all the world and preach the gospel," etc.—Christ.

Letter from Rev. George E. Henderson, M. A., graduate at Madison University, New York, that years ago conferred the degree of doctor of divinity on him. Rev. G. E. Henderson is pastor of churches with a membership of 1,800, has been a member of the Jamaica Baptist missionary executive for 34 years, and was president of the Jamaica Baptist Union and chairman of missionary board when Rev. L. Ton Evans was under that society as its chief missionary in Haiti 18 years ago and previous to his resignation through his late wife's sickness. Mr. Henderson, who is considered a profound Bible student, prominent teacher of the higher spiritual life, and leader in the island's missionary activities, is well known in the United States among the following Baptist leaders, many of whom also are his old college mates: President W. H. P. Faunce (Brown's, R. I.), President G. E. Horr (Newton, Mass.), Dr. Henry L. Morehouse (A. B. H. M. S.), Dr. Robert S. MacArthur, Dr. Edward Judson, Dr. Bitting, Dr. W. Newton Clark (Rochester), Dr. Leighton Williams, Dr. J. A. Francies (Boston), Dr. Thomas S. Barbour (A. B. F. M. S.), Dr. Charles Watson, Dr. Seymour (Philadelphia), Dr. W. M. Lawrence, Dr. John S. Love, Hon. Mornay Williams (New York), and others.

THE CHAPEL,
Browns Town, P. O., Jamaica, West Indies, August 12, 1910.

Rev. L. TON EVANS.

MY DEAR BRO. TON EVANS: Having a keen interest in your desire to establish the gospel in the neighboring island of Haiti, and with the keen knowledge of your plans, your efforts, and discouragements in this great enterprise, and also with an intimate personal acquaintance with yourself for many years, I have thought that a letter from me may be of some use in helping you to overcome the difficulties that are likely to oppose you in the mission to which I believe God has called you for the extension of his Kingdom in a land hitherto almost neglected.

In saying this I know of the efforts put forth by the Wesleyan friends for many years, and also by the Baptists of England, and after of Jamaica, as I have taken my part in all that our society has done in Haiti. * * *

My heart goes out toward you, as I found that zeal and devotion which burned in your heart 18 years ago, when you were the missionary of the Jamaica Baptists to Haiti, is still undemarred and undiminished, but has constantly manifested itself through the intervening years (though much occupied with your own churches in South Wales, and after in Edwardsville, Pa.) in efforts to awaken others, both individuals and societies, to take up the evangelization of Haiti.

He who fed the fires through all these years will, I believe, still keep them alive until your efforts meet that success which we all desire, and Haiti at last, like her sister islands of Jamaica, Porto Rico, and Cuba, is not only opened to the gospel, but dotted over with churches from which God's message of salvation to all mankind is proclaimed to "every creature."

I could wish that your efforts to awaken some of the great societies of our Baptist denomination in Great Britain or the United States of America had been more successful, and trust that this will ultimately be brought about.

I say this as it is only natural that left to work alone as a sort of free lance (missionary at large) you are likely to be misunderstood and misinterpreted even by (certain) brethren. * * *

On this account I trust before long you will succeed in securing the cooperation of some responsible Baptist society to shoulder the (whole) work and carry it on to the success that awaits those who are ready to respond to our Lord's "Whom shall I send, etc?" This I know is your earnest desire also, and until it is brought about I can only encourage you to go on Isaiah-like alone in the work to which God has called you, and He will lead.

Some misunderstandings have already arisen and some criticisms made, and I have had the advantage of hearing these (and refuting them) from the Rev.

C. E. Wilson, etc., * * * who have misunderstood some of your actions. The publication of your accounts (1) that has recently been made, which is signed by auditors, will satisfy some and remove their strongest objection, and I am hoping a letter from myself to Mr. Wilson (London,) will satisfactorily explain some other points he entirely misunderstood, (2) and trust will tend to remove the unfavorable impression he had formed as to your generalship.

I am grateful that your visit to Jamaica (1908 and 1909) has tended to revive the efforts of our Jamaica Missionary Society in Haiti, our first foreign field, and resulted (on this account) already in our taking over the support of Brother L'Herisson (3), of Jacmel, etc. * * *

Let me assure you of my own deep interest in your work and my desire to cooperate with you to the extent of my ability, and allow me also to say that with an intimate knowledge of almost every step you have taken in this great work, I commend you to the confidence of Christian brethren who may not yet know you as well as I do.

God has directed you so far, and He will guide you still. I am not unknown to a good many of our brethren in the States, having been graduated from Madison University, now Colgate, in 1875, and if this letter can be of any service to you, please use it in whatever way you wish, and believe me always,

Your brother and comrade in the gospel,

GEO. E. HENDERSON.

" My hand is still shaky, but I hope you will be able to decipher what I have written."—G. E. H.

Bro. Henderson, who was resting in the country after a very severe illness when he wrote above, has since greatly improved.

In another letter from the Rev. George Henderson he says:

" I am so glad to see that your spirit is equal to the changed attitude of the B. M. S. (England). Mr. Wilson broached the matter when he and Mr. Penny stayed with us, so I was not surprised when I saw the decision in the Herald, etc. I don't think there is any ultimate loss in dissolving an arrangement that could only be temporary and that was likely to bring friction as long as it lasted.

"There is no doubt that God, who opened up India by Carey and China by Hudson Taylor, when the societies threw them over, is also equal to open Haiti as well by whomsoever He finds ready to be His instrument. ' It is nothing to Him to work by many or by few,' and when He works by few and by feeble instruments the glory is all the more conspicuously His."

(1) Three reports in all have been issued, viz, 1,000 in 1908, 1,500 in 1909, and 8,000 (2,000 English, 6,000 Welsh) in 1910, which were sent at the time to all contributing churches and friends in Wales, America, and Jamaica, at a cost of over £50 ($250) out of our scanty funds, not to mention the labor entailed on the field secretary in addition to his work as organizer, deputation, and missionary.

(2) So deeply did Mr. Henderson feel the injustice and injury inflicted upon the mission and missioner among contributing churches in Wales, Jamaica, as well as friends of Haiti, that he wrote a strong letter not only to Rev. C. E. Wilson himself, but to T. S. Penny, Esq., chairman of West Indian English Baptist missionary committee, and Rev. Leonard Tucker, M. A., of the B. M. Society, now one of the tutors at Calabar Baptist College, in Jamaica, complaining of his conduct toward a brother engaged in the same kind of mission work, only as yet without wealthy religious organization at his back.

(3) For 14 years Rev. L. Ton Evans has urged the Jamaica Baptist Missionary Society to support this brother, ordained by him in 1894, but through the extreme poverty of the churches, etc., they have not been able to do this until now and through the personal visits referred to, and the influence of Rev. George E. Henderson.

There are already two consecrated and certificated teachers from Edwardsville (Pa.) First Welsh Baptist Church studying at the Women's Missionary Training College, Chicago, preparing for Haiti, and two more, Miss Bailey and Miss Alice Henderson (latter from Browns Town, Jamaica, West Indies), who have recently graduated and taken their B. A. degree in the States, seeking to enter the same Chicago Baptist missionary school, with the intention of laboring in the Black Republic. This is in addition to Miss Alice Pierre Alexis, the native young sister taken by the field secretary to the United States, etc., and who is now studying for missionary work in her own island, at the National Missionary Training School for Girls, Lincoln Heights, Washington, D. C., under the able principalship of Miss Nannie Burroughs.

New Haitian Railroad—Ratification by Senate and President.

News has just been received in Kingston, Jamaica, and New York that the important contract between McDonald & Co., and the Haitian Government recently passed by the chamber of deputies has now been adopted by the senate and signed by President Simon. This carries with it a Government guaranty of an interest in the banana trade and other fruit interest and the central sugar factories. It will be proceeded with as soon as possible, and opens up large areas of undeveloped, rich land and create new industries. It is said that a large and bitter fight has been waged for this valuable concession sought by French, and especially German, firms, opposed to American and Protestant influence. The sum and substance of this is that the present is the most important epoch in the history of Haiti, and hence a special call to the great Baptist body to strongly establish themselves in the social, moral, and sp.ritual interest of these long-neglected people.

L. Ton Evans.

September 15, 1910.

An Island Sadly Neglected of Great and Unique Baptist Opportunity.

BRIGHT PROSPECTS OF A WELL-SUSTAINED AND ORGANIZED CHRISTIAN ENTERPRISE—PERSONAL TESTIMONY AND HEARTY RECOMMENDATION OF MISSIONARIES AND THE MISSION BY A POPULAR AND EMINENT COLORED MINISTER WHO HAS VISITED THE BLACK REPUBLIC ON SEVERAL OCCASIONS.

"And how shall they believe in Him of whom they have not heard?"—Paul.
"Your visits and touching appeals have awakened renewed interest in Jamaica. But what is one missionary among millions?"
Letter from Rev. Hon. and Rev. W. M. Webb, a member of the Jamaica Legislature, founder and managing director of Westwood College for Girls in the island, pastor of churches with a membership of nearly 1,000, ex-President of Jamaica Baptist Union, member of missionary board for 45 years, twice special deputation of the denomination to the island of Haiti, and oldest native (colored) Baptist minister in Jamaica, West Indies:

Woodlands, Stewart Town Post Office,
Jamaica, September 6, 1910.

Rev. L. Ton Evans.

Dear Brother Evans: Having visited the island on separate occasions, and twice as a deputation from the Jamaica Baptist Missionary Society, to inquire into the spiritual condition of the people and report on difficulties, needs, and status of the mission work there (many years ago) you will know how deeply interested I am in Haiti and the social, moral, and religious welfare of the inhabitants. I deeply deplore that the efforts of the B. M. S. of London, and subsequently those of the Jamaica Baptist Missionary Society—were spasmodic, inefficient, and short lived—and that such a large island, with over 3,000,000 people who are trying to find out the true system of Government and have hitherto failed for lack of the evangel among them, should be so entirely left until now in the cruel bondage of Romanism, witchcraft, etc.

I am, dear brother, greatly interested, therefore, to learn of your self-sacrificing efforts to give these people the pure gospel, and from my own personal knowledge of such natives (Christians) as Dutreville Lamour, Hector, Hypolite, Jaques, Osiris, and Sisters St. Aude, Lamour, Louise Holder, and others I met there I am sure that any well-sustained efforts put forth in the evangelization of this island and its interesting people and under God's blessing must bring abundant success.

As one of the oldest members of the Jamaica Baptist missionary committee I remember well how deep was the regret felt by us when, through your late dear wife's illness, we were compelled to accept your resignation of your post, which you had so loyally and enthusiastically filled some 18 years ago as missionary of our society.

During the intervening years, however (though actively engaged in pastoral work in Wales and America), I am thankful to learn you have had Haiti in your heart and kept in personal touch with the natives and given many proofs of your deep sympathy with the evangelization of that dark land.

Your visits also and touching personal appeals have awakened renewed interest among us in Jamaica, and only at our last annual union meetings our missionary society has resumed in a small way (after giving up entirely for a number of years and through sheer poverty, etc.) its work in Haiti by the engagement of our (native) Brother L'Herisson, etc. We recognize this as the direct result of your labors and answer from God to your faith and prayer. But, then, what is one brother (receiving a salary and devoting the whole of his time and energy), among the perishing priest-ridden and superstitious millions of that island? What everyone who loves the kingdom of God and prays the Master's first petition, "Thy kingdom come," desires to see for Haiti is a well-organized Christian mission founded upon a strong, sympathetic, and lasting basis.

This requires an organizer with funds behind him to employ best methods and best qualified native and sympathetic foreign agents (white missionaries) for this purpose until the people now waiting and longing get a chance to hear the gospel.

From my own personal knowledge of the Haitian (character) I am satisfied that as soon as they have received the gospel * * * they will not only prove a stable, happy, and prosperous people, but will largely and rapidly become self-supporting and assist in giving the (same) gospel to other parts of the heathen world.

To this end I therefore much regret that your request made to the Baptist Missionary Society (England) for a grant of £300 ($1,500) a year for five years (until a constituency had been created or the cooperation of a strong Baptist society secured) and to be made good from the collections of Welsh churches (already passed resolutions to do this) interested in the Black Republic through your visits and advocacy of the special and imperative needs of the island was not responded to.

To secure this amount and much more which is urgently needed I must heartily commend you and your efforts to all who know the grace of God in their own salvation and Protestant churches able and willing to help by contributions, sympathy, and prayer.

My own personal contact with you on several occasions, your residence with me for short periods at my home, your pulpit ministrations that I and my people have greatly enjoyed, as well as your deep sympathetic spirit with the Negro race and large hopes for their future material, social, and spiritual progress, have convinced me long ago of the high motive and good faith of your endeavor in the evangelization of the Black Republic.

I am sure, dear brother, that knowing Him and His power, in Whom you believe, as I know you do, no misunderstanding of your aim by some and opposition to your efforts by others will discourage you in what you conceive under the inspiration of the Holy Spirit to be a direct call from God.

You will no doubt find in our northern and southern Baptist brethren in the States large-hearted and most generous sympathetic helpers, who will not fail you in your times of need, but will sustain you by their organized gifts, counsel, and prayers in your high and noble aim to give poor Haiti the gospel.

As a Christian brother and missionary worker I highly esteem you and only really wish I were a younger man, so as to be able to show in a more practical way my real sympathy, etc.

May our gracious Master raise up for you generous helpers among Christian leaders in Great Britain and America.

I am, very dear Brother Evans.

Yours in Christ,

W. M. WEBB.

NOTE.—Words in parentheses are not a part of original letters, but inserted for elucidation of meaning.

INDORSED BY NEW YORK MINISTERS.

Report submitted and accepted by New York Baptist Ministers' Conference Monday, June 27, 1910. (See Examiner.) Revs. S. J. Arthur, Harvey Wood, Gorrell Quick, G. A. House, and E. T. Stanford, special Haiti committee, formed immediately after the delivery of a missionary address by the field secretary, in which he described the spiritual destitution of Haiti, proximity to America, and its strategic importance.

"Your committee appointed to consider and report on the matter of Baptist mission work on the island of Haiti beg leave to report that having listened to the story of the work presented by Rev. L. Ton Evans, and confirmed unto us by printed reports from the field, and the personal testimony of Rev. G. A.

House, who has spent 25 years on the adjacent Island of Jamaica (and who is intimately acquainted with Mr. Ton Evans and his work), and the work having already received the hearty indorsement of the northeast Welsh, Abington, and Huntingdon Associations of Pennsylvania, and the western Pennsylvania Welsh and the Turnbull Associations of Ohio, as well as the Wyoming and Louisville Ministers' Conferences. We, the New York Baptist Ministers' Conference, respectfully and earnestly petition the officers and executive committee of the Home Mission Society to respond to this call of semibarbarous but awakening Haiti, to the end that these two and a half millions at our very doors may enter on the heritage of a New Testament Christian life and the privileges of an enlightened civilization."

Contributions should be sent toward missionaries' salaries, new chapels, schools, or bells to Councillor W. P. Thomas (chairman of East Glamorganshire Welsh Baptist Association), Gorphwysfa, Treorkey, South Wales (Britain). Haiti mission, treasurer in Wales; or Rev. J. E. Daires, M. A. (clerk of Northeast Baptist Association of Pennsylvania), Nanticoke, Pa., United States of America, treasurer in America. French, Spanish, and English tests and tracts and periodicals to be sent direct to L. Ton Evans, field secretary, Jacmel. Haiti, W. I. All moneys, if forwarded to the latter, must be in registered letters

[Rev. L. Ton Evans's interview in Wilkes-Barre, Pa., Evening News, Aug. 21, 1911 (revised)]

A REMARKABLE CAREER OF A BAPTIST MISSIONARY—TELLS OF STRUGGLES IN HAITI—
FIERCELY ATTACKED BY DEVIL WORSHIPPERS—A WHOLE CITY AND HIMSELF
SAVED FROM BURNING AND BUTCHERY BY AMERICAN GUNBOAT—BLACK REPUBLIC
MAKING GREAT EFFORTS TO BATTLE WITH SOCIAL AND FINANCIAL PROBLEMS—
PROPOSED INDUSTRIAL COLLEGE.

Rev. L. Ton Evans, field secretary of the Haiti mission, is home from the Southern and Northern Baptist Conventions, and the World's Baptist Alliance in Philadelphia, at which he spoke as the official representative of Haiti.

Rev. L. Ton Evans left the Welsh Baptist Church of Edwardsville exactly five years ago to preach the gospel to 3,000,000 spiritually dark and socially destitute Negroes of Haiti.

Like George Whitfield, the eighteenth century evangelist, he was born in a saloon in Wales, and on account of family relations and other pecuniary advantages might have easily been to-day, had he chosen, one of the wealthiest liquor merchants and brewers in that principality.

His parents having quit the hotel, their youngest son became a strict abstainer, and after his conversion, college training, and entrance upon the Christian ministry he eschewed all, gave up entire property so as to devote himself wholly to his sacred calling and consecrate all his energy to the work of soul saving.

While in the large seaport town of Barry, as a pioneer in Christian and social work, and where he was the means of forming five Baptist churches, Mr. Evans was one of the best known temperance reformers in the whole of Wales. He has been the recipient in this capacity of many tokens of esteem and respect from leading men, irrespective of religious denominations and political parties, although he himself is a strong Baptist and a staunch radical or liberal, or what we here would term prohibitionist-democrat. He is a freetrader. The very active part he played while pastor of First Baptist Church of Edwardsville as temperance reformer will not be soon forgotten when, in one year, he and his friends closed up about one-half of the saloons and reduced the tax revenue from that source alone some $4,000. The dastardly dynamite outrage against the Congregational Church is well known to have actually been aimed against the Rev. L. Ton Evans's church and people.

Like the reformers of his type he has been bitterly attacked, and seriously threatened many times, but all of which simply act as a tonic to him and only strengthen him in what he conceives to be his duty to God and man.

INTERVIEWED AT HOME.

After locating the missionary at his West Side American home and having gone into certain preliminaries, he expressed his willingness to a News reporter to answer question relative to himself and his special work and prospects in the black Republic.

" How long have you been in the island and what is the nature of the work you are engaged in, Mr. Evans? "

"I first left my churches in Barry, Wales, to go to Haiti in connection with Jamaica Baptist Churches, 18 years ago. Owing to repeated sickness of my wife, I was obliged to leave and return in two years' time, but before I left I had an able and consecrated native brother, Nosirel L. Herisson, ordained and placed in charge of the church and southern portion of the island, and whom God has signally blessed, though until two years ago he had not been in receipt of anything like a salary. In 1906, without a society really at my back, I left here and have traveled some 60,000 miles over sea and land, and spoken at many hundreds of churches, associations, conventions, etc., in Wales, Jamaica, West Indies and here in the States in behalf of Haiti. I have during the same period traveled five times through the Haiti Republic, and part of the Dominican, spending days, weeks, and months at various cities, towns, and villages of the coast and interior. As field secretary, or general missionary, my special work, after endeavoring to secure some financial aid to college trained natives and other brethren on the island, has been to visit churches and stations systematically, preach, baptize, marry, ordain native brethren of special ability and reliable Christian character, and so as to arrange for regular preaching in our poor churches and out-of-the-way places in the interior. In addition to this, I have been able to render financial help for new church buildings, rent, and repair others, secured financial aid altogether for five missionaries, etc. When I state that there are very long distances between these churches and stations; no railroad facilities, nor even roads, and that one must go for days and often weeks on ponies or mules through deep mud, thick bush, flooded rivers, and on small sailing boats around the coast, sleeping during the nights on the hard wooden decks, it will give you some idea of the difficulties and hardships of a Baptist field secretary in Haiti, and also enable you to understand how the poor members and natives appreciated and enjoyed my going and living among them. Perhaps no other man, white or black, has traveled so much and experienced what I have among all classes, and is in a position to really understand Haiti from the inside. I have been openly and personally attacked by the priest of the devil worshippers, on top of Gros Morne, between Jacmel and Port au Prince, and the whole city of Jacmel in November of 1908, when about to be bombarded, and people cruelly butchered by soldiers and officers of late Alexis Nord, to spite them for not preventing ex-President Simon entering Port au Prince, was saved, under God, by the American gunboat *Eagle* that sailed with the Haitian man-of-war into the harbor.

"We have now three financially supported brethren on the field, and through visiting the churches of the Baptists of the island of Jamaica, I have succeeded also in getting them to financially support two more, making a total of five. We have in Haiti 14 Baptist Churches and 17 stations, 5 financially supported trained missionaries, 25 native preachers, 600 members, baptized last year 100, over 100 received for baptism, and 1,200 converts in our churches and stations at present and under instruction. Also a number of day schools in cities, towns, and very poor country districts, but the latter for some years and to our great sorrow have been closed for want of funds."

DEFINES PLAN.

"What plan had you in mind when starting out, and how far have you realized this?" was next asked.

"Knowing the inability of Jamaica Baptists, and difficulty with the Baptists of Wales, and the poverty of our Negro Baptists in the States, who have helped me so far and enabled us with the Baptist Churches of this valley (Wyoming Valley, of the Welsh Pennsylvania Baptist Association), to do what has been done, yet I felt that to do effective work in Haiti and develop the mission, one of our great and strong American Baptist missionary societies must take over the work and carry it on as they do their work elsewhere, with schools and colleges, where the best young men and women could be trained for work in their own island.

"Haiti, which has a population of 3,000,000, that is, 2,000 000 more people than Jamaica, and 1,000,000 more than even Cuba, is only 1,000 miles from New York City, and 300 miles off the coast of Florida. In addition to our proximity to Haiti, and growing American interests in the Caribbean Sea, the Baptists of this country are at present operating missions in Porto Rico, Cuba, and Canal Zone right around the island. Again, Haiti is a Republic, and so can be better understood by our American Baptists than by the more conservative, if not pessimistic Baptists of England and Jamaica. Our American missionary methods have the great advantage also of being more aggressive and scriptural both on the foreign as well as the home field.

" It may not be known the debt which the United States owes to Haiti, and the obligation this country is under to the black Republic. It was the downfall of Haiti and defeat of Napoleon and France by Toussaint L'Ouverture and his black forces in their securing freedom from slavery and independence from France at the end of the eighteenth century that compelled Napoleon to sell the 1,200,000 square miles France had in North America to our Thomas Jefferson in 1803 for 2 cents an acre. Apart from the Louisiana Purchase, we in the States to-day would not have had any Pacific slope, Alaska, Philippines, Porto Rico, nor Panama Canal to boast of. Hence, in the providence of God and as authentic history attests, Haiti has materially helped to make the United States the leading world power it is. Yes, I am perfectly satisfied, and in taking everything into consideration I really feel delighted at the bright prospects and real success so far achieved. I came up from Haiti through Cuba, where I saw the splendid work of our Northern and Southern Baptists, and so as to attend the convention held at Jacksonville, Fla., this May. After hearing the story of Haiti's needs, the convention immediately called the attention of their home board to this field, with authority to act. The board have planned for Dr. Gray, their corresponding secretary, to come down at once to visit the island in accordance with the convention's desire.

" Exactly a month after, namely, in June, our Northern Baptists at Philadelphia also decided to make an appropriation of from $5,000 to $10,000 annually out of their budget and through their Home Mission Board, and so as to extend their work to include Haiti."

SOCIAL PROBLEMS.

" What, in your opinion, are some of the reasons which account for the restlessness in Haiti and the constant revolutions on this island? "

" Perhaps there is not a people in the whole world misunderstood and misrepresented as a whole more so than the people of this black Republic. From my long experience and intimate knowledge I can safely say that there is not a more kind-hearted and generous natured people anywhere than the Negroes of Haiti. The immediate cause of discontent which crystallizes into political upheavals, undoubtedly is the widespread poverty arising through want of money, and industries in the country. Men and women in sheer want can be easily worked upon by certain political factions, and so-called leaders, most of whom themselves again are in penury ; and are used by certain whites or Europeans who have an eye to business, and make great profits to themselves through these revolutions and financial embarrassments of the Government. There is also a system of corruption and spoliation carried on often by those around the President, and people in official positions, especially at the administration of customs and finances. Hence the treasury becomes depleted, soldiers, officers, and many others are not paid, often robbed in other ways. The people become discontented, and even bitter, and at times driven to desperation.

GOSPEL THE REAL NEED.

" The chief want of Haiti is the Gospel, the religion of the Bible, and Christianity of Jesus and the New Testament.

" When dissatisfied with political and social conditions (and no thinking man, much less educated, and Christian man should be satisfied with conditions in Haiti) unfortunately instead of having recourse to the ballot and the polling booth, they begin to plan and plot a revolution and appeal to the gun and sword rather than to justice, reason, and common sense. The Gospel is the greatest civilizing factor of any age, and this alone in its wide and far-reaching range can satisfactorily solve the Haitian problem. When the teaching of the Word of God, and principles of Christianity find a lodgement by faith in the human heart they change conduct as well as character. There is a new vision, new hope, in fact, an altogether new life, finding expression not only in mental thrills and spiritual throbs, but in fresh and actual daily activities. The burden and drudge becomes something worth while ; and one's whole life through this new motive power is lifted entirely from its old ruts. The whole man is brought into harmony, morally, intellectually, physically, and socially with the heavenly will and divine purpose of God in Christ. New conception of duty, new relation to wife and family, and community follow as the day follows the night.

Hence, they become honest, sober, and thrifty. They want, however, to be helped, encouraged, and taught so as to make the best of these new powers and energies.

SCHOOLS THE BASIS.

" We endeavor by way of Sunday and day schools for the young and middle aged, and even those advanced in years, as well as in other ways to accomplish this. One of the objects of my being now in this country is to interest our leading educationists and Christian philanthropists in the States to establish a normal and industrial college on a large scale; and so that the most promising young men and women, many of whom will go out again as teachers to lead their own people by example on lands, in homes, etc., and create respect for honest labor and gradually build an industrial system of sound and practical education that will make them self-supporting and independent, thus materially helping in the formation of a complete Christian character."

CARE FOR SMALL NATIONS.

" Don't you really believe that Haiti should be annexed to the United States and that this is the only political solution of the problem?"

"Certainly not. Small nations, in my opinion, have a place in the plan and purpose of God; and very often, if not always, like Israel and Wales for instance, have an important destiny to fulfill. The United States has never yet done her duty by Haiti. Had she helped Haiti as she has helped Cuba, and even recently helped the Dominican Republic, I am certain America would have had better results. The great powers concede that the interests of the United States are paramount to the combined interests of all other nations in the Caribbean Sea; and that according to the Monroe doctrine and the doctrine of God and humanity, that the strong should help the weak—the United States Government should befriend Haiti, not only by restoring order, or confiscating the island against their will and by force, but by establishing permanent peace and thorough confidence. By a little effort on her part to explain to the Haitian Government the true situation, and the purity and nobility of America's motive, not only Haiti would raise no objection, but really welcome such friendly help and protection, and encouragement to open up industries, etc.

PROMINENT MEN ENLIST.

" I have nearly 3,000 signatures of senators, deputies, judges of supreme and every other court, generals, magistrates, merchants, inspectors, cultivators, etc. When I inform you that only 20 per cent of our people can read, and but 10 per cent write, you will see that the petition comprises actually the whole nation as far as it can be got at. When the objects of this school were explained many hundred of times by myself in French and patois (the speaking language of 90 per cent of the natives) as well by many of my helpers interested, namely to train young men and women in skilled labor, useful industry; pointing out that it would effect eventually great political, social, moral, and religious changes that would be far-reaching in its effect upon the island; and revolutions and bloodshed, send three out of every four of our starving, barefoot soldiers back to their homes and habitations (small farms) in the country, and inspire confidence in one another, etc., they became deeply interested and even enthusiastic at the very idea of such an institution for the training of their sons and daughters in Haiti with such benign influence. In addition to the signatures named and support mentioned, I have received official letters afterwards from mayors and councils of the leading cities and towns, thanking me officially for my deep interest and real love for their country and people, and expressing their sincere hope that the earnest prayer of the petitioners will be responded to and answered by educationists and Christian philanthropists of this country and true friends of the Negro. Though I admit the responsibility of this most important and further great undertaking in behalf of Haiti, I naturally feel a little proud of being the first white man entrusted with such a mission; and especially that this whole black nation, so diversified in character, so opposite in their religious creeds, so different in temperament and opposed in politics, should consider me worthy of their implicit confidence and a true and genuine friend of Haiti and its people."

"May I finally ask you the effects of the last disturbances in the island, or will the change of President and cabinet and overthrow of late government by the revolutionists since you left Ha.ti, in any way interfere with your work. or change your plans?"

"I think not. In fact, I expect the present new government to prove of greater help. It may not be known that though Romanism is the State religion. according to Haiti constitution, there is liberty for all, and none more than for the Baptists. It is true, however, that certain Roman Catholic priests have from time to time caused warrants to be served on me and my native brethren, for preaching on ground claimed by the Catholic Church to have been consecrated by them; and that they have seriously threatened us for publicly baptizing in rivers and sea those who once were prominent in the Roman faith. But it is only fair and just to state that never has the Haitian (Negro) himself been the instigator in these cases. Moreover, in every case we faced the court. or officials asserting our legal as well as moral rights as Baptists, and humble representatives of Christ, the authorities and Government, strange to say. have always stood by and supported the radical Baptist missionary.

"The leaders in Haiti are at least beginning to understand that Baptists stand for the liberty of the individual to think and to act in all matters of conscience and religion. The right to read the B.ble and interpret it by the help of the Holy Spirit and without the interference of State, priest, or person. His excellency, Leconte. and Senator Dr. Laroch, the new minister of public instruction, were the first to sign the petition and are ardent supporters of the college. Friends of Gen. Firmin are not a bit less in their desire and with Gen. Firmin himself, whom I know as a learned man, and an author of ability and depute. but was absent from the island when the petition was gotten up, will, with all his influence, support everything in the way of education and religion for the real emancipation of his country and people from ignorance, supersition, etc.

WILL DRAW HAITI TO UNITED STATES.

"In addition to the advantage of this industrial institution as mentioned above. such an excellent college as th's established among them in the language of the petitioners and which petition is written in French—will place this small, but heroic little nation under a lasting obligation to the generous benefactors. and more than all else draw Haiti closer than ever before in its history to the United States and serve as a means of uniting the two Republics together in real sympathy and genuine good will."

Rev. Condillac Jean Jacqus, Cape Haiti, a graduate from Newton Theological Seminary, Massachusetts, and also attending the Baptist world's alliance. was also seen and questioned:

"Do you know much about Mr. Ton Evans and his work in Hait!?"

"Most decidedly. We look at him there at Haiti's best friend, and he enjoys the esteem, Christian affection and confidence of all classes, and we look at his coming among us as God's direct answer to our prayers. No white man has traveled more extensively and become personally acquainted with our social, intellectual, and spiritual needs than Mr. Evans himself. Hence he can speak with real authority based on personal knowledge. The moment we heard of his project of a normal and industrial college to teach my countrymen the value and dignity of honest labor. we (myself and a number of other leading men) at once fell in love with the idea. and at great risk during the political troubles associated ourselves with him and rendered what support we could. I may add that Rev. L. Ton Evans, whom we often call, on account of his real love for Haiti, and esteem for him "Negrè blanc" (the white black man), has the support of all the leaders of the Haiti Republic. The success which he has attained through h's undaunted courage and incessant efforts which astonish us all in Haiti. has been most marvellous. As stated in the petition I am sure the President and Government and senate and chamber will only be too glad to give the necessary land required, as well as do everything else they can to encourage this grand project."

APPRECIATE THE MISSIONER'S WORK.

"You then agree with Rev. Ton Evans. that the people would really appreciate such an institution. and that as he maintains. it will go a long way to establ sh peace and concord in your island. and unite the two Republics in sympathy?"

"I am certain that a large number of our best young men and women are yearning for knowledge, and prepared to make great sacrifices so as to equip themselves for useful vocations in life, and I do not see how such a college as this would not be as successful as Hampton and Tuskegee, with which Mr. Evans is already acquainted. Such a training would enable my people to develop themselves as well as our rich soil, and give them a taste for something other than politics. It would bring contentment to the whole island and help in the development of industries, as well as make in my opinion all the educational and religious work more effective and permanent. I may also add that such a generous act on the part of educationists and Christian philanthropists of your great country would never be forgotten by my people. The college itself, with its training of young men and women, year after year would be a standing reminder among us of your generosity and good will toward us, and actually cement Haiti to the United States as nothing else could; remove all suspicion that sometimes exists among nations, and especially a small nation like mine toward a large and powerful one. On account of these blessings therefore we are all earnestly praying that God may give success to Bro. L. Ton Evans, and that friends of the Negro with you here will do what they can to assist him in this noble effort to free little Haiti and its people from ignorance and superstition by giving an institution that will give them a sound and practical education that shall enable them to take their stand among other civilized, yea Christian, nations of the western world eventually."

PRESENT STATISTICS OF HAITI BAPTIST MISSION (1911).

Churches in Haiti	14
Church buildings	8
Church houses for missionaries	2
Mission stations	17
Mission chapels	5
Church buildings now being built	2
Mission chapels being built	4
Missionaries at present paid	4
Missionaries, graduates of Baptist College, unpaid	2
Native preachers and assistant missionaries unpaid	25
Total membership	600
Baptized since last report	100
Accepted candidates for baptism	105
Professed converts at churches and stations	1,200

In addition to the above there are the following day schools languishing for help, and most of country schools among the very poor have had to be given up for lack of funds:

1. Jacmel (two higher boys' and girls') grades, conducted by missionary and teachers. Connected with Jacmel, six country schools.

2. Port au Prince (capital), one day school conducted by missionary. Has financial support from the Government.

3. St. Raphael, one girls' school conducted by aged wife of missionary and Christian, recently converted from Romanism. Received financial support from the Government.

4. Dondon, one girls' school conducted by member of Baptist Church. Given Government financial help.

5. Trou, one mixed school conducted by member of Baptist Church. Given Government financial help.

6. Cape Haitian, one young men's school conducted by Baptist missionary here. Can be developed into a preparatory school to train native preachers. At present receives Government financial help.

HEADQUARTERS NINTH COMPANY, G. D. 'H.,
District of St. Marc, June 25, 1918.

From: District commander, St. Marc.
To: Prison sergeant, St. Marc Prison.
Subject: Services on Sunday afternoons.

The bearer, the Rev. Dr. Evans, has permission to enter the prison at St. Marc every Sunday afternoon for the purpose of holding a service for the benefit of the prisoners. Services will be held in the mess hall and order will be maintained at all times. Prison cell doors will be opened, and all prisoners who wish will be allowed to attend services.

CHARLES E. KENNY,
Captain Ninth Company, G. D. 'H.

Mr. EVANS. May I put in letters from and to Senator Knox, Lansing, and others pertaining to matters here dealt with, etc.

Senator ODDIE. Yes.

(The letters referred to will be printed in appendix.)

Mr. EVANS. I would be decidedly opposed to any idea of withdrawing from Haiti, but urge through this committee the establishment of a civil occupation, with sufficient high-grade American marines for administration purposes.

That a scheme of popular instruction should be launched as soon as practicable with compulsory free education, and both in the English as well as the French language, being that Haiti is so closely allied to the United States, and so as to do away with need of interpreters.

The lands should be preserved for the people and developed under a supervision of the United States, but with hearty and active cooperation of the Haitian Government, functioning through its Senate and Chambers, and with its constitution restored.

Senator ODDIE. And you feel sure that in your opinion there are a number of marines down there who would make very worthy men, and it would be well to retain?

Mr. EVANS. Yes; I believe there are some excellent officers there, but many have degenerated through drink and other forms of vice, so prevalent, unfortunately, in such a backward country as Haiti is. These marine officers, however, should have a high-class gendarmerie and less expensive administration through the employment of more qualified Haitians all through the civil occupation, and fewer but stronger white American officials who are free from prejudice against the colored, and must have faith in the future of the race under proper and favorable conditions.

Senator ODDIE. But the conditions have been trying on many of these marines, have they not?

Mr. EVANS. Quite so. They have been neglected both by the United States Government and by the Christian churches of America and the Y. M. C. A. Prohibition should be extended so as to include the manufacturing as well as sale of all intoxicants, and to the civilian white and colored, as well as marines and gendarmes. Drink and immorality have been the serious undoing of many of our young men who have come to me at Cape and also at Port au Prince with their complaints.

If Col. Russell and Gen. Cole and others had a free hand in Haiti from corporations and the Roman Catholic influences there would have been a much better record to-day. Without separation of Protestant and Catholic Churches from the Government there can be no spirituality and power in the one, nor honesty and efficiency in the other. *This is absolutely necessary.*

If the civil occupation is established and the Haitian Government completely restored only such minor changes and modifications made to harmonize with new conditions, and the treaty is going to be carried out in its educational and industrial phases, the confidence of Haitians will again be restored and Haiti will, under the sympathetic and efficient leadership of capable American statesmanship, yet take her place before many years among the Republics of the West, prove a credit to our own Government, and cemented in the closest bonds of amity and good will with her fostering as well as protecting neighbor and true sister Republic of the United States.

Senator ODDIE. Well, I think that covers everything. We will take a recess until Tuesday at 10.30 o'clock a. m.

(Whereupon the committee adjourned until Tuesday, October 11, 1921, at 10.30 o'clock a. m.)

AGREEMENT REGARDING THE GENDARMERIE.

The undersigned, duly authorized thereto by their respective Governments, have this day agreed:

1. That the constabulary contemplated by Article X of the treaty between the United States of America and the Republic of Haiti, signed at Port au Prince on September 16, 1915, shall be known as the Haitian Gendarmerie;

that its strength and amounts to be expended for pay, rations, and expenses of operation, etc., shall be as set forth in the following table:

Per annum.

1 commandant, $250 per month	$3,000
1 assistant commandant, $200 per month	2,400
4 directors, $200 per month	9,600
9 inspectors, $150 per month	16,200
1 quartermaster, paymaster, director, $200 per month	2,400
2 assistant quartermaster paymasters, inspectors, $150 per month	3,600
1 surgeon director, $200 per month	2,400
2 surgeons, inspectors, $150 per month	3,600
18 captains, $150 per month	32,400
21 first lieutenants, $100 per month	25,200
3 first lieutenants (hospital corps), $100 per month	3,600
39 second lieutenants, $60 per month	28,080
8 second lieutenants (machine gun), $50 per month	4,800
6 second lieutenants (hospital corps), $60 per month	4,320
19 first sergeants, $25 per month	5,700
112 sergeants, $20 per month	26,880
262 corporals, $15 per month	47,160
40 field musicians, $10 per month	4,800
2,100 privates, $10 per month	252,000

Pay, personal		$478,140
Rations, 2,533 enlisted men, at 10 cents per diem		92,455
Clerical force:		
1 secretary, $100 per month	1,200	
1 clerk to commandant, $45 per month	540	
1 clerk to assistant commandant, $45 per month	540	
2 clerks, $50 per month	1,200	
11 clerks, $45 per month	5,940	
		9,420
Forage and remounts	40,000	
Uniforms	66,000	
Ammunition and target practice	15,000	
Hospital, medicine, etc., per month	10,000	
Transportation, maps, office supplies, intelligence service, etc., per month	35,000	
Miscellaneous rent and repair of barracks, tools, kitchen utensils, lights, etc., per month	20,000	
		186,000
Total land forces		766,015

Coast Guard, annual cost of maintenance:		
2 inspectors, $1,800		3,600
4 first lieutenants, $1,200		4,800
4 engineers, $276		1,104
4 quartermasters, $216		864
30 seamen, $156		4,680
		15,048
Fuel		20,000
Total		35,048

II. A coast guard service shall be established, operated, and maintained as a constituent part of the gendarmerie, under the direction and control of the commandant of the gendarmerie, and in addition to the annual expenses heretofore set forth, the sum of P75,000 shall be allotted for the purchase of the necessary coast guard vessels for this service. These vessels may be used for the transportation of troops, Government employees, and the supplies of all departments at the discretion of the commandant of the gendarmerie, subject to the direction of the President of Haiti.

III. All American officers of the gendarmerie shall be appointed by the President of Haiti upon nomination by the President of the United States, and will be replaced by Haitians when they have shown by examination, as provided in Article X of the treaty, that they are fit for command.

IV. The gendarmerie shall be considered the sole military and police force of the Republic of Haiti, clothed with full power to preserve domestic peace, the security of individual rights, and the full observance of the provisions of the treaty. It shall have supervision and control of arms and ammunitions, military supplies, and traffic therein throughout the Republic. It shall be subject only to the direction of the President of Haiti; all other officials desiring the services of the gendarmerie, shall be required to submit request through the nearest official of that organization.

The private guard referred to in article 175 of the constitution of Haiti shall be composed of 100 men of the gendarmerie, chosen by the President of Haiti, which men shall wear distinctive insignia while employed on that service.

V. All matters of recruiting, appointment, instruction or training, promotion, examinationß discipline, operation, movement of troops, clothing, rations, arms and equipment, quarters and administration, shall be under the jurisdiction of the commandant of the gendarmerie.

VI. The gendarmerie shall be organized and officered as provided for in Article X of the treaty. The clerical force of the gendarmerie shall be Haitian citizens.

VII. Rules and regulations for the administration and discipline of the gendarmerie shall be issued by the commandant, after being approved by the President of Haiti. Infraction of these rules and regulations by members of the gendarmerie may be punished by arrest, imprisonment, suspension from duty without pay, forfeiture of pay, or dismissal under regulations promulgated by the commandant of the gendarmerie and approved by the President of Haiti.

VIII. Other offenses committed by gendarmes will be investigated by the gendarmerie officers as directed by the commandant of the gendarmerie. If the behavior of a gendarme is unjustified, he may, at the discretion of the commandant of the gendarmerie, be discharged from the gendarmerie, and, after his guilt is established, be punished in the same manner as other Haitian citizens; or, if not discharged, he will be punished as provided for in Articles VII and IX of this agreement. Officers and enlisted men of the United States Navy and Marine Corps serving with the gendarmerie will continue to be subject to the laws of United States for the government of the Navy.

IX. A tribunal, consisting of five officers of the gendarmerie, is authorized for the trial of gendarmes charged with conspiracy against the Government of Haiti. This tribunal will be ordered by the commandant of the gendarmerie, and in case of conviction is authorized to inflict the punishment of death or such other punishment as the tribunal may adjudge and deem proper, in accordance with the laws of Haiti. All sentences of this tribunal, after being reviewed and approved by the commandant of the gendarmerie, must be confirmed by the President of Haiti before being carried into execution.

X. Persons violating the laws governing traffic in arms, ammunition, and military stores shall be punished by a fine not exceeding P. 1,000 United States currency, or imprisonment not exceeding five years, or both.

XI. The Haitian gendarmerie shall be under the control of the President of Haiti, and all orders from him pertaining to the gendarmerie shall be delivered to the commandant through the minister of the interior. All other civil officials desiring protection or the services of the gendarmerie will make application to the senior officer of the gendarmerie in the locality.

XII. The sum of P. 801,063, United States currency, shall be appropriated annually for pay and allowances, equipment, uniforms, transportation, administration, and other current expenses of the Haitian gendarmerie. Allotments for the various needs of the gendarmerie shall be made from this sum by the commandant, but the total of such allotments in any month shall not exceed one-twelfth of the total annual appropriation: *Provided, however*, That the surplus from one month may be allotted in subsequent months.

XIII. Reports of expenditures shall be made by the commandant as directed by the President of Haiti.

XIV. The laws necessary to make effective the above provisions shall be submitted to the legislative body of Haiti.

In witness whereof the undersigned have hereunto signed their names and affixed their seals in duplicate.

Done at Washington, D. C., this 24th day of August, 1916.

SOLON MENOS.
ROBERT LANSING.

The undersigned, duly authorized thereto by their respective Governments, have this day agreed that the engineer or engineers to be charged with the supervision and direction of the sanitation and public improvement of the Rpublic of Haiti and to be nominated and appointed as stipulated in article 13 of the treaty between the United States of America and the Republic of Haiti, signed at Port au Prince on September 16, 1915, shall each receive annual compensation not to exceed seventy-five hundred (P. 7,500) dollars United States currency.

It is also agreed, pending further arrangement between the high contracting parties, that should such official or officials as may be nominated by the President of the United States, pursuant to article 13 of the convention hereinbefore referred to be selected from the service of the United States and receive compensation as such from the Government of the United States, the Government of the Republic of Haiti shall be obligated to remunerate such officer or officers each in a sum not to exceed one-half of the above-mentioned total annual emolument of seventy-five hundred (P. 7,500) dollars.

It is further agreed that should such officer or officers be appointed other than from the service of the United States the total annual emolument of each such officer shall be defrayed by the Government of Haiti in the following proportions:

A sum not to exceed P. 4,500 United States currency per annum for salary.

A sum not to exceed P. 3,000 United States currency per annum for personal expenses.

In witness whereof the undersigned have hereunto signed their names and affixed their seals.

Done in Washington, in duplicate, this 27th day of June, 1916.

ROBERT LANSING.

The undersigned, duly authorized thereto by their respective Governments, have this day agreed that the following officials, to be nominated and appointed as stipulated in article 11 of the treaty between the Republic of Haiti and the United States of America, signed at Port au Prince on September 16, 1915, shall, pursuant to the provisions of article 5 of said treaty receive annually compensation as follows:

Financial adviser: $6,000 United States currency per annum for salary and $4,000 United States currency per annum for personal expenses.

General receiver of customs: $5,500 United States currency per annum for salary and $3,000 United States currency per annum for personal expenses.

Deputy general receiver of customs: $4,800 United States currency per annum for salary and $1,200 United States currency per annum for personal expenses.

It is also agreed that pending further arrangement between the high contracting parties the President of Haiti shall appoint, upon nomination by the President of the United States and at salaries fixed or the recommendation of the latter, such additional aids and employees as may be necessary to assist the general receiver of customs properly to collect, receive, and apply all customs duties of imports and exports accruing at the several customhouses and ports of entry of the Republic of Haiti: *Provided*, That the total salaries and expenses of all the officials and employees herein mentioned shall not exceed 5 per cent of the collections and receipts from the customs duties, unless by subsequent agreement between the two Governments.

In witness whereof the undersigned have hereunto signed their names and affixed their seals.

Done at Washington, in duplicate, this 27th day of June, 1916.

ROBERT LANSING.

INQUIRY INTO OCCUPATION AND ADMINISTRATION OF HAITI AND SANTO DOMINGO.

TUESDAY, OCTOBER 11, 1921.

UNITED STATES SENATE,
SELECT COMMITTEE ON HAITI AND SANTO DOMINGO,
Washington, D. C.

The committee met at 10.30 o'clock a. m., pursuant to adjournment, Senator Medill McCormick (chairman) presiding.

Present: Senators McCormick, Oddie, and King.

Also present: Mr. Ernest Angell and Mr. Horace G. Knowles in their representative capacities as hereinbefore indicated; and Maj. Edwin N. McClellan, United States Marine Corps, representing the Navy Department.

STATEMENT OF REAR ADMIRAL WILLIAM B. CAPERTON, UNITED STATES NAVY, RETIRED, 714 MONTAUK AVENUE, NEW LONDON, CONN.

The CHAIRMAN. Admiral, will you give your full name and rank?

Admiral CAPERTON. Rear Admiral William B. Caperton, United States Navy, retired.

The CHAIRMAN. In your own way, Admiral, will you tell the committee of your being ordered to land and the circumstances which attended not only your landing, but the receipt of the orders to land, in Haiti?

Admiral CAPERTON. I landed several times. I do not know to which particular time you refer.

The CHAIRMAN. I would start with the first and end with the last.

Admiral CAPERTON. Yes, sir. I did not know what you wanted. I do not suppose it is necessary to repeat verbally my orders?

The CHAIRMAN. If you will refer to them and give them to the stenographer for the record, if they are brief, that will be sufficient.

Admiral CAPERTON. Yes, sir. One is not very brief.

(The matter referred to is here printed in full, as follows:)

JANUARY 5, 1915.

To: Commander Cruiser Squadron, United States Atlantic Fleet, U. S. S. *Washington*, flagship, via Commander in Chief United States Atlantic Fleet.

Subject: Movement orders—*Washington.*

1. On January 10, or as soon thereafter as practicable, proceed with the *Washington* to San Domingo City, S. D., stopping at such ports en route as may be necessary for coal and men.

2. Upon arrival at San Domingo City, S. D., communicate with the diplomatic representative of the United States and acquaint yourself with the political conditions in San Domingo.

3. After such length of stay at San Domingo City as you may deem necessary for the purpose indicated, proceed to Port au Prince, Haiti, where you will also communicate with the American minister and acquaint yourself with the political conditions in Haiti. After such length of stay at Port au Prince as you may consider advisable, proceed to Habana, Cuba, via Guantanamo, for coal and stores, at discretion.

4. Upon arrival at Habana, communicate with the American minister and acquaint yourself with the political conditions existing in Cuba.

5. After such length of stay at Habana as you may consider necessary for the purpose, proceed with the *Washington* to Vera Cruz, via Tampico and

Tuxpam, acquainting yourself in each locality with the political conditions in Mexico.

6. The department desires that you conduct a military inspection of such units of your command as the *Washington* may fall in with from time to time and as opportunity offers.

7. The department will be pleased to receive any suggestions or recommendations you may consider it necessary to make in connection with the political situation in West Indian and Mexican waters.

JOSEPHUS DANIELS.

Also the following by radio on January 19, 1915:

Rush. Ten p. m. Tuesday. Department directs you proceed Cape Haitien, Haiti, without delay to report conditions. Under what orders did you sail to-day for Guacanayabo, Gulf of Cuba.

FLETCHER.

The CHAIRMAN. Let me ask when did you land first and where?

Admiral CAPERTON. I landed first at Cape Haitien.

The CHAIRMAN. And when? Was it in July, 1915?

Admiral CAPERTON. I was just thinking whether I landed before or not. It was in July; yes, sir. I do not think I landed before. I mean I did not land my forces before.

The CHAIRMAN. The report of the department reads that the American consul at Cape Haitien——

Admiral CAPERTON. That is what I was trying to find.

The CHAIRMAN (continuing). Requested that a warship be sent there. In compliance with this request, the U. S. S. *Washington* arrived at Cape Haitien on January 23, 1915.

Admiral CAPERTON. Yes, sir; I arrived at Cape Haitien at 9.30 a. m., January 23, 1915.

The CHAIRMAN. Had you had any communication with the department before that time relative to the landing or the prospect of landing?

Admiral CAPERTON. My original orders directed me to proceed to the West Indies and become acquainted with the political conditions in Santo Domingo, Haiti, Cuba, and Mexico. I proceeded with the U. S. S. *Washington* from Portsmouth, N. H., on January 10, 1915.

The CHAIRMAN. When did you reach Haitian waters?

Admiral CAPERTON. On January 19, 1915, I received a radiogram from the commander in chief of the United States Atlantic Fleet directing me to proceed to Cape Haitien without delay and report conditions.

The CHAIRMAN. Where were you when you received the radiogram?

Admiral CAPERTON. At sea.

The CHAIRMAN. En route to where?

Admiral CAPERTON. Well, I was en route first to Santo Domingo. My original orders, I may explain——

The CHAIRMAN. Admiral, you need not go into the orders particularly, but just give us a running story. You received a radiogram?

Admiral CAPERTON. Yes, sir.

The CHAIRMAN. While you were on board the *Washington?*

Admiral CAPERTON. I was on board the U. S. S. *Washington*.

The CHAIRMAN. You proceeded to Cape Haitien, did you?

Admiral CAPERTON. Yes, sir.

The CHAIRMAN. What transpired after your arrival at Cape Hatien?

Admiral CAPERTON. On the 20th of January, 1915, I received by radio code a message from the Department of State, for delivery to the American consul at Cape Haitien, Haiti, which was delivered on arrival there. I have the inclosure here, Inclosure C, if you wish it.

The CHAIRMAN. Is that the code or a translation of it?

Admiral CAPERTON. I do not know whether I have it translated or not. I think, perhaps, that would be the code, sir.

The CHAIRMAN. What is Inclosure C?

Admiral CAPERTON. By reference to my report before me, I see it is the State Department's code. I did not translate it.

The CHARMAN. Then, it is immaterial if you have not got the translation. What transpired when you reached Cape Hatien and met the consul?

Admiral CAPERTON. At 10 a. m., January 23, 1915, the *Washington* anchored off Picolet Point, Cape Hatien, Haiti. I immediately sent a staff officer to communicate with the American consul. As the weather was very rough, I did not ins'st on the consul's coming off to the ship, but I received a report of the conditions from the staff officer sent ashore. The consul sent off to me a copy of a letter he had written to the American minister, Port au Prince, Haiti, outlining the situation on the 20th of January, 1915.

The CHAIRMAN. Have you got the letter?

Admiral CAPERTON. I have, sir. Shall I read it?

The CHAIRMAN. If it is not very long you may read it at this time.

Admiral CAPERTON. It is two pages.

The CHAIRMAN. Well, read it.

(Admiral Caperton thereupon read the letter referred to, as follows:)

CAPE HAITIEN, HAITI, *January 20, 1915.*

Hon. ARTHUR BAILLY-BLANCHARD,
  American Minister, Port au Prince.

SIR: I have the honor to report that on last Friday, the 15th instant, Gen. Vilbrun Guillaume Sam, the delegate of the departments of the north and northwest, convoked a reunion of the civil and military officials and many of the notabilities of Cape Haitien, and exposed to them the situation, stating, as I have been informed, that the town was threatened by a revolutionary army which it was impossible for him to resist because the Government had failed to place in his hands the means of resistance; that the only arms and ammunition that he had at his disposal were those sent here to the minister of the interior and which he had seized; that in view of this condition of affairs he felt it to be his duty to convoke the influential citizens of the town in order that the necessary measures might be taken to safeguard the general interests. At the very outset he reminded his hearers that it was generally known, and should be borne in mind, that he was a candidate for the Presidency.

After some deliberation a proces-verbal was drawn up giving the delegate full powers to act for the general good, and this document was signed by all present, including several senators and deputies and int'mate personal friends of the President. The proces-verbal, with the names of the signers, was published the following day in the Cable, the local journal, a marked copy of which is herewith inclosed.

On Saturday morning Gen. Metallus, with about 1,000 men and a few pieces of cannon, entered the town, lined up the whole force in front of the cathedral, and, after a short visit to the temple of worship, made a tourney of the town. These troops, as well as those already present, have up to the present time observed the most perfect discipline, and I have not heard of a single act of disorder. The town remains in an entirely normal condition, no flags have been displayed, and business pursues its regular course. This is entirely exceptional as a revolutionary incident.

Yesterday morning (the 19th instant) Gen. Metallus fired a salute of 17 guns, and his army proclaimed Gen. Vilbrun Guillaume Sam as chef du pouvoir executif.

The Cable of yesterday (the 19th) published an ordre du jour by Gen. Vilbrun Guillaume (this is the name by which he is geenrally known), dated the 16th, stating that measures had been taken to preserve order and asking the public to be reassured. A marked copy of this paper is also inclosed.

It seems now that the whole of the Departments of the North, Northwest, and Artibonite are in arms and that Gen. Guillaume has been very generally accepted as the candidate for the presidency.

Gens. Peralte and Fradelhomme (?), of the Zamor party, and formerly the brother-in-law of the ex-president, have written him letters accepting his candidacy and offering their support. A delegation was sent on Sunday last to Gen. Vieux, who is occupying Fort Liberte, and Gen. Bertan Codio, who is holding Ouanaminthe, and it is expected that both will accept, as they have already been in correspondence with Gen. Vilbrun. The delegation is expected to return to-day.

Two days ago a telephone message came here from Gonaives stating that it had been reported that a Haitian warship would be sent there with troops to hold that place. The delegate there, Gen. Misael Codio, has also offered his services to Gen. Vilbrun.

Your telegram bearing date of the 18th instant was delivered to me yesterday (the 19th). I immediately went to the delegate and made a complaint. He admitted that he had recently given orders not to accept any telegrams without his authorization, but promises to give orders that all my telegrams be accepted. I came to my office and made up a long telegram to you in code. When I sent it to the office the operator refused to accept it. The young man who took it went to the office of the delegate and made a complaint. The delegate sent his son with him to the telegraph office with the necessary orders. The operator replied that there was no communication and returned the telegram to me this morning. I have no means of verifying the facts, and, as I am writing you the contents of the telegram, I do not deem it necessary to inclose a copy.

Mr. Marsh asked me to beg you to deliver the inclosed note to Mr. Berlin.

As the agents of the French steamer refuse to accept private correspondence, and the post office is not sending any mail to Port au Prince, I am taking the liberty of inclosing to your address one important business letter of my own, and three left by Mr. Marshand and Mr. Edwards, which I would thank you very much to deliver.

I am, sir, your obedient servant,

L. W. LIVINGSTON,
American Consul.

The CHAIRMAN. Admiral, will you tell us, without any unnecessary references to the record there, how you came into contact with the consul, and what led to your landing, whether it was events, or the suggestion of the consul, or a decision on your own part?

Admiral CAPERTON. Yes, sir. Well, as I recall it now—this was six years ago—as I recall it now, without looking at my notes here, I am of the opinion that I did not land any force at that time, on my first visit to Cape Haitien.

The CHAIRMAN. You left without landing any force at that time?

Admiral CAPERTON. Yes. I went myself—if you would like a little story of it—I went myself to call upon the consul, and we discussed the condition of affairs.

Senator KING. Mr. Chairman, has Admiral Caperton already testified at any hearing?

The CHAIRMAN. No.

Senator KING. Or has he submitted a full statement of what he did and said?

The CHAIRMAN. The only statement we have is the department's general statement, with which you are familiar, of the history of the occupation of the two Republics.

Senator KING. Yes.

The CHAIRMAN. You left without landing. When did you return?

Senator KING. May I inquire, is there any controversy as to the department's statement? Does not that embody all that Admiral Caperton would testify to, or any other witness?

The CHAIRMAN. Well, I would not have called the Admiral if I had not thought he might throw some light upon the circumstances under which he landed and upon the orders which led to his landing.

Admiral CAPERTON. I have all those orders, sir.

The CHAIRMAN. Now, tell us, Admiral, when was it that you returned to land? Was it in conjunction with the arrival of the French ship *Descartes,* in June?

Admiral CAPERTON. That was several months afterwards. In the meantime I had gone to Port au Prince, and I followed Mr. Gillaume Sam around the coast, in order to impress upon him the importance of carrying on a—I am trying to think of the word for the kind of warfare.

The CHAIRMAN. Moderate warfare or civilized warfare?

Admiral CAPERTON. Civilized warfare. That is the word I was trying to think of.

The CHAIRMAN. You mean he was not carrying on the electoral campaign for the presidency, but a military campaign?

Admiral CAPERTON. Yes, sir; but you will understand that their methods are quite different from those of civilized people.

The CHAIRMAN. That is interesting.

Admiral CAPERTON. I had been informed by the consul that it was the general habit, if any man disobeyed, or did anything to displease him—I do not know to what extent—he would order him shot.

The CHAIRMAN. You mean to displease the commanding officer?

Admiral CAPERTON. Yes; Gen. Vilbrun Gillaume Sam.

The CHAIRMAN. Who is the consul, L'vingston?

Admiral CAPERTON. Yes; Mr. Livingston.

The CHAIRMAN. Is he a white man or a colored man?

Admiral CAPERTON. A colored man.

The CHAIRMAN. So Livingston himself, who is a colored man, told you that it was habitual that if a man offended the commanding general he was shot?

Admiral CAPERTON. Yes, sir; words to that effect, and he suggested that I call on Gen. Gillaume Sam unofficially, because he did not wish to recognize him officially as the "chief of the executive power," and after discussing the matter I called.

The CHAIRMAN. Was there another president in Port au Prince at this time?

Admiral CAPERTON. Yes, sir. This was a revolution. He was forming a revolution where they usually form them, in Ouanaminthe.

The CHAIRMAN. They started in Ouanaminthe as a rule?

Admiral CAPERTON. In Ouanaminthe. The cacos live in the vicinity, and the chief of the revolutionists, who afterwards proclaims himself "chief of the executive power," proceeds to Ouanaminthe, gathers in the chiefs of the cacos, and they bring in their men, and in a short time he has formed a revolutionary army.

The CHAIRMAN. You followed him then, as chief of the executive power, around the coast?

Admiral CAPERTON. Yes, sir.

The CHAIRMAN. Where did you head in again, at St. Marc or some place like that?

Admiral CAPERTON. Gonaives is the first place I think I touched. Understand, sir, there is a regular procedure in this warfare.

The CHAIRMAN. They take one place after another?

Admiral CAPERTON. Yes, sir; and they take them consecutively along the coast.

Senator KING. Did you make it clear that this Gen. Sam was a revolutionary general, or was in charge of the army of the recognized de facto and de jure government?

Admiral CAPERTON. I do not think I have yet, sir.

Senator KING. Well, what was he?

Admiral CAPERTON. Shall I just read a few lines on that, that will explain the whole thing? It seems that shortly after Davilmar Theodore, the then president, became president at Port au Prince, Gillaume Sam, in view of his strength in northern Haiti, demanded to be, and had been appointed by Theodore, as a delegate of the department of the north and northeast, and had taken up his headquarters in Cape Haitien. About the middle of January a revolutionary force of about 1,000 men appeared before Cape Haitien. This is the force I spoke of a moment ago. And as it eventually turned out, he pretended that he could not defend the city; in fact, he had nothing to defend the city with, and he immediately appealed to them to make him the chief of the executive power. In other words, he appointed himself there, the chief of the executive power, after arranging with the generals in the north and northeast for this purpose.

Senator KING. Then he betrayed the President?

Admiral CAPERTON. Yes, sir.

Senator KING. And the Government, and organized a revolutionary party and designated himself as the head of it?

Admiral CAPERTON. Yes, sir.

Senator KING. And he was well on in his revolutionary movement around the island?

Admiral CAPERTON. Yes, sir.

Senator KING. Electioneering by force, and attempting in a revolutionary way to make himself president of the Government?

Admiral CAPERTON. Yes, sir; and carrying out the usual routine of taking the march that was taken by all revolutionary forces. Strange to say, they are all exactly alike.

Senator KING. Was the president able to do anything to preserve order and peace and to maintain the dignity of his office and the Government against this revolutionary movement?

Admiral CAPERTON. He was not, to a satisfactory extent.

Senator KING. Where was he during the movement?

Admiral CAPERTON. He was in Port au Prince, the capital.

Senator KING. But no attempt had been made up to this time to oust him; that is, physically oust him from the capital?

Admiral CAPERTON. No, sir. They, the Government, carried on the usual process of getting ready and waiting for him to come around. The President of the

Republic eventually sent troops around to meet him at these different places, and as he advanced he took these places, because the forces that the Government had were not sufficient to hold these cities.

The CHAIRMAN. Now, let us get, if we can, Admiral, as promptly as may be, to the events which led to your first landing. Gen. Vilbrun Gillaume Sam was on his military electoral campaign and moving toward the capital?

Admiral CAPERTON. Yes, sir.

The CHAIRMAN. He took the capital, did he, or not?

Admiral CAPERTON. He took these various cities all the way around the coast from Cape Haitien to Port au Prince, via Gonaives, St. Marc, etc.

The CHAIRMAN. I understand that.

Admiral CAPERTON. And finally, when a revolutionary general or commander reaches a place called St. Marc, about 60 miles from the city, if he wins and takes that city, the capital falls immediately, and the President then makes arrangements to get out.

The CHAIRMAN. To go to St. Thomas?

Admiral CAPERTON. To go anywhere he can, unless he is murdered in the capital.

The CHAIRMAN. Who took St. Marc?

Admiral CAPERTON. Vilbrun Gillaume Sam.

The CHAIRMAN. Then what?

Senator KING. Was there a real battle there?

Admiral CAPERTON. No, sir; there was no real battle. The forces simply withdrew after a slight battle, when Gillaume Sam arrived, and when he got in everybody was his friend. They turned and went to him.

The CHAIRMAN. There are analogies between Haitian and American elections after all. However, after he took St. Marc, then what?

Admiral CAPERTON. After he took St. Marc Gillaume Sam moved down toward Port au Prince. Everything was in great excitement, and about that time, at 9.30 a. m., on Wednesday, January 27, 1915, the U. S. S. *Washington* arrived at Port au Prince.

The CHAIRMAN. You arrived at Port au Prince, and what did you find there? You did not land at Port au Prince at that time?

Admiral CAPERTON. No, sir. I am trying now to follow up this revolution.

The CHAIRMAN. Had Gillaume Sam come into Port au Prince when you got there?

Adimral CAPERTON. Not at that time. He arrived much later. I shifted my headquarters from Cape Haitien, as things quieted there, as his army moved out in the circle of march, and as I saw that my presence was demanded in the capital, I went there with my flagship, leaving the other ships under my command to look out for the different cities where I knew there would be——

The CHAIRMAN. What were these ships, gunboats?

Admiral CAPERTON. Yes; gunboats.

The CHAIRMAN. You left them back in the various ports?

Admiral CAPERTON. I left them in the various ports and gave them orders to meet the general outside of the city and make him again promise me that he would not loot or burn down the cities or fire in the cities, because I considered that not humane. The cities were all undefended, and they were poor people, generally speaking, and unarmed.

The CHAIRMAN. These were campaign pledges that you were exacting of him?

Admiral CAPERTON. Yes, sir. He gave me the first one in Cape Haitien, but I was not satisfied with it. I met him at each one, and so he finally laughingly said to me, "I do not see how you know where I am going. Every time I go to enter a city I find your representative outside with some question, asking me to behave myself." He promised to do so, and upon the whole he did very well, considering everything. He kept his word very well in that respect.

Senator KING. Were your movements approved by the Government?

Admiral CAPERTON. Every movement, sir; every single movement.

Senator KING. And you were not interfering with the functions of the Government that was in control of the island?

Admiral CAPERTON. No, sir.

Senator KING. I do not speak of the revolutionary movement.

Admiral CAPERTON. No, sir; I understand.

Senator KING. And all that you were trying to do was to exact pledges from the revolutionary commander that he would not sack, burn, rape, destroy, and loot in the towns and cities which he conquered?

Admiral CAPERTON. Yes, sir. That is what they usually do.

Senator KING. Admiral, right at this point, did you familiarize yourself sufficiently with the antecedent history of the island to justify the statement which you just made, that they usually do those things in a revolutionary war?

Admiral CAPERTON. Yes, sir.

Senator KING. They did not have civilized warfare there in those former revolutionary movements?

Admiral CAPERTON. No, sir; to my knowledge there has never been one, and I have followed up the history of many and have heard of many and talked about many.

Senator KING. It was savage warfare?

Admiral CAPERTON. Savage warfare; that is, uncivilized warfare.

Senator ODDIE. Do you know whether in any previous revolutions there were battles fought at St. Marc, before taking the capital, in which men were injured or killed?

Admiral CAPERTON. Oh, yes, sir; later on, when the next general came around. I will give that in detail. I was ashore then, having landed my forces to "protect property and preserve order."

The CHAIRMAN. This excursion was taken later by another?

Admiral CAPERTON. Yes, sir.

In order to clear up several questions asked me in regard to fighting at various places before they were taken by the revolutionists, also concerning the action taken by the Haitian Government in regard to the "service of the treasury," and also my sudden sailing for Port au Prince on the 26th of January, 1915, I would like to add the following remarks: I had decided to remain in Cape Haitien for a time after the departure of Guillaume Sam in order to observe conditions at that time; but the commanding officer of the *Wheeling*, Commander Moody, reported that the Theodore government had declared a blockade of the ports of northern Haiti, but was unable to enforce the blockade, as its naval vessels had no coal; that the American schooner *Alice Pendleton*, of New York, was in the harbor alongside the wharf with 600 tons of coal contracted for by the Haitian Government. It was known that the Government's financial condition was still in a low state and that they had been unable to obtain money for the purchase of this coal. Moody further stated that the Haitian Government had made attempts to obtain money from the Haitian National Bank, and upon the refusal of the management of this bank to deliver the money it was rumored that the Government had made threats to seize the money by force. The *Wheeling* further reported that our minister had received requests from both French and German Legations for an American man-of-war to visit Gonaives for the protection of foreign interests. The *Wheeling* also requested instructions relative to landing an armed force to protect the bank property. In view of this threatening attitude on the part of the Haitian Government, I feared for the safety not only of the bank property but for American lives and property in general at Port au Prince, and especially for the schooner *Alice Pendleton*. In view of these conditions, and also in view of the appeal of the American minister to protect American and foreign interests at St. Marc and Gonaives, I decided to concentrate what forces I had available and proceed to Port au Prince. In reply to the *Wheeling*, I informed Commander Moody to consult with the American minister, use discretion relative to protection of bank property, and also to protect the schooner *Alice Pendleton*. I notified the Secretary of the Navy and commander in chief of the Atlantic Fleet of these facts immediately.

I arrived with my flagship on the morning of the 27th of January, 1915, at Port au Prince, visited the minister with my staff, and found that although the rumored threats of the Government to seize funds in the bank had not been carried out, the bank situation was far from easy. Previous to my arrival I learned that the Haitian officials had again visited the bank and demanded gold, claiming this money belonged to the Haitian Government as part of "retrait" fund. Williams, acting director of the bank, refused, and reported to the legation that it was rumored same authorities would return and again renew their demand, in which case he would again refuse, and was afraid the authorities would attempt to take the money by force.

In view of the financial condition of the Theodore Government their urgent and vital need of funds, the lack of coal for the gunboats, the exposed position of the *Alice Pendleton*, the approach of the revolutionists, and the general insecure conditions at Port au Prince, I decided to keep in constant touch with the American minister and watch events. In view of the distance of the

Washington from the legation, I mounted a field radio set at the American Legation for purposes of communication.

Because of the report that the Government forces were threatening to burn St. Marc if they were forced to retire from that place, our minister and the French and German ministers were somewhat worried and requested that I send a ship to that port.

On January 28, 1915, I received the following message from the Secretary of State, via the Navy Department, in reply to my request of January 26 for immediate instructions relative to the protection of bank property at Port au Prince:

"State to the Government of Haiti that the Government of the United States of America can not consent to the removal of funds that belong to bank and getting which funds it is not possible for the bank to comply with contractual obligations it has assumed. You will issue to that Government a warning that any attempt that might be made to remove the funds of the bank will compel you to take into consideration means to prevent such violation of foreign stockholders' rights."

Shortly after this I received the following message from the Secretary of the Navy: •

"If deemed necessary in cooperation with minister land marines and sailors."

I also received from the commanding officer of the *Wheeling* on this date the following message describing conditions at St. Marc, Haiti:

"Government force 300. Revolutionists greatly outnumbered are said to be fighting 4 miles from town back of hills. Consular corps in body called aboard. Is stated it is feared Government forces will be defeated again and fall back into town and then fear they will burn town to-night unless I can prevent. Government expects reinforcements about 2 p. m., Thursday. Ministers war and interior now in town and I will have interview this afternoon. Town itself quiet now but practically deserted by population except few foreigners on account of fear. More later.

MOODY."

On January 29, 1915, the Theodore Government published the following proclamation changing the depository for customs and tax receipts from the National Bank of the Republic of Haiti to such business houses or banks as it may designate, etc.:

[Translation.]

PROCLAMATION—JOSEPH DAVILMAR THEODORE, PRESIDENT OF THE REPUBLIC.

[See art. 97 of the constitution.]

See that the seals have been fixed to the National Bank of the Republic of Haiti, on a value of 95140 dollars (P or 95140) that by reason of the two laws of the 18th and 23d of December, permitting the running use of certain available values for the State.

Considering that it is of moment before the illegal opposition of the bank that these definite values should be at the disposition of the Government, and considering that the extreme rarity and scarceness of gold renders difficult the payment of taxes in gold, paralyzes the importation and exportation and creates a situation very prejudicial to the public treasurer, that it is necessary to provide against this case with major force of wh'ch the gravity is evident.

With reference to the second new paragraph of the first article of the law of the 23d of December, 1914, aiming at the resumption of the service of the treasury under the direction of the secretary of state of finance and of commerce and the advice of the councils of the secretary of state.

ARTICLE 1. After the publication of the present proclamation all of the customs duties of exportation and the additional 45 per cent tax of gold American on imports will be deposited to the credit of the State at Port au Prince, Jacmel, Cayes, Jermie, Aquin, Miragoane, Petit-Goave, and St. Marc, at such business houses and at such banks which will be des'gnated by the secretary of state of finance, th's and the amount of 95,140 dollars will belong to the State actually under the seals at the National Bank of the Republic of Haiti and of the value fixed by the two laws of the 18th and 23d of December, 1914, that portion of the mortgages deposited designated to the home debt will be deducted from the moneys received and held at the disposition of the bank. After the whole collection by the State of the value of the moneys before defined the bank w ll make reimbursement to the interested accounts by means of the moneys actually under seal and as fixed by the laws of the 18th and 24th of December, 1914.

ART. II. The exportations and the surtax of 45 per cent will be deposited one half in American gold, one half in treasury bonds, or in the notes of the new issue of $8,000,000 at the rate of 5 piasters for $1.

ART. III. The present proclamation will be published and executed under the direction of the secretary of state, of finance, and of commerce. Given at the nat'onal palace at Port au Prince, January 27, 1915, and the one hundred and twelfth year of the independence.

DAVILMAR THEODORE.

By the President:
D. DALINOIS,
The Secretary of State of Finance and of Commerce.

In the meantime I had been in consultation with the American minister relative to the situation at Port au Prince. On Saturday forenoon, January 30, I was informed by h'm that the final answer of the Theodore Government to his representations directed made by the State Department in its telegram of January 26, had not been received; that he expected such reply in a few days. In the meantime about 1,000 Government troops had collected at Port au Pr'nce, some arriving from the south.

On February 3 the American minister informed me that he was assured by the Theodore Government that no attempt would be made to forcibly remove the funds from the bank, and that in all dealings in connection with these funds legal proceedings would be followed exclusively.

On the afternoon of February 5 I received a radiogram from the commanding officer of the *Wheeling*, who, as stated previously, had gone to Gonaives, that Vilbrun Guillaume Sam, with about 1,000 men, had entered Gonaives without resistance at 9 a. m. that day and had been received with a 21-gun salute by the shore battery. The commanding officer of the *Wheeling* urged on Guillaume Sam to take necessary measures to avoid injury to life and property at St. Marc and Gonaives.

Since the end of that phase of the bank situation at Port au Prince relative to the forceful removal of funds Port au Prince had been quiet, in so far as disorders were concerned; there was a suppressed air of uneasiness among all classes, however. Prominent men were preparing to take refuge in the legations, and many fantastic rumors of the doings of the revolutionists and Government forces and the Government officials there in the town were constant. I was in constant touch with the minister relative to the situation.

About February 9 Gen. Monplaisir came to Port au Prince, and there was also in Port au Prince at this time Gen. Defly, at one time general of the Arrondissement. Both of these men were undesirable characters. Defly had an unenviable record while general of the Arrondissement, and Monpalisir, while strong, was high handed and arbitrary in his methods. Both were consequently disliked and feared by the best Haitians. There was coming to my notice constantly indications of plots by Defly and Monpalisir for getting control of the Government. I thought it possible from information that I had gathered in Port au Prince that Monplaisir or Defly might attempt to force intervention by the United States by creating such insufferable conditions in Port au Prince that I would be forced to land for the protection of foreign life and property. These men evidently, from what I could learn, thought that if they were in power at the time I landed and that if the United States should decide to intervene at this place that in view of their high official positions at the time we landed they would probably be kept in office by the United States and would then be assured of steady pay and support. Further, in connection with the above, a combination of 10 senators had attempted to approach me with the further proposition to prevent Guillaume from entering Port au Prince so that they might have a free election for President, their ideas being that the United States support them in a government to be. It is needless to say that I ignored all such advances and that I refrained from showing by any word or action any disposition to favor any man or party in Haiti.

Guillaume was a strong man, but feared by the better class of Haitians on account of his harsh methods and crooked tendencies. He had already served one year of a life sentence imposed for falsifying government financial statements and causing a large overissue of bonds the proceeds of which he had appropriated to his own use.

In view of the conditions in Haiti which I believed were unusually disturbed because of the excessive number of plots and counter plots among the Haitians, the excessive continuation of revolutionary movements and disorder throughout the country, the rapidly approaching fall of the Theodore government and the consequent chaotic conditions that would occur in Port Au Prince, the approach of Vilbrun Guillaume with about fifteen hundred men, among whom were many cacos, the lawless men of the north who were very much feared; in view of the representations made by the United States with reference to the customs and other matters; in view of the possible violation of Haitian neutrality by belligerent ships of European powers; in view, further, of the unsettled condition of the bank question which, although assurances had been received that no forcible attempt would be made to remove funds, was yet far from settled owing to the breaking of the contract by the Theodore government; the changing of the depository for customs receipts, and the action taken by the directors of the bank in connection therewith; in view of the disturbed conditions in Santo Domingo; and especially in view of my lack of knowledge of the policy of the United States Government, which, without warning, might demand of me to take prompt action in that vicinity; I requested that an expeditionary regiment of marines be sent to this naval station, Guantanamo Bay, Cuba, together with the necessary means of transportation to Haiti, and that both the Marines and the transport be subject to my immediate call.

On February 18, the commanding officer of the *Des Moines* reported that St. Marc was in the hands of the revolutionists; that about eight of them had taken the town during the night; that casualties were few; and that a number of the Government forces were drowned while trying to get off to the Nord Alexis; and that Monplaisir, the Theodore minister of the interior, was reported dead. It was afterwards found out that Monplaisir had been stabbed in the back presumably by one of his own men in the boat getting off to the Nord Alexis.

In the midst of the foregoing events on February 8 the commander of the *Wheeling* reported that ex-Minister Bobo was on board the *Pacifique* going to Monti Cristi and Ouanaminthe to organize and lead a new revolution.

During this time Port au Prince was becoming more disturbed, but up to this date, February 18, 1915, there had been no outbreaks. On that day several changes were made by Davilmar Theodore in his cabinet, among which was the resignation of Mr. Norno, minister of foreign affairs.

At 7 p. m., Saturday, February 20, the commanding officer of the *Des Moines* reported that the Dutch steamer *Prins Frederick Hendrik* had arrived at St. Marc from Cape Haitien with 70,000 gourdes for Guillaume, and had little; that all was quiet at Cape Haitien and Ouanaminthe; and that the *Pacifique* had recently been at Puerto Plata.

As I believed that Guillaume had the situation well in hand at St. Marc, and would preserve order, and as he now had received considerable money and had paid his troops, and as, therefore, the pressure on the customs money at St. Marc was relieved, and as the situation was rapidly approaching a climax at Port au Prince, I decided to concentrate all my forces at Port au Prince, and accordingly ordered the *Des Moines* to that place.

The arrival of the Dutch steamer *Prins Frederick Hendrik* had been expected for a day or so prior to arrival, and it was believed that President Davilmar Theodore would take passage on her, this being in accordance with the time-honored custom of procedure in the abdication of Haitian Presidents who were exiled.

After the departure of President Davilmar Theodore on the *Prins Frederick Hendrik*, and after the occupation of Port au Prince by the Guillaume forces on February 23, a beneficent effect was noticeable. Business was resumed. Stores, which had been closed for several days, were reopened; the market reopened and the country people began bringing produce into the city; the water was turned on in the city again; and excellent order was preserved. It was reported to me by men who have witnessed these revolutionary movements for many years that this change of government in Port au Prince at this time had been occasioned by the least disturbance of any time for many years.

On February 26 I received a radiogram from the commander in chief, quoting one from the department, directing that the *Tacoma* or some other suitable vessel proceed to Santiago de Cuba, meet Gov. Fort and Mr. C. C. Smith, representatives of the State Department, and then convey them from Santiago de Cuba to Port au Prince, Haiti, and stating further that these gentlemen expected to arrive at Santiago de Cuba on the evening of March 8.

On Thursday, March 4, the Haitian Congress, in a joint session of senators and deputies, elected Vilbrun Guillaume Sam President of Haiti.

At 11 a. m., Friday, March 5, the *Tacoma* arrived from Santiago de Cuba with Gov. Fort and Mr. C. C. Smith, commissioners to Haiti from the State Department.

The situation at Port au Prince and throughout the Haitian Republic had now become tranquil. A constitutional government was established on shore which was maintaining order and gaining the confidence of the people. The negotiations pending between the United States Government and the Government of Haiti were in the hands of the American minister and a special commission from the State Department. There seemed, therefore, to be no need at present for as large a naval force in the vicinity of Port au Prince as I had theretofore kept. However, I decided to leave one vessel at Port au Prince to watch the political conditions and report thereon and to furnish such aid to the State Department commission as it desired.

I left Haiti with the *Washington* on March 8. Throughout my operations in the island of Haiti I had endeavored to ascertain and follow the Government's policy with reference to that island, and in view of its great economic and commercial importance to the United States, its vital strategic importance to the Navy in future operations in this our most threatened area, and the complications that might arise with foreign powers growing out of its chaotic conditions I had devoted myself to especial care in all operations in that vicinity.

The CHAIRMAN. Well now, proceed, Admiral, to the events which led to your landing in July, if I remember rightly, at Cape Haitien.

Admiral CAPERTON. Then, as I understand, you do not care to hear any further details?

The CHAIRMAN. Well, not in detail. Sam took the capital and made himself president?

Admiral CAPERTON. Yes, sir.

Senator KING. If the chairman would not object, I would be very glad to learn how he took it and what became of the president, very briefly.

Admiral CAPERTON. Yes, sir. I have all that written down here, if I can just find it.

On the 22d of February, Washington's birthday, I remember—I would like to explain the reason why it takes me so much time to do this——

Senator KING. Do not do that.

Admiral CAPERTON. I want to do it, in justice to myself. Every move I made and every move that was made by the forces of the Government and the revolutionary forces I reported daily, and sometimes twice a day, to the department here in Washington, so that I have all this down chronologically. It is a little hard to refresh my memory, as I have about 20 of these volumes.

On the 22d I arrived. I have gotten down to when Guillaume Sam arrived. He came in, I think, about the 23d of February. I have not looked at these things for a long time, and I have not refreshed my memory because I have not had time. I wish to make it plain that there was fighting at these different places outside of the city generally, during Guillaume Sam's march from Cape Haitien to the capital.

Senator KING. Did he always vanquish the forces of the Government?

Admiral CAPERTON. Yes, sir; generally he was successful. He had more troops and he had money and he managed to get ammunition.

Senator KING. Where did he get his money and his ammunition?

Admiral CAPERTON. It was said that his uncle, a previous president, gave him $50,000 to make himself president. This I have heard discussed in Port au Prince, and I believe it is a fact. He did not have all of this at that time, but, as I recall, in one instance—I think it was St. Marc or Gonaives—he managed to borrow money from some of his friends who were bankers.

The CHAIRMAN. Foreign or native bankers?

Admiral CAPERTON. Well, they are very much mixed up, sir; it is hard for me to tell exactly. I know of some native people who loaned him money.

Senator KING. Were there any German bankers who loaned him money or from whom he obtained money?

Admiral CAPERTON. I think there were in St. Marc. I had quite an experience with them, which is all detailed here in my report. It would take some little time to find it.

Senator KING. He did not conceal the fact that he was trying to overthrow the Government, did he?

Admiral CAPERTON. No, sir. This was a regularly organized revolution, if it can be termed such. The moment he acclaimed himself " chief of the executive power " he became the chief revolutionist in the island and the next president, to-be if he were successful with his revolution.

Senator KING. That was a violation of their constitution—his movement?

Admiral CAPERTON. Yes, sir.

The CHAIRMAN. Well, he got to Port au Prince?

Admiral CAPERTON. Yes, sir.

The CHAIRMAN. Do you want to say anything about his actions in the capture of the city?

Admiral CAPERTON. Yes, sir; I would like to make a few remarks in regard to that. During Sunday, February 21, 1915, the three parties of revolutionists under Hilaire, Zamor, and Guillaume Sam, continued closing in on the city of Port au Prince. These people had joined with Guillaume Sam, one coming from the east and the other from the south, so that he had, finally, three armies or bodies of troops advancing on Port au Prince. At this time General Zamor, who was spoken of as the head of one of the parties of revolutionists, was in the French consulate or French Legation, having taken refuge when the previous president went into office, and he had been there for four or five or six months, not able to get out, during which time he was fed and clothed by the French minister's family, with whom I talked much about this subject at a later date.

At 11.30 o'clock Sunday evening, the minister of war, Vagues, sent an officer to the *Wheeling*, in Port au Prince, and through him applied for an asylum for Vagues on board that vessel the following night, stating he intended to go aboard a Dutch steamer, the *Prins Frederick Hendrik*, the next morning. It seemed that it was arranged to delay this entry into the city of Port au Prince until this steamer arrived, and it was presumably understood that the President was to leave on this steamer, which it turned out was a fact.

The CHAIRMAN. You mean that just as these revolutions are functionizing in their progress so also it is customary to allow the outgoing President to leave the country before the arrival and the inauguration of the new one?

Admiral CAPERTON. Yes, sir; sometimes he is allowed to do so, unless he is unfortunate, like President Guillaume Sam, who was assassinated in the capital.

The CHAIRMAN. Yes; I understand.

Senator KING. There have been others who have been killed, have there not?

Admiral CAPERTON. Yes, sir.

Senator KING. If they did not get out, they were killed?

Admiral CAPERTON. Yes, sir. They usually took asylum promptly in the French Legation, which was divided from the palace by a large wall, in which there was a door with a key about that long [indicating], and if the lock had not rusted between the time the previous President had run through he would make his escape all right, but on this occasion, with Guillaume Sam, they could not unlock the door, and he had trouble getting over the wall, but he finally got over; they assisted him over the wall. That I will come to later. The matter of asylum—I do not suppose you want to know how that was dealt with?

The CHAIRMAN. Did you receive the general?

Admiral CAPERTON. No, sir; we informed him that there were other vessels in the harbor, two of his own men-of-war, and he could go to them, besides this Dutch steamer was expected the next morning at daylight, and they usually arrived on time, and in this instance she did arrive on time, and he then went aboard from his hiding place that night. I did not consider it a case of sufficient danger to grant him an asylum. I knew he had other places to go, as stated to him above.

The CHAIRMAN. Let me interrupt, Admiral, to ask during all this time you were reporting, as you have said, to the department?

Admiral CAPERTON. Yes, sir.

The CHAIRMAN. Did you receive from the department messages approving your course?

Admiral CAPERTON. Yes, sir. They are all in the record here.

Senator KING. I would like to ask, if I may, what did you understand you were there for?

Admiral CAPERTON. For the protection of foreigners and foreign property.

Senator KING. Do you think that your presence and the presence of the American fleet did protect lives and property?

Admiral CAPERTON. Yes, sir; undoubtedly so.

Senator KING. If you had not been there, do you think that not only American lives but the lives of other foreigners would have been taken?

Admiral CAPERTON. I fear so.

Senator KING. Had former revolutions resulted in the massacre of foreigners as well as natives?

Admiral CAPERTON. Generally speaking, no. I think they had not been in the habit of killing foreigners. I think that is a matter of history. But they did interfere with the property and the business of the cities, and no one knew what they would do at the time. I will show you later, when I really landed, and will tell you the circumstances and things that did take place in the city at that time.

Senator KING. Did you have sufficient contact with the people, the Haitians who were loyal to the Government, and the foreigners, including Americans, to introduce into your mind the belief and the conviction that your presence there was necessary?

Admiral CAPERTON. Yes, sir.

Senator KING. For the protection of the lives and property of foreigners?

Admiral CAPERTON. Yes, sir; and especially property, because they always looted. When a man joins a revolutionary army, it goes without saying that he has the right to steal, loot, or do whatever he likes to the natives, which they generally do. They fed themselves all the way along, and lived on the country.

Senator KING. Did you talk with Americans there?

Admiral CAPERTON. Yes, sir.

Senator KING. Did they state to you that their lives were in danger, and their property?

Admiral CAPERTON. Yes, sir; they insisted upon my landing, and when I reached the point of landing I will tell you why I landed. I had a conversation with the French minister, with the chargé d'affaires of the English Government, and also our own, who was then really the secretary of our legation.

Senator KING. Were you in contact with the President of the Government from time to time?

Admiral CAPERTON. Yes, sir; I was, in a manner, but we had not recognized the then President. I had not met him, but my officers talked with some of his cabinet from time to time, but we had not recognized him, so that I had not called upon him officially; I had not called upon any of them officially.

Senator KING. But he was de facto as well as de jure President?

Admiral CAPERTON. Yes, sir; he was de facto President.

Senator KING. But any movements of your war vessel around the island there were with his approval, or were they not; what is the fact, from what you could learn?

Admiral CAPERTON. From what I could learn; yes, sir. He knew I was trying to make the revolution be as civilized in warfare as near as possible.

Senator KING. To protect life and property and to prevent massacre?

Admiral CAPERTON. Protecting property and protecting lives; and the President knew I was going out to beseech the then revolutionary chief not to do his fighting in the cities.

The CHAIRMAN. Let me interrupt there with a specific question that will go back to your colloquy with the Admiral.

What specific instances, of your own knowledge, were there, either in the Vilbrun Guillaume Sam revolution, or others, of injury to the property of foreigners, or loss of life by foreigners at the hands of the revolutionists? Can you tell of any case where a foreigner was killed by the revolutionary or Government forces or where property was destroyed?

Admiral CAPERTON. I do not believe I can, sir. You must understand that foreigners were not allowed to own property by the constitution.

The CHAIRMAN. They are not allowed to own real property?

Admiral CAPERTON. No, sir.

The CHAIRMAN. Do you know of any case where any of them were ever killed?

Admiral CAPERTON. I do not know that I can recall now, sir.

The CHAIRMAN. That is all on that point, Admiral.

Admiral CAPERTON. On the morning of the 22d of February I sent an officer ashore to the American legation to ascertain the news. From this officer I received the report that there had been considerable firing throughout the town during the night.

I might say that during this time they shut off the water from the city—the revolutionists did—so that the citizens were crying out for water in the city, and the French minister made a protest to the officer in control relative to the water and had received assurance that the water would be turned on again as soon as the revolutionists took control.

Furthermore, I was informed that Gen. Praedel and Gen. Polynice were in charge of the city and were making arrangements to turn same over to Vilbrun Gillaume, and that Davilmar Theodore had been informed by the revolutionary factions that he would be given until noon to make his departure. That was on the morning of the 22d of February.

I may say that Gen. Polynice and Gen. Praedel and four or five others were in the habit of taking charge when the President was about to leave. They assumed authority to handle the police and the soldiers as best they could in the city, constituting themselves a committee of safety.

The CHAIRMAN. That was their usual function there?

Admiral CAPERTON. Yes, sir. On many occasions before, and while I was there with two Presidents, they both had the same position.

The CHAIRMAN. Did they hold office in the intervals between the assumption of this authority?

Admiral CAPERTON. No, sir; Gen. Praedel, I think, did, but Gen. Polynice was a business man—I do not know his business, because none or few of them have any business. I do not think he was a lawyer, even. Many are professional men, but they are not business men.

The CHAIRMAN. Well, his business was to take charge in the intervals?

Admiral CAPERTON. At that time he always took charge. They always went to him; they looked to him to take charge.

The CHAIRMAN. Did he save enough during that short time to live in the interval?

Admiral CAPERTON. I suppose so. He had a very nice home there and was a very nice man. They always went to him and expected him to bob up, and when he came up things quieted down more or less in the city when the took charge. He was the man I went to later when I had to go in myself, as I will explain when I reach that part of my testimony.

At 11.45 a. m. on this same day, January 22, Port Alexander and the battery on the water front fired a salute, and Davilmar Theodore, accompanied by a guard, went aboard the *Prins Frederik Hendrik*, unoccasioned by disturbance of any kind. With him went only two or three of his cabinet.

The CHAIRMAN. Accompanied by whom?

Admiral CAPERTON. Accompanied by the ex-Minister of War Vagues. I saw them with my glasses. They made quite an imposing march down the street and wharf with their long frock coats and silk hats. He was then going aboard the *Prins Frederik Hendrik* leaving the country. He was accompanied by ex-Minister of War Vagues, as I said before, Locean Baptiste, Mr. Geradin Theodore, and two sons. I know it to be a fact that the old man, Mr. Davilmar Theodore, had hardly a sufficient amount of money to buy his ticket out of the country, as he appealed for money to help him to go where he wished to go. and as it turned out he only went to Santo Domingo.

The CHAIRMAN. Now, will you not move on to the events which led to the occupation? I think that is what we want.

Admiral CAPERTON. You wish to know how the President came in—how Mr. Gillaume Sam got in? The then President, as I have said before, Mr. Davilmar Theodore, left the country in the Dutch steamer.

The CHAIRMAN. In a plug hat, on a Dutch ship?

Admiral CAPERTON. Yes, sir; leaving the city without any government whatever, and the only people with any authority whatever were those two officers, Gen. Praedel and Gen. Polynice, who appointed themselves a committee of safety, as they usually called themselves.

The city became more quiet as soon as Theodore left, Gens. Praedel and Polynice being in charge, working until the arrival of Vilbrun Gillaume Sam.

Senator KING. Where were the revolutionary forces then; how near the city? Were they in the city then, some of them?

Admiral CAPERTON. Not yet. About 800 revolutionists arrived in the city the following day.

Senator KING. You said they had been firing.

Admiral CAPERTON. Well, on the outskirts, a mile or so out, but there was some firing in the city. Everybody fires there on an occasion of this kind.

The moment the President left, according to custom the Government forces occupying the city usually turned over and joined forces with the new man coming in, because they wanted to be paid, and they would be paid under this procedure. The Government had some forces at this time up in the northeastern part of the island around near Ouanaminthe, where they went after Gillaume Sam proceeded around on this tour of his.

On the afternoon of the 23d of February about 800 troops of Vilbrun Gillaume's forces entered the city from the north. A committee of administration took charge, pending the arrival of Vilbrun Gillaume, and publicly assured peace and order.

On the morning of the 25th of February, Vilbrun Gillaume entered Port au Prince with about 2,000 men on foot and 400 mounted. His entry was occasioned with no disturbance of any kind. It was now estimated that about 5,000 troops were in Port au Prince. These men, or troops, had very few clothes. They were ragged, hungry, dirty. irresponsible, with no education, and simply did what they pleased in the city to a certain extent.

Senator KING. The cacos constituted a large part of the troops, did they?

Admiral CAPERTON. Yes, sir; they are all cacos; all the revolutionary fellows are cacos.· They live in the northern hills, and they have chiefs, as I said, and they all come in to be paid by the new Government. I might say that in the course of a few days—not being on shore at this time I do not know how many days it was— but in a few days they paid them off a few gourds, 5 or 10 each. Eight gourds at that time were equivalent to our dollar. They pay these troops off, who generally turn in their rifles, and sometimes they pay them a gourd or two for a rifle, and then they proceed back to their hills again, waiting for the next presidential move.

The President was unable to get a quorum of the Congress. so that he was not elected President until several days afterwards.

The CHAIRMAN. Was that a formality usual under the c'rcumstances?

Admiral CAPERTON. Yes, sir. I might say there is always a kind of "permanent committee." This committee can meet and call the congress.

The CHAIRMAN. In special session?

Admiral CAPERTON. Yes, sir.

The CHAIRMAN. And it is usual for a man, when he has come to the end of his military excursion to the capital, to be confirmed in the position of power by the congress?

Admiral CAPERTON. Yes, sir. So this committee met and sent out a call for a meeting of congress, but they were not able to get the delegates together—they were scattered around—so that Guillaume was not inaugurated until the 7th, I th'nk.

The CHAIRMAN. Never mind the date.

Admiral CAPERTON. The situation at Port au Prince and throughout the Haitian Republic had now become tranquil. A constitutional government was established on shore, which was maintaining order and gaining the confidence of the other people. I merely mention this to explain my next move. I therefore considered the opportunity available for me to withdraw what vessels I could spare in this vicin'ty and order them to Guantanamo for target practice, which, in view of the lack of opportunity for such work during the year previous, was greatly needed by all vessels of the cruiser squadron.

I left on the 8th of March, two days after the President was inaugurated, and sa'led for Guantanamo. Upon arrival at Guantanamo the commander in chief of the Atlantic fleet informed me that conditions were not very settled at Vera Cruz and said he would have to order me to that station, so that that afternoon I sailed for Vera Cruz with two or three vessels.

On July 1, 1915, in accordance with orders of the Navy Department. stating that French marines had landed at Cape Hatien, Haiti, and that I was to proceed there with the Washington to thank the French commander and take the necessary steps to "protect property and preserve order." I arrived with the Washington at Cape Haitien at 9.30 a. m. on Thursday, July 1, 1915, coming from Vera Cruz, Mexico. In order to better estimate the situation at Cape Haitien and get in touch with the general situation in the Haitian Republic. I assumed authority of the department to send the Eagle to Port au Prince for news. Upon arrival at Cape Haitien I found the French cruiser Descartes anchored near the town and exchanged salutes with that vessel. At 10.30 a. m. the commanding officer of the Descartes, Capt. H. Lafrogne, paid an official call on me. The commanding officer of the *Descartes* stated that he had arrived at Cape Haitien, coming from Jamaica via Port au Prince, on the early morning of June 19, at the direction of the French minister at Port au Prince; that at that time a revolutionary force under Dr. Rosalvo Bobo, minister of interior in former President Davilmar Theodore's cabinet, was in charge of the town; that at noon on that day the revolutionary troops under Bobo evacuated the town and the Government troops entered; and that on that day, for the protection of foreign interests, the *Descartes* had landed a force of 50 men, stationing them at the French consulate, the French monastery, and the bank, Commander Lafrogne further stated that he kept these men on shore until June 24, guarding foreign interests and otherwise aiding foreigners. He stated that he had sent some flour ashore for the use of the French citizens.

The French commander further stated that when he arrived in Haitian waters the French minister at Port au Prince had received an official protest from the Haitian Government against the *Descartes* remaining in Haitian waters on account of the violation of neutrality. He further stated that the German minister in Port au Prince had protested to the same and to the Haitian Government.

Senator KING. All your inquiries supported the statements made to you by the French commander?

Admiral CAPERTON. Yes, sir.

Senator ODDIE. Were there any foreigners or Americans hurt or killed at Cape Haitien at this time?

Admiral CAPERTON. I think not, sir. The French commander stated that he placed himself at my disposal and orders.

The CHAIRMAN. Excuse me. May I ask about what time you are speaking now?

Admiral CAPERTON. July, when I was about to land.

The CHAIRMAN. Your ship is lying off——

Admiral CAPERTON. I had left Vera Cruz under orders, and I had arrived in Haitien waters.

The CHAIRMAN. Where?

Admiral CAPERTON. Cape Haitien, and there I met the *Descartes*.

The French commander stated that he placed himself at my disposal and orders while at Cape Haitien for the protection of foreign interests. He asked me if my instructions interfered with his remaining at Cape Haitien. I told him that they did not. He stated that he would probably have to leave shortly for coal.

The CHAIRMAN. Did he tell you that property had been injured when he landed?

Admiral CAPERTON. No, sir; but another revolution had started, and the Government troops had left, or vice versa, I do not know which, and one had come in and the other gone out, and when they do that they always sack everything, you know, and shoot up the town, and the people were fighting, so they asked for French aid, and he landed.

Senator KING. There were foreigners residing there?

Admiral CAPERTON. Yes.

Senator KING. Americans as well as French and Germans?

Admiral CAPERTON. Yes, sir; Americans, French, and Germans.

Senator KING. Many nationalities?

Admiral CAPERTON. Yes, sir; many nationalities.

Senator KING. The French had done nothing other than protect the property of foreigners?

Admiral CAPERTON. That is all, sir, and sent some provisions ashore because the people were starving generally.

The CHAIRMAN. You landed then?

Admiral CAPERTON. Yes, sir—not just yet, sir. I do not suppose you would care to know how the revolutionary forces came in. You understand that Dr. Bobo was the minister of interior under Davilmar Theodore, the President, who had just left Haiti. He became dissatisfied, I might say, in the meantime, and resigned from the cabinet and went north to become President himself.

Senator KING. He started another revolution?

Admiral CAPERTON. Yes, sir; he did. This was in about two months' time.

Senator KING. And he had gathered a considerable force, had he, of these vagabonds and cacos?

Admiral CAPERTON. Yes, sir. We will get to that. Even on the 2d of July, with a revolutionary force of 500 men under Gen. Bobo, he had arrived at

Cape Haitien and had on that day assumed control of the town. The town was afterwards blockaded by the Government gunboats *Nord Alexis* and *Pacifique* and approached from the south by a Government force. There was some pillaging when the Government troops entered, but most of these offenders were promptly punished.

During the time that Bobo occupied Capt Haitien there was some shooting in the vicinity, some bullets falling in the town, and a few shots from the gunboats fired at Fort Picolet, at the head of the cape; otherwise order had been maintained.

All the cables from Cape Haitien, namely, one to Puerto Plata, one to New York, and one to Mole St. Nicholas, were open and in working order.

At this time the town of Cape Haitien was in charge of the Government forces under Gen. Blot, assisted by the commandant of the fort, Gen. Parisien. Gen. Blot was special delegate in the north in charge of the military operations against the revolutionists—that is, against Gen. Bobo.

The commanding officer of the *Descartes* informed me that he had as refugees on board the chief of staff and one or two other members of the staff of Bobo, who fled to his ship when Bobo left the city upon the return of the Government forces.

I do not like to take up the time of the committee, but what I next wish to show is what relations I had with this man, Gen. Blot, and also with Gen. Bobo.

Senator KING. Can you not state it without referring to your memorandum?

Admiral CAPERTON. Not very well, sir; I can not get the names. I think I can give it to you.

The city of Cape Haitien is so situated that it is very easily protected from the outskirts of the city. That is to say, a vessel in the harbor is able to protect a small neck of land over which troops have to pass in order to enter.

The CHAIRMAN. The city is on a sort of peninsula?

Admiral CAPERTON. A peninsula; yes, sir. After several days of discussion with Gen. Blot and also with our consul there and the prominent people of the city I decided that I would not allow any fighting within the city walls.

The CHAIRMAN. Was this conformable with any general or specific instructions from the Navy Department?

Admiral CAPERTON. This was not, sir. I had orders to protect the lives and property of Americans and other foreign citizens, and knowing how these people act when one force comes into the city——

The CHAIRMAN. You had orders to preserve peace or to protect——

Admiral CAPERTON. No, sir; I had orders to protect lives and property of the foreign citizens. I had orders to protect the city and property.

The CHAIRMAN. Is there some one general order which laid down your policy, a general order of the department to you?

Admiral CAPERTON. Yes, sir. You mean upon occasions like that?

Senator KING. Did you have any special order here?

The CHAIRMAN. The admiral has testified he did not have a special order in the case of Cape Haitien.

Admiral CAPERTON. Yes; I read my orders here, sir. I will just repeat them. I was to proceed there with the *Washington*, thank the French commander, and take the necessary steps to protect property and preserve order. This is the order:

"French marines landed Cape Haitien. Proceed there with U. S. S. *Washington*, thank French commander, take necessary steps protect property and preserve order. Dispose of vessels on Mexican coast to best advantage. U. S. S. *Marietta* en route to Vera Cruz.

(Signed)   DANIELS."

As I said, after discussing this matter with our consul and the French consul, with Gen. Blot himself, and other prominent men in the city, I considered it my duty, in order to carry out my orders, to allow no fighting in the streets, because the city was entirely unprotected. Therefore I drew up an order, which I presented to Gen. Blot, and also managed to send my chief of staff, with an escort, out into the jungles to find Gen. Bobo, and I presented each one of them with this order. I sent my chief of staff on shore to have a conversation with Gen. Blot, the commanding officer of the Government forces in Cape Haitien. The chief of staff stated as follows:

"I am charged by my admiral to express to you his compliments and his good wishes for the peace and prosperity of Haiti. The admiral desires to state frankly the purpose of his visit here. The statement is made with kind feeling and without any desire to appear as a threat, but it is made so that you may know exactly what to expect of him. The admiral is here to protect the lives of foreigners. This he will do if necessary, but he sincerely hopes and believes that there will not be occasion for him to do anything. The admiral knows that there are armed revolutionists near Cape Haitien, and there is a possibility of a conflict between these revolutionists and the Government forces.

"The admiral believes that the lives and property of foreigners residing in Cape Haitien will be threatened and insecure should there be fighting in the city itself or near the city. Therefore the admiral states that there must be no fighting in the city or near it, or he will have to take means to protect the lives of foreigners. He therefore suggests that all fighting must take place at a reasonable distance from the city, and that under no circumstances shall foreigners be endangered in life or property."

In reply to this the commander stated as follows:

"I thank you for your kindly sentiments. Express to the admiral my compliments and my appreciation for his message."

Senator KING. That was the representative of the Government?

Admiral CAPERTON. Gen. Blot, the representative of the Government.

Afterwards I wished to confirm this, so I wrote the following letters to Gen. Probus Blot, commanding the Haitian Government troops at Cape Haitien, Haiti.

The CHAIRMAN. Put them in the record as they are. You do not have to read them.

(The letters referred to are here printed in full, as follows:)

CRUISER SQUADRON, UNITED STATES ATLANTIC FLEET,
U. S. S. WASHINGTON, FLAGSHIP,
Off Cape Haitien, Haiti, July 2, 1915.

Gen. PROBUS BLOT,
Commanding Haitian Government at Cape Haitien, Haiti.

SIR: In confirmation of the conversation you had with Capt. E. L. Beach, my chief of staff, this morning, I have the honor to state that the United States naval forces are present at Cape Haitien for the purpose of protecting the lives and property of American and other foreign citizens.

In view of the number of lives and quantity of foreign property in Cape Haitien, it is impossible for fighting to occur in that town without seriously endangering these lives and property. In vew of the situation of Cape Haitien, the whole attack and defense of that town can take place well clear of it; and victory to one faction or the other there decided. I must, therefore, insist that no fighting whatever take place in the town of Cape Haitien and that the contending factions fight their battles well clear of the town where bullets will not fall therein.

In furtherance of these ends, and to aid the local authorities in preserving order and guarding property, if it should become necessary, I am prepared to land United States forces at Cape Haitien.

I have no intention of questioning the sovereignty of the Haitien nation or of maintaining any but a neutral attitude toward the contending factions.

I trust that, by confining your military operations to the country, well clear of Cape Haitien and by continuing to maintain order in the town, you will make it unnecessary for me to take action.

A letter similar to this has been sent to Gen. Rosalvo Bobo, commanding the revolutionary forces in the vicinity of Cape Haitien. I am,

Respectfully,

W. B. CAPERTON,
Rear Admiral, United States Navy,
Commanding Cruiser Squadron, United States Atlantic Fleet,
and United States Forces in the vicinity of Cape Haitien.

Substantially the same letter was sent to Gen. Rosalvo Bobo, commanding the revolutionary forces in the vicinity of Cape Haitien.

Senator KING. Gen. Blot approved of your course, did he?

Admiral CAPERTON. He approved of my course.

Senator KING. And the foreigners approved of it as well, and the Americans?

Admiral CAPERTON. They were satisfied, I think, but I stated further to these gentlemen that if they would fight out on the plains outside of the city I would recognize the man who won, and I would see that he afterwards took possession of the city, but he would so so in an orderly manner. In other words, I did not wish to appear as wanting to stop this revolution, or as taking any sides one way or the other.

The CHAIRMAN. You were just establishing rules like those of the Marquis of Queensbury?

Admiral CAPERTON. Yes, sir.

Senator KING. Did you learn from the American consul, the French consul, and others that there was danger to the lives and property of foreigners, except for the landing of French marines, or the maintenance, at least temporarily, of an American war vessel in the harbor?

Admiral CAPERTON. Yes, sir. I do not think I can hardly describe the difference of conditions in the city by merely having a few foreign troops there to take charge. When they came in, these fellows, especially the revolutionists—in fact, they are all perhaps more or less revolutionists—the Government had some few forces—they did as they pleased, ransacked everything, took what they pleased, shot up the town, and were entirely unruly.

Senator KING. Looting and violence?

Admiral CAPERTON. Yes, sir; no order whatever.

Senator KING. And were the lives and property of foreigners jeopardized by those revolutionary movements?

Admiral CAPERTON. I should think so, sir. They are certainly a very disturbing element.

Senator KING. You sent an order to Gen. Bobo?

Admiral CAPERTON. Yes, sir; the revolutionary general.

Senator KING. I know who he is. Did he respond to your suggestion that if there was any fighting that it be removed from the town?

Admiral CAPERTON. I think he did, sir. I have his reply here.

Senator KING. Did he make any objection to your suggestion to him?

Admiral CAPERTON. No, sir.

(Whereupon, at 12.15 o'clock p. m., a recess was taken until 2.30 o'clock p. m.)

AFTER RECESS.

The committee reassembled at 2.30 o'clock p. m., pursuant to the taking of recess.

The CHAIRMAN. Now, Admiral, let me recapitulate. At the moment that you communicated your views to Blot and Bobo, the French marines had reembarked?

Admiral CAPERTON. Yes, sir.

The CHAIRMAN. But yours had not been landed?

Admiral CAPERTON. No, sir.

The CHAIRMAN. You did not land forces immediately upon the reembarkation of the French; there was an interval between?

Admiral CAPERTON. Yes, sir; an interval there of several days.

The CHAIRMAN. Had your forces been landed at the time that you dispatched this communique to Bobo and Blot? Were you in occupation of the city or the posts in the city at that time, do you remember?

Admiral CAPERTON. No, sir; my men had not landed. I landed them first on the 3d of July. I think this happened on the 1st of July, the 1st or 2d.

The CHAIRMAN. I want to be sure whether I have got the date of the communique to Blot and Bobo. Under what date did you write them?

Admiral CAPERTON. The letter was written on the 2d of July, about their not fighting.

The CHAIRMAN. In the city?

Admiral CAPERTON. Asking them not to fight in the city; yes, sir.

The CHAIRMAN. And you landed on the 3d?

Admiral CAPERTON. I landed my troops on the 3d, and I give my reasons here for the landing.

The CHAIRMAN. Go on and give them.

Admiral CAPERTON. This was on July 3. In order to facilitate the communication between the American consulate and the U. S. S. *Washington*, I established a field radio station at the railroad station on American property—we have a railroad there——

The CHAIRMAN. I understand.

Admiral CAPERTON. And landed a party of 1 officer and 11 marines, and 1 operator to guard and operate the radio set. I informed Gen. Blot of my intention to land these men, and he made no objection.

On July 3, 1915, I informed the commanding officer of the *Descartes* and Gen. Blot of my intention, and on July 5, the ship in full dress, fired a salute of 21 guns in honor of Independence Day, and in order to close this incident up, I might say that on the day I fired the salute I was very much surprised to see that the Guillaume Sam Government had two ships in the harbor and they fired a salute with us, being also in full dress.

The CHAIRMAN. What date was this—the 4th of July?

Admiral CAPERTON. On the 5th it was done; the 4th was Sunday. That showed that the feeling between the Government at that time and ourselves was——

The CHAIRMAN. Very good?

Admiral CAPERTON. Very good; yes, sir.

Bobo's minister was also seen. He stated that the revolutionists did not want to fight in or near Cape Haitien, and that they were very anxious to avoid injury to foreigners. The minister of war further stated that unless the Government forces came out to fight, the revolutionists would move up to Cape Haitien on Wednesday and attack the Government forces.

On July 8 Gen. Blot informed me that he had received orders from Gen. Guillaume Sam in Port au Prince to extend to us all courtesies. I expressed my appreciation of this message through an officer and myself.

As an engagement between the Government and the revolutionary forces had not taken place, and as the revolutionary forces were still within 3 miles of Cape Haitien, and as occasional shots were occurring in the vicinity, indicating possible further fights in the near future, and in view of my announced intention to prevent fighting within the town of Cape Haitien, I decided to take precautionary measures to prevent a sudden rush of both factions into the town and their consequent fighting therein before I could land to prevent same. The *Washington* could not lie closer than 3 miles of the town, and trade winds made boating difficult. I learned from residents of the town that on two occasions outside forces had entered the town without warning, and fighting resulted therein, and my experience of the past winter also indicated that a similar case occurred at St. Marc.

This is to show why I wished to establish that radio set, so that I could communicate 3 miles distant from Cape Haitien, and, in fact, the city was partly hidden by the cape from where I had to anchor.

On July 9th, in accordance with my intention to land an outpost detachment of Marines at Cape Haitien, I directed an officer of my general staff to see Gen. Blot and explain my intentions, and to obtain his assent if possible. This officer visited Gen. Blot, in company with the American consul, and under my directions stated to him my wish to land this force of Marines, to guard the railroad property and American and foreign interests, and that I would be pleased to have his assent to this landing.

In answer to that Gen. Blot withheld consent for the present, giving as his reason that in view of the revolutionists' propaganda that foreign powers were aiding the government, any landing of a force there would be interpreted by the revolutionists as a movement to aid the government, and that he could not see any reason for the landing at that time.

From this date up to July 27 I remained at anchor off Cape Haitien, watching closely the actions of the revolutionary forces and the government forces outside and near Cape Haitien.

On the morning of July 27th I received information from the manager of the French cable station at Cape Haitien that the Arrondissement and the palace at Port au Prince had on this morning been attacked by a revolutionary faction, and that fighting was going on at Port au Prince. I immediately sent a flag officer ashore to investigate that report. They visited the cable station and received a confirmation of this report. It was also learned that Guillaume Sam and the government had been overthrown, and that the revolutionary faction now controlled the city, and that the government officials, including Guillaume, had taken refuge in the French and Dominican legations, and that the leader of the revolution was not yet known.

These reports were confirmed by cable which was received while these officers were at the cable station, and also from private messages to the business houses and individuals at Cape Haitien.

I immediately sent a cable to the American legation at Port au Prince, directing the American chargé d'affaires to report the situation to me.

In reply to my message I received the following:

"Guillaume in French legation. Revolutionists in entire control of city. Outgoing government shot 70 political prisoners in their cells, including ex-

President Zamor, on account of which trouble is feared. Large number of soldiers killed and wounded in fighting this morning. Not known at present in whose favor is movement. City quiet, but under circumstances your presence and American ship desired.

· "DAVIS, *Chargé d'Affaires.*

Senator ODDIE. What date was that?

Admiral CAPERTON. That was on July 27th. This was in reply to the message I sent:

"French legation threatened. Forcible entry attempted for the purpose of taking out president. English Chargé and French Minister have cabled for ships. Situation very grave, and presence of warship as soon as possible necessary.

"DAVIS."

As soon as I could withdraw the landing force from Cape Haitien, I immediately sailed for Port au Prince, leaving only the U. S. S. *Eagle* to take care of the situation at Cape Haitien.

The CHAIRMAN. The *Eagle* had no force ashore, then?

Admiral CAPERTON. No, sir; I withdrew all my forces.

On July 27, 1915, while the U. S. S. *Washington* was en route from Cape Haitien to Port au Prince, I sent the following message to the Secretary of the Navy:

"Cable dispatch from Port au Prince reports a revolutionary faction attacked the Arrondissement and palace at Port au Prince Tuesday morning, and has overthrown Guillaume government. Revolutionary faction now controls city. Government officials, including Guillaume, have taken refuge in French and Dominican legations. Leader of revolution not yet known.

"American legation at Port au Prince reports outgoing government shot 70 political prisoners, including ex-President Zamor, and a large number of soldiers killed and wounded in fight. Latest cablegram from American legation just received as follows: 'French legation threatened and forcible entry attempted for purpose taking out President. English chargé and French minister have cabled for ships. Situation very grave.'

"Cape Haitien at present quiet but growing uneasy. Gen. Blot received message from Port au Prince, stating revolutionists had control of city, and asked him to join them. This message signed by Delva, Polynice, Delinois, Robin, Etienne, and Delencourt, and Zamor.

"Have withdrawn detachment from shore, and am proceeding with Washington to Port au Prince. Am leaving Eagle to tend situation Cape Haitien. Have requested marine company, naval station, Guantanamo Bay, stand by to embark on Jason for expeditionary service in Haiti; unless otherwise directed will use this company to reenforce Washington's battalion if situation requires."

Upon arriving at Port au Prince at 11.50 a. m. on July 28, 1915, I immediately assumed control of the situation, and confirmed the report which I had previously received, and informed the Secretary of the Navy as follows——

The CHAIRMAN. Admiral, what are you reading from?

Admiral CAPERTON. This is a copy of my dispatches here.

The CHAIRMAN. Is that your dispatch that you are reading now?

Admiral CAPERTON. I am going to read it now.

The CHAIRMAN. Where you say "Rear Admiral Caperton," did you write a dispatch in the third person?

Admiral CAPERTON. These are the quoted parts there.

The CHAIRMAN. What is that volume?

Admiral CAPERTON. This is a report that Maj. McClellan has gotten up from my reports. You see, it is a copy.

The CHAIRMAN. Do you not think you would do better just to tell us the story in your own language?

Admiral CAPERTON. Yes; I can tell you a good many things, but I think perhaps it is due me. I could tell you what I did, but perhaps I would not be able to give you my authority for acting.

The CHAIRMAN. Well, I want you to follow the course which seems good to you, but we are interested, as you understand, primarily to know the circumstances under which you landed marines, and the authority upon which you acted.

Admiral CAPERTON. I am endeavoring to give you that.

The CHAIRMAN. All right, sir.

Admiral CAPERTON. This is my message.

"Dominican legation violated Tuesday: Gen. Oscar, chief of Arrondissement, forcibly removed and killed. At about 10.30 this morning French legation invaded by mob of about 60 Haitians, better class; President Guillaume forcibly removed from upstairs room and killed at legation gate, and body cut in pieces and paraded about town "——

The CHAIRMAN. These were the Haitians of the better class, then, who invaded the legation and cut Sam to pieces?

Admiral CAPERTON. Yes, sir. If you will allow me, in a moment I will tell just a short story of that. It will take me a few minutes. The cablegram continues:

"No government or authority in city. Many rival leaders in town. Am landing force in city for purpose preventing further rioting and for protection foreign lives and property, and to preserve order. Have directed naval station Guantanamo, Cuba, to send company marines Port au Prince. Account large area city, will require regiment of marines from United States at once for policing and patrolling. Suggest U. S. S. *Montana*, U. S. S. *North Carolina*, or U. S. S. *Tennessee* as transport.

"CAPERTON."

When I arrived with the *Washington* at about 10.30 on the morning of the 28th, the circumstances which I have just related in these various messages were reported to me from the city, and while I was listening to these reports I had my glasses in my hand, and as I looked ashore I saw much confusion there. I was about a mile off, and I saw much confusion, people in the streets, and apparently there was a procession, as if they were dragging something through the city, and I afterwards found out from officers when I sent them ashore that this was the body of President Guillaume Sam, which had been mutilated—the arms cut off, the head cut off and stuck on poles, and the torso drawn with ropes through the city.

To go back a little, I learned from what I considered good authority that President Guillaume Sam had received many notices in regard to the revolution which might break out right under his nose, and it is said in Port au Prince that he gave the order to Gen. Oscar to execute all prisoners at the first sound or first shot in the palace grounds. He was to murder or kill all the prisoners, which he proceeded to do.

The CHAIRMAN. Chiefly political prisoners?

Admiral CAPERTON. No, sir; I understood and know, in fact, that many of these prisoners were the best people of the city.

The CHAIRMAN. That is what I mean; they were seized as political hostages.

Admiral CAPERTON. They were seized, but they were not political prisoners. A good many of them were business people, and were seized, as I have often heard discussed there, on reports, without being substantiated at all.

The CHAIRMAN. It is generally believed that these prisoners were seized as hostages and killed by Sam's order.

Admiral CAPERTON. Yes, sir: but I would like to state that they were the best people of the city, and a great many of them had never interfered or had anything to do with politics.

This report became current at once throughout the city, and people who had friends and relatives there rushed to the prison and found the center of the court filled with bodies lying dead. There were 5 out of about 170 who were still alive. They saved their lives, as I found out afterwards, by getting behind the prison doors, the little cell doors. They just shot and stabbed and cut and mutilated as they went along from one cell to another. There were three or four or five in each cell. Those who were saved had enough sense, when the attacking party came back, to fall over as if dead. One man was under this whole crowd of one hundred and sixty odd men, and came near smothering before they got him out. Finally they pulled him out, and he had not been hurt at all.

During this melee, or this attack on the palace by, it is said, 50 or 60 men under Delva—I do not know that it is necessary to give the names; I have not that list just now, but I know the five or six men who stirred up this affair, and headed by these men they ran to the palace, broke open the palace, and began to shoot and kill one another, and do all sorts of outrageous things.

In the meantime the President attempted to leave the palace. He attempted to leave by this large door which is in the wall which separates the French Legation from the palace. He could not unlock the door, and I believe was raised and pushed over the wall, but, anyway, he reached the legation in some way, but in doing so he was shot in the leg, so that when he arrived in the legation he was wounded. This was about 4 or 5 o'clock in the morning of the 27th.

Sometime that afternoon the soldiers, who I think at that time had all turned perhaps and joined the new chief of executive power, attempted to gain entrance to the legation; and some of them, I believe, did get in, and Gen. Zamor seemed to be the leader. This was told to me by one of the young ladies in the legation. As he rushed to go upstairs, where the President had hidden himself in a locker or bathroom, it was, really, she put out her hands to stop him, and plead with him, with her hands on his shoulder, and reminded him that for the past four or five months, while he was in exile in the legation, she, herself, had fed him with her own hands, and appealed to him in such a manner that he broke down and sat down on the steps and wept. Then he arose and passed out, and as he went out he said to her, " I will take all of this mob, or this crowd of soldiers, out now. This legation will not be entered again by any soldiers. I will be responsible for that." He left and took the soldiers out, and as far as we know carried out what he promised. That was on the afternoon of the 27th.

Then the next morning, while all the good people of the city were taking their dead to the cemetery to bury them, and were in the act of doing this, somebody passed the word that the *Washington* was coming; that they saw her smoke; and that the admiral would be there in a few minutes and would stop all of that; and that everybody must rush to the French Legation and get the President. So that was the crowd that went the second time and really got in and got the President. They found him upstairs in the bathroom, pulled him out, dragged him down, dragged him through the back of the house, along a cobblestone walk or driveway about 50 or 100 yards to the gate, and there attempted to throw him over the gate. The gate being iron, with spikes on top, his body in some way or some manner caught on the top. They succeeded in pulling him over anyway, and when he reached the outside of the legation they fired six or eight shots into him, and found that he was not dead; and, as I have been told, the next thing they did was to cut his throat, cut his head off, put a rope around his body, and started off. Then the cry was to stop. Then they proceeded to amputate his arms and his legs and his head and stuck them on poles and paraded his body around through the streets. And that was the procession that I saw.

Immediately upon my arrival I sent two officers of my staff to call at the American Legation and ascertain the news. There these officers were met by Mr. Davis, the chargé d'affaires; and after hearing his statement, Mr. Davis and the two officers went into the French Legation, where they found the French minister and the British chargé d'affaires.

The CHAIRMAN. Which legation were they in then?

Admiral CAPERTON. In the French Legation. The two officers, the American chargé d'affaires, the French minister, and the British chargé d'affaires returned to the *Washington* and held consultation with me.

There was no government or authority in the city, but a so-called " committee of safety," which, it was stated, was formed by Gen. Polynice and three other generals. They made no attempt to preserve order, nor did they inform me or any foreign legation of their assumption of authority. Polynice himself perpetrated the violence on the Dominican consulate. As three of his sons had been murdered by Gen. Oscar, he went himself to the Dominican Legation, entered it, found Gen. Oscar, and dragged him out to the street and shot him full of holes.

Senator ODDIE. May I ask you here, Admiral, if any Americans were injured or killed during this time?

Admiral CAPERTON. I think not, sir. There were not very many Americans in Port au Prince.

After a consultation with the American chargé d'affaires, the French minister, and the British chargé d'affaires, I decided to land American forces for the purpose of preventing further rioting and for the protection of the lives and property of foreigners and to preserve order.

In the meantime, at 3 o'clock p. m., on July 28, the Acting Secretary of the Navy sent the following message to me in Port au Prince:

" State Department desires that American forces be landed at Port au Prince and that American and foreign interests be protected; that representatives of England and France be informed of this intention—informed that their interests will be protected and that they be requested not to land. In acting on this request be guided by your knowledge of present conditions in Port au Prince and act at discretion. Department has ordered *Jason*, with marines at Guantanamo Bay, to proceed immediately to Port au Prince. If more forces are absolutely necessary, wire immediately."

On my way down from Cape Hatien, as usual, I made all preparations for landing our landing force. Under orders of the Navy Department, and in cooperation with the State Department, I landed a provisional regiment of two battalions, under command of Capt. George Van Orden, United States Marine Corps, at Port au Prince on the afternoon of July 28, 1915, and occupied that city.

This operation is described in the following radiogram sent by me to the Secretary of the Navy on July 28, 1915:

"Landing at Port au Prince decided on after consulting with American chargé d'affaires, French minister, and British chargé d'affaires. Informed Gen. Polynice and three others, who seemed to be leaders ashore, of my intention to land and protect lives and property and preserve order. They assented to this landing, but said they could not guarantee peaceful entry, but would do all they could to explain our intentions to the populace and prevent disturbance and would cooperate with us. *Descartes* (French warship) expected tonight. No foreign men-of-war in harbor excepting *Washington* at present. Considered immediate landing necessary. Landing made at Bizoton with two companies of marines and three companies of seamen at 5.30 p. m. U. S. S. *Eagle* reports conditions Cape Haitien quiet. *Eagle* has landed 20 men Cape Haitien to protect French consulate for fear of attack on refugees there. Landing made at request of French consul.

"CAPERTON."

I think that letter explains this.

The CHAIRMAN. It does. It is all very clear and satisfactory.

Admiral CAPERTON. In order to acquaint the chargé d'affaires of my intentions, after deciding to land I wrote the following letter:

"I have the honor to state that it appears that rioting and disorder in Port au Prince have gotten beyond control and the situation to have become such as to endanger the lives and property of Americans and other foreigners who are left without protection. As a result of our conference a naval force will land and afford such protection. To facilitate this you are respectfully requested to notify all Americans and all foreign diplomats, representatives, consuls, and others who desire protection to keep within doors, to hoist the flag of their nationality, and refrain from all actions which could possibly be interpreted as a hostile demonstration against the naval force.

"CAPERTON."

I think it but fair and just that I make some mention of the intense feeling and desire with which the French minister especially and the British chargé d'affaires insisted upon my landing immediately. The French minister has a family consisting of a wife and two daughters, and he said, "They are there at the legation with no one to protect them. Now, you see what is going on in the city." And he begged that I land as quickly as possible, as did also the British chargé d'affaires.

At 11.20 on the 29th of July I sent the following message to the Secretary of the Navy and Commander in Chief:

"Landing force established in city. Slight resistance during early part of night as advance was being made. This resistance easily overcome. No casualties our forces. As there is no government or authority in town, am required assume military control in city. Am proceeding disarm bodies Haitian soldiers and civilians to-day. Can not see how this can develop into any other than absolute military control of city. Regiment of marines absolutely necessary, and should be sent at once. Two Haitian gunboats at Cape Haitien and most of army in that vicinity. Earnestly recommend U. S. S. *Nashville* be ordered take station situation Cape Haitien and that U. S. S. *Castine* be made available as soon as possible.

"CAPERTON."

From the reports which I received on shore, the majority of the Haitians welcomed the landing of the American forces and were overjoyed at the prospect of relief from revolution and government by terror. The politicians and soldiers naturally were opposed to any action which would prevent them from securing to themselves the results of the overthrow of the government.

On the morning of the 29th I immediately sent the chief of staff, Capt. E. L. Beach, ashore to confer with the commander of the landing forces and prominent citizens with reference to disarming the Haitian soldiers and civilians in the town. The chief of staff and the commander of the landing forces met

Gens. Polynice, Delva, Charles Zamor, Noel, Nau, Samson Monpoint, and Robin, who had organized themselves as a revolutionary committee. I might add that at the time when the city was taken Gen. Robin was in command of the forces. After considerable parleying it was agreed that they would undertake to disarm all the soldiers and civilians and place the arms in the palace under guard of police, subject to my inspection as to the completeness of the disarming. I, of course, assumed the right, and exercised it, of placing a guard over these arms. The conference with the committee of safety was of some length. I explained to them my intentions relative to the preservation of law and order and the necessity of assuming military control of the city. They assented to this control and agreed to cooperate. This committee agreed to meet my representatives daily to insure cooperation. I make these remarks so as to show and emphasize their promises at the time.

The CHAIRMAN. This committee included these same gentlemen who acted during all of these interregnums?

Admiral CAPERTON. Some of them; the principal ones, Mr. Delva and Polynice. Mr. Praedel was not in this party at the time.

The department sent the following message on July 30, 1915, to me concerning the military occupation of Port au Prince:

"The department appreciates the excellent manner in which disturbance at Port au Prince has been handled and directs that you retain military control of city until further orders. Acknowledge.

" DANIELS."

At 7.40 p. m. on the 30th I sent the following message:

" In accordance State Department instructions, American chargé d'affaires informed French minister of my instructions relative requesting he not land French troops. This was done previous my consultation with French minister on subject. French minister naturally feels great humiliation for his country and flag over insult of violation of his legation. While he feels amply protected, and expressed gratitude to me and to United States Government through me for furnishing him guard, yet he says not landing French guard at his legation might indicate to Haitians that he was deserted by his Government and prestige of France thereby suffer. French minister will probably insist on landing legation guard. Suggest advisability of arrangements being made between State Department and French Embassy, Washington, D. C., relative this matter. French cruiser *Descartes* arrived Port au Prince 2 p. m. Friday.

" CAPERTON."

I would like to add here that the first thing that was done when the landing party reached the vicinity of the legations was to send guards immediately to these legations for protection before our troops bivouacked for the night.

On the 31st I sent the following message to the Secretary of the Navy:

" Port au Prince quiet during day, but still unsettled. French minister informed me he had received dispatches from Paris, France, Government stating that French Embassy, Washington, had been directed inform United States Government that France considered landing legation guard at Port au Prince necessity for national honor. French minister repeated his conviction that we were ably protecting life and property and assured me his guard would be confined to legation and that arms of French guard would not be carried by them outside of legation. He further stated that he wishes it understood he does not intend interfering in any way my actions in town. Press dispatches received to-day from United States indicate State Department evidently thinks de facto government exists Port au Prince. No de facto government exists Port au Prince. All government functions at present undertaken carried on by committee citizens acting practically under my direction. Chamber deputies asked permission elect president, but deferred in compliance my request. Time for election President not propitious for maintaining law and order. U. S. S. *Eagle* reports heavy firing outside Cape Haitien; reports Bobo will attempt enter Cape Haitien. Blot in full control there at present. Blot has taken Gonaives, Haiti. Army in north menace peace and order, both Port au Prince and Cape Haitien. May have to occupy Cape Haitien. Department may expect request for another regiment of marines.

" CAPERTON."

The CHAIRMAN. Had the first regiment arrived by this time in Port au Prince?

Admiral CAPERTON. No, sir; it had not arrived. I think it was about this time that a company came.

I desire to state, in order to make the record clear, that the Zamor killed was the ex-President Zamor, Charles Zamor's brother. Charles Zamor was the general who was in the French legation.

I have been asked the question as to whether or not I have ever heard of the killing of a foreigner by Haitians. The records of the Navy Department disclose that our vessels of war have been there at practically every disturbance since at least 1857. I have not gone back beyond that. This, in my opinion, caused the Haitians to hesitate before killing any Americans. In other words, no one can tell how many foreign lives would have been lost and foreign property destroyed if United States warships had not been continually present to prevent violence. I think the committee would be surprised to see how many vessels it has been necessary to send down to Cape Haitien since 1857, every year, just to stop these things.

The CHAIRMAN. If the department has a record of that sort, it would be interesting to have it presented to the committee at your convenience, Admiral.

Admiral CAPERTON. Yes, sir.

(Whereupon the committee adjourned until Wednesday, October 12, 1921, at 10.30 o'clock a. m.)

INQUIRY INTO OCCUPATION AND ADMINISTRATION OF HAITI AND SANTO DOMINGO.

WEDNESDAY, OCTOBER 12, 1921.

UNITED STATES SENATE,
SELECT COMMITTEE ON HAITI AND SANTO DOMINGO,
Washington, D. C.

The committee met at 10.30 o'clock a. m., pursuant to adjournment, Senator Medill McCormick (chairman) presiding.

Present: Senators McCormick, Oddie, and Knox.

Also present: Mr. Ernest Angell, Mr. Horace G. Knowles, and Maj. Edwin N. McClellan, United States Marine Corps, in their respective representative capacities as hereinbefore indicated.

STATEMENT OF REAR ADMIRAL WILLIAM B. CAPERTON, UNITED STATES NAVY, RETIRED—Resumed.

The CHAIRMAN. Will you take up your testimony, Admiral, at the point at which it was concluded yesterday when you were about to speak of the landing at Cape Haitien, I think.

Admiral CAPERTON. Yes, sir. At this time, about July 31, 1915, the Army in the north and the leaders, Blot and Bobo, were menaces to peace and order, both at Port au Prince and Cape Haitien. Cape Haitien was uneasy, and it was reported to me reliably in Port au Prince that trouble was feared at that place. The French minister was anxious that steps be taken to guard French interests in Cape Haitien. For these reasons it seemed that it might be necessary for me to occupy Cape Haitien, in which event the department might expect a request for another regiment of marines.

On August 1, 1915, I sent the following message to the Secretary of the Navy:

"Sending, on *Jason*, commission to Cape Hatien composed of following: Lieut. Coffey, ex-President Légetime, Archbishop Bronan, Gen. Polynice, ex-Minister Charles Zamor, Col. Chevalier. My instructions to commission are to require armies in north disarm and disband, soldiers to return to their homes, leaders Blot and Bobo to return Port au Prince with commission and join conference promoting order in Haiti. This commission is formed by my order and acting under my order.

" CAPERTON."

Upon the arrival of this commission, they were able to communicate with Gens. Blot, Bobo, and Bourand, the latter in command of the Government forces near Ouanaminthe, and the others prominent officials and citizens of Cape Haitien.

During this time the following message was sent to me from the commanding officer of the *Nashville:*

"Blot left on *Pacifique*, some other gentlemen on *Nord Alexis*, also some troops. Have landed and taken charge. Will prevent entering of armed persons until some leader can take charge. Blot troops from country entered town 6 a. m., Wednesday ; some firing. Have now gone back country. At present all quiet in town : expect Bobo will try to come in.

(Signed)   " OLMSTEAD."

The CHAIRMAN. May I interrupt a moment there?

Admiral CAPERTON. Yes, sir.

The CHAIRMAN. To what order of the department would you refer as laying down the policy under which that landing took place at Cape Haitien—your general order in which the State Department wished you to keep order?

Admiral CAPERTON. Yes, sir.

About this time, on August 4, the U. S. S. *Connecticut* arrived in Port au Prince, but after discharging her marines and stores, owing to the disturbed conditions in the north at Cape Haitien, she was sent to that point. After using my best efforts through the joint American-Haitian Committee, as it was termed, and after inducing as many of the leaders of the ex-Government and revolutionary forces to come to Port au Prince, the *Jason* was ordered to return on the 5th, at which time I received the following message from Lieut. Coffey, the chairman of this committee:

"Am returning Port au Prince on *Jason* with commission, Bobo and 26 generals, Bourand, La Roche, and 17 nuns. Bobo troops will remain in present position as per your desire. Disarmament can not be accomplished except by aid of troops, either our troops go to them or their troops come to us. You may expect demonstration when Bobo arrives; parades, and cheering occurred at Cape Haitien this morning. Nothing serious. Commission, Bobo, Bourand, and La Roche will probably wish to pay respects. Do you wish to see them? All generals have arms. Will let none land until question disarming them settled.
"COFFEY."

I think a few words of explanation are due in regard to having those nuns on board. In compliance with the earnest request of the church authorities at Port au Prince, through the chargé d'affaires, and in view of the unsettled conditions at Cape Haitien, I authorized the passage of about 17 sisters of St. Joseph from Cape Haitien to Port de Prince. They represented to me that they were uneasy and disturbed in their minds, and that they would like to go temporarily for the time being to Port au Prince.

On August 5 the following message was sent to the Secretary of the Navy:

"To-day Haitian Congress published notice it would elect President Sunday, but has postponed at my request because time is inopportune. Am informed congress would elect Menos. Haitian minister at Washington, if here. In absence of Menos am informed president of senate, Dartiguenave, will be elected. From many other sources hear Dartigeuenave is man of personal honor and of patriotism. Has never been connected with any revolution, is of good ability, and anxious for Haiti's regeneration, realizes Haiti must agree to any terms laid down by United States, professes to believe any terms demanded will be for Haiti's benefit, says he will use all his influence with Haitian Congress to have such terms agreed upon by Haiti. If elected must be sustained by American protection. Same condition applies to whoever else is elected. Bobo only other prominent candidate. Bobo said to be man of intellectuality, honor, and patriotism. Friends maintain would work solely for Haiti's good. Bobo could be elected only through fear of Cacos, and if elected revolution against him would undoubtedly start unless prevented by United States.

"Great relief expressed by all classes except Cacos at presence of American troops. Americans afford hope of relief from Government by terror. Universally believed that if Americans depart, Government will lapse into complete anarchy. My opinion is that United States must expect to remain in Haiti until native Government is self-sustaining and people educated to respect laws and abide by them. Should president be elected now there would be complete machinery for all Government functions. With American protection and influenced by United States, progress toward good government could be soon commenced. Haitian people anxious to have president elected, because at present no central Government in Haiti except as directed by me. Also people uneasy, fearing United States may not permit continuance of Haitian independence.
"CAPERTON."

The CHAIRMAN. That telegram, as far as I have followed the record, is the first forecast of the policy later pursued in Haiti, that with the election of Dartiguenave and the continuance of the American occupation foundations might be laid for the progressive development of civil order and civil institutions?

Admiral CAPERTON. Yes, sir; those were my views, obtained by discussing the situation and conditions with all prominent men in Haiti.

The CHAIRMAN. The initiation of that policy, then, was in Haiti and not in Washington?

Admiral CAPERTON. That I could not say.

The CHAIRMAN. Well, now, had the Secretary, by verbal messages or otherwise, intimated to you that that was the policy he had in mind prior to the sending of that dispatch?

Admiral CAPERTON. The following message was sent on August 2, 1915, to the Secretary of the Navy:

"Large number Haitian revolutions, largely due existing professional soldiers called Cacos, organized in bands under lawless, irresponsible chiefs, who fight on side offering greatest inducement and but nominally recognize the Government. Cacos are feared by all Haitians and practically control politics. About 1,500 Cacos now in Port au Prince, ostensibly disarmed, but retain organization and believed to have arms and ammunition hidden. They have demanded election Bobo President, and Congress, terrorized by mere demand, is on point complying, but restrained by my request. Present condition no other man can be elected account fear of Cacos. Believe can control Congress. Can prevent any Cacos outbreak in Port au Prince after arrival regiment of marines U. S. S. *Connecticut*. Stable government not possible in Haiti until Cacos are disbanded and power broken.

"Such action now imperative at Port au Prince if United States desires to negotiate treaty for financial control of Haiti. To accomplish this must have regiment of marines in addition to that on *Connecticut*. Majority populace well disposed and submissive, and will welcome disbanding Cacos and stopping revolutions. Should agreement with Haiti be desired, recommend Capt. Beach, U. S. N., be appointed single commissioner for United States, with full instructions and authority. He has conducted my negotiations on shore, and I believe has confidence generally of Haitians. As future relations between United States and Haiti depend largely on course of action taken at this time, earnestly request to be fully informed of policy of United States.

"CAPERTON."

Senator ODDIE. I would like to ask you a question there, Admiral. What was meant by this clause, "Such action now imperative at Port au Prince if United States desires to negotiate treaty for financial control of Haiti"?

Admiral CAPERTON. I do not know why I mentioned or specified "financial control." I have in my mind now, and I am sure I had then, that if we wished to form a treaty with Haiti for all purposes, and a treaty like we finally did succeed in getting ratified, the expression "financial control" would be one part of the treaty.

Senator ODDIE. Are you referring to the policy adopted with Santo Domingo in commenting on this wording, "the financial control of Haiti"?

Admiral CAPERTON. Somewhere in my dispatches here I did mention something about a treaty similar to the one which we had in Santo Domingo. I can not just put my hand on the message now to the department, but I am quite sure that I can find it somewhere in the record.

Senator ODDIE. Now, another thing, Admiral. In the last part of your telegram you said, "As future relations between United States and Haiti depend largely on course of action taken at this time, earnestly request to be fully informed of policy of the United States." Had you been informed of any policy from the Navy Department prior to this time?

Admiral CAPERTON. No definite policy.

Senator ODDIE. Did you receive instructions regarding the future policy in answer to this telegram?

Admiral CAPERTON. I did, sir.

Senator ODDIE. I will ask you to go on and give it.

Admiral CAPERTON. On August 7 the following message was received from the department:

"Conciliate Haitians to fullest extent consistent with maintaining order and firm control of situation, and issue following proclamation: 'Am directed to assure the Haitian people United States of America has no object in view except to insure, establish, and help to maintain Haitian independence and the establishing of a stable and firm government by the Haitian people. Every assistance will be given to the Haitian people in their attempt to secure these ends. It is the intention to retain United States forces in Haiti only so long as will be necessary for this purpose.' Acknowledge.

"BENSON, *Acting*."

Senator ODDIE. Is there anything else that occurs to you that would show the policy of the Navy Department prior to this?

Admiral CAPERTON. There is a great deal afterwards. At the present time I am unable to say whether there was anything definite before or not.

Senator ODDIE. Let me ask you in regard to that telegram of August 5. You said, in referring to this man you recommend as the best for President: "He realizes that Haiti must agree to any terms demanded by the United States, and he professes to believe that any demands laid down by us will be for Haiti's benefit."

Admiral CAPERTON. He must have received this from various conversations that my representatives had with him, perhaps, or he read it in the papers. I do not remember whether such were published or not, but it was, as I understood, the general impression.

The CHAIRMAN. Now, Admiral, as the basis of that general impression, as the basis for the conversations which your representatives had with him, who suggested that the United States Government was going to propose terms? Where originated the idea that under a new President new contractual relations were to be established between the Haitian Government and the American Government which would require the approbation of the new President?

Admiral CAPERTON. I think the answer to that question would be found somewhere in my notes. I can not just put my hand on it now.

The CHAIRMAN. This is the most important phase of this part of the testimony. Are you unable to recall, offhand, whether the State Department or the Navy Department, directly or indirectly, suggested to the naval commanders or the diplomatic agents in Haiti that any terms to which Dartiguenave would accede would be proposed to him by our Government?

Admiral CAPERTON. These were my opinions at the time. Just how they were formed at the present I am unable to answer.

The CHAIRMAN. Let me put it another way then. Is there in the record, or have you any recollection, of a statement of policy which indicates that it was the purpose of the department that American troops should land and restore order, as already indicated by your testimony, and then withdraw, or that it was at the same time the policy of the department that having landed for the restoration of order, then steps should be taken by treaty to assure the continuance of order?

Admiral CAPERTON. My first orders were as outlined in my testimony here, to land for the purpose of preserving law and order and the protection of property, etc.

The CHAIRMAN. Your allusion to these other matters was based on conversation current, originating in the negotiations between the State Department and the Haitian Government which had taken place prior to your coming to Haiti?

Admiral CAPERTON. Yes, sir.

On August 6, finding the presence of a large number of Cacos in Port au Prince extremely undesirable, I directed that they be ordered to disperse and return to their homes. All Cacos found in the streets after 11 a. m. were placed under arrest. There was some excitement in the city as the first arrests were made, but when the populace realized that the disbursing of the Cacos was for the good of the people of Port au Prince they appeared to welcome this movement. A detachment of marines, which was taking a number of Cacos to the detention camp, was fired upon from a crowd on the sidewalk near the customhouse.

This is to show the disorder, etc., and what I had to contend with there in keeping peace.

The CHAIRMAN. I wish we might know what constituted a Caco. Do Cacos come from one part of the island, or are they like the medieval condoterri of professional soldiers who travel in each invading candidate's train? I gather they are turbulent fellows, but I would like to know.

Admiral CAPERTON. I am under the impression that I had in my testimony described where they lived and something about them.

The CHAIRMAN. Up in the Grand Basin, you said.

Admiral CAPERTON. I have something further here in the way of a description, if I can find it. In the absence of a better description, I would like to express myself as follows: This northern section of Haiti, or more the northeastern section of Haiti, is the home of the Cacos, and to understand the modus operandi of a political campaign in Haiti it is essential that one have a clear idea of who and what the Cacos are. The numerous revolutions, in combination with the tribal instinct of their African forbears, have resulted in the formation of numerous bands of men, each band under its own chief, who are called Cacos. They know no law save that of brute force, and obey the commands of their chief only because he has the physical power to enforce them. The minor chiefs usually follow the direction of a head chief, but the organization is very loosely knit, and it is not uncommon for bands who have fought each other in one revolution to be on the same side in the next. As a general rule, the Cacos are on the side of the "outs," and the men who help a President to power often are instrumental in driving him out a few months later.

With regard to the question of the policy of the department, I would like to add the following: The activities of the revolutionary committee which had been established at Port au Prince for the purpose of assisting me in maintaining order were of such a nature that it was necessary to direct them to resign and to assist all the good forces in Haiti to restore peace and order.

The Secretary of State advised the American Minister in Haiti concerning the procedure which he should adopt toward me for the purpose of assisting the Haitian National Assembly to elect a president of the republic on August 10, 1915, as follows:

"In view of the fact that the Navy last night informed Admiral Caperton that he might allow election for the president whenever the Haitians wish, and of the impression which exists here that election may take place Thursday next, it is desired that you confer with the Admiral to the end that in some way to be determined between you the following things be made perfectly clear:

"First: Let Congress understand that the Government of the United States intends to uphold it but that it can not recognize action which does not establish in charge of Haitian affairs, those whose abilities and dispositions give assurances of putting an end to factional disorder.

"Second: In order that no misunderstanding can possibly occur after election it should be made perfectly clear to candidates, as soon as possible, and in advance of their election, that the United States expects to be entrusted with the practical control of the customs and such financial control over the affairs of the Republic of Haiti as the United States may deem necessary for efficient administration.

"The Government of the United States considers it its duty to support a Constitutional Government. It seems to assist in the establishment of such a government and to support it as long as necessity may require. It has no design upon the political or territorial integrity of Haiti. On the contrary what has been done, as well as what will be done, is conceived in an effort to aid the people of Haiti in establishing a stable government and maintaining domestic peace throughout the Republic.

                                                        " LANSING."

On August 10, 1915, I received the following message from the Secretary of the Navy:

"Allow election of president to take place whenever Haitians wish. The United States prefers election of Dartiguenave. Has no other motive than that establishment of firm and lasting government by Haitian people and to assist them now and at all times in future to maintain their political independence and territorial integrity. United States will insist that the Haitian Government will grant no territorial concessions to any foreign governments. The Government of the United States will take up the question of the cession of Mole St. Nicholas later along with the other questions to be submitted to the reorganized Government with regard to its relation to the United States. Acknowledge.

                                        (Signed.) BENSON, Acting."

The night of the 10th of August and the day of the 11th of August passed quietly at Port au Prince; but there was considerable uneasiness and some small demonstrations due to the approaching election and the desperate attitude of the Bobo and Zamor factions. Seventeen disorderly Cacos were arrested.

Referring to the dismissal of the revolutionary committee, the following letter was addressed to them by my order:

                                                        AUGUST 11, 1915.

The revolutionary committee, Port au Prince, Haiti:

GENTLEMEN: I am directed by Rear Admiral W. B. Caperton, commander in chief of United States forces in Haiti, to direct the revolutionary committee to resign and to assist all the good forces in Haiti to restore peace and order.

                                                        E. L. BEACH,
                        Captain, United States Navy, Chief of Staff,
        By direction of the Commander, United States Forces in Haitian Waters.

On August 11, 1915, the following message was sent to the Secretary of the Navy:

"In conjunction with American chargé d'affairs, informed senators and deputies assembled and presidential candidates of intention and policy United States Government as set forth by Secretary of State in cable message of August 10, midnight. Senators and deputies cordial. Election will be held to-morrow. To-day passed quietly, Port au Prince, but considerable uneasiness and small demonstrations, due approaching election and desperate attitude Bobo and Zamor factions. Revolutionary committee issued order dissolving Congress to-day, and attempted seal doors chamber deputies; anticipated their action by sending force to chamber of deputies, and informed committee their action without authority. For this reason and account hostile and disturbing influence of Bobo and Zamor factions, have dissolved revolutionary committee and informed them they have no further authority Port au Prince, and would be considered public enemies of United States if they attempted to give any further orders or further menaced United States policy. Have taken extra precaution against disorder during election; have placed *Castine* and *Eagle* at wharf and landed men from them to reenforce landing force. Have assumed control State telegraph office. Petite Goave quiet. *Connecticut* to-day held conference with ex-Bobo forces relative surrendering arms at Cape Haitien.

                                                              " CAPERTON."

On October 8 I arranged to have a meeting between the prominent candidates for election as President for the purpose of ascertaining, if I could, their views and their feelings toward the United States. I think it but fair to say that I do not believe—and I received no such reports from the various representatives that I had on shore from time to time—that Dartiguenave knew that the United States wanted him to be president. I gathered this from what my officers told me, and I do not know that he actually knew that we wanted him to be president.

According to arrangements, on Sunday, the 8th, I arranged a meeting at the American legation, at which were present Senator Dartiguenave and Deputy Cham, Dr. Bobo, John A. Laroche, and my two staff officers—my chief of staff, Capt. E. L. Beach, and Lieut. E. G. Oberlin. Dartiguenave and Bobo were addressed as follows:

"Gentlemen, it seems likely that one of you will be elected President of Haiti. Haiti is in great trouble; she has suffered much. The United States has come to Haiti as a good friend, interested only in Haiti's welfare, in her happiness, in her prosperity. The United States has determined that revolution and disorder and anarchy must cease in Haiti; that unselfish and devoted patriotism must characterize hereafter the acts of the Haitian Government. Senator Dartiguenave and Dr. Bobo, realizing this momentous crisis in Haitian history, with the eyes of Haiti and of the United States upon you, do you promise that if elected President of Haiti you will, in your official acts, be guided solely by earnest devotion to Haiti's honor and welfare?"

Senator ODDIE. Let me interrupt a minute. Who was asking this question?

Admiral CAPERTON. My representative, Capt. E. L. Beach, my chief of staff, acting under my orders.

"I will so promise," replied Dartiguenave. "I have no other ambition than to be of service to my country."

"I promise," exclaimed Dr. Bobo, rather theatrically. "I would be happy to lay down my life for my beloved country."

"Senator Dartiguenave, in case Dr. Bobo should be elected will you promise that you will exert every influence in your power to assist him for Haiti's good; that you will join with him heartily and helpfully and loyally?"

"If Dr. Bobo is elected president I will give him the most loyal, earnest support in every effort he may make for Haiti's welfare," replied Dartiguenave, with simple dignity.

"Dr. Bobo, if Senator Dartiguenave is elected president, will you help him loyally and earnestly in his efforts to benefit Haiti?"

"No; I will not!" shouted Bobo. "If Senator Dartiguenave is elected president I will not help him. I will go away and leave Haiti to her fate. I alone am fit to be president of Haiti; I alone understood Haiti's aspirations, no one is fit to be president but me; there is no patriotism in Haiti to be compared with mine; the Haitians love no one as they love me."

While I am upon this subject I might mention another meeting that I had, trying to ascertain the feelings and purposes, and what these gentlemen would do if they were elected president, because I did not know. I felt, as the talk grew about Senator Dartiguenave, that I desired to know something about him.   This, I might add, was previous to the other meeting. I sent two of my staff officers, one of them being Lieut. E. G. Oberlin, and the other my chief of staff, Capt. E. L. Beach, to converse with Senator Dartiguenave. They met by appointment in the pleasant home of Dr. Furniss, formerly American minister to Haiti, and at the time a resident of Port au Prince. Present at this interview were Senator Dartiguenave, Deputy Cham, Dr. Furniss, and my two staff officers. My particular purpose was to gain a personal knowledge of Senator Dartiguenave and of his views and attitude toward Haiti and the United States. My idea was that the man most suitable for the Haitian presidency was one in whom the Haitians had confidence, one whose animating purpose would be Haiti's welfare, to which purpose he would give unselfish devotion ; and, also, one who combined such qualifications with confidence in the United States, who was friendly disposed toward the United States, who wanted her help, and who would listen sympathetically to the intentions of the United States. There was never any bargaining of any kind whatever with Dartiguenave, as far as I know. No pressure of any kind was brought to bear upon any Haitian elector in Dartiguenave's interest. The Haitians themselves, without any outside influence or pressure or bargaining, made him, later, their president.

(Whereupon the committee adjourned until Thursday, October 17, 1921, at 10.30 o'clock a. m.)

INQUIRY INTO OCCUPATION AND ADMINISTRATION OF HAITI AND SANTO DOMINGO.

MONDAY, OCTOBER 17, 1921.

UNITED STATES SENATE,
SELECT COMMITTEE ON HAITI AND SANTO DOMINGO,
Washington, D. C.

The committee met at 10.30 o'clock a. m., pursuant to adjournment, Senator Medill McCormick (chairman) presiding.

Present: Senators McCormick and Oddie.

Also present: Mr. Ernest Angell and Mr. Horace G. Knowles, in their representative capacities as hereinbefore indicated, and Maj. Edwin N. McClellan, United States Marine Corps, representing the Navy Department.

The CHAIRMAN. Maj. McClellan, in order that the committee may have in its possession the record available to the admiral and prepared by the department, will you place in the hands of the committee before the day is over a copy of your record?

Maj. MCCLELLAN. I will present that to you right now; I have anticipated your request.

(Maj. McClellan thereupon presented to the committee the record referred to.)

STATEMENT OF REAR ADMIRAL WILLIAM B. CAPERTON, UNITED STATES NAVY, RETIRED—Continued.

The CHAIRMAN. Admiral, you may proceed.

Admiral CAPERTON. Mr. Chairman, as there has been much criticism in regard to this election, I think it necessary that I explain, in a few words, the things that really happened at that time.

The law-abiding citizens were very anxious that the Haitian Congress meet for the purpose of electing a president. These requests were always coupled with the request that it should take place so there should be no intimidation of the senators and deputies who were to vote at that time. At this time the most urgent demands were being made in favor of Dr. Bobo's candidacy for the presidency. They insisted that a " free election " be held, which practically meant that it be held with caco guns leveled at the head of every Haitian congressman as he cast his ballot.

The CHAIRMAN. What do you mean when you say that a " free election " should be held?

Admiral CAPERTON. The Bobo people were impressing me with the idea that they wanted a " free election," and I was explaining what a " free election " had heretofore been, under the revolutionary régime.

The CHAIRMAN. You mean you inserted the words " free election " in the quotation marks?

Admiral CAPERTON. Yes, sir. The most extravagant offers were being made by Dr. Bobo personally and by his friends, the idea being that the United States in its dealings with Haiti was actuated only by selfish, interested motives, and it was thought that the United States wanted the cession of St. Nicholas Mole. So the Bobo crowd offered this and anything else I wanted.

The CHAIRMAN. If you feel that you can, will you not tell us presently who made these offers in behalf of the Bobo faction and through whom they were made?

Admiral CAPERTON. These offers just referred to were made to my chief of staff, Capt. E. L. Beach, sometimes in the presence of one of my staff officers who were accompanying him. It was his almost sole duty at this time to look

319

out for this election business on shore. I might add that the so-called revolutionary committee of safety, self-appointed, were in favor of Dr. Bobo.

In the meantime good citizens, whose only animating purpose was to save Haiti from as much misfortune as it was possible, who had no selfish aims, kept me informed of the schemes which seethed through Port au Prince.

It was seen by me that if the Bobo crowd were permitted to control the election, it would be a sign that the cacos were still capable of directing Haiti's destinies by rifles, and that fear and not free choice would determine each ballot.

Some time before this the Haitians began to talk of Senator Sudre Dartiguenave, a man long in public life. At the time he was president of the senate. He had kept out of political quarrels, belonged to no faction, and he was universally esteemed.

Many willing candidates had presented themselves to me, with statements of their claims; their great friendship for the United States, what they would do for the United States if elected President of Haiti, etc. But not one of these, though listened to, received encouragement.

As I have stated before, it was announced that the election would take place on August 12. At this time I gave orders to Col. E. K. Cole, United States Marine Corps, who was then commanding the marines on shore, having arrived on the *Connecticut* on August 4, to take such steps as were necessary to prevent disorder of any kind on shore. Any Haitian who came within a block of the Chamber of Deputies on August 12 was to be turned back unless he had a pass signed by a senator or deputy or Col. Cole or myself. This effectually excluded the cacos. At the election that occurred on August 12 the galleries of the Chamber of Deputies were thronged by Haitians invited by the senators and deputies and a few marines and marine officers.

Matters seemed to take on a very serious turn about now, so that the committee of safety—that is, the revolutionary committee—rushed to the ex-minister, J. M. Leger, and tried to induce him to be a candidate. He declined to have his name considered. There are a few remarks I would like to put in right here. It is a little long, but I would like to have them go in the record at this point.

Mr. Leger was one of the most distinguished Haitians living, a gentleman educated in Paris, a famous traveler, author, and diplomat; former minister at Paris and at Washington; a gentleman at home in any society; a man of keen, alert, vivid, and remarkable intuition; in every way a cultured, high-minded gentleman. Of him Lord Pauncefote, at one time British ambassador at Washington, once said: " Mr. Leger is the ablest, most accomplished diplomat I have known in all my experience."

All Haiti was proud of Mr. Leger, easily in popular esteem Haiti's first citizen, and the United States undoubtedly would have been satisfied with his election for the Haitian presidency. But he peremptorily refused to have his name considered. I sent my chief of staff to discuss the matter with him. He replied, " Tell the admiral I will do everything in my power for Haiti; but I must watch and see what the United States will demand of Haiti, and be in a position to defend Haiti's interests in case the demands should be unreasonable. At this time I could not possibly accept the presidency. I am for Haiti, not for the United States."

The Haitian minister at Washington, Mr. Enos, was cabled to and asked to accept the presidency. He peremptorily declined. Then efforts were made to induce ex-President Legitime, a venerable, universally beloved Haitian, an ex-President of the Republic, to stand for the presidency. He refused to accept. Any one of these three men would have had the respect and confidence of all good Haitians, and would have received many votes, perhaps a majority of those cast.

So now at the last moment the Bobo adherents determined to prevent the election, which clearly meant Dr. Bobo's defeat. So they determined that early on August 12 there should burst fourth such a scene of disorder, riot, and bloosshed in Port au Prince that all thoughts of election would be driven from our minds. But law-abiding Haitians learned of this and informed me on the morning of August 11, the day before the election. That afternoon, as I previously stated, I went on shore and informed the committee of safety that they were no longer to exercise any authority whatever in the city. In dismissing the committee of safety, which I related in my previous testimony, I failed to state the following, which I addressed to the committee of safety:

" Further, you are informed that your conspiracy to plunge Port au Prince into riot and bloodshed to-morrow morning is known and will not proceed."

Previous to their being dismissed, they had made no pretense of denial or innocence. They were full of consternation for fear they might not be able to stop their intended riot—that is, all except Charles Delva. He simply laughed in, perhaps, an ordinary way, and exclaimed, "You have won."

Nothing happened on August 12 to interfere with the election. The Haitian senators, 39 of them, and 102 deputies met in the Chamber of Deputies. There were but few formalities. The galleries were packed with Haitians, who had been disarmed at the door, and a few marines were present. My representative, Capt. E. L. Beach, chief of staff, was present on the floor and mixed in with the senators and deputies. All senators and deputies were armed at their own urgent request.

But one ballot was taken. Each congressman when his name was called, unintimidated by the cacos, freely announced the name of the man he voted for. It was soon evident that the majority for Senator Dartiguenave would be overwhelming. Then the vote was announced as 94 for Dartiguenave, 16 for Bobo, and a scattering for Cauvin, Thegun, and others.

Then came exulting cheers, triumph, and order, and hope, for Haiti had won. But Senator Sudri Dartiguenave did not cheer. He sat in his chair overcome with emotion; tears gushed from his eyes. It was some moments before he regained his self-control. He then took the oath as Haiti's President, swearing to maintain the constitution and laws of Haiti and to administer his high office with justice, without partiality, and solely in the interest of Haitians.

After this, with deep feeling, he made a noble speech, touching on the disorders that had such a painful effect on Haitian reputation, Haitian prosperity, and Haitian life. Among other things he said, was: "I have been elected because I belong to no faction, to no political group; I am free from all obligations of a faction nature. I beg earnestly for the support of every Haitian in the efforts I shall make for Haiti's welfare. If I receive this support, Haiti will make a start for the good of things we all long for. If I do not receive it, I will accomplish nothing, and the uncertainties, disorder, and sadness of Haitian live that now environ us will be continued."

Coming down from the elevated place from which he spoke, he went directly to where my chief of staff, Capt. E. L. Beach, was sitting, and taking him by the hand, made an impromptu speech, in words as follows: Admiral Caperton came to us at a moment when Haiti was in complete despair. But two days previously hundreds of Haitians had been murdered in their cells in the jail, Haitians against whom no crime was charged except lack of friendship for the Haitian President. The day Admiral Caperton arrived a mob, frenzied with grief, killed President Vilbrun Guillaume. The Government was overturned; chaos ran riot. It seemed that everything good in Haiti had burst into nothingness, and black, hopeless despair laid heavy on our hearts, and at this moment Admiral Caperton came in and landed troops, only for our protection and the protection of foreigners.

He assured us that he came to help Haiti; that he came as a sympathetic friend, and he asked for the cooperation of all Haitians. His troops came not as conquerers, trampling on our hearts, our bodies, our properties, but only as friends. His kindness, his consideration, his goodness, so apparent in his every act, started hope in our hearts. We love our Haiti and our independence, but we accept the help so generously given us by the United States, represented by Admiral Caperton. It is with the understanding and knowledge of all Haiti that as President I am to have the support and help of the United States. Otherwise I could not accept office. But also, with the clear understanding that the only promise and obligation that I am under to anybody is expressed in the oath I took to defend the constitution and the laws of Haiti, and to govern and be governed by them.

The inaugural procession then occurred, passed through the streets of Port au Prince. and in one of the carriages, the leading carriage, was the President, Dartiguenave, and Capt. E. L. Beach, my chief of staff. They were escorted by marines, followed by many carriages. Haitian soldiers, resplendent in brilliant uniforms, 100 in number, were the immediate guard and escort of the President, the President's idea of this being that it would show to everyone that Haiti and the United States were together from the beginning of his administration. Then the President and Capt. Beach went to Deputy Cham's home, where the inaugural reception was held. Here the senators, deputies, foreign officials, foreign residents, and Haitians came to pay their respects to Haiti's new President, and all gave the most cordial greeting to the American officer with the President. There was in that reception joy and hope.

Senator ODDIE. Admiral, let me ask you this question: Was that speech taken down in shorthand?

Admiral CAPERTON. Not in shorthand; no, sir. The speech was not taken down in shorthand, but Capt. Beach has a wonderful memory. He is a very good writer, and immediately after he left there and could get to himself he sat down and wrote this out, and, as you noticed, I did not quote the speech, but I said " in words as follows." I am satisfied that the President said about those words, knowing Capt. Beach's memory and his knowledge of the subjects discussed. He sat down and wrote out the whole speech. That same sort of coincident had happened before with me at various conferences.

The election occurred on the 12th. In the meantime, President Dartiguenave was most anxiously awaiting to hear the national salute, which would announce his inauguration, and which had been arranged for. Haitian gunners were to fire the guns, loaded and prepared by American sailor men. But no salute came. The President grew anxious. So Lieut. Oberlin was dispatched to the fort, Fort Nationale, where the guns were located. After a while the salute began. There was a painful interval between each shot, but finally the twenty-first gun was fired. This of itself might not seem to have been important, but it is mentioned here because of the great importance attached to it by President Dartiguenave. He could not feel that he was President until he had received the national salute, which had been customary upon similar occasions.

I would like here to recapitulate a little bit and make some remarks in regard to what happened a few days before the election, which took place on the 12th.

On August 7th Port au Prince remained quiet during the day. I had information that a number of bandits had been pillaging plantations to the north of the city, in the vicinity of Croix des Bouquet. A marine detachment was dispatched and succeeded in capturing the bandit chief and 11 others, who were engaged in pillaging.

On this day I directed that ex-Minister Bourand, who was one of the late cabinet, and Mr. Laroche, another one, be landed from the *Jason*, and escorted under guard, to Minister Bourand's residence, as I did not know how he would be received, and as he had been in immediate command of the Government's troops in the northwest. Mr. Bourand was minister of interior under Guillaume's government. I therefore placed a guard about his residence and directed that he and Mr. Durand be especially guarded during their stay in Port au Prince.

On August 8th, the next day, the Haitian Government's gunboat *Nord Alexis* arrived at Port au Prince with 766 soldiers disarmed at Cape Haitien. These soldiers lived in the vicinity of Port au Prince and in south Haiti. Seven hundred and thirty-six of these soldiers were landed and sent to their homes. The remaining 30 were either sick or wounded, and were sent to the Haitian hospital on shore.

The CHAIRMAN. By whom had they been disarmed?

Admiral CAPERTON. They had been disarmed—these were Government troops—either voluntarily or by my troops in the north for the purpose of bringing them down to their homes. They had nothing to eat, and they were in a destitute condition. So I sent this Haitian gunboat, the *Nord Alexis*, up there for them and brought them down. Through the committee on shore—this was on the 8th—I paid each soldier 10 gourdes and informed him that he was no longer a soldier, must not appear in uniform, and must return to his home and keep orderly.

" Referring to the destitute condition of these men, they arrived about 7 a. m., shortly after which I learned that they had nothing to eat on board to speak of during the past 24 or 36 hours. The crew of the U. S. S. *Washington* heard of this, whereupon they volunteered to send over their breakfast, which was about to be served, to these destitute soldiers, which was done. These soldiers were paid as I have said before, about 10 gourdes each as they passed over the gangway. The *Nord Alexis* was at this time alongside the wharf in the navy yard and it was necessary for the soldiers to pass through the navy yard and in doing so to pass by two or three of our marine sentries. To show the custom of graft which prevailed even among the soldiers, each one of these destitute soldiers as he passed a marine sentry, tried to hand to the marine his money which he just received, saying in so many words, ' Take out your share and give me the balance.' "

On the 9th I had removed from the Haitian gunboat *Nord Alexis* all the arms and ammunition on board that vessel and turned them over to the commander of the landing force for safe-keeping, not knowing what the *Nord Alexis* might do under the then prevailing conditions in the city and harbor.

To explain the condition of Haitian finances at this time, I may say that last January the treasury service, by an arbitrary act, was taken from the National Bank of Haiti, the national treasury—this was done by the Guillaume Sam government—and given to private banking firms, the principal one of which is Simmond Freres. The Simmond Freres is under no control which will safeguard public interests. They merely make collections of the revenues and receive a certain percentage as their fee and turn the rest over to whomsoever may exercise sufficient force or persuasion in the name of a government or revolution to obtain it.

The result is that considerable money is being thus forced from Simmond Freres by the so-called revolutionary committees in various towns, and this money is being used to actively support revolutionary activity. I might add that in all these towns they have also a self-constituted " committee of safety."

On account of military necessity, therefore. I this day, on the 9th, informed the committee in Port au Prince, Simmond Freres, and the National Bank of Haiti that the treasury service would be resumed by the National Bank of Haiti. This bank is under legal and exacting contract for the handling of the treasury service for the Haitian Government.

Referring to my previous remarks about the treasury service being restored to the National Bank of Haiti, I sent the following message to the Secretary of the Navy. This is a message to the department to inform them with regard to the case. The cablegram was as follows:

"Account military necessity, restored treasury service to National Bank of Haiti. Last January treasury service taken from this bank; given to Simmond Freres. Money forced from Simmond Freres by so-called revolutionary committees various places, constituting menace against order and prolonging disturbances. Cablegram sent to-day Washington, D. C., by revolutionary committee recommending provisional government caused solely by definite knowledge Bobo will not be elected by Congress. No doubt absolute legality status of Congress. Forming provisional government would be government by unconstitutional means and in effect another revolution in Bobo's favor; would continue unrest and unsettled conditions for long time and make uncertain and delay desired treaty with Haiti. Recommend no consideration be given recommendations for provisional government. Haiti needs freedom from political unrest, and most of all settled government. While many prominent Haitians at first favored provisional government, sentiment in this respect has generally changed, and now practically all Haitians except adherents of Bobo demand immediate election of President.

" Yesterday met Dartiguenave and Bobo together in conference. Asked Dartiguenave would he, if Bobo elected. accept Congress choice and give assistance to Government ; answer, yes. Asked Bobo same question if Dartiguenave elected. Bobo replied would not accept Dartiguenave nor assist his Government.
                                                                    " CAPERTON."

The CHAIRMAN. This is still a recapitulation of the events before the election?
Admiral CAPERTON. Yes, sir. That cablegram was sent on the 10th.

Cape Haitien remained quiet during the day of August 8, but information was received that the ex-Bobo troops had looted in the vicinity of Grande Riviere. I only mention this to show the disturbances in the north at this time.

On the 9th the following message was sent to the commanding officer of the U. S. S. *Castine:*

" Have assumed military control Port au Prince and Cape Haitien ; am disarming and disbanding all Haitian troops I can get hold of. Reports here indicate an ex-Government force of about 200 men under Gen. Auguste approaching St. Marc ; prevent their attacking town and endeavor persuade them to deposit arms in your keeping and disband. Am not yet ready to permanently occupy St. Marc ; cooperate with de facto civil authorities. Acknowledge 15109.
                                                                    " CAPERTON."

Under date of the 10th of August the following message was received from the commanding officer of the *Connecticut:*

" Referring your 12508, proclamation will be published broadcast in French to-morrow and copies issued at outpost to people leaving town. Have received no word yet from revolutionary generals. No troops have presented themselves to surrender arms.

" Have opened customhouse for business and made good progress in establishing local government.

" The revolutionary troops interfere with the free ingress of market people. There has been no disturbance to-day.

" DURELL."

This tells about the first disturbance made by the revolutionary forces, the cacos, in preventing food from coming into the cities.

The CHAIRMAN. What date is this?

Admiral CAPERTON. The 10th of August.

The CHAIRMAN. What was the date on which they elected Dartiguenave?

Admiral CAPERTON. That was on the 12th, sir.

On August 10 Port au Prince was becoming more uneasy as the election approached. The Bobo faction, since the cacos had been driven from the town and it had thus lost its power to intimidate Congress, was growing desperate. Threats of assassination had been made against Dartiguenave and other senators, and Charles Zamor and his faction were doing little toward aiding to quiet matters.

On August 10 the following message was sent from the commander of the cruiser squadron to the commanding officer of the *Connecticut:*

" National Bank of Haiti has resumed treasury service. This bank has issued instructions to its representatives Cape Haitien to pay each soldier disarmed and dismissed there 10 gourde and each chief 10 gourde. Get in touch representatives bank Cape Haitien and make necessary arrangements for paying these troops. Supervise payment troops yourself. Information given to troops in country that they will be paid if they will disarm and disband in Cape Haitien, may aid you in persuading them to come to Cape Haitien. This applies to any troops who will lay down arms at Cape Haitien and disband either government or any other kind.

" CAPERTON."

I think I might add here in regard to paying these soldiers for their services if they would disband, I had many conferences with the generals of both factions in the north in regard to this matter and arrangements had been made looking to this disarmament.

The following message was sent from the commander of the cruiser squadron to the Secretary of the Navy on date of August 10:

" Port au Prince quiet during night. Cape Haitien quiet; ex-Bobo troops causing some disturbance vicinity Grande Riviere; none of these troops have arrived Cape Haitien. Ex-government forces about 200 under Gen. Auguste attacked St. Marc Saturday, but repulsed by forces under committee of safety; Auguste and four followers killed. St. Marc quiet now; am encouraging local authorities preserve order. U. S. S. *Eagle* arrived Mole St. Nicholas 7.30 p. m. Monday for news.

" CAPERTON."

The CHAIRMAN. I think that is sufficient of the preliminary matter. You may now proceed to the conditions which followed the election of the President.

Admiral CAPERTON. After the 12th?

The CHAIRMAN. Yes. But before you do that let me ask you this question, Admiral. Did Capt. Beach speak French?

Admiral CAPERTON. Yes, sir; very well.

(Thereupon, at 12.10 o'clock p. m., the committee adjourned subject to the call of the chairman.)

INQUIRY INTO OCCUPATION AND ADMINISTRATION OF HAITI AND SANTO DOMINGO.

WEDNESDAY, OCTOBER 19, 1921.

UNITED STATES SENATE,
SELECT COMMITTEE ON HAITI AND SANTO DOMINGO,
Washington, D. C.

The committee at 10.30 o'clock a. m., pursuant to adjournment, Senator Medill McCormick (chairman) presiding.

Present: Senators McCormick, Oddie, and King.

Also present: Mr. Ernest Angell and Mr. Horace G. Knowles in their representative capacities as hereinbefore indicated, and Maj. Edwin N. McClellan, United States Marine Corps, representing the Navy Department.

STATEMENT OF REAR ADMIRAL WILLIAM B. CAPERTON, UNITED STATES NAVY, RETIRED, 714 MONTAUK AVE., NEW LONDON, CONN.—Resumed.

The CHAIRMAN. Admiral Caperton, before you proceed, let me call your attention to page 255 of the annual report of the Secretary of the Navy, paragraph 52, for the fiscal year ending June 30, 1920. This is paragraph 52 of Gen. Barnett's report, which purports to quote from cables sent by you to the department. I refer more especially to the assertion attributed to you that " In the presence of congressmen, Dariguenave, president of the senate, stated that congressmen are agreed that Haiti must and will accede gladly to any terms proposed by the United States, ' including right of intervention when necessary, customhouse control, and cession outright without restriction of St. Nicolas Mole.' " I read so much of it in order that you may refer directly to the dispatch to which he alludes, and if you have it, you might read it directly into the record. You may answer that later.

Admiral CAPERTON. On August 7 I sent the following message to the Secretary of the Navy, parts of which are quoted in the chairman's question:

" Before landing Port au Prince to-day Bobo formally resigned position chief executive power and dismissed his cabinet ministers. Has telegraphed all his generals in north to deposit arms with American forces Cape Haitien. Promises use every effort for good order. Bourand has given similar promises and sent similar instructions to his troops in north.

" I have curtailed power revolutionary committee; it did not keep faith. This results in not having services committee. Civil officials late Government glad accept and execute my orders.

" All classes Haitiens ´clamoring for immediate election President. Legal congress with civil functionaries and all necessary organization except President and cabinet for regular Government now exists. Only two serious candidates—Bobo and Dartiguenave; latter will probably be elected. Have had daily conferences with president of senate and chamber deputies, with senators, deputies, ex-cabinet ministers, and many leading Haitiens. President of Senate Dartiguenave, in presence of congressmen, states congressmen are agreed that Haiti must and will gladly accede to any terms proposed by United States. They now say will ˇcede St. Nicholas Mole outright without restriction, grant customhouse control, right to intervene when necessary, and any other terms. They beg only as far as possible avoid humiliation. They insist no Government can stand except by United States protection; state without this protection there would be nothing but anarchy in Haiti. Most Haitiens now fear American forces may be withdrawn.

"Extremely desirable reestablish Government immediately. Unless otherwise directed I will permit congress elect President next Thursday.

"CAPERTON."

The CHAIRMAN. Now, you may turn to the period after the election.

Admiral CAPERTON. As an indication of how matters were shaping themselves at this time, on August 13 Gen. Polynice informed me of his intention to help the present Government maintain order. Charles Zamor informed me that he would use all his influence for peace.

On the same date Bobo was living in the British legation. He seemed to be overwhelmed in his disappointment. His nerve, pluck, and self-assurance had gone. He stated that he no longer had a country, and that he was going to France.

Also, on August 13 considerable destitution exists among the lower classes in Port au Prince. On the morning of August 13 a woman and child were found dead in the open market place in the vicinity of Rue de St. Honore and Rue de Centre, their deaths having been due, without question, to starvation. A very intelligent woman, claiming to be a school-teacher, appeared this morning and showed what purported to be an acknowledgment of indebtedness to her for pay as school-teacher for the month of January. She claims that neither she nor family have had anything to eat for two days.

The CHAIRMAN. I do not think we can go into this detail.

Admiral CAPERTON. I do not intend to give you all of it. Other cases similar to this have been brought to my attention, and some cases where families have been without food for 24 to 48 hours. The starting of public works and establishment of peace will, without doubt, furnish employment to many men who are now without food, but this will not, in all probability, reach the women and children who have no men to support them.

I requested that this matter be brought to the attention of the Red Cross Society, with the request that they send representatives and undertake relief work at Port au Prince.

The CHAIRMAN. Did they do that ultimately?

Admiral CAPERTON. Yes, sir. I might say they from time to time sent me $1,000 at one time and $2,000 at another time.

The CHAIRMAN. Did they send you any nurses or physicians?

Admiral CAPERTON. No, sir. I had doctors from the ships whom I detailed.

The CHAIRMAN. Did any of the missionary societies of the United States undertake to do anything?

Admiral CAPERTON. No, sir; not outside of the Red Cross. I was compelled to employ some missionaries there to take charge of the work.

The CHAIRMAN. But no American Christian organization did anything to aid you in the relief of the suffering or the destitution of the people?

Admiral CAPERTON. No, sir. I formed all sorts of committees or societies.

The CHAIRMAN. During the first few weeks after Dartiguenave's election, what was the condition of the country in reference to order?

Admiral CAPERTON. The country to the north was very much upset. From day to day I reported these facts in messages, copies of which I have here, about the Cacos collecting in various ports and sections of the north.

The CHAIRMAN. If you care to, you may incorporate the messages in the record, but do no take the time to read them now.

Admiral CAPERTON. Yes, sir; I would like to do that.

The CHAIRMAN. There were bands gathering in the north?

Admiral CAPERTON. Yes, sir. I would like to incorporate in the record the following messages:

CRUISER SQUADRON, UNITED STATES ATLANTIC FLEET,
U. S. S. "WASHINGTON," FLAGSHIP,
August 14, 1915.

From: Commanding Officer *Connecticut.*
To: Commander Cruiser Squadron.

Daguesseau Montreuil arrived this morning. He communicated with revolutionary committee at St. Marc and Gonaives and sent telegram to revolutionary committee here to the effect that Bobo was very strong politically. Strongly

suspect that he will urge Bobo troops to maintain present stand and not surrender arms. Think Bobo's absence from north Haiti strengthens new government. The committee of public safety appointed by Bobo declared itself to be
strong last night after the news of the election. No troops have presented themselves yet to surrender arms. There has been no disturbance to-day.

DURELL.

AUGUST 14, 1915.

From: Commander Cruiser Squadron.
To: Commanding Officer *Connecticut.*

No revolutionary activity any kind will be tolerated in Haiti and especially
within the limits of my command. It is duty all citizens support present government. If Daguesseau Montreul or any other Haitian attempts revolutionary
activity any kind arrest them at once. Bobo I believe is entirely eliminated
politics in Haiti for the present. He is in Brit'sh legation now in pitiable condition; am inclined to believe he is insane.

CAPERTON.

Admiral CAPERTON. Then, at about 4 p. m. on August 14 I received the department's——
The CHAIRMAN (interposing). This was two days after·the election of President; the President was elected on the 12th?
Admiral CAPERTON. Yes, sir. I received the department's sigcode radiogram
No. 02014, relative to the treaty between the United States and Haiti. The
translation of the message was completed by 9 a. m. on the 15th of August,
when it was sent ashore to Mr. Davis, the American chargé d'affaires, by
special messenger. Mr. Davis received this message at 9.45 a. m. on the 15th
of August:

" U. S. S. *Washington, 14 August, 1915.*

" No. 2 du Check 561 via cable 3.10 p. m.
" From: Washington, D. C.
" To: Government U. S. S. *Washington,* Guantanamo.
" Sigcode flag for American Legation, Port au Prince.
" For more than a year the Haitian Government has been familiar with the
terms of the treaty contained in department's instructions of July 1, 1914, with
which they have already expressed their agreement regarding the principal part.
Recently, however, assurances have been received that the Haitian authorities
are willing "——
The CHAIRMAN. Does it read "willing" or "unwilling"?
Admiral CAPERTON. It reads "are willing"; "are willing now to go farther
than before, including the cession to the United States of Mole St. Nicholas.
In view of that friendly attitude of the Haitian Government, as shown by
these proposals, you will please prepare forthwith a draft of treaty as outlined
in this cablegram. Without delay submit it informally to the President elect
and advise him that the department believes that as a guaranty of sincerity
and interest of the Haitians in orderly and peaceful development of their
country that the Haitian Congress will be pleased to pass forthwith a resolution authorizing the President elect to conclude, without modification, the
treaty submitted by you. When officially notified that such a resolution has
been passed by Congress extend to the President elect the formal recognition
of this Government and simultaneously conclude with the newly elected
President of Haiti, to the end that it may be forthwith submitted for ratification by the present Haitian Congress before its adjournment, a treaty in strict
accordance with the draft referred to, with the following alterations and
additions:

" ALTERATIONS.

" Omit from article 1 the words ' if he shall deem it necessary and expedient,
or if the Haitian Government shall request.' so that that portion of article
1, referring to the appointment of financial adviser. shall read as follows: ' and
the President of the United States shall designate a financial adviser to the
Republic of Haiti, who shall devise an adequate system of public accounting,
etc.' Make corresponding changes throughout the treaty, particularly in articles
4 and 8. Omit last two words ' of account' at end of article 1.

"In article 2 after the word 'receivership' add 'and to the financial advisor,' change 'its' before 'execute' to 'the.'

"In article 3 substitute 'financial advisor' for 'general receiver' in both instances.

"First paragraph, article 4, will read 'all sums collected and received by the general receiver shall be applied, first, to the payment of the salaries and allowances of the general receiver, his assistants and employees and expenses of the receiver shall include the salaries and expenses of the financial advisor; second, to the interest and sinking fund of the public debt of the Republic of Haiti; and, third, to the maintenance of the constabulary referred to in article 9, and then the remainder to the Haitien Government for the purpose of current expenses."

"Second paragraph of article 4 will end with the words 'previous month.'

"Additional after article 8 insert articles as follows:

"ART. 9. The Haitian Government obligates itself, for the preservation of domestic peace, the security of individual rights and the full observance of the provisions of this treaty, to create without delay an efficient constabulary composed of native Haitians. This constabulary shall be organized and officered by Americans designated by the President of the United States, which officers the Haitian Government shall appoint and shall clothe with the proper and necessary authority and uphold in the performance of their functions. The constabulary herein provided for shall, under the direction of the Haitien Government, have supervision and control of arms and ammunition, military supplies, and traffic therein, throughout the country. The stipulations in this article are necessary to prevent factional strife and disturbances.

"'ART. 10. The Government of Haiti agrees not to surrender any of the territory of the Republic of Haiti by sale, lease, or otherwise, or jurisdiction over such territory, to any foreign Government or power except to the United States, nor to enter into any treaty or contract with any other foreign power or powers that will impair or tend to impair the independence of Haiti.

"'ART. 11. The Haitian Government agrees to execute with the United States a protocol for the settlement, by arbitration or otherwise, of all pending pecuniary claims of foreign corporations, companies, citizens, or subjects against Haiti.

"'ART. 12. The Republic of Haiti being desirous to further the development of its natural resources agrees to undertake and execute such measures as in the opinion of the Government of the United States may be necessary for sanitation and public improvements of the Republic, under the supervision and direction of an engineer or engineers, to be designated by the President of the United States and appointed and authorized for that purpose by the Government of Haiti.

"'ART. 13. That the United States shall have authority to prevent any and all interference with the attainment of any of the objects comprehended in this convention as well as the right to intervene for the preservation of Haitian independence and the maintenance of a Government adequate for the protection of life, property, and individual liberty.

"'ART. 14. The present treaty shall be approved and ratified by the high contracting parties in conformity with their respective laws, and the ratification thereof shall be exchanged in the city of Washington as soon as may be possible.

"'ART. 15. The present treaty shall remain in full force and virtue for the term of 10 years, to be counted from the day of exchange of ratifications, and further for another term of 10 years at the request of either party.'

"In faith whereof the respective plenipotentiaries have signed the present convention in duplicate and have hereunto affixed their seals."

Dr. Bobo left Port au Prince on August 15 on the French steamer *Abdel Kader*, which is bound for Jeremie, south Haiti, and ports in San Domingo. Bobo states he is going to San Domingo.

Referring to conditions in the north again, information was received on August 15 that ex-Bobo forces under Gen. Morency were marching toward Gonaives. About this time I decided it was time to make some distribution of my ships and forces in the north of Haiti. I therefore issued campaign order No. 8, as follows:

T. No. 7645-15.

CRUISER SQUADRON,
UNITED STATES ATLANTIC FLEET,
U. S. S. "WASHINGTON," FLAGSHIP,
Port au Prince, Haiti, August 15, 1915—1.30 p. m.

Campaign order No. 8.

Forces:

(a) Northern detachment, Capt. E. H. Durell; *Connecticut, Nashville,* First Regiment marines, less Second Battalion and band; (b) main body, *Washington, Castine, Eagle,* First Brigade marines, less one battalion.

1. No further news.

2. This force will maintain military control of Port au Prince and Cape Hatien pending negotiations United States and Haiti.

3. (a) Northern detachment, maintain military control Cape Hatien; (b) main body will maintain military control Port au Prince. Troops on shore maintain military control Port au Prince and sufficient outing territory to insure food supply for city. Occupy St. Marc, Leogane, and Petionville.

Washington remain Port au Prince and support main body of troops.

Castine patrol coast St. Marc to Gonaives, both inclusive. Support troops St. Marc and vicinity.

Eagle patrol coast Leogane to Miragoane, both inclusive. Support troops Leogane and vicinity.

Protect life and property and preserve order.

4. Base is at Guantanamo Bay. *Osceola* will carry mail, stores, and provisions between various detachments and base. *Jason* and *Solace* remain Port au Prince for the present.

5. Squadron commander on *Washington.* Make 8 a. m. and 8 p. m. daily reports and at such other times as may be necessary to keep squadron commander fully and frequently informed of situation. Use seventy-fifth meridian mean time.

W. B. CAPERTON,
Rear Admiral, Commander Cruiser Squadron,
Commanding United States Forces in Haitian Waters.

Copies to: Operations, commander in chief, *Washington, Connecticut, Tennessee, Castine, Nashville, Eagle,* commandant Guantanamo.

Extracts to *Solace, Jason;* commander First Brigade; commander First Regiment.

I also issued letters of instruction as follows:

U. No. 7637-15.

CRUISER SQUADRON,
UNITED STATES ATLANTIC FLEET,
U. S. S. "WASHINGTON," FLAGSHIP,
Port au Prince, Haiti, August 15, 1915.

From: Commander cruiser squadron, commanding United States forces in Haitian waters.

To: Chief of Staff.

Subject: Orders.

1. Orders No. 7198-15 of August 3, 1915, issued by commander cruiser squadron are hereby revoked.

2. I will directly, in conjunction with the American chargé d'affaires, carry on the negotiations and have charge of the important relations with the Haitian officials. These duties will be carried on by me, either personally or through members of my staff.

W. B. CAPERTON.

V. No. 7643-15.

CRUISER SQUADRON,
UNITED STATES ATLANTIC FLEET,
U. S. S. "WASHINGTON," FLAGSHIP,
Port au Prince, Haiti, August 15, 1915.

From: Commander cruiser squadron, United States Atlantic Fleet, commanding United States forces in Haitian waters.

To: Capt. E. H. Durell, United States Navy.

Subject: Letter of instructions.

1. The commander cruiser squadron has assumed military control of the cities of Port au Prince and Cape Haitien. A national government has just

been formed at Port au Prince with Dartiguenave as President, and this Government is now organizing and assuming control of civil affairs throughout Haiti. Important negotiations are going on between the United States and Haiti, of which you will be kept informed.

2. It is my intention to support the present Haitian Government and to carry on negotiations with it, while maintaining military control of the cities of Port au Prince and Cape Haitien.

3. You will maintain military control of the city of Cape Haitien, and will protect life and property and preserve order.

4. The deployment of forces in Haitian waters will be as given in campaign order No. 8.

5. I will directly, in conjunction with the American chargé d'affaires, carry on the negotiations and have charge of the important relations with the Haitian officials at Port au Prince. These duties will be carried on by me, either personally or through members of my staff.

W. B. CAPERTON.

W. No. 7644–15.

CRUISER SQUADRON,
UNITED STATES ATLANTIC FLEET,
U. S. S. "WASHINGTON," FLAGSHIP,
Port au Prince, Haiti, August 15, 1915.

From: Commander cruiser squadron, United States Atlantic Fleet, commanding United States forces in Haitian waters.
To: Col. Littleton W. T. Waller, United States Marine Corps.
Subject: Letter of instructions.

1. The commander cruiser squadron has assumed military control of the cities of Port au Prince and Cape Haitien. A national government has just been formed at Port au Prince with Dartiguenave as President, and this Government is now organizing and assuming control of civil affairs throughout Haiti. Important negotiations are going on between the United States and Haiti, of which you will be kept informed.

2. It is my intention to support the present Haitian Government and to carry on negotiations with it, while maintaining military control of the cities of Port au Prince and Cape Haitien.

3. You will maintain military control of the city of Port au Prince and of such outlying territory as may be necessary to insure food supply for the city, and will protect life and property and preserve order.

4. The employment of the forces in Haitian waters will be as given in campaign order No. 8. You personally will have direct charge of the troops at Port au Prince and vicinity. Col. Eli E. Cole will have charge of the troops at Cape Haitien.

5. I will directly, in conjunction with the American chargé d'affaires, carry on the negotiations and have charge of the important relations with the Haitian officials. These duties will be carried on by me, either personally or through members of my staff.

W. B. CAPERTON.

X. No. 7667–15.

CRUISER SQUADRON,
UNITED STATES ATLANTIC FLEET,
U. S. S. "WASHINGTON," FLAGSHIP,
Port au Prince, Haiti, August 15, 1915.

The AMERICAN CHARGÉ D'AFFAIRES,
American Legation, Port au Prince, Haiti.

SIR: I have the honor to state that Col. Littleton W. T. Waller, United States Marine Corps, has this day relieved Col. Eli K. Cole, United States Marine Corps, of the military duties at Port au Prince.

Col. Waller will be in charge of maintaining the United States military control of the city of Port au Prince and of such outlying territory as may be necessary to insure food supply for the city, and will protect life and property and preserve order.

Col. Cole will be in charge of maintaining military control of Cape Haitien and of the protection of life and property and the preservation of order at that place.

I will directly, either personally or through members of my staff, and in conjunction with you, attend to such civil matters on shore and such important relations with the Haitian officials as may from time to time be undertaken by the Un'ted States forces.

You are requested to communicate these facts to all foreign diplomatic and consular representatives. I am, sir,

Respectfully,

W. B. CAPERTON,
Rear Admiral, United States Navy, Commanding Cruiser Squadron.

Y. No. 7666–15.

PORT AU PRINCE, HAITI,
August 15, 1915.

The COMMANDING OFFICER FRENCH CRUISER "DESCARTES,"
Port au Prince, Haiti.

SIR: I have the honor to state that Col. Littleton W. T. Waller, United States Marine Corps, has this day relieved Col. Eli K. Cole, United States Marine Corps, of the military duties at Port au Prince.

Col. Waller will be in charge of maintaining military control of the city of Port au Prince and of sufficient outlying territory as may be necessary to insure food supply for the city, and of the protection of life and property and preservation of order.

Col. Cole will be in charge of maintaining military control of Cape Hatien and of the protection of life and property and the preservation of order at that place. I am, sir,

Respectfully,

W. B. CAPERTON,
Rear Admiral, United States Navy,
Commander Cruiser Squadron, United States Atlantic Fleet,
Commanding United States Forces in Haitian Waters.

To show that I was making endeavor to quiet the revolutionary forces in the north, I went to Mr. Leger in Port au Prince and he informed me that Mr. Ademar Auguste and Bishop Kerzusan in Cape Haitien are prominent men who have great influence with the Cacos. I immediately got in communication with these men in the north.

On August 16 I received information, which was fairly reliable, that the Cacos forces were concentrating at Le Borgne, on the north coast of Haiti, west of Cape Hatien, and at Fort Sonde, just east of St. Marc, on the Artebonite River; that the Cacos were becoming restless, as they had not received pay for some time; and that the leaders appeared to fear that they will lose control over their men.

The Cacos question will be the most difficult one for the United States to solve in Haiti; as these men have long been used to the wandering life of a bandit and to a life without work. The Cacos question is a most serious one, and will probably not be successfully handled until a reliable constabulary is established and money comes into the country to provide work for these men.

I would like to insert the following report in the record. This is a report made by one of our officers who was entirely engaged in keeping track of the Cacos situation:

"HEADQUARTERS SECOND REGIMENT,
"UNITED STATES MARINE CORPS,
"*Port au Prince, Haiti, August 16, 1921.*

" From: Capt. George Van Orden, Marine Corps.
" To: Chief of staff, First Brigade.
" Subject: Report concerning location and condition of revolutionary forces.

" 1. The 'Caco' forces have been reported as concentrating at Le Borgne, on the north coast west of Cape Haitien, and at Point Sonde, just east of St. Marc, on the Artibonite River. The report of their concentration at Point Sonde was practically confirmed from another reliable source, and as it agrees with reports of activities in the vicinity of St. Marc it can be taken as true. I was also informed by an agent of the organization that the chiefs were having some considerable difficulty in maintaining discipline because of the delay in paying their men and sending them home, which they were told was the intention of the Government. He told me that the conditions were getting rapidly more threatening and requested me to urge that steps be taken toward paying off these men, in order that he and the other chiefs, who had given me their personal assurances that their men would make no trouble during negotiations, could continue their contract with me. The above information was not given in a threatening manner, and it was plain to be seen that the agent was considerably worried over the prospect of his men getting out of hand. He stated that it had been very difficult to convince the lesser chiefs and the men that the Government would play fair with them, and that it was only because they knew that the Americans were handling this question that they consider it at all. I was also informed that if the man named Filogene were appointed a member of any commission that had to do with their organizations, it would certainly cause a serious outbreak, as Filogene is considered by them a traitor and an all-around scoundrel."

That report is signed by Capt. George Van Orden, United States Marine Corps.

On the 17th of August the American chargé d'affaires, Davis, delivered to President Dartiguenave the draft of the proposed treaty and a memorandum relative to Congress passing a resolution directing the President to conclude the treaty.

It now became necessary for me to occupy one or two of the cities adjoining Port au Prince, as a further security for that city, and to protect an important area furnishing food for Port au Prince. It must be remembered that these revolutionary troops, the Cacos, were prohibiting the entrance of foodstuffs and, in fact, all traffic for the cities, so it became a question of supplying food to the people within the cities.

On the 16th of August the American consular agent at Port de Paix informed the commanding officer of the *Connecticut* that Port de Paix was entirely and openly hostile to the Government of President Dartiguenave, which has not been recognized at that place yet, and that the population was ready to join the Cacos. This is a city to the eastward of Cape Haitien, on the north coast of Haiti.

Touching upon the point of alleviating the starving poor at Port au Prince, I would like to say that the following committee was named to carry on that work.

Senator ODDIE. Who appointed that committee, Admiral?

Admiral CAPERTON. I did, sir. That committee consisted of Archbishop Pichon, Rev. Turnbull, United States Vice Consul Battist, Senators Harrison and Villard, Madame Vue Fils Aime, president, and Madame N. Solages, treasurer of St. Vincent de Paul's Hospital, under direction of Lieut. Oberlin. They were engaged in alleviating the suffering of the starving poor at Port au Prince with funds provided by the American Red Cross Society.

I would like to mention a few of the things this society was doing. They formed milk stations where they assured the poor that they would get fresh milk. At first we sold it for a small amount and afterwards gave it to the patients. We also formed a station with the aid of some French nuns who were there, where the poor women could leave their children in arms while they went out to procure work in the city. Then we had another station where they treated all sorts of diseases as the people would report. Our doctors and also some of the Haitian doctors were very active in this work.

It was on the 18th of August that the Haitian Government published a decree of amnesty to all political factions.

The CHAIRMAN. What date was that?

Admiral CAPERTON. That was August 18. In this connection I would like also to refer to the following letter, addressed to the American consul at Port au Prince, Haiti, in which I said: "I have the honor to request that you take the necessary measures to direct the consular representatives at Port de Paix, Aux Cayes, Jacmol, and Jeremie to publish the following proclamation to the people of their districts:

"'I am directed by the United States Government to assure the Haitian people that the United States has no object in view except to insure, establish, and help to maintain Haitian independence and the establishing of a stable and firm government by the Haitian people.

"'Every assistance will be given to the Haitian people in their attempt to secure these ends. It is the intention to retain United States forces in Haiti only so long as will be necessary for this purpose.'"

It has been shown here that I had agreed, through the President of Haiti, to pay these troops from the north certain sums if they would turn over their rifles and ammunition, and, incidentally, they were paid a certain amount for doing this, provided they would lay down their arms and return home.

In order to give further publicity to my offer to pay the soldiers upon coming within the United States lines, depositing their arms, and returning to their homes, 15 gourdes apiece, and to each chief 100 gourdes, I directed the commanding officer of the Castine to publish the department's proclamation and this information at Gonaives. The other commanding officers throughout Haiti were ordered to publish the same——

The CHAIRMAN. Throughout Haiti or at the several Haitian ports?

Admiral CAPERTON. At the ports occupied by the American troops.

There were many promises—papers signed—to the end that these leaders in the north would carry out this plan of disarming the Cacos. We received hundreds and thousands of arms, but the project failed, as will eventually be shown.

The CHAIRMAN. This sum was paid from the Haitian treasury, I presume?

Admiral CAPERTON. Yes; I said with the understanding and permission of the President.

It was about this time—on August 18—that I informed our Government of my intention to extend to the President elect of Haiti formal recognition of the United States Government, as directed in the department's radiogram 02014: "Unless otherwise directed, I will fire a national salute of 21 guns with the Haitian flag at the main if I ascertain that this salute can be returned by the Haitian authorities."

The CHAIRMAN. Do you mean if they had powder enough?

Admiral CAPERTON. Yes, sir.

In that connection, I would like to put the following in the record:

"AUGUST 18, 1915.

"From: Commander cruiser squadron.

"To: Secretary of the Navy, via wire.

"If American chargé d'affaires extends to President elect of Haiti the formal recognit'on of United States Government, as directed in department's radiogram 02014, unless otherwise directed, I will fire national salute of 21 guns with Haitian flag at the main if this salute can be returned by the Haitian authorities. 23318.

"CAPERTON."

On the 19th of August I received a radiogram from the Navy Department stating that the State Department desired that I assume charge of the customhouses at Jacmel, Les Cayes, Jerem'e, Miragoane, Petite Goave, Port au Prince, St. Marc, Gonaives, Part de Paix, and Cape Haitien. It further directed that the funds collected be used for the organization and maintenance of an efficient constabulary for conducting such temporary public works as will afford immediate relief through employment for the starv'ng populace and discharged soldiers, and finally for supporting the Dartiguenave government. I was further directed to confer with the Amer'can chargé d'affaires for the purpose of having President Dartiguenave solicit the above action; but whether the Pres'dent so requested or not, I was directed to carry out the State Department's desires. The Navy Department further directed that the American officials placed in charge of the customhouses "be furnished with the necessary customs guards." I am to direct these American officials to collect all the import and export duties, to immediately depos't them w'th the respective local branches of the National Bank of Haiti in separate accounts opened in my name, and to draw against these accounts for the purpose mentioned above, the surplus to be held for the time being by the United States Government in trust for the people of Haiti.

In that connection, I would like to put the following into the record:

"AUGUST 19, 1915.

"From: Secretary of the Navy.

"To: Commander cruiser squadron.

"State Department desires you assume charge of following customhouses: Jacmel, Aux Cayes, Jeremie, Miragoane, Petit Goave, Port au Pr nce, St. Marc, Gonaives, Port de Paix, Cape Haitien. Funds collected to be used for organization and maintenance efficient constabulary, for conducting such temporary public works as will afford immed'ate relief through employment for starving populace and discharged soldiers, and finally for supporting Dartiguenave government. Confer with chargé d'affaires for purpose of having President Dartiguenave solicit above action. Whether Pres'dent so requests or not, proceed to carry out State Department's desire; supply American officials place l in charge with necessary customs guards. Direct officials collect all import an:l export duties to be immediately depos'ted by them with respective local branches of National Bank of Haiti in separate account opened your name. Draw against this account for purposes mentioned above, surplus to be held for t'me being by United States Government in trust for people of Haiti. Acknowledge. 20019.

"DANIELS."

The CHAIRMAN. I want to ask you a question which may be answered some time later, as to the effect of the use of the funds so seized upon the payment of the interest on the foreign debt—that is, the effect of the sequestration of these funds on the payment of the interest on the foreign debt.

Admiral CAPERTON. In view of the more or less delicate situation existing with reference to American control of customhouses, which has been violently opposed by the Haitien people for a number of years and even at the present time ; and as there is a treaty under negotiation now in Port au Prince covering this customs control matter, I considered it extremely undesirable to aggravate the situation by announcing that we were going to forcibly seize the customhouses immediately. This we are not in a position to do at the present time on account of the lack of my forces, and I therefore believe that the military intention of seizing the customhouses be for the present not communicated to the Haitiens. We should, however, immediately assemble the necessary forces. In this way no time will be lost, the treaty will be signed with less opposition, and the matter of military occupation of the customhouses can probably be arranged without unduly increasing the hostile attitude.

The CHAIRMAN. Let me ask, Admiral, what was the object in seizing the customhouses at the ports of entry?

Admiral CAPERTON. The funds that were being collected were being used at different ports by revolutionary forces in some instances. There was no control.

The CHAIRMAN. Had it been the practice in Haiti for a revolutionary chief at the beginning of his movement to seize a customhouse as the financial basis of his movement?

Admiral CAPERTON. Yes, sir. When he became President ; of course, he always became President.

The CHAIRMAN. The seizure of a customhouse was the first step in the accomplishment of a successful revolution? When they began a revolution in the north they seized the customhouse, did they, at Cape Haitien?

Admiral CAPERTON. I do not know. They seized—in many instances they did, but not always, I think. When they could, they did. In these marches around from Cape Hatien to Port au Prince during the revolution I had occasion frequently to intervene in the matter and save them from taking money from the Haitian Republic, and also on one or two occasions, I think, from some private bank.

On the 18th of August, referring to the matter of customhouses, I informed the department that the United States had not actually accomplished a military intervention in the affairs of another nation ; that hostility exists now in Haiti and has existed for a number of years against such action ; that hostile contacts have only been avoided by prompt and rapid military action which has given the United States control before resistance has had time to organize; that we now hold the capital of the country and two other important seaports; that the total force at my disposal now is one armored cruiser, two gunboats, one converted yacht, and 1,500 marines ; and that this force is now employed at the maximum extension consistent with maintaining control of the occupied territory and prompt concentration for defense. The department now desires that the customhouses in seven other cities be occupied. These customhouses can not be taken charge of unless the cities in which they are located are occupied with sufficient military force to protect our customs officers and preserve order. A further extension of my present force is imperative to avoid.

No troops should be without the support and communication facilities of a naval vessel for the present at least. To occupy these seven additional ports means practically military occupation of the seacoast of Haiti, which is extensive. No attempt must be made to accomplish this until there are available sufficient forces and sufficient officers and an organization completed for assuming control of the customs service. This will require not less than one more regiment of marines of not less than eight compan'es, the Artillery battalion of marines, and three more gunboats or light cruisers. For the reasons given before, I informed the department that I considered it imperative that these contemplated operations be kept a secret for the present and undertaken only when force is available and customs service organized and ready. This secrecy is extremely important now, pending the treaty negotiations. While we are powerful enough without doubt to accomplish anything we desire by force, yet a due respect for the sensibilities of the Ha tians and a friendly attitude in our operations at this time will do a great deal toward accomplishing what we wish now, and will lay the foundation for good relations between the two Governments in the future. We are not at war with Hait', and hostile operations, except where they can not be avoided, should be replaced by peaceful methods, consistent with accomplishing our objects.

I recommended that not less than one regiment of marines of not less than eight companies, the battalion of Artillery, and three gunboats be immediately ordered to Ha ti and placed at my disposal, and Paymaster Charles Conard and 10 other pay officers not below the grade of lieutenant be sent immediately to organize and administer the customs service. Paymaster Conard is especially fitted for this duty on account of his previous experience at Vera Cruz, Mexico.

While at a later date, after be'ng sufficiently organized, our forces may be withdrawn, yet at the present moment the United States should take no chances of injury to its dignity and prestige.

The message I sent to the Secretary of the Navy in regard to this matter reads as follows:

AUGUST 19, 1915.

From: Commander Cruiser Squadron.
To: Secretary of the Navy and Commander in Chief, via wire.

United States has now actually accomplished a military intervention in affairs of another nation. Hostility exists now in Haiti and has existed for number of years against such action. Serious hostile contacts have only been avoided by prompt and rapid m'litary action which has given United States control before resistance has had time to organize. We now hold capital of country and two other important seaports. Total force at my disposal now, one armored cruiser, two gunboats, one converted yacht, and 1,500 marines. This force now deployed at maximum extension consistent with maintaining control of occupied territory and prompt concentration for defense. Department now desires that customhouses in seven other cities be occupied. Customhouses can not be taken charge of unless cities in which they are located are occupied with sufficient military force to protect our customs officers and preserve order. Further extension of present force imperative to avoid. No forces should be without support and communication facil:ties of naval vessels for the present at least. To occupy these seven additional ports means practically military occupation of seacoast of Haiti, which is extensive. No attempt must be made to accomplish this until there are available sufficient force and sufficient officers and organization completed for assuming customs service.

This will require not less than one more regiment of marines of not less than eight companies, the artillery battalion of marines, and three more gunboats or light cruisers. Consider it imperative that these contemplated operations be kept for the present secret and undertaken only when force is available and custom service organized and ready. This secrecy extremely important now pending treaty negotiations. Recommend not less than one regiment of marines of not less than eight companies, the artillery battalion of marines, and three gunboats be immediately ordered Haiti and placed my disposal, and Paymaster Charles Conard and 10 pay officers not below rank lieutenant be sent immediately to organize and administer customs service. Paymaster Conard especially fitted, due previous experience, Vera Cruz, Mexico. While at later date, after constabulary is organized, our forces may be withdrawn, yet at present moment United States should take no chance of injury to its dignity and prestige.

CAPERTON.

Senator ODDIE. I would like to ask why that secrecy was suggested.
Admiral CAPERTON. It was my suggestion. The country was in a state of uproar at that time, and of course it has always been known that they violently opposed any taking over of their customhouses, and I thought it was not the opportune time to do this; and also the fact that, as I had asked for 10 paymasters in addition to Paymaster Conard, it was necessary to get up an organization before taking charge of these customs.

On the 20th of August there were approximately 17 shots fired in the vicinity of the railroad station in the northern part of Port au Prince. One sentry

was fired upon by a native; the sentry returned the fire with one shot, but the
man escaped. I merely mention this to show the great unrest in the city at
that time. On the 20th I reported that there had been no disturbances at Cape
Haitien. The country people are still held up outside the town by the Cacos,
which prevented food from coming in. On the 20th of August the American
chargé d'affaires was continuing the treaty negotiations. All our efforts were
directed toward a speedy conclusion of this work.

Conditions became so unsettled at St. Marc, which is about 50 miles to the
westward of Port au Prince, that I found it necessary to issue the following
order to the commanding officer of the *Castine*:

" Seize and administer customhouse at St. Marc. Collect all import and export duties. Open account in local branch of National Bank of Haiti in my
name and deposit customs receipts therein. Acknowledge.

" CAPERTON."

The CHAIRMAN. When was the President elected?

Admiral CAPERTON. On August 12. On August 21 treaty negotiations are not
progressing satisfactorily. President Dartiguenave still continues his favorable
attitude toward the treaty, but there is a change in the attitude of certain
members of the cabinet and of the Congress apparent. An unfavorable sentiment has appeared in Congress in the form of inflammatory speeches against
the customs control and American occupation in general. This change of attitude has been made in spite of repeated and solemn assurances given me before
the formation of the present Government. Both the Congress and the members
of the Government are cowed and intimidated by fear of sentiment throughout
the country against the American customs control, propagated constantly during
the last few years by the faction leaders.

Senator ODDIE. Let me ask you, who gave you these assurances?

Admiral CAPERTON. They were given to my representative by the President
and some of the members of his cabinet. We got this information from them
voluntarily.

On the 21st of August, in accordance with the Navy Department's instructions,
I directed the commanding officer of the *Connecticut* at Cape Haitien to open
an account for customs receipts in the local branch of the National Bank of
Haiti and otherwise carry out the department's instructions relative to the
administration of customs. I have temporarily placed this account in Commander Olmstead's name until I can organize an office in Port au Prince to
take care of this business for the coast as a whole in my name. In that connection I would like to put into the record the following communication:

AUGUST 21, 1915.

From: Commander Cruiser Squadron.
To: Commanding officer *Connecticut.*

In accordance orders Navy Department you will keep control customhouse
at Cape Haitien, with an American officer as collector of customs. Collect all
import and export duties. Open account in local branch National Bank of
Haiti in name of Commander Olmstead, military governor, and deposit total
customs receipts therein daily from now on. Draw against this account for
the following purposes: First, for conducting such temporary public works as
will afford immediate relief through employment for starving populace and
discharged soldiers, and second, for supporting local military government. Surplus will be held by American military governor in trust for Haitian people.
Acknowledge.

CAPERTON.

The CHAIRMAN. This was on the 21st of August. When was the seizure of
the customhouses completed?

Admiral CAPERTON. I think Port au Prince was the last one I took. I do not
remember the date.

The CHAIRMAN. I am trying to get a picture of that. You were on the
station how long?

Admiral CAPERTON. For about 18 months.

The CHAIRMAN. You have now covered 2 or 3 months of the 18 months?

Admiral CAPERTON. Yes, sir. Many things happened in that interval with
regard to outbreaks. The customhouse at Port au Prince was taken over on
September 2.

The CHAIRMAN. Between the 20th of August and the 2d of September, when
the customhouse at Port au Prince was seized, what events of importance took
place?

Admiral Caperton. I could not answer that offhand without following my notes consecutively, as I am doing now. This happened six or seven years ago, since which time I have been busy at other things, and it is hard to answer questions without referring to my official notes made at that time.

On August 23 treaty negotiations are still unsatisfactory. The fear of the Government and the Congress of the faction leaders and the Cacos apparently grows more each day. This Government, of course, by its very nature, in which it consists of men not associated with factions and not supported by Cacos, is weak, unless supported by the United States. Politics in Haiti has been entirely in the hands of the faction leaders for the last 30 or 40 years, and anyone not a member of a faction and not a participant in these factional disturbances is not politically strong. This present Government is not getting the support of the various parts of the country, nor has it been able to establish local government in other cities to any extent.

The American chargé d'affaires received at noon on the 23d of August a note delivered personally by the minister of foreign relations, who stated that should the United States insist on any other action than that which the Haitian Government expressed itself willing to perform in the note, the President and cabinet would be forced to resign. In this note the Haitian Government says, after expressing its great desire to enter into an arrangement with the United States, that it holds itself at the disposition of the United States Government to commence pour parlers, and, further, as it is anxious to avoid all difficulties which would be of a nature to alter the good relations which exist between Haiti and the United States, that it would be disposed, since the United States insisted upon it, to suggest to the Congress the passage of a resolution expressing the desire to see the President of Haiti conclude a convention with the United States for best reciprocal interests of the two countries. There is apparently no doubt but what the question of customs control is practically the great and only question in obtaining a treaty with these people, and that these pour parlers will without doubt be directed on the part of the Haitian Government toward the avoidance of customs control, or a great modification of it.

I still made reports from day to day saying that the town of Port du Paix is strong for Bobo; that the Cacos are reported at Le Borgne and are on their way to Port du Paix, and that the town is without a government.

(Thereupon the committee took a recess until 2.30 o'clock p. m.)

AFTER RECESS,

The committee reassembled, pursuant to the taking of recess, at 2.30 o'clock p. m.

The Chairman. You may proceed, Admiral.

Admiral Caperton. On the 24th of August private interviews by the American chargé d'affaires with the President and members of the cabinet indicated a more conciliatory attitude toward the treaty. The President himself is apparently anxious to have the treaty matter settled and states that, with few minor changes not affecting the general principles, the treaty would be acceptable.

On the 25th of August the American chargé d'affaires, in an unofficial and private talk with the President, received from him what seemed to be a most sincere expression of his desire to conclude the treaty as soon as possible. The President stated that he believed the treaty could be signed, provided the United States would agree to the change of a few details which in no way affect the basic principles involved. The American chargé d'affaires told him that, while he was not authorized to sign any treaty other than the one submitted, he would not object to forwarding to Washington these desired changes, should they be of a detail nature and not affecting the basic principles.

Unreliable and irresponsible political enemies of the Haitian Government are attempting to stir up animosities against the Government and the American intervention. There are, both in the Congress and in the country, among the Cacos, irresponsible agitators, mostly the faction leaders, who are attempting to undermine the present Government and on every pretext to influence opinion against it. It is believed that the chances for successfully negotiating the treaty will be increased if we for the moment cease seizing the customhouses and conduct no further military operations except those necessary for preserving peace and order and for other important military reasons.

Senator Oddie. Was that your cablegram?

Admiral Caperton. Those are my notes.

I sent the following message to the Secretary of the Navy on the 25th of August:

" From: Commander cruiser squadron, August 25, 1915.
" To: Secretary of the Navy via wire and Commander in Chief.

" Referring American chargé d'affaires radiogram of August 25, 6 p. m.: For better supporting treaty negotiations, unless otherwise directed, will for the present cease seizing customhouses and will for the present conduct no further military operations except those necessary for preserving peace and order or for other important military reasons. In event resignation present Haitian Government I recommend that military government be established Port au Prince, Haiti, with American officer as military governor. Present is most critical time in relations with Haiti, and our decision now will, to a great extent, determine future course. If military government is established, we would be bound not to abandon Haitian situation until affairs of country are set at right and predominant interests of United States of America secured. Necessity for action on my part will come if Government resigns, and I should at that time know wishes of United States of American Government. 23425.

" CAPERTON."

The CHAIRMAN. At this point, Admiral, I will put into the record the following from the department's record:

" Under date of September 20, 1914, the Secretary of State informed the Secretary of the Navy that the conditions in Haiti had improved to an extent that would admit of the withdrawal battleships *New Jersey* and *Georgia*, now in Haitian waters, but felt that a gunboat should be retained there. In reply thereto, on October 2, 1914, the Secretary of the Navy informed the Secretary of State that the gunboat *Tacoma* would be held at Cape Haitien, awaiting orders. Immediately following this, however, the situation in Haiti grew steadily worse, and under date of October 28, 1914, letters were addressed by the Secretary of State to the President and to the Secretary of the Navy as follows:

" ' DEAR MR. PRESIDENT: In view of our conversation this noon relative to Haiti it seemed to me of first importance that the naval force in Haitian waters should be at once increased, not only for the purpose of protecting foreign interests but also as evidence of the earnest intention of this Government to settle the unsatisfactory state of affairs which exists. We have one vessel now at Cape Haitien and two others are needed on the south coast, one at Port au Prince and the other at Gonaives.

" ' In the absence of Secretary Daniels and Assistant Secretary Roosevelt, I took up the matter with Admiral Fiske, who thinks one vessel can be spared from Dominican waters, and with him I agree. As to the other vessel necessary, the Admiral suggests that one of the warships now at Vera Cruz might be ordered to Haiti. In view of the urgent need of increasing our force on the south coast at this time when a renewal of negotiations seems probable, will you please advise me whether or not I can say to Admiral Fiske that you approve of sending a battleship from Vera Cruz to Port au Prince?' "

" ' The SECRETARY OF THE NAVY.

" ' SIR: I have the honor to inform you that the political situation in the Republic of Haiti is such as to render necessary the presence of additional United States naval ships in Haitian waters. It is therefore requested, in order to carry out the policies of this Government, that two ships be sent to Haiti of sufficient size so that their landing complements will be able to take charge of and preserve order in the cities of Port au Prince and Gonaives, should occasion therefor arise. It is hoped that these two ships may arrive in Haiti as soon as practicable.'

" To the above letter the Secretary of the Navy replied on October 29, 1914, as follows:

" ' SIR: I have the honor to acknowledge the receipt of your letter of October 28 stating that the diplomatic situation in the Republic of Haiti is such as to render necessary the presence of additional United States naval ships in Haitian waters. It is noted that the Department of State requests, in order to carry out the policies of this Government, that two ships be sent to Haiti of sufficient size so that their landing complements will be able to take charge of and preserve order in the cities of Port au Prince and Gonaives should occasion therefor arise.

"'I have the honor to inform you that the U. S. S. *Hancock* now at Monte Cristi has been ordered to proceed immediately to Port au Prince and that the battleship *Kansas* has been ordered to proceed immediately from Vera Cruz to Port au Prince. The *Hancock* has on board a regiment of marines, which force should be adequate to preserve order in the cities of Port au Prince and Gonaives should necessity require it to be landed.'

"The foregoing letters were followed by further requests from the State Department as follows, on October 30, 1914:

"'SIR: I have the honor to request that the attached telegraphic instruction to the American minister at Port au Prince, Haiti, be sent through the radio communication of the U. S. S. *Hancock*, as this department understands that cable communication with Port au Prince is very uncertain.

"'It is requested that instructions be sent to the senior officer of the United States naval forces in Haitian waters to confer with the American minister at Port au Prince and to accede to any requests he may make for the movement of ships and landing of men.'

"The Secretary of the Navy replied to the above letter on October 30, 1914, as follows:

"'SIR: I have the honor to acknowledge the receipt of your letter of October 30, requesting that the telegraphic instructions attached thereto be sent to the American minister at Port au Prince, Haiti, through the radio communication of the U. S. S. *Hancock*. It is also noted that the Department of State requests that instruction be sent to the senior officer. United States naval forces in Haitian waters, to confer with the American minister at Port au Prince and to accede to any request he may make for the movement of ships and landing of men.

"'I have the honor to inform you that the telegraphic instructions to the American minister at Port au Prince have been sent as requested. The commanding officer of the *Hancock* has been directed to confer with the American minister at Port au Prince and to cooperate with him.'"

Admiral CAPERTON. On August 25 I issued instructions relative to the administration of the customs and civil affairs. I appointed Paymaster Charles Morris, United States Navy, as "administrator of customs" for the entire customs service of Haiti assumed by the United States forces. In that connection, Mr. Chairman, I would like to put in the record the following communications:

"No. 8186–15.

"CRUISER SQUADRON, UNITED STATES ATLANTIC FLEET,
"U. S. S. WASHINGTON, FLAGSHIP,
"*Port au Prince, Haiti, August 24, 1915.*

"From: Commander cruiser squadron, United States Atlantic Fleet.
"To: Commanding United States forces in Haitien waters.
"Subject: Letter of instructions.
"Reference: (*a*) Campaign order No. 9.

"1. The following instructions will be followed for the purpose of administering customs and such other civil duties as may be assumed by the United States forces in Haitien waters.

"CUSTOMS ADMINISTRATION.

"2. The squadron commander will administer the customs through an 'administrator of customs,' who will be established at Port au Prince. The 'administrator of customs' will have general charge of the collection of customs duties at all ports and the depositing of receipts, in accordance with instructions given by the squadron commander and in accordance with the Haitien law not inconsistent with these instructions. For the purpose of insuring uniformity of administration the 'administrator of customs' is authorized to issue directly to the local commander such detailed instructions as may be necessary relative to the customs collection, depositing of receipts, keeping of accounts, rendition of returns, and such other administrative matters as comes within his province.

"3. Detachment commanders will appoint from their respective commands for each port in which customs are to be collected a commissioned Navy pay or Navy line officer as 'collector of customs' and 'captain of the port.'

"4. Detachment commanders will exercise general supervision over the administration of customs within the limits of their respective commands, being guided by the instructions of the squadron commander acting through the 'administrator of customs.'

" CIVIL ADMINISTRATION.

"5. Detachment commanders will have charge of such other civil affairs as may be assumed within the limits of their respective commands and of the disbursement of funds allotted to them by the squadron commander to meet obligations incurred thereby.

"6. Disbursements will be made by detachment commanders only under the following appropriations:

"'Appropriation constabulary;' to be used for the organization and maintenance of an efficient constabulary. (For use at Port au Prince only for the present.)

"'Appropriation public works;' to be used for conducting such temporary public works as will afford an immediate relief through employment for the starving population and discharged soldiers.

"'Appropriation military and civil government of the United States forces;' to be used for the maintenance of the customs and port services and such military government as the United States may establish.

"7. Detachment commanders will submit to the squadron commander by radio not later than the 25th of each month, confirmed by letter, estimates covering the funds desired under each appropriation for each town for the coming calendar month.

"8. Funds will then be allotted by the squadron commander to each detachment commander from the funds on deposit in the local branch of the National Bank of Haiti in each town, and these funds so allotted will be placed to the credit of the detachment commander in these local banks.

"9. Each detachment commander will render the following returns covering funds allotted to them by the squadron commander as specified in paragraph 8:

"(a) At the end of each quarter, beginning September 30, 1915, an account current with all substantiating vouchers.

"(b) At the end of each calendar month a statement of cash received and expended.

"10. The commanding officer of the *Washington* will assume the duties of a 'detachment commander.' indicated herein under 'civil administration' for Port au Prince. He will in addition assume the duties of 'captain of the port' at Port au Prince.

"W. B. CAPERTON."

"No. 8282–15.

"CRUISER SQUADRON, UNITED STATES ATLANTIC FLEET,
"U. S. S. SHIP WASHINGTON, FLAGSHIP,
"*Port au Prince, Haiti, August 23, 1915.*

"From: Commander cruiser squadron, United States Atlantic Fleet, commanding United States forces in Haitian waters.

"To: Paymaster Charles Morris, United States Navy, U. S. S. *Washington* (via commanding officer).

"Subject: Appointment as 'administrator of customs' and 'collector of customs' at Port au Prince.

"1. There is inclosed herewith Navy Department's radiogram No. 20018, directing the seizure of certain customhouses and a letter of instructions relative to the administration of the customs service. Customhouses at St. Marc and Cape Haitien have already been seized. The customhouse at St. Marc is administered in exact accordance with department's radiogram No. 20018. The customhouse at Cape Haitien is administered in the same manner, except that the account with the local branch of the National Bank of Haiti has temporarily been placed in the name of Commander P. N. Olmstead. The seizure and administration of the remaining customhouses will be undertaken as soon as possible.

"2. You are hereby appointed 'administrator of customs' and 'collector of customs' at Port au Prince.

"3. You will establish an office at Port au Prince and administer the customs service in accordance with department's radiogram No. 20018, the letter of instructions No. 8186–15, of August 24, 1915, and the Haitian law where this law is not inconsistent with these instructions.

"4. This is in addition to your present duties.

"W. B. CAPERTON."

" No. 8283–15.

" CRUISER SQUADRON, UNITED STATES ATLANTIC FLEET,
" U. S. S. WASHINGTON, FLAGSHIP,
" *Port au Prince, Haiti, August 23, 1915.*

" From: Commander cruiser squadron, United States Atlantic Fleet, command-ing United States forces in Haitien waters.

" To: Paymaster Charles Morris, United States Navy, U. S. S. *Washington* (via commanding officer).

" Subject: Appointment as ' fiscal officer ' for 'civil administration.'

" Reference: (*a*) Navy Department's radiogram 20018.

" Inclosure: 1.

" 1. There is inclosed herewith a letter of instructions No. 8186–15 of August 24, 1915, relative to ' civil administration,' assumed by the United States forces in Haitian waters.

" 2. You are hereby appointed the ' fiscal officer ' for the squadron commander in connection with the funds placed to his credit by the various collectors of customs.

" 3. Funds will only be disbursed under the following appropriation:

" 'Appropriation constabulary'; to be used for the organization and main-tenance of an efficient constabulary.

" 'Appropriation public works'; to be used for conducting such temporary public works as will afford an immediate relief through employment for the starving populace and discharged soldiers.

" 'Appropriation military and civil government of the United States forces ; to be used for the maintenance of the customs and port services and such mili-tary governments as the United States may establish.

" 'Appropriation Haitian Government,' to be transferred to the Dartiguenave government as may be determined by the squadron commander.

" The funds remaining after such disbursements will be left in the admiral's account and held by him in trust for the people of Haiti.

" 4. You will keep the necessary accounts and files and the returns rendered by the detachment commanders.

" 5. You will each month after the receipt of the detachment commanders' estimates prepare a synopsis of those estimates and a synopsis of the allotment which you consider necessary for the different detachment commanders for the coming month, and will submit same to the squadron commander for his approval. Upon approval of these allotments you will make the necessary arrangements through the National Bank of Haiti to place the funds so allotted to the credit of detachment commanders.

" 6. This is in addition to your present duties.

" W. B. CAPERTON."

———

" CRUISER SQUADRON, UNITED STATES ATLANTIC FLEET,
" U. S. S. ' WASHINGTON,' FLAGSHIP,
" *Port au Prince, Haiti, August 25, 1915.*

" Capt. E. H. DURELL, United States Navy,
" *U. S. S. ' Connecticut,' Cape Haitien, Haiti.*

" DEAR DURELL: I am inclosing herewith a draft of campaign order No. 9, which I have not yet issued, but will in the immediate future as soon as the necessary reconnoissances are completed at the southern ports. I am sending this advance copy to you so that you may have a general outline of the deploy-ment of the forces in Haitian waters. It will be signed by me in a few days and your regular copy sent to you then. So far as your detachment is concerned you may consider it in effect now. I am inclosing herewith a letter of instruc-tions which will become effective immediately upon its receipt.

" Paymaster Charles Morris, United States Navy, has been appointed ' admin-istrator of customs,' and will immediately proceed with the administration of customs for the entire coast of Haiti. You are, of course, the detachment commander referred to in the letter of instructions, and will immediately assume the administration duties directed therein for your two towns. We may have to be a little patient for the first month or so, until we begin to get some funds to our credit. After that I think matters will run more smoothly.

" Under direction of the Navy Department, the customs receipts are to be placed to my credit in a single account in the National Bank of Haiti. You will open an account in my name at this bank both at Cape Haitian and Port de Paix. You will proceed to shift the money on hand at Cape Haitian from Commander Olmstead's account to my account, keeping out sufficient funds as you may need to cover expenditures for one week in that town. Please advise me when this has been done and how much you have placed to my credit.

" I suggest that you immediately send in for both towns estimates for the month of September as money desired, in accordance with the letter of instructions. I will then immediately make an allotment by transferring funds to your credit at each place. I intend to have each town self-supporting; that is, the customs receipts at each place must support the work at that place. You will for the present use two appropriations: (a) 'Public works' and (b) 'military and civil government of United States forces.' In these two I think you will have plenty of leeway to meet all expenses of your administration and undertake such sanitary and cleaning-up jobs as you wish.

" If you need funds for immediate uses at Port de Paix, take funds out of Commander Olmstead's account at Cape Haitien before transferring to my name and inform me of the amount so taken.

" It is very necessary that the method outlined in the letter of instructions and in the circular letter of the administrator of customs to the collectors of customs be followed in order to carry on the business uniformly throughout the Republic. The scheme is roughly to collect the customs, put then in my name, and then I allot to you what I can out of these funds to pay for your two towns. After that I leave it entirely to your business and as to how you spend your money. No further action is necessary on my part. The only restriction is that money must be spent only under the two appropriations mentioned. I think these will leave you plenty of leeway to give you anything you please.

" With reference to the *Nashville* controlling Port de Paix and Cape Haitien, I consider it necessary to have the *Nashville* touch in at Port de Paix frequently, at your discretion, in order to get news, investigate conditions, support as necessary the landing force there and maintain communication with it. I am not as yet ready to leave any detachments in isolated positions without their being in reach of the prompt support of a naval vessel. This may interfere with Commander Olmstead's present duties as 'military governor' at Cape Haitien. If it does you are authorized to relieve him from that duty and appoint Col. Cole or anyone else you may have available in his place.

"A battery of Artillery will be landed at Cape Haitien in the near future by the *Tennessee*. The force you will then have ashore at Cape Haitien, supported by the *Connecticut's* bluejacket battalion, will give you practically the number of troops that Col. Cole thought were necessary there. I would suggest that this bluejacket battalion be kept aboard the *Connecticut* as a reserve, ready to land at either Port de Paix or Cape Haitien.

" In this connection it is very desirable to have the bluejacket battalion— officers, petty officers, and men—given thorough instruction in their military duties on shore. The department available has no more troops available to increase the force in Haiti at the present time, and we must therefore be prepared to use our seamen to reinforce our marines at any threatened point. In Port au Prince I have directed Col. Waller to furnish instruction through one of the marine officers to the *Washington's* seaman battalion. He is running a school in the simple military duties for officers and petty officers under the charge of a marine captain. I think this is of highest importance.

" With reference to the 2,000 ex-Government troops in the vicinity of Ouans-minthe, I don't presume that the orders issued by the President that they board the *Nord Alexis* and come to Port au Prince will be effective. I told him of the situation there with reference to their not being able to reach the seacoast, but he holds that if his orders get through to these troops they would board the *Nord Alexis* all right: so I forwarded his radiograms and gave you your directions relative to the *Nord Alexis*, as it will do no harm to try.

" I have been investigating Montreuil's activities and am endeavoring to get a line on him which will give you something definite to work on. You, of course, have orders to arrest him immediately if he attempts to start any revolutionary trouble.

"Bobo is out of it, and neither he nor any of his so-called factions can be recognized by us. We are having our own troubles in Port au Prince endeavoring to get the treaty through. Things are not entirely satsfactory, and I may be forced to establish a military government here. My general plan with reference to you is to give you entire freedom consistent with carrying out the general ideas with which you are familiar.

" Very sincerely,

" W. B. CAPERTON."

During the day reports continued to be received indicating pillaging and disorder in the interior; that is, in the northern interior. At this time there were about 1,000 of the old Government troops in the northeast of Haiti near Ouanamine.

I took the matter up with the president of paying these soldiers a few gourdes each, giving them some clothes, and bringing them down to Port au Prince and disbanding them there, as they lived in the southern part of Haiti. To this the president consented, and I had them brought down.

On the 27th of August I had a conference with Mr. Charles Zamor and Gen. Robin, relative to the Caco question. These gentlemen made the proposition that a joint commission, consisting of Gen. Zamor, Gen. Robin, and one other Haitian, and three or four American officers, proceed into the interior and visit all Caco chiefs and their towns. Upon the arrival at each chief and their men, sums of money would be paid to them in the form of checks, which would be cashed in the National Bank of Haiti within the American lines, and could only be cashed upon the surrender of arms and ammunition to the American forces; the amount of money to be paid to depend upon the particular influence of the chief, the size of his detachment, and other local conditions to be determined by the commission on the spot. These gentlemen say that then the Cacos would return to their homes and cease marauding. They proposed to pay these chiefs, when they met them, and also the men. They would gather around and receive their arms and disband them.

The proposition of paying each soldier 15 gourdes if he will surrender his rifle and disband, and 100 gourdes to each chief, which is the standing proposition now, is, I understand, quite liberal, and at this rate not more than 200,000 gourdes, or about $35,000, gold, could possibly be spent. It is therefore evident that this proposition of Zamor's is, to a great extent, an attempt to bleed the Americans. His proposition was for a great deal more than this. I forget just the figure now.

On the 27th of August the American charge d'affaires received from the minister of foreign affairs the written reply of the Haitian Government to the latest treaty proposition. In this reply practically every stipulation of the original treaty was either omitted or so changed as to defeat its purpose. This was done in spite of the repeated assurances that the Haitian Government was in accord with the United States as to all principles involved, differing only as to slight matters of detail.

The CHAIRMAN. Did Zamor propose that the Americans or the Haitians pay this excessive sum?

Admiral CAPERTON. The sums were, of course, to be paid out of the Haitian treasury.

The CHAIRMAN. I only asked that because you referred to his bleeding the Americans.

Admiral CAPERTON. That is what I have here in my notes.

The CHAIRMAN. You meant to take advantage of American credulity?

Admiral CAPERTON. I think that was the idea. This money was all paid out by the consent and orders of the president at that time for these various arms at these different places.

Gens. Blot and Davilmar Theodore arrived at Cape Haitien on the 29th of August, and I was of the opinion that the providing of work to the Cacos in north Haiti will be a valuable aid in stopping the present disorders in the north, and will probably do more toward this end than a commission such as Mr. Zamor suggests. I understand from reliable sources that the National Railroad of Haiti can, under its present contract with the Haitian Government, immediately employ about 1,500 men on new construction between Bahon and Pignon; about the same number between St. Marc and Petit Riviere. d'

L'Artibonite, and about 1,000 men between Gonaives and Gros Morne. I believe that if the State Department will use its good offices to induce the National Railroad of Haiti to begin this work and will offer its help, that the work may be begun at once. Funds from the customs will not be available for me to begin public works as directed by the department for some little while, and an early employment of the men in the north is extremely desirable.

A message was sent to the Secretary of the Navy on August 29, as follows:

AUGUST 29, 1915.

From: Commander Cruiser Squadron.
To: Secretary of the Navy.

Believe providing work will do great deal toward stopping present disorders in north. Understand from reliable sources that national railroad of Haiti can immediately employ about 1,500 men on new construction between Bahon and Pignon, about same number between St. Marc and Petit Riviere de L'Aritbonite, and about 1,000 between Gonaives and Gros Morne, under present contract with Haitian Government. Recommend State Department use good offices to induce National Railroad of Haiti to begin this work at once. Funds from customs will not be available for me to begin extensive public works as directed in department's radiogram 20018 at once, and early employment men in north extremely desirable. 16029.

CAPERTON.

On the 30th of August the American chargé d'affaires had a consultation which lasted several hours with President Dartiguenave and his cabinet. They agreed only to sign the treaty in a modified form. They insist that customs control infringes on the bank concession, and this matter must be adjusted before further discussion. They also stated that they are willing to give customs control, but even after this difficulty is removed would not be willing to allow the United States the administration of customs.

The CHAIRMAN. How did they make a distinction between customs control and administration?

Admiral CAPERTON. I think they meant the collection of customs. The matter of collecting customs depended entirely upon the collector of the customs. I have been informed by high officers there that it was only necessary to appoint a Haitian as an official collector of customs in one of these ports to give him the opportunity of becoming a rich man. They seemed to be satisfied with the manner in which we went about collecting the customs, reducing the large number of employees in the office, and with the vast increase in the amount of money turned over to the Government, because formerly each man, in addition to his pay, received a rake-off, which they admitted. When we went in, in readjusting the pay for the fewer number of men we found it necessary to increase their pay to include their rake-off, which was not too much, I thought.

The CHAIRMAN. You mean the rake-off was reasonable?

Admiral CAPERTON. The president himself seemed sincerely desirous of reaching an agreement, but he does not appear to be a man of sufficient force to control the cabinet and the congress at this time.

On the 31st of August there were no encouraging developments in the treaty situation. I have therefore decided that, unless otherwise directed, I will occupy and begin administering the customhouse at Port au Prince at 10 a. m. on the 2d of September. I so informed the department of this decision.

In connection with this matter I would like to put in the record the following communication:

AUGUST 31 1915.

From: Commander Cruiser Squadron.
To: Secretary of the Navy.

Unless otherwise directed will occupy and begin administering customhouse at Port au Prince at 10 a. m., September 2.

CAPERTON.

On September 1 I appointed Paymaster Charles Conard "administrator of customs" and "fiscal officer" for the civil administration, relieving Paymaster Charles Morris of those duties. In that connection, Mr. Chairman, I would like to put into the record the following communications:

ZZ.
No. 8639.   CRUISER SQUADRON, UNITED STATES ATLANTIC FLEET,
U. S. S. "WASHINGTON," FLAGSHIP,
Port au Prince, Haiti, September 1, 1915.

From: Commander Cruiser Squadron, United States Atlantic Fleet, commanding United States forces in Haitian waters.
To: Paymaster Charles Conard, United States Navy.
Subject: Appointment as "administrator of customs."
Reference: (a) Commander Cruiser Squadron's letter of instructions No. 8186-15 of August 24, 1915.

1. You are hereby appointed "administrator of customs" and will immediately relieve Paymaster Charles Morris, United States Navy, of the duties of that office.

2. You will establish an office at Port au Prince and administer the customs service in accordance with department's radiogram No. 20018, reference (a), and the Haitian law where this law is not inconsistent with these instructions.

This shore duty beyond the seas is required by the public interests.

W. B. CAPERTON.

AAA   CRUISER SQUADRON, UNITED STATES ATLANTIC FLEET,
No. 8642-15   U. S. S. "WASHINGTON," FLAGSHIP,
Port au Prince, Haiti, September 1, 1915.

From: Commander Cruiser Squadron, United States Atlantic Fleet, commanding United States forces in Haitian waters.
To: Paymaster Charles Conrad, United States Navy.
Subject: Appointment as fiscal officer for "civil administration."
Reference: (a) Navy Department's radiogram No. 20018.

1. You are hereby appointed the "fiscal officer" for the squadron commander in connection with the funds placed to his credit by the various "collectors of customs," and will immediately relieve Paymaster Charles Morris, United States Navy, of the duties of that office.

2. Funds will only be disbursed under the following appropriations:

"Appropriation constabulary," to be used for the organization and maintenance of an efficient constabulary.

"Appropriation public works," to be used for conducting such temporary public works as will afford an immediate relief through employment for the starving populace and discharged soldiers.

"Appropriation military and civil government of United States forces," to be used for the maintenance of the customs and port services and such military government as the United States may establish.

"Appropriation Haitian Government," to be transferred to Dartiguenave government, as may be determined by the squadron commander."

The funds remaining after such disbursements will be left in the admiral's account and held by him in trust for the people of Haiti.

3. You will keep the necessary accounts and files and the returns rendered by the detachment commanders.

4. You will each month after the receipt of the detachment commanders' estimates prepare a synopsis of these estimates and a synopsis of the allotments which you consider necessary for the different detachment commanders for the coming month; and you will submit same to the squadron commander for his approval. Upon approval of these allotments, you will make the necessary arrangements through the National Bank of Haiti to place the funds so allotted to the credit of the detachment commanders.

5. This shore duty beyond the seas is required by the public interests.

W. B. CAPERTON.

On September 1, I informed the American Chargé d'Affaires that I proposed, in accordance with Navy Department orders, to assume charge of the customhouse at Port du Prince at 10 a. m. on the 2d of September, and requested him to inform the Haitian Government of this intention and to request that they take the necessary steps to inform the Haitian Administrator of Customs. I further requested that the Haitian Government direct the Haitian Administrator of Customs to meet Paymaster Conard at the customhouse at 10 a m. on the 2d of September so that an amicable arrangement could be made relative to the transfer. In connection with this, Mr. Chairman, I would like to put the following communication in the record:

EEE.
No. 8655–15.

CRUISER SQUADRON, UNITED STATES ATLANTIC FLEET,
U. S. S. " WASHINGTON," FLAGSHIP;
Port au Prince, Haiti, September 1, 1915.

The AMERICAN CHARGÉ D'AFFAIRES,
American Legation, Port au Prince, Haiti.

SIR: I have the honor to state that at 10 a. m., Thursday, September 2, 1915, in accordance with orders of the Navy Department, I will assume charge of the customhouse at Port au Prince, Haiti.

I request that you inform the Haitian Government of this intention and request that they take the necessary steps to inform the Haitian Administrator of Customs.

I further request that you ask the Haitian Government to direct the Haitian Administrator of Customs to meet Paymaster Charles Conard, United States Navy, at the customhouse at 10 a. m., Thursday, so that an amicable arrangement can be made in the premises.

I am, sir, respectfully,

W. B. CAPERTON,
Rear Admiral, United States Navy, Commander Cruiser Squadron.
and Commanding United States Forces in Haitian Waters.

In view of the uneasy situation, the possibility of disturbance, the apparent attitude of some of the members of the Cabinet toward the Government, trouble or outbreak at Port au Prince is possible. In such a case it may be necessary for me to declare martial law. That was on the 1st of September.

In reference to this I sent the following message to the Secretary of the Navy, under date of September 1, 1915:

MMM.   SEPTEMBER 1, 1915.
From: Commander Cruiser Squadron.
To: Secretary of the Navy and Commander in Chief.

Conditions Port au Prince Haiti uneasy. Continued reports of minor officials exercising unwarranted authority and committing other abuses which Government appears unable to control; newly appointed police in towns near Port au Prince overbearing and cause general complaint. Cabinet minister warned me to-day to be especially on guard against outbreak against Government to-day and to-morrow and intimated present Government would not be adverse to martial law. President states action taken by Haitian minister at Washington, D. C., Menos, relative treaty negotiations was done without knowledge or consent of President or counsel of cabinet; have reliable information Minister Foreign Affairs Sannon communicated with Menos relative this matter on his own responsibility. Will occupy customhouse Port au Prince to-morrow. Any outbreak or trouble Port au Prince may necessitate martial law. 23401.

CAPERTON.

On September 2 I requested the American chargé d'affaires to inform the Haitian Government of the necessity of assuming charge of the port services and the intentions of the United States Government relative to the administration of customs. I also informed the commanding officer of the French cruiser *Condé* of the action I had taken with reference to the customhouses. In that connection I would like to put this communication in the record:

YYY.
No. 8791–15

CRUISER SQUADRON, UNITED STATES ATLANTIC FLEET,
U. S. S. " WASHINGTON," FLAGSHIP,
Port au Prince, Haiti, September 2, 1915.

The AMERICAN CHARGÉ D'AFFAIRES,
American Legation, Port au Prince, Haiti.

SIR: I have the honor to state that the following appointments have been made by me to administer the customs and the port service at Port au Prince:

Paymaster Charles Conrad, United States Navy, administrator of customs for all customhouses taken charge of in Haiti.

Paymaster Herbert R. Stevens, United States Navy, collector of customs at Port au Prince.

Lieut. Commander Willis McDowell, United States Navy, captain of the port at Port au Prince.

I request that you inform the Haitian Government and all foreign diplomats and consular representatives of these appointments.

I am, sir, respectfully,

W. B. CAPERTON,
Rear Admiral, United States Navy,
Commander Cruiser Squadron, United States Atlantic Fleet, Haiti,
and Commanding United States Forces in Haitian waters.

Then the following letter was written under date of September 2 to the American chargé d'affaires at Port au Prince:

VVV.

No. 8759-15.

CRUISER SQUADRON, UNITED STATES ATLANTIC FLEET,
U. S. S. "WASHINGTON," FLAGSHIP,
Port au Prince, Haiti, September 2, 1915.

The AMERICAN CHARGÉ D'AFFAIRES,
Port au Prince, Haiti.

SIR: I have the honor to request that you inform the Haitian Government that, in the name of the United States Government, I will administer the customhouses of which I have assumed charge for the benefit of the Haitian people and for the support of the present Haitian Government.

The funds collected will be used for the organization and maintenance of an efficient constabulary, will be used for conducting such temporary public work as will afford immediate relief, through employment, for the starving populace and discharged soldiers, and for supporting the Haitian Government.

The surplus receipts will be held for the time being by the United States Government in trust for the people of Haiti.

I am, sir, respectfully,

W. B. CAPERTON,
Rear Admiral, United States Navy,
Commander Cruiser Squadron, United States Atlantic Fleet,
Commanding United States Forces in Haitian Waters.

On account of increasing uneasiness at Port au Prince, the apparent inability of the present Government to control conditions with which it is confronted, the propagation by newspapers and public men of inflammatory propaganda against the Government and the American occupation, the disloyalty to the present Government of some Government officials, the personal request of the President, and in order to better support the present Government, I decided to proclaim martial law in the city of Port au Prince on the 3d of September, 1915. Under date of the 2d of September I sent the following message to the Secretary of the Navy:

CCCC. SEPTEMBER 2, 1915.

From: Commander Cruiser Squadron.

To: Secretary of the Navy, and Commander in Chief.

On account of increasing uneasiness Port au Prince, present Government confronted with conditions apparently unable to control; propaganda by newspapers and public men of inflammatory propaganda against Government and American occupation; disloyalty to present Government of some Government officials; and in order to better support the present Government I will to-morrow, September 3, proclaim martial law in Port au Prince, Haiti. This action in accord with American chargé d'affaires. Proclamation follows by radio 22402.

CAPERTON.

I sent another message to the Secretary of the Navy under date of September 2, in which I said:

"In addition reasons for martial law given in my 22402, I was also this morning requested by President Dartiguenave, in informal interview, to establish martial law as soon as possible."

On the 3d day of September I issued the following proclamation:

OOOO.   CRUISER SQUADRON, UNITED STATES ATLANTIC FLEET,
                                          U. S. S. *"Washington,"* *Flagship.*

PROCLAMATION.

To the people of Port au Prince, Haiti:.

Information having been received from the most reliable sources that the present Government of Haiti is confronted with conditions which they are unable to control, although loyally attempting to discharge the duties of their respective offices ; and these facts having created a condition which requires the adoption of different measures than those heretofore applied ; and in order to afford the inhabitants of Port au Prince and other territory hereinafter described the privileges of the Government, exercising all the functions necessary for the establishment and maintenance of the fundamental rights of man, I hereby, under my authority as commanding officer of the forces of the United States of American in Haiti and Haitian waters, proclaim that martial law exists in the city of Port au Prince and the immediate territory now occupied by the forces under my command.

I further proclaim, in accordance with the law of nations and the usages, customs, and functions of my own and other Governments, that I am invested with the power and responsibility of Government in all its functions and branches throughout the territory above described; and the proper administration of such Government by martial law will be provided for in regulations to be issued from time to time, as required, by the commanding officer of the forces of the United States of America in Haiti and Haitian waters.

The martial law herein proclaimed, and the things in that respect so ordered, will not be deemed or taken to interfere with the proceedings of the constitutional Government and congress of Haiti, or with the administration or justice in the courts of law existing therein ; which do not affect the military operations or the authorities of the Government of the United States of America.

All the municipal and other civil employees are, therefore, requested to continue in their present vocations without change; and the military authorities will not interfere in the functions of the civil administration and the courts except in so far as relates to persons violating military orders or regulations, or otherwise interfering with the exercise of military authority. All peaceful citizens can confidently pursue their usual occupations, feeling that they will be protected in their personal rights and property, as well as in their proper social relations.

The commanding officer of the United States Expeditionary Force, Col. Littleton W. T. Waller. United States Marine Corps, is empowered to issue the necessary regulations and appoint the necessary officers to make this martial law effective.

Done at the city of Port au Prince, Haiti, this 3d day of September, A. D. 1915.

W. B. CAPERTON,
Rear Admiral, United States Navy,
Commanding the Forces of the United States of America
in Haiti and Haitian Waters.

Later I wrote the following letter to the chargé d'affaires of the American Legation at Port au Prince':

PPPP.
No. 8840–15.
                         CRUISER SQUADRON, UNITED STATES ATLANTIC FLEET,
                                           U. S. "WASHINGTON," FLAGSHIP,
                                 Port au Prince, Haiti, September 8, 1915.

The AMERICAN CHARGÉ D'AFFAIRES,
        American Legation, Port au Prince, Haiti.

SIR : I have the honor to request that all foreign diplomatic and consular representatives be informed that martial law has been declared in Port au Prince, and that copies of the proclamation be sent to them.

I am, sir, respectfully,

W. B. CAPERTON,
Rear Admiral, United States Navy,
Commander Cruiser Squadron, United States Atlantic Fleet,
Commanding United States Forces in Haiti and Haitian Waters.

I also requested that a copy of that letter be sent to the commanding officer of the French cruiser *Condé*, informing him of this fact.

To further refer to the conditions in the north, on September 4, the following day, the commanding officer of the *Connecticut*, Capt. Durell, reported that there was no information at Cape Haitien from the Cacos regarding the surrender of arms; that they still besieged the town; and that the prices of foodstuffs were exorbitant and were causing hardship and suffering among the poor citizens. The commanding officer of the *Connecticut* further reported that two generals, representing the troops at Ouanaminthe, had arrived at Cape Haitien to see him about rations and pay. The sum of 5,000 gourdes granted last week was insufficient to ration these troops for one week, and he stated that 7,000 gourdes a week were necessary.

I immediately asked the commanding officer of the *Connecticut* what outlying towns it would be necessary to occupy to insure the food supply for Cape Haitien, and if any troops in addition to what he had would be necessary for occupying these towns and conducting offensive operations in connection therewith. The minister of the interior, Mayard, on this day stated that provision had been made for rationing the troops at Ouanaminthe and Mont Organise for one month.

The Caco situation is becoming critical. These Cacos will not come within our lines and surrender their arms and d'sband on account of the leaders, who are endeavoring to obtain exorbitant bribes. The liberal offer of 15 gourdes per soldier and 100 gourdes per chief, to pay for their rifles and give them sufficient money to return to their homes, has not been accepted, after repeated efforts made both through channels in the north and through the'r leaders in Port au Prince. These Cacos are a source of annoyance in the north, and, if they continue investing Cape Haitien it may force active measures against them. I am of the opinion that furnish'ng work on the railroad construction in the vicinity of Cape Haitien, as recommended in my radiogram No. 16029, might induce many of these men to desert their chiefs and go to work. Unless some measures are taken in this connection, I will probably be forced to continue very soon offensive operations against these Cacos.

On this same day, September 4, I received a cable message from the American charge d'affaires at San Domingo City, stating that he had reliable information that deposits of mun'tions of war were being made in Haiti along the border at Mirebalais, Fonds Parisien, and Fonds Verettes. In connection with this matter I desire to put into the record the following communication:

XXXX.

" From: American Chargé d'Affaires, San Domingo.
" To: Commander cruiser squadron.

Have relieble information that deposits of munitions of war being made in Haiti at following places on border mountain near town of Bourg St. Louis or Mirebalais, houses in towns of Fonds Parisien and La Mission or Fonds Verettes; the latter place can be reached via railroad and Lake el Fondo.

JOHNSON, *American Chargé.*

Late that night I sent the following report to the Secretary of the Navy:

YYYY.   SEPTEMBER 4, 1915.

From: Commander cruiser squadron.
To: Secretary of the Navy and Commander in Chief.

Caco situation north Haiti becoming critical. These Cacos w'll not come within our lines and surrender arms and disband on account leaders who are endeavoring to obtain exorbitant bribes. Liberal offer of 15 gourdes per soldier and 100 gourdes per chief to pay for their rifles and give them sufficient money to return to their homes not accepted after repeated efforts both through channels in north and through their leaders in Port au Prince. These Cacos have aga'n begun infesting Cape Haitien and are preventing market people and foodstuffs entering town. Believe furnishing work on railroad construction vicinity Cape Haitien as recommended in my radiogram 16029 might induce many men desert the'r chiefs and go to work. Unless prompt measures are taken in this connection will be forced to consider very soon offensive operations against these Cacos. 11504.

CAPERTON.

———

ZZZZ   SEPTEMBER 4, 1915.

From: Commander cruiser squadron.
To: Secretary of the Navy and commander in chief.

Expedition consisting of *Marietta* and sixth company of marines will leave Port au Prince Sunday afternoon to occupy Jeramie and customhouse that place. Paymaster Manning H. Philbrick has been appointed collector customs and captain of the port of Jeramie. No further news. 22204.

CAPERTON.

On September 5, under my direction, the commander of the expeditionary force sent for Mr. Charles Zamor and requested him to go immediately to Cape Haitien and endeavor to persuade the Cacos to open the food supplies to that place. Mr. Charles Zamor was informed of the seriousness of this situation and of the great danger of serious consequences to the Cacos if they persisted in such methods of annoyance. Mr. Charles Zamor agreed to go as I requested. This expedition was finally arranged after much talk and discussion with Mr. Charles Zamor for several days previous.

On this same day, September 5, I received the department's radiogram No. 12005 that I should take no offensive action against the Haitians without first consulting the Navy Department. I am now investigating the feasibility of occupying the towns on the principal roads entering Cape Haitien to insure the food supply for the city. I will not undertake any offensive operations before referring the matter to the Navy Department. In this connection, I would like to put in the record the following radiogram:

A SEPTEMBER 5, 1915.

From: Secretary of the Navy.
To: Commander cruiser squadron.

11504. Take no offensive action against Haitiens without first consulting Navy - Department unless absolutely necessary to prevent loss of life or property. More detailed instructions will be sent you to-morrow. Inform department immediately of any conditions that would seem to make offensive action either desirable or necessary. Acknowledge. 12005.

DANIELS.

Further unrest was reported at Gonaives on account of the reported approach of the Cacos. Information was continually coming in of Cacos movements in various places in the north. I would like to give you for your information, in connection with that matter, the following:

D SEPTEMBER 5, 1915.

From: Commanding officer *Castine.*
To: Commander cruiser squadron.

Gonaines and St. Marc quiet. Plaisance reported quiet. Information that Cacos are moving from St. Raphael to St. Michel. 08005.

CARTER.

E SEPTEMBER 5, 1915.

From: Commanding officer *Castine.*
To: Commander Cruiser squadron.

Officer 5102 (Capt. Fay, Marine Corps) reports considerable unrest in Conaives over reported approach of revolutionary forces under Chief Rowean last reported near Ennery. U. S. S. *Castine* will proceed to Conaives to-morrow upon arrival of U. S. S. *Osceolo.* 19305.

CARTER.

I reported the situation to the Secretary of the Navy that evening by the following message:

SEPTEMBER 5, 1915.

From: Commander cruiser squadron.
To: Secretary of the Navy and commander in chief.

12005. Charles Zamor, at my request, agreed to go immediately to Cape Haitien and endeavor persuade Cacos open food supply to that place. Am investigating feasibility occupying towns on principal roads entering Cape Haitien to secure food supply for city. Will not undertake offensive operations before referring to Navy Department. Some unrest Gonaives over reported approach Cacos. 23205.

CAPERTON.

On the same day, September 5, I issued a campaign order, No. 9, covering the deployment of the forces in Ha'ti and Haitian waters for occupying and maintaining military control of the ports of entry and the collection of customs thereat, pending negotiations between the United States and Haiti. That campaign order which I have just referred to reads as follows:

CRUISER SQUADRON, UNITED STATES ATLANTIC FLEET,
U. S. S. "WASHINGTON," FLAGSHIP,
Port au Prince, Haiti, September 5, 1915—10 a. m.

Campaign order No. 9.

Forces:

(a) *First detachment.*—Capt. E. H. Durell, *Connecticut, Nashville.* First Regiment Infantry, less Second Battalion, one battery Field Artillery.

(b) *Second detachment.*—Commander J. F. Carter, *Castine.* Seventh and Twenty-fourth Companies Infantry.

(c) *Third detachment.*—Maj. N. H. Hall. Sixth and Twelfth Companies Infantry.

(d) *Fourth detachment.*—Commander L. McNamee, *Sacramento.* Fourth and Seventeenth Companies Infantry.

(e) *Main body.—Washington, Marietta, Eagle.* First Brigade Infantry, less one battalion and six companies. One battalion Field Artillery, less one battery.

1. The Cacos will remain in arms in north Haiti. South Haiti is at present quiet. Negotiations relative to the treaty with present Haitian Government are continuing. This Government without funds and not at present strong; efforts to strengthen and support it are continually under way.

2. This force will assume and maintain military control of the ports of entry of Haiti and collect customs thereat pending negotiations between United States and Haiti.

3. (a) *First detachment* maintain military control Port de Paix and military government Cape Haitien. *Nashville* patrol Port de Paix and Cape Haitien. *Connecticut* support these operations.

(b) *Second detachment* maintain military control St. Marc and Gonaives. *Castine* patrol St. Marc and Gonaives and support these operations.

(c) *Third detachment* occupy Jeremie. Maintain military control Petit Goave and Miragoane.

(d) *Fourth detachment* occupy Les Cayes (Aux Cayes) and Jacmel. *Sacramento* patrol Les Cayes and Jacmel and support these operations.

(e) Main body will maintain military control under martial law at Port au Prince. *Washington* support these operations. *Marietta* patrol Petit Goave, Miragoane, and Jeremie and support third detachment. *Eagle* continue repairs.

(z) Maintain military control and administer customs at all ports occupied. Protect life and property and preserve order. Disarm all Haitian troops encountered.

4. Base is at Guantanamo. *Osceola* will make trips between base and various detachments with stores, mail, and provisions. *Jason* and *Solace* remain Port au Prince for the present.

5. Squadron commander on *Washington.* Make daily and such other reports as may be necessary to keep squadron commander fully and frequently informed of the situation. Use seventy-fifth meridian mean time.

W. B. CAPERTON,
Rear Admiral, Commander Cruiser Squadron,
Commanding United States Forces in Haiti and Haitian Waters.

The *Castine* arrived at Gonaives at 5 p. m. on September 6. The town of Gonaives continues uneasy and there is much excitement among the natives. A force of about 150 Cacos are a few miles from the town under Chief Rameau. Cacos are endeavoring to stir up the inhabitants against the Americans. Many people are leaving Gonaives in small craft. The *Castine* disembarked her landing force of seamen to reenforce the marines on shore.

I would like to submit, in connection with the arrival of the *Castine*, the following report of the commanding officer of that vessel:

SEPTEMBER 5, 1915.

From: Commanding officer *Castine.*
To: Commander cruiser squadron.

Castine arrived Gonaives 5 p. m. Monday; immediately sent landing force to assist marine detachment in patrolling town. One hundred fifty Cacos a few miles from town under Chief Rameau. Cacos endeavoring to stir up inhabitants against Americans. It is reported that Cacos sympathizers having come into town in last few days, inhabitants fear town will be burned by Cacos sympathizers. Many people leaving Gonaives in small craft. Much excitement prevails. Can disperse Cacos difficult. Will maintain regulation patrol of town to-night and await developments to-morrow. 19006.

CARTER.

On the 7th of September the American chargé d'affaires had a conference with the President and his cabinet relative to the treaty. The minister of foreign affairs and public instruction, Mr. Pauleus Sanon, and the minister of agriculture and public works, Mr. Antoine Sansaricq, refused to accept the financial adviser stipulation. Upon this refusal the President requested and accepted their immediate resignation. The remainder of the cabinet agreed to accept the treaty substantially as submitted. The President then asked to be allowed a short delay to enable him to fill the vacancies in the cabinet, which was agreed to. The resignation of the minister of foreign affairs and public instruction removes a dissenting and undesirable element.

It was reported on the same day that the Cacos were outside of Gonaives under the command of Rameau.

The commanding officer of the *Castine*, Commander James Carter, stated that it was advisable to disperse the Cacos or drive them back without delay, in view of the present force being insufficient for outposts and patrols unless the Cacos were driven back.

On the same day I sent the following message to the commanding officer of the *Castine:*

SEPTEMBER 7, 1915.

From: Commander cruiser squadron.
To: Commanding officer *Casine.*

09007. Do not take offensive unless necessary to protect life and property and hold town. Charles Zamor should arrive Gonaives to-day. He has promised to consult with Rameau and arrange difficulty. Believe you can arrange conference with Cacos through Charles Zamor and obtain results in that way. Have already told Zamor we can not tolerate these Cacos' annoyance and unless they cease will be forced take strong measures. Acknowledge. 11507.

CAPERTON.

Later in the evening of September 7 I sent the following report to the Secretary of the Navy:

SEPTEMBER 7, 1915.

From: Commander cruiser squadron.
To: Secretary of the Navy and Commander in Chief.

Gonaives uneasy and much excitement among natives. About 200 Cacos close to town under Chief Rameau. Cacos endeavoring stir up inhabitants against Americans. *Castine* has landed seamen to reinforce marines. Zamor on way to Gonaives to endeavor induce Cacos to cease operations. Have directed *Castine* not take offensive unless necessary protect life and property and hold town. 11407.

CAPERTON.

SEPTEMBER 7, 1915.

From: Commander cruiser squadron.
To: Secretary of the Navy and Commander in Chief.

Passed Assistant Paymaster Fred E. McMillen and Passed Assistant Paymaster Henry R. Snyder appointed collectors of customs and captains of the port at Petit Goave and Miragoane, respectively. These officers sent to those ports on U. S. S. *Osceola* to-day. Pauleus Sanon, minister foreign affairs, and Antoine Sansaricq, minister agriculture, resigned to-day. 22407.

CAPERTON.

SEPTEMBER 7, 1915.

From: Commander cruiser squadron.
To: Secretary of the Navy.

National Bank of Haiti at Port au Prince has contributed $500 to Red Cross fund. 23107.

CAPERTON.

On September 9 Louis Borno and Paul Salomon were appointed ministers of foreign affairs and public works, respectively, filling the vacancies in those places.

The CHAIRMAN. Louis Borno was appointed minister of foreign affairs?

Admiral CAPERTON. Yes; Borno was appointed minister of foreign affairs, and Salomon was appointed minister of public works. President Dartiguenave informed me that Leconte, minister of war, had instructions to get in touch with the Cacos at Cape Haitien and endeavor to reach an agreement with them or ascertain their terms.   Leconte is not to pay any money or make an pecuniary arrangements with them.

The CHAIRMAN. You have omitted a dispatch of September 8 to the commanding officer of the *Connecticut*. The language of that message is: " Successful negotiation of treaty is predominant part present mission. After encountering many difficulties treaty situation at present looks more favorable than usual. This has been effected by exercising military pressure at propitious moments in negotiations. Yesterday two members of cabinet who have blocked negotiations heretofore resigned. President himself believed to be anxious to conclude treaty. At present am holding up offensive operations and allowing President time to complete cabinet and try again. Am therefore not yet ready to begin offensive operations at Cape Haitien, but will hold them in abeyance as additional pressure."

The plain implication is that under the direction of the department the naval forces of the United States in Haiti were using the military pressure to compel the acceptance of the treaty.

Admiral CAPERTON. I have that message in my record.

The CHAIRMAN. I think you ought to describe the character of the military pressure brought to bear to secure the ratification of the treaty.

Admiral CAPERTON. Well, the only pressure I can think of or consider was the fact of bringing pressure to bear, in order, if possible, to quiet the Cacos and keep them from intimidating the members of congress and the senate who were in favor of the treaty as has been previously stated in my testimony. The pressure, I should say, was more moral than military. As I have frequently referred to taking over these customhouses at times, I ceased taking them over because it seemed to militate against us in getting the treaty ratified at that time. Perhaps I would have taken the customhouses at some distant points thinking it necessary at that time, owing to the disturbed conditions, but that would naturally have had a moral effect on the congress. There was no actual military movement made against the congress.

The CHAIRMAN. I am only seeking the interpretation of your own cable.

Admiral CAPERTON. If there was any pressure brought to bear at all, it was only on the enemies of the government, which I was there to support.

(Whereupon, at 4.10 o'clock p. m., the committee adjourned until Thursday, October 20, 1921, at 10.30 o'clock a. m.)

INQUIRY INTO OCCUPATION AND ADMINISTRATION OF HAITI AND SANTO DOMINGO.

UNITED STATES SENATE,
SELECT COMMITTEE ON HAITI AND SANTO DOMINGO,
Washington, D. C.

The committee met at 10.30 o'clock a. m., pursuant to adjournment, Senator Tasker L. Oddie presiding.

Present: Mr. Ernest Angell, Mr. Horace G. Knowles, and Maj. Edwin N. McCellan, United States Marine Corps, in their respective representative capacities as hereinbefore indicated.

STATEMENT OF REAR ADMIRAL WILLIAM B. CAPERTON, UNITED STATES NAVY, RETIRED—Resumed.

Senator ODDIE. Capt. Angell has requested the committee to grant him the privilege of asking some questions of Admiral Caperton regarding his testimony, and if there are no objections, his request will be granted, but this must not be considered as a precedent.

Mr. ANGELL. Admiral, at the time that you went down to Cape Haitien in January, as I remember, 1915——

Admiral CAPERTON. Yes.

Mr. ANGELL. On your assignment of duty in the West Indies to observe the general political situation——

Admiral CAPERTON. Those were my original orders.

Mr. ANGELL. The original orders to which you testified, I think the first day last week, were you at that time familiar with the correspondence between the office of the Secretary of State and the Secretary of the Navy, which was introduced in the record by Chairman McCormick yesterday, that being specifically, if you remember, the letters of October 28, 1914, and the replies? You may have to refer to your memorandum to know specifically the letters to which I refer, appearing on pages 343 et seq. of the typewritten report of the hearing. My question was essentially whether you were familiar with that correspondence.

Admiral CAPERTON. No; in glancing over them, it is all new to me.

Mr. ANGELL. And had you at that time had any conferences with the responsible officials in Washington of the Navy or State Departments or any general instructions from them along the line of those letters, namely the desirability, as appearing to the State Department, of putting additional naval forces in Haitian waters in conjunction with the proposed negotiation of a treaty?

Admiral CAPERTON. No; I knew nothing about it. I did know that the *Georgia* and the *New Jersey*, I believe, were down there, because we were always getting news of them from the papers, and in this way I knew something about it, but I never saw any official correspondence.

Mr. ANGELL. You had no knowledge, then, of any purpose behind the presence of additional vessels in Haitian waters?

Admiral CAPERTON. No; I had not.

Mr. ANGELL. During that fall and winter?

Admiral CAPERTON. I had not.

Mr. ANGELL. Admiral, did you have any knowledge, or have you since acquired any knowledge, of the affairs of the *Machias* at Port au Prince on December 17, 1914, when the $500,000 were taken from the bank and brought up to New York?

355

Adm'ral CAPERTON. I do not think I have enough definite information to discuss the matter at all. I merely heard that this amount of money was taken from Port au Prince, and as I recall, the *Machias* was the vessel. I perhaps have discussed it a little bit, but I really know nothing about the particulars at all.

Mr. ANGELL. Did you ever have an opportunity to discuss it with the then commanding officer of the *Machias?*

Admiral CAPERTON. No; I had not; I do not yet know who he was. I do not recall.

Mr. ANGELL. You never discussed it, then, with anyone who had a direct and immediate connect'on with that affair?

Admiral CAPERTON. No.

Mr. ANGELL. With reference to your presence at Cape Haitien in June and July, 1915, at the time you established a field radio station, and later landed marines, as you said, to protect the railroad property, am I correct in remembering that your testimony on the first or second day was that the French marines had already been reembarked on board when you arrived there?

Admiral CAPERTON. As far as I remember, they had been withdrawn.

Mr. ANGELL. And was the French vessel in the harbor when you got there?

Admiral CAPERTON. It was inside, in the inner harbor. You could never take a big vessel in there until after I surveyed that harbor.

Mr. ANGELL. You arrived there about July 1, as I remember?

Admiral CAPERTON. The second time.

Mr. ANGELL. The second time, yes.

Admiral CAPERTON. From Vera Cruz.

Mr. ANGELL. Did you have any conference at that time, personally or through your staff officers, with the commander of the French vessel there, regarding the presence of the French marines or French forces at Cape Haitien?

Admiral CAPERTON. Oh, yes; I have stated in my testimony here that he paid me an official visit, of course, the moment I arrived, and told me the situation which I have outlined in my testimony. I returned the call, I think, the next day, as far as I remember now. I know I did, if the weather was good, and we discussed it further afterwards.

Mr. ANGELL. Was the discussion about the advisability of the presence of the French on shore?

Admiral CAPERTON. Yes; the captain, as I have stated here, said he had landed at the request of his own consul or consular agent. as I recall it now; and, as I have outlined it in my testimony, the commanding officer told me that he had been sent there by the French minister at Port au Prince on account of the French consular agent at that point being fearful of the safety of French interests.

Mr. ANGELL. Did you have any instruct'ons from the Navy Department on the point of whether or not it was deemed advisable and proper for the French to land in Haiti?

Admiral CAPERTON. I had no direct information as to that point. I can not recall my test mony exactly now, but my orders were to proceed there, and——

Senator ODDIE. I think it would be a good idea for the admiral to have time to prepare his answers, because he has to refresh his memory.

Admiral CAPERTON. I had orders for each move, which I have already given in my testimony, but I had so many things to do that I can not recall.

Mr. ANGELL. The purpose of my question was to find out if there was any general or, on this occasion, any special policy of the Navy or the State Department, as indicated to you, regarding the presence of foreign forces in Haiti. In connection with my question, let me call your attention to the message of July 28, 1915, from the Acting Secretary of the Navy to yourself, which appears as paragraph 9 of Gen. Barnett's report attached to the report of the Secretary of the Navy for 1920, reading as follows:

" State Department desires that American forces be landed at Port au Prince and that American and foreign interests be protected; that representatives of England and France be informed of this intention; informed that their interests will be protected, and that they be requested not to land."

That was, of course, later in the month, regarding the landing at Port au Prince.

Admiral CAPERTON. Yes; later in July.

Mr. ANGELL. Now, earlier in the month, when you were at Cape Haitien, were there any such instructions, general or special, as far as you remember?

Admiral CAPERTON. I will have to refer to my notes.

Senator ODDIE. That can be answered and put in the record. Admiral, that answer can be held in abeyance until you have time to prepare it. We will save time in that way.

After looking over my notes I find I received no additional orders or instructions, general or special, except the following, which is my original orders, received on June 22, 1915, at Vera Cruz:

"Flag French Marines landed Cape Haitien. Proceed there with USS *Washington* thank French Commander take necessary steps to protect property and preserve order. Dispose of vessels on Mexican coast to best advantage. USS *Machias* USS *Marietta* enroute Vera Cruz acknowledge 14022 Daniels."

Mr. ANGELL. Then, following the same line, Admiral, and jumping a month, if I may, down to Port au Prince, as I remember your testimony and the official reports, the French vessel *Descartes* arrived in Port au Prince three or four days after you got there, on the 1st or 2d of August. A very short time, a day or two after, did the French land marines or naval forces in Port au Prince, at that time on shore as a legation guard, or otherwise, do you remember?

Admiral CAPERTON. I would rather refer to my notes. I have stated this in the notes definitely and I do not just recall.

Mr. ANGELL. You do not remember whether or not they landed at all?

Admiral CAPERTON. Oh, yes; I think they landed a guard, and after a certain time relieved my guard, and I sent an officer to be present when they relieved the guard. After referring to my diary I find the French guard landed August 2, relieving the American guard at the French legation.

Mr. ANSELL. I find again in Gen. Barnett's report, paragraph 34, the following:

"Rear Admiral Caperton, on August 2, 1915, informed the Navy Department that the *Descartes* landed legation guard at 7 a. m."

Do you remember, roughly, how long their legation guard remained on shore? Was it a few days, or a few weeks, or months?

Admiral CAPERTON. They remained there for quite a while. I can tell you by referring to my notes the exact date they were withdrawn, and the date they landed.

Mr. ANGELL. I do not think the exact date is material. Was it weeks or months?

Admiral CAPERTON. I think it was weeks?

Mr. ANGELL. Several weeks?

Admiral CAPERTON. Yes; and possibly months, I think.

Mr. ANGELL. I believe it was Mr. Farnham, the National City Bank's vice president, who testified earlier here substantially to the fact that the French forces, such as they were, remained in Port au Prince on shore some six months. Is he mistaken in that recollection, do you think?

Admiral CAPERTON. I could not answer that without referring to my notes, and by doing that I could give you the exact dates.

Mr. ANGELL. Have you any idea or recollection how large a force that was that the French landed and maintained? In other words, was it a dozen men, or one hundred men?

Admiral CAPERTON. Well, it was a legation guard. Without referring to my notes, I would say there were about 25, perhaps, or 50, maybe more.

Mr. ANGELL. That is sufficient.

Admiral CAPERTON. I have the exact numbers in my notes or official reports.

Mr. ANGELL. During the period of your command in Haiti, that is from June, 1915, until November, 1916, did any other European nations have forces on shore in Haiti?

Admiral CAPERTON. I am quite sure there were no others; in fact, I do not think there were any foreign men-of-war that visited the port during this time.

Mr. ANGELL. Only the French?

Admiral CAPERTON. Yes; they depended entirely on the Americans, because the French minister, or the French captain, officially informed me that he would not interfere in any particular with the American occupation, and that he would keep his guard inside the legation, and that they would not be seen outside of the legation with arms.

Mr. ANGELL. And that, I suppose, was followed, as you remember?

Admiral CAPERTON. As far as I know, that was followed, leaving the entire protection of the other legations and the rest of the city to the Americans.

Mr. ANGELL. And, so far as you know, was the purpose of the French in having a legation guard at Port au Prince for the protection of the legation based upon the incident of its violation about the time of the murder of the President in July?

Admiral CAPERTON. Well, I can not go into their motives, as to how much they proposed to protect when they went ashore, but they landed as a legation guard for the protection of the legation.

I find here that, referring to incident in question, I made a report to the Secretary of the Navy something as follows, on the 31st of July:

" French minister informed me he had received dispatches from Paris, French Government, stating that French Embassy, Washington, had been directed inform United States Government that France considered landing legation guard at Port au Prince necessity for national honor. French minister repeated his conviction that we were ably protecting life and property and assured his guard would be confined to legation and that arms of French guard would not be carried by them outside of legation. He further stated that he wishes it understood he does not intend interfering in any way my actions in town."

Mr. ANGELL. That is the answer. I had not seen that before.

Admiral CAPERTON. That is already in my evidence, I think; I am quite sure I quoted it.

Mr. ANGELL. Do you think, Admiral, that there was on the part of the French in Haiti, or the British official representatives, any fear of the Germans using the island as a base for operations against them in the war which was then almost a year old, or using the island as a base for propaganda?

Admiral CAPERTON. Well, I can hardly answer that. On one occasion, while I was in Mexico—off Vera Cruz, Mexico—we heard something about the *Karlsruhe*, I think it was, one of those German ships having entered the St. Nicholas Mole at one time, which I investigated but never could find out the exact truth about it, or whether she was really there or not. Some vessel went in, but we never could find out what nationality she was.

Mr. ANGELL. Well, during your 15 or 18 months in Haitian waters did you, in the course of conversations with individuals or by reports which may have come to you, learn anything which would have given you grounds to suspect that the French or British had any such fears regarding the use of the island of Haiti by the Germans?

Admiral CAPERTON. Well, the commanding officer of the French ship that was there always kept very close guard and watch in port; that is to say, he carried out his orders and regulations in regard to protecting himself from danger outside, as we did not know—at least, he said he did not know—what time the Germans might appear, but I had no discussion with him at all because I was busy.

This will repeat my evidence given before, but I find that on the 27th of July the department informed me as follows:

" 23327· State Department desires that American forces be landed Port au Prince and that American and foreign interests be protected; that representatives England, France, be informed this intention; informed that their interests will be protected and that they be requested not land."

As I have stated before, after my arrival an hour or two afterwards, the French minister, the British chargé d'affaires, accompanied by our chargé d'affaires, Mr. Davis, came off to the ship with some of my staff whom I had sent on shore to find out the latest information and condition of affairs, and both the French and the British representatives requested me and pleaded with me earnestly to land forces and to do it as quickly as possible, as they had no idea as to what might or what might not happen on shore. This was on July 28.

Mr. ANGELL. At Port au Prince?

Admiral CAPERTON. At Port au Prince, immediately after my arrival in my flagship, the *Washington*.

Mr. ANGELL. Now, to come to one or two points in connection with the murder of President Sam and the events of the landing, did you hear of any foreigners, including Americans, who were at that time molested or actually threatened by the disturbing element in Port au Prince?

Admiral CAPERTON. When I landed I took possession of the city between the hours of 5 and 10 at night, when everything was settled. I had given orders for the commanding officer, as he passed the various foreign legations, to ask them if they needed any guard, and, as I recall it now, many or all of them asked for the guard. I even gave a small guard to the German minister who, upon being asked whether he wished them, replied that he would like to have them, and they remained there, as I recall it now, for several days.

Mr. ANGELL. When your forces landed did you hear of any actual instances prior to the landing when foreigners had been molested or harmed?

Admiral CAPERTON. No; things were in such a chaotic condition that I did not ask whether any of them had been hurt or murdered, and I did not know whether they had been or not.

Mr. ANGELL. Did you receive any reports, voluntarily given you, of foreigners having been hurt or molested?

Admiral CAPERTON. No; I do not think I did.

Mr. ANGELL. You or your representatives, of course, conferred with the French minister and the British chargé d'affaires and others, as you have said?

Admiral CAPERTON. Every day.

Mr. ANGELL. Did the French diplomatic officials at Port au Prince report to you that any person had been molested in their legation except the Haitian president who was taken out?

Admiral CAPERTON. Not as far as I remember now, there was no one else hurt.

Mr. ANGELL. So, as far as you can now remember, you received no reports at that time of any foreigners having been actually molested or harmed during the riot and disturbances immediately preceding your landing?

Admiral CAPERTON. No; I do not recall any.

Mr. ANGELL. And do you remember receiving any reports of the harming or molesting of foreigners, including Americans, at any time immediately following, or in connection with your landing, other than the casualties to the military forces?

Admiral CAPERTON. No; under my orders, they could not very well have been molested, because I gave orders strictly to protect everything in the city and keep absolute peace and quiet.

Mr. ANGELL. Were there any specific attempts to molest or harm civilian foreigners?

Admiral CAPERTON. Well, we had several attacks on the city at night. I do not know who these fellows wanted to shoot up. Apparently, they wanted to shoot up the town, but they never told me whether they were after the British or after the French.

Mr. ANGELL. There were no specific attacks on individual foreigners?

Admiral CAPERTON. The view that I took of it was that with a mob, with no leader except the various chiefs around the city, I considered that anybody and everybody was in more or less danger, because these fellows were drunk and ungoverned and did pretty much as they pleased about the city; they were a lawless mob.

Mr. ANGELL. When you landed had this so-called revolutionary committee, or the committee of safety, actually been formed?

Admiral CAPERTON. When my chief of staff landed, as I recall my testimony here and my records, at that time he found a committee on shore of three or four men. Polynice was one, and I think Delvar was another. There were three or four at that time. Later there was a committee of six or seven.

Mr. ANGELL. Whose names you gave?

Admiral CAPERTON. Whose names I think I gave here.

Mr. ANGELL. Yes; you gave those names.

Admiral CAPERTON. But these fellows, except Mr. Polynice, were all Cacos and Caco chiefs. Mr. Robin was a man, as I afterwards found out, in command of the revolutionary forces, or the Cacos, in the city. He is one of the big Caco generals.

Mr. ANGELL. This committee which you found, or your chief of staff found on landing, was the so-called revolutionary committee, and that was the committee which Capt. ——

Admiral CAPERTON. That is the committee that they usually formed every time these affairs took place.

Mr. ANGELL. And this was the committee which a little later Capt. Beach, acting under your direction, dismissed or——

Admiral CAPERTON. It may not have been this first committee, because they, as I said before, later either joined in or formed a committee; but it was a "committee of safety," and I think all the members who were in this first committee, three or four, were also in this final "committee of safety." As I recall it, he only found three or four, and so reported to me; that there was, I think now, Mr. Polynice, Mr. Delvar, and I do not know whether he said Robin was there at that first meeting or not; but he said he met several of the committee of safety, and it was this committee that he asked for permission to land, seeing that the——

Mr. ANGELL. That is August 3?

Admiral CAPERTON. No; the 28th.

Mr. ANGELL. I was just inquiring about what this committee was.

Admiral CAPERTON. I would like to add that they were about all there were that had any appearance——

Mr. ANGELL. Of authority or government?

Admiral CAPERTON. Had any appearance of order or authority, and this same committee agreed to my landing, but said they would not be responsible for my reception.

Mr. ANGELL. I find in your message of August 3, which is contained in paragraph 36a of the Barnett report—I do not know the page of the record there—in the middle of the second paragraph, you say:

" Revolutionary committee at first acted practically under my direct'on, but now frequently give orders w.thout my knowledge and act more independently."

I also find a similar message earlier, on July 31, which is paragraph 25 of the Barnett report, the last sentence of which reads:

"All Government funct ons are at present carried on by a committee of citizens practically under my direction."

The phrase " practically under my direction " appearing in each of those two messages, just what did that mean? How were they acting under your direction, sir?

Adm ral CAPERTON. They promised that they would not issue any orders or do anything contrary to my orders, you might say, or my ideas and wishes in the matter. In other words, they promised to cooperate with me in everything I did.

Mr. ANGELL. So that you had, pursuant to instruct ous from Washington, assumed both military and to a certain extent political control of affairs in Port au Prince?

Admiral CAPERTON. I did, because there was no political head, and these were the only people who apparently were trying to keep peace.

,Mr. ANGELL. Was there a Congress in session at the time you landed?

Admiral CAPERTON. Oh, no.

Mr. ANGELL. Congress was not in session?

Admiral CAPERTON. Not in session; no, because a few days afterwards——

Mr. ANGELL (interposing). When did the Congress meet, do you remember: how soon after the murder of Sam and your land.ng?

Adm.ral CAPERTON. I think I have the exact date here, but I think it was several days, about the 5th, 6th, or 7th, because the permanent committee which has the authority and power to call Congress together under such condit ons were unable to get a quorum, so that Mr. Guillaume Sam had to wait several days in the city before he was elected President, and it is usually done with'n a few hours if they can get a quorum of the Congress together.

Mr. ANGELL. Well, in th s Navy Department file there is a message from Admiral Caperton to the Secretary of the Navy on July 31, the end of which message reads: " Chamber Deputies asked permission elect President, but deferred in compliance my request." That would seem to indicate that the Chamber of Deputies were in session at that time or had convened.

Admiral CAPERTON. Well, as I recall it now, they were trying to meet because they wanted to elect the new President, and, as far as I could find out, the reason why they did not meet, which I have stated in here, was because they could not get a quorum. I knew that that was no time to have a meeting, on the 31st, because things were so unsettled, and I dare say that if they had been able to have gotten a quorum—I do not know, but it appears to me now—that I would have requested them to wait a day or two, so that things could have quieted down a little bit and so that I would have a better grasp of the situation and be able to protect foreign interests in case they had an outbreak in carrying on the elections, as I have been told it was their custom to do when a President was elected, with Cacos all armed all over the city, the galleries full of Cacos with their pistols, and as each representative was called upon to vote he would cast his eyes around and see everybody had a pistol aimed at him. This was what was told to me there by the people throughout the city. I do not mean to say that this was perhaps actually the case, but I was told that was the way elections were actually carried on.

Mr. ANGELL. Of whom did the chamber of deputies ask permission to elect a President? Your message reads, " Chamber deputies asked permission elect

President, but deferred in compliance my request." Did they ask you or your representatives on shore for permission to elect a President?

Admiral CAPERTON. I suppose they must have.

Mr. ANGELL. The message would so indicate.

Admiral CAPERTON. I would infer that.

Mr. ANGELL. You do not remember the incident specifically?

Admiral CAPERTON. I do not recall now, but I kept in touch with all these affairs on shore, trying to get order and to assist them.

Mr. ANGELL. The purpose of my question, Admiral, was merely to establish, so far as we could, the approximate date at which you had actually assumed the general direction not merely of the military affairs in the city, but of the march of political events which culminated in the election of the President.

Admiral CAPERTON. At the time referred to there was nothing, no government, nothing at all except these three or four self-constituted "committee of safety." There was no government, no President.

Mr. ANGELL. You do not remember, then, Admiral, when the Congress convened, do you?

Admiral CAPERTON. I have it here.

Mr. ANGELL. It must have been prior to August 5, because in the long cable of August 3 the following appears in the beginning of what apparently is the third paragraph: "Although Congress is in session, it has elective power only. there being no President. Upon the election of President Congress acquires legislative power and revolutionary committee loses all authority." So that is a specific statement of fact, which was undoubtedly an accurate statement of the constitutional situation. That is August 3. Then, Admiral, so far as you remember, and as indicated by this message of August 3, Congress was in session at that time?

Admiral CAPERTON. On the 29th of July I have this note:

"Considerable uneasiness, however, exists throughout city. Both houses of delegates met to-day. An effort is being made to elect a President. The session was stormy and although a government may be established in form, there are not at present in sight sufficiently strong candidates to alleviate uneasy conditions among the populace and to insure prevention from further outbreak. The leading candidates here at present appear to be Bobo and Cauvin."

That was on the 29th of July.

I would like to say here that in my previous answer in regard to there not being a quorum of the Congress, I was then referring to the previous President, Guillaume Sam, who entered the city about the 22d or 23d of February, and was not elected, as I recall it now, until a week afterwards anyway, for the lack of a quorum of the congress.

Mr. ANGELL. Now, coming down, Admiral, to the 5th of August when you reported to the Secretary of the Navy that the Haitian Congress had issued a bulletin that on the Sunday following they would elect a President, but at your request they had postponed the election, how, if you remember, was that request of yours communicated to Congress?

Admiral CAPERTON. I am quite sure through my chief of staff, and probably through the chargé d'affaires, perhaps. I am not sure whether he went through the state department, but I imagine he did.

Mr. ANGELL. What was the usual procedure in your diplomatic negotiations on shore at this time; that is, did Capt. Beach go direct to the leaders of the House, or did he move entirely through the chargé d'affaires?

Admiral CAPERTON. I always cooperated very closely with the chargé d'affaires. That was my usual order and custom.

Mr. ANGELL. Well, what form did that cooperation take?

Admiral CAPERTON. Consultation. I do not remember a special case.

Mr. ANGELL. Do you remember whether Capt. Beach went direct, for example, to the leaders of the two Houses?

Admiral CAPERTON. You mean on this occasion?

Mr. ANGELL. On this or similar occasions.

Admiral CAPERTON. That I can not recall now, but Capt. Beach will be able to tell you exactly his procedure on shore.

Mr. ANGELL. Coming now to the 9th of August, when the Acting Secretary of the Navy, I believe, Admiral Benson, sent the message to you, you remember, "Whenever the Haitians wish, you may permit the election of a President to take place. The election of Dartiguenave is preferred by the United States."

Admiral CAPERTON. Yes.

Mr. ANGELL. Did you communicate to the leaders of the two Houses this statement, or the substance of it, to the effect that the election of Dartiguenave was preferred by the United States.

Admiral CAPERTON. I did not.

Mr. ANGELL. That was simply information for your guidance?

Admiral CAPERTON. That was information for me and my officers, my staff; it was for me really.

Mr. ANGELL. It was not communicated to the leaders in Congress?

Admiral CAPERTON. Not to my knowledge.

Mr. ANGELL. Not to your knowledge?

Admiral CAPERTON. No; I do not think it was.

Mr. ANGELL. Either formally or informally?

Admiral CAPERTON. I think not. Of course, we had met these various candidates and had discussions with them, and talks, and found out what they would do and what they would not do; but, as I stated before here, as far as I know, Mr. Dartiguenave may have thought that he was the favorite candidate in the eyes of the United States, but he was never so informed by me or by my orders. I made up my mind about him from the answers which he gave me in various conferences which my chief of staff and other officers had had with him on shore.

Mr. ANGELL. What steps, if any, were taken, Admiral, so far as you now remember, to throw the weight of the United States influence in Port au Prince, either the influence of the military forces under your command or the influence of the chargé d'affaires, to the support of Dartiguenave as a candidate for the presidency?

Admiral CAPERTON. I think it was Mr. Dartiguenave himself. He was then president of the senate, and he had many friends. He had been president for some time—I do not know for how long, but for quite a little while for Haiti—and, as I have stated here, he was a man of a good deal of personal influence, and I think he swung these fellows himself. There was certainly no pressure brought to bear on them.

Mr. ANGELL. Well, was the election of Dartiguenave, then, in a substantial sense, a free election of the candidate popularly desired by the elective body?

Admiral CAPERTON. I think it was, perhaps, the only fair and free election that Haiti has ever had, as far as I know, not having read up all the elections; but it was free from all sorts of intimidation, free of Cacos, with their guns, and each man got up and spoke and voted without any fear of anyone shooting him or going to shoot him afterwards, as far as I was able to protect him. My chief of staff, as I said here before, and several of the Marine officers made reports to me of the election afterwards, and they were present there and saw what was going on.

Mr. ANGELL. Capt. Beach was present on the floor at the election, was he not?

Admiral CAPERTON. He was present on the floor; and perhaps you were here the day I recited the speeches they made and the little incidents that happened. The President, when elected, came down from the speaker's stand and shook hands with Capt. Beach, and it was absolutely an orderly election. Not even one gun was fired, as far as reported to me; and on previous occasions there was nothing but shooting over the whole town.

Mr. ANGELL. And such American influence as there was—military and diplomatic—in Port au Prince was not thrown in favor of or against any of the candidates?

Admiral CAPERTON. As far as I know, no sir. We had only been there a few days, and we would have been pretty good diplomats to have gained the influence that was required to elect a President.

Mr. ANGELL. Of course, several times, at your request, though, they postponed the election, so you had acquired that much influence?

Admiral CAPERTON. Yes; I had many friends in Haiti at that time. I was met and told on the streets time and time again that it was their salvation, and that they appreciated everything of the kind. They saw what we were doing, and it was the first time they had ever been able to walk down the streets without being in fear of being shot at.

Mr. ANGELL. I do not want to appear to insinuate that you went so far in your diplomacy as to have the electors approached in order to secure the election of the candidate we wanted, but you evidently were a good enough diplomat to secure the postponement of the election several times?

Admiral CAPERTON. That was always accomplished, as far as I know, in an orderly, diplomatic way, by requests, and by representing to them that the time was not opportune, as the city was still in a state of great unrest, and as soon as I determined or thought that things were quiet enough for them to really have an election, and I had made all preparations to preserve order and had my forces stationed throughout the city the election was held. My forces did nothing except in behalf of peace, to protect everybody. All sorts of people went into the senate chamber when the election took place, as I have said before, at the request of either senators or deputies, as their friends. They were disarmed at the door and allowed to go in. The representatives all wore their arms by special permission.

Mr. ANGELL. You said something, Admiral, in testifying on Monday last, October 17, which I frankly did not get thoroughly at the time, and I want to ask you about it. It undoubtedly is in the record there, but there was some mention made by you, if I remember correctly, of getting one senator to come at the time of this election. There was somebody who was absent, away at some other town?

Admiral CAPERTON. No; I never mentioned that, but there was a senator that was brought down from Cape Haitien, I think.

Mr. ANGELL. Was that for the election of the President or for the ratification of the treaty?

Admiral CAPERTON. Oh, I think that was it.

Mr. ANGELL. There was an incident of bringing down a senator from Cape Haitien for the ratification of the treaty along in October or November.

Admiral CAPERTON. Yes; but not for the President.

Mr. ANGELL. Not for the President?

Admiral CAPERTON. You see, at that time I did not know any of the people on shore except the few that I had met in the few days before the election took place.

Mr. ANGELL. In further connection with the election of the President, you remember yesterday morning, Admiral, there was a question which was put to you by Senator McCormick regarding Dartiguenave's statement that Haiti must and will accede gladly to any and all terms proposed by the United States, including the cession outright of Mole St. Nicholas, and he asked you, as I remember it, to put in there the message verbatim, as it was, because in the reports so far there was merely a paraphrase of it. Maj. McClellon found that message.

Admiral CAPERTON. He found it afterwards, and I quoted it and put it in afterwards.

Mr. ANGELL. It is not in the record, not in this stenographic copy I have.

Admiral CAPERTON. It is coming, I suppose; it has not been copied yet.

Mr. ANGELL. It ought to be inserted on page 301 of the typewritten copy.

Referring to your message, can you tell us why Dartiguenave, ostensibly a patriot and jealously interested in guarding the welfare of Haiti, should have voluntarily, as appears to be the case, made an offer in advance of his election to the presidency, to cede Mole St. Nicholas to the United States?

Admiral CAPERTON. No; I do not know what was in his mind to cause him to make that remark.

Mr. ANGELL. The message to which I refer was sent by you on August 7, the message containing this statement; that is, some 9 or 10 days after you had landed?

Admiral CAPERTON. Yes.

Mr. ANGELL. Had there been any discussion with him, so far as you know, or can now recollect, by your representatives, Capt. Beach or others, or by the American diplomatic representatives in Port au Prince, regarding the question of Mole St. Nicholas?

Admiral CAPERTON. Not by my orders. Capt. Beach, as my representative, was on shore, and one or two others, trying to arrange for the election. I knew about Mole St. Nicholas or St. Nicholas Mole, but I knew nothing about or gave no orders to go and tell Mr. Dartiguenave that we wanted that or would want it in case anybody was elected. I do not know what these officers said to Mr. Dartiguenave. We had several formal and informal meetings with Mr. Dartiguenave, as we did with all the other candidates that we heard proposed. As soon as we heard of one we would try to find out what kind of a fellow he was and whether he could be trusted or depended upon; whether he was a good citizen, and whenever we inquired about Mr. Dartiguenave we always heard that he was a good man. He had been distributing the spoils, you might say,

I believe that was the way it was done in Haiti. The President of the Senate dealt out the money—I do not know where they got it—or the funds or spoils. as they say, and I have heard it said by many, and by prominent men, that although Dartiguenave had been doing this according to the custom, they did not believe Mr. Dartiguenave had ever accepted a cent in that way or through that channel, and so, of course, I had a high regard for Senator Dartiguenave at that t.me. But as to why he made this remark and whether there was any pressure, you might say, brought on him to make this remark, I am unable to say. There was nothing, to my knowledge.

During this time, it is but fair to say, that I did not know everything that the State Department was doing through the chargé d' affaires. We were working very closely together, but I did not know that I ever told him everything that I did and I do not believe that he told me everything he did.

Mr. ANGELL. There was no treaty or draft of a treaty, of course, submitted to anyone at this time, prior to the election, was there?

Admiral CAPERTON. No. I had never seen one.

Mr. ANGELL. The first draft of a treaty submitted to the Haitians after your arrival, so far as you know, was that draft which the State Department ordered Davis, by telegraphic message sent through you, to submit on August.14?

Admiral CAPERTON. I have already so stated in my evidence here or else I am going to do it.

Maj. McCLELLAN. You did on the 14th, and the whole thing is included in there.

Mr. ANGELL. That is included in the testimony of yesterday.

Admiral CAPERTON. It was; so it was.

Mr. ANGELL. And the suggestions and corrections for the draft are in the testimony of yesterday.

Admiral CAPERTON. That is in my testimony of yesterday.

(Whereupon, at 12 o'clock m., a recess was taken until 2.30 o'clock p. m.)

The committee reassembled at 2.30 o'clock p. m., pursuant to the taking of recess, Senator Oddie presiding.

Mr. ANGELL. Referring, Admiral, to the message of August 14 from Washington, directed through you to the legation at Port au Prince, wh'ch commences. as appears on page 306 of the typewritten report of the hearing, " For more than a year the Haitian Government has been familiar with the terms of the treaty contained in department's instructions of July 1, 1914," I would ask you whether you were or are now famil ar with the terms of that treaty, as contained in the department's instructions of July, 1914?

Admiral CAPERTON. No; I am not familiar with it.

Mr. ANGELL. You do not know whether or not the terms of that proposed treaty, or the department's instructions, as referred to in this message, made any reference to Mole St. Nicholas's cession?

Admiral CAPERTON. No; I do not. That was a year before I went there.

Mr. ANGELL. In you testimony of this week, Admiral, you referred to your statement on August 9, I believe, to the revolutionary committee that the treasury's services would be restored to the national bank and would be taken from the banking firm of Simmond Freres. 1 wanted to ask you in connection with that, Admiral, whether the service was restored by you to the National Bank of Haiti?

Admiral CAPERTON. Yes.

Mr. ANGELL. What steps did you take or have taken to restore this service to the National Bank of Haiti? In other words, how did you accomplish the transfer of the treasury's service from Simmond Freres to the National Bank of Hait ? What I wanted to bring out, Admiral, is the general means by which you effected this transfer from one bank to the other.

Admiral CAPERTON. I do not recall at this time. I had a paymaster who was looking out for the financial arrangements on shore.

Mr. ANGELL. The financial arrangements with regard to the Haitian national fund?

Admiral CAPERTON. Yes; but without finding my notes here, offhand I do not remember the modus operandi, but, as I recall it, it was done through the chief of staff and the paymaster.

Senator ODDIE. I would like to ask a question here, Admiral. Who controlled the bank of Simmond Freres?

Admiral CAPERTON. It was reported to me that anybody got money, as I have stated in my testimony here, who had the power to go and demand it.

Senator ODDIE. But I mean who controlled the bank itself? What interests controlled the bank itself?

Admiral CAPERTON. Well, I do not know. It was a private bank, Simmond Freres, and there were two or three brothers of them, I think.

Senator ODDIE. Do you know whether it had any connection with any country other than our own and Haiti?

Admiral CAPERTON. I do not recall that now, sir. It was more of a banking house than a regular bank, as I understand it.

This was what I put in previously in my testimony:

"Last January the treasury service by an arbitrary act was taken from the National Bank of Haiti, the national treasury, by a proclamation of President Theodoré and given to private banking firms, the principal one of which is Simmond Freres. Simmond Freres is under no control that will safeguard public interests. They merely make collections of the revenues received, take a certain percentage as their fee, and turn the rest over to whosoever may exercise sufficient force or persuasion in the name of the government or revolution to obtain it. The result is that considerable money is being thus forced from Simmond Freres by the so-called revolutionary committee in various towns, and this money is being used to actively support the revolutionary candidate. On account of military necessity, therefore, I this day informed the committee in Port au Prince, Simmond Freres, and the National Bank of Haiti that the treasury service could be resumed by the National Bank of Haiti. This bank is under legal and exact contract for the handling of the treasury's service for the country."

Mr. ANGELL. Now, Admiral, are we to understand from this testimony that such funds as there were of the Haitian Government on deposit at Simmond Freres were seized or directly controlled by you and your officers between the time of your original landing and the election of the new President?

Admiral CAPERTON. We seized no money at all, and as far as I remember I do not think there was any fund that was transferred. I do not know whether there were any funds in the bank or not. I simply ordered the National Bank of Haiti to resume the service for the Government, with the idea of making deposits in future there and not making them with Simmond Freres.

Mr. ANGELL. Was there any order, for example, given to Simmond Freres not to pay out any funds which may have been on deposit there nominally in the name of the Haitian Government except upon your orders or subject to your countersign?

Admiral CAPERTON. No; there were no orders of that kind given at all. I did not have anything to do with the money that Simmond Freres had. I just heard and it was reported to me that everybody with authority who came along had access to it, or words to that effect.

Mr. ANGELL. If they were collecting it and paying it out and the different people were getting it, there must have been some funds which were nominally national funds on deposit somewhere?

Admiral CAPERTON. Yes; it was deposited there, I imagine.

Mr. ANGELL. With Simmond Freres?

Admiral CAPERTON. With Simmond Freres, yes; but I did not transfer any funds from there at all. I just issued an order that day that in the future the service would be resumed at the other bank, and then if there was any collection anywhere it would be deposited in the other bank. Of course, at that time I forget whether I had taken over any of the ports of entry or not.

Mr. ANGELL. I am speaking now of the point of activities up to the taking over of any of the customhouses?

Admiral CAPERTON. Yes. Understand, I had my officers detailed to look out for certain things on shore. I did not attend to these duties personally; I simply did it by orders, so that it is not quite fresh or clear in my mind as to how we did it or what the procedure was. I do know that I took no funds that were deposited to the credit of the Government.

Mr. ANGELL. Then, as far as you remember, Admiral, there was no seizure or control of any of the funds of the Haitian Government whatsoever, while you were there, prior to the seizure and control of the funds coming in from customs collections?

Admiral CAPERTON. Nothing prior to the time when I received orders to deposit whatever was collected (after I had seized or taken possession of the ports of entry in my name) in this National Bank of Haiti and its branches.

Mr. ANGELL. What you refer to as the funds collected at the ports of entry is the funds you collected through the customs?

Admiral CAPERTON. Yes; through the customhouses.

Mr. ANGELL. So that the sole control exercised by you over the financial matters and funds began with the customs seizure?

Admiral CAPERTON. Began with the taking over of the customs. As I remember, this was done simply to let the National Bank of Haiti (which had a regular contract, by law, or a regular agreement, to look out for the funds of Haiti) receive these funds again and not let them go to an outside bank, to which they had been transferred, as I said before, by some arbitrary act, not legal at all.

Mr. ANGELL. Did you receive any orders, Admiral, from Washington to make this shift of service from Simmond Freres to the National Bank of Haiti?

Admiral CAPERTON. I must have received such orders or I certainly would not have done so.

Here on the 19th of August I find the following cablegram, which says that I was directed to take charge of certain customhouses, and then how I was to spend the money, and all that sort of thing, and to collect the import and export duties, to be immediately deposited by me with the resident legal branches of the National Bank of Haiti, in a separate account opened in my name.

I have either testified to this before or else have it in my notes to do it when I come to it. I had probably received orders before that time. I handled no money in the hands of Simmond Freres. I simply wanted to divert the manner in which the duties or customs were being deposited at that time back to the National Bank of Haiti, which had a lawful contract to handle these duties.

Mr. ANGELL. So far as you remember, were the funds collected after the issuance of your orders to the National Bank of Haiti and to the Simmond Freres deposited according to your instructions?

Admiral CAPERTON. Do you mean here on the 8th or 9th?

Mr. ANGELL. Yes, sir. In other words, was the service resumed with the National Bank of Haiti?

Admiral CAPERTON. Without refreshing my memory, I am unable to answer this; I do not recall.

Mr. ANGELL. At that same time, namely, August 9, you will remember that the Acting Secretary of the Navy sent you a message, to which we have referred here a number of times, regarding the election of the President and saying that Dartiguenave was favored, and that message went on to say, as is already in the record, "You will assure the Haitians that the United States has no other motive than the establishing of a firm and lasting government by the Haitian people, and wishes to assist them now and at all times in the future to maintain both their political independence and territorial integrity unimpaired." That message was, as I read it, an order to you to assure the Haitians of these purposes of the United States?

Admiral CAPERTON. Yes.

Mr. ANGELL. Do you remember, sir, what steps you took to carry out that order to assure the Haitians of these avowed purposes?

Admiral CAPERTON. I think I issued several proclamations there. What was that date?

Mr. ANGELL. August 9, sir.

Admiral CAPERTON. Just taking them as I find them here, here is one message from the commanding officer of the *Connecticut:* "Referring to your 12,006, proclamation will be published broadcast in French to-morrow and copies issued at outposts to people leaving town.

"Have received no word yet from revolutionary generals."

That shows the proclamation was there.

Mr. ANGELL. What is the date of that? That is the 8th, is it not?

Admiral CAPERTON. No; that is the 10th, really the 9th, you know. It was sent to me on the 9th. Everywhere that I had any ships or any men in control I issued this proclamation throughout the country, and, as in this instance here, it was posted on the outside or near the entrances of the city, so that the people leaving the city could see it.

Mr. ANGELL. Now, Admiral, referring to your testimony yesterday, on August 15 you sent a message to your chief of staff, appearing on page 313 of the typewritten report of the hearings, in which you say in paragraph 2: .

"I will directly, in conjunction with the American chargé d'affaires, carry on the negotiations and have charge of the important relations with the Haitian officials."

And the substance of that is repeated in several other communications of the same date as this, as appears in the following pages of the record, to Capt. Durrell, to Col. Waller, to the chargé d'affaires, etc.

Admiral CAPERTON. What is the date of that?

Mr. ANGELL. August 15, immediately following the election, and at the time when the treaty negotiat ons were just be ng put under way. Can you tell us, sir, in a general way, what the respective parts were, played by yourself or your representatives in the negotiation of this treaty, which culminated in its signature in September, and the part played by the chargé d'affaires?

Admiral CAPERTON. Well, I do not know everything the chargé d'affaires did, but in running my work I cooperated with him and Capt. Beach. I had Capt. Beach visit the different Senators around through the town, and talked with them about the treaty, and discussed it with them to get their views, all of them. I think finally I had a talk w.th every one of them—that is, through Capt. Beach—and we worked together in trying to persuade them or to represent to them what the treaty was. The chargé d'affaires, of course, conducted it, you know; but I assisted him, and I went so far as to tell Capt. Beach to go and see these different Senators and talk to them about it. If I had spoken French I would have, perhaps, seen some of the Senators and deputies myself.

Mr. ANGELL. From the record it does not appear, you see, what respective part was played by your side in Haiti, and what part was played by the accredited diplomatic representatives.

Admiral CAPERTON. I had orders to cooperate with the chargé d'affaires and aid him all I could in every way, which I did.

Mr. ANGELL. If I understand you rightly, then, the chargé d'affaires really controlled and was the general directing head of the American side of the negotiations?

Admiral CAPERTON. Certainly. He made the reports and conducted the affairs, and I assisted him in every way I could. There is one thing I do not th'nk 's necessary to bring out; that is, where the radiogram was sent to me to be del'vered to him, giving him his power to sign the treaty, etc. He had no way to receive it, the cable being out of order, so I received it by radio and delivered it to him.

Mr. ANGELL. You testified, Admiral, yesterday, and it has already appeared in the record before, that on the 17th of August, Mr. Davis, the American chargé d'affaires at Port au Prince, delivered to President Dartiguenave a draft of a treaty, as outlined in a message which passed through you on August 14.

Admiral CAPERTON. Yes.

Mr. ANGELL. Do you know whether or not the draft of that treaty, as presented by Mr. Davis to the President, contained any reference to Mole St. Nicholas?

Admiral CAPERTON. Without looking at it I do not remember. It was a long message or treaty, and I read it at the time, but now I can not recall it. It is down in the treaty, and you have a copy of it. You can read it yourself and see.

Mr. ANGELL. That is what I wanted to find out, whether the original draft, as delivered by Mr. Davis to President Dartiguenave on August 17 contained any reference to Mole St. Nicholas.

Admiral CAPERTON. Without looking at it, I could not tell.

Mr. ANGELL. You testified yesterday, Admiral, that on August 17, 1915, five days after the election of Dartiguenave, and three days after the receipt by you of the message for the chargé d'affaires concerning the treaty, that Mr. Davis, the chargé d'affaires, delivered to President Dartiguenave the draft of a proposed treaty. Do you remember whether that draft contained any reference to Mole St. Nicholas?

Admiral CAPERTON. If he delivered the one that I received by radio, if that is the one he delivered, which I presume it is, the treaty itself, a copy of which I have here, would show of itself whether there is anything about Mole St. Nicholas in it. That is all in the record, and has all been submitted. I do not see why you can not go to that and get it.

Mr. Angell. Pardon me. Perhaps I misunderstand, but what is in the record of yesterday is the message of the 14th, which outlined a treaty, and that message of August 14 directed Mr. Davis to prepare a draft of a treaty on the following basis.

Adm.ral Caperton. That was the message of August 14.

Mr. Angell. Now, on August 17, as you testified yesterday, you had by that time evidently made a draft of a treaty and presented to Dartiguenave that draft of a treaty, a complete treaty in other words.

Admiral Caperton. That is not in the record of yesterday. In my answer I was referr.ng to the message that I received from the Navy Department—that is, from the State Department, I think it was, through the Navy Department and through me to Mr. Davis.

Mr. Angell. Now, what I am referring to is the actual draft, as delivered three days later by Mr. Davis to President Dart;guenave.

Admiral Caperton. That I am unable at th s time to answer, because I do not recall. No doubt I read the treaty before he presented it, but I do not recall now whether St. N;cholas Mole was mentioned or not.

Mr. Angell. Coming now, sir, to the message of August 19 wh:ch directed you, on the authority of the State Department to seize the 10 ma.n customhouses, you testified yesterday, on page 326 of the typewritten record of the hearings that you were directed to confer with the American charge d'affaires for the purpose of having President Dartiguenave solicit the above action, namely, the seizure of these customhouses, " but whether the President so requested or not, I was directed to carry out the State Department's des.res."

Do you remember whether you did confer with the Amer.can chargé d'affaires for the purpose of having President Dartiguenave solic.t the seizure of the customhouses?

Admiral Caperton. Oh, yes ; I conferred with him through my chief of staff. Before taking over any customhouses, I always conferred with the President, and informed him of what I was going to do, and requested his permission or agreement to the matter, and as far as I remember now, he never gave his consent. In each case where a customhouse was taken over, the order issued to do it was referred to the chargé d'affaires, to have him go to the President first, and in many instances I asked h.m if he would not aid me in taking it over by having his customhouse officials present to aid me when taking it over.

Mr. Angell. When you say " he," you mean the Pres.dent?

Admiral Caperton. Yes ; the President.

Mr. Angell. But, so far as you know, he never consented affirmatively to the seizure of any customhouses?

Adm.ral Caperton. Not that I recall now, but I did have some of his customs officials at different customhouses, several of them, who aided us in taking charge. If he did not assent, he naturally objected. I do not know what he said at the t.me, except that it was generally understood that he did not approve of it.

Mr. Angell. Do you remember whether or not he made any specific protest?

Admiral Caperton. No ; I can not recall that now, in the absence of my representatives who personally conferred with him.

Mr. Angell. Do you remember the protest which was published in the Moniteur on September 4, 1915, specifically regarding the se.zure of the customhouses at Port au Prince, wh ch was dated September 2? I want to offer this in the record, and I will read you the material portions of it, Admiral, and ask if it refreshes your recollect on on the general attitude of the Government :

" Haitians ! At the very moment when the Government, engaged in negot:ations to settle the question of the presence of American military forces on Haitian territory, was looking forward to a prompt solution in accordance with law and justice, it finds itself faced with the simple seizure of possession of the customs admin.stration of the capital.

" Prev.ously the customhouses of several other cit es of the Republic have been occupied in like fashion, and whenever the news of such occupation reached the national palace or the department of finances it was followed by an energetic protest, demanding that the d plomatic representative of the Amer can Government resid:ng at Port au Prince restore the customhouses and put an end to acts so contrary to the relations at present existing between the Government of Haiti and the Government of the United States of North America."

And it goes on to comment on this situation, and is signed by President Dartiguenave.

Admiral CAPERTON. So far as I recall now, I had no paper written to me containing any objection, nor do I remember the words of objection that were given at various times to my representatives but I know there was more or less of a protest, whether from the President himself, or whether from the press, I am unable to say.

(The balance of the protest above quoted is as follows:)

"Haitians! In bringing these facts officially to the attention of the country, I owe it to myself to declare further, in the most formal fashion to you and to the entire civilized world, that the order to carry out these acts so destructive of the interests, rights, and sovereignty of the Haitian people is not due to anything which can be cited against the patriotism, devotion, spirit of sacrifice, and loyalty of those to whom the destinies of the country have been intrusted. You are the judges of that.

"Nor will I conceal the fact that my astonishment is greater because the negotiations, which had been undertaken in the hope of an agreement upon the basis of propositions presented by the American Government itself, after having passed through the ordinary phases of diplomatic discussion with frankness and courtesy on both sides, have now been relieved of the only obstacles which had hitherto appeared to stand in their way.

"Haitians! In this agonizing situation, more than tragic for every truly Haitian soul, the Government, which intends to preserve full national sovereignty, will be able to maintain the necessary resolution only if all are united in exercising their intelligence and energy with it in the present task of saving the nation.

"SUDRE DARTIGUENAVE.

"Given at the National Palace, September 2, 1915, in the one hundred and twelfth year of our independence."

Mr. ANGELL. With further reference, Admiral, to this question of the customs, and the use of funds, and the seizure, and the like, you testified yesterday with respect to the funds that were being collected at the customhouses as follows—and I am quoting now from page 329 of the typewritten record of the hearings:

"Admiral CAPERTON. The funds that were being collected were being used at different ports by revolutionary forces, in some instances. There was no control."

Can you remember—appreciating the difficulty of remembering things that happened back six years—can you now remember any specific instances where the customs funds were being used by the revolutionary forces or bands of Cacos?

Admiral CAPERTON. No; I do not know that I can recall any specific instances at the present. I might be able to refresh my memory by looking over my notes, but I do not recall any now.

Mr. ANGELL. Is it a fact—and I am asking this for mere information—that, as I have been told, and as I understand it to be, many of the customs services from particular ports were specifically pledged to meet the foreign debt or foreign loan service or services?

Admiral CAPERTON. Yes; I think that is the case. I do not know about the various ports.

Mr. ANGELL. I have no particular port or ports in mind, but merely the fact that some of the——

Admiral CAPERTON. The money that was collected from customs on individual things was frequently allotted for certain purposes or for certain debts to be paid. On a certain amount of coffee sometimes they had one or two different allotments. A certain percentage of it was to pay for one thing, and a certain percentage for another thing.

Mr. ANGELL. Do you remember, Admiral, whether there were any pledges of customs receipts from a specific port for the service of a specific foreign loan?

Admiral CAPERTON. No; I do not know of that detail.

Mr. ANGELL. At the time the customs services were seized by you, pursuant to the State Department's request, as contained in the Navy Department's telegram of August 19, were you informed officially by the Navy Department, or the American diplomatic representatives in Port au Prince, that the customs services were in some instances, and on some types of exports and imports, specifically pledged to certain foreign loans?

Admiral CAPERTON. Yes; as I recall it now, the National Bank of Haiti looked out for it, and had been looking out for it all along except when the services were taken from the bank as referred to previously. That was their duty. That was a part of their obligation, to devote so much of the customs money to this, and so much to that.

Mr. ANGELL. Do you know whether the seizure of the customs, as carried out by you, contemplated the honoring of these pledges?

Admiral CAPERTON. I do not know about that. I only know what was done with the money after I collected it; it was paid out in accordance with instructions from the Navy Department.

Mr. ANGELL. You have no idea whether the Navy Department or the State Department accepted these customs receipts to be used to carry out the pledges previously made by the Haitian government?

Admiral CAPERTON. No; I do not. I made several recommendations, or many recommendations, to pay out this money that was collected, and I remember that several hundred thousand dollars were paid out for the interest on the internal bonds. I was particularly interested in that, because it was explained to me on shore, what the internal bonds were. I was there such a short time, less than a year, after the time I took over the customs; however, we collected a good deal, and, as I remember, when I left there I left a million and a half or $2,000,000, something like that, in the Haitian National Bank, and I paid out $600,000 or $700,000 for interest on the internal bonds.

I might say that all these details were looked after and handled carefully by my officers whom I detailed for that specific purpose. For instance, the administrator of customs, Capt. Connard, looked out for all of this. He made a study of it. and was constantly in consultation and worked with the National Bank of Haiti, and he would come and report to me the results of what he was doing. so that I would know what was going on. He is thoroughly conversant with every step that was taken with regard to the finances of the country after his arrival and after his appointment under me.

Mr. ANGELL. During the period of your assignment to duty in Haitian waters, which was up until November. 1916, as I remember——

Admiral CAPERTON. No; until July 18, 1916.

Mr. ANGELL. July 18, 1916, there was no payment made, was there, of interest on the foreign debt?

Admiral CAPERTON. No; I think you will find in the records here somewhere frequent mention of this subject, but, as I recall it now, we paid no interest on the external or foreign debts.

Mr. ANGELL. There was no direction from Washington to you to pay such interest on the foreign debt?

Admiral CAPERTON. Not that I recall now.

Mr. ANGELL. In connection, Admiral, with the negotiation of the treaty or financial matters such as the customs control, did Mr. Farnham appear as interested in any way in these questions, or did he assist in any of the councils?

Admiral CAPERTON. I never saw Mr. Farnham. I heard a lot of talk about him, promiscuous talk. I appealed, I presume it was to him, or to the National City Bank, or some one in New York, to try to start up work on this railroad to keep the people from starving, which was outlined in my testimony, or will be before I finish, but as far as having any intercourse with him at all, I had none whatever. .

Mr. ANGELL. Do you remember or not whether he was in Haiti during the summer of 1915?

Admiral CAPERTON. I do not recall now; I do not believe he was. He may have been, but I never met him. Of course, there was a great deal of talk about him. The people on shore did not seem to like him; a great many did not, especially the people who were against the occupation. In that way they would frequently bring up his name, but I paid no attention to it, because I had my own orders and business to attend to.

Mr. ANGELL. Coming back again now to the customs, sir, it is a fact, is it not, that the customs service was the chief source of revenue of the Government?

Admiral CAPERTON. Oh yes; as far as I know, it was the only source.

Mr. ANGELL. There was none or practically no internal-tax revenue?

Admiral CAPERTON. No; they said they collected them, but when I went to look for them after I took charge, I could not find any.

Mr. ANGELL. Referring still to the customs seizure, you testified yesterday. on page 330 of the typewritten record of the hearings, that on August 18, as it appears here—I think it should be August 19—you sent a message to the Secretary of the Navy, stating that the United States had now actually accomplished a military intervention in the affairs of another nation. Referring, sir, to that message, you testified yesterday, and it appears in the message, that you said, "This secrecy extremely important now, pending treaty negotiations," the secrecy referring to the proposed seizure of the customhouses. Do you remember whether secrecy was maintained at that time? Were you permitted to carry out your own idea of maintaining secrecy?

Admiral CAPERTON. Yes; to a certain extent I was. It came through me, and unless it was intercepted it was kept more or less secret by me. To the best of my power the secrecy was maintained.

The secrecy referred to in this message refers to the secrecy covering the arrival of a regiment of marines. I think it refers generally to all my activities there. I had recommended the bringing down of a lot of marines, additional marines, and I think now, look.ng at it, as I recall it, I meant that my general activities would be kept secret, because I was not ready to do much then. If you will notice, these places were taken over one at a time for a while, because I had not the force to do otherwise. When I took one I had to have a sufficient force there to protect myself, to protect the act, and look out for the customhouse and see that that was properly protected.

Mr. ANGELL. The taking over of an individual customhouse was not a matter of secrecy in itself, was it?

Admiral CAPERTON. Oh, no.

Mr. ANGELL. That was done entirely openly?

Admiral CAPERTON. After the act commenced, and, as I have stated before, I always informed the Government of the fact and asked them if they would not assist me in turning over the archives.

Mr. ANGELL. So that as soon as you seized an individual customhouse that fact became known generally and broadcast at once?

Admiral CAPERTON. Oh, yes; as fast as news traveled at that time in Haiti.

Mr. ANGELL. Because I notice that in your testimony yesterday, on page 336 of the typewritten record of the hearing, you quote a message or note of yours of August 21, which was the date, I believe, that the first of the customhouses was taken over, that at St. Marc saying, "an unfavorable sentiment has appeared in Congress in the form of inflammatory speeches against the customs control and American occupation in general." That is on August 21, the date of the first taking over of any of the customhouses.

Admiral CAPERTON. Then the 21st was the date on which the first one was taken over without looking at my notes?

Mr. ANGELL. Referring to this statement in there with regard to the unfavorable sentiment appearing in speeches against the customs control, that would indicate, would it not, that this whole question of customs control was being agitated, and had been agitated, in and out of Congress, even before the customs were actually seized? In other words, was there any general discussion inside of Congress or outside on the question of the customs control or seizure of the customs prior to the first actual seizure by you on or about the 20th or 21st of August?

Admiral CAPERTON. Not that I recall now.

Mr. ANGELL. So that the storm broke regarding the seizure of the customs only after the first of the seizures?

Admiral CAPERTON. It would appear that way.

Mr. ANGELL. On August 23 you reported, Admiral, to the Navy Department, I believe, as appears on page 338 of the typewritten record of the hearings, in a message which begins, "Treaty negotiations are still unsatisfactory," and that phrase or words are substantially the same or indicating the same idea, appears in various other messages of this general period. Can you tell us what you meant by such expression or expressions as "treaty negotiations are unsatisfactory?"

Admiral CAPERTON. Yes. Of course, I kept track every day of the discussions and what was going on in Congress. I knew exactly nearly everything that took place in there, and I was able to tell when they were opposing it violently, or whether they were coming around, so to speak. In other words, if the speeches and the procedure in congress were satisfactory, they were satisfactory; if they were unsatisfactory, they were unsatisfactory, favorable to the treaty or unfavorable.

Mr. ANGELL. Whether they were favorable or unfavorable to the acceptance of the treaty is what I am trying to ascertain.

Admiral CAPERTON. One day we would have a senator with us, and then the next day he would be against us.

Mr. ANGELL. What was the main ground of such opposition as there was? Was it the opposition to the customs control?

Admiral CAPERTON. Oh, the customs control, no doubt, had something to do with it, but I think the whole American occupation. These people who were bitterly opposed to it were against the occupation, and many of them were—I do not know what you would call them, Cacos, perhaps; they were certainly very sympathetic with the Cacos.

Mr. ANGELL. The opposition in general was to the principle of the American occupation of Haiti?

Admiral CAPERTON. Well, the customs, I suppose, also had something to do with the opposition.

Mr. ANGELL. Including the customs?

Admiral CAPERTON. Yes; otherwise there would have been, as far as I can see, no opposition to it at all.

Mr. ANGELL. And those who opposed the acceptance of the streaty and the American occupation in general were the Cacos?

Admiral CAPERTON. Well, there were some men who opposed it; I would not like to say they were all Cacos, but they were sympathetic with the Cacos at that time. I think what I intend to infer is, that many of them, deputies, senators, were really Cacos.

Mr. ANGELL. You read into the record yesterday, Admiral—and they appear on page 347 and following of the typewritten record of the hearings—your instructions regarding the customs administration.

Admiral CAPERTON. What is the date?

Mr. ANGELL. The particular letter which I have in mind being dated the 24th of August, your letter of instructions to the United States forces in Haitian waters, where, under the heading of " Civil administration," it says:

" Detachment commanders will have charge of such other civil affairs as may be assumed w.thin the limits of their respective commands."

Can you tell us what those other civil affairs were intended to be, and what charge was actually assumed by detachment commanders over other civil affairs beyond the customs?

Admiral CAPERTON. I have in my previous testimony shown that in taking over the affairs of Haiti I said that the civil affairs would still be maintained and run by the Government, and that we would only take charge of such civil affairs as interfered with my military operations. That, I am sure, is already in the record, and was possibly in the proclamation, as I remember, or the order to my representatives on shore when they took over a place, namely, that the civil authorities would not be interfered with except where they interfered or clashed with my military operations.

Mr. ANGELL. The military operations, of course, were regarded as paramount in case of any conflict?

Admiral CAPERTON. Those were my operations; yes. When I did interfere, as I recall it, I usually informed the Government, or informed the locality, that it was necessary to do that. That was my intention to always do that, and I think I did.

Mr. ANGELL. On August 31, as you testified yesterday on page 363 of the typewritten record of the hearings, you sent a message to the Secretary of the Navy, saying: " On the 31st of August there were no encouraging developments in the treaty situation. I have, therefore, decided that, unless otherwise directed, I will occupy and begin administering the customs house at Port au Prince at 10 a. m. on the 2d of September." Was your determination to occupy the customhouse at Port au Prince made with a view to forcing or assisting by that act in the general aim of bringing about an acceptance of the proposed treaty?

Admiral CAPERTON. No; I think, as I stated there, whatever the words were there, that the developments were not encouraging for the treaty, I had been waiting and waiting to take over this customhouse, because I had my orders some time before to do so, and as the paymaster had only arrived a short time before that, I decided to take it over the next day and not to wait any longer. I think if the conditions under which the treaty was being considered had been taken into consideration I would not have taken over this customhouse if I had wanted to improve the treaty negotiations, because every time I took over a station there was a howl, and I lost a great many senators and representatives. On a round-up they went against me. They said they would vote now the other way on the treaty.

Mr. ANGELL. Admiral, there has already been placed in the record Maj. McClellan's memorandum which was submitted back here in August, containing a general outline and, of course, a great many specific details. In that memorandum now appearing on page 67 of the printed record appears your proclamation of martial law of September 3, in which in the second paragraph I note you say that " I am invested with the power and responsibility of government in all its functions and branches throughout the territory above described, and the proper administration of such government by martial law will be provided for in regulations to be issued," etc. That proclamation and the language of it would hardly seem to be reconcilable, would it, with the previous proclamation of political independence as ordered from Washington through you?

Admiral CAPERTON. I do not quite get that.

Mr. ANGELL. Do you remember, sir, the message which has been referred to a number of times to-day of August 9, in which you were directed by the Secretary of the Navy to assure the Haitians that the United States wished to assist them now and at all times in the future to maintain both their political independence and territorial integrity unimpaired? I was asking you, in a question which was somewhat argumentative, possibly, whether the purposes of that order of August 9 could be reconciled with the fact of the issuance of the proclamation of martial law and the language of the proclamation?

Admiral CAPERTON. I think that is answered in the next paragraph, which is a modification, which reads as follows:

" The martial law herein proclaimed and the things in that respect so ordered will not be deemed or taken to interfere with the proceedings of the constitutional Government and Congress of Haiti or with the administration of justice in the courts of law existing therein which do not affect the military operations or the authorities of the Government of the United States of America."

Mr. ANGELL. In other words, the military operations or the authorities of the United States were to be regarded as supreme?

Admiral CAPERTON. No; I will not say that at all.

Mr. ANGELL. It says that martial law would not interfere with the proceedings of the constitutional Government or Congress or the courts that did not affect the military operations of the United States.

Admiral CAPERTON. That is the theory, I think, of martial law. On page 68 of the printed hearings appears a legal opinion rendered by the judge advocate general of the Navy with reference to the status of the marines in Haiti, which reads as follows:

" The military forces of the United States have not displaced the civil government of Haiti and established a military government of the United States in that country, but are engaged, pursuant to law, in lending sufficient aid to the Republic of Haiti," etc.

That is here. You can read it on that page.

Mr. ANGELL. The opinion is based, as I read it, sir, upon the treaty and upon the status of the United States forces in Haiti subsequent to the treaty of September 16, 1915, whereas your proclamation of martial law was made and martial law went into effect 13 days before the treaty was signed, so that the opinion of the judge advocate general is hardly in point, it seems to me. That is more a statement for the record than a question to you, sir, because that is a fairly technical question of constitutional and international law. I simply asked you whether in your opinion there was a conflict between the avowed purposes to maintain the political independence and territorial integrity unimpaired of the Haitian people and the acts which were taken by you in accordance with your instructions received from Washington.

Admiral CAPERTON. Well, if you will recall my testimony, it was by the request of the President of Haiti that I declared martial law. I announced I would do it, and I had the approval of the department.

Mr. ANGELL. Am I to understand from your answer that you believe there was no conflict between the announced purpose to take no steps to impair the political independence of Haiti and the steps which were actually taken?

Admiral CAPERTON. Well, I found it necessary to declare martial law in order to exist there or get along. No one seemed to pay any attention to the laws. The newspapers were defaming us and me individually, and everything was running riot, so in order to handle matters and keep peace at all I really did it, you might say, to support the constitutional government of Haiti.

Mr. ANGELL. I am not asking you personally to defend it, and I am not criticizing or attacking it, but I am just trying to get the official view, if I can, of the accordance of these acts with our avowed purposes.

Admiral CAPERTON. I informed the department before that I would do this unless matters got better, and I had their approval, and I let the people know that I would not interfere with their civil government in any way, provided they did not affect the military operations or the authorities of the Government of the United States.

Mr. ANGELL. In other words, in accordance with the discretion which was vested in you, or with the instructions, you regarded the step of proclaiming martial law as an act necessary and proper to assist in the maintenance of the political independence of Haiti?

Admiral CAPERTON. And to preserve law and peace; yes; and I was so complimented by and had the approval of many of the best people in the city. Of course, a great many acts arising from this they disapproved, but the good things I did for them they all agreed to. They came to me and said it was the best thing. They could not live there without martial law, and I do not believe they could exist there without it at the present time.

Mr. ANGELL. You have referred in your testimony, Admiral, and it appears also in the record in the memorandum prepared by Maj. McClellan, that martial law, as proclaimed by you on September 3, 1915, in Port au Prince, was requested of the American forces by President Dart'guenave. Can you tell us when, where, to whom, and under what circumstances that request was made?

Admiral CAPERTON. I can not at the present time. It came to me officially. I would say very likely it came through my chief of staff. He reported it to me. Just how I received the message now I can not recall, but it was official and came from him, and I reported it to the Secretary of the Navy, and it is all a matter of record, and I think it is already entered in my testimony. Military intervention was required because there was no existing or prospective Ha tian authority, either civil or military, to cope with the existing state of anarchy. As the only poss ble means of establishing order and bringing peace and protection to the mass of the people, martial law was declared. This mart al law was, in fact, the martial law of the Republic of Haiti put into effect at the request of the President of that Republic and for the preservatiton of the lives and property of law-abiding Haitians as well as to avoid the necessity of the various units of the military forces adopting their own means for self-protection and for the preservation of order in their immediate vicin'ty.

(A supplemental statement filed by Rear Admiral William B. Caperton is here printed in full, as follows:)

STATEMENT OF REAR ADMIRAL WILLIAM B. CAPERTON.

(In accordance with the previous understanding between the chairman and Admiral Caperton the following was introduced in written form on November 10, 1921, by Mr. Howe, counsel for the committee, on behalf of Admiral Caperton, as a continuation of his former testimony:)

On September 9 I received the following report from Mr. McLean, the American deputy receiver in the Dominican frontier customs service, via the *Connecticut:* "Town quiet. Minister Leconte will send out a committee to-morrow to interview Cacos. Following message received this afternoon. Was sent to me by Beall, United States deputy receiver of customs, by boat leaving Monte Criste at 8 p. m. September 7: 'Haitian revolutionists are attacking the town of Ouanaminthe. They desire the loyal troops to unite with them to go to the cape and attack the Americans. When the troops at Ouanaminthe refused they began a siege and then the attack. The revolutionists are being aided from this side. The Dominican authorities have taken a stand against the loyal troops, but allow the rebels privileges here. In short, the Haitian revolutionists being maintained and sustained by the Dominican Government this side. Prisoners taken by both sides are put to death in most frightful manner. Troops at Ouanaminthe are willing to turn in arms to Americans and disband if they can find a way to do so. The revolutionists of Bobo and Theodore government preventing them going to the cape for that purpose.' (Signed) McLean, deputy receiver frontier customs service. 19306. Durell."

On this same date Louis Borno and Paul Salomon were appointed ministers of foreign affairs and public works, respectively, filling vacancies in those places.

On September 10 I received the following message from Commander James F. Carter, commanding officer of the *Castine:* "Between 300 and 400 Cacos

Morne that Cacos left there for Gonaives. Small bands scattered on roads leading to Gonaives. It is reported that Cacos intend to make demonstration at Gonaives. Since visit of Zamor revolutionists pretend that opposition is to the Government and not aga'nst the United States. Previously their threats were against Americans. I have no faith in good offices of Zamor. Consider it advisable to suppress any attempt of demonstration here. No coffee coming in now. 20110. Carter."

On September 12 the Caco general, Morancy, appealed to Zamor for funds to aid his sick and wounded, on which I d'rected the commanding officer of the *Connecticut* to inform Mr. Zamor and the Cacos that we have now established a hospital in Cape Haitien and would be glad to render medical assistance to their sick and wounded. It was on th's date that I decided to send Col. Waller on a trip of inspection and reconnaissance to·St. Marc, Gonaives, and Cape Haitien. I decided to await his report before taking any action in these Caco annoyances.

It was on the 13th of September that the Amer'can consul at Santiago de Cuba reported Dr. Bobo in that place; that he was keeping watch on him and would keep me advised as to his movements.

Late on the 13th I made the following report to the Secretary of the Navy: "Cacos continue 'nterfere food supply at Gonaives. *Connecticut* reports Leconte has offered Cacos vicin ty, Cape Hait'en, 50,000 gourdes for disarmament. Leconte informed that Cacos would disarm for 60,000 gourdes. Government accepted this offer, which included surrender all arms. General amnesty, and chief proceed Port au Pr nce. This apparently only appl'ed to Cacos in vicinity Cape Haitien. Government's message to Leconte advised him come to quick terms, 'because United States forces may take offensive act'on.' American consul Santiago de Cuba reports Bobo at Santiago de Cuba. 22313. Caperton."

On September 14 a conference was held between the min'sters of foreign affairs and finance and the American chargé d'affaires and Paymaster Charles Conard, my representative, concerning which I sent the following report to the Secretary of the Navy: "In conversat on held between ministers foreign affairs and finance on one hand and American chargé d'affa'res and Paymaster Charles Conard, my representative, on the other hand it was agreed that treaty, now being translated into French, would be signed and ratified and modus vivendi entered into. In order to assure prompt ratification Ha t an Government desires 'mmediate assurances in such shape as to be effective for use in Chamber of Deputies to the effect that the United States will exerc'se its good offices to obtain a temporary loan of $1,500,000 for the Haitian Government to cover expenses; first, for approximately three months, pending settlement of details of receivership, and, second, back salaries and unpaid expenses. Of th's sum, $500,000 is estimated as necessary for covering first head and $1,000,000 for second. In connection with amount last mentioned, the Haitian Government will agree to refrain from em tting paper to value of 5,000,000 gourdes, now authorized, of which 500,000 gourdes are said to be now in trans't. In view of the fact that the collection of practically all the revenues is at present in my hands, as the receipt from these revenues after deduct on made by me in accordance Navy Department's radiogram 20018, August, will for some t'me yet not be sufficient to meet current expenses of the Ha tian Government, espec'ally as funds should remain in national bank to move coffee crops and as the Haitian Government has at present insufficient revenues ava'lable to meet these expenses, I recommend that the assurances be given as above requested. Opinion was expressed by United States representative to effect that bonded indebtedness will be consolidated into one loan, including temporary loan referred to above and back unpaid interest on public debt. Confirmation of this is requested. 23414. Caperton."

About 8 p. m., September 16, the treaty as signed by the plenipotent'aries of the United States and Haiti, Mr. R. B. Davis, American chargé d'affaires, and Mr. Louis Borno, secretary of fore'gn relations of Haiti, was forwarded to the United States. It was understood that the modus vivendi would be held in abeyance pending a resolution relative thereto to be passed by the Congress.

On September 17 I was informed by the American chargé d'affaires that the present Haitian Government had been recognized by the United States. I accordingly at 9 a. m. fired a national salute of 21 guns to the Haitian flag at the main. This salute was immediately returned from the guns by the Haitian shore battery. After this salute, in company with my staff, I called officially on the Haitian President, which I at once reported to the Secretary of the Navy. On this day the treaty was presented to the Chamber of Deputies and was referred to the committee of 11 deputies. This committee consisted of five mulattoes and six blacks, five from North Haiti, two from the Artibonite region, and four from South Haiti.

On September 17 I called the attention of the department to the fact that since the establishment of martial law conditions at Port au Prince relative to disturbances have become greatly improved, so that the city is now entirely quiet and well regulated.

It was reported on the 17th that interference with the food supply at Gonaives by the Cacos continues. The Cacos levied illegal tax on coffee outside the town and had cut off the town water supply.

On September 18 the President of Haiti and his cabinet called officially on board the *Washington* during the forenoon. Full honors according to the Navy regulations were given. The Haitian congress was formally dissolved on the 17th of September on account of its being the end of the session; on this day the President convoked an extraordinary session of both bodies to meet September 20. I was informed that on the reconvening of congress on the 20th the Senate would appoint a committee and the deputies would reappoint the committee mentioned above to consider the treaty and make recommendations to their respective bodies. It was understood that after this report the request for a modus vivendi would be passed. I was informed that the President felt confident that there would be no opposition to the ratification of the treaty, but desired a full discussion to take place in order that acceptance might be made nearly unanimous.

The report formerly received that the Dominican authorities at Dajabon were aiding the Haitian Cacos to lay seige to the loyal troops at Ouanaminthe and openly aiding the Cacos was confirmed on September 18 by the American receiver of customs at Santo Domingo city.

On September 18 I was informed by Col. Waller of the conditions at Gonaives. He reported that with my approval he would take Maj. Butler and adjutant to Gonaives on the *Osceola* on the following day; that the situation would be cleared by direction from the chiefs outside Cape Haitien; that the water and food supplies were most important for Gonaives; that our prestige was involved and that if necessary he would stop at Gonaives in person; that he believed pressure necessary on the small bands; that no offensive movement was involved, and that protection of movements at a point like Gonaives was necessary. I immediately approved this contemplated action of Col. Waller's.

Commander Carter, the commanding officer of the *Castine*, reported that on the morning of the 18th he sent a working party, accompanied by a guard, to repair the water main broken by Cacos at the reservoir near Pierrehead; that the Cacos fired on our men when landing, but were quickly dispersed to the mountains when we returned fire with machine guns; that the water pipe was then repaired; that on the afternoon of September 18 the Cacos advanced a force against our outpost at Gonaives, but retreated to the bushes upon the approach of a patrol. It is reported that the Cacos received reinforcements and it is estimated that their force now amounts to 600 men. The *Castine's* landing force is still on shore. Interference with the food supply continues and is a great hardship on the poor people.

The commanding officer of the *Castine* earlier in the day reported that a patrol of 8 men and 1 officer encountered 75 armed Cacos outside of Gonaives at 9 a. m., September 18; that the Cacos attempted to surround the patrol, who then fired a few shots; and that the Cacos returned the fire and then withdrew to the bushes. There were no casualties at this time.

I decided to await a report from Col. Waller, who was en route to Gonaives, before taking any active measures at that place which could not be taken by him on the spot under his instructions.

On September 19 the Caco chiefs failed to appear for a conference with Col. Waller, which had previously been requested by them, but instead the commanding officer of the *Connecticut*, Capt. Durell, stated that they would send a letter stating their views. On this day the water main at Gonaives, which had been repaired by our forces the day before, was again broken by the Cacos.

On this date I found it necessary, owing to conditions, to forward the following letter to the American chargé d'affaires:

The AMERICAN CHARGÉ D'AFFAIRES,
    American Legation, Port au Prince, Haiti.

SIR: I have the honor to state that reports from various towns which American forces have occupied show a dilatory attitude on the part of some Haitian officials in cooperating with the American authorities, amounting in some places to negative opposition.

I request that you bring this matter to the attention of the Haitian Government and state that it is necessary that instructions be issued immediately to all concerned to cooperate with and meet the wishes of the American authorities in the various official matters under consideration without delay.

Unless this is done it may be necessary for me to take action in order to carry on necessary business and to safeguard the interests of the Haitian people in these various localities.

I am, sir, respectfully,

W. B. CAPERTON,
    Rear Admiral, United States Navy,
Commanding United States Forces in Haiti and Haitian Waters.

The Secretary of the Navy on September 18 informed me that the State Department stated that informat on received from the British vice consul at Sanchez, Santo Domingo, indicated need of protection for lives and property at that place and Macoris, Santo Domingo, and requested me to send a vessel to investigate and report cond.tions there. I accordingly directed the *Marietta* to proceed to Sanchez to carry out these duties.

A short t me previous to September 18 I received a report from the American consul at Cape Hatien, stating that Bobo had sent a cablegram from Santiago de Cuba to a friend of his in Cape Hatien urging the Cacos to hold out.

On September 20 I rece ved the following reply from the American chargé d'affaires to my letter of the 19th, relative to the dilatory tactics of the Haitian officials in the various towns:

LEGATION OF THE UNITED STATES OF AMERICA,
    September 20, 1915.

MY DEAR ADMIRAL: I am inclosing a copy of the treaty. As you will notice, it is the French-Engl sh text, but I suppose this will serve as well for your purposes as the Engl sh-French.

With reference to your letter received this morning with regard to lack of cooperation by certain Government officials in the different ports, I have brought its contents to the attention of the min ster of foreign relations, and he assures me that he will see that the action requested be at once had.

I have the honor to be, sir, your obedient servant,

R. B. DAVIS,
    Chargé d'Affairs ad in

Upon the return of Col. Waller from his reconnaissance and inspection trip to the north and after having received h s report I made the following report to the Secretary of the Navy, describing the situat on on September 21:

"Col. Waller returned Monday from reconnaissance and inspections trip to north Ha ti. He visited and consulted with Caco chiefs in north, explained intent ons of United States in regard to Haiti. Cacos found to be interested in United States intentions, but opposed Dartiguenave government. They were told it was necessary to open railroad from Cape Haitien to Grand Riviere to secure food supply for Cape Haitien, but were opposed to departure of train. On September 18, with three squads marines, two machine guns, and wreck ng mater.al, Col. Waller opened railroad to Grand Riviere without difficulty. Cacos much excited but offered no resistance, and finally accepted situation apparently in good humor. At one point train was dera led by Cacos, where two rails had been removed where track was hidden in grass. Cacos were little threatening at this point, but four marines tak ng position to guard men working on track Cacos ran, although under immediate command of Morenci and Petion. Country people along road and at Grand Riviere greatly pleased our action. Condition Cacos miserable and not to be considered any value as troops; they now live by robbing inhabitants and market people. Same class Cacos exist vicinity Gonaives, but are much bolder, due to excitement created by their proximity. Have directed commanding officer *Connecticut* keep railroad to Bahon open and secure free access market people and coffee to Cape Haitien, 13421, Caperton."

Col. Waller brought a report from the north that it is possible the Cacos would accept the Government's proposition relative to disarmament, if they could be assured that the money involved would be handled and paid to them by the Americans. I accordingly sent Col. Waller to see the Government, in company with the American chargé d'affaires, and come to a definite understanding relative to this matter. As a result of this conference the Government agreed to guarantee payment of 50,000 gourdes to every 1,000 Cacos soldiers who would proceed to Cape Haitien or Gonalves and surrender 1,000 serviceable rifles and ammunition to the American officers at those places within a period of eight days, beginning the day this notification reached the Cacos chiefs. The Government agreed to deposit to my credit the sum of 100,000 gourdes, and more if necessary, for th's purpose.

I informed the commanding officers of the *Connecticut* and *Castine* that this money would be deposited to the credit of the collectors of customs at Cape Haitien and Gonaives; that the disbursement would be controlled by them and made personally by American officers appointed by them; that no payment would be made unless the Caco chiefs agree in writing that hereafter they and their men will not oppose the present Government or interfere in any manner whatsoever with commercial, agricultural, or any other industries, and agree to return to their homes and take up peaceful occupations, I directed the commanding officers of the *Connecticut* and *Castine* to inform the Caco chiefs that the proclamation of general amnesty made by the President would be insisted upon by the United States forces. I then definitely withdrew all pecuniary propositions made by me relative to the surrender of arms and disbanding.

Preparations were made September 20 to open the railroad from Gonaives to Poteau. When the Cacos learned of these preparations they endeavored to destroy the railroad track, and a detachment of marines sent out to induce the Cacos to desist were fired upon. The fire was returned, the Cacos retreating into the bushes, though sniping from the bushes continued at intervals. The Caco chief was warned on the morning of September 21 not to interfere with the food and water supply. I immediately afterwards gave orders that the railroad be kept open to Ennery and that such steps as necessary be taken to secure food and water supply for the town and a free entry for coffee, and that no further tampering with these necessities be permitted.

I was informed about this time that the steamer *Fauna*, due to arrive Port au Prince on September 24, had on board unsigned bank notes for the Haitian Government to the amount of 500,000 gourdes. In view of our recognition of the Dartiguenave Government I, on September 21, requested instructions as to the disposal to be made of these bank notes upon their arrival.

On the 21st Maj. Butler, with a detachment sent out to keep open the railroad, held a parley with Gen. Rameau, who agreed to withdraw his force from the neighborhood of Gonaives and promised not to interfere with the food and water supply or injure the railroad or telegraph lines.

In connection with the expected arrival of the *Fauna* with unsigned bank notes for the Haitian Government and in reply to my request for instructions in the premises, I received the following from the Secretary of the Navy:

"15221. State Department has sent full instructions to chargé directing him consult with you. Hold gourdes for present and be guided by State Department wish as expressed in instructions to chargé. Acknowledge. 17022. Daniels."

On September 23 I learned that the Cacos at Cape Haitien were disagreeing among themselves and holding out for a much greater sum of money than they had been promised by the Haitian Government through Charles Leconte.

On the same date I learned that Rameau was informed that he and his chiefs would be held personally responsible for any further interference with the water and food supplies or the interruption of railroad and telegraphic communication or the collection of taxes on coffee or other products. Rameau promised to prevent further interference and to keep his men beyond Poteau.

The Haitian Senate met on this day in closed session and appointed the following committee to study the treaty: MM. Fouchard Martineau, Edward Pouget, Morpeau, Edmond Roumain, St. Lafontant, Beauharnais, J. Francois, and Dr. Jaenty.

On September 24, 1915, I informed the commanding officer of the *Connecticut* that I desired trains to be sent frequently on the Grande Riviere, allowing detachments to remain at Grande Riviere over night occasionally, and that detachments should visit Limonade, Quartier, Morin, Haut de Cap, Plain du Nord, and other accessible towns. These scouting operations were in no way in the nature of offensive operations, but were necessary to insure the free entry of food and other supplies into the town of Cape Haitien, and, in addition, to give our forces a better knowledge of the surrounding country. On this day the steamship *Fauna* arrived at Port au Prince in the afternoon, having on board 10 cases of bank notes consigned to the Haitian Government. In accordance with instructions from the Navy Department, I directed that these bank notes be held in the customhouse pending disposition in accordance with instructions from the State Department to the American chargé d'affaires.

In view of the disquieting rumors received from Port-de-Paix, I directed the commander of the military forces at that place, on September 25, to report how far scouting operations had been conducted, and directed him to warn the Caco chiefs that interference with the food and natives must cease, authorizing him to take necessary action, but warned him to not fire unless fired upon.

On September 26 the Caco chief, Morenci, and Petion gave Charles Zamor and Eirbert St. Noel power of attorney to go to Port au Prince to see President Dartiguenave to negotiate conditions of disarmament, giving them full power to arrange conditions and pledged themselves to abide thereby. The commanding officer of the *Connecticut* informed Morenci and Petion that he would send out patrols, but with no offensive or hostile intent. On the next morning the commanding officer of the *Connecticut* and the American consul each received warnings and defiant letters not to attempt to patrol the Plain du Nord. The commanding officer of the *Connecticut* replied that he would continue to patrol but without hostile intent.

At 6 a. m. the 26th of September two patrols, about 40 men each, were sent out from Cape Haitien, the first to go to the town of Plain du Nord via Haut du Cap; the second to Haut du Cap via Petit Anse. The patrols had orders to push through to take no offensive action, but to defend themselves if attacked. The second patrol was ambushed and attacked between Petit Anse and Carrefour de Trous. They forded the Haut du Cap River and returned to Cape Haitien about 12.30 p. m. with 4 wounded, all horses having been killed. The commanding officer of the *Connecticut* stated that the work of this patrol was excellent. The first patrol met opposition at the Caco outpost, but went on toward Haut du Cap. About 8.30 a. m. firing became general near Haut du Cap, supports consisting of Col. Cole and marines were sent to reinforce the patrols, and the remainder of the *Connecticut's* landing force was put ashore.

I informed the commanding officer of the *Connecticut* that the operations at Cape Haitien were approved and that the *Eagle* would sail that night from Port au Prince with Col. Waller and staff for Cape Haitien.

The patrolling in the vicinity of Cape Haitien was not considered in the light of offensive operations, but was necessary to insure the free entry of food supplies to the town of Cape Haitien. In view of the attacks made upon our forces, I considered that no let up in patrolling could be permitted until the Cacos voluntarily agreed to disarm or until they were driven from the Plain du Nord.

At 9 p. m. September 25 information was received that the Cacos near Dessalines were stealing and pillaging residents. Capt. Underwood, in temporary command of the Twenty-fourth Company, at St. Marc, was directed to proceed to Petit Riviere de l'Artibonite with 50 men, all mounted, on the morning of September 26, to protect residents against Cacos and bandits. At 3 p. m. September 26 Capt. Underwood reported having arrived at Petit Riviere and engaged the Cacos, estimated at 150. Sergt. John Platt, of the Twenty-fourth Company of marines, was killed; no wounded. The number of Caco casualties is reported as being three killed and nine wounded. This force occupied a good position in Petit Riviere for the night, the Cacos retreating to the hills toward Dessalines.

Together with Col. Waller and our respective staffs, on September 25 I attended the Te Deum mass, celebrated in honor of the election of President Dartiguenave, and afterwards attended a reception at the palace. This was also attended by the American chargé d'affaires, the Cuban chargé d'affaires, and the Dominican consul general.

In connection with the disposition of the unsigned bank notes, amounting to 500,000 gourdes, previously mentioned, I sent the following to the Secretary of the Navy on September 26:

"The Haitian Government being desirous that the 500,000 gourdes now in customhouse ex steamer *Fauna* be issued, the following plan has been devised by Paymaster Conrad: National Bank of Haiti to sign notes, thus issuing the first installment of its own circulation in accordance with its contract. The required reserve to be set aside from funds in hand. The notes so signed to be turned over to the Haitian Government immediately after ratification of the convention. Rate of exchange of bank circulation being 5 to 1. The delivery of these notes will constitute the loan of $100,000 by bank mentioned in State Department dispatches to chargé d'affaires. Bank approved this plan and is cabling New York to-morrow for necessary authorization. Bank in conference with Conrad regarding further steps for retirement of Government paper and nickel currency, to be undertaken promptly if above plan is carried into effect. It is believed that the issue of notes under the conditions stated will satisfy the Haitian Government, since it is to the loss of prestige resulting from their suppression that they really object. Will also indicate desire of bank to assist in settling difficulty and to carry out contract. This matter has not been discussed with Haitian Government, and if plan is approved it is requested that chargé d'affaires be authorized by State Department to negotiate in conjunction with Conrad, as my representative, on that basis. This message was prepared without knowledge of chargé d'affaires' dispatch to State Department. 23525.

"CAPERTON."

The *Eagle* arrived at Cape Haitien at 9 p. m. the 27th of September with Col. Waller and his staff.

On September 29 I received the following report from Col. Waller and Capt. Durell, commanding officer of the *Connecticut*, concerning the agreement entered into, and signed between them and the Caco chiefs at Quartier Morin: "In accordance with agreement by Haitian president and cabinet, made in personal interview with me, agreement approved by you, I have to-day in conference with the Cacos chief, concluded following agreement: Cacos of Haiti will disarm immediately. All arms to be deposited at Quartier Morin as soon as possible. Cacos chiefs submit to the Government of Haiti, as represented by Dartiguenave, the president. Cacos delegates will visit Port au Prince, consult with president. No money transaction involved now. We stand ready to affirm former agreement made by Leconte of 50,000 gourdes. Nothing asked. Cacos withdraw to-day all outposts and guards as evidence of good faith and country is free to traffic. Agree that after this all armed bodies of Cacos shall be treated as bandits. This agreement effective after to-morrow. We agree to sustain the general amnesty proclamation. No arrests for political offenses committed since institution of Dartiguenave government. All armed opposition after date of this agreement to be treated as act of bandit. Cacos chiefs ask that the appropriation heretofore made for the army be diverted to public works. Agreed we urge that upon Government. Cacos ask representation in constabulary police and civil government. We will see to the first two propositions and urge upon Government the wisdom of the latter, especially in locality. I have asked that the many wounded Cacos be sent in for treatment in hospital here, we to pay for treatment. This is voluntary and outside of any agreement in conference. Day after to-morrow I shall visit ―――― and chief at Quartier Morin. Charles Zamor has been invaluable in all dealings with chiefs and has lived up to his promise to us. Request that money to be sent at once for payment quanaminthe troops. 17029. Waller Durell."

On the 29th I addressed a communication to the American consul at Santiago requesting any further information he might have regarding Dr. Rosalvo Bobo, and in reply was informed on September 30 that Bobo was still at that place and under close surveillance.

In view of the fact that the Haitian Government did not wish to enter into any joint agreement with the bank regarding the issue of the 500,000 gourdes, the plan proposed in my radiogram 23525 can not be accepted. I therefore on September 29 addressed the following message to the Secretary of the Navy: "As the Haitian Government does not wish to enter into any joint agreement with bank regarding issue of 500,000 gourdes, no such plan can be accepted. At the same time the Government claims to be seriously embarrassed, having counted definitely on using the bills now withheld by me. Need for immediate funds seems to be real. If the State Department does not intend to release bills without condition, nor provide loan prior to ratification of treaty, am I authorized to furnish Haitian Government such funds as can be spared from customs receipts? 22229. Caperton."

On October 1, I received a radiogram from the Secretary of the Navy regarding the organization of the Haitian constabulary, which reads as follows: "It is intended to proceed with organizing of Haitian constabulary. As soon as practicable report to department by radio number of men considered necessary to form both urban police and rural constabulay; also number, makes, and condition of arms in Haiti available for use of constabulary. Submit any suggestions that you can regarding mounts, houses, feed, and clothing, this force, and any additional suggestions as to comparative cost of this force and that formerly spent by Haitian Government on army and police force. It is proposed that this force officered from Marine Corps, including sergeants. 10001. Daniels."

To show the unreliability and duplicity of the Haitian Caco the following incident is reported. Gen. Christian Fish called upon me aboard the flagship on October 2 and showed a letter dated September 27, which was signed by Morenci and Petion, giving Fish full power to settle any question in regard to the Caco situation. I informed him that Col. Waller was conducting negotiations in regard to the Caco situation, but inquired upon what conditions the Cacos would agree to disband and remain peaceful. He stated that the only condition acceptable to the Cacos would be the removal of President Dartiguenave, and that without the removal of Dartiguenave from the presidency, there could be no peace in Haiti. I informed Gen. Fish that Dartiguenave had been elected after a free election; that revolution against the Dartiguenave government would not be tolerated; and that in case of further disturbance, the Cacos chiefs would be held personally responsible; that it was not the desire or intention of the United States to shed the blood of the common people of Haiti, but that no revolutionary movements could be tolerated. Gen. Fish informed me that negotiations in the north were being carried on only to gain time until the result of his negotiations in Port au Prince could be reported there. I did not tell Gen. Fish of the agreement between Col. Waller and the Cacos chiefs, signed on October 1. I informed Col. Waller of this interview.

In reply to my message to Col. Waller concerning Gen. Fish I received the following: " Your (17002) request provost marshal arrest Christian Fish immediately. He has no power with anyone. Hold Fish incommunicado. Waller. 00403. Olmsted."

This request was complied with.

The fact that Christian Fish presented to me credentials from the cacos leaders, Morenci and Petion, which, from the information received from Col. Waller, were not bona fide; the threats made by him of continued disturbances against the Dartiguenave government and his reported affilations with men hostile to that government and the American occupation convinced me that Fish was a dangerous character to have at large at this time. I therefore directed that he be confined incommunicado until the reutrn of Col. Waller. In ordering this confinement I directed that Fish be allowed all the comforts the circumstances would permit.

President Dartiguenave on October 3 requested an interview with the American chargé d'affaires and my representative, Lieut. E. G. Oberlin. He informed them that his government was practically without funds, and that with no funds to meet the current expenses the government could not continue and he would be forced to resign. In view of this I sent the following radiogram approving the recommendations contained in the dispatch of the American chargé d'affaires of this date, which I also quote: " Chargé consulted with me before sending his telegram of to-day, and in view of all the facts as they appear here I approve request and consider Haitian Government should have immediate financial assistance. Will report more fully to-morrow and submit estimates of receipts and expenditures. 21303. Caperton."

" October 3, 5 p. m. This morning at 10, and before receipt of yours October 2, 5 p. m., I had an interview with the President personally at his request. He stated that he had asked for this interview in order to ascertain what steps he could take under existing conditions; that the Haitian Government following its plan to pay back salaries and thereby strengthen its position before the people and relieve suffering now finds itself entirely without funds, and inquired as to the disposition of the United States Government to assist them in this financial crisis. I told him that I expected instructions as to the matter and would advise him on receipt thereof.

"After receiving yours October 2, 5 p. m., I told the President that, as before stated, funds would be immediately available upon ratification of the treaty. The President seemed utterly discouraged and pointed out once more that the delay was not due to any lack of effort by himself or his cabinet; that withholding of funds only gave another weapon to the opposition, and that if the United States Government persists in withholding all funds ratification becomes so difficult that he and his cabinet will resign rather than attempt the fight in the senate under this handicap.

"I fear that I have failed in my previous reports to make perfectly understood the existing situation, which is as follows: The vote on ratification by the deputies will take place probably to-morrow, the committe having unanimously recommended ratification. Under the mode of procedure, after ratification by congressmen, the treaty goes before the senate, and there it is referred to a senate committee, who, after considering, submit a report, which is then printed and distributed, and three days allowed for consideration before discussion on the floor of the senate begins. Therefore ratification can not be expected before the latter part of next week.

"The President and cabinet are using every possible effort to secure ratification and seem confident of securing the same if not embarrassed financially. The Haiten Government realizes that such ratification is absolutely necessary for the welfare of Haiti. Opposition in the senate is strong, due to the fact that many senators are unscrupulous politicians or fanatics and wish either to embarrass the United States by nonratification or to overthrow the present administration, hoping to secure possible personal gain thereby. Pressure is also being brought to bear by outside interests which desire a continuance of past conditions for reasons of financial gain and which will be glad to see the present administration which is already reorganized and supported by the United States forced to resign.

"It is most important that the present administration remain in power as it is not believed that one more favorable to the United States could be obtained, and in view of all facts as they appear here that a military government would probably have to be established should this Government fall.

"Inasmuch as it is necessary to secure a treaty ratified before any definite financial plan can be formulated or permanent peace and prosperity assured in Haiti it would seem advisable to support and maintain the present administration, which will fall unless the slight financial assistance which they have requested is immediately available, and further, the progress made during the last two months will be lost. Although funds collected from customs have been expended for the first three purposes named in the department's instructions as to the use of money collected, not one cent has been turned over to the Haitien Government for living expenses, which expenses have been met by use of gourdes then on hand and now expended. In view of the importance and the extreme urgency of the case it is recommended that Admiral Caperton be instructed to turn over needed sums out of customs receipts not necessary for the customs service, constabulary, and public works. Request earliest possible decision and reply. Davis"

In a report made to the Secretary of the Navy on October 4, after outlining total customs receipts in Haiti to September 30, and quoting expenditures for various public works, etc., I reiterated my concurrence in the recommendation of the American chargé d'affaires, that I be allowed to turn over to the Dartiguenave government such funds from the customs receipts on hand and unobligated as I might consider necessary for its support, in view of the financial crisis of the Dartiguenave government, the loss of prestige of United States should that government fall, and the inevitable detrimental effect upon the treaty the failure of that government would have had.

On October 4 the American consul at Santiago de Cuba reported that Dr. Rosalvo Bobo had left that place for Guantanamo.

On October 5 Cape Haitien and vicinity was reported as quiet, but the report stated that certain minor Cacos chiefs were still collecting taxes on food products entering Cape Haitien and that unarmed outposts were maintained outside that town by Morenci. The detachment commander at Cape Haitien and warned Morenci that these outposts must be removed, and that if not removed a patrol would be sent out to arrest the men in charge of the outposts.

I reported to the department that the chamber of deputies met on October 6 to consider the adoption of the treaty and voted to ratify it without change, the vote being 15 in favor and 6 against ratification.

On October 7 I informed Col. Waller that the matter of bringing the commission of Cacos chiefs to Port au Prince at that time was left to his discretion. I further informed him that Gen. Christian Fish was still under arrest and incommunicado. On this day the commandant of the naval station at Guantanamo reported that Dr. Rosalvo Bobo arrived at Guantanamo on October 4 and left the same day for Santiago de Cuba; the commandant informed the American consul at Santiago de Cuba of this fact. The mayor at Guantanamo had received instructions from the secretary of the interior to keep in touch with Bobo and to detail policemen to watch him while there.

On October 8 Zamor, Marpoint, Noel, Etlene, Mehu, and Belleirie, left Cape Haitien at 2 p. m. for Port au Prince via Plaisance on horseback. This commission represented the Cacos in the negotiations with the Haitien Government. Belleir.e was said to be a member of the chamber of deputies.

Col. Waller on October 8, with his staff, returned to Port au Prince from Cape Haiten.

On this date the American consul at Santiago de Cuba reported that Dr. Rosalvo Bobo left that place for Jamaica on the preceding night.

Upon the arrival of Col. Waller he reported north Haiti quiet; that movements for relieving Government troops at Ouanaminthe were well under way; and that he had provided for feeding and transporting them to homes.

In view of the recent disturbances in the north; of the fact that for a number of years the center of unrest had been in the vic.nity from Cape Haitien to the Dominican border; and of the reports that arms were being received from Santo Domingo; and that coffee and other products were being smuggled across the border from Haiti to Santo Domingo, I decided to occupy Fort Liberte and Ounanaminthe. The Eleventh Company of Marines, wh.ch were divided between Fort Liberte and Ounaminthe, was ordered to Ounanaminthe, and on October 8 I sent the Fifteenth Company of Marines from Port au Prince to Fort Liberte on board the *Nashville*. The *Nashville* sailed for Cape Ha.tien and Fort Liberte at 3 p. m. that date.

In reference to my message to the department of October 3, in which I recommended approval of the request of the American chargé d'affaires of the State Department of the same date that immediate financial assistance be extended to the Haitien Government, to which message the Secretary of the Navy on October 5 made the following reply: " 23103. Cable has been sent this date to 'chargé with full instructions. You are authorized to furnish Haitien Government weekly amount necessary to meet current expenses. Use funds collected Haitien customs. Question payment back salary w.ll be settled by department immediately after ratification of treaty. Report what weekly expenditure will be necessary under these instructions. What is full amount back salaries now unpaid? Acknowledge. 22004. Dan.els."

On October 9, in reply to these instructions given me by the Secretary of the Navy, I sent the following radiogram to the department: " Estimates submitted by Haitien Government for expenditures classed as absolutely necessary approximate $150,000 per month. This does not include salaries of President and cabinet and other expenditures of like character. These figures have been gone over in detail but are difficult to check accurately. It is recommended that a weekly allowance of $25,000 be made. This is all that customs receipts can assure for the present, in view of expenditures contemplated for constabulary, public works, etc. 18309. Caperton."

With reference to the 100,000 gourdes deposited to my credit by the Haitian Government and forwarded by me to the collector of customs at Cape Haitien and Gonaives for disbursement by American officers to the Cacos for turning in arms, etc., according to the agreement made with them, this money having been forwarded to the collectors of customs at Cape Haitien and Gonaives on September 21, I on October 5 addressed a letter to the National Bank of Haiti, as follows:

OCTOBER 5, 1915.

NATIONAL BANK OF HAITI,
Port au Prince, Haiti.

GENTLEMEN: You are requested to retransfer to the Haitian Government the sum of one hundred thousand (100,000) gourdes, recently deposited by them to my account under the heading "Arms and ammunition."

Very truly, yours,

W. B. CAPERTON,
Rear Admiral, United States Navy.

None of this money had been expended for the purpose intended, as the project had failed.

With reference to the loyal Government troops who had been left at Ouanaminthe, as there had been no means available for them to return to their homes I took the following steps to relieve them, their situation having been reported to me as most deplorable. On October 4 I ordered the Haitian gunboat *Nord Alexis* to be coaled from the U. S. S. *Hector* and to proceed to Cape Haitien with orders to report to the senior officer present at that place for the purpose of transporting the loyal Government troops at Ouanaminthe to Port au Prince. The *Nord Alexis* sailed at 9 a. m. October 4 and arrived at Cape Haitien at 8 a. m. October 5 and reported as directed. On October 6 Col. Waller arrived at Fort Liberte with the loyal Haitian troops, numbering about 370, where they were to embark on the *Nord Alexis*. In reply to a request for money for pay due these troops I had on October forwarded to the collector of customs at Cape Haitien for payment to them five weeks' pay, 10,000 gourdes, and for rationing them on the *Nord Alexis* 600 gourdes. Before leaving Ouanaminthe for Fort Liberte it had been necessary to clothe nearly all of them, as they were ragged and many of them naked. The *Nord Alexis* with the loyal Haitian troops on board sailed from Fort Liberte on October 9, touched at Cape Haitien, and arrived at Port au Prince on October 10, where they were disembarked and ordered to proceed to their homes in and near Port au Prince.

During October 11 reports from the north showed that rifles and ammunition were be ng turned in at various places in the north and that at other places the Cacos were failing to live up to their agreement.

On October 11, in view of the official request of the Haitian Government for information on the following subjects, (a) Are salaries of all customs employees being paid by the United States forces, and if so, have these salaries been increased over the salaries paid them by the Haitian Government and to what extent; and (b) the percentage cost of collecting customs duties for the different ports, I directed the administrator of customs to furnish this information in the following letter:

No. 11055–15.

OCTOBER 11, 1915.

From: Commander Cruiser Squadron, United States Atlantic Fleet, Commanding United States Forces in Haiti and Haitian Waters.
To: Administrator of customs.
Subject: Customs administration.

1. The Haitian Government has officially requested information regarding the following subjects:

(a) Are salaries of all customs employees being paid by the United States forces, and if so, have these salaries been increased over the salaries paid by the Haitian Government and to what extent.

(b) The percentage cost of collecting customs duties for the different ports.

2. You will please submit at the earliest practicable date a written report embodying this information for Port au Prince. The reports for other ports to be submitted as soon as you can obtain the necessary information.

3. In case the percentage cost can not be furnished at this time, submit a report of the amounts expended for the collecting of customs at the various ports since they have been under the charge of American officials, together with the total amount collected at such ports.

W. B. CAPERTON.

On October 12 I received the following message from the Navy Department:

"Report immediately what in your opinion is cause of delay in ratifying treaty. What steps should be taken to accomplish early ratification. Acknowledge. 21011.

"BENSON, *Acting.*"

There is no doubt but that there was active opposition to the ratification of this treaty, and, in addition to the delays caused by the legislative procedure, this opposition endeavored to prevent the treaty from being ratified and employed various means to delay its being acted upon. I believed that the Haitian Government was using its utmost endeavor to expedite the ratification of the treaty, and considered that any open interference in its methods would be productive of evil results. I informed the department of my opinion on this subject at 3 a. m. October 12, as follows:

"10001. Cause of delay in ratifying treaty due to legislative procedure and discussion in senate. Considerable opposition in senate due outside influences and selfish motives. Believe opposition can only employ dilatory tactics to delay vote but can not block ratification, as opposition much weakened by large majority vote of deputies. Haitian Government taking all steps possible to hasten ratification and expects favorable senate vote first part of next week. Believe for the present we should only support present Government awaiting senate action. Senate meets Tuesday, Thursday, and Saturday. 03012.

"CAPERTON."

In compliance with the department's radiogram No. 10001, regarding the organization of the gendarmerie, on October 12. I submitted the following recommendations in a message to the Secretary of the Navy:

"10001. Submit following recommendations regarding constabulary, gendarmerie, for Haiti:

"1· (a) Gendarmerie to consist of 1,530 men, officered by 55 marine officers, including sergeants. The gendarmerie will perform the duty of both urban police and rural constabulary. (b) There are no arms in Haiti suitable for this purpose. (c) Annual cost estimated, as follows: Pay including marine officers and sergeants as officers, $351,200; clerical force, $9,780; uniforms, $40,000; forage and remounts, $22,769; ammunition and target practice, $12,000; administration expenses, $43,099; total, $478,848.

"2. The saving during the first year on pay rations, and other estimated expenses of personnel will cover the necessary appropriations of barracks, and also for the first equipment, as the recruiting up to the full strength will take several months.

"3· This organization provides for two marine officers for each company and Haitian officers to be assigned when they are properly instructed in their duties, the number of marine officers to be gradually reduced as the Haitian officers are substituted.

"4· The cost of the gendarmerie, as proposed, will be about $40,000 less than Ha'tian budget for 1914–15 for army and police.

"5· The pay recommended for the American officers and gendarmerie is as follows: American officers to receive following additional monthly pay: Commandant, $250; assistant commandant, $200; quartermaster and paymaster, $200; assistant quartermaster and pymaster, $150; directors, $200; inspectors $150; medical officers, $150; captain of company, $150; lieutenant of company, $100. Haitian officers and men, monthly pay as follows: Captains, $90; lieutenants, $60; first sergeants, $15; sergeants, $20; corporals, $15; privates, $10. Enlisted men to receive ration of 10 cents per day. In addition to pay and rations, each enlisted man will have certain clothing allowances. 14412.

" CAPERTON."

On October 13 I received the department's authorization to establish a weekly allowance of $25,000 to the Haitian Government for the present, which reads as follows:

"18309. You are authorized to establish weekly allowance of $25,000 for the present as recommended. Acknowledge. 11013.

" DANIELS."

On October 12 the delegation, composed of Charles Zamor and five others representing the Cacos, arrived at Port au Prince.

On October 14 I reported the situation to the Secretary of the Navy as follows:

"Maj. Butler with detachment 50 men returned to Fort Liberte, having scouted to Coupe Michel to Le Trou to Fort Liberte. Coupe Michel is high hill near Le Trou and former Caco stronghold. Found no Cacos and met with no opposition. Seized and destroyed 116 rifles at Terrior Rouge. Caco delegation accompanied by Col. Waller was received by President Dartiguenave and cabinet to-day. Meeting amicable but no definite negotiations entered into. Committee appointed by Senate to report on treaty has expressed desire to reopen treaty negotiations. Cabinet to-day declined to discuss treaty with committee, and it is understood Government will endeavor to force committee to report at early date even if report is unfavorable desiring to bring treaty up before entire Senate where Government believes ratification will be voted. 22114.

" CAPERTON."

On October 14 the administrator of customs submitted a reply to my letter No. 11055–15, of October 11, 1915, in which I directed him to report the difference between the salaries of customs employees under United States supervision and salaries formerly paid by the Haitian Government and the percentage of cost for collecting customs duties. I transmitted this information to the Haitian Government informally. The administrator's letter follows:

OCTOBER 13, 1915.

From: Administrator of Customs.
To: Commander Cruiser Squadron, United States Atlantic Fleet commanding United States Forces in Haiti and Haitian waters.
Subject: Customs Administration.
Reference: (a) Commander Cruiser Squadron's letter No. 11055–15, of October, 11, 1915.

1. The salaries of all employees in the Haitian customhouses conducted by the United States are paid from custom revenues. While direct comparison between salaries paid by the Haitian Government and salaries paid under American administration is difficult, the following relative to Port au Prince will be of interest:

	Haitian.	United States.
Number of employees	86	55
Monthly pay (in gourdes)	10,425	7,805
(Gourdes calculated at 6.20.)		
Average per employee (in gourdes)	121.22	141.91

2. It is not believed that figures based on one month, during which the system was in course of development, will be found of much value. So far as they go, however, it would appear that while the total pay under American administration is less, the average per employee is higher, fewer men being employed. It was found that many employees under the Haitian Government received merely nominal pay, their income being increased by fees advanced to them by merchants dealing with the customhouse. These fees have all been abolished and rates of pay in some cases have been raised to allow a fair wage to the employees concerned.

3. The percentage of cost for collecting duties at Port au Prince for the month of September was 5.1 per cent. This cost, however, included items properly chargeable to capital account, covering repairs and improvements to property.

4. Reports on other ports will be made as soon as practicable.

CHARLES CONRAD.

In connection with conditions in the north, on October 15 I received the following report from Col. Cole:

"Sullivan returned this morning; reports resumption cultivation along route; quiet generally; priests Le Trou and Limonade state that people are generally returning to their homes; roads beyond Limonade generally in better condition than this side, though in wet season in present condition will probably be impassable for motor trucks; believed that if Government will adopt general repair and construction roads immediate improvements in general condition will follow. Campbell returned from Quartier-Morin new route: reports resumption cultivation and attitude inhabitants very friendly; have received some reports from Grande Riviere that some pillaging and enforced recruiting going on in vicinity St. Suzanne; am sending Campbell with 62 men automatic special train to-morrow morning to operate in section around and beyond Grande Riviere. Butler reports all quiet but no rifles turned in Fort Liberte. 14015.

"COLE."

On October 15 the report of the board ordered to submit a report on the organization of a constabulary for Haiti was submitted to me.

On October 16 rumors in Port au Prince were rife to the effect that the Government would force action in the Senate on the treaty during the coming week, regardless of the report of the committee. No definite information on this subject was obtainable.

On October 18 I received the department's radiogram stating that Capt. E. L. Beach, United States Navy, had been ordered to command the U. S. S. *Washington* and would arrive at Guantanamo, Cuba, October 22, 1915.

On October 19 the Haitian Senate convened and reelected Steven Archer as president of the senate. No action in regard to the treaty was taken. The reelection of Mr. Archer by vote of 21 to 17 was regarded as showing that the treaty would be ratified, as Mr. Archer was known to be in favor of the treaty.

I informed the Secretary of the Navy on October 19 that Col. Cole was unable to communicate with the Caco chiefs at Fort Capois on account of heavy rains. He left a letter to be forwarded to the local chiefs informing the Cacos at Fort Capois that if they remained under arms they would be treated as bandits. The regular local government in charge at that place was favorable to America. Further, at the request of the Haitian Government and upon the advice of the American chargé d'affaires, I authorized the payment from custom funds of current months' salaries to senators and deputies, amount allotted being $35,000.

The *Connecticut* on October 20 sent a boat expedition to Petit Port Francais on the west coast of Cape Haitien and arrested M connor, the leader of a gang of bandits that had just previously robbed and pillaged at Fort Francais, and turned them over to Col. Cole for trial.

On October 21 I received the following message from the Secretary of the Navy:

"Information from State Department that Governor Monti Cristi, S. D., has informed Dominican Government that armed Haitian discontents crossed frontier near Dajabon and had encounter with frontier guard. Several Dominicans killed. Dominican Government has ordered authorities capture and intern all Haitians who cross frontier and for author.ties to cooperate with military forces of United States. Acknowledge. 13020.

"DANIELS."

On October 20 I sent the following message to the Secretary of the Navy and C. in C.:

"Patrolling vicinity Cape Haitian Ouanaminthe, Fort Liberte, cont'nued. *Nashville* arrived Cape Haitien from cruise to Mole St. Nicholas, Port de Paix, Fond la Grange, having investigated conditions these ports. Situation unchanged elsewhere. 22220.

"CAPERTON."

On October 22 I sent the following message to the Secretary of the Navy and C. in C.:

"Detachment commanded by Capt. Campbell fired on at 1 a. m. Friday, at Bahon; fire returned; known casualties, one Caco chief killed; none of our men hit. 22022.

"CAPERTON."

Also forwarded the following message to the Secretary of the Navy and C. in C.:

"To day chargé d'affaires received assurances from president of Senate and minister of foreign affairs that Senate committee report will be submitted Tuesday. In case report is not received Tuesday Dartiguenave states that steps will be taken to force action by committee. Press and public criticizing Senate for delay. Inasmuch as I have received continual assurance that majority in Senate favors treaty, have refrained from taking any steps which might appear as using force to secure ratification, believing it to best interests of both countries that treaty be ratified after full discussion following Haitian rules of procedure. 22122.

"CAPERTON."

Col. Cole reported on October 24 that patrolling in the vicinity of Bahon and Grand Riviere was being continued. A patrol from Bahon was fired on the preceding afternoon while returning from that place, but there was no casualties to our forces. He further stated that it was proposed to garrison Le Trou and then to systematically clear the district in the vicinity of St. Suzanne and Bahon of bandits then operating in that section. This was reported to the Secretary of the Navy and C. in C.

On October 25 marines from the *Connecticut* were sent at 2 p. m. to Bahon to reinforce garrison; the first company of the *Connecticut* bluejackets left for Grand Riviere at 4.30 p. m.; second company *Connecticut* bluejackets had been landed at Cape Haitien.

Orders were issued on October 25 by the governor of Monti Cristi, Santo Domingo, that all Haitians be returned immediately to Haiti.

On October 25 I was assured that the Senate committee would that week submit a report favorable to the treaty, but with interpretations of certain articles. I was informed that the Senate would vote for the ratification of the treaty without change, regardless of the committee's report. The public opinion in Port au Prince seemed to be very much in favor of ratificat.on at an early date. The press was favorable to ratification, and within the last few days posters had been put up in various parts of the city, censoring the Senate for delaying the rat.fication.

Capt. E. L. Beach, Un.ted States Navy, arrived at Port au Prince at noon. October 25, on the *Osceola* with orders from the Navy Department to command the *Washington*.

On- October 26 Col. Cole returned from Grande Riviere. That afternoon patrol between that point and Bahon were fired on several times to-day, but always from hills.des considerable distance. Yesterday much of the firing was from western s.de of railroad; to-day almost entirely from hill to east; practically all firing has been beyond kilometer 30, except night attack on Grande Riviere. Conditions of unrest reported from time to time, but personally have seen nothing to indicate it except in local.ties reported on heretofore. There is much clearing of ground going on, and yesterday the former minister of war for Bobo sent h.s distillery apparatus to h s place, about kilometer 12, to resume operat.ons, it having been in store in Cape Ha.tien for some months for security. Patrol to Milot yesterday and to Quartier-Morin to-day reported conditions normal.

On October 26 I sent the following message to the Secretary of the Navy and C. in C.: "To-day President Dartiguenave aga.n personally assured me that treaty will be ratified and stated that he had fully expected ratificat on th.s week, but that in view of more favorable attitude of senate committee he had cons.dered it wise to wa.t a little longer before forcing action. States that under any c.rcumstances will secure ratification next week. Caperton."

On October 27 Col. Waller left Port au Prince at 7 a. m. on board the *Osceola* for Cape Haitian.

As I had heard nothing from my radiogram No. 22019 relative to the relief of the financial conditions in Haiti I, on October 27, informed the department by radio that unless otherwise directed I proposed to allow customs funds in excess of current needs to be used by the National Bank of Haiti for the purchase of New York drafts, thus facilitating shipments of coffee. This would result in transferring part of my credit to New York, subject to 15 days' order. This step was necessary in order that funds might be available for moving the coffee crop, and unless this or equivalent steps were taken the customs funds, which were kept apart in the bank, would soon accumulate to the extent that it would seriously disturb economical conditions in the country.

"22019. Unless otherwise directed I propose to allow customs funds in excess of current needs to be used by national bank for the purchase of New York drafts, thus facilitating shipments of coffee. This would result in transferring part of my credit to New York subject to 15 days' order. Unless this or equivalent steps be taken funds will be hoarded in bank seriously disturbing economic conditions. Request acknowledgment. 23027. Caperton."

On October 19, in order to temporarily relieve the situation in regard to foreign exchange, I suggested to the department that New York representatives of the National Bank of Ha.ti be allowed to deposit $26,000 in the subtreasury and the pay officer of the *Washington* be authorized to deposit the same amount in the bank here, this money to be used by the bank to cash New York drafts, which were then discounted at 2½ per cent. I requested permission to render assistance later by allowing the customs funds, which were then being segregated and held entirely subject to my orders, to be used for th's purpose. I therefore sent the following message: "After consultation with Haitian syndicate of exchange and later with national bank find that foreign exchange situation likely to become serious. New York drafts now discounted 2½ per cent. The reason for th!s is that the demands for foreign drafts usually experienced this season of year does not exist owing to the probable nonpayment of interest on foreign debt. Coffee exporters for the most part are compelled this year to sell drafts on New York to realize on the crop and will suffer considerable loss owing to the discount mentioned. Situation can be temporarily relieved if New York representatives of the bank be allowed to deposit $26,000 in subtreasury and the pay officer of the *Washington* be authorized by radio to deposit same amount in bank here, thus furnishing funds to cash New York drafts. Sufficient funds aboard Washington to do this and meet other demands. Can assistance be rendered later from customs funds, which funds are now segregated and held entirely subject to my order. 22019. Caperton."

On October 28, on account of the disturbances in certain sections in the north, it had become necessary to take action to clear the country of the marauding bands that were pillaging and disturbing conditions in that vicinity. If these bands had been allowed to continue their actions unchecked, the good accomplished by the pacification of the Cacos would not be lasting.

On October 28, in answer to the department's radiogram requesting information as to the total amount of United States currency on board vessels at Port au Prince available for deposit in the National City Bank to help out the exchange situation, I replied that $26,000 could be spared.

Due to the failing health of the chargé d'affaires, Mr. R. B. Davis, on October 28 I found it necessary to send the following message to the Secretary of the Navy: "I feel it to be my duty to report that Chargé d'Affaires Davis has been in failing health for six months and is now physically unfit for duty, due to persistent pus infection resulting in successive abscesses and marked lowering of resistance which do not respond to most active treatment. Loss of weight more than 30 pounds. Ten days ago a rapidly spreading blood poison started up right arm, requiring 24 hours of heroic treatment before it was checked. Medical officers believe it to be imperative that he proceed north at once to enable him regain resistance to disease. Recommend he be ordered home by first steamer, leaving about October 31, and that Surg. May be directed to accompany him, not awaiting report of relief. 14528. Caperton."

On October 29 the Haitian Senate did not meet, as there was no quorum present.

In reply to my message of the 28th relative to Mr. Davis going north on account of his health I received the following message: "14528 approved. Provided Charvé d'Affaires Davis comes north d rect, may report by telegram to Bureau Navigation on arrival. 13229. Daniels."

In view of the information contained in the State Department's cable of October 28, 7 p. m., to the legat on, that the Navy Department would direct me to des gnate an officer to take charge of the legation upon the departure of the chargé d'affaires, I designated Lieut. E. G. Oberlin for this duty, as stated in the following letter:

PORT AU PRINCE, HAITI, *October 29, 1915.*

From: Commander cru ser squadron, United States Atlantic Fleet, commanding United States forces in Haiti and Haitian waters.
To: Lieut. E. G. Oberlin, United States Navy, U. S. S. *Washington.*
Via: Commanding officer.
Subject: Orders.
Reference: (*a*) Navy Department's radiogram 18028.
Inclosure: One.

1. In accordance with reference (*a*), on the departure of Mr. R. B. Davis, Amer can chargé d'affaires ad interim, you will consider yourself temporarily detached from duty as senior engineer officer of the *Washington* and assigned to temporary duty in charge of the archives of the American legation, Port au Prince, Haiti, pending the arrival of the official designated by the State Department to assume charge of the legat on.

2. You will retain your duties as aid and squadron engineer officer.

W. B. CAPERTON.

Lieut. Oberlin had been one of my representatives ashore during the preceding few months. He spoke French fluently, and during the illness of the chargé d'affaires had assisted at the legation. He was closely in touch with the situation and conversant with any duties that might be required of him.

Owing to the disturbed conditions on October 29 throughout the north, I found it necessary to take act on, informing the Secretary of the Navy as follows: "Although country vicinity Cape Haitien and Fort Liberte is quiet and inhabitants resuming normal occupatons, conditions vicinity Bahon and St. Suzanne are disturbed. Bands of Cacos raiding and pillaging small towns and terrorizing country. Under agreement these Cacos are to be treated as bandits, and I have directed Col. Waller to take active measures to suppress them. This plan should be kept secret, as action to be effective must be complete surprise or bandits will escape to mountains and continue depredations. 18029. Caperton."

On October 30, 1915, I was informed by Col. Waller that all reports showed that there was a gathering of Cacos in the neighborhood of Capois. and that there was much d'scontent in the north due to the appointment to office by the Dartiguenave government of men formerly affiliated with the Vilbrun Sam government. and that unless the gathering in the vicinity of Capois was not broken up that discontent would spread and serious disturbances probably result. Col. Waller also submitted a general plan of operations to be taken aga'nst the forces in the vicinity of Fort Capois. which was approved of by me in the following message to him: "For Col. Waller. 21429. Plan approved. Conduct operations at discretion. 13130. Caperton."

Referring to the sanitary board consisting of Passed Asst. Surg. H. A. May and Passed Asst. Surg. P. R. Garrison. appointed by me to make a sanitary survey of the city of Port au Pr'nce, although their report was but a preliminary report and did not go into details as was contemplated for a later report, it was complete in itself and contained information which would be of much value in planning in the improvement of sanitary conditions. This report was forwarded by me on October 30 to the Secretary of the Navy.

On October 31 Col. Waller reported from Cape Haitien that all plans for the campaign against the bandits in the Fort Capois d'str'ct had been perfected and that troops would be in position to-morrow evening, weather permitting. He further stated that the general feeling in the north was much improved.

In v'ew of the report that Dr. Rosalvo Bobo was to return to Ha'ti, on October 31 I requested the commandant. Naval Stat'on, Guantanamo Bay. Cuba, to forward the following message to the American consul at Kingston, Jamaica. requesting him to investigate this rumor: "Informed Haitien Gen. Bobo will return to Haiti from Kingston. Please report if it is true and keep me advised of Bobo's movements. Caperton 20031."

I received the following message from the Navy Department on October 31 concerning the financial situation: "Flag, State Department, informed National Bank of Haiti can not purchase coffee draft on Paris now discounted at 12 per cent because you have made no rem'ttance of custom rece'pts from duty pledged to serv'ce of foreign loans of 1825, 1896, and 1910. Sta'e Department desires to furnish bank with funds to purchase draft on Paris to give confidence to bondholders of fore'gn debt and to fac'litate coffee export, thereby increasing customs receipts. In this connect'on you are informed active organz'ing constabulary will be commenced immediately modus vivendi is entered into. plan under consideration contemplates annually appropr'ation about $500 000. Provision should be made for appropriation to meet initial expenditure for organization. In view of the above is 't possible to pay to bank any part of duty now collected by you pledged to service of foreign loans above mentioned without substantially affect'ng expenditure constabulary, public works, etc., or curtail weekly advances to Hait'an Government? 16030. Benson, Act'ng."

In reply to th's radiogram from the department on November 1 I sent the following message to the Secretary of the Navy and C. in C.: "16030. Plan recommended in my 23027 is des'gned to correct high exchange rate and facilitate movement of coffee. It is possible. advisable to pay bank part of duty collected but impossible to guarantee sufficient funds in excess of all needs to meet serv'ce of foreign loans, if excess funds are transferred to New York by purchase of drafts as I suggested they will be later available for such service. Th's plan suits bank. Very few transactions in Paris exchange probable. everything financed through New York. Consider this matter urgent. 20101. Caperton."

On November 1 I reported the situat'on to the Secretary of the Navy and C. in C. as follows: "In pursuance plan of action aga'nst bandits in Capois district forces being disposed 'n north, all *Connecticut* and one-half *Nashville* landing force ashore. No news Bahon and Grande R'viere to-day. American chargé d'affaires and Surg. May sailed for New York via steamer *Venezuela*. 21001. Caperton."

On November 2 I received reports of skirmishes between our forces and Caco bandits near Le Trou and a report from Col. Waller stating that he had delayed operations against the band'ts in the Fort Capo's district for one day.

In connection with the financial situation, on November 2 I received the following message from the Navy Department: "Flag. 20101. State Depart.

ment is endeavoring establish satisfactory arrangement to meet Haitian financial situation with New York representative national band. Will inform you arrangement decided upon earliest possible date. Acknowledge. 120002. Daniels."

I sent the following messages to the Secretary of the Navy on November 2, relative to the situation: "Patrol yesterday encountered bandits pillaging village near Grande Riviere. Bandits driven off with serious losses. No injuries our forces. U. S. S. *Patuxent* sailed 8 a. m. Tuesday with Sixteenth Company Marines for Cape Haitien. 11402. Caperton." "Caco bandits attacked Le Trou this morning. Six were killed by our forces. No other particulars. 22002. Caperton."

On November 3 the *Patuxent* arrived at Cape Haitien and at 8.45 a. m. the Sixteenth Company of Marines left Cape Haitien in boats for Caracol, en route to Le Trou. The concerted operations in the Capois district were again postponed for one day. On this date I received the department's radiogram, stating that Minister Bailly-Blanchard had been ordered to resume duties as minister in Haiti and that he would arrive at Guantanamo about November 9, and directed me to send a vessel to transport him to Port au Prince.

Accompanied by Capt. E. L. Beach, on November 3 I called on the President of Haiti. The reception by President Dartiguenave and Minister Borno was most cordial. I explained the department's desire to cultivate friendly relations between the Republic of Haiti and the United States by telling the Haitian people of the benevolent intentions of the United States in Haiti and of its intention to support the Dartiguenave government. I suggested that my representative, Capt. E. L. Beach, United States Navy, and a representative of the President should visit the interior and coast towns, in order to explain this policy to the Haitian people. This suggestion was enthusiastically received and prompt and hearty cooperation promised.

During this interview I made a statement to the President of Haiti, substantially as follows:

"I have given Capt. Edward L. Beach, who is my senior captain, orders to do everything in his power to get the treaty ratified. Accordingly, he has repeatedly seen different members of the senate treaty committee, as well as other prominent and influential Haitians, and has earnestly and forcefully presented to these members my reasons why the senate committee should reconsider the report it has determined upon, and should recommend immediate ratification by the senate of the treaty as it has passed the House. Capt. Beach will continue to work for this ratification.

"I will be glad to have you, President Dartiguenave, give me the names of any Haitian senators whose attitude toward the treaty is doubtful for the purpose of having Capt. Beach present my arguments to them. These arguments are that President Dartiguenave needs support and is entitled to the support of all true friends of Haiti; the salvation of Haiti depends on the immediate ratification of the treaty; that the interests, prosperity, and honor of Haiti depend on this ratification; the present complete prostration of business, agriculture, and commercial activities requires it; the deplorable misery of so many poor people who are crying for food need it. The only objections are unimportant technical points and abstract principles. These and other details can be arranged later.

"The United States prefers no further modifications of the treaty. It desires the immediate settlement of the Haitian question. Failure to ratify will delay regeneration, and the tens of thousands who are crying for food will become hungrier. It must be clearly understood that the outside world will not invest money nor start business enterprises in Haiti until Haiti's relations with the United States are settled.

"Capt. Beach thoroughly understands these and other reasons of convincing force which I would be glad to have impress on any senators now in opposition, or whose attitude the treaty is in doubt, particularly and always showing why the absolute salvation of Haiti depends on Haitians supporting Dartiguenave. All of the energies of Haiti are needed for Haiti's regeneration; there is now no time or place for opposition to President Dartiguenave, nor for political dissension.

"I desire that Capt. Beach should explain my views where they would help President Dartiguenave to carry out his measures, and would be glad if the President will inform me unofficially in ways in which I can help to secure ratification and also help create and maintain confidence in the present Haitian

Government; and therefore I would like the names of any senators that I might possibly influence.

" I desire to inform President Dartiguenave that as soon as the treaty is ratified I wish to institute systematic methods to inform the people of Haiti of the benevolent, unselfish, and helpful purposes of my Government toward Haiti. When conditions are such that I can be spared from Port au Prince I intend to visit different ports of Haiti, either personally or by my representative, and perhaps at times go into the interior. My purpose will be to meet Haitians of all classes and to explain to them the friendly intentions of the United States. With this friendship, if there is genuine cooperation on the part of Haitians, Haiti will be a land free from violence, with President Dartiguenave guiding the destinies of his country. With the support of his people, justice and prosperity will mark the life in Haiti, the country's fertility and possibilities will be developed, there will be plenty of work with good wages for the country's peasantry, and employment for the abilities and intelligence of the upper classes. It is easy to see that instead of misery and desolation, with misfortune knocking at every door, Haiti will be a land of honor, peace, and contentment. Haitians will do this for themselves; the United States will stand by as an elder brother to help and support. I shall give Capt. Beach special duties in spreading this information amongst Haitians.

" I hope that President Dartiguenave will be interested in this matter and that he will designate some official to arrange plans and details with Capt. Beach. I further hope that President Dartiguenave will cordially approve of this plan and that he will see that in it there are possibilities for good to Haiti, and that one of its chief features is to make everywhere apparent the necessity of complete and cordial cooperation by all Haitians for the support of President Dartiguenave and his measures.

" Capt. Beach understands thoroughly my policies and is imbued with the spirit of what I wish to accomplish for Haiti and is in complete and cordial cooperation with me in working for the good benefit, honor, and prosperity of Haiti, as well as for the good relations between Haiti and the United States."

The Haitian Senate met on November 4, but the committee ordered to report on the treaty did not submit its reports, giving as an excuse that the arguments had not been prepared. It was expected that this report would be submitted the next day.

Fort Capois was captured on November 5 by a detachment under Capt. C. Campbell, United States Marine Corps. There were no casualties to the American forces. One more company was landed from the *Connecticut* on this date and another company sent to Grande Riviere. The *Connecticut* reported having ashore in various places 363 men and 15 officers.

The senate committee on November 5 presented its report on the treaty in substance, as follows:

Article 1: This article was accepted as being conventional and a necessary preamble to all treaties.

Article 2: This article is declared unconstitutional because only the President of the Republic can appoint.

Articles 2, 3, 5: Are contrary to the agreement now in force with the Bank of Haiti. The appointment of a receiver general is a political subordination of the President of Haiti to the President of the United States, who will be responsible for any malfeasance on the part of the receiver. In place of a receiver a bank is proposed.

Article 4: To be cut out and an expert appointed to advise the minister of finance.

Article 6: The substance of this article would better be included in such contract as it is proposed to make with a bank.

Article 10: Better to have commission of American instructors, not to control the gendarmerie.

Article 11: Accepted.

Article 12: Changed in some unimportant particulars.

Article 13: Republic wishes the United States to loan funds for the carrying on of public works. American and Haitian engineers to do the work.

Article 14: Added the word " constitutional."

Articles 15, 16: Accepted.

A new convention (treaty) was recommended.

The Haitian Government claimed to have a majority in the senate and repeated its determination to force ratification of treaty without modification in spite of the adverse report of the committee.

Col. Waller reported on November 6 that he would continue clearing the section around Le Trou of bandits, and on the same date I received the following message from the Navy Department:

"Secretary of State received following telegram from minister, San Domingo City, dated October 30: 'Confidential minister of Haiti tells me he has received following report from Borno: "With the idea of overthrowing the present Government in Haiti, which he accused of selling itself to the Americans, and to bring himself into our power. Zamor is playing a double game, pretending that he is in favor of the American policy in Haiti and that he is supporting it when in reality he is working for the power and to obtain money at the same time. Zamor about 15 days ago sent agents from Port au Prince, among them a deputy, to treat with Cacos for the above objects. The Cacos are surrendering to the American forces at Cape Haitien and are unarmed, but their arms have been hidden in Dominican territory near the frontier. It being impossible for him to overthrow the Government with the American forces in the island, he is plotting to assassinate Dartiguenave. The trouble makers in Haiti are acting in accordance with certain Dominicans of either political influence." The Dominican official referred to is Desiderio Arias. (Signed) Russell.' Acknowledged. 11006. Roosevelt, acting."

On November 7, Col. Waller reported that operations were progressing well aga nst the Caco bandits and that the band'ts were scarce at present. He also stated that in his opinion the north would be quiet, but that our troops would be active for a few days more. He expected to nterview several Caco generals the next day.

On November 7 I directed the commander of the fifth naval district to occupy the customhouse at Aquin in accordance w th orders previously ssued. Ensign P. J. Searles, United States Navy. U. S. S. *Sacramento*, was designated for temporary duty as collector of customs and captain of the port. Aquin.

Having been requested by the Haitian Government to furnish transportation for Mr. Antoine Francois from Cape Ha tien to Port au Prince (Mr. Francois was to be elected senator to fill the vacancy caused by the death of Senator Papillon), on November 8 I sent the following orders to the U. S. S. *Connecticut*: "Expect senate will vote on treaty Thursday. Absolutely essential all possible votes for ratification be secured. Haitian Government urgently requests Antoine Francois. Cape Hait en. who will be elected to fill vacancy, be sent Port au Prince. Direct *Hector* proceed November 9 to Port au Prince with Antoine Francois as soon as he comes aboard. Acknowledge. 221508. Caperton."

In connection with the excellent work performed by the U. S. S. *Eagle*. under command of Lieut. Aubrey K. Shoup, United States Navy, in Hait an waters, on November 8 I sent the following message to the Secretary of the Navy: "Referring departure *Eagle* from Haitian waters, squadron commander wishes take this occasion express to Navy Department his appreciation of efficient serv ces rendered by officers and crew that vessel while under his command in Haitian waters. He commends this personnel to department for its most favorable consideration. 22008. Caperton."

With reference to the financial situation, I received the following message from the department on November 9: "22019 Authority granted pay officer *Washington* depos t $26,000 with Haitian Bank for use in cashing drafts. This amount has been deposited to official credit of Paymaster Morris subject to check; $12,500 currency shipped by *Vulcan* for deposit with bank. Acknowledge. 16508. McGowan."

In connection with the treaty ratification I advised the department on November 9 that I strongly believed treaty would be ratified Thurs lay. but that powerful nfluences in the senate were against ratification; that should ratification fail the constitution requires a year's delay before reconsideration of the treaty, which would be by the same senate. There was a strong demand throughout the country from all classes for immediate ratification and no public sentiment anywhere against t. Tens of thousands were starving and the prostration of all industries demande l ratification. I also informed the department that delay would probably cause further outbreaks because of prevailing lack of work. The Dartiguenave government seemed earnest in working for the welfare of Hait an people, and I had heard no protests against the Government or treaty except from senators working against the treaty. In view of these facts I requested instructions from the department

In reply to my message to the department in reference to ratification of the treaty on November 10 I received the following reply from the Secretary of the Navy:

"23100. Arrange with President Dartiguenave that he call a cabinet meeting before the session of senate which will pass upon ratification of treaty and request that you be permitted to appear before that meeting to make a statement to President and to members of cabinet. On your own authority state the following before these officers: 'I have the honor to inform the President of Haiti and the members of his cabinet that I am personally gratified that public sentiment continues favorable to the treaty; that there is a strong demand from all classes for immediate ratification and that treaty will be ratified Thursday. I am sure that you gentlemen will understand my sentiment in this matter, and I am confident if the treaty fails of ratification that my Government has the intention to retain control in Haiti until the desired end is accomplished, and that it will forthwith proceed to the complete pacification of Haiti so as to insure internal tranquillity necessary to such development of the country and its industry as will afford relief to the starving populace now unemployed. Meanwhile the present Government will be supported in the effort to secure stable conditions and lasting peace in Haiti, whereas those offering opposition can only expect such treatment as their conduct merits. The United States Government is particularly anxious for immediate ratification by the present senate of this treaty, which was drawn up with the full intention of employing as many Haitians as possible to aid in giving effect to its provisions, so that suffering may be relieved at the earliest possible date. Rumors of bribery to defeat the treaty are rife, but are not believed. However, should they prove true, those who accept or give bribes will be vigorously prosecuted.' It is expected that you will be able to make this sufficiently clear to remove all opposition and to secure immediate ratification. Acknowledge. 22010. Daniels."

On the morning of November 11, in accordance to the above instructions, having asked for and obtained an audience, I appeared before the President and his cabinet and made the following statement:

"I have the honor to inform the President of Haiti and the members of his cabinet that I am personally gratified that public sentiment continues favorable to the treaty; that there is a strong demand from all classes for immediate ratification and for the belief that treaty will be ratified to-day.

"I am sure that you gentlemen will understand my sentiment in this matter, and I am confident if the treaty fails of ratification that my Government has the intention to retain control in Haiti until the desired end is accomplished, and that it will forthwith proceed to the complete pacification of Haiti so as to insure internal tranquillity necessary to such development of the country and its industry as will afford relief to the starving populace now unemployed. Meanwhile the present Government will be supported in the effort to secure stable conditions and lasting peace in Haiti, whereas those offering opposition can only expect such treatment as their conduct merits.

"The United States Government is particularly anxious for immediate ratification by the present senate of this treaty, which was drawn up with the full intention of employing as many Haitians as possible to aid in giving effect to its provisions, so that suffering may be relieved at the earliest possible date.

"Rumors of bribery to defeat the treaty are rife, but are not believed. However, should they prove true, those who accept or give bribes will be vigorously prosecuted."

Minister Bailly-Blanchard arrived at Port au Prince on November 10 at 10 a. m.

On November 10 the commander of the expeditionary force reported that Forts Selon and Berthol had been captured on November 8; that the Cacos had fired at the sight of our men; and that all the people in the Caco country were displaying white flags. He further reported that a band of 15 bandits were trapped near Grande Riviere and that 2 were killed and 9 wounded. He also reported Limonade quiet, and stated that he was satisfied that the movement crushed was more than an aggregation of ordinary brigands. The commander of the expeditionary force now expected to start operations to the west of the railroad and toward Renquitte.

The senate met at 10 a. m., November 11, and remained in session until 5.50 p. m., when it ratified the treaty by a vote of 26 for to 7 against. The debates were long, the opposition being led by Senator Pouget. Pouget, at the opening of the session, stated that he approved of the treaty in principle, but that he did not agree with the details. It was noticeable that there was a great relief and general rejoicing among the people upon the successful outcome of the treaty negotiations. I promptly reported the ratification of the treaty on this date to the department.

Shortly after having reported the ratification of the treaty I received the following message from the Secretary of the Navy, November 12: " 22111. Department wishes to express its gratification at the ratification of the treaty and to warmly commend the able manner in which you have handled this important matter and the ability you have shown in directing affairs in Haiti. Acknowledge. 11012. Daniels."

On November 12 I made the following report to the Secretary of the Navy: " Commander expeditionary force returned Cape Haitien November 11, having completed operations against bandits to eastward of Cape Haitien—Bahon Railroad. Operations to westward at railroad begin to-day and expect to end by night of November 14. First Lieut. Ostermann slightly wounded in arm while on patrol between Bahon and Grande Riviere. Secnav. Flag *Wyoming*. 06812. Caperton."

On November 13 I reported the following conditions to the Secretary of the Navy: " Conditions more quiet and more people going to work on farms near Grande Riviere, Bahon district. Secnav, Washington, and Flag *Wyoming*. 22013. Caperton."

On November 15 I sent the following dispatch to the department: " Mr. Bailly-Blanchard received to-day formal audience by President and cabinet and presented credentials as minister of the United States to Haiti."

On November 15 I also sent to the Secretary of the Navy the following proclamation of the President of Haiti, made in reference to the ratification of the treaty: FF Nov. 15.

Liberty. Equality. Fraternity.

Republic of Haiti.   Sudre Dartiguenave, President of the Republic.

ADDRESS TO THE PEOPLE.

FELLOW CITIZENS: At the meeting of November 11 the senate of the Republic has sanctioned the Haitien-American convention. This event, the most important in our national history, is the foundation of Haitien independence, of the solemn consecration of the new era of progress for the nation after the powerful dayse of 27th and 28th July, which days we can not think of without a shudder of horror.

It you will consider the vote of the convention by its merits and patriotism you will render with me legitimate homage to the honorable members of the legislative corps who have shown once more their sense of duty in the face of a situation exceptionally grave for this unhappy country. They have come together in large numbers to open finally the road of material and through evolution which has always been their object. "Honor, therefore, to the saviors of the country's glory of their act for which the magnanimity is only equaled by its heroism to have the right to the benediction of our posterity."

Fellow citizens. these pressing circumstances which have made known to you the urgency of the convention with all the unhappy sacrifices which go with it, of the ransom for the faults and errors of a century. it is not necessary that I remind you of this, nevertheless, for the safeguard of the future, that you impress yourselves during these days were the chaos, the anarchy, and the humiliation of the people resulting from our unscrupulous competitions of bad and doubtful passions, which disputes with one another for a power which was involved in the advance to bring about the sterility of the country, of awaiting the hopeful moment of the final breaking up of the above evil conditions.

W'thout entering into a discussion of facts anterior to the coming of the Americans, remember that in a moment of our supreme despair the powerful and generous nation of North America saw our unhappiness, taking pity upon us and came in the name of humanity and universal fraternity to offer us the hand of friendship and of succor. Was it necessary to repulse, even under a disguised form, as several people of the same type as many of my predecessors seem to think, this friendly aid.

Being persuaded of the loyalty of the Government of the United States and convinced that its people who, by means of their work, have become great as to become our ideal, des re fully to guide us in the route which centuries of civilization have made, we unhappy slaves of false mentality, brought by jealous prejudices, have never tried to find this way for our own nationality. I, therefore, have not a second of hesitation.

I wish here to thank cordially my official collaborators whose experience, wisdom, and imperturbable conviction, together with the ardent faith in their devotion have been the strong aids to my firm resolution.

You have not been strangers to the struggle brought about by the severity of opinion whereby people opposed to the convention struggled against the Government to prevent its acceptance. We have defended it foot by foot and have guaranteed its various clauses in order to overcome the imminent peril which lack of reflection and blindness was liable to threaten our national sovereignty. And who can affirm but that the formal refusal to accept the convention would have been the destruction of our independence?

It is, therefore, in regard to the acts of brutality which have been continued for so long a time, and also with the conscientious reflection that we have in your name signed the act of diplomacy which has but recently been sanctioned by your own republic.

If you have seen the executive power marching resolutely to the solution of these troublesome questions, it is because that the power had the feeling that your hearts beat in unison with their own, although far away from them the chimerical dreams dear to those people who had no common sense or any appreciation of events as they really were.

The people in the future will see that we have done the best thing and that we have acted for love of country.

Fellow citizens, by your new contract with true civilization there are the exigencies of living absolutely free which will appear before you and are destined to make of you a prosperous, honest, and laborious nation. Therefore, it is not your satisfaction to anticipate the happy effect of the new state of things implanted in our midst.

To the populations of the department of the north and the northwest and the Artibonite, who have been the most inflicted by our latest calamities, have shown themselves above all courageous and confident, what a joy it will be for them to return to a full existence made possible by the local appreciation of the convention which has been so unjustly attacked.

All those who have been longing for such a long time for a definition of this union are concerned so that this treaty alone can bring to them security, prosperity, and happiness, and they recognize that already there is a better future assured them by means of work which incurs agriculture, industry, and commerce. This is the end of your desires and has come after your long dreams of peace after your sad deceptions, the sacrifices of life which we have accepted in the hour of peril to our signification.

Therefore, fellow citizens, let us wish success to ourselves and glory for the world of civilization. I repeat that the new era has begun, but the fruits of our labors demand that you repudiate forever the past shame and nefarious past which has made a blot upon the immortal names of our ancestors.

If the generations which have preceded you are judged by history for accumulated crimes you will be more than pardoned if you refuse to consecrate to-day yourselves to the work of the nation's redemption.

Having thought well over this convention and with firm realization of the future, join in crying:

Long live peace and union.

Long live work.

Long live regenerated Haiti.

DARTIGUENAVE.

On November 18 I sent the following report to the Secretary of the Navy, describing the capture of Fort Riviere on November 17: "Fort Riviere captured by forces under Maj. Butler. All avenues of escape had been previously closed so that no Cacos escaped; 51 were killed, including Gen. Joseph, 3 division chiefs, and all others captured. No casualties our forces. Attack made by Thirteenth Company Marines, Capt. C. Campbell; marine detachment, *Connecticut*, Capt. Barker; Fifth Company Marines, Capt. W. W. Low; seaman company from *Connecticut*, Lieut. (Junior Grade) S. D. McCaughey, and automatic-gun detachment from Third Company. Assault made by Fifth Company. Hand-to-hand conflict in fort lasted 10 minutes. Forty-seven rifles, considerable ammunition, found. Fort made of masonry and brick of most substantial construction. Fort will be leveled to ground. The fact that this fort was taken without a single casualty on our side speaks well for ability and judgment all officers concerned. Marine patrols continue operations to southward. All other areas in Caco country quiet. 12018. Caperton."

In answer to the department's radiogram 13050, a copy of which follows, asking for comments and recommendations relative to the claims of the P. C. S. Railroad, Power & Light Co. at Port au Prince, on the Haitian Government, I, at 2.10 p. m., on this day, forwarded to the Navy Department information as to our dealings with this company, and recommended that the loan to the Haitian Government, of one and a half million dollars, which the State Department has mentioned in its dispatches to the legation and of which the Haitian Government has been informed, be immediately made after the signing of the modus vivendi, in order that the Haitian Government may settle many pressing claims, of which the railroad is one. I further recommended that the $100,000, promised upon the ratification of the treaty in the State Department's cablegram of September 15, 5 p. m., be cabled at once. In view of the promises made by the State Department, which have not yet been carried out, the fact that the enemies of the United States and of the treaty are taking advantage of this apparent lack of support of the present Haitian Government to its detriment and intend to carry such information to Washington to aid in the fight against the ratification of the treaty in the United States Senate, I consider that American prestige is involved in this mattter.

The following is the department's radiogram 13050: " P. C. S. Railroad, Power & Light Co. at Port au Prince prior to American intervention had formally notified Haitian Government that operations have to cease on October 1, 1915, on account of lack of funds if Government continued not to live up to its financial engagement toward them. Department now informed that as these companies are still without funds they will be unable to continue further operations. President Staude states he has so far continued to operate under direction given by United States naval authorities. In view of above companies having requested State Department to give them preference of speedy consideration of their claim so that arrangements can be made to assure operation of railroad and electric light company, comments and recommendations requested. 13015. Daniels."

The following is my reply to the department's radiogram forwarded on November 18: " 13015. Commencing middle of August electric light company is being paid by me $7,500 per month, contract price for light Port au Prince and Cape Haitien. P. C. S. Railroad has been paid $5,000 and later $2,500 more in order to maintain it in operation as a military necessity. Haitian Government owes both companies several month arrears. President Staude states that if amount now due railroad as balance of guaranty of interest, about $17,000, is not paid before December 1 the road will be forced into bankruptcy. Haitian Government acknowledges this debt but is unable to pay. Owing to peculiarity of contract under which Government guarantees annual interest at 6 per cent on bonds of road to amount of $688 I hesitate to recommend further payments by American authorities. Instead I recommend further that loan to Haitian Government of $1,500,000 which State Department has mentioned in its dispatches to legation of which the Haitian Government has been informed be made immediately available after signing modus vivendi in order that the Government may settle many pressing claims of which railroads is one. The $100,000 promised upon ratification in State Department September 15 5 p. m., should be cabled at once. American prestige involved in this matter. 14118. Caperton."

In order to acquaint the department with conditions on November 19, I made the following report to the Secretary of the Navy: " Operations against Cacos bandits in north Haiti during last three weeks has resulted in dispersing Cacos, capture many of their strongholds, destruction quantities arms and ammunition, and bringing peaceful conditions throughout Cacos country. This area is included within lines Cape Haitien, Dondon, San Rafheal, Pignon, Carice, Mont Organize, Ouanaminthe, Mouth of Massacre River, and Cape Haitien.

This area is now patrolled throughout by our forces, is now peaceful, and country people are now busy with their crops. Our patrols are also at present operating from Gonaives through Ennery, St. Michel, Marmalade, Plaisance, and Poteau, from Port de Paix for distance of 8 miles to southward and from St. Marc through Artibonite Valley. These areas are quiet. This last movement of Cacos appears to have been of revolutionary nature against present Government as well as brigandage. While petty brigandage will continue from time to time; yet it is hoped no more such organized brigandage or revolutionary activity will occur. Our casualties to date in this campaign one officer and one man wounded. Secnav, Washington, and Flag, *Wyoming*. 14419. Caperton."

On November 19 I received the following radiogram from the Secretary of the Navy referring to the capture of Fort Riviere: "12018· Department appreciates excellent work done and gallantry displayed. In view of heavy losses to Haitians in recent engagement department desires our offensive be suspended in order to prevent further loss of life. Acknowledge. 32018, Daniels."

In reply to this message on November 19, I sent the following dispatch to the Secretary of the Navy: "22018. Department understands that patrolling in north Haiti is now under way by American forces and that hostile contact with the bandits may unavoidably occur from time to time, resulting in loss of life. Operations being conducted are purely of defensive character for the preservation of law and order, suppression of revolutionary activity against present Government and military intimidation of people, and for protection of life and property of the innocent farmers and tradesmen, who form by far majority of population in these districts. The Cacos, against whom operations have been undertaken, are bandits pure and simple, owing no allegiance to the Government or any political faction, but organized under petty chiefs for sole purpose of stirring up strife against Government and robbing, pillaging, and murdering innocent people. The suppression of this brigandage and these activities is absolutely essential to peace and security in Haiti. It will be remembered that there is no Government authority in these areas at present, and that we have disbanded the Haitian Army, heretofore the only means of protection to the inhabitants. The operations now undertaken should continue until this brigandage is suppressed or the constabulary is ready to relieve our forces. Having undertaken this intervention any diminution in the protection and support offered the Government and people of Haiti by the United States will greatly harm our prestige. Our action is approved by Haitian Government. It is absolutely necessary that our present movement continue to southward, to include Hinche at least, where arms and ammunition have been collected for delivery to our forces in accordance with agreement of Quartier Morin, and if Hinche is not occupied it will therefore form base for further revolutions. It is possible some slight opposition may be encountered at Hinche, although we are assured there will be none. Unless otherwise directed will continue this movement. Secnav, Washington, and Flag, *Wyoming*. 16119. Caperton."

Referring to the financial condition, on November 19 I received the following from the Secretary of the Navy: "After setting aside sufficient of the revenue coming into your hands for support of Dartiguenave government, for public works, and for constabulary, you may, upon request of Haitian Government, apply remainder of revenue collected by you, for purpose of and in accordance with, pledges thereof, which have been heretofore made or given by Haitian Government. Acknowledge. 18018. Daniels."

In connection with this message from the department and also my message 14118 of November 18, I sent the following dispatch to the Secretary of the Navy: "18018 and my 14118. Strongly recommend that distribution of revenues in accordance with past pledges be not attempted, for following reasons: Current receipts much too small to satisfy arrears of creditors extending back many months. Computation complicated owing to retention of sums for purposes mentioned by you, and results obtained will be difficult to make clear. Treaty provides different and better method of handling revenues, so that it is unwise now to revert to old system. The immediate loan of sufficient funds to discharge all obligations and subsequent organizations of debt as provided by treaty considered the only satisfactory method to follow. 18019. Caperton."

On November 20 information continued to be received from reliable sources that active aid was being sent to the Cacos from the Dominican Republic. The latest reports stated that Dominican police were aiding the Haitian rebels; that the governor of Monti Cristi was entirely failing to take any steps to prevent this; that there were many Haitians on the Dominican side of the border; that there was considerable agitation going on to foment revolution; that the American chief of the Dominican frontier guard had made numerous reports to the governor of Monti Cristi, who made promises but did nothing in the matter; that notorious Haitian bandits were receiving protection, notably one Hara and Hose Rinito; and that officials in Dajabon were doing all in their power to prevent the American chief of the frontier guard from cooperating with our troops on the Haitian side.

On November 20 I received the following message from the Secretary of the Navy relative to the recent military operations: "16119. Department strongly impressed with number Haitians killed. Department feels that a severe lesson has been taught Cacos and believed that a proper patrol can be maintained to preserve order and protect innocent persons without further offensive operations. Should these measures prove inadequate, inform department before taking steps that would lead to loss of life on either side, except in case of urgent necessity. Acknowledge. 14020. Daniels." I immediately transmitted these instructions to Cols. Waller and Cole, who in turn issued the necessary orders to all organizations to the effect that all operations must cease except patrolling pending further instructions.

In reply to the following inquiry from the Secretary of the Navy: "12018. How many prisoners taken at Fort Riviera? 10019. Daniels." I replied as follows on November 22, 1915: "10019. Later reports from north Haiti indicate that when Fort Riviere was rushed by Fifth Company Marines 29 Cacos were killed in the mêlée. Many jumped over the parapet and attempted to escape. These were attacked by remaining companies and 22 were killed. Not known how many escaped. My radiogram 12018 was in error relative to captures made at Fort Riviere; none were captured there; 42 prisoners were captured that day, but elsewhere. 14322. Caperton."

At 2.10 p. m. November 22 I reported to the department the action taken relative to department's instructions to suspend active operations against the Cacos, as follows: "14020. All operations except protective patrolling have been suspended. Directions have been given that loss of life both sides be avoided if possible. 14122. Caperton."

In order to suppress smuggling along the coast, which had been brought to my attention, on November 24 I issued special orders to naval vessels and the expeditionary force to begin operations against smuggling at once, and to take all smuggling cases to the nearest provost court for adjudication.

In view of the statement of President Staude that his railroad would be forced into bankruptcy if the interest on the bonds, amounting to $48,000 was not paid, on November 24 I sent the following recommendation to the Secretary of the Navy: "13015 and my 14118. In view of statement of President Staude that his railroad will be forced into bankruptcy if interest on bonds, amounting to $48,000, is not paid by December 1, it is recommended that stay of proceedings be urged on National City Bank, chief bondholder, or money furnished to tide over emergency. Haitian Government acknowledges indebtedness to various corporations controlled by Staude considerably exceeding sum stated, but can not pay at present. Bankruptcy proceedings which might be ascribed partly to American occupation deemed inadvisable at this time irrespective of actual merits of case. Status quo of this and all other concession holders should be maintained pending settlement of differences by commission under terms of treaty. Acknowledgment and information action taken requested. 22324. Caperton."

On November 25 Dessource, minister of war, was dismissed from the cabinet. The President states this was done on account of Dessource's grafting. This was promptly reported to the Secretary of the Navy.

On this day President Dartiguenave called at the French legation and formally apolized for the violation of that legation on July 28, 1915. The Haitian shore battery fired a salute of 21 guns to the French flag. This salute was returned gun for gun by the French cruiser *Descartes*, with the Haitian flag at the main. Shortly afterwards the *Descartes* got under way and stood to sea. These facts were reported to the Secretary of the Navy.

During the past few days the American minister and I had been in daily conference with the Haitian Government relative to the modus vivendi.

At 6 p. m., November 29, the modus vivendi embodying the exact terms of the treaty was signed by Mr. Bailly-Blanchard and Mr. Louis Borno, plenipotentiaries of the United States and Haiti, respectively. This now put the treaty into full working effect, and I therefore immediately recommended the following officers for nomination by the President of the United States in accordance with the terms of the treaty to act in a pro tem capacity pending the arrival of the regular appointments: Financial adviser, Capt. E. L. Beach, United States Navy; general receiver, Paymaster Charles Conard, United States Navy; senior American officer of constabulary, Col. L. W. T. Waller, Marine Corps; engineer for public improvement, Lieut. E. G. Oberlin. United States Navy; engineer for sanitation, Passed Asst. Surg. P. E. Garrison, Unitted States Navy.

This would continue the work heretofore done by the same officers that had been doing it, with the exception of Capt. Beach and Lieut. Oberlin. The financial duties had theretofore been done by Paymaster Conard and the public improvement duties had been done by the marines under Col. Waller. I was informed these nominations would be acceptable to the Haitian Government. I reported these facts and made these recommendations to the Secretary of the Navy and the commander in chief at 6.30 p. m. November 29.

On November 28 I received the following message from the Secretary of the Navy, which is self-explanatory:

"Loan of $1,500,000 can not be arranged until after arrival of commission and settlement of difficulties with bank. Advance of $100,000 upon ratification of treaty proposed to furnish funds for current expenses in the place of 500,000 gourdes held by you, but Haitian Government declined offer and stated they desired that conditions of affairs with National Bank of Haiti remain in status quo. Weekly payments of 25,000 was authorized in lieu of this proposed advance and was intended to supersede it. If, however. Haitian authorities still consider 100,000 due upon ratification of treaty, the amount may, in order to maintain prestige, be paid from funds in your hands, provided advance from this source is agreeable to Haitian Government. Owing to strained relations understood to exist between National City Bank and Central Railroad of Haiti. it is not desired to attempted to make arrangements for staying of proceedings unless it is absolutely necessary. Central Railroad informs State Department Haitian Government has requested you to pay $48,000 to railroad company. Can you not do this under authority granted in 18018? It would seem that you would be protected in such payment at request and with consent of Haitian Government. Desirability of plan suggested by you appreciated, but delay in getting loan can not be avoided and prompt compromise action appears necessary. To protect entire responsibility on Haitian Government suggest following procedure: If it requests that payment be made to prepare receipt for signature of proper officials acknowledge receipt from you of $48,000; also receipt from you for your signature acknowledging receipt from Haitian Government of $48,000, to be paid over to the Central Railroad of Haiti in accordance with request of Haitian Government. If you will direct purchasing paymaster New York to make payment to New York representative of railroad upon notice from you that $48,000 of Haitian funds has been turned over to Paymaster Morris, to be taken up under general account of advances for official use offsetting payment. Above sent after consultation State Department and conforms in views expressed in its cable of November 23 to American minister. Acknowledge. 14027.

"Victor Blue."

On November 29 the department again sent me a message concerning the foregoing, as follows:

"Very urgent department's 14027 should be settled by November 29. Please expedite action. Acknowledge. 11029.

"Roosevelt, Acting."

In reply to these messages on November 29 I reported the following action taken, my report reading as follows:

"14027 and 11029. One hundred thousand dollars were transferred to Haitian Government to-day from funds in hand. Haitian Government has requested $48,000 to pay Central Railroad and amount will be turned over to Paymaster Morris to-morrow. Immediately thereafter purchasing paymaster New York will be notified that he may make payment to New York representative of railroad. Regarding loan of one and a half million dollars, Haitian Government fully expects to receive this amount immediately, as State Department dispatches have indicated that temporary loan would be arranged immediately after signing of treaty and modus vivendi. Earnestly recommend that such temporary loan be made as soon as commission sails and prior to negotiations in Washington, to be afterwards included in final adjustment of all outstanding obligations. 23129.

"Caperton."

On November 29 I sent the following dispatch to the Secretary of the Navy:

"French Government has officially recognized Dartiguenave. British chargé d'affaires has instructions to recognize Dartiguenave government. Sec. Nav. Washington and flag *Wyoming*. 231529.

"CAPERTON."

On November 30, in accordance with my report to the Secretary of the Navy of November 29, I sent the following instructions to the Navy pay office, New York:

"For Navy Pay Office, New York:

"By direction of the Navy Department, pay immediately to Central Railroad of Haiti, 25 Broad Street, $48,000. Same amount has been deposited with Paymaster Morris under general account of advances. Acknowledge. 15030.

"CAPERTON."

On December 1 I sent the following dispatch to the Secretary of the Navy:

"*Connecticut* sailed from Port au Prince to rejoin battleship squadron noon Wednesday. Commander cruiser squadron takes this occasion to express his appreciation of excellent service and support rendered by the commanding officer, officers, and crew of *Connecticut* to the cruiser squadron and marines during operations of last four months in Haiti. He regrets that the lack of large cruisers in the cruiser squadron forced the temporary withdrawal of a battleship from her most important war training duties with the battleship squadrons. 14401.

"CAPERTON."

On December 2 I received reports from the north to the effect that conditions between San Raphael and Dondon were excellent; that the priests had reported the country absolutely quiet. There were many men at work clearing the ground and the district recently infested with outlaws. Patrols from Grande Riviere to Limonale, Fort Liberte to Perches, and from Ouanaminthe to southwest and to north report all quiet. There was considerable cleaning of the land and resumption of work between Perches and Terrier Rouge.

On December 6 the Haitian treaty commission to consult with the State Department relative to the details and operations of the treaty was announced as consisting of Solon Menos, Haitian minister at Washington, president; August Magloire, administrator of finance, Port au Prince; and Pierre Hudicourt, lawyer and plenipotentiary to second peace conference at The Hague, as members; and Leon Dejean, chief of bureau of ministry of foreign affairs, and Edgard Laroche, attaché of the ministry of finance, secretaries. I reported the sailing of this commission to the United States on December 6 to the Secretary of the Navy as follows:

"*Prairie* sailed 7 p. m., Monday, from Port au Prince for Annapolis, Md., with following gentlemen of Haitian treaty commission: Pierre Hudicourt and August Magloire members, and Edgar Larouche, secretary. Recommend representative State Department, who speaks French, meet commission upon arrival Annapolis, and that accommodations Annapolis and Washington and special transportation Annapolis to Washington be arranged. Request *Prairie* be informed arrangements made in advance arrival Sec. Nav., Washington, and flag *Wyoming*. 21106.

"CAPERTON."

Again on December 6 in further connection with the Haitian treaty commission I sent the following to the Secretary of the Navy:

"Commission has now sailed for United States. Urgently recommend loan of $1,500,000 be made immediately, as previously recommended in my 231229. Haitian Government has inherited months of unpaid debt and has incurred expenses in educating country to realize necessity of ratifying treaty. Salaries, debts, and obligations amounting to $500,000 must be paid before December 20. Otherwise Government prestige will be lost amongst Haitians and serious conditions will result. Expect part of cabinet will resign unless Government can meet its obligations by this date. Settlement of existing problem will be delayed and purpose of Unied States impeded under present conditions. Believe immediate favorable action on this recommendation vital and imperative. 22206.

"CAPERTON."

In reply to my recommendation relative to a loan to the Haitian Government, made on December 6, the Secretary of the Navy on December 8 sent me the following:

"22206 and 231229. In view of article 1, section 9, paragraph 8, of the Constitution, officers nominated in your 18329 can not be appointed by President until special authority obtained from Congress, which may take some time. Treaty negotiations did not provide for arranging for loan until after arrival of commission in Washington, D. C., and there are certain matters which should be adjusted by commission. State Department averse to loan being made unless assured it will be properly disbursed. Can you assure disbursement will be made under supervision naval officer pending appointment by President officer provided in modus vivendi? Loan negotiations will be expedited after arrival commission subject to foregoing. For information, State Department, submit by radio statement from occupation to November 30, showing total collected. also amount collected from each general source, total payment to Haitian Government payment for work done under your direction by general object. and balance on hand acknowledged. 10008.

"DANIELS."

Information as to the intentions of the United States Government with reference to executing the terms of the modus vivendi was very desirable in guiding me in the administration of Haitian affairs, and I therefore on December 10 sent the following message to the Secretary of the Navy:

"1008. Information as to United States Government intentions with reference to executing terms of modus vivendi very desirable in guiding me in administering Haitian affairs at this time. Is it intention to ask Congress to pass necessary resolution authorizing naval and marine officers to accept offices under Haitian Government or will civilian nominations be made. If latter, when may these appointees be expected to arrive Port au Prince? 15410.

"CAPERTON."

In reply to the department's radiogram 10008 of December 8 requesting information relative to the question of expenditures and collections of customs duties since the occupation I forwarded the following:

"10008. Total collections to end of November, $953 372. Include exports coffee, $366,098; miscellaneous exports, $144.227; imports and miscellaneous duties, $443,047. Expenditures, $179,519, divided as follows: Constabulary. 22,099; public works, $66,763; military and civil government, $64,210; customs service, $26,447. Transferred to Haitian Government, $393,000, which includes $48,000 to Central Railroad; balance, $308,853, of which $325,972 was in account of Admiral Caperton and $54,681 in hands of disbursing officers. Figures given closely approximate, as returns not all in for November. 23011.

"CAPERTON."

On December 11, 1915, there was considerable unrest on the Dominican side of the border in the vicinity of Monti Cristi and Dajabon. The American customs officials in the Dominican service stated that the Dominicans were hostile to the Americans, particularly to the Americans occupying Haiti; that the Dominican officials used to visit Haiti, but that now they never cross the border owing to the presence of the Americans; and that the people of Santo Domingo were much agitated over the reported pressure being brought to bear for making an addition to the present treaty between the United States and Santo Domingo, especially as to the clause for the formation of a constabulary. The formation of a constabulary would affect the politicians and persons connected with the rural police, who would lose their present graft. It seemed to be fairly well established that the Dominican authorities were harboring Haitian criminals and aiding Haitian bandits.

With reference to the question asked by the Navy Department in 10008, as to whether or not I could assure that disbursements of a loan made prior to the completion of the work of the commission would be made under the supervision of a naval officer, pending the appointment by the President of the officer provided in the modus vivendi, I made the following report to the Secretary of the Navy: "10008. Can assure disbursement of $500,000 will be made under supervision Capt. E. L. Beach, United States Navy, under following written agreement of the Haitian Government: 'With regard to the disbursement of the advance loan of $500,000 gold desired to be received by the Haitian Government by December 20, 1915, it is agreed that the advice of Capt. Beach will be necessary for the expenditures to be made from the $500,000, and that the concurrence of Capt. Beach will be required by the depository bank in honoring drafts on this amount. This procedure applies to this advance only and shall not be considered as an application to the terms of the treaty of September 16, 1915. It is equally agreed that in order to facilitate the payments, Capt. Beach will be at his office at the hours of service, and that he will give no advice contrary to the payments regularly ordered by the law fixing the budget. (Signed) Louis Borno.' Recommend this sum be deposited in National Bank of Haiti. This bank already agrees in writing as follows: 'With regard to the $500,000 proposed to be deposited with this bank as a repository, for the expenses of the Haitian Government, the bank agrees that on all withdrawals on such particular deposit the prior signature of Capt. E. L. Beach, United States Navy, will be required; provided, however, that instructions to this same effect be passed to the bank by the depositor when the above said deposit shall be made. (Signed) Reine.' Secretary of the Navy, Washington, and flag *Wyoming.* 10412. Caperton."

On December 14 the situation in north Haiti was quiet. Many people were at work and everyone apparently friendly.

In connection with the temporary appointment of financial adviser and other officials without congressional action, the department on December 13 advised me as follows: " On account of constitutional restriction impossible to appoint financial adviser and other officials without congressional action. The department assumed that in the meantime officers are discharging these duties. Report whether or not such is the case. Acknowledge. 21013. Daniels."

In reply to this I advised the department as follows: "21013. Status of administration of affairs here the same as prior to signing of modus vivendi. It has not been considered practicable to proceed under the terms of the modus vivendi owing to the nonappointment of necessary officials. Instructions requested Secretary of the Navy, Washington, and flag *Wyoming.* 11414. Caperton."

As the United States, by the signing of the modus vivendi was now under obligation to appoint the officials provided by the treaty to carry the same into effect, as I had already recommended officers for these offices, and as there was nothing further that could be done by me or by the Haitian Government, I considered it necessary to request further instructions in the matter.

In reply to my request for further instructions in the matter the department on December 14 advised me as follows: "11414. Department has assumed that pending regular appointments of financial adviser, general receiver, engineer for public works, and engineer for sanitation these duties were being performed under your authority by Capt. Beach. Paymaster Conrad, Lieut. Oberlin, and Passed Asst. Surg. Garrison, respectively. Is such the case or not? 18014. Roosevelt, acting."

In reply to the foregoing message I on December 15 advised the department as follows: " 18014. Officers mentioned are not performing duties mentioned as defined by the treaty, nor are any other officers performing these duties. Capt. E. L. Beach, Paymaster Charles Conrad, Col. L. W. T. Waller, Marine Corps, and Passed Asst. Surg. P. E. Garrison are performing duties somewhat similar to those provided in the treaty for financial adviser, general receiver, engineer for public works, and engineer for sanitation, respectively, under the status of subordinate officers aiding me in maintaining military control of the situation. under authority department's radiogram (20018), August, and such other military instructions as have been issued. The terms of the treaty as placed into effect by the modus vivendi are not being carried out by anyone. Haitian Government has made repeated requests that United States carry out their part of modus vivendi agreement and urge immediate appointments be officially made. Have explained constitutional restriction preventing naval officers accepting appointments, have stated that civilian appointments could be made at once, and have offered to recommend such appointments. Haitian Government earnestly requests appointments of naval officers and requests that special efforts be made to expedite these appointments. Can not joint resolution be immediately obtained from Congress authorizing in general terms naval and marine officers to serve temporarily under Haitian Government. Secretary of the Navy, Washington, and Flag *Wyoming.* 11315. Caperton." (For the benefit of the committee it is stated that the department's radiogram (20018), August, mentioned in the foregoing will be found in my testimony covering the date Aug. 19, 1915.)

In explanation of the foregoing I desire to make the following remarks: The status of our administration in Haiti was at this time purely one of military control. The terms of the treaty as placed into effect by the modus vivendi were not being carried out by anyone, nor could they be until appointments were made which would give a legal status to the appointees. For the protection of the United States' interests and the officers concerned, in order to gain the benefits to accrue from the treaty and prevent misguided interference on the part of the Haitian Government, no officer should attempt to carry out the duties defined in the treaty until their legal status and their authority and responsibility could be definitely assured by proper appointments. Until that time the present military control should continue.

The Haitian Government had made repeated requests that the United States carry out their part of the modus vivendi agreement and urged immediate appointments be officially made. I had explained the constitutional restriction preventing naval officers accepting appointments, had stated that civilian appointments could be made at once, and had offered to recommend such appointments. The Haitian Government earnestly requested appointments of naval officers and requested that special efforts be made to expedite these appointments.

From a cablegram received by the American minister on December 20 it appeared that the possibility of making the loan of $500,000 to the Haitian Government was very slight. I therefore made the following recommendations to the department: "Dispatch received by American minister to-day indicates that possibility of making loan of $500,000 to Haitian Government is very slight. It is now recommended that I be authorized to transfer to Haitian Government funds in my possession to meet immediate pressing demands, such funds to be disbursed under agreements similar to those contained in my 10412. If this be done, it will be necessary to arrange payment of interest of debt and similar obligations from funds to be later loaned to the Haitian Government. Secretary Navy, Washington, and Flag *Wyoming.* 22220. Caperton."

(NOTE.—The message 10412, mentioned above, may be found quoted under my testimony covering December 12, 1915.)

It having been decided to turn over to the Haitian authorities the control of all activities now being undertaken by the American forces for which expenditures were then being made under the heads "Military and civil government" and "Public works," with the exception of such activities as were necessary to maintain military control under martial law for the purpose of preserving peace and order. I, on December 20, issued the following instructions to carry out this decision in a letter to the expeditionary commander, which is quoted, as follows:

"1. It has been decided to turn over to the Haitian authorities the control of all activities now undertaken by the American forces for which expenditures are made under the heads "Military and civil government" and "Public works," with the exception of such activities as are necessary to maintain military control under martial law for the purpose of preserving peace and order.

"2. To this end you are directed to proceed with the preliminary arrangements necessary.

"3. (a) You will designate officers at each of the places where we now have control of these activities, who will make an inventory of the utilities, public works, repairs, etc., in progress and who will confer with the representatives appointed by the Haitian Government who are to receive control of these activities.

(b) Furnish squadron commander with the names of the officers so designated.

(c) The terms of the arrangements will be forwarded to the squadron commander in each case, together with your recommendations, before this control is actually surrendered.

(d) For your information Mr. Price is designated by the Haitian Government to receive the Hydraulic Service at Port au Prince. W. B. Caperton."

On December 21 a band of outlaws was reported to have been holding up women near Maissade. A marine patrol was sent to investigate. Other patrolling continued in north Haiti. A marine patrol while investigating robbery by a Caco band in the vicinity of Perches had a slight skirmish with a small Caco band. Five thousand rounds of ammunition were captured by the marines near the Dominican border, having been buried there. The location was ascertained through the secret service. Incriminating papers had been captured in north Haiti from a Caco chief, one Darius Davilmar, including one from Bobo from Cuba written in September, in which he styled himself as chief of the forces operating against the Americans. It was rumored that he was implicated in the recent Caco troubles.

In accordance with the decision to turn over to the Haitian authorities the control of the public works, etc., I on December 22 transmitted to the American minister the names of the officers who would consult with the Haitian officials at the various ports to make the necessary arrangements.

On December 22 I received the following radiogram from the department: "Desirable have as many marines as possible sent north at earliest practicable date. Report conditions and make recommendation. 13021. Daniels."

In reply to the foregoing, on December 22 I advised the department as follows: " 13021. In view of present unsettled relations between United States and Haiti and necessity of maintaining present military control of situation until appointments under modus vivendi are made, in view of public work carried on by marines under present status of military occupation, and in view noncompletion of organization, training, and arming of constabulary and their present inability to assume duties of maintaining peace and order unassisted, I recommend that marine force now ashore in Haiti be not reduced at this time beyond detachment of Twelfth Company, and that Col. Waller remain here until situation clears up. Recommend that twelfth company of marines be detached from duty Second Regiment and ordered proceed north on *Washington* when that vessel leaves Haiti. This company has been on continuous cruising and tropical shore service for about one year without leave or recreation, and is as much in need of leave and recreation as crew of *Washington*. Secretary Navy, Washington and flag *Wyoming*. 16122. Caperton."

On December 24 Annulyse Andre was appointed secretary of war and navy in the Haitian cabinet, and I so reported this fact to the Secretary of the Navy on the same date.

With reference to the turning over to the Haitian Government of the activities being carried out by me under " Public works " and " Military and civil government," on December 27 I made the following recommendations to the department, as quoted in the radiogram: " Control of public works and civil expenditures which have been assumed by me is now to be turned over to the Haitian Government. As weekly payments of $25,000 now authorized was not estimated to include expenses under the activities to be transferred, it is recommended that additional allowance be authorized. Expenditures made by me for public works and civil government have averaged $12,700 per week, and similar expenditures for which funds are to be transferred should be limited to this amount. Detailed estimates from Haitian Government will be required for expenditures to be made for these purposes. Secretary Navy, Washington, and flag *Wyoming*. Caperton. 14127."

On December 28 I received a letter from the President setting forth what he considers a serious situation due to the lack of funds, etc. I transmitted this letter to the Secretary of the Navy, as follows: .

" Have just received following letter from President Dartiguenave : ' Mon cher amiral, Il ne reste plus que quatre jours pour la fin de l'annee. Toutes nos conversations, depuis plus de deux mois, vous ont suffisamment reseigne que, moine aux pires epoques, les pires Gouvernements n'ont pas laisse le peuple aux prises avec la faim, quand l'annee se renouvelle. C'est le pays entier qui, par lettres et telegrammes, me le rappelle. Hier, Je voussai ecrit et jusqu'a ce moment, je suis a attendre votre reponse au sujet de l'argent qu'il nous ressources sont retenues par l'occupation. Jr dois ajouter que, dans la situation de crise aigue que le Gouvernement traverse, par manque de moyens de subvenir aux obligations les plus imperieuses de l'Etat, J'ai de serieuses raisons de craindre que le Conseil des Ministres ne se disloque, si la question d'argent pour la fin de l'annee n'est pas reglee. Et je crains aussi qu'il ne me soit difficile, dans ce cas, de reformer le cabinet. En attendant votre reponse, jr vous renouvelle, mon cher Amiral l'expression de mes meilleurs sentiments. Signed, Dartiguenave.' 19428. Caperton."

MY DEAR ADMIRAL: There are only four more days before the end of the year. All our conversations for more than two months have sufficiently shown you that even at the worst periods the worst Governments have not left the people to struggle with hunger when the new year began. The entire country is reminding me of this fact by letters and telegrams. Yesterday I wrote to you and am still awaiting your reply on the subject of money, as our resources are retained by the occupation. I must add that in the acutely critical situation through which the Government is passing, due to lack of means of meeting the most pressing obligations of the State, I have serious reasons to fear that the council of ministers may be dissolved if the question of money is not settled before the end of the year. And I also fear that it will be difficult for me in this case to form a new cabinet. Awaiting your reply, my dear Admiral, I am,

Yours, very respectfully,

DARTIGUENAVE.

On December 30 I received from the department the following radiogram transmitting to me a message to the American legation from the Secretary of State relative to the loan to the Haitian Government:

"'Your December 18, 6 p. m., eliminating the appropriation for war, public work, public debt, and service of the armistice contained in the Haitian budget for 1914–15, that budget, although contemplating a large deficit, made provision for an average monthly expenditure of about $150,000 gold a month.

"'Inasmuch as the Haitian Government had to make no expenditure for war, public work, public debt, and service of the bank during the months of October, November, and December, it should have needed on a basis of the 1914–15 budget the sum of $450,000. During these months the Haitian Government has actually been in receipt of $385,000 advanced to it by officer No. 17. It should therefore require but $65,000 to cover the deficit. The department believes that the law of December 2 contemplates the expenditure of nearly $1,000,000 for these three months is unwise and is not prepared to consent to the use of an advance of $500,000 upon any loan to be made for the purpose contemplated in that law and will not under the terms of the treaty approve also increasing the foreign debt of the Republic of Haiti for any such purpose. Commission informs department that Minister Menos has received telegram from President Dartiguenave instructing him to request department to authorize officer No. 17 to pay over all the funds in hand to be reimbursed by loan of two million, and states that situation of Government is critical and ministerial crisis imminent.

"'The department's opinion regarding such loan is stated above and it considers the funds held by officer 17 to be in the nature of a trust fund, as these moneys do not belong to the Haitian Government but to the holders of different debts of the Government. In view, however, of alleged urgency, you will report immediately by cable the amount in your opinion absolutely necessary to defray salaries of public employees for months of November and December while, notwithstanding advance of $25,000 per week, the department is surprised to learn have not been paid. Lansing.' 19029. Daniels."

In answer thereto I forwarded for the American minister to the Navy Department for transmission to the Secretary of State, the following:

"For Secretary of State. 'Your December 29, 7 p. m., Navy Department. It is impossible to obtain at once from the Haitian Government as the urgency of the situation requires, the information necessary to enable me to form an opinion and report immediately the amount absolutely necessary to defray salaries of public employees for months of November and December, but the Government now states that to avoid crisis by covering most pressing demands for November in the Provinces and December in Port au Prince, $50,000 imperatively needed. Immediate favorable reply urgently requested. Blanchard.' 19140. Caperton."

On December 31 I received the department's radiogram, which is quoted below, answering my messages of December 26 and 27, requesting instructions, etc.:

"22220 and 14127. National Bank of Haiti, which is operating only sources from which an immediate unsecured advance could be obtained, stipulated for restoration of contractual right before it would consider making an advance. This was not acceptable to Haitian commission. Offer of a temporary loan stipulated for guaranty by United States which can not be given. Prospects for securing any funds in the near future in addition to current revenue are not bright and probably nothing can be done until after a thorough investigation of liabilities and probable resources. The State Department as evidenced in its dispatch of the 29th to Minister Blanchard is not satisfied with the purpose it is purposed to apply the additional funds. For the above reason it is deemed inadvisable to authorize the payment to the Haitian Government of the reserved funds in your custody. Delay in securing advance or loan is not due to cause which can be controlled by the United States, but to unsatisfactory conditions of Haitian finances. Do not turn over control of public works or any other duties pertaining to civil government which have been assumed by you to the Haitian Government until so directed by the department, because State Department desires that status quo be maintained until the officials provided for in treaty and modus vivendi have been appointed and are ready to assume their duties. Modus vivendi provides for settlement of certain questions by Haitian commission and State Department in Washington, D. C., before money in addition to $25,000 per week be paid over to the Haitian Government unless department specifically authorizes. The foregoing has been submitted to the State Department, which concurs. Acknowledge. 10130. Daniels."

On this date I also received the following message from the department: "Confer with Minister Blanchard regarding message 15081 to him sent this date authorizing disbursement of $50,000, etc. Obtain verbatim copy of this message; carry out its provision as outlined by State Department. Acknowledge. 14081. Daniels."

On January 1, 1916, I received the department's radiogram 15031, transmitting a State Department message to the American legation. This message stated that I would be authorized to make use of $50,000 of the funds in my possession to defray unpaid salaries of the public employees referred to in Minister Blanchard's message of December 30, 5 p. m. It was directed that this money should not be paid to the Haitian Government, but should be drawn against the principal by me or my representatives, who shall pay salaries direct to the individual public employees, from whom they will obtain receipts presented in person. Preference shall be given to minor employees who are said to be in great want. This message further directed that all salaries to the military should be discontinued, including that of the minister of war and marine; that the so-called palace guard should be immediately disbanded; and that after January 1, 1916, and until arrangements could be made by officials appointed under the modus vivendi, I should have complete control of disbursements of the weekly allowance for maintenance of the Haitian Government and should make use of my representatives in the various ports to see that a proper proportion of the money reached the public employees in the Provinces.

On January 3 conditions were quiet throughout Haiti. The commanding officer of the First Regiment at Cape Haitien reported that conditions in North Haiti were better than they had been for many years; that cultivation was being resumed; that new habitations were being built; and that the land, more or less abandoned for a long time, was being occupied again. Rumors were heard from time to time of projected revolutions and hostile propaganda at different places in the country but nothing serious seemed to develop. Some slight brigandage in the north occurred but was quickly suppressed. Bandit leaders were now in hiding or in Santo Domingo. The attitude of the governor of Monte Chisti and the Dominican authorities at Dajabon was apparently more friendly, and they seemed to be aiding our forces in maintaining order on the frontier. There was some slight disturbance between the police and the soldiers in Monte Cristi on December 25. Patrolling by our forces in North Haiti was being continued.

In view of the department's instructions contained in the department's radiogram 10130 of December 30, orders were given to the commanding officers of all marine detachments on January 3, informing them that the public works and activities under military and civil government would not be turned over to the Haitian authorities and directed them to cease the arrangements previously ordered relative thereto.

The following report was made to the Secretary of the Navy on January 5 relative to disturbances which occurred in Port au Prince early on that date: "At 2.30 a. m. Wednesday barracks occupied marines at Port au Prince fired upon by small party of Haitians. This was followed by firing in other parts of city. Patrol officer was fired on several times. All disturbances suppressed in about one-half hour. One Haitian killed and some wounded. Corpl. Wedor,

Marine Corps, slightely wounded in foot. Disturbance apparently of political nature against Dartiguenave government and American occupation. Sixteen arrests of leaders and bad characters made to-day by marines and some arms and rifles captured. Precautionary measures under martial law taken. Port au Prince now quiet. Secnav, Washington, and Flag *Wyoming*. 22205. Caperton."

With reference to preparing a system for paying Haitian employees and creditors as directed in the department's radiogram of December 31, I sent the following to the Secretary of the Navy:

"In preparing system for paying Haitian employees and creditors as directed in 15081. It is important to know whether system is to be continued under treaty after appointment of necessary officials. Plans laid now should be comprehensive in character in order to insure efficiency, but if system is to be later discontinued such plans must be less comprehensive with partial sacrifice of efficiency. It is recommended that, if practicable, treaty arrangements include this method of disbursements. 15107. Caperton."

In connection with the disturbance on the morning of January 5 at Port au Prince, it was discovered that the outbreak was part of a well-organized plot, etc., and on January 8 I sent the following message relative thereto to the Secretary of the Navy:

"Disturbance Wednesday morning, Port au Prince, part of well-organized plot covering Port au Prince, Les Cayes, and South Haiti in general. Those engaged belong to black party as distinguished from mulatto. Leaders in Port au Prince were Pierre Paul, Misael Codio, Pradel, Annabel Hilaire, and Philogene. Latter three, with several other minor leaders, have been captured and confined. Pierre Paul and Misael Codio escaped. This movement appears was made in favor of ex-Senator Paulin or Pauleus Sannon for President. Plot contemplated assassination of President. North Haiti entirely quiet; does not seem to be concerned in this affair. No cause for alarm. Situation well in hand. Secnav, Flag *Wyoming*. 14108. Caperton."

On January 9 I received State Department's message "Bomky," in State Department code, by radio and transmitted it to the American Legation. I also received the department's 18008, directing me to cooperate and carry out the provisions of State Department's "Bomky," quoted as follows:

"Flag *Attention* invited to State Department Bomky to American Legation; cooperate carry our provision. 18008. Daniels."

During this time our patrols continued to work in north Haiti, where all was reported quiet with the exception of some petty stealing.

The municipal elections were now due in various parts of the country. Minor disorders were to be expected as the result of them here and there. At Petit Goave the election lists were stolen, so that the election could not take place, and in order to avoid disturbance at that place I found it necessary to place the mayor of the town, who was responsible for the safety of the election lists, under arrest and take entire charge of the town. I reported the incident to the department on January 10, as follows:

"Municipal elections now due; expect minor disorders. Election list Petit Goave has been stolen; to avoid disturbance have found it necessary to place Mayor Petit Goave under arrest and take entire charge that town. Reward 5,000 gourdes has been offered for Pierre Paul and Misael Codio, Secnav *Wyoming*. 22010. Caperton."

The *Prairie* arrived at Port au Prince on January 10 from the United States. Commander K. M. Bennett, United States Navy, on this day relieved Commander J. F. Carter, United States Navy, in command of the *Castine*.

In accordance with a request dated January 10, I, on January 11, received from the American minister a paraphrase of State Department's "Bomky." This message related to the disbandment of the so-called palace guard and the State Department's wishes and instructions relative to the gendarmerie taking its place, and is in substance as follows:

LEGATION OF THE UNITED STATES OF AMERICA.
January 10, 1916.

Rear Admiral W. B. CAPERTON, United States Navy,
Commanding United States forces in Haiti and Haitian waters,
U. S. S. "Washington."

SIR: Referring to your note of January 10, 1916 No. 434-16, I have the honor to inform you that the following message sent by the Department of State at 6 p. m., January 8, 1916, referring to the legation's telegram of 5 p. m., January 5, 1916, which I communicated to you and which stated that reforms desired were agreed to by the Government and that you were carrying out the provisions as instructed, has been received and a paraphrase thereof is herewith forwarded for your information:

It is understood in Washington that it has been accepted that the so-called palace guard be abolished.

The Department of State proposed to the Haitian Commission, in arranging with them for the organization of the gendarmerie, that the following provision be included: "The gendarmerie shall be the sole police and military force of Haiti." The Haitian minister maintained this would be contrary to the Haitian constitution, which provides for a president's personal guard. He objected to the words "the sole military" and now says that he has telegraphic instructions under dated of January 6 which permit him to accept the department's proposed wording if the words "excepting a palace guard not to exceed 250 men" be added, claiming this would allow conformance with the Haitian constitution, article 175. The palace guard is an unnecessary extravagance, and its continuance may in the future well develop into a source of danger to the Government. With it in existence it would be impossible for the gendarmerie properly to guard the palace. And if the palace guard remains in existence it would be impossible for any members of this gendarmerie to be detached on special duty in personal attendance on the President. I am instructed to bring these facts orally and discreetly to the attention of the President and to show him that his personal safety may be at stake. The department therefore believed it desirable that the commission accept the following phraseology: "Members of the gendarmerie shall form the personal guard of the President of Haiti, and the gendarmerie shall be the sole police and military force of the country." This meets objection raised by the Haitian minister.

I am instructed to furnish the department with a copy of the telegram accepting the above, which I am also instructed to suggest to the President to send to the commission, and to hasten my reply in order that on Monday next the department can conclude this matter with the commission. I have the honor to be, sir.

Your obedient servant,

A. BAILLY-BLANCHARD,
American Minister.

Pradel, who was recently arrested in connection with the outbreak in Port au Prince, was released on January 12 and this fact so reported to the Navy Department.

The department's radiogram 17012 in answer to my 15107 of January 7, was received on January 13 and is quoted as follows:

"Flag 15107. Any system for paying employees and creditors of Haiti that may be formulated at the present time can only be of a test nature and would probably be subject to revision and amplification by the financial adviser as contemplated in the treaty. It is much to be desired, however, that the method of disbursement now to be put in force shall be as comprehensive and as efficient in character as the means at your disposal will permit. In this connection and in view of the fact that no expenditures are now being made for the army and navy, for the services of the public debt, and for the treasury service of the bank, and as the disbursement for the public works and the cost of collecting customs revenue are being met from other sources, it is hoped that the sum of $100,000 per month or its equivalent in gourdes, which you have been authorized to use for necessary current expenditures of the Haitien Government, will prove more than sufficient for this purpose. It is intended that $50,000 special advance authorized in department's 15021 shall be used only to pay salaries in the Provinces for November, and salaries in Port au Prince for December. Dating from January 1, 1916, it is desired that you shall not make use of the monthly payment of $100,000 to pay the salaries of public employees or the creditors of the Haitien Government for services rendered previous to that date except the salaries of public employees in the Provinces for December, 1915, and that payment shall be limited to actual necessary expenditures for service and supplies incurred subsequent to January 1. Every effort should be made to prevent salaries from being paid to Haitiens whose services are only nominal, and also to eliminate the present pernicious system of discounting salaries and Government orders. From information in the possession of the State Department it appears that many of the expenditures contemplated in former budgetary law, and particularly in the budgetary law of December 2, 1915, are ill advised and probably in excess of the revenues which may be available for such purposes in the future. It is des'red that you use own discretion as to the payments which are to be made, and you are not bound to be governed by the budgetary law in mak ng these disbursements. The funds are in the nature of trust funds and it is highly desirable that proper receipts and vouchers be obtained covering disbursements in order that the interest of those for whose benefit the revenues have been pledged may be protected as fully as practicable. The foregoing has been prepared after conference with and with the concurrence of the State Department. An outline of the system adopted should be transm'tted by radio if practicable, otherwise by mail, and a copy of the detailed instructions issued by you should be forwarded when available; acknowledge. 17012. Daniels."

In reply to the above, on January 14, I forwarded the following radiogram to the Secretary of the Navy giving a paraphrase of the scheme devised for the payment of salaries, etc.:

"17012. Haitian Government is now forwarding all salary lists to administrator of customs. These are being checked against the budget and duplications, absentees, etc., are eliminated. Corrected lists are then prepared and individual receipts having functions of checks, but not negotiable, are to be delivered to individual employees who will obtain the funds after proper identification at the bank. Instructions have been issued to commanders of Marine detachments in the Provinces to investigate lists of employees, and after insuring that individuals are entitled to pay, to deliver receipts to them to be cashed at local branch of national bank as above stated. Entire system of payment is being carried out under direct supervision my representatives. Report covering system forwarded in mail to-day. 14014. Caperton."

In connection with the above I wish to add that on the same day I forwarded to the Secretary of the Navy by mail a letter describing in detail the system proposed for carrying out the provisions of the department's radiogram of the 12th instant; this letter containing four inclosures, including my detailed instructions to the National Bank of Haiti, the expeditionary commander, and instructions from the administrator of customs to the collectors of customs along the same lines, covering the payment of Haitian employees.

Upon the receipt of the department's radiogram of December 31, the President of Haiti and the members of his cabinet were informed of the instructions contained therein, that no further funds would be turned over to the Government directly, but that necessary payment of salaries would be made to the individuals concerned under the supervision of Rear Admiral Caperton or his representatives. This information caused much dissatisfaction, and the first reply was to the effect that such a method could not be accepted by the Haitian Government, in view of the implied insult contained in the proposal. Various plans were suggested by the American authorities, intended to soften or mitigate the implied insult. But as they all included the cardinal principle that the money should actually be placed in the hands of those to who it was due, under the supervision above referred to, none were acceptable. Finally the representative of the Haitian Government agreed to turn the business of paying salaries, etc., completely over to Rear Admiral Caperton, and to lend their assistance in furnishing the lists of employees to whom payments were due. As this appeared to be the most direct method of arriving at the desired end it was decided to so proceed.

Referring to the above objection by the President and cabinet I think it but fair to make a few remarks for the information of the committee showing why I considered it necessary to pay each individual employee personally by my representatives. It will be remembered that I had been instructed to pay $25,000 weekly to the Haitian Government to meet its current expenses, such as salaries to Government employees, etc. As I recall the circumstances at this late date there came to me many complaints from employees, both of high and low positions, that they were not receiving their salaries, and I also learned that much of this weekly allowance was going for purposes not intended. To insure the actual payment of this money to the people and for the purpose for which it was intended, the foregoing recommendations and plans were inaugurated. Much pains and many instructions were taken in order to make the first payment under the new régime successful and pleasing to the people. A special reception or writing room was fitted up in the National Bank of Haiti, and arrangements made for paying promptly, and at the same time using care to issue new bills in any denomination requested. I was much gratified shortly after this to receive many letters from people who had strongly objected in the first place to this mode of payment, and throughout the country the method was highly praised by everyone, as the employees found out that in this manner they received all of their pay and not a part of it as heretofore. It had been the custom to pay to certain "paymasters" (I believe was the term they used) the whole amount due certain districts, which resulted in the said "paymasters" retaining a large percentage of the pay and the individuals receiving what was left. I believe the first payment of about 14,000 employees was effected by the third or fifth of the month, which was very gratifying to the Haitian Government.

Misael Codio, military leader and one of the chief men in the attack of January 5 at Port au Prince, was arrested near the Dominican border by Maj. Dunlap on the morning of January 16, and was brought to Port au Prince, where he was confined.

On January 25 Dartigue, the minister of public works, resigned from the cabinet. The situation otherwise remained unchanged.

In answer to my request that the balance due the gendarmerie on January 31 from the date of its authorization at the monthly rate agreed upon be placed to the credit of the gendarmerie to cover expenses of equipment and stating that funds were available, the department answered that this request would be approved as soon as the Haitian commission signed the necessary agreement. It directed that in the meantime to proceed under previous authorization relative to the gendarmerie.

On January 26 I received the department's radiogram 18025, in which it was stated that in a conversation with the State Department Minister Menos referred to the alleged pressing needs of the department of the interior. He was informed at Washington that as the State Department had no means of deciding as to the necessity for meeting these needs the matter might properly be submitted to me. The department requested my consideration and recommendation in this connection and directed that I be guided by previous instructions. This message follows:

"Flag. In conversation with State Department to-day Minister Menos referred, among other matters, to alleged pressing needs of the department of the interior and was informed that as the State Department had no means of deciding as to the necessity of these payments the matter might properly be submitted to you. Your consideration and recommendation in this connection should be guided by previous instructions. Acknowledge. 18025. Daniels."

I also recommended on this date to the Secretary of the Navy that the palace band be authorized in the capacity as a band for the gendarmerie. The cost per annum would be $20,000, including pay, uniforms, instruments, and music. This cost would be additional to the allowance for the gendarmerie. The President requested the reorganization of this band to add to the dignity of the Government. My message follows:

"Recommend that palace band be authorized in capacity of band for gendarmerie. Cost per annum, $20,000, including pay, uniforms, instruments, and music. Cost to be additional to allowance for gendarmerie. President has requested organization of this band to add to dignity of Government. 22426. Caperton."

I give herewith a statement of the customs receipts and expenditures to December 31, 1915:

OFFICE OF ADMINISTRATOR OF CUSTOMS,
PORT AU PRINCE, HAITI.

Customs receipts and expenditures.

	Gold.	Gourdes.	Gold.	Gourdes.
Customs receipts to Dec. 31			$1,266,932.46	1,026,945.26
Total expenditures to Dec. 31:				
Constabulary	$33,140.70	68,814.85		
Public works	56,634.73	295,084.07		
Military and civil government	44,862.80	281,934.33		
Customs service	15,821.12	103,945.96		
Transferred to Haitian Government[1]	553,000.00	138,750.00	703,459.35	888,529.21
Balance to Jan. 1			563,473.11	138,416.05

[1] Includes $28,000 P. G. S. Railroad.

NOTE.—The account current for Les Cayes for the month of December, 1915, had not been received. Expenditures include the December allotment.

CHAS. CONRAD.

The commander in chief, Admiral F. F. Fletcher, arrived at Port au Prince on the *Wyoming* at 8.30 a. m. January 27. He paid official calls on the President of Haiti and the American minister and held a conference with the commander cruiser squadron. The commander in chief left for Guantanamo at 5 p. m.

In answer to the department's radiogram 18025 of January 25, I reported at 8.10 p. m. January 27 that the department of the interior wished to obtain lump sums for undefined payments; for example, about $4,000 for secret service and other expenses for December. I have insisted on detailed lists giving names and amounts for salaries only prior to January 1, and so informed the Secretary of the Navy, as follows:

"18025. Department of interior wishes to obtain lump sums for undefined payments; for example, about $4,000 for secret service and other expenses for December. Have insisted on detailed lists giving names and amounts for salaries only prior to January 1. 20127. Caperton."

On January 29 Capt. E. L. Beach, United States Navy, assumed command of the *Tennessee* and Capt. B. C. Decker, United States Navy, assumed command of the *Washington.*

The flag of the commander cruiser squadron was on January 31, 1916, shifted to the *Tennessee,* and so reported to the Secretary of the Navy, commander in chief, and forces in Haiti.

On February 2, 1916, local military officials under the titles of commandants of arrondissements, chiefs of sections, and commandants of communes, were discharged throughout Haiti. Military and police functions were to be carried on by the gendarmerie. On the preceding day, February 1, 109 different detachments occupied 109 different stations throughout Haiti, with instructions which would suppress brigandage, disorder, etc.

On this date I sent the following radiogram to the Secretary of the Navy, reporting conditions, etc.:

" Dr. Audin appointed minister of public instruction. Public works transferred to charge of Minister Borno. Government discharging many unnecessary officials in all departments. New method of paying Government employees is being received with general satisfaction. This method of paying direct and on time should break up pernicious system of discounting salaries. Many demands being made for back debts, but am not considering these at present. 13402. Caperton."

On February 5, in reporting conditions to the department. I sent the following radiogram:

" Everything quiet. Thirteen hundred enlisted constabulary and 400 rural guards not enlisted but under constabulary authority now performing all patrol and police duty throughout Haiti. Brigandage and pillaging stopped. Complete order everywhere exists. Peasants now have feeling of security and are planting their farms. General feeling of relief throughout country and contentment with American occupation and intentions except amongst few discontented politicians. Government and people eagerly awaiting American action on treaty and introduction of American capital. 23105. Caperton."

The Haitian Government, though well aware of the orders of the United States Government regarding the payment of expenses of the Haitian Government, and of the amounts that were available, was constantly sending mandates of expenditures entirely beyond the amount allotted for the Government's support. This forced me to return such mandates to the Haitian Government as they were not payable under my orders.

In a message to the department on February 6 I described the situation as follows:

" Office of commandant arrondissement declared abolished by Government. Civil duties assigned to them are now being discharged by Government court attorneys. President informed me personally this morning that matters are looking much better now for Haitian Government in the sense that agitation against it by discontented politicians is noticeably losing force. People throughout Haiti glad of assurance of security that detachments of gendarmes will give. 22206. Caperton."

On February 8 I reported the financial situation and made recommendations to the department in a message as follows:

"Am paying salaries public employees by nonnegotiable nontransferrable checks. Injunction brought on bank in many cases attaching salaries. Law permits not more than one-third salary attached any month. If attachments allowed and but two-thirds salary paid employee, system of discounting salaries will continue to flourish. Should attachments be not allowed, Government and judges say act would show United States had but little regard or respect for Haitian law and custom. Recommend that I be instructed to inform Government that as these attachments interfere with purpose of United States they will not be regarded and bank w ll be given military order to that effect. This matter of discounting salaries has been engaged in by comparatively few speculators. It is believed that this system would entirely stop if it became known that those who discount will not be aided by Un.ted States in collecting their claims. 22408. Caperton."

After some correspondence with the department on this question the department finally, on February 20. sent the following instructions in regard thereto:

"Flag 22408 and 00312. Authority granted; issue mil.tary order disregard any form of attachment of salary of Government employees, especially attachment by opposition. It is desired to respect Haitian law so far as relates to honest debts and you may recognize attachment of one-third salary by court injunction if based upon act on for legitimate debt with discounting of salary. Acknowledge. 18019. Josephus Daniels."

As matters at this time were more or less quiet, I took this occasion, in company with the American minister and the administrator of customs, to make an inspection trip of the north and accordingly left Port au Prince on February 15, inspecting the following-named places: Mole St. Nicholas, Port de Paix, Cape Haitien, Fort Libertie, Ouanaminthe, Grande Riviere, Bahon, Milot, etc., and returned to Port au Prince on February 22, 1916. I found conditions quiet in all places visited and was received most cordially everywhere by the natives. After this inspection trip of north Haiti I became convinced that the constabulary must be increased about one-third its present number, and so recommended to the department that it be considered by the commission and included in the treaty estimates.

With reference to the desire of the Haitian Government to send diplomatic and consular representatives to the various countries, on February 28 I sent the following message to the department:

"Haitian Government proposes to send diplomatic consular representatives to various European and American posts, in most cases relieving those now on duty. Each appointee and each one relieved entitled by law to three months' pay for expenses. Cost of these changes, $17,725. Recommend that all changes be postponed for the present and that expenditures be limited to bringing home representatives not needed abroad. 12428. Caperton."

A committee of citizens called on me on March 1 and requested that I forward a communication to the department stating that the resident investors in the three interior loans were suffering on account of nonpayment of interest. These bonds were held by many poor people who depended on this interest to meet expenses. There was no market for the sale of these bonds, largely due to the lack of currency in circulation as pointed out by me before in messages to the department. This committee requested that payment of this interest, amounting to about $100,000, be made immediately, thus relieving those dependent on it and also assisting business conditions by placing money in circulation. I reported these facts and approved this committee's request in a message which I immediately sent to the department.

With reference to the financial situation, on March 4 I sent the following message to the department:

"16301. Since all customs funds to my credit are held by bank separate from other funds, they are not now available for banking operations. If bank were permitted to transfer part of balance to New York, it could purchase good drafts when offered and transmit them to New York for credit there, always at bank's own risk. In this connection attention is invited to desirability of paying interest on foreign debt. Recommend that semiannual interest now overdue be paid as fast as funds are available and that the bank be directed to commence immediately in order of dates past due. This would cause demand here for foreign drafts and lower the discount rate and would release funds now impounded. Consideration should be given to the question whether service of foreign debt is to be handled entirely through New York or whether drafts on Europe can also be purchased for this purpose. notably to cover coffee shipments. Latter would make a more free market here, but might conflict with plans of State Department for reorganizing national debt. Owing to lack of information here regarding financial plans for Haiti being developed in Washington it is difficult to make more definte recommendations, but suggest that this matter be referred to financial adviser as soon as selected.

" No room for unfavorable public opinion if funds are to be used for service foreign debt. Bank has used funds forwarded to purchase drafts, but in absence of demand for transfer of credits abroad can not help situation much. 11104. Caperton."

In reply to the foregoing messages and recommendations the department on March 15 sent me the following instructions:

" Flag 21129, 14101, 11104, and 21413. You are authorized, with the concurrence of the Haitian authorities, to apply $500,000 of surplus revenue of Haiti now held by you on a per cent basis to the purposes for which the revenue had been lawfully pledged by the Government of Haiti prior to July 27, 1915. Statement furnished by the National Bank of Haiti shows the amount which should have been applied to each purpose during period of American occupancy and proration should be made on basis of these figures. As payments have been made under your direction for some objects to which revenues were pledged, such payments should be deducted from the pro rata share now available for these objects, and in cases where actual payments have exceeded the pro rata share nothing should be paid at this time. It is believed that March 1 would serve as convenient for prorating these payments, this distribution being authorized at present time more to relieve financial stringency than to settle outstanding claims against Haitian Government, and with this object in view the money should be placed in circulation in Haiti with least possible delay. Should it be impossible to purchase in Haiti sufficient drafts on Paris or Le Havre promptly to remit money for service of foreign loans, arrange to have manager of bank undertake purchase drafts on New York and have money transmitted to France through New York agent of the bank. It was stated in department's 10130 (December) National Bank of Haiti probably only source from which an immediate unsecured advancement could be obtained, and it would seem no steps looking toward securing such a loan should be taken prior to settlement of controversy between bank and Haitian Government which is now subject negotiations with Haitian commission. Assessment of loan and other financial matters mentioned in your 21413 should await appointment of financial adviser, which will be made as soon as possible. Trade adviser of State Department states it would seem that during the present high price on logwood will probably be maintained until dyes can be obtained from Germany. If method of prorating not thoroughly understood, further instructions will be given. Acknowledge. 15016."

In connection with the foregoing, my message to the department on March 13 is quoted as follows:

" 14409 and my 16110. Balance in my account February 29, $850,000. Collections in February were $300,000, and transfers for disbursements were $180,000. It is believed that revenues will not fall appreciably during next six months, as coffee shipments will continue to some extent during summer and heavy shipments of logwood are now waiting transportation. Information requested from Department of Commerce as to probability of logwood market holding at present high prices, with special reference to possibility of aniline dye industry interfering. Exchange between gourdes and gold now 5 to 1, and effort will be made to hold it there. This can be done if present uncertain conditions can be remedied. Extremely important that immediate steps be taken to settle all valid claims against Haitian Government and thus restore feeling of confidence. It is earnestly hoped that bonded indebtedness will be consolidated and that all special liens on various custom revenues will be abolished; otherwise it will be impossible to properly revise tariff. If this be done, prorating of available balance as contemplated would be unnecessary, as all just claims should be paid regardless of particular affectations involved. If possible, recommend immediate short-term loan of $500,000, to be expended by American occupancy in settling Haitian debts, to be used in addition to balance of custom receipts available for that purpose. A commission should be appointed as soon as possible to pass on all claims. This loan should later be included in consolidated debt, and any balance should be available for public works. Delay in appointment of financial adviser and general receiver is having bad effect, as no permanent steps can be taken pending their arrival. 21413. Caperton."

Conditions in Mexico having become acute, the following messages have been received from the department: " In case circumstances should make it necessary, U. S. S. Prairie will be sent Mexico with regiment marines. 13011." And: " Do not relinquish any part military control now exercised by you in Haiti nor put end to martial law as now in force without receipt further instructions. Answer. 12011." I on March 12 advised the department in a message as follows: " Shore forces now in Haiti not more than 1,700 men. This force minimum possible to maintain present military control of country and can not be reduced by single unit without greatly prejudicing United States control and prestige here. Constabulary are neither sufficiently trained nor reliable to be depended upon without support of all forces present. Urgently advise against weakening our present position this island. 23512. Caperton."

In connection with the approaching session of Congress, which was to assemble during the first part of April, campaigning was going on amongst senators and deputies to embarrass the Government. This information came to me from various reliable sources. It was well appreciated that with the American forces present a revolution was impossible, so other means were adopted to force the Dartiguenave government out, being planned somewhat as follows: When Congress met in April, if the enemies of the Dartiguenave government were strong enough to do so, a vote of censure and lack of confidence in the Government was to be passed and the President impeached. The charges were to be, "violations of the constitution."

In connection with this campaigning President Dartiguenave made a statement to my representative, Capt. E. L. Beach, United States Navy, late in February, which was substantially as follows:

"I do not expect the enemies of the Government will be in sufficient force to cause such a vote to be passed, I expect to be able to control Congress. I have enemies because of the reforms I have instituted, which have been to curtail unnecessary expenses and discharge unnecessary employees, cut fraud out of the pension list and out of Government contracts. Because I have not acceded to demands made by some who rated high the value of their services and for other personal reasons. Because I have suppressed the war department, army, and palace guard. Every refusal made was for Haiti's good and with the advice and confederation of American officers. There is but one thing to do—to revise the constitution and make it fit the present needs. The following changes are imperative: There are 39 senators and 102 deputies—double the number needed. Their salaries alone amount to one-seventeenth of the entire revenue of the country. The number must be reduced to less than half the present number. Article 6 of the present constitution provides that no foreigner may acquire or hold property. This prevents foreign capital from entering. Article 6 must be suppressed. The revised constitution must suppress the war department and army and substitute the gendarmerie. The magistracy and civil service must be reformed. And there are other needed reforms. My government will urge the chambers to take the necessary steps to revise the constitution on these lines. Should Congress be hostile and refuse there will be but one thing to do. I do not ask the American Government to advise me to do this, nor to express any opinion on this matter, but I request the forward assurance of Admiral Caperton that my Government will receive complete military protection. I shall declare both chambers dissolved. I will call for a constituent assembly which will be formed of about 50 representatives, patriotic Haitians, who will revise the constitution according to present needs. I request you to explain this situation to Admiral Caperton and state that I desire from him an assurance that should I be forced to disolve the chambers my Government will receive the protection of the United States, if needed."

Minister Borno, who was present when the President made the foregoing statement to Capt. Beach, stated to Capt. Beach that the President hoped that Admiral Caperton would have Capt. Beach explain the situation and purposes of the Haitian Government in detail to American officials in Washington. This was just prior to Capt. Beach's trip to the United States on the *Tennessee.*

The above facts were reported to the department in substance, and in reply I was authorized to support the Government.

About the 10th of March the President sent copies of the following letter to the various representatives of the Government in the various civil districts and to the various commissaries of the Government near the various civil courts:

10TH OF MARCH.

To the representative of the Government in the civil district of ———.

MY DEAR COMMISSIONER: The president of the premanent committee of the Senate, doubtless in accordance with the agreement of a majority of his colleagues, has made public call to the members of the legislature with a view of assuring their meeting on the first Monday in April for the accomplishment of work which the President has not yet been able to fully understand the character.

In view of this unusual act, I have thought, and am in agreement with the members of my cabinet, that it is desirable to anticipate a misunderstanding by making known through you to the senators and deputies who live in your district the reasons why it will be desirable, in spite of the opinion of the permanent committee, that the opening of the session of Congress for 1916 should not take place until the Government is in possession of full information in regard to the legislative work for the year. No member of the legislature may ignore the facts that since the meeting of the convention a commission has left for Washington with all instructions and powers necessary in order to find, with the assistance of the good offices of the United States, moneys to liquidate the debts of the Government for 1914 and 1915, to provide to the public services sufficient resources for 1915 and 1916; to find capital to redeem the interior debt and pay the budget of 1916 and 1917; to organize the new public service of Haiti; to ascertain a method of reconciling the duties of the receiver general with the privileges guaranteed to the bank by its contract; to reconstitute the office of the secretary of treasury; to adjust the disagreement with the national railroad; to harmonize our laws with the rule of the convention; and in a loyal effort, undertaken in common with the officials of the American Government, to prepare the solutions of problems essential to national work, which should have the favorable attention of the legislature this year.

But although it has in no sense neglected its mission and although it has already made appreciable progress, the commission has not yet reached the end of its work, and before it returns the President can not be fully informed as to its intentions.

Who under these conditions will compose the legislative body? Is it desired that we shall again have a session of eight or nine months entirely given over to useless agitations? And, furthermore, where may the money be obtained which will be necessary in order to pay the salaries of the representatives?

All these considerations, Mr. Commissioner, appear to me to be sufficient to decide me, in agreement with the cabinet, to recommend to you that you bring to the knowledge of the members of the legislature actually present in your district that the President has not been convinced by the permanent committee of the senate of the advisability of a meeting of the Congress in April, and he will not accept any responsibility for anything that may result from such a meeting.

The President does not ignore his obligations to the National Congress and he has no idea of taking away their prerogatives. But at a time which is so completely dominated by the circumstances under which we live at present, why should we consider inflexible rules which have never before appeared to have the inflexible character which it is now considered oppportune to accord to them? And while nothing can relieve the responsible officials of their duty to account for the business of the Republic, to prepare the budget for the State, and to reassemble the elements of the national forces, is it not right that they should be permitted to choose the time when this work can be best accomplished?

It is with the certainty that these wise reflections will be appreciated by the members of the assemblies who live in your district that I renew, monsieur the commissioner, assurances of my high consideration.

                                                        DARTIGUENAVE.

Notwithstanding the efforts of the President to have Congress postpone its meeting until the return of the commission, then in Washington to consult with the United States relative to the details and operation of the treaty, etc., the Haitian Congress met on April 3 and 4, but no quorum was present.

The official journal of Haiti, Le Moniteur, issued on April 5, published two decrees of the President of Haiti dated April 5, 1916. One dissolved the senate and decreed that the chamber of deputies shall be convened exclusively as a constituent assembly to, in cooperation with the executive power, revise the constitution of October 9, 1889, and perform such legislative work as may be called for by the President. The other decree created a council of state, composed of 21 members appointed by the President, whose duties shall be: First, to give its advice on all projects which the Government deems fit to send to it; second, to prepare and formulate laws, decrees, and other acts on matters on which the Government shall desire its action; third, to give its advice on all questions which may be submitted to it by the President and his cabinet. It was understood that this constituent assembly would revise the constitution to accord with the recent treaty and that the council of state would act with the Government in drawing up and preparing such changes and laws as might be necessary for this purpose. I therefore, on April 5, informed the Secretary of the Navy and Commander in Chief of the following by radiogram.

(The following is a translation of the decrees of the President of Haiti as published in Le Moniteur on April 5 dissolving the senate and creating the. council of state:)

DECREE CONCERNING THE COUNCIL OF STATE.

Dartiguenave, President of the Republic.

Whereas it has been shown by experience that legislative business requires a special preparation, which consequently necessitates the presence of a suitable organ with the political assemblies and with the executive authority: ·

DECREES.

ARTICLE 1. A council of state is appointed whose functions are:

1. To give advice on all plans which the Government may consider fit to submit to it.

2. To prepare and draw up bills, decrees, decisions, or other documents concerning subjects in regard to which the Government requires its attention.

3. To give advice on all questions submitted to it by the President of the Republic and the secretaries.

ART. 2. Councilors of state may be charged by the executive authority to support before the legislative body the bills which have been passed by the council of state.

ART. 3. The council of state is composed of 21 members, appointed by the President of the Republic. The secretaries of state have the power to participate as a deliberative body at the meetings of the general assembly and sections.

ART. 4. The bureau of the council of state, composed of a president and two secretaries, is elected by the council by secret ballot.

The mandate of the bureau lasts for one year and may be indefinitely renewed. In the absence of the President the council is presided over by the senior section president.

ART. 5. The functions of councilor of state are incompatible with every other public salaried function. Nevertheless, specialists, engineers, jurists, or others may be detached from a public service to take part in the work of the council as extraordinary councilors, with a consulting voice; and in this case, during their special mission, they retain the rights, prerogatives and salary belonging to their former positions but are not able to draw their salary with that from the council of state.

ART. 6. The council of state is divided into four sections. A public administrative regulation will decide on the interior order of the operations of the council. on the division of these operations among the sections, on the functioning of the general assembly, on the rotation of members between the sections, on the organization of the personnel which will be nominated by the President of the Republic, and in general on all the measures necessary to the satisfactory running of the institution.

ART. 7. A monthly remuneration of $150 will be handed to each councillor of state.

Issued at the National Palace, Port au Prince, April, 1916, the one hundred and thirteenth year of the independence.

DARTIGUENAVE.

By the President:

CONSTANTIN MAYARD,
The Secretary of the Interior.

EMILE ELIE,
The Secretary of Finance and Commerce.

E. DORNEVAL,
The Secretary of Justice and Public Worship.

LOUIS BORNO,
The Secretary of Foreign Affairs and Public Works.

LEON AUDAIN,
Secretary of Public Instruction.

A. ANDRE,
Secretary of War, Navy, and Agriculture.

DECREE.

Dartiguenave, President of the Republic.

Whereas the life and development of nations obey the natural laws to which the public law must adapt itself;

Whereas for a long time public opinion and the directing authorities have recognized the necessity of reforming the existing constitution; and the two former legislatures have formally manifested their willingness to do so;

Whereas to the reasons generally admitted up to last year there have been added others of still more urgent a nature, created by the new conditions imposed upon the Nation;

Whereas it is indispensable, in order that the convention of September 16, 1915, may be properly applied and may produce the advantages embodied in it, to accomplish the revision at as early a date as possible, of a large number of constitutional texts, notably those concerning public defense, finances, local institutions, reports of the public authorities, the number of deputies, and of senators, the right of real estate property;

Whereas with the present procedure of this revision it is in nowise possible to accomplish, in the proper time, these urgent reforms and a decisive measure of a character conforming best to the national necessities and to the democratic principles governing our institutions, must be introduced without delay;

Whereas the present chamber of deputies was formed by a special popular consultation which invested it directly with constituent authority, and this distinctive fundamental character is not possessed by the senate of the Republic:

For these reasons and on the advice of the council of the secretaries of state.

DECREES.

ARTICLE 1. The senate of the Republic is dissolved.

ART. 2. The chamber of deputies will be convened in exclusive capacity of constituent assembly to revise, in cooperation with the executive authority, the constitution of October 9, 1889, and take in hand organized decrees of public administration and all other acts of an urgent character the plans of which will be presented to it by the executive.

It will consist of an absolute majority of its members. (A majority of one more than half the number of members.)

ART. 3. A salary of $300 per month will be allowed to the constituents present in their seat.

ART. 4. The present decree will be published and executed by the secretaries of state, each acting with respect to that which concerns him.

Issued at the National Palace, Port-au-Prince, April 5, 1916, one hundred and thirteenth year of the independence.

DARTIGUENAVE.

By the President:
CONSTANTIN MAYARD,
    Secretary of the Interior.
LEON AUDAIN,
    Secretary of Public Instruction.
EMILE ELIE,
    Secretary of Finance and Commerce.
A. ANDRE,
    Secretary of War, Navy, and Agriculture.
E. DORNEVAL,
    Secretary of Justice and Public Worship.
LOUIS BORNO,
    Secretary of Foreign Affairs and Public Works.

The Senate did not meet on April 6, as on coming to the senate building it found the doors locked. The permanent committee met in the house of a member and decided to request the keys from the secretary of the interior. The Chamber of Deputies did not meet. On this date the President of Haiti directed a lieutenant of gendarmerie to lock the doors of the senate building. This lieutenant, A. August Daumec by name, locked the building at about 9.45 a. m., and then took the keys to the President, who then directed Lieut. Daumec to give them to the minister of interior, who was present. This Daumec did at about

10.30 a. m.   The Senate considering this measure rather irregular decided to meet on April 7 at 10 a. m. at a private dwelling.   What action was contemplated by it was not then known.   I took no action in this matter other than to preserve peace and order.

I reported the above facts to the Secretary of the Navy in a message as follows:

"In accordance with orders of the President, the senate building was locked on April 6.   The president of the permanent committee of the Senate have informed me that the legislative body views this procedure as an attempt upon national sovereignty and that they have decided to meet at a private dwelling, preserving all legal rights.   Am taking no action except preserving peace and order.   11308.

"CAPERTON."

On April 7 I received a message from the department asking if the Haitian Government had agreed to the distribution of the surplus revenue as authorized by the department, and in reply thereto I advised the department as follows:

"Haitian Government agrees to distribution, although opposed to payment interest foreign debt at this time.   Government has published in newspapers fact that distribution is being made and money has been transferred for that purpose.   21407.

"CAPERTON."

On April 8 members of the permanent committee of the dissolved Senate and several other senators met in the house of one of the members and decided to protest against the action of the President in dissolving the legislative bodies. Some of the deputies collected in the yard of the Senate and decided to take the same action as the Senate.   Some of these deputies were intoxicated.

On April 11 about 60 members of the dissolved Chamber of Deputies, who were to be convoked in accordance with the President's decree as a constituent assembly, met in the yard of the senate building.   No work was done except the preparation of a "procès verbal," stating that no quorum was present.

On this date the President issued a statement in the official newspaper, Le Moniteur, in which he stated that if the deputies would not perform their duties as a constituent assembly he would call a general election for a new constituent assembly.

On April 17 at a meeting of the "notables" of the city a committee was formed, with ex-President Legitime as president of the committee, to interview President Dartiguenave.   This committee of prominent nonpartisan citizens visited the President in an endeavor to bring about an amicable understanding between the President and the legislative bodies.

On April 19, by appointment, I held a conference with the President of Haiti in regard to the possibility of the Government reaching an agreement with the legislative bodies in connection with the necessary changes to the constitution of Haiti.   There were present at this conference, besides myself, the President of Haiti; the secretary of state for foreign affairs; the commander of the expeditionary forces ashore; Lieut. Col. Charles G. Long, United States Marine Corps; Lieut. Commander W. D. Leahy, commanding officer of the Dolphin, flagship, who since February 23 had been acting as my chief of staff; and the official Government interpreter, Depuy.

I pointed out the extreme desirability that the Government and the opposition to the Government should reach an amicable agreement.   I stated to the President that I had been told by presumably reliable persons of the opposition, as well as by members of the nonpartisan citizens of Haiti, that such an agreement was not impossible.   The President agreed to receive suggestions from the opposition and to give such suggestions full and honest consideration with a view of taking such action as was possible for the welfare of Haiti.   In order that any negotiations which might be started might not be interfered with, the members of the dissolved chambers were requested not to meet in their assumed capacity as legislative bodies.

On April 23 Mr. Borno, secretary of state for foreign affairs, came on board the Dolphin for an interview.   Mr. Borno at this conference discussed the basis of agreement proposed by the opposition and made a verbal statement of a "basis of agreement" which would be satisfactory to his Government.

On April 25, at a conference consisting of ex-President Legitime, Minister Bailly-Blanchard, M. Leon, president of the Chamber of Deputies, Col. Waller,

Lieut. Commander Leahy, and myself, a proposed basis of agreement between the Government and opposition, which had been previously prepared by the Chamber of Deputies, was discussed at length. The opposition made no material concessions to the Government. Following this an appointment was made with the President, at which the following were present: Ex-President Legitime, Minister Borno, M. Mathon, member of citizens' committee, Col. Waller, Lieut. Commander Leahy, and myself. After reading the opposition's proposed basis of agreement the President of Haiti informed ex-President Legitime that it was not possible for him to consider it, and that further discussion of the paper was useless. At the completion of this discussion, the President prepared a modified statement of the Government's proposed basis of agreement, which seemed to concede to the opposition in every material point which they desired, except that his decree of April 5 should not be revoked and that the two houses of the legislature should in this session make a complete revision of the constitution in order that it might be placed entirely in agreement with the American-Haitian convention and fit the new conditions which had arisen in the country because of the convention; and that the two chambers after organizing as a national constituent assembly and appointing a committee to formulate the necessary changes in the constitution, should adjourn for two months in order that information necessary for the formulation of changes might be received from the Haitian commission then in Washington. This last stipulation was made by the Government in order to avoid the large expenditures of public money which would be necessary in order to keep Congress in session pending the receipt of information from the Haitian commission in Washington, when there would be no useful work for them to perform.

After extended conferences with the two sides of the controversy, it was evident that the President justified his decree and action subsequent thereto on the necessity for obtaining a prompt and complete revision of the constitution in order that it might agree with the American-Haitian convention, and the new conditions which had arisen in virtue of this commission and also other reforms which had for many years been recognized as necessary. He was also influenced by the necessity for economy in the expenditure of the public funds.

On April 27 the dissolved Senate and Chamber of Deputies met in a rented house and organized as a national assembly. This was done contrary to an agreement. I have since been assured by the president of the dissolved Chamber of Deputies that the meeting was due entirely to a misunderstanding in regard to the necessity for permission to meet. No work was done other than that of forming a national assembly. It was then stipulated and understood by the dissolved legislative bodies that there would be no further meetings until an agreement was reached by the opposing factions.

At 8 o'clock p. m. on the 29th of April the president of the Senate and the president of the Chamber of Deputies, with several of their colleagues, arrived at the place of meeting and the president of the Senate showed me a letter signed by a majority of the Senate directing him to refuse acceptance of the basis of agreement, unless it could be stipulated that the legislative bodies should retain all their legislative functions. The president of the Chamber of Deputies at the same time informed me that his chamber could not agree to the proposal without the concurrence of the Senate.

I then informed the President that the failure of my efforts as a friendly intermediary to obtain an agreement between the Government and the opposition made it necessary, in order to insure the maintenance of peace and order, that I should comply with my orders to support the Government of Haiti, and of my intention to support it.

This information was then given to the president of the senate and to the president of the chamber of deputies, with the request that it be communicated to the members of the two dissolved legislative bodies.

During many conferences with the opposition to the Government the opposition had stated that there was much dissatisfaction to certain members of the cabinet, but none in regard to the President himself. I therefore fully informed the President of this matter, and he stated he was aware of this dissatisfaction and had already prepared the necessary papers for the dissolution of his cabinet.

At 11 a. m., May 2, the minister of foreign relations, Borno, called upon me by appointment to discuss the present situation. He informed me that the President of Haiti had completed arrangements for dissolving his cabinet, but had not yet definitely selected all of the members of the new cabinet. He also informed me that the President was considering the names of men to serve on his council of state, which was to be formed in accordance with the provisions of the decree of April 5. and that it was the President's desire to obtain in this council of state the services of some prominent members of the opposition to the Government, if they could be induced to serve, his idea being to demonstrate that he wished all factions to be represented in the work of revising the constitution.

At 2.30 p. m., on May 2 I also met on board the flagship, by appointment, the president of the senate. the president of the chamber of deputies, and several members of the two chambers. These men requested that I make a further effort to continue negotiations looking toward an agreement between them and the President, and assured me that the two chambers were now willing to sign the basis of agreement, which they had refused to consider on April 29. In view of the fact that I had informed both the Government and the opposition on April 29 that the failure of the opposition at that time to agree had made further conciliatory efforts on my part useless, and that I would therefore support the recognized and established Government, and in view also of the fact that the Government had already taken steps, which could not easily be withdrawn, to carry out its work of reform with the assurance that I would support it, such as dissolving his cabinet, etc., I informed the visiting members of the opposition that it would not be possible for me to inaugurate any further negotiations, and that I regretted extremely the failure of my efforts to bring about an amicable agreement.

With reference to the dissolution of the cabinet by the President, on May 3 I was informed in writing by Minister Borno that the President's cabinet had tendered its resignation.

During the past few days the reports from Santo Domingo showed that the situation there was fast approaching a crisis; therefore on May 9 I reported the conditions to the Secretary of the Navy and stated that I would proceed with the *Dolphin* to Santo Domingo at daylight on May 10, to arrive there the evening of May 11.

On May 11, while en route to Santo Domingo on the *Dolphin*, I sent the following message to the department, the information contained therein having been reported to me by radio from Port au Prince:

"New cabinet announced in papers. Borno foreign affairs. public works, public instruction temporarily ; Edmond Hereaux, finance ; Constant Vieux, interior ; Dorneval, justice, agriculture. No communication with San Domingo City. 02211.

"CAPERTON."

I arrived at Santo Domingo City on the *Dolphin* at 6.05 a. m., May 12, 1916.

On July 7 I received by cable a message from the department stating that the department desired me to relieve Admiral C. McR. Winslow and asked what was the earliest date possible for me to get away in case my relief was sent down. They further added that owing to the peculiar conditions it was desired that my staff remain with my successor, at least, for the present.

On July 18, 1916, at 9 a. m., I turned over the command of the cruiser squadron to Rear Admiral Charles F. Pond, my successor, and proceeded via Washington. D. C., to take command of the Pacific Fleet, in accordance with my orders, and on July 28 relieved Admiral Winslow as commander in chief of the Pacific Fleet, assuming the rank of admiral.

Mr. ANGELL. It is entered in there as a statement that it was requested. and I was trying to find out the details of the request, if you could recall.

(Whereupon the committee adjourned until Monday, October 24, 1921, at 10.30 o'clock a. m.)

INQUIRY INTO OCCUPATION AND ADMINISTRATION OF HAITI AND SANTO DOMINGO.

MONDAY, OCTOBER 24, 1921.

UNITED STATES SENATE,
SELECT COMMITTEE ON HAITI AND SANTO DOMINGO,
Washington, D. C.

The committee met at 10.30 o'clock a. m., pursuant to adjournment, Senator Medill McCormick (chairman) presiding.

Present: Senators McCormick, Oddie, and Pomerene.

Also present: Mr. Ernest Angell and Maj. Edwin N. McClellan, United States Marine Corps, in their respective representative capacities as hereinbefore indicated; and Mr. Walter Bruce Howe, as counsel for the committee.

STATEMENT OF MAJ. GEN. GEO. BARNETT, UNITED STATES MARINE CORPS, COMMANDING THE DEPARTMENT OF THE PACIFIC, SAN FRANCISCO, CALIF.

The CHAIRMAN. General, will you give your name and rank to the stenographer of the committee?

Gen. BARNETT. George Barnett, major general, United States Marine Corps, commanding the Department of the Pacific; station, San Francisco, Calif.

The CHAIRMAN. During what period were you commandant of the Marine Corps?

Gen. BARNETT. From February 25, 1914, to June 30, 1920.

The CHAIRMAN. This covered the entire period of the American occupation in Haiti?

Gen. BARNETT. Until that time. They are still there; yes, sir.

The CHAIRMAN. You began your service before we landed in Haiti?

Gen. BARNETT. I did; yes, sir.

The CHAIRMAN. So that what transpired in Haiti up to the time of your transfer to San Francisco was during the period of your command of the Marine Corps?

Gen. BARNETT. It was.

The CHAIRMAN. I think, General, if you will proceed to comment upon your report and upon your communications regarding the allegations of harsh usage of the natives of Haiti by the Marine Corps, in your own way, that that would be the shortest road to what we have in mind.

Senator POMERENE. Mr. Chairman, has that report been incorporated in our proceedings here?

The CHAIRMAN. It has been published by the department.

Senator POMERENE. How long is it?

Gen. BARNETT. It is 110 pages in this report of the Secretary of the Navy. It is in there I have not doubt.

Maj. McCLELLAN. It is published in the report of the Secretary of the Navy for 1920.

Senator POMERENE. Can we each be furnished a copy of that report?

Gen. BARNETT. There were plenty of them at headquarters; I have no doubt there are plenty yet.

Senator POMERENE. I saw at the time newspaper abstracts from it.

Gen. BARNETT. They took a very few abstracts from that.

Senator POMERENE. But I would like to have the opportunity to read it.

Gen. BARNETT. Yes, sir.

The CHAIRMAN. Let me, then, ask that Maj. McClellan supply to the committee copies of all reports to which reference is made—the Mayo report and Maj. Turner's report—in so far as that has been printed or mimeographed.

Maj. McCLELLAN. Yes, sir.

The CHAIRMAN. I do that seeking to economize in the printing.

Senator POMERENE. That is, Admiral Mayo's report?

The CHAIRMAN. Yes.

Gen. BARNETT. Admiral Mayo was the president of the court of inquiry.

Senator POMERENE. Has Maj. Turner's report ever been printed or mimeographed?

Maj. McCLELLAN. No, sir. Maj. Turner's report, from what I can gather as to what is in the committee's mind, consists of all the investigations which were initiated by Gen. Barnett's order——

Gen. BARNETT. That is right.

Maj. McCLELLAN. After he had read certain court-martial records.

Gen. BARNETT. That is right.

Maj. McCLELLAN. A naval court of inquiry was carried on both in Haiti and in the United States.

The CHAIRMAN. I want all that correspondence.

Gen. BARNETT. I will say here, Senator, that the Turner report which you mentioned had not been received up to the time I was relieved as commandant of the Marine Corps; but since I was relieved, in the headquarters of the Marine Corps I saw a copy of Maj. Turner's report, as forwarded by Col. Russell. What action was taken on that report I do not know; I was not informed.

The CHAIRMAN. We want all the correspondence, and that we will incorporate in the record.

Gen. BARNETT. As I remember, an investigation was ordered by Col. Russell immediately upon receipt of my letter, and a report by Maj. Turner was afterwards forwarded to headquarters after I left, and I think in that report, as I remember it—I just casually glanced over it one day after I was relieved, as a matter of information—I think Maj. Turner's report was pretty explicit and recommended certain trials by court-martial.

The CHAIRMAN. Did Col. Lay have to do with that investigation?

Gen. BARNETT. Col. Lay had this to do with it. In the organization of headquarters of the Marine Corps when I was commandant, as always, all court-martial records, when marines are tried, first are sent to the Judge Advocate General of the Navy, who, before forwarding them to the Secretary of the Navy for approval or disapproval, sends them to the commandant of the Marine Corps, who, by indorsement, returns them to the Judge Advocate General before they go to the Secretary of the Navy. Col. Lay was in the office of Gen. Haines, who was adjutant and inspector of the Marine Corps at that time and therefore in charge of the records of the Marine Corps, and Gen. Haines had detailed Col. Lay to read all court-martial records. Of course, I did not have time enough to read all the court-martial records carefully, but it was Col. Lay's duty to read all the court-martial records carefully, and if they contained any matter of importance, out of the ordinary, routine matter, instead of just preparing a formal indorsement upon them and returning them directly to the Judge Advocate General, before making any indorsement he would bring them to my attention, and I would read the records then.

The court-martial cases of Pvt. Johnson and Pvt. McQuilkin were considered by Col. Lay of such an unusual character that, after he read them, he brought them to Gen. Haines, his superior in his own department, and Gen. Haines read them and brought them to me. I read those two cases.

Senator POMERENE. Let me ask you a preliminary question there. You used the expression, "to read all court-martial proceedings"?

Gen. BARNETT. Yes, sir.

Senator POMERENE. How many of them were there?

Gen. BARNETT. A great many.

Senator POMERENE. Arising——

Gen. BARNETT. Not in this case. I mean all court-martial records in the Marine Corps. If a general court-martial any place in the world tries a marine, the record is sent to the Judge Advocate General's office, and then, according to routine, it comes to me as commandant of the Marine Corps.

Senator POMERENE. These two cases were our own cases, were they?

Gen. BARNETT. Our own cases, the cases of two marines who were tried in Haiti by a general court-martial. Those cases were brought to me, and I read them over, and was so startled by the disclosures shown in the evidence, and particularly by the statement of the counsel for the accused, who was a Lieut. Spear, at that time in the Marine Corps——

The Chairman. Incorporate in the record Lieut. Spear's argument.

Gen. Barnett. Lieut. Spear in his argument for his client stated that these marines—I think he was counsel for Pvt. Johnson—that in this case where they were tried and convicted, the court should not judge them too harshly, because they were following a general custom, and that he, Lieut. Spear, had himself seen many similar cases of executions of that kind.

The Chairman. Executions without trial?

Gen. Barnett. Yes, sir.

Senator Pomerene. You mean down in Haiti?

Gen. Barnett. Yes, sir. Now, I wish to say right here, which has, in my opinion, a very decided bearing on my act in that case, that in the first place I was commanding officer of the whole Marine Corps. A certain condition was brought to my attention by the records in these two cases, and particularly by the statement of counsel for the accused, and I considered that some drastic action was necessary at once. I, being commanding officer, it was up to me to act, and I took the action that I thought at that time, and still think, regardless of any report of the court of inquiry or anybody else, that I had to take. I settled that case myself, and I settled it promptly and quickly, and I settled it efficiently. I wrote an official letter on the 27th day of September, 1919, the day these records came to my attention.

The Chairman. A letter to whom?

Gen. Barnett. A letter to Col. Russell, the brigade commander of the marines stationed in Haiti. I took what I considered at that time, and what I still consider, proper action. I claim that nobody had a right to question my mode of doing that work as long as my work done efficiently. It was done efficiently for this reason, because Col. Russell got my letter, and got my personal letter which I wrote five days later, because I had reread the cases in the meantime and was so impressed with the importance of these two cases that I wrote another letter, which I have copied in my report, stating to Col. Russell in the second letter, or reiterating, what I said before, the absolute necessity for investigation.

Senator Pomerene. Nearly all of this is Greek to me.

Gen. Barnett. I will be glad to enlighten you.

Senator Pomerene. Tell me who Johnson and McQuilkin were and what the charges were.

Gen. Barnett. Pvt. Johnson and Pvt. McQuilkin were two privates in the Marine Corps stationed in the province of Hinche, under the command of a temporary lieutenant in the Marine Corps in Haiti named Brokaw. According to the evidence produced in these two cases, these——

Senator Pomerene. What was the charge against them?

Gen. Barnett. The charge was murder.

Senator Pomerene. Of some native?

Gen. Barnett. Of two or three natives. The record, which you will have, shows that these two or three people who were killed—two at least were Haitian prisoners—and that they were taken out by order of Lieut. Brokaw, in charge of these two marines, Johnson and McQuilkin, and put alongside of their graves, and Johnson and McQuilkin were ordered to shoot them, which they did.

The Chairman. By whom?

Gen. Barnett. Brokaw. Brokaw has since been committed to an insane asylum, and he is there, I think. I stated in my report, as will appear in this report, that no action could be taken in the case of Lieut. Brokaw because he was in an insane asylum at that time.

The Chairman. Who was commandant of the marines or constabulary, or both, in Haiti at the time?

Gen. Barnett. At that time the commandant of the marines was Col. Russell, John H. Russell, and in charge of the gendarmerie, as they call it in Haiti, was Col. A. S. Williams.

Senator Pomerene. What was the pretended reason for the execution of these natives?

Gen. Barnett. That I have no knowledge of.

Senator Pomerene. By Johnson and McQuilkin?

Gen. Barnett. They never tried to show any reason for it whatever. I would suggest there, Senator, that it would be better to get the records of the courts-martial and read the exact charges rather than rely on my memory, because this was two years ago last September.

The CHAIRMAN. We have the records.

Gen. BARNETT. That was, as I say, over two years ago; but I am perfectly convinced in my own mind, knowing this case from A to Z, that it was the first case of any unlawful action by any Marine in Haiti—the first knowledge that ever came to my desk.

Senator POMERENE. How soon did you learn about it after it occurred?

Gen. BARNETT. A very short time. The case was forwarded to the Judge Advocate General immediately after the trial, and on the same day or the day after, probably—a few days, anyhow—he forwarded the case to me. That was on the 27th day of September, 1919, that I got the record. On that same day I read it carefully and put an indorsement on it returning it to the Judge Advocate General; and knowing that that case, in the ordinary course of events, would in a very few days be presented by the Judge Advocate General to the Secretary of the Navy for approval or disapproval, having put a formal indorsement on it, and having written the same day to Col. Russell, the commanding officer in Haiti, telling him my views, as formed on account of this testimony and the statement of counsel for the accused. I went to the Secretary of the Navy and told him that I had gotten two cases from Haiti which disturbed me very much, but that I had written the necessary order to Col. Russell for complete correction of the faults, as disclosed by those two cases. He said all right.

Senator POMERENE. It was pretty hard to correct them if they were dead?

Gen. BARNETT. I know; but to prevent anything of that kind in the future. Those cases were, as a matter of fact, a very few days later taken to the Secretary of the Navy, and he signed them, approving both cases. By that act, of course——

Senator POMERENE. Approved them?

Gen. BARNETT. No; approved the action of the court.

Senator POMERENE. That meant a disaffirmance of your position?

Gen. BARNETT. No; not at all. There was no question of affirmance at that time at all—none whatever. I put a formal indorsement on it, just returning it to the Judge Advocate General. That is all I could put on a case like that, because the case was finished—settled. I simply showed by my indorsement that it had passed before me and that he had carried out the naval regulations in presenting it to the commandant of the Marine Corps for any remarks he wished to make.

Senator POMERENE. In what respect were those two men, Johnson and McQuilkin, to blame if they were simply carrying out the orders of their superiors?

Gen. BARNETT. That was not for me to decide; that was for the court. I did not have any witnesses before me at all.

Senator POMERENE. But I am asking you for your judgment about it. In what respect did they offend?

Gen. BARNETT. No man in the service is compelled or has a right to carry out an illegal order. That is the one case in the service where anybody is justified in disobeying orders—if he gets an illegal order.

Senator POMERENE. Who is to decide what is an illegal order?

Gen. BARNETT. The man himself must decide and take responsibility.

Now, as I say, knowing these cases would come before the Secretary of the Navy in a very few days, and not wanting him to think I had just passed two such important cases in a pro forma way, I spoke to the Secretary of the Navy. Two or three days later—maybe a week later—those two cases went before him, and he approved them, thereby taking the same action I had. I only mention this because the public press has done a lot of printing about this matter, and it was stated that the Secretary of the Navy did not know about these cases until after my final report was published. He passed judgment on both of those cases and approved them absolutely a few days after——

The CHAIRMAN. Approved these decisions?

Gen. BARNETT. Approved the findings of the court.

Senator POMERENE. What was that finding?

Gen. BARNETT. That I do not remember. That was of no importance to me whatever, because I had no remarks to make upon the cases.

Senator POMERENE. Has this record been briefed in any way, or must I wade through that whole record in order to find out what the facts are[

Mr. Howe. It has not been briefed. It did not reach my office until last week, and I have been unable to take it up or touch it so far.

Senator Pomerene. Is it your purpose to brief them?

Mr. Howe. Yes, sir.

Gen. Barnett. But I want to say, and say most positively, that I wrote that letter on October 2, which is called the confidential letter, and I marked it "confidential," because it was upon the same subject as the letter which I had written him five days before, the official letter, and I wanted Col. Russell to know how important I considered these cases, and I wanted him to strain every effort to make a complete investigation of this affair.

Col. Russell got both of my letters. Here is my letter. First, I had better read the letter of September 27, 1919. This was the official letter. I marked that "confidential" also, not personal, but confidential, because I did not want that letter to arrive in Col. Russell's office in Haiti and have all his clerks see it and be able to warn anybody of what might be expected in the line of an investigation. This letter reads as follows:

[Confidential.]

SEPTEMBER 27, 1919.

From: The major general commandant.

To: The brigade commander, First Provisional Brigade, Marine, Port au Prince, Haiti.

Subject: Unlawful acts by members of the gendarmerie d'Haiti and marines in Haiti.

1. It appears from the testimony in the general court-martial cases of Pvts. Walter E. Johnson and John J. McQuilkin, jr., Marine Corps, and from the argument of the counsel for the defense in the case of Pvt. Johnson, First Lieut. F. L. Spear, that unlawful executions of Haitians, called Cacos, have occurred in Haiti. You will issue immediately necessary and proper instructions regarding these unlawful actions.

2. It appears that Sergt. Brokaw, lieutenant of the gendarmerie, has been transferred north to the hospital, so no action can be taken in this case.

3. Make an investigation and submit a confidential report regarding the actions of Lieut. Spear, as stated in his argument as counsel for the defense in the court-martial case of Pvt. Johnson. A copy of this argument is attached hereto.

4. Such unwarranted and unlawful actions on the part of officers and men of the Marine Corps or of the gendarmerie d'Haiti can not be tolerated under any circumstances.

GEORGE BARNETT.

Senator Pomerene. Now, General, you use the expression there, "executions of this character."

Gen. Barnett. Indiscriminate killing.

Senator Pomerene. Indiscriminate killing?

Gen. Barnett. Yes, sir.

Senator Pomerene. To what extent had that been going on?

Gen. Barnett. I knew only of these two cases, and I formed my whole opinion on what was before me when I wrote that letter, that being the evidence in those two cases of Johnson and McQuilkin, particularly the statement of the counsel for the accused, who stated, in effect, that these men should not be punished for their acts, because they were following the general custom, and that he himself had seen many similar cases.

Senator Pomerene. Was that all the information that you had, and all the knowledge upon which you based your letter?

Gen. Barnett. That was all the information I had.

Senator Pomerene. After you had written that, did you make any further investigation to ascertain what the particular facts were upon which the lieutenant had based his statement?

Gen. Barnett. That I ordered Col. Russell to make.

Senator Pomerene. Are you coming to that later on?

Gen. Barnett. I am; yes, sir.

The Chairman. Then, General, will you proceed to answer Senator Pomerene's question now, or, if you prefer, make a note of it and go on with your story.

Gen. BARNETT. My letter was received by Col. Russell. Here is the answer of Col. Russell to my letter:

[Personal.]

HEADQUARTERS FIRST PROVISIONAL BRIGADE,
UNITED STATES MARINE CORPS,
Port au Prince, Republic of Haiti, October 17, 1919.

Maj. Gen. GEORGE BARNETT,
Major General Commandant United States Marine Corps,
Headquarters United States Marine Corps, Washington, D. C.

MY DEAR GENERAL: I received your letter in the last mail, and am answering it at once to assure you that I have taken up the matter you mention most seriously and will go into it thoroughly. I am inclosing herewith a copy of a confidential order which I have just issued, as well as a proclamation. The proclamation will be published in all the newspapers in Haiti, posted in all towns, and read at the markets to the people of each town by the majistrat (mayor).

I have gotten out several other proclamations since my arrival, with a view of quieting the fears of the people regarding the bandits.

Almost immediately upon my arrival things began popping here right and left and, together with an unsatisfactory political situation, kept me on the jump.

I wrote Gen. Long the other day regarding conditions here, and I have no doubt he has informed you.

We have now completely cleared the plain of the cul-de-sac of bandit groups, and at present they appear to be gathering in Honda Valley, with a view, possibly, of crossing the border and going to northern Haiti or of another descent in the plains. The latter I hardly believe, as we get at them too readily when they are in the plains.

I am now making preparations to strike the band from Belladare, Las Cohobas, Savanette. It will be unable to cross the border if our plans work out, but those that get away will be forced to scatter and retreat toward the Grand Bois.

It is estimated that about 2,000 bandits infest the hills. They are under Charlemagne Peralte, who styles himself the supreme chief. I estimate that they are mostly armed with machetes, knives, pikes, a few pistols, and some 200 or 300 rifles. I don't believe that in all Haiti there are more than 400 to 500 rifles, if that many. They are very short of ammunition. They use our ammunition and the Krag by tying a piece of goatskin on string around the base of the cartridge. I have consequently issued very strict orders regarding the accounting of our own and gendarmerie ammunition.

The Haitians, as you no doubt know, are a very hysterical people. Hundreds of rumors are circulated among them daily that are simply ridiculous, but, like children, they believe them and completely lose their heads. It is very hard, in consequence, to quiet them; however, I believe I have now succeeded in bucking them up. Of course, the officials seized the opportunity to make as much as they could out of the affair until I sent for the President's brother (minister of interior), told him plainly that the Government, instead of cooperating with me, was obstructing my work and that I would not stand for it; then things brightened up as far as the officials were concerned.

Yesterday I accompanied the American minister on a visit to the President, with the result that one of the cabinet members who has been a great obstructionist has resigned, so that the political situation is also much brighter.

As you know, General, I shall give my very best to the situation here, which is far from satisfactory; and with the backing that I know I may expect from headquarters, I feel confident I can clear it up and make a record for the corps.

With kindest regards to Mrs. Barnett and yourself,

Very sincerely,

JOHN H. RUSSELL.

Then here is the proclamation. It is written in French and then translated. The translation is not in the original report, as printed, but I have the translation here.

(The proclamation referred to, both in French and English, is here printed in full, as follows:)

NOUVELLE ADRESSE A LA POPULATION.

HEADQUARTERS FIRST PROVISIONAL BRIGADE,
UNITED STATES MARINE CORPS,
Port au Prince, Republic of Haiti, 15 Octobre, 1919.

CITOYENS: Vous etes tous convaincus maintenant que le régime de la corvée a été définitivement aboli. A une certaine éqoque, un tel travail par votre gouvernement a été juge nécessaire, ce afin de vous ouvrir certaines parties de votre Pays qui étaient presque inaccessibles; mais il y a de cela plus d'un an qu'il a été décidé que la nécessité pour de tels travaux n'existant plus, la corvée conséquemment a été abolie et ne sera plus envigueur en Haiti.

L'occupation entend établir pour vous, dans votre Pays, une paix permanente, afin de bous permettre de vous engager dans les travaux agricoles et autres et de gagner par la une existence honnete.

A cela je vous adjure de continuer à vaquer à vos occupations usuelles, dans la persuasion que vous estes entiérement et sincérement protégés par l'occupation.

L'occupation est déterminée à faire que les lois d'Haiti soient respectées et elle assurera de son entiére protection tous les bons et paisibles citoyens, tandis qu'elle pourchassera les bandits.

JOHN H. RUSSELL,
Colonel du Corps d'Infanterie de Marines Commandant de la Brigade.

NEW ADDRESS TO THE POPULATION.
HEADQUARTERS FIRST PROVISIONAL BRIGADE,
UNITED STATES MARINE CORPS,
Port au Prince, Republic of Haiti, October 15, 1919.

CITIZENS: You have now all been assured that the reign of corvee has been definitely abolished. At a certain time a certain form of work had been judged as necessary by your Government, which was the means of open certain parts of your country which was almost inaccessible, but a year ago it had been decided that the need for such work was not necessary. Corvee, consequently, has been abolished and will never be in usage in Haiti.

The occupation intends to establish for you, in your country, a permanent peace, in order that you may engage yourself in your agricultural enterprises and others, and thus be able to earn an honest living.

To this I pray you to continue your former occupation with zeal in the persuasion that you are entirely and sincerely protected by the occupation.

The occupation is determined to enforce only the laws of Haiti and have them respected, and it will assure its entire protection to all the good and peaceable citizens while it will drive out the bandits.

JOHN H. RUSSELL,
Colonel, United States Marine Corps,
Commandant of the Brigade.

HEADQUARTERS FIRST PROVISIONAL BRIGADE,
UNITED STATES MARINE CORPS,
Port au Prince, Republic of Haiti, October 15, 1919.

Confidential Order:

1. The brigade commander has had brought to his attention an alleged charge against marines and gendarmes in Haiti to the effect that in the past prisoners and wounded bandits have been summarily shot without trial. Furthermore, that troops in the field have declared and carried on what is commonly known as an "open season," where care is not taken to determine whether or not the natives encountered are bandits or "good citizens" and where houses have been ruthlessly burned merely because they were unoccupied and native property otherwise destroyed.

2. Such action on the part of any officer or enlisted man of the Marine Corps is beyond belief; and if true, would be a terrible smirch upon the unblemished record of the corps, which we all hold so dear.

3. Any officer, noncommissioned officer, or private of the Marine Corps, or any officer or enlisted man of the United States Navy attached to this brigade, or

any officer, noncommissioned officer, or privaae of the gendarmerie d'Haiti, guilty of the unjustifiable and illegal killing of any person whomsoever will be brought to trial before a general court-martial or military commission on a charge of murder or manslaughter, as the case may warrant.

4. The unjustifiable malteatment of natives and the unlawful violation of their person or property will result in the trial and punishment of the offender.

5. All officers and noncommissioned officers are enjoined to see that the provisions of this order are most strictly enforced, and anyone having a knowledge of the violation of this order and not promptly reporting it will be considered an accessory to the crime.

6. This order will be furnished all commanding officers, and the contents of this confidential order will be carefully and fully explained to every officer, noncommissioned officer, and private in the Marine Corps and gendarmerie d'Haiti in Haiti.

7. Commanding officers will report in writing to the brigade commander when every officer and enlisted man in their respective commands have been thoroughly informed and are fully aware of the contents of this order.

8. The chief of the gendarmerie d'Haiti will report in writing to the brigade commander, when every office and enlisted man in the gendarmerie and coast guard is fully conversant with the contents of this order.

9. Upon arrival in Haiti, all commissioned officers and enlisted men of the Marine Corps will immediately be fully informed of the contents of this order and the commanding officer of units to which they are assigned will report in writing to their immediate senior in command that this has been done.

10. The chief of the gendarmerie d'Haiti will have the contents of this confidential order carefully explained to all officers and men joining his organization and will be held strictly responsible that all officers and men in the gendarmerie d'Haiti are at all times thoroughly familiar with it.

JOHN H. RUSSELL.

The CHAIRMAN. General, I think it would be useful if you would indicate, provided you can, how the committee may pursue an investigation to determine the truth of the general allegations that there were punishments or killings without trial.

Gen. BARNETT. As I stated before, the two cases that I know of positively are these two cases of Johnson and McQuilkin. In my opinion, no progress can be made, and no legitimate report by a court of inquiry or anybody else can be made, as to the justification for my letter, without the testimony of Lieut. Spear. Whether they had him or not I do not know, but, in my opinion, a report of anybody as to whether or not I was justified in writing that letter is foolishness, unless the testimony of Lieut. Spear can be obtained.

The CHAIRMAN. Now, General, we know where Lieut. Spear is. The case at issue is not the justification for your letter.

Gen. BARNETT. Not a bit, sir.

The CHAIRMAN. You mentioned Lieut. Spear. Are there other persons, officers of the Marine Corps or not, for whom this committee ought to send to find information bearing on this subject?

Gen. BARNETT. As I stated before, the only cases I knew of were those two cases. Now, as I said in answer to my letter to Col. Russell, an investigation was ordered, as I understand, by Col. Russell, in direct compliance with my letter, and was ordered made by Maj. Thomas C. Turner. That report was received. As I stated to you a moment ago, I saw that report after I was relieved as commandant. The report was not received until afterwards. That report was made by order of Col. Russell, and forwarded by him to the Marine Corps headquarters. I read that report over very carefully several days after I was relieved and after this whole business was up. As I remember it, Maj. Turner, in accordance with the report forwarded by Col. Russell, recommended the trial by court-martial of certain people. I have not the records in the case, because they never came to my notice. I was not commandant of the Marine Corps at that time, consequently the papers did not come to me, but I was shown that report at headquarters, and I know that certain people were recommended for trial by court-martial. I do not remember definitely who they were, except, I do think, Maj. Wells was one man recommended for trial by court-martial.

The CHAIRMAN. What Maj. Wells?

Gen. BARNETT. Clark H. Wells. I think Maj. Clark H. Wells was ordered tried by court-martial by the Navy Department, and the court was ordered, but whether he has been tried or not I do not know. I will state, prompted by Maj. McClellan, that he was not tried; for what reason I do not know.

I have heard rumors—I do not even know where they came from—but this whole question was talked about a great deal at headquarters, and I heard rumors at that time that Lieut. J. P. Adams or Capt. J. P. Adams, who is now out of the service, and probably at Charleston, S. C., would make a very good witness before the committee. I do not know what he would testify to. I never knew him, and never saw him in my life, never had a word with him. I have heard that Maj. Woodworth knows something about it.

With the permission of the committee, I would like to continue my statement just enough to show what communications I had with the Secretary of the Navy about this.

The CHAIRMAN. Continue.

Gen. BARNETT. When I wrote my original letter I said that I spoke to the Secretary of the Navy about the two cases in general terms. No more knowledge came to me of this case until in the summer of 1920. When I was on leave at home I got an order from the Secretary of the Navy to come to Washington and make a report of what I knew about the trouble in Haiti. Thinking that he meant about these two cases, I brought with me copies of my letters of September 27, 1919, and October 2, 1919, and took them to the Secretary of the Navy and sat down with him at his desk. He read that letter absolutely from "whereas" to "amen," and we discussed it fully, giving full knowledge to him of my letter and what had been done in Haiti.

A few days later the Secretary of the Navy told me to make a report on Haiti. I made a report, and my two letters were attached to that report, which only dealt with these two cases of Johnson and McQuilkin, and those two letters were on there as appendages, Appendages A and B. The Secretary of the Navy said he did not have time to read it then, but that he would take it home with him and see me the next day. He sent for me the next day and said to me, "General, this is all right as far as it goes, but what I want is a complete report on Haiti, showing in that report everything that has happened, every order that has been given, every letter that has been written or received at the headquarters of the Marine Corps or Navy Department from the first occupation in 1915-to the time when you were relieved on June 30, 1920." Those two letters, as I have said, were appendages. He went on to say, "When you make your final report, instead of putting these letters on as appendages, put them in the body of your report, so that whoever reads the report will not have to look back and see what the appendage is, but can read it with the report."

When I made this final report I put them in the report.

A few days after that the Secretary of the Navy sent for Gen. Haines and me to discuss affairs in Haiti again, and again and in Gen. Haines's presence I showed these two letters to the Secretary of the Navy. In my final report, as I say, I put that letter in the body of the report as directed by him, because he told me to put everything I had received or written with reference to Haiti, or anybody else had written or received from Haiti, in the report.

The CHAIRMAN. In the report?

Gen. BARNETT. In this report; yes, sir; in my final report. After I had handed in this final report of 110 pages the Secretary of the Navy said to me, "This is too long to read now; I will take it home with me to-night and read it and see you to-morrow." I was under orders then to San Francisco and I was simply waiting his permission to go, in accordance with my orders.

The next day, about 3 o'clock in the afternoon, he sent for me, and he had this report in his hand, and he said, 'General, this is all right. You may carry out your orders to San Francisco." Again, this letter was in this report. Whether or not the Secretary of the Navy read my report that night I do not know, but I imagine that he had turned it over to Mr. Jenkins, his publicity man, who was on duty in the Navy Department, because Mr. Jenkins——

The CHAIRMAN. His publicity man?

Gen. BARNETT. Well, whatever he called him. He was a newspaper man originally from the Baltimore American. I do not know in what capacity he was in the Navy Department, but he attended to a great deal of personal matter for the Secretary.

The CHAIRMAN. The Secretary's personal publicity?

Gen. BARNETT. I do not know what it was. Maybe Maj. McClellan can tell us what his duty was there.

Maj. McCLELLAN. It was not personal, although he may have done personal work. He is a well known man there.

Gen. BARNETT. He was on duty in the department and is a well known man—a fine fellow.

The CHAIRMAN. What was his correct duty?

Gen. BARNETT. I do not know. Immediately when I saw the Secretary he said to me, "You may carry out your orders and proceed to San Francisco." Immediately when I left the office Mr. Jenkins came up to me and shook hands with me and said, "General, that is the most complete report I ever read since I have been in the Navy Department." He shook hands, congratulated me, and said good-bye to me. That lead me to believe that Jenkins read the report and reported to the Secretary that it was all right.

I left that evening for San Francisco. I was called back from Chicago because the morning papers had published my letter and made a considerable furore about this. I was surprised to find by the morning papers that the Secretary of the Navy had stated that he had never seen my letter until this report was published that morning. I immediately took the newspaper article and went to the Secretary's office and in the presence of Gen Lejeune and Asst. Secretary of the Navy Mr. Woodbury I said, "Mr. Daniels, I see in the morning papers that you have stated that you never saw my letter until it was published." He said, "I never saw it." I said, "Excuse me, sir, but you did see it." And then I said to him just what I have said to this committee, that he saw it in my presence, read it, and discussed it fully the first time. He said, "I never saw it." I said, "Again let me say to you, you did see it. I showed it to you again when you told me to make a report. I made the report and had these two letters appended, and you, in your own words, told me that when I made a final report to put these letters in the body of the report instead of as appendages, so that whoever read it would not have to look back and read the appendages but would see them in the body of the report." He said again, "I never saw it." I said, "Again excuse me, but you did see it another time. You sent for Gen Haines and me to come here to your office and discuss affairs in Haiti, and again, in Gen. Haines's presence, I handed you those letters and Gen. Haines saw me hand them to you." He said, "Of course, General, if you say I saw it I must have seen it, but I forgot it." I said, "You did not say that you had forgotten it, but that you had never seen it."

I simply make this statement to show that I was not making any secret of this business, but I was informing the Secretary of the Navy of everything I did, because I thought it was a most important matter.

While you said a moment ago that this was not an investigation to show the justification for my letter, I do want to say to this committee that I took the very best means that I knew of as commanding officer to correct a fault which had come to my notice in an official manner. I was the one to judge, and I judged and acted, and my letter was thoroughly understood by my junior, Col. Russell, who acted so promptly and so well that a few months later when Gen. Lejeune, the commandant of the Marine Corps, went to Haiti to make an inspection he found everything correct and in apple-pie order, and I say that largely responsible for that was my letter which had brought the facts to Col. Russell's attention, and his prompt action, showing that he thoroughly understood my letter, was the result.

The CHAIRMAN. This condition, subsequently corrected, grew up then under Russell's command before it was brought to his attention?

Gen. BARNETT. Yes, sir. Col. Russell was one of the best officers I knew, and would always take every action possible to correct every fault which he——

The CHAIRMAN. I did not ask that. Please answer my question, General. These killings, indiscriminate or otherwise, took place under Col. Russell?

Gen. BARNETT. Yes, sir.

The CHAIRMAN. He did not bring them to your attention; you brought them to his attention?

Gen. BARNETT. They were brought to my attention by——

The CHAIRMAN. He did not clean things up and put them in apple-pie order until you called the matter to his attention?

Gen. BARNETT. I do not suppose he ever knew of them until it came to his attention through me, and then he took prompt action. Senator Pomerene a few moments ago asked a question about what these people were tried for. On page 236 of the Navy Department's record I find the following:

PRIVATES ACCUSED WERE PROMPTLY BROUGHT TO TRIAL.

Johnson and McQuilkin, the privates named in Gen. Barnett's letter, were charged with being members of a firing squad which "unlawfully shot and caused the death of" two Haitian prisoners on May 22, 1919. Johnson was brought to trial June 26 and McQuilkin July 1, 1919. At the court-martial it was in evidence that Louis A. Brokaw, a marine who was serving as a lieutenant in the Haitian gendarmerie, ordered Johnson and McQuilkin, with three gendarmes, to shoot the two prisoners; that they, doubting his authority to order such an execution, but fearing to disobey orders, shot "wide" so as not to kill, and that, seeing the prisoners were still alive, Brokaw with his own pistol shot and killed them. The privates on trial were convicted of striking the prisoners, but it was testified that this was done by Brokaw's orders.

That is what Senator Pomerene asked a few moments ago—about the trial and what they were tried for.

The CHAIRMAN. Maj. McClellan, will you learn how it was that Brokaw appears not to have been tried?

Maj. McCLELLAN. He is insane.

The CHAIRMAN. I want to find out by whom he was adjudged insane.

Maj. McCLELLAN. All right, sir.

Gen. BARNETT. In this connection, I wish to state that when this conversation took place with the Secretary of the Navy and the Assistant Secretary of the Navy, both the Secretary and the Assistant Secretary said to me that I was at fault in my statement that certain testimony and the statement of the counsel for the accused showed me that illegitimate killing had taken place. They said it could not show me that, because this statement of counsel for the accused was not evidence but was a statement of counsel, and it was perfectly well known that counsel in criminal cases often made statements which could not be taken as evidence. I want to say here that I felt, and still feel, that I was perfectly justified in taking his word, which was an official report made to that court-martial by the counsel for the accused, and because he was an officer in the Marine Corps it was a statement made to me, because he knew, and everybody else in the service knew, that the record would come to me, and I would read his statement; he also knew that it was a statement made to the Judge Advocate General of the Navy, because he knew the record would go to him, and it was a statement made to the Secretary of the Navy, because he knew that the record would go to the Secretary of the Navy for final action. I therefore claim that I was justified in taking the word of a commissioned officer and in believing what he said was true.

The CHAIRMAN. Where was this court-martial held?

Gen. BARNETT. I do not remember the exact place; in Haiti.

The CHAIRMAN. Did it pass through the hands of the Judge Advocate?

Gen. BARNETT. It had.

The CHAIRMAN. And the occupation in Haiti?

Gen. BARNETT. It did.

The CHAIRMAN. Did he make any indorsement on it?

Gen. BARNETT. No, sir; not to my recollection.

The CHAIRMAN. Will we get the name of the judge advocate in Haiti who thought it was not important enough to call to the attention of Col. Russell, or of the Judge Advocate General in Washington?

Gen. BARNETT. That would be on those two cases. I say that I took this statement as true because, in all my experience of 44 years in the service I have taken it as a matter of course that a statement made to me by a commissioned officer was true. I will admit that in civil cases or criminal cases counsel may make statements prejudicial or in favor of a certain man whom he is defending, but I can not conceive of an officer acting as counsel for an enlisted man or other officer making a statement other than true. I took that statement as true, and therefore I wrote my letter, believing that it was true.

Now, to go on, when this whole thing was over, as far as these letters are concerned, and this report came in from Maj. Turner, forwarded by Col. Russell, which I never saw until afterwards, after this thing was brought to public attention, a court of inquiry was ordered to investigate the Haitian affair. I was before that court about five minutes and asked three or four questions with respect to why I wrote this letter, etc. I was also asked three or four questions with reference to the number killed, etc., and a correction was made because Maj. McClelland, who had compiled the data for me from the Navy Department files, had made a mistake in addition, and instead of being 3,250 there were 2,250 killed. I never saw the precept of that court of inquiry, but from their report I judge that one of the things they were ordered to report on was whether or not I was justified in using my phrase that indiscriminate killing had gone on for some time. They found in their report that I was not justified, although that is a question of opinion. As I stated a moment ago, my opinion is entirely different, as well as entirely different from the evidence that was before me, largely because of the fact that I think I was justified in believing as true the statement of the officer.

In the final paragraph of that report they said that the publishing of these charges and the statement with reference to indiscriminate killing in Haiti was most regrettable, unwarranted, and everything of that kind. That statement was taken by every newspaper in the United States, and by every individual, especially outside of the service that I know about myself, as a severe censure of me for having written this letter. Knowing the Navy regulations, I knew that no court of inquiry could censure an officer without having made him a party to the trial and allowing him to appear and introduce evidence. I was not made a party to the trial, and my conduct was not under investigation; but the concluding paragraph of their report was so badly worded—and I say that advisedly, because a thing must be badly worded that is misunderstood by everybody, and a report on anything can only be for the purpose of giving the idea in the minds of those making the report—as I say, it was so badly worded that every paper in the United States, especially the Army and Navy Register and the Army and Navy Journal, took it up as meaning severe censure of me. They were not justified in that, well knowing that after I was furnished with an official copy of this report of the court of inquiry, containing this so-called censure of me which the papers had taken to be a censure, I wrote a formal letter to the Secretary of the Navy, of which I will give a copy to the stenographer, and I stated in that letter that I had read this report of the court of inquiry——

The CHAIRMAN. If you are going to give the letter to the stenographer, do you want to summarize it for the committee?

Gen. BARNETT. I think you had better hear it right here in general terms. In that letter I stated to the Secretary of the Navy that I had read this report of the court of inquiry, and that I was shocked to find that every paper in the United States, and hundreds of friends of mine who had written to me condoling with me for having been censured by this court, had taken it for granted that I had been censured. Well knowing that this could not be so, and could not be intended so by the court, I requested him, as Secretary of the Navy, as an act of justice to one of the oldest officers in the service, to disavow this statement and give it publicity the same as the other had been given publicity, because I had been seriously injured by this report of the court of inquiry.

The Secretary of the Navy received this letter, and after some time wrote me an answer, failing to comply.

The findings and conclusions of the court of inquiry and my letter to the Secretary of the Navy are as follows:

[Navy News Bureau. Release morning papers of Sunday, Dec. 19, 1920.]

Secretary Daniels authorizes the following:

"The court of inquiry which convened on October 19, 1920, by order of the Secretary of the Navy to inquire into the conduct of the personnel of the naval service that has served in Haiti since June 28, 1915, has submitted its findings, which Gen. Lejeune, major general, commandant of the Marine Corps, and Secretary Daniels to-day approved."

Following are the conclusions of the court:

"The court, having thoroughly inquired into all the facts and circumstances connected with the allegations contained in the precept and having considered the evidence adduced, finds as follows:

"FINDING OF FACTS.

"1. The court finds that two unjustifiable homicides have been committed, one each by two of the personnel of the United States naval service which has served in Haiti since 28 July, 1915, and that 16 other serious acts of violence have been prepetrated against citizens of Haiti during the same period by individuals of such personnel.

"2. The court finds further that these offenses were all isolated acts of individuals and that in every case the responsible party was duly brought to trial before a general court-martial, convicted, and sentenced.

"3. The court has found no evidence of the commission of any other unjustifiable homicides or other serious, unjustifiable acts of oppression or of violence against any of the citizens of Haiti, or unjustifiable damage or destruction of their property, caused by any of the personnel in question.

"4. In view of the fact that the only unjustifiable acts found by the court to have been committed are those wherein disciplinary action has already been taken and where no further proceedings could be had in the matter, the court has not deemed it necessary to report further upon the question of responsibility.

"CONCLUSIONS.

"Referring to paragraph 2 of the precept, it is the conclusion of the court that there have been no proper grounds for the statement that 'practically indiscriminate killing of natives has been going on for some time,' as alleged in the letter from Brig. Gen. George Barnett, United States Marine Corps, to Col. John H. Russell, United States Marine Corps.

"Referring to the amendment to the precept calling for the conclusions of the court as to the general conduct of the personnel of the naval service in Haiti since July 28, 1915, the court does not consider that the small number of isolated crimes or offenses that have been committed by a few individuals of the service during the period in question are entitled to any considerable weight in forming a conclusion as to the general conduct of such personnel. It was inevitable that some offenses would be committed. However, considering the conditions of service in Haiti, it is remarkable that the offenses were so few in number and that they all may be chargeable to the ordinary defects of human character, such defects as result in the commission of similar offenses in the United States and elsewhere in the best-regulated communities.

"The general conduct of our troops of occupation can be fairly judged by the results of that occupation.

"Now, for the first time in more than a hundred years tranquillity and security of life and property may be said to prevail in Haiti.

"The Haitian people themselves welcomed the coming of our men and are unwilling to have them depart.

"The establishment and maintenance of tranquil conditions and the security of life and property all over the Republic of Haiti has been an arduous and dangerous and thankless task. That task our marines have performed with fidelity and great gallantry.

"The court can not refrain from recording its opinion of much, and that the most serious part of the reflections which have been made upon the officers who have served in Haiti.

"The outstanding characteristic of those officers, from the brigade commander down, has been their sympathetic attitude toward every step that would lead to a betterment of the country and to improvement in the physical, mental, and moral conditions of the population.

"With slender resources and inadequate administrative authority they have accomplished much, where anything more than suppression of organized insurrection seemed impossible.

"The above remarks apply with particular force to those officers and enlisted men of the Marine Corps who have been serving as officers of the gendarmerie of Haiti.

"After a careful study of the matters in issue, based not only on the evidence in the record but also upon other original and reliable sources of information, and the court's own observations while in Haiti, the court regards the charges which have been published as ill considered, regrettable, and thoroughly unwarranted reflections on a portion of the United States Marine Corps which has performed difficult, dangerous, and delicate duty in Haiti in a manner which instead of calling for adverse criticism is entitled to the highest commendation.

"The record of the proceedings of this twenty-first day of the inquiry was read and approved; and the court having finished the inquiry, then, at 11 o'clock a. m., adjourned to await the action of the convening authority.

"H. T. MAYO,
"*Rear Admiral, United States Navy, President.*
"JESSE F. DYER,
"*Major, United States Marine Corps, Judge Advocate.*"

UNITED STATES MARINE CORPS,
San Francisco, Calif., December 30, 1920.

From: Brig. Gen. George Barnett, Marine Corps.
To: The Secretary of the Navy.
Via: The Major General Commandant.
Subject: Findings and conclusions of the Haitian court of inquiry.

1. I have read carefully the " Navy News Bureau release morning papers of Sunday, December 19, 1920," authorized by Secretary Daniels and containing the findings of facts and the conclusions of " the court of inquiry which convened July 28, 1920 " and " approved December 19, 1920," by Gen. Lejeune, major general commandant, and Secretary Daniels.

2. I note the first paragraph under " Conclusions " reads as follows:

" Referring to paragraph 2 of the precept, it is the conclusion of the court that there have been no proper grounds for the statement that 'practically indiscriminate killing of natives has been going on for some time,' as alleged in the letter from Brig. Gen. George Barnett, United States Marine Corps, to Col. John H. Russell, United States Marine Corps."

3. No officer in the Marine Corps can be more pleased than I am that these allegations of indiscriminate killings have been disproved.

4. In this connection I invite attention to the fact that while the phrase "indiscriminate killing" was my own, the allegation of such misconduct was not made by me, and I preferred no charges against any person, nor did I publish or authorize the publication of anything.

5. In reviewing a court-martial case I read a statement of a commissioned officer, Lieut. Spear, in substance that he had personal knowledge of numerous cases where Haitians had been executed without any legal process. I immediately directed the local commanding officer to fully investigate and report, and in order to avoid unnecessary publicity I sent these directions in an envelope marked " Personal and confidential."

6. It is, of course, evident that I would have been neglectful of my duty as commandant of the Marine Corps had I failed to order an investigation.

7. I note also paragraph 11 of the " conclusions " of the court (next to the concluding paragraph), which reads as follows:

"After a careful study of the matters in issue, based not only on the evidence in the record but, also, upon other original and reliable sources of information, and the court's own observations while in Haiti, the court regards the charges which have been published as ill considered, regrettable, and thoroughly unwarranted reflections on a portion of the United States Marine Corps which has performed difficult, dangerous, and delicate duty in Haiti in a manner which, instead of calling for adverse criticism, is entitled to the highest commendation."

8. Unfortunately (for me) numerous newspapers and numerous individuals, having read in conjunction paragraphs 1 and 11 of the conclusions of the court of inquiry, have construed them to mean, in substance, that " Brig. Gen. George Barnett has made ill-considered, regrettable, and thoroughly unwarranted reflections on a portion of the United States Marine Corps which has performed difficult, dangerous, and delicate duty in Haiti in a manner which, instead of calling for adverse criticism, is entitled to the highest commendation."

9. I am constrained to believe that this is not the construction intended by the court or the reviewing authority. Otherwise it is certain that I would have been made party to the inquiry and accorded the right of an attempt at vindication, as provided by Navy regulations.

10. The record will show that I was not made a party to the inquiry and that I received no intimation that my conduct was under investigation. Hence I must assume that neither the court nor the reviewing authority intended that the court's findings and conclusions should convey the impression that I had been guilty of making unfounded, unwarrantable, and ill-considered charges against others of my corps who were entitled to commendation rather than censure.

11. I am thoroughly convinced in my own mind that the court did not have me or my conduct in mind when they drafted the eleventh paragraph of their conclusions, but that they had in mind the numerous newspaper articles published, with the publication of which I had nothing whatsoever to do.

12. The records will show, and the Secretary of the Navy has personal knowledge, that on numerous occasions, in my annual reports and in other ways, I have accorded and in my capacity as commandant of the Marine Corps awarded

praise and commendation for the conduct of marine officers and men in Haiti; that I thoroughly realized the dangerous and delicate nature of their duties and pointed with pride to their accomplishments. This especially in my final report to the Secretary of the Navy.

13. The published report of the conclusions of the court of inquiry has been construed to mean that my personal conduct in connection with the case has been severely animadverted upon by the court and through their approval by the major general commandant and the Secretary of the Navy.

14. I have read in a number of newspapers (vide attached clippings from the Army and Navy Register, dated December 25, 1920), this construction of the court's findings and have received dozens of letters from friends and acquaintances offering condolence that I should be so censured.

15. If my assumption is correct I request as an act of simple justice to an officer of 43 years' honorable service that the Secretary of the Navy give out a statement to the press to correct the impression that has gone broadcast over the country in effect that the court found me guilty of misconduct and the commandant of the Marine Corps and the Secretary of the Navy approved the findings.

GEORGE BARNETT.

The Secretary's reply to that letter is as follows:

NAVY DEPARTMENT,
Washington, January 10, 1921.

From: The Secretary of the Navy.
To: Brig. Gen. George Barnett, United States Marine Corps, commanding Department of the Pacific, No. 36 Annie Street, San Francisco, Calif.
Via: The Major General Commandant.
Subject: Findings and conclusions of the Haitian court of inquiry.
Reference: (a) Brig. Gen. George Barnett's letter 12–30–20.
Enclosure: (1).

1. In connection with reference (a), there is transmitted herewith for your information a copy of the Navy News Bureau release of December 19, 1920. It will be noted that this release does not contain any news items other than the findings and conclusions of the court of inquiry and the fact of their approval by the Major General Commandant and the Secretary of the Navy.

2. The comments complained of by you which appeared in certain newspapers did not emanate from the department, and the department therefore will take no action with reference to them.

3. With reference to paragraphs 4 and 5 of reference (a), your attention is invited to the fact that your official report of Haitian affairs shows that the investigation of the affairs mentioned in the general court-martial proceedings in the cases of Pvts. Walter E. Johnson and John J. McQuilkin, jr., was directed in your official letter to the brigade commander in Haiti, dated September 27, 1919, while your personal and confidential letter was not written until October 2, 1919, five days later; also, that the following allegations are contained in your personal and confidential letter above mentioned, namely:

"The court-martial of one private for the killing of a native prisoner brought out a statement by his counsel which showed me that practically indiscriminate killing of natives has gone on for some time."

And—

"I think this is the most startling thing of its kind that has ever taken place in the Marine Corps, and I don't want anything of the kind to happen again. I think, judging by the knowledge gained only from the cases that have been brought before me, that the Marine Corps has been sadly lacking in right and justice, and I look to you to see that this is corrected, and corrected at once."

4. Your attention is also invited to the fact that while you did not publish your personal and confidential letter above mentioned, yet you did include it in your official report, a public document, which you had been informed and which it had been publicly announced would be given to the press in its entirety upon its completion and submission by you.

5. In conclusion, you are informed that, although the court of inquiry was instructed in its precept to investigate and determine whether there had been practically indiscriminate killing of natives in Haiti for some time, as alleged in your personal and confidential letter to Col. John H. Russell, it was not directed to inquire into your conduct, and that, therefore, the court did not make you a party to the inquiry.

JOSEPHUS DANIELS.

The CHAIRMAN. The controversy between you and the Secretary does not concern the committee.

Gen. BARNETT. Entirely so; I understand that. I am simply showing this to show that he did have knowledge, the same knowledge that I had; that is all. As I have stated before, this letter shows that he refused to accede to my request to, state whether or not that finding referred to me, which he well knew it did not, because it was one of the most positive regulations that it could not refer to me in any possible way. I thought, and still think, that a fair-minded man, appealed to officially by one of the officers who had at least done honorable service for 45 years nearly, was entitled to a statement from the Secretary of the Navy——

Senator POMERENE. With regard to these executions, is it claimed now that these men were shot by direction of this sergeant who was demented at the time?

Gen. BARNETT. Oh, no, sir; that has nothing to do with the case at all. The only question that ever came up at all about the whole affair was whether or not there had been any indiscriminate killings in Haiti, and how many.

Senator POMERENE. Your opinion is, I take it, that these two were illegitimate?

Gen. BARNETT. Yes.

Senator POMERENE. Has your futher investigation enabled you to state how many others there were?

Gen. BARNETT. Only as I have stated in my letter, only the ones referred to as having been seen personally by Lieut. Spear, counsel for the accused, and then from the report on file at the Marine Corps headquarters by Maj. Turner, who was directed by Col. Russell to make a report. I do not know how many are in that.

Senator POMERENE. Are you able to state just briefly here what, in your judgment, were the causes which led up to this state of affairs?

Gen. BARNETT. No, sir; I was not there, and the only knowledge I have of the cases were these two court-martial cases.

Senator POMERENE. Who can give us that information?

Gen. BARNETT. Col. Russell, I have no doubt.

Senator POMERENE. Have you any one else to suggest?

Gen. BARNETT. Maj. Wells, I have suggested, while you were out. I was asked and I mentioned three or four while you were out.

Senator POMERENE. I will not ask you to repeat them, then. Are these men in this country now, or down there?

Gen. BARNETT. Some of them are here and some of them are down there.

Senator POMERENE. You, I believe, made the statement before we were called to the Senate Chamber that you took charge down there at the beginning of our occupation; did I understand you correctly?

Gen. BARNETT. The marines?

Senator POMERENE. Yes.

Gen. BARNETT. Yes; they were landed at once.

Senator POMERENE. What were the general orders which were given to you at that time? In other words, what were the reasons for sending you down there, if you know?

Gen. BARNETT. That was given to Admiral Caperton, who was in command. He has been before this committee for a week and probably stated everything of that kind.

Senator POMERENE. Well, I was not able to attend the hearings, because I have been attending two or three other committees.

Gen. BARNETT. The orders were given from the Navy Department to Admiral Caperton, who was in supreme command down there.

Senator POMERENE. You have not been down there?

Gen. BARNETT. Yes; I was down there on a tour of inspection in January, 1917, with the Assistant Secretary of the Navy, Mr. Roosevelt.

Senator POMERENE. And how long was that after the marines had landed there?

Gen. BARNETT. They landed in 1915, and I was there in 1917.

Senator POMERENE. What condition did you find then?

Gen. BARNETT. I found an excellent condition. It is so stated in my report made to the Secretary of the Navy, when I got back. I went from one end of Haiti to the other on horseback through the mountains.

Senator POMERENE. Did you have any knowledge at that time that there were any undue aggressions by our marines or others against the natives?

Gen. BARNETT. I had no knowledge, nor did I hear of any case, and I discussed the matter with the President of Haiti and with other prominent men in Haiti, with the parish priests and the local officials in the different towns through which we passed.

Senator POMERENE. They were nearly all Negroes, were they?

Gen. BARNETT. All of them, and I heard no complaints whatever.

Senator POMERENE. Was there any objection at that time to our possession of Haiti?

Gen. BARNETT. I heard none. I heard many remarks to the contrary.

Senator POMERENE. Was there any outbreak, revolutionary or otherwise, while you were there?

Gen. BARNETT. None whatever.

Senator POMERENE. Or have you learned of any since the time the marines took charge?

Gen. BARNETT. There had been many occasions.

Senator POMERENE. That was early after they took possession?

Gen. BARNETT. Yes. Once after that there was a concerted attack on Port au Prince in the night.

Senator POMERENE. By natives?

Gen. BARNETT. By natives, and was repulsed by the marines, and followed up pretty ruthlessly, and properly so.

Senator POMERENE. From a military standpoint, did you see anything to criticize in the defense by these marines?

Gen. BARNETT. I did not, and so stated in my report to the Secretary of the Navy. In fact, I came back very much pleased. I heard it stated by numerous people in Haiti that for the first time in a long, long time the people felt at liberty to go to the markets, and the markets were full of Haitians. Theretofore they had felt unable to go to market because they would be robbed, etc., or held up.

Senator POMERENE. Then the burden of your complaint grows out of these alleged illegal or improper executions?

Gen. BARNETT. Entirely from those two court-martial cases and the statement of the counsel for the accused. That was the only knowledge I ever had, as commandant of the Marine Corps, of any trouble in Haiti.

Senator POMERENE. Has the department made any further investigation?

Gen. BARNETT. The department sent Gen. Lejeune down there. I made this final report in the summer of 1920, and Gen. Lejeune went down later on and made an investigation, and reported everything in good shape. I understand—and I think it is true—that the Secretary of the Navy has been down there since. I know that the court of inquiry, of which Admiral Mayo was president, went there.

Senator POMERENE. You mean Secretary Denby, do you?

Gen. BARNETT. Yes, sir. Of course, I do not know what they found. I have never seen their report, or heard any statement from them, but I have read in the public press that they found things in good shape.

Senator POMERENE. Well, did you find any objection at that time that you went down there to our marines being there?

Gen. BARNETT. I found none whatever, and I am sure that Secretary Roosevelt, if he were here, would make exactly the same statement, because we made our trip together.

Senator POMERENE. You think, then, it was the consensus of opinion up to the time you were there that the marines were a good influence there for law and order?

Gen. BARNETT. I think entirely so, with a very large portion of the population.

Senator POMERENE. Did you find any sentiment there to the effect that the United States were trying to take possession of the island for the purpose of keeping control of it, or anything of that kind?

Gen. BARNETT. I never heard any such remark.

Senator POMERENE. Of course, you knew there was no such disposition on the part of the United States authorities?

Gen. BARNETT. I certainly felt it, and think so yet. I think the landing was originally made, and the marines have been kept there ever since, in my opinion, for what the United States considered was for the good of Haiti. And, far from criticizing in any way the Marine Corps for their action in Haiti, no man has ever given them more praise than I have given them in my annual reports and in my report of my inspection down there, and in my final report. I saw the construction of roads, I saw prisons cleaned up as clean as a table——

Senator POMERENE. You speak of the construction of roads. Were those roads being constructed under the supervision of the marines?

Gen. BARNETT. The gendarmerie.

Senator POMERENE. How was the labor performed, and who paid for it?

Gen. BARNETT. They were under the corvee system at that time.

Senator POMERENE. Who was it that issued these orders for that? Did the marines do it?

Gen. BARNETT. The gendarmerie, which was a part of the Haitian Government; that is accordinbg to Haitian law.

Senator POMERENE. As I understand, under that system down there, the natives may be directed to do a certain number of days' work on the roads?

Gen. BARNETT. That is the corvee system.

Senator POMERENE. And did you find any opposition to that order?

Gen. BARNETT. I heard none.

Senator POMERENE. How were these men fed?

Gen. BARNETT. Fed by the gendarmerie.

Senator POMERENE. Who furnished the provisions?

Gen. BARNETT. The gendarmerie.

Senator POMERENE. And that was by the Haitian Government?

Gen. BARNETT. That is a part of the Haitian Government; it is an institution of the Haitian Government.

Senator POMERENE. No part of that was furnished by our marines?

Gen. BARNETT. The officers of the gendarmerie were marines.

Senator POMERENE. Were they furnished good food?

Gen. BARNETT. As far as I saw. I only saw one meal. I saw one road gang working on the road, and when I passed there it was lunch time. That was the only meal I saw.

Senator POMERENE. There have been conflicting statements made before this committee, so far as I have heard them. One was to the effect that these men were eager to work there on the road, because they got better food than otherwise. The other was to the effect that many of these men were forced to work there under what was something akin to a peonage system, and under protest. Did you observe anything which would——

Gen. BARNETT. I heard nothing and observed nothing to that effect. As I have stated in this final report of mine, I had heard rumors only, but I had no substantiation for them whatever. I do not even remember who it was that said it, but I heard rumors to the effect that the corvee system was the cause of trouble, on account of abuse by having natives from one province working on the roads in another, contrary to the law. I do not know whether that was true or not.

Senator POMERENE. We had a rule, or did have until very recently in this country, in different States, that the taxpayers or men who were voters would work a certain length of time on the roads?

Gen. BARNETT. At one time I remember the Secretary of the Navy got word about some objection to the corvee system, and I happened to be in his office at that time, and the Secretary of the Navy made practically the same statement that you have made, that that was the common custom in this country. It was done under Haitian law. Whether or not the corvee system was ever abused I have no knowledge whatever except these rumors, and I can not substantiate them in any way whatever. I do not even know where they came from. But the officers who were on duty in Haiti with the gendarmerie ought to be able to state fully about that.

Senator POMERENE. Let me ask you another question. As I understand it, we have charge of the customs down there, have we not?

Gen. BARNETT. That, Senator, I can not answer any questions on legitimately, because it was under a different department entirely. We had nothing whatever to do with it.

Senator POMERENE. You got no information which would lead you to express an opinion as to whether it was satisfactorily administered or not?

Gen. BARNETT. None whatever, because I never had the slightest report or the slightest knowledge with respect to the customs. That was because it was under the—I forget what they call him—I think it is the receiver.

Senator POMERENE. Well, from the standpoint of law and order, at the time you were down there last was there then a necessity for our marines staying there?

Gen. BARNETT. I think so undoubtedly.

Senator POMERENE. Why?

Gen. BARNETT. Because I think that Haiti has the best Government and the best administered that it has had in 100 years. I think the improvements we made in the orphan asylums, in the prisons, in the schools, and in the hospitals were very marked, and almost entirely due to the marines.

Senator POMERENE. Well, you had the different revolutionary factions there, I take it?

Gen. BARNETT. I think so.

Senator POMERENE. And you think the demoralized condition of the island was due to that fact?

Gen. BARNETT. It seemed so to me. I think it got to be in a condition where it was absolutely necessary to have a stable government.

Senator POMERENE. Is it your judgment from what you have seen down there that it is necessary for us to continue our marines there?

Gen. BARNETT. For the present I unhesitatingly say so.

Senator POMERENE. For how long a time would you say?

Gen. BARNETT. That I think is utterly impossible to answer. It depends on conditions entirely.

Senator POMERENE. Did you discover that the nationals of other countries, for instance, the Germans, or British, or French, had any objection to our having our marines there?

Gen. BARNETT. I heard none. I went to a dinner given by the American minister, and I went to another luncheon given by the President.

Senator POMERENE. Who was the American minister at that time?

Gen. BARNETT. Mr. Bailly-Blanchard, a man from Louisiana. He had been for many years secretary of the legation in Paris, and was afterwards made American minister at Haiti.

As I was going on to say, I went to a dinner given by him, and to a luncheon given by the President, where we met practically all the different representative people in Port au Prince, and I heard of no complaint whatever.

Mr. HOWE. Since the interchange of letters between yourself and Col. Russell in September and October, 1919, have you heard anything from which you could judge whether Lieut. Spear's statements before the court-martial gave an exaggerated or an accurate account of the conditions there on which he was commenting?

Gen. BARNETT. I have not heard. As I say, shortly after these letters were written, in September and October, 1919, Col. Russell was ordered to make this investigation. Up to the time that I was relieved as commandant of the Marine Corps, his report had not been received, and I have not seen, except in a casual way, a copy of his report, and that is the only information I have had, because I have not seen the report of the court of inquiry, of which Admiral Mayo was president.

Mr. HOWE. General, you understand my question was wider than one directed to your knowledge of reports. What I would like to know is if since the time in September and October, 1919, you have heard from any source whatsoever any facts which would allow you to judge as to the accuracy of Lieut. Spear's statement?

Gen. BARNETT. I have heard no facts whatever. I have heard rumors that certain people knew of certain affairs down there, but they were the merest rumors.

Senator POMERENE. Let me ask you in that connection, General, following along the line that was just being asked you, how long has Lieut. Spear been in the corps?

Gen. BARNETT. I do not know. I do not know when he resigned.

Senator POMERENE. Is he a West Pointer?

Gen. BARNETT. No, sir; he came in the Marine Corps during the war.

Senator POMERENE. He was a civilian before that?

Gen. BARNETT. Yes, sir; and I think he is a civilian now.

Senator POMERENE. Do you know him personally?

Gen. BARNETT. No, sir: I never saw him.

Senator POMERENE. You have no means of judging of him temperamentally, then?

Gen. BARNETT. None at all. I never saw the man and never heard of him except in that connection.

Senator POMERENE. Do you know what his business was prior to going into the service?

Gen. BARNETT. No.

Senator POMERENE. Do you know whether he had any experience in court-martial matters or legal matters?

Gen. BARNETT. No knowledge whatever.

Mr. HOWE. Do you know what Lieut. Spear's duty had been in Haiti before the time he acted as counsel for these accused?

Gen. BARNETT. I do not.

Mr. HOWE. Do you know what regulations, if any, there were calling for the report by the Marine Corps of any occasions when natives met their death at the hands of members of the Marine Corps, either by authorized execution or by battle casualty?

Gen. BARNETT. I only know the custom of the service which would require, of course, a report of any deaths. Even after an engagement, a report would contain the number killed, as far as they could get at it; killed and wounded, as far as it was possible to find out, of course, in a short time, and the general regulations, without any specific orders whatever, would absolutely call for reports as to killings.

Mr. HOWE. Did you understand Lieut. Spear's remarks to the court-martial to refer to killing by marines not subsequently reported officially?

Gen. BARNETT. I did.

Senator POMERENE. You have referred to these illegal killings, etc. Of course, that statement seems to apply to the higher or more severe class of penalties which were inflicted upon these prisoners. Did you see anything or hear anything that would lead you to believe that there were other cases, so far as the lower grade of penalties are concerned?

Gen. BARNETT. No. My letter contained everything that I knew.

Senator POMERENE. Let me ask you another question. In answer to a question which I asked, you said that you discovered what you regarded as an improvement in their educational facilities, etc. I wish you would go more into detail and tell the committee what led you to believe that, or on what facts you based that conclusion. Let me say that I ask this question particularly because it would appear from the testimony of one or more witnesses before this committee that there was no improvement in educational matters, etc., and that the marines and our occupancy there was simply a drain upon the island's revenues.

Gen. BARNETT. I think that statement is absolutely wrong. I think undoubtedly that improvement has been made in many ways. I said in my report, and I say to you now, that during this trip across Haiti that I made with the Assistant Secretary of the Navy, Mr. Roosevelt, we stopped at every little village and town we passed through and sent for the head man of that village, and for the parish priest, and we discussed these matters with the physicians at the hospitals, and we discussed them with the nurses and with the people in charge of the hospitals, and we visited the prisons and inspected them ourselves, and we who had been in Haiti before saw the improvement ourselves.

Senator POMERENE. And you had been there before?

Gen. BARNETT. I had been there before, and I did not need anybody's statement to show me whether or not improvements had been made.

Taking the matter of the prisons alone, I know that years before the prisons at Port au Prince and Cape Haitien were very vile places. I know that when I inspected them, you could eat your dinner with perfect safety in any part of the prison, off the floor or off any bed. The beds were bunks made of boards. And I talked with numerous people, as I say, the parish priests, and the head men of every village, and we invited any criticism or question that they wanted to ask. Mr. Roosevelt was very much interested in this thing, and, of course, he being my senior, he conducted these questionings wherever we went, of the parish priests and the head men of these villages. I do not think he had ever been there before, but I say that any man who had ever been there before would see himself the improvement in these places, in the market places, in the prisons, and in the hospitals.

Senator POMERENE. Did these priests there have charge of the education of the children?

Gen. BARNETT. Yes, sir.

Senator POMERENE. They had control of that, I suppose? Were they parochial schools, do you know, or were they public schools belonging to the island?

Gen. BARNETT. I think probably they were parochial schools, because all that I saw were Catholic priests.

Senator POMERENE. Did any of these priests or other head men make any complaints with respect to educational facilities, or hospital facilities, or anything of that kind?

Gen. BARNETT. I do not think so, from the fact that.when we came back, the Secretary of the Navy and I were both very much pleased with our inspection trip, and very much pleased with the conditions down there.

Senator POMERENE. Then, as I understand you, the statements you got from these priests and head men were merely corroborative of what your own eyes showed you to be the condition?

Gen. BARNETT. Yes, sir.

As far as the school and hospital business is concerned, I do not know of a better man to have as a witness than Gen. E. K. Cole, who was in command at Port au Prince at that time when we made our inspection there.

Senator POMERENE. He is of the marines?

Gen. BARNETT. A marine—one of the best officers in the Marine Corps. He was there and devoted his whole undivided time to it, and went from one end of Haiti to the other frequently, and he was very well thought of throughout Haiti, because on that trip wherever we went he was received most heartily and kindly.

Senator POMERENE. Well, is it your belief that these people down there are anxious to advance and appreciate the benefits to be derived from increased educational facilities?

Gen. BARNETT. I do not think the mass of the people have a thought on that subject even. I do not think the whole mass of the people have a single thought, or have ever gotten that far in thought at all. They are absolutely illiterate. I think the only people to-day who would vote for a change in the conditions in Haiti would be the people who are of a little higher class in education, etc., and want to run the Government themselves.

Senator POMERENE. Then you think it is a sort of conflict between the high brows down there, do you?

Gen. BARNETT. I do entirely. I do not think the mass of the people have any more thought on the subject than children would.

Senator POMERENE. And, in your judgment, they are sort of treated as such, is that the idea?

Gen. BARNETT. That is my idea. They should be given every consideration compatible with good government, and should be given every facility for improving and possibly in the future coming into control, but the people are certainly, in my opinion, not fitted for it yet.

(Whereupon, at 12.30 o'clock p. m., a recess was taken until 2.30 o'clock p. m.)

AFTER RECESS.

The committee reassembled at 2.30 o'clock p. m., pursuant to the taking of recess.

Senator ODDIE. I understand there is a matter you would like to put in the record regarding education in Haiti.

Gen. BARNETT. In the session this morning I was asked whether any improvement had been made in the educational facilities in Haiti. I stated that there had been. I wish to state that my knowledge of that came from this trip that I made through Haiti with the Assistant Secretary of the Navy, Mr. Roosevelt.

Senator ODDIE. What year was that?

Gen. BARNETT. That was in January, 1917, and with Gen. Cole, who was in command of the marines in Haiti at that time. I wish to say that the improvement was largely, if not wholly, due to the general uplift of conditions in Haiti, and particularly, as far as I could see, from the warm personal regard in which Gen. Cole was held by everybody wherever we went, and the influence he had for good in lending his personal assistance and general approval of this work of the priests wherever we went. They were largely, as far as I could see, as I said this morning, Catholic schools. There was no law for it. We had no right, as I understand it, to take charge of education at all, no more than we had in the hospital work, but I wish to state that at a big hospital in charge of the head man of the Catholic Church in northern Haiti—we visited this hospital, and I have never seen greater affection displayed than what Gen. Cole got for what he had done, not officially, but for the general help he had given them in the way of moral help, moral uplift, and little things he had been able to do in a personal way.

I think I stated very explicitly what knowledge I had with reference to the educational system. The school there was not, in my opinion, in the same status as the hospital part. They did a great deal of work there, but not because of any treaty provision; it was done by general good feeling and uplift.

Senator ODDIE. What is your opinion regarding the action of the Marine Corps in the matter?

Gen. BARNETT. I can say that outside of the knowledge that I gained from the two court-martial cases of Johnson and McQuilkin, together with the statement of Lieut. Spear, the counsel for the accused, it is the only thing I have heard in my official career against the action of the marines in Haiti. Their work, in my opinion, has been splendid, and nobody has praised them more than I did in all of my annual reports, and in my report which I made to the Secretary of the Navy when I came back from my visit to Haiti, and I say unreservedly that I think they have done the country a great deal of good, and that the country is much better off for their presence there than it would have been without them.

Mr. HOWE. General, going back to the statement made by Lieut. Spear in the Johnson-McQuilkin investigation, was it ever proved that the facts alleged in that statement of Lieut. Spear were actually facts?

Gen. BARNETT. I have no investigation to prove that, one way or the other.

Mr. HOWE. Has it ever been shown by any reliable information that indiscriminate killings by marines had ever taken place in Haiti?

Gen. BARNETT. That is all the knowledge I have on the subject. As I stated in my original letter, and in my final report to the Secretary of the Navy, the whole knowledge that I have is the simple statement by Lieut. Spear on that record. I have no other corroborative evidence whatever.

Mr. HOWE. And the subsequent investigations you are familiar with, are you not?

Gen. BARNETT. I am not familiar at all with the court of inquiry. I have no knowledge of that. I have not seen their report or had reported to me what they found.

Mr. HOWE. Were there any other proceedings besides the proceedings of the court of inquiry, which would have a bearing——

Gen. BARNETT. Yes; as I stated this morning, after I was relieved as commandant of the Marine Corps I saw the report of Maj. Turner, but it was not before me as an official paper. I never passed on it, and therefore it is not as clear in my mind as it probably would have been if I had been in charge of it; and I suggest, of course, that the committee get that report and read it, because my opinion is that in that report Maj. Turner stated some cases of killings other than these; I am not sure of that.

Mr. HOWE. Were there any other investigations?

Gen. BARNETT. No; I know of no others.

Mr. HOWE. This, then, is really your statement and testimony; you refer the committee to those published reports, making no comment of your own on them?

Gen. BARNETT. None whatever. I have no comment to make, because I have not seen them, except in the most casual way.

Mr. HOWE. And you have no independent knowledge of your own as to that state of affairs or facts?

Gen. BARNETT. None whatever.

Mr. HOWE. Did the entrance into the war of the United States have the result of changing the personnel of the higher Marine Corps officers in charge in Haiti?

Gen. BARNETT. It did change a great many; it changed the officers and men, because it was my desire, when the war came on in Europe, to send as many of the older, deserving officers and men to France as possible, because I recognized the fact that they had had a couple of years or three years' pretty active service in Haiti, and therefore they were well fitted for the work in France.

Mr. HOWE. Those officers who had been in charge up to the time we went into the war were experienced officers of the Marine Corps, were they not?

Gen. BARNETT. Certainly.

Mr. HOWE. And, in your opinion, well qualified for their duties in Haiti?

Gen. BARNETT. That is the reason I sent them there, sir.

Mr. HOWE. After we went into the war, and after this necessary change in personnel, were their successors down there men of equal experience, in your opinion?

Gen. BARNETT. I should say almost; yes, sir. I did not weigh them in the balance at all. Like all details in the Marine Corps, they took their turn, as far as possible, for foreign service.

Mr. Howe. Let me just ask it in this way: Those then who were there before and after our entry into the war had about the same rank, did they not, when they were there?

Gen. Barnett. Very near.

Mr. Howe. Is it true, however, that those who came there after our entry into the war had received more rapid promotion than their predecessors; in other words, were younger men?

Gen. Barnett. That applied particularly not until about 1918, when our first big increase came, and the promotions came along with that, and naturally the officers then of the rank of colonel would not have been of the rank of colonel in 1916.

Mr. Howe. They had had shorter periods of service in the different grades?

Gen. Barnett. Yes; but God knows they had all been long enough.

Mr. Howe. Do you know whether the important steps during the occupation of Haiti, such as the dispersal of the Haitian Senate in 1916 and 1917, were originated in the State Department, or in the Navy Department, or in the Marine Corps?

Gen. Barnett. I know it was not in the Marine Corps; otherwise I have no knowledge of it, because that was done by the admiral, and the orders did not come through me.

Mr. Howe. And you do not know where that determination originated?

Gen. Barnett. I have no knowledge whatever. My people were there simply as military people, to obey the orders which were received through the Navy Department.

Mr. Howe. And that reply would be the reply to questions about most of the important policies taken?

Gen. Barnett. All with reference to finances, all with reference to the occupation, all with reference to everything except the purely military handling of the situation.

Mr. Howe. On all those things you have no knowledge as to what department of the Government the orders originated in?

Gen. Barnett. The orders did not come through me at all. I only got the orders that referred to the marines.

Mr. Howe. Take a slightly different question. Was the employment under American auspices of the institutions of the corvée ever referred to the headquarters of the Marine Corps?

Gen. Barnett. Never.

Mr. Howe. Do you know whether it was ever referred to the Navy Department?

Gen. Barnett. I think not. I can not answer positively as to that. I know it was never referred to the Marine Corps.

Mr. Howe. When your Marine Corps officers down there were in doubt as to how to proceed, whom did they consult? Did they consult through Marine Corps channels, or did they ask information of the naval authorities?

Gen. Barnett. Up to a certain point they would ask their own superior officers, and if it was a thing beyond his power to decide, he himself would refer it to the senior naval officer.

Mr. Howe. To the senior naval officer in Haiti?

Gen. Barnett. In Haitian waters.

Mr. Howe. It is possible, then, that the employment under the United States authorities of the corvée system may have been referred to the Navy?

Gen. Barnett. That I am utterly——

Mr. Howe. I say it is possible it may have been; you have no knowledge as to whether it was or not?

Gen. Barnett. I have no knowledge as to whether it was or not. I do not even know whether it was possible, because I have no means of stating one way or the other. Possibly it might have been referred to the financial advisor, but I do not think it would. As I stated a while ago, my understanding of it is that the corvée system was, under proper conditions, carrying out a Haitian law, and it was done under Haitian law by the Haitian troops, the gendarmerie.

Mr. Howe. And the question may never have been raised and presented to higher authority?

Gen. Barnett. It may not.

Mr. Howe. As far as you know?

Gen. Barnett. As far as I know. I know that certain orders were issued about doing away with the corvée system by the marine officers.

Mr. Howe. To what extent was the gendarmerie under the control of the Marine Corps?

Gen. Barnett. The gendarmerie was officered by Marine Corps officers. The commissioned officers were of the Marine Corps.

Mr. Howe. And what authority was there for that arrangement?

Gen. Barnett. It was a treaty arrangement, approved by Congress, by the Haitian Government and by order of the Secretary of the Navy, which, I understand, was approved by the Secretary of State, and certain additional pay was allowed the officers in Haiti and Santo Domingo, and that was passed upon by Congress, too. That is an act of Congress.

Mr. Howe. To what treaty do you refer?

Gen. Barnett. I refer to the treaty between the United States and Haiti.

Mr. Howe. Of what year?

Gen. Barnett. I have forgotten the year. It never came to me before or after its adoption, but I know there was a treaty, and I know Congress passed an act in 1916 authorizing the employment of marine officers in the Haitian gendarmerie, and stating definitely that their increased compensation would be from the Haitian Government. They got their regular pay as marine officers, and then this additional compensation. The act of Congress authorized them to receive compensation, because an officer in the United States service can not receive remuneration from a foreign Government without a special act of Congress.

Mr. Howe. Do you know who gave the order for the original landing in Haiti at Port au Prince and at Cape Haitien?

Gen. Barnett. I have understood it was Admiral Caperton. I never saw the order.

Mr. Howe. You have no personal knowledge of that?

Gen. Barnett. No.

Mr. Howe. Do you know whether the Navy Department or the Marine Corps ever advanced any plans in connection with the promotion of education in Haiti?

Gen. Barnett. I do not think they had authority to, according to law. I think it was all done by moral suasion, by general example, and by personal encouragement of the officers.

Mr. Howe. Do you know of any recommendations which were made, if any, to obtain the authority of law?

Gen. Barnett. They have tried to get authority of law, but it has not been granted yet, according to my understanding.

Mr. Howe. By "they" whom do you mean?

Gen. Barnett. Congress.

Mr. Howe. Who has tried?

Gen. Barnett. The Navy Department.

Mr. Howe. What did you understand to be the function of the Marine Corps in Haiti, General?

Gen. Barnett. I understand the function of the Marine Corps in Haiti to be two things: First, that a portion of the officers and the men of the Marine Corps are detailed to the gendarmerie by special order. That is one function. Although the gendarmerie officer gets pay from the Haitian Government, in general term in any emergency he is still a marine and still under the command of the senior marine officer there. The senior marine officer there functions with all the marines under his command, and the function of the marines in Haiti is for the preservation of general order, which would mean putting down any attack by the Cacos, so called, who are a sort of bandits, and for the general preservation of order throughout the country.

Mr. Howe. What is the relation, for instance, between the Haitian Government and the marines?

Gen. Barnett. So far as I know, there is no principle connection between the Haitian Government and the marines proper, except the marines were employed in the gendarmerie. I do know that the senior marine officer in Haiti has, while in Haiti, been in frequent conferences with the President of Haiti and his cabinet, giving them advice, but how strong the advice was I do not know.

Mr. Howe. Did the American minister exercise any control over the marines?

Gen. Barnett. No, sir.

Mr. Howe. Did any of the American-appointed civilian officials exercise any control over the marines?

Gen. Barnett. Only the financial advisor, with reference to the allotment of money. The gendarmerie and the marine officers of the gendarmerie got their money, their pay, through the financial advisor, and the financial advisor from time to time, in fact, I think, quarterly, allotted to the chief of the gendarmerie, who was a marine officer, an allocation of funds for the upkeep of the gendarmerie in every capacity—military stores, building equipment, arms, ammunition, horses, and everything for the quarter.

Mr. Howe. But the financial advisor was not authorized to give any directions to the commandant of the marines down there?

Gen. Barnett. None whatever.

Mr. Howe. To the commanding officer, I mean.

Gen. Barnett. None whatever.

Mr. Howe. What were the general or specific instructions issued through your office to the American forces in Haiti, regarding armed conflicts and dealing with bandits and similar subjects?

Gen. Barnett. I did not give the order. A man was sent down there to take charge, and the country, most of the time, if not all the time, was under martial law, and the man on the spot, where there is martial law, has absolute control of the military situation, and he reported to headquarters, the Navy Department, and only reported to the Marine Corps practically through headquarters, and with reference to the orders I gave. We did not attempt in any way to dictate the individual action of any body of troops in Haiti. That was under the military commander, who was a naval officer. The naval officer, however, as I understand it, did not in any way attempt to take charge or interfere with the military procedure, per se. That was left to the senior marine officer.

Mr. Howe. Your last direct knowledge or opportunity to judge of the feeling of the Haitians toward the American occupation was in 1917, during your visit there?

Gen. Barnett. That was the last time I have ever seen or talked to a Haitian.

Mr. Howe. Have you any means of judging or saying whether or not there has been any change in the attitude of the Haitians since that time?

Gen. Barnett. I have not.

Mr. Howe. General, is there any matter which you think you could or should testify to at the present time which would be of assistance to the committee in getting a thorough understanding of the affairs in Haiti?

Gen. Barnett. I do not think so. I think I have stated everything that came within my knowledge, and the action that I took on the things which reached me. I do not know of anything. As I have stated before, I have no first-hand knowledge of any trouble in Haiti. I know simply from official reports that came to me, and I have told you this morning the action I took with reference to them.

In further reply, Mr. Howe, I will say that naturally, being given orders from the Secretary of the Navy to make a report on everything that happened in Haiti from the time the marines first landed there until I was relieved as commandant of the Marine Corps, I made this report, which certainly contained about everything I could find in the Navy Department, assisted by Maj. McClellan, of the historical section, everything relating to what occurred in Haiti while I was commandant of the Marine Corps.

Senator Oddie. Capt. Angell has asked permission to ask some questions, and he is doing this as he did the other day, and we are not establishing any precedent by doing this, but it is simply as a matter of courtesy.

Gen. Barnett. I am willing to answer any questions anybody asks me.

Mr. Angell. As to the gendarmerie, General, you have testified that the officers of the gendarmerie were of the Marine Corps, and so provided for under the treaty. Do you know who chose, or rather, who was responsible for the choice and organization of the personnel of the gendarmerie? I do not mean of the specific officers of the Marine Corps.

Gen. Barnett. I was responsible for it, I think. I signed the orders, but I naturally got the suggestions from different officers and different members of the profession. From time to time officers were sent to Haiti, and from time to time the officer in command of the gendarmerie in Haiti would state to the commanding marine officer in Haiti that there were certain vacancies in the gendarmerie, and the senior marine officer in Haiti would make a report to me recommending certain people. These people had to be mentioned by name to get authority from the President of the United States to be detailed to the gendarmerie before they could draw the extra pay as gendarmerie officers. In every case where an officer was detailed to the gendarmerie the final order had to be approved by the President of the United States.

Mr. ANGELL. When you used the expression "these people," you meant the members of the Marine Corps who were detailed to duty as officers in the gendarmerie?

Gen. BARNETT. Certainly.

Mr. ANGELL. I referred more to the whole plan of organization and training and choice of the general personnel of the gendarmerie.

Gen. BARNETT. That was sent by the senior officer of the gendarmerie to the senior marine officer and approved by him and sent to me and approved.

Mr. ANGELL. In other words, it was done by the Marine Corps, not by the Haitian Government at all?

Gen. BARNETT. Not at all; it was done by the Marine Corps, of course.

Mr. ANGELL. Did the officers of the gendarmerie choose the enlisted personnel of the gendarmerie?

Gen. BARNETT. Undoubtedly; they were all Haitians.

Mr. ANGELL. Did they take and train men from among the Haitian population?

Gen. BARNETT. I do not know what their scheme of enlistment was, but they had that in charge the same as officers here who were in charge of enlistments for the Marine Corps.

Mr. ANGELL. Do you know what attempts, if any, was made, General, to make native Haitian officers in the gendarmerie, as provided or suggested by article 10 of the original treaty?

Gen. BARNETT. Our intention was originally as fast as possible to make the Haitians junior officers and see if they could not soon be in a position to become captains of companies. That was thought of at that time.

Mr. ANGELL. Do you know how far that original plan was pursued?

Gen. BARNETT. I do not know. That was left entirely to the gendarmerie; it was under Haitian control entirely.

Mr. ANGELL. When you say under Haitian control——

Gen. BARNETT. I mean under Haitian control according to the treaty. They were essentially Haitian troops and they were paid by the Haitian Government.

Mr. ANGELL. And the choice?

Gen. BARNETT. Entirely with the marines.

Mr. ANGELL. This morning you made reference, General, to the building of roads?

Gen. BARNETT. Yes.

Mr. ANGELL. In Haiti?

Gen. BARNETT. Yes.

Mr. ANGELL. By or under the direction of the marines or gendarmerie?

Gen. BARNETT. Yes.

Mr. ANGELL. And for what purpose were those roads built?

Gen. BARNETT. For the general purpose that they would be built in any country in the world. You can not have good military control; you can not have good business; you can not have good anything in any country without roads. It took me four days to go from Port au Prince to Cape Haitien, riding through the mountains, over a road which originally had been a splendid carriage road, according to history, and in many places it was almost impossible to get over it on horseback, and it was utterly impossible for any sort of traffic to go over, except the roughest sort of pack animals. A trip was made from Port au Prince, up through St. Marc, up around the coast, to Cape Haitien and Ouanaminthe, and they made such a good road there that it was reported to me later that the chief of the gendarmerie took the President of Haiti from Port au Prince to Ouanaminthe in 13 hours in an automobile.

Senator ODDIE. How many miles is that?

Gen. BARNETT. I do not remember the number of miles, but it is a good many. It took us four days, traveling on horseback, on a hard ride, riding 11 hours a day.

Mr. ANGELL. Was the principal purpose of building the roads that of military necessity?

Gen. BARNETT. I think that was the first thing that would naturally occur to a military man, and did occur to them, that before they could keep up any posts out in the interior they had to have roads whereby they could supply the commands with the necessary equipment and food, and everything that goes to keep up a military establishment, and it was much easier for us to supply our troops in the interior by truck than it was by pack animal, and therefore we had to get the roads in such a condition that a truck could go over them.

Mr. ANGELL. Was the statement contained in paragraph 3 of a letter or report of the brigade commander, dated June 19, 1919, appearing in paragraph 234 of your report to the Secretary of the Navy of October 11, 1920, and reading as follows: " Soon after the American occupation of Haiti it was realized that good roads between the principal towns were a military necessity," according to your understanding, an accurate statement?

Gen. BARNETT. I think so. I think that is the first thing that would occur to any military man.

Mr. ANGELL. Do you know why the building of roads was stopped, or largely given up, in 1918?

Gen. BARNETT. As I stated in my report, you will remember, in one paragraph of my report, I had heard rumors about trouble on account of the abuse of the corvee system, but I had no official report whatever; I had no statement of anybody, except I do remember that some rumor was to the effect that there was trouble with regard to the corvee system, and the corvee system was all stopped about that time you mentioned.

Mr. ANGELL. In 1918, had sufficient roads been constructed under the direction of the marines and the gendarmerie to meet the major requirements of the military necessity?

Gen. BARNETT. I think so. That road I spoke of, from Cape Haitien to Port au Prince—I mean via St. Marc to Cape Hatien and Ouanaminthe—was finished some time in the spring or summer of 1917.

Mr. ANGELL. Is it your understanding, General, that the so-called abuse of the corvee law or custom came into being after your trip to Haiti in 1917?

Gen. BARNETT. That I do not know. I say I have no reports whatever on that subject.

Mr. ANGELL. At the time of your trip in January, 1917, you heard no complaint then about the corvee law?

Gen. BARNETT. No.

Mr. ANGELL. It was only after that that complaints came to you directly or indirectly?

Gen. BARNETT. No; I had heard some rumors before that.

Mr. ANGELL. Before January, 1917?

Gen. BARNETT. Yes; but where they came from or anything about it I knew not.

Mr. ANGELL. You do not remember what those rumors were?

Gen. BARNETT. No; just simply some trouble about the corvee system was all I heard, and there was no report made about it, so I never heard anything more about it.

Senator ODDIE. General, may I ask a question here in regard to the roads? Did you consider the ultimate benefit to the country from an economic standpoint in laying out these military roads?

Gen. BARNETT. I did, and you will see every evidence of the good of it, because I do not know whether you happen to know it or not, but a large part of the produce of Haiti consists of logwood, which is used for dye purposes, and with the roads they had there at the time when the marines first went there the only way these people could get this into market at all would be in small amounts on pack animals. It is very heavy stuff. From an economic point of view I think it is absolutely essential that the roads should be in such a condition there that they could haul this stuff on wheel vehicles.

Mr. HOWE. Then, General, one of the purposes of the military control of the island was to permit commerce to proceed unhindered, was it not?

Gen. BARNETT. I do not think there was a single officer who went down there who was not thoroughly imbued with the fact that that was one of his principal duties, to see to the well-being of the country not only peacefully but commercially.

Mr. HOWE. So that the roads, then, naturally followed the proper arteries for the commercial development of that country?

Gen. BARNETT. Entirely.

Mr. HOWE. That was where there had to be military protection, and that was where, when peacefulness was established, there should be the means of transportation?

Gen. BARNETT. I think Haiti is no different from any country in the world, and the world is full of cases, especially France, where they have the good of the roads built by Napoleon, built for military purposes, and they are just as good now as they were then and just as essential for commercial purposes.

Mr. ANGELL. In your report, General, in paragraphs 169 to 171, you refer to reports from Gen. Cole in May, 1917, discussing the changed attitude toward the

Americans on the part of many classes of the people. Do you recollect, or can you give us any of the causes of that changed attitude in the spring of 1917?

Gen. BARNETT. I have no doubt that the report referred to in those paragraphs was largely the result of the trip Gen. Cole made with us when we went from Port au Prince to Cape Haitien overland on horseback in January, 1917, which gave Gen. Cole a chance to see all parts of Haiti with us. I think at that time he saw the changed conditions, and saw they were as I reported when I came back, very favorable indeed.

Mr. ANGELL. Paragraph 171 reads:

"On May 29, 1917, Brig. Gen. Cole reported that he had made efforts to locate causes for hostile attitude, but without success; and while admitting its presence "——

Gen. BARNETT. It was constantly changing from day to day. We had reports all the time that there would be an uprising here and an uprising there, when things had been very quiet.

Mr. ANGELL. Have you any recollection, then, as to what the causes were for this change, this newly hostile attitude?

Gen. BARNETT. No; I would not have known.

Mr. ANGELL. At the time of your trip to and through Haiti in January, 1917, when you, as you testified this morning, spoke to a great many people in the towns, was there no mention made to you and did you hear of no complaints of the forcible closing and dispersal of the Haitian Senate and Legislature in 1916?

Gen. BARNETT. It was never mentioned to me. Secretary Roosevelt was with me, but whether or not he discussed anything of that kind with the Haitian officials or Haitians in general I do not know. I was not present at any such discussion.

Mr. ANGELL. Did you converse directly with the natives or through an interpreter?

Gen. BARNETT. Through an interpreter entirely. Secretary Roosevelt spoke French very often, and very often he conducted the questioning.

Mr. ANGELL. To come back once more to the question of the improvement in educational conditions in the schools, can you give us specific instances of such improvement as you say took place or along what lines was the improvement?

Gen. BARNETT. We visited the big hospital and school particularly, to mention one of the most pronounced cases, in north Haiti. I have forgotten the old gentleman's name now, but he was one of the old type of Catholic priests, and he collected around him all of the sisters, and had charge not only of the hospital work but of the school work, and he was most enthusiastic about the improved conditions and what Gen. Cole personally had done for them.

Mr. ANGELL. Do you know what Gen. Cole had done, or what this gentleman said he had done?

Gen. BARNETT. No; I only know that he was expressing himself as perfectly delighted with Gen. Cole's attitude and what Gen. Cole had done for them.

Mr. ANGELL. So far as you know there was no fund placed at the disposal of the marines or gendarmerie for educational purposes, was there?

Gen. BARNETT. I do not think so.

Mr. ANGELL. So that Gen. Cole could not have done anything except by personal influence or——

Gen. BARNETT. Sympathy.

Mr. ANGELL. Sympathy?

Gen. BARNETT. Yes.

Mr. ANGELL. Nothing tangible that could have been accomplished in the building of schools or——

Gen. BARNETT. I think not.

Mr. ANGELL. Or the hiring of additional teachers?

Gen. BARNETT. He had no authority for that. I stated in my testimony some time ago that the Navy Department had been trying to get something through which would give them authority to allocate money for that, but I do not think they have gotten it yet.

Mr. ANGELL. It is true, is it not, General, that a number of marine officers in Haiti have made recommendations or requests for permission to be allowed to attempt to improve educational facilities in Haiti?

Gen. BARNETT. I think so; undoubtedly.

Mr. ANGELL. General, scattered through your report are various official reports of engagements between the marines and gendarmes, on the one hand, and Haitian natives, principally cacos, upon the other hand, as the result of which conflicts there were casualties amounting to 2,250, I believe are the official figures?

Gen. BARNETT. Yes.

Mr. ANGELL. For the natives and either 14 or 16——

Gen. BARNETT. A very small number.

Mr. ANGELL. A very small number for the marines and gendarmes during the period covered by your report, which is five years?

Gen. BARNETT. Yes.

Mr. ANGELL. What have you to say, if anything, regarding the striking contrast between those figures covering the casualties?

Gen. BARNETT. It was largely like it was in the Philippines. There were a great many natives down there who would be friends to-day and so-called Cacos to-morrow. They had no uniform, and it was hard to distinguish one from the other, and they were not well armed. They were brave, but they would have no show against well-armed troops, especially with machine guns, and it is perfectly natural to suppose that the contrast would be very marked and that a very great number should be killed in comparison with the number of white people who were killed.

Mr. ANGELL. To what extent were machine guns used, do you know?

Gen. BARNETT. I do not. They had them there and used them if they found necessity for it.

Mr. ANGELL. Was there an artillery battalion?

Gen. BARNETT. Yes; and they likewise used airplanes.

Mr. ANGELL. Do you know to what extent they used airplanes?

Gen. BARNETT. No.

Mr. ANGELL. Were airplanes used to bomb out supposed nests of Cacos?

Gen. BARNETT. I do not know the particular uses to which they were put. The reports which came to the commanding officer from them would not necessarily come up here at all.

Mr. ANGELL. So, in your opinion, the contrast between the figures of the respective casualties on both sides were due largely to the superior military armament and equipment of our forces?

Gen. BARNETT. Entirely so, I think. Every marine is a good shot, almost of necessity got to be.

Mr. ANGELL. To what extent, if you know, were offensive operations, in the narrow, military sense, taken by our forces in Haiti against the natives?

Gen. BARNETT. One particular one was the capture of Fort Riviere. That was really quite an affair.

Mr. ANGELL. That was the affair when there were 51 Haitians killed but no casualties on our side?

Gen. BARNETT. It was quite an affair. The Haitians were not well armed, but they stood up and fought to the best of their ability.

Mr. ANGELL. That is covered by paragraph 118 of your report?

Gen. BARNETT. Fort Riviere was captured on November 17, 1915, the message of Col. Cole to Col. Waller containing the following description:

"Capture of Fort Riviere effected by four columns. Campbell, Thirteenth Company; Barker, marine detachment Connecticut; Low, Fifth Company; McCaughey, seaman company from Connecticut; and automatic machine-gun company from Twenty-third Company. All companies were in their position at the time specified and Butler and Low's company made the assault, supported by five other companies. Hand-to-hand conflict in fort lasted 10 minutes. Twenty-nine killed and twenty-two jumped parapet, but all were killed by fire from the automatics, all avenues of escape being blocked. Forty-seven rifles and considerable ammunition found in fort after capture. Fort of mortar and brick of most substantial construction. The fact that this fort was taken without a single casualty on our side speaks worlds for the ability and good judgment of all officers concerned. Have sent to the cape for dynamite to destroy fort, as its complete destruction by blowing up will have great moral effect. All quiet Bajon; people returning to town."

Mr. ANGELL. Was that operation fairly characteristic of the operations in general conducted by our forces against the natives?

Gen. BARNETT. I should say that was a sample. They had a little better protection there than they would have ordinarily, it being an old fort on a high mountain.

Mr. ANGELL. The operations conducted by us were, in the strict military sense, offensive operations?

Gen. BARNETT. Yes; except in one case, where the natives attacked Port au Prince one night.

Mr. ANGELL. Do you know what the approximate casualties the natives suffered in that attack on Port au Prince were?

Gen. BARNETT. In the attack itself and the subsequent operations, where they were followed out into the mountains, etc., I think the exact number was 1,763 killed.

Mr. ANGELL. Those operations extended over a considerable period of time afterwards?

Gen. BARNETT. Several months.

Mr. ANGELL. In your opinion, General, was the method of operations pursued by our forces against the natives as typified by the attack on Fort Riviere, genuinely necessary in the best interests of the maintenance of order in Haiti?

Gen. BARNETT. I think it was. I have great confidence in the particular officer who was there at that time, Gen. Cole, and Gen. Waller also.

Mr. ANGELL. Referring to the proclamation which was published in Haiti on August 22, 1919, by the brigade commander, as appears and is reproduced in the record on page 83, reading, "Citizens of Haiti: The time has come to put a stop to further bloodshed. It has been necessary to use stern measures to repress the disorders in the north, and with the recent arrival of military engines we can use even sterner methods." Do you know to what that proclamation makes reference when it says, "The time has come to put a stop to further bloodshed"?

Gen. BARNETT. The time to close the thing out, to stop this thing of the cacos coming down from the hills.

Mr. ANGELL. What is meant by the recent arrival of military engines?

Gen. BARNETT. I imagine that means airplanes that arrived about that time.

Mr. ANGELL. If I understood you right, General, this morning you testified that largely as the result of your two letters to Col. Russell a correction of that state of affairs was made in Haiti. Can you tell us what correction or what specific steps were taken to correct such abuses as they had existed?

Gen. BARNETT. That was in the hands of Col. Russell, and, as I have stated this morning, the evidence that correction had been made was that in October or November, 1920, Gen. Lejeune and Gen. Butler went there, under orders of the Secretary of the Navy, and made an inspection and found things in fine shape.

Mr. ANGELL. You have no knowledge as to what particular steps Col. Russell took to change the state of affairs in Haiti?

Gen. BARNETT. He issued this proclamation and made it very drastic. As I read it to you this morning, it was a very drastic proclamation indeed, which, as he said, was to be read personally to every marine in Haiti, or marine officer, and to every marine arriving in Haiti at any time, and must be carried out. He got out his proclamation as the result of my letter and stated that if anything of that kind had existed, it must cease or they would all be court-martialed. That is probably just what the result was.

Mr. ANGELL. Referring now, sir, to the corvee system, can you tell us in any detail what abuses there were of that system?

Gen. BARNETT. I can not. As stated in my report, I had simply heard rumors that there was trouble about the corvee system, but I had no report whatever of any specific cases as long as I was commandant of the Marine Corps.

Mr. ANGELL. Do you know whether or not men were taken, native Haitians were taken and forced to work outside of the district in which they lived?

Gen. BARNETT. I do not.

Mr. ANGELL. Do you know whether they were forced to work more than a period of three days?

Gen. BARNETT. I do not. That I have stated in my report. The rumors were that there was trouble on account of the abuse of the corvee system, but where it came from, or what it was, I do not know.

Mr. ANGELL. So, you have no knowledge as to how widespread that abuse was, or in what particular it consisted?

Gen. BARNETT. I have not.

Mr. ANGELL. Nor who was responsible for it?

Gen. BARNETT. I have not.

Mr. ANGELL. Have you any knowledge at all as to why the corvee system was continued, as seems to be the case from official correspondence and reports, in the Hinche district?

Gen. BARNETT. I have understood from the reports I have seen since that time and the report I spoke of this morning, the report made by Maj. Turner, that in one particular Province, Hinche, it was continued contrary to orders, and the officer who was responsible for it probably was the officer in command of the troops in northern Haiti.

Mr. ANGELL. Who was that?

Gen. BARNETT. Maj. Wells, I think.

Senator KING. Do you know definitely that it was continued in violation of orders?

Gen. BARNETT. Senator, when you were not here this morning I stated that this report that I just mentioned, which was made by Maj. Turner, did not come to my office up to the time I left the Marine Corps headquarters, but since that time, and this committee is going to request it, and that will probably show. I have no knowledge whatever first hand of the abuses of the system.

Mr. Angell, in connection with what I stated a moment ago about Fort Riviere, I think it might be well to read here paragraph 119 of my report:

"General Order No. 319, August 25, 1917, announces the award of medals of honor to certain officers and enlisted men for gallantry in capturing Fort Riviere. The general order reads in part as follows."

Then it shows for what they were given this medal of honor. There are four of them, thus showing the approval of the Navy Department of that action.

Mr. ANGELL. General, do you know how thorough an inquiry the court of inquiry presided over by Admiral Mayo made into the Haitian question?

Gen. BARNETT. I have no knowledge of that. I only know, as I stated this morning, with reference to their finding, that that was the only part that came to me, but the record of the court of inquiry is before this committee.

Mr. ANGELL. Who were the members of that court?

Gen. BARNETT. Admiral Mayo. Admiral Oliver, and Gen. Neville.

Mr. ANGELL. Gen. Neville was of the Marine Corps?

Gen. BARNETT. Of the Marine Corps, and Maj. Dyer was judge advocate.

Mr. ANGELL. Where was Gen. Neville on duty at that time he was assigned to this court?

Gen. BARNETT. On duty at the headquarters of the Marine Corps as assistant to the commandant.

Mr. ANGELL. That was after you were relieved as commandant?

Gen. BARNETT. After I was relieved; yes, sir. I was relieved on June 30, 1920.

Mr. ANGELL. Had Admiral Oliver been governor of the Virgin Islands?

Gen. BARNETT. He had two of three years—two years, I think.

Mr. ANGELL. Do you know whether there were any charges, official or unofficial, which had been made or suggested against him arising out of his administration of the Virgin Islands?

Gen. BARNETT. I heard rumors. I never saw any trouble or paper on the subject at all. I never heard anything definite at all. I never saw any official paper of any kind.

Mr. ANGELL. So you do not know whether in that particular he was to a certain extent an interested party?

Gen. BARNETT. I had no knowledge of any trouble in the Virgin Islands at all. My only interest in the court of inquiry—I do not know how they conducted their affairs or anything of that kind—but my only interest in it was in their faulty wording of their report. It was worded so badly that everybody misunderstood it. I do not say a few people, but I say that everybody misunderstood it, and thought it was a severe censure of me.

Senator KING. While Mr. Angell is looking at his notes I would like to ask a question. When I was in Haiti a little over a year ago I was told that a number of marines had been butchered, and their bodies had been devoured, in part at least, by the natives. Did you, when you went down there, learn anything of that?

Gen. BARNETT. I did not. I heard nothing up to the time I left. I do know that there was a report that two American engineers down there were tied up to trees and hacked to pieces by the natives. Those people were tried by military commission, sentenced to be shot—or hanged, I have forgotten which—but the sentence never was approved in this country.

Senator KING. Did you not discover that a number of marines had been killed in ambush?

Gen. BARNETT. I have, undoubtedly.

Senator KING. You reported that?

Gen. BARNETT. Yes; I reported it in here. That was to be expected in any country where war was going on.

Senator KING. This was told me by the natives as well as by Americans, that one marine in particular had his head cut off, and his skull had been used in some of their incantations there; did you hear of that?

Gen. BARNETT. I did not hear of it, but I can well understand it might be true.

Senator KING. In performing their libations they had used the skull of the marine. I was told also that there were a number of natives in the prison at Port au Price—possibly in some other city, I am not sure which—awaiting trial for the butchery of one or more little children, whose blood was necessary in their rituals, in their pagan, religious ceremonials.

Gen. BARNETT. Yes.

Senator KING. Did you learn what became of those natives that were held awaiting trial?

Gen. BARNETT. No, sir; I did not; I have no report on that subject at all.

Mr. HOWE. General, in answering Mr. Angell's questions concerning these engagements and casualties in Haiti you, of course, rely on the reports of your officers down there?

Gen. BARNETT. Entirely; it is all in here.

Mr. HOWE. You had no personal knowledge of it?

Gen. BARNETT. None whatever; I took the official reports.

Mr. HOWE. Mr. Angell used the expression " offensive operations " in the strictly military sense, and that was the expression used in connection with his question to you with regard to the capture of Fort Riviere?

Gen. BARNETT. Yes.

Mr. HOWE. You did not conceive that to mean an unprovoked operation or unnecessary operation?

Gen. BARNETT. Not at all. I used " offensive " in the strictly military sense, meaning that they went after them; they did not wait to be attacked, but went after them.

Mr. HOWE. And the operation being carried out had the approval of the Navy Department?

Gen. BARNETT. Not only the approval of the Navy Department, but had such approval of the Navy Department that for that affair alone they awarded four medals of honor.

Mr. HOWE. You were asked a question by Mr. Angell as to whether that operation was characteristic of the many other operations in Haiti and you said it was. In what respect was the capture of Fort Riviere characteristic of the other operations?

Gen. BARNETT. Simply because they went after them. They went after the Cacos wherever they met any of them.

Mr. HOWE. Not after the Haitians in general?

Gen. BARNETT. Not at all. They only went after the Cacos, and it was not typical in that, as I said, at Fort Riviere the Haitians had much better protection than they had in most cases, because it was an old fort up on top of a high mountain.

Mr. HOWE. General, in connection with a question asked by Mr. Angell concerning Gen. Cole's investigation for a hostile attitude toward the United States, I would like to read you sections 169 and 171 of your report. Section 169 reads as follows:

" On May 28, 1917, Brig. Gen. Cole reported that the British charge d'affaires had informed him that he was much worried over the propaganda that was being spread against the Americans and the changed attitude toward the Americans on the part of many classes of people."

" 171. On May 29, 1917, Brig. Gen. Cole reported that he had made efforts to locate causes for hostile attitude, but without success, and while admitting its presence believed the belief of the British charge to be caused by the fact that he lived with an ' alarmist.' "

Do you not think those two sections which I have just read you constitute a full reply to the question asked you by Mr. Angell?

Gen. BARNETT. I think undoubtedly they are a very good answer, indeed. We heard rumors constantly about propaganda started by German citizens down there.

Mr. HOWE. But the fact remained that a rumor of a grievance against the Americans led, on an investigation, to the discovery of no specific cases?

Gen. BARNETT. No specific cases. I find here in the report, in reply to the question asked by Senator King about marines being cut up, that there is one case reported as follows:

"All clothing had been removed from the body of Lieut. Muth. The body had been badly mutilated, heart cut out, and head cut off. The underclothing had been replaced. The head and heart had been taken away, and the latter probably eaten."

That is a part of paragraph 251 of my report.

Senator KING. May I inquire, relative to the same military operations to which Mr. Angell directed your attention, whether those against whom you were operating were seeking the overthrow of the existing government, and whether the operations of the American troops or marines was with the knowledge, consent, and approval, if not the direction, of the Haitian Government?

Gen. BARNETT. It was in both cases.

Senator KING. Were any of the military operations there contrary to the wishes of the President and the native officials?

Gen. BARNETT. I think not.

Senator KING. Were they in harmony with their views?

Gen. BARNETT. As far as I know.

Senator KING. And aimed at the protection of law and order?

Gen. BARNETT. I think that without a force of marines there they would not have lasted long, and they knew it.

Mr. ANGELL. In connection with Senator King's last question, do you know whether or not the military seizure of the customhouses in August and September, 1915, met with the approval of the President and Government of Haiti?

Gen. BARNETT. I do not. You will have to ask, if you have not already, Admiral Caperton that. I was not there, and Admiral Caperton was.

Mr. HOWE. In one of Mr. Angell's questions he asked you about the abuses of the corvee system. You know that the corvee did exist there as a system, do you not?

Gen. BARNETT. I do.

Mr. HOWE. But have you any knowledge of any abuse of that system?

Gen. BARNETT. Not the slightest first-hand knowledge at all, sir.

Senator KING. Did it exist as a system before the American troops went there?

Gen. BARNETT. It is Haitian law. Just when it had been invoked I do not know, but I imagine whenever it became necessary to build roads.

Senator ODDIE. Do you know whether there is any comparison between that system and the poll-tax system in some of the States?

Gen. BARNETT. I have understood it is largely the same, where a man may work so many days or pay so much tax. I know out West it was quite a common custom when I was a boy.

(Whereupon, the committee adjourned until Wednesday, October 26, 1921, at 10.30 o'clock a. m.)

62269—21—PT 2——23

INQUIRY INTO OCCUPATION AND ADMINISTRATION OF HAITI AND SANTO DOMINGO.

WEDNESDAY, OCTOBER 26, 1921.

UNITED STATES SENATE,
SELECT COMMITTEE ON HAITI AND SANTO DOMINGO,
Washington, D. C.

The committee met at 10.30 o'clock a. m., pursuant to adjournment, Senator Tasker L. Oddie presiding.

Present: Senators Oddie and Pomerene.

Also present: Mr. Ernest Angell, Mr. Horace G. Knowles and Maj. Edwin N. McClellan, United States Marine Corps, and Walter Bruce Howe, Esq., in their respective representative capacities as hereinbefore indicated.

STATEMENT OF MAJ. T. C. TURNER, UNITED STATES MARINE CORPS.

Senator ODDIE. Major, give your full name and rank and your position in the Marine Corps.

Maj. TURNER. T. C. Turner, major United States Marine Corps; in charge of marine aviation, headquarters, Marine Corps.

Mr. HOWE. Major, how long have you been in the Marine Corps?

Maj. TURNER. Since January, 1901.

Mr. HOWE. Were you in Haiti in the years 1919 and 1920?

Maj. TURNER. I arrived in Haiti October 1, 1919, and left there on November 12, 1920.

Mr. HOWE. Did you, while down there, make an investigation of certain alleged irregularities in Haiti?

Maj. TURNER. I did.

Senator POMERENE. Were you the commanding officer?

Maj. TURNER. I was not; I was the brigade adjutant and acting chief of staff.

Senator POMERENE. Who was the officer in command at that time?

Maj. TURNER. Col. John H. Russell.

Mr. HOWE. Will you state, please Major, in connection with this investigation you conducted, when you received your orders and when you began the investigation?

Maj. TURNER. The orders came through Col. Russell, from the headquarters of the Marine Corps. I started the investigation about October 5, and I think I completed it——

Mr. HOWE. Of what year?

Maj. TURNER. 1919. I think it was completed sometime during the month of November of the same year.

Mr. HOWE. The investigation which we are now talking about, covered, did it not, among other things, the actions of Lieut. Williams, Lieut. Freeman Lang, and included testimony by Lieut. Van Horn?

Maj. TURNER. I do not remember that Lang's name was mentioned. Williams's was, but I do not remember that Van Horn's was.

Mr. HOWE. I think there is a sworn statement of Lieut. Van Horn's here in the record; I am not certain whether it was taken by you. I merely asked the question in order to identify this report.

Senator POMERENE. You made a written report?

Maj. TURNER. I did.

Senator POMERENE. To whom?

Maj. TURNER. To Col. Russell.

Mr. HOWE. We have that report here. Will you please give us a full description of your methods of making this investigation and taking the testimony?

457

Maj. TURNER. As I remember it, Col. Russell called me and showed me a letter received from the major general commandant, and at the same time issued an order to me to make an investigation on the contents of the letter from the major general commandant.

Mr. HOWE. Does this document which I hand you contain the results of your investigation [handing document to Maj. Turner]?

Maj. TURNER. It does.

Mr. HOWE. Is this the original?

Maj. TURNER. No; it is not.

Mr. HOWE. I notice here that there appears to be the signatures of witnesses to some of the sworn statements. It occurs to me to ask, Is this a duplicate original in so far as these sworn statements go?

Maj. TURNER. This is a part of the second part of the investigation, in which Lieut. Col. Hooker and myself took part. This is not the first investigation at all.

Mr. HOWE. Will you, taking that document by pages, indicate where your report begins and where it ends—where the first part begins and where the second part begins?

Maj. TURNER. This is in reference to an investigation made by Col. Hooker and myself.

Senator POMERENE. I would like to have the major give the substance of the charges made, which he was to investigate, and give us a general résumé of the conditions as he found them. I can understand how he will want to verify his memory by referring to the record later, but he can give us the substance of that, which will give us a bird's-eye view of it, and then he can give us a reference to the record afterwards and read such parts of the record as will be of assistance.

Mr. HOWE. As I understand it, a part of this document which constitutes this report will be put into the record later?

Senator POMERENE. Yes; but he can state what the charges were.

Maj. TURNER. As I remember the letter, it stated that during a court-martial the counsel for the accused had made various statements about killing Cacos. I took this letter and attempted to investigate the contents of the letter, but was unable to get anything on that one particular case.

My invesigation brought me to other matters that looked as if there had been irregularities committed by marines down there.

Senator POMERENE. Now, be more specific. That is a very general term. What kind of irregularities were they?

Maj. TURNER. The killing of prisoners.

Senator POMERENE. Go ahead.

Maj. TURNER. I went to Col. Russell and spoke to him about it, and he told me to go to the bottom of it and get everything out of it I could get, it made no difference what happened.

I examined a great number of witnesses, and the more I examined these witnesses the more firmly convinced I became that there was little or nothing to the whole thing.

The reports would come to me that certain prisoners had been killed, and the deeper I went into it it looked as if the killings were a fact. As a matter of fact——

Mr. HOWE. The killing of prisoners?

Maj. TURNER. The killing of prisoners. As a matter of fact, there is only one case, and that is in the case of Lavoie, where I considered that prisoners had been killed in an irregular manner.

Senator POMERENE. Give us the particulars of that case.

Maj. TURNER. That was some time in January, 1919, where it was alleged that Lavoie had machine-gunned some 15 or 19 prisoners in a graveyard outside of the town of Hinche, but there was no evidence, nor could I find any witnesses to that.

Senator POMERENE. Was this man Lavoie a marine?

Maj. TURNER. Lavoie was a sergeant of marines, and during the time mentioned, in January, 1919, he was a captain in the Haitian gendarmerie.

Senator POMERENE. How many were killed at that time?

Maj. TURNER. I am inclined to believe it was 19.

Senator POMERENE. Nineteen native prisoners?

Maj. TURNER. That was the report.

Senator POMERENE. What was the irregularity about it?

Maj. Turner. The irregularity was that Lavoie was alleged to have taken these men out of jail and shot them in the graveyard outside of Hinche.
Senator Pomerene. What was their offence?
Maj. Turner. None.
Mr. Howe. Proving there had been no trial; is that it?
Maj. Turner. They were captured caco prisoners.
Senator Pomerene. Do I understand you to say that a marine had done this without any court-martial proceeding?
Maj. Turner. That is what was alleged.
Senator Pomerene. Where is this man Lavoie?
Maj. Turner. Lavoie left Haiti, and I do not know where he is now.
Senator Pomerene. Is he still with the Marines?
Maj. Turner. No, sir; he is not; he left Haiti some years ago.
Senator Pomerene. That is one instance, and there were 19 men killed?
Maj. Turner. So it is alleged.
Senator Pomerene. That was something of an irregularity, was it not?
Maj. Turner. Yes, sir.
Senator Pomerene. Now, did you talk with Lavoie yourself?
Maj. Turner. I did.
Senator Pomerene. What did he say about it?
Maj. Turner. I would like to take a look at his testimony before saying that. I do not remember exactly just now. This was a couple of years ago.
Senator Pomerene. I can understand how you will want to be accurate about that, and we want it accurate. I thought perhaps you could give us, in a general way, what his claim was, and then you could supplement that later.
Maj. Turner. As I remember it, I think he denied it, but I am not sure of that.
Senator Pomerene. Then you had better look that up and get all the facts with regard to it. You say there were other irregularities complained of. What other irregularities were there?
Maj. Turner. Everything, Senator—everything; but, traced down, it was nothing.
Senator Pomerene. Go into the details as to what they were.
Maj. Turner. Rape, murder, and robbery.
Senator Pomerene. Did you satisfy yourself that there was nothing in these charges, or are we to understand that you were not able to get any proof as to whether or not they occurred?
Maj. Turner. I was satisfied after the investigation that they were untrue. The witnesses would tail off to an end without being able to give me any definite proof.
Senator Pomerene. When you speak of your witnesses, do you speak of natives or marines?
Maj. Turner. Natives and whites. Quite a number of these were not called before the investigation because after talking to them I was convinced that their testimony was of no value whatever. I put in the investigation the testimony of those which was of value. The rest was all hearsay.
Senator Pomerene. Did you trace that hearsay evidence down to get hold of the man who had primary knowledge of it?
Maj. Turner. Yes, sir; and could not get them; there was not anybody.
Senator Pomerene. Let us go back to this Lavoie matter again. Did his superior officers have any knowledge on this subject?
Maj. Turner. I do not think so at the time; no.
Senator Pomerene. Did they make any attempt to investigate this matter?
Maj. Turner. That I do not know. I think there was an investigation by Gen. Catlin in March, 1919. I believe—this is my belief—that that matter was taken up at that time, but how deeply he went into it I do not know.
Senator Pomerene. I think you ought to go very carefully into that record. This is a mighty grave matter and we ought to know exactly what the facts are with regard to it.
Maj. Turner. Yes, sir. Lavoie was discharged from the Marine Corps in Haiti and accepted a position with the sugar company down there, and later was with the Government in the customs service, and later on left Haiti.
Senator Pomerene. What other investigation did you make? You say there were a lot of other alleged irregularities, and you found nothing.
Maj. Turner. I investigated to find if I could put anything in this report of mine that would be of any value. But there was nothing else found.

Senator POMERENE. What was the substance of your conclusion?

Maj. TURNER. I made no conclusions. I was ordered to make an investigation, but not to give an opinion or a conclusion. The conclusions were made by Col. Russell.

Senator POMERENE. Have you since gone over his conclusions?

Maj. TURNER. Col. Russell's?

Senator POMERENE. Yes.

Maj. TURNER. Yes, sir.

Senator POMERENE. Do you agree with them?

Maj. TURNER. Yes, sir.

Senator POMERENE. Col. Russell, in his letter says:

HEADQUARTERS FIRST PROVISIONAL BRIGADE,
UNITED STATES MARINE CORPS,
Port au Prince, Republic of Haiti, March 13, 1920.

Confidential.

From: The brigade commander.

To: The Major General Commandant.

Subject: Report of investigation of certain irregularities alleged to have been committed by officers and enlisted men in the Republic of Haiti.

1. From a careful reading and study of the attached testimony, statements, and other reports, I am reluctantly forced to the opinion that Maj. Clarke H. Wells, formerly gendarmerie department commander in northern Haiti, is responsible for the conditions in northern Haiti as found by Brig. Gen. Catlin on his inspection of the Hinche-Maissade districts in March, 1919. If such conditions were not actually due to his orders and instructions.

2. I am further of the opinion that these gendarmerie officers under Maj. Well's command who were enlisted men in the Marine Corps, on duty in said districts, were acting in accordance with what they believed to be the policy of their department commander.

3. It is difficult to believe that Capt. Doxey was not fully aware of Maj. Well's policy and of the existing orders and conditions in the Hinche-Maissade district.

4. There is no doubt, however, in my mind, as to whether or not the evidence as here brought out is sufficient to warrant a trial before a general court-martial on charges of such a serious nature. It is extremely doubtful if further evidence can be procured.

5. The event referred to herein occurred over a year ago. Many changes have taken place in the personnel of the gendarmerie since that time. Nearly all the interested parties have either returned to the United States or have been discharged from the service. Mr. Lavoie, former captain G. D. H. and private Unitd States Marine Corps, has left the service and Haiti, and his whereabouts is unknown.

6. It is therefore recommended that these papers be referred to the office of the Judge Advocate General, United States Navy, where the sworn statements and other evidence may be carefully sifted and weighed with a view of determining whether or not it is sufficient to warrant a trial.

7. If the decision is in the affirmative, it is requested that specimen charges and specifications be prepared by the Judge Advocate's General's office, and that a competent officer be assigned to temporary duty with this brigade to act as judge advocate of the court. At present, there is no officer attached to the brigade who is considered to have sufficient legal knowledge to conduct a trial, to the best interest of the Government, where skilled opposing counsel is present.

8. The return to Haiti of all witnesses and interested parties would, of course, be necessary.

JOHN H. RUSSELL.

This sergeant certainly did not use the machine gun himself, but he must have had some privates doing it; did he not?

Maj. TURNER. I do not remember whether the gendarmerie privates did it, but I am inclined to believe that Lavoie was supposed to have done it, as I remember.

Senator POMERENE. I wish you would look up that record and refresh your memory about that. We want to know what did occur down there, and we ought to have the facts.

Maj. TURNER. Yes, sir.

(Thereupon a recess was taken until 2 o'clock p. m.)

The committee reassembled, pursuant to the taking of the recess, at 2 o'clock p. m., Senator Medill McCormick (chairman) presiding.

Mr. HOWE. Maj. Turner, how many investigations did you make down there in Haiti, or could you subdivide any of your investigations?

Maj. TURNER. There was one main investigation, and later on, in January or February, 1920, Col. Hooker was ordered to assist me in making further investigations, due to the fact that my duty at that time would not permit me to go into the hills and visit the different points where information might be gained. The main investigation was made by me between October—I think about the 5th or 7th—and I think it lasted until the latter part of November.

Mr. HOWE. Your first investigation was begun at the direction of Col. Russell, was it not?

Maj. TURNER. Yes, sir.

Mr. HOWE. And in connection with that letter sent by Gen. Barnett to Col. Russell, the letter being dated September 27, 1919?

Maj. TURNER. Yes.

Mr. HOWE. That was referred to you and you were told to investigate, with that letter as a starting point or basis——

Maj. TURNER. Of the investigation; yes.

Mr. HOWE. Then, as I understand it, major, you investigated during the remaining part of the month of October and began to take written testimony on the 3d of November?

Maj. TURNER. Yes.

Mr. HOWE. And that written testimony, when it was completed, you turned over to Col. Russell, did you not?

Maj. TURNER. I did.

Mr. HOWE. It was after that had been turned in that Col. Hooker was directed to cooperate with you in the taking of further testimony?

Maj. TURNER. Yes; considerably after—two months.

Mr. HOWE. I am going to ask you if this document which I hold in my hand, from pages 109 to 131, is not the written testimony to which we have referred as having been begun to be taken on November 3, 1919?

Maj. TURNER. Yes, sir.

Mr. HOWE. Mr. Chairman, I offer for the record pages 109 to 131, inclusive, of this report.

The CHAIRMAN. Without objection, that will be inserted in the record.

(The matter referred to is as follows:)

Confidential.   NOVEMBER 3. 1919.

From: Maj. Thomas C. Turner, A. A. & I., U. S. Marine Corps.

To: The brigade commander.

Subject: Report of investigation of certain irregularities alleged to have been committed by officers and enlisted men in the Republic of Haiti.

Reference: (a) Major general commandant's confidential letter dated September 27, 1919.

1. On receipt of reference (a) I immediately proceeded to investigate the alleged irregularities. I called in Sergt. Richard R. Siegert, United States Marin Corps, who was duly sworn as stenographer.

2. Capt. LAURENCE BOLTE, Gendarmerie d'Haiti (corporal, United States Marine Corps), was called as the first witness, was duly sworn, and testified as follows: •

1. Question. State your name, rank, and present station.

Answer. Laurence Bolte, corporal, United States Marine Corps, and a captain in the Gendarmerie d'Haiti, stationed at Hinche, Republic of Haiti.

2. Question. Statements have been made that both marines and gendarmes have been in the habit of having wounded cacos shot. Do you know anything about this?

Answer. No, sir.

3. Question. You never issued an order of that kind?

Answer. No, sir.

4. Question. Do you know that this has been done?

Answer. I don't know about it, but I have heard of it being done.

5. Question. Where did you hear this, and from whom?

Answer. I heard it from Lieut. Floyd, Gendarmerie d'Haiti; Mr. Baker; and Maj. Hayes, Gendarmerie d'Haiti.

6. Question. Who was in command at Hinche when the last rebellion started?
Answer. Capt. Kelly had it in October.
7. Question. Who relieved him?
Answer. Capt. Lavigne.
8. Question. Who relieved him?
Answer. Maj. Doxey.
9. Question. Were you ever instructed to make private reports to anybody in reference to operations in the Hinche district?
Answer. Not private reports, but telegrams received through Ouanaminthe by telephone were to be kept on file at the third company office under lock and key.
10. Question. Who gave this order?
Answer. Col. Wells.
11. Question. Why was this order issued?
Answer. I do not know if it was caused by this investigation which took place at Hinche.
12. Question. Did Col. Wells ever instruct you to disregard certain orders received from the chief of the Gendarmerie d'Haiti?
Answer. No, sir.
13. Question. Do you know whether these or any other orders were disregarded?
Answer. No, sir.
14. Question. Do you remember when the first order against corvee came out?
Answer. The first order came out in the latter part of August.
15. Question. Was this order ever disregarded?
Answer. I do not know that this was done. I heard it from the priest at Hinche (Belliot) and a chief of section named Joseph Marcellin, and one named Albert.
16. Question. Did the priest at Hinche ever inform you that before you came there that Cacos had been killed after they had surrendered?
Answer. Yes.
17. Question. Did anybody at Hinche tell you that?
Answer. No one at Hinche; but a marine named Sasse told me that prisoners had been taken out of the prison at Hinche and shot, and the priest at Hinche told me the same thing.
18. Question. Who issued the order for the shooting. Do you know?
Answer. No, sir.
19. Question. You do not know whether this was reported to Col. Wells or not, do you?
Answer. No, sir.
20. Question. While you were at the cape did a telegram show that there was any considerable trouble at the district of Hinche?
Answer. Yes.
21. Question. Between what months were those telegrams coming in?
Answer. From the 1st of January to the middle of March.
22. Question. Do you know what became of those telegrams?
Answer. They were left in the desk of the district commander at the cape.

3. Second Lieut. EDWARD J. SIEGER, Gendarmerie d'Haiti (corporal, United States Marine Corps), was called as a witness, was duly sworn, and testified as follows:

1. Question. State your name and rank.
Answer. Edward J. Sieger, second lieutenant, Gendarmerie d'Haiti, corporal, United States Marine Corps.
2. Question. How long have you been with the Gendarmerie d'Haiti?
Answer. Since October, 1916.
3. Question. What duty were you performing between the months of January and March, 1919?
Answer. Patrol duty in the Hinche district.
4. Question. Did you ever see wounded Cacos killed by marines or gendarmes?
Answer. No.
5. Question. Did you ever hear that it had been done?
Answer. No.
6. Question. Did you ever hear of an order abolishing corvee?
Answer. Yes.
7. Question. When was it issued?
Answer. September or October, 1918.
8. Question. Did you know of any corvees after that time?

Answer. I understand they were running corvee in Maissade.

9. Question. Who told you that?

Answer. Only Haitians.

10. Question. Who was in command of Maissade at this time?

Answer. Lieut. Williams.

11. Question. What were your reports to Haj. Wells as to the conditions of the natives during your time in command at Thomassique?

Answer. I only made reports to Capt. Lavoie. I reported conditions very bad.

12. Question. Did you ever hear that Maj. Wells had ordered Lavoie or anyone else at Hinche to disregard Maj. Wells's orders at Hinche?

Answer. No.

13. Question. Do you know that they had corvees at Maissade after the order abolishing it had come out?

Answer. Just from what Haitians had told me.

14. Question. Do you approve of killing wounded prisoners?

Answer. No, sir.

15. Question. Do you really think that conditions were good in the gendarmerie in the early part of 1919?

Answer. No.

16. Question. Why not?

Answer. Messages came in that telephone lines were being cut and houses burnt.

17. Question. Do you consider the Gendarmerie d'Haiti responsible for this condition?

Answer. Not absolutely responsible.

18. Question. But in a way?

Answer. Well, I don't know.

4. Captain FRANK VERDIER, Gendarmerie d'Haiti (sergeant, United States Marine Corps), was called as a witness, was duly sworn, and testified as follows:

1. Question. State your name and rank.

Answer. Frank Verdier, captain, Gendarmerie d'Haiti (sergeant, United States Marine Corps).

2. Question. Did you ever hear of any prisoners—that is, Cacos—being shot without proper trials?

Answer. No, sir.

3. Question. Where were you stationed in 1919, up to date?

Answer. I have been in Ouanaminthe since September, 1918.

4. Question. Did you ever hear that Caco prisoners were being treated roughly?

Answer. I never heard any remarks about it.

5. Question. When did the order against corvee come out?

Answer. October 1, 1918.

6. Question. Did you ever hear that this order has been disobeyed?

Answer. I heard that it had been disobeyed at Maissade by the magistrate.

7. Question. During early part of 1919, did you have any trouble with cacos in the Ouanaminthe district?

Answer. Yes; in July, 1919.

8. Question. Did you ever hear that caco prisoners had been shot in the cemetery at Hinche?

Answer. I heard that some people had been shot in the cemetery at Hinche, but I don't know whether they were prisoners or cacos.

9. Question. Who told you?

Answer. Some Haitian; I don't know his name.

10. Question. Did you ever speak to anyone about it?

Answer. I spoke to Capt. Kelly about it, but he said that it was not so.

11. Question. This was the only conversation you had on this subject?

Answer. Yes.

12. Question. Who told you of the corvee at Maissade?

Answer. I don't remember.

13. Question. Was he white or Haitian?

Answer. I think he was white.

14. Question. Did you ever have any conversation with Capt. Bolte about shooting prisoners or maltreating them?

Answer. I think that I told Capt. Bolte that I had heard a rumor that they had not been shot at Hinche.

5. Second Lieut. P. JULES ANDRE, gendarmerie d'Haiti, was called as a witness.

Mr. Alfred J. Holly was called as interpreter and was duly sworn.

Lieut. Andre testified as follows:

1. Question. What is your name and rank?

Answer. P. Jules Andre, second lieutenant, Gendarmerie d'Haiti.

2. Question. It has been reported that there has been a lot of killing of caco prisoners. Do you know anything about this?

Answer. I never witnessed any shooting, as I was at Thomonde; but I heard there was some executions at Hinche and at a suburb of Hinche called Latte.

3. Question. Who was in command at these places?

Answer. Capt. Lavole.

4. Question. Did you ever hear of any other murders of any prisoners in the district of the north?

Answer. Yes; at Maissade, one named Garliner.

5. Question. By whose orders was the murdering done by at Maissade?

Answer. I don't know.

6. Question. Wasn't it generally known throughout the gendarmerie that these murders were the result of orders from Maj. Wells?

Answer. No.

7. Question. Can you give any reasons for these killings?

Answer. These officers acted pretty much as they liked, as they were not seriously controlled by their superior officers.

8. Question. Do you know whether they had corvee at Maissade during the months of January, February, and March of this year?

Answer. They had it in December last year and in January and February of this year.

9. Question. By whose orders was this corvee ordered?

Answer. I don't know, but I presume it was by the order of Maj. Wells.

10. Question. Is it not generally known that this corvee was ordered by Maj. Wells?

Answer. I presume it was as he was in command of that district and the orders came from him.

11. Question. What effect did this corvee have on the feelings of the people of the north?

Answer. A very bad effect, and I think that it was the cause for the revolution in the north.

12. Question. Did you see much of Maj. Wells?

Answer. I know him very well because he was my captain, major, and colonel.

13. Question. Was he in the habit of using intoxicating liquor very much?

Answer. I never saw him intoxicated, but I know he drank.

14. Question. Do you know Maj. Doxey?

Answer. Yes, sir; very well.

15. Question. Was Maj. Doxey responsible in any way for the corvee?

Answer. I think not, because he never had anything to do with corvee.

16. Question. Did Maj. Doxey know anything about the killing of the prisoners at Hinche?

Answer. I don't know, because I was at the Cape and so was Maj. Doxey.

17. Question. Is there any bad treatment of prisoners in the north at the present time, and if not, what is the last case of that kind that you have heard of?

Answer. No; not at the present time. The last case was in March, this year.

18. Question. Did the maltreating of prisoners stop when Gen. Catlin issued that order?

Answer. Yes.

6. FREDERICK C. BAKER was called as a witness and was duly sworn and testified as follows:

1. Question. What is your name?

Answer. Frederick C. Baker.

2. Question. Have you ever been connected with the gendarmerie d'Haiti, and if so, for how long?

Answer. I have; I was attached to and serving with the gendarmerie d'Haiti for a period of three years, my service terminating April 1, 1919.

3. Question. It has been reported that marines and gendarmes have been killing caco prisoners. Do you know anything about this?

Answer. Only from hearsay.

4. Question. During your time in the gendarmerie, were you ever ordered to "bump off" or not to take any prisoners?

Answer. I was on one occasion. About November 1, 1918, while serving as district commander, District of Gonsivee, Haiti, Maissade was attacked by cacos and certain destructions committed there. On the date following this attack my then department commander, Maj. C. E. Wells, called me by phone from Cape Haitien to Gonaivos, and related the details of. the attack and ordered that I proceed with a patrol from Gonaives to Maissade. He further ordered that prisoners, if any were undesirable, useless, and he desired them bumped off, by this expression of course meant to kill them. I followed out his orders so far as going to Maissade and making a general patrol; no prisoners were captured, therefore none killed.

5. Question. Do you know of anyone else who received like order?

Answer. From Capt. Ernest Lavoie, G. D'H., Lieut. Sieger, G. D'H., and Lieut. Williams, G. D'H., I learned that they had received the same and similar orders.

6. Question. Did you ever hear that any of the above-named officers carried out those orders?

Answer. I have been informed and believe that Capt. Lavoie carried out these orders and was acting under the orders of Maj. Wells when he executed 19 prisoners at Henche in January, 1919.

7. Question. Was it generally talked about, among the marine officers and gendarmerie officers, that prisoners were being "bumped off"?

Answer. In close circles among the gendarmerie officers whom I knew best and with whom I most associated it was understood, I believe, to be the popular thing to "bump off" as nearly as possible all prisoners taken. It was more or less discussed by them all and it was generally understood among them.

8. Question. Was this understanding caused entirely by orders received from Maj. Wells?

Answer. To the best of my belief the whole incentive behind the executions referred to were the orders and sanction given the act by Maj. Wells.

9. Question. Were you very well acquainted with Maj. Wells?

Answer. I was. I was closely associated with Maj. Wells from November, 1917, until January, 1919, serving as his assistant on road construction in the district of the north, and by virtue of nature of this I became close to him, spending, as it were, weeks at a time continually in his company and with him in the country.

10. Question. What was the attitude of Maj. Wells with reference to reports of trouble in the north?

Answer. Maj. Wells often instructed me, along with others, to use the soft pedal on all reports, and except in cases of necessity or to comply with some regular order to make no reports at all. He often explained this by saying that Port au Prince was too busy and had no time to receive or read reports on details. He stated that he would be satisfied as long as the country was in a state of good police, and he neither cared nor wanted to hear of the details of executions to accomplish this end.

11. Question. Did Maj. Wells ever express any desire not to hear of these killings?

Answer. He often stated that he did not want to hear of these things.

12. Question. Have you ever seen Maj. Wells under the influence of liquor?

Answer. I have, numerous times.

13. Question. Is it possible that some of these "bumping-off" orders were due to the fact that he had been drinking?

Answer. I would think it possible that some were, although at the time he gave the order to "bump off" prisoners taken in or around Maissade, I do not believe that he was in the slightest affected by the influence of liquor.

14. Question. Was Maj. Doxey entirely familiar with everything that was going on in the north?

Answer. It is my opinion that he was. He was closer to Maj. Wells than any other officer in the department of the north, and appeared always to counsel and advise with Maj. Wells in all matters of importance pertaining to service. He was in and out of Hinche frequently, and it would seem inconceivable that he was entirely unconscious of the things that were going on.

15. Question. Did he ever express any orders as to bumping off prisoners?

Answer. Not to my knowledge.

16. Question. Was it generally known or talked about that all the conditions that you referred to had been explained and gone over by Gen. Catlin on his visit to St. Michel in March, 1919?

Answer. It was. From others and all practically who had been interrogated by Gen. Catlin I learned that practically every phase of the conditions which I have related were brought to the attention of Gen. Catlin at some time during his investigation at St. Michel and Hinche.

17. Question. At any time after Gen. Catlin's conference was an order issued by either Gen. Catlin or Lieut. Col. A. S. Williams or Maj. Wells that these conditions must change?

Answer. There was. I received an order from the chief of the gendarmerie prohibiting in detail the execution of Caco or other prisoners.

18. Question. What date was the order against corvee issued?

Answer. October 1, 1918.

19. Question. Was this order ever disobeyed?

Answer. It was. This order was disobeyed in the districts of Maissade and Hinche from October 1, 1918, until some time in March, 1919.

20. Question. Was this order disobeyed by instructions from anybody?

Answer. Capt. Lavoie and Lieut. Williams, when I inquired of them in my capacity as inspector of roads in the north as to by whose authority and from whence funds were coming to carry on their work, informed me that Maj. Wells had ordered them to construct roads between St. Michel and Maissade and between Maissade and Hinche with corvee labor, and that he had induced the magistrates of Maissade and Hinche to make a certain contribution from which the corvee would be fed.

21. Question. What effect did the breaking of this order against corvee labor have on the people in the north?

Answer. It is my opinion that the corvee illegally formed after October 1, 1918, and after the Haitian public generally knew and well understood that all corvees and forced labor had been ordered suspended constituted the chiefest factor in the dissatisfaction which led to revolution, and it is well understood that the first Caco forces were largely recruited from the last-formed corvee. This opinion is based on my experience of handling corvee labor during the fall of 1917 and the spring of 1918, when I had under me and personally directed the largest corvee ever formed in Haiti, numbering 3,000 men.

Under the then existing conditions the members of my corvee, knowing that they were subject legally to be called up to do road work, offered no resistance and seemed contented during the entire operation—that is, the construction of the road from Gonaives to the Limbe River—and the first discontent over this subject had its inception in the district of Maissade and Hinche when these people learned that they were being forcibly detained, worked under guard, and knowing that the President of Haiti as well as the chief of the Gendarmerie d'Haiti had ordered the suspension of corvee labor throughout the Republic.

22. Question. From your conversation with Marine and gendarmerie officers, can you give an estimation of illegal executions in the district of the north?

Answer. Aggregating all reports and rumors, I would judge the number to exceed over 400 at least, and in this number there are included a large percentage of persons suspicioned or whose identity was never known.

23. Question. Was this estimate a low or high estimate?

Answer. This is a low estimate.

7. First Lieut. HAROLD H. WOOD, Gendarmerie d'Haiti (corporal, United States Marine Corps), was called as a witness, and was duly sworn and testified as follows:

1. Question. What is your name and rank?

Answer. Harold R. Wood, first lieutenant, Gendarmerie d'Haiti (corporal, United States Marine Corps).

2. Question. Do you know anything of the unlawful killing of caco prisoners?

Answer. No, sir.

3. Question. Have you heard in any way of the unlawful killing of caco prisoners.

Answer. I had heard of some of them being killed.

4. Question. Where?

Answer. In Hinche and Maissade.

5. Question. Did you ever hear by whose instructions this was carried out?

Answer. I know nothing of instructions about actual killings of any prisoners, but instructions were said to have been issued not to take any prisoners.

6. Question. By whom were these orders issued?
Answer. They were said to have been issued by the department commander, Col. Wells.
7. Question. Was Maj. Doxey cognizant of these instructions which you had heard had been issued?
Answer. As to that I don't know, because at that time I saw Maj. Doxey but once, having passed him on a road.
8. Question. Do you know whether Maj. Doxey was in or around Hinche about this time?
Answer. No, sir; Maj. Doxey was not there.
9. Question. Do you know Lieut. Spier?
Answer. No, sir.

8. Capt. JOHN L. DOXEY, United States Marine Corps, was called us a witness, and was duly sworn and testified as follows:

1. Question. State your name and rank.
Answer. John L. Doxey, captain, United States Marine Corps.
2. Question. What duty were you performing between the month of October, 1918, and March, 1919?
Answer. I was district commander of the district of Cape Haitien.
3. Question. Did this work take you into the Hinche district; that is, into the towns of Maissade and Hinche?
Answer. I was directed to go into the Hinche district on about October 18, 1918, and remained there until October 30 or 31. Again, I was ordered to Hinche about February 17 and remained there until March 31, 1919.
4. Question. While in the Hinche district did you at any time hear of the unlawful killing of caco prisoners?
Answer. Some time in March I heard rumors of this.
5. Question. What were these rumors?
Answer. All that I remember was killing of prisoners, and that there would be an investigation.
6. Question. Where did rumors say these prisoners had been killed?
Answer. Just in the Hinche district.
7. Question. Not in Hinche?
Answer. No; not necessarily in the district of Hinche.
8. Question. Can you give the approximate date?
Answer. No, sir.
9. Question. What attempt, if any, did you make to investigate these rumors?
Answer. None.
10. Question. Can you give any reasons for not investigating these rumors?
Answer. None, except that I was not directed to investigate these rumors, and I understood there would be an investigation.
11. Question. Your theory is, then, that if you heard of something wrong in your district that you would not investigate it unless ordered. Is that correct?
Answer. No, sir; that was not in my district at that time.
12. Question. Do you say that some time in March you were ordered out in the Hinche district again?
Answer. About the 17th of February until the 7th of March.
13. Question. Then you did not hear these rumors in the Hinche district but at the cape?
Answer. Yes, sir.
14. Question. Did you ever mention these rumors to Maj. Wells?
Answer. Not that I remember.
15. Question. Did you ever hear that certain gendarmerie officers had received orders to bump off prisoners?
Answer. No, sir.
16. Question. Was the killing of prisoners you referred to the killing of nineteen men who were shot in the cemetery at Hinche?
Answer. No, sir; I do not recall any particular incident in regard to these rumors, but understood that there was to be an investigation of conditions in the district of Hinche.
17. Question. There was an investigation, was there not?
Answer. Yes, sir.
18. Question. You had nothing whatever to do with the district of Hinche when you heard these rumors?
Answer. No; I can not recall just when I heard these rumors. I don't know whether it was before or after.

19. Question. Well, had it been while you were in charge of that district would you have investigated it?

Answer. Yes; I would have if I were in charge of the district.

20. Question. Do you know Capt. Lavole, G. d'H.?

Answer. Yes.

21. Question. Do you know Capt. Bolte, G. d'H.?

Answer. Yes.

22. Question. Do you know Lieut. Williams, G. d'H.?

Answer. Yes.

23. Question. Do you know Mr. Baker, formerly of the gendarmerie?

Answer. Yes.

24. Question. Have you ever had any conversation with the above-named people with reference to the killing of Caco prisoners or the unlawful killing of any Haitians?

Answer. On about March 10 I received written orders in regard to what disposition would be made of prisoners, and I personally instructed Lavole and Williams and others in district, as I recall now in this order, and explained its meaning to each officer and each gendarme before they left on patrol. There may have been a conversation that I can not recall at this time.

25. Question. You state positively, then, that you do not remember of any conversation held with the gendarme officers aforementioned with regard to the killing of prisoners or Cacos in the Hinche district?

Answer. I don't recall any, as I stated that I did not have anything to do with any killings.

26. Question. If you had had any conversation with any one of the aforementioned gendarmerie officers before March, it would surely have arrested your attention, would it not?

Answer. Not necessarily, because during this time there was a great deal of rumor and gossip going on, and I did not go in for either.

27. Question. Did you not consider it necessary, then, to consider the rumors or gossip in the district you command?

Answer. I did not command the district of Hinche until about March 7 or 8. and did not interest myself in anything that happened prior to this date, but did after this date, and every rumor or report of killing had made an investigation or report of it.

28. Question. Did you ever find that on an investigation that any of these rumors were true?

Answer. I remember of one prisoner who was killed—I believe March 13— while on a detail getting sugar cane. I investigated this and made a written report of it, as required then by regulations, and later was directed to make a more detailed report, which I submitted and was accepted.

29. Question. Who did the killing?

Answer. A private in the gendarmerie.

30. Question. What duty were you performing at Hinche between October 18 and October 31?

Answer. To operate patrols and try to capture Charlemagne.

31. Question. Were you in command of the Hinche district at this time?

Answer. No, sir.

32. Question. Were you the senior officer present?

Answer. After the 22d I was.

33. Question. The second time you went to the Hinche district was about February 17, was it not? What was your duty then?

Answer. To see that there was no friction between the gendarmerie and the marines.

34. Question. Were you the senior officer present then?

Answer. No, sir; not at all times. Col. Hooker would come in and out.

35. Question. If you heard any rumors of killings of prisoners between February 17 and March 7, would you have investigated them?

Answer. Not necessarily. I would have reported it to Maj. Wells.

36. Question. Did you ever make any report to Maj. Wells with reference to killing of cacos, or prisoners, before the investigation of Gen. Catlin?

Answer. I would have, perhaps, told him that I heard rumors of killings in the district.

37. Question. Do you know of any investigation he ever made on your reports?

Answer. I don't recall if he did or did not make an investigation.

38. Question. Would you know if he made an investigation?

Answer. No; not necessarily.

39. Question. Will you state positively that you knew absolutely nothing of the killing of certain prisoners in Hinche in January, 1919, by Capt. Lavoie?

(Capt. Doxey was informed of his rights in this question and that he had a perfect right to refuse to answer it if it in any way incriminated him.)

Answer. I heard rumors, but of no specific case. It was reported that Capt. Lavoie had something to do with the killing of prisoners in January, and, if I remember, it was in conversation with Gen. Catlin.

40. Question. Will you make the positive assertion that you did not know of this occurrence before your conversation with Gen. Catlin?

Answer. No, sir; but I believe it to be correct.

9. Mr. ERNEST J. LAVOIE was called as a witness, was duly sworn, and testified as follows:

1. Question. What is your name?

Answer. Mr. Ernest J. Lavoie.

2. Question. Have you ever been connected with the Haitian constabulary?

Answer. Yes.

3. Question. During your connection with the gendarmerie, were you ever cognizant of the fact that there was any unlawful killing of cacos?

Answer. Yes.

4. Question. Can you state whom these instructions with reference to the unlawful killing of cacos were given by?

Answer. That is a very difficult question to answer.

5. Question. Were you ever given instructions to bump off prisoners?

Answer. Yes.

6. Question. Who gave you these instructions?

Answer. Col. Wells.

7. Question. Please state the circumstances.

Answer. It was in conversation at Hinche the first night I was back from leave, in the presence of Capt. Verdier. "The only way to stop the uprising was to make it as hard as we could for them, as the gendarmerie had to handle the situation. Such men as Saul Peralte should be bumped off. On your return to Ouanaminthe you can tend to that Verdier." And he said, "Never mind sending any prisoners into Cape Haitien; you can handle them yourself at Hinche."

8. Question. Will you state positively that you never received any instructions from Col. Wells to bump off prisoners?

Answer. In substance, he told me that I shouldn't send any prisoners on into the Cape; that I could handle them right in Hinche, and not take them to the Cape; that they could be bumped off.

10. Lieut. Col. RICHARD S. HOOKER, United States Marine Corps, was called as a witness, was duly sworn, and testified as follows:

1. Question. State your name, rank, and present station.

Answer. Richard S. Hooker, lieutenant colonel, United States Marine Corps, and serving as assistant chief of Gendarmerie d'Haiti, Port au Prince, Haiti.

2. Question. What duty have you been performing since your arrival in Haiti in January of this year?

Answer. From January, 1919, to July 20, 1919, I resumed my duties at Cape Haitien as regimental commander of the Second Regiment and district commander of northern Haiti when I was appointed assistant chief of the Gendarmerie d'Haiti. I continued the same duties until October 9, 1919, when I took up my duties in the gendarmerie in Port au Prince.

3. Question. State fully all you know of the disturbances in northern Haiti as they came to your knowledge as district commander, stating particularly of any killing of prisoners, corvee, or other treatment which would be likely to cause discontent and tend to continue the trouble.

Answer. When I arrived in Port au Prince from the United States, January 15, 1919, Gen. Catlin told me that he was not satisfied with conditions in the north and stated that his information was not direct. He directed me to look into affairs in the north and let him know. I arrived in the cape January 20.

From rumors and general gossip I gathered that in the district of central Haiti some rough treatment was going on and from several Haitians that corvees was still in force. Maj. Wells, then colonel in the gendarmerie, practically told me in the presence of Maj. Doxey that they, meaning the bandits, were getting hell and were being bumped off, and that no official reports were being made. I did not take this seriously at the time. I went to Port au Prince in the latter part of January or early part of February, and in conversation with Gen. Catlin told him that I knew there was too much rough work and that the corvee was still in existence. Gen. Catlin then gave me verbal instructions to go into the Hinche district and submit a report to him as to what I found there. This report I forwarded about the middle or latter part of February, in writing, and in which I stated that I had seen 150 men actually doing corvee labor and had seen gendarmes maltreating inhabitants. In Hinche I stopped a gendarme from whipping a woman in the open market because her price for tobacco was more than he thought it should have cost. I reported this case to Capt. Lavoie in Maj. Doxey's presence. I saw a prisoner being beaten by three gendarmes with the butts of their rifles. I heard from Pere Belliot, of Hinche, and from Pere Lerue, of San Michel and Maissade, that the inhabitants were in a state of terror and being killed ad libitum. The bishop of the cape told me the same thing. This I did not see nor could find at that time witnesses to prove, but I could see that a reign of terror existed. When my report was received by Gen. Catlin I was sent for and had a discussion, in which Gen. Williams and Maj. Wells were present.

My report was discussed and the existence of corvee was denied by Maj. Wells. From this time to March 6 or 7 verbal reports and conferences were held, when Gen. Catlin, on account of conflicting testimonies, decided to make a personal investigation himself. On March 7 he arrived in San Michel, accompanied by Gen. Williams and Mr. Holly, where I met him. Maj. Wells and Maj. Doxey were also there. We all started the next morning; we went to Maissade. On coming into the town there were some workmen on the road. Gen. Catlin stopped and after being told by several that they had been working for nothing, that some had been working since February, and that in the early part of their work they spent the night in pr son. They stated that some of them had received 30 cents Haitian a day for about a week, but that L'eut. Williams had promised them a gourde a day on the coming Monday. Gen. Catlin told them that those who were not there voluntarily to step to the other side of the road. All but three d'd so. Two of these three stated that they were chiefs of the work and well paid and the other stated that he had not stepped over because he lived in Maissade proper. The general took verbal testimony for about three or four hours, and the gist of the whole testimony was that corvee had been going on and that several persons had been k lled through the false testimony of the magistrat, Martial Preval, to L'eut. Williams There was no direct proof to many of the stories, but L'eut. Williams admitted to having executed three or four and later five or s'x. Several witnesses testified to the death of Garnier, the notary, and L'eut. Williams admitted that the man had died. A report made against the magistrat by five citizens of Maissade. They were confined in Hinche and tr'ed in Maissade without being present. Garnier stated in the court that this was not justice, or words to that effect. That night about 7 or 8 o'clock Garnier was taken to Williams's house with the magistrat, and at 2 o'clock the next morning was found dead in a chair in the barracks yard, beaten with a club.

In Hinche that same day testimony was received from the priest, Père Belliot, the magistrat, Savique Perlate, and Juge de Paix Moncey Malary that many persons had been executed with a machine gun and that the corvee had been continually in operation. The first statement was corroborated by Mr. Lang in a statement to Gen. Catlin and myself at the San Michel plantation. Capt. Lavoie admitted to having taken six prisoners and executed them for disobeying orders. Both L'eut. Williams and Capt. Lavoie were silent as to where their instructions came from allowing maltreatment during Gen. Catlin's investigation. Marines were placed in all the towns as garrisons and to give more men for patrols to the gendarmes in March, and I issued instructions to them dated March 12 concerning their treatment of inhabitants.

(Copy of order attached, A. Copy of commanding officer, Fifty-third Company, B.)

These instructions were repeated on many occasions and all officers and men thoroughly understood them. Such maltreatment of inhabitants as came to notice or were subject to proof and not idle rumors were punished by general court-martial. On June 7 I investigated a report made against Capt. Hamilton as to his giving orders to shoot prisoners if sure they were Cacos. On questioning him he stated to me before Col. Wise that he had an order in his files from Gen. Williams dated March 10, forbidding the shooting of prisoners, but that Maj. Wells had verbally told him that that order did not apply unless the prisoners were actually in pr'son, and that he should go ahead executing prisoners and say nothing about it. I recommended and Capt. Hamilton was brought to trial before a general court-martial for murder. This is the only direct case where I personally was told by one who had himself received Maj. Well's order to execute prisoners. There were many rumors and the impression throughout the north was that such orders existed. I have heard many stories of prisoners being wantonly killed, but upon investigation I have found that they were untrue and usually circulated by men who were trying to make themselves out to be bad men. I heard that Lieut. Ryan had killed two natives without cause and recommended and brought him to trial before a general court-martial for murder.

4. Question. Do you know anything of Lieut. Spear's actions?

Answer. No; I was at Hinche and in the north. He was in the south. I know nothing about him except that there was such an officer.

5. Question. Do you know of any order forbidding corvee?

Answer. Yes. On October 1, 1918, the chief of the gendarmerie issued such an order, and later, on October 18, he issued an order stopping it all over. This was because the corvee was going on in the Hinche Maissade, San Michel district, because these places were not mentioned in his first order. There was a proclamation or notice from the brigade commander to the same effect.

6. Question. Do you know positively that the corvee continued after the order?

Answer. Yes. In February, 1919, I myself saw the corvee in operation near Maissade. Two groups of between 50 to 75 men each were working on the roads, and a third group of about 45 in the market place at Maissade.

7. Question. Do you know if Maj. Wells gave orders or knew that the corvee was still in operation there?

Answer. I don't know; but Maj. Wells was in command of that department, and the roads were being built, which Maj. Wells knew; therefore he must have known that there was corvee.

11. Mr. ALFRED HOLLY was called as a witness and testified as follows, after being duly sworn:

1. Question. What is your name and occupation?

Answer. John Alfred Holly; translator at brigade headquarters, United States Marine Corps, Port au Prince, Republic of Haiti.

2. Question. In March, 1919, did you act as interpreter for Gen. Catlin in an investigation at Maissade?

Answer. Yes.

3. Question. Repeat as nearly as possible the conversation you translated for Gen. Catlin.

Answer. At Maissade the greater part of the investigation was devoted to the hearing of evidence as to the continuance of and manner of conducting compulsory corvee, as to the treatment of the men, and the manner in which they were recruited, and as to the wages paid them.

Briefly stated, the evidence tended to show that the peasants were " invited " (convened) to assemble at a certain place to attend an "audience" to be given by Lieut. Williams, then in command at Maissade. When the country folks arrived at the place of rendezvous the lieutenant was not there and they were told to go on to Maissade. When they arrived at this place they were locked up in prison for the night, and the next morning they were put to work on the roads. At the time the general was speaking to them the majority of the men had been kept at work for two months or more. Every night they were locked up in prison to keep them from running away.

Some of the men declared that, as a matter of fact, they had been invited (asked) to come and work on the roads; that they considered the invitation as an order, because such was the custom in Haiti and because they knew of instances where those who refused to respond to the invitation were beaten and compelled to go, and that some who tried to run away were fired at.

All of the men of the gang, with one exception, on being asked the question by the general, replied that they would much prefer to return home and work in their gardens, which, they said, were going to ruins. All of them owned lands in their own rights. The exception was the gang leader, who explained that he was, to a certain extent, responsible for bringing the men there; he could not consistently say that he preferred to be at home. In this case his presence with the gang was entirely voluntary.

It was found that up to the time that the general was speaking to the men none of them, with the possible exception of the gang leader, had been receiving wages to which he was entitled.

On being given permission to do so, the whole gang broke up and went home.

There were complaints of illtreatment of the natives, and of persons being beaten to death. One instance is that of the public notary of the place, an old man by the name of Garnier. This man was arrested at the investigation of the justice of the peace and of the mayor of the commune (magistrate communal) taken to the bureau of the gendarmerie at about 7 o'clock in the evening and was beaten by the lieutenant himself until after 9 o'clock, when he was put in a rocking chair in which he died sometime during the night. The notary's offense was that of having remonstrated with the judge as to the severity of a sentence rendered by him in a case in which the magistrate communal was the plaintiff. I can not recall the particulars of the case, but I do remember that the sentence was heavy fine plus imprisonment, and the notary thought that, in view of the fact that there were serious doubts as to the justice of the case, the fine should have been considered to be a sufficient penalty.

Lieut. Williams's action in this matter seemed to have been due to his friendship or sympathy for both the mayor and the judge.

There were complaints of unlawful capture of cattle and other animals, that were sent to the pound and which, under various pretexts, the lieutenant refused to return to the owners. Many, and among them all the gendarmes stationed at Maissade at the time, testified that Lieut. Williams had summarily executed some 12 or 16 persons, some with his own hands, and buried their bodies in the yard back of his office. The spot where the bodies were buried was pointed out, but the grass had been leveled down when it was learned that Gen. Catlin was coming to hold an investigation.

Maissade was the only place among those that was visited where the gendarmes bitterly complained of being illtreated by their chief.

All the evidence taken at this place showed that the lieutenant, the mayor, and the judge all worked together and that the one was the accomplice of the others.

The above is, to the best of my recollection, a true and faithful relation of the conversation that took place at Maissade in the month of March, this year, between Gen. Catlin, then chief of the occupation, and the inhabitants of that place, that nothing has been added or withheld that in one way or the other might alter the value of the facts as they were given to the general.

11. The undersigned question many others, both civilian and commissioned, but while they all admitted of hearing many rumors of murdering caco prisoners none of them were able to testify under oath that such was so, and where they had heard it. Almost everyone stationed in Haiti during the early part of this year seemed to have some knowledge of the fact that both marines and gendarmes were killing prisoners. It was very difficult to get any witnesses to testify directly as, in the opinion of the undersigned, they were all equally culpable. As far as Lieut. Spear is concerned, no one seemed to know anything about him, and I am inclined to believe that his statement before the court, that he had killed prisoners, was deliberately untrue.

12. That there were killings and many of them is undoubtedly true, but I believe that all of these can be directly traced to Maj. Clarke H. Wells, who was in command of the district.

13. The gendarme officers in the district were all noncommissioned officers of the old Marine Corps, men who believed in their officers and to whom an order was to be obeyed to the letter. These officers received instructions from Maj. Wells to bump off caco prisoners, and they carried their orders out to the best of their ability. I do not feel that under the circumstances they should be held responsible, and that the responsibility should be placed where it belongs, on the shoulders of Maj. Wells.

14. Capt. Doxey's testimony was undoubtedly colored by the fact that he was attempting to shield himself, and even if his testimony was true he showed the greatest disregard for his duty when he neglected to report all rumors to Maj. Wells. His work in Hinche seemed to be to get by and do nothing.

15. I am convinced that Corpl. Edward J. Sieger, United States Marine Corps, deliberately lied in his testimony. Sufficient evidence was brought out to show that he was included in the ones who received the "bump-off" order.

16. Sergt. Dorcas R. Williams, United States Marine Corps, who was in charge of Maissade as a lieutenant of the gendarmerie, could give quite a lot of evidence, if he desired, but he is now in the United States, probably discharged.

17. Further, the fact that Gen. Catlin made an investigation at San Michel would tend to prove that something wrong had happened. I have searched the files for any correspondence on this subject, but found none.

18. Attached marked "A," "B," and "C" is the only data on this subject in the files of the brigade.

T. C. TURNER.

Maj. TURNER. I am not sure of this, but, as I remember, a letter came from the headquarters of the Marine Corps directing Col. Russell to make further investigation, and that is why Hooker was called in, because of his knowledge of the Haitians. He probably had a better knowledge of the Haitians than any other man down there. And it was also due to the fact that I could not go out into the hills.

Mr. HOWE. You could not go out into the hills because you were acting as brigade adjutant and chief of staff?

Maj. TURNER. Yes; because of my duties I could not be away for any length of time.

Mr. HOWE. I wish to offer for the record, Mr. Chairman, a copy of letter dated February 12, 1920, from the brigade commander, Col. Russell, to Col. Hooker, directing him to investigate. That is on page 30 of the report. I also desire to offer a letter dated January 11, 1920, from the same to the same, which is found on page 31 of the report, directing the cooperation of Col. Hooker with Maj. Turner.

The CHAIRMAN. Col. Hooker was in command where at the time?

Maj. TURNER. He was assistant chief of the gendarmerie at the time.

(The letters above referred to are as follows:)

HEADQUARTERS FIRST PROVISIONAL BRIGADE,
UNITED STATES MARINE CORPS,
Port au Prince, Republic of Haiti, February 12, 1920.

From: The brigade commander.
To: Lieut. Col. R. S. Hooker, United States Marine Corps.
Via: The chief of the gendarmerie d'Haiti.
Subject: Investigation by adjutant and inspectors department.
Reference: (a) Letter from this office, No. 5–18, dated January 11, 1920.

1. The brigade commander desires that every effort be made by you to expedite the investigation mentioned in reference (a).

2. This investigation will be completed before the end of the present month.

3. If your present duties are such as to interfere with this work you will so inform the brigade commander in writing, and the necessary action will be taken.

JOHN H. RUSSELL.

Copy furnished Maj. T. C. Turner, assistant adjutant and inspector, United States Marine Corps.

JANUARY 11, 1920.

From: The brigade commander.
To: Lieut. Col. Richard S. Hooker, United States Marine Corps.
Via: Chief of the gendarmerie d'Haiti.
Subject: Investigation by adjutant and inspectors department.

1. You are hereby ordered to cooperate in the investigation of certain irregularities now being conducted by Maj. T. C. Turner, assistant adjutant and inspector, United States Marine Corps.

2. Your report will be made direct to the brigade commander.

JOHN H. RUSSELL.

Mr. HOWE. Major, I will show you pages 55 and 59 of this report and ask you if, to the best of your knowledge, that is the written testimony which resulted from Col. Hooker's investigation?

Maj. TURNER. Yes.

Mr. HOWE. Then, Mr. Chairman, I offer that for the record.

(The matter referred to is as follows:)

GONAIVES, HAITI, February 19, 1920.

JOSEPH O. VAN HORN, lieutenant, gendarmerie D'Haiti, was called as a witness, was informed that he need not answer any incriminating questions, testified as follows:

1. Question. What is your name?

Answer. Joseph O. Van Horn, lieutenant, gendarmerie d'Haiti, stationed at St. Michel, Haiti.

2. Question. Where were you stationed in the letter part of 1918 and the early part of 1919?

Answer. At Ouanaminthe, Haiti.

3. Question. During the trouble at Hinche from October, 1918, was Ouanaminthe used as a relay station for telephone messages to and from Hinche?

Answer. Yes, sir.

4. Question. Do you remember the nature of those messages?

Answer. Some messages were written and placed on file at Ouanaminthe and some were verbal over the phone and relayed to their destination. They related to transportation activities and some were reports from Capt. Lavoie to Col. Wells.

5. Question. Did these reports from Levole indicate that he was having trouble in his district or not?

Answer. Yes; some did and some were to the effect that all was quiet.

6. Question. What were the nature of these reports during January, February, and March, 1919?

Answer. I don't remember exactly what the reports were, but I knew that things were not quiet. This was during December, when I was stationed at La Meille, Haiti.

7. Question. Do you remember any instructions from Col. Wells to any officer as to the treatment of Cacos or Caco prisoners?

Answer. No; I never heard him say anything about that, because when he came up here he always told me he had to tell to the district commander.

8. Question. Have you spoken to other officers on the treatment of Cacos or Caco prisoners; and if so, what was their idea on the subject?

Answer. I remember speaking to several officers, but I can't recall who they were now or exactly what was said. But I was under the impression that when I went out after an armed band of bandits I was supposed to go and get them and get rid of them. When the prisoners were taken I always treated them the same as other prisoners, like prisoners in the civil prison, and I brought them in to stand trial.

JOSEPH O. VAN HORN,
Lieutenant Gendarmerie d'Haiti.

Subscribed and sworn to before me this 19th day of February, 1920.

R. S. HOOKER,
Lieutenant Colonel, United States Marine Corps,
Sous Chief Gendarmerie d'Haiti.

A true copy:

R. S. HOOKER,
Lieutenant Colonel, United States Marine Corps.

STATEMENT OF SERGT. LAMARTINE TOUSSAINT, FIFTEENTH COMPANY GENDARMERIE D'HAITI.

FIFTEENTH COMPANY GENDARMERIE D'HAITI,
Ouanaminthe, Haiti, October 26, 1919.

Lieut. Van Horn, Gendarmerie d'Haiti, had turned over to me one prisoner, named Saul Peralte, to conduct to Mount Organise. On arriving at the River Canarie he asked me permission to drink some water. I refused him. On crossing said river he tried to escape. I cried out " halt " on him three times; he did not want to stop. Seeing that he was gaining ground from me, I fired four times, the first time in the air and the last three times upon him. The bullets attained him in the back and went through his stomach, under which he fell, and in the space of three he expired.

Certified a true copy:

JOSEPH O. VAN HORN,
Lieutenant, Gendarmerie.

CAPE HAITIEN, February 17, 1920.

FRANK VERDIER, captain, Gendarmerie d'Haiti, was called as a witness, was informed that he need not answer any incriminating questions; testified before me as follows:

1. Question. What is your name?

Answer. Frank Verdier, captain, Gendarmerie d'Haiti, stationed at Ouanaminthe since September, 1918.

2. Question. Were you present at a conversation between Col. Wells and Capt. Lavoie? If so, state the subject matter of this conversation, as far as you can remember it.

Answer. Yes, sir; I was present at this conversation, and most of the conversation was on the Caco situation. I don't remember the exact conversation, but Col. Wells did say that such men as Saul Peralte should be gotten rid of.

3. Question. Was any mention made to the effect that either you or Capt. Lavoie should handle your district and that it would not be necessary to make reports on your activities?

Answer. It may have been mentioned, but I can't recollect.

4. Question. Were any instructions given to make it as hard as possible for the Cacos?

Answer. Yes sir; instructions were given to make it hard for the Cacos, but I don't know exactly what they were.

5. Question. In your opinion, what was meant by making it hard? What did you think was meant?

Answer. I think that Col. Wells meant to convey the idea to get rid of them, to bump them off.

6. Question. Have you spoken to other officers on this subject; and if so, what opinion did they have relating to these instructions?

Answer. I think I spoke to Bolte on this subject, and he had the same opinion as myself.

7. Question. During this trouble in Hinche, from October, 1918, on was not Ouanaminthe a relay station for messages from the cape to Hinche?

Answer. Yes.

8. Question. Do you remember any reports from Hinche to the department commander at the cape relative to the situation in Hinche?

Answer. I remember receiving some telegrams regarding activities.

9. Question. Were those messages confidential?

Answer. Yes; some to and from Col. Wells and Lavoie at Hinche, and perhaps some to Kelly at Cerca la Source. They referred to operations against Cacos and detailing of officers. I had verbal instructions not to let you see them if you came through Ouananminthe.

10. Question. Have you copies of those messages?

Answer. I'm pretty certain I have. I will try to find them and give them to you if they are still there.

11. Question. Did these Caco telegrams state that the situation in Hinche was serious or not?

Answer. I should consider so.

12. Question. Do you remember whether Lavoie was nervous over the situation or whether he thought he could handle it without outside aid?

Answer. At the time I was in Hinche, in November, 1918, Lavoie thought he could handle it without aid, but later he requested that machine guns be sent him with marine crews.

13. Question. Did you transmit any messages from Maj. Doxey to the department commander at the cape after he went to Hinche in January or February, 1919, to relieve Lavoie?

Answer. Yes, sir.

14. Question. What were the nature of those?

Answer. Mostly regarding the shipment of supplies.

15. Question. Nothing regarding the Caco situation?

Answer. I think there was something regarding the Caco situation, but I can't think what it was.

16. Question. Do you remember if these messages said that all was quiet, or that he was having trouble with the Cacos?

Answer. He reported all was quiet.

Captain Gendarmerie d'Haiti.

Sworn to and subscribed to before me, this 17th day of February, 1920.

Lieutenant Colonel, United States Marine Corps,
Sous-Chief de la Gendarmerie d'Haiti.

A true copy.

R. S. HOOKER,
Lieutenant Colonel, United States Marine Corps.

Mr. Howe. Now, Major, I want to go into your method of pursuing this inquiry, beginning in October, 1919, and beginning with the letter of Gen. Barnett dated September 27, 1919. How did you go about it, Major?

Maj. Turner. I interrogated everybody I could find. I started out by asking if they had heard of any of these things, and particularly that part referring to the letter.

Mr. Howe. That part of what?

Maj. Turner. The part that the letter referred to about Lieut. Spear.

Mr. Howe. In his statement in reference to killings?

Maj. Turner. Yes; before a general court-martial. I could find nothing about Lieut. Spear. I did find rumors and statements that there had been killings. So I considered, in view of the major general commandant's letter, that I should continue with that, and I did so.

Mr. Howe. Did you, in the course of your investigations, run down any facts which were alluded to or may have been alluded to by Lieut. Spear?

Maj. Turner. No.

Mr. Howe. Did you see Lieut. Spear?

Maj. Turner. No.

Mr. Howe. Did you find anybody who knew Lieut. Spear?

Maj. Turner. No.

Mr. Howe. You did, however, run across other rumors of killings?

Maj. Turner. Yes.

Mr. Howe. What were the prinicpal ones of those rumors?

Maj. Turner. The only ones I could seem to get any information on was the alleged killing at Hinche in January, 1919.

Mr. Howe. In order to identify that, what was the name of the marine officer who was supposed to have directed this killing?

Maj. Turner. Capt. Lavole, of the Haitian gendarmerie; Ernest L. Lavole.

The Chairman. Was he an enlisted marine?

Maj. Turner. He was a private in the Marine Corps, detailed for duty as an officer in the Haitian gendarmerie.

Mr. Howe. Was the name of Lieut. Williams, of the gendarmerie, connected with any one of these rumors?

Maj. Turner. Yes; at Maissade.

Mr. Howe. Was there any connected with the alleged killing of one Garnier?

Maj. Turner. Garnier was a notary; yes.

Mr. Howe. You then proceeded to try to trace down these two rumors and any other rumors you came across?

Maj. Turner. Yes.

Mr. Howe. Did you, as a matter of fact, learn of any other definite rumors beside these two?

Maj. Turner. No. There were many rumors, but you would run them all down and there would not be any foundation for them. You would go as far as you could—I remember one case where a man told me he had heard of two murders at Grande Riviere, and I ran it down and found his mother-in-law had told him, so he said, and his mother-in-law had been dead for 10 years, which would have been about six years before it possibly could have happened.

Mr. Howe. Was that sort of luck you had in tracing a rumor typical of what you ran into as to many of these statements made to you by witnesses?

Maj. Turner. In almost all of them, yes.

Mr. Howe. If, for instance, some one down there whom you were interrogating mentioned an occurrence or killing, and said some one had told it to him, what would you then do?

Maj. Turner. I would try to get the person who was supposed to have told him.

Mr. Howe. If you got that person, what would he, in general, say?

Maj. Turner. That some one else had told him, in almost every case.

Mr. Howe. Did you, under those circumstances, follow out as far as you could, in turn, everyone who was quoted?

Maj. Turner. Yes.

Mr. Howe. Did this written testimony, which appears on the pages of the report which you have seen, embody the most definite part of what you learned?

Maj. Turner. Yes; it was the only definite part I could learn, and I took that testimony in writing.

Mr. Howe. And that is all the definite part of it that you learned?

Maj. Turner. Yes.

Mr. Howe. Can you give us an idea as to about how many individuals you interviewed, whose written testimony you did not take during this investigation?

Maj. Turner. Yes; I think about 50—probably 40; it may be 40.

Mr. Howe. The report states, as an instance of these hearsay reports which you ran across the testimony of Bolte at the bottom of page 109:

"2. Capt. Laurence Bolte, gendarmerie d'Haiti, corporal, United States Marine Corps, was called as the first witness, was duly sworn, and testified as follows:

"1. Question. State your name, rank, and present station.

"Answer. Laurence Bolte, corporal, United States Marine Corps, and a captain in the gendarmerie d'Haiti, stationed at Hinche, Republic of Haiti.

"2. Question. Statements have been made that both marines and gendarmes have been in the habit of having wounded Cacos shot. Do you know anything about this?

"Answer. No, sir.

"3. Question. You never have issued an order of that kind?

"Answer. No, sir.

"4. Question. Do you know that this has been done?

"Answer. I don't know about it; but I have heard of it being done.

"5. Question. Where did you hear this, and from whom?

"Answer. I heard it from Lieut. Floyd, gendarmerie d'Haiti, Mr. Baker, and Maj. Hayes, gendarmerie d'Haiti.

"6. Question. Who was in command at Hinche when the last rebellion started?

"Answer. Capt. Kelly had it in October.

"7. Question. Who relieved him?

"Answer. Capt. Lavigne.

"8. Question. Who relieved him?

"Answer. Capt. Doxey.

"9. Question. Were you ever instructed to make private reports to anybody with reference to operations in the Hinche district?

"Answer. Not private reports, but telegrams received through Ouanaminthe by telephone were to be kept on file at the Third Company office under lock and key.

"10. Question. Who gave this order?

"Answer. Col. Wells.

"11. Question. Why was this order issued?

"Answer. I do not know if it was caused by this investigation which took place at Hinche.

"12. Question. Did Col. Wells ever instruct you to disregard certain orders received from the chief of the gendarmerie d'Haiti?

"Answer. No, sir.

"13. Question. Do you know whether these or any other orders were disregarded?

"Answer. No, sir.

"14. Question. Do you remember when the first order against corvee came out?

"Answer. The first came out in the latter part of August.

"15. Question. Was this order ever disregarded?

"Answer. I do not know that this was done. I heard it from the priest at Hinche (Belliot) and a chief of section named Joseph Marcellia and one named Albert.

"16. Question. Did the priest at Hinche ever inform you that before you came there that cacos had been killed after they had surrendered?

"Answer. Yes.

"17. Question. Did anybody at Hinche tell you that?

"Answer. No one at Hinche but a marine named Sasse told me that prisoners had been taken out of the prison at Hinche and shot, and the priest at Hinche told me the same thing.

"18. Question. Who issued the order for the shooting? Do you know?

"Answer. No. sir.

"19. Question. You do not know whether this was reported to Col. Wells or not, do you?

"Answer. No, sir.

"20. Question. While you were at the Cape did a telegram show that there was any considerable trouble at the district of Hinche?

"Answer. Yes.

" 21. Question. Between what months were these telegrams coming in?

"Answer. From the 1st of January to the middle of March.

" 22. Question. Do you know what became of these telegrams?

"Answer. They were left in the desk of the district commander at the Cape."
Did you find and interrogate Floyd, Hayes, or Baker?

Maj. TURNER. I did.

Mr. HOWE. All of them?

Maj. TURNER. All of them; yes.

Mr. HOWE. What did you learn from Floyd?

Maj. TURNER. From Floyd—he stated that he had heard rumors; he did not
know where they came from, and he did not know anything about it.

Mr. HOWE. You do not include Floyd's testimony among your written testimony.

Maj. TURNER. No; neither Floyd's nor Hayes's. Hayes stated the same as
Floyd.

Mr. HOWE. That he really did not know about it?

Maj. TURNER. Yes.

Mr. HOWE. And Hayes's written testimony was not taken?

Maj. TURNER. No.

Mr. HOWE. What about Baker?

Maj. TURNER. I took Baker's testimony. Baker's testimony was mostly
hearsay, too.

Mr. HOWE. And that you included, because there was something in it more
definite?

Maj. TURNER. Yes.

Mr. HOWE. Is that example typical of the way you went at the investigation,
and of the thoroughness with which you went at it?

Maj. TURNER. Yes.

Mr. HOWE. Did you have any instructions from Col. Russell as to the extent
and thoroughness of your investigation?

Maj. TURNER. I did. When I first took up the investigation, the rumors
were so bad that I went to him and told him what these rumors were and
asked his advice on the subject. He told me, never mind, to go straight ahead
and get to the bottom of it and get everything in hand on that subject.

Mr. HOWE. And you proceeded to do so?

Maj. TURNER. Which I did.

Mr. HOWE. Did anybody direct you to discontinue your investigation?

Maj. TURNER. No.

Mr. HOWE. Never?

Maj. TURNER. Never.

Mr. HOWE. Then why did you stop investigating?

Maj. TURNER. Well, I could not find anything more. I could have filled thousands of pages with just that kind of stuff, hearsay. There was no use going
any further because I could not get anything definite.

Mr. HOWE. Major, as a matter of fact, were you trying to get something
definite there?

Maj. TURNER. Yes; I was. I had a feeling at first that there had not been
fair treatment to the Haitians. I thought it was up to us to straighten it out,
but I did not know who was responsible, and it did not make any difference,
and, as I say, I had had this talk with Col. Russell, and I went as far as I
could into the case and got everything out of it that I could.

Mr. HOWE. And when you handed in this written testimony which begins
with the date of November 3, you felt you had pursued the investigation as
far as you profitably could?

Maj. TURNER. Exactly; as far as it could possibly be taken by me.

Mr. HOWE. Now, I am going to read from page 130, paragraph numbered 11
of this report of your written testimony:

" 11. The undersigned questioned many others, both civilian and commissioned
but while they are admitted of hearing many rumors of murdering Caco prisoners none of them were able to testify under oath that such was so, and where
they had heard it. Almost everyone stationed in Haiti during the early part
of this year seemed to have some knowledge of the fact that both marines and
gendarmes were killing prisoners. It was very difficult to get any witnesses to
testify directly as in the opinion of the undersigned they were all equally
culpable."

The CHAIRMAN. Who were equally culpable?

Maj. TURNER. Everybody who was telling these yarns down there, if they were true.

The CHAIRMAN. They were culpable of misrepresentation or culpable of having killed Haitians?

Maj. TURNER. Just telling rumors that might have been true or might not have been true.

Mr. HOWE. Did you mean here that they were equally culpable of killing natives?

Maj. TURNER. Yes; if it had been true, they were.

Senator ODDIE. Or culpable of misrepresentation?

Maj. TURNER. The people I had been able to get who had talked would not give me any information, so I felt they were all equally culpable if it had been true.

Mr. HOWE. There were some of these witnesses you d'd not believe in their denials of knowledge or denials of crime?

Maj. TURNER. Yes.

Mr. HOWE. Paragraph 11 continues: "As far as Lieut. Spear is concerned, no one seemed to know anything about him. and I am inclined to believe that his statement before the court that he had killed prisoners was deliberately untrue." Have you any further comment to make on paragraph 11?

Maj. TURNER. No.

Mr. HOWE. Paragraph 12 says: "That there were killings and many of them is undoubtedly true, but I believe that all of these can be directly traced to Maj. Clarke H. Wells, who was in command of the district."

Maj. TURNER. I would like to state that these killings were in the corvee and escaped corvee prisoners. They were people who attempted to escape, and in my opinion they were killed.

Mr. HOWE. And those were the many killings to which you referred?

Maj. TURNER. Yes.

Mr. HOWE. You are certain that in this paragraph 12 you did not refer to the deliberate and cold-blooded removing of a prisoner from prison and shooting him?

Maj. TURNER. No.

Mr. HOWE. But to the killing of escaped prisoners or people escaping from the corvee?

Maj. TURNER. People escaping from the corvees or people who had jumped and were running and were killed, in these different Caco bands throughout the country.

Mr. HOWE. Paragraph 13, at page 131, says:

"The gendarme officers in the district were all noncommissioned officers of the old Marine Corps, men who believed in their officers, and to whom an order was to be obeyed to the letter. These officers received instructions from Maj. Wells to bump off Caco prisoners, and they carried their orders out to the best of their ability. I do not feel that under the circumstances they should be held responsible, and that the responsibility should be placed where it belongs, on the shoulders of Maj. Wells."

Have you any comment to make at this time on paragraph 13?

Maj. TURNER. No.

Mr. HOWE. Are you at the present time of the belief that Maj. Wells did issue these orders to bump off prisoners?

Maj. TURNER. No; I am not.

Mr. HOWE. Were you, at the time you submitted this report. of that opin'on?

Maj. TURNER. Yes.

Mr. HOWE. What, if anything, have you learned which has changed your opinion?

Maj. TURNER. I had only been in Haiti a short time when I made this investigation, and I was not thoroughly familiar with the character of the Haitians down there. The more I saw of them the more I became convinced of their unreliability, as far as any statement was concerned.

Mr. HOWE. Any statement they might make?

Maj. TURNER. Any statement they might make, yes. All their statements were made for their own benefit or to gain something.

Mr. HOWE. What is your present idea as to the extent to which the killings of natives down there went on, without reference to the shooting of natives in battle or in pursuit?

Maj. TURNER. I have no doubt there were many killed in the corvee.

The CHAIRMAN. You mean that many were killed in attempting to escape from work under the corvee?

Maj. TURNER. Yes.

The CHAIRMAN. When they would jump and run they would be shot?

Maj. TURNER. They were shot.

The CHAIRMAN. Do you think that there were any executions without trial?

Maj. TURNER. Yes; I think there have been executions without trial. That is my opinion, but I have no facts to substantiate that.

The CHAIRMAN. Does your report cover the harsh treatment, the brutal handling of any prisoners, apart from killings?

Maj. TURNER. Yes; as far as I could find out; yes, sir.

The CHAIRMAN. Were prisoners frequently or habitually roughly used?

Maj. TURNER. Not that I could find out.

Mr. HOWE. If you had heard any rumor or accusation of brutal treatment of prisoners, would you have investigated that?

Maj. TURNER. I would.

Mr. HOWE. You would have conceived that to have been in the scope of your investigation?

Maj. TURNER. I would. The word was "irregularity," and I considered any ill treatment of prisoners as coming under that word.

Mr. HOWE. What is your present impression or belief as to the incident at Hinche, where it was said that from 15 to 19 prisoners were taken to a cemetery and machine-gunned by Capt. Lavoie?

Maj. TURNER. I believe something actually happened there.

Mr. HOWE. Is it not true that a further investigation of that incident was made later on?

Maj. TURNER. Yes.

Mr. HOWE. Was that Gen. Lejeune's investigation?

Maj. TURNER. Gen. Lejeune and I also believe the Mayo Board made an investigation of that.

Mr. HOWE. You took the testimony of Lavoie yourself, did you not?

Maj. TURNER. Yes.

Mr. HOWE. As I recollect it, in that testimony it does not appear that you asked Lavoie the direct question as to whether or not he had killed these people at Hinche. That is so, is it not?

Maj. TURNER. No. There is a lot that did not go into the testimony, in talking back and forth, which was not put down, and I know Lavoie denied having done any of that killing.

Mr. HOWE. Your present recollection is that although it does not appear in the written testimony, the question was asked as to whether he had killed natives?

Maj. TURNER. I do not know whether it was asked in a question, but I do know he denied it.

Mr. HOWE. He denied it to you?

Maj. TURNER. Yes.

Mr. HOWE. Do you know whether or not in any of the other investigations he admitted or partly admitted that occurrence?

Maj. TURNER. No; I do not.

Mr. HOWE. Some of these witnesses made a more favorable impression on you than others, did they not, as to telling the truth?

Maj. TURNER. Yes.

Mr. HOWE. How would you characterize the testimony of Jule André?

Maj. TURNER. I was very favorably impressed with André's testimony.

Mr. HOWE. He was a Haitian, was he not?

Maj. TURNER. Yes.

Mr. HOWE. And a second lieutenant in the gendarmerie?

Maj. TURNER. Yes.

Mr. HOWE. He states in his testimony——

Maj. TURNER. I would like to state right there that I questioned André as to whether or not he could give me the names of anybody who had actually seen these murders or killings, and he told me he could not.

Mr. HOWE. He made a statement in his testimony that there was no serious control of the officers of the gendarmerie by their superior officers in some of the districts of Haiti, did he not?

Maj. TURNER. Yes.

Mr. HOWE. What comment have you to make on that answer of his—I mean from knowledge gained in your investigation?

Maj. TURNER. I should say some of the officers had positions that they were not capable of holding. They were young in the service or did not have the capability of handling these jobs they had.

Mr. Howe. What period of time is most closely connected with these rumors of killings?

Maj. Turner. Between October 15, 1918, and March 13, 1919.

Mr. Howe. Was the date of October 15 after some particular outbreak down there?

Maj. Turner. October 15 was after Charlemagne had started his revolution in the north of Haiti—after the attack on Hinche by Charlemagne.

Mr. Howe. During that time prisoners were taken and safely sent back, were they not?

Maj. Turner. Yes; lots of them.

Mr. Howe. And at other times many prisoners were taken, were they not?

Maj. Turner. Yes.

Mr. Howe. And that fact appears in certain records, does it?

Maj. Turner. It appears in my testimony in the Mayo Board investigation.

Mr. Howe. Have you gained any impression as to what was the custom down there when a patrol would come upon Cacos with guns in their hands?

Maj. Turner. The Cacos would jump immediately; they would never stand, and there would be firing on both sides right away. Most all of the attacks were surprise attacks. They would find out where the bands were and would look for them and jump them.

Mr. Howe. How many prisoners were taken who had guns in their hands?

Maj. Turner. I do not know, but I do know that not just at this time, but later on many thousands were taken who had guns.

Mr. Howe. Who had guns in their hands?

Maj. Turner. Yes.

Mr. Howe. Did you investigate any abuses of the corvee that you might have heard of in this investigation?

Maj. Turner. Yes.

Mr. Howe. You questioned individuals and witnesses about that?

Maj. Turner. I did.

Mr. Howe. Did you find difficulty there in locating witnesses who had actually seen the corvee in operation?

Maj. Turner. No.

Mr. Howe. In your opinion the corvee was in operation, and after it had been ordered discontinued?

Maj. Turner. Yes.

Mr. Howe. Where was that?

Maj. Turner. In the Maissade and Hinche district.

The Chairman. Who were the commanding officers there?

Maj. Turner. Lieut. D. L. Williams at Maissade and Lavoie at Hinche.

The Chairman. What became of Lavoie?

Maj. Turner. I do not know, sir.

Mr. Howe. Have you any direct knowledge of your own as to the employment of the corvee system?

Maj. Turner. No.

Mr. Howe. But you did come across witnesses and interrogate them who had seen it?

Maj. Turner. Yes.

Mr. Howe. You also came across witnesses who reported it from hearsay only. Is that correct?

Maj. Turner. Oh, yes; many of them.

Mr. Howe. In his testimony Lieut. André refers to the corvee as the direct cause of revolutionary outbreaks there. Would you agree with him in that?

Maj. Turner. No. The corvee, I believe, might have made conditions harder for the occupation down there, but it had nothing to do with the outbreak.

Mr. Howe. It was an aggravating circumstance always, was it not?

Maj. Turner. Yes; they were able to recruit lots better, because there was the corvee to recruit from.

The Chairman. Was that due to the corvee or to the use of corvee workers away from the neighborhoods in which they lived?

Maj. Turner. I think it was due to the fact that they were taken away from the neighborhoods in which they lived.

Mr. Howe. The testimony of Frederick C. Baker appears in your report, and in that testimony he refers either as of his own knowledge or by hearsay to orders issued by Maj. Wells to bump off prisoners. Did you yourself examine Maj. Wells?

Maj. Turner. No; Maj. Wells was not in Haiti at the time. He was later examined by Col. Lay, I believe.

Mr. Howe. In this country?

Maj. Turner. In this country, yes.

Mr. Howe. That was the reason you did not examine Wells?

Maj. Turner. Yes.

Mr. Howe. Did other witnesses besides Baker corroborate the statement that Wells had issued orders that he did not want prisoners sent in?

Maj. Turner. Yes; I think Lavoie corroborated it, and probably Bolte.

Mr. Howe. Let me ask you this question: In other words, this written testimony you took includes all such statement as to Major Wells's responsibility for any such order?

Maj. Turner. Yes.

Mr. Howe. No information you got on that phase of the subject was omitted from your written testimony?

Maj. Turner. No.

Mr. Howe. You also examined Capt. Doxey, did you not?

Maj. Turner. I did.

Mr. Howe. How would you characterize his testimony? Did you believe it or not?

Maj. Turner. I did not.

The Chairman. Was he another enlisted man who was detailed to the gendarmerie?

Maj. Turner. No; he was a captain of the Marine Corps, a Regular.

Mr. Howe. He denied knowledge of conditions there pretty generally, did he not, in his testimony?

Maj. Turner. Yes.

Mr. Howe. And would not say whether or not Maj. Wells was familiar with those conditions?

Maj. Turner. He was very evasive in his testimony.

The Chairman. These incidents which you were investigating took place during the period of the command of the gendarmerie by whom?

Maj. Turner. You mean the chief of the gendarmerie?

The Chairman. Yes.

Maj. Turner. By Col. A. S. Williams.

The Chairman. They did not antidate his command?

Maj. Turner. No; because I do not think anything I was told to investigate antedated October 15 ,1918.

Mr. Howe. Major, if you had that investigation to make over again, would you go at it in any different way; would you have been more thorough?

Maj. Turner. I would have gone at it in an entirely different way. I do not know that I would have been any more thorough, but I would not have placed as much faith in some people as I had placed at that time, and I might have placed more in others.

Mr. Howe. In general, which one would you not have placed more faith in?

Maj. Turner. One or two of the witnesses I called, and I would put very little faith whatever in any of the Haitians' testimony.

Mr. Howe. Tell us a little bit more about that, about the untrustworthiness of the Haitians' testimony.

Maj. Turner. I was chief of staff down there, and we would get letters and reports from Haitians on different subjects, mak'ng requests, and want'ng investigations. Almost invariably it turned out that their reports were false.

Mr. Howe. Do you know the methods that Col. Hooker pursued when he began to cooperate with you in th's investigation?

Maj. Turner. Yes. Col. Hooker went all through the north. He knew more about the Haitians, I think. than any officer down there and was more popular with them than any officer down there. He went all through the north looking for information. He took the matter up with the gendarmes, who were supposed to be stationed around Hinche and Maissade and attempted to find out something definite. All he found was letters from Van Horn and Sieger and a sergeant named Toulssant. Sieger had already been examined by me.

Mr. Howe. Do you know whether or not he interviewed other people besides those three men?

Maj. Turner. Lots of them; yes.

Mr. Howe. About how long was he on that investigation?

Maj. Turner. I do not remember; I could not even state approximately.

Mr. Howe. Was it a few days or a couple of weeks?

Maj. TURNER. It must have been a couple of weeks, because he received his orders on the 11th and 12th of January. His first report came in on the 1st of February, 1920, so he must have been quite some time on that.

Mr. HOWE. That is more than six weeks after he got his orders?

Maj. TURNER. Yes. That was his first report.

Mr. HOWE. Let me say this for the record: This report, the pages of which have been quoted in putting certain matter into the record, is a carbon copy and not an original. The original of Maj. Turner's report, as I understand it, was lost. There was a carbon copy of that brought up by Gen. Lejune to Washington. This document which we have had actually before us to-day is not that copy. This copy has been introduced here for the convenience of the witness and of the reporter. That copy of Gen. Lejune's, I am informed, is in the Navy Department and it is now being searched for, and when it is found it will be offered itself.

Maj. TURNER. This is a correct copy. however.

Mr. HOWE. But the original carbon will be produced and offered and will become a part of the record. That is the copy brought up by Gen. Lejune, but the original of Maj. Turner's report, as I understand it, was lost in transit from Haiti to the United States.

Now, Mr. Chairman, I will offer in evidence pages 64 to 106, inclusive, of this same compilation, or report, being the testimony taken by Lieut. Col. H. R. Lay, of the Marine Corps, including a sworn statement by Gen. Catlin, and consisting of the testimony of Lieut. Col. A. S. Williams, Maj. Clarke H. Wells Capt. John L. Doxey, Sergt. Dorcas L. Williams, and also a sworn statement by Col. A. S. Williams in addition to his testimony.

(The matter referred to is as follows:)

JANUARY 12, 1920.

From: Lieut. Col. H. R. Lay, assistant adjutant and inspector, Marine Corps.
To: The Major General Commandant, via the adjutant and inspector.
Subject: Confidential investigation.

1. In obedience to verbal instructions from the Major General Commandant, I submit the following sworn testimony of Lieut. Col. A. S. Williams, Maj. Clark H. Wells, Capt. John L. Doxey, Sergt. Doreas L. Williams.

2. There is also submitted the sworn statement of Lieut. Col. A. S. Williams, Marine Corps, regarding conditions existing in Haiti during his service as chief of the Haitian gendarmerie.

STATEMENT OF BRIG. GEN. A. W. CATLIN, UNITED STATES MARINE CORPS, RETIRED, RELATIVE TO CERTAIN IRREGULARITIES ALLEGED TO HAVE BEEN COMMITTED BY OFFICERS AND ENLISTED MEN OF THE REPUBLIC OF HAITI.

I relieved Col. John H. Russell, United States Marine Corps, in command of the First Brigade of Marines in Haiti, December 1, 1918. At this time marines were stationed only at Port au Prince, Cape Haitien, and Guanaminthe, while the gendarmerie of Haiti were scattered all over the island and were handling the policing of the island. Bandits had been causing trouble in the Hinche district and the gendarmes were operating against them. The chief of gendarmerie, Col. A. S. Williams, United States Marine Corps, assured me that the gendarmes could handle the situation. Toward the end of January, 1919, rumors reached me that "corvee" was still being used in the Hinche district, although it had been ordered stopped on October 1, 1918, and also that the gendarmes were treating the country people in such manner that many of them were joining the bandits. Col. Williams denied this and assured me that there was no "corvee" being used in the country. Rumors continued to come in and I sent Lieut. Col. Hooker, United States Marine Corps, to Hinche to investigate and report to me the actual conditions there. He reported to me that he found "corvee" going at both Maisade and at Hinche, and that the gendarmes used the natives so brutally that many had left their gardens and either joined the bandits or had come into the towns for safety.

Col. A. S. Williams, chief of gendarmerie, and Maj. Clarke H. Wells, district commander of northern Haiti, were shown the report, and both denied that conditions were as reported. I questioned Maj. Wells as to the manner of obtaining labor and the methods of payment; he did not seem to be sure, although he stated that he had inspected within a week. I then directed Maj. Wells to proceed to Hinche and investigate thoroughly the labor question and to report to me the number of men being worked, the manner of obtaining the laborers, what they were paid, and who actually paid them. About 10 days later Maj. Wells returned to Port au Prince and reported to me verbally that he had made the investigation directed, and that he found only 45 men working on the road at Maisade, and that these men were all voluntary laborers; that they were paid a half gourde a day, and that the gendarme officer at Maisade paid them personally; that at Hinche there were no laborers except prisoners. Col. A. S. Williams and Lieut. Col. R. S. Hooker were present when this report was made. Maj. Wells stated on being questioned that he felt sure that there was no "corvee" in force anywhere in his district.

This report was so contradictory to the one made by Col. Hooker, who stated that he found at least 150 men working at Maisade and that many of them on being questioned by the interpreter stated that they were brought there and forced to work, that I decided to go to Hinche in person and find out the true conditions there. Accompanied by Col. A. S. Williams, Lieut. Col. R. S. Hooker, Maj. Clarke H. Wells, and Maj. Doxey I visited St. Michel, Maisade, and Hinche. I found conditions as Col. Hooker had reported, except that the force of workmen had apparently been cut down, as I found only about 45 men working on the road near Maisade under guard of several armed gendarmes. I stopped and questioned these men, and they all stated that they were not working voluntarily; some claimed to have been brought there by gendarmes, while others said that the chief of section had brought them. The gendarme officer denied this, but on being told that they were at liberty to go to their homes or remain and work at a gourd a day they all but three left. At Maisade I interviewed the local priest, as well as the magistrate communal, the judge de pais, and a number of the inhabitants, also a number of gendarmes. The priest accused the gendarme officer, Lieut. D. B. Williams (sergeant, United States Marine Corps), with having killed a number of prisoners and also with having beaten a notary of Maisade to death in his office. The only substantiating testimony of this latter charge was from three privates of gendarmes, who also claimed to have been beaten by Lieut. Williams.

The charge was denied by Lieut Williams, as well as by the first sergeant, the magistrate, and the judge de pais, all of whom stated that the said notary was shot the night before during an attack by bandits on the town and had died from the effect of the wound. Lieut. Williams admitted that he had killed several prisoners, but only when they attempted to escape.

At Hinche I found a modified "corvee" had been in force, both of the roads and in building the gendarme barracks. All the inhabitants of a certain section (Zeb Guinea) had been rounded up and brought into Hinche as suspected bandits and had been put to work without pay, but had been allowed 30 cents Haitien (6 cents gold) per day for food; they had been released a few days before my arrival. I also found that practically all the gardens and farms outside of the towns had been abandoned and the inhabitants had disappeared, many probably having joined the bandits. The priest, Father Belliot, stated that this was partly on account of their fear of the gendarmes and of the "corvee." The appearance of a gendarme uniform was sufficient for the peasant to take to the brush and hide.

The priest and the magistrate of Hinche stated that a number of prisoners had been shot. On being questioned Capt. Ernest J. Lavoie (private, United States Marine Corps) admitted that six prisoners had been shot. He said that the cacos had attempted to escape several times; that they were a bad lot and had caused trouble among other prisoners. They were taken to the cemetery outside of the town and shot by gendarmes. He stated that he had no orders to shoot prisoners, and he had not reported the matter to anyone. Maj. Wells stated that no report had been made to him, but admitted that he would not expect a report in case of shooting of prisoners.

Upon the admission of Capt. Lavoie that prisoners had been shot, Col. Williams immediately wrote an order, a copy of which he had sent to all gendarme officers in Haiti, forbidding the killing of any prisoner, even if attempting to escape, and directing that in case a prisoner should be killed a full report with names of witnesses be submitted at once.

I considered that the action of the gendarmes in this section had had a very bad effect on the inhabitants, and I directed Col. Williams to transfer the officers, Capt. Lacoie and Lieut. Williams, and all gendarmes at Hinche and Maisade to Port au Prince, and replace them with others from a quiet part of the island. I also directed that marines be stationed immediately in Hinche, Maisade, San Michel, Cerca La Source, and Thomond, with an officer at each place, and directed Col. Hooker to assume command of all troops in the field.

I directed that all officers and men be instructed to treat the natives kindly and to make every effort to regain their confidence. I also directed that all patrolling by gendarmes cease and that they be restricted to the towns (in this section). I found that the gendarme officers had made no attempt to propitiate the priests; in fact they were in most cases antagonistic to them and treated them without any respect and had gained their ill will, when they might have had their good offices in dealing with the natives.

I questioned Maj. Wells carefully, and while I was unable to get anyone to state that he had given any orders for "corvee" or the killing of prisoners, I was satisfied that the officers under him understood that they were to get results, but were not expected to make any reports. I considered Maj. Wells principally responsible for the conditions as found. He stated that he made frequent inspections of all posts, and it is inconceivable that he should not have known something of the conditions. I directed that Maj. Wells be relieved of the command of the northern district. Maj. Meade arrived about this t.me and was assigned to command at Cape Haitien. Maj. Wells applied to be relieved from the gendarmerie and was ordered to the States.

In my opinion the young gendarme officers performed their duties to the best of their abilities according to the orders they received. They were all marines and, according to. the custom, never questioned any orders given them by regular officers. It is also my opinion that the actions of many of the young gendarme officers in treatment of natives is due to the methods taught them in handling the "corvee" workmen.

A. W. Catlin.

Headquarters Marine Corps, Washington, D. C.

Subscribed and sworn to before me this 31st day of December, 1919.

H. C. Haines,
*Colonel, Assistant Adjutant and Inspector,
United States Marine Corps.*

Washington, D. C., *January 8, 1920.*

John L. Doxey, captain, United States Marine Corps, having been called as a witness, and having been informed of his right to decline to answer any criminating question, was duly sworn, and testified before me, Lieut. Col. H. R. Lay, assistant adjutant and inspector, United States Marine Corps, as follows:

1. Question. Please state your name, rank, and present station.

Answer. John L. Doxey; captain, United States Marine Corps; stationed at Marine Barracks, navy yard, Philadelphia, Pa.

2. Question. Have you recently been on duty with the Haitien Gendarmerie; and if so, what was your rank and title while on such duty; also, where were you stationed and what duties were assigned to and performed by you and between what dates?

Answer. From January 25, 1916, to about June, 1918, I held the rank of captain or inspector, but my principal duties have been as a captain. From June 25, 1916, to about February, 1917, I was stationed at Port au Prince; from about February, 1917, to February 13, 1918, I was stationed at Hinche; from February 13, 1918, to March 8, 1919, at Cape Haitien; from March 8 to June 28, 1919, at Hinche; from June 28 to September 17, 1919, Cape Haitien; from September 17 to November 8, 1919, Port au Prince; from about October 18, 1918, to October 30 or 31, 1918, at Hinche; from about February 22 to March 8, 1918, I was in and out of Hinche, but not assigned as district commander at that place at that time.

3. Question. During your service with the Haitian Gendarmerie in Hinche and Maisade and elsewhere, were you aware of the existence of any compulsory "corvee" subsequent to the receipt of the order of October 1, 1919, suspending the corvee law? If so, please state particulars.

Answer. To my knowledge there was none. I personally questioned D. L. Williams, the lieutenant at Maissade, the magistrate of Maissade, Martial Breval, and a number of natives working on the road at this time, and all told me that no forced labor was going on. I questioned these people some time between the 1st and 5th of March, 1919. In this connection I would like to state that corvee is a Creole expression for any work by either a small or large body of men, whether they are working for the gendarmerie, the Marine Corps, or for themselves or other natives, and in case you should ask if corvee were going on the natives would naturally answer "yes," whether it was voluntary or forced labor. My understanding of corvee when questioned by an inspecting officer is that a body of men are working against their wishes and that they may be paid or not paid, while it may or may not be with a native. The native, when questioned, thinks that any work, whether paid or not paid, whether voluntary or not voluntary, is corvee. To my knowledge of the definition of the word "corvee" it was not going on in the district at this time.

During my investigation, which was about March 3, 1919, I personally questioned natives working on the road at that time near Maissade, about 15 men out of 45, and each one told me in substance that he was glad to work on the road, because he could not work his garden on account of the bandits, and that he would rather make a little money until the banditism was over. A few days later I was with Gen. Catlin, and through his interpreter some of these same men personally told him that they were forced to work, although they were paid, and would rather be at home working on their gardens. At this particular time in that section there was no particular work for them to do, even in preparing their gardens to be planted, as it was very dry. During my duty with the natives I have found that practically all, educated and uneducated, will work for you just because they like you, and at the same time it may be against their wishes, and you would not know about it. Another cause would be through fear that they might displease the chief, and later the chief might persecute them, would influence the native to work for you. However, in this case, if an opportunity occurred, another inspector might find out that the natives had a dislike for this work. At this time, as far as I know, every one was being paid for the work performed. At this time I personally carried up 600 or 800 gourds to pay the native road workmen, and at this time, and before this time, there were about 3,000 gourds available for paying these road workmen, and after my trip, as I remember it, there were 1,200 gourds left at Hinche. This money was kept at Hinche for safe-keeping only—it belonged to the commune of Haissade.

4. Question. Did you at any time observe personally, or receive any report, of instances of abuse or ill treatment of members of corvee by members of the gendarmerie?

Answer. No, sir.

5. Question. Did you ever see or hear that caco prisoners had been taken out and executed without trial?

Answer. I never did see this, and I don't remember of ever hearing of it up unt:l March 19, 1919, when Gen. Catlin's investigation was made.

6. Question. In your position which you occupied, did you ever hear of any cases where any persons were shot without trial in or near Hinche or Maissade?

Answer. No, sir. However, when Maj. Turner made his investigation, I did hear from Maj. Turner that 19 prisoners had been killed in January in Hinche. I personally did not believe this; for, in numerous conversations with the natives, they never mentioned that anything of this kind had occurred. I had personally known the natives in the district of Hinche, and the priest, and if anything of this kind had been on their minds they, perhaps, would have brought it up in some of these conversations. From all my dealings with the Haitian, it is absolutely impossible to tell whether an occurrence actually took place or not; they may tell you that an incident took place, which is absolutely incorrect; they may tell you that an incident happened and implicate other natives; and upon investigation ylu will find their statements untrue.

7. Question. Did you hear it spoken of among the gendarmerie that it was customary to execute, "bump off," caco prisoners and to make no report of such affairs to higher authority?

Answer. No, sir.

8. Question. Have you any knowledge of the circumstances attending the death of Garnier, the notary, at the house occupied by Lieut. Williams at Maissade?

Answer. Only from hearsay, after Gen. Catlin's investigation. Gen. Catlin investigated this case himself.

9. Question. What, in your opinion, were the principal causes for the spirit of unrest prevalent in the Republic of Haiti?

Answer. The natural dislike of the Haitians toward any white man (foreigner) in Haiti and the changing of article 6 of the constitution, which in substance allows a foreigner to own land in Haiti. This change was made in June, 1918. My personal feeling and the intimate knowledge I have of the natives leads me to believe that the changing of article 6 of the constitution was the cause of this banditism in Haiti.

10. Question. Do you consider that the Haitians residing in the district of Hinche were subjected to ill treatment or were unduly oppressed by the Haitian gendarmerie?

Answer. No, sir.

11. Question. Did you ever see or hear of any confidential reports, confidential telegrams, or confidential messages being received in Maj. Well's office relating to the alleged killings and the corvée after the order abolishing corvée had been given, in the vicinity of Hinche or Maissade?

Answer. No, sir; so far as I know no such messages ever came to his office.

12. Question. Would you have been in a position to have known had such confidential messages or telegrams been received?

Answer. Not necessarily, although Maj. Wells usually gave me all reports to read.

13. Question. Did you ever hear of any confidential reports, confidential telegrams, or confidential messages of any kind disappearing from Maj. Wells's office?

Answer. No, sir.

14. Question. Were you intimately associated with Maj. Clarke H. Wells while he was department commander?

Answer. Yes, sir.

15. Question. During that time did you live with him?

Answer. No, sir; but I lived in the same town with him and saw him practically every day.

16. Question. During this time did you ever see Maj. Wells under the influence of intoxicating liquor?

Answer. No, sir.

17. Question. Do you know Mr. Frederick Baker, formerly an officer in the Haitian gendarmerie?

Answer. Yes.

18. Question. Please state what you know in regard to his character and general reputation among his associates in Haiti?

Answer. By hearsay from American business men and gendarmerie lieutenants, he is an agitator and is not loyal to his superior officers and always **exaggerates** any incident that he may have personal knowledge of. I personally would not believe any statement he ever made to be a fact, and I have heard of statements made by him that were absolutely incorrect, according to different sources of hearsay information.

HEADQUARTERS MARINE CORPS.
Washington, D. C.

Subscribed and sworn to before me this the 8th day of January, 1920.

H. LAY,
Lieutenant Colonel, Assistant Adjutant and Inspector,
United States Marine Corps.

WASHINGTON, D. C., *January 7, 1920.*

CLARKE H. WELLS, major, United States Marine Corps, having been called as a witness, and having been informed of his right to decline to answer any incriminating questions, was duly sworn, and testified before me, Lieut. Col. H. R. Lay, assistant adjutant and inspector, United States Marine Corps, as follows:

(NOTE.—Before commencing the testimony of Maj. Wells attention is invited to the confidential report of the brigade commander, First Provisional Brigade, United States Marines, Port au Prince, Haiti, to the major general commandant, dated December 7, 1919. In paragraph 2 it is stated that from an investigation of the report it appears that in the north of Haiti, in violation of the order of October 1, 1918, suspending the application of the corvee law, this law was put in effect in certain sections after that date by order of the gendarmerie district commander, Maj. Clarke H. Wells, United States Marine Corps. This is misleading, as Maj. Wells at that time was department commander and Capt. Lavoie was the district commander where this corvee was alleged to have been put into effect. Maj. Wells was in command of the entire department, comprising seven d.stricts, and was 90 miles away from this district at this time.)

1. Question. Please state your name, rank, and present station.

Answer. Clarke H. Wells, major, United States Marine Corps, in charge of the Marine Corps recruiting station, Washington, D. C.

2. Question. Have you recently been on duty with the Haitian gendarmerie, and if so, what was your rank and title while on such duty? Also where were you stationed and what duties were assigned to and performed by you and between what dates?

Answer. I was detached from the Haitian gendarmerie on May 17, 1919. At that time I held the rank of colonel in command of the Department of the North, with headquarters at Cape Hait:en, Haiti. To the best of my knowledge, I joined the gendarmerie on May 6, 1916, and was on duty all the time between those dates. I joined the gendarmerie first as an inspector, and had charge of the road system in north Haiti and also in command of the civil pr son at Cape Ha:tien, which was then in process of construction. I was also assigned to regular inspection duty in that department. I was appointed colonel in the gendarmerie on the 16th of December, 1918.

3. Question. Can you give the names and rank of some of the gendarmerie officers under your command and subject to your orders?

Answer. In the north I had Capt. Bartel as inspector, Capt. Chaffee as quartermaster, Maj. Hayes as quartermaster, Capt. Doxey in command of the Third Company at Cape Haitien, and Lieut. Bowley, his assistant; at Grande River, Capt. Hamilton at Ouanaminthe, Capt. Verdier; at Hinche, Capt. Lavoie; Lieut. Williams at Maissade; Capt. Howell at Port de Paix; Capt. Hannigan at the remount stat'on; Capt. Hartman at Letrou; Lieut. Cates at the civilian prison, Cape Haitien; and Capt. Gibbons at Gonaives.

4. Question. During your service with the Haitian gendarmerie in Hinche and Maissade and elsewhere were you aware of the existence of any compulsory " corvee " subsequent to the receipt of the order of October 1, 1918, suspending the corvee law? If so, please state particulars.

Answer. After the receipt of the order of October 1, 1918, abolishing corvee, to the best of my knowledge, as far as I could find out during my inspections, there was no compulsory labor, meaning " corvee."

5. Question. Between what dates, approximately, were corvee lawfully operated in the department under your charge?

Answer. Corvee was first started when the road system of Haiti was in process of construction, by order of the chief of the gendarmerie; that was the latter part of 1916.

6. Question. Did you at any time observe personally or receive any report of instances of abuse or ill treatment of members of corvee by members of the gendarmerie?

Answer. I visited Hinche as frequently as my other duties would let me, and no complaint ever reached me from any civilians or anybody in authority there of the ill treatment of natives or members of the corvee, nor were any members of the corvee ill treated by members of the gendarmerie.

7. Question. Did you at any time subsequent to October 1, 1919, issue any orders or give your tacit consent for the convening of compulsory corvee for construction work in your district?

Answer. No; I had personal charge of 65 miles of road between Cape Haitien and Gonaives. After the corvee was abolished these laborers were paid by me each week. The road to Hinche was in charge of the district commander of Hinche, Capt. Lavoie, who as a member of the communal council at Maissade used the taxes which the people were required to pay for bringing in their goods to sell for the purpose of paying for this labor. This was with the consent of the magistrate there, as the people were very desirous for this road.

8. Question. Did you ever see or hear that Caco prisoners had been taken out and executed without trial?

Answer. When Gen. Catlin made his inspection in Hinche the latter part of March, 1919, it was found that several prisoners had been shot. This was told to Gen. Catlin by several natives, who were interrogated by him at that time. This was the first intimation that I had had of anything of this nature. No compla'nts ever reached me from any source as to any shootings up to this time.

9. Question. Following the attack by bandits upon Maissade on or about November 1, 1918, did you express the wish to any of your junior officers that Caco prisoners, if undesirable or worthless, be " bumped off "?

Answer. Never.

10. Question. Did you hear it spoken of among the gendarmerie that it was customary to execute "bump-off" Caco prisoners and to make no report of such affairs to high authority?

Answer. Never.

11. Question. Was any report made to you, or did you ever hear, that Capt. Ernest Lavois had executed some 19 caco prisoners in or near Hinche in January, 1919? If so, was any investigation made by you at the time and what action taken?

Answer. Gen. Williams and myself visited Hinche in January, 1919, and found things in good order, with the exception that roving bands of bandits in that district who robbed the market workmen, burned the houses, and in general terrified the natives, was reported. The strength of the gendarmerie detachment on duty there in central Haiti was approximately 100 men and officers. Hinche was 90 miles from Cape Haitien; all supplies had to be sent through on pack trains. It was my opinion that the officers on duty there were very active. They had completed one of the finest barracks buildings in the gendarmerie. An electric-light plant was installed there, and the place was generally in excellent condition. Numerous bands of bandits were reported from time to time; some of these reports were numerous, and rumors travel very fast in that country, while other reports were actual facts. I think the natives had the habit, in fact I know they had the habit, of exaggerating and lying to a great extent. The garrison was reenforced by the cavalry from Port au Prince, and several additional officers would come up for two or three weeks for patrol duty and then return. On my numerous visits to Hinche the officers seemed interested in their work; especially the construction work of building up the country. The natives seemed contended in the vicinity of Hinche, and there were no reports or evidences of any forced labor, except by prisoners. The jail contained approximately 60 men and women during my trips there. I never saw any mistreatment of prisoners or the inhabitants.

12. Question. Were you well acquainted with Capt. Doxey, and, if so, what was your opinion of his ability as an officer and reputation for veracity? Were your personal relations friendly or otherwise?

Answer. Capt. Doxey and myself were good friends; we were together in northern Haiti during all of our service down there, and I would not doubt what he said for a minute. He was always truthful and conscientious in his work; he was very thorough, painstaking, and a good all around dependable man. My personal relations with Capt. Doxey were always very friendly. He is of a retiring nature, sensitive, and a man of few words. He was respected by the better element of natives. The bad element during his service in Hinche tried to kill him because he was doing his duty. On account of his upholding the law and looking out for the interests of the better element of the people, he was attacked in his house one night at Hinche by bandits who were armed with rifles and knives. At this time he displayed great courage. He was by himself, and finally succeeded, after the alarm had been sounded, in quelling the disturbance and driving the bandits out into the country. He sent a report to Cape Haiten recounting the circumstances, saying that he was all right and did not need help. A number of bandits were killed during this attack. I consider Doxey one of the most dependable officers in the service. He was very patient with the Haitians, listened to all their troubles, and had many friends among the better element.

13. Question. Have you any knowledge of the circumstances attending the death of Garnier, the notary, at the house occupied by Lieut. Williams in Maissade?

Answer. It was reported to me verbally that this man had been shot during a daylight attack on that town. The officer in charge, Lieut. Williams, seemed to think that Garnier was implicated in the attack, as the bandits came into the town through his house and were firing from his house. Lieut. Williams was alone in Maissade at this time. This affair took place about 3 o'clock in the afternoon. Lieut. Williams was in his own house, across the square; he heard the shots and immediately went outside to find out what was going on. He stated to me that the bandits were firing all around him, and that in order to protect himself he got his men in the best shape he could on short notice and returned the fire, and finally succeeded in driving them off after a number had been killed. Just how many actually were killed I do not remember. It was during this attack, it was reported, that Garnier was killed. He was found dead in his house.

14. Question. What was the attitude of Frederick Baker toward you while he was a gendarmerie officer?

Answer. He was my assistant in the road business; had command of the district of Gonaives, which is 65 miles from Cape Haitien, over the mountains, and our relations were always pleasant. When his enlistment expired from the Marine Corps he was released from the gendarmerie and joined the Haitian Products Co., which was then organizing in Haiti. I saw him very seldom after this, as he was working in a different part of the country. I did notice, however, and it was talked about among the other officers of the gendarmerie, that he seemed to avoid further relationship with any of the officers attached to the gendarmerie.

15. Question. What, in your opinion, were the principal causes for the spirit of unrest prevalent in the Republic of Haiti?

Answer. The principal cause, I think, when Charlemagne escaped from prison at Cape Haitien by bribing a gendarme. This man had great influence over a large number of people. He was educated, and circulated all kinds of propaganda about the American occupation. There was no trouble, except the generl police cases, throughout the north until his escape from jail. The people were all afraid of him and he got recruits every place he went by telling them that he was there to drive the whites out of Haiti. Before the corvee was abolished he spread great discontent by circulating the report that the Americans were there to make slaves out of them. The Haitians are very excitable, rumors and news travel very fast, and they have the habit of lying. Northern Haiti composed six districts of the most mountainous part of the island, about 150 miles across and about 90 miles wide. The quota of gendarmes for this territory was about 960 men divided between the different districts.

16. Question. Do you feel justified in stating that there were no illegal executions of native prisoners in the department under your charge?

Answer. Yes; except in the instance of the investigation at Hinche by Gen. Catlin in March, 1919, of which I never knew the outcome, what the final decision was, or the attendant circumstances. About this particular instance I knew nothing, it having never been reported to me, if it took place at all.

17. Question. Admitting that natives were in some instances executed without trial and without official report of same being made to higher authority, is it your opinion that such killings were justifiable under the circumstances?

Answer. I do not think that any killings are justifiable without trail, except in the case of bandits in the hills who are armed and trying to escape with rifle and ammunition in their possession, as happened in numerous cases.

18. Question. Do you consider that the Haitians residing in your Department were subjected to ill treatment or were unduly oppressed by the Haitian gendarmerie?

Answer. I do not; I think they were better treated than they had ever been before in their lives. During the time that I commanded in the north nobody was put in jail without a trial, as had been done before the gendarmerie was established; the communes had more money; the taxes were collected regularly; the trails and roads were made passable both for automobiles and carts; bandits were stopped from pillaging the inhabitants; disputes among the natives were setted; and everything was done to improve conditions.

(At this point the witness submitted to the examining officer certain letters which he requested be made a part of his testimony. The letters are as follows:)

GENDARMERIE D'HAITI, QUARTIER GENERAL.
Port au Prince, February 14, 1917.

From: Chief of the Gendarmerie d'Haiti.
To: Commandant Clarke H. Wells, inspector, Gendarmerie d'Haiti.
Subject: Road work.

1. The following indorsement, signed by the commander, Department of the Cape, appears on your road report for the month of January, 1917:

"The attention of the chief of the gendarmerie is invited to the fact that under the supervision of Maj. Wells the amount of work accomplished in road repair has greatly increased per month. This is undoubtedly due to the constant attention given the work by this officer and to the efficient manner in which he has expended the funds given him."

2. Gen. Cole, to whose attention this indorsement was brought by the undersigned, stated to me that you are doing exceptionally fine work at the cape, and it gives me great pleasure to add my approbation to that of all others who have visited your Department.

3. Upon good road work largely depends the future of this country, and it is for that reason it is particularly gratifying to hear such praise as is given your work.

4. A copy of this letter will be appended to your official gendarmerie record.

S. D. BUTLER.

GENDARMERIE D'HAITI, QUARTIER GENERAL,
Port au Prince, March 3, 1917.

From: Chief of the Gendarmerie d'Haiti.
To: Commandant Clarke H. Wells, inspector, Gendarmerie d'Haiti.
Subject: Inspection of barracks, prisons, etc., at Cape Haitien.

1. The following extract appears in a report made by Col. H. L. Roosevelt, general inspector, G. d'H, on a recent trip made through your district:

"I found the prison in a most excellent condition; in fact, it is easily the finest institution of its kind in Haiti and would be a model anywhere. It was absolutely spotless, and the buildings are admirable for the purpose and the discipline was remarkable. The greatest credit is due to all who have been in any way connected with the maintenance and operation of this prison and special credit is due to Commandant Clarke H. Wells, G. d'H, who is in charge."

2. The excellent condition of the Cape Haitien prison is a subject of enthusiastic comment by everyone who has seen it, and I take pleasure in thanking you for your work in connection therewith.

3. A copy of this letter will be appended to your official gendarmerie record.

S. D. BUTLER.

[First indorsement.]

HEADQUARTERS DEPARTMENT OF THE CAPE,
GENDARMERIE D'HAITI,
Cape Haitien, March 9, 1917.

To: Maj. Clarke H. Wells, G. d'H.

1. The undersigned is much pleased to note the contents of this letter, which reflects great credit upon you.

J. M. TRACY.

GENDARMERIE D'HAITI,
QUARTIER GENERAL,
Port au Prince, Haiti, December 21, 1917.

From: Commanding officer, constabulary detachment, United States Marine Corps.
To: Capt. Clarke H. Wells, United States Marine Corps.
Subject: Commendatory letter.

1. Attached hereto is a radio from the major general commandant, United States Marine Corps, transmitted to these headquarters by the brigade commander.

2. A copy of this will be appended to your Marine Corps record.

S. D. BUTLER.

[First indorsement.]

HEADQUARTERS DEPARTMENT OF THE CAPE,
GENDARMERIE D'HAITI,
Cape Haitien, December 27, 1917.

From: Department commander, Department of the Cape.
To: Capt. Clarke H. Wells, United States Marine Corps.

1. Forwarded.

J. K. TRACY.

HEADQUARTERS FIRST PROVISIONAL BRIGADE,
UNITED STATES MARINE CORPS,
Port au Prince, Haiti, December 20, 1917.

From: Brigade commander.
To: Chief of gendarmerie.
Subject: Road repair.

1. The following radiogram has been received in reply to one sent from this office reporting the successful run of an automobile from Port au Prince to Cape Haitien on the 17th instant.

"Brigade Port au Prince, information contained radiogram 09518 most gratifying. My sincere congratulations to all who have been instrumental in doing this great work. 13319.

"MARCORPS."

2. It is with great pleasure that I am able to forward this congratulatory dispatch to the organization which is solely responsible for the successful accomplishment of the work in question.

JOHN H. RUSSELL.

GENDARMERIE D'HAITI, QUARTIER GENERAL,
Port au Prince, Haiti, December 20, 1918.

From: Chief of the Gendarmerie d'Haiti.
To: Maj. Clarke H. Wells, G. d'H.
Subject: Letter of commendation.
Inclosure: One.

1. This office takes pleasure in forwarding to you the attached copy of a letter dated November 16, 1918, from the American minister, Port au Prince, Haiti.
2. A copy of this letter and inclosures will be appended to your record.

ALEX. S. WILLIAMS.

LEGATION OF THE UNITED STATES OF AMERICA,
November 16, 1918.

Gen. ALEXANDER S. WILLIAMS.
Chief of the Gendarmerie d'Haiti, Port au Prince.

SIR: In reply to this legation's dispatch transmitting your report for the week ending August 5, 1918, addressed to the Secretary of State, in which you stated that "the road work is progressing satisfactorily and that Maj. G. H. Wells, Capt. C. F. Baker, and Capt. Ernest Lavo'e, of the gendarmerie, can not be praised too highly for their energy and resourcefulness," the Department of State directs me to inform you that because of its desire for the improvement of conditions in Haiti it is particularly pleased to learn of the progress which is being made in road construction and to request you to express to the officers aforementioned the real appreciation of the department for their work in connection with the road between Cape Haitien and Hinche.

I am, sir, your obedient servant,

A. BAILEY-BLANCHARD,
American Minister.

GENDARMERIE D'HAITI, QUARTIER GENERAL,
Port au Prince, Republic of Haiti, January 31, 1919.

From: Chief of the Gendarmerie d'Haiti.
To: Col. Clarke H. Wells, G. d'H.
Subject: Inspection of the Department of the Cape.

1. On the completion of my recent inspection of the Department of the Cape, which you command, I have to inform you that I found little to criticize and much to commend. The great improvements made in barracks and quarters, in enl'sted personnel, in roads, in prisons, in hospitals, and in the communes administered by your officers reflect great credit on your conduct of affairs, especially as much of the improvement, even allowing for the work of your predecessors, is evidently due to your ability, energy, and initiative.
2. A copy of this letter will be attached to your record.

ALEX. S. WILLIAMS.

19. Question. Did you ever receive any confidential messages as to conditions existing in your department; and if so, were those confidential reports ever taken from your files or lost?
Answer. I never received any confidential reports.
20. Question. Did you ever receive any confidential telegrams or messages reporting the actual state of affairs at Hinche and Maissade in regard to corvee being carried on after the order was issued abolishing it, or about any unlawful killing of natives in or near those towns?
Answer. No; no telegrams of this nature were ever received by me.

HEADQUARTERS MARINE CORPS,
Washington, D. C., January 12, 1920.

Maj. CLARKE H. WELLS, United States Marine Corps, was recalled as a witness, and having been informed that his previous oath was binding, and of his right to decline to answer any criminating question, further testified, as follows:

1. Question. Did you ever intimate to any member of the gendarmerie that you did not care to receive reports about prisoners?

Answer. I never intimated that I did not care to receive such reports. The gendarmerie regulations called for regular inspections and reports about prisoners by the inspecting officers attached to the department, and these reports of inspection were always written up and remain in the department commander's files at Cape Haitien. The district commanders made written reports of the conditions existing in their districts at the end of each month through me to the chief of the gendarmerie. These reports are on file, by the month, with the records of the gendarmerie.

2. Question. Did you ever receive any messages?

Answer. Lots of messages were received each day over the telegraph from outlying stations and districts.

3. Question. It has been stated by witnesses that the telegrams and orders in the department of the north have disappeared. Do you know what became of them?

Answer. At the time I was detached from Cape Haitien, May 17, 1919, all orders and telegrams were there as I had received them. I know nothing about the loss of any of them.

4. Question. Why were the papers referred to kept under lock and key?

Answer. The drawer of the department commander's desk was kept locked, and papers relative to watching the activities of certain natives were kept there; also personal letters from the chief of the gendarmerie, all of which remain there.

5. Question. You stated, in answer to question 20, that no confidential telegrams were received by you. How do you account for the discrepancy between the answers to questions 9 and 10 in the testimony of Capt. Laurence Bolts?

Answer. Upon visiting the Third Company's office one time, which was used as a police station also, in which there were always a number of natives lounging. I instructed Lieut. Bolts to keep the telegraph file out of sight, as it often related to watching the movements of certain natives who were under suspicion, and I thought that it might be read by those about.

6. Question. After Gen. Catlin's visit to your department, in which he found that it was alleged that corvee was practiced after the issuance of the order of October 1, 1918, and also that some prisoners had been unlawfully killed, what steps did you take to correct this?

Answer. In order that there would be no further doubt about how the work was carried on, all work was suspended. Gen. Williams, who was also present, issued written orders on the spot that no prisoners under any circumstances would be unlawfully shot, and these orders were dispatched by me, by special messenger throughout the department.

7. Question. Lieut. Williams has testified that certain escaping prisoners had been killed and that he had made written reports of these killings, and any operations, to the district commander; were any of these prisoners killed ever reported to you by the district commander under whom Lieut. Williams was serving, and if so, did you make any report to Col. Will'ams?

Answer. I remember certain reports of operations made by Lieut. Williams; I can not say whether they mentioned any killings of prisoners, but I forwarded these papers to Col. Williams. These reports were concerning the general bandit situation, so far as I remember. I also made several trips to Port au Prince during this time and talked over the situation with Gen Williams.

8. Question. Did you ever tell Capt. Hamilton that Gen. Williams' orders prohibiting shooting of prisoners did not apply unless the prisoners were actually in prison?

Answer. No; I gave no instructions whatsoever to Capt. Hamilton concerning this, as he already had the gendarmerie orders.

9. Question. Did you tell Capt. Hamilton that he should go ahead executing prisoners and say nothing about it?

Answer. No; I never mentioned to any officer or man during my tour of service in Haiti anything about executing anybody. The question never entered my head.

In this connection I would like to supplement my answer to quest'on 19, in my former testimony, by saying that I did receive confidential reports and telegrams in code, all of which remain on file.

Subscribed and sworn to before me this January 12, 1920.

———— ————,
Lieutenant Colonel, Assistant Adjutant and Inspector
United States Marine Corps.

————

WASHINGTON, D. C., *January 6.*

ALEXANDER S. WILLIAMS, lieutenant colonel, United States Marine Corps, having been called as a witness, and having been informed of his right to decline to answer any criminating questions, was duly sworn, and testified before me, L'eut. Col. H. R. Lay, assistant adjutant and inspector, United States Marine Corps, as follows:

1. Question. Please state your name, rank, and present station.

Answer. Alexander S. Williams, lieutenant colonel, United States Marine Corps, stationed at Marine Barracks, navy yard, Philadelphia. Pa.

2. Question. What duty were you performing from May, 1915, to July, 1919?

Answer. I was chief of the Haitian gendarmerie from May, 1918, until July, 1919, and I was assistant chief from organization of the gendarmerie in 1915 until May, 1918.

3. Question. Did you ever hear that Caco prisoners had been taken to a cemetery in or near Hinche and shot; if so, please state what steps were taken by you to verify this statement.

Answer. Yes; during a visit of inspection made by Brig. Gen. Catlin and myself to Hinche in January, 1919, Gen. Catlin interrogated gendarmerie officers, local officials, the local priest, enlisted gendarmes, and inhabitants, relative to certain reports which he told me had been received by him. These reports alleged that certain prisoners involved in banditism had been taken from a prison in Hinche, led to a point outside of Hinche, near a cemetery, and there executed by a detachment of enlisted gendarmes. This allegation was supported by the statements of one or more gendarmes interrogated by Gen. Catlin. To the best of my recollection, Capt. Ernest Lavole who was at the time district commander at Hinche, acknowledged that such an execution had taken place. He offered in explanation of this action the fact that it was impossible to obtain conviction in the local civil courts, and that after their trial by a provost court in Cape Haitien and the expiration of the sentences adjudged by such court, that they would return to the neighborhood of Hinche, rejoin the bandits with whom they had been originally identified and make the pacification of the region more difficult. The entire investigation was conducted by Gen. Catlin, and the allegations seemed supported, except as to the exact number executed. No steps were taken by me to verify this statement or to investigate the allegations, for the reason that Hinche at that moment, and up until the date of my departure from Haiti, was under the direct military control of the commander of the district of north Haiti, who received his orders from the brigade commander, First Provisional Brigade, United States Marines, Port au Prince. I was not a party to this investigation, but was present during part of it.

4. Question. What duty was Maj. Clarke H. Wells, United States Marine Corps, performing during the latter part of 1918 and the beginning of 1919?

Answer. Maj. Clarke H. Wells at that time was department commander, department of the cape, which department included the district of Hinche.

5. Question. Did you consult with Maj. Wells from time to time as to how matters were going on in his department; and was the killing of prisoners or others ever mentioned?

Answer. Yes; the killing of prisoners in custody was never discussed, but instructions were given that every effort should be made to distinguish between those who were actually involved in operations against bandits and those who were in the vicinity of the operations or who might have become associated with the bandits against their will.

6. Question. Would it have been possible for 6 or 19 prisoners to have been executed at any one time in the Hinche district without your knowing about it?

Answer. Yes.

7. Question. In conversation with Capt. Lavoie and Lieut. Williams was the question of execution of prisoners ever mentioned?

Answer. No; except along the broad lines of general treatment of natives and the suppression of banditism.

8. Question. During your service with the Haitian gendarmerie did you ever see Maj. Wells under the influence of intoxicating liquor?

Answer. No.

9. Question. What is your opinion as to the character and veracity of Maj. Doxey?

Answer. I consider Capt. Doxey—then major in the gendarmerie—to be an officer of very fine feeling. He was noted among gendarmerie officers for his understanding of and sympathy with the natives. He was successful in his administration of gendarmerie affairs, and had the confidence and respect of the natives to a marked degree. This was not due to his temperament entirely but to his thorough understanding of the native dialect (Creole), which he spoke and understood better than any commissioned officer of the Marine Corps serving in the gendarmerie. I have found in every official and personal dealing with Capt. Doxey this officer to be very careful in his statements, and have never had any reason to suppose or believe that he was not absolutely truthful in all of his statements.

10. Question. Did you ever see or hear of any order being issued by Maj. Clarke H. Wells putting into effect the corvee law, after October, 1918, in his northern department where he was commanding?

Answer. No.

11. Question. It has been stated that corvee was seen in operation in February, 1919, near Maissade, where two groups of between 50 and 75 men each were working on the road and a third group of about 45 men in the market place near Maissade; please state what you know about this?

Answer. Gen. Catlin informed me that Col. Hooker had reported the existence of corvee in the neighborhood of Maissade, and directed me to have an investigation made. I assured him at the time that no corvee was in operation, and that my orders relative thereto were being carried out throughout Haiti. I had passed through Maissade two or three times and had seen no road gangs the composition of which, or the attitude of which, led me to believe that corvee was being carried on. I had seen road gangs working under the charge of a single gendarme who was in charge of the road construction. The belief inspired by my observations was borne out by reports to the effect that the road work in this neighborhood was being conducted by volunteer labor, and that the cost of this labor, which was not paid for from federal funds, was being paid from communal funds. On the occasion of Gen. Catlin's visit in January, when I was present, a road gang of perhaps 50 men were working to the westward of Maissade. Members of this gang were interrogated by Gen. Catlin through the interpreter, a Mr. Holly, a Haitian, and practically all stated that they were forced to work. Gen. Catlin asked those who had been forced to work and wanted to return to their farms to step to the front. Practically the entire gang stepped to the front.

While the party was still present, Capt. Doxey, if I remember correctly, without the aid of an interpreter, reinterrogated them; and Capt. Doxey told me at that place and time, that with the exception of a very few men all had stated that they were not forced to do this work; that they were free to leave when they wished, and that from time to time they took advantage of this freedom and returned to their farms in the vicinity. The report as to the number stated in this question I believe was made by Lieut. Col. R. S. Hooker. As a result of the contradictory statements made by the men in the road gang I could form no definite conclusion at that time as to whether or not these men had been as alleged forcibly collected, forcibly detained, or forcibly worked; and as stated in an earlier question the military control of this district having devolved upon the district commander of the district of the north of Haiti, I made no further investigation. I did, however, direct that all road work in that neighborhood cease. I further directed Lieut. Williams, an enlisted man of the Marine Corps serving as officer of the gendarmerie, to let me know how many men of this gang returned to work or wanted to work at the beginning of the following week. My recollection is that he reported that a fair percentage had shown up the following week for road work.

12. Question. Do you know if Maj. Wells knew that corvee was still in operation after October, 1918?

Answer. Assuming that corvee was in operation after the date stated, with the exception of corvee which, due to a misinterpretation of my order, was carried on for about a week subsequent to that time, I can not state.

13. Question. Would it have been possible for corvee to have been in use after October, 1918, without the knowledge of Maj. Wells in his department?

Answer. To a very limited extent: yes.

14. Question. Do you know of any confidential telegrams or messages having been sent to the gendarmerie department commander of the north reporting the actual state of affairs at Hinche and Maissade; if so, please state the substance of such confidential telegrams or messages?

Answer. That question can only be answered in a general way. Much of the gendarmerie telegraphic work, especially that involving troop movements and the operations of patrols, are transmitted in code. Every department commander and district commander had a copy of this code, and I presume that messages were received by Maj. Wells that were confidential to an extent at least of warranting coding. I have no knowledge of messages sent by district and department commanders, except where the message was sent in duplicate to me or a report based upon the message referred to the message or incorporated the message in a communication. I have no knowledge of confidential communications to which I might not properly have had access.

15. Question. Please state what you know of Maj. Wells's duty in connection with the gendarmerie.

Answer. Maj. Wells served under me from early in the organization of the gendarmerie until early in 1919; for the first part of this period he was in general charge of the road construction in north Haiti; this was during the operations of corvee. He relieved Maj. R. O. Underwood, United States Marine Corps, as department commander at a date subsequent to the abolition of corvee. During Maj. Wells's incumbency he devoted himself to road construction, barracks and prison construction, and the general well-being of the gendarmerie and the civil inhabitants in the north. He brought about marked improvements in the roads, prisons, and barracks, and the welfare of the prisoners. The improvement of conditions in the gendarmerie of north Haiti and in the administration of the communals was marked. To accomplish these results he worked harder and worked his officer under him harder than any senior officer in the gendarmerie.

16. Question. Do you consider that he efficiently occupied his position as department commander of the north?

Answer. Maj. Wells I consider the most efficiently and successful department commander who has ever served in the gendarmerie.

17. Question. Did you know Mr. Frederick Baker, formerly in the gendarmerie; and if so, please state his attitude toward Maj. Wells?

Answer. Mr. Baker, who had a commission finally as captain in the gendarmerie, and who was, I believe, a sergeant in the Marine Corps, was associated with the gendarmerie almost from the beginning. As a junior officer and as district commander of Gonaives he had a model command and post. He was assigned to road work, I think, by Gen. S. D. Butler, but this assignment may have been made subsequent to my assuming command. He was in charge of the road work from Gonaives over the mountains toward Cape Haitien, and during this work operated what was probably the largest corvee ever used. He was highly successful in his conduct of road work, and, except for such abuses as were incidental to the operation of corvee, I never heard any complaint of his action. Latterly he was associated with Maj. Wells as his assistant in road work, and to the best of my knowledge his relations with Maj Wells were amicable, as they were with all officers of the gendarmerie—myself notably. He was considered at that time one of the most efficient officers in the gendarmerie, so much so that I endeavored to obtain for him a temporary commission in the Marine Corps. Some time in 1918 Capt. Baker, who extended his enlistment from one year on the strength of my promise that he would be put in charge of growing castor beans, which the gendarmerie was to undertake at the request of the War Department, was offered a position in civil life in Haiti which was very attractive. He was discharged from the Marine Corps upon my recommendation and took up his new work. From his entry into civil life Mr. Baker stopped practically all relations with the officers under whom and with whom he had served. This attitude was so marked as to cause comment, and no reason was ever advanced for it.

Statement of Lieut. Col. A. S. Williams, United States Marine Corps, relative to certain irregularities alleged to have been committed by officers and enlisted men in the Republic of Haiti:

1. I was placed on duty in connection with the organization of the gendarmerie in August or September, 1915; I was commissioned by the President of Haiti as assistant chief of the gendarmerie about the middle of 1917. In that capacity I served until May, 1918, when I was commissioned chief of the gendarmerie, relieving Gen. S. D. Butler at that date. Gen. Butler had been on leave for about two months prior to this, so that my actual conduct of gendarmerie affairs began about March, 1918. I served as chief of the gendarmerie until July 19, 1919, when I was relieved and ordered to the United States.

2. In order to build certain public roads which were considered necessary for the commercial development of Haiti and also for the military control of the Republic, free labor, known as corvee, was used. This free labor was available by virtue of certain provisions of the Haitian laws contained in the Code Rural. The necessities of the public works demanded a greater supply of labor than was available in any one locality, and it was therefore necessary in obtaining the supply of labor to ignore, to a certain extent, the letter of the law bearing on this matter. This consisted principally in ignoring that provision of the law which provided that country people were to work in or near the locality in which they lived, in holding them for longer periods than the law permitted, and on work not contemplated by law.

The results of this exploitation of labor were two: First, it created in the minds of the peasants a dislike for the American occupation and its two instruments—the marines and the gendarmerie—and, second, imbued the native enlisted man with an entirely false conception of his relations with the civil population. As the corvee became more and more unpopular, more and more difficulty was experienced in obtaining men; and this difficulty caused the gendarme to resort to methods which were often brutal but quite consistent with their training under Haitian officials. I soon realized that one of the great causes of American unpopularity among the Haitians was the corvee and determined to put a stop to the practice. For various reasons it was not considered a good policy to stop it before certain road work had been completed. After consultation with the military commander, the American minister, American treaty officials, the President of Haiti, and his cabinet, I announced that corvee would shortly entirely cease. This announcement, if my memory serves me, was followed by a formal announcement that corvee would cease; and in October, 1918, I think, I issued an order definitely stopping all corvee of any sort throughout Haiti. This order was not issued by the President of Haiti, but was issued by myself, on my own responsibility. The order was enthusiastically received not only by the Haitians but by the gendarmerie officials in general, practically all of whom realized the evils which corvee had brought about, and welcomed the opportunity to reestablish themselves in the good graces of the inhabitants as well as to take up their more legitimate work of organizing and training a military police.

On the date set, so far as my personal investigation, official reports, and information from other sources could inform me, all corvee stopped with one exception. The original order stopping corvee was drawn so as to indicate certain road work, and the road work listed in the order did not cover, although it was intended to cover, road work being carried on with local funds. It must be understood that the road work in general was being carried on with what might be called Federal funds. I found that my order, despite the general knowledge that it was intended to stop corvee throughout the island had been misinterpreted by the department commander of the Department of the Cape. I think at that date that this officer was Maj. R. O. Underwood, United States Marine Corps. As soon as this was brought to my knowledge, perhaps a week after corvee had stopped throughout the island, I directed the department commander of the Cape by telephone to cease all corvee of whatever nature, paid for from whatever funds. This order was carried out to the best of my knowledge. The work which was being carried on with the aid of communal funds, and which was in violation of my order, was road work on the road Maissade-Hinche. From that date on I heard no report or any knowledge of corvee being used in Haiti.

8. Some time subsequent to this Gen. Catlin told me he had reports of corvee being used in the neighborhood of Maissade—this, I believe, was during November, 1918. He directed that I make an investigation or have an investigation made; I directed the department commander, Maj. Wells, to investigate. Between the date when corvee was stopped, by order, and November, 1918, work had been continued on the Maissade-Hinche road, but with paid labor and prisoners. During this period I had been over this road two or three times and saw no evidence of corvee being used. I saw gangs of natives, aggregating, perhaps, 50 or 60 men, working on the road without other guard than the single gendarme, in charge of the work. These gangs in no way resembled the corvee gangs working in this region or in any other part of Haiti; and their manner of working, their remoteness from the towns, and the absence of guards found so necessary in corvee work, led me to believe that these were volunteer paid laborers. If coercion was used at all it is probable that the coercion consisted simply in the issuance of an " invitation " which is the only word that could have been used in French or Creole for men to work. How this notice was conveyed to the country people I do not know positive, but I presume it was made known to them by enlisted gendarmes and local representatives of the Haitian Government. This would be perfectly regular, and provided they were adequately paid, and free to leave the work when they chose, would not be open to criticism. It is alleged that force was used in bringing these men to work; that they were restrained by force, and kept at work long after their little farms called for their presence.

Aside from the difficulty of defining just what is forced labor under these circumstances, I am not convinced that corvee was actually used on that road. Maj. Wells reported that no corvee was used, but in view of reports submitted to Gen. Catlin, Gen. Catlin decided to investigate himself, and informed me that he wished to visit northern Haiti, and further, that he desired me to go with him. I do not remember whether or not any notice of the proposed visit was given; I think it must have been, however, for Maj. Wells met us at Gonaives. Together with Gen. Catlin the party visited St. Michel, Maissade, and Hinche. At all three places Gen. Catlin interrogated gendarmerie officers, local officials, priests, and gendarmes, prisoners, and certain inhabitants. I was not present at all of the investigations, but enough was brought out, even allowing for the unreliability of native testimony, to indicate that very severe measures had to be taken to put down banditism; and even allowing for the inexperience and youth of the officers involved, they did not always exercise good judgment. Without entering into a defense of such errors of judgment, it must be borne in mind that a single white officer placed in military and police control of a district embracing 400 or 500 square miles and 50,000 Negroes, swarming with bandits, and having at his disposal a very insufficient number of ill-trained native police, was apt to take the most direct course under any circumstance.

The case of Lieut. Williams, at Maissade, is a case in point. Gen. Catlin asked if there were any gendarmes who wished to complain of the treatment they had received, and one at least testified that he had been kicked or struck by Lieut. Williams. This would seem an inexcusable exhibition of brutality, but when it is considered that Williams was living in a town situated in a country full of bandits, which had been jumped twice by bandits (on one of which occasions the gendarmerie garrison had been driven out), his action in striking this man, who was the only sentinel by night over the gendarmerie barracks, and who was found by him to be asleep on post, the action finds an explanation. I can not remember that I ever issued up to this time any formal or informal order bearing on the killing of prisoners. The gendarmerie regulations provided for this, and gendarmes who were guilty of ill-treatment of prisoners, or killing of prisoners, were always tried by either the gendarmerie court-martial or by the civil courts of Haiti. The sentences adjudged were always very severe, as I controlled the policy of the gendarmerie courts, and to a certain extent could influence the civil courts. Several sentences of death were adjudged, and these sentences upon my personal presentation of the case to the President of Haiti were always approved by him and the sentences carried out by firing squads. The action of these courts is referred to because the president invariably commuted the death sentence of civilians to life imprisonment, and in this matter realizing the racial defects of his own people aided me in enforcing discipline in the gendarmerie in the one matter which gave us the greatest trouble; that is, the abuse of authority by Haitian officials when free from superior control.

4. While every order issued from gendarmerie headquarters and bearing upon the relations of the gendarmerie with the civil population was designed to create good feeling between the gendarmerie and the civil population, and every attempt was made by myself and many others to cultivate such good feeling, the allegations made to Gen. Catlin on this inspection trip were such as to cause the issuance of an order bearing directly upon the treatment of prisoners. Whether or not the suggestion of such an order be issued came from Gen. Catlin or myself I can not say, but an order was issued which in its phraseology was considered foolproof. The expression " in custody " was used in the order, if I remember correctly, and this expression was used in the order to cover the cases of prisoners actually confined, prisoners being taken over the trail, and prisoners captured during a fight. To the best of my knowledge no report or rumor worthy of credence had ever been received to that date which would warrant the issuance of such an order; and, as before stated, by example, by advise, and by order, the policy of the gendarmerie to gain the good will of the people had been stressed. It is practically certain that prior to this time gendarme patrols operating against bandits and not led by an American had killed prisoners, and such patrols were therefore not sent out unless absolutely necessary. Wherever possible an American officer went with all patrols. During the visit of inspection of Maissade several of the inhabitants complained of brutal treatment; some of them could not substantiate their statements, which is not remarkable considering the utter ignorance of the Haitian countryman; others I believed at the time, and still believe, were inspired in making these reports by the local priests. This priest, it may be stated, was not on good terms with the gendarmerie officer, in consequence of the gendarmerie officer having cut off certain allowances which the church received from the commune. It may be stated at this time that the relations between the priests generally and the officers of the gendarmerie, while personally pleasant, were officially very unsatisfactory. The lack of good official feeling was due to the fact that with the coming of the American gendarme the priest lost the prestige which had been his before. In the department of the north this feeling, I believe, was largely due to the influence of the bishop of north Haiti, Mons. Kersusan. I am more convinced of this regrettable relationship and the causes which led to it, for the reason I succeeded myself in establishing pleasant personal and official relations with the archbishop of Haiti, the bishop of Port au Prince, and the papal legate. As a result of these relations I was able to bring about a certain amount of teamwork between the priests and the gendarmerie officers in central and southern Haiti. I have often discussed with the papal legate the attitude of the northern priests, and particularly that of the bishop of the north. From what they said I am led to believe that the bishop of the north was considered to be by his colleagues an " infant terrible."

It was specifically charged at this time that Lieut. Williams had executed a number of prisoners in his own back yard, but such testimony as I heard bearing on this was indefinite and contradictory. Williams did acknowledge having killed one escaping prisoner under circumstances which in the absence of evidence to the contrary would seem to have justified the act. It was also alleged, and not contradicted, that one man at least had been killed incidental to making an arrest in the country. In this particular case it is difficult to decide whether or not the arrest could have been made without shooting. Allegations were made that Williams had collected cattle which he impounded and either held for exorbitant fees or else refused to give up. I do not know whether or not the communal laws bearing on lost, strayed, or stolen animals were properly enforced, but it may be stated that these laws were not enforced with any uniformity in Haiti, and that their application ran from neglect of the law to using it as a means of graft. This is a matter which lies largely with the local civil officials though subject to gendarmerie control.

5. The mayor of Maissade, Martial Preval, was complained against by the inhabitants. He was accused of extortion, of grafting, of misappropriating communal funds, and of what was more important from a gendarmerie viewpoint, of using corvee on his private properties. It was alleged specifically, though perhaps this allegation was made at a later date, that he used forced labor for the construction of a house for one of his various women. Preval is a very high type of Haitian and remarkably well educated for interior Haiti. He belongs to the ruling class, and his family has always been identified with civil affairs in that region. His father is or was mayor of a small town in northern Haiti. This man, from the very beginning of American occupation, showed himself more than friendly to the Americans, and was first brought

to our favorable notice by his action in organizing a posse and capturing a number of people who participated in the first attack on Hinche. His action in this matter won him a commendatory letter from the President of Haiti. Having thus definitely identified himself with the Americans he incurred the dislike of his countrymen, and as time went on and the communal revenues were collected with greater regularity, the local laws enforced as they had been enforced before, Preval's attitude gained him the native hostility of the 14,000 or 15,000 Haitians in his commune. It is more than probable that Preval was guilty of extortion and that he did use forced labor on his outlying properties.

These faults I found to be prevalent among Haitian communal officials. Just what efforts were made to control his actions I can not say, but until this visit I had no reason to suppose that anything was radically wrong with the conduct of communal affairs in Maissade. I did know, however, from a personal inspection, that the entire aspect of the small town was changed. The streets were clean, a proper market established, and the communal revenues increased. If, however, Preval was guilty of all with which he was charged his actions must have borne heavily on the inhabitants; and as he was apparently doing these things with the knowledge, consent, and active aid of the gendarmerie officers any feeling of hostility held by the natives against the gendarmerie must have been intensified.

6. While visiting Hinche, Gen. Catlin interrogated people of every class, including the officers and men of the gendarmerie. It was alleged that a number of natives had been executed in an open space in front of the gendarmerie quarters by machine-gun fire. This allegation was denied by the district commander, Capt. Levoie, and all knowledge of such an occurrence was denied by enlisted men of the gendarmerie who should have been cognizant of such an affair.

At the time the alleged execution took place two enlisted men of the Marine Corps were stationed at Hinche with a Lewis machine gun. I can not state positively whether or not these two men were in Hinche at the time of Gen. Catlin's visit. I do not remember at the time who made these allegations, but I believe they were made by a local official. It was further alleged and substantiated, as I remember, that a number of prisoners were taken from the jail where they had been confined and executed about a half a mile outside of town. I believe the gendarmes who took part in this execution were examined by Gen. Catlin and acknowledged the charge in part, differing from the allegation in respect to the number of prisoners.

7. While the use of corvée on road work had been alleged, its use in the neighborhood of Hinche was alleged mostly in connection with the construction of the gendarmerie barracks. Specifically it was stated that all the male inhabitants of a certain rural section called "New Guinea" had been collected, brought to Hinche, placed at work on the construction of a barracks well, and kept on this work for a considerable time. There was some question as to the amount of money paid these men, but they were paid something. This action had been taken by Capt. Lavoie as a military measure and designed to clear out a section touching on the no man's land between Haiti and Santo Domingo, which was an asylum for bandits for both Haiti and Santo Domingo. Capt. Lavoie stated that working these men on barracks construction was simply incidental.

8. It was alleged generally by the civil officials, and I believe by the priests, that the banditism in central Haiti was the result of the illegal acts committed by the gendarmerie in this region, and that between the bandits and the gendarmes the inhabitants did not know which way to turn. This to a certain extent is true. The bandits were only partly armed, wore no uniform, and would scatter usually at the approach of a gendarmerie patrol. When such a patrol established contact with a group of bandits a few shots would be fired by these and the bandits would scatter in all directions and with them would go the inhabitants of that particular locality, especially those who had willingly or otherwise furnished food to the bandits and who felt that they were guilty with them. In the pursuit it is more than probable that innocent inhabitants were killed. So far as my own orders were concerned and so far as concerns those orders issued by officers under me, every attempt was made to distinguish between bandits and those who were involved in banditism against their will. I have no knowledge that Maj. Wells, the department commander, ever issued any order contravening mine or of his own initiative issued any order contrary to my expressed and generally known wishes regarding the treatment of natives, whether under arms or not.

9. On the return of Gen. Catlin and myself to Port au Prince in January, 1919, Gen. Catlin desired that Capt. Levole and Lieut. Williams be removed from Hinche and Maissade. I ordered to Hinche Capt. Doxey, whose disposition and reputation was that of kindness, sympathy for the natives, and more perfect knowledge of native dialects than any other senior officer of the gendarmiere.

10. Meantime marines had been ordered to Hinche and outlying posts, the gendarmes restricted to ordinary police work within town, and Lieut. Col. R. S. Hooker placed in military command of the affected central region. What investigations were made subsequent to that by Gen. Catlin, by Col. Hooker, or by other marine officers I do not know.

11. Knowing Haiti as I do it is difficult for me to believe that the banditism, which had its origin in or about Hinche and was spread rapidly north, east, south, and west from there, attaining its maximum in Mirabaldis and Lascahobas, was due to specific misconduct or misadministration on the part of any officer. Hinche, even during Spanish colonial times, has been a nexus of revolution and banditism. Long before corvee was used in this region Hinche was attacked by organized bands, the first attack taking place while Capt. Doxey, who, as before stated, enjoyed the confidence and liking of the natives to a marked degree, was in command. It is impossible for me to believe that the application of corvee within a limited area would have such an effect. I am therefore led to believe, and my belief is founded on most careful thought, that the banditism in central Haiti, which grew almost to the proportions of a revolution, was due to other causes.

12. The first of these causes was the illegal general application of the corvee; second, the racial antagonism between the Negro and the white; third, the virtual loss of national independence; fourth, the economic conditions brought about by the war.

In assigning these reasons I wish to make it clear that had these causes for dissatisfaction not been stressed and played upon by Haitian leaders the recent outbreak would never have occurred and the natives would have remained quiescent under almost any system of abuse, as they rested quiescent for over a hundred years under graver abuses inflicted by their own people.

13. Assuming that the corvee was illegally applied in the neighborhood of Hinche and Maissade, and in defiance of my clear orders on the matter, and, further, assuming that the allegations of indiscriminate and unjustified killings are true, it is not difficult to understand how these things could have been done without the knowledge of responsible seniors. With the best of will in the world the amount of administrative work thrust upon all gendarmerie officers made it impossible to properly supervise the details of local administration. If reports and rumors seemed to justify an investigation into any complaint, the investigation itself was attended with every difficulty.

Generally, in the interior the native has no knowledge of the time, dates, or distance (his stupidity as a witness caused me to approve gendarmerie courts-martial with more or less reluctance), and the amount of work involved in any investigation was very often out of all proportions to the results obtained. It was therefore necessary in making an inspection trip to judge conditions by what one saw and what one was told. Another index, and one upon which I myself depended largely as showing the mental attitude of the natives, which attitude was of necessity a reflex of the attitude of the gendarmerie toward them, was whether or not the natives when met on the road showed no desire to avoid meeting my party. This was not true where the corvee had been worked. At the very time when corvee was alleged to have been terrorizing the natives in Hinche and Maissade, the weekly markets in Maissade were crowded by country people as they never had been before. Than this attendance on market days there is no better barometer of the state of feeling among the natives with regard to protection and security. If there were any underlying signs of dissatisfaction among the well disposed country people I failed to see them; and while the inspection trips of my subordinates could and should have gone more into detail it is quite possible that they too failed to note any reasons for suspecting that affairs were not well.

14. In conclusion, it may be stated that the efforts of practically all gendarmerie officers were devoted to improving the condition of the natives and to gain their good will. This they did because of a liking for, and sympathy with, the natives, and to make the conditions of their own service more pleasant. Officers who failed to conduct themselves in this fashion, whether commissioned

or enlisted in the Marine Corps, were detached from the gendarmerie. I have no knowledge of corvee carried on contrary to orders, or of the killing of prisoners, except as stated, nor have I knowledge of any orders which would encourage or justify any such action.

HEADQUARTERS MARINE CORPS,
Washington, D. C.

Subscribed and sworn to before me, this 7th day of January, 1920.

——— ———,
Lieutenant Colonel, Assistant Adjutant and Inspector,
United States Marine Corps.

WASHINGTON, D. C., *January 9, 1920.*,

DORCAS L. WILLIAMS, sergeant, United States Marine Corps, having been called as a witness, and having been informed of his right to decline to answer any criminating question, was duly sworn and testified before me, Lieut. Col. H. R. Lay, assistant adjutant and inspector, U. S. Marine Corps, as follows:

1. Question. What is your name, rank, and present station.

Answer. Dorcas Lee Williams, sergeant, United States Marine Corps, stationed at Marine Barracks, Navy Yard, Brooklyn, N. Y.

2. Question. Have you recently been on duty with the Haitian gendarmerie and, if so, what was your rank and title while employed on such duty; also where were you stationed and what duties were assigned to you and performed by you?

Answer. Yes, sir; as a second lieutenant of the Haitian gendarmerie. I was stationed in the district of Hinche from November 12, 1918, to March 18 or 19, 1919, was performing patrol duty. I was in Maissade from December 28, 1918, to some time in March, 1919; the rest of the time I was in Cerce Corjal, which is in the district of Hinche, guarding the town and performing patrol duty. While I was in Maissade I was in charge of road work; I was subdistrict commander and looked out for the duties of the district in general.

3. Question. Who was your immediate commanding officer while serving with the gendarmerie; if more than one state names and dates between which you served under each? Did you at any time have independent command of any forces or any commune or district?

Answer. Capt. Ernest Lavoie; he was the only one who was really my immediately commanding officer. I never had any command that could be called independent.

4. Question. While serving with the gendarmerie, did you ever see, or hear, of the killing of any caco prisoners; if so, state particulars?

Answer. No, sir; except prisoners trying to escape.

5. Question. While serving with the gendarmerie, were you aware of the convening of any corvee, compulsory or voluntary, subsequent to the receipt of the order of October 1, 1918, suspending the corvee law? If so, state your knowledge of the facts in the premises.

Answer. There was no corvee as I would call it, as the people who worked were all paid for the work they did. My understanding of corvee is compulsory work or labor, feed, and imprisonment. The men who were working on the road or for the commune were paid by the magistrate from communal funds, and I witnessed all payments. From the time I came into the Maissade district all work which was being performed by native labor was paid for and was not corvee.

6. Question. Did you, personally, subsequent to October 1, 1919, issue any orders, directly or indirectly, for the convening of any compulsory corvee for construction work in your district?

Answer. No, sir; I never did.

7. Question. It has been alleged that you had personal knowledge of the killing of a number of caco prisoners near Maissade. Is this allegation founded on fact, and, if so, what were the attendant circumstances?

Answer. There were no prisoners killed except escaping prisoners; that is, prisoners who were attempting to escape. Several prisoners were killed in attempting to escape. Between December, 1918, and March, 1919, there were several attempts by prisoners to escape, and quite a number escaped—I think 15 or 20. During that time we probably killed between 10 and 15 men who were trying to escape.

8. Question. Do you know of any other prisoners being killed in or near Maïssade during your duty there?

Answer. No, sir.

9. Question. Have you any knowledge of the circumstances attending the death of one Garnier, a notary, who, it is alleged, was found dead in your office under peculiar circumstances?

Answer. Yes, sir; I have some knowledge of this man. He was found wounded in his house, concealing his wound with a towel wrapped around his abdomen. He was brought to the barracks and I questioned him, asking him why he had not reported for treatment; why he had not made some report of his being wounded, so that we could have treated his wound, and all he would say was that "I don't know." He wanted to go back to his house, and would not talk of his wound, so I left him sitting in front of the barracks in a chair. The sergeant gave him first-aid treatment. He would not agree to anything being done for him. At first he denied being wounded.

During the attack that came through Garnier's house, or about 3.30 o'clock in the afternoon, there was an attack by the bandits on the town, and the barracks were attacked. The bandits came through Garnier's house and took cover behind his house—we were firing from the barracks and they were firing from Garnier's house. After the skirmish was over, I chased the bandits out of the town, and it was dark when I returned to the town; so I went into my house and shortly after I went into my house the sergeant came over and told me that he believed Garnier had been wounded. I sent the sergeant to see if he could find Garnier.

When the sergeant returned he brought Garnier with him. I asked Garnier if he was wounded and he said that he was not. The sergeant unbuttoned his vest and I saw blood on the towel. I asked Garnier who had wounded him and he replied that he did not know. I asked him why he didn't report so that we could give him treatment, and all he would say was that he didn't know. I asked him if he knew anything about the attack and he said he didn't know. I asked him if he wanted to lie down and he said he would rather sit up. I left him sitting in front of the barracks. I went to bed and left the sergeant to look out for him and do what he could for him. Some time in the night they awoke me and said that Garnier was dead. The sergeant awoke me again the next morning and asked what I wanted done with Garnier's body; I told him to inform the Judge de Paix, which was done. Everything was done to save Garnier's life that could be done. I gave him the best I had in medical treatment to save his life.

Garnier was a very good inhabitant of the town and friendly toward us. He must have gotten in the way of a stray bullet during the fight. After this fight, I would like to state, all the civilians left the town.

10. Question. Was any order, written or verbal, ever received by you, or did you ever hear of such an order, to summarily execute (bump off) caco prisoners and to make no report of such executions to higher authority; and, if so, from whom did you receive such orders; or, if no order was received, what led you to assume that such actions would meet with the approval of your superior officers?

Answer. No, sir; I never heard of anything like that; the orders we had were to scatter, disband, or capture organized bandits. The bandits were all thieves, traveling from place to place in bands of from 30 to 150 men, and when I went into the district we were instructed to scatter these people and capture as many as we could, and any stolen property that was recovered I was instructed to return it to the owners, if the owners could be found. These bandits were all armed with machetes and rifles, and when attacked, or when you came up to them, they would always fire on you.

11. Question. Did you ever hear that Capt. Ernest Lavoie had executed some 19 caco prisoners in or near Hinche, in January, 1919; and, if so, from what source was your information gained?

Answer. While I was in the district I did not hear that any prisoners had been killed by Capt. Lavoie, but after I left the district and returned to Port au Prince I did hear rumors—sometimes that 40 prisoners had been killed, and sometimes that 8 or 10 prisoners had been killed in the district of Hinche. There were always rumors floating around that bandits had attacked this town and that town, and more false rumors than anything else; every man that came in had a different tale to tell.

12. Question. Did your duties place you in direct contact with Maj. Clarke H. Wells?

62269—21—PT 2——26

Answer. Only during inspections and his passing through the place.

13. Question. Then you saw him quite a number of times during your tour of duty?

Answer. Yes. sir.

14. Question. During these times did you ever see Maj. Wells drunk or under the influence of liquor?

Answer. No, sir; I never did.

15. Question. During your talk with Maj. Catlin, at the time of his investigation at Hinche and Maissade, you acknowledged that some prisoners in your district had been killed.

Answer. The only prisoners that were killed were those prisoners attempting to escape.

16. Question. Gen. Catlin has made the statement that on his visit to Maissade he found about 45 men working on the road near Maissade under guard of several gendarmes. He further stated that they stopped and questioned these men and that some of them stated that they had been brought there by gendarmes and others said that the chief of section had brought them. Can you explain this?

Answer. The chief is known as a justice of peace or some official assistant to the justice of the peace. This chief of section would send to me from time to time as many men as were needed to work on the road. He would notify the people that I had work, and that if they would report to him he would send them into town. Some would work and some wouldn't. Every Saturday or Sunday the sergeant would notify the magistrate as to how many men he had, and the magistrate would come to me to get the money, and I would go with the magistrate to pay the men. They were all paid in my presence. The sergeant was the timekeeper and figured out how much each man had due him, and after payment everybody went home or stayed over for the next week's work, whichever they preferred. The forty-five men that Gen. Catlin questioned were all paid, to my personal knowledge, from my house on Sunday. Some of these forty-five men had not been paid up to the time when Gen. Catlin was talking to them because they had not been working long enough—only two or three days—in other words, they were paid once a week and pay day hadn't come round.

17. Question. Did you ever know an officer in the gendarmerie by the name of Frederick Baker; and if so, please state your opinion as to his general reputation?

Answer. He was known as an agitator; he was not sincere; he would give information he thought people wanted to have to them. In other words, he was referred to by all the people who knew him as a man not to be depended upon for truthfulness. He was known as a squealer, and after he got out of the service he turned against the gendarmerie and has been a great agitator; that is the general talk of everyone in Haiti that knows him.

18. Question. During your service in the gendarmerie you had frequent conversations with the natives?

Answer. Yes, sir; I was associated with them continually.

19. Question. Did you ever hear the natives refer to Capt. Doxey, of the Marine Corps?

Answer. Yes, sir; I have had all kinds of natives tell me that they liked Capt. Doxey; in fact, he was referred to by them as " the old man," as he was always ready to accommodate them and assist them in any way he could.

HEADQUARTERS MARINE CORPS,
Washington, D. C.

Subscribed and sworn to before me this the 9th day of January, 1920.

——————,
Lieutenant Colonel, Assistant Adjutant and Inspector,
United States Marine Corps

Sergt. DORCAS L. WILLIAMS was recalled as a witness, and having been informed that his previous oath was still binding, and having been informed of his right to decline to answer any criminating question, further testified as follows:

1. Question. Referring to your answer to question 5, of your previous testimony, wherein you stated that the natives working in your district were paid, state how much they were paid?

Answer. They were paid 40 cents a day, Haitian money, and their meals.

2. Question. Could labor not be paid and still be compulsory?

Answer. It could be if it was that way, but I obtained the labor the same as I did before corvée ever existed by notifying some good inhabitant that I had work, or the chief of section.

3. Question. Were any of the prisoners referred to in your previous testimony killed after recapture?

Answer. No, sir; not after recapture—none.

4. Question. Referring to question 7 of your previous testimony, was any report of the killing of these prisoners made to the higher authority?

Answer. All prisoners killed were reported to my district commander, and all operations were reported in the same way.

5. Question. What was the name of the sergeant who gave Garnier first aid?

Answer. Absalo Kies.

6. Question. Did you ever receive any hint, directly or indirectly, from Maj. Wells, that he did not care to receive reports about prisoners?

Answer. No, sir; I never did.

7. Question. What reports, if any, were made to your superiors regarding the conditions in your district?

Answer. All reports, even down to rumors reported.

8. Question. Were any or all of these reports confidential?

Answer. All reports were in writing and forwarded to my district commander; they were not marked confidential. They were all written and sent through by messenger.

9. Question. Do you know personally of any brutal or improper treatment of natives by either the gendarmes or the marines during your tour of duty in Haiti?

Answer. No, sir; I wish to state here, however, that on several occasions while my men were working they were molested by bandits, and on one occasion the working men chased the bandits. Any of the workmen captured by the bandits were badly treated, and even some were killed.

HEADQUARTERS MARINE CORPS,
Washington, D. C.

Subscribed and sworn to before me, this the 12th day of January, 1920.

HARRY LAY,
Lieutenant Colonel, Assistant Adjutant and Inspector,
United States Marine Corps.

Mr. ANGELL. Major, did you hear rumors or reports of any connection of Lieut. Cukela with killings?

Maj. TURNER. None that I remember; no.

Mr. ANGELL. You do not remember any specific investigation being pursued by you in regard to any such rumors?

Maj. TURNER. I am under the impression that I wrote an order to Col. Little to investigate somebody, but I have forgotten now who it was; I do not believe it was Cukela. I do not remember who it was. I am inclined to believe it was not Cukela, but the leader of a patrol of a district somewhat in the north of Haiti, where it was reported that some killings had happened.

Mr. ANGELL. Turning back now, Major, to the alleged killings at Hinche, under Capt. Lavoie, will you tell us a little more in detail than you did upon direct examination just what investigation you made of those reports, so far as you can now remember.

Maj. TURNER. I questioned everyone who seemed to have any knowledge on the subject or whose names were mentioned.

Mr. ANGELL. Do you remember whether or not you learned of the names of the gendarmes serving under Capt. Lavoie, who were alleged to have actually performed these killings?

Maj. TURNER. I tried at the time to get the names of the gendarmes from the gendarmerie, but the records were such that I was unable to get them.

Mr. ANGELL. You did interview Capt. Lavoie?

Maj. TURNER. Yes.

Mr. ANGELL. And he denied to you having committed the killings?

Maj. TURNER. Yes.

Mr. ANGELL. You were not present at the prior investigation of this instance made by Gen. Catlin and Col. Williams?

Maj. TURNER. No.

Mr. ANGELL. So you have no knowledge of the declarations made at that time by Capt. Lavoie, except——

Maj. TURNER. Except through investigation and through testimony of one or two of the witnesses.

Mr. ANGELL. Did you make any investigations of any rumors or allegations of killings by or under the direction of Lieut. Freeman Lang, of the gendarmerie, in and about the district of Hinche?

Maj. TURNER. No.

Mr. ANGELL. In October and November, 1918?

Maj. TURNER. No; that was one which never came to my notice.

Mr. ANGELL. Did you make any investigation of any allegations regarding the supposed killing of Garnier by Williams at Maissade?

Maj. TURNER. Yes; I tried to connect up the Garnier killing at Maissade, but was unable to get any information on that subject. I tried to get the names of some of the gendarmes who were there, but the records at Port au Prince were such that at that time I could not get any. Williams was not in the country at the time.

Mr. ANGELL. Had Williams been in the Marine Corps service?

Maj. TURNER. Yes.

Mr. ANGELL. But he had left Haiti at the time you made your investigation?

Maj. TURNER. Yes.

Mr. HOWE. He had also been in the gendarmerie?

Maj. TURNER. He was a lieutenant in the gendarmerie.

Mr. ANGELL. He was an enlisted man in the Marines?

Maj. TURNER. He was a sergeant.

Mr. ANGELL. So you never had an opportunity to interview Williams?

Mr. TURNER. No.

Mr. ANGELL. You said you believed that something actually happened at Hinche in regard to this supposed killing of natives under Capt. Lavoie's orders or command?

Maj. TURNER. Yes.

Mr. ANGELL. What is your belief regarding that incident?

Maj. TURNER. I believe somebody was killed at Latte. Latte is a section of Hinche.

Mr. ANGELL. You say that somebody was killed? What is your belief as to the number that were killed?

Maj. TURNER. That I do not know.

Mr. ANGELL. What is your belief as to the circumstances under which they were killed?

Maj. TURNER. That I do not know.

Mr. ANGELL. When you say somebody was killed at Latte, do you refer to combat?

Maj. TURNER. Oh, no; I mean——

Mr. ANGELL. You mean unlawful killing?

Maj. TURNER. Yes.

Mr. ANGELL. Unlawful killing under the direction and with the connivance of Capt. Lavoie?

Maj. TURNER. Yes.

Mr. ANGELL. Is it a fact, then, that you believe his denial of such killings made to you was not true?

Maj. TURNER. Yes.

Mr. ANGELL. And of course an admission by him of such killings would have been self-incriminatory?

Maj. TURNER. Yes. I told them all in any questions they were asked that they did not have to incriminate themselves; that they could refuse to answer any questions which might incriminate them.

Mr. ANGELL. You said a little while ago in answer to a question that you heard, but could not get any definite information regarding brutal treatment of prisoners. In answering that question did you have in mind prisoners who were taken from the Cacos or did you refer to men working under the corvee, or both?

Maj. TURNER. I had in mind the idea of prisoners from the prison more than anything else.

Mr. ANGELL. You were not referring to those working under the corvee?

Maj. TURNER. Yes; I was, in a way, too. Yes; that was considered, too.

Mr. ANGELL. Did you find any definite information regarding brutal treatment of men working under the corvee as distinguished from prisoners?

Maj. TURNER. No.

Mr. Howe. You are distinguishing brutal treatment from the killings you have discussed?

Maj. Turner. I was thinking that taking them on the corvee might be considered brutal treatment, but I did not consider that part as brutal treatment.

Mr. Angell. In the course of your investigation and of the performance of your duties in Haiti, did you learn of the extent, if any, to which airplanes were used in combating the native force?

Maj. Turner. Yes.

Mr. Angell. Do you know how many airplanes our forces had down there which they used in combat against the natives?

Maj. Turner. Approximately——

Mr. Angell. How many were there?

Maj. Turner. Three to five. There was one case where as many as three were out at one time.

Mr. Angell. For what purpose were those airplanes used?

Maj. Turner. For information and scouting, locating the bands of Cacos, and I believe in one case they attacked them.

Mr. Angell. Attacked them with what?

Maj. Turner. With machine guns.

Mr. Angell. Were they ever used for bombing, as far as you know?

Maj. Turner. I believe some homemade bombs were used, but that was immediately stopped.

Mr. Angell. Was the use of bombs upon orders from headquarters or upon the responsibility of officers immediately in charge of the airplanes.

Maj. Turner. I do not believe that any orders were ever issued to use bombs; that is, orders from headquarters. In fact, I am sure none were issued while I was there.

Mr. Angell. Why was it stopped, if you know?

Maj. Turner. I do not know why they were stopped, but I do not believe they were effective anyway. There were not enough Haitians together to make it worth while to drop a bomb.

Mr. Angell. Did you know of specific instances where bombs from airplanes were used?

Maj. Turner. No.

Mr. Angell. Your knowledge on that point is confined to knowledge of the fact in general, that airplanes had been on some occasions used as a means of dropping bombs?

Maj. Turner. Yes; I know of only one case, and I do not believe it happened while I was there—I know it did not—but they dropped a bomb, I heard talk about it.

Mr. Angell. Did it result in any deaths, as far as you know, in that particular instance?

Maj. Turner. I do not remember. I remember the talk among the aviators down there; they had no success whatever with bombs. They never got enough Haitians together to make it worth while to drop bombs.

Mr. Angell. Were the bombs dropped on villages?

Maj. Turner. Oh, no.

Mr. Angell. You testified that when our marine or gendarmerie forces came upon the Cacos they jumped them, and that there was firing on both sides?

Maj. Turner. Yes.

Mr. Angell. That, you say, resulted sometimes in the death of natives—of Cacos?

Maj. Turner. Yes.

Mr. Angell. Have you any idea of the number of Cacos killed under those circumstances?

Maj. Turner. Altogether, you mean, throughout Haiti from the time we occupied it?

Mr. Angell. What is your understanding of those figures?

Maj. Turner. I should say about 2,100. I know almost exactly how many were killed between October 1, 1919, and October 1, 1920.

Mr. Angel. Can you tell us what that number was, approximately?

Maj. Turner. It was 1,132.

Mr. Angell. That is the number of Haitians killed between October 1, 1919, and the following October, 1920?

Maj. Turner. Yes.

Mr. Angell. Those are the official figures?

Maj. Turner. Those are the official figures.

Mr. ANGELL. You think those figures are accurate?

Maj. TURNER. Except probably for the first two months, October and November, and they are approximately accurate. You can call the figure of 1,132 accurate. They were all killed in action, every one of these.

Mr. ANGELL. You testified, if I remember correctly, that you had no doubt there were many killings of men working under the corvee while they attempted to escape. Have you any idea, even approximately, of the number killed in this manner?

Maj. TURNER. At first I thought there were quite a lot, but later I have been paring it down, and I should say probably a hundred or less.

Mr. HOWE. During the whole occupation?

Maj. TURNER. Yes. I have no figures to prove that at all; it is merely my opinion on it. At first, in taking the testimony, it was a good deal worse than it was later. As I got to learn them better I scaled down my figures a lot on everything.

Mr. ANGELL. Those would be native Haitians who had been killed, presumably, while trying to escape from the forced labor on the roads?

Maj. TURNER. Yes. I would like to say that the 2,100 approximately were what our figures gave when I was down there. I am also of the opinion that that is exaggerated, particularly the number of deaths that happened prior to October 1, 1919. I happened to know of a case where it was reported that 50 were killed, and on investigation only one dead body was found at the scene of the action. Before we took these records and made them correct, quite often reports would come in that cacos had been jumped and a certain number killed, and the number killed seemed to be such a great percentage of the number supposed to be in the band that orders were issued that the reports of killings would include only dead bodies found, and the percentage then dropped back to normal or below normal, considering the actual number of deaths.

Mr. HOWE. The estimates turned out to be higher than the actual number?

Maj. TURNER. Yes. As I say, in this case where a major was killed down there a report came in that they had been attacked and that they had killed about 50, and that was accepted on the records. An investigation was made, and when they looked it up they found one dead body and no sign of anybody else having been hurt. I also know that reports had come in that, for example, 75 Cacos were met at a certain point and 25 were killed, and on investigation I found sometimes that they found straw hats, and considered that the men who lost their hats were killed.

Mr. ANGELL. Referring to the letter signed by Lieut. Col. Hooker, which is addressed to the brigade commander, dated February 28, 1920, which was the report of your investigation, and particularly referring to paragraph 2 of that letter [reading]:

"We are of the opinion that Maj. Wells and Capt. Doxey knew that corvee existed; that inhabitants were being maltreated and killed; and to a certain extent we are convinced that some reluctance was shown in keeping Port au Prince fully posted as to the true conditions."

I would ask you whether that represented your final opinion as to those points or whether you have had any occasion whatever to change your opinion?

Maj. TURNER. Yes; I am quite well satisfied that the inhabitants were taken in the corvee and some were killed in jumping the corvee. There is no question about that.

May I go back again and say also that between October 1, 1919, and October 1, 1920, there were exactly 298 encounters with bandits, and in those 298 encounters there were 1,132 killed, which averages less than 5 killed per engagement.

Mr. ANGELL. During the course of your investigation of the corvee system, were you able to learn for how long a period the natives were kept at work under forced labor?

Maj. TURNER. Yes; I think some of them were kept at work as long as two months.

Mr. ANGELL. And were you able to form any opinion as to the general way of keeping these natives at work in districts other than those in which they lived?

Maj. TURNER. The corvees existed only at Maissade and Hinche. I think that was after the order of September 1, 1918, forbidding the corvee. I did not take the corvee into consideration before that at all.

Mr. ANGELL. So, as to the corvee, your report deals with its continuance after October 1, 1918?

Maj. TURNER. Yes.

Mr. ANGELL. In your opinion, based upon your investigation of the corvee system, did the men who were laboring under the system as you found it, or learned of it, in the Hinche or Maissade district, after October, 1918, object to being kept at work there for periods running up to two months?

Maj. TURNER. Yes; I think they did object.

Mr. ANGELL. Their labor then under those conditions was not in any proper sense voluntary labor?

Maj. TURNER. No.

Mr. ANGELL. Did you hear rumors or reports of cruelty or abuses or killings attributed to one Capt. Fitzgerald Brown at St. Marc?

Maj. TURNER. Yes; that was Fitzgerald Brown. I did hear something about that, but it all turned out—this was after my investigation that I came on Fitzgerald Brown—that Fitzgerald Brown was a boaster and just a plain fool. He had no standing whatever.

Mr. ANGELL. Did you hear any reports of complaints by natives that he had killed or abused prisoners at the prison in St. Marc?

Maj. TURNER. No.

Mr. ANGELL. Was he an enlisted man or a noncommissioned officer of the marines and a captain of the gendarmes?

Maj. TURNER. He was a sergeant; yes.

Mr. ANGELL. And a captain of the gendarmes?

Maj. TURNER. Yes.

Mr. ANGELL. Have you had occasion to see the Haitian memoir printed in the record, in which, on pages 30 to 32 of the printed record, are 25 specific alleged cases of killings and abuses of natives on the part of gendarmes and marines?

Maj. TURNER. No; I never saw that before.

Mr. ANGELL. Glance over this list, and refer particularly to the instances numbered on these pages, 1, 2, 4, 5, and 11. I will ask you whether you heard at the time of your investigation of afterwards any complaints or reports regarding those specific instances, and if so, what investigation you made of them.

Maj. TURNER. No; I have never heard of any of them. If they had been reported, I certainly would have heard of them. If anything of that sort was heard of, it was reported and investigated.

Mr. ANGELL. Major, have you read the statements or are you familiar with the statements of Gen. A. W. Catlin, dated December 31, 1919, and of Lieut. Col. A. S. Williams, dated January 6, 1920, both sworn and contained in the Lay report on pages 65 to 67 and 85 to 99, respectively?

Maj. TURNER. I have read them, but I am not familiar with them.

Mr. ANGELL. From your recollection, having read them, can you state whether or not you agreed substantially with the statements and conclusions therein made and reached?

Maj. TURNER. I would like to read them over again before answering that question. I read those a year and a half ago, and I do not remember the matter at all at this time.

(Thereupon, at 4 o'clock p. m., the committee adjourned to meet to-morrow, Thursday, October 27, 1921, at 10.30 o'clock a. m.)

INQUIRY INTO OCCUPATION AND ADMINISTRATION OF HAITI AND SANTO DOMINGO.

THURSDAY, OCTOBER 27, 1921.

UNITED STATES SENATE,
SELECT COMMITTEE ON HAITI AND SANTO DOMINGO,
Washington, D. C.

The committee met at 10.30 o'clock a. m., pursuant to adjournment, Senator Tasker L. Oddie presiding.

Also present: Mr. Walter Bruce Howe, Mr. Ernest Angell, and Maj. Edwin N. McClellan, in their respective representative capacities as hereinbefore indicated.

STATEMENT OF BRIG. GEN. SMEDLEY D. BUTLER, UNITED STATES MARINE CORPS, COMMANDING MARINES, QUANTICO, VA.

Mr. HOWE. General, will you give your name, rank, and present station, please?

Gen. BUTLER. Smedley D. Butler, brigadier general, United States Marine Corps, commanding marines, Quantico, Va.

Mr. HOWE. General, how long have you been in the Marine Corps?

Gen. BUTLER. I have been in the Marine Corps 23 years and 6 months.

Mr. HOWE. Were you in Haiti in 1916?

Gen. BUTLER. I was.

Mr. HOWE. About when did you go to Haiti at that time?

Gen. BUTLER. I landed in Haiti on the 10th of August, 1915, and remained there continuously until the 9th day of March, 1918.

Mr. HOWE. You were commander of the gendarmerie of Haiti?

Gen. BUTLER. I was the first commander and organizer of the gendarmerie of Haiti.

Mr. HOWE. When did you assume those duties?

Gen. BUTLER. I was detailed by the commanding officer of the naval forces operating in Haiti on the 3d day of December, 1915, to organize the gendarmerie. Subsequent to the passage of the act of Congress in June, 1916, authorizing officers of the United States service to serve with the Government of Haiti, I received my regular appointment in an order from the commandant of the Marine Corps, dated September 1, 1916, and during the period between December 3, 1915, and September 1, 1916, I served as such, but only under the orders of the commander of the naval forces, Admiral Caperton.

Mr. HOWE. Between August, 1915, and December, 1915, what were your duties?

Gen. BUTLER. I was commanding the forces in the field in the north in various places.

Mr. HOWE. In the north?

Gen. BUTLER. My forces operated from Gonaives to Cape Haitien, and from Cape Haitien to the Dominican border, and south to the line running east and west through Gonaives, known as the district of the north.

Mr. HOWE. When you, in September, 1916, got your orders from the commandant of the Marine Corps, was your status then changed; and if so, how, by the operation of those orders?

Gen. BUTLER. My status was simply changed in this respect, that what I had been doing previously, under the orders of the occupation, I proceeded to do under the orders of the President of Haiti. I had always acted under the President of Haiti, but had consulted with the American commander.

Mr. HOWE. Before those orders in September, 1916?

Gen. BUTLER. Yes, sir. After that I still considered myself, due to the presence of martial law in Haiti, a member of the forces of the occupation, but did nothing with respect to the Haitian people without first discussing the matter with the President of Haiti.

Mr. HOWE. And receiving his directions?

Gen. BUTLER. And receiving his directions.

Mr. HOWE. During the time you were organizing the gendarmerie—that is to say, from December, 1915, to September, 1916—will you please give us a little more definite idea as to the extent to which you consulted the President of Haiti and took his directions?

Gen. BUTLER. During the period from the 3d of December, 1915, to the 29th of January, 1916, the gendarmerie performed no functions whatsoever except those necessary to its own organization. It was assembled in a number of towns for drill and organization and equipment purposes only. It performed no police functions; it was nothing but a school.

Mr. HOWE. And consequently you, as its organizer, were in charge of no police functions?

Gen. BUTLER. No police; and had no connection whatsoever with the Haitian President, except as to its future development and status. During this period, with the assistance of the President of Haiti, we wrote and prepared for promulgation, upon the confirmation of the service by our own Congress, a set of rules and regulations for the government of the gendarmerie, in accordance with the treaty, which rules and regulations were promulgated and enforced in the name of the President of Haiti, and the whole conduct of the force of the gendarmerie during the whole time I was in it was directly in accordance with the directions and orders given by the President of Haiti himself.

Mr. HOWE. And in the preparation of those orders he was consulted?

Gen. BUTLER. Every day.

Mr. HOWE. Did those early orders and regulations meet with his approval?

Gen. BUTLER. Absolutely, or they could not have been published, because the treaty stated that they had to be promulgated by the President of Haiti.

Mr. HOWE. You are referring to Article X, no doubt, of the treaty?

Gen. BUTLER. I am referring to the gendarmerie agreement here, which has the same effect with us as the treaty.

Mr. HOWE. Will you give a reference to that gendarmerie agreement?

Gen. BUTLER. It is an agreement dated the 24th of August, 1916, in which appears this provision:

" Rules and regulations for the administration and discipline of the gendarmerie shall be issued by the commandant after being approved by the President of Haiti."

That was strictly carried out. That is article 7 of the protocol of the 24th of August, 1916.

Mr. HOWE. While you were organizing the gendarmerie did you perform any other duties?

Gen. BUTLER. I did not.

Mr. HOWE. After you were duly appointed commandant—is that the correct term, or commander?

Gen. BUTLER. I would like to bring this in. On the 1st day of February, 1916, the following proclamation was issued by Admiral Caperton:

PROCLAMATION.

Whereas the President of Haiti and his cabinet have decreed that on this date the commandants of communes and the chiefs of sections are abolished, and also that all military and police duties of the commandants of arrondissements are taken away, it is hereby ordered that from this date all the military and police duties heretofore performed by those officers be performed by the gendarmerie of Haiti, supported by the expeditionary forces under my command.

By order of Rear Admiral W. B. Caperton, United States Navy, commanding United States forces in Haiti and Haitian waters.

LITTLETON W. T. WALLER,
Colonel, United States Marine Corps,
Commanding United States Expeditionary Forces Ashore in Haiti.

PORT AU PRINCE, HAITI, February 1, 1916.

Mr. HOWE. The date of that proclamation was February 1, 1916?

Gen. BUTLER. Yes.

Mr. Howe. How did that affect you, sir?

Gen. Butler. That made me chief of police in Haiti. I assumed all responsibility for the safety and proper policing of the Republic of Haiti.

Mr. Howe. Through what instrumentality did you operate?

Gen. Butler. The gendarmerie.

Mr. Howe. Then the gendarmerie did begin to operate before September, 1916?

Gen. Butler. Yes, sir.

Mr. Howe. I had misunderstood you. I thought I understood that they did not operate until September, 1916.

Gen. Butler. I thought I put that in there; I intended to put it in; until the 1st of February.

Mr. Howe. Then the gendarmerie, as a going operating institution——

Gen. Butler. Commenced to perform its legal functions——

Mr. Howe. On February 1, 1916. Is that correct?

Gen. Butler. Yes, sir; to perform its functions, under Article X of the treaty, on the 1st of February.

Mr. Howe. So the formative period, as such, lasted from December, 1915, to the 1st of February, 1916?

Gen. Butler. Under my control. Previous to my control it had been in process of organization for six weeks, but when I took command of the gendarmerie it had a total personnel of about 600, and on the 1st of February, when we assumed police charge, we had 1,500.

Mr. Howe. Will you describe the organization of the gendarmerie, please?

Gen. Butler. It is organized exactly as laid down here in the protocol which is in evidence.

Mr. Howe. As in the protocol of August 24, 1916?

Gen. Butler. Yes.

Mr. Howe. How soon after that protocol came into effect did the organization conform with it?

Gen. Butler. About seven months.

Mr. Howe. Early, then, in 1917?

Gen. Butler. Yes; late in 1916, if I remember correctly, on the 1st of October, 1916, the gendarmerie was completed.

Mr. Howe. Then from February 1, 1916, up until that time in 1917 the gendarmerie was in course of organization?

Gen. Butler. 1916, sir; the 1st of October, 1916. There were only six or seven months in there.

Mr. Howe. Let us get this straight. You were detailed to organize and command the gendarmerie in December, 1915?

Gen. Butler. Yes, sir.

Mr. Howe. By proclamation on February 1, 1916, the gendarmerie began to operate and function?

Gen. Butler. Right.

Mr. Howe. On August 24, 1916, the status was somewhat changed by the protocol, was it not?

Gen. Butler. Yes.

Mr. Howe. Which outlined the extent of the organization and made definite many of its functions; is that right?

Gen. Butler. Correct.

Mr. Howe. And some seven months later——

Gen. Butler. No, sir; only two months later.

Mr. Howe. Two months later on, in October, 1916, the gendarmerie attained its——

Gen. Butler. Its full strength.

Mr. Howe. Its full strength.

Gen. Butler. Yes, sir; that is right.

Mr. Howe. I will just ask you, General, to describe how you went about building that up, how you recruited and how you selected your officers.

Gen. Butler. The marine forces in Haiti were distributed throughout the Republic, different sized organizations, from a platoon to a battalion, being stationed in the smaller towns, preserving peace. There was no Haitian police force; there was no Haitian order; there was nothing but pillaging and riot until the marines arrived, when they took over this police, and martial law was declared by the United States.

Mr. Howe. You took over the police duties?

Gen. BUTLER. We took over the police duties and performed them until the formation of the gendarmerie made it possible for them to take it over.

Mr. HOWE. General, I want to get back later on in the examination to a few of the facts about the selection of your forces—enlisted men and officers.

Gen. BUTLER. That is, the organization of the gendarmerie and how it was done?

Mr. HOWE. Yes.

Gen. BUTLER. In each town where a considerable force of marines was stationed—that is, a company or more—one commissioned officer of marines and certain noncommissioned officers and privates were detailed by the commander of the marines in Haiti to enlist and organize and train Haitians for this gendarmerie, so that each body of marines resolved itself into a little training camp.

Mr. HOWE. And recruiting station?

Gen. BUTLER. And recruiting station, the Haitians voluntarily enlisting on enlistment papers similar to those used in our corps. They were dressed in our clothes. The Haitian Government bought the excess marine clothing, in order that we might have some distinguishing mark for them, and dressed them just as marines were dressed, with the exception that we did not give them the Marine Corps device. They had no Marine Corps devices, and they had plain Haitian buttons.

That system continued until the 1st of February, 1916, when it was necessary for the gendarmerie to stand on its own feet. On the 29th day of January Gen. Waller, commanding the marines in Haiti, notified me that the Haitian Government had decided to give up trying to maintain law and order and had said, " Now, you Americans do it with your gendarmerie "; and Gen. Waller gave me two days to garrison Haiti.

Mr. HOWE. With the gendarmerie?

Gen. BUTLER. With the gendarmerie.

Mr. HOWE. What did the Haitians mean, then, by saying to the Americans to preserve law and order with their gendarmerie, when the gendarmerie was the Haitian gendarmerie?

Gen. BUTLER. It was the Haitian gendarmerie. We understood it to be an effort on their part to embarrass us, because they well knew that our gendarmerie, or their organizing for them under the provisions of a treaty already confirmed, was not complete; but in two days we established 117 posts around Haiti, and on the night of the 1st of February I reported to the commander, to Col. Waller, that the police force of Haiti was complete, but in reduced numbers. We did not have a sufficient force.

Mr. HOWE. Did you have any difficulty in getting recruits?

Gen. BUTLER. Absolutely none. We took the best men in the country.

Mr. HOWE. Was there competition among them for recognition?

Gen. BUTLER. Very great competition. An actual blood test taken by me of 1,200 gendarmes selected at random, which gendarmes had been previously selected from 50,000 of the best Haitians, showed that 95 per cent of them were diseased. That is the material with which we worked.

Mr. HOWE. But you had plenty to select from, and you tried to select the best?

Gen. BUTLER. Yes; and we made every effort to cure those that we had, so that they would not go to sleep standing up in the daytime. That was the one test. I have frequently found a sentry on a post in front of an important building sound asleep, standing up with the sun shining in his face. That is not his fault. He was diseased. An examination showed that 95 per cent of them had blood diseases and 85 per cent had intestinal worms, and we took immediate measures to cure it, and before I left Haiti the gendarmes could keep awake for two or three hours.

Let me say something about the faithfulness of the gendarmes; I have said something about what they can not help. Never during the time I was in Haiti, nor from any reports I have received since, has any disloyalty on the part of a gendarme occurred. I never heard of a case. I gave the Haitian medal of honor to three gendarmes who gave their arms and their legs for their white officers. They are sergeants and kept at headquarters on light duty as show pieces or examples of the most devoted loyalty. The action of one of them is particularly affecting.

Mr. HOWE. I think we would like to hear that.

Gen. BUTLER. At a little place called Circa la Source a gendarmerie officer named Kelly—this was in the early days, early in 1916, shortly after the occupation of the country by the gendarmerie and the taking over of the police duties—Kelly was stationed at this town in a little native hut that we rented for police purposes. With him were 16 gendarmes as the police force of that subdistrict. He personally lived in a small mud hut next to the police station. One night while asleep his house was attacked by a large number of bandits. The gendarmes in the station next door were surprised, and the sentry, due to physical or other reasons, was asleep, and they fled. They did not run away, but they just fled out into the bushes and re-formed. But the bandits were not after the gendarmes; they were after the American officer, so they attacked his little house. Kelly was a very bold, gallant fellow. He grabbed his pistol when he heard the firing, and rushed toward the door. His gendarme orderly, who was sleeping in the same room with him, got up and threw his arms around Kelly and spoke to him in Creole. It must be remembered that none of us spoke their language, yet we taught them to drill in English. All the commands were in English. Kelly was unable to understand all that this gendarme said to him, but he gathered enough to know that the gendarme did not wish him to go out of that door to be killed. Kelly did not agree with him, but threw him to one side and grabbed the door and pulled it open. The gendarme knew the habits of his friends. He had been a Caco himself. My orderly in Port au Prince was the worst Caco in Haiti, and I picked him out because he was the ugliest brute I ever saw, and I trusted him with my children, my wife, and everything. He was the most faithful man I have ever known. This gendarme knew the habits of the men outside, and that they would fire through that lighted door the moment Kelly appeared in it, and when Kelly opened the door he threw himself in front of him and they put five bullets through him. They did not kill him, but he had to have one leg amputated, and one arm.

Now, you see why the American officers like these gendarmes. They will give their lives for you any time, and there has never been one instance of their failing loyalty to us, never once.

There is a major here at Quantico who with five of them was beset by 250 Cacos, and these five stuck right by him. Never once have they gone back on us.

Whenever I had an inspection to make in the woods, I left my family with this ugly Caco sleeping on a couch on the front porch of my house, and he never would move for two weeks. They would take his food to him. And nobody would come into the yard either. I trusted him absolutely. It is a great army that gendarmerie.

Mr. Howe. What kind of a country did you have to operate in? Tell us how Haiti looks.

Gen. Butler. Haiti has about 190,000 acres of flat land, and the rest is mountains. Haiti looks like a crumpled-up piece of paper, as a French admiral said when Napoleon sent him over. The highest peak in Haiti is 7,000 feet, and it is divided into three sections. There are the plains of the north along the Atlantic Ocean, facing to the north. They run in width from a quarter of a mile to 10 miles. Then you come to a range of mountains running east and west, mountains about 3,000 feet high, a ridge range. You cross those, make a slight dip, and arrive at another range of peaks, 4,000 feet high. You drop on the other side to what is known as the valley of the Artibonite River, which is approximately 90 miles long and 8 miles wide. It is not flat, but it is rolling country. It could not be characterized as flat, tillable land, without a great deal of work, not all of it. Then you come to a small range of hills—this is going south—which you cross, and you come to the plains of Cul de Sac, at the eastern end of which lies the city of Port au Prince. The plains of Cul de Sac are 10 miles wide and 20 miles long, and they are perfectly flat. Then you cross another high range of mountains, running from 1,500 feet to 7,000 feet. It is there you find the highest mountains, and you drop from there over to the South Atlantic, over the top right down. There is practically no flat land on the other side at all.

Mr. Howe. How much flat land is there in the whole place?

Gen. Butler. About 190,000 acres absolutely flat land.

Mr. Howe. The rest of it is up and down hill?

Gen. Butler. I will take that back; 180,000 acres.

Mr. Howe. How many people live in the country?

Gen. Butler. Two million and a half, approximately.

Mr. Howe. Are they getting more numerous?

Gen. Butler. No; I should say the population will never become very much larger. Perhaps it will go to 3,000,000. They increase very rapidly, but they die off very rapidly. They are not a hardy, sturdy race at all.

Mr. Howe. Are they all colored people?

Gen. Butler. They were originally brought over from Africa. The importation of the black man into Haiti commenced about 1565, or the importation of slaves from Africa, about the same date as the founding of St. Augustine, according to my recollection of it—it has been several years since I read the history—and the importation continued during the whole of the French régime, and by 1789, when the French Revolution broke out in France, with its reflection in Haiti, the first overt act in France, you remember, was on the 14th of July, the fall of the Bastile, and the first outbreak in Haiti was in October, on the plains of the north. At that time the black population was about 400,000 and the white or foreign population about 40,000. Of course, there had been considerable mingling of the whites and blacks, and about 20 per cent of the 400,000 were mulattoes.

Do you want the caste system? Would that help you any?

Mr. Howe. Yes; I would like to have it. At the present time how many whites are there in Haiti? I mean living there.

Gen. Butler. Counting the American occupation?

Mr. Howe. Not counting the American occupation.

Gen. Butler. Not counting the military people?

Mr. Howe. Not counting the military people.

Gen. Butler. Two hundred or two hundred and fifty.

Mr. Howe. And the rest are colored or various degrees of mulatto?

Gen. Butler. Various degrees of dark blood.

Mr. Howe. Now, how about the caste system that you mentioned?

Gen. Butler. What we tried to provide for in the formation of our gendarmerie was a system which could be passed over to the Haitians, because it was well understood by us all that there was a limit to our treaty, and the country did not belong to us, and I never heard any American officer in Haiti express the desire to take it. We were all embued with the fact that we were trustees of a huge estate that belonged to minors. That was my viewpoint; that was the viewpoint I personally took, that the Haitians were our wards and that we were endeavoring to develop and make for them a rich and productive property, to be turned over to them at such time as our Government saw fit, before the expiration of the treaty. So in order to profit by the mistakes of the French we, of course, read the history of their gendarmerie and their caste system, which was the cause of their downfall.

As I told you, the original colored man in Haiti was a black African slave. The French settlers in the early days were adventurers. For 50 years no French women came to Haiti, and the blood became mixed until in 1789 about 20 per cent of it was mulatto. By that time the French had set up their caste system: that is, the rich plantation owners formed one set. They only came to Haiti during the sugar and coffee harvest season, and indigo was another part of the crop. They spent the rest of their time spending the proceeds of their labor, or the other man's labor, in Paris. A certain number of poor French farmers lived in Haiti all or most of the time. They were known as colonists. The French plantation owner, or Frenchman as he called himself, would not associate with the planter. That made the planter more or less unhappy, and it kept down his associates, and he had a tendency then to seek a person nearest his own color, and gradually an association sprung up between the mulatto and the French colonist which tied them together, and they intermarried. The blacks were out of it, the pure blacks. They were the best, and are still the most reliable, but they were entirely out of it, just pure slaves.

It had been a custom on the part of the French planter when a child appeared who had his blood in his veins to free that child and perhaps the mother. That gave the mulatto or the octoroon—the name depending on the degree of black blood in his veins—property. According to the law in Haiti, a person with one thirty-second black blood in his veins was a black; if he had one sixty-fourth black blood, he was white. That is published in the decrees of the King. That gave a certain number of mulattoes property, due to this freedom, and they soon became quite prominent and prosperous, and they formed a league with the colonists. The planter was busy traveling back and forth to Paris and caring very little for what occurred in Haiti until the French Revolution. Then the legislative bodies in Paris, the revolutionists, called on Haiti to equalize and not have any color line or any quality. They said, "We are all free and equal," and they took over to France a lot of representatives of the mulattoes, who told their grievances, and the French rulers—I do not remember just who they were, Robespierre, perhaps—who were in charge at the time sent over orders to abolish all distinction.

The planters resented that, and in the end the planters and the blacks made a combination against the mulattoes and the colonists. That is the way the line-up occurred. Among the mulattoes was the gendarmerie for the maintenance of law and order, in addition to the regular French garrison. It was composed of the better mulattoes, but they had mixed blood among their officers. The troops were black and some mulatto, but their officers were natives with black blood, and when the test was put upon them they did not stand. So, in forming ours we had but three colored officers until we could teach the Haitians to obey an order, irrespective of the giver, profiting by the failure of the previous gendarmerie and the subsequent massacre of women and children that followed, due to their turnover. We followed that principle. The three colored officers were appointed by the President, as he appointed us all, as officers in his personal bodyguard; and they were the three most trustworthy noncommissioned officers that we have had after six months drill.

Mr. Howe. That you have developed in six months drill?

Gen. Butler. That we developed in six months. We assisted him in selecting them. They were all men of so-called good family, and most desirable to the President. We had very little success with the Haitian officer. I tried two or three others, without success. I did not give them regular commissions, in order not to bruise their feelings by having to reduce them, so we gave them the position without any of the emoluments to try them out, and gave them districts; and we found they were brutal with the people, unnecessarily harsh; that a little authority encouraged them to square old accounts with any person with whom they had had any difficulty, which they remembered for years, so it was not entirely successful, although as noncommissioned officers, controlled by the marines, they were most excellent. When independent authority was handed them, they became too brutal. I do not mean that they ever killed anybody, but they were always imprisoning people and causing us considerable worry. Never once during the time I was in command of the gendarmerie did I ever fail to severely punish, even going so far as to execute, gendarmes who abused the people. The executions, of course, required the sanction and approval of the President of Haiti. He signed the death warrants. On one occasion we shot a gendarme for shooting a prisoner. We never tolerated abuse of prisoners or the public.

Mr. Howe. What about the public there? How could you describe those, General, the Haitians?

Gen. Butler. The Haitian people?

Mr. Howe. Yes.

Gen. Butler. The Haitian people are divided into two classes; one class wears shoes and the other does not. The class that wears shoes is about 1 per cent. I should say that not more than one-fifth of 1 per cent of the population of Haiti can read and write. Many of those that wear shoes can not read and write. In fact, many of the teachers can not read and write. I remember one instance, in sending to a certain district money to pay a school-teacher who had a claim against the Government, the gendarmerie officer took the money to the school-teacher, and he said, " I can not sign that receipt; I can not sign my name." He said, " You are a teacher, are you not?" He said, " Yes; I am a teacher of reading, but not of writing."

Ninety-nine per cent of the people of Haiti are the most kindly, generous, hospitable, pleasure-loving people I have ever known. They would not hurt anybody. They are most gentle when in their natural state. When the other 1 per cent that wears vici kid shoes with long pointed toes and celluloid collars, stirs them up and incites them with liquor and voodoo stuff, they are capable of the most horrible atrocities; they are cannibals. They ate the liver of one marine. But in their natural state they are the most docile, harmless people in the world.

Mr. Howe. What were your relations with the ones that did not wear shoes?

Gen. Butler. Those that wear shoes I took as a joke. Without a sense of humor you could not live in Haiti among those people, among the shoe class.

Senator Oddie. What else did they wear besides shoes and collars?

Gen. Butler. They wore cut-away coats, brass-head canes, stove-pipe hats 3 inches in diameter, and anything they could put on to make themselves conspicuous. But the people who were barefooted, the women wearing mother hubbards and the men dungarees half way up to their knees, with scarred feet, indicating the hardest kind of toil, and with great blisters on their hands, and with the palms of their hands as hard as a piece of sole leather—those people you could absolutely trust. I went all over Haiti, living with them in their shacks, and they always gave you the best they had—food and anything they had in the world. They did not know the value of anything. They did not know anything about time, distance, or value.

Mr. Howe. How did you protect yourself when you went among them?

Gen. Butler. I never carried a gun the whole time I was there; it was not necessary. They would not hurt you. I took the President all over Haiti without a gun. He made speeches to them, encouraging them, and in every public work we wanted to undertake the President led the procession. I was his chauffeur. We rode in a Ford, but we carried an enormous Haitian flag in front, with the President's coat of arms, and we went with a great fanfare of trumpets, in a modest car, to be sure, but it was just exactly what they wanted. My object down there was to do what they wanted, not to make out of Haiti an America, but to make out of Haiti a first-class black man's country, and instead of import'ng our style of architecture down there, to develop a style of architecture suited to the colored man and to the country. When you go to Haiti, Senator, as you should, in order to properly understand this, you must see Christophe Citadel, which is one of the wonders of the western hemisphere. It is a perfect piece of Ha'tian architecture, designed by a Frenchman and an Englishman, both engineers and architects, but built to match the country. The average Haitian who gets a little money goes to France, and brings back some conception of a French palace and builds it, and destroys Ha'ti. What we wanted was clean little towns, with tidy thatch-roofed dwellings. That is what the country can afford, and that is what it ought to have, and then there would never be any temptation to anybody to grab it either.

Mr. Howe. Whom did you have to contend with down there—whom were you fighting?

Gen. Butler. We were not really fighting anybody. We were endeavoring to overcome certain obstacles created by the polit'cal element, obstacles in the road of accomplishment of the object I have just pointed out.

Senator Oddie. What percentage of the Cacos wore shoes?

Gen. Butler. None of the Cacos except the leaders and the politicians and the officers who put up the money, etc. They were the only ones.

Senator Oddie. How was a Caco created, trained, and developed, General?

Gen. Butler. He just grew; he had no training at all.

Senator Oddie. How did he grow?

Gen. Butler. How did the revolution run?

Senator Oddie. Yes. The revolution developed the Cacos; is that it?

Gen. Butler. All the discontented element that had nothing else to do and wanted a little loot would join up at this little town called Bodeaux, about 1 mile to the westward of the Massacre River, and there have a season of drinking, carousing, and debauchery, which would correspond in our m'litary service to a training period, and then this force would move on 14 miles to Fort Liberte.

Senator Oddie. Who would start this, General?

Gen. Butler. This would be started by anybody who wanted to be President, and could get enough money to provide rum and the sustenance of war, and get enough rifles together.

Senator Oddie. Where did he get them from?

Gen. Butler. They would be brought over from Santo Domingo, and loaned for this revolution, and when Santo Domingo had one they would be sent back. Being near the boundary line between autonomous Republics side by side, a man was perfectly safe in jumping over the boundary, so they established themselves right near the boundary, so that in case they got caught with the goods they could jump over the river and be safe, and likewise they could be supplied from the rear. Then, when the movement received sufficient strength, it passed on to Fort Liberte, which they captured, and published all over Haiti that the customhouse was in their hands, which would indicate to us a certain amount of revenue, but, as a matter of fact the customhouse had no revenue, because there were no exports or imports, as it was a closed port. But it gave them a certain prominence, and attracted more recruits to the colors, and the army would then move on to a town called Le Tron. After spending about a week in Fort Liberte, burning the town and getting some more rum, they would move down to Le Tron, which they would burn and announce the capture of. Then in order to get to a railroad and save some walking, and to give them more prominence, they would cross the mountains on the trail, and stop at a place called St. Suzanne where they would establish headquarters, and the government. would send out a proclamation for three or four days, a notice to join them. They then went down and into the valey of the Grande Riviere and took and captured the town of Grande Riviere. That was the regular course of events.

By this time the President in power would be thoroughly alarmed, and he would take the Haitian navy, consisting of an old Ward liner called the *Nord Alexis*, and put on board his army of 600 or 700 men, and send them up to Cape Haitien, the principal town in the north. There they would disembark, and would march out, or ride out on the railroad, the officers or leaders in little hand cars, or with a locomotive, if they could persuade the American authorities to give them one.

Mr. Howe. The American authorities?

Gen. Butler. This railroad is owned by Americans.

Mr. Howe. Not the American Government authorities?

Gen. Butler. No. And they would march out to the crossroads, which was at the kilometer post 17, where a battle would occur, and you will see the evidence of the battles by the graves all around, hundreds of them, and the Government forces in the last seven revolutions were always licked. I do not know whether there were any previous accounts of a victory or not, but in the last seven revolutions they got licked there, and those that were too tired to run would go over to the revolutionists, and those that could get transportation on the way back to Cape Haitien, would take what was left in the customhouse, quite a good customhouse, board the *Nord Alexis*, and sail back to Port au Prince with the discouraging news that their army had not been successful. The President then would organize another army, and lie in wait for them. In the meantime the revolutionists would advance on Cape Haitien, and of course, there would be no fighting, and they would capture Cape Haitien and take over the customhouse, issue more proclamations, have a great many speeches, and set up another government.

By this time the movement would be quite large. Then it was a question of marching across the mountains that I have described to you, those ranges, down to the valley, to Gonaives. At one time, in one revolution, at Gonaives there was a fight, but generally there was very little trouble encountered there, and they would progress farther down along the railroad track to the town of St. Marc. They would progress overland to St. Marc, take that with its customs house, and then down the railroad track to a place called Arcahaie, which was the approved jousting place for the final scene of the revolution. There the President's army—not the President, but his army—would meet the victorious revolutionists, and be defeated and absorbed and the tragedy would be reported to the President, who, if he were fortunate and were agile, would get on a ship and leave with the treasury for Paris. If he were not very agile, or if he had some personal friends near him who did not care much about him, they killed him, as the record of the Presidents shows.

Here is a list of the Presidents of Haiti. I might give you a few of the figures. Between 1911 and 1915 they had seven Presidents. Those are the seven revolutions of which I speak.

Mr. Howe. Did those seven revolutions follow this general course you outlined?

Gen. Butler. Yes; they followed the general course, but sometimes there would be a little diversion. In the last revolution the slaughter by Vilbrun Guillaume Sam of the prisoners in the jail brought it to a head before the army came in from Arcahaie, and he could not get away. He took refuge in the French legation, but was finally pulled out. A mob searched the French legatiton, took him out and threw him into the street, where he was cut up into 200 pieces and dragged around the streets on pieces of string, what was left of his body. That was when we landed.

Mr. Howe. During the American occupation have any such revolutions broken out—any organized revolutions?

Gen. Butler. No.

Mr. Howe. What was the nature of the active operations of the gendarmerie during your time there?

Gen. Butler. Just the ordinary police duty. We had two instances such as I spoke of in connection with the heroism of that gendarme, little local affairs, those two, during my period.

Mr. Howe. Were there any Cacos around then?

Gen. BUTLER. No; there were these bands that might be called Cacos, but they went up in thin air. They were very small, and there was no concerted movement.

Mr. HOWE. Were they troublesome?

Gen. BUTLER. No. After that one attack on Kelly the whole thing disappeared, the whole band disintegrated, and after the attack on Hinche, about a year following that, the band dispersed, and we never heard anything more of it.

Mr. HOWE. Was the attack on Hinche before or after you left; you left in March, 1919?

Gen. BUTLER. That was before I left. I will describe that to you. A captain named Doxie, a captain of the gendarmerie, had brought $1,200 gold in Haitian money, which made an enormous pile of Haitian bills. This money was to pay his gendarmes and to pay the police of his post. It was in a wooden box, and on the day he received it he counted it, and while counting it the lid of the box was open and in walked some Haitian citizens and saw this money. The next morning at 2 o'clock, a large number, approximately estimated at 57, of Haitians attacked this little house in which he was living, and he was awakened by a hammering on the front door. He thought it was a drunken man, and called, "Go on away," in Creole. As he did so the hammering became more violent and the door fell in just as he got out of his bunk, and he saw in the bright moonlight a number of men armed with spears, rifles, and swords, pushing into the room. The door was narrow, so that not a great number could come in at one time, and he reached for his pistol and shot three of them dead.

This provided a little discouragement to the rest, and they hesitated just long enough to give him an opportunity to face about and fire into the crowd which had broken in the rear door. I do not remember how many he killed, but two or three. His pistol was then empty, and the crowd moved on in in front, but fortunately he had a riot gun at hand, with which he shot a few more. The crowd then scattered. The gendarmes were in their barracks two squares up the streets, and it only lasted two or three minutes. The gendarmes then pursued the scattering band, and the leader was shot by a sergeant of the gendarmes. The next day the whole thing was over, and there was no further trouble, and the investigation through our own secret service indicated that it was an effort to get the $1,200; that Doxie was very popular with the people, and that nobody had any desire to kill him if he would hand out the $1,200.

Those were the two instances of any serious trouble until I left Haiti.

Mr. HOWE. Was it necessary for you to send out patrols with any frequency?

Gen. BUTLER. The whole of the country was patrolled every day, for various reasons. One was to obtain from every citizen any complaint that he might wish to make. The patrols were both mounted and on foot. They went along the trails, and listened to the stories of the natives, and they had a certain system of little cards, by which we could keep a record of their movements, but not an accurate record.

Mr. HOWE. Of the movements of the patrol?

Gen. BUTLER. Of the patrol. They would be ordered to a certain man's plantation, and the man would be asked to indorse on the card that the patrol had been there. That was the system that we tried to carry out. Of course, it was not entirely successful in certain places.

Mr. HOWE. Then, outside of these two outbreaks that you mentioned, the instances that you have mentioned, there was no serious disorder for the gendarmerie to cope with during the time you were its commander?

Gen. BUTLER. No.

Mr. HOWE. That would carry us back, then, to December, 1915?

Gen. BUTLER. Between December, 1915, and March, 1918, there were just the two instances I spoke of. At Arcahaie, in January, 1918, five shots were fired, but the firers were not seen, and although it created a sufficient excitement to warrant a telephone call, we never found out who did it, and no one was hurt. They were the only shots that were fired.

Mr. HOWE. Now, General, who was responsible for health, education, and public works on the island, the Americans or Haitians?

Gen. BUTLER. The Americans.

Mr. HOWE. Now, let us take them one at a time. First, let us take health.

Gen. BUTLER. That was handled by the Americans. Under the treaty of 1915 there was a sanitary engineer who was responsible for the health of Haiti.

Mr. HOWE. Who was in charge of carrying out any health regulations that were in existence?

Gen. BUTLER. During my time the wishes of the sanitary engineer were carried out or enforced by the gendarmerie, provided they did not in any way endanger the public peace. Frequently I considered that certain wishes of the sanitary engineer were unreasonable and put an unnecessarily heavy burden upon certain individuals, and I would not carry them out, not have the police enforce them.

Mr. HOWE. Illustrate that.

Gen. BUTLER. For instance, on John Brown Avenue in Port au Prince was a poor woman who lived in a house on a sloping hill. She was ordered by one of the local sanitary inspectors, a subordinate of the sanitary engineer——

Mr. HOWE. A Haitian?

Gen. BUTLER. A Haitian—to have her yard filled up to a certain level. This would have cost her considerable money, and she was very poor, so I notified the sanitary engineer that I thought it was unreasonable and could not see my way clear to have the police arrest and punish this poor woman.

Mr. HOWE. Officially to whom did the sanitary engineer report?

Gen. BUTLER. The minister of public works.

Mr. HOWE. A Haitian?

Gen. BUTLER. A Haitian. The chief of the gendarmerie did not report to anybody but the President.

Mr. HOWE. The health department?

Gen. BUTLER. That was a public work.

Mr. HOWE. Was under the Haitian Government, directed by the Americans, as provided in the treaty?

Gen. BUTLER. As provided in the treaty; yes.

Mr. HOWE. Whence came the funds for the health department?

Gen. BUTLER. Those were derived from the collection of the external revenue, the customs. They were provided by the general receiver, who comes under the direction of the financial adviser.

Mr. HOWE. They did not come from American appropriations, then?

Gen. BUTLER. No.

Mr. HOWE. You had this much money to spend, that you could get from that one source, and no more?

Gen. BUTLER. In the beginning we had a certain amount.

Mr. HOWE. I mean for health work.

Gen. BUTLER. For health work we had just as much as was allotted.

Mr. HOWE. But that was not your business, except in so far as your gendarmerie had to carry out the directions of the sanitary engineer?

Gen. BUTLER. Yes; with several exceptions. Out in the smaller towns, where it would have been too expensive to maintain a direct sanitary representative, the officers and noncommissioned officers of the gendarmerie acted as sanitary officers to save expense, and their reports were made to the sanitary engineer, through the chief of the gendarmerie.

Senator ODDIE. What policy, if any, was definitely adopted in regard to improving the health conditions?

Gen. BUTLER. Up to the time I left Haiti the steps were these: All towns were cleaned up, sewers were opened, drainage effected, wells were covered in order to keep the water as pure as possible, little dispensaries, wherever possible, were set up, with American doctors or members of the Hospital Corps of the American Navy to administer to the people. The quarantine service had been started and was in operation to guard against the introduction of diseases from other countries.

Mr. HOWE. How were the dispensaries paid for, and the quarantine stations?

Gen. BUTLER. Generally the dispensary was in the police station, because it cost less money than maintaining it elsewhere, or if the town owned a public building the police would be in one part, the judge in one part, and the dispensary in one room. Every gendarmerie post had a certain amount of medicines and supplies on hand, and frequently there was no American person to dispense them, but we had a native hospital corps consisting, as I remember, of 24 Haitians, who showed an aptitude for medicine and whom we had trained, and they were distributed around, in addition to the Americans.

Mr. HOWE. When the Navy doctors furnished their services there were they in the employ of the Haitian Government?

Gen. BUTLER. They were in the employ of the Haitian Government.

Mr. HOWE. As part of the gendarmerie?

Gen. Butler. No; some of them. Three of them only were commissioned officers of the gendarmerie. The rest were with the sanitary engineer. Then, of course, all the medical officers and all the medical personnel of the marines there on duty, who had nothing whatsoever to do with the Haitian Government, were constantly caring for and improving the condition of the Haitian people. Everybody was working for the same end, no matter who employed him.

Senator Oddie. In this matter of conserving and improving the public health and sanitary conditions do you consider that everything was done that could have been done, in the light of modern science and energy and thoroughness?

Gen. Butler. With the funds on hand; yes, sir. I might mention that the hospital in Port au Prince, which was in a deplorable condition upon our arrival, was restored and was conducted by Americans, with the Haitian assistants and nurses. That is true also of the hospital at Cape Haitien, and in addition we had little gendarmerie hospitals in the principal towns which were open to all civilians, where they were taken in case of emergency.

Senator Oddie. I want to diverge a little, General, and ask you for your definition of a caco.

Gen. Butler. Well, you can get fifty different definitions. The one popularly given to me by the Haitians in whom I had the greatest trust was this, that the caco was a bird of prey that lives off the weaker fowl. It has a red plume and makes a sound " caco," as it is called, and these bandits live entirely off the weak, so they adopted that name. They wear a patch of red on their clothing, either a little red stripe on their trousers, or a red hatband, or something to indicate the fact that they are cacos. You can get, Senator, any number of reasons for the term. There is a bird that says " caco." I have heard the bird and seen it.

Senator Oddie. How about the prisons?

Gen. Butler. The prisons were under the gendarmerie, I think, under some presidential order.

Mr. Angell. I have here two petitions in the form of letters from the Union Patriotique, addressed to the committee, regarding particularly that portion of the investigation which the commitee expects to make in Haiti. The petitions are in French, and, in substance, they are based upon the existence of martial law in Haiti at the present time, and the censorship of the press. These petitions stress the opposition which, as is there claimed, is now being offered by the military and civil agents of the United States to a full, fair, and thorough investigation by the committee with testimony adverse to the American occupation of the island. What the specific facts are on which the Union Patriotique officials rely I am not personally informed. Whatever be the reasons for it, and whether the reasons be justified or not by past events, particularly the events surrounding the inquiry conducted by the Mayo court last year, it is a fact, of the existence of which I am personally convinced from all that I can learn, both from Haitians and from disinterested Americans, that the Haitian people generally do not at this moment feel free to come forward before this committee with testimony adverse to the American occupation of the island. The existence of martial law at the present moment obviously plays a large part in such a feeling.

As an example of how martial law operates at the present time to suppress the legitimate acts of a people jealous of any infringement upon their political rights throughout 100 years of absolute independence, I respectfully call your attention to the fact disclosed by the second petition to the committee, which I present herewith, dated October 9 of this year. This petition and the letter accompanying it discloses the fact that the officials of the Union Patriotique have made a respectful request of Col. Russell, the brigade commander of the marines in Haiti, couched in the most moderate terms, for permission to hold a public manifestation at Port au Prince in honor of the arrival of the committee, the manifestation to consist of a parade, but without speeches or any other demonstrations which could be in any wise conceived as inflammatory. This request was made in writing to Col. Russell on September 28, and I present herewith a copy of that letter of request. In reply Col. Russell says—and I have here his original letter, which I will offer:

" I have to inform you that I have received no official information regarding the visit you mention, and until such is received no action will be taken by me."

The visit he refers to in that letter is the visit of your committee to Haiti.

A similar request addressed by the Union Patriotique officials to the Haitian department of the interior has brought a reply, under date of October 1, likewise postponing any decision, upon the same ground.

I submit, in all confidence, that it is inconceivable that the Haitian people, the attainment of whose entire political independence the United States has solemnly pledged by treaty and by repeated assurances to maintain and to respect, should be continued to be subjected to such humiliation. The investigation now being made by this committee can be a great step forward in regaining the confidence of the Haitian people as to the aims and methods of the United States in Haiti, but this investigation can not in that respect be a success if the Haitian people, during the visit of the committee to the island, continue to be bound by the repression and fear of martial law. To the end, therefore, that the visit of the committee to Haiti may be regarded by the people as a genuine earnest of the desire of our Government to regain the confidence of Haiti and to accomplish permanent benefits of an absolutely constructive character, I, as counsel for the Union Patriotique, respectfully urge upon the committee the present immediate need for such action initiating with your committee as will result in an official proclamation from the headquarters of our military forces in Haiti, announcing, following the pending arrival of your committee in Haiti, the raising of martial law for the period of its stay there, and publicly inviting a free appearance before the committee of all Haitians who have reasonable complaints to make regarding the occupation or testimony of value to offer without fear of let or hindrance, and without such a proclamation I am convinced that the Haitian people will not regard the investigation made by this committee as fair and full as to them.

(The petitions and letters above referred to by Mr. Angell are here printed in full, as follows:)

UNION PATRIOTIQUE.

PORT AU PRINCE, *17 Septembre 1921.*

MONSIEUR LE PRÉSIDENT, MESSIEURS LES COMMISSAIRES: Le 5 Août dernier, notre Délégué, M. Sténio Vincent, à la fin de son Exposé, avait l'honneur d'attirer l'attention de votre Commission sur les conditions spéciales et très regrettables faites au peuple haïtien par le régime de terreur qu'entretient l'application de la Loi Martiale. Il nous incombe aujourd'hui le devoir de vous signaler le danger qu'entraîne une telle situation pour le succès de l'Oeuvre de vérité et de justice que l'on attend universellement de l'initiative prise par le Sénat des Etats-Unis. Nos populations ont depuis six ans tellement souffert que leur défiance s'étend à tout ce qui est Américain. Les gens les plus intéressés à l'Enquête sont obligés à toutes sortes de précautions, puisque beaucoup d'entre eux se rappellent les persécutions dont ils avaient été l'objet pour avoir seulement demandé, sans succès d'ailleurs, à être entendus par la Commission Mayo.

Les agens militaires et civils des Etats-Unis, sachant que l'Enquête du Sénat sera autrement sérieuse que celle de l'Admiral Mayo et tenant beaucoup (ce qui de leur part est assez naturel) à ce qu'elle n'ait pas de résultat, s'ingénient à démoraliser complètement les populations par la propagande, la corruption et la terreur. L'Union patriotique serait, en conséquence, reconnaissante à la Commission d'enquête de faire dès maintenant une déclaration publique au aujet des garanties qu'elle compte offrir aux citoyens haïtiens et à toutes personnes qui se présenteront devant elle pour déposer sur les atrocités et aux autres abus commis dans ce pays par les agens militaires et civils des Etats-Unis.

Cette déclaration pourrait être contenue dans la réponse que la Commission voudra faire à la présente supplique de l'Union patriotique. Elle serait portée à la reconnaissance du public haïtien par la publication des deux pièces.

Dans l'espoir que nous n'aurons pas fait inutilement appel à la prévoyance et à la loyauté de la Commision d'enquête, nous vous prions d'agréer.

Monsieur le Président,
Messieurs les Commissaires,
l'assurance de notre haute considération et de notre profond respect.
Pour le Comité central de direction:

GEORGES SYLVAIN,
Administrateur-délégué.

Monsieur le Sénateur MACCORMICK,
    Président de la Commission.
MESSIEURS LES MEMBRES DE LA COMMISSION
    D'ENQUÊTE SÉNATORIALE SIÉGEANT AU CAPITOLE,

Washington.

RÉPUBLIQUE D'HAITI,
SECRÉTAIRERIE D'ÉTATDE L'INTÉRIEUR,
Port au Prince, 1 Octobre, 1921.

Monsieur GEORGES SYLVAIN,
Administrateur Délégué de l'Union Patriotique, En Ville.

Monsieur LE DÉLÉGUÉ : Je vous accuse réception de votre lettre en dâte du
29 Septembre écoulé, m'informant que l' "Union Patriotique" se propose
d'organiser, avec le concours de la population de Port au Prince, une grande
manifestation en l'honneur de la Commission d'enquête sénatoriale et cette
manifestation consistera en un défilé à travers les rues de de la ville, du
Champ de Mars, au bord de mer avec fanfares et bannières, sans discours ni
vivats.

Mon Département en prend bonne note. Relativement au concours que vous
lui demandez, en la cirsconstance, il vous informe qu'il n'est pas encore saisi
officiellement de l'arrivée de la Commission Senatoriale Américaine en Haïti.
En attendant, veuillez lui faire avoir un programme de cette manifestation.

Recevez, Monsieur le délégué, l'assurance de ma parfaite considération.

B. DARTIGUENAVEZ.

UNION PATRIOTIQUE HAÏTIENNE.

PORT-AU-PRINCE, *9 Octobre 1921.*

Monsieur le PRÉSIDENT,
*et Messieurs les Membres de la Commision
d'enquête sénatoriale siégeant au Capitole. Washington.*

MONSIEUR LE PRÉSIDENT, MESSIEURS LES COMMISSAIRES : Nous avions l'honneur,
le mois dernier, de signaler à votre haute attention les difficultés que le maintien
de la loi martiale oppose à la préparation de l'Enquête sénatoriale en notre
pays. Ces difficultés s'aggravent chaque jour du fait que les Agents militaires
des Etats-Unis, affectant de considérer comme des atteintes à l'ordre public les
manifestations d'opinions contraires à leurs intérêts, usent de tous les pro-
cédés d'intimidation pour fausser l'esprit de nos populations et les éloigner de la
Commission d'enquête. C'est ainsi qu'à la date du 3 de ce mois, Monsieur
Eugène Vieux, administrateur du Courrier Haïtien, journal dont les deux
directeurs, Messieurs Jh. Lanoue et Jolibois fils subissent pour délit d'opinion,
depuis bientôt 6 mois, une condamnation imméritée aux Travaux forcés et à
l'amende, a été arrêté pour un article que nous expédions ci-joint à votre
adresse, afin de vous permettre d'en apprécier par vous-même le caractère
inoffensif.

Monsieur Vieux est un vieillard de 67 ans, des plus honorables, à qui personne
n'a jamais eu à rien reprocher jusqu'à ce jour. En même temps que lui a com-
paru devant le Tribunal militaire de l'Occupation un autre citoyen haïtien.
auteur de l'article incriminé, Monsieur Étienne Mathon, connu pour ses opinions
modérées, ancien Bâtonnier de l'Ordre des avocats de Port-au-Prince, ancien
Ministre des Relations Extérieures et de la Justice. Le seul crime à tous les
deux est d'être des militants de notre cause nationale et des membres dévoués
de notre Union Patriotique, dont Monsieur Mathon est un dirigeant.

Par les deux lettres dont nous vous envoyons également ci-joint communication, vous constaterez qu'à l'occasion d'une manifestation que projette la population de Port-au-Prince pour faire accueil à votre Commission, le jour de son
arrivée, le Colonel Russell, Chef des forces expéditionnaires des Etats Unis à
Haïti et Monsieur B. Dartiguenave, Secrétaire d'Etat de l'Intérieur, conviés à
nous prêter leur appui, se sont rencontrés pour déclarer qu'ils s'en abstiendraient
tant qu'ils n'auront pas reçu notification officielle de la visite de la Commission
d'Enquête. C'est une situation certainement anormale. Le voyage de la Commission en notre pays devrait-il jusqu'à cette heure constituer un sujet de doute
pour les autorités locales?

En se piquant de n'en rien connaître, ne contribuent-elles pas a en faire
suspecter la sincérité et par là à entraver toute préparation sérieuse a l'enquête
que vous comptez diriger sur les lieux?

Du jour ou l'Union Patriotique, représentant le Peuple Haïtien, a été admise
à déposer les plaintes et les désiderata de sa Nation devant la Commission
d'Enquete formée par le Sénat des Etats-Unis et qu'en même temps les repré-
sentants du Département de la Marine ont eu à y produire leurs répliques, la
situation juridique s'est trouvée la suivante : d'une part, le Peuple Haïtien,

partie plaignante: de l'autre, le Département de la Marine Etats-Unis, partie défenderesse, et comme arbitre entre les deux part'es, le Sénat des Etats-Unis, actuellement représenté par votre Commission. Il n'est pas adm'ssible, dans ces conditions, que la balance ne reste pas égale entre les deux parties, au moment où les arbitres poursuivent leurs investigations. Il est particulièrement intolérable que, dans l'intervale du déplacement de la Commission d'Enquête, les Agents du Département de la Mar'ne, abusant de l'autorité dont ils sont les dépositaires, s'emploient de toutes les manières à entretenir le trouble dans les esprits à l'égard de l'Oeuvre de la Comm's'ion sénatoriale, sous prétexte que sa venue leur reste officiellement douteuse.

Il nous suffira, espérons-nous, Monsieur le Président, Messieurs les Commissaires, de vous avoir signalé cette anomalie, pour que vous y mettiez bon ordre, car elle tend à ruiner toute confiance dans la justice et la loyauté qu'on doit attendre de l'intervention su Sénat des Etats-Unis, et dont nous sommes heureux, pour notre part, de vous renouveler l''nébranlable attestation.

Veuillez agréer, Monsieur le Président, Messieurs les Commissaires, les assurances de la haute considération avec laquelle nous avons l'honneur d'être vos bien dévoués et obéissants serviteurs.

> Pour les Comités réunis de l'Union Patrit'que L'Administrateur-délégué du Comité central, George Sylvain, ancien E. E. et Ministre plénipotentiaire d'Haiti en France et auprès du St siège, officier de l'Instruction Publique, officer de la Légion d'honneur; Le Secrétaire général: P. Thoby, ancien Secréta're de Légation d'Ha'ti a Washington, Délégué de l'Un'on Patriotique aux Etats-Unis; L'Archiviste: Ch. Rosemond, Notaire; F. L. Cauvain, ancien Secrétaire d'Etat, ancien Sénateur, ancien Bâtonnier de l'Ordre des avocats de Port-au-Prince; Léon Nau, anc'en Doyen du Tribunal Civil de Port-au-Prince, avocat, ancien Juge au Tribunal de Cassation de la Républ'que; D. Jeannot, ancien Secrétaire d'Etat, avocat; Stenio Vincend avocat, anc'en Secrétaire d'Etat, ancien Président du Sénat, Délégué de l'Union Patritoque aux Etats-Unis, ancien ministre l'Haïtien Hollande.

UNION PATRIOTIQUE.

PORT AU PRINCE, *28 Septembre, 1921.*

MONSIEUR LE COLONEL RUSSELL,
    Chef des forces expéditionnaires des Etats-Unis en Haiti.

MONSIEUR LE COLONEL: Neus avons l'honneur de vous informer que l'Union patriotique so propose d'organizer avec le concours de la population de Port-au-Prince une grande manifestation en l'honneur de la Commission d'enquete sénatoriale,—au moment de son débarquement—Cette manifestation cons'stera en un défilé à travers les rues de la ville, due Champ de Mars au berd de mer, avec fanfares et bannières, sans discours ni vivats.

Elle sera une attestation de nos sentiments patriotiques et un hommage de confiance en la justice et en l'impartialité du Sénat fédéral.

Tenant essentiellement à ce que nos futurs hotes so'ent, dès leur première prise de contact avec le pays, favorablement impressionnés par l'accueil de la population, nous nous plaisons à comptr sur l'appui de toutes les autorités et vous prions d'agréer, Mons'eur le Colonel, l'assurance de mes sentiments de haute considération.

(Signeé)   GEORGES SYLVAIN,
Administrateur-délégué.

UNITED STATES MARINE CORPS, FIRST BRIGADE.
OFFICE OF THE BRIGADE COMMANDER,
Port au Prince, Haiti, October 3, 1921.

SIR: Replying to your letter of 29 September, 1921, I have to inform you that I have received no official information regarding the visit you mention and until such is received no action will be taken by me.

Very truly, yours,

JOHN H. RUSSELL.

M. GEORGE SYLVAIN,
    Port au Prince, Haiti.

Senator ODDIE. Let me ask a question. Do you not think that that request assumes that this committee will have rendered its decision to a certain extent before completing its investigation? In other words, you realize that the investigation is to be a very complete and thorough one, a part of which is being made now, and the balance of which will be made in Haiti, and that the issuing of such an order may be begging the question somewhat?

Mr. HOWE. And committing this body to a conclusion in advance of the completion of its investigation?

Mr. ANGELL. In reply to your question, Senator, I would say that I do not think that such a request or move emanating from this committee looking toward the raising of martial law in Haiti for the period of the visit of the committee there, accompanied by the other declarations which I have suggested, would be in any sense a decision, nor even suggesting a decision in any ultimate and final sense on the part of the committee. Such a move looking toward the temporary raising of martial law, and the publishing of such a proclamation as I have suggested, would only be taking proper and, as I regard them frankly, necessary steps by this committee in order to obtain a fair opportunity to ascertain in Haiti what has taken place during the occupation, to afford the Haitian people a full and fair opportunity to come before the committee with whatever testimony they deem pertinent and important, and therefore such a move by the committee would not presage in any sense its final conclusions; it would only be a step taken by it to afford it an opportunity to pursue its inquiry in Haiti.

Mr. HOWE. How would a fair opportunity for this committee to continue its investigations in Haiti be prevented by the continuance of martial law? Please develop your reasons on that.

Mr. ANGELL. As I have not been in Ha'ti personally, I am at a disadvantage, naturally, when called upon to give specific reasons or detailed facts. I am, in the first instance, advancing the request of the organization which I represent before this committee; in the second instance, I venture to express my personal conviction, somewhat in support of those requests, to the effect that a large portion of the Haitian people do not feel free at the present time to come forward and offer testimony.

Mr. HOWE. For fear of what?

Mr. ANGELL. They fear—whether justified or not, I am unable to state—reprisals of some nature on the part of either the American forces there, the gendarmes, or the Haitian Government officials and those who sympathize with the Haitian Government and with the American occupation, reprisals directed against those who may testify adversely to the occupation.

Mr. HOWE. What would be the effect of the removal of martial law? Would it not be to remove from authority the American gendarmerie commander and officers, and the control of all other military officers in Haiti?

Mr. ANGELL. I fail to see why the raising of martial law would result in such a state of affairs, because the presence of the marine forces there is, at least as stated in the opinion of the Judge Advocate General of the Navy in 1920, authorized in the treaty of 1915, and that the gendarmerie forces are specifically provided for by that treaty and the subsequent conventions, and by the act of Congress of June 3, 1916, so the raising of martial law would not have the effect, as I understand it, of suspending the legality of the presence of the marines and marine officers and gendarmes.

Mr. HOWE. That was not what I meant to get your opinion on. Would not the suspension or termination of martial law permit arrests, trials, and imprisonments without the supervision or control of our military authorities, or of our officers of the gendarmerie in the employ of the Haitian Government?

Mr. ANGELL. I do not think so. I think that the gendarmerie would still continue to be the local police of the country, and the suspension of martial law would be merely the restoration of civil as distinguished from military law.

Mr. HOWE. And such civil law to be administered by whom, Haitians or—

Mr. ANGELL. By the Haitian Government. the Haitian native and civil courts, and by the gendarmes as the police force of the Government.

Mr. HOWE. Do the organizations which you represent prefer the administration of civil law by the present Government to the administration of law under martial law as it is now being carried on?

Mr. ANGELL. Speaking. generally, I believe they do.

Mr. HOWE. In your opinion, is there more danger of persecution of witnesses who appear before this committee from the uncontrolled authorities of the present Government or from the military officers in control of the administration of martial law?

Mr. ANGELL. Your question calls for an answer based on facts of which I have not sufficient knowledge to form a personal judgment.

Mr. HOWE. In your opinion, has this committee carried its investigation far enough along to have a knowledge of the facts on which to base its recommendation for the suspension of martial law? I understand you have been present at most of the hearings before this committee?

Mr. ANGELL. All of the hearings. I do not think that question has been touched on, one way or the other, so far as I can recollect.

Senator ODDIE. If martial law were withdrawn, do you consider that there would be danger of various factions in Haiti taking advantage of that condition and starting their factional fights again?

Mr. ANGELL. Such as disturbances?

Senator ODDIE. Yes.

Mr. ANGELL. Subject to the limitation which I have previously referred to in my own particular unfamiliarity with the detailed facts there arising from the unfortunate fact that I have not had the opportunity to be in Haiti, I would answer that question to this effect, that I can not conceive that the Haitians who are in large part pressing for a restoration to them of the essence and substance of Government now controlled by the United States would be so foolish as to give way to factional disturbances, riots, and the like at the very time of the committee's visit to Haiti, and thus afford the more food for the claim that the Haitians are not fit to govern themselves, and that martial law must be continued there indefinitely by the presence of our military forces.

Mr. HOWE. Is your recommendation, or the recommendation of the society that you represent, for the suspension of martial law only for the visit of this committee to Haiti?

Mr. ANGELL. Entirely. They do not go beyond that, and the publication of some sort of a proclamation such as I referred to in the beginning of my statement.

Mr. HOWE. Would you, on your own responsibility, with no more information than you now have, order the suspension of martial law during the visit of this committee?

Mr. ANGELL. If I were in a position of authority to do so?

Mr. HOWE. Yes.

Mr. ANGELL. And based only on such knowledge as I have and such representations as have been made to me?

Mr. HOWE. Yes.

Mr. ANGELL. Yes; I think I should. In doing so I might concededly err on the side of laxity from the military point of view, but since you ask the question of me personally I will reply that from my own personal point of view I would prefer to err upon that side rather than do anything or refuse to do anything which would, even apparently, and whether I agreed with the opinions of the native Haitians or not, militate against their feeling that the investigation now being conducted by this committee will be full, fair, and thorough as to them.

Mr. HOWE. Now, do you think that this committee has sufficient knowledge of present conditions down there, gained from its investigations which you have heard, to justify any request from it for the suspension of martial law?

Mr. ANGELL. As I have said before, I recollect no testimony which has been offered thus far on that subject, so that it is really a question de novo which I have presented here this morning, and simply based upon the two petitions presented in the record here and the letters to and from the Union Patriotique, the Department of the Interior, and Col. Russell.

In fairness to the question asked and to such responsibility as might attach to the committee in making such a request, I should say that I feel that the committee might, very properly hear some evidence upon that point at this time. I do deem it of vital importance, on the psychological ground—that is, as to the feelings of the Haitian people regarding the investigation being conducted by this committee—that if such a request is to emanate from this committee it must be done very shortly. Here we are at the end of October and the committee proposes to go to Haiti in about three weeks, as I understand. It takes some time to get these things done, and if the committee delays until a few days before its departure from the United States any decision on this point or the taking of any testimony which it might feel necessary in order to arrive at any fair conclusion, then I feel fairly confident that the opportunity would have slipped by to make the Haitian people feel that this is going to be a thorough investigation down there. In other words, if it is to be done, it must be done now or in the very immediate future.

Mr. Howe. Have you any witnesses immediately available who could give such testimony?

Mr. Angell. Yes; I have; not here in Washington, that I know of, but there are some witnesses—civilian witnesses—disinterested Americans in New York, who are willing and ready to offer information on that point based upon their knowledge of Haitian conditions.

In connection with the question which you put to me, Mr. Howe, I think I should say that the request is not merely for the raising of martial law but is a little wider or further than that. For example, the letter of Col. Russell which I read—possibly you did not hear it at the moment—said he had received no official advice as to the coming of this committee to Haiti and consequently he could not take any action at all upon the request of the Union Patriotique for permission to stage a parade in honor of the arrival of the committee. My request, then, would be as much addressed to the desirability of having the military forces in Haiti informed officially of the arrival of the committee, so that such a reasonable request as that for permission to stage an honorary demonstration upon the arrival of the committee could be granted. Col. Russell refused to grant it, saying he has no knowledge of it.

Maj. McClellan. As I understand, the date of the request made on Col. Russell to ascertain the date of the visit of this committee antedated by some time the date on which this committee decided tentatively on November 19 as the date of sailing.

Mr. Angell. I believe so.

Maj. McClellan. Then the reply of Col. Russell to that request was bona fide and proper, was it not?

Mr. Angell. I have no doubt but what it was. I have no criticism whatever to make of Col. Russell's reply.

Mr. Howe. Has the society which you represent made any request through the Government of Haiti for it to make a request of the Government of the United States to suspend martial law?

Mr. Angell. Not that I know of. It has made a request in this particular instance of the Department of the Interior for permission to hold this parade which they desire to stage there, and the Department of the Interior has replied likewise that it has no official knowledge of the arrival of the committee and can do nothing.

Senator Oddie. I would like to ask Gen. Butler for an opinion as to the raising of martial law.

Gen. Butler. If you raise martial law down there, Senator, while there are any United States troops at all in Haiti, you are going to have some of them murdered.

Senator Oddie. Some of the United States troops murdered?

Gen. Butler. Yes, sir. We are only paid soldiers; we have nothing to do with the policy of our Government. We are only sent to these places to perform acts. We have nothing to do with the reason for which we are sent, and if we have no method of protecting ourselves you had better keep us home. I feel strongly, because I have seen men cut up on the streets when I was in Port au Prince last year, unarmed marines, two of them, cut with bolos from the rear. Of course the Haitian courts did nothing. Why would they punish their own people for jumping on us? You raise martial law, and you will have a fight, because the marines are human and they will not be butchered. Wherever the flag goes we have got to have protection for the soldier, otherwise you should bring us away.

Senator Oddie. Another question, General. In your opinion, is there danger of the rival factions in Haiti starting trouble if martial law is raised?

Gen. Butler. No, sir; I do not think the rival factions will start trouble, but any person who has been harboring a grudge against a marine would take it out of him. The marines would be the ones that would suffer. The marines have the strictest orders about the use of their arms. They are not allowed to go at liberty under arms; they are perfectly helpless.

(Whereupon the committee adjourned until Monday, October 31, 1921, at 10.30 o'clock a. m.)

INQUIRY INTO OCCUPATION AND ADMINISTRATION OF HAITI AND SANTO DOMINGO.

MONDAY, OCTOBER 31, 1921.

United States Senate,
Select Committee on Haiti and Santo Domingo,
Washington, D. C.

The committee met at 10.30 o'clock a. m., pursuant to adjournment, Senator Medill McCormick presiding.

Present: Senators McCormick and Oddie.

Also present: Mr. Walter Bruce Howe and Maj. Edwin N. McClellan, United States Marine Corps, in their respective representative capacities, as hereinbefore indicated.

STATEMENT OF BRIG. GEN. SMEDLEY D. BUTLER, UNITED STATES MARINE CORPS, COMMANDING MARINES, QUANTICO. VA.—Resumed.

Mr. Howe. General, at the end of the hearing last Thursday we were, as I recollect it, about to take up the so-called corvee system in Haiti, and I think the best way to get at it would be for you to tell us briefly what the corvee system was by law, and how the gendarmerie proceeded, with the knowledge of that law, to build roads.

Gen. Butler. The rural code, which was one of the Haitian laws, contains a law which requires every citizen of Haiti to either pay a road tax or work for the maintenance of the roads a certain length of time each month on the roads which he uses. It is the same law which we have in the United States. You either pay a tax or work. The law had not been enforced for some time prior to our arrival, and they had no roads. When we landed in Haiti there were 3 miles of roads built, at a cost to the Haitian Government of about $51,000 a mile. This was told me by members of the Haitian cabinet. This road was hardly passable. In order to facilitate the bringing of products to market, and to bring the north and south closer together, we decided to build roads. There was a very distinct feeling of antagonism on the part of the people in the north against the people in the south, mainly because they could not communicate with each other. There were no roads. There were rivers that they could not cross, except at great danger to themselves, and this feeling had caused one revolution after another until, as I said before, they had had seven in four years, resulting in the death of thousands of people. The Haitian Government had no money for the construction of the roads, and without roads you could get no money except by borrowing it, and nobody would lend them any money, which was perfectly proper. They were unable to pay the interest on the national debt they already had, and it was perfectly reasonable that no one else would lend them any money except under the old system of getting concessions, which we stopped. That is, a collection of bankers would lend them money with the provision that they should have all the revenue from a coffee crop, and that system of borrowing money was ruinous to the country, so we stopped it. We decided that we would attempt to market what products we had and try to raise money in that way. The only way to get those products down to the seacoast where they could be sold was over the roads. We then counted our money and found that we could afford $8,000 a month for the construction of roads.

Mr. Howe. Where did that money come from?

Gen. Butler. That money came from the collection of external revenues in the hands of the general receiver of customs, an American official. That amount was allotted monthly. We did not build one new road in Haiti. You could not build a new road in Haiti, because the French had had a complete network of roads.

The CHAIRMAN. How many years ago?

Gen. BUTLER. The French were driven out in 1804, but the signs of the grading and of the old bridges and old culverts were still evident everywhere, so it required no new engineering on our part. We simply repaired and put into condition the old roads as provided for in the rural code.

The CHAIRMAN. Let me interrupt to ask if the general can supply the committee with a map, at this or a subsequent session, which will show the roads passable for motor traffic before this work was undertaken, and after it was undertaken?

Gen. BUTLER. I can show you right here on that map. There were just 3 miles of road before we started, from the city of Port au Prince to a place 3 miles from Port au Prince called Mardissant.

The CHAIRMAN. How many roads did you build?

• Gen. BUTLER. During the time I was there we repaired approximately 470 miles of road.

The CHAIRMAN. How much money did you expend on that work?

Gen. BUTLER. The roads cost about $205 a mile. We had a certain amount of hired skilled labor to build culverts, and we bought our cement and used what road machinery we owned, and the rest of the money was used for food for the corvee.

Mr. HOWE. General, what was your source of information for the statement that the 3 existing miles of road cost $51,000 a mile?

Gen. BUTLER. The statements made to me by members of the Haitian cabinet.

Mr. HOWE. During what period were these 470 miles of road rebuilt or built?

Gen. BUTLER. From the 1st of July, 1916, until the date on which we left Haiti—the 9th of March, 1918.

Mr. HOWE. Does the revival of the corvee system, or the employment of the corvee system, date from about July, 1916?

Gen. BUTLER. From July, 1916.

Mr. HOWE. Will you describe the working of the corvee system?

Gen. BUTLER. The corvee worked in this way while I had charge of it. We had little cards printed, notification cards, and lists of the names of citizens who should work on the roads given the gendarmerie officers of the Haitian civil offic als of that district, and the gendarmes then delivered these little cards notifying them that on a certain date they would report at a certain place and do their work or pay a certain tax.

The CHAIRMAN. They had the option?

Gen. BUTLER. They had the option. Nobody had any money, so they reported for work. During the period they were working they were housed and fed, and in order to amuse them dances were given them in the evenings, and it was somewhat like a barn raising here in America. I took the President and members of his cabinet at least once a week to call on the corvee parties and to make speeches to them, and impress upon them that they were doing this for their own country and not for the white men.

On the 7th of November, 1917, the road work on the main highway, Route Dartiguenave, named after the President of Haiti, had progressed to such an extent that 75 miles of the 182 had been completed between Port au Prince and Cape Haitien.

The CHAIRMAN. Did the barn raising method and the speech making method of preserving the esprit de corps of the corvee continue; did that go right straight through to the end of your tour?

Gen. BUTLER. To the end of my time. We opened the Las Cahobas Road with great ceremony, the President and all the members of his cabinet and 18 automobile loads of distinguished citizens being present, on the Sunday before I left Haiti or about the 3d of March.

The CHAIRMAN. And during all that time had the corvee been fed?

Gen. BUTLER. Fed?

The CHAIRMAN. And housed?

Gen. BUTLER. And housed; and not a single complaint on the part of anybody had ever reached my ears.

The CHAIRMAN. Were there during that time instances of inhabitants of one district performing work in another district?

Gen. BUTLER. Not to my knowledge, and there were the strictest orders against it. I was well aware that this thing was acpable of tremenduous abuse, and had been abused by the Haitians previously, and was determined that there should be nothing of that kind, and the men were only used on the roads that they themselves used. There were plenty of people to do it, and there was no object in taking them from one place to another.

The CHAIRMAN. There was a density of population along the line of these roads?

Gen. BUTLER. There was a density of population all along the line of these roads to do this work. May I give some instances of the enthusiasm of the people for this road work?

The CHAIRMAN. Yes.

Gen. BUTLER. We had little prizes of flags to hang on the gate posts where the roads were particularly well done, in front of the properties. The President, when traveling with me, would stop at my request and make speeches to the families that had done particularly well in front of their property, and that encouraged them very greatly. Men, women, and children would lay stone on the road to keep the little holes filled up.

I would like to give an instance. On the 7th of November, when we had reached this stage where 75 miles had been built, and about 100 more had to be completed to the cape, war had broken out in the United States, and I was anxious to go home, and I wanted to see the road finished.

On the 7th of November, 1917, I took the President and two members of his cabinet and many other members of the Government to Gonaives on the Government yacht and sent a band up ahead. He had been invited by the town of Gonaives, although no President had ever been there before, and they said they would shoot him if he came. But we all went up without any firearms and had a big demonstration. We went to church on Sunday morning, and on Monday morning we all rode out to the end of the road being then constructed. We walked up along the road where all the corvee were working, and the President made a speech to each gang of the corvee. They had the internal revenue. I said to him, " If you will trust me with some of your money, in addition to the $8,000 a month I am getting, on the 1st of January I will take you and your cabinet and anybody else you want to Cape Haiti en. We have 100 miles of road to build, but we will build it in six or seven weeks, if you will give us that money out of the taxes and take this additional road on your shoulders and issue a proclamation." They promptly voted at a meeting of the cabinet to turn over $400,000, which was given me on Wednesday morning, for additional food and additional effort, and after a lot of noise, dancing, and praying the soldiers and the Government started immediately to put their shoulders behind the wheels, and on the 17th of December, five weeks and four days later. I went to Cape Haitien in an auto, and on the 1st of January the President and the Government, 27 truck loads of people, went to Cape Haitien, for the first time that wheeled vehicles had ever traveled that distance, for in the French days there was a gap about 6 miles across a swamp, where they had to get out of their carriages and ride over on horseback.

The CHAIRMAN. You filled that in?

Gen. BUTLER. Yes, sir; we drained it and cut the water off and embanked it.

Mr. HOWE. Who first proposed the use of the corvee?

Gen. BUTLER. I do not know, but I think it was a member of the Haitian cabinet who produced this old law. The Government was heartily in favor of it, and I would like to introduce a letter of congratulation from the President of Haiti to me which indicates his approval.

The CHAIRMAN. By all means.

(Gen. Butler thereupon read the letter referred to, as follows:)

PRÉSIDENCE DE LA RÉPUBLIQUE,
Port au Prince, le 10 janvier, 1918.

Gen. S. D. BUTLER,
Chef de la Gendarmerie d' Haiti, En Ville.

MON CHER GÉNÉRAL: Ma courte tournée du Nord s'est accomplie dans des conditions trop agréables pour que je n'éprouve pas le plaisir de vous exprimer toute ma satisfaction et de vous remercier de la part que vous avez que dans cet heureux résultat. C'est, en effet, grâce aux grands travaux de réfection et de réparation des routes publiques entrepris sous votre intelligente et énergetique direction que j'ai pu, en un si court espace de temps, me rendre dans le Nord où j'ai constaté, à ma vive satisfaction les progrès réalisés dans les régions visitées et l'excellent esprit qui anime leurs population. J'en augure pour mon pays un brillant avenir de prospérité dans l'ordre et la paix.

En vous adressant mes plus cordiales félicitations, il m'est impossible de ne penser à vos dévoués auxiliaires à qui vous voudrez bien transmettre l'expression de toite la gratitude de mon Gouvernement.

Veuillez agréer, mon cher Général, mes meilleurs remerciements joints à mes sentiments toujours cordiaux.

DARTIGUENAVE.

[Translation.]

PRESIDENTIAL SEAT OF THE REPUBLIC,
Port au Prince, January 10, 1918.

To Gen. S. D. BUTLER, ·
    Chief of the Gendarmerie,
        d'Haïti, City.

MY DEAR GENERAL: My short tour of the north has been accomplished under conditions so agreeable that I hasten to express my entire satisfaction and to thank you for the part that you have had in this gratifying result. It is, in fact, thanks to the extensive work of reconstruction and repair of the public roads undertaken under your intelligent and energetic direction, that I was able in so short a time to reach the north, where I witnessed, to my lively satisfaction, the progress realized in the regions visited and the excellent spirit that animates their inhabitants. I predict for my country a brilliant future of prosperity, amidst surroundings of order and peace.

Whilst tendering you my cordial felicitations, it is impossible to forget your devoted assistants, to whom I beg you to express the gratitude of my Government.

Kindly accept my sincere thanks and kind regards.

DARTIGUENAVE.

Mr. HOWE. During the continuance of this system, until your departure, did you ever receive any protest against the use of the corvee?

Gen. BUTLER. I never did, except in the case of employers who would come and ask that the dates of the working of the men might be shifted from one date to another in order that they might work on the plantations.

Mr. HOWE. But there was no protest against the system?

Gen. BUTLER. No.

Mr. HOWE. How long did the corvee workers have to work?

Gen. BUTLER. I do not remember the exact time prescribed by the law.

The CHAIRMAN. That is in the record, in the statement originally filed by the department.

Gen. BUTLER. They worked exactly according to the Haitian law, no longer and no less.

Mr. HOWE. Did they ever attempt to escape or run away before their time was up?

Gen. BUTLER. No; and, in fact, after the completion of the road to Cape Haitien, it was with the greatest difficulty that we got 4,000 of them to go home. They were on our hands for a month, and it worried me to death to get food to feed them. They enjoyed this dancing; they enjoyed the food; and they enjoyed the housing.

Mr. HOWE. How far away did they live?

Gen. BUTLER. Right around in the neighborhood; but they liked this collection, they liked the big assembly, they liked the voodoo dancing, they liked the visits, and, in fact, when I visited Haiti last year I visited a cotton plantation run by a former gendarmerie officer, who had had these 4,000 men building the road from Ennery to St. Michel, and he still had in his employ and had never been able to get rid of 1,200 of the original corvee laborers. I went out and made speeches to them through an interpreter, and there was great shouting and yelling. He had never been able to get them to go home.

There was not one single thing we ever did relative to the inhabitants of Haiti that did not have the full knowledge and consent of the President of Haiti, because I took it all to him; I saw him daily.

Mr. HOWE. Do you know of any instances where people escaping from the corvee, or attempting to escape, were shot?

Gen. BUTLER. I do not.

Mr. HOWE. Did you ever hear of such instances?

Gen. BUTLER. I did, but upon investigation I found them to be groundless rumors.

Mr. HOWE. Through what instrumentality did you recruit the corvee?

Gen. BUTLER. The corvee was hardly recruited; it was notified, and it came.

Mr. HOWE. Who notified it? Who carried the cards?

Gen. BUTLER. The cards were carried around by the local patrols, by the gendarmes who went out every day, but, as I said before, in this connection we worked entirely with the local Haitian officials, who knew the people much better than we did.

Mr. HOWE. When you left the corvee system was in full blast?

Gen. BUTLER. In full blast, and, as I said before, just before I left we made a trip of 125 miles, the President and his cabinet and myself, in order to see it.

Mr. HOWE. You have no particular knowledge of anything which might have happened to lead to the stopping of the corvee system?

Gen. BUTLER. I have not, except that I have heard it was abused.

The CHAIRMAN. That is not your personal knowledge?

Gen. BUTLER. No; that is not my personal knowledge. I have no personal knowledge. It was stopped about seven or eight months after I left. I know nothing about that.

The CHAIRMAN. You were present in Haiti when the legislature was disbanded in 1916, were you not?

Gen. BUTLER. I was, sir.

The CHAIRMAN. The testimony of other witnesses has indicated that if men working on the corvee, or prisoners, were harshly used, that harsh usage was attributable in great part to the native gendarmerie. How were the gendarmes recruited? What method did you have for selecting men for service in the gendarmes?

Gen. BUTLER. We had recruiting regulations and requirements. We took the very best applicants.

The CHAIRMAN. What was the standard?

Gen. BUTLER. The standard was 5 feet 4 inches, if I remember correctly, to 6 feet. We started originally to take only those who could read and write, but we could not find sufficient men to fill the gendarmerie. We examined them physically and mentally, and as nearly as we could, morally, and inquired about them from the people among whom they lived in order to get the best material we could.

The CHAIRMAN. How much were they paid?

Gen. BUTLER. They were paid $10 a month and food and clothing—that is, privates.

The CHAIRMAN. How would that compare with the going wage in Haiti?

Gen. BUTLER. That was 50 gourdes a month, and the wage for an ordinary laborer was a gourde a day, or about 25 gourdes a month.

The CHAIRMAN. And he fed himself?

Gen. BUTLER. And he fed himself; but we fed them.

The CHAIRMAN. You had every reason to get the best men obtainable at that wage?

Gen. BUTLER. Yes, sir. It cost us $275 per gendarme per year to feed, house, and clothe him, and give him his medical and dental attention.

The CHAIRMAN. The noncommissioned officers of the gendarmerie were drawn from the gendarmerie?

Gen. BUTLER. From the best class of privates.

The CHAIRMAN. The greater part of the commissioned officers were enlisted men or noncommissioned officers of the Marine Corps?

Gen. BUTLER. Originally, sir, all the captains and their seniors in the gendarmerie were commissioned officers of the Marine Corps. All the lieutenants were noncommissioned officers in the Marine Corps, first and second lieutenants.

The CHAIRMAN. Have any Haitians been made commissioned officers of the gendarmerie, do you know?

Gen. BUTLER. During my time there were two or three who were made, at the request and solicitation of the President, to act as lieutenants of his personal bodyguard. They were not in command of the bodyguard. We had American officers and noncommissioned officers, but these were additional lieutenants.

The CHAIRMAN. Since your departure do you know whether any Haitians have been made commissioned officers of the gendarmerie?

Gen. BUTLER. I believe there have been some, but I am not sure.

The CHAIRMAN. If under the treaty the American Government remains responsible for the gendarmerie, have you any idea about the establishment of a school for the training of officers of the gendarmerie?

Gen. BUTLER. American officers?

The CHAIRMAN. Well, Americans, or natives?

Gen. BUTLER. If I had charge, I would appoint no Haitian officers of the gendarmerie, because they will abuse the natives. It is instinctive with them to abuse the inhabitants whenever they are given power. I would not have them, except as personal aids to the President.

The CHAIRMAN. In that connection, will you not give the committee your impressions of the administration of justice in Haiti, whether in the magistrates' courts or the courts of general jurisdiction of first instance?

Gen. BUTLER. You mean, sir, whether it is well done?

The CHAIRMAN. Whether justice is sure——

Gen. BUTLER. No, sir.

The CHAIRMAN. And prompt?

Gen. BUTLER. No, sir.

The CHAIRMAN. And easy to be had by the poor man as well as the rich?

Gen. BUTLER. No, sir. In numbers and numbers of instances prisoners had been in jail years without trial, we discovered when we took over the prison system.

The CHAIRMAN. When you took over the prison system you found in the prisons, held by the Haitian authorities, numbers of prisoners who had been there for years pending trial?

Gen. BUTLER. There was no record of when they had been put in, but, judging by their physical condition, they had been there for years, with no records of trials and charges of any kind.

The CHAIRMAN. And in civil cases are the courts intelligent and impartial?

Gen. BUTLER. No, sir. May I give you an instance?

The CHAIRMAN. Certainly.

Gen. BUTLER. When an owner of a house desires to recover his property from a renter——

The CHAIRMAN. A delinquent tenant?

Gen. BUTLER. A delinquent tenant, who has paid no rent probably for years, the court will and has, to my knowledge, made several decisions of this kind, that the tenant can not be evicted until the tenant has found a suitable other place to live, and the court has fixed as much as six years for a tenant to find other accommodations.

The CHAIRMAN. Do you think the whole judicature ought to be reformed?

Gen. BUTLER. I do, sir.

The CHAIRMAN. Do you believe it can be reformed without American assistance?

Gen. BUTLER. It can not.

The CHAIRMAN. Is there anything more important to the development of Haiti and its progress than the reformation of the judicature?

Gen. BUTLER. No, sir; it is the most important thing they have to do.

The CHAIRMAN. You regard the establishment of order, the opening of communications, and the impartial administration of justice as the three fundamental things that are necessary?

Gen. BUTLER. The three fundamental things that are necessary.

The CHAIRMAN. Is there any officer among the Judge Advocate General's subordinates, who, through his experience, is competent to give the committee a report on the administration of justice in Haiti?

Gen. BUTLER. Not that I know of, sir. The Haitian courts, we did not trifle with. We never investigated them.

The CHAIRMAN. You mean you had nothing to do with them?

Gen. BUTLER. Nothing to do with them. We kept our hands entirely off the Haitian courts. We advised with the President, and urged him to appoint proper judges, but we never interfered with the Haitian courts.

The CHAIRMAN. You do not know of any officer who might, outside of the regular line of his duties, have observed the administration of justice in Haiti, so that he might render an informed opinion?

Gen. BUTLER. No, sir; no officer any more than any other. They all witnessed the functioning of the Haitian courts.

The CHAIRMAN. I thought that possibly somebody under the Judge Advocate General, with a natural bent for the profession, might have studied it?

Gen. BUTLER. No, sir. The provisions of the treaty and the gendarmerie agreement gave us no control over the Haitian courts, and we did not attempt to exercise any.

The CHAIRMAN. General, a moment ago you agreed that the establishment of order and the opening up of communications, and the impartial administration of justice were the three bases of any progress. You have spoken of the 470 miles of highways which have been opened up. I have been interested to learn what, if anything, had been done during the occupation for the improvement of agriculture, including the improvement of live stock, whether any breeding animals had been brought in, whether any experts in cotton or cane growing had been brought in by the occupation to improve the quality of the live stock owned by the peasant, and to improve the methods of agriculture in the country?

Gen. BUTLER. During my time, sir, the American Government sent down from the Department of Agriculture two agricultural experts who spent, if I remember correctly, two months in Haiti, and traveled all over it, accompanied by a gendarmerie officer. They pointed out to us certain sections of land that should grow certain products. On the strength of their recommendations, the gendarmerie then took government land in those sections and set up, or attempted to set up, model farms for the growing of beans and potatoes. We grew potatoes at an altitude of 6,800 feet, and made a number of experiments. The gendarmerie had two principal big farms, one near Cape Haitien in the north, which you will see when you go down there, and one outside of Port au Prince. These two farms were very successful during my period, and, as I understand now, but one of them is continued. The smaller district farms all disappeared, as there was no money to support them, and there may have been a lack of interest; I do not know. For the breeding of cattle we made several efforts to import breeding stock, but we were never able to get sufficient funds.

The CHAIRMAN. From the Haitian Government?

Gen. BUTLER. From the Haitian Government, to bring in the cattle, but we did have cotton men and cane men, and private cotton concerns establish plantations.

The CHAIRMAN. Well, the sum, then, of the official effort was the study of the country for some 8 or 10 weeks by two representatives of the Department of Agriculture in Washington, and the creation of the experimental farms of which you spoke?

Gen. BUTLER. You see, sir, the Department of Agriculture took a part of the funds of the gendarmerie. We were doing this.

The CHAIRMAN. I understand that.

Gen. BUTLER. What funds we had we had to take from the gendarmerie in order to do this. We had no support from the Department of Agriculture. It was an independent effort on our part.

Mr. HOWE. Had anything of the sort ever been undertaken by the Haitian Government, to you knowledge?

Gen. BUTLER. Not that I ever heard of. The Haitian Government, except on the part of the President himself, was not interested in our efforts.

Mr. HOWE. Now, as to the assembly, as I understand it, ordinarily there are the senators and the deputies in the Haitian Congress? When they function separately, they are known as the legislature, is that correct?

Gen. BUTLER. Yes, sir; they have the legislative corps.

Mr. HOWE. And sometimes they meet together, and then they are known as a national assembly, is that the correct term?

Gen. BUTLER. That is correct, the national assembly.

Mr. HOWE. And then sometimes they have met in a constitutional assembly?

Gen. BUTLER. That is correct.

Mr. HOWE. And in April, 1916, there was a national assembly terminated by the President of Haiti?

Gen. BUTLER. That is correct.

Mr. HOWE. And in 1917 there was a constitutional assembly terminated by the President of Haiti?

Gen. BUTLER. That is correct.

Mr. HOWE. Did you have any personal part in, or have any personal knowledge of, the termination in 1916 of the national assembly?

Gen. BUTLER. I did not.

Mr. HOWE. The assembly met in Port au Prince, is that right?

Gen. BUTLER. That is correct.

Mr. HOWE. Were you in Port au Prince at the time?

Gen. BUTLER. I was.

Mr. HOWE. But, in your official duties you had no official connection with that?

Gen. BUTLER. No official connection.

Mr. HOWE. Or private connection?

Gent. BUTLER. No private connection either.

Mr. HOWE. In 1917, when the constitutional assembly was terminated, did you have any connection with it?

Gen. BUTLER. I did.

Mr. HOWE. In 1916, what American officer or officers had anything to do with the termination of the national assembly?

Gen. BUTLER. I do not remember. I think a lieutenant of the gendarmerie serving directly under the orders of the President of Haiti, had something to do with the keys of the assembly room. but I do not remember. It did not come under my notice, officially or privately. .

Mr. HOWE. Did you order officers on any detail connected with the closing of that assembly?

Gen. BUTLER. No; I did not order any one, and I knew nothing about it.

Mr. HOWE. And if any of your officers had been employed on any such work, you would have known it, is that correct?

Gen. BUTLER. Officially; yes. No order passed through me. Anything that a gendarmerie officer did at the palace under the personal direction of the President might not have come through me at all. They were under his personal orders, his bodyguard.

Mr. HOWE. In 1917, will you describe what the President ordered, and what part you took in carrying out his orders?   .

Gen. BUTLER. Shall I give you a detailed description, Senator?

About 10 o'clock, on the morning of the 19th of June, 1917, two members of the Haitian Cabinet, Dr. Heraux, Minister of Finance, and Mr. Cham. Minister of the Interior, came to the headquarters of the gendarmerie, and Dr. Heraux, speaking English very fluently, or quite fluently. said to me: " The constitutional assembly is making nasty remarks about the President."

Mr. HOWE. Would that be the constituent assembly?

Gen. BUTLER. That is the constituent assembly. He said: " The constitutional assembly is making nasty remarks about the President. They are saying he is a bad man, and he is dishonest, and that he is pro-American, and that at 1 o'clock they are going to impeach him, and the President, he do not want to be impeached, and he say to me, ' You tell Gen. Butler to take the gendarmerie and go down there and break them up.' " I said, " That is none of my business, Dr. Heraux, and you know it. I can not take the gendarmerie and go down there and break up your legislature. If the President wants that done, he will have to do it himself. However, if he issues a decree dissolving the assembly, that is his own business." He said, " Let us go to the palace and see what the President wants."

So we went to the palace, and on going upstairs an aide met us in the hall and whispered that the President was sick, but that he ordered me to go down with the gendarmerie and dissolve the assembly. When I saw the President he said, " Good morning," and said he was sick. I said I was very sorry, but that I would like to find out what these orders were he was trying to issue to me relative to the use of the gendarmerie. He came out of his room and went across the hall into the Cabinet room and he said, " I want the assembly dissolved." I said, " All right, sir, then you must write a decree. It is none of my business. I can not use the gendarmerie for that purpose without your written order." He said, " I give you my order." He said he could not sign a decree without the presence of the members of his cabinet, but that the assembly must be dissolved. I said, " Then secure the members of the Cabinet, and sign the decree." He said that was impossible because one of the members was in Cape Hatien, and the simplest way would be for me to go down with the military force and dissolve it. I positively refused to do it. He then sent out and secured four of his five ministers, and a decree which had been previously written, the original of which I have here in my hand, was brought in to the Cabinet room, and the President and his four cabinet ministers signed it, the President being the last one to sign it. He held it in his hand and said, " How shall we deliver it?" I said,

"Mr. President, it is customary for a member of your cabinet to take this and read it to the assembly."

The cabinet ministers looked from one to the other, and Dr. Heraux said, "They do not want to take it. They will be hissed, and maybe they will be shot." The President looked at me and said, "You take it." I said, "I am perfectly willing to take it; I am just a messenger, but there may be bloodshed." There were gendarmes in the assembly room, sent there each morning before the session to preserve order, at the request of the presiding officer, Mr. Stenio Vincent, who was president of the Senate, and a man named Hillaire, who was the presiding officer of the House of Deputies. When meeting as a constituent assembly Vincent presided, but the two sat together behind the speaker's desk, and at the request of the presiding officer the gendarmes were sent each morning as police to preserve order; and that same force—the police force—was at that moment in the assembly room.

The CHAIRMAN. Under the command of an American officer?

Gen. BUTLER. Under the command of an American officer, a captain of Marines and a major of gendarmes. When I said I was willing to carry this message, I knew full well there might be shooting, as on one occasion a revolution started over the casket of a murdered President right in the church, so they never stood on ceremony when they started to shoot. It was not desired to have a cabinet minister shot, so I offered to take this down, which I did. I walked into the assembly amid hisses and jeers, which had no effect, of course, and notified Mr. Vincent that I had a communication from the President of the Republic. He came down from behind the speaker's desk, walked over to me and said, "Let me see it," and I handed it to him and he read it and said, "I would like permission to read this to the assembly." I said, "That is the reason I brought it down here, so that you might read it." He went up behind the desk, and instead of reading it he entered into a vicious assault upon me and all other Americans, and referring to us as foreign dogs and devils dissolving the assembly. The gendarmes, who had previously been Haitian soldiers, and who had taken part in this dissolving function about every six months, had always been accustomed to shoot at this stage of the game, and when the President was criticized they all commenced to load their rifles, which created considerable confusion, and we had to suspend operations until we ran around and took all the cartridges out of their guns. I was their chief, and they were interested in my cause, because I paid them and fed them and treated them squarely. Again we started, after the cartridges were withdrawn, and the members settled in their seats.

The members were quite alarmed, and some of them took refuge under their chairs, because on previous occasions a number of them had been shot by the President's soldiers. He started in again to make remarks derogatory to the Americans, and the second time the gendarmes thought to themselves, as was told me by one of their sergeants, "Surely the time has now come to shoot," and they loaded the second time, which resulted in much confusion. We unloaded them a second time and told the officers not to allow them to do that any more; that we wanted to finish with the meeting. And then Mr. Vincent read this, at the conclusion of which he came down from behind the desk and advanced upon me. The others were milling around and picking up their hats and their notes and going out of the door. The meeting was out, and the presiding officer came toward me waving this paper, and with a look of intense hatred upon his face, and I thought to myself, "Now I am in for a cussing." Instead of that he rushed at me and said, "General, I am hungry." It was the end of his political career, that remark. He was waiving the paper around, and realizing that sooner or later the Haitian Government down there would dodge the issue and put the blame of this on the Americans, I just reached over and took it out of his hand, and here it is.

The CHAIRMAN. He said, "I am hungry?"

Gen. BUTLER. "I am hungry," which was an invitation for me to invite him out to lunch.

This original decree belongs to the files of the Government of Haiti but not caring to be held responsible or charged with exercising undue force in dissolving the assembly, and well realizing they might deny the existence of this, I have kept it, and wish to place it in the files of the United States Senate, if you will allow me to do so.

The CHAIRMAN. File the original and the copy.

Gen. BUTLER. This is the original and the translation.

(The original of the decree referred to was filed with the committee, a translation of which is as follows:)

[Translation.]

DECREE—DARTIGUENAVE, PRESIDENT OF HAITI.

Considering that in order to efficiently develop its agricultural, mineral, and commercial resources, and to prepare a better chance of success for the generations to come, the Republic of Haiti has signed a convention with the Republic of the United States.

Considering that in order to arrive at the application of this convention and to derive all the benefits that it admits, certain constitutional reforms are necessary, free of party spirit and inspired by the desire to launch the nation into the channels of progress and civilization.

Considering that it is with this purpose that the two branches of the Legislative Corps have been organized and called upon to achieve the constitutional reform in the National Assembly, and that, far from being inspired with the idea which gave birth to the convention of September 16, 1915, and (far from) offering to foreign capital the guaranty which it has the right to expect, the National Assembly has had no other preoccupation than to give free rein to political rancor and to hinder the realization of the regenerative program undertaken jointly by the two Governments.

Considering that the national welfare makes it imperative to end the spirit of anarchy which animates the National Assembly and to adopt fitting measures in order to facilitate the development of agriculture, to organize seriously the public education, and to stabilize the finances of the nation.

With the advice of the council of the Secretaries of State.

DECREE.

ARTICLE I. The Chamber of Deputies and the Senate of the Republic are dissolved.

ART. II. The present decree will be published and enforced with dispatch by the Secretaries of State wherever concerned.

Delivered at the national palace at Port au Prince the 19th day of June, in the one hundred and fifteenth year of independence.

DARTIGUENAVE, *President.*
OSMIN CHAM,
Secretary of State of the Interior and Justice.
FURCY-CHATELAIN,
Secretary of State of Foreign Affairs.
Dr. EDMOND HERAUX,
Secretary of State of Finances and Commerce,
Charge par interim with Public Works and Agriculture.

Secretary of State of Public Instruction.

Mr. HOWE. Were there any subsequent developments to this prorogation of the constituent assembly?

Gen. BUTLER. There were. One member of the cabinet resigned the next morning, and all the members called upon the President in large bodies for several days asking for other jobs. He was much worried by them. He had no other jobs to give them. There was no disorder. I was present when they called, and saw the show. The old gentleman was much worried because he had no positions for them. There was no disorder. In fact, the majority of the people were well contented, as they expressed it.

Mr. HOWE. Was there any need for any action by the gendarmerie?

Gen. BUTLER. Not the slightest.

Mr. HOWE. Did any other members of the United States Marine Corps take any action independent of the action of the gendarmerie in connection with this prorogation?

Gen. BUTLER. No; there were no marines present except those who were serving as officers in the gendarmerie.

Mr. HOWE. Were you personally armed when you went down there?

Gen. BUTLER. I was not.

Mr. HOWE. You carried no weapons of any kind?

Gen. BUTLER. I carried no weapon, and never did while going around Haiti.

Mr. Howe. Did you while you were at the chamber, during the time when Vincent was talking or at any other time in the chamber, have a weapon in your hands?

Gen. Butler. I did not, nor on my person. None of the other officers, except as marks of the uniform, ever carried firearms except in line with troops. The country was perfectly peaceful, and I went everywhere without arms and took the President personally without firearms and never had a guard for him. I took him all over Haiti in a Ford automobile without firearms of any kind.

Mr. Howe. What do you know about the state of the prisons down there before the occupation, and what, if anything, was done about the condition of the prisons during the occupation?

Gen. Butler. When the prisons were turned over to us by the President, they were vile beyond description. There were no records to show when the prisoners had been confined, and why they were confined, and when they were to be released. They were rotten with disease and filth, and it is impossible to describe them.

We rebuilt every prison in Haiti. We had an allotment of $8,000 a month for the maintenance of the prison system, that allotment being made by the financial advisor from funds under his control derived from customs receipts. We started two prison schools, one in the penitentiary in Port au Prince and one in the prison at Cape Haitien. We reorganized the prison system, so that prisoners with long terms to serve were transferred to the penitentiary in Port au Prince under my personal observation, and I personally visited that prison on an average of once a day. Those with over 30 days and less than 6 months to serve were placed in the prisons at Cape Haitien and Aux Cayes, the two very big ones. Those with 30 days to serve, the short timers, were placed in the local district lockups. In the two big prisons at Cape Haitien and Port au Prince we started industrial schools. The prisoners built the prisons themselves. We taught them to do concrete work, and you will see when you go down there, Senator, that it is a model prison, with concrete cells. We taught them to make furniture, to repair automobiles, to make shoes, to make clothing, to make baskets, and taught them the tinner's trade.

The Chairman. Parenthetically, are there any trades in the island? Are there any handicraftsmen?

Gen. Butler. Yes; those that I have mentioned.

The Chairman. You taught them, but there were none before?

Gen. Butler. Oh, yes; they had certain trades, not very well performed, any of them, but under the instruction of the commissioned or noncommissioned officers of the Marine Corps who had known these trades on the outside before entering the service, these men were taught. The prison system developed to such an extent that we granted prisoners liberty in the evening to go home, and nearly every morning the roll call showed more prisoners than we were entitled to.

Mr. Howe. How do you account for that?

Gen. Butler. Because they were well fed, well cared for, and well housed and attended to medically. We attended to them and took care of them. There was a regular uniform given them—to the liberty prisoners—and all except the murderers would go home in the evening and spend the night with their families and come back. The earnings which we derived from the sale of their products we gave to their families, that were naturally destitute during the time they were in jail—such earnings as we could get. We made all the clothing for the gendarmerie, shirts, trousers, and blouses, and made ourselves nearly self-supporting.

Mr. Howe. Did you correct the records so that everybody in prison had a record as to when he got in and as to when his term was up?

Gen. Butler. Unless there was some charge against a man or something definite, we released him and started afresh.

Mr. Howe. And thereafter kept these records?

Gen. Butler. And thereafter kept very accurate records.

It might be interesting for the Senate to know that during the year 1917, when most of this prison work was done, there were about two violent deaths in Haiti, which was considered by the President and all Haitians with whom I talked as indicating a remarkably quiet state. Those were not shot by the gendarmes; those were murders.

Mr. Howe. During that year, 1917, were there any engagements between the gendarmerie and marauders or Cacos?

Gen. Butler. Not that I remember.

Mr. HOWE. To go back again to the prorogation of the constituent assembly, I have one more question to ask. Did you at any time, or any one acting under your orders, search the archives of the two chambers and remove certain documents?

Gen. BUTLER. I did not nor did anybody under my orders.

Mr. HOWE. On June 20 or on any other date?

Gen. BUTLER. No.

Mr. HOWE. The document which you have produced here this morning, the order of the President, you obtained from Vincent?

Gen. BUTLER. Vincent himself.

Mr. HOWE. At the moment?

Gen. BUTLER. At the moment.

Mr. HOWE. And in the presence——

Gen. BUTLER. Of all the assembly.

Mr. HOWE. Of all the assembly?

Gen. BUTLER. Yes.

The CHAIRMAN. There are three points we want to cover—education, sanitation, and a word about the physical condition and aspect of a town before and after taking it.

Gen. BUTLER. Senator, I wonder if I might be permitted to go back and read this decree of the President, dissolving the senate?

The CHAIRMAN. We had it once; it is in the record.

Gen. BUTLER. Will you read it?

The CHAIRMAN. Yes; I read it in French just now.

General, will you say something, first, about the physical condition of the towns when you assumed command and at the termination of your command of the gendarmerie, something about the sanitation, and, finally, something about education?

Gen. BUTLER. When we took over the police of Haiti on the 1st of February, 1916, we found no sanitary precautions in any town in Haiti. There was no sewerage system even in Port au Prince.

The CHAIRMAN. Had the streets of Port au Prince at that time been paved?

Gen. BUTLER. Partially paved, sir, under a concession, and the paving was continued throughout the time I was there. There was no water system in any of the towns, with the exception of Port au Prince and Gonaives. There was a water system in several of the larger towns, but very poor pressure. There was one fairly good hospital in Haiti, and that was run by the sisters at Cape Haitien. The others were abominable. There was absolutely nothing of a sanitary nature. We immediately commenced to influence the people in the little towns, as well as the large ones, to clean up their habitations. In many of the little towns, whenever the communal magistrate would allow us a little money from his internal receipts and when we could spare any from the gendarmerie funds, we bought little hand pumps and made little covered wells, instead of the open bucket well which was filled with disease. We put up little street lanterns so that they might be able to see and go about to a certain time at night; we built gutters and did whatever we could in a poor way, without the expenditure of money, to make the towns more sanitary and inhabitable.

The CHAIRMAN. Would they do any work, under your influence, in surfacing the streets?

Gen. BUTLER. Yes; they worked very well under our influence.

The CHAIRMAN. Did they surface the streets in the towns?

Gen. BUTLER. Yes, sir; we surfaced the streets in the towns and built little sidewalks, and we found in 90 per cent of the cases the heartiest cooperation on the part of the civil officials and of the townspeople.

Mr. HOWE. Who did the actual labor?

Gen. BUTLER. The people of the towns themselves. We had no money to pay them, and they would simply fix up in front of their habitations. It was their own movement, just like the roads. Then, when a town had reached a certain degree of cleanliness, and when they were very proud of it, the civil officials invited the President to come to see it, and it was an occasion of great rejoicing. That was one of the methods used by us in encouraging them to clean up—the promise of a big fête day, with the presence of the President and the gendarmerie there. They would make great efforts to clean up.

Mr. HOWE. Under whose supervision was that work done, under the local gendarmerie officer?

Gen. BUTLER. Under the local gendarmerie officer. We had little dispensaries, with medicine, in every town, in which we had a medical officer or a member of the Hospital Corps of the Navy.

Rather to show the confidence of the poorer people, the peasants, in our gendarmerie officers, one instance I would like to quote: In a town called Las Cohobas a native woman brought her baby to the gendarmerie office for safekeeping while she went to market. That became in the towns quite the custom, and we set up little nurseries where we took the babies and cared for them while the women went out to work. The women do all the work; the men do not work. The women are the hard workers.

The men do not do any work except what they have to do in accordance with the law. They sit around and toast in the sun. Our sympathies were entirely with the women, because they really did work. They walked miles and miles to the markets. The life of the market women is rather interesting. One of the curses of Haiti is the market system, because they are on the road all the time. A woman left Las Cohobas one morning with a bunch of bananas, and after traveling a whole week she came back one night with a bunch of another fruit very s'milar to the banana. She spent a whole week, and she had one less bunch of bananas when she got back than when she started out, but she had all the gossip of that end of the world and she was well repaid.

The CHAIRMAN. Was there any complaint of the corvée system on the part of the women?

Gen. BUTLER. No; the women enjoyed seeing the men work; they had been sitting around so long. In fact, the market women developed this. They were so anxious to have decent places to walk, instead of scrambling down the stream beds, that when they came along they would almost invariably stop and throw stones on the roads. They were not required to work. They kept the nation running while the men built the roads.

The school system was deplorable. In fact, there was no school system. They had one on paper, with thousands of instructors, and the other day I quoted the instance, to show the character of the instructors, of sending a check for delivery to a school-teacher at Fort Liberté and instructing the gendarmerie officer to get a receipt, and the school-teacher could not sign the receipt. He said he was not a teacher of writing; he was a teacher of reading. From that you can judge the character of their school system. We brought from Louisiana a man who had knowledge of the Creole language. There are two languages in Haiti, one Creole and one French.

The CHAIRMAN. Could he speak the Creole pato's?

Gen. BUTLER. Quite well.

The CHAIRMAN. Where did he learn that?

Gen. BUTLER. In Louisiana. It is similar to the Louisiana Creole. He had to make a few changes, due to the distance. It changes a little. He became a commissioner of education and an adviser to the minister of public education. His work was not very successful, because advising a minister, unless you have some power, is futile. So we in the gendarmerie branched out as we did in agr'culture, and began to erect modest little schoolhouses of material which we could obtain on the ground.

The CHAIRMAN. Where di'l you get the labor?

Gen. BUTLER. The labor was provided in the same way that we built the streets.

The CHAIRMAN. The people volunteered?

Gen. BUTLER. They volunteered, and it was a long process. We hired one stonemason to put it together, and then the rest, in the afternoons or some time, would deposit b'g piles of stone, and he would work the next day. I hunted around and found quantities of scrap, corrugated iron from burnt buildings, some of them Government buildings, and collected that at the jails, and what was left after rebuilding the old jails, we used in the construction of the schoolhouses. We had no windows or doors, but simply high-walled tent houses. During the time I was there we built 17 of the schoolhouses.

Mr. HOWE. How about the teachers?

Gen. BUTLER. We had no direct control over the teachers. We simply made recommendations when the teachers were unfit to teach, but, of course, you. could not get a very good teacher for 80 cents a month. Some of the salaries were only 4 gourdes, or 80 cents a month, and you could not expect a very good teacher for that. They recommended that their pay be increased, but there was no money to do it.

Mr. HOWE. Who brought about the sending of that adviser on education that you have mentioned?

Gen. BUTLER. That was done by Gen. Cole, who commanded the American marines there.

Mr. HOWE. Are there any other matters which you believe the committee should hear about as to the administration of the occupation in the island?

Gen. BUTLER. I do not think of a thing. I touched the question of martial law. That is the one danger point we have, Senator. You were not here.

The CHAIRMAN. You might take that up again. In connection with what I have said with respect to the administration of justice, you might tell the committee whether you believe, in the event of a re-formation of their judicature, the continuance of martial law would be necessary, provided, of course, that the civil magistrates would do their duty without favor and without fear.

Gen. BUTLER. As long as the American troops stay in Haiti, and their courts are as they are and will remain, unless you change the Haitian characteristics, it is unfair to our soldiers not to give them the protection of martial law. The modified martial law that is now in existence makes a marine comparatively safe. That is, only offenses against the safety of our troops are triable or punishable by the martial law courts.

The CHAIRMAN. Do you not think it might be interesting, in this connection, to study the capitulations between the foreign bureau of Turkey on the one hand, and Egypt on the other, and the system of the administration of justice in Egypt, before the administration commits itself to a policy?

Gen. BUTLER. I think that might be well. I am not familiar with the Egyptian system.

The CHAIRMAN. It is a long time since I have studied it, but I am under the impression that in Egypt an assessor sits on the bench with the Egyptian judge, and advises him in the formulation of his decisions.

Gen. BUTLER. That system is all right. Under the present system in Haiti, the murder of a marine would call for nothing but commendation on the part of the Haitian courts.

(Whereupon the committee adjourned until Thursday, November 3, 1921, at 10.30 o'clock a. m.)

INQUIRY INTO OCCUPATION AND ADMINISTRATION OF HAITI AND SANTO DOMINGO.

THURSDAY, NOVEMBER 3, 1921.

UNITED STATES SENATE,
SELECT COMMITTEE ON HAITI AND SANTO DOMINGO,
Washington, D. C.

The committee met, pursuant to adjournment, at 10.30 o'clock a. m., Senator Medill McCormick (chairman) presiding.

Present: Senators McCormick and Oddie.

Also present: Mr. Walter Bruce Howe, Mr. Ernest Angell, and Maj. Edwin N. McClellan.

STATEMENT OF LIEUT. COL. ALEXANDER S. WILLIAMS, UNITED STATES MARINE CORPS, ARMY WAR COLLEGE, WASHINGTON, D. C.

Mr. HOWE. Colonel, will you give your name, rank, and present station, please?

Col. WILLIAMS. Alexander S. Williams, lieutenant colonel, Marine Corps, Army War College, Washington.

Mr. HOWE. You, as an officer of the Marine Corps, succeeded Gen. Smedley Butler as commandant of the Haitian gendarmerie, did you not?

Col. WILLIAMS. Yes.

Mr. HOWE. At what date?

Col. WILLIAMS. I was appointed chief of the gendarmerie on the 2d of May, 1918.

Mr. HOWE. How long did that term of duty last? When did you cease to be chief of the gendarmerie?

Col. WILLIAMS. I left Haiti on the 19th of July, 1919.

Mr. HOWE. How long before you left did you cease to be chief of the gendarmerie?

Col. WILLIAMS. I was chief until the date of my departure.

Mr. HOWE. Is that the correct title, chief of gendarmerie?

Col. WILLIAMS. That is the exact translation of the French title.

Mr. HOWE. Had you been serving in Haiti before you became chief of the gendarmerie?

Col. WILLIAMS. I landed in Haiti on the 15th of August, 1915, and was in Haiti continuously, except for two periods of leave, until the date of departure.

Mr. HOWE. That means just short of four years, then, Colonel?

Col. WILLIAMS. Just short of four years.

Mr. HOWE. The gendarmerie, when you succeeded Gen. Butler, was recruited up to substantially its full strength?

Col. WILLIAMS. Practically its maximum authorized strength.

Mr. HOWE. Had you served with the gendarmerie before you became its chief?

Col. WILLIAMS. Yes; I was appointed assistant chief of the gendarmerie on the 31st of August, 1916.

Mr. HOWE. So you were assistant chief for a little less than a year and chief for a little more than a year?

Col. WILLIAMS. Assistant chief for nearly two years; but prior to that I had been associated with the native police, which was developed into the gendarmerie, from the 2d of September, 1915.

Mr. HOWE. At the time you became chief of gendarmerie, what were the methods in use by which the chief could receive reports and communicate with his subordinates throughout the country? Can you give us a general description of your methods of communication and your methods of reporting?

Col. WILLIAMS. When the organization of the native police, with a view to its development into a national military police, was begun, the methods of communication available throughout the Republic were by telegraph, telephone, mail, and mounted messenger. The wire communications were extremely inefficient, the mail communications were utterly unreliable, and courier service was very slow and not dependable. The post did not increase in efficiency notably until about three years of American occupation had passed. Wire communications increased in efficiency from the very beginning, because the lines were put in repair by the marine personnel, and certain wire lines were erected and operated by marine personnel, so that the wire communications increased progressively in efficiency from the very beginning until the end, when they were normally fair. Communication by courier increased——

Mr. HOWE. Just before you get off the subject of the wires, what type of circuit was there in use there? Did you have a metallic circuit?

Col. WILLIAMS. No; all the wire lines were ground return—that is, a single wire, with an earth return--and subject to constant interruption because of the climatic conditions. The insulation would be largely lost because of rain; and as in many stretches the wires were fastened to trees rather than to poles, a windstorm would carry them away. In addition to that, the wires themselves were in a very bad state through constant breaks and splicing. I counted between two poles at one time 110 splices.

Mr. HOWE. Why was not a more efficient system installed, do you know?

Col WILLIAMS. Because the Haitian administration was not competent to install one.

Mr. HOWE. Were the funds available to the gendarmerie for the restoration or improvement of the lines?

Col. WILLIAMS. The military commander, who disbursed certain Haitian funds turned over to him by Admiral Caperton, I believe, allotted a small amount for the purchase of material and for labor, but most of the repair was done with marine expeditionary material and by marine personnel.

Mr. HOWE. Is it correct to say that it was a lack of funds which really prevented a further improvement in the wire communications?

Col. WILLIAMS. By the Haitian Government, you mean?

Mr. HOWE. By the Haitian Government or by our military authorities?

Col. WILLIAMS. In the case of the Haitian Government, funds could have been found for this purpose. In the case of repairs made by the American military authorities, we were undoubtedly hampered by the lack of funds and personnel.

Mr. HOWE. You were going on to speak of the road communications, or the messenger communications.

Col. WILLIAMS. As we became familiar with the geography of Haiti and the existing road system, and found that certain couriers were reliable, and others were not, and had determined approximately the necessary time for the transmission of messages by courier, we were able to more efficiently conduct a courier service, and also hold up the couriers themselves to a better standard of performance.

Mr. HOWE. How would you characterize the development of your courier service? Did it become efficient?

Col. WILLIAMS. Its development to the point of efficiency was never reached, because we finally brought about a fairly satisfactory system of wire communication. In the interior, however, we were dependent upon couriers to a great extent, especially when the wire lines went out, and for limited distances the courier service might be said to be fairly efficient.

Mr. HOWE. Colonel, with these means at your disposal, what system was possible by which you could supervise your command, and by which you could learn of the performance of its duties by your command? How did you keep in touch with it?

Col. WILLIAMS. In the very beginning the headquarters of the gendarmerie can hardly be said to have kept in touch; communications were so bad, and access to the more remote posts so difficult. With the improvement of the service certain reports were called for. All officers who were charged with any individual responsibility were required to make, first, a monthly report, which gave every contact which the gendarmerie made with the Haitian society or with Haiti. That report was divided into heads and subheads, and was very complete, and was designed to give the chief of the gendarmerie a cross section of the gendarmerie activities in any area.

In addition to that, the ordinary military reports of strength, health of the command, progress of barrack construction, progress in road work, condition of the prisons, the inmates, etc. Also reports were obtained informally from every available source. It was customary, for instance, for travelers of the better class visiting Pourt au Prince to call on the chief of the gendarmerie, and when they did this they were cross-examined so far as possible regarding conditions. In addition, the Haitian Government received from its various officials reports covering their administrative work, and from time to time, where these reports touched on the activities of the gendarmerie, either in the way of favorable or unfavorable comment, excerpts from the reports would be forwarded by the minister of the interior to the ch'ef of the gendarmerie for his informat'on, and sometimes with the request that an investigation be made. The best means, however, that the senior officers of the gendarmerie had of obtaining knowledge of what was going on in the country was by visits. These visits were unannounced, followed no particular schedule, and were cons'dered the most valuable means of keeping in touch with the work. On these visits the chief of the gendarmerie, or the department commander and the assistant chief, who also inspected, was called upon by all the local officials, and he discussed with them the conditions obtaining in their districts, with particular reference to the work of the gendarmerie. These occasions were considered very valuable indeed as a means of obtaining information, and the local officials never hesitated to speak frankly, and often in a critical fashion, of anything to which they might object.

Mr. HOWE. Did the district commanders make reports of these meetings to the chief and the senior officer as a rule? Say, if a district commander held one of these meetings which you have described was that meeting and anything that developed in it, reported to headquarters?

Col. WILLIAMS. Yes; if anything of note developed, mention would be made of it. Ordinarily, however, there would be perhaps three or four of these meetings in one day, and they were, in certain respects, rather tiresome. No formal report would be made that a meeting had been held in such a State and location.

Mr. HOWE. If anything unusual, however, came up, it would be reported?

Col. WILLIAMS. It should have been reported, and it usually was.

Mr. HOWE. And were these visits comprehensive? Did they cover all posts?

Col. WILLIAMS. In my own case, I visited all but three, I think, of the gendarmeries posts, and they were so remote and of so little importance that I could not spare the time for the detour necessary to visit them.

Mr. HOWE. Did the district commanders, however, visit the posts in their command with fair frequency?

Col. WILLIAMS. The district commanders were required to visit all posts in their commands quite frequently. I have forgotten what the regulation said in the matter. The subdistrict commanders made more frequent visits than the district commanders, and the department commander visited all headquarter posts in his department at certain intervals, and all subdistrict posts in his department at certain intervals—just what they were I have forgotten.

Mr. HOWF. But these visits were systematized?

Col. WILLIAMS. The visits were systematized in that they must be made within certain periods, but they were not on a schedule of dates.

Mr. HOWE. In case any emergency came up, were there no means available for the officer in the outlying country to receive instructions or to ask them from headquarters?

Col. WILLIAMS. In the large cities it was comparatively easy to get in communication with headquarters. In many of them it was possible to get into direct telephonic communication. I speak now of the later development of the wire lines. In the smaller posts it was sometimes very difficult, but unless the methods of communication had been interfered with by hostile natives, there would be but one post, I think, more than two days beyond communication with headquarters. That means that a courier from that post would probably take two days to reach the nearest reliable wire station.

The CHAIRMAN. How many of such posts were there?

Col. WILLIAMS. I think there was but one. I may say, however, that an officer might wire with full confidence of receiving an answer and the message never go through. There were a good many relay points on these wire lines.

The CHAIRMAN. Who were the operators?

Col. WILLIAMS. The operators were Haitians.

Mr. HOWE. Under those conditions, Colonel, what confidence could headquarters have of knowing of all cases of irregularity in the conduct of the gendarmerie?

Col. WILLIAMS. Its confidence in knowing of the regularities immed'ately following their occurrence was fairly good; of knowing of them eventually it was excellent. No irregularity, and I speak from recollection of personal instances, could obtain over any considerable period without knowledge coming to headquarters from unofficial sources, or from the Haitian Government itself.

Mr. HOWE. When serious irregularities were heard of, or reported at headquarters, was an investigation always made?

Col. WILLIAMS. An investigation was made of any report, however absurd it might seem on its face. A great part of our officers' work was investigating reports which on their face were unworthy of credence.

Mr. HOWE. In general, all these answers of yours would apply to the time during which you were chief of the gendarmerie?

Col. WILLIAMS. Yes; except where I spoke specifically of the great inefficiency of the wire communications.

Mr. HOWE. During the time you were commander how many instances were reported to you of the killing of natives who, at the time they were killed, had already been taken prisoner, and without trial?

Col. WILLIAMS. I can remember two instances. The dates I can not give, but the location and the attendant circumstances I remember fairly well.

Mr. HOWE. Those are the cases of which you heard, as distinguished from cases investigated and either disproven or confirmed?

Col. WILLIAMS. These were both investigated.

Mr. HOWE. Is two the total number of which you heard?

Col. WILLIAMS. Oh, no.

Mr. HOWE. Let me qualify that question a little bit more. Killings for which the responsibility was attributed to white officers of the gendarmerie? I am excluding any killings which you may have heard of, unauthorized killings by native members of the gendarmerie, but I am referring to reports of unauthorized killings of native prisoners on the responsibility of white officers of the gendarmerie. How many such reports did you receive? If you can not remember exactly an approximate answer would suit my purposes for the present.

Col. WILLIAMS. I am trying to remember whether or not any came to my notice. I do not remember any report ever having been made of the killing of prisoners on the responsibility of a white officer.

Mr. HOWE. You mentioned a moment ago two cases of which you could not remember the precise dates, but where you could describe the attendant circumstances. Which were those two cases? Can you give the names of the officers involved for the purpose of identifying them?

Col. WILLIAMS. In neither case was a white officer involved. They were unjustified killings of prisoners by gendarmes, and in both cases the gendarme was court-martialed and punished. I think in one case sentenced to death and executed, but in the other case I do not remember what the punishment was.

Mr. HOWE. Before we get to those, let me ask you if you are, in general, familiar with the contents of the investigation conducted by Maj. Turner, Col. Hooker, and Col. Lay, with the investigation conducted by Gens. Lejeune and Butler, and with the Mayo court of inquiry?

Col. WILLIAMS. I am familiar with the investigation conducted by Maj. Turner to the extent to which I was a party. I was personally interrogated by Col. Lay. I was at that time given an opportunity to hastily look over the testimony of other witnesses. Of the proceedings of the Mayo court and of the investigations conducted by Gens. Lejeune and Butler I know nothing.

Mr. HOWE. Then, let me ask you this: In those three investigations there were charges investigated and testimony taken which brought in the names of Lieut. Brokaw, that, in the first instance, came up in the Johnson court-martial record, the case of Capt. Lavoie, charged with having prisoners killed; of Lieutenant, I think it was Lang, who was charged with killing a native unjustifiably; Lieut. Williams, charged with killing the notary, Garnier—I do not mean in the strict sense charged, but accused in some manner—and an officer about whom a resident called Liftshitz testified, he referring to that officer by the name of Koskoski. Did you learn anything of the circumstances connected with these accusations against those officers whom I have mentioned?

Col. WILLIAMS. Your question makes it necessary that I amend my answer to a previous one where I stated that I had received no reports of any unauthorized killings under the authority of a white officer. I meant by that that I had received no reports of such killings when action lay in my hands. With the cases you mention I am more or less familiar.

Mr. HOWE. Will you please explain a little bit further just what you mean by that?

Col. WILLIAMS. The status of a gendarmerie officer in Haiti was rather anomolous. He was serving under a commission issued by the President of Haiti on the nomination of the President of the United States, and in this capacity he was subject to such control as the Haitian Government chose to exercise. At the same time he remained a member of the American naval forces. As such he was included in the personnel of the Marine brigade serving in Haiti, and all American officers and noncommissioned officers serving with Haitian commissions were organized as the constabulary detachment of the United States Marine Corps and were a part of the brigade organization.

The CHAIRMAN. They were subject to the orders of the commandant of the gendarmerie?

Col. WILLIAMS. They were subject to the orders of the commandant of the gendarmerie, both under the gendarmerie regulations which had Haitian sanction and as members of the constabulary detachment, which was an organization of the Marine Corps.

The CHAIRMAN. The commandant of the gendarmerie, then, was responsible for the discipline and the conduct of the Marine Corps officers and men detached for service in the gendarmerie?

Col. WILLIAMS. Within the limitations of the authority laid down in the Navy regulations for the commanders of small organizations when included in larger ones. The authority of the chief of the gendarmerie with respect to the American personnel of the gendarmerie was that of the commander of a company post. He could, for instance, order summary courts on the enlisted personnel, and he could punish officers to the extent permitted by the Navy regulations.

The CHAIRMAN. What steps were necessary for him to bring offenders before general courts-martial?

Col. WILLIAMS. He would have to recommend their trial to the brigade commander, who was authorized to order general courts.

The CHAIRMAN. Who was responsible for the regulations of the department governing the conduct and discipline of officers in this detachment? Whence were they issued?

Col. WILLIAMS. They were never issued; they always existed. We were still officers and enlisted men of the Marine Corps and were governed in that status by the existing Naval regulations and orders.

The CHAIRMAN. Who, then, was responsible for the orders governing the discipline of the gendarmerie?

Col. WILLIAMS. The gendarmerie regulations were prepared largely by Gen. Butler and myself, and after approval by the President of Haiti became operative for all who were serving in the gendarmerie, either American officers or enlisted men.

The CHAIRMAN. Then you and Gen. Butler were responsible, or if he was in command at the time he was responsible, for the regulations of the gendarmerie?

Col. WILLIAMS. If you mean the regulations of the gendarmerie——

The CHAIRMAN. Well, for the rules governing their discipline?

Col. WILLIAMS. The rules were prepared by Gen. Butler and myself with the advice and counsel of various people, and submitted to the Haitian Government, and the Haitian Government approved them, an approval which was required, I believe, by the treaty, or the gendarmerie agreement, and then became the regulations for the interior administration of the gendarmerie.

The CHAIRMAN. The rules governing the discipline of American officers serving with the gendarmerie, then, were those of the American Navy in force before the occupation began, of course?

Col. WILLIAMS. Yes.

The CHAIRMAN. Supplemented by those authorized by yourself, Gen. Butler, and others, and sanct'oned. by the President of Haiti?

Col. WILLIAMS. Not supplemented, Senator; they were concurrent.

The CHAIRMAN. Well, concurrent, if you please.

Col. WILLIAMS. There were two sets of regulations for the regulation of the personnel.

Mr. Howe. The gendarmerie regulations did not authorize a general court-martial. Was that right?

Col. Williams. They did.

Mr. Howe. For American officers?

Col. Williams. Not for American officers, but for members of the Haitian gendarmerie whose conduct merited such trial.

Mr. Howe. Would that include American officers?

Col. Williams. One test case was made, and a lieutenant whose name I have forgotten was tried by a gendarmerie general court-martial, and I believe sentenced to dismissal. He protested against this. How far his protest was carried I do not know—I was not chief at the time—but it was not sustained, and he was separated by the sentence of the court from the gendarmerie and reverted to the status of an enlisted man in the Marine Corps. He was then transferred from the constabulary detachment 'to the brigade and continued to serve, I assume, as an enlisted man in the brigade. No other officer was tried. We did not have the available material for their trial.

Mr. Howe. Now, Colonel, to illustrate that explanation which you gave a while ago as to your knowledge of these cases which I mentioned, as I understand it, you said that none of these cases was reported to you during the time in which you could take action?

Col. Williams. I meant by that that the report was either investigated by the brigade commander who assumed jurisdiction, and that was true in the case of Brokaw——

Mr. Howe. Who was brigade commander?

Col. Williams. Gen. Catlin.

Mr. Howe. He assumed, as I understand it, jurisdiction before the report had reached you or before you had had an opportunity to investigate. Was that correct?

Col. Williams. That was true in the case of Brokaw. In the case of Lavoie, Williams, and Lang Gen. Catlin made the investigations himself and assumed jurisdiction. Of Lang's case I do not know, except as I heard incidentally.

Mr. Howe. Then the first report, or the first action in the case of these officers whose names I have mentioned, Brokaw, Lavoie, Lang, Williams, and one more mentioned by Lifshitz, was taken, in the first place, by the brigade commander?

Col. Williams. By the brigade commander.

Mr. Howe. Did you learn officially, or at first hand otherwise than officially, of any of the circumstances in any of these cases? For instance, take the Brokaw case, Brokaw being the officer alleged to have directed Pvts. Johnson and McQuilkin to shoot prisoners.

Col. Williams. In the case of Brokaw I know nothing at first hand. The investigation of that case was conducted by the brigade commander, and final action was taken by him. Do you want the circumstances of that case? Investigation of that case was conducted by the brigade commander, and ordered the court-martial of Pvts. Johnson and McQuilkin?

Col. Williams. The brigade commander. I had no authority to order general courts on members of the marine personnel.

Mr. Howe. Did the brigade commander, however, take action in those cases on your report or suggestion?

Col. Williams. I know nothing whatsoever about those cases, except as I have heard.

Mr. Howe. Did the killings alleged in those cases take place while you were commander of the gendarmerie?

Col. Williams. Yes; but the men involved were not members of either the gendarmerie or the constabulary detachment.

Mr. Howe. That is it, they were out as members of the Marine Corps, on telephone duty, is not that it, and not under your jurisdiction?

Col. Williams. On what duty they were I do not know; they were not under my command.

Mr. Howe. In the case of Capt. Lavoie, as I understand it, he has never been court-martialed. What did you learn directly about the case of Capt. Lavoie? Will you go into that fully?

Col. Williams. Early in March, 1919, I visited central Haiti with Gen. Catlin. Gen. Catlin wished me to go along, and led me to believe that he had received reports in regard to conditions in central Haiti which warranted an investigation. I accompanied him on this trip, but was not present at his examination of

Williams or Lavoie. In fact, his investigation was conducted without my presence designedly.

The CHAIRMAN. How designedly—designedly on his part or yours?

Col. WILLIAMS. Designedly on his part, and I agreed with h.m. It was thought that the presence of the chief of the gendarmer,e, who had considerable prestige among the natives, would perhaps influence the native witnesses to reticence. I agreed with Gen. Catlin in this, and also pointed out to him that the exclusion of the chief of the gendarmer.e would have a reflex so bad as to more than offset, in my opinion, any benefits which followed my absence. That reflex would be in the minds of the natives, that the chief of the gendarmer,e, the biggest man they ever met, was now ent.rely d.scredited, and the Haitian being an opportunist by tradition and dispos:tion, would see an opportunity to place himself in favorable light in the eyes of the new man by telling things discreditable to the old one and his administration.

The CHAIRMAN. As a matter of fact, how was this tour of investigation or inspection conducted?

Col. WILLIAMS. Gen. Catlin first sent for the local officials and questioned them regarding conditions in the district. He sent for the local priest and questioned him.

The CHAIRMAN. Were you, as a matter of fact, excluded from most of these investigations?

Col. WILLIAMS. I was, as I said, designedly excluded.

The CHAIRMAN. Now, in the case of Capt. Lavoie, did you take any part in that investigation whatsoever?

Col. WILLIAMS. I took no part in the investigation, but after Gen. Catlin had interviewed Lavoie over a considerable period, privately, Gen. Catl'n sent for me and told Lavoie to repeat before me that which he had told him relative to the execution of certain prisoners.

The CHAIRMAN. And what did Capt. Lavoie say then in your presence and that of Gen. Catlin?

Col. WILLIAMS. Lavoie stated that he had caused to be executed a certain number of prisoners. Six or seven is in my mind—how many he exactly stated I do not remember. That concluded the investigation so far as I was involved.

The CHAIRMAN. Did he say nothing of the circumstances under which the execution was done?

Col. WILLIAMS. He explained how this execution had been carried on.

Mr. HOWE. And where?

Col. WILLIAMS. And where.

Mr. HOWE. Will you tell us what he said as well as you can recollect it?

Col. WILLIAMS. He said these men——

The CHAIRMAN. Where was he stationed, at Hinche?

Col. WILLIAMS. At Hinche. He said that the men were well known Cacos, as he called them; that they had been captured redhanded; that the civil courts of Haiti gave no assurance that they would be punished; that the only agency for their punishment was the marine provost court in Cape Haitien.

Mr. HOWE. The marine provost court?

Col. WILLIAMS. The marine provost court, and that that court had been limited by recent orders to six months confinement, and a very considerable gold fine, which would be beyond the capacity of any Haitian to pay, that is any Haitian of the peasant class; that if sentenced to six months, good conduct would reduce it to four, and then they would be back on his hands and augment the bands which he was then trying to put out of business. That was his explanation of his reason. He did not go into the details of the execution, but said that it had been carried out a short distance from town.

Mr. HOWE. From what town?

Col. WILLIAMS. From the town of Hinche, on the road leading to Maissade, and that it had been carried out by a detachment of gendarmes. That was, as far as I recollect it, what he said.

The CHAIRMAN. By his orders?

Col. WILLIAMS. Yes; the execution.

Mr. HOWE. The execution had been carried out by gendarmes by his orders?

Col. WILLIAMS. By his orders.

Mr. HOWE. Did he fix this by date at all?

Col. WILLIAMS. I do not think he did; if he did I do not remember.

Mr. HOWE. It was, however, the only occurrence of that kind of which he spoke to you and Gen. Catlin?

Col. WILLIAMS. I do not know what he said to Gen. Catlin.

Mr. HOWE. To you and Gen. Catlin together, I mean.

Col. WILLIAMS. Together, that was the only case of which he spoke.

Mr. HOWE. Before you and Gen. Catlin?

Col. WILLIAMS. The only case of a killing that was spoken of.

Mr. HOWE. Is that all that you recollect of the talk there between Capt. Lavoie, you and Gen. Catlin?

Col. WILLIAMS. I think Gen. Catlin and I discussed the extraordinary aspects of this case.

Mr. HOWE. But was that in the presence of Capt. Lavoie?

Col. WILLIAMS. No.

Mr. HOWE. So that was all of what Lavoie said at that time, in your presence?

Col. WILLIAMS. Yes.

Mr. HOWE. Then you did have a discussion with Gen. Catlin thereafter?

Col. WILLIAMS. I believe we did.

Mr. HOWE. Do you know why charges were not then preferred against Lavoie? What is the reason they were not? Why did you not prefer charges at that time?

Col. WILLIAMS. I did not prefer charges because the case was out of my hands, my immediate military senior having taken cognizance of it. Why Gen. Catlin did not prefer charges I can not state, because he never told me directly. From the general tenor, however, of the entire investigation, I am led to believe that, despite Lavoie's statement, who is a wild talker, Gen. Catlin was not convinced of the truth of it. That, however, is an assumption on my part.

Mr. HOWE. Mr. Chairman, Gen. Catlin will be called as a witness, I hope next week, before this committee, and will, of course, be interrogated on this point when he appears as a witness.

As to L'eut. Williams, did you make any investigation yourself, or were you present at any investigation in his case? I mean the Lieut. Williams who was charged with killing the native notary, Garnier?

Col. WILLIAMS. Lieut. Williams is the subdistrict commander at Maissade. Gen. Catlin and I, with several other officers, Gen. Catlin's interpreter, and a priest from St. Michel, went to Maissade by motor. There Gen. Catlin interrogated certain of the civil officials and asked if there were any gendarmes who wished to make any complaint against Lieut. Williams, their commanding officer. What Gen. Catlin heard from the civil officials I do not know. I was again des'gnedly excluded. In the case of the gendarmes I was also excluded designedly, but was asked by Gen. Catlin to be present when they repeated what they had told him. Their complaints about Lieut. Williams were not pertinent to Catlin's investigation of conditions, so the allegations made against Williams were founded upon an investigation at which I was not present. I must modify that. One of the witnesses whom Gen. Catlin interrogated was also directed by Gen. Catlin to repeat what he had told them. That was in reference to the death of Garnier Jean. The allegations made against Williams were not, as far as I could make out from my part in the investigat'on and subsequent investigations, substantiated in any degree by the witnesses, but the investigat'on having been taken over by Gen. Catlin, I made no official investigation in the sense of having a board investigate it; I investigated it myself.

Mr. HOWE. The Lang case you know nothing about?

Col. WILLIAMS. Of the Lang case I know nothing.

Mr. HOWE. The Mayo court of inquiry heard the Lang case, and, as I understand it, Mr. Chairman, exonerated Lieut. Lang entirely, but the facts of that will appear when the record of the Mayo court is put in evidence here, as it will be.

These cases, I believe, Colonel, that I have mentioned are all of the principal cases which were developed in the course of these investigations. Do you know whether the statements made by these witnesses before you, when requested to do so by Gen. Catlin, were substantially the same statements as they had made before Gen. Catlin previous to mak'ng them before you?

Col. WILLIAMS. In the case of Lavoy, Gen. Catlin did not indicate in any way that what he told me differed substant'ally from what he had told him. In the case of those witnesses who were asked to repeat before me that which they had told Gen. Catlin in the case of Williams, I think there were some differences, and I think they were substantial. I do not remember just what the details were. There were some questions that came up in regard to the interpretation. If I may explain at this time, Creole is the language of the Haitian peasant, but Creole differs in the different parts of the country. There is the south Creole, the north Creole, and central Creole. The interpreter, a Haitian named Holly, at that time did not seem to well translate central Creole, but whether the differences in statement between those made to Gen. Catlin alone and to Gen. Catlin and me together were due to the interpreter or to being entirely different, I do not remember.

Mr. Howe. These were, of course, the cases of native witnesses that you are referring to now?

Col. Williams. These were all native witnesses. There were no other witnesses.

· Mr. Howe. Then, aside from Brokaw, Lavoy, and Williams, you know of no other accusations having been made against any of the white gendarmerie officers in connection with the killing of native prisoners; is that it?

Col. Williams. I believe one officer was tried by general court-martial in connection with a killing. That was Hamilton.

Mr. Howe. Then, adding the name of Hamilton, those were all that you heard of?

Col. Williams. Yes.

Mr. Howe. Then the only killings of prisoners under the orders of white officers down there or by white officers are the ones of which these people that I have mentioned were accused, these officers that I have mentioned?

Col. Williams. Yes.

Mr. Howe. Do you believe there were any more killings than those, supposing even that those took place?

Col. Williams. From my knowledge of the gendarmerie American personnel, a very intimate knowledge gained during the close association of four years, my belief is that the gendarme American was inspired by a very high sense of duty; that he considered his paramount duty, first, to do everything which would advance the interests of the Haitians; second, to do everything which might reflect credit on the Marine Corps. Aside from this conception of duty, they all showed the greatest friendliness and sympathy for the natives. They identified themselves with every local movement for the betterment of their districts, and not only developed an acquired national spirit but a district pride, which made them jealous and resentful of what they would consider favoritism shown in allotting more funds to one district than to another. Their relations with the natives were very friendly; they were spoken of highly by all classes, though criticized from time to time for what might not meet with the approval of the people, and it is difficult for me to believe that any gendarme officer would deliberately kill or cause to be killed a native who was under his control. I except those when in military operations.

Mr. Howe. And you referred to what might be described as cold-blooded killings of natives after they had become prisoners?

Col. Williams. Yes.

Mr. Howe. And you, therefore, do not believe that, aside from these possible cases which have been mentioned, that there were any of those cold-blooded killings under the direction or by gendarmerie officers?

Col. Williams. I not only do not believe that there were any others, but I am far from convinced that the ones alleged occurred.

Mr. Howe. As alleged?

Col. Williams. As alleged. I may say in this connection that I have no doubt whatever that many natives were killed by the native personnel of the gendarmerie. I say that because I had occasion to try a number by court-martial, and turned over to the civil authorities for trial by the criminal courts a number who, without any good reason, had killed prisoners or people whom they were about to make prisoners.

Mr. Howe. I want to come back to that branch of your testimony and go into it thoroughly. Before we get there, there is just one other matter I want to ask you about, Colonel, in connection with the white officers of the gendarmerie. Had you reason to suppose while you were chief of the gendarmerie that any officers under your command directly or indirectly encouraged the killing of prisoners?

Col. Williams. I had no reason to believe it and every reason not to believe it. I attempted by personal conversation and in written communications to indoctrinate all the officers, and I hoped through them to indoctrinate the native personnel with the idea that no life must be taken and that no suffering must be inflicted unless it was absolutely necessary to the legal carrying out of police duties or military operations.

Mr. Howe. To be more specific, have you any reason to believe that Maj. Wells encouraged officers under his command to kill natives after the natives had been taken prisoner? I refer to Maj. Wells, who was, I believe, a district commander.

Col. Williams. He was a department commander in north Haiti. From an intimate association with Maj. Wells, I do not believe that Maj. Wells ever encouraged, much less directed, the killing of prisoners. I say that from a knowledge of his character, from a realization that such things would be counter to gendarmerie policy, and, thirdly, because Maj. Wells would have considerable difficulty in having such orders carried out. The subordinate officers I do not believe would lend themselves to any such program. And, moreover, the fact that such orders had been issued or such things resulted would sooner or later come to me.

Mr. Howe. And it did not come to you?

Col. Williams. And it did not come to me.

Mr. Howe. Later on in the course of some of these investiagtions, the investigation by Maj. Turner, some witnesses testified that Maj. Wells had used language to this effect to them: "I do not want to have any prisoners taken; you know what to do with the prisoners." You never heard of Maj. Wells using such language to his subordinates, or giving such directions to his subordinates, or making such suggestions to his subordinates, during all the time he was under your command?

Col. Williams. No.

Mr. Howe. Or at any other time?

Col. Williams. Such parts of the investigation that have come out or come to my knowledge informed me of that allegation.

Mr. Howe. But that is your only information?

Col. Williams. That is all I know of it.

Mr. Howe. On the subject?

Col. Williams. On that subject.

Mr. Howe. Is there any further statement you care to make about Maj. Wells or the accusations against Maj. Wells? What was his first name—which Maj. Wells?

Col. Williams. Clarke H. Wells.

Mr. Howe. That is the Maj. Wells to whom we have been referring here?

Col. Williams. Yes. Maj. Wells, I understand, is further alleged to have informed his district and subdistrict commanders that they were to report tranquillity in their districts, whereas, in fact, conditions were far from peaceful. I can not reconcile that with the common sense which distinguishes Wells. It was unnecessary. I knew, and it was a matter of common knowledge, that conditions were not tranquil in these districts, and, moreover, it would be impossible for the attack of a small gendarmerie post and the killing of several gendarmes to be passed over in that fashion. A knowledge of that would have to come to me. Wells could not conceal it, and I therefore do not believe that he issued such orders.

Mr. Howe. Now, as to killings of natives by native members of the gendarmerie, have you any reason to believe that such killings occurred—I mean, of native prisoners?

Col. Williams. I know they occurred. I had occasion to investigate a great many; and where there was any hope of obtaining evidence sufficiently credible to warrant trial, these gendarmes were brought to trial. Sometimes they were convicted and sometimes acquitted.

Mr. Howe. Before what tribunal?

Col. Williams. Before the gendarmerie general court-martial, authorized by the gendarmerie regulations, which could give the death sentence. subject to the approval of the President.

Mr. Howe. The President of Haiti?

Col. Williams. The President of Haiti.

The Chairman. Were any men executed as the result of these trials?

Col. Williams. My recollection is that only one man was executed, and he was executed, I believe, in the town of Ouanaminthe. He had been convicted by the gendarmerie general court-martial of murder. Whether it was a prisoner, or what not, I do not remember. You must understand, Senator, that I had hundreds and hundreds of courts to look over, and I do not remember the details.

The CHAIRMAN. In that connection, Colonel, I want to ask if, in killing prisoners without trial, the gendarmerie did something which had never before been done in Haiti, or if, in your judgment, they did that which, under the old administration, had been done by the forces subject to the command of the generals arrondissement, etc.?

Col. WILLIAMS. For the unauthorized killing of prisoners, there is an uninterrupted series of precedents running back to that established by Cacique Caonabo in 1492.

The CHAIRMAN. Is that a Caribbean chieftain?

Col. WILLIAMS. Columbus discovered Haiti in 1492, and the *Santa Maria* was lost in the waters near what is now Cape Haitien, and out of the timbers of the *Santa Maria* he built Fort Nativity. He left in that fort, not being able to accommodate them on his reduced fleet, about 29 Spaniards. These Spaniards were so brutal in their treatment of the natives, a very harmless lot, and so exigent in their demands that gold be produced that the natives in the north, under the leadership of the Cacique Caonabo, massacred every last one of them, and destroyed the fort.

The CHAIRMAN. You think, then, that certainly during the period of the existence of the Haitian Republic executions without trial were customary?

Col. WILLIAMS. I would not say customary; I would say they were very usual. Our greatest problem in the organization of the gendarmerie was the gendarme. Our little experience with him had led us to believe that he was utterly indifferent to the value of human life; that he was prone to make the most of his police authority, and very liable to exceed it. His treatment of prisoners was generally brutal. The earlier arrests were attended by great ill treatment of the prisoner, usually by clubbing, and it was with the greatest difficulty, by the infliction of the severest punishments, that his attitude toward prisoners became materially modified. One of my best noncommissioned officers, an English-speaking gendarme, made an arrest in the town of Leogane. For some reason which I have forgotten I was interested in this particular arrest, and sent for the corporal when he returned to the capital. He said that the prisoner had been left by him in Leogane. Why? Because the prisoner had attempted to escape, and he had shot him in the leg. I had him explain the circumstances of the attempted escape, and the corporal told me, and they seemed reasonable and would have justified firing on the escaping prisoner. I then asked him what measures he had taken to hold the prisoner, and he said he had arranged for his burial, and it developed then that he had shot him in the leg, and not being able to stand the sight of his suffering, he shot him through the head as he lay on the ground. This early instance was a great shock because this man was a representative of the 3,000 with whom we would have to police Haiti.

The CHAIRMAN. Did you have that case investigated?

Col. WILLIAMS. That case was investigated in more or less of an informal manner, because in the beginning it was impossible to investigate everything that came up. I was satisfied, however, that the occurrence was substantially as I have stated.

The CHAIRMAN. That the prisoner really was trying to escape?

Col. WILLIAMS. Yes; that statement was later substantiated when I visited Leogane and made an informal investigation.

The CHAIRMAN. Did you ever turn over your native gendarmes for serious offenses to any tribunal than the gendarmerie general court-martial?

Col. WILLIAMS. The Haitian law did not provide for military courts, as I remember it, and the institution of gendarmerie courts-martial not subject to review by the civil courts created considerable opposition among the lawyer class and the jurists of Haiti. We, however, believed that it was essential that the conduct of discipline in the gendarmerie must be under the control of the American officers, because the only regenerative influence in the gendarmerie was the American influence, and if we were not free to organize, train, discipline and operate the gendarmerie according to our American conceptions of what was right and proper, we felt that the gendarmerie would remain what the Haitians desired it to remain, a Haitian organization, and consequently of little efficiency, so we insisted, in discussions with the Government, the Haitian Government, that the gendarmerie courts be not subject to review by the Haitian civil courts. First, the limitation of punishment was life imprisonment at hard labor.

I subsequently, in view of the bad conduct of the gendarmes on several occasions, used my influence with the President to have him approve a modification of the regulations which permitted the gendarmerie courts-martial, subject to presidential approval, to adjudge the death penalty. That was because life imprisonment was not bringing the disciplinary results which we had hoped for. However, as a matter of policy I exercised my discretion, and turned over to the civil courts several cases where the evidence against the gendarme was so complete and the crime had been attended by such publicity, that I thought conviction would follow, and the death penalty be adjudged and the good faith of the American officers shown. The only case of which I recollect the details was that of a gendarme in the town of St. Michel, which comes within the jurisdiction of the criminal courts of Gonaives. The district attorney, as he may be called, in Gonaives was one of the most efficient I had met.

The CHAIRMAN. Among the Haitians?

Col. WILLIAMS. Among the Haitians. The judges seemed good and the town had a rather high cultural development. This gendarme had shot and killed a woman about 60 years old. She was a professional beggar. She was an idiot, and she begged about the streets of the town, half naked, and was a nuisance. The gendarme's defense before the court was self-defense in that this woman had thrown a handful of pebbles at him. The gendarme was acquitted. This acquittal was in what I thought probably the best judicial district of the Republic. I think that was the last important case that I turned over to the Haitian courts.

The CHAIRMAN. Have you any idea, or have you any means of estimating, how many native prisoners were illegally killed by Haitians in the gendarmerie without or against the orders of their white superior officers?

Col. WILLIAMS. So far as my recollection serves me I think 9 or 10 were brought to trial. I think I caused to be investigated perhaps 50 reports of such killings, but most of them, because they were not true or because it did not seem possible to obtain sufficient evidence, were handled in some other way than by taking disciplinary measures, such as the transfer of the man accused from the post where he was serving to another post, or his discharge from the gendarmerie.

The CHAIRMAN. You refer now to cases where you felt you could not prove a capital crime?

Col. WILLIAMS. Could not prove any crime. Investigations in Haiti are conducted with so much difficulty, and the native witness is so utterly unreliable that an investigation of a serious charge was, according to our American ideas of what an investigation should be, almost impossible. I think I am safe in saying that at least 50 per cent of the gendarmerie officers' time was spent in investigating. A native witness, in the first place, while not meaning to lie, but simply because he argues directly from cause to effect without in any way considering the modifying intervening circumstances jumps to conclusions. What he hears once or twice becomes a belief. If he hears it more than that, it is a firm conviction, and he is prone to relate as a fact that which has come to his knowledge only as a bit of gossip.

In connection with the killing of native by a gendarme, a case where the circumstances seemed to warrant the trial of the gendarme by court-martial, the principal witness for the defense testified that he had been standing beside the gendarme during the events leading up to the killing, at the time of the killing, and immediately subsequent thereto. He stood cross-examination on the details of his testimony, and when he had completed his testimony, following our American system of court-martial procedure, his testimony was read aloud to him, and he was asked if it was correct, and to correct it, if necessary. He said, yes; that those were exactly the words of his friend, so nearly as he could remember them, and he tried to stick to his friend's statement.

It then developed that he had not been anywhere near the neighborhood at the time of the event, but that his friend, who was the real witness, was about to draw irrigating water for his little farm on that particular day, and if he missed it the week would go by and all of his bananas die, and he had asked this witness to testify in his place, and the witness, in perfect good faith, permitted himself to be identified as the real witness and sworn, had testified and stood cross examination, and it was only by the merest accident that his utter ignorance of all the facts in the case became evident.

That was a striking instance, but there were many others less striking, which led us to believe that the native's testimony was not reliable unless it could be substantiated by many witnesses.

The investigations themselves were conducted under the greatest difficulties, especially in the case where the officer charged with the investigation did not speak Creole fluently. Even a knowledge of French would not help much, because the native in the interior did not understand French. Two gendarmes were put in charge of a prisoner one day, a prisoner who had stated that he knew where arms were hidden. He was a civil prisoner, but we promised him his pardon, knowing we could persuade the President of Haiti to pardon him, if he would show where the arms were buried. The two gendarmes, accompanied by a local civil officer, went to the town of Croix des Missions, and they came back the following day and reported that the prisoner had attempted to escape and was about to run into the cane fields where they could never get him, and they fired on him and killed him, and they buried him.

They had a list of witnesses to this. Not only because it was the proper thing to do, but in order to get a side light on the gendarmes, I ordered a board of three officers, who proceeded to the place of the killing, and interrogated the witnesses through an interpreter. At that time few, if any, of the gendarmerie officers spoke Creole fluently. The witnesses testified substantially to the same facts, and the board then proceeded to the place where the man was buried, and dug up the body. They submitted a written report. The only thing suspicious in their conclusion that the gendarmes had been justified in this shooting was that the body was rather badly decomposed. We sent for a prominent undertaker at Port au Prince, and asked him about this, and he said that perhaps the condition of the soil and the drainage might bring about such a decomposition in three or four days, but it was rather doubtful. However, there was no time to make a further investigation. Three officers of the very few available had spent two days on this, and their services were badly needed in the rather amorphous organization we had at the time. About six months later the prisoner was arrested 30 miles from the place where he had been buried. I sent an officer who spoke Creole fluently to Croix des Missions. He collected most of the original witnesses, who stated that they had not told the truth at the time of the first investigation; that they had told what the gendarmes told them to tell, but that now that they had satisfied the curiosity of the American, would the American be good enough to tell them what had bothered them for many months, that is why the three white men had insisted on digging up the body of a man who had been buried, having been run over by a train three months before.

That investigation in all its phases is characteristic of the investigations that were carried on to the very last. Witnesses were willing to identify themselves as anybody. They would try to determine what the court wanted to find out, and then try to please the court or the board. If they disappeared from the control of the investigating officer, it was difficult to get them back, because the name under which they identified themselves was just the name of the day. On the following day they would perhaps have another name. They drifted around the country so much that it was hard to find them. They knew the meaning of an oath, and they were informed of the pains and penalties of perjury, but they would recite as facts things which they imagined.

Mr. Howe. Is perjury a crime in Haiti?

Col. Williams. Perjury, as I remember the code, is not defined as such, but, of course, false testimony is punishable.

Mr. Howe. Colonel, were all reports of unauthorized killings by the gendarmerie investigated?

Col. Williams. Every report against the gendarmerie body or its individual members, however foolish the reports seem on its face, was investigated as thoroughly as we could possibly investigate them, and in many cases we found that the complaints were justified.

Mr. Howe. And in the case of justified complaints there were trials where you felt them to be proven?

Col. Williams. If the circumstances justified a trial, they were tried.

Mr. Howe. And there were, as you say, about nine convictions there, you think?

Col. Williams. My recollection is that the gendarmerie courts convicted somewhere in the neighborhood of ten people for serious crimes.

Mr. Howe. For the killing of prisoners and other crimes?

Col. Williams. They must have been for the killing of prisoners, because otherwise I would not have brought them to trial by general court. We had other courts, departmental courts and districts courts, with more limited jurisdiction and more limited power of punishment. They handled the minor offenses.

Mr. Howe. There were other classes of killings down there, were there not, where the individual resisted arrest, or where he was out in that way, and he ran away and was shot as he was running, classes of killings which would come under the head of killings incident to military operations? That is, of course, true, is it not, that there were in those military operations many killings?

Col. Williams. The repression of banditism involved the killing of very many Haitians.

Mr. Howe. What was the attitude of the white officers in the gendarmerie, in general, toward the killing of natives in the field?

Col. Williams. Of extreme regret. It was realized that the bandits, or, as they came to be called, the Cacos, were probably 75 per cent natives who did not want to do what they were doing. The bandit leaders had a system of selective draft which worked about in this way: A bandit leader with a few ex-criminals or bad men would come to the remote house of a native and they would offer him his choice between joining the bandits, the patriot army, as they called it, or having his head cut off.

The Chairman. Colonel, upon what evidence or report do you make that statement? Did the peasantry tell this to your marines or officers?

Col. Williams. The peasants in many instances told it. It was a matter of common knowledge among the educated Haitians that this was the method employed in gaining recruits. It was the direct testimony of certain natives who had elected to remain peaceful and in whose cases haste or some other consideration had interfered with the completion of the head-cutting job, and we fixed them up in our hospitals. I have spoken of the unreliability of Haitian testimony, but the testimony regarding this particular point was so universal that one could not but believe it. Few resisted this form of recruitment and the bands grew very rapidly, and as they grew the recruiting capacity increased; and I think it is conservative to state that at least 75 per cent of the natives in the field were there against their wills, but, of course, as soon as they became committed by having operated in this fashion, then they felt they could not desert. Deserters from a band or gang were looked upon with a natural degree of suspicion and they had to prove their case before they were permitted to go loose, and when they were turned loose they were quickly murdered by the members of the gang or some other gang which they deserted; so we realized that in an attack on a bandit gang or in a stand-up fight between bandits and gendarmes, if there were 10 men killed on the side of the natives, probably 7 of them were innocent of any real animosity or hostility to the Americans.

Mr. Howe. So the natural result from that was that your officers were loath to kill unless it seemed to them necessary, is that correct?

Col. Williams. They were loath to kill, but it must be understood that in the jungle and in the morning twilight it is impossible at 200 yards to tell exactly what a man's inclinations are.

The Chairman. When you captured bandits what disposition was made of them?

Col. Williams. Various dispositions. The most usual disposition was to try them by the American provost courts. We had found that the Haitian courts generally were not able, where willing, to punish in such a fashion that the punishment would act as a deterrent. The sessions of the criminal courts were held at points very distant from the scene of the bandit activities; the cases were tried months, perhaps, after the occurrence, and the deterrent effect of the criminal court's action, where it could be obtained at all, was nil. The provost court acted promptly and the punishment was, I think, limited to hard labor—six months at hard labor. I am not quite sure of that.

Mr. Howe. Were there any killings that came to your knowledge in connection with natives escaping from corvee gangs?

Col. Williams. I had reason to believe, and received reports, that natives had been killed in avoiding corvee work, but in no case was I ever able to collect sufficient data to justify more than such investigation as I made myself or directed some other officer to make. In other words, I never made such a thorough investigation as is incident to the trial of an accused by court-martial. I have no doubt, however, knowing the native personnel as I do, that men were killed.

Mr. Howe. Were the corvée gangs guarded by gendarmerie?

Col. Williams. The corvée gangs were always guarded by gendarmerie.

Mr. Howe. For what purpose, to protect the gang or to prevent their escape?

Col. WILLIAMS. I know of only one instance where the gang had a guard for the purpose of protecting it, and that was in the Massade district.

Mr. HOWE. And in the other case it was——

Col. WILLIAMS. In the other cases they were guards to insure the continued presence of the laborers and to furnish subbosses for the road work.

Mr. HOWE. What were the instructions of the guards? What were they instructed to do in case some of the gang made a break and started to run away?

Col. WILLIAMS. To recapture them.

Mr. HOWE. Did their instructions justify them in shooting them?

Col. WILLIAMS. No.

Mr. HOWE. As they ran away?

Col. WILLIAMS. No.

Mr. HOWE. Then, any killing of a member of a corvée gang who was running away was an illegal killing, was that right?

Col. WILLIAMS. Any killing of a member of a corvée gang who was engaged in some other crime than a criminal assault on a member of the guard or a member of the gang, would be a crime.

Mr. HOWE. You refer to killings or to possible killings of escaping members of the corvée. You mean those killings were by native guards?

Col. WILLIAMS. By native guards.

Mr. HOWE. Did you ever hear of such instances in which such a killing was countenanced, ordered, or accomplished by the white officer of the gendarmerie?

Col. WILLIAMS. No.

Mr. HOWE. Or in the marines?

Col. WILLIAMS. The possibility of those killings was recognized, and such supervision as was possible was given.

Mr. HOWE. To prevent them?

Col. WILLIAMS. To prevent them; not specifically to prevent those, but to prevent all abuse of authority by the gendarmerie.

Mr. HOWE. Did you hear of any cruelty by the native gendarmerie to the corvée gangs.

Col. WILLIAMS. I heard of cruelty; that is, the beating of corvée men by gendarmes. Where it was possible to do so, those cases were punished. This inherent tendency to abuse authority was the subject of constant effort toward repression. We never succeeded in repressing it entirely.

Mr. HOWE. Your officers were directed to use their efforts to repress any of their subordinates' acts of oppression against the natives, is that correct?

Col. WILLIAMS. As I said before, our greatest problem in organizing and administering the gendarmerie was the gendarme, and we realized that the good will of the people could not be gained if the gendarme were to comport himself according to his inclinations.

The CHAIRMAN. I may interject that that is a difficulty which confronts every organizer of constabulary in the Tropics the world around.

Col. WILLIAMS. I think it is characteristic of the lower races to exceed authority, if they are invested with it. We had the same trouble in the Philippines.

Mr. HOWE. Can you estimate the number of natives who were killed by the native gendarmerie while trying to escape from the corvée?

Col. WILLIAMS. I can not, because I do not know of any.

Mr. HOWE. But you believe that such killings were possible?

Col. WILLIAMS. I believe that such killings were possible and probable.

(Whereupon, at 1 o'clock p. m., a recess was taken until 2.30 o'clock p. m.)

AFTER RECESS.

The committee reassembled at 2.30 o'clock p. m. pursuant to the taking of recess.

Mr. HOWE. Colonel, can you give us a brief definition of the term "corvee" as it is known under the Haitian law?

Col. WILLIAMS. Corvee, in a general sense, is forced manual labor, or perhaps I had better put it nonvoluntary manual labor.

Mr. HOWE. In Haiti was there a law authorizing that?

Col. WILLIAMS. The code rurale provided that the repair of the roads, and I believe also the repair of dikes, was to be performed by the labor of the inhabitants; that whenever the commandant of a certain commune or department wished this work done he would take the inhabitants of the district in which the repairs were to be made and put them on this work. There were other improper uses made of the corvee under the Haitian administration, and in the more remote districts frequently it was the custom of officials to collect the men of a certain neighborhood and put them to work on their private property.

Mr. Howe. You are speaking of times previous to the occupation?

Col. Williams. The code rurale was adopted, I think, in 1863, or in the early sixties.

Mr. Howe. And these abuses of the law of the corvee that you refer to were before the American occupation?

Col. Williams. Before and during.

Mr. Howe. Was the term "corvee" ever used except in its strict legal sense which you have defined?

Col. Williams. Yes; the word had such general currency in Haiti that it became an expression descriptive of anything a person did not care about doing. An unwelcome reception would be referred to by a Haitian perhaps as a corvee which he must go through. The usual sense, however, in which it was used was work on the public roads.

Mr. Howe. Was it used in common parlance for work on the public roads whether that work was being done for wages or whether it was being done strictly as a legal corvee?

Col. Williams. The natives almost always referred to road work, whether paid or unpaid, as corvee.

Mr. Howe. Paid road work was not corvee?

Col. Williams. Was not corvee in any sense.

Mr. Howe. A previous witness, Gen. Butler, has given the committee a description of the use of the corvee law by the occupation, and of the repair or reconstruction of a considerable road system under the corvee, and he brought his description up to the time of his relief. Will you begin with the time you became chief of the gendarmerie and tell the committee as to the operation of the corvee from that time on?

Col. Williams. The inspiration for the application of the corvee was the definite recognition that the commercial and social regeneration of the Haitian people and Haiti called for roads which would bear wheeled transportation. Such roads, except in small stretches, hardly existed. The French had built a splendid system of roads, uniting nearly all the principle towns, but this had fallen into such disrepair that in many places it was difficult to find even the traces of the roads.

Mr. Howe. May I interrupt you? Gen. Butler devoted a good section of his testimony to informing the committee as to the necessity for the repair of roads. Just let me perhaps go over the ground of some of his testimony. With a few questions we can take up your observations of the corvee work from the time you became chief.

First of all what is your view as to the necessity for reconstructing the old French system of roads?

Col. Williams. As I say, the commercial and social regeneration of the people called for communication. When we landed in Haiti, while the inhabitants were homogenous, the north Haitian knew nothing of the central Haitian, nor the central Haitian of the southern Haitian, and local interests had become so strong because of isolation that there was no national unity other than that founded upon a common race. I believed that the roads were very necessary. The military aspects of the case also appealed to me strongly, because, as I have stated this morning, the most reliable means of keeping in touch with what was going on in Haiti was by personal inspection. That on horseback was utterly impracticable, and some more rapid means of getting around must be devised. That, in my mind, however, was incidental to the main object.

Mr. Howe. As I understand it, your chief military mission in Haiti was the preservation of law and order, was it not?

Col. Williams. That was why the gendarmerie was organized.

Mr. Howe. And when you speak of the roads being a military necessity, the implication is strong, is it not, that roads were necessary for the preservation of law and order by the gendarmerie?

Col. Williams. For the development of the gendarmerie into an efficient organization, personal contact with all parts of Haiti was necessary. This could only be facilitated by the construction of roads, but, as I say, the conditions which obtained during most of my tour of duty made it possible for me to consider this as an incidental result of the road building, rather than that which was my reason for believing them necessary.

Mr. Howe. And your reason for believing them necessary was——

Col. Williams. The social and commercial regeneration of Haiti.

Mr. Howe. Is there any distinction to be drawn between work done on roads as a national project and work to be done on roads as a communal project?

Col. Williams. The law, as I remember it, classified the roads, but the classification can not very well be applied because there are no physical differences between what might be called a communal road and what might be called a national highway. None of them was passable for wheeled vehicles.

Mr. Howe. This work on the roads under the corvée required also, however, a certain amount of money, did it not?

Col. Williams. Yes. The central Government appropriated, starting, I think, with $30,000 a month, and dropping finally, toward the end of my tour, to $10,000 a month, for the repair and upkeep of the roads.

Mr. Howe. In addition to that, were any of the communal funds available or made available for the construction or repair of roads?

Col. Williams. The Federal appropriations were quite insufficient, and a communes appropriated money for the work on roads which would immediately benefit that particular town, and, in addition to that, a good-roads campaign was conducted, which led to the receipt of very substantial contributions from civilians. In the town of Aux Cayes, for instance, in one meeting the people subscribed over $1,800 in gold, which is quite a bit of money in Haiti.

Mr. Howe. Was that money allotted out in connection with corvée labor?

Col. Williams. It was allotted out in connection with corvée labor, or in connection with paid labor, or in connection with both.

Mr. Howe. As the case might have been in the particular locality?

Col. Williams. Yes.

Mr. Howe. Is it not a fact that during the time when the corvée was in operation some road construction was also done by paid labor?

Col. Williams. Oh, yes.

Mr. Howe. In more than one instance?

Col. Williams. Yes. We found it necessary where the work approached real road work, I mean excellent road work and rock work, to have organized gangs which we had to train and keep together by the only possible means; that is, by paying them.

Mr. Howe. Do you recollect how many days' labor the corvée law exacted from the individual?

Col. Williams. Without the code rurale I would not care to state exactly, but my recollection is that it did not cover the entire week, and that when the repairs were completed the corvée, or the workers, were dismissed.

Mr. Howe. Was the recruiting, as we might call it, of the corvée more difficult as time went on, or less difficult under the occupation?

Col. Williams. It became more difficult. The population of Haiti is very irregularly distributed. Along the coast it is relatively dense; in the interior it is very, very small. In those districts where water is available for irrigation the population is dense; in the arid stretches it is very sparse. Naturally, the first roads constructed were those through the more populous districts. They were the more important roads, and there was little difficulty found in obtaining a sufficiency of labor for them, but where the road stretches passed through districts where the population was only a few to the square mile—I could not say how many—the labor supply did not begin to meet the labor requirements.

Mr. Howe. And the recruitment became increasingly difficult?

Col. Williams. And the recruitment became increasingly difficult, because it was necessary then to go well back from the roads into the hills and mountains and forests to get the people to work on these particular stretches.

Mr. Howe. And they came less willingly?

Col. Williams. And they came less willingly as the work continued.

Mr. Howe. Was this operation under the corvée conducted by the gendarmerie?

Col. Williams. Our first attempts at recruitment were conducted largely by the lowest civil officer, who is known as the chief de section, or by the marshal de champs. This led to so many abuses, and so much bribery, corruption, and dissatisfaction that we ceased using these agents, and collected these laborers with the gendarmes. These gendarmes were sent to the various localities to notify the people who were due for road work.

Mr. Howe. When that recruitment came to be conducted by the gendarmes, was it conducted without abuse, in your opinion?

Col. Williams. Knowing the gendarmes, I do not see very well how it could have been conducted without abuse, and instances came to my knowledge where the gendarmes had committed abuses.

Mr. Howe. Will you give us one or two illustrations?

Col. Williams. In the town of Arcahaie the gendarme was to collect laborers for a stretch of road in the immediate vicinity. He went to a brickyard and collected the entire personnel of the brickyard, thereby, of course, making it impossible to attend the baking, or whatever you call it, of the bricks. In the same neighborhood a gendarmerie sent out to collect corvée men for work on the roads collected the entire crew of a small coasting schooner. I must say, in the first place, that there has never been a census made in Haiti. The election laws provide for a registration, but the law has never been carried out, so it was impossible, except in a very rough fashion, to estimate the labor supply in any one district, and as for listing the population for work, so that the work could be properly distributed among the inhabitants who were due to perform it, we tried that, and the only result was that the natives thought the registration was a preliminary step to placing them in slavery, and they took to the woods. We issued cards to corvée men who had completed their tour of duty. These cards stated, in effect, that so and so had completed so many days corvée, and was not available for further work. I am afraid these cards did more harm than good, because the native furnished with such a card, having had its meaning explained to him, instead of trying to evade work, when he saw a gendarme in that district charged with the duty of recruiting, would come forward confidently and show his card to the gendarme. The gendarme's reasoning in that case was. "Well, this is easy: I do not need to go any further." And he would take the man's card and tear it up, and send him on to work.

Mr. Howe. Did you learn of instances of that happening?

Col. Williams. I was unable to prove any instances of it, but the report was so general as to the practice that I was convinced that it existed.

Mr. Howe. What effort did you make to put an end to this abuse of recruiting in the corvée?

Col. Williams. By the instruction of the gendarmes as to their duty in relation to recruiting, by talks with the officers, who realized even more clearly than I did what the dangers were, and by the punishment of any gendarme whom we could prove guilty of any sort of abuse.

Mr. Howe. When the gangs were recruited were they harshly treated in any instance that you know of?

Col. Williams. I do not know of a specific instance of harsh treatment. There undoubtedly were instances. There were many thousand men engaged at a time, and they were working over hundreds of miles of road. They were under native foremen, and in some cases they were under gendarme noncommissioned officers who had qualified as road builders after a fashion, and I have no doubt that they committed abuses, but there was no way of listing these laborers. A certain stretch of road would necessitate the employment, we will say, of 100 men. They came and they went without registration. There were no pay rolls, there was no time to make them up, and no one could have signed them had we had them, and the identity of individuals in the gang was absolutely lost, and I have been present when gendarmerie officers directly in charge of road gangs have attempted to investigate cases of alleged ill treatment, and if we found the witnesses we could not find the gendarme, and if we found the gendarme we could not find the witnesses. That was about the way it ran. It was an extremely difficult thing to do.

Mr. Howe. With the number of white gendarmerie officers at your disposal, was it physically possible to closely supervise the corvee work and at the same time keep your territory patrolled and policed?

Col. Williams. The gendarmerie officers were given such stretches of road to supervise that it was utterly impossible for them to closely supervise the work, except in those instances where rock work was being done, and in those cases the gendarmerie officer was usually present, because the native foreman of labor could not be trusted with the handling of explosives.

Mr. Howe. Under the occupation there was far more corvee work done per month or per year than had been customary under the Haitian Government before the occupation; is that correct?

Col. WILLIAMS. That is correct.

Mr. HOWE. I had understood so from Gen. Butler's testimony.

Col. WILLIAMS. The repair of roads under the Haitian administration was carried on in a most casual fashion. They would throw a lot of rocks into a mud hole, and that is all it amounted to.

Mr. HOWE. We learned from Gen Butler's testimony the other day that at the outset of this repair work under the corvee the gangs were fairly contented and were ready to stay and work, and at the outset there was no dissatisfaction among the workers themselves. Would you concur in that view?

Col. WILLIAMS. That is absolutely true. There was a campaign for good roads. The local officials were encouraged to take part in the work, and they were given credit always for what had been accomplished, even though the gendarmerie officer had done it. The laborers were brought together, and the code rurale, which prohibits public dances on work days and cock fighting except, I think, on Sundays and holidays, was suspended in the labor camps, so that the pleasant evenings and the companionship during the day made the work rather attractive to the Negro, who is a gregarious creature.

Mr. HOWE. Were the Haitian laws against public dancing and against cock fighting, except on Sundays and holidays, rigidly enforced by the Haitian Government at all times?

Col. WILLIAMS. No; they were not enforced. The laws were on the statute books, but under the Haitian administration it was simply a means of oppression or extortion. Even during the day drummers were provided so that the road work, the pick and shovel work, was syncopated. The men were paid a small sum, based upon the value of the gendarmerie ration, or else were furnished food. That was not called for by the code.

Mr. HOWE. Did that contentment lessen and disappear as time went on?

Col. WILLIAMS. Yes; it lessened very materially. As the road system became developed and it was necessary to call laborers a second time to work on a road which to their eyes was a magnificent boulevard, they could not see the point and they objected to doing the work.

Mr. HOWE. It became drudgery?

Col. WILLIAMS. It became drudgery and the old-time attractions disappeared.

Mr. HOWE. Did the continuation of the corvee, in your opinion, act as a serious irritant, and was that irritation a serious factor to be considered by those directing the occupation?

Col. WILLIAMS. It would be interesting to note to what extent it was a serious factor had the corvee existed as the sole basis for anti-American propaganda, but there were factors which came into action at the same time and which, to all seeming, joined in with the corvee and made a complete whole, upon which was based a very strong anti-American feeling.

Mr. HOWE. After you became chief of the gendarmerie, did you reach any conclusion as to the continuance of the corvee system?

Col. WILLIAMS. I had reached a conclusion regarding the corvee system before it was put in operation. I did not believe in it. I believed that it was an uneconomical way of producing results and I did not believe that the people had reached a sufficiently high cultural state—and I speak now of the peasantry—to realize the benefits which would accrue from their labor. On becoming chief of the gendarmerie I immediately took under consideration the question of stopping it. That was the first time I had been in a position to do so. I discussed the matter with everyone, officers of the gendarmerie, officers of the Marine Corps, the Haitian Government, the President, and civilians all over the country, and the other treaty officials. I wanted to stop it at once, but among other things that I had in mind was to disabuse the Haitian from the idea that a change of chiefs meant a complete reversal of policy. That, of course, was what obtained in their own administration. I wanted them to realize that the coming of the Americans meant a continuing policy; that they need not play up one official and then play up the next. In other words, I wanted the administration to appeal to them as impartial, so far as the policy was concerned. At that time the road system had been projected to a point which I believed would serve the material and social needs of the people and the country fairly well, and I thought that the time to stop the corvee would be when its reason for being no longer existed.

Mr. HOWE. That is to say——

Col. WILLIAMS. When the projected road system had been virtually completed. I figured out that that would be in October and issued an order stopping all corvee of whatsoever sort throughout Haiti.

Mr. Howe. May I call your attention to this letter and ask if that is a copy of that order to which you refer?

- Col. Williams. It is nearly three years ago. I think it is.

Mr. Howe. You might take a moment to look through it to make sure.

Col. Williams. Yes; that is mine.

Mr. Howe. Was the order issued on the day it was dated?

Col. Williams. No; my recollection is that the order was issued sometime prior to that, and even before its issuance I had been lessening the employment of corvee and increasing the amount of paid labor.

Mr. Howe. This letter which I have just shown you, or the order, rather, General Order No. 22, is dated September 2, 1918, and it refers to General Order No. 21, dated May 10, 1918. As far as you know, is that a correct copy of General Order 21?

Col. Williams. I believe that is correct. It sounds right.

Mr. Howe. I should like to have this order and the order to which it refers in the record.

Senator Oddie. Without objection, we will put them in the record.

(The orders referred to are here printed in full, as follows:)

FROM GENERAL ORDER NO 22, SEPTEMBER 2, 1918.   (SINCE REVOKED.)

1. Beginning October 1, 1918, the use of corvee on the national roads as listed in General Order No. 21, of May 10, 1918, will be discontinued, and the maintenance and improvement of these roads will be carried on with paid labor and prison labor except when a real emergency calls for emergency repair beyond the available appropriation, in which case corvee will be used.

2. The paid labor will be organized into gangs and every effort will be made to keep together a permanent personnel. A maximum of 1.10 gourdes per day, without food, or 1 gourde per day, plus a meal at cost—10 centimes—will not be exceeded, and wherever possible labor will be obtained at a lower per diem. Shelter, to be constructed by the labor gangs themselves, will be always provided, and the better the shelter, keeping in view its temporary nature, the more contented and efficient will be the workers.

3. Holidays and fêtes will be recognized and celebrated with moderation, the idea being to take advantage of all possible means to build up an organization which will be attractive to the Haitian laborer.

4. The use of corvee for other roads than those listed will be restricted by the provisions of articles 52 and 65, Code Rural.

5. The use of corvee or free labor for other road building will be conducted under the restrictions of law, and care will be exercised that none is called by local officials for illegal work.

6. When prisoners are used, only prisoners physically capable of hard work will be employed, and gangs of prisoners will be put on work separated from that performed by paid gangs. The cost of feeding and clothing prisoners will be paid for from prison funds.

7. Upon the receipt of this order the district and subdistrict commanders will inform the officials and notables that its issuance is made possible only by the patriotic and earnest efforts of the inhabitants of the rural sections who have so fully given of their labor, and that to each and every one of these the gendarmerie owes a debt.

Alex. S. Williams,
Chief of the Gendarmerie.

EXTRACT FROM GENDARMERIE GENERAL ORDER NO. 21, MAY 10, 1918.

(8) For the present, funds for road repairs alloted from these headquarters will be used as far as possible on the following roads:

Department of the Cape.	Gros Morne-Port de Paix.
Mapou-Gonaives.	Cap Haitien-Ouaneminthe.
Gonaives-Ennery.	Ouanaminthe-Fort Liberte.
Ennery-Saint Michel.	Post Chabert.
Gonaives-Gros Morne.	

(9) Such other roads and trails as serve to define general economic needs will be repaired when there exists a condition which seriously impedes the trans-

portation of goods or passengers by horse, pack, or cart. When communes and public-spirited individuals are contributing to the repair or development of certain roads, such work will be continued and every encouragement given to the end that such contribution increase.

Mr. Howe. Now, that General Order No. 22 orders work stopped on the roads mentioned in General Order No. 21; that is the gist of it, is it not?

Col. Williams. Yes.

Mr. Howe. Were these roads mentioned in General Order No. 21 all the roads on which corvée was in progress at the time of the issuance of Order No. 22.

Col. Williams. I believe so.

Mr. Howe. Was work-stopped, as a matter of fact, on all those roads after the issuance of your order No. 22?

Col. Williams. Free labor was discontinued on all those roads; corvée labor was stopped on all those roads.

Mr. Howe. As a matter of fact, did this order have the effect of stopping corvée labor absolutely in Haiti at that time?

Col. Williams. No; it did not.

Mr. Howe. Will you tell the committee, please, about instances of where the corvée labor continued after the issuance of this order, and what steps were taken in that connection?

Col. Williams. Shortly after the order had been issued, and, as I said, it was welcomed by all the gendarmerie officers who had operated under the old system, I should say within a week of its issuance reports came to me from various sources that corvée labor was continuing on the road which we referred to as the Maissade-Hinche road. I called up on the telephone the department commander at the Cape—I had a very good connection—and asked him about it, and he said, " Yes," that corvée labor was continued on this stretch of road—it was not a large stretch—because he had not understood the order to refer to that particular road, where corvée had always been used, and the expense incidental to feeding or paying the men came from communal funds, and not from the funds which I myself allotted from headquarters.

Mr. Howe. It may be noted, may it not, that the Maissade-Hinche road does not appear as one of the roads listed in General Order No. 21?

Col. Williams. It was not listed. I thought my order was foolproof, but it was not. I remember the instance very well, because the officer who made the mistake was very much chagrinned over the mistake, and did not care for the way in which I spoke to him over the phone, and protested against it. That was the only instance where the corvée continued on any of the public roads in the gendarmerie project, or the roads leading into them, so far as I was ever able to find out.

Mr. Howe. I have here a copy of a telegram as follows:

Department Commander,

Gendarmerie, Cape Haitien.

From letter dated October 8 from magistrate, Maissade, believe order stopping corvée after October 1 may not have been reeceived at Hinche. If order not received, notify Hinche of same by telephone. 120112.

Tracy, *Acting.*

Who was Tracy?

Col. Williams. Tracy was assistant chief of the gendarmerie.

Mr. Howe. And these figures, 120112, would be the serial number of a telegram?

Col. Williams. I think that is the time and date cipher. We had some sort of a date and time cipher, but just what it was I could not translate it now.

Mr. Howe. The presence of those figures in the telegram would indicate to you that it was an official telegram sent on official gendarmerie business.

Col. Williams. Yes. I think we can clear something up there. Maissade is a subdistrict of the district of Hinche, and so when they referred to the corvée not being understood at Hinche, the way in which Maissade would be informed of its cessation would be through Hinche.

Mr. Howe. Then here is another telegram from the department commander of the cape to the chief of gendarmerie:

Your 120112. Corvée labor has not been stopped on the Hinche-Maissade and St. Michel Road, for the reason that this road is not included in General Order No. 21. Unless corvée is worked on this road little can be done toward opening up this section of the country. Request its continuance. 10114.

UNDERWOOD.

Who was Underwood?

Col. WILLIAMS. Underwood was the man who misunderstood the order in the first place, and with whom I had the telephone conversation relative to it.

Mr. Howe. And on this piece of paper I see the typewritten entry, in parenthesis, at the bottom of this telegram, in Col. Williams's handwriting, in pencil, the following: "October 8. Orders given by telephone to cease all corvee. A. S. W."

Does that recall that incident to you?

Col. WILLIAMS. We were our own file clerks largely in the gendarmerie. It is quite possible that I may have made a notation of that sort on the telegram.

Mr. Howe. Then, by the issuance of that order, all corvée on the Hinch-Massade road was finally stopped; is that correct?

Col. WILLIAMS. That is my belief.

Mr. Howe. Did you learn of any other instance where the corvee was employed thereafter?

Col. WILLIAMS. When I say the corvee stopped on October 1 I speak in a Haitian fashion. It took some days, we will say, after that for the order to filter down to the more remote road gangs, and I have no doubt that in certain instances it may have continued for a week or 10 days.

Mr. Howe. We will say, then, that by October 15, 1918, corvee had ceased in Haiti?

Col. WILLIAMS. Yes; and on October 1 it had practically ceased.

Mr. Howe. And thereafter did you hear of any instances of its being revived?

Col. WILLIAMS. Yes.

Mr. Howe. During your administration?

Col. WILLIAMS. During my administration I visited central Haiti with Gen. Catlin, in March, 1919. Gen. Catlin, among other things, wished to investigate the reports that corvee, despite orders, had continued on the Massade road, particularly in the vicinity of the town of Massade. I motored into Massade over the incompleted road, on which a large gang were then working. Gen. Catlin, through his interpreter, interrogated first the gendarmerie officer, Lieut. Williams, then the foreman of the gang, and then individuals of the gang. The gendarmerie officer stated that 'these men were not corvee men; that they were paid from communal funds; that they were free to come and go as they chose. The foreman, a native foreman, stated substantially the same thing. Several individuals stated they were not paid; they were not allowed to go home when they wished, and they were forced to work. The entire gang was then lined up and they were asked or told that those who were corvee were to step forward. I think all but one slow thinker stepped forward. The conclusion which Gen. Catlin very naturally arrived at was that corvee was in existence on the road, contrary to orders. At the same time Capt. Doxie, of the gendarmerie, an officer who enjoyed the confidence and esteem of the natives to a very high degree, and one senior officer of the gendarmerie, who spoke creole very fluently, interrogated the men in my presence, and they all declared that they were well paid; they were contented, and they were perfectly free to attend to their domestic affairs, gathering the crops and attending to their wives and children. The difference of statement, I think, was not due to any intention of the men to deceive Gen. Catlin, but simply because of the use of the word "corvee." Corvee was road work. If you work on a road you belong to a corvee gang. And I investigated it further and asked other questions and was convinced at the time—and am convinced to-day—that so far as any investigation, at least, determined, corvee was not in existence at that time at that place.

Mr. Howe. Were you, at the time you and Gen. Catlin were out to see this gang at work, aware that road repair was going on in that district?

Col. WILLIAMS. Yes.

Mr. Howe. And was it your impression that that road repair work was being done by paid labor?

Col. WILLIAMS. I knew what was going on, and I knew it was being paid for largely through the very much increased revenues of the town of Massade, an increase brought about by the municipal administration conducted or supervised by the gendarmerie subdistrict commander.

Mr. HOWE. In other words, Colonel, is this what we should understand, that these particular men who were interrogated were unable to distinguish between paid labor and nonvoluntary labor, when the word used in the question to them was "corvee," meaning road work?

Col. WILLIAMS. That is the only way in which I can explain the discrepancies.

Mr. HOWE. Were there other gangs of paid laborers working in that district?

Col. WILLIAMS. No; that was the only gang that was doing it. In the other parts of the district the gendarmerie was altogether too busy with the bandit situation to go in for road building.

Mr. HOWE. Were the gendarmerie officers in charge of disbursing those communal funds? In other words, would there be any record? Was there any record at that time in existence which would show the payment to those men?

Col. WILLIAMS. Only the disbursement of lump sums, and the bookkeeping was very crude.

Mr. HOWE. Was a pay roll possible?

Col. WILLIAMS. A pay roll was not possible.

Mr. HOWE. Even where there was paid labor?

Col. WILLIAMS. Even where there was paid labor.

Mr. HOWE. Please tell the committee why it was impossible.

Col. WILLIAMS. Because none could sign it had one been in existence. I may say in connection with these gangs working on the Massade road that there were no guards about it. The only gendarmerie representative present, I think, was a gendarmerie sergeant who had either been enlisted and promoted to sergeant because of his ability in this line—road building—or had been detailed from the command because of his ability.

Mr. HOWE. Under the real, true corvee under the law, or forced labor, was it your experience that the gang could be left working by itself without guards, and still remain a gang?

Col. WILLIAMS. There was no uniformity in the practice. It depended upon the amount of work to be done, the character of it, and the date on which we consider it.

Mr. HOWE. Were there any other instances, or seeming instances, of the violation of your order than the.ones you have mentioned?

Col. WILLIAMS. I heard of none. Subsequent to that investigation the only report of corvee that was made was made by the inhabitants of a certain district, who protested against the fact that the French priest had corveed them to either build or repair the church.

Mr. HOWE. If that was so, it would not be any shortcoming of the gendarmerie?

Col. WILLIAMS. It was a shortcoming of the gendarmerie, because upon investigation I found that in this village, garrisoned by, I think, a corporal and two privates of gendarmerie, a very remote place, the priest was of so strong a character, and so great was his prestige that he was enabled to use the gendarme corporal as an agent in the collection of these workers. That was promptly stopped.

Mr. HOWE. Were there any other instances that came to your knowledge?

Col. WILLIAMS. I know of no others.

Mr. HOWE. Was there any abuse of the corvee consisting in having an individual do work on roads outside of the district in which he lived?

Col. WILLIAMS. Yes; the law was exceeded in that it was impossible from certain districts to draw the labor for the roads which passed through that district, and men had to be brought from other districts. I speak of political districts.

Mr. HOWE. And that was done, was it?

Col. WILLIAMS. That was done.

Mr. HOWE. Was there any law in Haiti prohibiting the taking of corvee laborers from the district of their residence into another district to work?

Col. WILLIAMS. No.

Mr. HOWE. Simply the law of corvee did not authorize that?

Col. WILLIAMS. The law provided they should work in their own district.

Mr. HOWE. Since the corvee was abandoned, has it been possible, in your opinion, to keep up the roads in repair?

Col. WILLIAMS. So far as labor is concerned, yes; but the money available, even when I left, had to be spread very thinly over the system.

Mr. HOWE. A thin spreading of money, plus plenty of free labor, made it possible, is that correct?

Col. WILLIAMS. Yes.

Mr. HOWE. Was there less money, when available for a certain length of time, at the time you left than there was available earlier in the occupation?

Col. WILLIAMS. Yes; I think the original monthly allotment was about $30,000; I am not sure of that.

Mr. HOWE. A month?

Col. WILLIAMS. Yes; and it dropped to $10,000 before I left.

Mr. HOWE. And at the time you left that $10,000 were the only funds available for road repair?

Col. WILLIAMS. The only funds available, except such as the communes might allot and some which public-spirited individuals turned over.

Mr. HOWE. Then the greater part of your money would, of course, have to go for wages; is that correct?

Col. WILLIAMS. It would have to go for wages.

Mr. HOWE. Instead of for supplies, as formerly?

Col. WILLIAMS. Instead of for supplies, as formerly. In the very beginning the labor demanded of the peasant was of the very simplest kind, ditching, carrying dirt, filling in holes, chopping a way through the jungle, and after some instruction we were able to have them use the ordinary tools, the pick, the ax, and wheelbarrow with some success, and for that work the corvee was suitable, but after the roads approached virtual completion, when they became real roads, and they required surfacing, draining, ditching, the placing of culverts, and the building of bridges we found corvee labor was very unsatisfactory. They simply did not know how. And we gradually as the roads improved, placed them, for repair purposes and final completion, under paid labor, and it worked very well.

Mr. HOWE. Up to the end of your administration, were the roads kept in fair repair—such as had been restored?

Col. WILLIAMS. The roads were becoming better daily.

Mr. HOWE. What can you tell us about the vote for the adoption of the constitution, how it was conducted, and if it was conducted under your direction or under the direction of the gendarmerie?

Col. WILLIAMS. Who decided and when and how it was decided to have a plebiscite to determine whether or not the constitution should be adopted, I do not know; but when the question came up about holding the plebiscite there was but one agency by means of which the mechanics of the operation could be carried through. The administrative system of Haiti is so nebulous that no uniformity of performance can be expected from the minor officials in the various parts of the Republic, but the gendarmerie had in nearly every commune an American gendarmerie officer who, by this time, had learned to speak Creole in most cases very well, always sufficiently well to make himself understood, he had learned the people, he had learned the officials, he knew his way around, and it was proposed, by whom I do not know, that the gendarmerie conduct the plebiscite. The President informed me that this was the decision of the Government, and I had several discussions with him and with his ministers, notably the minister of the interior, regarding the methods to be followed. They had no suggestions to make, because such things as a plebiscite was unknown in Haiti, and I had no suggestions to make, because I had never heard of one.

However, it was necessary, in my opinion, that a constitution of some sort should be adopted, and I sent circular letters to all gendarmerie officers informing them that they would soon be called upon to supervise a vote of the people for or against the adoption of the projected constitution; told them that it was desirable that this constitution pass, but that in presenting it to the people they must inform them that while there might be valid objections to the constitution as published, that it provided for its own amendment, and that however they might dislike the constitution, it was better than no constitution at all, and that the stability of the Republic called for such an instrument. I do not remember how long before the plebiscite was held that these instructions were given, but there was a considerable time, ample time, to enable the gendarmerie officers to conduct this campaign, which was frankly proconstitutional.

I also sent out other circular letters, furnishing them with arguments for and against the constitution. I allotted from gendarmerie funds a small amount which enabled each gendarmerie district and subdistrict commander to have a popular meeting prior to the date on which the vote was to be held; and, I think, of I recollect correctly, that I made some references to earlier American political campaigns where barbecues were features of the meeting. On these occasions the gendarmerie officer mixed with the people, sometimes addressed them, freely advocated the adoption of the constitution, told them of the conditions which would obtain when the vote was taken; and insisted, in season and out of season, that every voter would be perfectly free to vote as he chose, and that, moreover, he might be certain that he would not suffer because of making a negative vote.

The plebiscite was held on the same day throughout Haiti. At every voting place there was a gendarmerie officer, except at four or five where I was unable to supply officers and where I placed marines, whom I borrowed from the brigade, and who were thought qualified to act in such a capacity. The gendarmes were not allowed near the voting places but were allowed to vote. The gendarmerie officer, I believe, was directed to remain in the voting place during the entire period. Some question came up about meals, and, I think, I directed that they should make arrangements to have their meals brought to them, and their duties were to see that every person who appeared to vote had not voted before on that day, and to see that he received the ballot which he asked for. The ballots were roughly printed: "Oui," and "Non." I do not remember whether they were of different colors or not; but the voter would come in and ask for a ballot, negative or affirmative, and the gendarmerie officer——

Mr. HOWE. All the "Yes" votes or affirmative votes were printed on paper of the same color, were they not?

Col. WILLIAMS. I think so.

Mr. HOWE. And all the "No" votes were printed on the same colored paper?

Col. WILLIAMS. That is my recollection.

Mr. HOWE. Do you remember whether the "Yes" and the "No" were on different colored paper?

Col. WILLIAMS. I do not think they were; I do not remember. I may say that the ballots themselves were turned over to me by the minister of the interior or delivered by the public printing office and sent by me in sealed packages to the various gendarmerie officers who would have to act in the voting places. They were not to be opened until the day of the election, when they were turned over intact to the Haitian officials who were directly charged with the conduct of the voting—I believe the judge de paix, the local police judge, the local mayor, and some other official. I think that was the composition of the voting committees. All the ballots reached their destination, except one batch intended for a little town in the north, and the gendarmerie messenger who was to deliver these ballots—we found his horse, rifle, and stuff but never found him or the ballots. Whether he was murdered or bribed to desert I do not know.

The balloting was conducted with the utmost order. I spent the day in Port au Prince, going from one balloting place to another, and, so far as I could determine, everything was running perfectly smoothly. There was considerable drunkenness, as there always is on an election day in Haiti, but from all points I received reports that the plebiscite had gone through very nicely, without any trouble, except in one town, the town of Aquin, where a drunken row resulted in some disorder, but it was in no way connected with the political situation.

Mr. HOWE. How did the vote come out?

Col. WILLIAMS. The ballots were counted after the closing of the polls, in the presence of the gendarmerie officer and. after having been counted, were sealed and kept until orders were issued for a recount, in case of a dispute, or their destruction after a time. They were finally all destroyed, I believe. The count came out roughly, 98,000 in the affirmative and seven hundred and odd in the negative. Those figures would seem on the face of them to indicate fraud or coercion, but, as a matter of fact, they do not indicate anything except a very peculiar feature of the Haitian disposition. It was believed by all hands that the plebiscite would go through without a large dissenting vote, and this belief was so generally held that the Haitian who wanted to vote negatively, rather than identify himself with a losing cause, failed to vote at all. In Cape Haitien, the largest city after Port au Prince, the number of votes cast, both affirmative and negative, was ridiculous in comparison with the size of the electorate.

Mr. Howe. So much smaller?

Col. Williams. So much smaller. The plebiscite I considered in every phase, those which led up to it, and the phase of operation, and the events subsequent, to be absolutely and entirely creditable to the gendarmerie. I am really very proud of the plebiscite. So far as supervision, orders, instruction, indoctrination could go, it was conducted as honestly as anything possibly could be. I have no doubt there were many repeaters, but there was no miscounting, no ballot stuffing, or any such practice.

Mr. Howe. You endeavored to guard against repeating?

Col. Williams. I endeavored to guard against repeating; but the registration did not amount to anything, and it very often occurs in the interior of Haiti that not only are there many men of the same name but the same man will not have the same name two days.

Mr. Howe. What was the attitude of the Haitian courts toward the occupation? How did they administer justice, both civil and criminal? Can you tell us, Colonel, briefly what your observations were on those matters and on kindred subjects?

Col. Williams. The administration of justice in Haiti would be a farce if it were not a tragedy. The lower-court judges with whom the people are mostly brought in contact and with whom we as policemen were mostly brought in contact, are, as a class, ignorant, venal, and utterly and entirely incompetent. There are exceptions, of course. I speak generally. The next class of judges show themselves to be excellent jurists, but their verdicts, because of the uniformity with which these verdicts are decided in favor of the Haitian party to the case, excite suspicion. The very highest court, the court of cassation, is a body of dignified jurists known for their legal lore even outside of Haiti, and these men are so wedded to the law, as law, that they have completely disassociated themselves from the life of the people. This last court is held in very high esteem, and the most radical political demagogue in Haiti has never accused the court of cassation, as a whole, or its membership, of doing wrong, but they do not qualify to pass upon conditions arising from the occupation. Have you time to hear an instance that is pertinent?

Mr. Howe. Yes.

Col. Williams. Admiral Caperton, in first landing, found that there was deposited to the credit of the Haitian Government, in the national bank, something under a million dollars gold. This he seized and directed the bank that it was to be paid out only on his order. In other words, the Haitian Government was not permitted access to the funds deposited to its credit. The administration of this fund and other funds was conducted generally along the lines provided for in the Haitian law. In 1918, I think it was a prominent lawyer that presented a Government check which called for the payment of 75 gourdes, the Haitian monetary unit, for the rental of a house which was occupied by the Government. The bank had shortly before that received orders that certain classes of payments were to be made in gold. That was in order to stabilize the exchange which, at that moment, was fluctuating in such a fashion as to greatly interfere with the conduct of business. Mr. Francis, who presented the check, refused to accept payment in gold, and brought suit in the courts against the bank, represented in the person of Mr. Scarpa, the manager. The bank's defense was simply the production of an authenticated copy of Admiral Caperton's order and the subsequent order bearing on the exchange situation. Of course, other things came into it, but, in the main, that was the defense of the bank. The court of cassation declined to take judicial cognizance of the occupation and of Admiral Caperton's order, and found for the plaintiff.

Mr. Howe. In what amount?

Col. Williams. To pay the check in gourdes, as the writing called for, and for punitive damages, I think, of 100,000 gourdes; I am not certain of that amount. It was, like all punitive damages, for a very large amount.

Mr. Howe. That being the decree of the court, what happened, if you know?

Col. Williams. Of course, it would be impossible to permit such a decree to be carried out, because, if so, the whole structure upon which was built the occupation would fall, so the manager of the bank was told that he would be protected. I think the case is in that status now.

Mr. Howe. If he did not pay the 75 gourdes and the damages?

Col. Williams. If he did not. I have mentioned that as an instance of the complete detachment of the one reliable court.

Mr. Howe. Did you ever make any observation as to what was the percentage of convictions in the ordinary police cases which were brought into the lower courts?

Col. Williams. The number of convictions in the lower courts obtained by the police was largely a reflex of the gendarmerie officer's influence.

Mr. Howe. Where did he have a chance to bring his influence to bear on the police court?

Col. Williams. By winning the confidence of the people and the officials by making himself popular with them, and by proving to them what we are all trying to prove, that we are there to help them. Whenever this influence was not exerted, the percentage of convictions was very small. The Haitian judges did not care for the new gendarmerie, and they did not care for it mostly because they were subject to a surveillance which they had never before experienced. This surveillance was not only carried on by taking an active interest in the work of the courts, but was carried on by having present in each of these police courts a gendarmerie representative known as the ministre publique. This gendarmerie representative was provided for by an obscure passage in a very long law. I discovered it, and realizing what a powerful agency this might be for the betterment of conditions in the courts, immediately installed them whenever a gendarme of sufficient intelligence and reliability could be found. In some instances I enlisted ex-ministres publique, old men in many instances, to service as gendarmes in the courts. Their duties were somewhat comparable to those of a district attorney, if you can conceive of a district attorney in a police court. They rather presented the police side of the case, and recommended a punishment. The judge was bound to listen to their presentation of the police side of the case, but was not bound to accept their recommendation. In fact, he usually did not. But by having these more or less reliable agents in every court for every trial, we increased the percentage of convictions, because in an open-and-shut game, such as police trials usually are, they hardly dared run counter to the evidence.

Mr. Howe. In the presence of the ministre publique?

Col. Williams. In the presence of the ministre publique, who would promptly, of course, report what he considered without or with reason as a miscarriage of justice. The presence of these agents, who were authorized by law, and who, so far as I know, never exceeded their authority except in individual instances, was a source of constant irritation to the whole judiciary, and particularly the lawyer class. They felt that the gendarmerie was trespassing on their preserves in having this Haitian institution active, and the Government itself did not like it, and when a new judiciary law was passed by the conseil d'etat I found, to my dismay, that no mention was made of the ministre publique, and I was forced to send telegraphic orders all over Haiti, withdrawing these people. My order was followed by a flood of protests from the gendarmerie officers who realized his value.

Mr. Howe. Was there a falling off in convictions after that withdrawal of the ministre publique?

Col. Williams. I do not know, because it happened so late in my administration that there was no opportunity to ascertain.

Mr. Howe. In your opinion, are the Haitian lower courts capable of themselves, under Haitian conditions, and without assistance or suggestion from the occupation, of so administering justice as to make the carrying out of law and order and progress possible?

Col. Williams. The Haitian judge, working after the French fashion, has little discretion. If the evidence indicates that the crime was committed, he must find the man guilty, and the various classes of crimes are described with great minuteness in the code. Therefore, if the Haitian Government could place in the lower courts Haitians of education, and pay them sufficient to make it worth their while to attend to their business, and to ignore the temptations to which they are subject, I do not see why the lower courts can not be reformed.

Mr. Howe. Under the conditions which you have named?

Col. Williams. Under the conditions which I have named.

Mr. Howe. How about the higher courts?

Col. Williams. I think the higher courts must undergo an educational process which will bring them closer in touch with the actual needs of the people. Whether or not that can be done, and the Code Napoleon still remain the Haitian code, I am not enough of a lawyer to say.

Mr. Howe. And the conditions which you stipulate as to the lower courts, however, did not prevail, did they, at the time of the occupation, or during the occupation?

Col. WILLIAMS. They did not.

Mr. HOWE. And did the courts, the lower courts, do their fair share in upholding the hands of the police, and in maintaining order and progress in Haiti?

Col. WILLIAMS. Speaking generally, when working under the personal influence of the gendarmerie officer, whom they may have learned to respect, and checked by the presence of the ministre publique, they did. Where these influences and these checks did not exist I do not believe they functioned any differently from the way in which they functioned years before we came.

Mr. HOWE. In his testimony the other day Gen. Butler indicated in a general way, and with some illustrations, the work which the gendarmerie carried on in straightening out and carrying on the affairs of the communes. Can you give us some statement of your observations on that?

Col. WILLIAMS. I think they once reported that the most definite social results had been accomplished in Haiti by the communal administration conducted under the direct supervision of the gendarmerie officers. Early in the occupation the minister of the interior, under whose administration and control the communes worked, issued a letter to all the communes, stating they must place their financial operations, and some other operations, under the supervision of the gendarmerie officers. This meant a tremendous amount of work, but the gendarmerie officers undertook it gladly, and succeeded in time in changing materially the appearance, the sanitation, and the financial condition of every commune with which they were brought in contact. Some of them increased the revenues a hundredfold. In all cases their work was directed along the lines of developing civic pride. It would be too much to say that he developed a civic pride, but I could see glimmerings of it in all the towns. A better class of Haitians was willing to accept public office in the communes. The books, if crudely, were at least accurately kept. The revenues were in their collection supervised by the gendarmerie officers, and extortion was not permitted.

Mr. HOWE. Had extortion been at all prevalent before that?

Col. WILLIAMS. Yes; extortion in a negative sense. That is, the people without influence had to pay, and the people with it did not. The disbursements were made only on the approval of the gendarmerie officer, and the Haitian official made to show results. The Haitians themselves took to this enthusiastically, and supported, except in the capital where there was a great deal of friction, the efforts of the gendarmerie officers for the betterment of conditions in the town. The work was enthusiastically carried out and was definitely productive of tangible results of a very important nature.

Mr. HOWE. What kind of results?

Col. WILLIAMS. The town was cleaned up, in the first place, and proper market places would be built, and rough slaughterhouses, or, at least, a slaughtering place would be provided, and stray animals were kept off the streets. The gutters were cleaned out, the people were encouraged to trim their hedges and put up fences and whitewash their houses; sanitary measures of a very, very rudimentary sort were carried out with some success; the operations of the office charged with the collection of vital statistics were supervised to a degree which resulted probably in at least one-half of the births and deaths being registered.

Mr. HOWE. Was that better than previously?

Col. WILLIAMS. That was much better, but mostly the gain was in civic pride, so that towns began to compete with neighboring towns, and, as I say, I saw the beginning of this pride which I considered so essential to a rejuvenated Haiti coming to be.

Mr. HOWE. Did this undertaking of the rejuvenation of the communes in itself create any friction in any quarter?

Col. WILLIAMS. Naturally, tactless officers sometimes tread on the toes of sensitive officials, but those could ordinarily be straightened out. The only cases of serious friction that occurred were in the capital itself, which is probably the only town where the municipal revenues are really worth going after.

Mr. HOWE. Will you compare the prison conditions as you found them wtih the prison conditions as they became after the occupation?

Col. WILLIAMS. The condition of the prisons in Haiti when we landed were unspeakable. In the large cities, where they should have been the best, they were probably the worst. There was no provision made for the feeding of the prisoners, the sanitary arrangements were practically nonexistent, and records were so poorly kept as hardly to serve as a guide in the segregation and in the release and treatment of prisoners. A man with influence or with family or w'th money woul:l have a cell to himself, from which he would conduct all his affairs, and the people without money or influence would be jammed like sardines in other cells that were extremely dirty.

Mr. Howe. Were the sexes segregated there among the prisoners?

Col. Williams. Yes; except in the smaller prisons. The prison reform was one of our chief interests, and the officers l ked it very much. The prison in the capital became, I believe, a model for what the prisons of a small country might be. We not only made a sanitary, livable prison out of it, but had a trade school and workshops which made all the gendarmes' uniforms, all the gendarme hats, an·l made a part of the shoes and a lot of miscellaneous equipment. We had an automob le repair shop in there, a blacksmith's shop, a brass workers' shop, a carpenter's shop that turned out far better furniture than the native craftsmen did, and not only were the natives whose term was sufficiently long to make it worth while taught a trade, but they were paid a percentage of what their production brought in. The gendarmerie, for instance, bought its un forms from the prisons. It did not commandeer this stuff, and it was often the case tha a prisoner would be discharged with $15 or $20 gold, a very considerable sum for a poor Haitian.

Mr. Howe. Did they receive a fair ration while they were in there?

Col. Williams. The ration was as much as we could buy. The Haitian Government, of course, after discussion, allotted 8 cents gold for the rationing of the prisoners.

Mr. Howe. That ration means per day per man?

Col. Williams. Per day per man. In normal times this would have been sufficient, but under the conditions brought about by the war it was——

Mr. Howe. By the World War?

Col. Williams. By the European war; it was very difficult, indeed, to make this ration work out. We had a scientific ration of 2,400 calories worked out as well as we could on the calorific value of the native products, and it resulted, this scientific ration, in a marked increase in the general good health of the prisoners, but I must say that the prison mortality, while less than it was in the beginning, was still very high.

Mr. Howe. Even in the prisons where these good conditions prevailed?

Col. Williams. Even in the prisons where these good conditions prevailed. In the prison of Port au Prince we had a medical officer of the gendarmie who had practically nothing else to do but look after the prisoners, and we had a good infirmary or hospital, and every care was given them. That was our model prison, but even there the death rate was too high.

Mr. Howe. As compared with the death rate among people who were at liberty—the same kind of people?

Col. Williams. There was no way of telling what the death rate among the people was, because the vital statistics were not sufficiently well kept.

Mr. Howe. Do you know whether or not the prison death rate was higher than the death rate outside of the prison?

Col. Williams. I have no figures to compare.

Mr. Howe. Nobody knows what the death rate in Haiti is, then?

Col. Williams. Nobody knows what the death rate in Haiti is.

Mr. Howe. Have you any means of knowing what the prison mortality was before the occupation?

Col. Williams. Before the occupation they had exactly the same prisoners, with miserable prisons, no sanitary arrangements, no medical care, and no rationing. I must assume that the death rate was very much higher than it was under the American direction.

Mr. Howe. What, if any, progress was made in popular education as a result of and during the occupation?

Col. Williams. The Haitian Government spends a large percentage of its revenues on education and the money is practically all wasted. There is no training school for teachers worthy of the name, and therefore the school-teacher is utterly and entirely incompetent. Again I speak generally. The superintendents of school districts are equally incompetent to teach, know nothing about scientific educational methods, and hold their positions largely through political influence. They are, however, well educated.

Mr. Howe. Do the gendarmerie, or any of the treaty officials, have the legal right to change the personnel of the teaching force or the school system?

Col. WILLIAMS. The only relations we had with the personnel of the schools were two. The monthly report, to which I referred earlier, had a section devoted to the schools, and on which the gendarmerie officer made such observations on the conduct of the schools as appeared to him pertinent, and if the case seemed to warrant it, I would send an excerpt of this to the minister of education. I never received any other answer than a flat denial.

Mr. HOWE. But it was a supplementary kind of inspection system?

Col. WILLIAMS. It was not an inspection; it was simply an observation. The other contact with the personnel of the schools was that established by the fact that the gendarmerie delivered the cash, the monthly payment of each teacher to that teacher, and before paying him or her, required the teacher to sign a little slip which certified that he or she had conducted his or her duties as such and such a sort of teacher during the month or portion of the month.

Mr. HOWE. How did that work out?

Col. WILLIAMS. That worked out to this extent that the teachers were present on the school days during school hours, but as to their competency, that was not affected in any way, and my personal experience when, in order to get a line on the personnel, I paid off a number myself, resulted like this: One woman teacher came forward to receive her check, which was not much—10 gourdes—$2 for the month, and she could not sign the receipt. I asked her why not, and she said that she did not have to write; that she was a teacher of reading, as I could see for myself, if I read her ticket. That sort of teacher was not uncommon.

Mr. HOWE. There were really a number of illiterate teachers?

Col. WILLIAMS. There were illiterate teachers.

Mr. HOWE. And did the American occupation have any legal authority to change that?

Col. WILLIAMS. It had no legal authority whatsoever, and never did anything because of it.

Mr. HOWE. Was the occupation responsible for building some schoolhouses? Gen. Butler told us something about that, but was that work carried on after he left?

Col. WILLIAMS. Yes; a small sum allotted originally by the military commander, when he had control of certain disbursements, permitted the erection of what we liked to call model schoolhouses in several of the more important communes. With this money we put up a substantial building of a simple type, with a center partition to separate the sexes and provide the rudiments of sanitary facilities.

Mr. HOWE. Could the school system be improved without a radical reformation?

Col. WILLIAMS. The school system could not be improved; it will have to be done over again.

Mr. HOWE. Does the Haitian Government spend a substantial amount of money on it?

Col. WILLIAMS. A very creditable proportion of the revenues. I have forgotten what it is.

Mr. HOWE. So its reconstruction is necessary?

Col. WILLIAMS. Absolutely.

Mr. HOWE. And the treaty officials and the Marine Corps and the constabulary did not have the legal right to bring about any such reconstruction, is that correct?

Col. WILLIAMS. We had no legal right. We were all interested in it, and I believe that one treaty official—who it was I am not sure, but I think it was the financial adviser—persuaded the Haitian Government to engage under contract a qualified American educator. He came to Haiti under a contract, and started out by presenting to the Government a very ambitious program of school reform. His program was utterly impracticable and fell of its own weight. He then came around and made such reformation as he could with the material at hand, but being engaged in a purely advisory capacity, he was never able to put across any of his recommendations, and subsequently left without accomplishing anything.

Mr. HOWE. There would be necessarily a long wait before competent teachers could be supplied? They would first have to be educated, would they not?

Col. WILLIAMS. There must be a normal school; there must be a source of teaching personnel.

Mr. HOWE. You will have to wait for your first crop of teachers, will you not?

Col. WILLIAMS. Or else import them.

Mr. Howe. Has there ever been any financial irregularity attributable to the gendarme officers in the administration of these communal funds or the pay of the school-teachers that you know of?

Col. Williams. The only two cases when an American has been even suspected of dishonesty in connection with the public funds were these: A sergeant of marines in charge of some work—I do not know just what it was—appropriated to his own .use something in the neighborhood of $20, I think. He was court-martialed for that. The other concerns the seizure of $1,000,000 by Admiral Caperton. It was currently believed that Admiral Caperton, when he left, had taken with him that part of the $1,000,000 which he had not turned over to Col. Waller.

Mr. Howe. Currently believed by whom?

Col. Williams. It was a matter of gossip in Port au Prince, and people who related this to me—several did—told me they were eminently satisfied with the action of the United States Government in shooting Admiral Caperton and hanging Col. Waller for the part they had played in this.

Mr. Howe. You believed them equally well informed on both heads of the news they gave you—as to Admiral Caperton's peculation and his later violent death?

Col. Williams. I can not answer that. But. seriously, there has never to my knowledge been the slightest hint of a suspicion on the part of any Haitian regarding our administration of finances.

Mr. Howe. Gen. Butler has told us of what efforts were made under the circumstances toward demonstrating agricultural possibilities down there. You were assistant chief of the gendarmerie during that time, I believe. Were those expermental farms, or what efforts that were being made, continued during your incumbency as chief?

Col. Williams. No; they were not, except unofficially by individual officers who, in many instances, being farmer boys who had enlisted, attempted to teach the Haitians something about better methods, particularly in the preparation of the soil.

Mr. Howe. Were early efforts toward instruction in agriculture by the occupation discontinued?

Col. Williams. We attempted to raise potatoes and improve the standard of potato raising in Haiti, but our efforts were not successful.

Mr. Howe. In 1917 the constituent assembly was prorogued. Did you have anything to do with that or any direct knowledge of the process?

Col. Williams. I was Gen. Butler's assistant at the time, but except from what was common knowledge and what he told me himself I know nothing.

Mr. Howe. You took no active part in that yourself?

Col. Williams. I had no active part in closing it.

Mr. Howe. There was a s'milar prorogation in 1916.

Col. Williams. The key, however, which I believe has become prominent in the discussions of the matter, came into my possession.

Mr. Howe. The key to the chamber?

Col. Williams. The key to the chamber. I had a great deal of difficulty in persuading any Haitian minister to accept it. I did not want it. I have forgotten whom I finally persuaded to take it.

Mr. Howe. How did they get it into your hands?

Col. Williams. I was assistant to Gen. Butler, and many details fell to me.

Mr. Howe. Did Gen. Butler hand you the key?

Col. Williams. I do not know, sir.

Mr. Howe. You do not know how you got it?

Col. Williams. I do not remember how I got it.

Mr. Howe. There was a similar occurrence in 1916, the prorogation of the legislature. Did you have any direct knowledge of that, or take any part in that?

Senator Oddie. In your opinion, what would be the effect of an order abolishing martial law temporarily while this committee is in Haiti investigating?

Col. Williams. It would permit every liar in Haiti to go to the limit in his imaginings.

Senator Oddie. Do you think it would do real harm?

Col. Williams. I think it would do a great deal of harm.

Senator Oddie. Do you think it would endanger lives?

Col. Williams. No.

Senator Oddie. The lives of our marines?

Col. Williams. No.

Senator Oddie. In what respect would it do harm?

Col. Williams. As I mentioned before, the Haitian is a direct thinker; what he hears he believes. The raising of martial law, which has never operated except for the suppression of untrue newspaper articles, would permit the publication of anything that any Haitian wished to say. It would result undoubtedly——

Senator Oddie. Say or print?

Col. Williams. Or print. It would result in a mushroom growth of newspapers that would all find circulation, and what the Haitian read in these papers he would accept as gospel. I can see that no useful end would be gained.

Senator Oddie. Would it have any effect on the testimony given before this committee?

Col. Williams. I do not think so. On the witness who would appear before you—and I take it that your visit there will permit only of the interrogation of the better qualified witnesses—the effect would be slight. The Haitian, high class, does not fear punishment or imprisonment, especially if any tinge of martyrdom goes with it. I do not believe that the better class of Haitians would feel honestly that they would suffer because of any testimony, however disparaging it might be, that they gave before the committee. The censorship, it must be understood, so far as I was able to exercise it—and I exercised most of it—was directed only against the publication of libelous articles, libelous as a marine understands it.

Senator Oddie. Untrue?

Col. Williams. Untrue. There was not the slightest attempt made to stop criticism. That was fully discussed by me in a conference I had with representatives of all the papers in the capital. That interview was reported and printed in extenso, and I do not remember a single instance where the papers were suppressed or their editors punished for printing a critical article that could be even read as being truthful. I was one of the few officers who read French, and not only was a good deal of suppressing done but a good deal of reading was done by me. I tried to get through all the papers every day. It was not difficult because there were only a few.

Mr. Howe. To what extent would the existence of military tribunals be affected by the suspension of martial law?

Col. Williams. It would depend upon the phraseology modifying the martial law or suspending it in whole or in part.

Mr. Howe. It would not suspend the laws of courts-martial, of course?

Col. Williams. If martial law were lifted without qualification, it would stop the operation of the military courts; I mean the provost courts.

Mr. Howe. And that would leave only the civil Haitian courts?

Col. Williams. The civil Haitian courts.

Mr. Howe. Are those, as they are now constituted, adequate for the administration of justice during the occupation?

Col. Williams. They are not adequate for the administration of justice, so far as justice is involved in the adjudication of cases where the United States or its representatives are a party.

Senator Oddie. There is one more question I wanted to ask in connection with what I asked you before. If martial law were abolished temporarily, and our marines were still there, do you think there would be any danger of vengeance being worked against them?

Col. Williams. No; the Haitian is not an assassin. I think in four years there in Port au Prince, a city of 100,000 people, there were not more than five or six murders.

Senator Oddie. What would be the effect of suspending martial law temporarily while this committee is investigating matters in Haiti? Would it result in vengeance being taken on the marines and result in harm to the marines, who would then be unarmed, as far as the law is concerned?

Col. Williams. I do not believe that for a period of two weeks the suspension of martial law would result in any crimes or violence.

Mr. Howe. If the question referred to a longer period would your answer be the same?

Col. Williams. No; an indefinite suspension of martial law would make extremely difficult the working of the occupation.

Senator Oddie. If conditions remain as they are in regard to martial law, do you think that it would mean any trouble in getting fair and truthful and unbiased statements from the witnesses?

Col. WILLIAMS. I do not. The class of Haitians whom I assume you will mostly interrogate have never had any reason to fear the operation of martial law and are perfectly familiar with its application, and they realize as well as we do the limitations which we ourselves place on its application.

Mr. ANGELL. In connection with these questions in regard to martial law, the questions here put to the witness, Col. Williams, regarding the lifting of martial law would seem to take their origin in the request or grow out of the request which I made last week or 10 days ago for the temporary raising of martial law during the presence of the committee in Haiti, and I therefore wish it to appear on the record, in order that there may be no doubt or ambiguity in this connection, that the request was for the lifting of martial law only during the period of the visit of the committee to Haiti, which would not be in any event, as I understand the present plans, above two weeks, and possibly less than that.

(Whereupon, at 4.35 o'clock p. m., the committee adjourned until Monday, November 7, 1921, at 10.30 o'clock a. m.)

INQUIRY INTO OCCUPATION AND ADMINISTRATION OF HAITI AND SANTO DOMINGO.

UNITED STATES SENATE,
SELECT COMMITTEE ON HAITI AND SAN DOMINGO,
Washington, D. C.

The committee met, pursuant to adjournment, in room 131 Senate Office Building, at 10.30 o'clock a. m. Senator Tasker L. Oddie presiding.

Present: Senator Oddie.

Also present: Mr. Walter Bruce Howe, Mr. Ernest Angell, and Maj. Edwin N. McClellan.

STATEMENT OF MR. FREDERICK L. SPEAR, ATTORNEY AT LAW, FREMONT, NEBR.

Mr. Howe. Mr. Spear, how old are you, please?

Mr. Spear. Twenty-nine years old.

Mr. Howe. You went to a law school?

Mr. Spear. Yes, sir.

Mr. Howe. Before that, did you have university training?

Mr. Spear. Just the law school; that was all.

Mr. Howe. Where was that?

Mr. Spear. The University of Nebraska.

Mr. Howe. Were you ever a member of the United States Marine Corps?

Mr. Spear. Yes, sir.

Mr. Howe. In what capacity?

Mr. Spear. Well, from private to first lieutenant.

Mr. Howe. When did you enlist?

Mr. Spear. Sometime in July, 1917.

Mr. Howe. How soon after that were you commissioned?

Mr. Spear. July, 1918.

Mr. Howe. That was a commission in the United States Marine Corps?

Mr. Spear. The Marine Corps Reserves, first, and a month later in the Marine Corps.

Mr. Howe. As second lieutenant?

Mr. Spear. Second lieutenant; yes, sir.

Mr. Howe. Were you afterwards promoted to first lieutenant?

Mr. Spear. Yes, sir.

Mr. Howe. When was that?

Mr. Spear. I think in about March or April, 1919.

Mr. Howe. That was first lieutenant in the Marine Corps?

Mr. Spear. Marine Corps; yes, sir.

Mr. Howe. There has been testimony before the committee here of individuals who, being members of the Marine Corps, had rank in the Haitian gendarmerie. These commissions and promotions of which we have been speaking in your testimony here refer to Marine Corps promotions and grades, do they not?

Mr. Spear. Yes, sir.

Mr. Howe. Where was your service?

Mr. Spear. From the start.

Mr. Howe. From the start?

Mr. Howe. In the United States?

Mr. Howe. You served in the United States and Haiti?

Mr. Spear. Yes.

Mr. Howe. When did you go to Haiti?

Mr. Spear. I think I landed in Port au Prince on April 18, 1919.

Mr. Howe. What duties did you perform?

Mr. Spear. The next day I was sent into the field, in the mountains.

Mr. Howe. With what organization?

Mr. Spear. I think I was attached to either the Sixty-seventh or Sixty-ninth Company, but I was not with them; I was detached. I was carried on their roster.

Mr. Howe. When you took the field what outfit were you with?

Mr. Spear. I think with the One hundredth Company; I am not certain.

Mr. Howe. Did you perform any duty as an officer of the gendarmerie?

Mr. Spear. I had command of some gendarmerie, but I was not an officer of the gendarmerie.

Mr. Howe. Explain that, will you please?

Mr. Spear. I was sent out by the major in command at Mirebalais to a town called Sautenu, and there I had charge of the town with, I think, about 8 or 10 marines and 3 or 4 gendarmes in the barracks there—a little barracks.

Mr. Howe. You therefore had some gendarmerie under your direction?

Mr. Spear. At that time; yes.

Mr. Howe. But you were never given any separate command of the gendarmerie?

Mr. Spear. No, sir.

Mr. Howe. About when was it that you had these few gendarmes under your orders?

Mr. Spear. It must have been the latter part of April and the first part of May.

Mr. Howe. Of 1919?

Mr. Spear. 1919.

Mr. Howe. When were you discharged from the Marine Corps?

Mr. Spear. About the 1st of August, 1919, I think.

Mr. Howe. Why were you discharged?

Mr. Spear. I asked for it, I guess; yes, I asked for it. The war was over.

Mr. Howe. How was your health at that time?

Mr. Spear. I had malaria and I weighed 135 pounds, and my average weight was 175.

Mr. Howe. Are you suffering from some after effects of that malaria now?

Mr. Spear. I just got out of bed a little while ago.

Mr. Howe. From malaria?

Mr. Spear. Yes.

Mr. Howe. On June 26, 1919, did you act as counsel for the accused in the general court-martial of Pvt. Walter E. Johnson, United States Marine Corps?

Mr. Spear. Yes, sir.

Mr. Howe. Mr. Chairman, I want to introduce into the record the court-martial proceedings of the Walter E. Johnson general court-martial case, of which I have here the original record. My suggestion would be that the record, typewritten, possibly printed later on, contain the charges and specifications, the summing up of counsel for the accused, and the findings of the court in full, and the action of the convening authority in full, but as to the testimony, for purposes of the record of the committee, I believe that a carefully prepared digest of the testimony will serve all purposes equally well, and in the preparation of the digest I should, before submitting it to the committee, submit it to Mr. Angell, counsel for the Haitian societies, to obtain his assistance in seeing that it is a sufficiently full and impartial digest.

Senator Oddie. With a reference made to the place where this can be found?

Mr. Howe. With a reference made to the place where this can be found, so that although it will be one of the records introduced in evidence before this committee the committee by that means will avoid unnecessary typewriting and printing. Will that be satisfactory, Mr. Angell?

Mr. Angell. Quite satisfactory.

Senator Oddie. If that is satisfactory, it will be so ordered.

(It was understood that the records referred to would be later printed in the record.)

Mr. Howe. I will remind you that Johnson was tried on charges and specifications as follows: summarizing: Charge I: Assault. Specification: Assaulting Leonard Placide, a native. Charge II: Absence from station and duty without leave. Specification: Absence without leave on or about May 22, 1919. Charge III: Conduct to the prejudice of good order and discipline. Specification 1: That Pvt. Johnson, serving with the One hundred and forty-eighth Company, Second

Regiment, of the First Provisional Brigade, United States Marine Corps, on detached duty at Croix des Bouquets, in Haiti. unlawfully became a member of a firing squad that unlawfully shot the said Leonard Placide. Specification 2: That Johnson unlawfully joined a firing squad which unlawfully killed another native named Destine Jean, a native prisoner.

I will remind you that the result of the court-martial was that the accused was found guilty of the first charge; that the second charge, of absence without leave, was not proved; and that the third charge, with both specifications thereunder, were held to be not proved, and that the sentence was confinement for six months and dishonorable discharge.

Th convening authority of this court-martial was Col. L. McCarty Little, of the United States Marine Corps.

Now, having identified the proceedings in that way, I will read to you the transcript of your summing up or argument before the court-martial in that case, which appears on page 41 of the record of the court-martial.

(Mr. Howe thereupon read the closing argument of counsel for the accused in the record of the court-martial of Pvt. Walter E. Johnson)

Mr. Spear, is the transcript of your summing up, to the best of your recollection, a correct one?

Mr. SPEAR. Practically so. The reporter was rather slow, and a few words he missed, but it is practically the meaning of the thing.

Mr. HOWE. I draw your attention to your remark to the court: " I myself have ordered one or two Cacos shot upon notification of a chief of section." Was your language there reported substantially correct?

Mr. SPEAR. Practically; yes, sir.

Mr. HOWE. You accept that as a transcript of what you said, which would not be misleading?

Mr. SPEAR. Yes; if explained.

Mr. HOWE. Please explain and also state to the committee what, if any, occurrence you had in mind when you made that statement to the court.

Mr. SPEAR. I was in the field in command of about 30 men.

Mr. HOWE. You are now describing the occurrence which you had in mind?

Mr. SPEAR. Yes. About half of them were incapacitated with the fever. I was supposed to go out and make a certain patrol, looking for this band of Cacos. Understand me, a Caco means the people that were fighting us.

Mr. HOWE. Fighting against you?

Mr. SPEAR. Armed forces, yes; not natives, armed forces. When I went out on this morning I took five men, a Negro guide and myself, all the men that were available for me at that time.

Mr. HOWE. When you speak of men do you mean enlisted personnel of the United States Marine Corps?

Mr. SPEAR. Yes; except the Negro guide that I speak of.

Mr. HOWE. What was the Negro guide's position?

Mr. SPEAR. He was chief of section there.

Mr. HOWE. That is a civil office, is it not, under the Haitian law?

Mr. SPEAR. Yes; something like our sheriff here. We came up with the armed Cacos at about 5 o'clock in the morning, after marching two or three hours. As soon as it was daylight we turned loose with our Lewis gun and the rifles.

Mr. HOWE. How many pieces did you have there?

Mr. SPEAR. One Lewis gun, four rifles, and a pistol. I carried a pistol, and the other men had pistols. These Cacos were in houses and behind trees down in the valley, and we were on top. We drove them out of the valley; at least, when we got down in the valley there were various dead and wounded Cacos lying there.

Mr. HOWE. At this point. what was the date of this occurrence, as nearly as you can recollect?

Mr. SPEAR. Sometime in May or June, 1919.

Mr. HOWE. About how long before you acted as counsel for Johnson?

Mr. SPEAR. Possibly six weeks.

Mr. HOWE. And where did this action take place that you are now describing?

Mr. SPEAR. The same place, to the east of the little trading point called Petit Fond.

Mr. HOWE. Where is Petit Fond; what part of Haiti?

Mr. SPEAR. I think it is some 45 miles to the northeast of Port au Prince, I should say.

Mr. HOWE. Will you continue with your description of the action?

Mr. SPEAR. We were firing as we ran down into the valley, they firing back at us.

Mr. HOWE. The Cacos?

Mr. SPEAR. Yes; we chasing them up the hill, consequently our positions were reversed; we were in the valley and they were on·the hill. These wounded men—I do not know how badly they were wounded or whether they were faking, these Cacos. I rushed ahead and grabbed the machine gun myself at that time—the Lewis gun—and detailed two of my men to watch the rear. That left me with three men.

Mr. HOWE. Let me get this correct in my own mind, as far as I can. You had at the time that you took charge of the Lewis gun yourself passed with your command in your advance beyond the point where lay the dead and wounded who were struck down in your opening volley; is that right?

Mr. SPEAR. Yes.

Mr. HOWE. And you were pursuing the others?

Mr. SPEAR. Pursuing the others.

Mr. HOWE. Up the hill?

Mr. SPEAR. Yes; sending two of my men back to watch my rear.

Mr. HOWE. Having at that time passed over and beyond the original position of the Cacos?

Mr. SPEAR. Yes.

Mr. HOWE. Go ahead, please.

Mr. SPEAR. One of the men came forward and said, " What are we going to do with these wounded fellows? " And I said, " Go back and shoot them and protect my rear. Do not bother with the wounded men."

Mr. HOWE. How many Cacos were there in the forces opposed to you at that time?

Mr. SPEAR. About 100.

Mr. HOWE. Is that an estimate or an actual count?

Mr. SPEAR. An estimate.

Mr. HOWE. How did you estimate them?

Mr. SPEAR. Our intelligence department had said that there were 100 in that band I was to attack; between 80 and 100, they said.

Mr. HOWE. Were you able to judge by the volume of their fire whether they were numerous or not?

Mr. SPEAR. No; except that they were unusually skilled riflemen in that bunch. They were coming very close to my men all the time. Ordinarily, they did not.

Mr. HOWE. At the time you gave that direction to your soldier to kill the wounded in your rear, where were the rest of the enemy with relation to your force?

Mr. SPEAR. They had almost completely surrounded us at that time. They went up on the hills and went around us.

Mr. HOWE. Was there firing from front and both sides?

Mr. SPEAR. Yes, sir.

Mr. HOWE. Had there been any firing from the rear?

Mr. SPEAR. I do not know right at that time whether there had or not. They were going there. We could see them getting behind us.

Mr. HOWE. You could see these people?

Mr. SPEAR. Once in a while a flash through the trees.

Mr. HOWE. You say you could see them working around to the rear of your position, some of them?

Mr. SPEAR. Yes.

Mr. HOWE. How were these Cacos armed?

Mr. SPEAR. Well, those we killed were armed with rifles, swords, and knives.

Mr. HOWE. Did you see arms in the hands of any of the Cacos you observed running?

Mr. SPEAR. No; but I could see them shooting.

Mr. HOWE. Could you hear the bullets coming near by?

Mr. SPEAR. Yes, sir.

Mr. HOWE. And were you able to judge how near the bullets were coming?

Mr. SPEAR. Well, some of them hit right between my men sometimes. I could see the dust fly.

Mr. HOWE. How long did this action last?

Mr. SPEAR. About an hour.

Mr. HOWE. Was the firing of the Cacos fairly sustained during that hour?

Mr. SPEAR. Yes.

Mr. HOWE. How near were your supports or reserves?

Mr. SPEAR. We had none; there were none.

Mr. HOWE. You had made a two or three hours' march before you met with this band of Cacos?

Mr. SPEAR. Yes.

Mr. HOWE. In your opinion, how important was it to disperse and drive off the Cacos at the earliest possible moment?

Mr. SPEAR. Of supreme importance. That was the object of the campaign.

Mr. HOWE. How many dead were there that you counted as the result of the engagement?

Mr. SPEAR. I have forgotten now; I suppose half a dozen, that is that were there, and the rest of them, some wounded, running. I could see the blood trails. They carry off their wounded, those Cacos. They think that if a man is killed on the battle field and lies there overnight he goes to hell, so that they are very anxious to carry their wounded and dead with them when they retreat.

Mr. HOWE. How many wounded were there, do you know?

Mr. SPEAR. I do not know, a couple or three.

Mr. HOWE. Two or three?

Mr. SPEAR. Yes.

Mr. HOWE. You knew, however, from the report of your subordinate that there were wounded there behind?

Mr. SPEAR. Oh, yes; I passed over them when I went up.

Mr. HOWE. Where were they when you passed over them; were they in a village?

Mr. SPEAR. Yes; in some houses; small, scattered houses; it was not a village; they were outside of the inhabitants.

Mr. HOWE. Were there any peaceful inhabitants around in the houses?

Mr. SPEAR. No.

Mr. HOWE. Do you know whether or not, as a matter of fact, your subordinate did kill those wounded?

Mr. SPEAR. No.

Mr. HOWE. You assumed that he did?

Mr. SPEAR. I assumed that he did; yes; they were dead.

Mr. HOWE. They were later found dead?

Mr. SPEAR. Yes.

Mr. HOWE. What was the nature of the country there; was it wooded?

Mr. SPEAR. Wooded and mountainous; very mountainous.

Mr. HOWE. How near could an enemy have approached to your rear and still have kept under cover?

Mr. SPEAR. Fifty yards.

Mr. HOWE. These were modern rifles they were armed with, were they not?

Mr. SPEAR. No.

Mr. HOWE. What was the range of these rifles they were armed with?

Mr. SPEAR. I have no idea.

Mr. HOWE. More than 50 yards?

Mr. SPEAR. Oh, my, yes; they were .45-caliber rifles—old French rifles.

Senator ODDIE. One of those would kill a man as far as you could see him?

Mr. SPEAR. Maj. John L. Mayer was hit with one of them, and it killed him instantly.

Senator ODDIE. At how close a range?

Mr. SPEAR. At close range. It tore his whole side out instantly.

Mr. HOWE. A pistol's range is good for more than 50 yards, is it not?

Mr. SPEAR. You will have to shoot better than I can. I would say yes.

Mr. HOWE. You can hit at 50 yards?

Mr. SPEAR. You can hit at 200 yards and can kill a man with a pistol; yes.

Senator ODDIE. Those guns would be absolutely fatal at a thousand yards, at least?

Mr. SPEAR. I should think so. I am not a technical expert, but I should think so.

Mr. HOWE. How did you come out?

Mr. SPEAR. We carried only the ammunition that we could carry on our backs, and, of course, that does not go very far in a Lewis gun, consequently I had to clear the way and get out of there. My ammunition was about gone, and I could not risk the lives of my men any further, of course.

Mr. HOWE. So what did you do?

Mr. SPEAR. We fired and cleared the way and got out of this valley, and as soon as we backed out of there we were safe again. We were on the high land and we could watch them.

Mr. Howe. That was open ground?

Mr. Spear. More or less open ground.

Mr. Howe. Did you retrace your steps any in order to get to the open ground or did you go to the other side of the valley?

Mr. Spear. No; we went back; we could not get to the other side.

Mr. Howe. Did you make a report of that engagement?

Mr. Spear. Yes, sir.

Mr. Howe. Reporting the casualties to the enemy?

Mr. Spear. Yes, sir.

Mr. Howe. In that report did you make any mention of your order to kill the wounded?

Mr. Spear. No; I did not suppose that was necessary.

Mr. Howe. You counted those as dead?

Mr. Spear. I had to kill them; I could not leave them there. .

Mr. Howe. Had you at the time or have you now, any doubt as to your justification in giving that order?

Mr. Spear. Absolutely none—no doubt.

Mr. Howe. You believe you were justified?

Mr. Spear. I certainly was.

Mr. Howe. And if you had not given that order and those wounded had killed or hurt any of your men, would you have then felt responsible for them?

Mr. Spear. I would have felt responsible and I would have been court-martialed. It was my duty to bring my five men home.

Mr. Howe. And your reason for that feeling is that this was a critical situation in the field?

Mr. Spear. A critical situation in the field.

Mr. Howe. The circumstances of which justified the killing of these wounded men?

Mr. Spear. Absolutely.

Mr. Howe. When you were addressing the court-martial in the Johnson case did you have any other instances of the killing of wounded in battle in mind?

Mr. Spear. No, sir.

Mr. Howe. That was the basis of your remark?

Mr. Spear. Yes.

Mr. Howe. And the sole basis of your remark?

Mr. Spear. The sole basis.

Mr. Howe. Where I left off quoting your remark goes on, " and I also doubt whether a treacherous guide need expect a trial if made prisoner." Had you any occurrence in mind when you made that remark?

Mr. Spear. Not to my personal knowledge.

Mr. Howe. That remark is, in general, correctly quoted by the reporter?

Mr. Spear. Yes, sir.

Mr. Howe. What caused you to make that remark? Have you any explanation to give of it further than that you made it?

Mr. Spear. Yes; I understand that a lieutenant in the section next to me was betrayed by his guide one morning and I do not know whether they hit him on the head and killed him or shot him or what, but I know there was something doing there.

Mr. Howe. On the spot you heard it?

Mr. Spear. Yes.

Mr. Howe. But you have no further knowledge than what you heard, is that correct?

Mr. Spear. That is it; and if the guide did betray him, I think he was perfectly justified; there was no other way he could do with him.

Mr. Howe. That is to say, out in the field and in the presence of the enemy?

Mr. Spear. Yes; you understand we were out in the field.

Mr. Howe. Your views are limited by that circumstance, are they not, when you expressed them, of the treatment of unfaithful guides in the presence of the enemy in the field?

Mr. Spear. Certainly.

Mr. Howe. I will continue the quotation: " I merely mention these things to show that marines in the field live in this atmosphere and that it is nothing surprising to receive orders to kill a man. I myself have been second in command of forces in the field to which prisoners were sent and who—the captain so notified me—we had orders to execute. The captain detailed one man to shoot at the prisoner, which he did without question, close beside me; the other one was taken back to Mirebalais through mistaken orders regarding his execution."

What, if any, incident did you have in your mind when you made that statement to the court?

Mr. SPEAR. You mean the times.

Mr. HOWE. If you will give us your recollection, I will, with your permission, interrupt you to make as precise as possible the time and the circumstance.

Mr. SPEAR. This was, I think, in May or June sometime that I was in the field, under the command of Capt. Edwards.

Mr. HOWE. This was 1919?

Mr. SPEAR. Yes.

Mr. HOWE. Capt. Edwards?

Mr. SPEAR. Yes.

Mr. HOWE. Do you know Capt. Edwards's first name?

Mr. SPEAR. No; I do not.

Mr. HOWE. Do you know what outfit his command belonged to?

Mr. SPEAR. I think he commanded the One hundredth Company at that time.

Mr. HOWE. The One hundredth Company?

Mr. SPEAR. I believe so; yes.

Mr. HOWE. Are you certain of that?

Mr. SPEAR. No, sir.

Mr. HOWE. That is your best recollection?

Mr. SPEAR. Yes, sir.

Mr. HOWE. Will you continue what you were going to say?

Mr. SPEAR. This was in May or June, 1919, I think, and Capt. Edwards and myself were stationed at this town, Petit Fond, he, of course, being superior in command. We stayed there at 10-day intervals, and with relief sent out and they convoyed two prisoners out there.

Mr. HOWE. What was that date?

Mr. SPEAR. I say it was May or June; I could not say which.

Mr. HOWE. How long before your relief at Petit Fond had you been with Capt. Edwards?

Mr. SPEAR. Well, you see, a part of the time I was in command at Petit Fond, and a part of the time Capt. Edwards. If you will state your question again, I will try to answer what you are trying to get at.

Mr. HOWE. You said some time ago in your testimony that you left for the field with a contingent from the One hundredth Company?

Mr. SPEAR. Yes.

Mr. HOWE. And your departure was very soon after your arrival in Haiti, about a week, was it not?

Mr. SPEAR. The next day.

Mr. HOWE. And was Capt. Edwards the commanding officer of that detachment with which you went?

Mr. SPEAR. Well, in the meantime I was out at this little town I spoke about, when I had command of the gendarmerie, Sauteau. Then I came right back and went out with Capt. Edwards after that.

Mr. HOWE. He was your superior officer?

Mr. SPEAR. Yes, sir.

Mr. HOWE. You occasionally performed duty separate from him, did you not, or did you?

Mr. SPEAR. Yes; he sent me out on patrols, of course.

Mr. HOWE. But you reported back to him after those patrols?

Mr. SPEAR. I reported to him; yes.

Mr. HOWE. So at the time of your relief you were under Edwards's orders directly?

Mr. SPEAR. At the time of my relief from Haiti, you mean?

Mr. HOWE. No; at the time of your relief at Petit Fond.

Mr. SPEAR. Oh, yes, sir.

Mr. HOWE. How many men did you have there? Were you there under Capt. Edwards's orders?

Mr. SPEAR. Thirty-three, about.

Mr. HOWE. Those were all marines?

Mr. SPEAR. All marines, except our guides.

Mr. HOWE. And the marines were not on gendarmerie duty there?

Mr. SPEAR. No, sir.

Mr. HOWE. And neither were you?

Mr. SPEAR. No, sir.

Mr. HOWE. And neither was Capt. Edwards?

Mr. SPEAR. No, sir.

Mr. HOWE. Now, go ahead please.

Mr. SPEAR. Our relief brought these prisoners out, and I saw them there. Capt. Edwards saw me and said, " You are responsible for these prisoners."

Mr. HOWE. How many were there?

Mr. SPEAR. Two.

Mr. HOWE. Do you remember the names of the prisoners?

Mr. SPEAR. No; they were Negroes.

Mr. HOWE. Haitians?

Mr. SPEAR. Yes. He detailed me to guard the prisoners. He said, " I am to shoot one of these fellows, but you are responsible. Watch them. They may try to get away from you." So I very carefully walked right behind them on the way, personally myself, as a guard.

Mr. HOWE. All the way from where to where?

Mr. SPEAR. To the place I am going to tell you about, and we arrived at a place there, and he detailed a man to execute this prisoner, and while I did not personally witness it, he did execute the prisoner.

Mr. HOWE. What is your basis for saying he did execute the prisoner? What did you observe there from which you concluded he executed that prisoner?

Mr. SPEAR. I heard the rifle shot, and when I went back there I saw the fellow there dead.

Mr. HOWE. Do you know any of the other circumstances—that is, how many men were in the firing squad?

Mr. SPEAR. One man.

Mr. HOWE. How do you know that?

Mr. SPEAR. I guess the captain told me afterwards—no; I saw him taking the fellow away. I saw the marine taking the Negro out.

Mr. HOWE. You saw the marine taking the Negro out?

Mr. SPEAR. Yes.

Mr. HOWE. To the point where shortly afterwards the shot came from?

Mr. SPEAR. Yes.

Mr. HOWE. The sound of the shot came from?

Mr. SPEAR. Yes, sir.

Mr. HOWE. And the marine was taking the Negro out in the direction of the place where you subsequently saw the Negro dead?

Mr. SPEAR. There was no question about it; he shot him, as far as that is concerned.

Mr. HOWE. Is there any question but that he shot him under the orders of Capt. Edwards?

Mr. SPEAR. I could not say. I did not hear the captain give him the order.

Mr. HOWE. The captain however, told you he had ordered him shot?

Mr. SPEAR. Yes.

Mr. HOWE. Did he tell you on whose authority those orders were given?

Mr. SPEAR. No; he did not.

Mr. HOWE. These two prisoners were brought out by this relief?

Mr. SPEAR. Yes, sir.

Mr. HOWE. Where were they brought from, do you know?

Mr. SPEAR. Mirebalais, I think.

Mr. HOWE. Do you recollect who was in command, what marine officer was in command at Mirebalais at that time?

Mr. SPEAR. No; I can not. If you can refresh my memory, perhaps I can remember. He was a major in the Marine Corps, a colonel in the gendarmerie; I do not know.

Mr. HOWE. How could you refresh your recollection?

Mr. SPEAR. I believe if somebody mentioned his name I could say whether he was the man or not; I do not know. He wore a mustache.

Mr. HOWE. Have you with you or at home any notes, correspondence, or other material in which you could hope to find the name of this major?

Mr. SPEAR. No; I could not—I could not tell.

Mr. HOWE. What were the names of the officers coming out with the relieving force to Petit Fond?

Mr. SPEAR. Capt. Brecker or Becker, I do not know which.

Mr. HOWE. Brecker or Becker?

Mr. SPEAR. Yes.

Mr. HOWE. Of the marines?

Mr. SPEAR. Yes.

Mr. HOWE. Was there another officer with him?

Mr. SPEAR. Yes, sir.

Mr. HOWE. Do you recollect the name of the other officer?

Mr. SPEAR. I do not know. I know he went down to the military academy last year, the Virginia Military Institute. He was a great football player. I can not think of his name.

Mr. HOWE. He went to Virginia Military Institute last year as a student?

Mr. SPEAR. Yes.

Mr. HOWE. Have you any notes or other material from which you could refresh your recollection as to the names of those relieving officers?

Mr. SPEAR. No, sir.

Mr. HOWE. Do you know how the orders to kill these prisoners had been transmitted to Capt. Edwards?

Mr. SPEAR. No, sir.

Mr. HOWE. In point of time, how near did Capt. Edwards's remark to you coincide with the arrival of Capt. Becker or Brecker?

Mr. SPEAR. Oh, it was after.

Mr. HOWE. How soon after?

Mr. SPEAR. Well, he told me to guard these prisoners, and it was half an hour afterwards, as soon as we started back.

Mr. HOWE. Would it be fair to suppose that the orders to execute these prisoners were carried by Capt. Brecker to Capt. Edwards?

Mr. SPEAR. Yes.

Mr. HOWE. Did Capt. Edwards have any other means of receiving an order from Mirebalais at that time?

Mr. SPEAR. Yes; it is possible by native he could have received those orders.

Mr. HOWE. A native messenger?

Mr. SPEAR. Yes, sir.

Mr. HOWE. Would you have known of the arrival of a native messenger with orders?

Mr. SPEAR. I believe so.

Mr. HOWE. Were you aware of the arrival at that time, or just before that time, of any native messenger with orders?

Mr. SPEAR. No, sir; but I could not say for certain, of course.

Mr. HOWE. What happened to the other prisoner? You mentioned two.

Mr. SPEAR. We took him back to Mirebalais with us.

Mr. HOWE. Did you have any conversation with Capt. Edwards about this?

Mr. SPEAR. That night, yes; after we were back in Mirebalais.

Mr. HOWE. About the return of the second prisoner?

Mr. SPEAR. Yes.

Mr. HOWE. What was that?

Mr. SPEAR. I can not give his exact conversation, but he said he was supposed to have executed that man, but he made a mistake, and did not do it.

Mr. HOWE. Before he learned of his mistake and informed you of it, had he been to any headquarters at Mirebalais?

Mr. SPEAR. I think he had; yes.

Mr. HOWE. Before your arrival back in Mirebalais had Capt. Edwards told you that it was a mistake not to have killed that prisoner?

Mr. SPEAR. Oh, no.

Mr. HOWE. So it is fair to assume that he learned that he had mistaken his orders for the first time when he got to Mirebalais?

Mr. SPEAR. Oh, yes; that is the fact.

Mr. HOWE. Can you think of any circumstances by which you could fix the execution more nearly in point of time? Had you cashed a pay voucher anywhere near that time, or was there any outstanding fact by which you could give us the date?

Mr. SPEAR. I was not paid for six months there.

Mr. HOWE. Did you have any other incident in mind of the execution of prisoners when you told the court that you had been second in command of forces in the field to which prisoners were sent with orders to execute them?

Mr. SPEAR. I do not understand your question.

(The stenographer read the question as above reported.)

Mr. SPEAR. No, sir.

Mr. HOWE. That was the only incident that you had in mind

Mr. SPEAR. Yes, sir; except hearsay, you understand, as I told you.

Mr. Howe. By hearsay you refer to rumors of similar occurrences?

Mr. Spear. Well, I would not say similar. I have heard of rumors of people being executed. I suppose they were bandits; I do not know.

Mr. Howe. Did the rumor which you heard go into particulars as to whether those executions were before or after the trial?

Mr. Spear. No, sir; I do not know whether this particular one of Capt. Edwards was before or after a trial either.

Mr. Howe. Did you ever inquire of Capt Edwards whether this execution was authorized after trial?

Mr. Spear. No, sir; I never asked any questions.

Mr. Howe. Do you recollect whether the Capt. Edwards to whom you referred was named Thomas L. Edwards?

Mr. Spear. Yes.

Mr. Howe. Have you in mind anything about the commanding officer at Mirebalais, the major, acting as colonel in the gendarmerie, which would help the committee to identify that commanding officer?

Mr. Spear. Well, Gen. Catlin was the commanding officer at Port au Prince at that time.

Mr. Howe. Had you heard of any previous service in the marines that this major had performed?

Mr. Spear. Yes; Capt. Edwards was under him in Mexico as a sergeant.

Mr. Howe. In Mexico?

Mr. Spear. Yes, sir.

Mr. Howe. At what time in Mexico did you hear?

Mr. Spear. About 1914, was it, when they had the trouble there at Vera Cruz that time?

Mr. Howe. Are there any other particulars that you can give us about this commanding officer by which we could identify him?

Mr. Spear. Well, if I could think of the name of that lieutenant in the gendarmerie that was there, I could identify him by him, but I can not think of his name.

Mr. Howe. There was a lieutenant of gendarmerie at Mirebalais?

Mr. Spear. Yes; the commander of that district there, and that was the field headquarters for this major.

Mr. Howe. If you should think of any other circumstances by which we could identify the commanding officer there, while you are here as a witness, please speak of it.

Mr. Spear. I will.

Mr. Howe. Now, as to Capt. Edwards, had you any information up to this morning as to his present whereabouts?

Mr. Spear. No, sir.

Mr. Howe. What was the last you saw of Capt. Edwards?

Mr. Spear. I saw him in Port au Prince just before the trial of these men.

Mr. Howe. The trial of Johnson?

Mr. Spear. Yes.

Mr. Howe. Which was on the 26th of June, 1919?

Mr. Spear. Yes.

Mr. Howe. And you have not heard from him or seen him since then, is that correct; Edwards, I mean?

Mr. Spear. Yes, sir.

Mr. Howe. Was there any subordinate of this commanding officer at Mirebalais whose name you recollect?

Mr. Spear. Maj. Pearce.

Mr. Howe. Was it the same Maj. Pearce who was called as a witness in the Johnson court-martial case?

Mr. Spear. Yes, sir.

Maj. McClellan. That is Jacob M. Pearce.

Mr. Howe. J. M. Pearce was the witness in the Johnson case. Is that the one to whom you have reference?

Mr. Spear. Yes, sir.

Mr. Howe. Where was Maj. Pearce stationed at the time of the execution of these prisoners; do you know?

Mr. Spear. I can not remember the name of the town; it was a town east of Mirebalais some miles.

Mr. Howe. Do you know whether he was in Mirebalais or in that town to the east at the time when you got back to Mirebalais with Capt. Edwards?

Mr. Spear. I have no idea.

Mr. Howe. Have you any reason to assume that if this commanding officer whose name you do not recollect was not at Mirebalais, that Maj. Pearce would have been at Mirebalais?

Mr. Spear. That was the usual custom, yes; and if Maj. Pearce could not come, Capt. Edwards took charge.

Mr. Howe. In the absence of the colonel, whose name you can not remember, and Maj. Pearce, Capt. Edwards would go into Mirebalais and take charge?

Mr. Spear. Yes. ⁻ I think he was called adjutant; I do not know.

Mr. Howe. Adjutant of what?

Mr. Spear. I do not know the whole thing there. I do not know what it was; the whole field.

Mr. Howe. Adjutant of the district?

Mr. Spear. Yes.

Mr. Angell. Mr. Spear, do you remember in general the substance of the testimony in the Johnson trial, in which you acted as counsel for Pvt. Johnson, the accused?

Mr. Spear. Yes, sir.

Mr. Angell. And that testimony in substance was that a native Haitian, one Placide by name, had been taken out by gendarmes, under the orders of Lieut. Brokaw, and, with another native Haitian, had been shot by a firing squad without trial?

Mr. Spear. Yes, sir.

Mr. Angell. Was it your belief at the time of the trial that these one or more native Haitians had been shot under orders of Lieut. Brokaw without trial?

Mr. Spear. Yes, sir.

Mr. Angell. Was it your belief that the killings were unlawful and illegal?

Mr. Spear. In so far as Brokaw was concerned.

Mr. Angell. In so far as Brokaw was concerned?

Mr. Spear. Yes.

Mr. Angell. Have you since that time learned anything to change your belief in the fact of the shooting, or the illegality thereof, so far as Brokaw was concerned?

Mr. Spear. Not as regarding the fact of the shooting. However, Brokaw was adjudged insane afterwards. That would be a defense, of course.

Mr. Angell. Have you learned anything since then to change your belief that these men had been killed under orders of Brokaw, without previous conviction and sentence of death by lawful trial?

Mr. Spear. No.

Mr. Angell. Do you remember the comments on the findings and sentence of the court-martial in the Johnson case, by Col. L. McCarty Little, the convening authority?

Mr. Spear. I never heard them.

Mr. Angell. These findings are a part of the record?

Mr. Howe. They are the ones that will be printed in full.

Mr. Angell. I just want at this point to refer to them, to emphasize the view of the convening authority, Col. Little saying: "The reviewing authority, after careful consideration, is at a loss to understand how officers of the service and experience of some of those who constituted this court could so disregard their oaths and obligations to enforce the laws and regulations "——

Mr. Howe. Just a second, Mr. Angell. Would it not be better to read the whole of that, until we get it printed in the record as a whole? Would it convey the proper idea?

Mr. Angell. All right, I will read the preceding sentence. It was just to save time, that is all.

Mr. Howe. Were you going to ask a question of the witness, based upon that?

Mr. Angell. Yes.

Mr. Howe. I think it would be better if you would read the whole thing.

Mr. Angell. Very well. [Reading:]

" The proceedings of the general court-martial, in revision, in the foregoing case of Walter E. Johnson, private, United States Marine Corps, are approved: the findings on the first charge and specification thereunder are approved; and the findings on the second and third charges and specifications thereunder and acquittal, are disapproved. The reviewing authority, after careful consideration, is at a loss to understand how officers of the service and experience of some of those who constituted this court could so disregard their oaths and obligations to enforce the laws and regulations of the military service of their country, as to find the accused not guilty of the third charge and specifications thereunder, after the testimony which was presented. The plea of the defense that it was in obedience to the order of a superior officer is untenable. All regulations state that the order must be lawful. The fact that the accused claimed he did not aim at the executed man, does not relieve him from responsibility in the man's death. He made no protest. The very fact that he aimed and fired led the other members of the firing squad to believe he was shooting at the man, and the example thus set by him certainly makes him a party to the execution. Subject to the foregoing remarks the sentence is approved."

Did you, as counsel for the accused in that case, believe that the order of Lieut. Brokaw was lawful?

Mr. SPEAR. Yes, sir.

Mr. ANGELL. You believed that Lieut. Brokaw, then, had the right to order these one or more Haitians to be shot without trial?

Mr. SPEAR. No, sir; I meant lawful as regards to the privates.

Mr. HOWE. You mean lawful authority to the privates?

Mr. SPEAR. Yes; that is what I mean.

Mr. HOWE. For their actions?

Mr. SPEAR. Yes.

Mr. ANGELL. Did you believe it was lawful in the marine service for an enlisted man to obey the order of a superior officer to execute a prisoner without trial?

Mr. SPEAR. Yes, sir. I do not want to get in an unfair position here, Mr. Angell. I mean that a private should always obey the orders of his superior officer under all conditions. That is what I meant to say to you.

Mr. ANGELL. Do you think that the belief which you have just stated, that it is the duty of enlisted men to obey orders of a superior officer under any circumstances was common in the marine personnel in Haiti?

Mr. SPEAR. Absolutely.

Mr. ANGELL. And irrespective of whether or not the order, as in the Brokaw instance to which we have just been referring, was that prisoners, though never lawfully convicted, should be executed?

Mr. SPEAR. It was the duty of a subordinate to carry out the orders of his superior.

Mr. ANGELL. And that was the common and usual belief among the marine personnel in Haiti?

Mr. SPEAR. In a military force.

Mr. ANGELL. Referring now to the instance of the shooting of the wounded prisoners at the time of the attack to which you have just testified, can you say whether or not, in your belief, the shooting of wounded prisoners under similar circumstances was or was not common in engagements with the bandits in Haiti?

Mr. SPEAR. Personally, I can not say; that is, as to my personal knowledge.

Mr. ANGELL. Have you any belief on that question, based upon your experience in Haiti, your conversation with brother officers, and the like?

Mr. SPEAR. Yes; I think it was the custom. When you are out there surrounded, you have to do the best thing you can do to get your men out.

Mr. ANGELL. And that best thing, under such circumstances, may require, in the judgment of the officer so engaged, the shooting of prisoners?

Mr. SPEAR. Well, they were not prisoners. They were there on the field. They were not taken charge of yet, you see. I will say wounded, not prisoners.

Mr. ANGELL. Had you not in this particular instance instructed your two men to go back and shoot those wounded?

Mr. SPEAR. Well, the one man came up and asked me what they should do back there in the rear with those prisoners who were still alive.

Mr. HOWE. Wounded prisoners?

Mr. SPEAR. Yes; they were afraid. They did not know whether they were faking or what they were doing. I said: "Get them out of the way, and get back to the rear and watch there, and watch out for your own lives."

Mr. ANGELL. It is correct. is it not, to refer to them as wounded prisoners?

Mr. SPEAR. No; they were not prisoners. They were there. They might have a knife or a gun or something and shoot me or shoot anybody there.

Mr. ANGELL. You had captured them, had you not?

Mr. SPEAR. No; they were not captured—they were there.

Mr. ANGELL. You passed by them on your way up to leave this collection of huts and go up the hill after the Cacos?

Mr. SPEAR. Yes; passed over them, you might say, and went right on. There seems to be a lot of confusion in this whole thing between a Caco and a peaceful native, and I can not understand it. A Caco is a man in the field, a revolutionist, a bandit, or whatever you want to call him. I do not know what to call them. They were the fellows who were fighting us. They were Cacos, and the rest of them were called just Haitians.

Mr. ANGELL. Was it your understanding of the general situation in Haiti, at the time of the instances referred to, that our forces there were engaged in regular warfare against the Cacos in the hills?

Mr. SPEAR. Yes.

Mr. ANGELL. And that the rules and customs of regular modern warfare prevailed?

Mr. SPEAR. Not entirely.

Mr. ANGELL. In what respects did they not prevail?

Mr. SPEAR. Well, those Cacos were very savage men, and if they had captured one of our marines they would probably have skinned him alive.

Mr. ANGELL. Did you ever know of such circumstances?

Mr. SPEAR. No; I never knew of such.

Mr. ANGELL. Did you ever hear of any such instances?

Mr. SPEAR. It was reported to me that one of the native guides was found neatly stacked up by the road one morning in pieces this long.

Mr. HOWE. You mean cut into pieces?

Mr. SPEAR. Yes; I knew what to expect from them.

Mr. ANGELL. That was hearsay, so far as you were concerned?

Mr. SPEAR. Yes; of course, I had viewed those Cacos, too, at close range. I knew what kind of men they are.

Mr. ANGELL. You never knew, did you, of any formal declaration of war by this country against Haiti, or the bandits of Haiti?

Mr. SPEAR. No, sir.

Mr. ANGELL. There was none, as far as you knew?

Mr. SPEAR. I do not know anything about it. I did whatever I was told to do.

Mr. ANGELL. What were the general instructions that you had upon arrival in Haiti as to the operations against the Cacos?

Mr. SPEAR. I had no instructions. I was sent out with the other officers first to show me how to take charge.

Mr. ANGELL. What was your understanding, derived from your conversation with these other officers and instructions from them, as to the attitude to be observed toward the Cacos?

Mr. SPEAR. The attitude, from instructions and observations, was that we were there to kill the Cacos, and the quicker the better; but to be very careful about peaceful natives. When I went out to this town to take command, they instructed me, regardless of any belief that I held toward the black race, to be very careful and go to the chief magistrate and take him into consultation in this town.

Mr. HOWE. Before doing what?

Mr. SPEAR. Before taking command of the town, and work with him, and not to be antagonistic toward peaceful men. But all Cacos were to be killed. It was guerilla warfare, as I understood it.

Mr. ANGELL. Did I understand you correctly to say that you went out into the field the day after you reached Haiti?

Mr. SPEAR. Yes, sir.

Mr. ANGELL. And what general instruction was given, if any, in your case or in any other case that you know of, to newly arrived officers in Haiti, regarding the general conditions there?

Mr. SPEAR. Well, I do not just exactly remember the distinction between the instructions and the general way of doing things, but I knew that the thing was to get rid of these cacos. They figured there were from 3,000 to 7,000 of them, they told me, and the quicker we got them killed the better the whole country would be off. They had devastated this country where I was.

Mr. ANGELL. That was the substance of the instructions you had, or the understanding which you acquired, upon your arrival in Haiti and during the early weeks of your duty there?

Mr. SPEAR. Yes.

Mr. ANGELL. And you believe that was the general understanding and the general instructions that were given at that time to newly arrived officers like yourself?

Mr. SPEAR. Yes, sir.

Mr. ANGELL. Were there any general or specific instructions given to you or to your brother officers about the time of your arrival there, so far as you remember, regarding detailed conditions in Haiti; that is to say, the political condition, the social condition of the people, their attitude toward the native government and toward the American occupation; in other words, details which might assist you in dealing with the people and performing your duty there?

Mr. SPEAR. No; no more than what I picked up from Capt. Edwards. I expect he was my tutor; I do not know.

Mr. HOWE. He was your commanding officer?

Mr. SPEAR. Yes.

Mr. ANGELL. In other words, there were no detailed instructions about conditions in Haiti given to newly arrived officers?

Mr. SPEAR. No, sir.

Mr. ANGELL. How long after your arrival were you placed in command of a town or subdistrict or other area?

Mr. SPEAR. Two days; but it was supposed to be a peaceable area.

Mr. ANGELL. Was that a fairly common practice; that is, to give newly arrived officers command duty in the country within a very short time after they arrived?

Mr. SPEAR. No, sir; I do not think it was. They picked me out of a bunch of lieutenants to take command of that town. I was senior lieutenant, I think; senior first lieutenant there.

Mr. ANGELL. Do you know whether many or most of the marine officers, as they arrived in Haiti, spoke French?

Mr. SPEAR. Very few of them. It is a kind of a patois there, anyway, but a Frenchman can understand it.

Mr. ANGELL. Referring now to the second instance of which you testified this morning, did I understand you correctly to say that prior to the shooting of this one man whose body you saw shortly after the rifle shot, Capt. Edwards said to you that the man was to be shot?

Mr. SPEAR. About two hours before that. I was to guard him until he was ready to shoot him.

Mr. ANGELL. Capt. Edwards said nothing to you, either before the shooting or afterwards, as to whether or not the man had been convicted by trial or sentenced to death?

Mr. SPEAR. No; he said nothing.

Mr. ANGELL. You had no knowledge on that subject?

Mr. SPEAR. No, sir.

Mr. ANGELL. How far had the man been brought under guard, to your knowledge, for his execution?

Mr. SPEAR. Well, they sent him out there. They made him carry some stuff out to us. I do not know how far it was.

Mr. ANGELL. Out from Mirebalais?

Mr. SPEAR. Sixteen miles or so, I think, or whatever it was.

Mr. ANGELL. Do you believe that this man had been lawfully tried, convicted, and sentenced to death?

Mr. SPEAR. I do not know anything about it. I believe he was a caco, though.

Mr. ANGELL. And that was sufficient justification?

Mr. SPEAR. I was not in it.

Mr. ANGELL. No; I am asking merely for your belief. I understand you were not in it.

Mr. SPEAR. Well, it was claimed they found this man with a rifle in his hand. I think he should have been shot right there.

Mr. HOWE. Before being taken prisoner?

Mr. SPEAR. Before being taken prisoner.

Mr. ANGELL. Is it your belief that the decision to shoot this man in question was made by Capt. Edwards on his responsibility, or came from higher up?

Mr. SPEAR. Came from higher up.

Mr. ANGELL. There is no doubt about that in your mind?

Mr. SPEAR. No.

Mr. ANGELL. You said that you had heard rumors of people being executed. Were those rumors common among the marine personnel in Haiti at this time?

Mr. Spear. What do you mean by common? Do you mean hundreds of them, or scores, or tens, or ones?

Mr. Angell. Well, how current were such rumors? How often did you come across them?

Mr. Spear. Well, I suppose I heard it four times while I was in Haiti.

Mr. Howe. What rumor?

Mr. Angell. The rumor that people were being executed.

Mr. Howe. Well, illegally?

Mr. Angell. All right, I will make it specific. What were the rumors which you testified to having heard about people being executed?

Mr. Spear. I had heard that they had executed people, that was all.

Mr. Angell. Do you mean lawful executions as the result of trial and conviction and sentence to death, or unlawful executions?

Mr. Spear. Well, they did not state that to me. I could not tell, you see.

Mr. Angell. Were these rumors those of the death of Cacos in battle?

Mr. Spear. I do not know; I do not think so. It was after they were captured.

Mr. Angell. There were executions, then, of prisoners?

Mr. Spear. I suppose they were prisoners, yes; that is, I do not say that of my own knowledge, now, you understand.

Mr. Angell. Referring now to the Johnson court-martial record and to the examination and the testimony of the accused, Walter E. Johnson, and particularly to question 38, which appears on page 21, I want to read you the question and answer, as follows:

"Question. Is it your duty to kill Cacos if taken prisoner and if you recognize them as such?

"Answer. The American forces in Haiti are in war against these Cacos. I consider it my duty to shoot a Cacos."

Mr. Howe. Whose testimony is this, Johnson's own testimony?

Mr. Angell. Johnson's own testimony; yes.

Mr. Howe. Questions asked by his own counsel?

Mr. Angell. Yes; questions asked by his own counsel.

Mr. Howe. That would be question 38 by yourself?

Mr. Angell. Yes; that would be your own question. Do you regard that answer which I have just read to you in answer to the question put by yourself at the trial, as counsel to Johnson, as a fair reflex on the attitude of the marine personnel in Haiti toward the Cacos?

Mr. Spear. Yes.

Mr. Howe. You said you had not seen the action of the convening authority of Lieut. Col. Little?

Mr. Spear. Yes, sir.

Mr. Howe. You left Haiti very shortly after the court-martial?

Mr. Spear. A week after.

Mr. Howe. And the findings of the convening authority are not, under the practice, referred to accused's counsel, are they?

Mr. Spear. Not that I know of.

Mr. Howe. They certainly were not referred to you?

Mr. Spear. No.

Mr. Howe. And you know the action of the court must be reviewed by the convening authority?

Mr. Spear. Yes, sir.

Mr. Howe. And that even the prisoner himself, or the accused himself, is kept in ignorance of the action of the court?

Mr. Spear. Yes, sir.

Mr. Howe. Until the convening authority has acted on the court?

Mr. Spear. Yes.

Mr. Howe. You left Haiti on what date, about?

Mr. Spear. I think about the 2d of July.

Mr. Howe. The action of the reviewing authority which was read by Mr. Angell is dated July 18, 1919. You certainly were out of the country at that time?

Mr. Spear. Yes, sir.

Mr. Howe. And a copy of this was not later furnished to you?

Mr. Spear. No, sir.

Mr. Howe. You answered some questions on cross-examination as to the duties of marines to obey the orders of their superior officers?

Mr. Spear. Yes, sir.

Mr. Howe. You know that to be a general rule of military service, whether in our Marine Corps in our Army, or Navy?

Mr. Spear. A fundamental rule.

Mr. Howe. And not one peculiar entirely to the service of the United States, the military service?

Mr. Spear. No, sir.

Mr. Howe. You know, of course, that as a matter of law it is no justification for a subordinate to carry out an illegal order of a superior, do you not?

Mr. Spear. No; I did not know that.

Mr. Howe. But you do know, or it was your feeling when you were a Marine officer, that you were to presume the legality and authority of the orders of your superiors?

Mr. Spear. Yes, sir.

Mr. Howe. Did you yourself, when Capt. Edwards directed you to guard this prisoner until he should be executed, inquire of Capt. Edwards whether the prisoner had been duly convicted and sentenced, or ask him for any of the circumstances of the proceedings leading up to that?

Mr. Spear. No, sir.

Mr. Howe. Why did you not?

Mr. Spear. I expect I would have got whacked on the head if I had.

Mr. Howe. It was not customary for you to question the orders of your superior officers, is that it?

Mr. Spear. Certainly not.

Mr. Howe. By your answers you did not mean to state that a subordinate, being clearly aware of the illegality of the orders of a superior, would be justified to carrying them out?

Mr. Spear. I do not think it is for him to judge whether it is illegal or not.

Mr. Howe. You made some answers about the shooting of wounded in action. You would not say, would you, that the killing of wounded was justified under all and any circumstances?

Mr. Spear. Of course not.

Mr. Howe. You answered that the shooting of wounded would be justified, in your opinion, under circumstances similar to the circumstances under which you gave your orders to shoot these wounded?

Mr. Spear. Yes, sir.

Mr. Howe. Did you hear of many cases of similar circumstances of the detachment of 5 men and 1 officer surrounded by 100 Cacos firing at them?

Mr. Spear. In the district next to me there were 33 men who fought 800 of the others until their ammunition ran out. I think they killed 120. I do not know whether they killed any of the wounded, or what they were, but I know they were outnumbered all the time.

Mr. Howe. Is it your opinion that the responsibility is on the commanding officer in a unit in battle under those circumstances to take all steps necessary for the safety of his men?

Mr. Spear. Yes, sir.

Mr. Howe. And if in his opinion the killing of wounded enemies in his rear would remove an element of danger to his command, it would be his duty to order it?

Mr. Spear. It certainly would.

Mr. Howe. But you would say, would you not, that each of those circumstances, each case, must be judged on its own circumstances?

Mr. Spear. Of course.

Mr. Howe. Entirely?

Mr. Spear. Certainly.

Mr. Howe. You would agree with me, would you not, that there are circumstances when it would be clearly the duty of a commanding officer to shoot a wounded enemy?

Mr. Spear. Certainly. They had their rifles there yet. We could not carry their rifles with us or take their arms away from them, or anything.

Mr. Howe. How many men would be a proper prisoner's guard for two Cacos?

Mr. Spear. I should say——

Mr. Howe. The minimum, the least that you could get along with?

Mr. Spear. It would depend upon the circumstances. One of these Cacos could lick 10 of our men if he got hold of them with a knife.

Mr. Howe. Let us assume the circumstances that existed there.

Mr. Spear. They are powerful men.

Mr. Howe. How many men would it require safely to guard two wounded Cacos in the presence of 100 armed and unwounded Cacos?

Mr. Spear. I should say two or three men.

Mr. Howe. Well, subtracting two or three men from your forces that you then had at your disposal, how many would that have left, including yourself, to fight the other 100?

Mr. Spear. Three. In that case I do not see that there was any question about it. They were there.

Mr. Howe. How much time did you have within which to make up your mind on this?

(The witness snapped his fingers.)

Mr. Howe. As long as it would take you to snap your fingers?

Mr. Spear. Yes, sir.

Senator Oddie. And the element of a few seconds or minutes might have meant the annihilation of all your men?

Mr. Spear. It may have meant the death of two or three of them at least.

Mr. Howe. Let us say the reduction of your force by 50 per cent?

Mr. Spear. The reduction of the whole thing.

Mr. Howe. Or by 100 per cent. When you arrived in Haiti you were first lieutenant?

Mr. Spear. Yes, sir.

Mr. Howe. Did your experience as first lieutenant give you any basis for learning what the instructions of a colonel or a brigadier general were in arriving at Haiti—on the social and political conditions in the island?

Mr. Spear. No, sir.

Mr. Howe. You can not, therefore, say and you do not mean to say what instructions were given to lieutenant colonels, majors, and brigadier generals on their arrival in the island?

Mr. Spear. Of coure not.

Mr. Howe. You were assigned to duty in the field the day after you got there?

Mr. Spear. Yes, sir; the day I got there the adjutant called me up and said: "Take charge of a convoy going out to a certain camp and report to a certain officer there."

Mr. Howe. And you reported to a certain officer there and there came under his orders?

Mr. Spear. Yes, sir.

Mr. Howe. He gave you sufficient directions to let you know what your course of action would be as circumstances came up?

Mr. Spear. He did not say anything; but, of course, I knew what they were, and would be in the command of a convoy if I took it, of course.

Mr. Howe. Irrespective of whether the United States was at war with Haiti?

Mr. Spear. Yes. I presumed they were at war.

Mr. Howe. What was your reflex on that question when the bullets were striking around you on the day you have told us about, as to whether a state of actual warfare existed or not?

Mr. Spear. I rather considered it did.

Mr. Howe. You were asked whether you believed that the rules of regular warfare were applied there in Haiti, and you said you did not believe they were applied in all respects, and you later on said that this was guerilla warfare.

Mr. Spear. I did.

Mr. Howe. In your opinion, does the kind of guerilla warfare which was being followed there modify the rules of regular warfare?

Mr. Spear. Yes.

Mr. Howe. In what respects?

. Mr. Spear. No; I could not say it would, either. I will take that back. I would not say it does, either.

Mr. Howe. Therefore, the actual conditions of warfare which must govern one in those circumstances is self-preservation and the preservation of the forces under his command?

Mr. Spear. Yes; that is what I am trying to get at.

Mr. Howe. Did the enemy observe all the rules of civilized warfare?

Mr. Spear. What do you call civilized? The warfare at the beginning of the German war was not civilized, and at the end it was civilized, with respect to poison gas, for instance. It depends on what the other fellow does. We understood we should expect no quarter from the Cacos.

Mr. Howe. Did you ever hear of Cacos ordering a wounded American shot, or shooting or killing wounded Americans?

Mr. Spear. I do not believe I ever did, personally; no.

Mr. Howe. Did you form any opinion as to what would happen to you or your men if you had been wounded or left by the rest of the party there?

Mr. Spear. We would have been killed, of course.

Mr. Howe. You have not any doubt of that?

Mr. Spear. No.

Mr. Howe. Who are the Cacos the enemies of?

Mr. Spear. Of the United States and Haiti.

Mr. Howe. And of law and order in the island?

Mr. Spear. Yes, sir.

Mr. Howe. Were they a good or a bad influence on the country?

Mr. Spear. Very bad.

Mr. Howe. Did you know of any other way to deal with a Caco who was trying to kill you than to kill the Caco?

Mr. Spear. Certainly not.

Mr. Howe. Your experience in Haiti was entirely out in the field, was it not, substantially so?

Mr. Spear. Yes; except for the last week, when I was in the barracks. I was sick in the field a part of the time and sick in quarters in town a part of the time, and then, about a week before I left, I was put on duty as officer of the day.

Mr. Howe. Do you know, at the time you were down there on duty, over how large a part of Haiti this guerilla warfare with the Cacos extended?

Mr. Spear. I do not just know the distances there. I should judge in a circle 30 miles across each way—or 40.

Mr. Howe. And all the time you were there the brigade commander of Marines was Gen. Catlin?

Mr. Spear. No, sir; I think he came there after I was there. I think there was a colonel in command when I came there; I do not know.

Mr. Angell. Do you think, Mr. Spear, that your beliefs and opinions, as set out in your testimony this morning regarding the duties of our marine forces in Haiti at this time, and the duties of marine officers and marine personnel when engaged in conflict with the Cacos, fairly conforms to the general opinion on such subjects by your brother officers and the remaining personnel of the Marine Corps in Haiti at that time?

Mr. Spear. Well, I think so. Some thought they ought to go a little stronger with them than I thought. I was a kind of middle-of the-roader in those lines.

Mr. Angell. What have you in mind when you say some of them thought they ought to go a little stronger?

Mr. Spear. Well, some of them thought the warfare should be more intensive; that there should be more troops there, and harder fighting; to kill them all and get rid of them; kill all the Cacos.

Mr. Angell. What were the beliefs of the others who, if I understand the inference of your answer right, had the view to the other extreme, or in the other direction from you?

Mr. Spear. No; I do not know of anyone, except some of the marines accused an officer or two of being more partial to the native troops than he was toward his own troops; that is what I mean.

Mr. Angell. Generally speaking, you think your opinion was fairly representative of the general opinion of the other marine officers in Haiti toward these questions?

Mr. Spear. Yes, sir.

Mr. Angell. So far as you can remember, did you or your brother officers in Haiti believe that the application and enforcement of the corvee law had contributed to the numbers of the Cacos operating, or against whom the marines were operating, or to the attitude of these Cacos?

Mr. Spear. I never heard of the corvee law until I came back to the United States again and saw it in the paper. I did not know how they recruited those fellows.

Mr. Angell. So that so far as you know or knew at that time, the attitude of the bandits or Cacos was not affected by the existence or application of the corvee law?

Mr. SPEAR. No, sir; I did not know anything about it. I knew that Charlemagne III, who called himself the chief of them, broke out of prison some place.

Mr. HOWE. Do you know Maj. Walter N. Hill, or Maj. Woolman G. Emery, of the Marine Corps?

Mr. SPEAR. I think I knew Hill. I do not know Maj. Emery that I remember of.

Mr. HOWE. You do not know whether either of those officers whom I have just mentioned was the commanding officer in Mirebalais at the time of the execution of this native?

Mr. SPEAR. No; I believe Hill was, but I do not know.

Mr. HOWE. It may have been Hill?

Mr. SPEAR. It may have been Hill.

Mr. HOWE. Or it might have been Emery?

Mr. SPEAR. Yes, and it might have been Pearce. I do not know. I never went to headquarters when I came in. The captain reported.

Mr. HOWE. Now, in your views with the views of your brother officers in Haiti as to the methods of warfare to be employed against the Cacos, you are referring to brother officers of about your own rank?

Mr. SPEAR. Yes, sir.

Mr. HOWE. You have no means of knowing the attitude of the senior officers down there?

Mr. SPEAR. Well, I knew the commanding officer in the field wanted me to kill all the Cacos. That is all I knew. And he was very friendly toward the natives.

Mr. HOWE. As a matter of fact, the Cacos were very unfriendly toward the natives too, were they not?

Mr. SPEAR. Yes.

Mr. HOWE. Unfriendly to the extent of killing them?

Mr. SPEAR. Yes.

Mr. HOWE. Were you able to judge whether the native population in general was frightened of the Cacos, or not?

Mr. SPEAR. Very much. They were all gone when we were out there. They had to hike out to the cities, in other words.

Mr. HOWE. Did you ever hear anybody express regret at the death of Cacos killed in battle?

Mr. SPEAR. No.

(Whereupon, at 12.30 o'clock p. m., a recess was taken until 2.30 o'clock p. m.)

AFTER RECESS.

(The committee reassembled at 2.30 o'clock p. m., pursuant to the taking of recess, Senator Tasker L. Oddie presiding.)

STATEMENT OF LIEUT. COL. ALEXANDER S. WILLIAMS, UNITED STATES MARINE CORPS—Resumed.

Mr. HOWE. Mr. Chairman, at the end of the committee meeting last Thursday, we had completed the direct examination of Col. Williams, and I would suggest now, if Mr. Angell has any questions, that he proceed to ask them. There may be, in the course of the examination, some points that may come up that the committee or its counsel may want to further question Col. Williams about, I will postpone that to the end.

Senator ODDIE. Very well; you may take the witness, Mr. Angell.

Mr. ANGELL. At the beginning of your direct testimony the other day, Colonel, you said, if I remember correctly, that you could remember only two instances of the killing of prisoners without trial, and you then went on to say that you received no reports, except where action by way of investigation or disciplinary measures would lie in your own hands. That is substantially correct?

Col. WILLIAMS. That is substantially correct.

Mr. ANGELL. Was your position, and were your duties in Haiti such that there could have been other reports made of killing of prisoners without trial, which would not have come to you personally?

Col. WILLIAMS. It is, of course, possible that reports of killings were made to my subordinates, and those subordinates did not inform me. Of that I can not speak. When I answered the question you have quoted, I answered it in that fashion in order to exclude the Lovole, Williams, and Lang allegations.

Mr. ANGELL. Because those reports did not come to you as head of the gendarmerie?

Col. WILLIAMS. Because they did not come to me as head of the gendarmerie, but became known to Gen. Catlin and myself at the same time.

Mr. ANGELL. Whereupon Gen. Catlin assumed direction of the investigation?

Col. WILLIAMS. Whereupon Gen. Catlin, in virtue of his seniority, assumed charge, or, to put it in another fashion, I took no action.

Mr. ANGELL. Referring now to the Lovole case at Hinche, and the alleged shooting of the six or more at the cemetery outside of Hinche, on the Maissade road, do you know why Gen. Catlin, after his personal investigation of those allegations, took no disciplinary measures against Capt. Lovole other than to have him transferred to duty in some other part of Haiti?

Col. WILLIAMS. I do not know.

Mr. ANGELL. Did you ever hear of Gen. Catlin having said that the reason why he took no action in this case was because this was during the period of the consideration of the Versailles treaty, and that he did not wish to embarrass our President by having stories of cruelty appear about our own soldiers while we were taking a position on the side of humanity, or words to that effect?

Col. WILLIAMS. I can not recollect any statement by Gen. Catlin to that effect.

Mr. ANGELL. Did I understand you correctly the other day, Colonel, to say that from your own hearing of the statements of the witnesses in the Lovole case, at the time of Gen. Catlin's investigation, that you were not convinced that there had been such an illegal execution?

Col. WILLIAMS. So far as I remember, any testimony given, and I am not certain that I was even present when such testimony was given, I was not convinced that the allegation was supported.

Mr. ANGELL. There has already been introduced at least formally into the record the so-called Turner report, which is somewhat misleading in terms, and is called the Turner report for the purpose of identification lagely, but includes, for the purposes of the record, the testimony of several witnesses which was taken in Washington by Lieut. Col. Lay, including your own testimony at that time, your statement before Col. Lay being dated January 6, 1920. Referring now to your testimony, as taken by Lieut. Col. Lay on January 6, 1920, or thereabouts, I quote now from your own statement:

"These reports alleged that certain prisoners involved in banditism had been taken from a prison in Hinche, led to a point outside of Hinche near a cemetery, and there executed by a detachment of enlisted gendarmes. This allegation was supported by the statements of one or more gendarmes interrogated by Gen. Catlin. To the best of my recollection, Capt. Earnest Lovole, who was at the time district commander at Hinche, acknowledged that such an execution had taken place. He offered in explanation of this action the fact that it was impossible to obtain conviction in the local civil courts, and that after their trial by a provost court in Cape Haitien and the expiration of the sentences adjudged by such court, that they would return to the neighborhood of Hinche, rejoin the bandits with whom they had been originally identified and make the pacification of the region more difficult. The entire investigation was conducted by Gen. Catlin and the allegations seemed supported, except as to the exact number executed."

Does that statement, assuming it to be, as read, a correct copy of your statement before Col. Lay, refresh your recollection on that point?

Col. WILLIAMS. I do not recollect exactly what I told Col. Lay. I believe I talked without interruption for an hour or more, but assuming that that is correct, the seeming discrepancy is explainable. When I say that the allegation was supported I meant to convey only the fact that it was testified to. Does that answer your question? And you will further note in the quotation I say "seemed to be."

Mr. ANGELL. Having refreshed your recollection by the reading of this statement, assuming it to be a correct copy, you are still of the opinion that the allegations were not satisfactorily proved, so that you became convinced that such illegal executions had been ordered and had taken place at that time, substantially under those circumstances?

Col. WILLIAMS. Reserving always an open mind in the matter, I was then unconvinced and remain unconvinced.

Mr. ANGELL. You testified on direct examination that on the trip of investigation upon which you accompanied Gen. Catlin you were excluded from the presence of the general and the witnesses upon the first examination and that you agreed thereto, and that the thought was expressed that your presence as chief of the gendarmerie might influence the native witnesses to reticence. Will you explain why you felt that would be the result of your presence?

Col. WILLIAMS. I do not remember whether or not Gen. Catlin stated specifically why I was to be excluded, but I knew that it was because he thought that my presence would have a tendency to restrict the witnesses' testimony. I agreed with Gen. Catlin as to this being a fact. I believed that my presence would affect the witness in testifying, because it was perfectly evident to even the most ignorant that the final responsibility for misconduct on the part of junior officers must fall on the responsible senior, and that to a certain extent I was a party to the investigation and to any charges which might be advanced. The Haitian witness in that case, looking to his own future, might be tempted to avoid antagonizing a man who, with the exception of Gen. Catlin, had been the biggest man he had seen.

Mr. ANGELL. Speaking generally and without reference to that particular instance or any other instance, do you or do you not think that it was the feeling of the Haitian population generally that the ultimate responsibility for what was done by the gendarmerie must, in the last analysis, come back to or rest upon the titular head of the force?

Col. WILLIAMS. To what extent a peasant could work that out in his mind I do not know, but the better-educated Haitian was fully able to come to such a logical conclusion. I presume in such an outstanding matter as the allegations against Lovole or Williams that the peasant might be able to trace the connection.

Mr. ANGELL. Take, for example, the history of the later phase of the corvee law. Do you think that the Haitian population generally regarded the senior officers or the chief of the gendarmerie, and ultimately the brigade commander of the marines and the American occupation in general, as responsible for the policy of the later corvee law, and, in a general sense, responsible for whatever abuses may have occurred under it?

Col. WILLIAMS. The Haitians generally, both ignorant and educated, seemed, so far as I was able to make out in the many conversations I held with them on this subject, to hold the occupation—by which they meant the gendarmerie, the marines, the treaty officials, etc.—jointly responsible with the Haitian administration for the corvee. It was well known that the corvee, in its inception and its continued use, had the tacit approval, at least, of the Haitian Government.

Mr. ANGELL. Did you have any personal knowledge, Colonel, of the Hamilton court-martial case—the case of Capt. G. D. Hamilton?

Col. WILLIAMS. No personal knowledge whatsoever. I believe that happened subsequent to my detachment; at least the development of the case did.

Mr. ANGELL. Did you have any knowledge of the general court-martial of one Lieut. Ryan?

Col. WILLIAMS. I do not think I did.

Mr. ANGELL. There has been just one passing reference to that somewhere in the record or the testimony, but I do not think we have any specific testimony on that yet.

Mr. HOWE. Certainly the court-martial record is not in the record before this committee yet, and I do not recall any mention of it.

Mr. ANGELL. There is just one. I am trying to find out what it is. The colonel has no knowledge of it.

Col. WILLIAMS. I never heard of it.

Mr. ANGELL. At this point I think it becomes necessary to refer to the court-martial record of Capt. Hamilton, because in there is a matter which I presume is within the personal knowledge of the witness, and I would therefore like to offer that in the record, subject to such digesting and shortening as may be desired.

Mr. HOWE. Counsel refers to the court-martial record of Capt. George D. Hamilton. The court-martial record in that case, and in the cases of Johnson and McQuilkin, will be offered to the committee in evidence, but, with the suggestion that instead of being admitted in full, that it be incorporated in the printed record by a summary or a digest satisfactory to all parties represented.

Mr. ANGELL. Mr. Howe and I discussed that general question already, and we have agreed on that.

Senator ODDIE. Very well.

Mr. ANGELL. For the purposes of further identification merely, the court-martial of Capt. Hamilton was the court-martial which took place at the marine barracks in Cape Haitien on August 4, 1919, and the days subsequent thereto.

Charge I, preferred against Capt. Hamilton, upon which he was tried, was for disobedience of a lawful order of his superior officer, of which the material portions, for our present purposes, are the specifications thereunder, reading as follows:

"In that Capt. George D. Hamilton, United States Marine Corps, while serving in the Constabulary Detachment, First Provisional Brigade, United States Marine Corps and in the Gendarmerie D' Haiti, at Grande Riviere, Republic of Haiti, having on or about March 10, 1919, had addressed to him by Col. (then lieutenant colonel) Alexander S. Williams, United States Marine Corps. commanding the constabulary detachment, aforesaid, and chief of the Gendarmerie D' Haiti, an order of which he was conversant, in words and figures substantially as follows:

"1. No prisoner while in custody, whatever his or her status, will be shot. executed, or permitted to be shot.

"2. In case of an attempt to escape every reasonable effort will be made to prevent the escape before shooting is resorted to.

"3. A report will be submitted to headquarters gendarmerie of all prisoners shot under any circumstances. This report will contain all available data brought out by careful investigation."

Do you remember that order, Colonel?

Col. WILLIAMS. I remember an order which I believe to be that.

Mr. ANGELL. Do you remember the reasons why that order was issued?

Col. WILLIAMS. Yes. Incident to Gen. Catlin's inspection trip to central Haiti, and the investigation of the allegations made against Lovole and Williams, it transpired that there was no written order ever issuing from the headquarters of the gendarmerie which forbade the killing of prisoners. Gen. Catlin suggested that such an order should be issued. I protested against issuing such an order, but did issue it in the form in which it has been presented. It was delivered personally to Lovole by me, and on my return to Port au Prince, I believe, the order was sent out immediately in regular form.

Mr. ANGELL. Do you know why Gen. Catlin felt that the issuance of such an order was required or proper? Did he give any reasons for that at that time?

Col. WILLIAMS. I do not remember that he gave any reasons, but it is a strong tradition in the military service that every offense is followed by the issuance of an order forbidding every one else to do the same thing.

Mr. ANGELL. So far as you know, did the fact of prior reports and allegations as to unlawful killing of prisoners by gendarmes motivate in any way the issuance of this order?

Col. WILLIAMS. So far as I was concerned, no. What Gen. Catl'n thought I can not say. You mean by that reports prior to these particular ones?

Mr. ANGELL. No; I meant by that question reports coming in prior to the date of the issuance of this order. In other words, was the cause for the issuance of this order the mere fact that no such order had ever been issued. or was it, in addition, the fact that there had been reports of unauthor zed killings of prisoners by gendarmes?

Col. WILLIAMS. The order was issued immediately following the investigation of the allegation aga'nst Lovole. But I issue:l it because Gen. Catlin wished it issued. What I mean is that I did not believe that such an order was necessary any more than one that housebreaking should not be carried on, but he seemed to think differently, so I issued it.

Mr. ANGELL. Referring still to the record of the Hamilton court-martial, particularly the test'mony of Lieut. Col. Hooker, on pages 4 and 5 of the record. I will read you a part of the answer to the third question, and ask you a question based on that:

"I asked the accused (that is, Capt. Hamilton) what he meant by stating that a prisoner had been shot, and the accused told me that he had been shooting all Cacos captured if he was positive that they were Cacos. I spoke to him about an order issued by Gen. W:lliams, chief of the gendarmerie, dated March 10, the gist of which was that no prisoner, no matter what his or her status, would be shot or allowed to be shot under any circumstances, and that in case of a prisoner escaping every possible means would be taken to recapture before resorting to firing upon, and further, that in case anyone was shot, no matter what the cause, a full report would be made. I looked through the files of his office and found th's order, which the accused informed me he had read and knew, but that he thought the order simply prevented him from taking prisoners out of a prison and shooting them, that he did not consider that the order applied to prisoners taken on the trail. He told me that he had been carrying out this policy s'nce the order had been issued."

Of course, the order, as framed and intended and issued by you, was not designed to be so interpreted as Capt. Hamilton stated to Col. Hooker, but was intended to apply to all cases, was it not, Colonel?

Col. WILLIAMS. It was intended to apply to all cases.

Mr. ANGELL. Turning now to your testimony of the other day concerning the general att:tude of the gendarmerie officers toward the native population, where you said in substance that they showed the greatest friendliness and sympathy for the natives, and identified themselves with every measure for the betterment of the districts and the general welfare, do you think that the gendarmerie officers succeeded in gain'ng the good will, generally speaking, of the native population?

Col. WILLIAMS. Almost without exception, the gendarmerie officers, senior and junior, enjoyed the confidence and the liking of the natives.

Mr. ANGELL. Would you make the same answer regarding the enl'sted personnel of the gendarmerie?

Col. WILLIAMS. Generally, the enlisted personnel mixed freely and in a friendly manner with the class from which it had been drawn. In certain instances noncommissioned officers in charge of small posts conducted themselves in such a fashion as to be disliked. The gendarmerie represented to the Haitian peasant to a great extent the old gendarmerie military, and the gendarme had to prove to the native, before he made his friendship, that he was not operating on the lines which the old Haitian soldier followed.

Mr. ANGELL. In your testimony before Col. Lay, referr'ng to that again, you said, substantially, that the difficulty of getting men in the later stages of the corvee law application caused the gendarmes to resort to methods that were often brutal, but quite consistent with their training under Ha:tian officials. That is a fair statement of their relations, is it?

Col. WILLIAMS. It is a fair statement of their relations in that part'cular phase of the gendarme duties, but I must explain that the gendarmerie personnel had had no training generally under Haitian officials. It is possible that many of the gendarmes had served in the old army, but probably a small percentage.

Mr. ANGELL. How would that use of brutal methods, then, be consistent w:th the training under Haitian officials?

Col. WILLIAMS. That statement, as quoted, did not express my thought. What . I meant to convey was that this brutality was in line with that which the Hait:an police and army had learned under Haitian officials. The precedents were there.

Mr. ANGELL. Perhaps an inheritance from the slave days of the eighteenth century?

Col. WILLIAMS. The reflexes of slavery were relatively few and did not seem to manifest themselves in any important fashion. The only relic of slave days that I was ever able to isolate was the universal habit of carrying a very large club. This, I always believed, was due to the fact that the code noir prohibited Negroes from carrying a stick greater than a certain diameter.

Mr. ANGELL. In Gen. Catlin's statement before Col. Lay, taken about the same time, December 31, 1919, in speaking of the corvee as it existed in the later time in the Hinche district, he says: "All the inhabitants of a certain section had been rounded up and brought into Hinche, and that all the gardens and farms outside of the towns had been abandoned, and the inhabitants had disappeared, many probably having joined the bandits," and Gen. Catlin goes on to say that the priests stated this was largely on account of the fear of gendarmes and of the corvee; and further, that the appearance of a gendarme uniform was sufficient for the peasant to take to the brush and hide. I want to ask you whether that conforms with your own personal experience and views of the interrelations of the gendarmes and the population?

Col. WILLIAMS. In part I am in agreement, that central Haiti was largely deserted.

Mr. ANGELL. At what time?

Col. WILLIAMS. During the period of the bandit activities.

Mr. ANGELL. 1918 and 1919?

62269—21—PT 2——32

Col. WILLIAMS. 1918. This was due to the fact that the native had to join the bandit gang or else be killed, so those who did not join came into the towns.

In regard to the peasants taking flight on the appearance of a gendarme uniform, I do not think that was generally true unless there was a bandit gang in the immediate vicinity. The natives, I may say, although they abandoned their farms, did sneak out to them and made some attempts to cultivate them, perhaps to save their crops. If bandit gangs were operating in the neighborhood and gendarmes came along, it is highly probable that the natives took to flight, because they feared to be identified or mistaken for bandits. Generally, throughout Haiti this condition did not obtain. I personally have ridden over nearly all the roads in Haiti on horseback or by motor, and only once do I remember a native running away, and that was in a section of the country where corvee had never operated.

Mr. ANGELL. Is it your impression that the natives take to the brush, or otherwise make themselves scarce, because of the fear of being impressed into the corvee gang?

Col. WILLIAMS. In central Haiti, no; because at the time Gen. Catlin inspected it is my belief that there was no corvee there.

Mr. ANGELL. Prior then, to the time that Gen. Catlin inspected, do you believe that the natives disappeared or took to the brush to avoid being impressed into the corvee?

Col. WILLIAMS. No; because my personal experience tells me differently. I have been over that road between St. Michel, Maissade, and Hinche any number of times, once alone, and I never saw anyone run.

Mr. ANGELL. Why, then, did it become more and more difficult to obtain labor for the corvee as time went on?

Col. WILLIAMS. The reluctance of the natives to work on the roads.

Mr. ANGELL. If it was the practice of the gendarmes to bring these men in for forced labor, how would their reluctance make any substantial difference in the ability to obtain labor unless their reluctance caused them to avoid the presence of the gendarmes?

Col. WILLIAMS. All gendarmes were not bad. Many of those sent out to collect the corvee conducted themselves in a perfectly proper manner. If the natives failed to come in when ordered, or broke away from the gendarme who had gathered them, that gendarme would bring in no recruits. It was not a question of finding labor so much as it was a question of bringing it in, and if the recruits of labor did not want to come in, in very many instances the properly conducted gendarme was unable to bring them in. In speaking of the personnel of the gendarmerie in the condemnatory way in which I did, it must not be understood at all that all gendarmes were badly conducted. A great many were, within the limits of their intelligence and training, perfectly good native police.

Mr. ANGELL. Is it your understanding that the gendarmes used force of intimidation to gather in workers for the corvee gangs as well as keeping the men at work, once they were there?

Col. WILLIAMS. I have no doubt at all but that in many instances force, intimidation, and brutal methods were used by the gendarmes.

Mr. ANGELL. To get the men to the roads as well as to keep them there?

Col. WILLIAMS. To get the men to the road; yes. I had occasion to investigate a number of these reports, but rarely found sufficient evidence to warrant the trial of a gendarme. In some instances, if my memory serves me correctly, they were punished.

Mr. ANGELL. From what class of the Haitian population were the gendarmes generally drawn?

Col. WILLIAMS. From the lower class almost entirely. The old Haitian police had enjoyed such a reputation that anyone who joined it practically announced his criminal tendencies. This made it very difficult for us in the beginning to even recruit the necessary educated material which we had to have in order to develop noncommissioned officers, who must know how to read and write.

Mr. ANGELL. Do you think that the reluctance of the upper Haitian class toward service in the gendarmerie was based to any considerable degree upon opposition to the intervention and presence of the United States in Haiti?

Col. WILLIAMS. Absolutely not. One of the things which astonished me was the fact that the Haitians realized that the American development of the gendarmerie would be an excellent thing, and there was no reluctance at all on the part of the higher class to come in as officer, that is as commissioned officers. In fact, we had no end of applicants. The feeling generally of the better class toward the gendarmerie was a friendly one. They realized, of course, that we were making mistakes. Some of us did not know the language, others did not know the laws, others were tactless, but, as the President himself told me, the mistakes of the gendarmerie have been well-intentioned mistakes, and it is not held against them.

Mr. ANGELL. To what extent were the native Haitians sworn into the gendarmerie as commissioned officers?

Col. WILLIAMS. When the gendarmerie first came into beginning, in virtue of the gendarmerie agreement, an annex to the Haitian-American treaty, it was considered very desirable that Haitian officers be included in the personnel. With this idea in mind, a number, I think about 20, young Haitians of good family and education were put in a training school, but the scheme did not work out well. The training of these young officers naturally was conducted along the lines of that which we give our own, and the first requirement, that they strip for a physical examination, was objected to so strenuously that we had to release many from semiengagement. The next difficulty concerned the grooming of horses. A gendarmerie officer, an American, qualified to instruct in the care of animals, in which the Haitians are notably deficient, gave them a practical illustration of the methods, and then told one of them to groom the horse. The man refused. They all refused. So that school stopped almost before it had begun.

Mr. HOWE. When you say a practical demonstration there, do you mean that the instructing officer groomed the horse himself?

Col. WILLIAMS. The instructing officer groomed the horse himself, rubbing with the hair, the way it lay, and not rubbing against it, and turning it in, making a sore skin, all the practical work of grooming.

There were, however, four or five Haitians commissioned with an acting commission issued by Gen. Butler. Only one of these four or five lasted throughout my tour. The first one to go out was detailed as subdistrict commander at Dame Marie, and acting in that capacity he borrowed the communal funds, telling the magistrate in whose charge they were that he needed them for the pay of the gendarmes. I caused him to resign.

Another one, having had an ordinary police report made against him, which report came to me, and which I in turn sent out to have investigated, as we did all reports, promptly brought suit in the civil courts against the man who made the complaint, for, I think, 20,000 gourdes damages. I got rid of him.

Another one who was in charge of Fort Nationale, a little fort that overlooks the city of Port au Prince, I found had diverted the water supply of the fort for the purpose of irrigating his garden, which was down on the side of the hill. I got rid of him.

Another one, having been reported for debt by almost everyone who would give him credit, I had to get rid of.

That left but one, a perfectly splendid young Haitian, who did very remarkable work against the bandits, but his value was limited to that, because as soon as he was put in a position where he was brought in contact with the civil officials, friction came about, and we could not remove him because the officials did not like him, and we could not keep him there because he could not get along with the officials, so we put him in the field. I think that was all the Haitian officers whom I inherited, and of those I got rid of all but one.

Mr. ANGELL. Was there any further attempt, Colonel, to obtain the services of native Haitians as officers in the gendarmerie?

Col. WILLIAMS. Not during my time. I believed then as I believe now that the gendarmerie will be good only to the extent to which it is driven by American ideas, not that there is not good material in Haiti, but the material will be Haitian naturally, and with the Haitian's way of looking at things, and they will not bring about a condition of police efficiency such as we sought.

Mr. ANGELL. Do you think that a reasonable degree of police efficiency is dependent upon an exclusively American personnel of all commissions?

Col. WILLIAMS. Judging from the administrative history of Haiti in the past, I should say yes.

Mr. ANGELL. You think, then, there is no reasonable possibility of the Haitians qualifying as efficient officers, even junior officers, of a gendarmerie which would, let us say, be officered in its higher ranks entirely by Americans?

Col. WILLIAMS. I do not believe—I will not say that it is not a possibility. Almost anything is possible. But I doubt very much if an efficient military police can be maintained in Haiti with the commissioned personnel largely Haitians.

Mr. ANGELL. Do you know whether any of these young Haitians who made applications for commissions in the gendarmerie, and you testified there were a good many of them, if I remember correctly, were graduates of the French military academy of St. Cyr?

Col. WILLIAMS. I have a vague recollection of one man—I do not think he was a young man—who had attended St. Cyr. I would not say whether or not he was an applicant.

Mr. HOWE. Could you say whether or not he was a graduate of St. Cyr?

Col. WILLIAMS. I can not say that. I do not know.

Mr. ANGELL. Were there actually any examinations conducted under the direction of a board to be selected by the senior American officer of the constabulary for native Haitians as commissioned officers?

Col. WILLIAMS. No; you refer now to that treaty?

Mr. ANGELL. I am referring to the treaty, to Article X of the treaty of September 10, 1915, and to Articles II and V of the subsequent gendarmerie convention of the following year—I have not the exact date.

Is it proper, Colonel, to refer to the operations of our forces in Haiti against the cacos as being divided into two periods; first, the period in the early days of the occupation as one of preliminary pacification; and the second, from 1918 to 1920, as one of a second period of caco activity, and of operations by our forces against the cacos, the two periods of the caco activity and the operations by our forces against them being separated by a period of comparative quiet and calm in 1916 and 1917?

Col. WILLIAMS. The early operations conducted by marines in Haiti were brought to a close by the native leaders agreeing to cease. I will put it that way, because there was no surrender.

Mr. ANGELL. And that was about what time?

Col. WILLIAMS. Those operations took place in 1915, and if they extended into 1916, not very long. I do not just remember. If they extended into 1916, it must have been for a short time. The operations conducted by the gendarmes against the bandits in central Haiti, and latterly by the gendarmes and marines, constituted a distinct phase.

Mr. ANGELL. This affects the days of 1918 to 1920?

Col. WILLIAMS. 1918 and 1919. What happened in 1920 I do not know.

Mr. HOWE. Have you been using the term "Caco" and the term "bandit" interchangeably?

Col. WILLIAMS. I have not. I have very much not used them in that way. They connote two entirely different things.

Mr. ANGELL. Gen. Cole, in his report to the Secretary of the Navy, dated September 23, 1920, which appears, as I believe, as Exhibit 4 appended to the record of the Mayo court of inquiry, and which I should like to offer in the record, or refer to now——

Mr. HOWE. Mr. Chairman, as to the record of the Mayo court of inquiry, I hope that may be introduced in the record in connection with the testimony of Maj. Dyer, who was the judge advocate of that court, and introduced into the record, in full, and some of it summarized for the printed record, and there can be no objection at the present time, in view of the certainty that it must be in the record——

Senator ODDIE. There is no objection to the witness referring to it?

Mr. HOWE. No, sir. It will be entirely proper, and not confusing, if he refers to it, with sufficient explanation as to what part he is referring to.

Senator ODDIE. There is no objection to that.

Mr. ANGELL. Continuing my question, then, and referring specifically to paragraph 26 of the report, which is dated September 23, 1920, reading:

"When the undersigned relieved Maj. Gen. (then Brig. Gen.) L. W. T. Waller as brigade commander on November 22, 1916, conditions throughout the Republic of Haiti were generally peaceful, there being no armed opposition to the United States forces or to the Gendarmerie d' Haiti, though from time, but at increasingly rare intervals, reports would be received of cattle lifting or of robbing of market women by armed robbers, almost invariably along or in the vicinity of the border between Haiti and Santo Domingo."

Does that conform, Colonel, with your own recollection of conditions in the latter part of 1916?

Col. WILLIAMS. I can not place the date, but after the operations by marines in north Haiti had ceased there was a condition of general peace, except in that no man's land between Haiti and Santo Domingo. There cattle lifting, robbery, and offenses of that sort were reported from time to time.

Mr. ANGELL. That was up in the central and north central region, near the border?

Col. WILLIAMS. The east central.

Mr. ANGELL. How long did that general condition of relative peace and quiet continue after the latter part of 1916?

Col. WILLIAMS. Something under two years, I should say. It is difficult to say when the relative peace became general disturbance. One condition merged into the other.

Mr. ANGELL. But for a period of approximately two years relative peace and quiet continued?

Col. WILLIAMS. Continued.

Mr. ANGELL. And that situation, then, was not changed until some time, well, along in 1918?

Col. WILLIAMS. It did not develop in an important way until some time in 1918.

Mr. ANGELL. What, in your opinion, Colonel, were the reasons for the change in the situation, or the recrudescence of the caco or bandit activity, or our operations against Cacos or bandits?

Col. WILLIAMS. It is necessary in order to answer that question to go back a bit. The boundary between Haiti and Santo Domingo has never been defined, or has never been agreed upon by the representatives of the two republics. The result is that over a great part of its length it was a true no-man's land. The country is sparsely settled; it is generally very mountainous, and very heavily wooded. This from time immemorial has been the resort of the Haitian and Dominican bad man. I believe that the growth of the bandit movement was because of the success of several of these bands, and also to a great extent because of the personal popularity of one Hait'an named Charlemagne Perolte. Perolte belonged to an influent'al and very large family, which lived generally in east central Haiti. He was a very large man, which carries a strong appeal to the Haitian, and he was well educated. I bel'eve he was insp'red by race hatred. He found men in plenty available for his purposes in no-man's land, and his system of recruitment, which I described the other day, enabled him to soon gather important forces.

Mr. ANGELL. May I interrupt to ask what you mean by race hatred?

Col. WILLIAMS. Black against white.. He was able to point out a number of things which ranged themselves very logically to base his claim, which was that the Americans were conquering Haiti; and the bases of his statements were fairly well known to most of the people in that region.

Mr. ANGELL. Did he claim, as far as you know, to speak for the population either of Haiti generally or of that portion of Haiti where he had his activity?

Col. WILLIAMS. I bel'eve he did.

Mr. ANGELL. Did he purport to have a cabinet and attempt to enter into diplomatic relations with foreign governments?

Col. WILLIAMS. He sent a letter to the British chargé requesting that Great Britain assist in the liberation of Haiti. I think he generally signed himself as commanding the patriot army.

Mr. ANGELL. His request for assistance and the liberation of Haiti meant assistance——

Col. WILLIAMS. From the Americans.

Mr. ANGELL. Assistance to him as leader of the native patriotic Haitian army against the Americans?

Col. WILLIAMS. Yes. I believe that the offer included a proposition by which he would aid Great Britain against the Germans.

Mr. ANGELL. Do you believe that race hatred specifically—h's opposition as a black man, as a Haitian, to the presence of the white man, the American in Haiti—was the real motive of the organization and continuation of his resistance to our forces and the occupation there?

Col. WILLIAMS. I believe that he was inspired to a great extent by race hatred. My recollection is that he invariably referred to us not as the Americans but as the whites, which is rather unusual in the case of a Haitian of education. I also came across a copy of a play written by Charlemagne Perolte when he was younger, in which he was pictured lying on a divan with a beautiful white girl fanning his feet and another beautiful white girl, described with considerable detail, fanning his head.

Mr. ANGELL. He was in alliance or supported, was he not, by the other Caco leader at that time in the south, Benoit, and then after his death succeeded by Benoit?

Col. WILLIAMS. Benoit was one of Charlemagne's generals. He came into prominence well after Charlemagne had commenced his operations.

Mr. ANGELL. Did he succeed Charlemagne as the recognized leader of the irregular forces after Charlemagne's death?

Col. WILLIAMS. Charlemagne's death occurred subsequent to my leaving Haiti.

Mr. ANGELL. Do you remember whether it was Benoit who belonged to the 10th Haitian regiment, whose members had sworn not to lay down arms until they had driven the white man from the island?

Col. WILLIAMS. I never heard of the regiment or the oath.

Mr. ANGELL. There is reference to it somewhere. I have seen it, and I was wondering whether you had heard the story.

Col. WILLIAMS. Benoit's father was an armorer. I think, in the Haitian army.

Mr. ANGELL. Do you know what forces were available to Charlemagne in the course of his operations and of our operations against him?

Col. WILLIAMS. You mean the numbers?

Mr. ANGELL. The numbers.

Col. WILLIAMS. I do not believe that Charlemagne could have subsisted over, perhaps, 2,000 men under the conditions which obtained at the time. These, of course, were broken up into bands of various size and scattered all over central Haiti.

Mr. ANGELL. Referring to a report by Gen. Russell, which is attached to the Mayo court records and dated August 15, it appears, according to Gen. Russell's statement, that the numbers on which Charlemagne and Benoit could draw were about 17,000. Do you think that is a fair figure?

Col. WILLIAMS. If he means the available man power in central Haiti, I should say that that was not far wrong.

Mr. ANGELL. I think he does mean that figure to mean the man power on which they could draw.

Col. WILLIAMS. If he means the men whom he controlled, or had enlisted, or could enlist, that is a different proposition; but there were that many people living around there.

Mr. ANGELL. In answer to a question by Mr. Howe a few minutes ago, Colonel, you said you had meant to differentiate between Cacos and bandits. Will you explain that difference?

Col. WILLIAMS. Caco is a Haitian word, and it has never been used in Haiti in any other connection than this. When a revolution occurred, which in the last 60 or 70 years has almost invariably taken place in north Haiti, the people who were identified with the movement called themselves and were called by others Cacos. The derivation of the word I was never able to find out. The people who were operating against the gendarmerie, or against whom we were operating, more properly, in central Haiti, were not Cacos in the true sense, because, in the first place, they were not from north Haiti, and, in the second place, whatever political motives they may have had developed after their disorders had been initiated were not the inspiration of the disorders. I referred to them as bandits as being most descriptive.

Mr. ANGELL. Were our activities, for example, in the year 1915, when, according to official records, as appears by the letter of Maj. McClellan of October 25, 1920, in the Mayo court records, the Haitian official casualties are given as 212—were they against Cacos or against the bandits?

Col. WILLIAMS. When was the date?

Mr. ANGELL. In the year 1915.

Col. WILLIAMS. The people who opposed the marines in north Haiti after our first landing in 1915 had started out by being Cacos. In other words, there was an uprising already under way, and, originating as it did in north Haiti, and having a political motive, the people identified with it could be. called Cacos. Just what they could be called when the marines were operating against them I can not say. I would say they were not Cacos, but that is rather quibbling.

Mr. ANGELL. Now, for example, in 1919, when the casualties, according to this same McClellan letter, are reported to have been 1,861, were the natives against whom our forces were operating and upon whom those casualties were inflicted bandits in the ordinary sense of robbers and persons guilty of all sorts of crimes or were they principally the native irregular forces operating under the leadership of Charlemagne or other leaders actuated by similar motives?

Col. WILLIAM. I used the word "bandit" because it seemed more descriptive of these people than any other word that I know. It is not entirely descriptive. It does not bring out the bandit as we think of him. These people were bandits to the extent that they did rob and burn throughout central Haiti, and, of course, the sufferers were always their own countrymen. They were not under the leadership and they did not operate under the leadership of Charlemagne, but Charlemagne, being a man of a great deal of force, served as a personality to which they could be tied and with whom they could be associated. Whether or not Charlemagne ever attempted to coordinate the activities of these various generals and their bands I do not know, but there never was any particular evidence of it.

Mr. ANGELL. Do you regard, then, these natives against whom we were operating in 1919, and upon whom we inflicted these casualties, as, primarily, ordinary criminals, or, on the other hand, rather irregular troops who incidentally preyed upon their own countrymen, but whose primary purpose and organization and operation was to drive out the whites?

Col. WILLIAMS. I could not regard them as in any sense irregular troops; they were too irregular for that. I could not regard them as criminals, because I knew or believed that the percentage of criminals among them was relatively small and that the great proportion of them had been forced to join these bands, and, having been forced, of course, were unable to get out. They did not dare in many instances.

Mr. ANGELL. Were these bands making offensive warfare of any sort, regular or irregular, against the gendarmes and marines, or were they solely operating against their native, civilian countrymen?

Col. WILLIAMS. They necessarily depended upon the countryside for their subsistence, therefore they robbed their own people. Without any appearance of unified command, different bands all attacked from time to time the gendarmes. They killed a number, and they burned several gendarmerie barracks.

Mr. ANGELL. Coming now to the corvee, I want to ask you certain general questions about that, Colonel. You testified that the code rurale of 1863 provided for this labor in connection with the repair of roads and the like. Do you know whether or not the corvee law or custom went further back than 1863?

Col. WILLIAMS. Yes; I found a reference to it in Moreau St. Mery's book, published in 1789, in which the inhabitants of the parish of Grande Riviere protested against the fact that if they built the roads which they were required to build in that parish there would be no slaves available for work in the fields. I take it that was substantially a corvee.

Mr. ANGELL. Then your understanding is that the corvee went back into the eighteenth century?

Col. WILLIAMS. I believe it did; and the code rurale, I might say, is taken from the French code.

Mr. ANGELL. Do you know whether there were traditions among the Haitian people of abuses and hardships under the old corvee law or custom dating from the slave days?

Col. WILLIAMS. How far back the traditions ran I do not know, but I heard from various Haitians that the corvee had often been accompanied by abuses.

Mr. ANGELL. There is a book here published in 1818, from which I would like to read one sentence, called the History of the Island of Santo Domingo, of which the author is Sir James Bashett, published in London, and it says on page 110, regarding the blacks:

"On attaining the age of manhood (they were compelled) to serve three years in a military establishment called the marechaussee, and on the expiration of that term they were subject, great part of the year, to the burthen of the corvees—a species of labor allotted for the repair of the highways, of which the hardships were insupportable."

That conforms with your understanding of the manner in which the corvee had been applied in the past?

Col. WILLIAMS. Only in certain instances. I said that the corvee, I understood, had been accompanied in the past by certain abuses, but that it was accompanied by insupportable hardships I had never heard, except in its use by the King Christophe.

Mr. ANGELL. In the early years of the nineteenth century?

Col. WILLIAMS. In the early years of the nineteenth century.

Mr. ANGELL. Did the code rurale of 1863, under your understanding, provide for the building of roads as well as the repair of roads by this species of labor?

Col. WILLIAMS. My recollection of the text is that it provided for the repairs.

Mr. ANGELL. Not specifically for the building of new roads?

Col. WILLIAMS. I think it provided for repairs. That is the only way I can remember it.

Mr. ANGELL. You testified, Colonel, if I remember rightly, that you were opposed at the outset to the institution or reapplication of the corvee law. Why were you opposed, and what efforts did you make or what opposition did you express?

Col. WILLIAMS. I was opposed because I did not believe that it was the proper way or the economical way of getting the work done. I was opposed because I did not like the idea of a corvee. It seemed to me rather un-American. I made no effort to have it stopped, because I was not in a position to do so.

Mr. HOWE. You were a subordinate?

Col. WILLIAMS. I was a subordinate officer.

Mr. ANGELL. Who was, then, responsible for its institution by our forces in Haiti?

Col. WILLIAMS. The Haitian Government and the American occupation.

(Whereupon the committee adjourned until Tuesday, November 8, 1921, at 11 o'clock a. m.)

INQUIRY INTO OCCUPATION AND ADMINISTRATION OF HAITI AND SANTO DOMINGO.

TUESDAY, NOVEMBER 8, 1921.

UNITED STATES SENATE,
SELECT COMMITTEE ON HAITI AND SANTO DOMINGO,
Washington, D. C.

The committee met, pursuant to adjournment, in room 131, Senate Office Building, at 11 a. m., Senator Tasker L. Oddie presiding.

Present: Senator Oddie.

Also present: Mr. Walter Bruce Howe, Mr. Ernest Angell, and Maj. Edwin N. McClellan.

STATEMENT OF MAJ. GEN. LITTLETON W. T. WALLER, UNITED STATES MARINE CORPS, RETIRED.

Mr. Howe. General, give your name and present rank and station, please.

Gen. Waller. Littleton W. T. Waller, major general, United States Marine Corps, retired; 2500 South Twentieth Street, Philadelphia.

Mr. Howe. How many years ago did you join the Marine Corps, General?

Gen. Waller. Forty-two.

Mr. Howe. How long ago were you retired; that was quite recently, was it not?

Gen. Waller. I was retired a year ago.

Mr. Howe. In August, 1915, what was your rank in the Marine Corps?

Gen. Waller. I was colonel commanding the brigade.

Mr. Howe. Did you land in Haiti in August?

Gen. Waller. I did.

Mr. Howe. Was that August 15?

Gen. Waller. I landed there August 15; yes.

Mr. Howe. At the time you landed were you senior marine officer present?

Gen. Waller. I was senior marine officer, and my orders detailed me to command the United States forces ashore in Haiti.

Mr. Howe. That included command over the seamen, did it not, as well as the marines?

Gen. Waller. On shore; yes, sir.

Mr. Howe. To whom did you report directly?

Gen. Waller. To the commander of the cruiser squadron, Rear Admiral Caperton.

Mr. Howe. You got your orders, however, directly from the Secretary of the Navy?

Gen. Waller. From the Secretary of the Navy; this refers to my original orders.

Mr. Howe. Or through the major general commanding the Marine Corps?

Gen. Waller. They were sent through the usual form, but they came directly to me—telegraphic orders.

Mr. Howe. How long did you remain in Haiti?

Gen. Waller. I left in the first part of December, 1916, but I was still attached to that expeditionary force until the 10th of January, 1917, but I was in this country from, I think, the 15th of December, 1916.

Mr. Howe. Therefore, during your last months in that tour of duty you were in this country?

Gen. Waller. I was in this country.

Mr. Howe. Were you continuously in Haiti from August 15, 1915, until December, 1916?

Gen. Waller. Except once for three weeks, when I was brought to Washington to consult with the State Department.

Mr. Howe. But during all of that time you were commanding the brigade?
Gen. Waller. Yes.
Mr. Howe. From the time there was a position of brigade commander there, were you brigade commander at first?
Gen. Waller. Yes.
Mr. Howe. You had that designation?
Gen. Waller. That was my brigade. It was sent down, so I simply retained the command I had—the First Brigade.
Mr. Howe. And after a while the bluejackets were withdrawn from shore?
Gen. Waller. Yes.
Mr. Howe. Then, your command consisted entirely of marines?
Gen. Waller. After the completion of the campaign we had in the north, then it was entirely marines.
Mr. Howe. You were succeeded by what officer in command?
Gen. Waller. Col. E. K. Cole.
Mr. Howe. How long before you landed was President Dartiguenave elected?
Gen. Waller. Two days, I think.
Mr. Howe. Maj. McClellan, when was he elected?
Maj. McClellan. He was elected on August 12.
Mr. Howe. That would be three days?
Gen. Waller. Three days.
Mr. Howe. What was the situation there when you landed, with especial reference to peace and order?
Gen. Waller. Conditions were very bad, and the town of Port au Prince was being controlled by the landing party that had landed from the *Washington*, and also the regiment that Col. Cole had brought down a few days before I arrived.
Mr. Howe. You landed at Port au Prince, did you not?
Gen. Waller. Yes.
Mr. Howe. What shape did the disturbing conditions take?
Gen. Waller. Gatherings of mobs, threatening disturbances, and much propaganda.
Mr. Howe. American propaganda?
Gen. Waller. Not as much so as against the Haitian Government itself?
Mr. Howe. You are referring to conditions in town in Port au Prince?
Gen. Waller. In town in Port au Prince. The country at that time was more or less quiet in the central part.
Mr. Howe. What was the condition in the north?
Gen. Waller. Dr. Bobo had been made President by the Cacos, and they claimed him as their President, and refused to have anything to do with the Dartiguenave government. Dr. Bobo came to Port au Prince and remained probably 10 days, and then, at his own request, was permitted to go to Jamaica. He was never in any danger there at any time, but could go and come as he saw fit. He had some fear of violence, and I saw that he was escorted on board the steamer, with the British chargé.
Mr. Howe. Do you know if before the time you landed there were any armed conflicts in which the seamen or marines took part?
Gen. Waller. I think there was one in which two of our men were killed. That occurred the night of the original landing.
Mr. Howe. At Port au Prince?
Gen. Waller. At Port au Prince.
Mr. Howe. After you landed how soon was there any armed conflict?
Gen. Waller. There was a little trouble at Gonaives early in September. Then, on the 26th of September they ambushed two of my patrols near Cape Haitien, one of them at Haut de Cap and one a little south of that. There was no name for this place.
Mr. Howe. Before the 26th of September had you gone out to talk with the so-called Caco leaders?
Gen. Waller. I did. I went to Cape Haitien and got in communication with them, and they said they would permit me and two others to come out to Quatier Morin and interview them. They absolutely refused to come to Cape Haitien, because they said it was only a trap to catch them.
Mr. Howe. Let us go back to your reasons for that interview with the Cacos. First of all, was there any request on the part of the Haitian authorities or President Dartiguenave?
Gen. Waller. Yes; from President Dartiguenave.

Mr. Howe. For you or some one else to make an arrangement with the Cacos in the north?

Gen. Waller. He had authorized me.

Mr. Howe. President Dartiguenave?

Gen. Waller. President Dartiguenave; to conclude any treaty I could make with them, even to the extent of purchasing their arms from them. My recollection is that he limited the price of the arms, or the negotiations, anyhow, to $400,000, which was to my mind perfectly absurd.

Mr. Howe. Too much?

Gen. Waller. Entirely.

Mr. Howe. What need was there for reaching any agreement with the Cacos?

Gen. Waller. Well, they were the king makers of Haiti.

Mr. Howe. Do you mean that under the conditions wh'ch prevailed at that time the Haitian Government existed during the pleasure of these Caco leaders?

Gen. Waller. That had been the case before we landed. What I mean is that an aspirant for political power, a man who wanted to be President, would go to the north and make an agreement with these Caco leaders, and for a certain sum to be paid from the Haitian treasury after he was successful; also the privilege of looting some of the towns on the way down. They would descend from the mountains and put the President in power.

Mr. Howe. To what extent were these Caco bands at this time a menace to the Haitian Government?

Gen. Waller. They had been for a hundred years a menace to it.

Mr. Howe. But at the time you landed were they a menace to the then Government?

Gen. Waller. Unquestionably, because they were back of the man, Dr. Bobo, whom they claimed they had appointed president. They had not marched upon Port au Prince; they had not done so because our people had landed.

Mr. Howe. Were they doing any actual damage at the moment?

Gen. Waller. They were stopping all food going to Cape Haitien; they cut off the water supply of Gonaives, and were levying taxes on all the market people, and the business of the country without any authority and treating them brutally. When the marines were permitted to come into the market places the Cacos would seize them and take their money from them when they returned to their homes. To understand that you would have to understand that the market places in the towns were rather peculiar. For instance, the populat'on in Port au Prince on Saturday would probably be increased by something like 20,000 people, and these people had marched from the interior, some of them for three or four days, bringing their produce into the market places. The different towns through the central portion and the northern portion had other market days, and they would proceed from one to the other. Almost all this work was done by women.

Mr. Howe. Then the existence of these Caco bands tended to paralyze the commerce from the interior, in the northern part?

Gen. Waller. Yes.

Mr. Howe. And the immediate effect of that was felt in the towns in the northern part?

Gen. Waller. It was felt in the towns in the shortage of food. It did not affect us, because we had our own provisions.

Mr. Howe. Will you describe your trip out and what transpired when you met these Caco leaders?

Gen. Waller. The officers were bitterly opposed to my going out, because they thought I would be killed; but I took Col. Cole and an interpreter and proceeded to Quartier Morin, I think it is about 8 miles from Cape Haitien.

Mr. Howe. Without any further escort?

Gen. Waller. No.

Mr. Howe. What is the name of that place?

Gen. Waller. Quartier Morin.

Mr. Howe. That was about 8 miles from where?

Gen. Waller. About 8 miles from Cape Haitien, as I recollect it. They met me some 2 miles from this place and escorted me in. Their delegation consisted of 136 generals.

Senator Oddie. How many privates?

Gen. Walker. Not many privates. Any one who had command of five or six men was called a brigadier; if he had 15 or 20 men he was a major general, so there were quite a number of generals there.

Mr. Howe. Let me ask you, sir, did these generals who met you at that place in turn travel a considerable distance to the meeting place?

Gen. Waller. Some had. Some had come down from Grande Riviere and others from farther south.

Mr. Howe. How was the time and place of meeting announced to them, do you know?

Gen. Waller. They had gathered there prior to my arrival at Cape Haitien.

Mr. Howe. You knew of that gathering there?

Gen. Waller. Yes.

Mr. Howe. How did you find out? Who informed you?

Gen. Waller. Col. Cole had informed me that Cape Haitien was surrounded, and the conditions were very bad, and our orders were to take no overt action. Anything that happened must come from them first. I went out to see these people and explained to them our purpose in coming to Haiti. They had in their minds a very fixed idea that we were going to seize naval bases, one of them being Mole St. Nicholas. They referred to that many times during this consultation. I explained to them that Mole St. Nicholas was absolutely worthless as a naval base, and we never contemplated it for a moment; it was not our purpose to take one foot of territory from Haiti; that if, during the time of the occupation, it became necessary for us to take buildings other than the Government buildings, that we would pay a reasonable monthly rent, and we did.

Mr. Howe. To the owners?

Gen. Waller. To the owners; yes.

Mr. Howe. And you did so?

Gen. Waller. We did so always.

Mr. Howe. What else did you say to them and they to you?

Gen. Waller. They told me that Bobo was their president, and they would not have any other. Dartiguenave had failed—well, I suppose, had gone back really on the party. They wanted Bobo and no one else. They had been informed that I had him imprisoned. I had great difficulty in convincing them of the fact that he had left Haiti at his own request, without hindrance of any sort, and, as far as I was concerned, he could return; that we did not regard him as a menace in Haiti. They refused to have any dealings with us, and I told them that I was very sorry; that I would give them a couple of days to think the matter over, and the next day I proposed to open the railroad from Cape Haitien to Grande Riviere, and I would be very glad, indeed, to take any of them on the train with me. They became very indignant and said that we held Cape Haitien, but that they held the north country and we would not be allowed to go. But the train left and we went on to Grande Riviere, and, except for some menacing attitude on their part, there was no trouble. Probably three or four hundred of their men had gathered under their generalissimo and made menaces, but there was not a shot fired at all. When I returned they agreed to come into Cape Haitien and have a further talk.

Mr. Howe. General, what date was this first conference you had with them, how long before the written agreement?

Gen. Waller. About a week.

Mr. Howe. Do I understand that you had a second conference after the railroad had been opened?

Gen. Waller. Yes; they came into Cape Haitien. That was where the second conference was held, and at that time they were joined by Gen. Charles Zamor, and the agreement was made.

Mr. Howe. Was the agreement formulated in writing at the time of that second interview?

Gen. Waller. Yes; that is, the English of it, and it was translated afterwards into French for them.

Mr. Howe. I have here a copy of that agreement, which, Mr. Chairman, is short, and I would like to read it aloud.

Senator Oddie. Very well.

Mr. Howe. General, is this the text of the agreement, which I am about to read:

" Cape Haitien, Haiti, *September 29, 1915.*

"Agreement between Col. L. W. T. Waller, United States Marine Corps, commanding United States expeditionary forces on shore, representing the United States and the Haitian Government, and Gens. Antoine Morancy and Jean Baptiste Petion, representing the Cacos of Haiti.

" Part 1.

"1. It is hereby agreed on the parts of the Caco chiefs as follows:
"(a) To disarm immediately, turning in all arms and ammunition at Quartier Morin.
"(b) Caco chiefs and men to go to their homes, not to oppose in arms the present Government of Haiti, not to interfere with the railroads, commerce, agriculture, and industries of the country.
"(c) Caco chiefs agree to send delegation to Port au Prince to consult and confer with the Dartiguenave Government concerning participation in the civil government of Haiti and to abide by such terms as may be agreed upon.
"(d) Cacos found in arms against present Government after signing of this agreement to be treated as bandits.

" Part 2.

"2. It is hereby agreed on the part of the United States and Haitian Government:
"(a) That the general amnesty granted by the Haitian Government to those Haitians now in arms be guaranteed by the United States forces to all Cacos turning in their arms and observing the requirements laid down in part 1.
"(b) The United States expeditionary forces agree to guarantee the terms made with the Dartiguenave Government as may be.agreed upon as indicated in (c), part 1. Such terms being consistent with the mission of the United States and any treaty made between the United States and Haiti.
"(c) That when practicable, Cacos who have observed part 1 may have representatives in such constabulary or police as may or be organized in Haiti.
" Littleton W. T. Waller.
" Witness:
"Eli Cole.

" Ant. Morancy.
" P. Jn. Baptiste.
" Witness:
" C. Zamor."

Senator Oddie. What was the date of that?
Mr. Howe. September 29, 1915.
Gen. Waller. These two paragraphs, part 1, paragraph (c), there was considerable discussion about at the second meeting.
Mr. Howe. What were those paragraphs?
Gen. Waller. This one, paragraph (c): " Caco chiefs agree to send delegation to Port au Prince to consult and confer with the Dartiguenave Government concerning participation in the civil government of Haiti and to abide by such terms as may be agreed upon."
They were very much in doubt about the frankness of the Haitian Government in connection with their participation in the civil government, and the other paragraph was put in.
Mr. Howe. Meaning which paragraph?
Gen. Waller, Paragraph b, under part 2. We agreed to guarantee the terms made with the Dartiguenave Government as may be agreed upon as indicated in paragraph (c), part 1.
Then they took much interest in the concluding paragraph, paragraph (c), part 2: " That when practicable, Cacos who have observed part 1 may have representatives in such constabulary or police as may or be organized in Haiti."
As a matter of fact, some of the best men we have in the constabulary to-day came——
Mr. Howe. Came from those Caco bands who were represented by these generals?
Gen. Waller. Represented by these generals at that time.
Mr. Howe. That, then, is the text of the agreement which was reached by you at Cape Haitien, as you have described?
Gen. Waller. Yes; but the French of this was not signed at that time.
Mr. Howe. The French copy?
Gen. Waller. It was signed subsequently at Quartier Morin.
Mr. Howe. How long after?
Gen. Waller. It was after the 26th, because they had ambushed the American patrols on the 26th of September, but I found that these men were not concerned in that.

Mr. Howe. Not concerned in the ambush?

Gen. Waller. Not as far as I know, and they have, even to this day, kept to their agreement.

Mr. Howe. The signers of this agreement?

Gen. Waller. Yes. During the campaign in the north I consulted frequently with Baptiste Petion, or Petion Jean Baptiste, just as you like. They call it either way.

Mr. Howe. Did Morancy and Baptiste represent these Cacos?

Gen. Waller. Yes; they practically had vice regal powers.

Mr. Howe. You were convinced they were the individuals who actually represented the Cacos?

Gen. Waller. They were so acknowledged by all of them.

Mr. Howe. To what extent and for how long was this agreement observed by the Cacos?

Gen. Waller. A number of them broke it on the 26th of September when they ambushed my patrols.

Mr. Howe. Now, I notice this agreement here is dated September 29?

Gen. Waller. Yes; that would be the date of the actual signature of the French.

Mr. Howe. Of the French version?

Gen. Waller. Yes.

Mr. Howe. How long before that ambush on the 26th had you formulated the English version?   -

Gen. Waller. The date of the last meeting in Cape Haitien.

Mr. Howe. How long before the ambush was that, do you believe?

Gen. Waller. I think that was about five or six days.

Mr. Howe. And that ambush was on the 26th?

Gen. Waller. On the 26th.

Mr. Howe. Of September?

Gen. Waller. Yes. It is positively fixed in my mind, because it was my birthday, and I thought it was a nice present to receive.

Mr. Howe. The English version was signed before the ambush?

Gen. Waller. That was signed in pencil. I think the original copy, or possibly one of them, may possibly be in the hands of our consul in Cape Haitien now. He was present at the time.

Mr. Howe. Have you any means of knowing how far the news of the signing of the English version was spread among the Cacos?

Gen. Waller. Considering the time between the actual signing, there must have been at that time at least 500 of them in Cape Haitien besides the generals.

Mr. Howe. And did they all know about this agreement?

Gen. Waller. They all knew of it. It was very rapidly spread through the country, carried by the market people.

Mr. Howe. Did they begin to comply with any of the requirements before the 29th?

Gen. Waller. They claimed that they had.

Mr. Howe. Had they turned in any arms?

Gen. Waller. They claimed that some arms in the immediate vicinity of Cape Haitien had been turned in, and, of course, arms were turned in at Port au Prince. I can hardly say they were turned in. More properly speaking, they were collected.

Mr. Howe. But, as the result of this agreement, I mean, were arms turned in before the 26th, before the ambush?

Gen. Waller. Very few. They hesitated for a long time, I mean the peasants, about turning in their arms, because they claimed they were liable to attack at any moment, and should be allowed to have these arms; I mean attacked by their own people.

Mr. Howe. Aside from this ambush, were there any breaches of that agreement?

Gen. Waller. At Gonaives.

Mr. Howe. When.

Gen. Waller. That was, I should say, two days after this agreement.

Mr. Howe. After the English version of the agreement?

Gen. Waller. Yes.

Mr. Howe. What was that occurrence?

Gen. Waller. They had cut off the water supply of Gonaives, and had practically surrounded the town. When I left Cape Haitien I took Maj. Butler, now Gen. Butler, with me to Port au Prince. Stopping at Gonaives I found this condition. It was necessary for me to go on immediately to Port au Prince and report to the Government what I had done, so I left Maj. Butler at Gonaives with instructions to protect the water supply and open the railroad, and I gave him three days in which to do it, and as soon as this was done, he was to report to Port au Prince. He completed this work in two days.

Mr. Howe. In those two days he restored the water supply?

Gen. Waller. He restored the supply, and he came to terms, under my authority, with this commanding general who was there, who also called himself the secretary of state for war under the Bobo government, and he promised faithfully, if he were not put under arrest, that he would carry out these instructions. Instead of doing so, however, he moved back into the interior, attacked a small town and treated the natives very badly, and it was necessary to send a column after him.

Mr. Howe. When was this?

Gen. Waller. It was probably 10 days later.

Mr. Howe. Then this column which was sent up to restore order back of Gonaives had an engagement with the Cacos?

Gen. Waller. They had an engagement with the Cacos, and four or five, I think, were killed or wounded. One of my first sergeants was killed.

Mr. Howe. That was on the 26th of September?

Gen. Waller. That was on the 26th of September also. That report I received just prior to going back to Cape Haitien.

Mr. Howe. Tell us something more, then, about the ambush on the 26th, at Haut de Cap, on the 26th of September.

Gen. Waller. After opening the railroads I instructed Col. Cole to patrol the town of Cape Haitien for a radius of 16 miles every day, and he sent out two patrols of probably 30 or 40 men each to and from that point constantly, in order to permit the food supply for the natives of Cape Haitien to come in freely without interruption. For some reason it was not done immediately, and the first patrols were sent out on the 26th of September, and they were ambushed at two different points. At Haut de Cap the ambush was very much larger, and there were 10 of our men wounded, no one killed, but two died from their wounds afterwards. I do not know how many of the Cacos were killed at that time; I think probably quite a number, but it has been my experience that young officers going into action for the first time are very apt to greatly exaggerate the damage they do to the enemy. Certainly there were comparatively few bodies found after the ambush was over.

Mr. Howe. Why, do you suppose, did the Cacos set this ambush and bring this on?

Gen. Waller. They had received information about these patrols we sent out that day.

Mr. Howe. Why did they want to attack the patrols?

Gen. Waller. Apparently there had been disagreement between some of the subordinate people and the commanding generals about the terms of surrender.

Mr. Howe. After these two engagements, one back of Gonaives and the other at Haut de Cap, were there for a while any other clashes or conflicts?

Gen. Waller. Not until during about the latter part of October, I think it was.

Mr. Howe. In the meantime?

Gen. Waller. In the meantime there were no clashes between our troops and the natives. Many depredations had been committed by these different bands, and they had robbed the towns and villages and the market people, and had interfered with the produce coming into these towns.

Mr. Howe. Did that continue?

Gen. Waller. That continued. My idea was to round up these people, if possible, in the mountains of the north, and to find out exactly where their headquarters were. There were certain forts that had been built along the old Santo Dominican border by the French Government, but were used as points of incubation really for these revolutions. One of them was at Ouanaminthe, on the Santo Dominican border, and there were three forts in the mountains. It was very difficult to find out the exact location of these, so I ordered th's reconnaissance made, which covered somewhere between 300 and 500 miles really around, and Maj. Butler's column was attacked, I think, on the second day of this march.

Mr. Howe. And was that in October?

Gen. Waller. That was in October.

Mr. Howe. Along toward the end of October?

Gen. WALLER. Yes; because as soon as the reports came in to me I went on to Cape Haitien with the plan of campaign that I had arranged.

Mr. HOWE. Why d'd you order that long reconnaissance by Maj. Butler?

Gen. WALLER. For the purpose of finding the exact location of these forts, and finding the exact location of these bands who would descend into the plains and go back into the mountains.

Mr. HOWE. The continuance of these depredations by these bands was in itself a violation of this agreement, was it not?

Gen. WALLER. Absolutely.

Mr. HOWE. Did the American and the Haitian Governments keep their side of the agreement?

Gen. WALLER. To the letter.

Mr. HOWE. Did the campaign of November, 1915, start with the long reconnoissance of Maj. Butler?

Gen. WALLER. No; the plan was not made until after h's report on that reconnaissance. It was necessary for me to get this information before I could make this plan. I wanted to get them into the mountains, and then establish these different bases in the mountains, and operate from the different bases each day, with rap'd moving columns, small columns. I seldom sent out more than 40 men in a column, but as they moved in different directions it kept the other people guessing as to our actual intent and was very successful. I do not think the campaign lasted more than three weeks altogether.

Mr. HOWE. That was a campaign, then, to keep the cacos stirred up and on the run?

Gen. WALLER. Yes.

Mr. HOWE. Moving from place to place?

Gen. WALLER. Moving from place to place. In the meantime we communicated with Jean Baptiste Petion, and told him that he must communicate with these people and say that it was our intention as soon as order was restored to see that work was started on the roads, and work would begin on the railroads, and that these men would have employment at the proper pay, and I know that he did so communicate with them, because I captured afterwards letters from h'm to these other alleged generals.

Mr. HOWE. With the substance of that offer incorporated in those letters?

Gen. WALLER. Yes.

Mr. HOWE. The reason you began this campaign was on account of these depredations?

Gen. WALLER. Yes.

Mr. HOWE. To put a stop to them?

Gen. WALLER. Yes.

Mr. HOWE. How many killed did the Haitians suffer, do you believe, in that three weeks' campaign?

Gen. WALLER. Officially, I think I reported about 182. Personally, I did not see more than 60. They attacked me at my base the morning after I arrived.

Mr. HOWE. That was at Le Trou?

Gen. WALLER. That was at Le Trou. They made a mistake in thinking that I had moved in there with only 18 men. It was true that I had only 18 men when I had moved in from the base, and they sniped me from Caracol up to La Trou, but it did not even halt the march. But they did attack in the morning with a large force, but unfortunately they did not know that three companies and five machine guns had arrived the night before. The engagement was of very short duration.

Mr. HOWE. How many dead did you count after that?

Gen. WALLER. Thirty.

Mr. HOWE. Thirty dead Haitians?

Gen. WALLER. Yes.

Mr. HOWE. Was this 182 total the actual counted number of dead or the estimated number?

Gen. WALLER. Well, I suppose it was the actual count. Of course, I had to depend on the reports of my subordinates in the mountains. I imagine they counted them, because they reported so many dead and so many wounded.

Mr. HOWE. And first to last that campaign was carried out along the lines laid down by you, namely, patrolling columns based on several different points?

Gen. WALLER. Yes.

Mr. HOWE. And constantly patrolling?

Gen. WALLER. I have here the plan of campaign, with the original orders.

Mr. HOWE. Did you have the authority of President Dartiguenave for your conference and agreement with the cacos?

Gen. WALLER. Yes; and not only his authority, but he requested me to take charge of it originally. He made the original request that I take charge of it, and I received a telegraphic dispatch from him conveying the thanks of the Haitian Government for the services which were performed in the north in connection with this agreement, and subsequently the thanks, publicly expressed, of the Haitian Government for the successful campaign in the north which had freed these people of the terror that had existed for so many years.

Mr. HOWE. General, these letters from the President of Haiti to which you have referred appear in a compilation of orders, etc., which compilation is already in the record of this committee, and so we have before us a record of those letters to which you have referred. They appear on page 57 of that compilation.

Now, General, you spoke of having your campaign orders there.

Gen. WALLER. Yes, sir.

Mr. HOWE. May I look at them? General, I have looked over this order, and will you please correct me as I summarize it? It made disposition of your forces?

Gen. WALLER. Yes, sir.

Mr. HOWE. It directed the capture of certain fortified points in the hands of the cacos?

Gen. WALLER. Yes.

Mr. HOWE. And it directed the constant patrolling from designated points?

Gen. WALLER. Yes.

Mr. HOWE. And in field order No. 9, in order to complete this summary, I will read paragraphs 1 and 2:

"1. The territory inclosed between Le Trou, Ste. Suzanne, Grande Riviere, Bajon, Gross Roches, Le Trou is infested with outlaws and bandits; their operations also extend to the west of the Grande Riviere and to the south of Bajon. They have strongholds in the mountains south of Ste. Suzanne and a camp, Berthol to the eastward of the trail Le Trou, Ste. Suzanne; one fort, Capois, their stronghold, is reported to have stone parapets and is situated south of Ste. Suzanne. Strength of the hostile forces is not known, but probably not less than 1,000. Gen. Pinede Pierre is to occupy La Valliere with 100 Haitians, in support of our troops in that vicinity. U. S. S. *Connecticut* in support at Cape Haitien.

"2. Our troops will occupy positions in readiness to clear the above district of outlaws, the movement being started Monday morning, November 1, 1915; natives with arms in their possession are bandits and are to be treated as such. Particular attention will be paid to the capture or destruction of the chiefs."

Mr. HOWE. Paragraph 2 of your orders described the mission of your forces, did it not?

Gen. WALLER. Yes.

Mr. HOWE. These orders also contain a letter of instructions which had principally to do with the details as to distinguishing marks of the soldiers?

Gen. WALLER. For the safety of our own people in night work.

Mr. HOWE. And with water and water facilities, the care of animals, and all the other details of a campaign in the field in an unusual country?

Gen. WALLER. Yes.

Mr. HOWE. That is a fairly correct summary of those orders, is it not, sir?

Gen. WALLER. I think so.

Mr. HOWE. Mr. Chairman, I suggest that these orders, dated at Cape Haitien October 29, 1915, by order of Col. Waller, Field Order No. 9 of the same date, and general instructions accompanying the field order, as well as Field Order No. 9a, and a letter from Col. Waller to Col. Cole, dated October 31, 1915, form a part of the record, and be kept in the records of this committee, but that they be not printed in full in the record, as that seems to be unnecessary.

Senator ODDIE. It will be so ordered.

Mr. HOWE. How successful was that three weeks' campaign in obtaining its objective?

Gen. WALLER. Entirely so. At the end of that time they had given up. Many of them came in, and we gave them work immediately.

Mr. HOWE. Were arms turned in in large numbers?

62269—21—PT 2——33

Gen. WALLER. Arms came in rather rapidly at first, but then, as I say, the peasants held on for a little while, and they were coming in for probably a month afterwards.

Mr. HOWE. A month?

Gen. WALLER. Yes.

Mr. HOWE. About how many rifles were turned in, can you estimate?

Gen. WALLER. I do not remember exactly. I do not remember exactly what price we paid for those rifles, for each one. It was according to the condition of the gun.

Mr. HOWE. So the total amount paid would give no indication as to the number of arms?

Gen. WALLER. No; because we certainly got quite a large number of them.

Mr. HOWE. Perhaps it would be more interesting to know your estimate as to how many firearms were left in the country after this turning in?

Gen. WALLER. It was pretty difficult to say, but there were not very many in the north. At the same time, it was a very easy matter to run arms across from Santo Domingo into Hinche, across the Santo Dominican border in that way.

Mr. HOWE. After the end of this campaign, were there any more armed conflicts for some time?

Gen. WALLER. Nothing for some time. There was an attempted abortive revolution in Port au Prince.

Mr. HOWE. But that was started later?

Gen. WALLER. That was next year.

Mr. HOWE. Then there was a period of quiet?

Gen. WALLER. Entirely so.

Mr. HOWE. And with the exception of this abortive revolution to which you have referred, how long did that period of quiet last?

Gen. WALLER. As long as I was there.

Mr. HOWE. At least, then, until December, 1916?

Gen. WALLER. Over a year.

Mr. HOWE. When you speak of the revolution do you speak of the disturbance called the Pierre Paul revolution?

Gen. WALLER. Yes.

Mr. HOWE. Where was the center of that?

Gen. WALLER. In Port au Prince.

Mr. HOWE. Did you have any intimation in advance that this trouble was coming?

Gen. WALLER. I had. I knew it was coming and the President kept me very actively informed. He was reporting something about it every day and was very anxious for me to arrest the people before any overt acts were committed.

Mr. HOWE. What course did you take?

Gen. WALLER. I told him I was inclined not to do it. I was going to let the revolution start. I said, " I am going to let them begin shooting and I will finish it."

Mr. HOWE. What was your purpose in adopting that plan?

Gen. WALLER. I wished to find out exactly who the leaders were and who the people were who were financing this thing and who were back of it.

Mr. HOWE. Did you gain any information on those points?

Gen. WALLER. I captured two letters. I know that some of the German houses were financing it, and, also, when Pierre Paul escaped the night of the revolution, he was assisted in his escape by a German, and I have reason to believe that he was taken into the German Legation for awhile. Of course, I could not violate that. I should have unhesitatingly arrested any German subject outside, but the legation was sacred.

Mr. HOWE. The legation was sacred?

Gen. WALLER. Yes; the Haitians did not regard it so in the case of the French Legation when they killed the President.

Mr. HOWE. But you had to regard it as sacred?

Gen. WALLER. I did; yes.

Mr. HOWE. Did you capture any of the leaders of this outbreak?

Gen. WALLER. Yes; we captured the commanding general in his escape from Port au Prince. In Port au Prince he escaped from prison.

Mr. HOWE. Who? Pierre Paul did?

Gen. WALLER. No; Codio did—the commanding general. We captured also another general by the name of Metallus, who was probably one of the most desperate of characters on the face of the earth. He was a bodyguard of the former President and betrayed him to the revolutionists. He was accidentally shot at that time, shot in the arm, and we treated him; but he left Port au Prince and went up to Fort Liberté and there committed one of the most dastardly murders ever committed and escaped and got down to Port au Prince and was employed by Codio in this revolution.

Mr. Howe. And was captured?

Gen. Waller. He was captured.

Mr. Howe. Is he alive or dead?

Gen. Waller. He is dead, and so is Codio.

Mr. Howe. And were there any other important prisoners captured there?

Gen. Waller. When they broke out of prison after the revolution, and probably 150 men got away, some of them political and others criminal prisoners, but the majority of the political prisoners simply hid and gave themselves up the next day. They hid because they were afraid they would be shot.

Mr. Howe. Was Codio taken in that way?

Gen. Waller. Codio was recaptured just as he was making his way to the Santo Dominican border with Gen. Metallus and another man. I have forgotten his name just now. He was not of very great importance. He was a bandit and a political disturber. And there were some pirates who had been captured. They had killed the captain of their ship and were awaiting trial. These people, on the march back to Port au Prince, were sent down to get water one morning, and they attempted to break away from the guards and get across the shallow stream and escape. Of course, they made the mistake of thinking the American riflemen were something like the Haitians. The result was that they were killed.

Mr. Howe. By the marines?

Gen. Waller. Yes.

Mr. Howe. As they were attempting to escape?

Gen. Waller. Yes.

Mr. Howe. Did that account for the end of all your principal captures in the Pierre Paul revolution?

Gen. Waller. All except Pierre Paul himself.

Mr. Howe. What happened to Pierre Paul himself?

Gen. Waller. He got away, and subsequently communicated with me, probably after four or five months, and asked for terms of surrender, which I refused to give. I sent word to him that he would have to throw himself on my mercy altogether and surrender unconditionally. He complained that his wife was starving, and we were withholding the rent for a building that we were using as barracks up at Ouanaminthe, so the rent was paid to Madame Paul.

Mr. Howe. This building was owned by Pierre Paul?

Gen. Waller. The rent was regularly paid to her. He came in and I told him that I was going to pardon him, as far as the occupation was concerned, but it would be necessary to have action on the part of the Haitian Government; otherwise a charge might lie against him at any time.

Mr. Howe. Was he pardoned by the Haitian Government?

Gen. Waller. I took him over to the President, and the President pardoned him, and he was released immediately. He was not in confinement an hour; he was not in confinement at all; he was in my office, or in the President's office, and came right out.

Mr. Howe. After he returned he was not in confinement?

Gen. Waller. No.

Mr. Howe. What happened to him after that, when he was turned loose?

Gen. Waller. He was politically dead. Our action in not regarding him as a dangerous character had a wonderful effect, as we knew it would.

Mr. Howe. And there was no more trouble from Pierre Paul?

Gen. Waller. Not at all. There was an alleged political trouble. The information was given to me by the President. Mr. Pradel, who was one of the leading Haitian lawyers and a very intelligent man, the President kept informing me was holding communication with people who were opposed to the Government and particularly in the salon of one of the Haitian ladies who was a political disturber. I had no reason to believe that he was in any way concerned in it, but they were so insistent in their reports that finally I said, " I will have his house searched and see what there is." So the house was searched, and they did find some arms that were not allowed. I think there were four guns, four rifles, but they were found in the stable which opened on the street. Mr. Pradel was brought to my office and stated he knew absolutely nothing about it, and I am quite convinced that he did not. I think it was a plot on the part of his political enemies.

Mr. Howe. Did that trouble incident to the Pierre Paul revolution constitute the only instance of that kind, the only disturbing incident?

Gen. Waller. That is all.

Mr. Howe. During the rest of your tour there?

Gen. Waller. That is all.

Mr. Howe. Did you have any active part in the negotiations of the treaty with the Haitian Government?

Gen. Waller. Simply to carry out the instructions of the State Department that were given to me through Admiral Caperton.

Mr. Howe. The customhouses were seized?

Gen. Waller. Yes.

Mr. Howe. Before the negotiations for the treaty, before your participation in the negotiations for the treaty became effective; is that correct?

Gen. Waller. I knew that would be agreed upon, that they would take over the customs.

Mr. Howe. You knew that the Haitians would agree to the taking over of the customs?

Gen. Waller. That was understood.

Mr. Howe. Was that agreement reached before the customhouses were taken over?

Gen. Waller. The verbal agreement?

Mr. Howe. Yes.

Gen. Waller. Yes.

Mr. Howe. The treaty later on provided for the taking over of the administration of the customs; is that right?

Gen. Waller. Yes; and the appointment of a receiver general and a financial adviser.

Mr. Howe. General, these negotiations in which you took part lasted over a considerable period of time, did they not?

Gen. Waller. Yes.

Mr. Howe. The treaty was signed in September, 1916, I believe?

Gen. Waller. I think so.

Mr. Howe. On behalf of Haiti?

Gen. Waller. Yes.

Mr. Howe. How soon after your arrival in August, 1915, did you begin the negotiations?

Gen. Waller. They were going on when I got there, two days after the President was elected.

Mr. Howe. During that time did you observe any compulsion being brought to bear on the Dartiguenave government, forcible or otherwise, to sign this treaty?

Gen. Waller. None whatever.

Mr. Howe. There were, however, prolonged negotiations on many of the details of the treaty?

Gen. Waller. One paragraph of the treaty would take up sometimes a week or 10 days, arguing pro and con.

Mr. Howe. Who took part in those discussions?

Gen. Waller. The Haitian Government, our minister, our admiral, in communications from the State Department.

Mr. Howe. Where did you come in, sir?

Gen. Waller. I came in the Naval Establishment there.

Mr. Howe. Were you and the admiral present, both of you, at the same negotiations frequently?

Gen. Waller. Frequently; yes.

Mr. Howe. Did you sometimes take the place of the admiral and represent him in the negotiations?

Gen. Waller. Yes; occasionally.

Mr. Howe. Under his instructions?

Gen. Waller. Oh, of course, in a case of that kind I reported immediately afterwards what was done.

Mr. Howe. Were you present at most of the negotiations, or were you absent from a considerable number of the meetings?

Gen. Waller. No; because a great many of these were going on when I was in the north.

Mr. Howe. You have not, then, from your own knowledge, any complete information as to the negotiations of the treaty?

Gen. Waller. No; I have not—only what I would read over and hear discussed afterwards; from my own knowledge, nothing.

Mr. Howe. I want to ask you now, s'r, about the administration of affairs by the Americans from the time you got there, and I mean by that the collection of customs, the administration of justice under martial law, and any other functions of government performed by Americans, or in which Americans directly intervened. When were the customhouses seized, do you know?

Gen. Waller. I do not remember whether it was the latter part of August or the first part of September.

Mr. Howe. Is this, according to your recollection, correct—that the seizure of the customhouses went on in the last 10 days of August and on the first one or two days of September, 1915?

Gen. Waller. Yes, sir; according to the distances of the places.

Mr. Howe. According to the distances of the customhouses from Port au Prince?

Gen. Waller. Yes. It was very difficult to reach some of those in the south. If we did not have a cruiser available, we would have to send people overland, and the trails were in wretched condition.

Mr. Howe. I understand that martial law was put into effect on September 3, 1915?

Gen. Waller. Yes.

Mr. Howe. So the seizure of the customhouses was practically completed by the time martial law went into effect?

Gen. Waller. Yes.

Mr. Howe. What Americans were the agents of this seizure?

Gen. Waller. The officers of the Pay Corps of the United States Navy.

Mr. Howe. And were they under the orders of some one officer in the Pay Corps?

Gen. Waller. The receiver general.

Mr. Howe. The receiver general was in the Pay Corps?

Gen. Waller. Yes.

Mr. Howe. And the different customhouses were administered by other pay officers under him?

Gen. Waller. Under his instructions, and he received his instructions from Admiral Caperton.

Mr. Howe. What did they do when they seized the customhouses? What did they collect?

Gen. Waller. They collected the export and import customs.

Mr. Howe. All of them?

Gen. Waller. Yes.

Mr. Howe. What did they do with the money they collected?

Gen. Waller. That was turned in to the Haitian bank, the National Bank of Haiti, the depository of the Haitian Government. You see, there is no banking system in Haiti. The bank of Haiti is in Port au Prince.

Mr. Howe. Let us say, then, General that the funds were put in the best available place for safe-keeping, but I was more interested to know how the funds were disbursed or disposed of.

Gen. Waller. They were disbursed in this way. At first the Haitian Government was given a lump sum, and they were supposed to do the disbursing.

Mr. Howe. And over and above the lump sum, was there any money left?

Gen. Waller. There was never any money left.

Mr. Howe. After the lump sum was paid over to the Haitian Government, was there any money left, any balance?

Gen. Waller. Yes; there was a balance left. That was used for educational purposes, and for the hospital, for the external debt, and for sanitary purposes—that is, keeping the towns absolutely clean.

Mr. Howe. What was the lump sum turned over to the Haitian Government supposed to cover?

Gen. Waller. All the salaries of the Hatian officials, from the President down. That included his salary and his allowance. His salary, as I recollect, was $25,000 gold, and he had 3,000 gourdes for his table.

Mr. Howe. How long did the arrangement last by which the receiver general turned over a lump sum to the Haitian Government?

Gen. Waller. Four or five months, I think.

Mr. Howe. Then was that arrangement changed?

Gen. WALLER. Yes.

Mr. HOWE. In what respect?

Gen. WALLER. We paid all the bills.

Mr. HOWE. Instead of handing the money over to the Haitians in a lump sum?

Gen. WALLER. Yes; we took their pay rolls, audited them, and paid the bills.

Mr. HOWE. Without the money passing through the hands of the Haitian Government?

Gen. WALLER. Yes.

Mr. HOWE. Why was that necessary, if it was necessary?

Gen. WALLER. Because we were convinced, as well as the general public was also convinced, that there had been not a proper administration of affairs by the Haitian Government.

Mr. HOWE. Was there reason to doubt that the money turned over for salaries did not reach those who were entitled to the salaries in all cases?

Gen. WALLER. Very strong reason, because many of the clerks and employees in the Government offices were simply given a certificate of indebtedness or chit for a month's salary, and those would be held back.

Mr. HOWE. The payment of those would be held back?

Gen. WALLER. The payment of those would be held back, and it came to my notice that there was a sort of exchange in the different cafés of the town, quoting prices for the value of these chits according to the month in which they were issued. These were bought up by the capitalists at anywhere from 30 to 40 cents on the dollar, and then the secretary of state or the treasurer would decide that such and such months would be paid, and these chits would be sent in.

Some of them had been bought up, I think, by the president of the senate, who was a large investor.

Mr. HOWE. In these chits?

Gen. WALLER. Yes, of course; the secretary of the treasury got something, I suppose.

Mr. HOWE. Did this practice which you have described prevail through these four or five months during which the lump sum was paid over?

Gen. WALLER. It was not a new practice.

Mr. HOWE. But it continued on?

Gen. WALLER. Simply continued on.

Mr. HOWE. Therefore, in addition to the salaried officers not receiving their salaries, this condition did not tend to keep political conditions stable; is that right?

Gen. WALLER. That is right.

Mr. HOWE. It was a disturbing factor?

Gen. WALLER. Always. There were many little things in that line, very little things. I did not consider that a very small item, but, as an illustration, the concession to the ice plant, which was a German concession, by the way, required them to furnish 300 pounds of ice a day to the hospital in Port au Prince. I sent our medical officers into the hospital to take charge of it. There were probably 10 or 12 patients. Some of the sisters of the different orders were acting as nurses in a way, with no provision for food and no provision made for the preservation of such food as they might have. Inquiring into this, the proprietor of the ice plant informed me of the fact that this 300 pounds of ice that was supposed to be delivered at the hospital was delivered at the palace and to the administrative officers—to the houses of the secretaries of state, interior, finance, justice, etc. I ordered him to stop it, and he said they would come down on him and put him out of business.

Mr. HOWE. Who was this—the ice-plant manager?

Gen. WALLER. Yes; I told him I would seize his ice plant as a military necessity and administer the thing myself. After that the ice was properly and promptly delivered to the hospital. That is just one of the illustrations.

Another little incident was in the formation of the gendarmerie. I had appointed Maj. Butler as acting commandant of them until his appointment could be approved here, and he came to me on one occasion and said he would like to have about 2 pounds of scratch paper; that he had seen some in the official storehouse, which is under the department of the interior. I told him that he could have it, but that, of course, he would have to go through the usual official channels, but I would write to the secretary of the interior and ask him if he would not permit him to take 2 pounds of paper.

Mr. Howe. Two pounds of paper?

Gen. Waller. Two pounds of paper for use with the gendarmerie for printing his orders. About a week later the paymaster, Conard, called me up and said the secretary was in his office at that time, and stated that I had authorized him to get $1,000 for stationery. I had forgotten this incident at the time and told him to put him out. There was not anything else to be done. Then I recalled this item, and I said, "That must be what he is talking about." I interviewed him again to see if he could explain. He came back again and said that it was arranged between us that I had agreed that the secretary of the interior was to purchase all of the supplies for the gendarmerie, and he wanted this $1,000 to begin to purchase stationery.

Mr. Howe. Who was this you are talking about—the secretary of the interior?

Gen. Waller. The secretary of the interior; yes. He was the gentleman who was put out afterwards.

Mr. Howe. These paymasters were succeeded in their duties by civilians. Was that after the adoption of the treaty or before?

Gen. Waller. Yes; that was after the formal adoption of the treaty.

Mr. Howe. And thereafter the so-called treaty officials came in?

Gen. Waller. They came in at that time.

Mr. Howe. And the treaty was formally promulgated after your departure; was that not so?

Gen. Waller. Yes; I think at that time. There was a great deal of delay on account of the organization of the gendarmerie. There were different things that came up from time to time.

Mr. Howe. I want to ask you, General, about the beginning of martial law on September 3, 1915. To what extent was martial law imposed at that time?

Gen. Waller. The proclamation was issued, and all police had been abolished, all of their military had been abolished, and it was absolutely necessary that martial law should be employed for the protection of the Government and for the protection of our own men.

Mr. Howe. And for preserving peace?

Gen. Waller. And for preserving peace.

Mr. Howe. Is it correct to say, and please correct me if it is not, that the system of martial law at that time took over the administration of criminal justice but left the administration of civil justice alone?

Gen. Waller. Left it alone, although we were besieged by the people, requesting us to take jurisdiction in that also.

Mr. Howe. But it is so that it was an assumption of the administration of criminal justice?

Gen. Waller. Yes.

Mr. Howe. The administration of all criminal matters in the courts but of no civil matters?

Gen. Waller. No civil matters. There were some instances in the north. For instance, I have heard much about executions that took place but I never knew of one. I never heard of any sentence of execution except one that was given by the Hatian court itself, in the north, and when it was brought to my attention by the officer in that district—the offense was really a minor one—not a capital offense, and I wrote to the President and told him that it would be a disgrace if this judgment of execution was permitted to take place.

Mr. Howe. This was an execution ordered by a Haitian court?

Gen. Waller. By a Haitian court.

Mr. Howe. During the time martial law was in existence?

Gen. Waller. When martial law was in existence, but it had not taken cognizance of this thing. It was something like petit theft, petit larceny, or a little thing like that.

Mr. Howe. Was the action of that court then set aside?

Gen. Waller. It was set aside by the President.

Mr. Howe. By the President of Haiti?

Gen. Waller. By the President of Haiti.

Mr. Howe. But, with a few sporadic exceptions like that, martial law took over the administration of the criminal law?

Gen. Waller. Yes.

Mr. Howe. Why was that necessary?

Gen. Waller. It was necessary largely for the protection of our own men there and for the protection of the Government itself.

Mr. HOWE. Was there not a system of criminal courts provided for by the Haitian law?

Gen. WALLER. Yes; I suppose there was.

Mr. HOWE. Prior to September 3, 1916, had those Haitian courts been functioning in the administration of the criminal law?

Gen. WALLER. They had existed, but they were not functioning.

Mr. HOWE. To any extent?

Gen. WALLER. They were not interfered with by us.

Mr. HOWE. Were they functioning to a sufficient extent for the maintenance of law and order and of the Government?

Gen. WALLER. No.

Mr. HOWE. And for the safety of our marines?

Gen. WALLER. Not at all.

Mr. HOWE. Was that failure to function demonstrated by actual occurrences?

Gen. WALLER. Every day.

Mr. HOWE. The proclamation of martial law to which you have referred appears on page 67 of the printed record of this committee, part 1. What tribunals administered the martial law?

Gen. WALLER. The provost courts.

Mr. HOWE. Was there any higher court?

Gen. WALLER. Yes; there was, but I never found it necessary to convene the higher one.

Mr. HOWE. What would the higher one have been called?

Gen. WALLER. The military commission.

Mr. HOWE. The military commission is provided for by law, but during your time none was convened?

Gen. WALLER. It was not convened. I had the power to do so, but it would only be convened in capital cases.

Mr. HOWE. So the provost courts were sufficient for the purpose?

Gen. WALLER. Yes. The action of the provost judge, of course, had to be approved by me.

Mr. HOWE. In all cases?

Gen. WALLER. Yes.

Mr. HOWE. Of punishment?

Gen. WALLER. Yes.

Mr. HOWE. Or of acquittal?

Gen. WALLER. Yes. Acquittal goes without saying. It would be approved by me.

Mr. HOWE. In other words, all the cases were submitted to you for action?

Gen. WALLER. Yes.

Mr. HOWE. And your approval was necessary to sentence or conviction?

Gen. WALLER. Yes; the execution of the sentence.

Mr. HOWE. Who were the officers or the people who conducted the provost courts?

Gen. WALLER. In Port au Prince, Col. Williams.

Mr. HOWE. I did not mean their names, but were they marine officers?

Gen. WALLER. Oh, yes.

Mr. HOWE. In every case?

Gen. WALLER. Yes.

Mr. HOWE. How many such provost courts were instituted?

Gen. WALLER. One at the headquarters of each district.

Mr. HOWE. How many districts?

Gen. WALLER. Or each post, really.

Mr. HOWE. How many provost courts were there?

Gen. WALLER. Roughly, about 20.

Mr. HOWE. In your opinion, was the operation of the provost courts satisfactory and effective?

Gen. WALLER. I am very sure it was very effective, and I have a very strong opinion of the fact that martial law, humanely administered, is the best form of government I know for the country.

Mr. HOWE. Was it humanely administered in Haiti?

Gen. WALLER. Absolutely; I mean as far as I know.

Mr. HOWE. On April 6, 1916, the Legislature of Haiti, consisting of the Senate and the Chamber of Deputies, was prorogued, was it not?

Gen. WALLER. Yes.

Mr. HOWE. By whose order?

Gen. WALLER. It was done at the order and upon the strong personal request of the President.

Mr. HOWE. But did not the prorogation require some formal, legal order?

Gen. WALLER. Usually the proclamation of the President of Haiti.

Mr. HOWE. The President of Haiti issued the proclamation?

Gen. WALLER. Yes, sir.

Mr. HOWE. Do you know why the President issued the decree?

Gen. WALLER. He told me that it was on account of the tremendous opposition that he was meeting from members of the legislature in the organization and formation of the council of state.

Mr. HOWE. The council of state was necessary for what purpose?

Gen. WALLER. For the adoption of the new constitution.

Mr. HOWE. Do you believe that was his real reason?

Gen. WALLER. It may have been. There may have been something in it, but I think the general impression was, and it was my own also at the time, that he feared impeachment. In fact, he said so on one occasion.

Mr. HOWE. Let me ask you this question, sir. Did that desire to prorogue the legislature originate with the President of Haiti or was it inspired by the United States,

Gen. WALLER. It originated with the Haitian Government, the President and his secretaries.

Mr. HOWE. As far as you know.

Gen. WALLER. As far as I know.

Mr. HOWE. As far as you know, was the prorogation of this legislature desired by our Government?

Gen. WALLER. Only to carry out the request of the President.

Mr. HOWE. Of Haiti?

Gen. WALLER. Personally, I was bitterly opposed to it.

Mr. HOWE. To the prorogation?

Gen. WALLER. Absolutely; and I worked over it even after the prorogation with the greatest efforts to get them together again, but I was always confronted——

Mr. HOWE. Upon whom did you bend your efforts?

Gen. WALLER. On the Haitian Government.

Mr. HOWE. The President of Haiti?

Gen. WALLER. The President of Haiti and his secretaries, but was bitterly opposed all the time.

Mr. HOWE. By what means was the President's decree carried out?

Gen. WALLER. By the locking of the door—the gates of the inclosure.

Mr. HOWE. Do you recollect who locked the doors and the gates?

Gen. WALLER. I do not know, personally, who did it. I gave the order myself to Maj. Butler to carry out and he probably sent some marines to preserve order, as I have a letter here from the President requesting that it be done.

Mr. HOWE. I was asking a slightly narrower question than that, as to who, if you know, locked the doors and at whose orders?

Gen. WALLER. At that time there was a lieutenant by the name of Daumet who was connected with the gendarmerie, who was acting as aid to the President. I think that he was the one who did the actual locking.

Mr. HOWE. And at whose orders, do you know?

Gen. WALLER. Maj. Butler's, but if he was aid to the President, it would be the President.

Mr. HOWE. At the President's orders?

Gen. WALLER. Maj. Butler also received the notice from the President, because it came through me.

Mr. HOWE. What was that notice from the President to Maj. Butler, through you?

Gen. WALLER. To close the doors of the chamber.

Mr. HOWE. You, however, did give Maj. Butler directions to make disposal of his forces to see that there was no disorder?

Gen. WALLER. Yes.

Mr. HOWE. But do you understand that the actual closing of the gates was done at the orders of the President of Haiti?

Gen. WALLER. I know it was.

Mr. HOWE. And the marine forces and such gendarmerie forces as were then in existence were disposed around under the orders of Maj. Butler, to preserve order?

Gen. WALLER. Yes.

Mr. Howe. Was there any disorder?

Gen. Waller. None whatever. The marines were not in the inclosure at all.

Mr. Howe. Do you know if at any time any of the forces under Maj. Butler used any force against the members of the legislature?

Gen. Waller. No; it was not necessary at that time.

Mr. Howe. Were marines or gendarmerie employed to keep them out of any inclosure?

Gen. Waller. The gendarmerie were at the gate, and told them they could not go in the doors, that is the members of the legislature.

Mr. Howe. Do you know whether any gendarmes or marines put any members of the legislature out?

Gen. Waller. I do not think so. I should certainly have heard of it, because I was in very close connection both with members of the Senate and the deputies at that time.

Mr. Howe. Did the Senate or Chamber of Deputies attempt to reconvene elsewhere?

Gen. Waller. Yes.

Mr. Howe. Many times, or more than once?

Gen. Waller. Four or five times. They stopped it at my request.

Mr. Howe. Who stopped it at your request?

Gen. Waller. Both the deputies and the senators.

Mr. Howe. You requested them to stop meeting?

Gen. Waller. I requested them to stop meeting until the final arrangements could be made. I was confident we could get over this and reestablish them.

Mr. Howe. I see; your idea was that they should be reconvened or reestablished?

Gen. Waller. That is what I thought.

Mr. Howe. And you used your influence with them to stop these irregular meetings until some conclusion could be reached along those lines?

Gen. Waller. Yes.

Mr. Howe. Was there any disorder that you know of incident to these attempted meetings?

Gen. Waller. Not at all. The senators would come from their meetings to me, and the deputies also, and tell what had happened. I had particularly asked them if they would take up only matters concerning the council of state, for instance, and they agreed that they would take up nothing, that is the deputies agreed, and I am sure the senators did. I have a letter here from Camille Leon, the speaker of the House, in which he agrees to do this, to the holding of these meetings, but to take up only certain questions until this final arrangement could be made, but Mr. Borno, the secretary of state for foreign affairs, was so bitterly opposed to it that finally all measures failed.

Mr. Howe. Did you have anything to do with the preparations for the election of January, 1916?

Gen. Waller. I wrote the orders.

Mr. Howe. What orders?

Gen. Waller. For the conduct of the election.

Mr. Howe. Who called the election; who decided that there should be an election?

Gen. Waller. The Haitian Government—President Dartiguenave.

Mr. Howe. How did you come to be charged with the duty of conducting an election?

Gen. Waller. Because, in addition to the occupation, I was also in charge of the gendarmerie, not as a Haitian officer, but all the instructions had to come from me.

Mr. Howe. What provisions did you arrange for the conduct of the election?

Gen. Waller. I have it here.

Mr. Howe. You have what there, sir?

Gen. Waller. I have this proclamation, or my order.

Mr. Howe. That is in French, is it not?

Gen. Waller. In French.

Mr. Howe. That proclamation to which you refer appears here in an issue of Le Nouvelliste, dated Wednesday, the 15th of November, 1916. Your proclamation is dated November 10, 1916, at Port au Prince. I offer this in the record, Mr. Chairman, and will furnish a translation for the purpose of printing in the record.

Senator Oddie. It is so ordered.

(A translation of the proclamation referred to follows:)

HEADQUARTERS OF UNITED STATES
EXPEDITIONARY FORCES OPERATING IN HAITI,
Port au Prince, Haiti, November 10, 1916.

Having been informed that considerable anxiety exists in the minds of the people regarding the attitude of the occupation (expeditionary forces) in respect to the elections for the month of January, 1917, the following instructions will be given to the expeditionary forces and to the gendarmerie serving with them during the existence of martial law:

The firm intention of the Haitian Government and of the occupation is that the elections shall be free and honest; therefore the rôle of the expeditionary forces and of the gendarmerie will be—

First. To maintain order, to prevent any obstruction in the voting, and to see that no one shall be hindered in the exercise of his right to vote by any individual or by any party.

Second. No gathering of persons shall be permitted at a distance less than 30 feet from the places where the ballots are cast, and no gathering shall be permitted where it can constitute an obstacle to the free exercise of voting.

Third. A representative of the occupation or of the gendarmerie shall be present at each place where the voting takes place, in order to insure the full execution of the present instructions. He shall decide all disputes which may arise at the places where the voting takes place, and shall see to it that the voting or the emptying of the ballot box shall take place without interruption, making written note at the same time of formal protests which may be made on the subject of any disputes.

Fourth. Gendarmes who have the right to vote shall do so as ordinary citizens without arms. They shall vote promptly and return immediately to their duties.

Fifth. The decree of September 22 having been modified by the instructions to the commissaries of the Government, each candidate or party will be represented in the bureau of assessors by one individual of his own choice nominated by the judge de paix. It is understood that where there are several candidates from the same party, they must agree upon the choice of one person to represent the party in the bureau of assessors.

The officers of the occupation and of the gendarmerie will see to the execution of this plan, and especially that the nominations shall be made by the judge de paix, or by his deputy, as the case may be, before the elections.

Sixth. In order to prevent any fraud in the elections, very special attention shall be given to the question of the true residence of each voter. No one shall have the right to vote except in the ward where he resides.

Any individual who shall attempt to vote outside of his ward will be arrested and brought before the court of the high provost.

LITTLETON W. T. WALLER,
Brigade Commander, United States Marine Corps.

Mr. Howe. In general, what did you aim at, sir, in your provision for this election?

Gen. WALLER. The preservation of order and a fair election.

Mr. Howe. This election took place after your departure, did it not?

Gen. WALLER. It took place after my departure, but there was no disturbance.

Mr. Howe. That election was for members of the legislature, was it not?

Gen. WALLER. Yes.

Mr. Howe. And your orders contemplated those elections being supervised by the gendarmerie?

Gen. WALLER. Yes.

Mr. Howe. As far as law and order went?

Gen. WALLER. As far as law and order went.

Mr. Howe. Now, your proclamation provides that a representative of the occupation or of the gendarmerie shall be present at each of the voting places. What is that distinction there, General?

Gen. WALLER. The distinction is due to the fact that it was impossible to furnish a representative or officer of the gendarmerie at every polling place in the country.

Mr. Howe. And to fill his place when you did not have enough to go around——

Gen. WALLER. The occupation.

Mr. HOWE. What do you mean by the occupation?

Gen. WALLER. I mean an officer of noncommissioned officer of the United States marines. I will have to explain the real reason for some of those paragraphs, perhaps. In Port au Prince alone it took 25 days to hold an election; I mean before the establishment of these rules it took 25 days to have an election.

Mr. HOWE. In previous elections?

Gen. WALLER. Yes; such as they had. I think at Cape Haitien it took five or six days, but the result of it all was that the rival candidates were working up their following to such a pitch that before the election actually took place there were quite a number of casualties, and always rows and disturbances going on. So I changed the number of polling places, of course, and we made districts of Port au Prince, in other words, wards, from which residents would vote, and a resident in a certain ward would vote in that ward, and nowhere else. That is accounted for.

The only difficulty we had at any time during the election, I understand, and I have every reason to believe it is true, was from the people in the north, who came down from the mountains to vote, and insisted on voting for the marines for deputies. I know that is the attitude they had toward me always when I went through the country after this trouble was over, because they are a very lovable people and very happy if they are properly treated, but, of course, they have been under this tremendous misrule for so long that they are suspicious of everything.

(Whereupon, at 1 o'clock p. m., a recess was taken until 2.30 o'clock p. m.)

AFTER RECESS.

The committee reassembled at 2.30 o'clock p. m., pursuant to the taking of recess.

Mr. HOWE. General, the employment of the law corvee was begun in your time down there, was it not?

Gen. WALLER. Yes.

Mr. HOWE. And you were in command down there at the time it was begun?

Gen. WALLER. It continued during my whole stay.

Mr. HOWE. In order to save time, may I repeat my understanding of the law of corvee to be that before the American occupation there, there was in existance a Haitian law by which the inhabitants of a district could be required to work for a limited time in the repair of roads in their district without compensation to themselves?

Gen. WALLER. Yes, sir.

Mr. HOWE. My further understanding, derived from the testimony of preceding witnesses, is that the general use of the word " corvee " in common parlance down there applied to any work on roads, whether it was paid work or not; that is correct, is it not, sir?

Gen. WALLER. That is correct.

Mr. HOWE. But when you answered my first question, which related to the corvee, you meant, did you not, the work under this old law, work without compensation?

Gen. WALLER. Yes, sir. While we employed other men, and took them out of their own districts to work, those were the men who had excelled in the work, and they were regularly paid and went perfectly willingly. It really was not corvee, because they were paid and went willingly.

Mr. HOWE. In your opinion, was it necessary to employ this Haitian law?

Gen. WALLER. Not only necessary, but greatly desired by the Haitians themselves.

Mr. HOWE. It was for the purpose of building roads?

Gen. WALLER. Rebuilding roads.

Mr. HOWE. There had been, as the committee has learned from other witnesses here, quite an elaborate system of roads built under the French?

Gen. WALLER. A really very wonderful system of roads.

Mr. HOWE. Which had been neglected to the point of almost disappearing?

Gen. WALLER. Impassable, practically.

Mr. HOWE. What was the need for roads down there?

Gen. WALLER. Intercommunication with the towns for the market people themselves, bringing their produce into the markets, and also for the quick movement of troops and gendarmes.

Mr. HowE. Was there immediate need for the quick movement of troops and gendarmes?

Gen. WALLER. Not at that time, because they were very generally distributed throughout the island. The gendarmes, after they were thoroughly organized, were distributed in small detachments through the island, so that they were not very far apart, and the patrols would meet.

Mr. HowE. How about the supply of those detachments?

Gen. WALLER. That was done by pack animals.

Mr. HowE. They could be supplied on the existing paths or roads?

Gen. WALLER. You could not use a wagon on those roads at that time; it was absolutely impossible.

Mr. HowE. How soon after you got there was the corvee revived or employed by the occupation?

Gen. WALLER. I think we began it early in 1916.

Mr. HowE. And as I recollect your earlier testimony. that was a period of comparative quiet?

Gen. WALLER. Yes.

Mr. HowE. Did the employment of that system proceed uninterruptedly throughout your tour down there?

Gen. WALLER. Yes, sir.

Mr. HowE. Did you hear of its leading to any dissatisfaction among the natives, the peasants?

Gen. WALLER. On the contrary, they volunteered in such numbers that I could not possibly use them. The only difficulty was that it was impossible to furnish the tools and material, as evidenced, for instance, in the correction of the irrigation system, which had been built by the French in the Cul-de-Sac, one of the most fertile valleys of Haiti. This system had been neglected, and large landholders had deprived the small landholders, the peasants, of the use of this water by leading it off on to their own places, so that probably 8,000 varas of land were practically a desert and produced nothing. It became necessary to do something with these, and the Haitian engineer estimated that the cost of repair would be $60,000 gold. As that alleged engineer was an architect, I was not prepared to accept his estimate, and I sent out my own engineer for an estimate, and he came back again and said that the native had told him that they would furnish 1,000 or 2,000 men, or just as many men as we could furnish tools for, to do this work, and the work was completed and the land restored at a cost of $800 in material.

Mr. HowE. With the aid of that native labor?

Gen. WALLER. Yes. We could not get the tools to employ all. They were perfectly willing to do it.

Mr. HowE. Did this oversupply of labor for the roads continue during the time you were there, or did it become difficult later on to obtain the necessary amount of labor?

Gen. WALLER. It continued all the time. I have seen hundreds of men applying for that species of work.

Mr. HowE. Applying for it?

Gen. WALLER. Applying for it at the public works' office. that is my public works office.

Mr. HowE. That is uncompensated?

Gen. WALLER. Yes; uncompensated. You know, that sounds a little peculiar and I would like to tell you.

Mr. HowE. I would like to hear your explanation of that.

Gen. WALLER. Frequently, with the Haitian prisoners who were working on the streets, a guard would take out 15 or 20 of them, and it seldom happened that he would turn in less than 18 or 22. They would simply fall in and go back.

Mr. HowE. Why?

Gen. WALLER. Well, they got something to eat and they could not get it outside.

Mr. HowE. In the employment, what is the connection between that and the corvee on the roads, and your supply of labor on the roads?

Gen. WALLER. The willingness of these people to do the work.

Mr. HowE. Did you supply them with food while they were working on the corvee?

Gen. WALLER. Not those that were paid.

Mr. HowE. Did you have an oversupply of volunteers for the unpaid corvee?

Gen. WALLER. Yes.

Mr. Howe. And what was the inducement to them to do their work for nothing?

Gen. Waller. The improvement of the road itself, for the communication.

Mr. Howe. The unpaid corvee worker—did you give him his subsistence?

Gen. Waller. No; we did not. Under their law it is not required at all. You know, they subsist largely on mangoes, bananas, and that sort of thing, which are plentiful everywhere; also sugar cane, a little rice, and occasionally it was fish and very small portions of meat. They eat very little meat.

Mr. Howe. While at work on the roads were the corvee gangs contented, or otherwise?

Gen. Waller. If you could judge by the singing, I should say they were thoroughly contented.

Mr. Howe. Were attempts made to escape from the work of the corvee in any large numbers?

Gen. Waller. Nobody escaped. I never heard of an instance of anyone escaping.

Mr. Howe. Or trying to get away?

Gen. Waller. No.

Mr. Howe. Do you know of any negotiations or discussion about the new constitution of Haiti?

Gen. Waller. Yes; I had a great deal to do with that—a number of the articles.

Mr. Howe. With whom did you consult?

Gen. Waller. With President Dartiguenave and members of the cabinet, with the senators and deputies, and also with what they called the advocates, who correspond to our bar association.

Mr. Howe. Did you have any conferences with other American officials on the subject?

Gen. Waller. Only from time to time, when, sometimes the Admiral would come and I would talk matters over with him; but during the time this constitutional change was taking place he was in Santo Domingo, and, while I was also ordered to command the troops in Santo Domingo, as well as Haiti, the department informed me that my presence was required in Haiti, so I could not go to Santo Domingo.

Mr. Howe. Were there any particular difficulties encountered in your consideration of this proposed constitution with President Dartiguenave?

Gen. Waller. I do not recall any, except the question of the right of foreigners to acquire property, and there we had considerable difficulty. They were willing to put in this article, but I objected to the phraseology very seriously for the simple reason that it threw everything into the hands of the Germans and cut out all of the other nations.

Mr. Howe. How would that have been brought about by the language of the article?

Gen. Waller. Because the article they wished to adopt permitted the acquisition of real property after a residence of five years. What I wished to put in, and what was finally put in, was after a residence of five years after the enactment of this article.

Mr. Howe. Did you have any instructions from the United States Government as to what it wanted in the constitution?

Gen. Waller. A general outline, and communications were held also with the Haitian Government, through their minister here in Washington, and through our minister.

Mr. Howe. Through what channels did you get this outline of which you speak?

Gen. Waller. From the State Department, through the Navy Department, and also through the minister. Sometimes a dispatch would come which would tell me to confer with him on the subject.

Mr. Howe. Did you take up these discussions of the new constitution independently of our diplomatic representative?

Gen. Waller. We were all together.

Mr. Howe. In what capacity, General, were you in those discussions?

Gen. Waller. I was in the capacity of commander of the occupation—that is, the expeditionary forces. It was rather difficult to say exactly what the minister's position was.

Mr. Howe. You spoke about this one clause in the constitution, as originally drafted, being advantageous to the Germans?

Gen. Waller. Yes.

Mr. Howe. Was that because there were more Germans of long residence there?

Gen. Waller. That, and the fact that under the Haitian laws the Haitian woman has control of her own estate, and the Germans married the Haitians.

Mr. Howe. Rather more than nationals from other countries?

Gen. Waller. I do not know of any others at all.

Mr. Howe. Except Germans?

Gen. Waller. I say I do not. I do know of one American; but that is the only instance I know of.

Mr. Howe. Are we to understand, then, that there were more Germans there who had had a long residence?

Gen. Waller. They have had a long residence, and, under that clause, they would have had a very great advantage over any other nation.

Mr. Howe. Had you any reason to suppose that that clause in that form was inspired by Germans?

Gen. Waller. I think that everything that was against us was inspired by them; I mean as far as the treaty and as far as the constitution was concerned.

Mr. Howe. What, if any, efforts were made to improve sanitary conditions under the occupation?

Gen. Waller. We originally started in with a house-to-house inspection to clean up each town. Port au Prince, I think, took about two months to clean up. We built incinerators in many parts of the town, and we compelled them to bring their refuse to these incinerators and burn it; and I must say that after they saw the operation, they did so very, very willingly.

Mr. Howe. Elsewhere were there operations?

Gen. Waller. Elsewhere the same thing.

Mr. Howe. How about out in the country, in the smaller towns?

Gen. Waller. In the smaller towns, when the gendarmes were located in them they were required to do the same thing.

Mr. Howe. But that was later on when the gendarmes got in there?

Gen. Waller. Yes; after we had the forces distributed. After we had the gendarmes organized and had them large enough, we distributed them throughout the smaller towns.

Mr. Howe. Did the natives take kindly to this operation on the part of the occupation to make the conditions more sanitary?

Gen. Waller. Wonderfully well, I thought.

Mr. Howe. Did any friction develop out of these sanitary regulations?

Gen. Waller. None whatever. In one case we built a rest house so that the women who were coming in from the interior would have a place to rest at night, at the end of the day's march, you know, when their animals, if they had any, were cared for. There was a guard put there to protect these people, and I do not know when I have ever seen as much gratitude shown as was shown by these people.

Mr. Howe. Would you regard that as a sanitary measure?

Gen. Waller. Absolutely.

Mr. Howe. A rest house for the market women?

Gen. Waller. Yes.

Mr. Howe. What was the condition of the prisons at the time of the occupation and what, if any, efforts were made to improve the conditions?

Gen. Waller. When we first got there, of course, they had not yet removed the bodies from the prison where they had a massacre of 150 people in their cells. They put them in one large room and fired on them until they was no more movement at all, and about 150 of them were killed. It became necessary to practically rebuild this prison, reventilate it, put in water and other sanitary measures, establish the kitchen, because before they had to get their food in any way they could, and of course we fed them.

Mr. Howe. Did feeding the prisoners represent a change in prison management?

Gen. Waller. Very much. That was one of the reasons why so many volunteered to be prisoners, you know, when the workmen were being brought in from the street.

Mr. Howe. What I was trying to find out was did the Haitians before the occupation feed their prisoners?

Gen. Waller. No. They allowed their families to feed them, but gave them nothing themselves.

Mr. Howe. In general, what was the condition of the prisons outside of Port au Prince, if you know?

Gen. WALLER. It was very much the same as the others, except they were about as sanitary as the old-fashioned pigsty.

Mr. HOWE. Was that sanitary condition in the prisons remedied to any extent under the occupation?

Gen. WALLER. The prisons were made models.

Mr. HOWE. What about the prison records, I mean as to the length of time the people would remain in prison, and the records of prisoners on hand under the Haitians?

Gen. WALLER. They were kept in each prison.

Mr. HOWE. Under the Haitians, I mean.

Gen. WALLER. I do not think there was any. I never heard of it.

Mr. HOWE. Were such records instituted under the occupation?

Gen. WALLER. Yes; very complete records, and the same was true about the hospitals.

Mr. HOWE. There was an improvement in the hospitals, was there, under the Americans?

Gen. WALLER. Yes.

Mr. HOWE. Or attempt to improve them?

Gen. WALLER. We took over the hospitals, for instance, at Port au Prince. I think there were 20 or 30 people in there. When I left there must have been two or three hundred who were coming there for treatment every day, surgical operations, etc. They were carried on by American doctors.

Mr. HOWE. What funds were made available for the hospitals?

Gen. WALLER. Haitian funds for the Haitian hospital. Of course, our own hospitals were financed out of our own funds from the Navy appropriations.

Mr. HOWE. Were native Haitians treated in the Navy hospitals supported by United States funds?

Gen. WALLER. That was not allowed, except in an emergency case. If an accident happened and a man was brought in, near a hospital, he would receive first aid there, and be transported by ambulance down to the native hospital.

Mr. HOWE. Did the Navy personnel do anything in the way of care of the sick of the natives?

Gen. WALLER. In the native hospitals?

Mr. HOWE. In the native hospitals.

Gen. WALLER. Yes; they had hospital apprentices, stewards, and all of the medical officers. There was an American medical officer in charge of the hospital, of course; the native doctor practiced there also.

Mr. HOWE. Did the gendarmerie have anything to do with the care of the sick, or hospital assistance, or anything of that sort?

Gen. WALLER. Only in bringing them in. They had nothing to do with it outside, except in the country, where they had a medical officer attached. Then they looked out for them.

Mr. HOWE. The gendarmerie did?

Gen. WALLER. Yes.

Mr. HOWE. Looked out for the sick Haitians?

Gen. WALLER. Yes. We had a great deal of difficulty at first in getting them into the hospitals. The voodoo practice had been very general, and, of course, they told these people that our idea was to get them in there and torture them, and do all sorts of things, so that even in the case of those we picked up wounded, those that they could not hide away from us, they resisted going to the hospitals, but we had a great deal more trouble getting them out of the hospitals afterwards.

Mr. HOWE. Did the practice of voodoo have any influence on the course of events down there during the occupation, or was it a thing to be reckoned with?

Gen. WALLER. Yes; it had a wonderful effect over the peasants and the lower class of the people, and had some over the higher classes. It is against the Haitian law, this practice, but they never enforced the law. We did, and we broke up all their meetings, seized all of their drums, etc., and wherever a voodoo drum was heard we immediately got on the trail and captured it, and broke it up, as far as we could.

Mr. HOWE. What was the voodoo drum used for, in connection with what?

Gen. WALLER. In calling them to these meetings, in the first place, and also in the dances that they had. They used three or four or five drums. Some of the drums were 5 feet high, and as big around. It is a wooden log, hollowed out, with a cowhide over the top.

Mr. Howe. What is voodoo?

Gen. Waller. It is very difficult to say exactly what it is. It comes really from the West Coast of Africa originally.

Mr. Howe. Of what does it consist?

Gen. Waller. There it consists in the belief that human sacrifice was a cure for all evils, but I do not think that human sacrifice had been resorted to in Haiti for some years, but they do sacrifice the goat and sheep, and they do it in a very cruel way.

Mr. Howe. In general, with respect to the material side of life down there, what was the effort of the American occupation?

Gen. Waller. Uplifting in every direction. That was our attitude toward them.

Mr. Howe. That was your aim?

Gen. Waller. Absolutely so. I am sorry that I have not a copy of an address that was made to them there when I came away to show you exactly what the attitude we had toward them was. Home influence in Haiti is unknown. Adopting the same mode of expression that the French did, they refer to the communities as the families, and as long as there is peace in the families there is peace in the communities, but I am sorry to say that the majority of the men down there, even the educated men, paid comparatively little attention to the family.

Mr. Angell. Did I understand you correctly this morning, General, to say that Bobo had been made president by the Cacos?

Gen. Waller. They called him president.

Mr. Angell. That was simply their declaration of an entirely informal election or nomination?

Gen. Waller. It had been the usual form they adopted.

Mr. Angell. You did not mean that remark to be understood that there had been a formal election under the Haitian constitution of Bobo as President?

Gen. Waller. No.

Mr. Angell. You spoke of the conditions when you arrived and first landed in Port au Prince in August, 1915, as being those of threatening disturbances. Apart from battle casualties during these disturbances were there ever any Americans or foreigners killed or molested, to your knowledge?

Gen. Waller. No; only Haitians.

Mr. Angell. At the very beginning of your testimony, when you were giving the dates of your tour in Haiti, you spoke of coming back to the United States in December, 1916, and having had a conference with the State Department?

Gen. Waller. Yes.

Mr. Angell. Can you tell us briefly what those conferences were and what reports, if any you made, and what officials you saw?

Gen. Waller. The official was the one who is in charge of the Latin American Bureau.

Maj. McClellan. Sumner Wells?

Gen. Waller. No; Wright. He is now the secretary of the embassy in London.

Mr. Howe. Butler Wright?

Gen. Waller. Yes; Butler Wright. He had charge of that department of the State Department, but the consultation was largely at that time in connection with the organization of the gendarmerie.

Mr. Angell. Did you consult with Mr. Lansing?

Gen. Waller. No; only through Wright.

Mr. Angell. With President Wilson?

Gen. Waller. No.

Mr. Angell. Did you discuss the affairs of Haiti with Mr. Daniels?

Gen. Waller. Yes; to some extent. I do not recall what, though, because he had really no jurisdiction over those affairs, over the State Department affairs, but I had been ordered up here by the Navy Department for this consultation with the State Department.

Mr. Angell. And the consultation was chiefly regarding the gendarmerie organization?

Gen. Waller. They were regarding the gendarmerie, yes.

Mr. Angell. Coming now to the operations in the fall of 1915 against the Cacos, the campaign which was conducted, do you know whether Admiral Caperton received, on or about the 20th of November, 1915, an order or message from the Secretary of the Navy informing him that the Navy Department was strongly impressed with the number of Haitians killed, and felt that a severe lesson had been taught the Cacos, and believed that a proper control could be maintained to preserve order and protect innocent persons without further offensive operations, this appearing on page 78 of the printed record?

Gen. WALLER. Did I know of that message?

Mr. ANGELL. Yes, sir.

Gen. WALLER. Yes; my own radio picked that up.

Mr. ANGELL. Was that message then communicated to you by Admiral Caperton?

Gen. WALLER. Yes; but I picked it up before he did.

Mr. ANGELL. It was communicated to you, however, officially by Admiral Caperton?

Gen. WALLER. Yes; but we appealed from that because the campaign had not been completed. I wanted to finish it successfully and capture another town which I stated could be done, I thought, without firing a shot, but the answer was that I was to cease all hostile operations. The town, however, surrendered. The commanding general met me outside, and he surrendered without firing a shot, but the message I remember very, very distinctly, for the simple reason that we soldiers who have taught and trained our men as we have, and lived with them and go through all the hardships that they do, resent very much, indeed, the fact that it is always the enemy's casualties that are spoken of and pitied and not those to our own people.

Mr. ANGELL. What had been the casualties of our own personnel down to that time, do you remember?

Gen. WALLER. Approximately, about 45, I think.

Mr. ANGELL. Of those how many were killed?

Gen. WALLER. I do not recall exactly; probably 10 or 12 killed, and some died afterwards. Others would have died but for our medical care.

Mr. ANGELL. You said that Bobo was opposed to the Dartiguenave Government. Did he ever make a statement to you why he was opposed to the Dartiguenave Government?

Gen. WALLER. He never made a statement. I think everybody knew that he wanted to be President. Zamor would have been the same way.

Mr. ANGELL. What was Bobo's attitude toward the presence of the United States forces in Haiti, if you know?

Gen. WALLER. When he was at Port au Prince at the meeting of the Senate— I think when he was elected—I was not there, but after my arrival I saw him on one or two occasions and he was very much depressed, but he was perfectly free to go and come wherever he chose.

Mr. ANGELL. You say when he was elected?

Gen. WALLER. When Dartiguenave was elected.

Mr. ANGELL. Did Bobo ever express to you opposition to the presence of the United States forces in Haiti?

Gen. WALLER. No.

Mr. ANGELL. Do you know whether he was publically or personally opposed to our presence there?

Gen. WALLER. Only from the attitude of these people in the north.

Mr. ANGELL. Would that lead you to believe that he was opposed?

Gen. WALLER. Yes; he was communicating with them. After he left Haiti he went to Jamaica, and from Jamaica to Cuba. I was communicated with from Cuba concerning him.

Gen. ANGELL. Is he still alive; do you know?

Gen. WALLER. I do not know. He probably is. He was a comparatively young man.

Mr. ANGELL. Referring again to the campaign which was conducted in the fall of 1915 against the Cacos, did you regard the opposition of these Cacos to be one against the Haitian Government or against the American occupation?

Gen. WALLER. Their own statements were that it was against both the Haitian Government and the occupation.

Mr. ANGELL. Speaking practically, were our troops down there engaged in warfare against these Cacos during this period?

Gen. WALLER. It depends on what you call warfare. Actual war had not been declared. We were operating under the agreement. Naturally, when you get into an engagement of that kind both sides think there is war going on, although it is not formally declared.

Mr. ANGELL. Did you receive, on or about the end of March or early in April, 1916, a letter from the Secretary of the Navy, which appears as paragraph 144 of the Barnett report, attached as an exhibit to the report of the Secretary of the Navy for 1920, one paragraph of which, No. 2, reads as follows:

"Col. Waller, during the operations of October and November in north Haiti, with the expeditionary force of marines and seamen from the squadron, effectively crushed all armed resistance to the American occupation and the Haitian Government, and has maintained peace and order in all parts of the country."

Gen. WALLER. I did not receive this, but I did receive a letter from the Secretary of the Navy of commendation and congratulation. This is a letter that was addressed by Gen. Barnett to the Secretary. The letter the Secretary sent me was very much shorter, the letter of commendation and congratulation was very much shorter, and I think you have the speech of the President, giving me the thanks of the Haitian Government.

Mr. ANGELL. There are one or two points I want to ask you about in connection with these campaign orders which have been presented to the committee to-day. I note in paragraph 1 of your letter of October 29, 1915, to Col. Cole, constituting the formal campaign order, I take it, the Cacos are referred to as rebels, the language reading:

"The following disposition of troops is directed preparatory to the movement against rebels in the vicinity of Fort Capois, and the forces indicated must be in the positions indicated at the time specified below:"

You regarded the Cacos as rebels, both against the Haitian Government and against the American occupation?

Gen. WALLER. They were so designated by the President in communications with me. He spoke of them as the rebels.

Mr. ANGELL. President Dartiguenave?

Gen. WALLER. Yes.

Mr. ANGELL. The purpose of my question was to find out whether or not you regarded the Cacos as rebels both against the Haitian Government and the American occupation?

Gen. WALLER. I regarded them as violating the agreement of the Caco generals, and regarded them more or less as bandits, and I stated they would be treated as such.

Mr. ANGELL. Did you or did you not regard them as rebels both against the Haitian Government and against the American occupation?

Gen. WALLER. They were absolutely opposed to the American occupation forces. Those forces were what the Dartiguenave government was using.

Mr. ANGELL. Do you remember the letter of instructions for the campaign against the Cacos, which seems to be attached to these so-called campaign orders? Was that drawn up by you, or under your direction?

Gen. WALLER. Under my direction; written by my adjutant general.

Mr. ANGELL. And formed a part of the instructions and orders which went out at that time?

Gen. WALLER. Yes.

Mr. ANGELL. On page 2 of this letter of instructions, as so headed, under the paragraph "Sanitary arrangements," I find this language:

"1. Medical Corps will be prepared to care for wounded on firing line, at all bases, and transport them via Grande Riviere or Carncol routes to the U. S. S. Connecticut. Stretchers will be prepared and will be carried by natives, who will be impressed if possible to hire."

What was the intention of giving such an order? Was it, as the language seems to imply, that they were to be compelled to carry stretchers if they would not voluntarily agree to do so?

Gen. WALLER. They certainly were. I would give them an opportunity to do so willingly, but when we were there to protect them I was going to make them do something to aid themselves.

Mr. ANGELL. Do you know, General, whether or not it was necessary to impress the natives as stretcher bearers?

Gen. WALLER. No; we had a number of volunteers when the occasion arose. We never at any time had to use stretcher bearers to carry the wounded back. In the operations in the mountains the wounded men were carried on horseback or by their own people.

Mr. ANGELL. Referring now to the treaty negotiations, the negotiations which preceded the signature to the treaty on September 16, 1915, you said this morning, if I understood you correctly, that there was a verbal agreement prior to the signature of the treaty for the taking over of the customs?

Gen. WALLER. Yes, sir.

Mr. ANGELL. Do you know who made such an agreement, and when and where?

Gen. WALLER. President Dartiguenave and the minister and Admiral Caperton.

Mr. ANGELL. The American minister?

Gen. WALLER. Yes.

Mr. ANGELL. President Dartiguenave agreed to the taking over of the customs?

Gen. WALLER. Yes.

Mr. ANGELL. That was after his election as President?

Gen. WALLER. Oh, yes.

Mr. ANGELL. Were you present at the meeting when that was agreed on, or was it just a meeting between the admiral, the minister, and the President?

Gen. WALLER. I do not know that I was present at the original meeting, but I was present one time when it was clearly understood, at any rate.

Mr. ANGELL. And the President consented?

Gen. WALLER. Yes. He subsequently wrote a communication to others that it was a dreadful thing for us to do.

Mr. ANGELL. Do you remember his proclamation, as published at Port au Prince, in the early days of September, 1915, protesting specifically against the taking over of the customs at Port au Prince?

Gen. WALLER. Yes.

Mr. ANGELL. That was published, was it not?

Gen. WALLER. That was published; yes. We also knew what his agreement was at that time. You will find the same attitude, as far as martial law was concerned.

Mr. ANGELL. I am glad you mentioned that point, General. Admiral Caperton, on the stand, testified that President Dartiguenave had either requested or consented in advance to the declaration of martial law. He said he, Admiral Caperton, was unable to remember the circumstances under which that request or consent was given. Do you remember those circumstances?

Gen. WALLER. Very distinctly, because the request was most urgent.

Mr. ANGELL. Was it made to you, or, if not, to whom?

Gen. WALLER. It was made in my presence; it was made to the admiral. Admiral Caperton did not wish to proclaim martial law.

Mr. ANGELL. Do you remember when it was made?

Gen. WALLER. When this request was made?

Mr. ANGELL. Yes.

Gen. WALLER. At different times, from 10 days to 2 weeks before the proclamation was actually issued.

Mr. ANGELL. In the President's palace, or where?

Gen. WALLER. In the palace; that is the one he was occupying at that time, the temporary palace.

Mr. ANGELL. Was it held that the customs constituted the chief or practically the exclusive source of national funds?

Gen. WALLER. Yes. They have very little internal taxation; it is almost all from the export and import duties.

Mr. ANGELL. Did the great proportion of the internal taxes go to the local communes?

Gen. WALLER. They were supposed to go there.

Mr. ANGELL. It did not come to the National Government?

Gen. WALLER. No; it was not paid at any time to our representative.

Mr. ANGELL. Is it a fair statement to say, for example, that over 90 per cent of the national revenues came from the customs receipts?

Gen. WALLER. I do not know exactly. I have no means of reckoning what their receipts were for licenses, and things of that sort, merchants' licenses, and other little taxes of that kind, but there was no tax on real estate. Their charges for water and that sort of thing were practically nil, and very few of the aristocrats paid any bills at all we found when we took over the water.

Mr. ANGELL. Is it substantially true, however, that the great proportion of the national funds came from the customs?

Gen. WALLER. Yes.

Mr. ANGELL. Did you say, in your testimony this morning, General, that there was no compulsion on the Dartiguenave Government to induce the signing of the treaty which was signed in September, and subsequently ratified in October and November by the two chambers?

Gen. WALLER. I never heard of any. I never dreamed there was any such thing going on. I knew the trouble we were having in different discussions.

Mr. ANGELL. Would you not regard the seizure of the customs funds and the withholding of the funds derived from the customs as compulsion exercised on the Government?

Gen. WALLER. Why should it be? We were paying the regular salaries they got right along.

Mr. ANGELL. Did we pay them at first salaries?

Gen. WALLER. We paid them afterwards. We found out some of the salaries were not being paid.

Mr. ANGELL. And we paid the salaries until after the treaty was ratified?

Gen. WALLER. Oh, yes. That is the salaries of the Haitian officials. There was no salary paid to the legislative branch, after their prorogation.

Mr. ANGELL. At this point, may it please the chairman, I want to offer specifically in evidence certain messages appearing in this compilation, which have not yet been referred to at any point specifically in the testimony.

Senator ODDIE. Is that in the record at all?

Mr. ANGELL. I have never been able to find out whether this whole compilation is per se and verbatim in the record. I should imagine not, because it includes, for example, practically all the Barnett report, and a good deal of other matter which would probably not be necessary to print, to the extent of 260 long typewritten pages. I think it has been the practice hitherto to offer specifically certain parts of this, or various messages In fact, Senator McCormick himself on one or two occasions read into the record various messages out of this compilation. I want at this time also to have in evidence, specifically as bearing upon the testimony we are just having regarding the negotiation of the treaty and the ratification of it. certain messages appearing in this compilation.

Senator ODDIE. Well, there will be no objection to that.

Mr. ANGELL. Specifically, then, I wish to offer in evidence the message appearing on page 47 of this compilation, from Admiral Caperton to the Secretary of the Navy, on September 14, where he says that in order to assure prompt ratification, the Haitian Government desires immediate assurances in such shape as to be effective for use in Chamber of Deputies to the effect that the United States will exercise its good offices to obtain a temporary loan of $1,500,000 from the Haitian Government to cover expenses, and goes on to ask authorization for that.

(The message referred to is here printed in full, as follows:)

"In conversation held between ministers foreign affairs and finance on one hand and American chargé d'affaires and Paymaster Charles Gonard, my representative, on the other hand; it was agreed that the treaty, now being translated into French, would be signed and ratified and modus vivendi entered into.

"In order to assure prompt ratification Haitian Government desires immediate assurances in such shape as to be effective for use in Chamber of Deputies to the effect that the United States will exercise its good offices to obtain a temporary loan of $1,500,000 for the Haitian Government to cover expenses, first, for approximately three months, pending settlement of details of receivership, and, second, back salaries and unpaid expenses. Of this sum $500,000 is estimated as necessary for covering first head and $1,000,000 for second.

"In connection with amount last mentioned the Haitian Government will agree to refrain from emitting paper to value of 5,000,000 gourdes, not authorized, of which 500,000 gourdes are said to be now in transit.

"In view of the fact that the collection of practically all the revenues after deduction made by me in accordance Navy Department radiogram 20018, August, will for some time yet not be sufficient to meet current expenses of the Haitian Government, especially as funds should remain in national bank to move coffee crops, and as the Haitian Government has at present insufficient funds available to meet these expenses; I recommend that the assurances be given as above requested.

"Opinion was expressed by United States representative to effect that bonded indebtedness will be consolidated into one loan including temporary loan referred to above and back unpaid interest on public debt. Confirmation of this is requested. 28414.

"CAPERTON."

Mr. ANGELL. I wish to offer in evidence also that message of Admiral Caperton on the following day, September 15, to the Secretary of the Navy, where he informed the Secretary that if definite assurances can be given

Haitian Government, that work on national railroad will commence immediately after ratification of treaty, such assurances will aid materially in securing ratification.

I wish to offer also specifically certain messages appearing on pages 53 and 54 of this compilation, particularly one from Admiral Caperton to the Secretary of the Navy, of October 3, in which he refers to a message from the chargé d'affaires, saying, " I approve request and consider Haitian Government should have immediate financial assistance."

(The message referred to is here printed in full, as follows:)

"Chargé consulted with me before sending his telegram of to-day, and in view of all the facts as they appear here I approve request and consider Haitian Government should have immediate financial assistance. Will report more fully to-morrow and submit estimates of receipts and expenditures.   21303.
                                                                                                   " CAPERTON."

Mr. ANGELL. I also wish to offer a long message on pages 53 and 54, from Davis, the chargé d'affairs, presumably through Admiral Caperton, to the Navy Department.

Gen. WALLER. That, I think, went direct to the State Department.

Mr. ANGELL. Was it customary to radio up direct to the State Department?

Gen. WALLER. They sometimes sent a radio in the State Department code.

Mr. ANGELL. Without reading all of this, I simply wish to call the attention of the committee here to one or two paragraphs in the message, where it says he told the President, that, as before stated, funds would be immediately available upon ratification of the treaty.

"The President seemed utterly discouraged and pointed out once more that the delay was not due to any lack of effort by himself or his cabinet, that withholding of funds only gave another weapon to the opposition and that if the United States Government persists on withholding all funds, ratification becomes so difficult that he and his cabinet will resign rather than attempt the fight in the Senate under this handicap."

Also a further paragraph, in which Mr. Davis says:

"It is most important that the present administration remain in power, as it is not believed that one more favorable to the United States could be obtained, and in view of all the facts as they appear here that a military government would probably have to be established should this Government fall."

(The message referred to is here printed in full, as folows:)

"Confidential, urgent, October 3, 5 p. m. This morning at 10 and before receipt of your October 2, 5 p. m., I had an interview with the President personally at his request. He stated that he had asked for this interview in order to ascertain what steps he could take under existing conditions, that the Haitien Government following its plan to pay back salaries and thereby strengthen its position before the people and relieve suffering, now finds itself entirely without funds, and inquired as to the disposition of the United States Government to assist them in this financial crisis. I told him that I expected instructions as to the matter and would advise him on receipt thereof.

"After receiving your October 2, 5 p. m., I told the President that as before stated funds would be immediately available upon ratification of the treaty. The President seemed utterly discouraged and pointed out once more that the delay was not due to any lack of effort by himself or his cabinet, that withholding of funds only gave another weapon to the opposition, and that if the United States Government persists on withholding all funds ratification becomes so difficult that he and his cabinet will resign rather than attempt the fight in the Senate under this handicap.

" I fear that I have failed in my previous reports to make perfectly understood the existing situation, which is as follows: The vote on ratification by the deputies will take place probably to-morrow, the committee having unanimously recommended ratification. Under the mode of procedure after ratification by congressmen the treaty goes before the Senate and there it is referred to a senate committee who, after considering, submit a report which is then printed and distributed and three days allowed for consideration before discussing on the floor of the Senate begins. Therefore ratification can not be expected before the latter part of next week.

" The President and cabinet are using every possible effort to secure ratification and seem confident of securing the same if not embarrassed financially. The Hait'an Government realizes that such ratification is absolutely necessary for the welfare of Haiti. Opposition in the Senate is strong, due to the fact that many senators are unscrupulous politicians or fanatics and wish either to embarrass the United States by nonratificat on or to overthrow the present administration, hoping to secure possible personal gain thereby. Pressure is also being brought to bear by outside interests which desire a continuance of past cond'tions for reasons of financial gain and which will be glad to see the present administration, which is already reorganized and supporte l by the United States, forced to resign.

"It is most important that the present administration remain in power, as it is not believed that one more favorable to the United States could be obtained, and in view of all the facts as they appear here that a military government would probably have to be established should this government fall.

"Inasmuch as it is necessary to secure a treaty ratified before any definite financial plan can be formulated or permanent peace and prosperity assured in Hait', it would seem advisable to support and maintain the present admin-lstration, which will fail unless the slight financial assistance which they have requested is immediately available, and further the progress made during the last two months w'll be lost. Although funds collected from customs have been expended for the first three purposes named in the department's instructions as to use of money collected, not one cent has been turned over to the Haitian Government for living expenses, which expenses have been met by use of gourdes then on hand and not expended. In view of the importance and the extreme urgency of the case, it is recommended that Admiral Caperton be instructed to turn over needed sums out of customs receipts not necessary for the customs service, constabulary, and public works. Request earliest possible decision and reply.

" DAVIS.

" OCTOBER 3, 1915."

Mr. ANGELL. I also wish to offer a message on page 55 from Admiral Caperton to the Secretary of the Navy, of which the last paragraph reads:

" In view of present financial crisis of Dartiguenave government, the loss of prestige of United States should that government fall, the inevitably detrimental effect upon the treaty the fa lure of that government will have, I reiterate my concurrence in the recommendation of the American charge d'affaires that I be allowed to turn over to the Dartiguenave government such funds from the customs receipts on hand and unobligated as I may consider necessary for its support."

(The message referred to is here printed in full, as follows:)

" 14002 and 20018, August. Total customs receipts Haiti to September 30, $170,000. Total expend tures $31,500, under following heads: Constabulary, $1,500; public works, $9,000; customhouse expenditures, $5,000; military and civil government, $16,000, which covers expenditures made necessary by military and public policies in ports occupied by Un'ted States, such cost of electric lighting, expenses of provost martial, prisons, and hospitals. No funds have been given to Dartiguenave government.

" Estimate for October under heads " Constabulary," " Public works," " Customhouse expenses," " Military and civil government," amounts to $62,000. Increase due to added expense of constabulary now being introduced as rapidly as possible and to all ports being occupied for entire month. Unobligated balance of customs funds, $76,000.

" In view of present financial crisis of Dartiguenave government, the loss of prestige of United States should that government fall, the inevitably detrimental effect upon the treaty the failure of that government will have, I reiterate my concurrence in the recommendation of the American charge d'affaires that I be allowed to turn over to the Dartiguenave government such funds from the customs receipts on hand and unobligated as I may consider necessary for its support. 18204.

" CAPERTON.

" OCTOBER 4, 1915."

Mr. ANGELL. I also wish to offer the following message from Secretary Daniels to Admiral Caperton, dated October 5, appearing on page 55 of this compilation:

" 23103. Cable has been sent this date to Charde with full instructions. You are authorized to furnish Haitian Government weekly amount necessary to meet current expenses. Use funds collected Haitian customs. Question payment back salary will be settled by department immediately after ratification of treaty. Report what weekly expenditure w ll be necessary under these instructions ; what is full amount back salar'es now unpaid. Acknowledge. 22004.

" DANIELS."

Do you know, General, whether the back salaries actually were paid until after the ratification of the treaty? Just to refresh your recollection, if necessary, the treaty was ratified in December.

Gen. WALLER. I do not think they were. I recall an interview with Vincent, who came to my office to see about the back salary for himself and. I think, his brother.

Mr. ANGELL. Vincent was president of the Senate?

Gen. WALLER. Yes; and also the secretary of the interior. H's brother, I think, had been the minister to Belgium. He thought it was a great hardship that he should be over there without any money, and he wanted me to pay him when the Haitian Government had dismissed h'm. Naturally we did not take up the question; that is, we declined to pay it.

Mr. ANGELL. Do you know whether, as a matter of fact, the back salaries ever were paid until after the ratification of the treaty?

Gen. WALLER. No.

Mr. ANGELL. You do not know?

Gen. WALLER. No. The salaries we paid were the salaries of the people who were working after we took it up.

Mr. ANGELL. I also wish to call attention on the record at this time to the paragraph on page 63 of this compilation, which seems to be a paraphrase from a message from the Secretary of the Navy, reading here as follows:

"On October 18. 1915, the Secretary of the Navy authorized Rear Admiral Caperton to establish a weekly allowance of $23,000 for the present as recommended."

On that same page the further paraphrase, saying:

"On the same date (referring to October 19) the Secretary of the Navy was advised by Rear Admiral Caperton that he had authorized the payment of salaries from customs funds to senators and deputies for the current month."

I wish at this time also, with the consent of the committee, to offer upon the record the messages appearing on page 65 of this compilation, the long one from Secretary Daniels dated November 10, 1915, being numbered 22010, to Admiral Caperton, apparently. I should say the treaty was ratified by the Senate on November 11, Armistice Day, 1915. This message from Secretary Daniels to Admiral Caperton is dated November 10, the day before. It reads as follows:

"28109. Arrange with President Dartiguenave that he call a cabinet meeting before the session of senate which will pass upon ratification of treaty and request that you be permitted to appear before that meeting to make a statement to President and to members of cabinet. On your own authority state the following before these officers: 'I have the honor to inform the President of Haiti and the members of his cabinet that I am personally gratified that public sentiment continues favorable to the treaty; that there is a strong demand from all classes for immediate ratification, and that the treaty will be ratified Thursday.

"'I am sure that you gentlemen will understand my sentiment in this matter and I am confident if the treaty fails of ratification that my Government has the intention to retain control in Haiti until the desired end is accomplished and that it will forthwith proceed to the complete pacification of Haiti so as to insure internal tranquillity necessary to such development of the country and its industry as will afford relief to the starving populace now unemployed. Meanwhile the present Government will be supported in the effort to secure stable conditions and lasting peace in Haiti, whereas those offering opposition can only expect such treatment as their conduct merits.

"'The United States Government is particularly anxious for immediate ratification by the present senate of this treaty, which was drawn up with the full intention of employing as many Haitians as possible to aid in giving effect to its provisions, so that suffering may be relieved at the earliest possible date.

"'Rumors of bribery to defeat the treaty are rife but are not believed. However, should they prove true, those who accept or give bribes will be vigorously prosecuted.

"'Confidential. It is expected that you will be able to make this sufficiently clear to remove all opposition and to secure immediate ratification. Acknowledge.' 22010.

"DANIELS."

There follows in this compilation a message from Admiral Caperton, dated November 11, presumably to the Secretary of the Navy, reading as follows:

"Carried out instructions in department's 22010 this forenoon. Treaty ratified by Senate by vote 26 to 7 at 6 p. m. to-day. General rejoicing among populace. 22111.

"CAPERTON."

· Finally, a message from Secretary Daniels, apparently, to Admiral Caperton, on November 12, the following day, reading as follows:

"22111· Department wishes to express its gratification at the ratification of the treaty and to warmly commend the able manner in which you have handled this important matter and the ability you have shown in directing affairs in Haiti. Acknowledge. 11012.

"DANIELS."

Were you present, General, at the interview which Admiral Caperton, according to these messages, seems to have had with the President and cabinet, in which he read them, on his own authority, this message from the Secretary of the Navy?

Gen. WALLER. Yes; at the palace, at the temporary palace, I mean.

Mr. ANGELL. Was that, do you remember, on the date of the ratification of the treaty by the Senate?

Gen. WALLER. I think that was the date.

Mr. ANGELL. Was anything else said, so far as you can remember, by Admiral Caperton?

Gen. WALLER. Oh, there was a general rejoicing. I think the chargé was there and several officers of the Navy.

Mr. ANGELL. Were any members of the Haitian Senate there?

Gen. WALLER. No.

Mr. ANGELL. Just the President and the cabinet?

Gen. WALLER. And the cabinet.

Mr. ANGELL. Did you have any discussion with the President or the members of the cabinet about the situation?

Gen. WALLER. I had nothing to do with it at all at that time.

Mr. ANGELL. Do you remember whether the minister had any discussion with the President and the cabinet at that meeting?

Gen. WALLER. I do not think so. I think all the talking was done by Admiral Caperton at the time.

Mr. ANGELL. Just how was it handled? Was it done through Capt. Beach, his chief of staff, and the interpreter?

Gen. WALLER. Capt. Beach was there, but Admiral Caperton made the talk.

Mr. ANGELL. In English?

Gen. WALLER. In English, and it was interpreted by the official interpreter.

Mr. ANGELL. Then and there?

Gen. WELLER. I think at that time it was a man whom I had supplied the President, because the cabinet refused to let him have an interpreter.

Mr. ANGELL. When I say then and there I mean the putting of this declaration into French was made at that time at that meeting, on the morning of the 11th, prior to the ratification of the treaty by the Senate?

Gen. WALLER. Yes.

Mr. ANGELL. Do you know whether or not, apart from the seizure of the customs and the customs receipts, there was any seizure by Admiral Caperton or the officers under his direction, of any national funds of the Haitian Government?

Gen. WALLER. I do not.

Mr. ANGELL. You do not know one way or the other?

Gen. WALLER. No.

Mr. ANGELL. The particular reason I asked you was that I asked that question of Admiral Caperton here in cross-examination, and he said he could not remember, but he did not think so. But Col. Alexander S. Williams, in testifying the other day, made a reference to the seizure of the Haitian national funds in such manner as to give me the belief that it was not the customs he was referring to.

Gen. WALLER. It would depend. In the first place, Williams would not know anything about it at that time. He must have referred to something else. Williams had nothing to do with any of the negotiations of either the treaty, or the constitutional work, or the organization of the gendarmerie.

Mr. ANGELL. Williams had nothing to do with the organization of the gendarmerie?

Gen. WALLER. He was simply on the board, the second member, I think, on the board. This board received its instructions and considered the suggestions that were sent out from my headquarters to them. I also received suggestions from them, and they were discussed.

Mr. ANGELL. Coming now, sir, to this proroguing, or dissolution, of the legislature in 1916, do you know whether or not, under the Haitian constitution, it was provided that the President could dissolve the legislature in the manner in which he did it by the decree of April 5, 1916?

Gen. WALLER. I do not think so.

Mr. ANGELL. You do not believe that the constitution gave the President that power?

Gen. WALLER. That was one of the reasons why I opposed it, but there might have been necessity for it.

Mr. ANGELL. Do you know whether or not that decree of April 5, 1916, was made the subject of court action in the native courts of Port au Prince at that time?

Gen. WALLER. It was made the subject of discussion with this corps of lawyers, and the President wrote me on the subject, stating that they were opposing him in every way, and wished me to take action, which I declined doing, but I interviewed them, and they assured me they would give every assistance in their power.

Mr. ANGELL. So far as you know or remember, then, there was no decree in the civil court of Port au Prince, about April 15, authorizing the deputies and senators to open the gates of the legislative building, on the ground of the alleged unconstitutionality of this decree?

Gen. WALLER. I do not remember it, but even if it had been issued no attention would have been paid to it.

Mr. ANGELL. Do you remember two lawyers, Luxembourg Cauvin and Edmond Lespinasse, coming to you about this decree and the question of the unconstitutionality of the decree?

Gen. WALLER. I remember a number of interviews that we had with Cauvin, Lespinasse, Bailly, and others, but this was after the legislature was closed.

Mr. ANGELL. That is some time subsequent to May?

Gen. WALLER. It followed almost immediately afterwards.

Mr. HOWE. The legislature was closed on April 6, was it not?

Mr. ANGELL. The decree was on April 6.

Gen. WALLER. It closed on that day, I think. I have a notice here from the dean to the deputies, by which I can fix that absolutely. My impression is that that meeting was on the 8th—two days afterwards.

Mr. ANGELL. What meeting, sir?

Gen. WALLER. With Cauvin, the first meeting I had with Cauvin.

Mr. ANGELL. On the 8th or 18th? The decree, I believe, was on the 15th of April.

Gen. WALLER. It was two or three days after the dissolution of the legislature.

Mr. ANGELL. After the President's decree?

Gen. WALLER. Yes.

Mr. ANGELL. Then, it would have been April 8?

Gen. WALLER. April 8 it would be.

Mr. ANGELL. The decree of the President was that of April 5?

Gen. WALLER. It is in here somewhere—a placard from the dean to the deputies.

Mr. ANGELL. I just suggest, General, it is not of sufficient importance, perhaps, to fix the date of this thing exactly. Perhaps we can proceed.

Mr. HOWE. What fact are you trying to fix? Perhaps we can stipulate on that.

Mr. ANGELL. I am just trying to find out what representations, if any, were made to the General by these Haitian lawyers about the alleged unconstitutionality of the decree.

Mr. HOWE. Can we not fix that by bringing up the question of how long before or how long after the decree was passed these representations were made?

Mr. ANGELL. There seems to be confusion somewhere, for the reason that the General has it in mind that he had this interview with these men—Cauvin and Lespinasse—three days after the President's decree, which would have been April 8. In the Haitian memoir the statement is made that the decree of the civil court authorizing the opening of the legislative chambers was obtained on the 15th of April, 10 days after the President's decree; thereupon these two lawyers went to the General with this decree.

Gen. WALLER. They came to me at that time, too; but, as I say, I had several interviews with them on the subject.

Mr. Howe. The witness has testified that he knows nothing of the decree anyhow.

Gen. Waller. I do not know anything of the decree having been issued at all, because I had told them I had received instructions.

Mr. Angell. Instructions from the President?

Gen. Waller. From the President.

Mr. Angell. And you would have carried those out, do I understand you rightly, whether there had been a court decree as to the unconstitutionality of the President's order, or otherwise?

Gen. Waller. Yes; as long as martial law existed.

Mr. Angell. Appearing on page 24 of the printed record, there are two letters that I would just like to ask you to look at, General, one of them being apparently, as printed here, from you to Mr. Laroche, dated April 27, and an apparent reply from him to you, dated April 28. I will ask you, for the purpose of identification, whether you sent and received those two letters. I am just asking you whether that is substantially correct.

Gen. Waller. That is substantially correct.

Mr. Angell. Those two letters?

Gen. Waller. I have not read Laroche's yet, but we were having a good deal of communication at that time.

Mr. Angell. I just want to identify these two letters, to show they were sent and received, there being no formal proof on that subject at all thus far.

Gen. Waller. Yes; that is correct.

Mr. Angell. Then may I consider that these two letters, as identified by the General, and stated by him to be substantially correct, as having been sent and received by him, are offered in the record as so identified. They are already parts of the printed record, but have never been identified or proved.

Gen. Waller. They were sent, and as the Government feared impeachment, that was the point I made there, that they were to consider those matters only.

Mr. Angell. Now, the specific order for the closing of the legislative chambers was received, as I understand it, by you from the President, and transmitted by you to Maj. Butler?

Gen. Waller. Yes.

Mr. Angell. The chief of the gendarmerie, for execution?

Gen. Waller. Yes.

Mr. Angell. How far was it customary, General, for you to receive and carry out orders from the President of Haiti?

Gen. Waller. They were not orders; they were always considered as requests and we usually discussed them beforehand. This was not discussed at this time, the date of his signing of this proclamation, becaue he knew I opposed it.

Mr. Angell. He transmitted it to you, with the request that it be enforced?

Gen. Waller. He transmitted it in a letter, in which he states that he relies upon me for my entire support in the preservation of order, inclosing at the same time a copy of the proclamation.

Mr. Angell. If that is not in the record already, I suggest that it be put in the record, the proclamation of April 5, dissolving the legislature.

Mr. Howe. If it is not in the record, I think it should be, and also the letter of the President, accompanying the proclamation.

(The letter referred to is here printed in full as follows, the proclamation having been introduced as a part of Admiral Caperton's testimony.)

PRIVATE OFFICE OF THE PRESIDENT OF HAITI,
Port au Prince, April 5, 1916.

To Col. LITTLETON W. T. WALLER,
City.

MY DEAR COLONEL: For the good of the Haitian people, the Government intends, with the indispensable aid of the occupation, to resolutely carry out the work of regeneration (uplifting) that it has begun. But, from the very outset as you yourself have witnessed, it has met with obstacles that have been thrown in its way by those who see in the new order of things the destruction of the baneful state of things which had served their selfish and personal ends.

Among the measures demanded by this state of things, I have decided, in accord with the members of the Government, to publish in to-day's official journal the two executive orders (decrees) of which I have inclosed a copy. I have added an expose setting forth the determining reasons which explain and justify said two orders. I must not let you ignore that a like communication had been made to Admiral Caperton and to Mr. Bailly-Blanchard.

After taking into consideration all possible contingencies, I am relying absolutely upon all your help to assure public order and security by paralyzing, if needs be, the evil actions of those who might wish to create popular agitation for their own personal advantage which they set above the public weal.

In the meantime, I send you, my dear colonel, the renewed assurances of my very cordial consideration.

DARTIGUENAVE.

Mr. ANGELL. Are we to understand, General, from your statement about the corvée law, that the natives flocked in to work upon the roads from the sole motive of their desire to see the roads improved?

Gen. WALLER. I presume so.

Mr. ANGELL. And that it was not the food and it was not the pay which they were after?

Gen. WALLER. No.

Mr. ANGELL. They were not paid and they were not fed?

Gen. WALLER. Some of them were paid, and a number of the people may have thought that there was the hope of advancement later.

Mr. ANGELL. Have you any idea, sir, how long these men were apt to continue to work in this manner without pay and without food?

Gen. WALLACE. When the repairs went through a district the people worked in that district.

Mr. ANGELL. Which would have been several weeks, upon the average?

Gen. WALLER. It depended largely upon the weather. You see, in the evenings, they had torrential downpours, and sometimes considerable work would be washed away that had been done during the day, if the work had not been completed.

Mr. ANGELL. Did the work continue in any given district on an average for a period of several weeks?

Gen. WALLER. Yes.

Mr. ANGELL. Sometimes several months, perhaps?

Gen. WALLACE. Yes. In the district of Port au Prince, for instance, we were working on both sides at the same time.

Mr. ANGELL. Now, sir, in reference to the new constitution, you said that with reference to the proposal for the acquisition of the right to acquire land by foreigners, that they were willing to put it in?

Gen. WALLER. I mean the Government.

Mr. ANGELL. The executive branch of the Government?

Gen. WALLER. Yes.

Mr. ANGELL. Did that apply to the constituent assembly?

Gen. WALLER. That had not met.

Mr. ANGELL. That had not met at the time you speak of?

Gen. WALLER. The Government, the plans they were formulating to put before the constituent assembly.

Mr. ANGELL. So the individuals who were willing to put this in were merely the Dartiguenave government?

Gen. WALLER. Yes.

Mr. ANGELL. That is the President and his cabinet?

Gen. WALLER. The President and his cabinet. There were some members, for instance, Camille Leon, the chairman of the deputies, who was in favor of it.

Mr. ANGELL. Had the conseil d'etat been organized at the time you are speaking of?

Gen. WALLER. During the discussion?

Mr. ANGELL. At the time of the discussion of the proposed new treaty?

Gen. WALLER. Partially so; yes. He requested them to serve on this.

Mr. ANGELL. Was there any authorization for such a body in the constitution, if you know, any authorization for the body of the conseil d'etat?

Gen. WALLER. I think so; either in that or the prior constitution.

Mr. ANGELL. The constitution which was then in force was the constitution of 1889, was it not?

Gen. WALLER. Yes. I say either that or the one before. I have forgotten which of the two; but they had ample authority for it, it seems to me.

Mr. ANGELL. After the treaty went into effect in June, 1916, by ratification of this treaty by the United States Senate, was there any single responsible American, civil or military, head in Haiti or was it a responsibility divided among a number of military and civilian representatives?

Gen. WALLER. Financial affairs were controlled by the financial adviser, who was appointed under the treaty.

Mr. ANGELL. To whom did he report in this country?

Gen. WALLER. The State Department, I presume.

Mr. ANGELL. To whom did the receiver general of customs report?

Gen. WALLER. To the financial adviser.

Mr. ANGELL. To whom did the commander of the brigade—yourself, for example—report?

Gen. WALLER. When anything arose to report it was sent in duplicate, one to the commander in chief of the cruiser squadron of the Atlantic Fleet and the other to Washington, to headquarters of the Marine Corps.

Mr. ANGELL. The brigade commander, of course, did not report to the State Department directly?

Gen. WALLER. No; except in personal communications.

Mr. ANGELL. To whom did the engineer of public works, the American official, report, if you know?

Gen. WALLER. His final appointment did not get there until after I left.

Mr. ANGELL. Until after you left, in November, 1916?

Gen. WALLER. Yes.

Mr. ANGELL. His office was provided for by the treaty?

Gen. WALLER. Yes; there were two engineers provided for. One of them was called the sanitary engineer and one called the public works engineer. I used up to that time my own engineer.

Mr. ANGELL. Do you know what accounting was made to the Haitien Government of the Haitien national funds by our civil and military representatives in Haiti, speaking, of course, up to the time that you left?

Gen. WALLER. Yes. The military, strictly speaking, had absolutely nothing to do with this, except to disburse the funds, except at the request of the financial adviser and the receiver general.

Mr. ANGELL. The military made no report or accounting to the Haitian Government; that was not their function?

Gen. WALLER. It was not their function.

Mr. ANGELL. Did the military or naval officers make any report to the Haitian Government prior to the appointment of the receiver general?

Gen. WALLER. I do not know whether Admiral Caperton did or not. I know the man who acted as receiver general made the reports to him.

Mr. ANGELL. To Admiral Caperton?

Gen. WALLER. To Admiral Caperton. I saw these reports from time to time, considering the resources. The budget was prepared each month, and it was necessary to see exactly what funds they had in hand.

Mr. ANGELL. I show you what purports to be, General, a copy of a letter from you, dated June 30, 1916, addressed to the American minister at Port au Prince, and ask you whether that is substantially accurate?

Gen. WALLER. Yes; I am sure that letter was written.

Mr. ANGELL. I would like to offer in evidence this letter, as identified by the general.

Gen. WALLER. I can relate to you why the letter was written.

Mr. ANGELL. I want to read this letter to the Senator.

(Mr. Angell thereupon read the letter referred to, as follows:)

HEADQUARTERS UNITED STATES EXPEDITIONARY FORCES
OPERATING IN HAITI.
Port au Prince, Haiti, June 30, 1916.

From: Expeditionary commander.
To: The American minister, Port au Prince, Haiti.
Subject: Public works.

1. Acknowledging and complying with your note of June 28, 1916, forwarding copy of a formal protest from minister of foreign affairs concerning the alleged beginning of certain public works by the occupation, I have the honor to state that I have already explained the status of the work to the department concerned.

2. The work in question is a continuation of work begun by us early in December, 1915. It became necessary for two reasons:

First. To furnish employment to starving Haitians.

Second. In order that there might be communication between towns, by land, for military as well as commercial purposes.

3. If, as stated by the minister of foreign affairs, the treaty has been in operation since May 3, 1916, I know nothing of it. I must receive my information through proper military channels before I can relax our established rules under which we have been operating.

4. I was not aware that the agreements had been signed; in fact, I have been informed that this Government would not agree to them.

LITTLETON W. WALLER.

I want to ask you, in this connection, if you remember when you were officially notified of the ratification by the United States of the treaty which is dated September 16, 1915?

Gen. WALLER. No; I do not recall the date.

Mr. ANGELL. You had not been notified at this time, on June 30, 1916, that the treaty had been ratified by the Senate on May 3, 1916?

Gen. WALLER. No; on the date of that letter I did not know the United States had ratified the treaty.

Mr. ANGELL. So that, so far as you, the brigade commander, was concerned, the treaty was not yet formally in effect?

Gen. WALLER. The Haitian Government had claimed from time to time the treaty had been in effect for months when it had not been ratified by our Government.

Mr. HOWE. When did the treaty become formally in effect, on its promulgation or ratification?

Mr. ANGELL. It was ratified on May 3, and I believe it was promulgated on the 3d of June.

Mr. HOWE. That is when it became effective, is it not?

Mr. ANGELL. That is a question of constitutional law. I do not think it came into effect at that time. Prior to that time there had been, had there not, a modus operandi?

Gen. WALLER. Yes.

Mr. ANGELL. Which was soon after or immediately following the signature of the original treaty in September?

Gen. WALLER. Frequently they had stated to me that they considered the treaty was in operation before our ratifying it.

Mr. ANGELL. The modus operandi was, however, in terms identical with the treaty, was it not, or substantially so?

Gen. WALLER. Not entirely so, because we had charge of public works at that time. It was after this that they made this claim. When this letter was written it was because they had sent an architect up to look out for the water supply of a suburb of Port au Prince, and he had driven away our public-works officer, and I had sent an officer up to him and apprehended him, and had communicated with the Government. They then wrote to the minister, and he wrote me on the subject, and I replied in that way. That was the cause of that.

Mr. ANGELL. When were the public works taken over by the occupation?

Gen. WALLER. We took them over at first.

Mr. ANGELL. In the early days of the occupation?

Gen. WALLER. In the fall of 1915. We took them over as soon as we took over the customs.

Mr. ANGELL. Was the occupation requested by the Dartiguenave government to take over the public works, or was that done as a matter of military necessity?

Gen. WALLER. It was done for military reasons, but it was done with the approval of the Dartiguenave government. Many suggestions came from them.

Mr. ANGELL. And the administration of public works was continued by the officers of the military occupation until the engineer provided for by the treaty was nominated and sent down to Haiti?

Gen. WALLER. Yes.

Mr. ANGELL. And was that prior, do you remember, to the time when you left in November, 1916?

Gen. WALLER. He came down just before I left, but he did not assume the office exactly. I think he was there probably a month or so.

Mr. ANGELL. So at the time you left in November, 1916?

Gen. WALLER. It had not been taken over.

Mr. ANGELL. The military officers of the occupation were still administering the public works?

Gen. WALLER. Yes.

Mr. ANGELL. What funds were being used for such expenses as were neces-sary?

Gen. WALLER. Haitian funds, of course. All of the expenses of the occupa-tion, you see, were paid for by our own Government.

Mr. ANGELL. When you say expenses of the occupation you mean the pay of the officers and men?

Gen. WALLER. House rent, supplies, transportation, and everything of that sort.

Mr. ANGELL. The building of roads, public works, sanitation, and such mat-ters, came——

Gen. WALLER. From the Haitian Government, the funds.

Mr. ANGELL. As administered by, first, our military representatives?

Gen. WALLER. Yes.

Mr. ANGELL. And then the receiver general and financial adviser?

Gen. WALLER. We had pretty much the same plan there that we did in Cuba, very much the same as we did in Mexico. In fact, that proclamation of martial law was almost identical with the one in Vera Cruz.

Mr. ANGELL. To what extent during the time you were brigade commander in Haiti did the American military forces interfere, if at all, with local municipal administration?

Gen. WALLER. We never interfered with them at all, except probably once in Port au Prince, when a man had been appointed or suspended by the President and a new man appointed, and there was a little resistance to his occupation of that office.

Mr. HOWE. What office was that, sir?

Gen. WALLER. It corresponded practically to mayor.

Mr. ANGELL. Was his name Auguste Magloire?

Gen. WALLER. Yes.

Mr. ANGELL. Was that the case?

Gen. WALLER. Yes.

Mr. ANGELL. Do you remember whether or not he was arrested and im-prisoned?

Gen. WALLER. He was arrested.

Mr. ANGELL. By whom, by the marines, or by the gendarmerie, or native court?

Gen. WALLER. I do not remember whether it was the marines or gendarmerie, but in either case he would have been arrested, because he drew a revolver on the incumbent in office.

Mr. ANGELL. He was the lawful incumbent in office, was he not?

Gen. WALLER. He was arrested for creating a disturbance and carrying a weapon, which he was not allowed to do.

Mr. ANGELL. Do you know how long he was imprisoned?

Gen. WALLER. A very short while. I do not remember whether it was over-night. He was released when the matter was brought to me.

Mr. ANGELL. Do you remember, General, the difficulties which seemed to have taken place regarding the proposal to place under the control of the gen-darmerie the telegraphs, telephones, public works, the lighthouse service, such as there may have been, and the postal service?

Gen. WALLER. The lighthouse service was always ours. The postal service and the postal telegraph was the principal thing.

Mr. ANGELL. Give us, General, in brief, that story, will you please?

Gen. WALLER. The proposition was made and accepted by President Darti-guenave and his Government. It was made because we would save the Govern-ment a very large sum of money, and we would give efficient service. We had our own experts, men who had operated everything in Vera Cruz for nine months without any hitch, or anything of that sort, and we were prepared to rebuild and carry the lines all the way through Haiti, so that communication could be correctly carried on. We also wished to stop the graft in the post office. The employees of the post office had stolen quite a large amount of money. The President said he would do this. He also asked for an engineer at the same time; that is, an additional engineer, and he told me that he would issue instructions to his minister in Washington that day. He failed to do so. I saw him the next day, when he made me a solemn promise.

Mr. ANGELL. Who made, the President?

Gen. WALLER. Yes. He then said that he would send the cable to the min-ister, and I informed him that I would be very glad to have it sent down by our messenger, but he had it coded and sent down, and it was exactly the reverse of his promise.

Mr. ANGELL. It was in code, was it?

Gen. WALLER. It was in code.

Mr. ANGELL. How could we tell it was exactly the reverse?

Gen. WALLER. Because it is our business to decipher any code. Very frequently it does not take them but a very few minutes to get hold of the most intricate code, either in the air or on the wire.

Mr. ANGELL. You were saying the message was exactly the reverse of what he promised?

Gen. WALLER. Yes; exactly the reverse; and when I went to him about it he said that there had been an error in coding it, but I told him I knew there had been no error and that I would be obliged to say to my Government that he was insincere and unstable; that his Government was insincere and unstable. The question of removing martial law had arisen, and I said, "Do you wish that done?" He said, "No; under no circumstances."

Mr. ANGELL. This all happened during the summer of 1916?

Gen. WALLER. Yes.

Mr. ANGELL. Early in August, was it not?

Gen. WALLER. Yes.

Mr. ANGELL. Was it finally agreed that these various services were to be put under control of the gendarmerie?

Gen. WALLER. Not at that time; no.

Mr. ANGELL. Subsequently it was agreed in the final gendarmerie agreement?

Gen. WALLER. That was a long time after.

Mr. ANGELL. After your departure?

Gen. WALLER. Yes.

Mr. ANGELL. So that you have no particular knowledge of the final accomplishment?

Gen. WALLER. I have no knowledge of that. In fact, I think it had hardly been done. I mean the postal service. It was not done at the time I left; that is, they had not been turned over to the gendarmerie. I believe that in a later agreement it was agreed to, but I do not think it had yet been done.

Mr. ANGELL. Was Mr. Augustus Scholle, the chargé d'affaires, present at this conference in early August, do you remember?

Gen. WALLER. He was present at the first one. He was not present at the final one. There were several interviews that took place about that time.

Mr. HOWE. I now offer a certificate by Maj. Jesse F. Dyer, dated November 8, 1921, containing true copies of extracts from the muster roll of the One Hundredth Company, Second Regiment, First Provisional Brigade, United States Marine Corps, which extracts show that Capt. Thomas L. Edwards, commanding that company, was stationed at Mirebalais, Haiti, throughout the months of May and June, 1919; also an official copy of the report of the death of Capt. Thomas L. Edwards, United States Marine Corps. The report states that death took place as the result of an airplane accident, and that Capt. Edwards died at Port au Prince on August 10, 1920.

(The papers referred to are here printed in full, as follows:)

HEADQUARTERS UNITED STATES MARINE CORPS,
Washington, November 8, 1921.

This is to certify that the muster rolls of the One hundredth Company, Second Regiment, First Provisional Brigade, United States Marine Corps, for the months of April, May, and June, 1919, show the following remarks opposite the name of Capt. Thomas L. Edwards, United States Marine Corps, as designated below, and that the remarks so shown are a true copy of the original muster rolls:

Muster roll of One hundredth Company, Second Regiment, First Provisional Brigade, United States Marine Corps, for April, 1919. Company at Port au Prince, Haiti, 1 to 30.

Name: Capt. Edwards, Thomas L.

Remarks: 1 to 30 commanding company, 6 to 30 participating in operations against bandits in central Haiti.

Muster roll of One hundredth Company, Second Regiment, First Provisional Brigade, United States Marine Corps, for May, 1919. Company at Mirebalais, Haiti, 1 to 31.

Name: Capt. Edwards, Thomas L.

Remarks: 1 to 31 commanding company participating in operations against bandits in central Haiti; 8 received requalification bar.

Muster roll of One hundredth Company, Second Regiment First Provisional Brigade, United States Marine Corps, for June, 1919. Company at Mirebalais, Haiti, 1 to 30.

Name: Capt. Edwards, Thomas L.

Remarks: 1 to 30 commanding company.

JESSE F. DYER,
Major, United States Marine Corps.

FORM N.

From: Field hospital, First Provisional Brigade, Port au Prince, Republic of Haiti:

To: Bureau of Medicine and Surgery, Navy Department, Washington, D. C.

Subject: Report of death in case of—

Edwards, Thomas Louis, captain, United States Marine Corps, enlisted Marine Barracks, Port Royal, S. C., July 24, 1917. Relation, name, and address of next of kin, mother, Martha Edwards, 2496 Carter Street, Baker City, Oreg. Born: Place, Ogden, Utah. Date, December 10, 1889. White, United States. Eyes, brown; hair, brown; complexion, ruddy; height, $67\frac{3}{4}$; weight, 133. Psc. forehead. Sc. $\frac{3}{4}''$ R. cheek; $\frac{3}{4}''$ up. lip.

Died Port au Prince, Haiti, August 10, 1920, 2.15 p. m. Embalmed at field hospital; to be transferred to United States by first available transportation. Immediate cause of death, fracture at base of skull. Key letter, G–R. Origin is in the line of duty. Disability is not the result of own misconduct. Original diagnosis of last disease or injury causing death or resulting in complications causing death; and ship or station to which attached at that time. Fracture at base of skull, Eighth Regiment, First Provisional Brigade, United States Marine Corps.

Facts are as follows: Patient was passenger in plane which stalled at 500 feet altitude and crashed. Brought to hospital unconscious. Strong evidence of fracture of base of skull; left hip dislocated upward and backward. Lacerated wound in inner aspect of left knee. Many bruises and scratches. Dislocation reduced and wound sutured. Put to bed; ice cap to head; Murphy drip. Patient continued to improve during the night, but at 11 a. m. pulse and temperature rose and he died at 2.15 p. m. from complete dissociation of medullary centers.

J. R. POPPEN,
Lieutenant, Medical Corps, United States Navy.

Approved:

JOHN H. RUSSELL,
Colonel, United States Marine Corps.

(Whereupon the committee adjourned until Wednesday, November 9, 1921, at 10.30 o'clock a. m.)

INQUIRY INTO OCCUPATION AND ADMINISTRATION OF HAITI AND SANTO DOMINGO.

WEDNESDAY, NOVEMBER 9, 1921.

UNITED STATES SENATE,
SELECT COMMITTEE ON HAITI AND SANTO DOMINGO,
Washington, D. C.

The committee met, pursuant to adjournment, at 10.30 o'clock a. m. in room 131, Senate Office Building, Senator Tasker L. Oddie presiding.

Present: Senator Oddie.

Also present: Mr. Walter Bruce Howe, Mr. Ernest Angell, and Maj. Edwin N. McClellan, United States Marine Corps.

STATEMENT OF BRIG. GEN. ALBERTUS W. CATLIN, UNITED STATES MARINE CORPS, RETIRED, WASHINGTON, D. C.

Mr. Howe. Gen. Catlin, will you give your name, rank, and present station?

Gen. Catlin. Albertus W. Catlin, brigadier general, United States Marine Corps, retired; 1401 Webster Street NW., Washington, D. C.

Mr. Howe. How long ago did you retire, General?

Gen. Catlin. I retired in December, 1919.

Mr. Howe. How long before that had you become a member of the Marine Corps?

Gen. Catlin. I was appointed in the Marine Corps on the 1st of July, 1892.

Mr. Howe. You saw active service overseas, did you not, during the war?

Gen. Catlin. I was over there for about eight months.

Mr. Howe. What was your command in France?

Gen. Catlin. I had command of the Sixth Regiment of Marines.

Mr. Howe. Until you were wounded?

Gen. Catlin. Until I was wounded.

Mr. Howe. Then you returned to this country?

Gen. Catlin. I spent about six weeks in the hospital in Paris, and then returned.

Mr. Howe. Where was it that you were wounded?

Gen. Catlin. In the first attack on Belleau Wood, June 6, 1918.

Mr. Howe. It was after your return from France that you were sent to Haiti; is that correct?

Gen. Catlin. Yes; I was sent to Haiti in November, 1918, after returning from France.

Mr. Howe. What was your assignment down in Haiti?

Gen. Catlin. I was assigned as brigade commander of the marines in Haiti.

Mr. Howe. Which officer did you succeed?

Gen. Catlin. Col. John H. Russell.

Mr. Howe. That was Col. Russell's first tour down there?

Gen. Catlin. Yes.

Mr. Howe. How long did you remain brigade commander?

Gen. Catlin. I remained from the 1st of December, 1918, to the 15th of July, 1919. I came away on leave on the 15th of July, 1919.

Mr. Howe. And were you relieved, and when?

Gen. Catlin. I was relieved in September.

Mr. Howe. Without, however, returning to Haiti?

Gen. Catlin. Without returning to Haiti.

Mr. Howe. You were succeeded by?

Gen. Catlin. By Col. Russell, whom I had succeeded.

Mr. Howe. What was the state of Haitian affairs when you got down there? Was it tranquil or was there trouble in the field?

Gen. CATLIN. Affairs in Port au Prince were very quiet. Trouble had started shortly before I arrived in the Hinche district, or in the surroundings of Hinche, and about the date of my arrival, I think it was about November 24, there had been an attack upon the town of Hinche by bandits, and gendarmes, extra gendarmes, had been sent up from Port au Prince to pursue the bandits.

Mr. HOWE. Lieut. Col. Williams was the commander of the gendarmerie at that time?

Gen. CATLIN. He was during my whole tour.

Mr. HOWE. What did you estimate the situation to be around Hinche as to whether it was possible for the gendarmerie to control it?

Gen. CATLIN. Well, of course, my estimate at that time would be entirely upon information I received from the officers who had been around there, as I knew nothing of the country myself, and Col. Williams assured me that he could control it.

Mr. HOWE. Did you later on send a detachment or company of marines to Hinche?

Gen. CATLIN. Yes; in February, the latter part of February, Col. Hooker, who was in command of the northern district and the regiment stationed at Cape Haitien, sent a company of marines on a hike to Hinche, at the same time making a report to me of conditions he had found up there, and made recommendations which I afterwards approved, and they were kept there until the marines finally took over operations themselves.

Mr. HOWE. When was it that the marines took over operations themselves?

Gen. CATLIN. Active operations were started about the 1st of May, and the marines were sent in there during March.

Mr. HOWE. When did you first visit the Hinche district?

Gen. CATLIN. I do not know the exact date, but it was somewhere about the second week in March.

Mr. HOWE. What were conditions up there when you went there?

Gen. CATLIN. I found conditions were very bad. I found that the country outside of the town was practically depopulated. All of the little huts, etc., were empty, and the occupants had disappeared.

Mr. HOWE. What had brought that about?

Gen. CATLIN. As far as I could gather from this information, it was brought about by two reasons: One was the bandits, the fear of the bandits, who had been recruiting throughout the district, forcing the people to join them, and the other one, I came to the conclusion, was fear of the gendarmes.

Mr. HOWE. Please say a little more about that second reason there, the fear of the gendarmes.

Gen. CATLIN. Well, the gendarmes were scattered all over the island in small detachments, generally with one white officer, who was a marine; and it was necessary, of course, to send out patrols through the districts, of gendarmes, under a sergeant, corporal, etc., and I found that the native gendarme was very prone to use his position against other natives; if he was given any authority at all he was very prone to exceed it, and that the patrols would abuse the people, and a number of cases were reported where natives were abused and robbed, and women carried off, and shot, and things like that. And that was the reason I said I came to the conclusion that one reason was fear of the gendarmes. Many of them had disappeared, having either gone with the bandits or gone into the towns for protection.

Mr. HOWE. If a native in or near his own house saw another native coming, armed, what was his guess as to whether it was a bandit or a gendarme?

Gen. CATLIN. I do not think he stopped to guess; he generally took to the woods.

Mr. HOWE. And if a peaceful native was seen taking to the woods by a gendarme, with no white officer present, what would the gendarme generally do at that time in that place?

Gen. CATLIN. At that time, with bandits in the field, the gendarme would generally shoot at him, because it was found that the bandits had spies and lookouts all over the country and had their own men scattered around, and they would have them out three or four hills ahead of the bands; so that the chances were that if you saw a man running he was one of their men running to give them notice. That was the general supposition whenever a man was seen running.

Mr. HOWE. Was the overbearing attitude of a gendarme who was not under the immediate control of a white officer sufficient in itself to drive the inhabitants away; I mean at that time and under those conditions up there?

Gen. CATLIN. I do not know that it was; but there were other things, of course. There was the corvee, too, which probably had an effect on that, too.

Mr. HOWE. In March, 1919?

Gen. CATLIN. Well, in March, 1919, there was a modified corvee working in that district.

Mr. HOWE. And that contributed also to the unsettled conditions?

Gen. CATLIN. Undoubtedly.

Mr. HOWE. Do I understand that it was on account of those unsettled conditions and the mistrust of the gendarmerie that you sent the marines in there for station?

Gen. CATLIN. Yes; I sent the marines in there on account of that; and my first order was that they were simply to go in and take station in the town, not to operate in the field in any manner whatever, leaving that entirely to the gendarmes.

Mr. HOWE. Did you take any other steps to restore confidence there?

Gen. CATLIN. In March?

Mr. HOWE. Yes.

Gen. CATLIN. Yes. When we took over the operations the first thing we did was to send out a notice or proclamation by means of the priests, market women, and all means we had all over the island, or that district of the island, requesting all natives to come in and give themselves up and they would receive protection; and we issued a sort of a pass to them which guaranteed protection, et cetera, and there were something over 3,000, as I remember it, who came in and received those passes.

Mr. HOWE. How many of those that came in were armed?

Gen. CATLIN. None of them brought arms at that time. Later men came in with arms and received passes. That was a period of about two weeks which was given them to come in.

Mr. HOWE. And that was in March?

Gen. CATLIN. That was in March.

Mr. HOWE. You spoke of taking over operations. From whom did you take over operations?

Gen. CATLIN. From the gendarmerie. Up to that time Col. Williams had assured me that he could handle the situation, and it was a gendarmerie job, not a marine job, but the bandits increased to such an extent that he found, although he withdrew troops from Port au Prince, and sent about 500 additional gendarmes up there, that he could not handle it, and about the middle of March, or a little later than that, he informed me that he could not handle it any longer. Then I sent the rest of the marines in and took over operations personally.

Mr. HOWE. How long did those operations remain active?

Gen. CATLIN. Until some time after I left; I do not know the exact date, but it was going on when I left.

Mr. HOWE. What form did the operations of the marines take?

Gen. CATLIN. Well, the operations were not strictly military, in a military sense. The marines were stationed at all the different towns in the district. A company was divided up. For instance, the Fifty-fourth Company, with headquarters at Hinche, had detachments at Maissade, St. Michel, and later at other little places. Another company which came from Ouanaminthe, was over at Thomaseau and Thomusique, and three or four towns in there, and a little later, when it spread down toward the south, companies were sent to Mirebalais and Las Cohobas. These companies there were divided into different detachments, and patrols were sent out from these towns. There were no roads. They were sent out by the trails over the mountains. At first they went out in search of the bandits, but it was found that it was impossible to find them in that way. We used native guides, and the farmers wherever we could get them, and it finally became necessary to locate a camp, and then march at night. The patrols would do their marching at night and jump the camp at daylight. That was the only way we could get in touch with them.

Mr. HOWE. What was the effect of this patrolling and these morning surprises on camps?

Gen. CATLIN. The effect was that the small bands joined in with other bands, and a number of men came in and gave themselves up. A lot of them claimed they were captured by the bandits and forced to serve with them. But it had no appreciable effect on the bands themselves. Charlemagne, who was in command of the outfit, and entitled himself commander in chief of the forces fighting against the Americans, sent over the island trying to recruit more. I got a number of letters that he had sent, one to the magistrate of Plaisance, which is up near Cape Hatien, and to Gen. Aspelly, telling him that now was the time for all good Haitians to join in, stating he had 30,000 men in the field.

Mr. Howe. Did he have 30,000 men in the field?

Gen. Catlin. No; it was impossible to tell how many he had, but I estimated at that time that there were about 5,000 bandits in the field, not over that, and of those probably not over one-quarter, or less than that, had arms.

Mr. Howe. How many marines were there in the field then?

Gen. Catlin. There were less than 2,000 in the island. I could not give the exact number, but I imagine probably 500 or 600 in the interior.

Mr. Howe. Actively engaged in the interior?

Gen. Catlin. Yes.

Mr. Howe. Were the gendarmes cooperating at that time?

Gen. Catlin. Yes; to a certain extent. I had stopped all patrolling in that district by the gendarmes, for the reason which I gave before, but in the districts farther to the west, toward Gonaives, I still allowed them to patrol over there; it was outside of the district where the conditions had been as I stated.

Mr. Howe. What was the area of these operations?

Gen. Catlin. I imagine from St. Michel to the border was approximately 50 or 60 miles, and it was probably 15 miles across the hills to Mirebalais, the other way, so I should say, roughly, that ti was about 50 miles by 15 or 20 miles, something like that.

Mr. Howe. That region might be described as being in the center of Haiti?

Gen. Catlin. Yes. It belongs to the northern district, but it is practically in the center of Haiti, I should say.

Mr. Howe. Had Charlemagne been captured or killed before you left?

Gen. Catlin. No. Before I left I had a letter from the bishop at Cape Haitien, requesting that I allow Charlemagne and Norde, one of the principal leaders there, to escape from the island.

Mr. Howe. You spoke of the bands of natives getting larger; that is, by the small bands joining up together?

Gen. Catlin. Yes.

Mr. Howe. On their part, what did the bandits do?

Gen. Catlin. Well, the bandits—most of their activities, although they said they were fighting against the Americans, were against the peaceable natives. They would jump a little town and burn the houses, take all the men they could gather with them as recruits, and all the provisions and things like that which they could get.

Mr. Howe. Did they commit any brutalities on the women and children?

Gen. Catlin. Not that I know of; I know of nothing of that kind. In a number of cases where there were small gendarme posts they would jump the gendarme posts to get the arms and ammunition, principally, and they used the uniforms which they captured. There were a number of fights there where gendarme uniforms were seen with the bandits.

Mr. Howe. You spoke of them jumping small towns. Do you mean that gendarme posts were in those towns?

Gen. Catlin. Not necessarily; no.

Mr. Howe. Sometimes with posts in the towns and sometimes not?

Gen. Catlin. Yes. It would not necessarily be a town. It would be a small community, like, for instance, near Ennery. They went through a district there, which is on the road from Ennery to St. Michel—that is, on the main road up to Cape Haitien—went through one night and burned all the houses in the district for about 3 miles, destroyed the growing crops, and carried everybody off.

Mr. Howe. Then, from March until the time you left, did the same characteristics mark the operations in the fighting up there?

Gen. Catlin. Practically.

Mr. Howe. In Port au Prince what were the conditions?

Gen. Catlin. Conditions were apparently comparatively quiet in Port au Prince. There were, of course, the usual rumors always going around that there was going to be an attack on Port au Prince, but it never materialized; and there were in Port au Prince undoubtedly a lot of people who were assisting the bandits in a way, both with money and with information.

Mr. Howe. There were no outstanding political occurrences in Port au Prince at that time; that was, not during your tour?

Gen. CATLIN. Nothing at all; and there was absolutely nothing political in the uprising of the bandits in the field.

Mr. HOWE. Will you explain that a little further, please?

Gen. CATLIN. By that I mean that there was nothing against the Government or the Americans really. The bandit uprising was started by Charlemagne, who had been a Caco leader before he had been imprisoned in Cape Haitien, and he escaped in September, 1918, and took to the woods and gathered a few of the outlaws around him, and most of the leaders of the bandits were old bandits, old Cacos.

Mr. HOWE. He described his operations as being against the Americans?

Gen. CATLIN. He did that for recruiting purposes, principally, as far as I could gather.

Mr. HOWE. What do you think started this trouble, aside from the escape of Charlemagne?

Gen. CATLIN. I doubt if there would have been any trouble if Charlemagne had not escaped. I think he started the whole thing.

Mr. HOWE. What feeling existed among the people whom he recruited which enabled him to induce them to take up arms and operate against the Americans?

Gen. CATLIN. Well, that I do not know. As I say, he was one of the old Caco leaders, and I have been told that there was a feeling among the natives that they must follow their old leaders. A lot of the ignorant natives and many of the natives in the hills there are really almost savages. You see them up in the hills naked, where they never come down, many of them. They are really savages.

Mr. HOWE. Would you say that the operation of the corvee had anything to do with the creating of discontent which would have made this outbreak possible.

Gen. CATLIN. I think the operation of the corvee possibly aggravated the situation. I do not think the corvee had anything to do with the original starting of it. I think the operation of the corvee undoubtedly sent a number of recruits to the bandits.

Mr. HOWE. Where were you personally during the greater part of the tour of your duty in Haiti?

Gen. CATLIN. In Port au Prince.

Mr. HOWE. Under whose direct immediate control were the operations in the interior?

Gen. CATLIN. Lieut. Col. Richard Hooker.

Mr. HOWE. You made, however, General, an inspection trip?

Gen. CATLIN. I made several inspection trips.

Mr. HOWE. I am referring particularly to one up to Hinche and the Hinche-Maissade district.

Gen. CATLIN. I went to Hinche about four times.

Mr. HOWE. You made an inspection trip in which you were principally interested in finding out whether the corvee was going on?

Gen. CATLIN. Yes, sir.

Mr. HOWE. When did that trip start?

Gen. CATLIN. That trip took place about the middle of March; I do not remember the exact date.

Mr. HOWE. Will you please tell us what led up to your taking that inspection trip?

Gen. CATLIN. Rumors had reached me that conditions were unsatisfactory in that district, and that the corvee was still running. I questioned the gendarme commander and he stated that it was not; he had issued an order in October abolishing the corvee; but I believe it was worded so that it covered certain roads, and had failed to cover the road to Hinche, and he had discovered that in November, and issued an order to the commanding officer up there to stop the corvee; but, according to rumors, it was still going on up there. I sent Col. Hooker up to make a trip through that district, and find out the actual conditions and report to me. After his report, or upon the receipt of his report, I sent for Col. Williams and showed him the report, and also Maj. Wells, who was in command of the gendarmerie of the northern district, which Hinche was in, and they disagreed entirely on the report of Col. Hooker.

Mr. HOWE. What was the substance of Col. Hooker's report?

Gen. CATLIN. I have it here. You can see it, although it is a personal report.

Mr. HOWE. General, this letter from Col. Hooker, which you have just handed me, is the report which you have been speaking about?

Gen. CATLIN. That is the report of the investigation.

Mr. HOWE. And on which you invited the comment of Col. Williams and Maj. Wells?

Gen. CATLIN. Yes.

Mr. HOWE. Mr. Chairman, I think this report should undoubtedly go in the record. I offer this report of Col. Hooker's for the record, and will read it:

Personal.   FEBRUARY 15, 1919.

MY DEAR GENERAL: I left for Hinche Tuesday last, arriving back here to-day. I inspected the whole district south of San Michel. I am sending this to you by special messenger, as I consider immediate action most urgent. The Fifty-fourth Company will leave here for the Hinche district Tuesday at the latest on a hike, arriving in Hinche next Friday or Saturday. This will give you time to approve or modify my recommendations given later in this letter.

I found the following conditions existing: The corvee is still going on, camouflaged either accidentally or otherwise by the payment of one gourde to not more than one gourde forty per week per man. Men are kept for long periods of time on this work, and in order to escape the draft they take to the hills, joining the so-called Cacos. The magistrate of Maissade is a bad egg and should be removed, being back of the corvee and using about 50 for his own garden. This can be taken up later. It was very hard for me to find out anything from the gendarmes themselves, as the entire district was expecting me. I questioned all the natives I could get to come to me, and together with information I received from the priests I am certain that the corvee is at the bottom of the whole trouble, as it was in 1917 when Hinche was attacked the first time. The other cause, which is equally as important as the corvee, is the indiscriminate strong-arm work being pulled off. A great many innocents have suffered; and those who are outside the towns, not necessarily with the Cacos, are remaining in the bush through fear of the gendarmes, who are given and helped in their methods by officers of the gendarmerie unqualified by intelligence or experience to act in executive capacities. I am sorry to have to state that I got the impression that the officers higher up were approving these methods.

I ran into a horrible condition in San Michel. On Wednesday or Thursday I had a talk with Lieut. Haug. He was in a frightful mental condition and on the verge of a nervous breakdown. He volunteered and told me the following, which I corroborated by the magistrat, his interpreter, and the priests: On the 4th of February he ordered some prisoners to work on the "place." When 15 or 20 minutes had passed and the prisoners had not arrived he went personally to investigate. A corporal was standing in front of the prison door, and when questioned, refused point blank to either let the prisoners out to work or to obey any order from Haug. Haug then told him to give him the key to the prison, and when he reached to take the key from the corporal, the corporal caught him by the throat, and assisted by two other gendarmes, held him against the wall. Haug tried to pull his gun and found that other gendarmes had secured their rifles and had them pointed at him threatening to shoot. Haug is over 50, and he is in horrible physical condition, his mentality is not strong, and he does not yet realize the enormity of the mut'ny. The next day, while I was out of San Michel, Capt. Gibbons, of Gonaives, arrived to make an investigation. Gibbons was supposed to have made an investigation much sooner, as he knew at least seven days previously that mut'nous or similar conditions existed at San Michel. He claims that he knew nothing of the assault. When I arrived in the evening I found that he had conducted his investigation by informing Haug that he was going to do his best to drive him out of the gendarmerie and other like remarks. This was while my orderly, Sasse, was present. He conducted the investigation by calling each gendarme in separately, excluding Haug, and making him stand outside. My confidential interpreter told me later that the gendarmes were very much pleased because they had put their officer in a bad hole and would get a new officer, which they wanted. I, unfortunately, was too late to be present before the investigation started and to prevent Haug from being placed in the position of the accused. I took charge later to the extent of ordering Gibbons back to Gonaives, with instructions to return with sufficient men to place the mutineers under arrest and to regarrison the place with reliable men. Wells now knows of it, and if the gendarmerie does not act immediately and properly I will take charge. The news of the affair has spread rapidly and may become serious, although at present I do not believe so if action is immediately taken.

The situation in that whole district is, to say the least, out of hand, and I strongly recommend the following:

One squad stationed in San Michel, for the present at least.

One squad at Maissade.

The rest of the Fifty-fourth Company at Hinche.

I will personally go to Hinche primarily as nearly all the people know me, and I believe to a certain extent trust me.

Give the men now out two weeks to return to their farms and towns excepting, of course, those who through leadership have placed themselves outside the law.

Promise and see that these men who return are not proceeded against as the majority of them have been forced through fear to take to the bush and not important.

Stop the corvee.

In my opinion, I do not believe it would be proper to start a military campaign immediately until all efforts to regain the lost confidence of the people in us are tried out.

Very sincerely,

R. C. HOOKER.

In reading this letter over in some respects it does not seem strong enough and in others too strong, but I can not impress too strongly on you that in my opinion a change of régime is most necessary and do not believe any gendarme change will help.

P. S.—Private Sasse, the bearer of this letter, was with me and can give you any details not included.

Mr. HOWE. Was Sasse a white?

Gen. CATLIN. He was a private of marines.

Mr. HOWE. In what respect did Col. Williams and Maj. Wells differ in their conclusions on the report of Col. Hooker?

Gen. CATLIN. In regard to the corvee, they both stated that there was no corvee; that all work was being done voluntarily, and that the men were being paid. As I remember now, they said they were being paid half a gourde a day.

Senator ODDIE. How much is a gourde?

Gen. CATLIN. A gourde is 20 cents.

Mr. HOWE. That was the general average exchange of the gourde, was it?

Gen. CATLIN. Yes; that was settled by Admiral Caperton down there, at 5 gourdes for a dollar, and it has practically been that ever since, although the exchange has varied a little. I found when I went up through there that they were paying the men, and the day before I arrived they told him they would get a gourde a day.

Mr. HOWE. Before we go on to your inspection trip, which we do want to hear about, let us hear, please, in what other respects there was disagreement with Col. Hooker's report?

Gen. CATLIN. Well, as I said, in regard to the corvee, and Gen. Williams did not believe that the action of the gendarmes had any effect on men going to the bandits.

Mr. HOWE. Do you know how this mutinous incident was handled or disposed of?

Gen. CATLIN. The mutineers were tried by court-martial. I do not remember what was finally done with them, but that was a gendarme trial.

Mr. HOWE. Do you remember whether the court-martial found them guilty of anything?

Gen. CATLIN. I think they did. I can not say positively. I had nothing to do with it.

Mr. HOWE. Is it your recollection that this report of Col. Hooker as to this mutinous outbreak was later on approved substantially at the court-martial?

Gen. CATLIN. Oh, yes; undoubtedly.

Mr. HOWE. There is no doubt, then, that the circumstances were accurately reported by Col. Hooker?

Gen. CATLIN. None whatever.

Mr. HOWE. After referring this matter as you described to Col. Williams, what was the next step you took?

Gen. CATLIN. Maj. Wells stated that he had just been through the district, and I asked him if he was satisfied that there was no corvée. He stated positively that he was; that he had seen the men paid off by the gendarme officer,

Lieut. Williams, at Maissade, and stated that there were not over 40 men on the pay roll or working—no; I am wrong there. It was not at that time that he stated that. He stated he did not know how the men were paid, but he was satisfied there was no corvée. I then sent Williams up personally to find out who paid the men, as there was some talk of the money being turned over to the magistrate to pay them, and to investigate on his part and make a report, which he did.

Mr. Howe. Wells, you mean?

Gen. Catlin. Wells.

Mr. Howe. You sent him back?

Gen. Catlin. I sent him back for his side, for the gendarme report side. That report was made verbally, not in writing, and when he came back Col. Hooker and Col. Williams were also present at the time, and he stated the manner in which the men were paid, and that he found that there were only that many working, or they were all on the pay roll, and that there was no corvée.

Mr. Howe. Was this verbal report made at Port au Prince?

Gen. Catlin. At Port au Prince; yes. The two reports were so diametrically opposite that I decided to go up into the district myself and find out, if possible, what the conditions actually were. So that, I think, it was about the middle of March that I took Col. Williams with me and went up to Hinche.

Mr. Howe. Your investigations there, as I have heard, were investigations of the corvée, and incidentally to that you heard reports of killing of prisoners, and made investigations along that line?

Gen. Catlin. Yes; my object in going was to investigate the general conditions. As I was practically new to the country and found I could not get from reports a very good idea, I went up to satisfy myself what the conditions were, and to satisfy myself in regard to the corvée.

Mr. Howe. Was that your first visit to the Hinche district?

Gen. Catlin. My first visit; yes, sir.

Mr. Howe. General, will you please describe your inspection trip and just how you went about it and what you found out?

Gen. Catlin. Well, I went up to St. Michel, and was joined there by Maj. Wells and Col. Hooker, and then proceeded to Maissada first. Just before arriving at Maissada I found a gang of about 45 men working on the road, with gendarme sentries over them, and I stopped, and, through my interpreter, questioned the most intelligent looking members of the gang, and they all stated that they were not there of their own free will but were there because they had been ordered there. Several of them stated that they had been brought by the chief of section. There was no chief of section at that time, but he had been changed to the chief of agriculture. The old chief of section in Haiti used to have a great deal of authority in his section.

Mr. Howe. He was a civil Haitian officer?

Gen. Catlin. He was a civil Haitian officer, and most of the natives felt that they had to do whatever the chief of section told them to do, and they had been directed to report to the point there for work, and had come because they did not dare not to come. A number of them stated they had been working in their gardens, and had been ordered out to come, and their gardens had gone to the bad because they had not been able to work there.

Mr. Howe. Let me interrupt you there. Did you gather that these people had been ordered by the chief of section or the chief of agriculture, and not by the gendarmes?

Gen. Catlin. Most of them; yes.

Mr. Howe. Did you find or did some of them tell you that they had been ordered there by the gendarmes?

Gen. Catlin. Yes; in one or two cases the men had been brought in by gendarmes.

Mr. Howe. That is what they said?

Gen. Catlin. Yes; they said gendarmes had come out and told them to come in to work and they had come along. I asked them if they had used any force, and they said no; they did not have to use force, because when a gendarme told them to that was enough for them.

Mr. Howe. According to the answers you got, what proportion were directed to come by the gendarmes and what proportion were directetd to come by other officers?

Gen. Catlin. I can not remember that, but there were only a few that were directed by gendarmes, as I remember it.

Mr. Howe. And the rest?

Gen. Catlin. The rest were mostly ordered by the chief of section. There were a few who claimed that they had been told to come into a meeting or something in town, at Maissade, and when they got in there they were locked up for the night and then put on the gang.

Mr. Howe. Now, will you go ahead, please?

Gen. Catlin. After questioning a number of these men, I then asked all who were there involuntarily, not of their own free will, and who did not want to work on the road to step across the road, and all but three stepped across. These three I questioned, and they said they were overseers and they lived in Maissade and they could not say anything else. I then told them that all those that wanted to do so could go home, and did not have to work unless they wanted to; that if they wanted to come back and work for money they could do it, and the following Monday I understood that six men came to work.

Mr. Howe. What happened on that particular occasion when you told them they could go home and leave work if they wanted to?

Gen. Catlin. They stopped work; work was stopped.

Mr. Howe. What time of day was that?

Gen. Catlin. It was in the morning, about 10 o'clock, I should say, 10 or 11 o'clock.

Mr. Howe. That was the end of work there for that day?

Gen. Catlin. That was the end of work there for that day.

Mr. Howe. Was the next working day Monday?

Gen. Catlin. The next working day was Monday.

Mr. Howe. And it was on the next working day that only six of them returned?

Gen. Catlin. Yes.

Mr. Howe. What else developed on that occasion?

Gen. Catlin. I then proceeded into Maissade.

Mr. Howe. Excuse me just a second. I mean at the time you were questioning the road gang, were there any other features developed by your questioning?

Gen. Catlin. Not then.

Mr. Howe. Did you learn at that time in questioning the gang as to the residence of the members of the gang? Were they working in their own district or were they there from other districts?

Gen. Catlin. As far as I remember, the majority of them were working in their own district. They all came from the vicinity—in the district around there.

Mr. Howe. Did you strike any cases where they said they came from districts farther away?

Gen. Catlin. As I remember it, there was only one man who claimed he had been captured by gendarmes in the foothills, and as far as I could gather from the information, apparently he was a bandit.

Mr. Howe. What did you learn from them as to the amount of their pay?

Gen. Catlin. They stated they had been receiving half a gourde, and that they had been promised the following Monday that they would get a gourde a day.

Mr. Howe. They had been receiving half a gourde a day?

Gen. Catlin. Yes.

Mr. Howe. Do you know what the prevailing labor wages were in that district?

Gen. Catlin. A gourde a day was fair pay.

Mr. Howe. And half a gourde a day was less than fair pay?

Gen. Catlin. It was a little less, yes. Although there were districts where half a gourde a day was paid.

Mr. Howe. Did that pay include subsistence?

Gen. Catlin. No; the men fed themselves.

Mr. Howe. How many sentries were there, General?

Gen. Catlin. Two, as I remember it.

Mr. Howe. Armed?

Gen. Catlin. Yes; armed.

Mr. Howe. Gendarmes?

Gen. Catlin. Gendarmes.

Mr. Howe. Could they have been performing any other duty than that of guarding the corvée gang?

Gen. CATLIN. The officers stated they were there to guard the corvée gang from the bandits.

Mr. HOWE. Which officer was that?

Gen. CATLIN. Williams.

Mr. HOWE. Col. Williams?

Gen. CATLIN. No; Lieut. Williams.

Mr. HOWE. Dorcas Williams?

Gen. CATLIN. Doras Williams.

Mr. HOWE. What conclusion did you reach on that, General? Were they there to protect the gang or to prevent the gang from running away?

Gen. CATLIN. Well, my idea at the time was that they were there to keep the gang from running away.

Mr. HOWE. What led you to that conclusion?

Gen. CATLIN. Simply the fact that the men were there involuntarily; and that there was as I say, one man who apparently was a bandit, a caco himself, that had been captured near the foothills, running off some cattle, I believe, and he would probably take to the woods when he got a chance.

Mr. HOWE. Was Col. Williams present at this time?

Gen. CATLIN. Col. Williams was standing beside me; yes.

Mr. HOWE. What, if any, comment did he make on the developments there?

Gen. CATLIN. None whatever at that time.

Mr. HOWE. Did he offer any explanation of the apparent inconsistency between the facts as you found them and his report?

Gen. CATLIN. Yes. A little later he stated that his idea was that these men had made the statements to me because they thought that was what I wanted; that that was the Haitien custom.

Mr. HOWE. Did you regard that incident of that gang working there as a violation of the orders stopping the corvee?

Gen. CATLIN. I did; yes.

Mr. HOWE. And you still so regard it?

Gen. CATLIN. I do.

Mr. HOWE. In the course of that inspection trip, or other inspection trips, did you come across other states of affairs which you regarded as a violation of that order against the corvee?

Gen. CATLIN. Yes; I found in Hinche that same day among other things that the gendarmerie had been building a prison and barracks at Hinche. I believe they were very short of money, and the gendarme officer had rounded up all the inhabitants of a certain district called Zebguinea and brought them into Hinche and presumably for protection. Zebguinea being at the foothills, also claiming that it was a bad district and that no one but bandits were left there anyway and these men were either bandits or in favor of the bandits, and that these men had all been worked on these barracks to build the barracks and the prison, and paid nothing, but were fed.

Mr. HOWE. Were these men prisoners?

Gen. CATLIN. They were not prisoners, but they were kept in a compound there. They had all been released or let go before my arrival.

Mr. HOWE. Were they detained in the compound against their will?

Gen. CATLIN. I assumed so. They had no other place to sleep, probably. The town was full of people. They were detained in the town. They were not allowed to leave the town.

Mr. HOWE. How many days' work did they work there, do you know? What was the extent of that job?

Gen. CATLIN. I do not know that. It was quite a building that was put up there.

Mr. HOWE. Masonry?

Gen. CATLIN. Masonry.

Mr. HOWE. What part did they take in the construction of the building, did you hear; what kind of labor?

Gen. CATLIN. Well, the stone all had to be carried from the quarry some distance.

Mr. HOWE. What did you find out about the magistrate at Maissade who Col. Hooker said was using 50 men for his own garden?

Gen. CATLIN. I was unable to get any information on that. The only person who would mention it at all was the priest of Maissade, who apparently was afraid of his life and would not go into the town. I saw him at St. Michel. He claimed the magistrate had two men hired to kill him and he would not go to the town. I think he was crazy, because his statements were wild. But

In Maissade I was unable to get any information, because there was no one working. If they had been there, they left before I arrived.

Mr. Howe. Aside from these instances, were there any further violations of that order stopping corvee?

Gen. Catlin. Not that I know of—not that I heard of.

Mr. Howe. Do you believe these instances marked the end of the corvee in Haiti?

Gen. Catlin. I think so.

Mr. Howe. General, in your investigation there did you learn how this road gang was paid and who paid them?

Gen. Catlin. Yes; the road gang was paid personally by the gendarme officer.

Mr. Howe. And, in your opinion, was there any chance for the chief of section or of agriculture to come in on the pay of these men in any way?

Gen. Catlin. No; when I say they were paid in that way, I mean they were paid that way when I got there, but how long before they started that I do not know.

Mr. Howe. Did you form any idea as to why these chiefs of section were sending in recruits for the road gang?

Gen. Catlin. I did not go into that, because I was satisfied myself that the corvee was going on, and my main object was simply to stop it, but my idea was that they were probably acting under the orders of the magistrate of the town.

Mr. Howe. Was there anything in it for the magistrate?

Gen. Catlin. No; except it was a very nice thing to get a good road put in there. It was hard communication in that country. I would like to say here that in regard to this corvee it covered only a very small section of Haiti; that this was only in this one locality, not in any other part of Haiti.

Mr. Howe. That is the breach of the orders?

Gen. Catlin. Yes.

Mr. Howe. That leaves me to ask how much of Haiti the corvee system extended over when it was at its height?

Gen. Catlin. Well, I was not there at that time, but, as far as I know, it only extended over on the road from Port au Prince to Cape Haitien. The principal corvee was in putting through that road. As far as I know, the corvee was never used in the southern part of the island.

Mr. Howe. I want to go back again and ask you about the chiefs of section. Was there anything you learned which would lead you to believe that before you got up there and inspected any money had been paid to the chiefs of section for wages for the corvee gangs?

Gen. Catlin. No; I had no reason to believe it had been.

Mr. Howe. Is there anything more that you might add about your investigation of the corvee at that time?

Gen. Catlin. Nothing.

Mr. Howe. What other subjects did you investigate?

Gen. Catlin. Well, I called for the magistrate, the judge de paix, and the principal leaders of the town to come before me, and questioned them on conditions, etc. The magistrate and the judge de paix said everything was all right and working nicely. There were some complaints, of course, against the magistrate by natives, but those were things which I did not take up. It was the business of the gendarme officer, not mine.

Mr. Howe. Did you hear reports of the killing of prisoners?

Gen. Catlin. At Maissade I questioned a lot of gendarme privates. In fact, two or three wanted to come before me; and they came and at least two stated that their officer, Lieut. Doras Williams, had killed a native named Garnier, who was, I believe, a local lawyer or something like that there.

Mr. Howe. When you say a local lawyer, would he be described down there as a notary?

Gen. Catlin. A notary, yes; and these two men, two privates, stated that this man Garnier had been sent for on the day after the attack by the bandits on the town, had been brought to the office, and had been beaten to death with a club. The first sergeant denied it, and Lieut. William denied it, and the magistrate denied it, and so did others. I found out upon further investigation that these two men who made the original report had both had a grudge against Lieut. Williams for treatment which they had received from him. One of them, I believe, was found asleep on a post, and he had been kicked up because he had been lying down asleep, and the other man something else; so I decided that there was probably nothing in it, as those two men who had the grudge were the only ones who said anything about it. The others denied it absolutely, although Williams admitted that the man had died in his office, but he and the first sergeant both claimed that he had been shot. He had been in a house which was between the gendarmes and the bandits on the night before, and he had been shot in the stomach, and when he came over he was wrapped up with a towel, and he died from the effects of the wound.

Mr. Howe. Therefore, in this Garnier case, where the accusation was made against Lieut. Williams, you took no action because you did not believe the accusation?

Gen. Gatlin. I took no action because I could get no testimony except from two men who had a grudge against the lieutenant—two gendarmes.

Mr. Howe. You mentioned talking to other witnesses, and I gathered that they testified in a way contrary to the statement of the two gendarmes?

Gen. Catlin. Including the first sergeant of the detachment and the magistrat of the town and the judge de paix.

Mr. Howe. Do you know whether this case of the killing of Garnier and the accusation against Lieut. Williams was one of the subjects taken up by the Mayo court of inquiry?

Gen. Catlin. I have been told so. I do not know it personally.

Mr. Howe. Maj. McClellan, is it your recollection of the Mayo court of inquiry record, which we are going to put in the record as soon as we have an opportunity to call Maj. Dyer, that Lieut. Williams was exonerated of this charge of killing Garnier?

Maj. McClellan. Yes; to such an extent that there is in the record of the Mayo court, I believe, a copy of a Haitian document which states that it is not known how he met his death; in other words, it was an accidental death. They do not know whether it was a caco bullet or an American bullet that killed him in this scrap around there. It is very definitely stated that his death is not attributable to Lieut. Williams.

Mr. Angell. What is that Haitian document, do you know, Major?

Mr. Howe. It is in the record here.

Mr. Chairman, I asked Maj. McClellan that question at this time because it seemed to me that there should be some mention of the findings of the Mayo court in the record in connection with this testimony of Gen. Catlin about Lieut. Williams. In other words, in justice to Lieut. Williams, if he was later exonerated after investigation, it would be better for it to appear in the record at this time.

I will read from page 205 of the record of the Mayo court of inquiry a letter which, it is there testified, was written by the judge de paix on February 15, 1919, to the commissary government of the city of Gonaives:

"Commissary: I am in haste to inform you that the bandits took the village yesterday noon. During the fight the notary, Garnier Jean, who was at home and whose house was between two fires, was wounded. No one can say if the bullet was fired by the gendarmes or by the cacos.

"After the battle he was sent for to come to the office of the gendarmerie, where he died a short time after. During this time his house and effects were put under seal. The bandits were repulsed.

"I salute you, commissary, with respect."

General, in addition to this accusation against Lieut. Williams, did you hear accusations against other officers of the gendarmerie for the killing of prisoners?

Gen. Catlin. Yes; upon my arrival at Hinche I sent for the priest, the magistrat, the judge de paix, and several other natives and questioned them separately in regard to conditions and their knowledge. Their statements were rather wild. The priest stated that over 50 persons had been killed at Hinche, but he had not seen any of the killings; he only heard it from hearsay. The magistrat, as I remember, stated that a number had been killed. He did not state how many, but other people placed the number anywhere from 2 to 10. After talking with all of these people, I went into the house. I had this hearing outside on the porch. I went in the house and questioned Capt. Lavoie, who had been in command of the gendarmes at Hinche. At first he stated there had been no killings, but when I informed him of what I had heard from the magistrate and the priest, he said there had been six persons killed there at Hinche. He stated that they were bandits and had been captured in a fight up in the hills; they had since tried to escape several times, and caused a good deal of trouble in prison and had been killed. I questioned a lot of the gendarmes, but none of them would admit that they knew anything about any killings.

Mr. Howe. This is Capt. Ernest Lavoie?

Gen. Catlin. Capt. Ernest Lavoie.

Hr. Howe. Of the gendarmerie?

Gen. Catlin. Of the gendarmerie at that time.

Mr. Howe. He was an enlisted man?

Gen. Catlin. An enlisted man in the Marine Corps.

Mr. Howe. Did Capt. Lavoie make any statement as to whether these six prisoners who had been shot were shot at his orders, or with his previous knowledge?

Gen. Catlin. I do not remember that any absolute statement was made to that effect, but that was the understanding, that he was responsible for their being shot, although he stated that he was not present at the shooting.

Mr. Howe. Did he state whether or not those six killings took place while he was in command there?

Gen. Catlin. He did; yes.

Mr. Howe. Did you bring any charges against Capt. Lavoie?

Gen. Catlin. I did not.

Mr. Howe. Did it seem to you that the other witnesses whom you interviewed there furnished corroboration of the admission of Capt. Lavoie that prisoners had been shot?

Gen. Catlin. Not entirely. The statements made by the other witnesses were also wild, and a number of statements made were, on the face of them, false, and I did not consider that the'r statements amounted to anything, one way or the other, as far as corroboration went.

Mr. Howe. However, did you believe Capt. Lavoie, when he told you that six prisoners had been killed there while he was in command?

Gen. Catlin. I partially believed it, and partially d'd not, because Capt. Lavoie is a man who sort of loved the theatrical part of it, and liked to brag about what he had done, and I do not think that the man was entirely right in his mind; I d'd not think so at that time. I think he was queer, and without further other corroboration, I would hesitate to believe that they had been killed. I talked the thing over very carefully with Gen. Williams for several hours, the whole matter, and finally came to the conclusion that a court-martial was not the thing.

Mr. Howe. What reasons led you to that conclusion?

Gen. Catlin. Well, in the first place, I did not believe that it could be proved by witnesses. Undoubtedly if he had been brought to trial he would have pleaded not guilty, and I did not believe that any court would accept the testimony of these witnesses that I had heard. I considered that if the man was brought to trial and acquitted it would have a very bad effect with the natives particularly, who would say that we had whitewashed the man, and I thought it was better not to try him. It was a question of policy more than anything else.

Mr. Howe. Do I understand you to say that you feared an acquittal would have an unfortunate effect?

Gen. Catlin. At that time; yes.

Mr. Howe. At that time, on the natives?

Gen. Catlin. On the natives.

Mr. Howe. At that time what effect do you think a conviction would have had?

Gen. Catlin. I could not imagine a conviction would have affected matters one way or the other—much.

Mr. Howe. To what extent then, General, did reasons of policy prevail in your mind, and also to what extent did doubt as to the ability to convict Capt. Lavoie influence you in bringing no action at that time?

Gen. Catlin. I can not say exactly to what extent, because they were both considered and both entered into my final decision.

Mr. Howe. Was there any other aspect to your decision not to bring charges against Capt. Lavoie which you would like to mention?

Gen. Catlin. Not that I know of.

Mr. Howe. What action, other than bringing charges, did you take in the case af Capt. Lavoie and Lieut. Doras Williams?

Gen. Catlin. I considered that their services were no longer of any use in that district; that they were simply harmful, and I directed Col. Williams to detach them at once, and ordered them to Port au Prince, and to take steps to have them removed from the gendarmerie, because I did not think they were proper officers for the gendarmerie.

Mr. Howe. How soon afterwards, do you know, did they get out of the gendarmerie?

Gen. Catlin. They did get out, but I do not remember now the exact date. It took some little time. It had to be done in the States; orders came out from the States.

Mr. Howe. Orders to relieve them from gendarme service?

Gen. Catlin. Yes; but they were taken to Port au Prince very shortly, and were kept in Port au Prince under the colonel's eye all the time, in barracks.

Mr. Howe. When they finally were relieved of duty with the gendarmerie, they reverted to duty as members of the enlisted forces of the marines?

Gen. Catlin. Yes.

Mr. Howe. Do you know anything of the subsequent history of either Lieut. Williams or Capt. Lavoie?

Gen. Catlin. Personally, no.

Mr. Howe. Do you know how long either of them stayed in the Marine Corps?

Gen. Catlin. I do not. The records will show that, but I do not know.

Mr. Howe. Did you, on that inspection trip, hear of any other cases of the killing of natives?

Gen. Catlin. No.

Mr. Howe. Subsequent to that inspection trip, did you hear of cases of the killing of native prisoners?

Gen. Catlin. The case I heard of was the case at Croix des Bouquets, which is near Port au Prince, where a man was taken out, a man was captured one evening and executed that night.

Mr. Howe. Under whose order?

Gen. Catlin. Lieut. Brokaw.

Mr. Howe. That was the incident which was the subject matter of the courts-martial of Pvts. Johnson and McQuilkin?

Gen. Catlin. It was.

Mr. Howe. What about the case of Ryan?

Gen. Catlin. Ryan was an officer of the marines stationed at St. Michel. He was reported for having shot two natives near Grande Riviere. After investigation by Col. Hooker, I directed his trial by court-martial, and he was being tried when I left the island. I understood afterwards he was acquitted.

Mr. Howe. Were there any other cases of alleged killings that you heard of during that time there?

Gen. Catlin. There was a case of a gendarme killing some prisoners, I believe, one or two being Santo Dominicans, which took place several months before my arrival but for which I ordered a military commission for the trial of one man, and he was acquitted by the military commission.

Mr. Howe. That military commission met at?

Gen. Catlin. At Cape Haitien.

Mr. Howe. Was that the only military commission you appointed?

Gen. Catlin. The only military commission during my régime.

Mr. Howe. Was the case to which you refer the only case in which you appointed a military commission?

Gen. Catlin. That was the only case in which I appointed a military commission.

Mr. Howe. I understand that the provost court can not inflict the death penalty.

Gen. Catlin. No.

Mr. Howe. The military commission is the only body under martial law which can sentence to death?

Gen. Catlin. A court-martial could sentence to death, but only for military people, people under their jurisdiction, not for civilians.

Mr. Howe. Not for civilians?

Gen. Catlin. No.

Mr. Howe. Could a gendarme have been tried—a gendarme private—by a court-martial?

Gen. Catlin. He could have been tried by a gendarmerie court-martial, not by a marine court-martial.

Mr. Howe. Why was it that this gendarme, accused of killing prisoners, was tried before a military commission?

Gen. Catlin. Because—well, it was directed by Admiral Snowden. The probability is it was because one or two of the people supposed to have been killed belonged to a different country, belonged to Santo Domingo. It was right on the border where it took place.

Mr. Howe. So there may have been some doubt as to the jurisdiction of the gendarmerie court-martial?

Gen. Catlin. Yes.

Mr. Howe. Is this a correct statement: After you heard these accusations against Lavoie, did all other accusations of illegal killing of natives lead to charges and court-martial?

Gen. Catlin. Yes; every one that was heard of.

Mr. Howe. There are no exceptions to that statement?

Gen. Catlin. No exceptions.

Mr. Howe. Every one that was heard of? .

Gen. Catlin. Yes.

Mr. Howe. Do you know of any death sentence imposed by gendarme general courts-martial?

Gen. Catlin. No.

Mr. Howe. Do you know whether there were any or not?

Gen. Catlin. I am positive there were not.

Mr. Howe. During your time you know of no death sentences imposed by any commission?

Gen. Catlin. There were none imposed by any court with which the Americans had anything to do.

Mr. Howe. General, the other day here before the committee Lieut. Spear, formerly in the Marine Corps, testified that at a point about 16 miles from Mirebalais, at a time probably in the month of May, 1919, he was on duty with, as his commanding officer, Capt. Thomas Edwards, commanding the One hundredth Company of Marines, or a part of it, and that a relieving force of marines under other officers came out near the station of this One hundredth Company, or a part thereof, and the relieving force brought two native prisoners, and that Capt. Edwards informed him, Lieut. Spear, that those two prisoners were brought with orders for their execution, or words to that effect—probably words not to that direct effect, because one of these men was returned alive to Mirebalais. Lieut. Spear testified that his commanding officer, Capt. Edwards, told him to guard these two prisoners, which he did for two or three hours, and that thereafter one of the prisoners was marched out in front of one of the marines and shot; that is to say, one of these prisoners to whom Capt. Edwards had referred when he said they were received with orders to execute them, and that May, 1919, was during your tour of duty down there, was it not?

Gen. Catlin. It was.

Mr. Howe. Did you hear in any way of any sentence of death emanating from any tribunal, passed on any native during that time?

Gen. Catlin. I did not.

Mr. Howe. Whether in the district of Mirebalais or anywhere else?

Gen. Catlin. Anywhere in the island.

Mr. Howe. You are able to state positively that during your time no sentence of death was passed by a commission?

Gen. Catlin. Positive.

Mr. Howe. Do you know whether or not military commissions had been convened by your predecessor, or by any of your predecessors?

Gen. Catlin. Not to my knowledge.

Mr. Howe. Would you have known of the existence of a prisoner under sentence of death passed by a military commission previous to your arrival?

Gen. Catlin. Previous to my arrival?

Mr. Howe. I mean if there had been in custody during your tour a native under sentence of death you would have known of it?

Gen. Catlin. Certainly ; I would have known of it.

Mr. Howe. Can you state whether or not there was any such?

Gen. Catlin. There were none, and previous to my arrival there were no troops or prisoners or anything else in the districts you have referred to, Mirebalais and Las Cohobas.

Mr. Howe. The truth is that this One hundredth Company and others to which I referred were some——

Gen. Catlin. Were sent there by me.

Mr. Howe. Were put in by you or came in there after 1919?

Gen. CATLIN. May probably is the period.

Mr. HOWE. Do you know who was in command at Mirebalais at that time?

Gen. CATLIN. I can not state exactly now. Lieut. Col. Walter N. Hill was in command a part of the time.

Mr. HOWE. Was there a Maj. Emery in command there at any time?

Gen. CATLIN. No; Maj. Emery belonged to the gendarmerie and was on road work, etc., but was not in command.

Maj. McCLELLAN. This man referred to was a gendarmerie officer, was he not?

Mr. HOWE. Was Hill a gendarmerie officer?

Gen. CATLIN. Hill was a gendarmerie officer, but I had him report to me for temporary duty and had put him in command of that district of the marines.

Mr. HOWE. When Hill was absent from headquarters was there another officer there subordinate to him who would act in his place?

Gen. CATLIN. Certainly. The next senior officer would act in his place.

Mr. HOWE. Do you recollect at this time who was his next senior officer?

Gen. CATLIN. I do not at this time.

Mr. HOWE. It would be the purpose of the committee to question all officers who could have given that order for the execution there at Mirebalais. I was wondering if, besides Maj. Hill or possibly Maj. Emery, there were any others?

Gen. CATLIN. Maj. Emery could not have given orders to the marines, as gendarme officers were not allowed to issue orders to the marine officers. There was a Maj. Pearce at Las Cohobas.

Mr. HOWE. Was he on gendarme duty or with the marines?

Gen. CATLIN. No; he was a marine.

Mr. HOWE. Was Pearce ever performing duty which would permit him to act in place of Hill during the temporary absence of Hill?

Gen. CATLIN. Yes.

Mr. HOWE. How far away would Maj. Hill have to be from his headquarters to make it proper for his next in command to act?

Gen. CATLIN. As soon as he was out of sight, if he was going anywhere.

Mr. HOWE. Do you know whether Maj. Jacob M. Pearce was ever acting at Mirebalais in the absence of Maj. Hill?

Gen. CATLIN. No; I do not know. I imagine, though, he must have been a number of times.

Mr. HOWE. Is there anybody else there who could have been during the month of May or the early part of June, 1919, acting in command?

Gen. CATLIN. Yes; any officer who might have been left. You see, the detachments were being sent out at different times. Capt. Edwards would go out to his company or a part of it, and some officer would be left with the troops in Mirebalais. Now, during that time, whenever Col. Hill found it necessary to go to a different part of the country—Las Cohobas, or anywhere—the senior officer left would be in command temporarily of the town.

Mr. HOWE. Where would be any records from which we could learn who was in command, or acting command there, during the month of May, 1919?

Gen. CATLIN. Those records would all be in Port au Prince in the brigade headquarters. All records were there in regard to operations and where the troops were.

Maj. McCLELLAN. They would not show the temporary commands, though.

Gen. CATLIN. No; they would not show the temporary commands, but they would show what officers were out there.

Mr. HOWE. And what officers could have been in temporary command?

Mr. ANGELL. You testified, General, that to the best of your knowledge the corvee had actually been in operation only on the Port au Prince-Cape Haitien road. Was that just your understanding of it, or are you reasonably confident of that?

Gen. CATLIN. That is my understanding. I know nothing personally of it; it is only from hearsay, what I heard in regard to it.

Mr. ANGELL. Are you able to give us any estimate of the number of men who had been engaged at any one time in forced work on the roads under the corvee?

Gen. CATLIN. No; absolutely. As I say, all my information is hearsay. I heard of camps of 2,000 men, etc., but that is all. As to the actual number I have not any idea. Gen. Butler would be the only man I know of who could give the actual number, probably.

Mr. ANGELL. Did you see any of those camps yourself, or what was left of them, when you came there?

Gen. CATLIN. I saw places which were said to have been camps, one or two.

Mr. ANGELL. Did you ever hear whether or not those camps were surrounded by barbed-wire inclosures? You never heard of any such rumor?

Gen. CATLIN. Not barbed wire; no. I heard they had inclosed camps, and the men were kept in them.

Mr. ANGELL. And kept in them by armed guards?

Gen. CARLIN. Yes.

Mr. ANGELL. Were those guards, so far as you heard, always gendarmes, or were they sometimes marines?

Gen. CATLIN. Always gendarmes. All the corvee was worked by the gendarmerie, as far as I know.

Mr. ANGELL. Were these camps, so far as you know, in charge of white gendarmerie or marine officers?

Gen. CATLIN. Yes. As I say, my information is all hearsay on the corvee, because it all took place before I went down there.

Mr. ANGELL. All you know of your own personal knowledge of the corvee was what you found out on this inspection tour at Maissade and Hinche?

Gen. CATLIN. Yes.

Mr. ANGELL. What is your understanding of the meaning of the word "corvee"?

Gen. CATLIN. The meaning of the word "corvee" in the corvee law of Haiti was that men could be taken to work in their district upon the roads for a certain length of time each year, and upon the completion of that time they were given certificates that they had so worked and completed their work.

Mr. ANGELL. Do you remember what that period of time was?

Gen. CATLIN. I do not remember; roughly, I should say, two weeks, but I do not remember. As I said, the corvee did not interest me, the corvee itself. It was simply a question of stopping the corvee that interested me.

Mr. ANGELL. Was it your understanding that the corvee administered prior to your time had been in conformity with the old Haitian law or custom?

Gen. CATLIN. As I understood it, the corvee, as first started, was in compliance with the law, and that later, in building the road to Cape Haitien, it was found, in going through a district where very few people lived, that there was not enough labor to do the work, according to the law, and that natives were brought in from other districts.

Mr. ANGELL. And was it your understanding that these natives were kept beyond the statutory period of service?

Gen. CATLIN. I have heard so. These statements I have made in regard to the corvee are absolutely from hearsay evidence, not from any knowledge on my own part.

Mr. ANGELL. Can you tell, General, from your conversations with Haitians and other American officers in Haiti, particularly from any conversation with Col. Russell and among our marine officer. that there had been the policy in the later period of the corvee of taking men and making them work in districts other than their own and keeping them beyond the statutory period of time, etc.?

Gen. CATLIN. No; I do not know who did that. All I ever heard was that the corvee was started under Gen. Butler's régime, and presumably carried on during his régime as gendarmerie officer.

Mr. ANGELL. What do you believe that Charlemagne and the other Caco leaders against whom the operations were conducted in 1919 intended and hoped to obtain by their operations or activities out there in the hills?

Gen. CATLIN. It is impossible for me to state what they believed; I have not any idea. Of course, they were outlaws. They could not come in themselves without being imprisoned.

Mr. ANGELL. How are they outlaws; in what sense?

Gen. CATLIN. Well, Charlemagne was an outlaw, because he was serving a prison sentence as an outlaw, and escaped at the time. Norde was an outlaw.

Mr. ANGELL. For the same reason?

Gen. CATLIN. Norde had not escaped. Norde had always been an outlaw in the hills, as far as I could gather.

Mr. ANGELL. He never had been brought to trial?

Gen. CATLIN. To my knowledge he never had been.

Mr. ANGELL. Was that generally true of the other Caco leaders?

Gen. CATLIN. Of the principal ones, I think. Some of them were new. One of the principal ones down on the southern side of Mirebalais was a young fellow.

Mr. ANGELL. Had Charlemagne, by the way, been tried and imprisoned by our forces?

Gen. CATLIN. By the provost court.

Mr. ANGELL. For some violation of the criminal law?

Gen. CATLIN. No; banditry, in 1917.

Mr. ANGELL. For being in armed opposition to the Hatian Government and the American occupation?

Gen. CATLIN. Yes.

Mr. ANGELL. And sentenced to imprisonment?

Gen. CATLIN. For a certain period; I do not remember the period.

Mr. ANGELL. From which sentence he had escaped?

Gen. CATLIN. He had escaped from the gendarme sentry working over him on the road, and disappeared.

Mr. ANGELL. To what extent do you believe the opposition to the presence of the American military forces in Haiti contributed to the existence of the opposition under the lead or inspiration of Charlemagne and his immediate followers?

Gen. CATLIN. None.

Mr. ANGELL. You believe, then, that the sole motive for the activity of these irregulars, the Cacos out in the hills, was criminal banditism?

Gen. CATLIN. The sole motive at first was that, and their motive afterwards, and their fighting against the Americans, was to protect themselves in the hills.

Mr. ANGELL. Protect themselves from what?

Gen. CATLIN. From the Americans who were trying to chase them down.

Mr. ANGELL. Did you ever hear, General, that Charlemagne was actuated by a very strong feeling of racial hatred against the whites, the Americans?

Gen. CATLIN. I never did.

Mr. ANGELL. Did you ever hear his forces referred to as the patriot army?

Gen. CATLIN. No. He called himself the commander in chief of the forces operating against the Americans in several letters which I saw of his.

Mr. ANGELL. Did he attempt to get into diplomatic communication with the British chargé d'affaires down there?

Gen. CATLIN. Yes; and with different people, and he wrote letters to different public officials, asking them to come out.

Mr. ANGELL. Did he purport to have a cabinet?

Gen. CATLIN. Yes; a cabinet.

Mr. ANGELL. Is there any distinction, in your mind, between the term "Cacos" and the English word "bandits"?

Gen. CATLIN. Yes; a Caco is not the proper term for these people.

Mr. ANGELL. For which people?

Gen. CATLIN. For the people who were out in the field at the time, in 1918 and 1919.

Mr. ANGELL. Who were Cacos?

Gen. CATLIN. They were improperly called Cacos. The Cacos, as I understand it, were the old leaders of bands which were not necessarily bandits. They were really simply separate bands who lived by themselves, while the people who were in the field in 1918 and 1919 were bandits, according to the English idea of a bandit.

Mr. HOWE. The English-language idea, you mean?

Gen. CATLIN. The English-language idea.

Mr. ANGELL. Referring, General, to the case which was mentioned in a long question put to you by Mr. Howe regarding Lieut. Spear's testimony of an execution of one man, under orders of Capt. Edwards, can you say, from your own personal knowledge of the sentences of courts-martial and the military commissions, either immediately prior to the time when you took command in Haiti or during the time when you were in command, that such an execution as was mentioned by Mr. Howe in his question, assuming it to have happened, could not have been lawful?

Gen. CATLIN. I can not, as no military commission or court-martial could have been ordered except by me.

Mr. ANGELL. So that if, then, such a killing, in fact, did take place?

Gen. CATLIN. It was unwarranted.

Mr. ANGELL. It was unwarranted?

Gen. CATLIN. Yes.

Mr. ANGELL. General, do you remember the sworn statement which you gave before Lieut. Col. Lay, I believe, in Washington, at the end of December, 1919?

Gen. CATLIN. Before Col. Lay; no.

Mr. ANGELL. Can you find that, Major?

Maj. McCLELLAN. Yes; it is here.

Gen. CATLIN. That was a statement I made to the Secretary of the Navy.

Maj. McCLELLAN. Yes; he put it under oath afterwards.

Gen. CATLIN. I remember making a statement to the Secretary of the Navy.

Mr. ANGELL. There are two reports or statements. I just want to identify them.

Mrj. McCLELLAN. Did the general make two of them?

Mr. ANGELL. Yes; he made a statement to Gen. Lay, which it attached to what we call the Turner investigation, on December 31, 1919 and he also wrote a letter, at the request of the Secretary of the Navy, dated September 20, 1920. Do you remember having made such a statement?

Gen. CATLIN. Yes; I remember now.

Mr. ANGELL. Could you have written a letter to the Secretary of the Navy, under that later date, about September 20, 1920?

Gen. CATLIN. Yes.

Mr. ANGELL. I wonder if you can and will possibly in the intermission just read over those two, of which there are copies here, and then just state on the record whether the testimony there given or the statements there made are substantially correct as you now recollect.

Gen. CATLIN. That is correct—the testimony I gave there.

Mr. ANGELL. I want to ask you a few questions, further, General about the conditions at Hinche and the alleged Lavoie incident there. In your statement before Col. Lay you said: "I consider Maj. Wells principally responsible for the conditions as found. He stated he made frequent inspections of all posts, and it is inconceivable that he should not have known something of the conditions." That is, as you now recollect it, an accurate statement of your convictions at that time?

Gen. CATLIN. Yes; although this statement was made, of course, after I came back from Haiti, and my idea in regard to the responsibility of Maj. Wells was not what my idea was at the time of the inspection at Hinche. Things came up afterwards which caused me to change my idea in regard to Maj. Wells and to consider him more responsible than I did at that time.

Mr. ANGELL. When you say "at that time," you mean at the time of the investigation at Hinche?

Gen. CATLIN. Yes.

Mr. ANGELL. And later, if I understand you, you became convinced that there was a greater degree of responsibility attached to Maj. Wells?

Gen. CATLIN. Yes.

Mr. ANGELL. Do you mean by that answer to refer to the causes or to the general conditions, which?

Gen. CATLIN. No; I mean the general conditions and the lack of supervision and inspection which I found Maj. Wells had.

Mr. ANGELL. Maj. Wells was a major of marines and colonel in the gendarmerie?

Gen. CATLIN. Yes; he was colonel in the gendarmerie and had charge of the northern district. which took in Hinche at that time.

Mr. ANGELL. Did you, as brigade commander in Haiti, consider that the gendarmerie officers, and ultimately the marine officers not of the gendarmerie, were generally responsible for conditions as they existed?

Gen. CATLIN. No; I could not say that.

Mr. ANGELL. To what extent, then, would you say that the gendarmerie officers, for example, were responsible for general conditions?

Gen. CATLIN. I would not say the gendarmerie officers were responsible for conditions. I do say that I consider Maj. Wells principally responsible for his lack of supervision.

Mr. ANGELL. In that district?

Gen. CATLIN. In that district. I think the conditions in the rest of the island were undoubtedly very good.

Mr. ANGELL. That was on the other side, then, to the credit, to your mind, of the gendarmerie officers, and ultimately the marine direction?

Gen. CATLIN. It might have been; it might not. It may have been that the people were different in the gendarmerie. I do not know whether the conditions were different or not.

Mr. ANGELL. Did you regard the conditions in the gendarmerie and the general action of the gendarmes to be the ultimate responsibility of the gendarme officers and, in a military sense, the final responsibility of the higher officers of the marine occupation?

Gen. CATLIN. Yes; the conditions in the gendarmerie was the responsibility of the gendarmerie officers, undoubtedly.

Mr. ANGELL. And the gendarmerie was, in the last analysis, responsible to and generally directed by the marine officers of the occupation?

Gen. CATLIN. The marine officers were in command of the gendarmerie; they were the upper officers of the gendarmerie.

Mr. ANGELL. Was the ultimate responsibility that of the Haitian civil Government, or of the marine occupation?

Gen. CATLIN. Really, the marine occupation had nothing to do with the policy of the gendarmerie—that is, with their actual work in the field. They were theoretically under the brigade commander—that is, the general of the gendarmerie—but the brigade commander had nothing to do with the troops in the field or with the under officers except through the head of the gendarmerie.

Mr. ANGELL. Did the brigade commander confer with the chief of the gendarmerie as to matters of gendarmerie policy and discipline?   •

Gen. CATLIN. No; that was entirely a Haitian matter.

Mr. ANGELL. How was it, then, that, for example, you, if I understood you correctly, had Lieut. Doras Williams and Capt. Lavoie transferred from the Hinche district to Port au Prince?

Gen. CATLIN. I did that because I was going into a district with marines to take command and considered that they were not the proper men to have there, and the officers of the gendarmerie are still attached to what they call the constabulary detachment of the brigade. They are under the control of the brigade commander for disciplinary purposes only, not for other purposes.

Mr. ANGELL. What effect do you think the change of Article VI of the old constitution, the article which prohibited the ownership of land by foreigners, had in the general feeling of the population toward the United States and the American occupation in Haiti?

Gen. CATLIN. I am unable to state. My personal idea is that it probably had a bad effect in a way.

Mr. ANGELL. The change?

Gen CATLIN. Yes; I think not so much in the feeling of the natives as in the feeling which was engendered by certain leaders.

Mr. ANGELL. I do not understand the difference.

Gen. CATLIN. What I mean to say is that the people themselves, I do not really think, cared very much, the majority of the people.

Mr. ANGELL. You spoke of the feeling engendered?

Gen. CATLIN. Yes; engendered by the leaders.

Mr. ANGELL. Engendered among the Haitian people?

Gen. CATLIN. Among some of the Haitian people. Some of the propaganda issued by Charlemagne was along that line.

Mr. ANGELL. Was that feeling very strong?

Gen. CATLIN. Well, I am unable to state, because I was not in touch with the Haitian people, and I could not say.

Mr. ANGELL. You were not in touch with the Haitian people?

Gen. CATLIN. No. I, of course, had certain dealings with the people in Port au Prince, but outside of that I was not in touch.

Mr. HOWE. Mr. Chairman, it has been the intention all along to get the entire record of the Mayo court of inquiry and exhibits on the record here, but that has not been formally put on the record because it was hoped it would be put in in connection with the testimony of Maj. Dyer, who was judge advocate of that court of inquiry, and we are having difficulty finding time to put in Maj. Dyer here as a witness. I, therefore, suggest that the whole report be admitted in evidence now, with the understanding that later on such parts of it as may be a duplication of other matter which has already been admitted, may be left out from the printing of the record, and that perhaps a summary or digest of the testimony there may be printed in lieu of printing the whole testimony, but my present proposition is to admit it in evidence so that it may be referred to now as one of the exhibits.

Senator ODDIE. If there is no objection it will be so ordered.

Mr. ANGELL. You testified, General, that you did not believe that a conviction in the event that Capt. Lavoie had been court-martialed would have affected matters very much?

Gen. CATLIN. Yes.

Mr. ANGELL. Why?

Gen. CATLIN. Well, I do not know that I can give any particular reason, except a conviction would be expected in case of a man being guilty in the service, and if a man is convicted you would naturally suppose that everything is carried through all right, while if a man is acquitted there are always a lot of people who are willing to say that it was a whitewash.

Mr. ANGELL. Do you not feel, though, that a conviction, if a man had been tried and proven guilty, would have had or might have had a beneficial effect on the attitude of the natives toward the gendarmes in that district?

Gen. CATLIN. I did not consider it so. If I had considered his conviction as probable, I would undoubtedly have ordered the court-martial.

Mr. ANGELL. In this large compilation of the Mayo court of inquiry records, attached thereto as Exhibit 5, is an official report from Gen. Lejeune and Gen. Butler of their investigation in 1920 into conditions in Haiti, and as a part of that Lejeune-Butler report, Exhibit 5, there is attached a résumé of testimony taken by those officers wherein, at page 5, I find the résumé of the testimony of Lieut. Col. Richard S. Hooker. Col. Hooker at that time was not assistant chief of the gendarmerie?

Gen. CATLIN. No. You mean at the time of this?

Mr. ANGELL. At the time you were brigade commander in Haiti?

Gen. CATLIN. No; he was in command of a regiment of marines stationed at Cape Haitien in the north of Haiti.

Mr. ANGELL. He was later assistant chief of the gendarmerie?

Gen. CATLIN. He was assistant chief after I left.

Mr. ANGELL. I want to read from one paragraph of this report and ask you about it. This is Col. Hooker's testimony, or a résumé of his testimony, in which, referring to the investigation which he made upon your order, he says, " That he wrote a note on a Corona typewriter to Gen. Catlin, setting forth the result of his investigation ; that he kept no copy of his notes ; and that no record of it could be found in the files of the brigade headquarters at Port au Prince, Haiti." That, presumably, is the typewritten letter which you have introduced?

Gen. CATLIN. That is the letter which has been introduced to-day.

Mr. ANGELL. " Col. Hooker further states that Gen. Catlin, before leaving Haiti, said to him (Col. Hooker) in substance as follows : ' I suppose you wonder why I never did anything about the Hinche matter.' Hooker said, ' That he did.' Whereupon Gen. Catlin further stated in substance : ' That he did not do anything because it was during the period of the consideration of the Versailles treaty ; and that he did not wish to embarrass our President by having stories of cruelty appear about our own soldiers when we were taking a position on the side of humanity,' or words to that effect."

Do you remember whether or not you did make such a statement to Col. Hooker?

Gen. CATLIN. I do not remember making any such statement.

Mr. ANGELL. Would you say that you did not make such a statement?

Gen. CATLIN. To the best of my knowledge and belief I did not, because I can say that no such statement had any influence on my action in regard to the case. To the best of my knowledge and belief no such statement was made.

Senator ODDIE. I would just like to ask you one question. I want to ask what is your personal opinion of the value of Haitian testimony?

Gen. CATLIN. I do not think it has any value, sir. My idea, from seven months down there, is that a Haitian, as a rule, will testify to whatever he thinks is to his best interests.

Mr. ANGELL. Were you called before the Mayo court?

Gen. CATLIN. I was not.

Mr. ANGELL. Do you remember where you were on duty in the fall of 1920?

Gen. CATLIN. I was living in Washington at that time.

Mr. ANGELL. You were retired at that time, and were living in Washington?

Gen. CATLIN. I have been in Washington since I retired in December, 1919; I have not been out of the city.

Mr. HOWE. Why did you retire, General?

Gen. CATLIN. I was retired by a medical board as being not fit for active service on account of wounds received in France.

(Whereupon, at 1 o'clock p. m., a recess was taken until 2.30 o'clock p. m.)

The committee reassembled at 2.30 o'clock p. m., pursuant to the taking of recess.

STATEMENT OF BRIG. GEN. ELI K. COLE, UNITED STATES MARINE CORPS, PARIS ISLAND, S. C.

Mr. HOWE. General, will you give your name, rank and present station?

Gen. COLE. Eli K. Cole, brigadier general, Marine Corps, Paris Island, S. C.

Mr. HOWE. How long have you been in the Marine Corps, General?

Gen. COLE. Since 1890; in the Naval Academy before that.

Mr. HOWE. General, you went down to Haiti in 1915, did you not?

Gen. COLE. I sailed on the 31st of July and arrived there on the 4th of August.

Mr. HOWE. On what ship?

Gen. COLE. The *Connecticut*, and took about 500 men.

Mr. HOWE. You were in command?

Gen. COLE. I was in command of the Second Regiment.

Mr. HOWE. When did you land in Haiti?

Gen. COLE. On the 4th of August.

Mr. HOWE. Were you at that time the senior marine officer on land in Haiti?

Gen. COLE. Yes; until August 15, when Col. Waller arrived.

Mr. HOWE. And then he was senior to you?

Gen. COLE. He was senior to me. I had taken down a regiment and Col. Waller had followed on the *Tennessee* with another regiment, and upon landing he took command of the brigade, which was then formed, and I was then transferred to Cape Haitien and took command of the Second Regiment there and acted as military governor of northern Haiti and conducted the operations in northern Haiti.

Mr. HOWE. You remained with that assignment until when?

Gen. COLE. I remained with that assignment until early in November, as I remember it, 1916, when I went to Port au Prince to relieve Gen. Waller, possibly the latter part of November; the 22d of November I think was the exact date on which I relieved him and on which he sailed.

Mr. HOWE. From that time what was your position?

Gen. COLE. From that time I was in command of the brigade. and was termed there "chief of the occupation." That was the name the Haitians had for me.

Mr. HOWE. Until when?

Mr. HOWE. Until about the 1st of December, 1917. As a matter of fact I was actually attached to the brigade until the end of January, 1918, I having been sent up here with the constitution for the State Department about the 1st of December, 1917.

Mr. HOWE. So after the first few days after the landing you were about 16 months in the north?

Gen. COLE. Approximately.

Mr. HOWE. And approximately a year after that as brigade commander?

Gen. COLE. Yes; a little over a year; very little.

Mr. HOWE. What was the situation in Haiti at the time you landed in Port au Prince?

Gen. COLE. In Port au Prince?

Mr. HOWE. Yes.

Gen. COLE. The landing force of the *Washington* was on shore and in possession of the city. There were Government troops and revolutionary troops around there. Conditions were quiet but unsettled in the city itself. There was no government whatsoever other than the committee of safety.

Mr. HOWE. There was no President of Haiti at the time?

Gen. COLE. There was no President of Haiti.

Mr. HOWE. The last President of Haiti had just before that been killed, had he not?

Gen. COLE. Yes; he had taken refuge, I think, on the night of the 27th or morning of the 28th in the French legation, which was right next to the then palace, and had been wounded, as a matter of fact, that same night. On the morning of the 29th a mob of about 60 Haitians, under the leadership of Charles Zamor, had entered the legation—I might go back a little bit. The day before the mob had gone in the legation, but the French minister and his two daughters, h the possible assistance later of Mr. Cohn, the British chargé, and Mr.

Meyer, our chargé, had protected the President. The next morning, the 29th, Zamor, with these same 60 people, actually invaded the legation, pushing aside the one or two Mademoiselles Gireau, the daughters of the French minister, and going through the bedrooms and bathrooms they found him I think under a bed, and he was taken out and cut to pieces and his body dragged through the streets. This cutting into pieces, as far as I know, was done actually outside of the legation compound.

Mr. Howe. How long after that occurrence did you learn that the *Washington* landed her party?

Gen. Cole. Well, I was in the United States, and the first I knew of it was on the morning of the 30th.

Mr. Howe. Here is what I am getting at. How long had the *Washington's* landing party been on shore when you got there?

Gen. Cole. The *Washington's* landing party—I think I have the date, or I probably could get it. I got there about five days later, approximately; it may have been four or five days. I got there on the 4th.

Mr. Howe. Was there active disorder going on at the time you landed?

Gen. Cole. The city was quite quiet, although there was a decidedly tense atmosphere there, and during the time I was there there were disorders. There was some shooting at our people, but after the landing there was very little of it.

Mr. Howe. What, if any, Haitian was in authority or control in the city?

Gen. Cole. The only control was the revolutionary committee, called the committee of safety, of which I think Mr. Polynice and Gen. Zamor were the two principal members. Mr. Polynice was a merchant but not, so far as I know, a member of the revolutionary forces.

Mr. Howe. Under whose direct orders were you after you landed?

Gen. Cole. Admiral Caperton's.

Mr. Howe. You spoke of revolutionary troops being in the vicinity of the city. Where were they and what were they?

Gen. Cole. I never saw many of them. They were around outside of the city, but we did not go outside of the city, except on one or possibly two occasions. About August 7 I sent Capt. Fay some 12 or 15 miles outside of Port au Prince, to the Plain of the Cul de Sac, to hunt up a bandit by the name of Desgantes, who was said to have 15 or 20 followers and who was pillaging and robbing on the plains, and Capt. Fay captured him and a lot of his followers. They were armed.

Mr. Howe. Were there any other troops other than the United States forces near by?

Gen. Cole. There were Government troops in the city, and Government troops and revolutionary troops on the plain, and particularly around St. Marc and Gonaives.

Mr. Howe. That was farther north?

Gen. Cole. That was farther north.

Mr. Howe. Was there any fort or garrison in the city of Port au Prince?

Gen. Cole. There was Fort Nationale, which was on a commanding eminence right close to the city and which was occupied by the Haitian forces.

Mr. Howe. As distinguished from the revolutionary forces?

Gen. Cole. As distinguished from the revolutionary forces. I landed on the 4th, and on the 5th we took Fort Nationale. There we found 14 cannon, 450 rifles, and 1,000,000 rounds of ammunition. We tried to do everything we could to prevent bloodshed or armed resistance, and I got hold of one of the leading generals left in Port au Prince, and after considerable discussion and a great deal of hesitation on his part, and a promise to do it, and a backing out, and then a promise to do it—and we in the meantime were making preparations to take the fort if it became necessary, because it dominated the city, and with the ammunition, etc., there, it would do untold harm—he agreed to surrender the fort, and a lieutenant of the Navy, who had command of two of the companies from the *Washington*, was detailed as the officer to receive the surrender, and he and this general entered the fort by the drawbridge, and the surrender was made. However, quite a good many of the people jumped over the parapet and ran away, but we did nothing in regard to them, because what we were after was the arms, so that there would be no fighting.

Mr. Howe. As a matter of fact, what disposition was made of such of the garrison as did stay to surrender?

Gen. Cole. Those that surrendered, as I remember it, were placed for a short time in the old barracks, the Dessalines Barracks. On the 6th we disarmed all the soldiers we could find in the city. We rounded them up. There was a general division of the city into sect'ons, and a rounding up in those sect ons of the soldiers, and the taking of their arms, and they were held for a short time; those who belonged to Port au Prince were sent to their homes, and those who belonged outside were held for a time and then sent to their homes. As a matter of fact, it was rather a laughable situation at one time, because whenever we counted the prisoners we always had more. We turned them loose and they would find their way back, because they were getting fed, and Port au Prince at that time was almost on the verge of starvation. As a matter of fact, it was very badly undernourished and there were a considerable number of deaths from starvation, so much so, and the situation was so bad, that I recommended to Admiral Caperton that a dispatch be sent to the United States to the Red Cross requesting that funds be furnished so that we could have money to spend.

Mr. Howe. For feeding the population?

Gen. Cole. For feeding those who were in actual want. The Haitian officials had not been paid for a long time. The school-teachers had not been paid for an exceptionally long time, because education was the last thing they thought of, and I remember one case of a family of some 12 or 13, the mother a school-teacher, as I remember it, or the sister, possibly, and it was apparent to me that this family was practically starving, so we provided food from our own supplies in all cases of that sort where we found them. But she had been a school-teacher and had not received any pay for 18 months. Nobody could live under conditions of that sort.

Mr. Howe. In the occupation of the fort no shots were fired, and there were no casualties; is that correct?

Gen. Cole. There were no casualties, and I do not think any shots were fired. If there were any shots fired, they were shots fired from the fort. I do not think there was any resistance whatever, and no attack whatsoever on the fort.

Mr. Howe. In the disarming of the other soldiers in and around the city were there any casualties?

Gen. Cole. There were two. Two Haitians were killed, one at the custom-house and one on a street outside what they call the Ecole Normale.

Mr. Howe. That brings you up to the day——

Gen. Cole. That brings us up to the 6th.

Mr. Howe. To the 6th of August?

Gen. Cole. Yes.

Mr. Howe. What was your mission in landing, General?

Gen. Cole. My mission in landing was to preserve peace and order in the city of Port au Prince, to protect property, and protect lives; knowing or suspecting the irresponsibility of those people who had arms, the only thing to do was to get the arms away, and there were vast quantities of arms in the city, and a steamer came in just about that time and it had a lot of arms on also, which we naturally did not allow to get to the Haitian authorities.

Mr. Howe. What conditions were there prevailing which justified, if you think they did justify, the landing of the marine forces there or American armed forces there at all?

Gen. Cole. That, of course, is a question to be decided by the State Department. I can give my own opinion in the matter.

Mr. Howe. That is what the committee wants.

Gen. Cole. First and foremost, right then and there, was the fact that within a few days there had been a massacre of some 240 prisoners, mostly political, in the municipal prison of Port au Prince, and a condition of anarchy which existed throughout the whole of Haiti. In 1908 a President was elected, and in 1911 he was deposed or poisoned. If I may turn to some notes I have, I can give you——

Mr. Howe. Will you refresh your recollection from them and state what those condit'ons were prevailing?

Gen. Cole. I have the following memorandum: "In Haiti in 1915 the country was in a state of anarchy, with all attendant ills.

"A. Some 240 Haitians, including many of education and influence, were massacred in the prison at Port au Prince on the night of July 27, 1915, for political reasons, by order of the then president of Haiti, Guillaume Sam, in an endeavor to stamp out revolution, which apparently was going to overthrow his administration.

"B. Owing to constant civil warfare, the crops had not been equal to the needs; produce was seized by armed bands whenever the owners tried to get to the larger towns, particularly Port au Prince and Cape Haitien, and in these towns many were without adequate food, and some were actually starving to death.

" C. Roads had ceased to exist, being impassable for vehicles at all seasons, and in rainy seasons only donkeys could go over the trails, and then only with small loads and in danger of being drowned in mudholes.

" D. Telegraphs and telephones were practically destroyed.

" E. The postal service was dishonest and inefficient and the mails unsafe, due to dishonesty of employees and to the operation of revolutionary bands.

" F. Prisons were pestholes and filled with prisoners whose only sources of food were charity and relatives and whose only offenses were enmity of officials.

" G. Hospitals were nonexistent or absolutely lacking in means of support and for providing treatment to the sick.

" H. Practically no sanitary measures were taken by the Haitian officials, and with few exceptions funds collected were used for benefit of officials and their followers.

" I. Practically all male persons were under arms (forced levies) or in hiding.

" J. The school system was entirely a political affair, and, with the exception of the schools maintained by the church, there were practically no educational facilities for the poorer classes, and these in a few localities only; probably 95 per cent were illiterate.

" K. Such police as there were were politico-military in their character and tools in the hands of their chiefs.

" L. The judiciary was venal and generally only responsive to political favor or to litigants who could pay for decisions.

" M. Revenues, including customs, were spoils of political success.

" N. Voudauxism was rampant.

" O. But for the fact that a great war was raging in Europe, there seems but little doubt but what a European country would have attempted control in Haiti—at least unless we took control ourselves. German influence was going to predominate, and unless conditions set forth above were checked we would have faced an aggressive enemy at our doorstep or have given way to one, with the attendant ills of such a procedure or backdown."

Mr. Howe. Was that paragraph 3 you just read?

Gen. Cole. Paragraph 2.

Mr. Howe. Will you read paragraph 3?

Gen. Cole. Paragraph 3 is a question as to how the situation has changed now.

Mr. Howe. You need not go into that.

Gen. Cole. I did not think you wanted to go into that at this particular time.

(Thereupon, at 3 oclock p. m., a recess was taken until 4 p. m.)

AFTER RECESS.

The committee reassembled at 4 o'clock p. m., pursuant to the taking of recess.

Gen. Cole. I think you had asked me a question as to my opinion of the reasons for landing, and I think I had stated that there had been this massacre, that the President had been killed, and that there was no government.

Mr. Howe. And you gave a number of items as to the——

Gen. Cole. As to the general condition of the country.

Mr. Howe. Which, as I take it, would demonstrate a lack of systematic government.

Gen. Cole. There was no government at all. The courts had practically ceased functioning, and it was a state of each man for himself so far as he had a chance. Foreign lives had never been troubled by the Haitians. They had been very careful in regard to that. Foreign property was generally——

Mr. Howe. Please let me interrupt there. Do you think if there had been no active intervention there that foreign lives would have been taken?

Gen. Cole. Not at that time; but it was a case of disorder piling on disorder, and conditions were getting worse and worse, and the longer anarchy and where a condition of that sort exists the worse it is going to become, and it probably would have been a question of time only before there would have been destruction of foreign lives and, without any question, destruction of foreign property; but the past history of Haiti had been that they had been very careful in all their revolutionary activities not to direct them against the property of foreigners or against the lives of foreigners. They had milked the foreigner whenever they could in their courts and in their demands—this is what I am told—in demands for contributions, etc., in the way of payments for concessions, but they had been very careful in regard to property. I do not know how much this had to do with it—this is simply one of my opinions—but the World War was on, and the condition of anarchy existing in a country of that sort at our front door, in the first place, made an intolerable condition against everybody, and, in the second place, the German influence in Haiti predominated. It was greater than our own influence and it was beyond the French, although the French were the owners of practically all of the Haitian loans; but the submarine campaign was getting along about that time, and I believe that one justification of it would be that we could not have our commerce attacked by submarines from submarine bases in the West Indies. Of course, that is simply a personal opinion.

Mr. Howe. That was, of course, before our entry into the war?

Gen. Cole. That was before our entry into the war, but signposts were pointing that trouble was going to come sooner or later. Well, it was simply a general conglomeration of intolerable conditions, a civilization which had gone absolutely to ruin.

Mr. Howe. In your opinion, was some intervention necessary?

Gen. Cole. Absolutely, unless you wanted to allow what I think to be almost the richest part of the globe to become an African jungle. In the time of the French the whole country had been the richest and best-cultivated colony in the world. It had financed one or two of the French wars. It was wonderfully cultivated, and the French had mile after mile of fine roads, and when we landed the whole thing was a jungle. As I say, the roads had gone to ruin. The men had either become soldiers or were Cacos. The lands alongside the roads were desolate. The people had moved back into the hills, because either the Government or revolutionary forces going along the roads would pillage them. Men were never seen in the towns, except those who lived there. The women did all the marketing and things of that sort. On the road between Fort Liberté and Ounaminthe, about 15 or 16 miles, on the trip when we went over there we did not see one single habitation, we did not see one single hut, and yet it was said that that stretch of the road on either side of it had supported a population of about 3,000, and before I left Haiti approximately 10,000 people had come back into the area surrounding Ounaminthe.

Mr. Howe. Were there any other foreign Governments who were interested directly in that state of affairs in Haiti?

Gen. Cole. The French were materially. They were the only ones besides Germany. As I said, the French were the owners of the Haitian loans.

Mr. Howe. After you landed there what did you learn about the movement of Bobo?

Gen. Cole. Bobo had been in the north of Haiti, around Cape Haitien; and under arrangements made by Admiral Caperton he was embarked, as I remember it, on the Jason, some time about the 3d or 4th of August, because he arrived in Port au Prince on the 5th.

Mr. Howe. Who was Bobo?

Gen. Cole. Dr. Bobo was a Haitian physician, a man who was educated abroad, of considerable ability, inordinately, I understand, vain, and I guess he stood away above the majority of the Haitians in intellect.

Mr. Howe. Was he a presidential candidate at that time?

Gen. Cole. He was a presidential candidate at that time and had declared himself the possessor of the executive power. I have forgotten the term he used for it, but he had declared himself in that position; and, without any question, if we had not landed in Port au Prince I think Bobo would have been the President of Haiti and that he would have brought his revolutionary army into Port au Prince; and, as always was the case, the national assembly would have elected him as President. The successful revolutionary leader usually declared himself the possessor of the executive power, and then, upon his arrival in Port au Prince, the national assembly gave legality to his claim by electing him President. They had to do it.

Mr. Howe. Had the town and the fort been disarmed by the time they had arrived?

Gen. Cole. The town was disarmed, I think, the day after Bobo arrived, and the fort was taken the day he arrived. That is my recollection of it.

Mr. Howe. What relations did Bobo establish with you or Admiral Caperton?

Gen. Cole. Personally, there was practically no relation between Dr. Bobo and myself. I gave him protection and gave him a guard. He came there under the safeguard of Admiral Caperton, and I had instructions to safeguard him, and he was informed that I would safeguard him. A few days later, I think probably at the time of the election, he took refuge. He left the place where he was safeguarded—we did not interfere with his movements at all—he left his place and went to the British Legation. The British chargé d'affaires, Mr. Cohn, came to me and begged me to dispose of Dr. Bobo; that he did not want him; and I told Dr. Bobo that we absolutely would protect him; that there was no danger to his life, and I think the arrangement was that he went on board a steamer leaving for some other port in the West Indies and went to Jamaica that day or the next day. At no t me, so far as I have any knowledge whatsoever, was there any attempt on our part to do bodily harm to any of them. We tried to handle the thing without bloodshed and without interference with personal liberty. We stopped license.

Mr. Howe. When was the election called?

Gen. Cole. The election was called on the 12th of August.

Mr. Howe. When was notice of the election given?

Gen. Cole. Notice was given on the 11th of August, and on that day a revolutionary committee issued instructions dissolving the national assembly, and they were informed, I believe, by Admiral Caperton, that such action was not permissible, and they were rather obstreperous, as I remember it, or some of them were, and they were ordered dissolved.

Mr. Howe. The revolutionary committee?

Gen. Cole. The revolutionary committee. I think that was on the 12th.

Mr. Howe. Dartinguenave was elected on the 12th, was he not?

Gen. Cole. Dartinguenave was elected on the 12th.

Mr. Howe. Was there any military activity?

Gen. Cole. In connection with the election?

Mr. Howe. Yes. No; I did not mean that. Was there any military activity at the time of the election, in town or out?

Gen. Cole. The only military activity on the day of the election was this: There had been repeated reports of attempted disorders in case of an election, and as military commander I was responsible for the peaceful holding of the election, so I made arrangements with the president of the Senate and the speaker of the Chamber of Deputies that admission to the assembly place of the National Assembly should be by card, signed cards. He gave me the list of people that wanted to come, including the deputies, and the number that were allowed to attend as spectators, as I remember it, was limited, and we required the people who entered the inclosure where the National Assembly met to have these signed cards.

Mr. Howe. Who signed the cards?

Gen. Cole. The cards were, to the best of my recollection, signed by either the president of the Senate or speaker of the Chamber of Deputies and countersigned by me. That is my recollection of it.

Mr. Howe. Were they issued to all members of the Senate and the Assembly?

Gen. Cole. They were given, to my recollection, to the Haitian officials of the Senate and the Chamber for delivery. They had to sign these cards, and I countersigned them and kept the list of the people that went in. That is my recollection of it now. All of the area for one square around the place of assembly was held by troops in order that there could be no overt act against the Assembly.

Mr. Howe. Which was during the election?

Gen. Cole. Which was during the election. There were no American soldiers inside of the Chamber at the time, to the best of my knowledge and belief. I was at the front gate myself all the time to see that the people who entered had the proper cards, and in the case of any dispute the highest military authority would be there to settle it; but there was no attempt to prevent those people who had any right to get in from going in. The only thing was to prevent any disorder.

Mr. Howe. Then, after the election?

Gen. Cole. After the election Mr. Dartiguenave held a reception and insisted on being accompanied by one Gunner Sergt. Miller, who was afterwards called the Vice President of Haiti. The President could not go anywhere without Mr. Miller.

Mr. Howe. Did Miller stay with him?

Gen. Cole. He stayed with him until almost before I left. Shortly before I left, Miller wanted to get back to straight duty, and he went back to duty as lieutenant of the gendarmerie. Dr. Bobo left about that day—the day of the election—or the next day. I think it was the next day. Bobo, when he arrived, was allowed to parade through the streets with his followers, about 50 or 60. I took precautions to see that there was no trouble or interference with him. He was told that he could not start any revolutionary propaganda, or anything of that sort, but so far as his ability to see his friends, or anything of that sort, was concerned he was free.

Mr. Howe. Was there any firing on patrols outside after the election?

Gen. Cole. Yes; once or twice, as I remember it. I have a note of once: "On August 14 a patrol was fired on."

Mr. Howe. But otherwise?

Gen. Cole. Quiet.

Mr. Howe. Col. Waller arrived on the 15th and you left the next day; is that correct?

Gen. Cole. I left the next day for Cape Haitien.

Mr. Howe. What was your position at Cape Haitien?

Gen. Cole. In command of all military forces in the north and military governor.

Mr. Howe. When did you arrive at Cape Haitien?

Gen. Cole. The 17th.

Mr. Howe. What was the situation when you got there?

Gen. Cole. The landing forces from the *Connecticut* and from the *Nashville*, as I remember it, were occupying the town of Cape Haitien. The cacos were outside of the town. There are two roads into Cape Haitien only, one by way of Haut de Cap and one by way of Petite Anse. There are two roads entering Cape Haitien, one by way of Haut de Cap from the south, and the other from the Dominican border, and they go off like that [indicating]. The approach to the town is quite limited, and those approaches were held by Cacos.

Mr. Howe. How near in?

Gen. Cole. Their outpost toward Petite Anse was about a mile and a half, and the other way it was three-quarters of a mile. The other entrance was farther out of the town, and at Haut de Cape it was about 3 miles out.

Mr. Howe. How long had the American forces been in occupation there?

Gen. Cole. I think they had been there for a little over two weeks.

Mr. Howe. What was the situation in town as to food?

Gen. Cole. Very scarce. Nothing could come in. The Cacos did not allow it to come in.

Mr. Howe. What disposition did you make when you got there? Did you take troops there with you?

Gen. Cole. Yes; I went right on board the Tennessee and went up with a battalion and came down toward the station on the *Tennessee.*

Mr. Howe. With about 500 men?

Gen. Cole. Four hundred or five hundred. My orders were to preserve peace and order in Cape Haitien for the time being, and not to start any conflicts with the Cacos, and I simply took the necessary steps to protect Cape Haitien, established outposts at the entrances to the town, and patrolled the immediate vicinity within the outposts.

Mr. Howe. What did you do about the food situation?

Gen. Cole. Well, that kept getting worse and worse, but some little stuff came in, but very little, and there was a very decided shortage of foodstuffs, and we could do nothing in regard to it, except to bring it in by sea, so long as that condition was allowed to exist.

Mr. Howe. Was that condition allowed to exist?

Gen. Cole. That condition was allowed to exist until about the end of September.

Mr. Howe. The end of September?

Gen. Cole. Yes.

Mr. Howe. Then what happened?

Gen. Cole. Now, wait a second. About the middle of September, from the middle to the end. The thing was not opened up until after the 1st of October, as a matter of fact, but some things did come in, some little amount, but nothing like the amount that was needed. There was a sort of truce, you might say, understood, and some little stuff did come in, but it was very little.

Mr. Howe. Was there any Haitien Government in Cape Haitien?

Gen. Cole. No; there was no communal government. They had resigned. There were some representatives of the Government but there was no government.

Mr. Howe. Were any courts there functioning?

Gen. COLE. No courts were functioning.

Mr. HOWE. Col. Waller told us that an agreement was signed with the Cacos in September there, or about that time. Will you tell us what you know about that, General?

Gen. COLE. Col. Waller came up about the middle of September—the 18th, I think it was—and he and I, and I think one or two orderlies, met the Caco chiefs at a place called Carrefour, a mile and a half or 2 miles outside of Cape Haitien. Gen. Zamor, I think, was instrumental in bringing about that meeting. At that time my recollection is that Col. Weller stated it was necessary that the orders of Bobo and the other people that had been given prior to the election be honestly carried out, Bobo having given instructions that his followers in the north should turn in their arms, disband, and go to the their homes. They had not done that, and Col. Waller informed them that that would have to be done, and that he proposed to start patrolling; that it was necessary for foodstuff to come into Cape Haitien. After that conference he decided to open up the railroad, at least to go to Grande Riviere, which, as I remember it, was about 18 miles from Cape Haitien. We started out with some three squads of men, I think, and got to the cross-roads at Carrefour, near Quartier Morin, where we were halted by an obstruction placed on the track, and we were met by the Caco leaders and told that we could not go on. Col. Waller said we were going on, and we went on, and they promptly derailed us, they having drawn the spikes of some of the rails. I put the men out at once alongside of the track, and these Cacos were across the road at Carrefour, behind the hedges, etc., but there was no shooting, and we got our train back on the track after a while, and they were informed that we were going to Grande Riviere. But we went back to Cape Haitien, and it was decided that the situation was sufficinetly charged with dynamite that we better have more than three squads, so we took about 60 men, with a machine gun, put sand bags on a flat car and built up a parapet, etc., and started out, and we went to Grande Riviere that night. It was one of the wildest rides I ever took.

The road had not been used for a period of five or six months, and it was simply a line going through a young forest. We never knew what was going to happen. One time the engineer let her go lickity-split down grade, and we were going 35 miles an hour on this road where you could not see the track in front of you. We got up to Grande Riviere at about 9 o'clock in the evening, and there was a lot of obstructions on the track there. We were halted right under a bluff which we found out later the Cacos had occupied with some cannon, and had them trained on us, but fortunately Col. Waller induced the Caco general not to oppose our entry, and we went on into Grande Riviere. We spent the night there and a part of the next day, loaded up all the produce that was in the station awaiting shipment, and took that back to the cape, mostly coffee. Then Col. Waller went back to Port au Prince and I had instructions not to start patrolling until I got orders; along about the 23d, I think, or the 24th, I got instructions to start patrolling, and to notify the Caco leaders that we were going to start this patrolling; that we did not intend any harm to them, but that we were going to patrol; that we must have the food coming in, and that while we were making these patrols we did not intend to open fire on them, but that they must not open fire on us; that if they did we would then certainly take forceful action.

On the 25th of September I sent two patrols out, one to Haut de Cap about 3 miles outside of the town, in the morning. They went through some of the Caco patrols and they did not stop us. Our patrol went to Haut de Cap. On the way back there was considerable shouting at one point, and apparently they were about to fire upon our men, so our troops just put their machine gun in position, the Cacos quieted down, and we came on in.

The same afternoon I took a patrol out to Petite Anse, and we rode by their outpost. As a matter of fact, their outpost was at the crossroads, Petite Anse being off the main road. I took one company past their outpost, and the other company went on through Petite Anse and came back. This day they had evidently been surprised and their outpost commanders evidently did not know what to do about these patrols.

The second day I sent out two patrols of about 40 men with a machine gun in both cases. One, I remember, was to go to Haut de Cap, and then on to the town of Plain du Nord. The other patrol was to go past Petite Anse and then across the Plain, and eventually join with the other column at Haut de Cap on its return from Plain du Nord. They had the same instructions as the others, and we sent interpreters with them so that there could be no question as to the thing being understood, that we were going to make this patrol; that we did not intend to start offensive operations against them but that we must make the patrol; that if they attempted to stop us by force or opened fire on us, we, of course, would return the fire.

About 9 o'clock I got word from Haut de Cap that the Cacos had said that if we advanced they would fire on us, and was asked for instructions. I said the instructions were plain, to go ahead. And our men went ahead and they were fired on. Our men dropped alongside of the road, and opened fire with their machine gun. The Cacos scattered through the town of Haut de Cap. There was considerable firing going on there. I sent out three squads as a reinforcement, and shortly after that went out myself. There was firing going on all along out there, and up to three o'clock in the afternoon desultory firing was kept up, principally from across the river at Haut de Cap, and considerable firing had been heard in the distance, from Capt. Campbell's column. The Cacos had attacked him, and had caught him in a rather nasty place, and he had a number of his men wounded, but he had successfully extricated them. We do not know how much loss he inflicted on the Cacos. He inflicted some, without any question, because they gave it up and left him.

As soon as they got back to the Cape I had a conference with the senior naval officer present, Capt. Durell, and said that my proposition was that I was going to Quartier Morin the next morning with all our troops, with the exception of just a few to hold Cape Haitien; that I would like him to land a couple of companies to hold the Cape, my idea being that if the troops at Quartier Morin, which was their headquarters, would stand, we would have 'the issue decided then and there; that if they would not stand, we would ride over the town to show them we would go anywhere we wanted to.

We started out the next morning. Quartier Morin was 8 or 9 miles away. We went out there, and there was only one shot fired by us that day. At Carrefour, about half or three-quarters of a mile from Quartier Morin, we were met by a Gen. Fouche, a Haitien, who was surgeon general, and he said that the war was over; that they wanted to be good, and welcomed us to Quartier Morin. As we were going up toward Quartier Morin there was one shot fired by a Caco at our column and one of our men took a shot at the man who had fired and killed him.

We went to the town of Quartier Morin, and I asked for Gen. Moranoy, and was told that he had business elsewhere and had left the town a few minutes before, so there were none of their soldiers there. The population of the town, such as it was, largely women, turned out to greet us, and was very pleasant, and so on, and Dr. Fouche, the only officer who was present, said that the war was over without any question; that they had had enough; that the day before had been a very severe lesson to them, and that they realized it would not pay to attack us again.

Gen. Waller, I think, came up about the 28th. I am not certain just as to the sequence of events there. I am inclined to think that Gen. Petion came in to Cap Haitien, and a few days later Gen. Waller and I, with some others, went to Quartier Morin, and Gen. Waller signed the copvention with the Caco chiefs for them to carry out their instructions to turn in their arms and disband and go to their homes and take up peaceful pursuits. That is my general recollection of it.

Mr. HOWE. That, by the way, went into our record here. It was read in as Gen. Waller was testifying. Did you have any negotiations yourself with these Cacos at or about that time?

Gen. COLE. I do not think you could call them negotiations. They would not come into Cape Haitien for preliminary negotiations unless I agreed to go out to their outpost with one orderly to meet them, and I went out there to meet them, but Gen. Morancy would not come in. He evidently was afraid.

Mr. HOWE. Who did?

Gen. COLE. Gen. Petion, with a considerable number of his followers, I think, came into town, and they insisted that I should accompany them everywhere.

Mr. HOWE. You mean back into their own country; back of their own outposts?

Gen. COLE. Not only through the town, but back into their own country; back to their outpost. As a matter of fact, I accompanied them out to their headquarters at Quartier Morin, which was about 8 or 9 miles out, with an orderly.

Mr. HOWE. What happened there?

Gen. COLE. Well, they brought out some champagne, and had a band and a few other things, and I distributed some gourdes among the band, and they cheered me, and then they escorted me back to their outpost.

Mr. HOWE. It was a friendly visit?

Gen. COLE. It was a friendly visit. Gen Petion said that if I would go out—I had no idea of doing it—he said that if I would go out with them that it would do more to bring about peace in the north of Haiti than anything else.

Mr. HOWE. Did it have a good effect?

Gen. COLE. It had a splendid effect. It gave me a very big influence with the chiefs in the north of Haiti.

Mr. HOWE. I fancy you must have been more comfortable after the receipt of this hospitality than on the way out to it.

Gen. COLE. Yes; I was. I was not particularly anxious to go, but it was one of the things you had to decide like that. They evidently saw that I was hesitating, and I suppose that they thought that I thought of treachery, which I did, and I thought, " Well, the best thing to do is to go."

Mr. HOWE. In general, what were your relations thereafter with the Caco chiefs?

Gen. COLE. Very friendly; very friendly. Gen. Morancy, who was supposed to be the big chief, used to come into my office and prink himself before the glass—we always had one of these big mirrors in the office, one of the signs of Haiti, and he would step up there before that and prink himself. And sometimes he would come in crying. They arrested him time and again, and he would come in crying like a child, and look up in the mirror and see himself crying, and would straighten up and get along very well. He was a good deal of a bucco, but he had a good deal of force withal. He was a child in certain ways, but I got along splendidly with Morancy, and exceptionally well with Petion, who really had the brains of that outfit.

Mr. HOWE. Did those two keep the terms of that agreement fairly well?

Gen. COLE. To the best of my knowledge and belief, absolutely. I had more support from Petion than I did from Morancy. Morancy was an entirely different type of man from Petion. Gen. Petion was a man of a great deal of intelligence, and we discussed things very frequently, and he became convinced after I was there, at least I though he did, that there was a great deal more for him and for his country through peace than there was through disorder, and at that time there was a big boom in logwood. German dyes were kept out of our country, and logwood was selling away up to the skies, and Petion had large properties, so he started in cutting logwood, and I think he cleared a good many thousands of dollars.

Mr. HOWE. Then, we are now up to the point, after the attacks on those patrols, where you took Quartier Morin, and where the agreement with the Cacos had been signed. Now, will you outline the developments after that?

Gen. COLE. During October and November there were a considerable number of arms turned in. They came in slower than we thought they should come in, but they came in. The arrangement was that they should be paid for their arms after they were turned in, and possibly, in part, for the reason that they were not paid for as turned in, some of the minor chiefs thought that their head chiefs were taking the money, and as they were not getting anything, they did not turn in their arms. Some of them were opposed to the Americans. You see, there had been revolution after revolution in Haiti, and they had lost the habit of work. They did not want to work, they did not want peace, and some of the bad men, I think I could call them, took to the hills, more or less. They went up in that area which lay between the Grande Riviere and the Dominican border, and more particularly up in and around what was called the Capois district. I tried to meet them. I went up in that vicinity two or three times, and they would promise, but they would not meet us; they attacked our forces in one or two places; there was robbery going on all the time, and conditions gradually got worse in that area; so it became necessary to clean it up, and we started a systematic campaign of running down these bands.

Mr. HOWE. Let me interrupt right there. How would you characterize the people with whom you came into conflict at first there on the 26th of September? Were they Cacos or bandits?

Gen. COLE. They were Cacos. They were what I would call mercenaries. I think that is about as good a definition of what a Caco is as anything I know of. They were people who sold their arms, that is the use of their arms, military arms, to any revolutionary candidate. They were, generically, people who lived in the north of Haiti, and a certain type of peasant and his chief.

Mr. Howe. Later on, up near the border, at the time when you said it was necessary to clear that country up on account of the bandits, those were not Cacos any more that you were opposed to?

Gen. Cole. They had been Cacos, and they were Cacos in the sense of the word that they belonged to that ilk. There were good Cacos and there were bad Cacos. Most of the Cacos that I ran across I rather liked. I liked them better than the other Haitians. They were more sincere. The Haitian politician I never had much use for, but I did have a good deal of liking for the Caco chiefs.

Mr. Howe. Then, were these people that you did have to proceed against good ex-Cacos or bad ex-Cacos?

Gen. Cole. I would say they were bad ex-Cacos, most of them. There may have been some of them who were actuated by patriotic motives. One of their principal leaders, Joseph, was very bitterly antiwhite, and said that the Americans had come there to enslave the country. He inflamed a good many people, and got a good many together, a considerable number. He was in command of For Riviere. The day before our final attack on Fort Riviere he took some of his principal followers and certain minor followers into the fort with orders to defend it, and he went off to save his own skin. That was the sort of patriot he was. He left them there with orders to fight, and defend it to the last, and they did. They were not in the habit of giving mercy, and they had no idea that mercy would be given them. That was their system of warfare, and they fought to the very end in the fort.

Mr. Howe. General, will you give us an outline of the campaign beginning up at the border there and ending in the capture of Fort Riviere?

Gen. Cole. Well, we sent troops up to Grande Riviere, and then we sent them on to Bahon, which was 10 or 12 miles beyond Grande Riviere. We sent two or three squads—three squads, I think. They were fired on from across the river. They were at the railroad station there. Our troops returned the fire and evidently did some damage, although they never knew how much, because the next morning they examined the place and they found trails of blood. They were withdrawn to Grande Riviere, and the report was received that Grande Riviere was to be attacked, and there were only about 20 men there. I took a company to Grande Riviere, I think, that night. Along the border somewhat the same conditions prevailed, and there was a good deal of bandit activity, but that was cleared up, and Capt. Campbell at Grande Riviere was directed to operate through that country and find out what he could about the country, and Gen. Butler, then Maj. Butler, was directed to make a reconnaissance from Fort Liberte, by way of Terrier Rouge, Le Trou, St. Suzanne, Grande Riviere, Bahon, to a place called Valliere, thence back to Ounanaminthe. There was some trouble around Terrier Rouge, as I remember it, and we seized some 50 rifles there. Butler's detachment was mounted, but they found the trails so bad that they could not get through, so the horses were left at Grande Riviere. I had information that the principal stronghold was at a place called Fort Capois, but we could get no information as to its exact locality. Gen. Butler, at St. Suzanne, was given information that he believed its location could be determined from the northern trail from Bahon to Valliere.

The informant said that there were probably three people who could lead us to Fort Capois. He was one, and he could not do it, and the other two would not, without any question. I changed Gen. Butler's route to go by Fort Dipiti, with the idea of locating Capois. He was attacked when near Dipiti in the night by what was estimated to be about 400 Cacos but drove them off; held them off. I think we had a couple of wounded, and continued to Gros Roches. In the meantime Col. Waller had come north and be joined Col. Waller and me at Cape Haitien, and as the result of this reconnaissance a plan of action was drawn up to attack Fort Capois. The operations were to be divided into two parts, (a) cleaning up the country east of the Grande Riviere, and (b) the cleaning up of the Fort Riviere district to the west of the Grande Riviere. The country east of the Grande Riviere was cleaned up, but owing to the failure of a part of the troops to get to the fort at the proper time most of its garrison escaped.

Mr. Howe. The fort was occupied?

Gen. Cole. The fort was occupied. It was very well defended. It could have been held if they had gone about it properly, without any question. Some of those people fled across the Grande Riviere. We tried to stop them, but the advance was very slow through that section, and it had to cover a very wide area, and a considerable number got across and took station in Fort

Riviere; after that area was cleaned up of the bandits our troops refitted at Grande Riviere. I, in the meantime, had been getting a good deal of information about Fort Riviere; a plan was drawn up and the place was attacked by four columns coming from widely different directions, but the time was fixed·so that each column got to the place at the right time, and the attack was made at daylight on a certain morning; the fort was occupied after considerable firing, and some of the people escaped but I do not know how many. There were about 50 dead counted in the fort and in the vicinity of the fort. There was only one entrance. It was on a high mountain, and it was a masonry fort, with embrasures and a moat, and places inside, cells inside where they could shoot in every direction, and they simply fought to the end. They would not surrender.

Mr. Howe. What was the character of the fighting there?

Gen. Cole. Hand to hand, cons'derable.

Mr. Howe. How was entrance gained?

Gen. Cole. The report was—and I presume it is correct, there was no reason to doubt it—that our assaulting troops got under the cover of the wall of this fort at the entrance and they had difficulty in getting in, so Pvt. Gross and Sergt. Iams climbed in through a small sally port and held the entrance, followed by Butler and the rest of his men.

Mr. Howe. Gen. Butler got a medal of honor for that, did he not?

Gen. Cole. I do not think so. Iams did, and Gross.

Maj. McClellan. Yes; he did.

Mr. Howe. There was a brief resistance then by the Haitians inside the fort?

Gen. Cole. Apparently, and then we blew up the fort, got dynam'te from the Cape and blew up the fort.

Mr. Howe. That was on November 17?

Gen. Cole. November 17.

Mr. Howe. Did that mark the end of the campaign?

Gen. Cole. Yes; 't ended the campaign, but my plan had been, just as soon as troops could be refitted, to start a detachment to Hinche. That was Gen. Waller's orders, and my plan was to send out other troops and to go all through the area between the Grande Riviere and the Dominican border, not with the idea of any offensive action, but with the idea that if any wandering bands were in that area they would be disposed of, captured, dispersed or killed, whatever had to be done, and to show the Haitians in that area, in the first place, that the Americans would go anywhere.

The Haitian Government troops had never been in the Fort Riviere and Fort Capois districts. It was absolutely an unknown land to them. It was the Caco's stronghold all through there, and my idea was that by sending troops all through that country they would see, in the first place, that so long as there was no resistance we would treat them kindly, and in the second place, that we went anywhere we wanted to go. I do not think they had any doubt about it, because we had gone all through that country, but I thought a second going through it in a peaceable sort of way would be a very good thing; but the department dec'ded that there had been enough lesson given to them and that probably they would be good.

Mr. Howe. So you abandoned that reconnaissance?

Gen. Cole. We sent troops to Hinche, but in very much smaller numbers, to get arms down there which were to be turned in. They were not turned in, all of them, by any manner or means. They kept a lot of them at Hinche. If we had sent right away a column in there, I think we would have gotten more arms.

Mr. Howe. How soon after was absolute quiet restored?

Gen. Cole. There was quiet from then on. except for bands of robbers, small bands of four, five, or six, just here and there and anywhere between St. Suzanne, Le Trou, Limonade, and the border. They usually robbed the market women. That was their best bet. They always avoided our patrols if they could; sometimes they did not.

Mr. Howe. And to that extent there was unrest and trouble there?

Gen. Cole. To that extent there was unrest, but it grew smaller and smaller, and I adopted the policy wherever a man who had been out would come in and present himself and state that he would be good and would go to his place to live and keep in touch with us, that unless there was some crime alleged against him, an actual crime, he would not be confined but given his liberty and the opportunity to make a good citizen of himself. That was the general principle. There were practically no punishments, practically no imprisonments, on account of that. Joseph some time later was captured, and I think myself, in view of the cowardly way in which he left his followers in Fort Riviere, he ought to have been hanged. He was given 10 years.

Mr. HOWE. By the provost court?

Gen. COLE. By the provost court.

Mr. HOWE. That brings you up to March, 1916?

Gen. COLE. That brings us up to March, 1916. There were a considerable number of small outbreaks directed against the gendarmerie. The gendarmerie had, in the meantime, been established, and had been sent out for some political reason from Port au Prince—that is, for some political reason in Port au Prince had been sent out to take over the policing of the interior to as great an extent as possible. They were not fit for it, they had not had sufficient training to do it, and it was not a good thing to do, except as it may have affected the political situation, of which I have no knowledge. So far as the military proposition of this order was concerned, it was not the best thing to do, but it was done, and soon there was trouble. I sent white troops, a couple of white soldiers to each detachment, or something of that sort, and with the white man they were stiff—they would stand. Without the white man they were not apt to do it. I was afraid to send one white man, and I sent from two to four to six to eight, depending upon the isolation of the post, but during the month of December, 1916, there were three or four skirmishes. On December 6, at Gros Roches, there were several captures, and on December 12, at Perche and Terrier Rouge, several were killed, and on December 21 one was killed at Perche in an attack there.

Mr. HOWE. General, as you look over your notes there, can you summarize the number of engagements there then, in the first months of 1916?

Gen. COLE. Well, that was the end of 1916. During December there were four.

Mr. HOWE. In the first months of 1916?

Gen. COLE. In 1916 I have notes showing 17 little attacks on the gendarmerie.

Mr. HOWE. Between what dates?

Gen. COLE. Between March 6 and April 11 St. Michel was attacked and the gendarmes fled.

Mr. HOWE. Did that end the disturbances?

Gen. COLE. On May 1 there was a serious attack on Hinche. That ended it. All of these things, except St. Michel, amounted to very little. At St. Michel there was quite a serious repulse. I had this policy in regard to conditions of that sort: I believed that prevention was very much more valuable than cure; we could not keep troops in all parts of the country, and, as a matter of fact, they did not want it done, but I did have white troops in what I considered strategic points, and whenever trouble showed its head in any one section, I immediately sent military detachments of white troops, and at every place they surrounded them and went right in.

Mr. HOWE. In order, if possible, to prevent the trouble from becoming active?

Gen. COLE. Always before it did, because it did not become active; we always stopped it. There were seven attacks in 10 days on different places, and we sent troops in from along the border towns and in from the other places.

Mr. HOWE. But the attack on Ouanaminthe ended things, and that was in May?

Gen. COLE. Yes; that was in May.

Mr. HOWE. Had you by that time been able to begin building public works?

Gen. COLE. Oh, yes; it had been going on.

(Whereupon the committee adjourned until Thursday, November 10, 1921, at 10.30 o'clock a. m.)

INQUIRY INTO OCCUPATION AND ADMINISTRATION OF HAITI AND SANTO DOMINGO.

THURSDAY, NOVEMBER 10, 1921.

UNITED STATES SENATE,
SELECT COMMITTEE ON HAITI AND SANTO DOMINGO.
Washington, D. C.

The committee met pursuant to adjournment, in room 131, Senate Office Building, at 10.30 o'clock a. m., Senator Tasker L. Oddie, presiding.

Present: Senator Oddie.

Also present: Mr. Walter Bruce Howe, Mr. Ernest Angell, and Maj. Edwin N. McClellan.

STATEMENT OF BRIG. GEN. ELI K. COLE, UNITED STATES MARINE CORPS—Resumed.

Mr. HOWE. General, yesterday, when the hearing closed I had just asked you a question about what you were able to do in the way of internal improvements and restoring the various undertakings of government, such as hospitals.

Gen. COLE. In the North?

Mr. HOWE. Yes.

Gen. COLE. I think probably I can do that more quickly with my notes. You might try that, if you feel disposed to do so.

Mr. HOWE. Will you go ahead, and let us have the heads of what you undertook there.

Gen. COLE. There was no civilian administration whatsoever in Cape Haitien, and the various things pertaining to a town administration were taken up and carried on by us. The Hospice, in charge of the French Sisters, was in a very dilapidated state, and without supplies or proper appliances, and even shelter for people who were there for care. In the course of our stay in the north of Haiti this building was thoroughly overhauled, supplies were obtained from the United States, the question of proper food was taken up and solved, and generally it was placed in a very satisfactory and efficient condition.

Along the same lines, the people of the rural districts of Haiti had absolutely no medical attention whatsoever, and in order to eliminate as much of this as possible, I had established, wherever we had American troops, small dispensaries, furnishing the medicines for a long time from the United States supplies, and later purchasing them in the United States, and had either medical officers or Hospital Corps men detailed in charge of those dispensaries, where people who had physical troubles could receive such examinations and treatment as the limited facilities would allow, medicines being dispensed, and in serious cases the people being sent to one of the large ports where they received as good hospitalization care as we could give them. This was without question of great value to the people, and it did much to establish our influence for good with the people of Haiti.

The prison at Cape Haitien was a national affair, and was about as disreputable an institution as it would be possible to find. The place was thoroughly gone over, rebuilt in many places, repaired, put in sanitary condition, exercise grounds were prepared, the men incarcerated therein were taught trades, and they were fed, the former procedure being that if the prisoner had no friends or relatives to feed him, he was apt to die of starvation, and generally the place was placed in a condition where one could see that it was as clean and sanitary a place as one could find anywhere.

The water works had been allowed to go entirely to pieces. Fresh water possibly was available in some houses for a period of from one to two hours a day. This water system was thoroughly overhauled, and while there never was a sufficient amount of water to meet all the requirements, there was ample water for the immediate purposes of human life.

The streets had not been cleaned for years, and no street repairs had been made. First the main streets, and then the secondary streets in the town of Cape Haitien were overhauled and put into a good state of repair.

The roads outside of Cape Haitien, and, as a matter of fact, outside of all towns, had been allowed to go utterly to ruin. In the dry season passable for donkeys, but not for vehicles, and in the wet season the donkeys would frequently be drowned in mud holes. For mile after mile of road in the wet season, if you rode over it, you would have to pull your feet up to keep them out of the mud, the mud rising up practically to the horses' belly. We employed a large number of ex-Cacos and farm laborers on these roads, paying them at the rate of a gourde a day, the idea being that they would get money in that way to purchase seed, etc., to start planting, and that the men who were working would not engage in revolutions. Up to that time the Haitian officials or Haitian laborers had practically never been paid, and we made it the absolute rule, of course, that they should be paid not only the full amount but actually on time every week. At first the people did not want to work, because they feared they would not be paid, but when they found they were being paid we had many more applicants than we had funds to employ.

The road between Cape Haitien and the border was put in a state, within a few months after we arrived there, when an automobile could go over it, and eventually it was made into a well-graded and maintained highway.

The national schools hardly existed. There were some in the Cape, and there were so-called schools in a good many different places, but they were not functioning as schools. The school system was a political one. The school teachers were very inadequately paid. They were generally appointed as the result of some friend being in power, and they were actually not expected normally to do any work in regard to teaching school. The state did not own these buildings but rented them. I inspected a school in a little settlement outside of Limbe, on a tour of inspection I was making, and it was built of wattle, and when I went inside I found that it was a hog wallow. There were no windows, just one door, and a sow with a litter of pigs was inside of the building, and it never could have been occupied in any way, shape, or form as a school building, yet the government was paying for it. That is an extreme case, but it is a sample of the conditions existing in the schools of rural Haiti.

One schoolhouse where there were supposed to be two school rooms was probably 12 by 8 feet. It had two rooms, the second room being a closet without windows about 3 by 8 feet. The reports of that school showed about 45 or 50 pupils in daily attendance. I asked the teachers where they could get anything like that number in the school, and they said they could not. As a matter of fact, at the time I arrived there the school was not open and the school-teacher was not present until the following day. There had been no regular school held there, at least for some time, the place being used as a coffee broker's office.

Mr. Howe. What were you able to do about the schools, if anything?

Gen. Cole. The only real schools, outside of some in Cape Haitien, were the church schools, run either by the Catholic priests or by the sisters. They had fairly good schools in Cape Haitien and in nearly all the communes. In all the communes where there were priests they had schools which were quite good. They were far better than anything else in Haiti.

Mr. Howe. Who were those priests? Were they Frenchmen?

Gen. Cole. They were Frenchmen, and the sisters were French women almost entirely. There were a few of other nationalities. If it had not been for the church schools, in my opinion, Haiti would have relapsed absolutely into barbarism. It was the one source, the one ray of educational light in the whole country There can be no question about that, because outside of a few of the larger towns, the public schools were absolutely of no use whatever. There might be one here and there. We did find people here and there who were trying to do with the things they had as best they could, but it was little. We gave assistance to the church schools wherever we could. We assisted them in making repairs. They were supposed to receive a subsidy from the

Government, and we investigated those as far as we could, and paid them, and where possible paid the arrears, in order that the work of repair might go on. And generally, during my stay in Haiti, I had the utmost support of the church, from the priests and from the sisters, because wherever we went, realizing the fact that they had done so much, and that they were the points from which we could do something in regard to education, we gave them such support as we could, and they were very grateful. The bishop of northern Haiti, an old man by the name of Kerquzan, made two extensive trips on horseback through the north of Haiti, in order to preach cooperation with the American occupation in Haiti.

In the latter part of my stay an expert from the United States has been obtained to give advice and assistance in regard to building up the school system. The archbishop of Port au Prince rather opposed that proposition. He was in favor of national schools, but entirely under the Catholic Church, and that caused a little antagonism on the part of some toward the American occupation, and pressure may have been brought to bear on officials to interfere with the work of the expert we brought down to help build up the national school system.

Sanitation in all the towns was entirely neglected. Refuse of every description was thrown on vacant lots. There were no sewers and no toilets. The result was that the town stunk to heaven. The yards were cleaned up, public toilets were built, drainage was instituted; areas where mosquitoes had been breeding were drained or filled, as we could do it, and generally the place was put into a state of good sanitation.

We did everything we could to get the peasant to return to the farm and go to work cultivating, and with the exception of a few, a very few of the chiefs of the rebellion against us during October and November, they were allowed when they came in to go to their farms and go to work. We told them that we did not care for anything except their being good, honest citizens, and that so long as they behaved themselves we would not interfere with them, but that they must keep absolutely clear from any robberies or banditry, or anything of that sort.

The sugar mills we did nothing about, but, as a matter of curiosity, the same type of sugar mill which you see in picture books as being in use in ancient Egypt were in use in Haiti at that time, and I presume are generally in use to-day, the long pole, with the oxen tramping around the grinders.

We took up, under orders from Admiral Caperton, the payment of Haitian officials, and our officers personally paid the officials the amounts due them, something that had never been done before.

Practically nothing was done in regard to the postal system at that time. The telegraph and telephone lines were practically down and out of existence, the telegraph entirely. Here and there there were some single wires. We reconstructed the lines in the north of Haiti, extending them into the interior and along the border, very frequently without proper material. For many miles on the telegraph poles we used beer bottles and other bottles for the purpose of insulation.

The judiciary did not exist at the time we landed, and did not function for a considerable period thereafter. I had no authority over that, except under the power of military rule. There were no judges, and practically nothing was done in regard to that, though after a few months one of the higher courts was opened. As soon as we could we had a judge de paix appointed, but until that time offenses against sanitation were punished in the provost courts, usually by a fine or a certain number of days work, and generally the people were not taken before the provost court for first offenses. For a repetition of offenses after warning they were sometimes fined 2, 3, or 5 gourdes, and sometimes the fine was waived. The military court was functioning, and where robbers were captured they were brought before the military court, but it never weighed heavily on any honest citizen in Haiti, and it did not weigh heavily enough very frequently on the dishonest citizen, because we were trying to get the good will of the people of Haiti in the north, because, in my opinion, such good will was absolutely necessary, if we were going to successfully accomplish our mission.

Those same things were done to a greater or lesser extent in the towns of Fort Liberte, Ouanaminthe, Le Trou, Limonade, Grande Riviere, Port de Paix, Leborgne, and other towns.

Mr. HOWE. Were similar undertakings begun and carried on in the other parts of the island in the south of Haiti?

Gen. COLE. In the larger towns, to the best of my knowledge and belief. I know they were.

Mr. HOWE. And when you became brigade commander down there, you found similar undertakings in operation?

Gen. COLE. Yes.

Mr. HOWE. Under your command were these undertakings, such as the schools, hospitals, prisons, etc., continued and maintained?

Gen. COLE. Yes; there was considerable done. You are speaking of the time after I got to Port au Prince?

Mr. HOWE. Yes; in other words, was this general work carried on during that year during which you were brigade commander?

Gen. COLE. Yes; and in addition there were a good many other things done in addition to what I have mentioned here.

Mr. HOWE. I would like to get to those, but let me ask you did you encounter, as brigade commander, any difficulties in carrying on this work?

Gen. COLE. Yes; some, but the difficulties were hidden to a great extent. For instance, take the school proposition: The president, I think, was really in favor of good schools. The minister of public instruction was an educator—was not a politician; that is, except incidentally, as every educated Haitian is, and he promised to "beat the band" to do things to help build up the school system. I might preface this a little bit. I had caused a comprehensive survey to be made of the actual conditions in the schools in Haiti, the number of children that were attending them, the size of the schools, the condition of the buildings, the teachers, whether they went to the places or not, and we found that conditions were simply intolerable.

As I said, there was no public-school system outside of the large towns. In conversation with the president, on a number of occasions, the question of the school system was taken up, and, eventually, I was requested by the president to procure the services of a school expert, and I set the requirements that he was to be a man who could speak French, and, if possible, have some knowledge of Creole, should be a Catholic, should have dealt with colored people, should be a man of tact, and one who had handled a reasonably large school system. We found a man by the name of Bourgeois, from Louisiana, who had been county superintendent of schools, and spoke Creole and French, etc. Mr. Bourgeois came to Haiti. Considerable difficulty was experienced in regard to the contract. It was finally agreed that he should receive a compensation of $3,000 a year, and should be employed for a period of three years, as I remember it. They had wanted to employ him for a year. I said, "No," because conditions were such that in one year the man can do nothing; he will simply have started. It will take him six months to get familiar with the proposition, and at the end of the year, if conditions are such that you want to get rid of him, he has no contract, and it is not fair to that man to have him come down here for one year with the expense of moving at that salary, so it was agreed to give him a contract for three years.

Mr. HOWE. Did Mr. Bourgeois run into any difficulties there?

Gen. COLE. Mr. Bourgeois had them all the time.

Mr. HOWE. Just in general, describe what kind of difficulties those were.

Gen. COLE. Well, Mr. Bourgeois did not get there very long before I left. He found inertia and objection to a white man working in their bureau. While I was there he was able to make some headway in his preliminary work, because he came to me when he had trouble, and I went to the president, and the president usually straightened it out.

Mr. HOWE. Who caused the trouble?

Gen. COLE. Subordinates in the office of the minister of public instruction and assistants to him. I think he (the minister) did himself at times, and it is possible that the church may have had something to do with it.

Mr. HOWE. In other undertakings other than schools, like sanitation, prisons, or hospitals, were you hindered in your efforts?

Gen. COLE. No; I can not say we were hindered, because we went ahead and did the things. Generally they wanted the things done, but just as soon as anything was done they wanted Haitians to take it over. All we could do in most of these cases was to have, as, say at the hospital in Port au Prince, which was built up into a really exceptionally good institution—we had one or two American surgeons and one or two Hospital Corps men or something of that sort, but they wanted to put the Haitian in charge of it. The Haitian can work under the American and can do good work, and they had some exceptionally good medical people down there along certain lines, but just the minute the Haitian takes hold of anything that I ever saw in the way of executive work and keeping an organization together and keeping it in shape, it goes to pieces.

Mr. Howe. When you were in the north did you find that you had a freer hand than when you were later on in Port au Prince? In other words, I would like to know whether your remoteness from Port au Prince in the center of government there made it easier for you or not to carry on these works of internal improvement.

Gen. Cole. No; I can not say it did make any difference. In the north of Haiti I was very fortunate in having, apparently, the confidence of the people who were in Port au Prince. my recommendations were generally accepted and I was never interfered with; and in Port au Prince I was in charge of the brigade—I was chief of the occupation. as they called it, and I had no interference. The only time in which I did have interference was when the terms of the convention were put into effect in regard to the civil engineer and the sanitary engineer and when the distribution of funds was placed entirely in the hands of the financial advisor. We had used the gendarmerie officers as our agents through the country. They were people that we could rely on; we could not rely on a Haitian. That was absolutely out of the question. Occasionally we could rely upon one, but he is apt to go off at a tangent without any warning. He may be honest, but we had in the white officers of the gendarmerie people who were honest, people who would do what they were told, people who believed that they were doing a big piece of constructive work, people who put their heart and soul and everything else into the work they were doing and who were trying to build a fine system in Haiti, trying to benefit the people of the country. There is no question about it. And they were making every dollar they were allowed for repairs and improvements do the work of two or three, because they were eternally on the job all of the time themselves. out day and night. There can be no question but what the subordinate as well as the higher officers of the gendarmerie in Haiti performed a magnificent piece of work under exceptionally trying conditions.

Mr. Howe. General, you mentioned that when you went down to Port au Prince later on you observed other undertakings in addition to those you described as having been put into effect in the north.

Gen. Cole. We will take agriculture. We did something in the North to aid agriculture, everything we could do. In 1917, the United States having declared war, the submarine campaign being extremely effective, all the French ships which ran to Haiti having been sunk to the bottom, the question of foodstuffs in Haiti, in my opinion, became very important. This came up possibly before our declaration of war, but it was just about—well, the sinking of the three French ships, the *Quebec*, the *Montreal*, and the other one were sunk just about the time we declared war, but the shipping conditions had been growing steadily worse from early in 1917, and it was early in 1917, though I do not remember the exact date, that I had a survey made to find out what I could about agricultural conditions, and what had been imported in the way of foodstuffs into Haiti, and I found that Haiti had been getting somewhere in the neighborhood of from 1.800 to 2,000 tons of foodstuffs.

Mr. Howe. A year?

Gen. Cole. Yes; and that if steps were not taken to provide this, to take the place of this foodstuff, that we might have serious difficulty in feeding the people of the country. Through the assistance of some Haitian societies, the President, the minister of agriculture, and the gendarmerie, we got started a campaign on agriculture, with the idea of not only providing food for the people but also possibly providing a reservoir for ourselves and for the Allies. This campaign was remarkably successful. In connection with it we established experimental farms, and had them in different parts of the country. We established an agricultural school outside of Port au Prince, and the result of this campaign was extraordinarily successful, and the question came up, "What are we going to do with the food after it is raised? How are we going to get all of this food from the interior to the coast?" And that started the intensive campaign to build up the roads, because I felt that if these people, at our instigation, had started in and cultivated a large quantity of land and obtained a large crop, and then their crops had to rot, because there was no transportation, or any way of getting it into the towns, and there was nothing to be done with the stuff. that we would be in a worse condition than before, because they would say, "Here is what the Americans have promised, and see what they have done to us."

The Panama Canal Zone sent agents to look into the question, and they started in buying very heavily.

Mr. Howe. Food?

Gen. Cole. Food. We were raising food and getting it into the ports, and Haiti was exporting large quantities of foodstuffs by the spring of 1918 and the end of 1917. The Panama Canal Zone along in the summer of 1917 was spending over $10,000 a month for food supplies in Haiti, and we were assisting our allies and our own country in that way, and by shipping that foodstuff to the Canal Zone it enabled a full ship to be brought to Port au Prince or to St. Marc, and this stuff would be put in the place of goods that were assigned to Haiti; otherwise they could not have gotten the stuff down there. The department at home was asked to get agricultural experts. This was at the request of the President, as the result of conferences. The President was apparently extremely anxious to do everything he could do to benefit his country in the way of building things up, and I do not know whether I suggested it, or whether he suggested it—probably I did—but he accepted the suggestion and requested that we get agricultural experts from our Department of Agriculture, and we went into the question of preventing the importation of diseased seed, etc. We arranged with the Department of Agriculture for inspections here and certificates and things of that sort in the United States.

Mr. Howe. How about irrigation; General? Have you mentioned that?

Gen. Cole. I have not mentioned that. There was very little irrigation. There had been irrigation in the north, but it had completely gone to pieces. The plains of the cul-de-sac had quite an extensive irrigation system in the time of the French, called the Grande Bassin, and that did at one time probably give water to the entire plains of the cul-de-sac. I made a personal inspection of the place and went over it very carefully, and in order to increase the supply of water so far as I could we started the system, under the law, of keeping the existing canals open, of preventing the big landowner from opening up the gates and taking all the water himself, simply because he happened to be nearer, and we started plans for the repair of the dam at the Grande Bassin, which was, in my opinion, in danger of being carried away, and we were about to start work on that project when the orders were received to turn over public works to the civil engineer.

Mr. Howe. One of the treaty officials?

Gen. Cole. Yes; and I thought that was one of the works which should be taken over, but when I left nothing had been done, and I was told that nothing has been done since. But the thing had been very thoroughly gone into, and a comprehensive plan had been drawn up to repair and rehabilitate this system of irrigation there, and to finish the urgent repairs in a month or six weeks.

Mr. Howe. General, did the work undertaken there tend to encourage the men to work generally, instead of making the women do all the work, as theretofore?

Gen. Cole. Yes.

There is one thing I would like to add in regard to Mr. Bourgeois. I understand that Mr. Bourgeois, upon leaving Haiti, made a very comprehensive report in regard to the school condition and the difficulties encountered by him. I have never seen it, but I believe it will probably contain very valuable information for the committee, as, in my opinion, it is very essential that the United States take some active predominating part in establishing proper schools in the Republic of Haiti.

Mr. Howe. Where do you think we could find Mr. Bourgeois's report, at a guess?

Gen. Cole. At a guess, the headquarters of the Marine Corps. Maj. McClellan could possibly tell about that.

Maj. McClellan. There are some papers in the papers here with reference to that report made by Mr. Bourgeois, and they are certainly available to the committee, if they desire them.

Mr. Howe. Will you be good enough to find out what is there and let us know, please?

Maj. McClellan. Yes.

Gen. Cole. There is one thing I would like to bring in in regard to the school proposition. I had plans drawn up, Gen. Butler and myself between us, of model schoolhouses for a climate like Haiti, with its particularly peculiar resources, and I allotted funds to build four of these model schoolhouses, the sites selected being in locations where the largest possible number of people from all parts of the country would pass by these schoolhouses and see what they were. For instance, one was placed at Croix des Missions. This place was selected because it was at a crossroads outside of Port au Prince, over which every one entering Port au Prince from the major part of the plains of the cul-de sac and from the Artibonite district and Laguna district passed by in entering Port au Prince. When we landed in Port au Prince no market women were coming in. On the big market day before I left there anywhere from five to eight thousand donkeys loaded with produce would be brought in over that one road.

Mr. Howe. And then all hands passing there saw the schoolhouse?

Gen. Cole. All hands passing there saw that schoolhouse.

Mr. Howe. Gen. Butler. as I recollect it, told us that the people in the immediate neighborhood were much interested in the construction of these schoolhouses?

Gen. Cole. They were; and then I had minor plans drawn up for very extensive schoolhouses, and through the gendarmerie had the information sent out that we would provide the plans, some one to supervise the work, and such material as could not be obtained locally to any commune that would do the rest of it themselves.

Mr. Howe. Was that offer taken up?

Gen. Cole. That offer was taken up, and Gen. Butler told me that approximately 40 communes had accepted that proposition. My recollection was that there had been some 36 or 38 started before I left.

Mr. Howe. Do the peasants down there want education for their children?

Gen. Cole. I believe they do. You would have difficulty in enforcing attendance for some time. but I do believe that the peasant does want education for his children. It may be because they want to go to the "patent-leather stage," but I do believe they want the education.

Mr. Howe. Is there any other feature of your time of command in the north that you think the committee should hear about?

Gen. Cole. I do not know of anything; I do not remember anything.

Mr. Howe. Then. General, what was the date again, please, of your going down to Port au Prince and becoming brigade commander?

Gen. Cole. I think it was the 22d of November is my recollection of it.

Mr. Howe. In 1916?

Gen. Cole. 1916. Now, of course, this latter discussion has gone a good deal into Port au Prince, you remember.

Mr. Howe. Yes; the latter part of it especially.

Gen. Cole. All of that latter part.

Mr. Howe. After you became brigade commander, what was the first event of importance that came up?

Gen. Cole. The question of elections.

Mr. Howe. Let me ask you on that, the elections for what offices?

Gen. Cole. For the Chamber of Deputies.

Mr. Howe. And those elections were conducted under the supervision of the gendarmerie; is that correct?

Gen. Cole. Under the supervision of the gendarmerie and of the Haitian Government. The plans had been worked out to a considerable extent—almost entirely, as a matter of fact—by Gen. Waller. in connection with, presumably, the Haitian Government; and immediately after Gen. Waller left I was asked to come to the palace and they wanted to make some changes.

Mr. Howe. In the arrangements?

Gen. Cole. In the arrangements.

Mr. Howe. Let us have that, will you, please?

Gen. Cole. I do not remember the details. They wanted to make arrangements. different arrangements, and it was a succession of desires to make different arrangements, apparently with the idea of having the Government able to exercise its former activities in connection with the results of the election. As a matter of fact. on a number of occasions afterwards the President said that we had forced them to have a fair election and that we could handle the national assembly ourselves; that the President formerly would have been in a position to have expended money, but we would not allow that, and consequently his hold over the national assembly was gone. As a matter of fact. the legislative bodies in Haiti prior to the occupation had been absolutely, completely subservient to the person who was in power, who held the power.

Mr. Howe. These changes which they suggested. General, did you agree with them?

Gen. Cole. Generally not.

Mr. Howe. Why not?

Gen. Cole. Because I was using my best judgment in trying to get as close to a fair, honest election as it was possible to get.

Mr. Howe. And these suggested changes would, in your opinion, have made that more difficult?

Gen. Cole. Yes. I do not say there were many of those changes. There were frequent requests, probably for local conditions, in regard to the instructions that had been issued. There was constant calling on me for investigations, one way or another, or reports of interference or of noninterference or things of that sort. We had to look after the registration to see that that was honestly conducted, and they tried to put over all sorts of things, but our people stopped them so far as they could. Sometimes they made mistakes, but when they were made they were rectified. Where they were not made, they were told that their actions were perfectly correct. We actually tried, to the best of my knowledge and belief—I know it, as far as I am concerned and as far as the people who were working under my immediate control were concerned—I can not, of course, answer for every man who was in the Republic of Haiti, but as far as those people were concerned, we were trying to have as honest and fair an election as we could possibly have, and I think that I can state that that was the attitude in every other activity that the Americans had during the years 1915, 1916, and 1917, and I presume since.

Mr. Howe. The election, then, took place?

Gen. Cole. The election then took place.

Mr. Howe. Did it pass off quietly?

Gen. Cole. It passed off quietly, without any disorders.

Mr. Howe. How soon after that did the assembly meet—or it would be the legislature, would it not—that you were electing?

Gen. Cole. The Chamber of Deputies.

Mr. Howe. About how long? What date did the assembly meet?

Gen. Cole. The Chamber of Deputies met on April 2, and for the information of the committee I will state that the Senators were elected by the Chamber of Deputies from certain lists of candidates, and that consequently the complete National Assembly was not formed until after the election and the organization of the Senate, and then the organization of the National Assembly and the two chambers, and that took place on April 19.

Mr. Howe. Between the election and the organization of the assembly there were more than two months?

Gen. Cole. Yes; it was three months: February, March, and April.

Mr. Howe. Now, in those three months what was the next important matter that came up after the election?

Gen. Cole. The question of the cabinet came up in February, and it came up at the same time as the extension of the terms of the treaty from 10 to 20 years, the terms of the convention.

Mr. Howe. Will you give us a descriptive outline of what you know in connection with the selection of the cabinet and with the extension of the time of the treaty?

Gen. Cole. As the result of the elections, I recommended to the department, and also to the President, that it would be well to have a cabinet which would be in accord with the different chambers and the National Assembly, somewhat along the same political lines as the National Assembly was. I also felt, somewhat later, in particular, that Dr. Herraux, the minister of finance, should remain in any cabinet formed. Herraux had been a strong supporter of the American occupation, and was known as probably the only minister who really was in favor of American intervention and American management of Haitian affairs. He had married a Cuban, and their only son had been killed in one of the recent revolutions, and she was probably the stronger member of the family, and very bitter against the revolutionary idea in Haiti. In addition to his having been a constant supporter of the American occupation, he also, as head of the department of finance, was the one Haitian who was familiar with the work that was being done to carry out the investigation of Haitian financial affairs and accounting affairs of the Haitians, and to have him removed from the cabinet in the midst of this work going on would have resulted, without any question, in a decided hindrance to the work that was being undertaken. At the request of the President of Haiti, I saw Gen. Legitime, probably the finest specimen of the best type of Haitian that I met in my sojourn in Haiti, with the idea that he might be able to form a cabinet of a more or less nonpolitical type, composed of the best men in the country that would serve with the President. He had a good many difficulties. People distrusted the President, but the main thing was that Dr. Herraux had to remain as a member of the cabinet.

Mr. Howe. Do I understand you to mean that that made Legitime's task in forming such a cab'net difficult?

Gen. Cole. Very difficult. He said he had no objection to Herraux personally; that he believed that he was honest, but that Herraux had the antagonism of all the political element of Haiti, and that he did not think that any cabinet that included him could be formed, of the type that had been suggested between the President and myself, or suggested to him. The antagonism to Dr. Herraux grew on the part of the politicians stronger and stronger, until he became, as you might say, the storm center, and with their vicious attacks on Dr. Herraux, if we had acquiesced in his being thrown aside, it would have destroyed, in my opinion, a great deal of the influence that we had there, in that we would have been unable to get anyone to work with us openly, because they would say, "There is the case of Dr. Herraux. He worked with the occupation, and the time came when he stood in their way, and they calmly threw him aside." And I felt, for that reason, in addition to the other ones, that Dr. Herraux would have to remain as secretary of finance, and that the department also agreed to.

About that time the question of the extension of the terms of the treaty from 10 to 20 years came up, and there was a good deal of discussion back and forth. The Haitian Secretary of State for foreign affairs in particular, Mr. Borno, who was really the dominating member of the cabinet, tr.ed to use it as a lever to get concessions toward the appointment of Haitians in the customshouses, and after it was agreed to there was constant delay, and the terms they made were not lived up to when they were put in writing, and the correspondence went back and forth, and Mr. Borno, Dr. Herraux, and one other man, as I remember it, were in favor of it. The President was in favor of it, and three other members of the cabinet were opposed to it.

Mr. Howe. To the extension of the treaty for 20 years?

Gen. Cole. To the extension of the treaty; and while it was passed on h's majority, the President having voted in case of a tie, that, among other things, in the main, caused the resignation of the cabinet. Vincent left the cabinet absolutely. The other five remained, and my recollection is that Dr. Herraux, or Mr. Borno, carried on the duties of two departments during the time when his vacancy had not been filled. The whole cabinet resigned but continued to function, upon the request of the President, until the new cabinet was formed, about the time that the National Assembly met, or just before.

Mr. Howe. I understand, then, that the treaty was extended?

Gen. Cole. The terms of the convention were extended to 20 years. The object I had in all the discussion in regard to the cabinet was to try to get people together who would work with us and with the Haitian Government to build up a government, and a proper government, in that Republic.

Mr. Howe. General, would you say that in this work you acted primarily as assistant to the President in the formation of his cabinet?

Gen. Cole. I considered I had two masters, as it were, or, at least, I had two sides to serve—I had to serve the United States and I had to serve Haiti—and anything I could do to serve the interests of those two I did.

Mr. Howe. And did you work in cooperation with the President of Haiti?

Gen. Cole. I did.

Mr. Howe. Close cooperation?

Gen. Cole. Close, very close.

Mr. Howe. General, you spoke of having two objects; that is, the interests of the United States and the interests of Haiti. Did those interests coincide or conflict?

Gen. Cole. In my opinion, they coincided absolutely.

Mr. Howe. What was the object of both of those interests?

Gen. Cole. The object of both of those interests was to establish peace and order and a proper government in the Republic of Haiti in order that there could be no cause by irresponsible people for foreign complications to arise. I believed that by building up the Republic of Haiti and improving the conditions of the people in the Republic of Haiti it was working for the benefit of the United States.

Mr. Howe. And your conception, then, of the interests of the United States and of the interests of Haiti——

Gen. Cole. Were absolutely coincident.

Mr. Howe. They coincided for that purpose?

Gen. COLE. Yes. I told the President from time to time that that was my idea. I also told him on one or two occasions, when there were serious discussions between us, or something arising between us, that I would have to consider primarily the point of view of the United States, but the whole thing was that the United States needed a proper government in the Republic, and that is what we were after.

Mr. HOWE. Why did the United States need a proper government in Haiti?

Gen. COLE. Well, in the first place, it is at our front door. The Carribean Sea is the entrance; that is, the islands of the Carribean guard the entrance to a considerable part of the United States and the Panama Canal, absolutely. We can not afford to have any foreign country obtain additional power and influence in that part of the world. Our policy is, and I think has been, that we do not interfere with the status quo, but that we do not propose to allow European powers to gain any further influence in that part of the world.

Mr. HOWE. Well, was there danger of that?

Gen. COLE. I think there was danger of that. We can not allow intolerable conditions to exist, or to grow, and say "Hands off" to everybody else, and let them stew in their own juice indefinitely. France had $150,000,000 worth of francs invested in Haiti in the loans, and she had other sums there. Germany had large sums invested in Haiti, and, as I have said yesterday in my testimony, I believed that the European situation was the one thing that prevented active operations in Haiti by either one or two European nations.

Mr. HOWE. Now, besides the United States policy, which you might describe as its following of the Monroe Doctrine down in Haiti, what other objects did the United States have?

Gen. COLE. Well, my own opinion is that its objects or object was to eliminate a state of chaos, and replace it by a condition wherein the Negro Republic of Haiti could continue to exist as an independent State and exercise its own functions of government. In other words, I believe it had a moral duty to clean that place up and establish decency down there, because it did not exist. You have no idea of the conditions, if you have not been there, that did exist when we landed in Haiti. The Aegean stables were Paradise compared to it.

Mr. HOWE. It would sound as if you believed that one of the objects of the United States going down there was to save Haiti?

Gen. COLE. I think it was. I think that we were compelled to land in July of 1915, and having landed and found the conditions that did exist, there was not anything else to be done but to say there and save Haiti. Always did I say to everybody that I talked to that, to the very best of my knowledge and belief, the United States had no design whatsoever against the independence of Haiti, but on the contrary, it had every design to maintain it.

Mr. HOWE. And you were closely in touch, as brigade commander, with the policies of our country?

Gen. COLE. I know that is the policy of our country; I got it in black and white, to maintain it and establish a proper government down there. There was no idea of taking away the independence of Haiti. I am certain of that. Establishing an influence; yes.

Mr. HOWE. And you have already told us as to what you believed your mission to be in establishing good material conditions down there. That was a part of the whole task?

Gen. COLE. Yes; by task, particularly after the national assembly was dissolved was to do everything I possibly could to aid—not that I had not been doing it before, but that became almost the sole task—to aid the Haitians in building up a proper government. It was difficult and required a long time to do. I do not know how much of an impression I even made.

Mr. HOWE. What was the next matter that came up? Was it the question of the declaration of war against Germany?

Gen. COLE. The question of the declaration of war against Germany, and that was made the object of the wrath of the national assembly against the United States.

Mr. HOWE. Was it desirable or even considered necessary that Haiti should declare war against Germany? That was in the spring of 1917, after we had gone in, was it not?

Gen. COLE. It was considered desirable. The President of Haiti considered it desirable, though they wanted certain guaranties. When I say he considered it desirable, I mean that he said he considered it desirable. We were a belligerent nation occupying a neutral country in an area where enemy operations were being conducted.

Mr. Howe. You refer to the submarine operations?

Gen. Cole. I refer to the submarine proposition. I do not believe the stories we heard in all cases were true, but Haiti might very well have become a base for German submarines. If German ships had been able to put to sea, Haiti might very well have been a place where they would have tried to base. An enemy country—Germany—had large material interests in Haiti, a neutral country which we, a belligerent, were occupying, and it was thought best to have Haiti become our ally. There were good reasons for it. For instance, Haitian lives had been lost through the sinking of French ships which plied between Haiti and France; numerous Haitians were in the French Army as volunteers, and when they came back to Haiti they were received as heroes; the Haitian civilisation was entirely French; their names were French; their education was French; the educated Haitian who could go to Paris to live was going to Paradise, and he had every sympathy with the French; and yet, in order to swat the United States, they voted absolutely against war with Germany.

Mr. Howe. The assembly?

Gen Cole. Yes. There can be no question about it that that was the case.

Mr. Howe. And that declaration of war was killed in the assembly?

Gen. Cole. They recommended the severance of diplomatic relations, and they wanted the President of Haiti to make claim for indemnity and so on.

Mr. Howe. Did the question of the declaration of war come up later?

Gen. Cole. In September I had a very long letter from the President, in which he made that proposition.

Mr. Howe. What did he propose at that time—that the assembly be asked again to declare war?

Gen. Cole. He proposed that the cabinet and the council of state should draw up a declaration of war, and then it should be submitted to a plebiscite, and they wanted a loan and everything else; and I replied to it, or advised in regard to it, that, in my opinion, it was entirely undesirable; that it was not necessary at that time; that if Haiti had done it in the beginning it would have had a good effect and would have probably aided Haiti very materially in her desire to get the loan. She needed financing, and I was very much in favor of it in the spring, because I felt it would have assisted Haiti in that line at that time, but in September, no. I have a long correspondence here about it.

Mr. Howe. You must have considered, then, the conditions to be very radically changed between April and September?

Gen. Cole. I considered they had changed. I think the United States policy was to have as many countries declare war against the Central Empire as possible, as a matter of morale, as a matter of showing that the world was in league against the Central Empires. It was the desire of the United States, without any question, that as many American States as possible join in this alliance. Cuba joined in. Of course, San Domingo was under our occupation. Some of the other countries took a stand, but Haiti wanted to swat us.

Mr. Howe. Then, that condition had changed by September?

Gen. Cole. I considered it had changed, and that there would be no moral effect in aid of the United States in the war with Germany, and I did not see that Haiti would get any benefit from it. She was coming in with the idea that having made this declaration of war she could get a loan, and I did not think the financial conditions warranted her in that belief. I believed she would have obtained the loan if she had gone in at the start, but when she was coming in, apparently with the idea of simply getting something out of it, I thought it was not good form for her to do it. As I say, I have a long correspondence here about it, if you care to have me read it.

Mr. Howe. Had the military situation changed by September? It is so, is it not, that the military situation required caution on the part of the United States in April?

Gen. Cole. In September of 1917 the conditions were pretty well drawn at that time. Cambrai, as I remember it, occurred about the 1st of December, when the British made the assault and were so badly broken up.

Mr. Howe. Cambrai was in——

Gen. Cole. November, 1917, was it not? That was the time the British made the advance and got caught there, and they were not prepared for an open movement at all, and got smashed back.

Mr. Howe. They got pretty well pushed back by a counter attack?

Gen. Cole. I will give you my résumé, if you wish, in a few words.

Mr. Howe. I wish you would, please.

Gen. Cole. My opinion is that the motives were: (a) Desire to obtain from the United States a loan on the ground that the country is one of the Allies; (b) desire to be placed in a favorable position, so that she may properly obtain the needed merchandise from the United States; (c) a market for her coffee, or, at least, to gain favorable consideration from France; (d) the question of gaining prestige and of getting an indemnity for the destruction of Haitian armed vessels by the Germans on December 6, 1897, and for various other arbitrary acts of Germany, including the loss of Haitian lives and property during the present war.

Mr. Howe. That 1897 is the correct date?

Gen. Cole. Eighteen hundred and ninety-seven. With this goes the expectation that they will be represented on the council when peace negotiations are started at the end of the war. I also hear they are talking of a commission to take charge of German sequestered property, if such a declaration of a state of war is made, but in that I can see absolutely no advantage for Haiti from the proposed move, but, on the other hand, I see some disadvantages for the United States. If the declaration is made, they will expect us to do many things for them, and if we do not do them as they expect, our position with the present Government will be made less satisfactory; they certainly can give no aid commensurate with the expenditures that would be involved.

It is also said that we are using our influence to press this matter, and, in general, it would be one more thing to distract the people from following peaceful pursuits, and would be a source of or cause for agitation. At present there is no real excuse for such a step on the part of Haiti, and, if taken, it would be considered as the result of pressure by us—if in the future more Haitians are lost through submarine activity, then there may be reason for such a step but at present, in my opinion, emphatically no.

Mr. Howe. Did the fact that the declaration of war had once been rejected have anything to do with your determination in September?

Gen. Cole. I think it had something to do with it; yes.

Mr. Howe. Was the next important event the revision, or the attempt to revise the Haitian constitution?

Gen. Cole. That was one of the outstanding features of that part of it.

Mr. Howe. Then, General, can you indicate in what respects this constitution needed change, and what was done about it, or what was attempted? Give us another narrative outline, please.

Gen. Cole. My recollection is that the thing was practically an outcome of the convention, necessary in order for the United States to carry out the duties it was to undertake under its terms—as the constitution then stood it would be very difficult, if not impossible, to get financial interests to loan money to Haiti, at least without our guarantee and we could not well give that without changes in the fundamental law of Haiti—a revision of the constitution was, at least, implied by the terms of the convention of August, 1916. This would be indicated by the fact that there had apparently been two or three commissions sent from the United States to take up formally and informally with the Haitian Government the question of a convention between the two Governments which would contain features that would require a modification of the constitution. Under the constitution of Haiti, as then existing, a foreigner could not own land. Through subterfuge, through marrying with Haitians, German subjects had become possessed of a good deal of land in Haiti. Our people did not intermarry with the Haitians, and the English did not intermarry with the Haitians. As a matter of fact, the only people who did were the Germans and the French. So, under the constitution as it existed then, there was no way for a foreigner legally to own real estate in Haiti, and that was one of the things that the United States Government desired to have modified. Do you want to go into the exact details?

Mr. Howe. On this land tenure?

Gen. Cole. Yes; compare the two constitutions. You have them before you, have you not?

Mr. Howe. We have not got those in the record, have we?

Mr. Angell. Yes; at least the article of the old constitution is in the record. I read it one time in the hearings.

Gen. Cole. I can take up the comparison of the two later, if you want it.

Mr. Howe. Yes; I think now, if you will go ahead and indicate any other changes, besides the land-tenure one, it would be well; changes of importance, I mean.

Gen. Cole. Article 4. We desired that fore'gners should have the same protection granted to Haitians, without exception, the difference in the preceding constitution being that foreigners were granted the protection accorded by law, and also denying the right of diplomatic intervention or discussion in case of damage to foreign property. It was desired that the condition of five years' residence be set aside. The intention to engage in business and to reside in the country should be added to the list of enterprises for which the right to hold property may be acquired, the exception concerning diplomatic intervention to be taken out.

Mr. Howe. In other words, did you favor a clause in the new constitution by which an absentee foreign landowner would, after a certain time, lose his right to hold land?

Gen. Cole. That does not concern what I was talking to you about over here, this particular thing. These were made by the American minister. I had nothing to do with that, this thing I am giving you. I am quoting this correspondence simply to show what the United States desired the Haitian Government to do in connection with this change in the constitution.

The constitution provided that secretaries of state should receive fees in addition to their pay. Our country desired that cut out, our Department of State. I desired to do away with the council of state, as it did not consider it was necessary, being an additional expense and, as a matter of fact, another cause of friction in the country. It desired that provision should be made for the prosecution of judges of the court of cassation and the judges of the courts of appeal. This had been made for the prosecution of the secretaries of state, in other words a procedure whereby the judiciary could be held to account for malfeasance in office. It desired that article 131 should read: "The examination and the liquidation of the accounts and of the general administration of all officers responsible to the public treasury should be determined by law," in the place of having it in the constitution, "On confirmation of a chamber of accounts," which was the prior constitutional provision.

Then there were three articles—132, 133, and 134—that it desired to be eliminated.

Article 133 refers to justices of the peace being named by the President of the Republic, under certain conditions.

Article 134 concerned judges also, judges of the court of cassation, the removability of the judges and the fact that they could not be removed from office other than by legal forfeiture, a judgment, or suspended only by an admitted accusation. They could not be retired.

And the next one, 135, provided that the appointment of judges of the peace be open to ratification.

Those things were apparently not considered proper in there, and the government wanted them eliminated.

Article 140. They desired that foreigners should enjoy the same protection granted to Haitians, without exception, and besides that the right shall not be denied them to claim indemnities for wrongs or losses sustained by them.

Mr. Howe. I have not got that quite clearly. The proposed change was to permit foreigners to claim indemnities?

Gen. Cole. Yes; the proposed change to the article followed substantially article 4 and we wanted inserted in the constitution an article similar to the appendix to the Cuban constitution, ratifying the acts of the United States in Haiti during the military occupation—a very important provision.

Mr. Howe. Affecting property rights and everything else vitally?

Gen. Cole. Affecting everything. Practically everything that had been done by the American military forces in Cuba could be set aside.

Mr. Howe. If it were not——

Gen. Cole. If it were not——

Mr. Howe. For such a provision in the constitution?

Gen. Cole. For such a provision in the constitution, an absolutely essential provision, the same as was made in the case of the Republic of Cuba.

Mr. Howe. Was not that essentially for the good of Haiti?

Gen. Cole. Essentially for the good of everybody—Haiti and the United States. No one could know where he stood.

Mr. Howe. Did you find more objection to some of these proposed changes than to others?

Gen. Cole. Yes; but I did not have anything to do with them other than advise them. I do not think I did very much in that, as a matter of fact, the revision of the constitution, so far as that was concerned. In discussions with the President and in discussions with the different members of the Senate and of the cabinet and the Chamber of Deputies, I advised them to give very careful consideration to the wishes of the United States, but I did not take any particular part in that particular feature of it. That was a question between the State Department and the Haitian Government.

Mr. Howe. Now, let me just ask you this question. What was the attitude of the Assembly toward these changes?

Gen. Cole. The attitude of the Assembly was very hostile.

Mr. Howe. To the United States?

Gen. Cole. To the changes and to the United States. They were particularly hostile, and this, I think, was something that they believed thoroughly—the question of land tenure they were afraid of; there is no doubt about it. The question of ratifying the acts of the occupation, the American military forces, martial law, the decisions of the military commander or the military courts——

Mr. Howe. They were very reluctant on——

Gen. Cole. They would not do it. They did not want to do it. They wanted that set aside, and it was absolutely essential.

Mr. Howe. For the best interests of Haiti?

Gen. Cole. I think for the best interests of Haiti.

Mr. Howe. How about foreign land tenure? Was that for the best interests of Haiti?

Gen. Cole. I think so, with certain reservations to bind the rights of Haiti.

Mr. Howe. You mean for the protection of the rights of Haiti?

Gen. Cole. For the protection of Haiti. That was a question that was very carefully considered by Admiral Knapp, Mr. Myer, and myself in the preparation of the form in which the constitution was finally passed.

Mr. Howe. Of what we might say was the new constitution?

Gen. Cole. Of the new constitution.

Mr. Howe. As distinguished from this attempt to revise the existing constitution?

Gen. Cole. As distinguished from this attempt to revise the existing constitution.

Mr. Howe. Now, General, some little time after that the assembly was prorogued, or dissolved?

Gen. Cole. I think if I gave a short résumé of the constitutional proposition it would be well. The council of state prepared a project for the constitution. That project was presented to the national assembly. It was also presented to the American minister, who also took it up with the United States, presumably. The American minister, after having the matter considered in the United States, I presume, communicated with the Haitian Government. and there was considerable correspondence with the executive branch of the Haitian Government. The Haitian Government, I always thought, to use a slang expression, deliberately spilled the beans. They took this whole correspondence and sent it, without comment, practically, to the national assembly. In other words, saying, " Here is not our recommendation, but here is what practically amounts to dictation from the United States. Now, see what you can do with it." There is not any question in my mind but what that was done with absolute malice aforethought, and it certainly did raise a rumpus, and the chambers naturally got angry, because it was inexcusable to do anything of that sort. They just simply shot this thing over to the national assembly, and that naturally made them all the madder.

Mr. Howe. That result is easily understood?

Gen. Cole. I think so. They just simply would not pay attention to what the United States considered necessary. The United States felt that certain things had to be done to carry on the work it had set itself in Haiti, and one of them was that a constitution which was absolutely at variance with every expressed wish of the United States should not be put into effect.

(Whereupon, at 1 o'clock p. m., a recess was taken until 2.30 o'clock p. m.)

The committee reassembled at 2.30 o'clock p. m., pursuant to the taking of recess.

Mr. Howe. Mr. Chairman, I will present certain testimony of Admiral Caperton written form, in the shape of a continuation of his former testimony, as was the understanding, I believe, when he was last here as a witness. This is received with the understanding that later on, if cross-examination is desirable, or further examination, Admiral Caperton will be recalled. This is a document of some 75 typewritten pages.

(The matter referred to was printed as a part of Admiral Caperton's original testimony.)

Mr. HOWE. General, I think at the end of the morning session we had arrived at the point where you were going to describe the prorogation or dissolution of the assembly. Will you give us an outline of that?

Gen. COLE. There were a number of conferences with the President. The President had conferences with the leaders of the national assembly, the Senate and House, in an endeavor to come to some amicable arrangement, but apparently without avail. The President had from time to time intimated or stated that he thought it would be necessary to dissolve the national assembly sooner or later, and he had asked me what attitude we would take, and I told him that it would depend on what developed; that at the times he had spoken before, in my opinion, the time was not yet ripe for any such action.

I notice here I have a comment on that question which I wrote at the time, which would probably express my opinion better about the thing than I could say now.

Mr. HOWE. Will you read that? Is that your idea?

Gen. COLE. Yes; I thought I might do that, if it is agreeable.

On June 5, 1917, the President asked me to come and see him at 10.30 a. m. I found him with Dr. Herraux. He stated that the national assembly did not seem disposed to act in accordance with the desire of the United States in regard to certain changes in the constitution, and that the opponents to the Government and to the United States are apparently endeavoring to prevent, by means of a claque, the expression of opinion of those favorable to the Government, and consequently to prevent a free discussion; that while he was trying, he did not appear to be able to get very much done, and wanted to know what attitude the United States would take in the matter of the national assembly failing to comply with the wishes of the United States. I told him that I was keeping the United States Government informed as to the conditions here; as to the attitude of the national assembly, and as to the various happenings; that I have made a long and fairly detailed report as to the general conditions in this country, and particularly as to the present situation, and that this report must now be in the hands of the State Department, I also told him that I felt that my Government felt that Haiti should have every chance to show her capacity for self-government, and to actually govern herself; that I believed that it considered that the national assembly should be given every opportunity to show that it was capable of relieving the actual state of affairs and capable or incapable of performing its duties in such a way as to aid in establishing a proper Government in this country; that there were a number of projects or agreements which required the approval of the national assembly, and that until this assembly showed that it actually was not going to approve such agreements, it would not be wise to have recourse to drastic action, particularly as there would be no assurance that another body would be any more amenable to reason, and in the meantime things most necessary for the development of this country would be held up.

In regard to the interference of which he spoke, I suggested that he endeavor to get his supporters to stop playing politics and come out in the open in favor of the various things he was supporting, and to demand their rights to be heard; that the balance of power had apparently been in his hands, and that if they really wanted to be heard they could force the opposition to act in a reasonable manner; I also told him that when disorder was feared before, the presiding officer had asked for gendarmes to preserve order and that as soon as additional gendarmes were asked for they would be furnished, and in sufficient numbers to clear the chambers of spectators if necessary.

That is all in regard to that.

Mr. HOWE. That conversation which you have just spoken of took place about how long before the actual time of the dissolution of the assembly?

Gen. COLE. Fourteen days, two weeks.

Mr. HOWE. Then what developed?

Gen. COLE. The reprt of the committee to the national assembly to prepare the new constitution provided that only Haitians could be landed proprietors or acquire real estate. They stuck to their safeguard that foreigners could enjoy the protection provided by law, etc.

Mr. Howe. They stuck to that—continued it?

Gen. Cole. Yes; they stuck to that.

Mr. Howe. Just what was that you referred to; they stuck to their safeguard that foreigners——

Gen. Cole. Should have the protection accorded them by law. The United States' demand was that foreigners should have the same protection accorded to Haitians, and they stuck to the provision that they should have the protection provided by law.

Mr. Howe. What was the difference there?

Gen. Cole. What was the difference?

Mr. Howe. Yes; between the two classes of protection?

Gen. Cole. Well, the one class of protection to foreigners gave a foreigner the same rights and the same protection under Haitian law that the Haitian law gave the Haitians, while under the provisions of the constitution of Haiti it gave them such rights only as the national assembly in the course of its law-making might see fit to grant them.

Mr. Howe. As a matter of fact, was there a different degree of protection provided by law?

Gen. Cole. There was. It was practically impossible for foreigners to get justice in the Haitian courts.

Mr. Howe. That word " protection " applied to more than physical safety of their lives?

Gen. Cole. I mean in litigation and things of that sort a foreigner had no chance in a Haitian court unless he was able to buy it.

Mr. Howe. Was he discriminated against in the constitution?

Gen. Cole. Offhand I would say yes; decidedly.

Mr. Howe. So there was more than a distinction in language in the two kinds of protection?

Gen. Cole. Oh, yes; it was considered very vital, and I considered it very vital myself.

Mr. Howe. And the assembly stood by the existing provision of the constitution?

Gen. Cole. Yes.

Mr. Howe. And would not change it?

Gen. Cole. And would not change it; and they would not consider the question of ratifying the acts of the occupation and the military government and martial law. I had reported the final project that the national assembly had proposed to put through and I received instructions to exert every endeavor to prevent the passage of such a project.

Mr. Howe. You have given us an outline of that project?

Gen. Cole. Yes. Now, here is a report that I made on the 15th of June:

"Antagonism national assembly to foreign ownership land and to all American influence such that no endeavor I can make short of dissolution assembly will prevent passage constitution along lines reported my 13107. Have discussed matters fully with minister and Gen. Butler. Suggest minister notify Haitian Government that, in opinion our Government, constitution prepared assembly will make impossible to bring about results contemplated under articles 1 and 14 of treaty, and consequently our Government can not accept such constitution. If national assembly refuses heed such warning, it will be necessary to dissolve assembly to prevent passage. The number marines in Haiti should be increased by at least eight full companies to prevent disorders that may follow dissolution assembly. See paragraph 16 my report May 17."

Mr. Howe. Did you anticipate trouble when you were considering dissolving the assembly?

Gen. Cole. I did not anticipate it, but I was prepared for it. I did not think it would create trouble. I did believe this: That it would create more trouble than the dissolution of the entire Haitian Government and the establishment of a military government there, because, on account of the antagonism between the two elements, if both were suppressed each would be pleased at the downfall of the other, but if one went down, one would be sore about the other.

Mr. Howe. For surviving?

Gen. Cole. For surviving.

Mr. Howe. You refer to the executive and the legislative branches?

Gen. Cole. Yes. The President had sent me a memorandum on the 16th, and I went to see him in regard to this memorandum, concerning a proposal he made in connection with the constitution. I went to see the President in regard to his memorandum and discussed matters with him very thoroughly.

and in the course of the conversation I learned a number of interesting things. In regard to his memorandum I told him that it was necessary, before it could receive further consideration, to follow out its results to an ultimate conclusion. He admitted that if the people decided, in the election proposed by him, to sustain the constitution prepared by the national assembly that unless the United States were willing to accept such a constitution and was willing that Haiti should remain in its present primitive and disorganized state that it would be necessary to suppress the national assembly. He also finally admitted that if the result of the elections was to reject the constitution prepared by the national assembly the fact that the national assembly would not change its attitude and that it would still, in his opinion, stick to its original scheme, and that if his suggestion that other representatives be elected were followed the consequence would be either two assemblies, each claiming to be legally elected or that the present national assembly would have to be dissolved.

He further stated that he could do nothing without the complete support of the United States and that his real belief was and is that the national assembly will have to be suppressed. As I have reported on a number of occasions, there is little doubt in my mind but what the President has consistently worked toward that end. He stated that, in his opinion, the dissolution of the national assembly was absolutely the only method that could be followed, but that he must have the approval of the United States before he could take that step. He also stated that at no time, as he believed, has this country been in condition to elect a proper national assembly, that the elections were engineered by a few politicians, and that the vast majority of the voters had no idea as to what they were voting for, but were simply brought in and voted by the candidate or his friends, having received money for such votes. He stated that in his opinion the only government by Haitians that would be satisfactory would be one of a President, with a council of cabinet ministers and a further council of state with legislative powers; that such government should prepare a constitution in accordance with the ideas of the United States, promulgate same to the country and carry on the government under such constitution until such time as the country had gotten out some of the influence of the politicians and had been able to realize by actual experience the benefits resulting from the various changes in the constitution that were suggested by the United States. He stated that such a government had been carried on in 1846. I stated to him that if the experience with the last and the present national assembly was a criterion of the capacity of a Haitian national assembly that I quite agreed with him as to the undesirability of such an assembly.

I also stated to him that while the present system seemed to be demonstrating its inefficiency, that for a year the system proposed by him had been tried and had not been a success; that if such system were continued, in order for it to succeed it would be absolutely necessary that the political element be practically discarded and a cabinet and council of state formed of people of education and ability who had not been active politicians, and, above all, by people who had the reputation of being thoroughly honest, so that the educated people of the country would realize that the Government was composed of people who were working to benefit the country and not to fill their own pockets at the expense of the country. I stated that the council of state had been almost entirely all politicians, and that they had not been able to command the respect of the country, and further, that if such experiments were again tried and found lacking there could be but one result, the administration of affairs of Haiti by Americans until such time as the younger generation could be trained in public affairs. He stated that he realized this fully and that if such government were permitted that he would make no appointments to the council of state or to the cabinet without the express sanction of the representative of the United States Government, and that, in his opinion, such a government would be successful. He further stated that he would employ expert assistants in the various departments, particularly of agriculture and of public instruction, as would be necessary to place these departments on a modern basis.

The President stated that since he had become President many people who had been former friends, became his enemies; but that outside of the political world he had numerous friends of high standing in all parts of the country, and that he believed he could get good citizens to work with him. As to this

I am somewhat uncertain, as the President has been in political life for many years, and I do not think he is particularly well or favorably known in any other parts of the country than Port au Prince and his home.

In discussing politicians he stated that the reason why the occupation and the United States influence was so bitterly hated by the politicians was that they were prevented from getting their livelihood from the public funds, adding that in former days all of the principal politicians expected to get enough money out of the public funds to enable them to live well and to take their families to Paris each year.

In discussing article 6 I stated that from the instructions I had received, I had no doubt whatever but what my Government would refuse to recognize or to accept a constitution similar to the one now being considered in the national assembly, and I referred to the fact that his brother had voted against the right of foreigners to own land, and the President explained it in this way: Prior to the first meeting of the national assembly to vote upon the constitution he had had a meeting of his friends and that one-half had been in favor and one-half had been opposed to the right of foreigners to own land; that he had information that payment was being made by those opposed to the change to have people in the chambers to howl down any attempt to speak in favor of the ownership of land by foreigners, and, consequently, not being able to keep his supporters lined up, he had suggested or stated that they could vote as they pleased, and consequently his brother, among others, had voted in favor of denying foreigners the right to own land. I reminded him of my suggestion, when he had referred to paid people being present in the national assembly chamber while voting was going on to intimidate voters, that that was a game at which two could play; that we would provide the necessary force to maintain order in the chambers, and that aggressive action on the part of government supporters would have resulted in a hearing for all concerned.

I think, possibly, it would be well to explain what that particular thing means. On one or two occasions, when they had feared disorder, the President of the chambers had asked for additional gendarmes to guard the chambers, and we had furnished them, and that was what was intended in that particular case, and if they asked for additional protection, or if they feared disorder or asked for protection, that we would furnish it.

Mr. Howe. Was that request made in this case by Vincent?

Gen. Cole. Certainly not. If it was, they were provided; but they were not. This was something the President was stating. I further stated that the whole trouble lay in the fact that most of the Government supporters were not acting in an aggressive manner; that they were all afraid of the political world in Port au Prince and that they would do nothing to oppose the things that were antagonistic both to our Government and to their government. He also stated that when the convention was passed he had adopted the same tactics that he claimed had been recently adopted by the opposition, but that now, having no money to spend, he was unable to follow that practice.

This is one of my reports.

Mr. Howe. On that situation?

Gen. Cole. Do you want that?

Mr. Howe. Yes.

Gen. Cole. I had an interview with the President.

Mr. Howe. Dated?

Gen. Cole. The 16th.

Mr. Howe. June 16?

Gen. Cole. June 16.

"Had interview, President, who stated his suggestion, present constitution, to people reported my 16014 Marcorps would only result in delay and eventual dissolution national assembly, as it will not grant foreigners right own land. He stated Government supporters in assembly were evenly divided regarding foreign ownership and feeling certain of defeat, and to avoid possible hostile demonstration, meeting assembly, his brother and others voted to deny foreign ownership lands, this apparently with his consent. He desires suppression assembly and Government by cabinet, with council of State with legislative powers, the latter to prepare and Government to promulgate a constitution to meet our views, such form government to continue until country realizes benefits and ready for self-government. He will promise anything. I believe conditions as stated, paragraph 16, my report May 17. Assembly about one-third through constitution."

Mr. HOWE. What developed after that?

Gen. COLE. On June 18 I notified Washington, "Unless contrary instructions received, if necessary to prevent passage proposed constitution, I intend dissolve national assembly, through President, if possible; otherwise direct."

Mr. HOWE. Was that proposal of yours approved?

Gen. COLE. It was approved and it was disapproved.

Mr. HOWE. Explain that, will you please?

Gen. COLE. "State Department is dispatching a message to Hatian Government in regard to this matter, which also refers to the changed aspect of the question due to the break in diplomatic relations with Germany."

Mr. HOWE. What is the date of that?

Gen. COLE. That is the 16th of June.

Mr. HOWE. From the State Department?

Gen. COLE. From the Navy Department. "The department vests you with full discretionary power. Endeavor to accomplish and desired without the use of military force."

I will read the whole of that message:

"Following message received evidently intended for Port au Prince.: Brigade's 15318. State Department is dispatching a message to Haitian Government in regard to this matter, which also refers to the changed aspect of the question, due to the break in diplomatic relations with Germany." (Haiti had broken her diplomatic relations with Germany.) "The department vest you with full discretionary power. Endeavor to accomplish end desired without the use of military force. Acknowledge."

On the 18th it had been concluded that the assembly would have to be dissolved—it may have been on the 17th—and the President was to draw up and did draw up a decree dissolving the national assembly. He was to give me a copy of it to examine. I did not get it on the morning of the 19th, having sent to him or having gone to him, I do not remember which, personally and got it. I was informed that it had been s'gned, the original, or was being signed. I had in the meantime drawn up a proclamation of my own, which I intended to put into effect in case the President did not exercise his powers as President. I did not want to use our military force, as it was contrary to the desire of the United States, but it was ready to use in case it became necessary.

Mr. HOWE. That was a proclamation to dissolve the assembly?

Gen. COLE. To dissolve the assembly.

Mr. HOWE. That you had prepared?

Gen. COLE. That I had prepared myself. That was prepared and in my possession, ready to use in case it became necessary.

Mr. HOWE. That is to say, in case the President d'd not dissolve it?

Gen. COLE. In case the President absolutely refused to do it. Suppose I read my report of June 19.

Mr. HOWE. I think that is very important.

Gen. COLE. "June 19, 1917. Early this morning the President sent a message to me that he proposed to go to the national assembly and, in a secret session, inform them that it was absolutely essential that they pass a constitution which conformed to the recommendations made by the Government of the United States; that he proposed to make this visit about 10.30, after he had received the American minister and Capt. Anderson, commanding the patrol force. I stated that I saw no objection to his endeavoring to get the assembly to change its stand but that I would communicate with him later.

"Saw the miniser and discussed matters with him, and then went to the palace and saw the President. I informed him that some time ago he had requested that I consider the question of dissolving the national assembly, but that I had informed him that, in my op'nion, the time was not quite ripe. Yesterday I had informed him the time had come to dissolve the national assembly and that he had agreed and informed me that he would furnish me, either last night or this morning, with copies of the decree for my consideration. Prior to its being promulgated he immediately gave me the decree; copy appended."

That does not seem to be particularly good sense.

"I asked the President what he expected to gain by seeing the chambers, and he stated that he had hopes that all the suggestions of the United States would be accepted by the national assembly with the possible exception of the one ratifying the acts of the occupation. I told him that the constitution of 1889, in the third paragraph of its one hundred and ninety-second article, had provided .that certain decrees and acts made by revolutionary committees were ratified, and that I considered that the new constitution of Haiti should have similar ratification of his decrees and of the acts of the occupation. His proposal was that the end desired could be accomplished by agreement between the two countries formally ratified by the national assembly. I informed him that, in my opinion, no constitution could possibly be accepted which did not conform generally to the one prepared by the council of state and which was submitted to our State Department for consideration, with modifications in accordance with the suggestions of our State Department. In the meantime he had informed me that, fearing he might be insulted, he decided to send for presiding officers and assistants of the two chambers in place of going to the national assembly himself. I informed him that the decree should be in readiness for immediate delivery, so that in case any tricks were tried by the national assembly they could be met by an immediate delivery of the notice of dissolution. I then left, as the American minister, with Capt. Anderson, was entering the palace. Capt. Anderson was received with honors of a vice admiral.

"Immediately after the American minister had left the palace the President saw the bureaus of the national assembly, after which they returned to the meeting place of the national assembly, when the national assembly went into secret session on the second floor of the building, the meeting lasting about one-half hour. After this they came downstairs and resumed their regular session, starting in at article 104, where they had left off the preceding day. Gen. Zamor then attempted to speak, starting his speech with a statement that, while he could not divulge what had taken place in the secret meeting, he considered that people should know what the situation was, and that it was useless for the national assembly to attempt to pass a constitution which they all knew could not possibly be accepted or put into effect. At this stage of proceedings various members interposed to such an extent that he resumed his seat. Shortly afterwards it became apparent that the chambers were endeavoring to rush the constitution through. I sent Gen. Butler to the palace to get the decree, and after his arrival there he reported that it had not been signed, and that one of the cabinet members could not be found, but that he had sent an automobile to search for him. I had told Gen. Butler that, in case the President did not sign the decree, he was to be informed, as coming from me, that I would suppress the national assembly myself and would recommend the establishment of a military government. The President then signed the decree. A short time afterwards it was reported to me that the national assembly was endeavoring to pass the whole constitution by skipping articles, so I sent immediately orders to the gendarmerie officer at the meeting place of the national assembly to prevent, by force if necessary, any further proceedings. The assembly had skipped various articles and endeavored to declare that the constitution had been passed. I directed that the doors be closed with the members and spectators being inside. The missing secretary of state was found; he signed the decree. I directed Gen. Butler to proceed immediately to the national assembly and deliver the decree to the President of the assembly.

"The president of the assembly refused to accept the message or to announce it to the assembly as it was not delivered to him by the cabinet or by a member thereof, announcing that he had a message from the President, but he did not know what it contained. Gen. Butler then took the decree, promulgated it to the national assembly, and directed, in accordance with my orders, that the chambers be cleared and members and spectators be released. The guards had been placed at the entrances to the chamber, and no further meetings of the deputies or senators will be recognized nor, if practicable, permitted. In any event they stand dissolved and no meeting of any considerable number can take place and then only in some private place."

Just prior, I think a couple of hours prior, to the dissolution of the assembly I was at the legation with the American minister and the commander of the patrol forces, and just about that time, after we had decided that the dissolution was necessary and must be done at once, a message was delivered, which stated: "Take no action until arrival of State Department's message. Acknowledge." There was nothing else to be done but dissolve the national assembly, and it was done.

Mr. Howe. Did Gen. Butler clear the hall, the legislative meeting room, or did he strike any difficulty in that; do you know?

Gen. Cole. As far as I know there was no clash whatsoever.

Mr. Howe. This report which you have just read was prepared after you had seen Gen. Butler, after the dissolution was accomplished; is that right?

Gen. Cole. Yes.

Mr. Howe. Do you know whether or not Gen. Butler was personally armed when he went down there?

Gen. Cole. I do not know; I would presume that he probably was.

Mr. Howe. But do you know?

Gen. Cole. I do not know. He may or he may not have been.

Mr. Howe. Do you know whether there were gendarmes inside there?

Gen. Cole. I think there were.,

Mr. Howe. Do you know why they were there?

Gen. Cole. To preserve order.

Mr. Howe. Do you know if they had been requested by the presiding officer?

Gen. Cole. My recollection is that they were invariably there.

Mr. Howe. Do you know whether they had been requested?

Gen. Cole. On that specific occasion I do not remember.

Mr. Howe. Had they been on previous occasions requested by the presiding officer or officers to keep order?

Gen. Cole. There had been requests made on previous occasions for extra numbers to preserve order.

Mr. Howe. A request made by the presiding officer?

Gen. Coe. Yes. I think, as a matter of fact, there was probably a request made by the cabinet that there be extra men there to preserve order.

Mr. Howe. Well, then, General, to sum this up, the assembly was dissolved?

Gen. Cole. The assembly was dissolved?

Mr. Howe. By the President?

Gen. Cole. By the President.

Mr. Howe. But you were prepared, in case the President did not take that action, to have it dissolved on your own orders, and in that you had the approval of the Navy Department, with the exception, perhaps, of that last dispatch which you read, and do I understand that that was received so late in the day that plans could not be changed?

Gen. Cole. It was received so late that we could not change our plans. If we had stopped, our usefulness there would have ended then and there.

Mr. Howe. Was that received before or after the President signed his proclamation?

Gen. Cole. I would say it was received after he had signed his proclamation, because it came in after it had been decided that the dissolution was to take place, that it must take place. It was received just a few minutes before the dissolution actually took place in the chambers. If I had gone to the telephone, or sent a mounted messenger, or automobile, I could have stopped it.

Mr. Howe. You could have stopped Gen. Butler?

Gen. Cole. I could have stopped Gen. Butler.

Mr. Howe. From delivering the President's proclamation?

Gen. Cole. Yes.

Mr. Howe. But you could not have done that unless you had acted quickly?

Gen. Cole. It was not a case that could be done. I had to take the responsibility of carrying out what I considered the best thing to do, being on the spot.

Mr. Howe. Were there attempts after that, on the part of the assembly, to meet?

Gen. Cole. No; it passed off as quietly as you please.

Mr. Howe. They did not gather in other places and attempt to function?

Gen. Cole. No.

Mr. Howe. From that time on until the end of your tour there were there any more political crises?

Gen. Cole. No; no more. That ended it.

Mr. Howe. Then how would you characterize the remaining months of your tour there? Were they tranquil?

Gen. Cole. Yes; very tranquil.

Mr. Howe. And how was the time used?

Gen. Cole. The time was used in building up, to the best of our ability, the Haitian Government, and improving conditions?

Mr. Howe. During all your tour there did you hear of any Haitian prisoners being killed by gendarmes or marines?

Gen. Cole. No.

Mr. Howe. And, to the best of your belief, during your tour were there any such occurrences?

Gen. Cole. There were no such occurrences, to the best of my knowledge and belief. There was a prisoner who escaped at Fort Liberte, or at Ouanaminthe.

sometime In 1916, and a considerable number of prisoners got away before the escape was discovered, and I am of the opinion that one man was killed at the time of that escape, by a guard who saw him getting away.

Mr. Howe. He was in the act of escaping?

Gen. Cole. He was in the act of escaping, one of a considerable number who had broken jail. They had started to tunnel and gotten under the walls of the prison, without being seen, but some were seen just as they were going, and my recollection is that one may have been killed at that time, though I would not state for certain.

Mr. Howe. General, during your time down there were the relations between the American occupation and its forces, and the people in general in the country, happy?

Gen. Cole. They were all given to understand that it was their business to make themselves so persona grata to the Haitians and the Haitian Government, that they were on their toes to do it, and they did a very great deal for the country, and they made their influence throughout the country very strong.

Mr. Howe. Now, in addition to this influence of the occupation over the people of the country, in addition to the steps taken to preserve law and order and to internally upbuild the country, could you say that the occupation has resulted in the increase of the wealth of the country in that strictly material sense?

Gen. Cole. Taking the end of 1917, when I left there; yes. The country, I do not believe, had been as prosperous as it was in the fall of 1917 for generations. The country people, the peasantry, were far ahead of any wealth they had ever had before. However, that did not apply so much to the merchant class, nor did it apply to the political class, for the reason on the part of the political class that they did not have the pickings, and on the part of the mercantile class that the war and the suspension of water transportation had materially affected their business, and they could not get material, so there was a considerable difficulty in regard to that. But we had absolutely the respect and confidence, I will venture to say, of 95 per cent of the country people of Haiti. On a number of occasions it was reported to me by priests and others that they had seen country women kneeling down beside the wayside shrines thanking God that the Americans were in Haiti.

Gen. Butler and I took the President and a number of the members of his cabinet out to a place called Morne a Cabrit, 20 miles outside of Port au Prince. on the top of a mountain on the road to Mirebalais, to see some road work that was going on, and while we were there a number of parties of country women with their produce came by, and I said to the President, " Suppose you and your minister of public works go off there by yourselves and stop some of those women and talk to them about what they think of conditions, and the American occupation, and the work they are doing." And he did, and he said that they all thanked God that we were there.

That was the attitude of the country people almost entirely.

There is one phase of the work that was done that I think may be worth while bringing up, and that is the improvement of the communes in the interior. We found from time to time that probably one-tenth of the funds that should be collected by the communes were being accounted for; that taxes were apparently being collected still, but that there were never any such sums as should have been collected accounted for by the communal books, and on one or two occasions, owing to the absence, the enforced absence or long absence of the magistrate of a commune, we had placed officers of the gendarmerie in charge of affairs of the communes, upon the request of the President, and on two of those occasions it developed that, under the law, collecting himself the things that the magistrate was supposed to collect, approximately 1.000 per cent more was collected, sometimes at least 1.500 per cent more, and so when a particularly good case came up, the matter was taken up with the President and he eventually signed a decree making the gendarmerie officers inspectors of the finances of the communes, each district commander. He had supervision and represented the central government in the commune, and saw how the funds were collected, etc.

Mr. Howe. Did that work well?

Gen. Cole. It worked splendidly.

Mr. Howe. Did it cause any friction?

Gen. Cole. It caused the resignation of the magistrate at the cape. Mr. Adehemar Auguste, but generally no friction. There were rubbings at times, but it straightened out, and the funds were properly accounted for, and the improvement in the communes was simply beyond belief. It was not accepted in good spirit by some people. They found that the President stuck to it in Haiti, so some one took it up with M. Menos, who was the Haitian minister to Washington, and he made complaints to the State Department, and the State Department took it up with us, and I took it up with the President. and the President said M. Menos had acted entirely without his authority; that he had acted on his own initiative entirely, without any authority from the Government, and the Government was thoroughly satisfied with the way in which the thing was working. There were one or two complaints from the Government, and the question was gone into, and it was satisfactorily arranged, I think, in both cases, it being shown to the President, to his entire satisfaction and to the satisfaction of the minister of the interior, that the reports that had come to him were misleading reports, and not correct.

Mr. HOWE. Was there anything else down there that you think we should know about, General, that you have not covered in your testimony?

Gen. COLE. There is that question of martial law that has not been spoken of at all, or at least very little.

Mr. HOWE. Will you make comment on that, please?

Gen. COLE. In my opinion, until the Haitian courts have been entirely reformed, and until an entirely improved government exists in the Republic of Haiti, martial law must continue. It certainly must continue so long as American troops are there under anyth'ng like the present conditions. It has not weighed heavily on the innocent; it has not weighed heavily on the poor; it has not weighed heavily on anybody, except on their fears. There were very few cases where provost courts were resorted to. There was one occasion when I took action in a purely Haitian case.

Mr. HOWE. Will you describe that?

Gen. COLE. A man died, leaving two sons. and also leaving some property. There was a dispute between the two sons as to a division of the property, and they were not friends. One brother sent to the other brother and said that he was ready to settle up, so the other brother went to him, and he was bound by h's brother and the brother's son. and then his wife and child were sent for, and they came. and for a period of approximately 12 hours, in the sight of the wife and the child, the man was gradually tortured to death by slow means—cuttings and bleedings, and ligatures—tied to a tree. It was a particularly atrocious, deliberate kill'ng of a brother. The matter was reported by the gendarme officer to the local judicial authorities, and the man was arrested and released. The gendarme officer took it up with the next higher judicial authority, and was informed that nothing could be done in regard to it; that the case was ended. he having been released by order of this judge de paix. The matter was reported to the chief of the gendarmerie, who brought it to my attention, and I took it up with the minister of justice and with the Pres'dent. I said that a condition of that sort could not be allowed to exist, and they took it up with the commissary of the Government. In the meantime I directed that the man be arrested. They sa'd that there was nothing that could be done. I said, "Very well, then, this is a case I am going to put before a military court," and the man was tried before a provost court and sentenced to confinement. After that was done, a short time afterwards, the minister for justice said he thought they could deal with the case; that they had made a mistake; they said they could not deal with it before, and after some discussion between the minister, the President, and myself, they having asked for jur'sdiction of the man, I told them that I preferred to have the man serve under the sentence of the Haitian court than serve under the sentence of a military court; that it was a Haitian offense. between Haitians, but I did not propose to allow·the man to escape punishment; that if they would prepare the proper legal papers in his case and would br'ng him to trial before the proper Haitian tribunal, that in case that tribunal acted in accordance with the evidence, the man would then be considered as a Haitian prisoner, but, so long as I remained in Haiti, and so long, in my opinion, as the Amer'can military authorities remained in Haiti, that man would have to remain in jail for the length of his sentence; in other words, he could not, having become a Haitian prisoner, be immed'- ately released.

Martial law was something that they feared, but it was something that did not touch them very often; very, very seldom. The newspapers generally behaved themselves pretty well. The only case in which I remember of having put a newspaper editor before the provost court was immediately after the dissolution of the National Assembly. The same day that the National Assembly was dissolved I gave Gen. Butler a notice to deliver to all the newspapers that there should be no comment on this particular thing, to inflame public opinion, and all the newspapers carried out those instructions.

Some two or three days later a Government newspaper came out with a vicious attack on the National Assembly, and I had the editor taken before the provost court, and he was tried and placed under a bond of $100 not to repeat his offense. Incidentally, it looked very much as though the article had been written by Dr. Heraux.

Mr. Howe. What was the attitude of the Haitian courts toward the occupation?

Gen. Cole. They were opposed to it; they did not want to recognize it.

Mr. Howe. Do you know about the case which has been mentioned here of the presentation of a check for gourdes?

Gen. Cole. Well, I know something about it.

Mr. Howe. It was testified here, General, that a Haitian presented a check calling for the payment of gourdes at the bank, and he was offered payment in dollars, but refused payment, whereupon he brought suit against the bank for the amount of his check in gourdes and punitive damages, and that the plea of the bank was that it was forced to take that action—forced by the officials of the occupation—and thereafter the court of cassation refused to recognize that plea and upheld the action of the lower court in finding for the plaintiff. Do you know who of the American officers ordered the bank to pay in gourdes?

Gen. Cole. I think Admiral Caperton. My note states the foundation of the case; that acting under an order of Admiral Caperton, with the end in view of preventing speculation in gold and gourdes, and the corresponding fluctuation in the rate of exchange, the bank made payment in gourdes at the rate of five for one for a check drawn in gold. This was a check drawn in gold.

Mr. Howe. Drawn in gold means in dollars?

Gen. Cole. Yes. Mr. Francis—his name is Francois—brought suit against the bank and attempted to execute the judgment. I issued instructions that the judgment could not be executed and that no interference with the operations of the bank on account of this case would be permitted.

Mr. Howe. Then I got my question hind part before as to what the check was for.

Gen. Cole. Mr. Francois made decidedly objectionable statements, according to this, against the occupation; and I was very much inclined to take action against him, but finally decided I would not, as he was an old man and had the reputation of being quite irascible and was apparently trying to get himself made a martyr, and I thought the best thing was simply to prevent any action being taken to put into effect the decrees. I took it up with the President, and he could not do anything, of course; it was beyond his power. And the minister of justice said it was beyond his power; but as it was done under an absolutely direct, positive order of Admiral Caperton, as far as I could tell, I had nothing to do but protect the bank. I have considerable papers about this proposition. I can give my instructions, if you would care to have them, in regard to that.

Mr. Howe. Let us have those.

Gen. Cole. This is to the financial adviser, dated April 28, 1917:

"Referring to your letter of April 26, 1917, with inclosures, whereby I am informed that one J. B. W. Francis has caused a summons to be issued for the 'National Banque de la Republique d'Haiti' through its representative, to appear before the tribunal civile of Port au Prince, to produce certain papers, or copies thereof, and to show cause why certain fines or penalties should not be imposed against the said banque, you are informed that, as the original action on which this complaint is based was performed by the banque as an agent of Admiral Caperton (in whose name the account was carried and by whose orders the funds concerned were disbursed) and in compliance with his orders, this case does not fall within the jurisdiction of the civil courts and consequently that no judgment of the civil courts against the banque in this case can be permitted to be executed, nor will any interference with the business of the banque on account of this case be tolerated. Please notify the banque accordingly and instruct it to inform this office immediately if any attempt is made to effectuate any judgment or execution against the banque or to interfere in any way with its operations on account of the action of the plaintiff in this case. Also instruct the banque to keep the military commander informed of the further actions of the plaintiff and of the civil courts in this case."

Mr. Howe. I think that probably is all that is really necessary about the facts in that case.

Gen. Cole. The court withdrew a part of its decision against the occupation, and a part of the fines against the bank, but they stuck to something else, but it was not put into effect.

Mr. Howe. In other words, the effect of that direction of yours was to disregard the order and decree of the court?

Gen. Cole. To set aside the decree in the civil court. That would be an example of a case where it was necessary to have ratified the acts of the occupation in the Republic of Haiti by the constitution before we could withdraw. That is simply a case in point.

Mr. Howe. Mr. Chairman, I understand that Mr. Angell would like to suggest the names of some witnesses to the committee. I told him that I hoped that the witnesses to be called by the committee at its own instance will probably have been examined by the end of Tuesday morning's session of the committee next week—that is to say, on the 15th of the month—and he, I think, will now suggest to the committee the names and addresses of some witnesses that he would like to have called.

Mr. Angell. All of these names, I believe, have been already given by me informally to Senator McCormick, at his request, as far back as August, the time when he called me down here from New York to go over with me the names of the witnesses and the general procedure, and these were the names that I suggested at that time.

Senator Oddie. Do you think that he had better give a list of them for the record?

Mr. Howe. Here is the point. You will probably not have time in the two or three days before we start down to Haiti to examine all of these witnesses.

Mr. Angell. I suggest, in view of the limited time at the disposal of the committee before we sail, that only two or three or possibly four of those be heard next week. I am particularly anxious to have the committee hear the testimony of a Mr. H. R. Pilkington, whose address is care P. W. Chapman & Co., 115 Broadway, New York City, or, if he happens to be away from New York at this moment, he can be reached in care of P. W. Chapman & Co., Chicago.

I would also like very much to have the committee hear the testimony of one Max Zurckerman, at 110 Crawford Street, Roxbury, Mass., care E. Levy, and the testimony either of Charles A. Burrows, 253 Belgrade Avenue, Roslyndale, Mass., or James W. Johnson, 70 Fifth Avenue, New York.

Mr. Pilkington and Mr. Johnson would come simply on any informal request from the committee or its counsel, Mr. Howe. Zurckerman is a young man who is in business, and he told me he could not get away without serious prejudice to his own position with his employer unless he had some kind of semiofficial notice from the committee.

Mr. Howe. I would suggest a telegram from the Sergeant at Arms.

Mr. Angell. Yes; some such form in his case. I do not think that will be necessary in the case of Mr. Pilkington and I am sure it would not be necessary in the case of Johnson, but I would suggest that a similar telegram be sent by the Sergeant at Arms to Burrows.

Mr. Howe. Which would you rather have, Johnson or Burrows?

Mr. Angell. I can tell that better when I get back to New York to-morrow. I know what Johnson has to say, in substance, but I do not know what Burrows has to say, although he has promised to write me and give me an outline of what his testimony will be.

Senator Oddie. You take that up with Capt. Angell, Mr. Howe?

Mr. Howe. Yes; I will take that up.

Mr. Angell. If in the meantime I may have Pilkington and Zurckerman notified definitely, when I get back to New York to-morrow morning I will be able to say whether I would prefer to have Johnson or Burrows, as the case may be.

(Whereupon the committee adjourned until Monday, November 14, 1921, at 10.30 o'clock a. m.)

INQUIRY INTO OCCUPATION AND ADMINISTRATION OF HAITI AND SANTO DOMINGO.

MONDAY, NOVEMBER 14, 1921.

UNITED STATES SENATE,
SELECT COMMITTEE ON HAITI AND SANTO DOMINGO,
Washington, D. C.

The committee met at 10.30 o'clock a. m., pursuant to adjournment, Senator Tasker L. Oddie presiding.

Present: Senator Oddie.

Also present: Mr. Walter Bruce Howe, Mr. Ernest Angell, and Maj. Edwin N. McClellan in their respective representative capacities as hereinbefore indicated.

STATEMENT OF BRIG. GEN. ELI K. COLE, UNITED STATES MARINE CORPS—Resumed.

Mr. ANGELL. You spoke in the early part of your direct testimony, General, concerning conditions relative to Cape Hatien and the Cacos of the north, and of good and bad Cacos. What was the distinction in your mind in using that term?

Col. COLE. The good Caco was by force of circumstances a member of the, from time to time, revolutionary forces, and between times was engaged in his occupation, generally that of small farmer, while the bad Caco was intended to designate those people who, from one cause or another, had become objectors to work and who when not engaged in revolutionary activities prefer living on the work of others to work performed by themselves; and in general it included those who lived by armed robbery.

Mr. ANGELL. Were the Cacos who refused to surrender their arms and accept the occupation in the fall of 1915 thereafter regarded as bandits by virtue of the fact of such refusal?

Gen. COLE. Only during the period when they remained under arms. After the campaign at Fort Riviere was finished we did what we could to get people to come into their homes and reestablish their farms; and it was our general policy to take no action against other than a few of the higher leaders, except in the case of people who still continued in bands under arms and were scouring the country robbing, in particular market women, their best prey.

Mr. ANGELL. Well, up to the time of the capture of Fort Riviere were those who in any way remained under arms regarded as ipso facto bandits and enemies of the occupation?

Gen. COLE. They were. They were regarded as bandits, because their leaders had entered into a formal convention for the delivery of arms and the return to their homes of their followers; and these people had disobeyed not only the orders of their leaders, up to and including the very highest. but they had taken to the woods with the announced determination of carrying on a war to drive us out of Haiti. A subordinate must in civilized warfare follow the instructions of those placed over him in the military hierarchy.

Mr. ANGELL. Were those operations—I am speaking now of the operations in the fall of 1915, which concluded with the capture of Fort Riviere—regarded by the occupation as practically warfare being conducted by our troops against the Cacos?

Gen. COLE. Yes; absolutely.

Mr. ANGELL. You spoke in considerable detail of the conditions at Cape Haitien in the summer and early fall of 1915 and of the work that was undertaken by our military forces under your direction, such as cleaning up hospitals, waterworks, sanitation, and public utilities generally. From what sources were the funds used in those works derived?

Gen. Cole. Almost entirely from funds allotted me by Admiral Caperton, as the senior naval officer present, through Col. Waller, the brigade commander and senior military officer on shore, although some small sums collected or on hand in the treasury of the commune were used to make payments for purely communal purposes and to make payments, as I remember it, for the rent of the communal building or buildings. But the amount involved in the latter class was very small, the funds being turned back as soon as a Haitian communal administration was formed at the Cape.

Mr. Angell. Were those communal funds seized by you or by Col. Waller or others under his direction or your direction? In other words, how were they made available for expenditures by the military forces?

Gen. Cole. There was no Haitian official of any authority remaining, and I found that there were funds belonging to the commune in what I considered a very precarious position, and——

Mr. Angell (interposing). Were those funds on deposit in the bank?

Gen. Cole. No; they were not.

Mr. Angell. They were in specie?

Gen. Cole. They were in specie, in a very insecure safe, in a very insecure building, and in charge of a man of whom I was somewhat suspicious; and those funds were placed in the bank at Cape Haitien, and receipt was given for them, and an account was kept of all funds that were received, and a receipt was received from the communal administration when these funds were turned back.

Mr. Angell. Were the funds in question deposited by you or under your orders and in your name?

Gen. Cole. They were, as I remember it, deposited by me personally and in my name, as representing the commune of Cape Haitien.

Mr. Angell. Do you remember the approximate amount of those funds?

Gen. Cole. I do not. And I have not got the data; I looked to see if I could find it. I have it somewhere, but I do not know where it is.

Mr. Angell. Was it a few hundred gourdes, or several thousand dollars, roughly speaking?

Gen. Cole. As I remember it, it was some hundreds of dollars at the start. Now, the time approached—or the time had arrived—when it was necessary to make up the tax list for the commune for the coming year. I knew nothing of this until very near the time to have the thing completed, and I ascertained from, I believe, the former mayor, Mr. Auguste, who had drawn up these papers before, and the same people were employed to draw up the tax notices for the ensuing year. And my recollection is that funds were not collected from those taxes during my administration. They may have been, however, like a good many other things, and I had placed an officer in direct charge of that work, carrying that on under my general directions. But the funds were, I am quite certain, absolutely secure without my signature. My records show funds of Commune of Cape Haitien were deposited in the Banque Nationale de la Republique d'Haiti in the name of Col. Eli K. Cole, pour compte de la Commune de Cap Haitien, as follows:

	Gourdes.
10 Oct., 1915	452.32
28 Oct., 1915	496.49
22 Nov., 1915	3,543.59
23 Nov., 1915	1,462.54
Total	5,954.94

The above total was turned over to and receipted for by the Receveur Communal of Cape Haitien on December 4, 1915.

Mr. Angell. The funds were secure without your signature?

Gen. Cole. They were absolutely secure unless I put my signature on something ordering them to be taken out of the bank.

Mr. Angell. Oh, they could not be disbursed except with your signature?

Gen. Cole. They could not be disbursed without my signature.

Mr. Angell. In the name of the commune?

Gen. Cole. I really do not remember, but I have no reason to doubt that it was in the name of the commune. It was a separate account; it was not an account lumped with anything else; but as to the exact name in which it was carried I do not know, though I did have a number of different accounts in the bank from time to time, though never a personal account there.

Mr. ·ANGELL. Who was responsible for determining the purposes for which these funds were expended in and around Cape Haitien?

Gen. COLE. The military governor himself.

Mr. ANGELL. Do you know the sources from which the funds turned over to you by Admiral Caperton were derived?

Gen. COLE. I always understood they were derived from the customs revenues.

Mr. ANGELL. Was martial law in effect in Cape Haitien in the fall of 1915?

Gen. COLE. It was.

Mr. ANGELL. By formal proclamation?

Gen. COLE. Yes.

Mr. ANGELL. Was that made substantially at the same time as the proclamation of martial law in Port au Prince?

Gen. COLE. Immediately following, or at the same time.

Mr. ANGELL. You spoke of the agricultural stations, experimental farms, and experiments conducted. Do you remember how many of those stations there were and where they were located?

Gen. COLE. The school was located outside of Port au Prince, beyond a place called Bizoton.

Mr. ANGELL. And when was that begun—that school—approximately, if you remember?

Gen. COLE. It was some time prior to the end of June, 1917.

Mr. ANGELL. Was that established and run by the marine forces of the occupation—by the military occupation?

Gen. COLE. It was run by the military occupation, and my recollection is that it was handled by officers of the gendarmerie. Now, there was an experimental farm at the same place; there was a farm started at Furcy, and there was a farm started, my recollection is, in the vicinity of the gendarmerie station near Le Trou; and a number, or practically a large proportion, I think, of the gendarmerie posts had been directed to start small farms with as up-to-date methods of operation as the officer concerned was capable of putting into effect.

I had the scheme of having a model cabin or farm buildings put up, but it never was done.

Mr. ANGELL. All of this work that you are just speaking of—this agricultural work—was undertaken upon the initiative of the military occupation?

Gen. COLE. Yes.

Mr. ANGELL. Rather than upon a suggestion from Washington?

Gen. COLE. Oh, yes. Washington never made any suggestions. All of this was being done—we had a certain mission to perform, to do the best we could to build up that country; to build up a stable government; to preserve peace and order; and to bring prosperity to the people; and we were all trying our best to do that; and anything that we could put our hands to that would help toward that result we tried to put over.

Mr. ANGELL. So far as you know, were agricultural experts ever sent down from this country?

Gen. COLE. Oh, yes.

Mr. ANGELL. When was that? Was that during your time in Haiti?

Gen. COLE. Yes. I find this under date of July 13——

Mr. ANGELL. 1917?

Gen. COLE. 1917.

"The delay in the arrival of the agricultural experts from the United States is unfortunate, as it was hoped through their advice to be able to secure a considerable quantity of nonperishable foodstuffs for export to the United States or to Cuba."

You see, we were up against the.proposition there of lack of transportation from the United States, and consequently we had to provide food in Haiti, not only for Haitians. but we wanted to go beyond that if we could and provide food for export, which would be to our benefit and to the benefit of the Hatians also.

Mr. ANGELL. What was the source of the funds that supported these little farms and stations?

Gen. COLE. Haitian funds; presumably collected, as I said, from the customs.

Mr. ANGELL. Have you any idea, General, of the attendance at the agricultural school? How widely did the idea spread? How much was it taken up by the Haitians?

Gen. COLE. It was an idea that grew. At first we paid them a little, I think——

Mr. ANGELL (interposing). During attendance?

Gen. COLE. During attendance; I think 10 gourdes a month, and we provided them with their food, such food as they could not raise on the farm. Later that was withdrawn—that is, the 10 gourdes—and my recollection is that they were required to pay small fees. But it was a thing that started out and increased. I have somewhere among these papers—I may be able to find it—an account of the visit of the President there, if you care to have it.

Mr. ANGELL. You might put it in afterwards if you think it of interest.

Gen. COLE. Well, I would have to hunt for it. I may not have it here.

Mr. ANGELL. Did the numbers in attendance at the schools run into the scores or the hundreds or——

Gen. COLE. No; my recollection is that there may have been 40 or 50 there. But unless I had something in my records to show I would not be able to answer that question very satisfactorily.

Mr. ANGELL. Did that school continue to exist so long as you were in Haiti?

Gen. COLE. Yes.

Mr. ANGELL. Do you know if it was continued after that, or was it given up?

Gen. COLE. I understand that it is still in existence, though I am not positive in regard to it.

Mr. ANGELL. Referring to irrigation and the cul de sac region around Port au Prince, I understood you to say that nothing had been done by the engineer appointed under the treaty prior to the time when you left Haiti in 1917?

Gen. COLE. Nothing had been done by him. We had the plan drawn up to repair the dam, I being afraid that in the winter freshets it might give way, and I believed then that we would have completed the work inside of a month or six weeks; but as I had orders to turn over the engineering work to the engineer of Haiti, and as I believed that the irrigation systems came clearly under his jurisdiction as a treaty official, I turned it over and said, "There is a job that you can go at."

Mr. ANGELL. Do you remember about when it was that you turned over those plans to him?

Gen. COLE. I think it was probably in September or October.

Mr. ANGELL. Of 1917?

Gen. COLE. Of 1917.

Mr. ANGELL. These plans were drawn up by you, or under your direction, and upon your initiative?

Gen. COLE. Yes.

Mr. ANGELL. Rather than by direction from Washington?

Gen. COLE. Yes; all of these things. I do not remember of anything of that sort that we ever got from Washington.

Mr. ANGELL. Did you make recommendations along that general line to Washington—that is, recommendations for irrigation, or agriculture, or education, or such matters—to Washington?

Gen. COLE. I kept a diary, and copies of that diary were sent to Admiral Knapp in San Domingo, to the Navy Department, to the State Department, and to headquarters of the Marine Corps; and I took up everything, day by day, that came up that was of any importance. In that diary there were numerous discussions in regard to what we were trying to do; what we wanted done; that I had gotten the President to ask for agricultural experts, school experts, or postal experts, or whatever it might be. So Washington was always informed during the year 1917 as to what was actually being done in the Republic of Haiti.

Mr. ANGELL. Did your diary also contain general notes which to a reader would set forth clearly conditions in Haiti as you have testified to them on direct examination here?

Gen. COLE. I think so, without any question.; because my memory in giving my testimony here has been refreshed by going over this mass of diaries.

Mr. ANGELL. Did you keep such a diary during the year 1915?

Gen. COLE. No.

Mr. ANGELL. Or 1916?

Gen. COLE. No.

Mr. ANGELL. In addition to this diary, copies of which were forwarded, as you have just said, did you make specific recommendations and reports to Admiral Knapp, the State Department, the marine headquarters, or the Navy

Department on such aspects of the whole situation as education, public works, the judiciary, Government administration, and the like?

Gen. COLE. Yes; but not extensively. The only way to get things done is to do them yourself. And the United States was pretty busy, with probably more important things for its Government than the administration of an experimental farm, or something of that sort, though they did send the agricultural experts; they sent one of their postal experts. I got the expert for the schools. They sent down some geologists; the Smithsonian Institution sent down some people. And generally those things that they were asked to do they did. But I did not ask them to do things that it was our business to do, or that it was the business of other treaty officials to do. I made comment from time to time in regard to what was being done, or as to what was not being done, by other treaty officials.

Mr. ANGELL. Are those comments contained in this file?

Gen. COLE. Yes; generally. Of course, there were brief, more or less daily, or, at least, frequent radio reports made, and impotant things were handled that way, or by cable very frequently.

Mr. ANGELL. Why did the people of Haiti disapprove of President Dartiguenave?

Gen. COLE. I imagine because he was a politician, had been in political life all of his life—that is, most of his life. And there are very few men in Haiti who could rise to prominence in political life and retain their integrity. You see, d'Artiguenave was well educated—quite polished; and I must say, in my opinion, a consummate politician. I have a great deal of respect for Mr. d'Artiguenave, and a great deal of personal liking for him. And he had the courage to accept a difficult position, when apparently very few others would. So you must give him the credit of being a man of considerable moral and physical courage.

Mr. ANGELL. When you say "to accept a difficult situation," do you mean accepting the American intervention as a fait accompli, as a necessary step in the development of Haiti?

Gen. COLE. Yes; I think that would be a correct way of putting it. The term "anarchy" best describes the condition of affairs in Haiti; our troops had been compelled to land; the President had been assassinated, murdered; revolutionary troops were at large throughout the extent of the Republic; generally the courts were in a very low state of morale, if any existed at all; a foreign government had landed troops in Haiti; and the Haitians had had no reason to think that European powers, that is, white powers, were particularly anxious to regard their rights. So any man that accepted and worked with a white occupation must have known that he would be a very decided object of suspicion and of hatred. Because there is no question that they were jealous of their independence. We were anxious to preserve their independence, but they did not realize that; they had the idea that were were going in there, for instance, as the Germans had gone in there, and were going to swat the deuce out of them.

Mr. ANGELL. Was the President's acceptance of the American intervention generally known among the people?

Gen. COLE. Oh, I think so, without any question.

Mr. ANGELL. Did the knowledge of that acceptance of such intervention have any part, in your judgment, in the distrust in which he was held by the people?

Gen. COLE. Now, do not go too far in regard to that, because Mr. Dartiguenave did not have the distrust of all the people, by any means. Mr. Dartiguenave had the distrust and the dislike of a considerable part of the Haitian politicians, the Haitian political classes, but Mr. Dartiguenave did not have the animosity of the people of Haiti. Mr. Dartiguenave went through the Republic of Haiti; and he went at times almost unattended, and he did not have their animosity; he had their liking, to a great extent.

Mr. ANGELL. Did he have the general support of the population?

Gen. COLE. I think Mr. Dartiguenave had as much of the support of the population as a population like that of Haiti was able to give anybody; as a matter of fact, the population of Haiti are like so many sheep in the hands of a few of their leaders; a few educated people, possibly 2 per cent of the total population, are the people who handle the affairs of Haiti, and who have manipulated the affairs of Haiti for the purpose of lining their pockets and maintaining their own standards.

Mr. ANGELL. Did the population of Haiti generally know, in your judgment, of the detailed facts leading up to our intervention and the signing of the treaty and its ratification and the subsequent steps?

Gen. COLE. No; only a comparatively small part of them did. Their idea was based on the fact that they were getting better treatment than they had ever gotten before; that their life and property were more secure; that they had much more consideration shown them; that they were not subject to being arb'trarily led off in droves to form part of a revolutionary band or the army of the Government. They had rights, and their rights were respecte'l, and they were given a chance to enjoy the benefits of their own labor, which they had never had before.

Mr. ANGELL. What was the general attitude of the Haitian population toward the United States and the military occupation at the end of 1916 and dur'ng the year 1917?

Gen. COLE. Fine. They used to kneel down by their wayside shrines and thank God that we were there. I have told about the President and Gen. Butler and I, as well as the cabinet, going up the mountains and seeing the people.

Mr. ANGELL. You remember the report which you made to the Secretary of the Navy, in an offic'al letter dated September 23, 1920, in which, speaking of the peaceful conditions in Haiti at the time you relieved Col. Waller in November, 1916, you went on to say: "I will venture to say that during the time in question" (that is, wh'le you were in command) "life and property in Haiti were as secure as in the United States, if not more secure?"

Gen. COLE. Yes. You take the little State of Georgia, and there are more murders, or more killings in a day, or in an average of 10 days in that State, than there were in a month in the Republic of Ha'ti at that period of time. I mentioned Georgia because I read the Savannah News; and that is a commentary on American civilization.

Mr. ANGELL. Did they ever have to use the marines in Haiti to guard the mails? [Laughter.]

Gen. COLE. No. But in order to prevent rifling of the mails we inaugurated a system whereby a gendarmerie noncommissioned officer or officer should go to the post office and seal sacks of mail and deliver those sacks sealed to another part of the Republ'c, getting the receipts therefor. I initiated that system of having gendarmerie messengers responsible for the carrying of the mail. And we shortened the delivery of the mail very materially, and at the same time mail that was intrusted to the charge of the gendarmerie was delivered invariably.

Mr. ANGELL. W'll you tell us briefly, General, what you did to support Dr. Heraux, the pro-American leader in the assembly?

Gen. COLE. Well, I gave you my reasons for the support of Dr. Heraux. In acting for the President in regard to getting together people who would serve in his cabinet, I invariably made the statement that it was necessary for Dr. Heraux to remain as a member of the cabinet, giving my reasons. I presume that is about the extent of my discussions in regard to Heraux; there were many of them, but they were along that same line. Heraux was the one Haitian who had consistently endeavored to aid us in building up a proper nat'onal government in Haiti, and he was the one Haitian who was familiar with the financial investigation and revision of system of accounts that was going on. The President, without any question, wanted at times to get rid of Dr. Heraux. As a matter of fact, I felt quite certain at times that the agitation against Dr. Heraux was traceable directly to the room occupied by his excellency.

We felt that in order to carry out our work in Haiti we had to have the cooperation of Haitians; unless we had the cooperation of Haitians, there would be no Haitians to occupy Government positions of Haiti under the education that we hoped they would get from an honest administration of affairs. If we had calmly thrown Dr. Heraux aside, because he was considered honest and a firm supporter of the United States, desiring to improve conditions in Haiti, we never would have been able to get anybody to stand up for us, because they would have said: "You use him, and when it seems better to you for your own purposes you cast him aside." And I would not do it.

Mr. ANGELL. Was the treaty of September, 1915, extended for a further period of 10 years upon the request of the United States?

Gen. COLE. Upon the request of Haiti, but presumably after conversations between the representatives. The United States had bound itself under that convention to do certain things. Among other things, was the rehabilitation of the finances; the procurement of a loan.

Now, the United States, or the fiscal agent nominated by the United States as financial adviser, had. I think, without any question, tried to get a loan for Haiti under the terms of the old convention. It was absolutely essential that such a loan be procured if the work was to be initiated that we wanted to have done there and the country built up. And the United States, I believe, notified the Haitian Government that such loan could not be obtained from the financial interests of the United States under the 10-year tenure in Haiti; and the Hatian Government then took up the question of asking the extension of the treaty; and it was passed by a divided cabinet. ,

Mr. ANGELL. The request, then, came from the Haitian Government, rather than from the United States Government, in the first instance?

Gen. COLE. The official request came from the Haitian Government. Now, as to whether or not the United States or the Haitian Government first started it I do not know, because I had nothing to do with that particular feature, as the matter was handled between the representatives of the State Department and of the secretary of state for foreign affairs of Haiti.

Mr. ANGELL. Do you know the period from which the treaty was extended for a further period of 10 years?

Gen. COLE. Nineteen hundred and seventeen. The school system and every other thing that we wanted to get built up in Haiti required financing, and to do the work that we had to do we had to have the funds, and we could not get the funds under the then existing conditions. In my opinion, if the Haitians had acted decently and aided us as we were trying to aid them, the funds could have been obtained long ago, and the affairs of Haiti could have been in a very much better state than they are to-day. And I lay the blame, to a great extent, on the Haitian people's or the Haitian Government's, or the Haitian politician's inability to do anything that seemed to aid in this particular work.

Mr. ANGELL. You say the funds might have been obtained if it had not been for this condition. What do you mean by saying the funds might have been obtained? Do you refer to a loan?

Gen. COLE. Yes. I think that if the Haitian Government, its representatives, the nat'onal assembly, and so on, had acted as honestly toward us as we were trying to act toward them, or as fairly as we were trying to act toward them, they would have done a great deal better for themselves; they would have retained the good will of the United States and they would have caused, through showing their desire to cooperate with the United States, such an attitude as would have enabled the Government at home to put over a loan to the Republic of Haiti to refund its debts, and to give it sufficient funds to enable the work that was to be carried on to be started, at least.

Mr. ANGELL. And you feel that the fact that no loan was made is due in large part to the political conditions in Haiti?

Gen. COLE. I think it was absolutely due to that. If, for instance. Haiti at the start had cooperated with us; if they had displayed a desire to cooperate, I have no doubt in my own mind but that in 1916, or the spring of 1917 at the latest, the Haitian loan could have been floated in the United States. But the people who had funds just simply would not advance funds, on the lack of knowledge as to what was going to be done in the Republic of Haiti. Then, of course, there was the war financing; loans to countries whe were to become our allies, etc. But largely, the thing is due to the attitude of the Haitian politicians.

Mr. ANGELL. Speaking of the United States interests in Haiti, you referred to the fact that the French had 150,000,000 francs——

Gen. COLE (interposing). In round numbers.

Mr. ANGELL. Yes; invested in Haiti. That was largely the sum invested in the Haitian foreign loan, was it not?

Gen. COLE. Yes.

Mr. ANGELL. And on that loan the interest had been paid regularly during all recent years, up to the time of the intervention, had it not.

Gen. COLE. Up to the time of the intervention.

Mr. ANGELL. And for five years following the intervention the interest was not paid, was it?

Gen. COLE. I am not able to answer as to five years. I can say it was not paid for two years and a half. But as an explanation, I think that you will find, if the matter is investigated, that the payments of the interest would not have been continued by Haiti any longer. I think that she had reached the limit of her paying or borrowing capacity.

I was very anxious to have the finances of the country put in order. I was very particularly anxious to have the internal debt, particularly the bonds held by the people of Haiti, put in the course of settlement at least, so that the income therefrom could be paid. These bonds had been taken, I suspect, very frequently forcibly, by the middle and upper middle classes of Haitians, and by some politicians as provision for their families when they died. And I felt that if those bonds could be settled, or if the interest on those bonds could be paid, it would relieve a very pressing necessity. Because the people who owned those bonds were generally the people that we were unable to help. We could help the countryman, the farmer, and so on; we could help the laborers. But with the war going on, with steamers not running, with goods difficult to secure, the commercial class, the city dweller who was living on what had been saved in one way or another before—we had no way of giving any particular financial benefit to those people.

Now, I said and reported that if the interest on these loans could be paid, we were at least going to get away from the antagonism and animosity of those people; and that that antagonism and animosity must grow the longer they were unable to get their interest with which to purchase the necessities of life. I wanted that paid, and I wanted it paid badly, because I wanted the support of those people; and I believe that if we had gone ahead and made an arrangement to pay the interest on the internal loans in particular, and paid all of them, it would have given us a great many more friends in Haiti than we had, and among a class of people who were able to influence public opinion.

Mr. Angell. Was the interest paid on the so-called interior bonds during the first two and one-half years of occupation?

Gen. Cole. No; it was not paid at all.

Mr. Angell. The question as to whether or not interest on that loan should be paid depended ultimately on Washington?

Gen. Cole. Possibly. There was the financial adviser. I had nothing to do with those things; but I observed those things only as they had to do with what I had in mind, which was to build up a Government in Haiti which they could work themselves.

Mr. Angell. You made an investigation and report?

Gen. Cole. I did, a number of times.

Mr. Angell. You made reports to Admiral Knapp and to the Navy Department?

Gen. Cole. Yes; I think that was in a long report that I made in May, 1917.

Mr. Angell. You said a moment ago that in your opinion Haiti would have been unable to continue to pay the interest on the foreign loan. Is such opinion based upon the feeling by you that the national funds would not have been sufficient to meet these obligations?

Gen. Cole. Yes; for, as I understand it, the national funds had practically disappeared, interest on the loans would become due within a short time, and there was nothing on hand or in sight sufficient to pay that interest.

Mr. Angell. After our intervention in July, 1915, and the seizure of the collection of the customs by us, were there, to your knowledge, or were there not funds that actually would have been sufficient to meet the interest on these foreign-loan obligations?

Gen. Cole. I really do not know, but I rather doubt it.

Mr. Angell. Do you mean when you say you doubt it that you think the surplus above and beyond the expenditures actually made for public improvements, constabulary, road building, etc., would have been insufficient?

Gen. Cole. Yes.

Mr. Angell. Or that the total receipts before any such expenditures would have been insufficient?

Gen. Cole. I do not know whether or not the total receipts would have enabled the interest to be paid. I presume they would, but government had to be reestablished; much starvation had to be warded off; the expenses of administering the government had to be met. And as the Haitian employee, dependent upon his stipend for his daily bread, had not been paid for months and months, it was necessary to provide these people with some means under the conditions existing of meeting their obligations and of reestablishing credit in the country. I think those are the things that must have been considered as necessary to place ahead of the payment of the interest on the loan.

Mr. Angell. You had no hand yourself in the determination of whether or not to pay the interest on the loan?

Gen. Cole. I had nothing to do with it at any time.

Mr. ANGELL. Do you think that the declaration of war on Germany by Haiti in the spring or early in the summer of 1915 would have been beneficial to Haiti?

Gen. COLE. I think it would have been very beneficial to Haiti. It would have made no difference in her expenditures; and it would have brought about, I believe, a feeling in the United States—that is, in the Government at Washington—that at last Haiti was willing to work with us. They were informed that we had no idea of calling upon them for assistance. All the arguments that I made in regard to Haiti entering the war with the President and members of the National Assembly were based on what, in my mind, were the best interests of Haiti; because, so far as the United States was concerned, we did not need Haiti in the war; it would have been much more expensive to arm her people than to arm ourselves, and we would not have made good soldiers out of them. The advice was absolutely given, I repeat, with the idea that it was to improve conditions in the Republic of Haiti, and incidentally it would have improved our relationship with Haiti.

Mr. ANGELL. When you say it would have improved the conditions in Haiti, do you mean by virtue of the——

Gen. COLE (interposing). I believe that they would have gotten their loan; I believe that that had something to do with it.

Mr. ANGELL. That it would have established a psychological rapproachement between Haiti and the United States?

Gen. COLE. A rapproachement, yes; but they just could not do it.

Mr. ANGELL. At the very beginning of your testimony the other day, in giving the dates of your tour of duty in Haiti, you said that you left there late in 1917 and came up to Washington, where you had conferences at the State Department regarding the new constitution. With whom did you hold such conferences? Will you tell us briefly about that?

Gen. COLE. Mr. Stabler, as I remember it.

Mr. ANGELL. Mr. Stabler was chief of the Latin-American Division of the State Department?

Gen. COLE. Yes, sir. My interviews with him were brief and far apart. I got here early in December, and the business was finished up by the end of January, when I thought that it would have been finished up long before. However, Haiti, as I say, was probably a small part of the large whole that had to be considered.

Mr. ANGELL. Were your interviews at the State Department with Mr. Stabler alone or with other officials?

Gen. COLE. With other officials. I think there was a Mr. Glen Stewart; there was another man there most of the time. I had interviews alone with him.

Mr. ANGELL. Did you acquaint the State Department through these gentlemen in these interviews with the general state of affairs in Haiti?

Gen. COLE. As much as was necessary. I think the State Department had a pretty fair idea—that is, the Latin-American Division head had a pretty fair idea.

Mr. ANGELL. Had a pretty fair idea of the conditions there?

Gen. COLE. Yes.

Mr. ANGELL. And of what was needed and what the occupation had been trying to do?

Gen. COLE. Yes.

Mr. ANGELL. Do you know who drafted or was in the main responsible for the principal changes desired by the United States in the then existing constitution of Haiti?

Gen. COLE. I had nothing to do with the projects of the constitution until the early summer of 1917, and I presumed the questions as to what changes were necessary had been discussed between representatives of the State Department of the United States and the Department of Foreign Affairs of the Republic of Haiti.

Mr. ANGELL. Of those preliminary discussions and projects you have no personal knowledge?

Gen. COLE. I have no personal knowledge. I know that there was correspondence on the subject; that the correspondence went to the Department of Foreign Affairs; that the Haitian Government—I have always felt with an idea of creating difficulties—sent the correspondence direct to the bureau of the National Assembly without comment, or with other than little comment.

Mr. ANGELL. That was the act which you referred to the other day as a faux pas?

Gen. COLE. I do not know that that act on the part of the President, or of his cabinet, really had any actual effect on what took place, because I believe that the members of the National Assembly were so antagonistic to the United States in every way, shape, and form, reasonable or unreasonable—if there were any reasons for it—that they would not have acceded to the slightest request of the United States Government in regard to the change in the constitution, although, through the convention, such changes had been clearly indicated as contemplated, as necessary, and as agreed to by the representatives of the Haitian nation.

Mr. ANGELL. Agreed to in so far as they were implied in the terms and the fact of the execution of the convention of 1915?

You referred to different articles which the United States desired to have modified in the old constitution, such as the land-holding question, and other articles which you named. Is it your understanding of the negotiations that the suggested changes initiated with the United States rather than with the Haitian Government?

Gen. COLE. I can not say. It was probably as the result of negotiations between the two departments of state, or discussions between them. In all probability, the United States took the lead; but I have no knowledge of it. The Council of State drew up the projet de constitution. That was the basis of the preliminary discussions. After the assembly had thrown aside the constitution recommended by the Council of State and prepared one of their own, which they were trying to put into effect, they were dissolved, and then the Council of State prepared another project.

And my first real connection with the constitution as a constitution, dated from immediately after the dissolution of the National Assembly, when the President asked me to come to the palace and discuss with him the question of a constitution which would meet the objections of the United States to the ones that had already been prepared. I told him that I had made full report to our Government, and that I could not do more than act in a friendly way with him in discussing the matter; and that I could in no way bind myself or the Government in any way without referring a question of this sort to the United States. And we had considerable discussion, and I made certain suggestions.

The thing, with my suggestions, as I remember it, did go to our legation. As a matter of fact, I think I took them there; became an intermediary between the President direct and the legation, and cut out the Department of State for the time being. I think that I was simply trying to get something in each instance which stood a reasonably good chance of meeting the approval of everybody concerned.

There was after that, to my knowledge, considerable correspondence, and the department sent back a project of constitution; and Admiral Knapp and the chargé and myself thought we probably were better informed as to the needs of Haiti than anyone else; and we decided to go into executive session and to take everything bearing on the constitution that we could, go over it and consider it from every point of view, and possibly finally arrive at a constitution which we hoped would be a satisfactory one to the United States and at the same time conserve the interests of the Republic of Haiti. We spent, as I remember it, some three weeks on it. We realized that there were various things——

Mr. ANGELL (interposing). This was in the fall of 1917?

Gen. COLE. This was in the fall of 1917.

Mr. ANGELL. After the dissolution of the assembly?

Gen. COLE. After the dissolution of the assembly; some months afterwards. This was in November. We felt that there were certain things wherein, Haiti had a right to feel disquiet, and we tried to fix it so that the rights of the Haitians would be safeguarded just as much as it was reasonable for them to be safeguarded.

Mr. ANGELL. In what particular did you feel that the Haitians had a right to feel disquiet?

Gen. COLE. I felt that there was in Haiti the idea that foreigners should not be given the right to own land. That was one thing.

Mr. ANGELL. Was that idea widespread and intensely felt?

Gen. COLE. I do not think that it was widespread or intensely felt, except among the political classes, and to a certain extent among the educated classes. The better they were informed, of course, the more they could think for themselves. And I really believe that they had an honest fear of——

Mr. Angell (interposing). Economic exploitation?

Gen. Cole. Economic exploitation, yes'; that is a very good term for it. I think they did have a real, honest fear; and we tried our best to give at least safeguard so that that fear could not materialize.

Mr. Angell. In what other particulars, if any, did the Haitians feel disquiet?

Gen. Cole. I think this is about the only one that they really had disquiet about. There was the question of so-called diplomatic intervention. Under the constitution of Haiti, carried to its logical conclusion, no Haitian official could allow or consider a question raised by a foreign government through its diplomatic representative concerning an indemnity for damages done in the Republic of Haiti to the foreigner or to his property. In other words, their constitution absolutely prohibited any such diplomatic representation or intervention. And I think that that was one of the things that they had in mind.

Mr. Angell. Was that provision finally done away with in the new constitution, do you remember?

Gen. Cole. That provision was done away with, yes. Our Government contended that the foreigner doing business in Haiti should have the same legal protection as was accorded a Haitian. A Haitian comes to the United States and he has the same legal protection that our people have. In addition, he has the protection due to diplomatic representations, which would without any question be made. And you can not expect the country of Haiti to be built up without funds and without security for property. And I know perfectly well that I would not put a cent, if I had a million dollars, into Haiti under the conditions that existed there.

Mr. Angell. You have referred several times recently to the council of state. That body was appointed exclusively by the President of Haiti, was it not?

Gen. Cole. Yes.

Mr. Angell. It was not elective?

Gen. Cole. It was not elective.

Mr. Angell. And since the dissolution of the national assembly in 1917, there has been no meeting of any legislative body in Haiti?

Gen. Cole. No; the only legislative body is the council of state, which, under the transitory provisions of the constitution which was adopted, exercises all the functions of the legislative branch of the Government of the Republic of Haiti.

Mr. Angell. It frames and passes laws?

Gen. Cole. Yes.

Mr. Angell. To use the inaccurate word "passes"?

Gen. Cole. Yes; as a matter of fact, I believe it would elect a President, if a vacany existed.

Mr. Angell. Do you know whether, under the constitution of 1889, which was still in force up to the adoption of the new constitution in 1918, there was any provision for a council of state which has functioned as you have just described?

Gen. Cole. I can not answer that directly. I will examine the book. It says, article 199, "The council of state is dissolved," under "Transitory dispositions" in the constitution of 1889. That seems to settle that; there was no council of state.

Mr. Angell. So that, under your understanding of the constitution of 1889, there was no constitutional provision for the existence or functions of such a body?

Gen. Cole. To the best of my knowledge I believe there was not; though a council of state did exist in 1917—though it was very quiet, and I do not think it was getting any pay; it very likely was an unofficial body.

Mr. Angell. That was the body presumably existing under the President's decree of April 5, 1916?

Gen. Cole. Yes. And I guess that must have been the time when they were dissolved; it was by presidential decree, to take the place of the legislative power though only in an advisory capacity. I was not in Port au Prince at that time and incidentally neither one of those dissolutions made the slightest ripple in Haitian affairs.

Mr. Angell. What instructions did you get, and from whom, and what was the approximate date, so far as you can remember, approving the adoption of a constitution adverse to the wishes of the United States? Were those

Instructions, in other words, that came from the Navy Department, or the State Department?

Gen. COLE. The Navy Department. I read them all into the record.

Mr. ANGELL. All right, if those instructions are in the record. Did you give us, in your direct testimony, the date of your cable showing that no steps short of dissolution by force would prevent the adoption of a constitution adverse to what was desired by the United States?

Gen. COLE. I think so, but I can very easily give it to you [examining papers]. That was the 15th of June.

Mr. ANGELL. June 15, 1917?

Gen. COLE. Yes.

Mr. ANGELL. Were you, as brigade commander of the United States Marines in Haiti at that time, prepared for the eventuality of the substitution of a military government for the then Haitian Government?

Gen. COLE. No, and yes. I had stated in the first long report (May 17, 1917) that I had made that I believed the results desired could be accomplished quicker through a military government, and more economically and more satisfactorily than in any other way. I had given four different methods which, in my opinion, could be followed by the United States Government.

Mr. ANGELL. In those suggestions of the method of accomplishing the desires of the United States, did you specifically recommend the substitution of an out-and-out military government for the Haitian Government?

Gen. COLE. I stated that, in my opinion, that was decidedly the best thing to do. We could not get cooperation from them; the minute we took our eyes off of them they were off doing something that was a waste of money, or a waste of time, or a grain of sand or two in the bearings.

Mr. ANGELL. Did you make actual preparations for a military government for the Haitian Government?

Gen. COLE. No; not at all. I had been told by members of the cabinet that they thought that the only way in which the matter was going to be straightened out in Haiti was through the exercise of the military government; and I believed it myself.

Mr. ANGELL. General, I do not want to put to you a question which by virtue of its legal and constitutional implications seems unfair, but, knowing your familiarity with conditions in Haiti, I would like to ask you whether, according to your understanding of the constitution of Haiti, the President's decree of dissolution in 1917 was constitutional or was provided for by the constitution?

Mr. HOWE. It seems to me, Mr. Chairman—Mr. Angell and I have just been talking about it—that perhaps it would be just as well not to ask the general those questions of Haitian constitutional law here—merely confining himself to the understanding of that law on which he was acting at the time.

Senator ODDIE. Yes; I approve of that point. I think that is going too far.

Mr. ANGELL. I think it is an intricate question of constitutional law. The practical question is, we have this constitution here, but it is in French and it consists of some two hundred and odd articles. Now, for any of us who are not familiar with it to go through with it and pick out the right article that bears or does not bear on a particular question is a difficult thing.

Gen. COLE. I can do it, but it will take some time, because you never can tell where a thing is stuck in that constitution.

Mr. HOWE. I want to say, Mr. Chairman, however, that I think the question asked by Mr. Angell is one of some importance and interest to this committee.

Senator ODDIE. Yes.

Mr. HOWE. But we are starting down to Haiti at the end of this week, and our time is very limited. I know that Gen. Cole has a mass of material, much of which may be of importance—I mean documents and copies, and his diaries that he mentioned this morning. The committee is going to hold sessions on its return from Haiti, as I understand it. Gen. Cole was in command in Haiti during a most important period. And it may very well be that the committee will need to have the general's knowledge put at its disposal on another occasion by having him here as a witness, or by having him give the committee the benefit of this collection of memoranda and papers of his, which could only be taken up on our return on account of the shortness of our time.

Senator ODDIE. Yes; I agree with you about that.

Mr. HOWE. And I believe that an arrangement can be made with Gen. Cole by which we can inform ourselves more at leisure as to what material he has got there, and if necessary we can have him as a witness again or at least have him furnish us with copies of these papers for our information.

Senator ODDIE. Yes.

Mr. HOWE. I would like to make that statement at this time, because I think it would be unfortunate to have the impression go out that the committee was hurrying through with Gen. Cole's testimony.

Senator ODDIE. Yes. I think unquestionably we must have it understood that Gen. Cole will have time to give us the material facts, and that Capt. Angell can question him on these matters, so that none of us will be unduly hurried.

Gen. COLE. To the best of my knowledge and belief I am entirely at the disposition of the committee, and I have nothing to hide that I know of.

Mr. ANGELL. Then would you make as an answer to that question which I put to you before, the question which started this last discussion, the answer that you are not prepared to answer the question specifically at this time, or words to that effect?

Gen. COLE. Yes; that will serve my purpose very well. I can add to it if it is wanted, if it is necessary.

Mr. ANGELL. You said in connection with martial law, General, if my recollection is correct, that it is and will be necessary in Haiti so long as American troops remain there. Why do you think it is and will be necessary?

Gen. COLE. From the attitude of the Haitian politicians and from the condition of the Haitian judiciary.

Mr. ANGELL. Do you think that the raising of martial law while American troops are there would result in an outbreak of crime, or rather in what the military occupation might regard as undue liberties or excesses on the part of the press?

Gen. COLE. I have never worried much about the press—never did myself while I was there. I would not tolerate the things that appeared in the press subsequent to my leaving there—absolutely. But I had no particular trouble with the press; occasionally they would slop over a bit and maybe be cautioned to be careful.

Mr. ANGELL. That, then, is your belief, is the actual practical function of martial law in Haiti?

Gen. COLE. A military force occupying another country has got to have a law of its own, and it can not get along without it, particularly under the condition where there is a venal judiciary system, and one that is absolutely, in my opinion, unreliable; no white man can get justice before a Haitian court, in my opinion.

Mr. ANGELL. Martial law, then, in Haiti enables a white man to obtain justice through the medium of our own military provost courts?

Gen. COLE. Our martial law in Haiti is more of a moral force than it is a physical force, but it is a physical force standing back of the shadow of the moral force.

Mr. ANGELL. The moral force being exerted——

Gen. COLE (interposing). Through the belief that, in case of necessity, the power back of that moral force would be exercised.

Mr. ANGELL. To the end that the white man may obtain justice in Haitian courts?

Gen. COLE. No; we have never interfered in the Haitian courts to amount to anything; we have prevented, on one or two occasions, through the power of military force, the Haitian courts from putting into effect judgments against institutions where the institutions were acting as agents of the occupying forces.

Mr. ANGELL. For example, the bank case?

Gen. COLE. The bank case. But if martial law were lifted. Tom, Dick, or Harry could go out and shoot at a white man, or at a member of the occupation, and unless the member of the occupation took the law into his own hands there would be no punishment for the Haitian. In other words, I believe that martial law is absolutely necessary, under the conditions existing Haiti, to enable peace to be maintained throughout that country.

Mr. ANGELL. Martial law operates, then, as a protection to the white man?

Gen. COLE. I believe that it operates as a protection to the white man and the black man, because the black man knows that, under the pains and penalties that martial law may invoke, he is being protected from his own people, in many cases. It is just as important for the black man as it is for the white man; it is a moral force which makes people behave themselves, a blessed sight more that the Haitian law. If there were no martial law, it would be possible for any man that wanted to start in and raise trouble, to do so, and there would be nothing for us to do but to go after them with military force to kill them; we could not deal with them under martial law, unless we put it back; and in the meantime, if we had raised it, something might come up, and our people might be shot and killed, and white people might be shot or killed. I do not think that it is really an important danger, but you have got to consider eventualities and possibilities, whenever you take any particular step, and particularly when you take any step to destroy a system which has been in existence. And if you had your martial law raised for even a period of 24 hours, you would really have no right to act or function as a military force, even if it was 24 hours later, on anything that had happened in between.

Mr. ANGELL. Except as to offenses by the military.

Gen. COLE. Offenses by the military are not tried by those courts.

Mr. ANGELL. By those—you mean the provost courts?

Gen. COLE. Yes; the provost courts. Our own courts function right straight along, and would function.

Mr. HOWE. The military is taken care of by the military courts?

Gen. COLE. The military is taken care of by the military courts, and the provost courts are different, though they are military courts; for instance, in the two cases of murder or killing by our men, in cases where it was a civil crime; that is, in one case a man got drunk in Port au Prince and started shooting, and killed somebody; I had him tried and charged with murder, by a military court-martial, not by a provost court.

Mr. ANGELL. Killed by a Haitian?

Gen. COLE. No; he killed a Haitian.

Mr. ANGELL. I mean the man that got drunk?

Gen. COLE. The man that got drunk was a sergeant of marines; he was tried by court-martial and got 10 years at hard labor.

Mr. HOWE. Before a general court-martial?

Gen. COLE. Yes. Another case came up at Cape Haitien, where a man was tried by general court-martial.

Mr. ANGELL. And not by the provost court?

Gen. COLE. Not by the provost court. Now, a man was killed in Cape Haitien. If I had gotten that man, he would probably have been tried by a military commission, and probably hanged, because it was cold-blooded murder, not under the influence of liquor, or anything of the sort, but just murder. In the same way, the man that killed Lieut. McNab would have been tried by a military commission, and not by a naval general court.

Mr. HOWE. Let me straighten that out: The members of our military forces are always subject to the military courts?

Gen. COLE. Are always subject to the military courts.

Mr. HOWE. But it takes the operation of martial law to subject the civil population to a military court?

Gen. COLE. Yes.

Mr. HOWE. That is, under the control of our forces?

Gen. COLE. Yes.

Mr. HOWE. And they are subject to the jurisdiction of certain other military tribunals, the provost courts?

Gen. COLE. Yes; and the military commission.

Mr. HOWE. And the military commission, for more serious offenses?

Gen. COLE. All offenses between members of the military organization are tried before the naval or military court, pure and simple.

Mr. HOWE. That is so in this country?

Gen. COLE. That is true everywhere; wherever the forces go there goes the right to use the military or naval courts. Now, when you are in conflict with the law in the United States, a civilian would be tried in the civil courts; a military man would be tried in the military courts or the civil courts, depending on which had taken jurisdiction first. Formerly the proposition was that a man in the military service who had committed an offense under the civil law was amenable to trial not only by the military courts but by the civil courts as well; and he might get one sentence by the military courts and then come out and have to take another trial by the civil courts. Now, in a foreign country, where the crimes are between members of the occupying forces and the members of the civil population, there is the provost court, and the military commission, and under certain conditions the provost court and the military commission can exercise jurisdiction over people who are exclusively civilians.

Mr. HOWE. Who are exclusively civilians?

Gen. COLE. Yes; it does not necessarily limit its authority to people who are in conflict with the military forces; they may be in conflict simply with the mission or with the promulgated decrees of the military force.

Mr. Howe. Thank you; that is all.

Mr. Angell. General, would you care to make any comment upon the degree of fulfillment by the United States, particularly through its civilian treaty officials, of the obligations assumed by the United States under the convention of 1915?

Gen. Cole. Well, I have made a considerable number of comments already in regard to it. I think that the financial situation could have been bettered; more could have been done, possibly, than has been done. But I also believe that you would have to go back to the fact that there were always difficulties, most serious difficulties, put in the way of the financial adviser in carrying out his part of the work, in endeavoring to get the finances straightened out, through the obstruction of the Haitians, and of the legislative branch of the Government in particular.

Mr. Angell. Referring particularly to article 1 of this convention of 1915, do you believe, from your understanding of the facts, that the United States has aided the Haitian Government in the proper and efficient development of its agricultural, mineral, and commercial resources?

Gen. Cole. It has, without any question, done a great deal; it has not done as much as it should have done had there been sufficient funds available. As I have stated, a country which was on the verge of starvation in 1915, for the country as a whole was absolutely undernourished, inside of two years, or two years and a half, had been developed into a country where the country people were richer than they had ever been before, and were not only producing enough food for the Haitians but were exporting food. I say it did a good deal to help develop agriculture. It did not do all it might have done had funds been available, but it did do a great deal. I say this, that without funds—and considerable funds—it was a mistake to create an engineering organization which was going to require for overhead practically all of the funds that could be allotted, and consequently that funds that had been theretofore actually available for improving conditions were going to get up here (in "overhead"). That was my objection.

Mr. Angell. To the overhead?

Gen. Cole. To the engineers going in at that time. I wanted to use the engineers; I offered to put them in a position where they could handle the work through other people, and where they could have gotten something done. But they wanted to have their organization. Each man naturally, I suppose, is working for his own position; he fights for his own position. And, under the treaty, they were independent branches, independent of the military, and they wanted to be independent. It did not matter to me whether they were independent or anything else. What I wanted was to get the results; and I did not believe they would get the results—and they did not. And they will not until funds are available and they get a different system. I do not know what they can depend on in the way of Haitian assistance under the present conditions.

Mr. Angell. Do you believe that the unification of the responsibility and direction of all American administration, civil and military, in Haiti would make for a greater accomplishment by the United States in the island?

Gen. Cole. I do. I think there is no question but what that is true. I would put selected Americans in positions where they could be responsible for what was being done, and I would put with them just as many Haitians as have shown by their attitude and by their work that they were the kind of men needed for that particular kind of work. In other words, I would start in with such American forces as were necessary to direct the work, supplemented by such Haitian forces as could be used to perform such details as could be entrusted to them; and I would gradually increase the number of Haitians employed, and gradually reduce the number of Americans employed.

Mr. Angell. Do you think the responsibility and direction of the Americans under the several different branches, military and civil, such as military commander, financial adviser, receiver general of customs, engineer, and the like, has militated against the effectiveness of the aid which the United States might have rendered Haiti?

Gen. Cole. I think so. Now, I do not know what has been done in Haiti in nearly four years beyond casual hearsay.

Mr. Angell. You have not been back to the island since 1917?

Gen. Cole. I have not been back to the island since the end of 1917. But I do know that when I lost control—just before leaving—over the sanitary engineer and the civil engineer, or at least when my control over them was reduced, the efficiency began to go straight down; and the funds, which theretofore had been put into actual work in improving conditions, a considerable part of them went up here—considerable number of engineers.

Mr. Howe. Went up to overhead?

Gen. Cole. Went up to overhead. They brought down their engineers from here, and there was not anything to be done with them; they did not want to go out into the country with them. I wanted the chief engineer to go out and make a comprehensive survey in the country.

Mr. Angell. When you say "the chief engineer," to whom do you refer?

Gen. Cole. I am referring to the civil engineer, who was a treaty official. I fought it just as hard as I could.

Mr. Angell. As a matter of fact, the civil engineer and the sanitary engineer were not responsible to the chief of the military occupation, were they?

Gen. Cole. They were only responsible to the military occupation in this sense: That I was the senior officer on the spot, and they had to be responsible up to a certain point. But instead of my having the final say in regard to the details of their work, in regard to the policy, etc., that they were to work out, that was practically taken away from me. That was the point. But so far as their not being under my control is concerned, they were under my control; but I had lost my power of saying: "This is what you have to do," or "this is what must be done." I could advise them, but they could do it or not.

Mr. Angell. The determination of questions was not under your control?

Gen. Cole. It had passed from my control.

Mr. Angell. I want to read article 5 of the convention of 1915, as follows:

"All sums collected and received by the general receiver shall be applied, first, to the payment of the salaries and allowances of the general receiver, his assistants, and employees, and expenses of the receivership, including the salary and expenses of the financial adviser, which salaries will be determined by previous agreement; second, to the interest and sinking fund of the public debt of the Republic of Haiti; and, third, to the maintenance of the constabulary referred to in Article X, and then the remainder to the Haitian Government for the purposes of current expenses.

"In making these applications the general receiver will proceed to pay salaries and allowances monthly and expenses as they arise, and on the 1st of each calendar month, will set aside in a separate fund the quantum of the collection and receipts of the previous month."

I want to ask you whether it is your belief that the first paragraph of article 5, which I have just read, giving the order of the disbursement of funds by the general receiver, has been carried out?

Gen. Cole. I will say that that is a question that should be answered by the people who have to do with it, because I did not know what the conditions were. I had nothing to do with that at all, absolutely nothing; and I had enough things to do with to make it undesirable for me to mix into the affairs of somebody else.

Mr. Angell. I think we understand that you had no direction in the spending of money.

Gen. Cole. Absolutely nothing in regard to that particular part. I did have direction for a long time in regard to the expenditure of such funds as were allotted to the Government of Haiti; that is, which were expended through the military occupation of Haiti; all of that I allotted. I was informed that there was a certain sum which I could employ for certain purposes of the Republic of Haiti; and reports were coming in all over the country of things that were needed, and I made up every month a budget of an allotment of funds for different purposes, roads, repair of hospitals, schools, irrigation, or whatever it might be; and that budget, signed by me, was sent to the financial adviser and he paid that. Now, that sum was not a sum which I fixed; it was simply a sum which I was authorized to expend, and I never went beyond that.

Mr. Angell. Well, upon the understanding that you had no control of the disbursement of funds, except such as were specifically allotted to you in the manner you have just described, is it your understanding that the sequence of disbursement and appropriation of funds provided for by paragraph 5 of the treaty was carried out?

Gen. Cole. Well, I would have to make my answer a qualified one. It is a question in my mind whether it has been carried out, but I do not know of my own personal knowledge.

Mr. Angell. All right; that is all.

Mr. Howe. You referred to those funds which were allotted to you. From those funds, were there any funds available for the necessary upkeep and building up of public works?

Gen. Cole. No; except that in——

Mr. Howe (interposing). Except for the communal funds which you have already mentioned?

Gen. Cole. Yes; that is correct.

Mr. Howe. But beyond the communal funds and the allotment there was no money available?

Gen. Cole. No money available.

Mr. Howe. The United States was not supplying funds for those purposes from its own Treasury?

Gen. Cole. No; nor was the Haitian Government, as reported, making any payment whatsoever to the support of the United States occupation.

Mr. Howe. In other words, the sustenance and the pay and the equipment of the marines who were in Haiti was borne solely by the United States?

Gen. Cole. Solely by the United States, except in so far as those people who were appointed to the gendarmerie of Haiti received the additional compensation allowed by law—and the sanitary engineers, etc. They got their compensation——

Mr. Howe (interposing). To what extent was agriculture down there dependent upon irrigation? Were there lands down there which could be cultivated without irrigation?

Gen. Cole. Yes; there were two or three irrigating systems; there were two irrigation systems, I think, that were in existence when I was there, one at the Plain of the Cul-de-Sac and the other one down near Mommance.

Mr. Howe. In those regions was irrigation necessary?

Gen. Cole. Irrigation was necessary for the raising of sugar cane; irrigation systems were formerly in quite a number of the plains.

Mr. Howe. Here is what I want to get at: The repair of these irrigation systems which you have spoken of—would the tendency of that be to put more lands under cultivation?

Gen. Cole. Yes; much more land. The work that was done in fixing up the existing system in the Plain of the Cul-de-Sac increased materially the acres of land that were under cultivation.

Mr. Howe. Now, was it necessary to increase the acreage at that time, or was there enough land susceptible of cultivation available without repair of the irrigation systems?

Gen. Cole. The people own the land, and they had their homes on this land. Now, in a country like Haiti, which is thickly populated, and where all the good lands are taken up, you do not want to make the people go out and move to another part of the country if you can avoid it—if, by repairing the irrigation systems, those people can grow their produce in the vicinity of the market.

Mr. Howe. Then, I take it that these irrigation systems which were repaired had been impaired comparatively recently?

Gen. Cole. There was only one that we did anything to, so far as I know, and that was the one in the Plain of the Cul-de-Sac.

Mr. Howe. Which had fallen recently into disrepair?

Gen. Cole. It was in a very bad state of repair. And the large landowner, near the source, had simply taken all the water, so that the people who were farther down, and who were generally the small landowners, did not get any. And we stopped that, and we opened up the ditches.

Mr. Howe. You made a comparison, for the purpose of illustration, between safety of life in Georgia and safety of life in Haiti. Did you mean that comparison, which was somewhat to the disadvantage of the Georgian, to apply to those times when the Cacos occupied Fort Reviere?

Gen. Cole. No; I did not.

Mr. Howe. And excluded food from the towns and robbed the market women?

Gen. Cole. No; I meant that during the major part of the year 1917.

Mr. Howe. Yes.

Gen. Cole. Now, I do not want to make any disparaging remarks about Georgia. Because I simply read the Savannah News——

Mr. Howe (interposing). Excuse me. I just want to say, Mr. Chairman, that I am asking this question, of course, as the question was asked the general and answered by him, and the time to which he meant it to apply was not made definite; and it might be construed as meaning that at the time of our occupation there——

Gen. Cole (interposing). No.

Mr. Howe (continuing). Conditions as to peace and quiet in Haiti compared favorably with those of enlightened communities in our own country.

Gen. Cole. Oh, this was in 1917.

Mr. Howe. After the suppression of the Cacos?

Gen. Cole. Yes, absolutely; and after we had been functioning there for a year and a half.

Mr. Howe. I think that clears that up, Mr. Chairman.

Senator Oddie. Yes.

Mr. Howe. Now, as to the interest on these different classes of loans, external and internal, do you know whether Haiti could have paid the interest on her foreign loans and maintained the necessary current expenses of her Government at the time of our occupation?

Gen. Cole. I do not believe so. I do not know from actual experience, but I do not believe so. She could not have paid, in my opinion, the interest on her loans at any time subsequent to the 30th of June, 1915.

Mr. Howe. Let me ask you this question for the record: Do you know, if the treasury was practically empty at the time of our occupation, how to account for the fact that up to that time Haiti had met the interest on her foreign loans?

Gen. Cole. I understood that it had been through borrowing from others, or forced loans from its own people.

Mr. Howe. Which practices were not continued during the occupation?

Gen. Cole. Which practices were absolutely discontinued during the occupation.

Mr. Howe. Do you know why no interest was paid during the two and one half years with which you were familiar?

Gen. Cole. I think they were trying to get the thing straightened out, an agreement reached between the parties, trying to find out what the bonds actually represented, and trying to get a loan to refund the whole business. It was not my business; but that was my understanding of what was going on.

Mr. Howe. I understand. But was it your recommendation that the interest on the internal loan should be paid by funds furnished by the United States?

Gen. Cole. I did not recommend how it should be done. I simply pointed out the political effect, or the social effect, that the nonpayment of these things would have, and why, in my opinion, the people who were in charge of the finances should, as soon as possible, make some arrangement whereby those things could be paid.

Mr. Howe. If you had been in charge of those matters yourself, and there had been money enough, then you would have done it; but you do not know why it was not done?

Gen. Cole. That I can not say, because no man in a position of high responsibility can say what would be done until he knew all the conditions that surrounded that thing.

Now, I picked out, as a person who was not materially active in the thing—I picked out a certain salient point which could be improved, and which, if certain action was taken, would cause good results to follow over a much larger place than that particular point. But I can not say that the people who had charge of that particular thing could have done what appeared to me the best thing to do; for instance, I could not say that if they had paid one creditor there would not have been such a howl from the other creditors whom, possibly, they would not have paid, that it would not have been wise to do that to incur the good will of one at the expense of the antagonism of many.

Mr. Howe. Did you see any rise in the revenues, and any benefits from the internal improvements on which you expended the allotment?

Gen. Cole. Oh, yes; materially. The exports for a time from Haiti were very large. And they were just as large as the transportation could handle, up to the time I left, though at one time the bottom dropped out of the logwood market.

Mr. Howe. Did you see any connection between the changes in the Haitian constitution and the possibility of commercial development and financial rehabilitation?

Gen. Cole. The changes, as I have said, were, in my opinion, absolutely necessary; nobody is going to go into a country like Haiti and be at the mercy of a constitution which says that he shall not have even the safeguards given their own citizens, but that he must have a safeguard which is whatever they may want to make it and never equal to that of their own citizens. He is not getting any. He can not get land; the land tenure is uncertain. The courts were venal, and the man who went in there and put a sugar mill on land leased from a Haitian, the Lord only knows whether he would ever be in a position to make anything out of it. All the provisions in the proposed constitution, to the best of my knowledge, were as much to the interest of Haiti as to that of the United States and were such that the terms of the convention could be carried out. I believe those terms were in such shape that proper safeguards were given to the Republic of Haiti and to its people.

Mr. HOWE. You have spoken of certain difficulties put in the way of improvements by certain Haitians, and to distinct opposition to changes in this constituition by members of the assembly. It must follow, then, that those who made those changes difficult did not look on them in the same way as you do, for the benefit of Haiti?

Gen. COLE. I am not going to give them that much credit, because I think that, in many cases, they were so obsessed with the idea that if they could get the Americans out they could get back to their old system of graft, and their old system of handling all the Government funds between the pockets of those who paid them into the Government and their own pockets, that they would do anything to get rid of us, and that they lost all sense of proportion in that regard.

Mr. HOWE. Then do you mean to say that you had the interest of the Haitians more at heart than the members of the Haitian Assembly?

Gen. COLE. Unquestionably; there is no question about it at all; it is unquestionable that I had.

Mr. HOWE. Let me ask you this: Do you think you understood better than they did the relation between these steps proposed by the United States and the rehabilitation of their country?

Gen. COLE. I think probably I did, though I also believe that many of them realized that many of the things that we asked them were for the best interests of their country; but they did not think they were for the best interests of themselves, or of their own individual and political life.

Now, understand this: In Haiti politics was a profession—almost a profession; that the politician was largely a class by itself; people came into it and people went out of it; but it was a class which had its own morals, its private morals and its public morals. Its public morals were absolutely lacking. There were some people who were all right. Legetime, I believe, was a very fine man; he was a politician; he had had the executive power; he had not enriched himself, and would not enrich himself at the expense of the country. I think Polynice was a very fine man. And there were some others who belonged in the political class. But, generally, the class of political parasite in Haiti—you can not describe them.

Mr. HOWE. Well, do you think the peasant—the country people, by and large—had an conception of the effect of these proposed changes?

Gen. COLE. No; I do not think so. The peasant was fed up, I believe, with talk to the effect that the Americans were trying to enslave them and trying to get possession of their lands, and that if the changes were made, Americans would get possession of their lands. But, as a matter of fact, we never believed that the country people were against us in any way, after, I will say, the middle of 1916.

Mr. HOWE. Now, as to martial law, on cross-examination you used some expressions, as I remember it, to the general effect that martial law there is necessary to obtain justice to the white man?

Gen. COLE. Safety and justice.

Mr. HOWE. Safety and justice to white men?

Gen. COLE. White military men.

Mr. HOWE. Yes; white military men. Now, does the martial law which we imposed have anything to do with what we call in this country civil cases, as opposed to criminal cases?

Gen. COLE. No. The biggest fine I ever had given in a provost court in Haiti was against a white American who occupied the position of general manager of the railroad.

Mr. HOWE. That was analogous to a criminal case?

Gen. COLE. Yes; a case of disorder and of defiance; he got drunk.

62269—21—PT 2——40

Mr. Howe. Now, the provost courts do not undertake to decide lawsuits between private plaintiff and defendant?

Gen. Cole. No; it deals entirely with public order.

Mr. Howe. Yes. While martial law is in effect there through the operation of the provost courts, is there any room there for the administration of criminal justice affecting natives or whites or anybody? Do the native courts still impose fines? Do they still sentence a person?

Gen. Cole. Yes.

Mr. Howe. What classes of cases, then, do they handle?

Gen. Cole. The provost courts?

Mr. Howe. No; the native courts.

Gen. Cole. The native courts handle all cases between Haitians.

Mr. Howe. Criminal cases?

Gen. Cole. Criminal cases; practically every criminal case.

Mr. Howe. Excepting the ones which are before the provost courts?

Gen. Cole. Yes.

Mr. Howe. Now, where is the line drawn?

Gen. Cole. The line is drawn that the provost court deals ordinarily with those things which directly affect the armed forces in the United States in its occupation; they do not ordinarily concern the gendarmerie. I do not think we would ordinarily put up cases before the provost courts against the gendarmerie unless it were in connection with the maintenance of peace and order in the country.

As I have said, the martial law is a moral force a great deal more than it is a physical force; but it is a very potent moral force on account of the physical force that stands behind and casts its shadow on the moral force.

Mr. Howe. You say it is necessary for the safety of our marines down there?

Gen. Cole. Yes. It is necessary for Haiti, in order that peace and security may not be flouted.

Mr. Howe. Are there any more questions, Mr. Chairman?

Senator Oddie. I have none.

Mr. Angell. I have one question, based upon your's. You said, General, that martial law did not operate to interfere in cases between Haitian civilians?

Gen. Cole. Yes.

Mr. Angell. There was the bank case?

Gen. Cole. Yes.

Mr. Angell. Martial law did in effect there operate to interfere to prevent the carrying out of the decree of the court of cassation, did it not?

Gen. Cole. The military commandant—not martial law. The officer commanding the military forces in Haiti said to the Haitian courts and to the president of the bank, "The actions of the bank in this particular case are done under direct orders and under duress of the naval commander, and consequently I, as military commander, can not permit the courts of Haiti, which are not my superiors, to interfere and prevent something which the naval commander has ordered done."

Mr. Howe. The justification of the act, or of the failure of the bank to act, as the case may be, would be in the existence of martial law?

Gen. Cole. Would be found in the facts that the bank, as the agent of the military or naval commander in supreme control, had done certain acts, and that as it had to do those acts it could not be held responsible for such acts by the Haitian courts.

Senator Oddie. Is that all?

Gen. Cole. I think so.

Mr. Angell. There is a practical arrangement for going over such portions of the general's data as are not personal and private to him, but are copies of reports, etc.

Mr. Howe. It was my suggestion that on our return from Haiti, the committee authorize me to take up with the general the consideration of what parts of his files should be available for the further consideration of the committee. The time at our disposal has not permitted us to learn from the general what those records are.

Senator Oddie. I think that can be done after we get back.

Mr. Howe. These are part of the records of the Navy Department; they are available to the committee; but it would be in the nature of asking the general a favor and assistance in guiding us through those reports to see what we need in them.

Gen. Cole. I make this suggestion: That through your investigation in Haiti you make record of such things as you feel I could possibly give you information about during the time I was there, and inform me as to those things and give me a chance to refresh my memory in regard to the particular things that you have in mind, because there is a whole mass of that in there, and it stands to reason that I can not remember everything that is in there.

Mr. Howe. Are these your own private papers?

Gen. Cole. These are private papers, kept for my own personal gratification and protection in case any such question as this ever did come up.

Mr. Howe. I feel a delicacy in asking the general to send those papers up to me en masse to look through them, but I am sure we can between us cut out everything there that we think would be useful to the committee. My feeling is that there is much valuable material there that the committee ought to know.

Gen. Cole. I will turn over that material to you as counsel for the committee during the rest of the time that you remain here, and I am not certain but that I will let you have them to take with you, but it will have to be on the understanding that they are not available as testimony before the committee unless I have something to say in regard to them.

Mr. Howe. Yes.

Gen. Cole. Because conditions might come up that you might find conditions in Haiti that I might have to take what was said here and there, and all through the papers, in order to give proper answers and to have proper interpretations placed upon them. You can take almost any bald statement and cut out certain parts and make a man out a liar, or anything else; and I do not want anything of that sort. But my understanding is that headquarters of the Marine Corps expects me to make available everything that I have. Is that true, Maj. McClellan?

Maj. McClellan. Yes; but with regard to most of these papers that Gen. Cole has with him, the originals are either in the Navy Department records, or the Marine Corps headquarters records; and Gen. Lejeune and the Secretary of the Navy have both already stated that everything in those records is available to the committee; and there are tons of such material. I merely want to make this statement so that the committee will know that all these papers and many others are officially available if the committee desire them. But the general is right in saying that he has been instructed to give the committee every assistance possible with reference to books and papers.

Gen. Cole. My papers there are generally arranged in chronological order; sometimes they are not, but generally they are. And in addition to that, I think there are certain things there that headquarters do not have.

Mr. Howe. It is my intention to get in touch with you on the return of the committee, to find out to what further extent you can add to the very valuable information you have already given.

Gen. Cole. I do not know what I can do, unless you want certain definite information.

(Thereupon, at 1 o'clock p. m., the committee took a recess until 2.30 o'clock p. m.)

AFTER RECESS.

The committee reassembled at 2.30 o'clock p. m., pursuant to the taking of recess, Senator Oddie presiding.

STATEMENT OF MAJ. JESSE F. DYER, UNITED STATES MARINE CORPS, HEADQUARTERS MARINE CORPS, WASHINGTON, D. C.

Mr. Howe. Major, will you give your name, rank, and present station, please?

Maj. Dyer. Jesse F. Dyer, major, United States Marine Corps, attached to and stationed at headquarters, Marine Corps, Washington.

Mr. Howe. Mr. Chairman, the purpose of calling Maj. Dyer as a witness is for him to give the committee an idea as to the scope and methods of the investigation conducted by him as judge advocate for the so-called Mayo court of inquiry in Haiti.

Major, I see by the record of the Mayo court of inquiry here that the first day was Tuesday, October 19, 1920. You had been appointed judge advocate of that court of inquiry, had you not?

Maj. Dyer. Yes.

Mr. Howe. Some of the meetings of the court were in this country, and others in Haiti?

Maj. Dyer. Yes.

Mr. Howe. And there is already in the record the precept of that court of inquiry. I gather from reading the proceedings of the court that it was your idea, as judge advocate, that the investigation and duties of that court were prescribed in the precept?

Maj. Dyer. That is correct. That was not only my idea, but that is the only authority a court of inquiry has to act, the precept.

Mr. Howe. Therefore within the authority of the precept it was your duty, as judge advocate, was it not, to assist the court to bring before the court the materials for an investigation?

Maj. Dyer. Yes.

Mr. Howe. Now, may I, for the sake of brevity, ask you a leading question to this extent: The record shows that some investigation was made by that court of the cases in Haiti which involved the names of Lieut. Brokaw, Capt. Lavoie, Lieut. Lang, Lieut. Doras Williams, and an officer named Rogoski, the latter being one whose name was mentioned by the witness Lifshitz. I believe I am correct in saying that the cases where these officers were accused, by rumor or in testimony, were the only specific cases which you came across in your investigation. Am I correct in that, that these are all the cases of improper treatment of Haitians that came within the scope of the precept?

Maj. Dyer. No; there were a number of other cases mentioned, by rumor or otherwise, which I attempted to run down. In the case of men who had been accused of offenses and tried by court-martial, I got the records from the Judge Advocate General's office and introduced them in evidence before the court of inquiry. In numerous other cases I spent considerable time trying to obtain some testimony to present to the court, but was unable to find it.

Mr. Howe. The record itself speaks of the cases of Brokaw, Lavoie, and the others whose names I mentioned, and of these court-martial records, but I understand from your last answer that there were a number of other reports which came to you in the course of the investigation, no mention of which is made in the record, and that you undertook to run those down, so far as you could?

Maj. Dyer. Yes.

Mr. Howe. What I want you to do now, Major, is to tell us the extent of such investigations which you were unable to run down, how many interviews they involved, to what extent there was correspondence on the subject, and to what extent you traveled around the country.

Maj. Dyer. While I was in Haiti I interviewed scores of people who had related what they had heard. I corresponded with scores of other people and traveled up into the interior somewhat to try to run to their sources indefinite rumors which I had heard. I found a number of people who claimed to have personal knowledge of alleged misconduct, but many of these were cases which had already been tried by general court-martial; or, I would say, several, in place of many. In other places the witnesses related facts which, under no interpretation could be construed as offenses, since they related to legitimate acts, for instance, the case of Haitians who had been killed while resisting arrest, and in one particular I recall there were five or six witnesses who came to tell me, or who wrote to me, about such a killing, and they admitted to me themselves that they had no charges to bring of illegal acts, but simply wanted to tell about the case as they knew it. In most instances the people who wrote to me or who came to see me had no personal knowledge of the cases of which they talked. I tried to get them to give me the names of their informants so as to run the thing back to the original relator, but they claimed that they got their information from general rumor, or that the thing was well known, etc. In a few cases I was given the names of people from whom they had heard the stories, and on communication with those people I found they, too, were dependant upon hearsay. Of course, I did not bring people before the court to relate hearsay, but wherever any person claimed to have any personal knowledge of any acts that could be construed as coming within the scope of our precept, I brought such a person before the court as a witness, so that the court could judge and weigh the testimony, which I never attempted to do.

Mr. Howe. I want to ask you also if you traced all such rumors, as far as possible, so that you could determine whether you could find a witness who could speak of his own knowledge or not?

Maj. Dyer. I did the best I could in that respect, and before I left Haiti I was convinced that I could get not further testimony to bring before the court in relation to the matters mentioned in the precept.

Mr. Howe. Now, as to these cases of Brokaw, Lavole, Lang, Williams and Rogoski, in all but the case of Rogoski you had some reports on them as the result of previous investigattion, did you not?

Maj. Dyer. Yes; there were possible witnesses mentioned in those cases.

Mr. Howe. What efforts did you make to extend the scope of the previous investigation with relation to those men?

Maj. Dyer. I went to the same source of information as the previous investigators did, and endeavored to get further information. Also, I made inquiries among the people mentioned as witnesses, and those people were brought before the court wherever they could be obtained. In order to make one thing clear, I wish to explain that a court of inquiry is purely a creature of statute, and has no power not granted to it by statute. It is empowered to subpœna witnesses, that is, the judge advocate is, provided such witnesses be situated within the same State or Territory or District as that in which the court is sitting. There was one witness who came before the Senate Committee that I tried to get before the court of inquiry. The court was then sitting in the District of Columbia, and the witness was, I think, in Kansas City. I wrote to him, as judge advocate, and requested his appearance, but we were unable to subpœna him, and he did not appear before the court.

Mr. Howe. Do you refer to Lieut. Spear?

Maj. Dyer. Yes.

Mr. Howe. In other words, the Senate committee had the power to subpœna him?

Maj. Dyer. I understand the Senate committee can subpœna anywhere within the United States.

Mr. Howe. But it was not within your power to subpœna him unless he was within the radius within which the law allowed your subpœnas to operate?

Maj. Dyer. Yes.

Mr. Howe. Did you make any efforts to find Capt. Lavole?

Maj. Dyer. Yes; but I was unable to find out where he was located. Just on a chance I wrote to him at his last known address, but the letter was returned "Address not known."

Mr. Howe. What did you ascertain as to Lieut. Brokaw?

Maj. Dyer. Lieut. Brokaw was at the time insane and was not competent to appear as a witness. In connection with the allegations against him, it was not possible to complete an investigation, due to his insanity and to his inability to defend himself or explain the circumstances as far as he was concerned.

Mr. Howe. I have here a letter from the Secretary of the Navy to Senator McCormick, dated October 29, in reply to an inquiry from this committee concerning the sanity or insanity of Lieut. Brokaw, and also replying to a question from this committee as to whether or not charges had been brought against Maj. Clark H. Wells; and if so, why the charges had been dropped. The letter of the Secretary of the Navy carries with it inclosures in explanation of the questions asked, and, in the case of Lieut. Brokaw, shows reports by medical boards as to the insanity of Lieut. Brokaw. I offer in evidence the letter of the Secretary and its inclosures. I think they should go in this record.

Senator Oddie. If there is no objection, they will be admitted.

(The letter and inclosures referred to are here printed in full, as follows:)

THE SECRETARY OF THE NAVY,
Washington, October 29, 1921.

MY DEAR SENATOR: In compliance with the requests contained in your two letters of the 25th instant I inclose herewith the following papers concerning the charges preferred against Maj. Clarke H. Wells, United States Marine Corps:

(A) Letter Major General Commandant to Secretary of the Navy, No. 53086, AQ–17–hdh, November 1, 1920.

(B) Letter Judge Advocate General of Navy to Major General Commandant, No. 5526–321, November 5, 1920.

(C) Letter Secretary of Navy to Major General Commandant, No. 5526–321, November 5, 1920.

(D) Letter Major General Commandant to Secretary of Navy, No. 53086, November 8, 1920.

(E) Letter Major General Commandant to Secretary of Navy, No. 53086, AQ–17–hdh, December 29, 1920.

(F) Letter Secretary of Navy to Major General Commandant, No. 26283-3725: 4, January 7, 1921.

(G) Letter Secretary of Navy to Judge Advocate General No. 26251-26072: R–sn, January 7, 1921.

(K) Charge and specification against Maj. Clarke H. Wells as preferred on November 1, 1920.

These inclosures will show that one charge was preferred against Maj. Wells and that it was withdrawn before trial. Inclosure (C) will show that Maj. Wells was first temporarily released from arrest in order that "he may not be unduly prejudiced before the court of inquiry" convened "to investigate conditions in Haiti," while inclosure (G) revoked the order for Maj. Wells's trial in view of the fact "that the exhaustive evidence adduced by the said court of inquiry fails to contain evidence upon which court-martial proceedings could be held in the case of Maj. Wells."

The questions regarding the mental condition of Lou's H. Brokaw, formerly private, United States Marine Corps, and lieutenant, Gendarmerie d'Haiti, are fully answered in the following inclosed papers marked.

(H) Report of Board of Medical survey. Naval Hospital, Washington, D. C., October 17, 1919.

(I) Report of Board of Medical Survey, Naval Hospital, Charleston, S. C., September 15, 1919.

(J.) Report of Board of Medical Survey, Port au Prince, Haiti. July 9, 1919.

The last address of Mr. Brokaw, as given by him on April 22, 1921, in a communication to the office of the Major General Commandant of the Marine Corps, was "Route No. 1, Fairview, Fulton County, Ill."

The following records requested in your letters have already been forwarded to the committee.

1. The record of testimony, taken by Lieut. Col. Lay and Maj. Turner, etc.

2. The record of proceedings of the court of inquiry of which Rear Admiral Mayo was president.

3. The record of proceedings of the general court-martial in the cases of Pvts. Johnson and McQuilkin and Capt. Hamilton.

Trusting that I have furnished you with the desired information and papers, I am,

Very sincerely, yours,

EDWIN DENBY.

Hon. MEDILL MCCORMICK,
    United States Senate, Washington, D. C.

(A)

HEADQUARTERS UNITED STATES MARINE CORPS,
    Washington, D. C., November 1, 1920.

From: The major general commandant.
To: The Secretary of the Navy.
Subject: Investigation of affairs in Haiti.
Inclosures: 22.

1. In September, 1919, the record of the proceedings of a general court-martial at Port au Prince, Haiti, in the cases of Pvts. Walter E. Johnson and John J. McQuilkin, jr., United States Marine Corps, were receiced in this office and were found to contain references by counsel to a practice of executing Haitian prisoners without trial. The Major General Commandant immediately referred the matter to the brigade commander in Haiti for a full investigation, with the object of bringing such practice, if it existed, to a stop, and of bringing all persons found to be guilty of such practice to punishment.

2. On December 9, 1919, the brigade commander, Col. John H. Russell, United States Marine Corps, forwarded the record of investigation, conducted by the assistant adjutant and inspector attached to brigade headquarters, with recommendation that the statements of officers and men in the United States be obtained. This was accomplished and all papers were returned to Haiti on January 12, 1920, with instructions that the investigation be completed as soon as practicable and the full report, together with recommendations of the brigade commander, submitted to these headquarters.

3. On March 20, 1920, the brigade commander mailed the complete report, but it was never received, being apparently lost in the mail. The fact that the report had not been received was not discovered until August last, and it was not until the return last months of Gens. Lejeune and Butler from a trip of inspection in Haiti and Santo Domingo that all of the report was available at these headquarters.

4. There are inclosed herewith copies of the first report of Maj. Thomas C. Turner, A. A. & I., November 3, 1919; of the forwarding letter from the brigade commander, Col. John H. Russell, December 7, 1919; statements taken by Lieut. Col. Harry R. Lay, A. A. & I., and submitted by letter of January 12, 1920; letter of Maj. Gen. Commandant Barnett to Secretary of the Navy January 12, 1920, stating that partial investigation had been made and that report was being returned to Haiti for completion of investigation and submission of report and recommendations (original); approval of action reported by Secretary of the Navy in own handwriting on above-mentioned letter (original); letter January 11, 1920, brigade commander directing Lieut. Col. R. S. Hooker to cooperate with Maj. Turner in conduct of investigation; letter February 12, 1920, from brigade commander directing Lieut. Col. Hooker to expedite investigation; joint report of investigation, February 28, 1920, Lieut. Col. Hooker and Maj. Turner; indorsement, brigade commander, Col. Russell, March 13, 1920, forwarding report of investigation; résumé of testimony taken by Gens. Lejeune and Butler in Haiti, including 12 statements of gendarmes, taken by Lieut. Bertol, Gendarmerie d'Haiti; and report of investigation made by Gens. Lejeune and Butler.

5. On or about August 25, 1918, the commandant of the gendarmerie issued an order abolishing the system of corvée (enforced labor) on the public roads. This was extended by another order, October 18, 1918, to include the Hinche-Maissade districts, which had been interpreted as being outside of the limits of the first order. The system was continued in those districts notwithstanding the said orders and caused a great deal of unrest and disturbance. The continuance of the corvée was repeatedly denied by Maj. Clarke H. Wells, the commander of the gendarmerie in the Department of the North, Haiti. Finally the brigade commander personally investigated the matter and found the corvée still in existence at Hinche and Maissade.

6. Lieut. Col. Alexander S. Williams was chief of the Gendarmerie d'Haiti, and from the evidence available it does not appear that he kept himself sufficiently informed of conditions. Moreover, it appears from the statement of Edward J. Seiger, formerly an enlisted man in the Marine Corps and a lieutenant in the Gendarmerie d'Haiti, that Lieut. Col. Williams, on November 1, 1918, told Capt. Lavoie, of the gendarmerie, that no provost prisoners were wanted; that if Lavoie found that any of the prisoners were "Cacos" and actually had arms in their possession to do away with them. These statements, if made, would show at least that the chief of the gendarmerie approved of the unlawful killings of prisoners, and such approval would have had a baleful effect in the indoctrination of his subordinates. There appears, however, to be insufficient evidence for bringing Lieut. Col. Williams to trial at this time, and it is recommended that action on his case be deferred until after receipt of the record of proceedings of the court of inquiry now in session.

7. There is evidence that Maj. Clarke H. Wells had knowledge of the continuance of the system of corvée in the Hinche-Maissade districts during the period November 1, 1918, to March 31, 1919, in the department under his command, and failed to suppress it, well knowing that the order of the chief of the Gendarmerie d'Haiti of August 25, 1918, and October 18, 1918, prohibited corvée; that on or about November 2, 1918, he gave orders over the telephone from Cape Haitien to Frederick C. Baker, at that time a private in the Marine Corps and a captain in the Gendarmerie d'Haiti, to "bump off," meaning to kill, prisoners; that on or about March 19, 1919, he gave Capt. George D. Hamilton orders to kill any man whom Capt. Hamilton thought to be a caco and not to bring him to prison; that at divers times during the period November 1, 1918, to March 31, 1919, he gave orders to his juniors to suppress reports of any unfavorable conditions in regards to the state of peace in the Department of the North, of which he was in command. In view of the foregoing I recommend that Maj. Clarke H. Wells, United States Marine Corps, be brought to trial by general court-martial for these offenses, and for such other offenses as may be warranted by the evidence.

8. From the statements in the attached papers it would appear that Doras L. Williams, now a sergeant in the Marine Corps at Quantico, Va., and then a lieutenant in the Gendarmerie d'Haiti, beat to death with a stick one Garnier Jean during the month of March, 1919, in the town of Maissade; that he had three prisoners, names unknown, shot to death during the month of March, 1919, at the same place; that during the period November 1, 1919, to March 31, 1919, he permitted work under the corvee system on the roads in the Maissade district in violation of the orders of the commandant of the gendarmerie. It is recommended that he be brought to trial for these offenses, and for such others as may in the opinion of the Judge Advocate General be warranted by the evidence.

9. From the statements available it appears that former Pvt. Ernest Lavole, formerly a captain in the Gendarmerie d'Haiti, was guilty of numerous offenses. He was discharged on July 30, 1919, upon expiration of enlistment, and his present address is not known. In case it is possible to bring him within the jurisdiction of a naval court-martial, it is recommended that he be brought to trial. While his present whereabout are unknown he could probably be located in case of necessity.

10. From the statements of certain native gendarmes it appears that former Sergt. Freeman Lang, while a lieutenant in the Gendarmerie d'Haiti, committed certain alleged offenses. He was discharged in January, 1919, and is now living in Haiti. In case it is possible to bring him within the jurisdiction of a naval court-martial, his trial is recommended.

JOHN A. LEJEUNE.

(B)

DEPARTMENT OF THE NAVY,
OFFICE OF THE JUDGE ADVOCATE GENERAL,
Washington, November 5, 1920.

From: The Judge Advocate General.
To: The Major General Commandant.
Subject: Investigation of conditions in Haiti and the trial by court-martial of certain officers of the Marine Corps.
Reference: Your letter of November 1, 1920, and inclosures.

1. Referring to the subject matter of above-mentioned reference, you are informed that one charge and specification of a charge were prepared against Maj. Clarke H. Wells, United States Marine Corps, and orders issued for the trial of said officer on November 1, 1920. This action was necessary to prevent ·the statute of limitations from preventing the prosecution of said case, as the offense upon which the charge and specification were based was alleged to have been committed on November 1, 1918. The two-year limitation prescribed by article 61, A. G. N., expired November 1, 1920, and would have barred the prosecution had not orders been issued for trial before the expiration of two years from the date of the offense.

2. In view, however, of the fact that a court of inquiry has been convened by order of the Secretary of the Navy to investigate certain alleged irregularities in Haiti, among which matters to be investigated are those contained in the above-mentioned reference, the Secretary of the Navy has directed that the trial of Maj. Wells be deferred until after the court of inquiry, which is now in session, has completed its work and rendered its report. The Secretary has also directed that no further charge and specifications be prepared against persons in the Marine Corps based upon the irregularities reported in the above-mentioned reference until after the court of inquiry has submitted its report.

The Secretary of the Navy has directed that the charge and specification prepared against Maj. Wells on November 1, 1920, be returned to the department, where they will be held pending further developments.

4. With reference to the case of Doras L. Williams, United States Marine Corps, you are informed that unless arrest is considered necessary to prevent escape he need not be placed under arrest until after the completion of the investigation now being conducted by the court of inquiry, unless otherwise ordered by the Secretary of the Navy.

GEO. R. CLARK.

(C)

DEPARTMENT OF THE NAVY,
·Washington, November 5, 1920;.

From: The Secretary of the Navy.
To: The Major General Commandant.
Subject: Investigation of conditions in Haiti and the trial by court-martial of certain officers of the Marine Corps.
References: (a) Your letter November 1, 1920.
        (b) Letter of Judge Advocate General to the Major General Commandant, dated November 5, 1920.

1. The charge and specification preferred by the department against Maj. Clarke H. Wells, United States Marine Corps, on November 1, 1920, have been temporarily withdrawn from the court and ordered returned to the department pending the completion of the investigation of other charges against said officer and other alleged irregularities in Haiti by the court of inquiry of which Rear Admiral Henry T. Mayo is president. The charge and specification are not to be regarded as having been quashed or abandoned by the department but merely as held in temporary abeyance.

2. It is directed that Maj. Clarke H. Wells, United States Marine Corps, be temporarily released from arrest and restored to duty pursuant to section 52. Naval Courts and Boards. The order temporarily releasing him from arrest should be in writing and should inform of the reasons for his release; also that his temporary release from arrest and restoration to duty will not be a bar to any subsequent investigation or trial of the case that the Secretary of the Navy may think proper to order on the charge already preferred or other charges now being investigated.

3.·The reasons for the temporary release from arrest of Maj. Wells are that he may not be unduly prejudiced before the court of inquiry convened by order of the department to investigate conditions in Haiti; that he may have every opportunity to defend himself as an interested party before said court; that the department may have opportunity to investigate other charges against him ; and in order that he may not be held an unreasonable length of time under arrest awaiting trial by court-martial.

JOSEPHUS DANIELS.

(D)

HEADQUARTERS UNITED STATES MARINE CORPS,
Washington, November 8, 1920. ·

From: The Major General Commandant.
To: The Secretary of the Navy.
Subject: Temporary withdrawal of charge and specifications against Major Clarke H. Wells, United States Marine Corps.
References: (a) Letter of Secretary of the Navy to Major General Commandant, forwarding charge and specifications, of date November 1, 1920. (b) Letter Major General Commandant to Maj. Clarke H. Wells, United States Marine Corps, of date November 6, 1920, placing him under arrest. (c) Letter of Secretary of the Navy to Major General Commandant, No. 5526–821, of date November 5, 1920, directing temporary withdrawal of charge and specifications preferred by the department against Maj. Clarke H. Wells, United States Marine Corps, on November 5, 1920, and release from arrest.

1. In compliance with reference (c), Maj. Clarke H. Wells, United States Marine Corps, has this date been released from arrest and restored to duty, pending completion of the investigations of the court of inquiry, of which Rear Admiral Henry T. Mayo, United States Navy, is president.

2. Maj. Wells has been informed that his temporary release from arrest and restoration to duty is not a bar to subsequent investigation of, or trial upon, the charge and specifications preferred against him by the department under date of November 1, 1912, or upon any other charges and specifications that may hereafter be preferred against him in connection with the case.

3. The receipt for the court, of which Brig. Gen. Eli K. Cole, United States Marine Corps, is president, bearing date of November 1, 1920, is returned here·with. Maj. Wells has been allowed to retain the copy of the charge and speci·fications furnished him at the time of his arrest.

JOHN A. LEJEUNE.

(E)

HEADQUARTERS UNITED STATES MARINE CORPS,
Washington, December 29, 1920.

From: The Major General Commandant.
To: The Secretary of the Navy.
Subject: Investigation of affairs in Haiti.
References: (*a*) Major General Commandant's letter November 1, 1920, same
subject. (*b*) Record of proceedings of court inquiry.

1. The court of inquiry convened October 19, 1920, to inquire into the conduct
of the personnel of the naval service that has served in the Republic of Haiti
since July 22, 1915, of which Rear Admiral H. T. Mayo, United States Navy,
was president, included in its findings of facts a paragraph as follows:

"4. In view of the fact that the only unjustifiable acts found by the court
to have been committed are those wherein disciplinary action has already been
taken, and where no further proceedings could be had in the matter, the court
has not deemed it necessary to report further upon the question of responsibility."

The court had before it all of the reports and evidence upon which my recommendations, contained in reference (*a*), were based. It is quite apparent that
the court considered all charges and found them, except those already subjected to disciplinary action, to be unsupported by sufficient evidence. The
court did not recommend any further action.

2. In view of the finding of the court after an exhaustive investigation, I
desire to withdraw the recommendation for trials of officers and enlisted men,
as contained in paragraphs 6, 7, 8, 9, and 10 of my letter of November 1, 1920,
reference (*a*), in respect to Lieut. Col. Alexander S. Williams, Maj. Clarke H.
Wells, Sergt. Dorcas L. Williams, former Pvt. Ernest Lavoie, and former Sergt.
Freeman Lang, and to recommend that no further action be taken.

JOHN A. LEJEUNE.

(F)

DEPARTMENT OF THE NAVY,
January 7, 1921.

From: The Secretary of the Navy.
To: The Major General Commandant.
Subject: Investigation of affairs in Haiti.
References: (*a*) Your letter December 29, 1920, 53086 AQ–17 hdh. (*b*) Letter
from the Secretary of the Navy to the Judge Advocate General, January 7,
1921, 26251–26072.

1. A court of inquiry, of which Rear Admiral H. T. Mayo, United States
Navy, was president, and consisting of high ranking officers of the Navy and
Marine Corps, was specially convened for the purpose of inquiring into the
conduct of the personnel of the naval service that has served in the Republic
of Haiti since July 22, 1915. In view of the finding of the court that the only
unjustifiable acts committed were those wherein disciplinary action has already
been taken, and that further fact that the exhaustive evidence adduced by the
said court of inquiry fails to contain evidence upon which court-martial proceedings could be held in the cases of Lieut. Col. Alexander S. Williams.
Maj. Clarke H. Wells, Sergt. Dorcas L. Williams, former Pvt. Ernest Lavoie,
and former Sergt. Freeman Lang, United States Marine Corps, the department
considers that no further action is warranted in their cases.

2. The department, on November 1, 1920, directed the trial by general court-
martial of Maj. Clarke H. Wells, United States Marine Corps, based upon certain alleged offenses, the facts of which were meager and questionable. The
trial, however, was directed in order that, if the offenses had been committed,
the statute of limitations would not bar subsequent trial. The department,
on November 5, 1920, directed the delay of Maj. Wells's trial pending the findings of the court of inquiry convened as above. The order of the department
that Maj. Wells be brought to trial has been revoked, under date of January 7,
1921, for the reasons set forth in paragraph 1 of this letter.

JOSEPHUS DANIELS.

(G)

DEPARTMENT OF THE NAVY,
Washington, January 7, 1921.

From: The Secretary of the Navy.
To: The Judge Advocate General.
Subject: Revoking order for trial of Maj. Clarke H. Wells, United States Marine Corps, by general court-martial.
Reference: (a) Letter from Major General Commandant to Secretary of the, Navy, December 29. 1920, 26283–3725: 4.

1. A court of inquiry, of which Rear Admiral H. T. Mayo, United States Navy, was president, and cons'sting of high rank'ng officers of the Navy and Marine Corps, was specially convened for the purpose of inquiring into the conduct of the personnel of the naval service that has served in the Republic of Haiti s'nce July 22, 1915. In view of the finding of the court that the only unjust'fiable acts committed were those wherein disciplinary action has already been taken and that no further proceedings could be had in the matter, and the further fact that the exhaustive evidence adduced by the said court of inqu!ry fails to contain evidence upon which court-martial proceedings could be held in the case of Maj. Wells, the department considers that no further action is warranted in his case. The previous order of the department dated November 1. 1920, that Maj. Clarke H. Wells, United States Marine Corps, be brought to trial by general court-martial is therefore hereby revoked.

JOSEPHUS DANIELS.

(H)

DISABILITY UNDER 10 PER CENT.

From: Board of Medical Survey.
To: Commandant navy yard, Washington, D. C., for transmission to the Bureau of Medicine and Surgery.
Subject: Report of medical survey.
Place, United States Naval Hospital, Washington, D. C. Date, October 17, 1919.
Name, Brokaw, Louis Abraham. Grade or rate, private, United States Marine Corps.
Attached to United States Naval Hospital, Washington, D. C. How long at this place? Sixteen days.
Admitted from naval hospital, Charleston, S. C. Date, October 1, 1919.
Born: Place, Fulton County, Ill. Date, December 21, 1889.
Enlisted: Place, Marine Barracks, Port Royal, S. C. Date, October 4, 1916.

Copy of abstract of health record.

[During present enlistment and subsequent to any prior survey.]

Name of ship or station.	Date of transfer.	Disease or injury.	Days on sick list.
Marine barracks, Port Royal	Dec. 27, 1916	None	0
Navy yard, Charleston	Jan. 14, 1917	....do	0
Marine barracks, Port au Prince	Sept. 17, 1917	Poisoning by alcohol	0
Field hospital, Port au Prince	Sept. 21, 1917	....do	4
Marine barracks, Port au Prince, Haiti	Apr. 4, 1918	None	0
Constabulary	May 29, 1919	....do	0
Territorial hospital, Port au Prince, Haiti	July 30, 1919	Dementia precox	0
U. S. S. Kittery	Aug. 14, 1919	....do	0
United States Naval Hospital, Charleston	Sept. 30, 1919	....do	47

PRESENT HISTORY OF CASE.

Diagnosis: Dementia precox.
Origin not in the line of duty. Disability is not the result of his own misconduct.
Facts are as follows: Predisposition existed prior to enlistment. Article 291.2, Navy Regulations, complied with. No statement.

Upon admission to this hospital patient was somewhat tense, nervous, and physical examination showed tremor of eyelids and vasomotor disturbance of the hands. However, he was oriented and in touch with his environment. Stated that he thought he had been poisoned while on duty in the Tropics. He admits having been a heavy drinker, which was probably responsible for his condition at this time. All symptoms have now disappeared and he is apparently reacting on his normal mental level.

W. M. M.

Present condition: Unfit for service.
Probable future duration: Permanent.
Recommendation: That he be discharged from the United States Marine Corps. No menace.

[SEAL.]   DALLAS G. SUTTON,
            Lieutenant Commander, Marine Corps, United States Navy.

[SEAL.]   .   V. E. HARMON,
                 Lieutenant, Marine Corps, United States Navy.

[SEAL.]   ALAN CHENERY,
                 Lieutenant, Marine Corps, United States Navy.

[First indorsement.]

OCTOBER 17, 1919.

From: Commanding officer.
To: Commandant navy yard, Washington, D. C.
   Forwarded.

PHILIP LEACH,
Captain, Marine Corps, United States Navy.

[Second indorsement.]

OCTOBER 20, 1919.

From: Commandant navy yard, Washington, D. C.
To: Bureau of Medicine and Surgery.
   Forwarded. Approved.

A. W. GRANT,
*Rear Admiral, United States Navy, Commandant,
                    and Superintendent Naval Gun Factory.*

[Third indorsement.]

OCTOBER 23, 1919.

From: Bureau of Medicine and Surgery.
To: Major General, Commandant, United States Marine Corps.
   Forwarded: Recommendation of board approved.   .

W. C. BRAISTED.

———

(I)

From: Board of Medical Survey.
To: Commandant sixth naval district.   For transmission to the Bureau of
   Medicine and Surgery.
Subject: Report of medical survey.

Place, United States naval hospital, Charleston, S. C.   Date, September 15, 1919.
   Name, Brokaw, Louis Abraham.   Grade or rate, private, United States Marine Corps.
   Attached to naval hospital.   How long at this place?   One month.
   Admitted from U. S. S. *Kittery*.   Date, August 14, 1919.
   Born: Place, Fulton County, Ill.   Date, December 21, 1889.
   Enlisted: Place, MB Port Royal, S. C.   Date, October 4, 1916.

Copy of abstract of health record.

[During present enlistment and subsequent to any prior survey.]

Name of ship or station.	Date of transfer.	Disease or injury.	Days on sick list.
Field hospital, Port au Prince	Sept. 21, 1917	Poisoning by alcohol	4
Field hospital, Port au Prince	July 30, 1919	Dementia praecox	62
U. S. S. Kittery	Aug. 14, 1919	Dementia praecox	15
Naval hospital, Charleston, S. C		Dementia praecox	

PRESENT HISTORY OF CASE.

Diagnosis, dementia praecox (217).
Origin, not in the line of duty. Disability is not the result of his own misconduct.
Facts are as follows: Article 2902, United States Navy Regulations, complied with. Patient has systematized delusions. He says that while on duty in Haiti he became unconscious, and when he regained consciousness he found himself in the brig. He says that he was poisoned by the natives in the highlands of Haiti. Patient seems to be normal otherwise, excepting that he is nervous; more marked at times, and while talking shows lack of concentration of thought on different occasions. It is recommended that he be transferred to United States naval hospital, Washington, D. C., for further observation and treatment. Serological test on blood, negative. Patient refused to have spinal puncture made.
Present condition: Unfit for service.
Probable future duration: Indefinite.
Recommendation: That he be transferred to United States naval hospital, Washington, D. C., for further observation and treatment, in care of medical officer and under guard.

[SEAL.]	S. M. TAYLOR, *Lieutenant Commander (M. C.)*.
[SEAL.]	L. L. ADAMKIEWICZ, *Lieutenant (M. C.)*.
[SEAL.]	A. D. BURNETT, *Lieutenant (M. C.)*.

[First indorsement.]

SEPTEMBER 15, 1919.

From: Medical officer.
To: Commandant.
Forwarded.

GEO. W. CALVER.

[Second indorsement.]

SEPTEMBER 15, 1919.

From: Commandant.
To: Bureau of Medicine and Surgery.
Forwarded.

E. THOMPSON, *Commander (M. C.), U. S. N,*
Medical Aid, Sixth Naval District, by Direction.

[Third indorsement.]

SEPTEMBER 19, 1919

From: Bureau of Medicine and Surgery.
To: Major General, Commandant, United States Marine Corps.
Forwarded: Recommendation of board approved.

W. C. BRAISTED.

(J)

From: Board of Medical Survey.
To: Brigade commander, First Provisional Brigade, U. S. M. C., for transmission to the Bureau of Medicine and Surgery.
Subject: Report of Medical Survey.
Place, Port au Prince, Haiti. Date, July 9, 1919.
Name, Brokaw, Louis Abraham. Grade or rate, private, United States Marine Corps.
Attached to field hospital. How long at this place? One year, 11 months.
Admitted from gendarmerie D'Haiti. Date, May 29, 1919.
Born: Place, Fulton County, Ill. Date, December 21, 1889.
Enlisted: Place, Port Royal, S. C. Date, October 4, 1916.

Copy of abstract of health record.

Name of ship or station.	Date of transfer.	Disease or injury.	Days on sick list.
Marine barracks, Port Royal, S. C.	Dec. 27, 1916	None	0
Navy yard dispensary, Charleston, S. C.	Jan. 14, 1917	....do	0
Marine barracks, Port au Prince, Haiti	Sept. 17, 1917	Poisoning by alcohol	0
Field hospital, Port au Prince, Haiti	Jan. 21, 1917	....do	4
Marine barracks, Port au Prince, Haiti	Apr. 4, 1918	None	0

PRESENT HISTORY OF CASE.

Diagnosis, dementia precox (217). Origin in the line of duty. Disability is not the result of his own misconduct.

Facts are as follows: Patient was admitted to hospital on May 29, 1919, for observation as to his mental condition, having been accused of an unlawful execution of two natives. Hearsay evidence is to the effect that he has been a heavy drinker for some time, and his health record shows one admission for poisoning by alcohol. Upon admission, he answered some questions in a very hesitating manner, but since then he has not answered questions or spoken a word. Patient is not oriented to his surroundings, and apparently sleeps or keeps his eyes closed all of the time. When aroused by sitting him up in bed he will pick at the bed clothes, look under the bed, and assumes facial expressions which would indicate to the onlooker that he is having very disagreeable hallucinations. Patient is unable to care for himself.

Present condition, unfit for service. Probable future duration, indefinite.

Recommendation, that he be transferred to a United States naval hospital via the first available Government transportation for further disposition.

[SEAL.]
G. P. SHIELDS,
Lieutenant, Marine Corps, United States Navy.
[SEAL.]
W. E. BEATTY,
Lieutenant, Marine Corps, United States Navy.

[First indorsement.]

JULY 9, 1919.

From: Brigade surgeon.
To: Brigade commander.
Forwarded.

A. J. GEIGER.

[Second indorsement.]

HEADQUARTERS FIRST PROVISIONAL BRIGADE, U. S. MARINE CORPS,
Port au Prince, Republic of Haiti, July 10, 1921.

From: Brigade commander.
To: Bureau of Medicine and Surgery.
Forwarded.

A. W. CATLIN.

[Third indorsement.]

JULY 28, 1919.

From: Bureau of Medicine and Surgery.
To: Major General Commandant, United States Marine Corps.
Forwarded. Recommendation of board approved.

W. C. BRAISTED.

(K)

NAVY DEPARTMENT,
Washington, November 1, 1920.
To: Maj. Edwin N. McClellan, United States Marine Corps, Judge Advocate,
General Court-Martial, Marine Barracks, Port au Prince, Haiti.
Subject: Charge and specification in case of Clarke H. Wells, major, United
States Marine Corps.

1. The above-named officer will be tried before the general court-martial of
which you are judge advocate upon the following charge and specification.
You will notify the president of the court accordingly, inform the accused of
the date set for his trial, and summon all witnesses, both for the prosecution
and the defense.
Charge: Conduct to the prejudice of good order and discipline.
Specification: In that Clarke H. Wells, then a major in the United States
Marine Corps, while serving as an officer of the Gendarmerie d'Haiti in command of the department of the north of the Republic of Haiti, did, on November 2, 1918, at Cape Haitien, Haiti, by telephone to Frederick C. Baker, then
a private, United States Marine Corps, while serving as a captain in the Gendarmerie d'Haiti at Gonaives, Haiti, willfully, maliciously, and without proper
authority or justification, deliver and cause to be delivered to the said Capt.
Baker an order to "bump off" any undesirable or useless Haitien prisoners
which he, the said Baker, might have captured or might capture in the operations at that time being conducted by the Gendarmerie d'Haiti against the
Cacos in the vicinity of Maissade, Haiti, by the words "bump off," used as
aforesaid, meaning and intending to kill such aforesaid prisoners; the United
States then being in a state of war.

------- -------.
Acting Secretary of the Navy.

Mr. HOWE. Did the court of inquiry come to any conclusion in the cases of
Lieuts. Lang and Williams?
Maj. DYER. Yes, sir. I think you have the record. The court found the alle-
gations against them not sustained.
Mr. HOWE. And as to the officer named Rogoski?
Maj. DYER. I believe the same findings in his case. As a matter of fact, I
think you will find that the court did not find any acts such as set forth in the
precept had been established.
Mr. HOWE. How many individuals do you suppose you interviewed or listened
to in connection with this inquiry while you were in Haiti?
Maj. DYER. At a guess, I should say probably between 250 and 300.
Mr. HOWE. What, if any, steps did you or the court take to let it be known
in Haiti that the investigation was on and that you were the proper person to
receive accusations or reports?
Maj. DYER. Shortly after we arrived in Port au Prince I drafted a notice,
under the instructions of the court, to be sent to the local newspapers, announcing the arrival of the court and the purpose for which it had come. That notice
was published. The fact of the court's coming was also pretty well known in
Haiti and had been a matter of discussion there for some weeks at least.
While we were holding sessions in Haiti a number of Haitians came to me and
said that some people thought they would have to wait until they should be
summoned and that I might not get in touch with them. I explained to them
that such was an erroneous idea, and that not only were they allowed to come
and give information to the court, but that I would consider it a favor if they

would come to me and let me know what they had to say in regard to our investigation. Some of the Haitian newspaper men asked me if they could publish a statement to that effect, and I told them that they not only had permission to do so, but I would be very glad to have them do so. As I recall it, however, they refrained from publishing that interview with me. In addition to what I have stated, word was transmitted through the occupation to notify any person who wished to testify to communicate with the judge advocate of the court at Port au Prince.

Mr. HOWE. There was no inquiry into the corvee by that court, was there, Major?

Maj. DYER. Not into the corvee as such, because the subject of corvee was covered by Haitian law, and corvee, which means public work, was carried on under the Haitian Government. The principal connection with that work on the part of any of the forces of the occupation was through the gendarmerie, who had charge of the actual work going on. I looked into the matter as far as I could, and tried to find out if in connection with the corvee any of the American forces had committed any of the alleged acts, but could find no evidence to that effect to bring before the court. We were not there to investigate into the question of the operation of the Haitian Government or any outrages that Haitian officials may have perpetrated upon their own people. As a matter of fact, numerous persons came to me offering to testify in regard to the fact that illegal acts had been perpetrated upon them by Haitians, but in those cases I had to tell them that that matter was not being investigated by the court of inquiry.

Mr. HOWE. Could you ascertain whether in those cases where the accusation was against Haitian officials there was more or less than the usual amount of hearsay?

Maj. DYER. Well, I can only judge from my experience with those people that practically none of them know the difference between real testimony and hearsay.

Mr. HOWE. So from what they told you——

Maj. DYER. They did not recognize the difference in their own courts.

Mr. HOWE. So from what they told you, you really gained no idea as to the extent to which Haitian officials abused the law; is that correct?

Maj. DYER. I never made any attempt to form an idea on that subject.

Mr. HOWE. Did you at any time discourage any witnesses from coming before you or from testifying?

Maj. DYER. No; I did not; although I understand I have been accused of discouraging them, based upon an incident which occurred while I was acting as judge advocate. I explained to a number of Haitians who were present for the purpose of giving me information that as a preliminary matter I was glad to hear even rumors, which I would try to trace down, but that when it came to testifying under oath that a witness should confine himself to facts within his knowledge, and that for any man to take the stand and swear that such a thing had been committed, that he knew it had been committed of his own personal knowledge, when, as a matter of fact, he was not present and only knew of the occurrence by the fact that some person had told him of it, would be perjury, and that I wanted them to understand what was required in our courts; that, as far as the court of inquiry was concerned, it followed the same rules as all the Federal courts of the United States, and only accepted sworn testimony as to facts or circumstances within the knowledge of the witness himself. I might say that several people who had come with the idea of being witnesses left after that explanation. If that was discouragement, then I may have discouraged some of them.

Mr. HOWE. Is that the only basis you can think of for any reports as to your discouragement of witnesses to appear?

Maj. DYER. I can not think of anything else, because my whole conversation and attitude was to dispel any such idea, if it existed. I do not believe that any such idea did exist, on account of the fact that people from different parts of the country, and widely scattered, communicated with me with the utmost freedom volunteering to testify. They seemed to have no fear of it at all. As a matter of fact, people came to me with complaints about civil suits being carried on in the Haitian courts and wanted our court of inquiry to take jurisdiction. One woman had a suit over a grocery bill, and she wanted our court to have a hearing on it and adjust it. They seemed to think they could get justice from the court of inquiry, and had confidence in it. I believe there were certain people there who pretended to believe and tried to create the atmosphere that witnesses were not wanted, but I think that was confined to a few people for a certa n special interest. The people at large, I feel sure, felt confident that they could come before the court, and they did.

Mr. HOWE. What action, if any, do you recollect that the court took in the case of Maj. Clark Wells?

Maj. DYER. The court took no action in h's case at all. There was no evidence to bring before the court, none which I could find, to show that any of the offenses named in the precept had been committed, with which he could be connected. It was necessary, of course, before you could bring Maj. Wells in, to show that some act had been committed, and then connect him up with it in some way. There were rumors in regard to him, but we were unable to verify the acts having been committed. In other words, there was no corpus delicti that we could start on.

Mr. HOWE. You did, however, invest'gate such rumors or reports as you did hear about Maj. Wells?

Maj. DYER. I traced them down as far as I could, trying to get something to start on, but was unable to get it.

Mr. HOWE. How long have you been in the Marine Corps, Major?

Maj. DYER. Eighteen years in the Marine Corps and about a year and a half in the Army before that.

Senator ODDIE. As a matter of curiosity, I would like to ask where you got your medal of honor?

Maj. DYER. Down in Vera Cruz, sir.

Mr. ANGELL. Major, have you the terms of the notice which you caused to be given out of the arrival of the court of inquiry in Haiti, and its mission?

Maj. DYER. No; I have not.

Mr. ANGELL. Was that notice published in full, as you remember, in the papers?

Maj. DYER. Yes; I know it was. It was translated into French and published in French in the newspapers. I read it myself.

Mr. ANGELL. Was it published anywhere, to your knowledge, except in Port au Prince?

Maj. DYER. Not to my personal knowledge; I do not know.

Mr. ANGELL. Were any steps taken, so far as you know, to have it published in other places in Haiti, or give out an official announcement?

Maj. DYER. I do not know whether there were or not, but the purpose of the court being there was well known in other places in Haiti, because I had letters from various parts of the country, for instance, from up in Cape Haitien, Gonaives, and several other places.

Mr. ANGELL. Was that notice the only public announcement made by the court or by the judge advocate of the court, concerning the function, purpose of the court, procedure, method of hearing witnesses, and the like, during its stay in the island?

Maj. DYER. Yes; that was the only official notice sent out. That court, the same as any other court in the United States, did not advertise itself. It was just like the Supreme Court of the United States, or any inferior court. They do not send out notices about what their purpose is, or their status, or anything else.

Mr. ANGELL. Was any announcement made, in your notice or otherwise, of the t'me and place where the court would hold its sessions?

Maj. DYER. Not in that notice, but it would have been impossible, because we held our sessions as we were able to get testimony to bring before it.

Mr. ANGELL. Are we to understand, then, that there was no public announcement of the times and places of holding these sessions?

Maj. DYER. No; there was no public announcement. There was no purpose in announcing it that I know of. The sessions of the court were open, but if any person wanted to know when he could appear before the court, he would have to come around and inquire.

Mr. ANGELL. He would have to know where to inquire, to find out when and where the court was going to sit?

Maj. DYER. They knew that. It sat in the same place, the barracks, every day, and arrangements were made for the public to have access. I personally saw that those instructions were given, because I knew there would be charges made that it was not open to the public, so I know orders were given, and I know they were carried out, that any person who came there to the barracks and wanted to attend the court was told where the room was and shown how to get up there and told he could come in, because, as I say, I anticipated there would be charges made about secret hearings, and all that sort of thing.

Mr. ANGELL. The sessions were, in fact, then, open to the public and attended by the public?

Maj. DYER. Yes. There were, of course, certain times when the court was closed.

Mr. ANGELL. Under the technical rules of procedure of military courts?

Maj. DYER. Yes; but not to take testimony.

Mr. ANGELL. Was there any official statement gotten out by the court or in its behalf, inviting persons who had complaints to make to present themselves either to the court or to the judge advocate?

Maj. DYER. No there was no advertisement other than what I have spoken about already. We did not advertise in the newspapers for possible witnesses to come or offer them any rewards for coming or anything like that, or hold out any inducements for them. They were all given the opportunity.

Mr. ANGELL. Where did the court hold sessions in Haiti?

Maj. DYER. In the library room in the barracks in Port au Prince. They also held, as I remember, one or two sessions on board ship, but not for the purpose of taking testimony. That was only to consider matters of procedure.

Mr. ANGELL. There were no sessions, then, held in any other place in Haiti besides Port au Prince?

Maj. DYER. No.

Mr. ANGELL. You said you went up into the interior?

Maj. DYER. Yes.

Mr. ANGELL. Where did you go? How many trips did you make? Can you give us some idea of the extent of the investigation you conducted on this trip or trips into the interior?

Maj. DYER. I made one trip, going to Hinche and St. Michael, and spent most of the time at Hinche, endeavoring to obtain some witnesses from that place, because that had been the center of rumors of numerous charges, and on the statements of one of the inhabitants of that town prior investigators had reported the possible occurrence of a number of outrages. I interviewed that man and endeavored to obtain from him the names of all possible witnesses. I also got into communication with Mr. Lang on that trip. I had intended to go Cape Hatien, and the court had originally intended to go there to hold sessions, but in view of the fact that it was impossible to obtain any testimony from people up there other than those who were brought down to Port au Prince to testify, I never proceeded there. I was gone on that trip, I think, about three days.

Mr. ANGELL. Did you go to Cape Haitien?

Maj. DYER. No; I just said I did not.

Mr. ANGELL. Admiral Knapp made a trip to Cape Haitien about this time, did he not?

Maj. DYER. Yes; he did.

Mr. ANGELL. Did he go officially or unofficially for the court of inquiry?

Maj. DYER. No; he had nothing to do with the court of inquiry.

Mr. ANGELL. Any investigations he may have made at that time was, then, entirely disconnected with the work of the court of inquiry?

Maj. DYER. So far as the court was concerned. He may have endeavored, and, as a matter of fact, I know he did give us several possible leads which we followed up, but he was not connected with the court of inquiry investigation any more than any other official down there.

Mr. ANGELL. You felt, then, that there was no necessity for the court itself to go to any other point, in Haiti to hear possible evidence?

Maj. DYER. No; there was no object in the court going to a place unless they knew they were going to get some testimony there.

Mr. ANGELL. And you felt that your trip or trips had covered the ground?

Maj. DYER. That, and in connection with the correspondence that I had and the interviews. In other words, we could not spend a couple of years down there going from one town to another and putting out advertisements for people to come and testify before this court. We could have spent months doing that, hoping that something might occur, or fearing that something might occur, but the court stayed there as long as they thought there was any possibility of getting any testimony in connection with their precept. It might make it a little more understandable to you if I would state that the investigation—the preliminary investigation preceding the hearings before the court and the action of the court—followed the same lines that would be followed in any United

States court which had a United States attorney to prepare the cases for the court.

Mr. ANGELL. That is as you conceived your function as judge advocate?

Maj. DYER. Not only conceived it; I knew it.

Mr. ANGELL. In this large volume I have before me, which is or purports to be the record of the Mayo court of inquiry and in evidence as such, I find on pages 2 and 3 a list of the names of witnesses. Glancing that over, can you by refreshing your recollection tell us whether those names include all the witnesses who appeared before the court?

Maj. DYER. No; I can not tell you from recollection. The record will have to speak for itself.

Mr. ANGELL. I will change the form of the question. This, then, is a complete record of the proceedings of the court, so far as you know?

Maj. DYER. The proceedings of the court, not of any of my preliminary investigations.

Mr. ANGELL. The court did not hear as a witness Gen. Catlin, did it?

Maj. DYER. No; Gen. Catlin never claimed to have any knowledge which would enable him to testify as to any of the acts mentioned in the precept having been committed upon any Haitians.

Mr. ANGELL. Did you interview Gen. Catlin or have any correspondence with him?

Maj. DYER. No; I read his reports and his prior statements, and he was not present on any occasion when any alleged offense was committed.

Mr. ANGELL. Was it for that reason that others of the higher Marine officers who had served in Haiti did not appear before the court, such as Gen. Cole, Gen. Waller, and Col. Williams?

Maj. DYER. I do not understand what you mean by that. Appear before the court for what purpose?

Mr. ANGELL. In other words, did you make any attempt, and if so, what attempt, to learn from these other Marine officers what knowledge they had, if any, of acts which would come within the scope of the precept of the court?

Maj. DYER. I did.

Mr. ANGELL. What attempts?

Maj. DYER. I read all the reports and other data on file in the Navy Department and headquarters of the Marine Corps before taking up the investigation—prior investigations which had been made—and interviewed some of the people personally.

Mr. ANGELL. You did not conceive or feel that under the precept of the court any possible irregularities or abuses of the corvee law came within the scope of the precept?

Maj. DYER. Oh, yes; if they involved any one of the acts alleged, any unjustifiable homicide or other serious acts against any of the natives of Haiti or their property; yes.

Mr. ANGELL. Did you interpret the precept of the court, then, to apply only to specific acts—unlawful acts—on the part of the personnel of the United States Navy or Marine Corps?

Maj. DYER. Yes; it was confined entirely to their acts, not to the acts of other people—foreigners.

Mr. ANGELL. And did not involve, under the precept, the question of responsibility, if any, for such acts committed by any persons other than the personnel of the Navy and Marine Corps?

Maj. DYER. It involved inquiry and finding the responsibility in case any person of the Navy or Marine Corps was involved, mediately or immediately. For instance, to illustrate, if a Haitian committed one of the acts under the directions of a marine, then the marine would be in part responsible, and we attempted to fix the responsibility in a case like that, but if it was a case of a Haitian acting not under the directions or orders of an American, we did not attempt to investigate all those cases; in other words, the court did not attempt to substitute itself for the Haitian courts.

Mr. ANGELL. You did not feel that it came within the purview of the court of inquiry to inquire into the possible question of responsibility of naval or marine personnel for the institution, conduct, or a possible general abuse of the corvée law?

Maj. DYER. Yes; we did as I explained before.

Mr. ANGELL. Did you hear any stories or rumors of forced labor under the corvée law?

Maj. DYER. All corvée is forced labor. I heard lots of rumors of it.

Mr. Angell. Did you understand from sources of information which came to you during your investigation 'there in Haiti that the corvée law, as applied since the occupancy, had been in accordance with the Haitian law, irrespective of any case of individual abuses?

Maj. Dyer. I can not answer that question as put, because I think it is inconsistent. The corvée was administered illegally, according to what I heard, but the illegality consisted of specific instances of not following out the laws.

Mr. Angell. And the specific instances of illegality were cases, were they, of alleged killings, or particular crimes?

Maj. Dyer. No. They were not alleged killings or particular crimes so much as they were the abuse of putting people under the corvée who were not subject to it at that particular time or place.

Mr. Angell. Did you make any attempt, then, to find who, if any, of the Navy or marine personnel were responsible for such a state of facts?

Maj. Dyer. Yes. And I found it was the Haitians that were responsible for it, the Haitian officials.

Mr. Angell. It was the Haitian officials, and not the Navy or marine personnel?

Maj. Dyer. Exactly. I am stating now that that was not a judicial determination, but I could find no evidence that the marines were responsible for that, and my personal opinion was that other people were responsible for it, and they were the people who administered that law.

Mr. Angell. Could you find any reliable or satisfactory evidence that marine officers or marines who were officers of the gendarmerie, had knowledge of such alleged illegal conditions in their own districts?

Maj. Dyer. Yes. They must have, because they issued orders to correct those abuses. I know that the chief of the gendarmerie issued orders to try to correct it, and they employed the method of having colored identification tickets issued to the men to show that they had performed their work and were not liable to it again, and so I take it from that that they must have known there were abuses under it, and were trying to correct them.

Mr. Angell. You say that you could not get ex-Lieut. Spear to appear voluntarily before the court?

Maj. Dyer. I wrote and asked him to come, as judge advocate, but got no reply, as I recall it, to the letter. I know he did not come.

Mr. Angell. Was that just one letter you sent to him? Was that followed up at all?

Maj. Dyer. No. It was not followed up at all, because, as I say, I had no authority to compel him to come.

Mr. Angell. Did you make any investigation into the case of Capt. George D. Hamilton, who was court-martialed in Haiti?

Maj. Dyer. The records of his court was introduced in evidence before the court of inquiry.

Mr. Angell. Was there any attempt to get him as a witness before the court, or any persons who testified at that trial?

Maj. Dyer. You mean to retry that case?

Mr. Angell. No; not to retry the case.

Maj. Dyer. For what purpose?

Mr. Angell. I am just asking you the question, whether any attempt was made to get him or any of the witnesses who testified at his trial before the court?

Maj. Dyer. I do not recall as to any of the other witnesses, but so far as he was concerned, I made no attempt to get him.

Mr. Angell. What attempt, if any, was made to look into the case of Lieut. Ryan, who was court-martialed?

Maj. Dyer. There was no attempt made to reopen any case which had been settled by a court-martial. Our court could have had no jurisdiction over a subject of that kind. The case was closed. We could not retry the man a second time. We accepted the finding of the court. When it said a man was guilty, we accepted that as evidence of the fact that the crime had been committed and that the man had committed it; and where the man had been acquitted, we accepted the finding of the court that he was not guilty of it.

Mr. Angell. It was not within the scope of the inquiry of this court, was it, to inquire into the general question of the American armed intervention in Haiti or the conduct of the occupation, except for specific unlawful acts?

Maj. Dyer. The court, as you will notice from the precept, had nothing to do 'i the policy there and could not call upon the President to explain why the

Government adopted any such policy, or the Secretary of State, or the Secretary of the Navy, or any of those people. The precept was not broad enough to go into that subject.

Mr. ANGELL. It would not include, for example, the question of the original intervention in July, 1915, apart always from individual cases of specific abuse or alleged acts?

Maj. DYER. No; it had nothing to do with the question of policy or the intervention at all.

Mr. ANGELL. Or the seizure of the customs, or the new constitution, or any of those matters?

Maj. DYER. No. The precept will speak for itself.

Mr. ANGELL. I know; but I want to get it in the record, that is all Major, the scope of the thing.

Did you speak French or Creole, Major, at that time?

Maj. DYER. I do not speak Creole at all, and I do not claim to speak French.

Mr. ANGELL. Did you have to converse with your witnesses who spoke French through an interpreter?

Maj. DYER. I used an interpreter, and used several of them. The majority of the people in Haiti do not speak French, and their dialects are so different that, for instance, a man can interpret for a native living in Port au Prince is not necessarily an accurate interpreter for one living 100 miles away. At any rate, we had four people interpreting before the court, to try to find out what the witnesses really wanted to say. We had one interpreter who was with the court all the time, who spoke, read, and wrote French excellently, and we had several, or one other, who attended all sessions of the court, as a Creole interpreter. I believe that all the members of the court read, write, and speak French with some fluency—I know that Admiral Oliver is an especially excellent French scholar—so that they were able to follow the witnesses who used French, with no difficulty, although everything was interpreted.

Mr. ANGELL. Had you served in Haiti before you were appointed judge advocate of this court?

Maj. DYER. No; I had never been there before.

Mr. ANGELL. Had you made any special study of Haitian affairs before being appointed to the court?

Maj. DYER. Not any special study. I had been familiar with the general situation down there, as I followed it, but not what you would call a special study of Haiti in particular.

Mr. HOWE. Is there any further statement that you think you should make, Major, in order that the committee may have any information that you have about your investigation and about your conduct of this court?

Maj. DYER. No; I have nothing to say, except I believe that a reference to the record of the court will show that it proceeded intelligently and thoroughly, and within the scope of its precept.

Mr. HOWE. The record of the court is in evidence before this committee, and it will, of course, with its appendices and exhibits, speak for itself. We were more particularly interested in hearing from you the practical methods you pursued in getting that record up.

Maj. DYER. I simply want to state that while I do not claim to anything near perfection as a judge advocate of a court, I have had a good many years' experience in that kind of work, and I have a legal education and I understand the duties of a prosecuting officer before a court, and where dissatisfaction was expressed in regard to our court it was largely through ignorance of the American judicial system. The criticism that was most frequently made was that the court would not accept hearsay testimony, and I explained to the people, among others being one or two Americans down there, that that was a rule followed in all United States courts, and that we had exactly the same rules that the Federal courts of the United States follow, and we only accepted hearsay when it fell under one of the regular exceptions to the general rule.

(Whereupon the committee adjourned until Tuesday, November 15, 1921, at 10.30 o'clock a. m.)

INQUIRY INTO OCCUPATION AND ADMINISTRATION OF HAITI AND SANTO DOMINGO.

TUESDAY, NOVEMBER 15, 1921.

United States Senate,
Select Committee on Haiti and Santo Domingo,
Washington, D. C.

The committee met at 10.30 o'clock a. m., pursuant to adjournment, Senator Tasker L. Oddie presiding.

Present: Senators McCormick (chairman) and Oddie.

Also present: Mr. Walter Bruce Howe, Mr. Ernest Angell, and Maj. Edwin N. McClellan, United States Marine Corps.

STATEMENT OF MR. RICHARD E. FORREST, RYE, N. Y.

Mr. Howe. Mr. Forrest, will you give your name and present address to the reporter?

Mr. Forrest. Richard E. Forrest, Rye, N. Y.

Mr. Howe. Mr. Forrest, you are a graduate of Yale, are you not, of the class of 1899?

Mr. Forrest. Yes.

Mr. Howe. You have had experience in the Philippines and Haiti. Before you went to the Philippines, what was your occupation?

Mr. Forrest. I was in financial work, in what is known as Wall Street, first with a large bond house there, and then with my own firm, and from that work I went into the financing of a very large company in the Philippines, which to-day is the largest producer of coconut oil under the American flag. We developed a very large industry there, and during the war were practically, or pretty nearly, the largest shippers of coconut oil into the United States.

Mr. Howe. In addition to the financing of that company in the Philippines, did you take an active hand in the development work there, and in the direction of its affairs in the Philippines?

Mr. Forrest. Yes.

Mr. Howe. Did you go to the Philippines?

Mr. Forrest. Yes.

Mr. Howe. How long were you in the Philippines; I mean from the time you went until the time you came away?

Mr. Forrest. About three months. That was in 1915, after this company had gotten under way, and then, after that, I was in charge of certain branches of the company's work, as its vice president, in New York.

Mr. Howe. When did you cease to be the vice president of that company?

Mr. Forrest. In January, 1918.

Mr. Howe. That company is still doing business?

Mr. Forrest. Yes; a very large business.

Mr. Howe. Did you have anything to do with the Philippine Society?

Mr. Forrest. Yes; in 1912 the questions which arose in regard to the political situation in the Philippines were of considerable moment, and those who were commercially interested in the Philippines banded together to endeavor to work out conditions which might help their interests in the Philippines, into the Philippine Society. I had talked with Mr. Taft and Gen. Wood, and Mr. Cameron Forbes, and others who had had to do with the development, politically and industrially, and so on, in the Philippines, and under their advice we organized the Philippine Society with myself as secretary, and I was the moving factor in the work of that society for upward of three years.

Mr. Howe. So it is fair to infer that you made a study of conditions in the Philippines, and the relations between our country and the Philippines?

Mr. FORREST. Yes.

Mr. HOWE. When you left the company in the Philippines, with which you were connected, did some of your associates leave at the same time with you?

Mr. FORREST. Yes.

Mr. HOWE. That is in stock ownership?

Mr. FORREST. Those who had been interested in the company by me retired at the same time I did.

Mr. HOWE. Then there was a prompt transition, was there not, from there to Haiti in association with the same people?

Mr. FORREST. Yes; in association with the same people.

Mr. HOWE. What was your project in Haiti?

Mr. FORREST. It started by taking a contract from the Aircraft Bureau to produce castor beans in Haiti, from which castor oil would be made for aviation. We were given a contract which was in the nature of an exclusive contract for the production of castor beans, and subsequently, by the fact that we were asked to enlarge our contract, our production, we were led to believe that we would have the exclusive right for the importation of castor beans from Haiti.

Mr. HOWE. About when was that?

Mr. FORREST. The first contract was taken in February, 1918, and the second contract was taken in September, 1918.

Mr HOWE. Will you go ahead now, Mr. Forrest, and outline your business and development experience in Haiti, giving us an idea as to how much time you spent there, whether or not you were interested in other projects when you were not actually in Haiti, and, in general, give the committee an idea as to what your opportunities for observation were?

Mr. FORREST. We organized our company, which was known as the United West Indies Corporation, with myself as president, in February, 1918. In March I went to Haiti and spent about two months. We devoted ourselves to the production of castor beans and the production of castor beans for the Government until December, 1918, about a month after the armistice was declared. I went again to Haiti in January, 1919, and spent about three and a half months in order to develop plans for the production of long-staple cotton. Then we devoted ourselves to this cotton industry until November. 1920, during which time I spent, I suppose, an average of from four to five months a year in Haiti.

That is condensing the whole thing. I do not think it is necessary to give the details.

Mr. HOWE. No; it is not. We just want an idea as to what your general experience was.

Mr. FORREST. And during all of that time, until May, 1921, I devoted myself entirely to the work of the company in Haiti, whether I was in Haiti or New York. I did nothing else.

Mr. HOWE. What results came from the long-staple cotton project?

Mr. FORREST. We had developed a very large plant on the plain of St. Michel.

Mr. HOWE. About how many acres did you have there?

Mr. FORREST. We had under cultivation there about 2,500 acres, and there was cotton there on the 10th of November which looked extremely good, and on the 20th of November we found that practically the whole of that crop had been attacked by an infection which apparently is a very unusual thing. In fact, there has been no record of that infection happening at any other place, except in the island of St. Vincent some years before. The calamity we met with in the destruction of that cotton, of course, meant that we were set back to an experimental stage, and our position now is that we are experimenting with sugar and cotton to see what further plans we should adopt.

Mr. HOWE. Has the company holdings of land outside of the St. Michel district?

Mr. FORREST. Yes; we own, altogether—perhaps it would not be well to put that in the record.

Mr. HOWE. I do not think that is necessary on the record.

Mr. FORREST. I will simply say that we have large tracts of land in other parts of the country besides St. Michel.

Mr. HOWE. You formed the acquaintance of many Haitians. I take it?

Mr. FORREST. I have been down there very frequently and met them not only in Haiti but also in New York, and I feel that I have a great many friends among the Haitian people.

Mr. HOWE. Have you also met our treaty officials and marine officers in Haiti?

Mr. FORREST. Yes.

Mr. HOWE. What were your relations with them?

Mr. FORREST. Complete cooperation. I have always been treated by the Haitians as if they were glad to have our company there, as if they looked toward us to help in the agricultural development of Haiti, and we have endeavored on our side to help them in giving them the benefit of our experts which we sent down there, and further in actually taking up to our plantation certain members of the agricultural schools to instruct them in the work that we were doing, which of course was done without any cost.

Mr. HOWE. You expect to be in the United States for the next few months, do you not?

Mr. FORREST. I do.

Mr. HOWE. The committee expects to go to Haiti, Mr. Forrest, starting in about a week and coming back in about a month after that. Its time for hearings is at present limited, although the committee wants all the information it can get. Do you believe that we could have the benefit of your information again on the committee's return to this country?

Mr. FORREST. I should be very glad indeed to do anything I can to assist in this very important question, either now or when the committee comes back.

Mr. HOWE. Mr. Chairman, Mr. Forrest has had great opportunit es for observation down there, I learn, and it would be impossible in the time at our disposal now to go into these matters in any great detail, but there are a few matters that I think he could touch on at the present t me, and with your permission I am going to lead him up to those matters and then get his free comment on them, but I am not going into an exhaustive examination.

Senator ODDIE. That can be taken up later.

Mr. HOWE. Is agriculture an easy matter down there in Ha't', or do you always have to be on the lookout for plant blights in cotton or in other crops?

Mr. FORREST. The conditions which make for the prospect of agricultural success in a country like Haiti also make for very dec ded dangers as to crop destruct on. Where you have conditions which favor very rapid growth of plants you also have conditions which favor the rapid growth of things wh ch will destroy the plants. If we were ever to have the boll weevil in Haiti, it would be very difficult to ever get any cotton out of Hait , because there would be nothing in Haiti to destroy the boll weevil as there is in this country where the winters come along and retard their production. If you have army worms to destroy the plants, you are going to have a tremendous number of them developing in a very short time. In agricultural production in Haiti, or in fact anywhere in the Tropics, the risks that are taken are not only on account of the rap d development of destructive influences but also the risks of transportation and all the difficulties of organization on the ground. To sum that up, I should consider that the profits from agriculture in Haaiti would be very large and the r sks also very great.

Mr. ROWE. You have had an opportunity since you went to Haiti early in 1918 to observe the results or accomplishments of the American occupation there. Will you please compare those results, not with what the conditions were before the American occupation began, because, as I understand it, you would have no direct knowledge of them; but compare them, please, with the obligations assumed by the United States in its treaty with Haiti, the treaty of 1915?

Mr. FORREST. I have the treaty, what is called the convention, here with me, and if I may be permitted to just read the first article of that treaty, it says:

"The Government of the United States will, by its good offices, aid the Haitian Government in the proper and efficient development of its agricultural, mineral, and commercial resources, and in the establishment of the finances of Haiti on a firm and solid basis."

That is a point of the convention which, it seems to me, is the most important point to be considered in regard to the questions which this commitee has to consider. It speaks of the efficient development of agricultural, mineral, and commercial resources, and the establishment of the finances of Haiti on a firm and solid basis. If we look back to the time when we made this convention in 1915, and consider the progress which has been made during four years and a half, we have to admit that the progress has not been at all satisfactory. In my opinion, to-day the agricultural and commercial resources of the country, while somewhat improved on account of the establishment of law and order, still have not been at all commensurate with what both the Haitians and the American business men who are interested in Haiti had a right to expect from the words of this convention.

Of course, the European war has had to do with the retarding of this program, but, nevertheless, it seems to me that the chances are that when this convention was made the people of Haiti had a right to believe that they were going to be lifted up into prosperity, and looked to the United States to help them in that. I regret to say that, in my opinion, the United States has not lived up to that faith which they gave the Haitians. And I consider that the feeling of disappointment and the indefinite policy on the part of the United States, and also on the part of the Haitian Government, has caused a great deal of friction, and has brought about a weakening of confidence on both sides. I think, if we look at that, as the basic situation with regard to the condition of Haiti to-day, we have got the main cause of the difficulties which exist.

Mr. Howe. You stress what you term the disappointing results of the American occupation in bringing about financial stability. What is needed?

Mr. Forrest. First, I should say that there was needed a definite policy on the part of the United States Government as to how the Government of Haiti can be established on such a basis that friction between the Haitians and the representatives of the United States Government can be entirely done away with, to the end that the words of this article may be adhered to, and after a firm policy of government has been established, capital will be encouraged to go into Haiti. We all know that capital is extremely timid, and we also know that if there are indications of governmental friction capital will not allow itself to become subject to the exigencies of a continual series of political misunderstandings.

Mr. Howe. To go back a minute to the material evidence of our occupation, what about the establishment of law and order? Has that been well done, or not?

Mr. Forrest. I consider that the work which has been done in establishing law and order in Haiti has been truly remarkable. The geographical formation of the country is such that to the person who sees these mountains and impassable districts it would seem quite impossible to ever preserve law and order throughout the country. The efficiency with which the marines have handled that is, I think, truly remarkable and very much to their credit.

Mr. Howe. What have you to say, Mr. Forrest, as to the development of roads and communications?

Mr. Forrest. I can not give the details. It is not perhaps, expected by the committee that I, a layman, would give the details as to what the roads were and how much had been constructed and what the expense had been.

Mr. Howe. Well, we knew from testimony which has been given to us here that between 400 and 500 miles of roads of various classes were reconstructed or constructed under the supervision of our military or naval authorities—our marines—down in Haiti. How good has that work been, how useful, and what purposes has it served? Let me ask you a question suggested by the testimony which the committee already has. In your opinion, were these roads located on a plan which would do the most for the commercial development of the country or, in your opinion, does the plan of reconstructed roads indicate military considerations as being better served by the roads as they were laid out?

Mr. Forrest. It is very difficult to discriminate between the value of a road for commercial purposes and for military purposes, except where the location of a road would be such that there would be no economic value whatever. The road from Ennery to Limbe is purely a military road, for the reason that the agricultural products of the Gonaives Valley and of the Ennery Valley would naturally go to Gonaives for export, and on the north side the agricultural products of the Plain du Nord would naturally go to the seaports of the north coast; therefore the most expensive, you might say the spectacular part, of that road is purely a military road, because it leads over the mountains, where there are no agricultural developments whatever and probably never could be.

Mr. Howe. Is there on either end of that road a district which could be economically served to other outlets, to outlets on the sea?

Mr. Forrest. Yes; but the building of the roads across the country can not have anything to do with the handling of the economic products of the country, because they would not go over the mountains.

Mr. Howe. They would not go to the sea?

Mr. Forrest. They would not go to the sea, but entirely in this direction instead of over the mountains the other way. I speak of that particular road because I think that is the most spectacular road in Haiti.

Another road on which I came to the same conclusion is the road from Pont Bed to Mirebelais, which has no economic value whatever, and must have been built in order to allow good access into the heart of the country, where the so-called Cacos were operating.

A third road is the road from Ennery to the St. Michel plain. In the building of this road it must be remembered that the headquarters of the Charlemagne insurrection were in the mountains surrounding the plains of St. Michel, and the construction of that road into the St. Michel plain was undoubtedly one of the means of eliminating the Charlemagne rebellion, for the reason that it could be approached from the south and also from the north.

The road from Miragoane to Jacmel is also purely a military road, for the reason that the products of Miragoane are on the shore, and the products of Jacmel are also on the shore, but those three roads are very spectacularly built, and, in my oipnion, are purely military roads.

Now, in order to facilitate military operations, it was really necessary to improve the condition of the roads which were already in Haiti. Whether you would say that the improvement of the road to Croix Des Boquets and to Leogane, and into the Gonaives district would be due to economic developement is also doubtful, because it must be remembered that the products of Haiti are carried by burro and oxcart, and can be carried over a road which is not what is known as an automobile road. It is perfectly true that the economic advantages of good roads have been very remarkable in Haiti, and I believe that the market people of Haiti recognize the fact that to-day they can transport their products three times as far with the same effort as they could before these good roads were built.

Mr. Howe. Let me interrupt there to ask if you think there was any benefit in building that road you mentioned over the mountains, in making it possible for the people of one part of the country to mingle with and meet the people of another part of the country?

Mr. Forrest. I believe that political stability and the progress of the intelligence of the country people is dependent upon communication, just as we know in China, or any other country, that you can not have a civilized, intelligent people who are separated from each other by impassable conditions of the country.

Mr. Howe. So that might be an incidental good from that piece of road building?

Mr. Forrest. Absolutely. The communication has been tremendously improved during the American occupation.

Mr. Howe. And that has brought forth greatly bettered conditions?

Mr. Forrest. A great deal better living conditions, and a decided advancement in the people of the outlying districts.

Mr. Howe. In other words, you would not call that work wasted work?

Mr. Forrest. No, I should not.

Mr. Howe. But if the plan had been purely for the economic development of the country at the earliest possible date, would you have devised a different road system?

Mr. Forrest. Entirely—I do not mean entirely, but I would have supplemented the construction of these important military roads over the mountains, which presumably were the most expensive part of the program.

Mr. Howe. What would be the central theory of a system of roads for the economic development of the country?.

Mr. Forrest. The proper construction of roads in the three large agricultural plains of Haiti; first, the Cul de Sac; second, the Plaine du Nord; and third; the plain of St. Michel.

Mr. Howe. And an outlet from those regions to what point?

Mr. Forrest. To the seacoast.

Mr. Howe. And then, after that, I take it you would be ready to link up these different plains, but your first avenue of transportation would be to the sea, is that correct?

Mr. Forrest. Correct.

Mr. Howe. How much of that has been done, giving these regions direct access to the sea over roads?

Mr. Forrest. That is a difficult question to answer, because it involves a knowledge of all of the little roadways that go through those districts.

Mr. Howe. I do not think it is going to be beneficial at this time to have a detailed answer to that, Mr. Forrest?

Mr. Forrest. I should say there has been considerable improvement in the facilities for transporting products to the markets and to the seacoast.

Mr. Howe. Would you say that considerable improvement remains yet to be done?

Mr. Forrest. A great deal remains yet to be done; yes.

Mr. Howe. What about sanitary conditions?

Mr. Forrest. Sanitary conditions in the towns have shown remarkable progress. It used to be such that when ships passed by Port au Prince without even stopping there, they knew that the sanitary conditions of Port au Prince were bad, because of the wind, which would carry the odors to them. To-day the towns, the large towns of Haiti are in an excellent sanitary condition, and this has been brought about by the expenditure of comparatively little funds.

Mr. Howe. By what agency?

Mr. Forrest. By the sanitary engineer of Haiti, assisted by the local Haitian magistrats and chefs de section, through the old rural police.

Mr. Howe. Have the gendarmerie or the marine commanders had any hand in that improvement?

Mr. Forrest. Yes; where the towns were under the command of the gendarmerie and the marines, the sanitary conditions were entirely in the control of those officers, and they are directly responsible for the improvement that has taken place in those towns.

Mr. Howe. Has progress in sanitation, then, been worth while?

Mr. Forrest. Not only worth while, but truly remarkable.

Mr. Howe. I suppose there is still more to be done along those lines?

Mr. Forrest. Yes; I should say that there was in a great many instances, but to-day I consider that Haiti is a very healthy place to live.

Mr. Howe. What changes has the occupation brought about in education in Haiti?

Mr. Forrest. The education has been improved by the improvement, of course, in the conditions of law and order. There are more children going to school now than there were when we first went into Haiti, but the progress could not be called satisfactory, in my opinion. Whether this is due to the fact that when we went into Haiti there was no school organization of a satisfactory character from which to build up, or whether it is due to the lack of finances or funds to carry on a proper organization of an educational development, is the question. My own idea is that the prospects for educational development in Haiti would not be bad if funds could be provided and a proper educational bureau, with funds at its command, established.

Mr. Howe. How long would it be before you could have teachers in sufficient numbers?

Mr. Forrest. I believe it would be a long time.

Mr. Howe. Would you have to train your own?

Mr. Forrest. You would.

Mr. Howe. What, then, is necessary for the carrying out of any educational system there, would be sufficient funds and sufficient time?

Mr. Forrest. Sufficient time to provide an organization. I can not give you the details of the number of children that are at school, but I would say it is really very small compared to the size and population of the country.

Mr. Howe. What has been effected in the way of improvement of agriculture?

Mr. Forrest. I feel that the improvement in agriculture has been developed by the work of companies which have started there in the last three or four years, but that the results, as far as economic progress of the country is concerned, 's to-day not of any consideration.

Mr. Howe. What is needed in order to make progress in agriculture?

Mr. Forrest. The first thing that is needed is the clearing up of the land situation in Haiti. It is not feasible for people to start to develop lands when they do not know who owns the land, and that is a subject which the committee will probably go into at length.

The second thing is intelligence of management and organization, and the third thing is the providing of equipment, and the fourth thing, of course, is a market for the products.

The land situation is a very difficult one to solve in Haiti. The organizations to-day down there who are in agriculture are comparatively few, and I think it will take a considerable time before Haiti really starts to get on a good footing in agriculture unless the finances of the country encourage the investment of proper capital down there.

Mr. Howe. Here again is a feature of development requiring capital?

Mr. Forrest. Yes.

Mr. Howe. So far you have made that comment on education, that it requ'res money, and on roads or transportation, that that requires money and capital, and now on agriculture. Would you deem :rrigation projects as another matter which requires capital and which projects themselves are necessary to a betterment of conditions in Haiti?

Mr. Forrest. I should say irrigation was a part of the equipment of a plantation, and therefore comes under the heading that I spoke of. It is just as much equipment as buildings or anything else which has to do with the improvement of soil conditions. I consider that in any agricultural operation in Haiti a large investment of capital would absolutely require irrigation.

Mr. Howe. The reclamation of land would also require irrigation, is that correct?

Mr. Forrest. Yes.

Mr. Howe. So an rrigation system would be an indispensable prerequisite to new agricultural projects in Haiti?

Mr. Forrest. Yes.

Mr. Howe. The development of new lands?

Mr. Forrest. You say new? I should say large agricultural developments in Haiti. There are a great many things that are produced that require no irrigation, but the important things in Haiti, such as sugar and cotton, should have irrigation. Of course, we deal with coffee and cocoa, and things of that kind. They do not require irrigation, but the important development in Haiti is in sugar, and irrigation is necessary for that, but not for cotton, because there are districts in Haiti where cotton could be grown without irrigation.

Mr. Howe. What has been done toward the restoration of irrigation systems and the development of new irrigation systems by the forces of our occupation?

Mr. Forrest. In 1919 an irrigation expert was employed by the engineer of Haiti to come down there and report on a complete system for the irrigation work of the Cul de Sac. He made a full and complete report, which is on file. As I understand it, nothing has been done further with regard to that plan, on account of the lack of funds, but it has been seriously considered in Haiti ever since we have been down there that a proper irrigation development was necessary.

I may say in this connection that there have been plenty of revisions of the irrigation laws of Haiti for some time past, and that the difficulties in the revision are very great, due to the uncertainty again of land ownership. It all comes down to the same thing. If a man is not sure as to who owns the land, he is not so much interested in how he is go'ng to put water on the land. Whereas in a great many instances of irrigation that has been carried on for a good many years the ownership of the water is established. still, with the situation in Haiti with regard to land titles as it is to-day, the land title situation is linked up with an irrigation system. For instance, if you are going to put in an irr'gaton system, and then put a tax on the lands which are benefited by the irrigation, the question is who is going to pay the tax—who owns the land?

Mr. Howe. And that is a question on which there is uncertainty in Haiti?

Mr. Forrest. On which there is and always has been and will be until some system of land surveys can be put in, and the ownership of land established. The irrigation projects and the land title situation are linked up together, in my opinion.

Mr. Howe. In your opinion, what should be the main channels of expenditure of the funds of the Haitian Government?

Mr. Forrest. The object of investing any money in Haiti would be to get back as quickly as possible a return on the investment.

With the land situation as it is to-day, it is impractical to place a land tax in Haiti, therefore I think that the thing that would yield the quickest revenue to the country, and also clear up all of these other indefinite projects which are so necessary, would be the establishment of a proper system of land titles, which means of course, a Government survey, and, after that, the establishment of land titles; in other words, the establishment of a proper bureau of lands, as we had in the Philippines. The Torrens system has worked out extremely well in the Philippines, and I think it might work well in Haiti.

Mr. Howe. Then you think that the existence of land surveys and Government machinery and the bureaus for the administration of land titles would be an appropriate expenditure of Government funds?

Mr. Forrest. I believe so, and not only appropriate, but would tend also to clear up a great many of the difficulties which have to be met now.

Mr. Howe. What else would you spend Government money on?

Mr. Forrest. I should say that the second thing would be the proper educational progress of the country. I do not believe the country can progress as rapidly as it should, without having the educational system very much improved.

Mr. Howe. What visible results would you expect from a better education of the Haitians?

Mr. Forrest. The whole welfare of the people would be greatly benefited. It would result in the development of a middle class in Haiti, which I think we can not say we have at the present time. It would tend to harmonize the political situation. I think the benefits of education, of course, could be discussed at quite a length but not necessarily here.

Mr. Howe. But it would be a direct and important benefit to Haiti?

Mr. Forrest. It would be a direct and important benefit to the situation.

Mr. Howe. What else would you spend Government funds on?

Mr. Forrest. Haiti is decidelly an agricultural country, and the most important factor in the development of agriculture is the handling on an economic basis of the products of the country. Wherever you are going into an industry which deals with things in bulk. the cost of transportation is a very important item in the proper conduct of the business. It applies especially to sugar and to cotton, and I think practically everything Haiti would produce. I should, therefore, say that the ability to get the products to a market at the lowest cost would be the next thing to handle and consider, and therefore, that the proper development of the road system which would go through all of the agricultural districts of Haiti, would be the next most important thing, by opening up those districts and also increasing the security of those who are going into agriculture, and also improving the intelligence of the farmers of Haiti.

Mr. Howe. Then, from what you say, I would gather that not only private enterprise but the Government of Haiti now needs capital and financing; is that correct?

Mr. Forrest. That I consider to be most important.

Mr. Howe. And if that should be accomplished would you look for satisfactory progress and would you expect satisfactory progress along the lines of the development of the country and the proper development of Government institutions?

Mr. Forrest. I think it would be the first step in the satisfactory progress of both the Government and economic development.

Mr. Howe. Would you consider that the negotiation of a loan was one of the duties and obligations which the United States Government assumed when it entered into that treaty?

Mr. Forrest. I think that is implied in this convention without any doubt, and I know that the sentiment in Haiti, or the feeling in Haiti, was one of absolute confidence that as soon as this convention was signed they would be provided with the funds, because it says here, "The Republic of Haiti, desiring to remedy the present conditions of its revenues and finances."

The Chairman. Do you think that the American Government has been delinquent by reason of its delay in making this loan?

Mr. Forrest. I consider that the American Government has not lived up to the terms of this convention, as generally interpreted by the Haitian people.

The Chairman. Apart from the interpretation of the Haitian people, in your own judgment, do you think our Government, as a matter of policy, has erred in postponing until this time the negotiation of a loan?

Mr. Forrest. I think so.

The Chairman. Let me ask you further: The authorized issue is $40,000,000. It will take some $14,000,000, in round numbers, to pay the French debt, and that on very advantageous terms, I think, to satisfy the local claims and refund the internal debt. That will leave somewhere between $1,000,000 and $2,000,000 free for expenditure on public work in Haiti. Do you think that sum is adequate at this time?

Mr. Forrest. I should say it was pitiably inadequate.

The Chairman. Do you believe that even at the high cost of money the Government would have done better to borrow $5,000,000 more?

Mr. Forrest. I am confident that it would; yes.

The Chairman. I ask that because, at 6 per cent. which is the rate borne by the loan ultimately and permanently, apparently the market for the bonds stays around 85, and naturally the conservators of Haitian credit are indisposed to make great borrowings at this discount. Nevertheless, you believe that despite the discount, it would have been better to have borrowed $5,000,000 more, let us say, now, in order to carry out energetically the program of public works?

Mr. FORREST. Senator, I feel that anyone who would think that they should delay in the borrowing of $5,000,000 at the present time, even if they paid such a high rate as you say, could not have the proper confidence as to what that investment means in Haiti. In other words, if we consider that this loan means an investment in Haiti for the improvement of Haiti, the more money that is put in there up to a certain limit will bring back more return, because those of us who believe in Haiti——

The CHAIRMAN. Well, more money put in, and the sooner the better?

Mr. FORREST. The sooner the better, because those of us who believe in the future of Haiti believe that we would not invest capital in Haiti if we would only get 9 or 10 per cent out of it. We believe that the prospects for investment of capital in Haiti are far in excess of 10 per cent, and what applies to the investment of private capital in Haiti would also apply directly to the investment of public funds in Haiti.

Now, as I have just explained, the most important thing in Haiti at the present time is the settling of the land situation, and until that is done——

The CHAIRMAN. By that you mean the clarification of titles?

Mr. FORREST. Yes; and until that is done I do not think you can start any proper economic development of Haiti, and that will take a great deal more money than the Senator has said would be available right there, in my estimation.

Mr. HOWE. Well, how about the negotiation of a loan, or the settlement of land titles when the relations of this country in Haiti are, as you have called them, indefinite? Can you obtain that loan or settle your land titles as long as those relations are indefinite?

Mr. FORREST. I think that capital, ordinarily being extremely timid, would hesitate to invest in a country where the political program or policy, we will say, was in any way indefinite, and that it would be essential to obtaining the proper confidence of the people who have the capital that they should know what the political conditions are in the country in which that capital is invested.

Mr. HOWE. And what they are likely to be?

Mr. FORREST. And what they are likely to be.

Mr. HOWE. How far can you go in the development of the country by private capital, or in assisting the Haitian Government along progressive lines, or lines of progress, without the confidence of the Haitian people?

Mr. FORREST. I do not believe that any project can succeed in a country which has not the sympathy of the people of the country. I think that the sympathy which I have gotten myself from friends in Haiti can be easily obtained by the representatives of the United States, once the program of a political policy has been determined. I believe the Haitians will cooperate. I think that it is essential in any agricultural development of a country to have, further, more than cooperation, almost a partnership with the people of that country. I think that is essential, and I believe that can be done in Haiti.

Mr. HOWE. In other words, the agricultural development of Haiti would carry with it necessarily benefits to the Haitians?

Mr. FORREST. Yes; and I think that the Haitians, who are extremely sensitive now on account of what has happened since this convention was made—I think that their confidence could be obtained.

Mr. HOWE. By what steps?

Mr. FORREST. First, by a development of policy which would show that their interests are properly safeguarded, and by a general cooperation between those who go down into Haiti to invest their money and those——

The CHAIRMAN. Has our Government had any policy in Haiti since it went in there?

Mr. FORREST. I should say no; I think things have been allowed to drift.

The CHAIRMAN. Has there been any responsible American official to whom all Americans, either in the service of the Haitian Government or in the service of the Government of the United States, could be held responsible?

Mr. FORREST. No; there has not been, because the authority has been undefined as to the standing of treaty officials, and as to their standing in their relations with the Haitian Government. There has been a confusion of authority which has deprived those who are in Haiti of confidence as to just what the Government of Haiti was, and where the responsibility lay, a problem that we all know.

The CHAIRMAN. Let me ask you, Mr. Forrest, to consider again for a moment the problem of a loan. The treaty was proclaimed in May, 1915, and runs for a period of 10 years, and may be extended for a per'od of 10 years, so that it will expire automatically, unless further renewed, in 1936. The period for which the proposed loan of $40,000.000 is to be made is 30 years.

Mr. FORREST. So I understood; yes.

The CHAIRMAN. Therefore, the treaty will expire at the end of 15 years, although the loan runs for 30 years. Let me ask you if you find in the eighth article of the protocol, and especially in the following language, adequate security for the loan:

"And it is further agreed that the control by an officer or officers duly appointed by the President of Haiti, upon denomination of the President of the United States, for the collection and allocation of the hypothecated revenues will be provided for during the life of this loan, after the expiration of the aforesaid treaty, so as to make certain that adequate provision be made for the amortization and interest on the loan."

I ask that question because I am disposed to believe that the rate of interest borne by the loan and the ability of the underwriters to place the bonds turns largely upon the interpretation of that provis'on of the protocol?

Mr. FORREST. Well, I think you have answered the question yourself, Senator. I believe that if I was one of a syndicate which was going to take up this loan, that I would try to make the loan as good as possible.

The CHAIRMAN. Well, under that language, is it good enough?

Mr. FORREST. Well, I could not answer that question, because I am not sufficiently in touch with the investment market to know how the people would feel in taking that loan, under those conditions.

The CHAIRMAN. Let me ask the question in another way: Does the language imply to you that for the service of the external debt proposed to be created, the receivership under control of officers appointed by the President of the United States will continue until the service of the debt is complete, and the loan is paid?

Mr. FORREST. I should say that 15 years was too short a time.

The CHAIRMAN. That is not the question I am asking. I am asking if this means that the receivership will continue for a subsequent 15 years?

Mr. FORREST. I should say yes.

The CHAIRMAN. After the expiration of the treaty?

Mr. FORREST. Yes; I do not bel'eve that Haiti could recover into a proper condition in 15 years.

The CHAIRMAN. Do you believe that she is bound by the terms of the protocol, whether she recovers or not, to agree to the appointment of a rece'ver by the President of the United States?

Mr. FORREST. I should say that she was; yes.

Mr. HOWE. How much progress can be made until the loan is a fact?

Mr. FORREST. Under the present world conditions, I should say almost no progress.

Mr. HOWE. Can the loan be a fact until the uncerta'nty of the relations of this country and of Haiti is turned into as great a certainty as possible?

Mr. FORREST. Well, that depends on the conditions, the chances which those who are subscribing to the loan are willing to take. It is not possible for me to say whether people are going to buy those bonds under the present conditions or not, but there is no doubt that there would be more chance of it——

Mr. HOWE. The greater the certainty, the greater the chances of a loan?

Mr. FORREST. Yes.

Mr. HOWE. Is there anything more, Mr. Forrest, that you would like to add which you think the committee should hear from you?

Mr. FORREST. No; I think that as the committee is going to Haiti, they will perhaps absorb more information, or so much information that anything I might say now further would be superfluous, but I would be very glad to hold myself available for the committee on their return.

Mr. HOWE. Mr. Chairman, I have now called the last witness which the committee has in mind to call before its departure for Haiti, unless the plan can be materially changed, with the exception perhaps of a short time with Col. Williams to complete his cross-examination, and I therefore now propose to the committee that Capt. Angell be permitted to call his witnesses and conduct the examination of his own witnesses.

STATEMENT OF MR. MAX ZUCKERMAN, ROXBURY, MASS.

Mr. ANGELL. Will you state your name and residence, Mr. Zuckerman?

Mr. ZUCKERMAN. Max Zuckerman, 110 Crawford Street, Roxbury, Mass.

Mr. ANGELL. Have you served in the United States Marine Corps?

Mr. ZUCKERMAN. Yes.

Mr. ANGELL. Will you give us the dates of your service?

Mr. ZUCKERMAN. From July 6, 1915, up until, I believe, October, 1919.

Mr. ANGELL. In October, 1919, did you receive an honorable discharge from the Marine Corps?

Mr. ZUCKERMAN. I did.

Mr. ANGELL. Did you serve in Haiti while a member of the Marine Corps?

Mr. ZUCKERMAN. Yes.

Mr. ANGELL. Between what dates?

Mr. ZUCKERMAN. From the 7th of November, 1915, up until the 22d of October, 1918.

Mr. ANGELL. Where were you on duty with the Marine Corps between the date of your enlistment and the time you went to Haiti?

Mr. ZUCKERMAN. What is the question?

Mr. ANGELL. Where did you serve in the Marine Corps between the time of your enlistment and the time you went to Haiti?

Mr. ZUCKERMAN. I served at Norfolk, and then went to Haiti, Cape Haitien, Fort Liberte, and Ouanaminthe.

Mr. ANGELL. Where were you on duty after your return from Haiti?

Mr. ZUCKERMAN. Quantico, Philadelphia and Quantico.

Mr. ANGELL. Did you go overseas?

Mr. ZUCKERMAN. I did not.

Mr. ANGELL. With what units did you serve in Haiti?

Mr. ZUCKERMAN. The Fifteenth Company, and then was transferred to the headquarters detachment, Second Regiment, as acting sergeant major to Col. Gulich.

Mr. HOWE. Was that what you were during the rest of your time in Haiti?

Mr. ZUCKERMAN. I left Haiti as sergeant major and came back to Philadelphia, and then went to Quantico.

Mr. HOWE. And did you serve as sergeant major in the headquarters of the Second Regiment during that time?

Mr. ZUCKERMAN. Yes; I was acting sergeant major up until the time I was made sergeant major at Cape Haitien.

Mr. ANGELL. What other officers of the Marine Corps did you serve actively with and under in Haiti?

Mr. ZUCKERMAN. Capt. Upshur, Col. Gulich, Col. Hooker, Col. Wadleigh, Col. Bannon, Col. Bab—that is all I can remember.

Mr. ANGELL. Gen. Catlin, did you serve with?

Mr. ZUCKERMAN. No, sir.

Mr. ANGELL. Where did you go when you first landed in Haiti?

Mr. ZUCKERMAN. Fort Liberte.

Mr. ANGELL. What indications, if any, did you have on going to Fort Liberte of the general attitude of the Marine forces in Haiti toward the natives?

Mr. ZUCKERMAN. We came down on the *Prairie* and got aboard a motor boat, and as we got on the motor boat there were two or three natives, as I remember, and we got the impression that these were the men we had to contend with on the island.

Mr. ANGELL. What impression were you given?

Mr. ZUCKERMAN. Well, "these are the sons of bitches that you would have to contend with while you are down here."

Mr. ANGELL. Who made that remark, if you can remember?

Mr. ZUCKERMAN. The man in charge.

Mr. ANGELL. Was that an officer?

Mr. ZUCKERMAN. Yes; he was an officer.

Mr. ANGELL. A Marine officer?

Mr. ZUCKERMAN. Yes.

Mr. ANGELL. You went to Fort Liberte first?

Mr. ZUCKERMAN. Yes.

Mr. ANGELL. What was the nature of your duties there?

Mr. ZUCKERMAN. I was private, attached to the Fifteenth Company.

Mr. ANGELL. What was the nature of your duties?

Mr. Zuckerman. Hiking details, guard duty, etc.

Mr. Angell. How long were you on duty at Fort Liberte?

Mr. Zuckerman. About five months, I believe; four or five months.

Mr. Angell. Then where did you go?

Mr. Zuckerman. Then I was assigned to headquarters, and went to Ouanaminthe as acting sergeant major for Col. Gulich.

Mr. Angell. How long were you at Ouanaminthe?

Mr. Zuckerman. I was at Ouanaminthe for about a year, I guess.

Mr. Angell. Then where were you transferred to?

Mr. Zuckerman. Back to Cape Haitien.

Mr. Angell. In what capacity were you there?

Mr. Zuckerman. As acting sergeant major of the regiment.

Mr. Angell. Did you remain at Cape Haitien the rest of your time?

Mr. Zuckerman. Until I was ordered back to the United States.

Mr. Angell. Did you ever serve in the gendarmerie?

Mr. Zuckerman. I did.

Mr. Angell. Where?

Mr. Zuckerman. Ouanaminthe.

Mr. Angell. In what capacity?

Mr. Zuckerman. Just detached from the Marine Corps to serve with the gendarmerie.

Mr. Angell. Were you an officer in the gendarmerie?

Mr. Zuckerman. No; I was not.

Mr. Angell. How long were you at Ouanaminthe in the gendarmerie?

Mr. Zuckerman. About seven months.

Mr. Angell. Did you come in frequent contact with the natives in and around Ouanaminthe?

Mr. Zuckerman. I did.

Mr. Angell. While you were serving in the gendarmerie at Ouanaminthe were there native prisoners brought in from time to time?

Mr. Zuckerman. There was.

Mr. Angell. What was the general attitude of our forces at Ouanaminthe toward the natives and how were they treated?

Mr. Zuckerman. Well, it was an individual attitude. As a unit they were treated fair, but it was the individual attitude of the different men who were bringing the prisoners in. They were generally grilled. There was a third degree. We brought them into the gendarmerie headquarters. The gendarmerie would take their prisoners to the gendarmerie headquarters and the marines would take theirs to the marine headquarters, and they were questioned there by the captain in charge of the gendarmerie—put through a third degree—in order to derive answers from them. They had two different treatments there. One was to gain information from them by beating them with just—I can not remember what it was, but it was a long thing filled with sand—and a gendarmerie would stay there, and if he would not answer just so he would let him have it. Another one was this: They had a stanchion there built about 6 feet over the ground, and they just strung a rope around him and tied him there so that his toes would just touch the ground, and if he would not answer the question he would pull the rope.

Mr. Angell. Who were those prisoners?

Mr. Zuckerman. Brought in by the gendarmeries.

Mr. Angell. Why were they brought in? Were they Cacos in active rebellion?

Mr. Zuckerman. They were brought in to get information as to where the Cacos were.

Mr. Angell. How often did you see these methods of treatment of prisoners which you just described?

Mr. Zuckerman. About twice a week.

Mr. Angell. Over a period of what length of time?

Mr. Zuckerman. During my period of duty with the gendarmerie. I just do not know how long it was. It was five, six, or seven months—something like that.

Mr. Angell. Was the information obtained from these men through an interperter or through direct questioning by the officers?

Mr. Zuckerman. Through an interpreter.

Mr. Angell. Were you yourself actually present to see these methods of treatment?

Mr. Zuckerman. Yes.

Mr. ANGELL. Did you ever see yourself or know of your own personal knowledge of any instances of shooting of prisoners?

Mr. ZUCKERMAN. No.

Mr. ANGELL. Did you go out on patrol duty or hikes in active operations against the natives, the Cacos?

Mr. ZUCKERMAN. I have often gone out on h kes, but was never jumped by any of them.

Mr. ANGELL. On these hikes did your detachment take active operations against the natives?

Mr. ZUCKERMAN. We did.

Mr. ANGELL. What was the nature of those operations?

Mr. ZUCKERMAN. Well, on several hikes out of Ouanaminthe we fired at several parties out in the fields supposed to be Cacos.

Mr. ANGELL. What were those parties you refer to doing?

Mr. ZUCKERMAN. They were out in the fields there a distance of about a thousand yards, I should say.

Mr. ANGELL. And doing what?

Mr. ZUCKERMAN. And apparently it was a large plantation there. On two distinct occasions there was a party of three or four that were fired at, and on another occasion. just coming over the top of Mount Capitan, we fired at a party.

Mr. ANGELL. What were these various parties doing at the time? Were they engaged in operations against your detachment?

Mr. ZUCKERMAN. No.

Mr. ANGELL. Were they working on a plantation, or what were they doing?

Mr. ZUCKERMAN. Well, they were quite a distance away. We could not tell just what they were doing. They appeared to be working on the plantation.

Mr. ANGELL. Do you know whether your firing at them resulted in hitting them?

Mr. ZUCKERMAN. I really could not say.

Mr. ANGELL. You could not tell?

Mr. ZUCKERMAN. No.

Mr. ANGELL. Was there or was there not common talk among the marines of shooting prisoners, referred to as bumping them off?

Mr. ZUCKERMAN. There was by a certain gendarme lieutenant.

Mr. ANGELL. Who was he?

Mr. ZUCKERMAN. Lavoie.

Mr. ANGELL. Lavoie?

Mr. ZUCKERMAN. Ernest Lavoie.

Mr. ANGELL. Did you know him personally?

Mr. ZUCKERMAN. I did.

Mr. ANGELL. Where have you seen him, under what circumstances?

Mr. ZUCKERMAN. Well, I used to see him at Cape Haitien quite often. He used to come in there. I believe he was stationed at Le Trou, in charge of the district at Le Trou.

Mr. ANGELL. Is Le Trou near Hinche?

Mr. ZUCKERMAN. It is quite a distance from Hinche. They operated from Le Trou up through Hinche. That was before they put a gendarme post at Hinche.

Mr. ANGELL. What conversation did you have with Lavoie along those lines?

Mr. ZUCKERMAN. We were all at the French Club one night, a party of five or six.

Mr. ANGELL. This was at Cape Haitien?

Mr. ZUCKERMAN. This was at Cape Haitien; and he came in and told us about bumping off a magistrat, I believe; that he finally caught him and bumped him off.

Mr. ANGELL. Did he give any particulars of this incident?

Mr. ZUCKERMAN. No; he just happened to pass that remark.

Mr. ANGELL. Can you fix the approximate date of this statement by Lavoie?

Mr. ZUCKERMAN. It was either the latter part of 1917 or in 1918; I just can not remember; but I remember distinctly his coming down to the French Club on this night. He drove in there with his horse and told us this story.

Mr. ANGELL. Did you ever see the corvee in operation?

Mr. ZUCKERMAN. I seen two corvee camps, and I saw them working on the roads.

Mr. ANGELL. Where were these camps?

Mr. ZUCKERMAN. One of the roads was from Cape Haitien to Ouanaminthe and one of the roads from Cape Haitien to Port au Prince.

Mr. ANGELL. How far, approximately, from Cape Haitien were these two camps?

Mr. ZUCKERMAN. One of them was about 12 or 15 miles and the other one was about 7 or 8 miles. They worked on the roads, and while building those roads they helped build the road from Cape Haitien to——

Mr. ANGELL. Will you describe these camps as nearly as you can remember them?

Mr. ZUCKERMAN. In one camp on the road to Ouanaminthe they had them quartered in these ordinary Haitian huts, and in the other one they had a shed about the length of this building, and barb wired off.

Mr. ANGELL. When you say "barb wired off," how do you mean—surrounded by barbed wire?

Mr. ZUCKERMAN. Just the front of it was barbed wired, not the back of it. The back of it was a wooden background and the front of it was barb wired.

Mr. ANGELL. Did you see the gangs actually at work on the roads?

Mr. ZUCKERMAN. I believe I did; yes.

Mr. ANGELL. Do you know whether or not you saw the gangs?

Mr. ZUCKERMAN. I believe they were working on the road there building the road—out on the road to Port au Prince. They were building the road there to transport logwood from the interior, and I believe the corvee system built that road coming out to the Plain du Nord, I believe it was.

Mr. ANGELL. Who were in charge of these men you saw working on this road?

Mr. ZUCKERMAN. Gendarmes.

Mr. ANGELL. Were they armed or not?

Mr. ZUCKERMAN. They had a gendarme guard there.

Mr. ANGELL. Were they armed?

Mr. ZUCKERMAN. Yes.

Mr. ANGELL. How many were in these gangs?

Mr. ZUCKERMAN. I believe 30 or 40; something like that.

Mr. ANGELL. Each gang?

Mr. ZUCKERMAN. No; that is the crowd that I saw working, about 30 of them.

Mr. ANGELL. What was the general attitude of the enlisted personnel and the officers of the Marine Corps toward the Haitians?

Mr. ZUCKERMAN. Well, among the enlisted personnel it was an individual attitude. Some of them had no use for the natives and others got along fine with them.

Mr. ANGELL. What was the attitude of the natives toward the marines and the occupation?

Mr. ZUCKERMAN. It varied. When they first went down there it appeared to be all right, but kind of went after we were there a while.

Mr. ANGELL. What did it become after you were there a while?

Mr. ZUCKERMAN. They got so they did not like us.

Mr. ANGELL. Do you know why there was that change in feeling?

Mr. ZUCKERMAN. Well, as I say, it was individual. The marines would go out and raise hell with them, and it got to be that they would take the other side of the street when they would see a marine coming.

Mr. ANGELL. Will you specify a little more what you mean when you say the marines would go out and raise hell with them?

Mr. ZUCKERMAN. They would go out and break up their furniture in their houses and beat them up.

Mr. ANGELL. Did you see such instances?

Mr. ZUCKERMAN. No; but several of them were tried by court-martial. That is how I know that.

Mr. ANGELL. Where were these courts-martial held?

Mr. ZUCKERMAN. At Cape Haitien.

Mr. ANGELL. How did you know about these courts-martial?

Mr. ZUCKERMAN. I was sergeant major, and drew the specifications.

Mr. ANGELL. Were there convictions in some of these cases?

Mr. ZUCKERMAN. There were.

Mr. ANGELL. Why did you get out of the gendarmerie?

Mr. ZUCKERMAN. Well, I requested a transfer to Cape Haitien, and I was ordered to put a priest under arrest.

Mr. ANGELL. Where?

Mr. ZUCKERMAN. At Ouanaminthe.

Mr. ANGELL. Ordered by whom?

Mr. ZUCKERMAN. By a captain of the Marine Corps in charge of the gendarmerie.

Mr. ANGELL. At Ouanaminthe?

Mr. ZUCKERMAN. At Ouanaminthe. I was ordered to put this priest under arrest, and there was some stir coming up about it, and when this thing came up I requested to be transferred back to the Marine Corps headquarters.

Mr. ANGELL. Why did you request to be transferred back?

Mr. ZUCKERMAN. I thought some investigation was coming out of it, and I wanted to get back to duty in headquarters; I did not want to be on duty with the gendarmerie.

Mr. ANGELL. Why?

Mr. ZUCKERMAN. Well, I did not like the doings down there at Ouanaminthe; I did not like the way things were carried out down there; and I wanted to get back to the Marine Corps.

Mr. ANGELL. When you say "doings," what do you mean by doings?

Mr. ZUCKERMAN. I saw there was going to be some investigation of some sort coming out of the arrest of this priest, and I did not want to get mixed in with it.

Mr. ANGELL. Tell us about the arrest of that priest?

Mr. ZUCKERMAN. I was sent over to place a priest under arrest, with five gendarmes.

Mr. ANGELL. That was at Ouanaminthe?

Mr. ZUCKERMAN. That was at Ouanaminthe.

Mr. ANGELL. Can you fix the date approximately?

Mr. ZUCKERMAN. No; I can not.

Mr. ANGELL. During what year?

Mr. ZUCKERMAN. 1917.

Mr. ANGELL. In 1917?

Mr. ZUCKERMAN. Yes; I was sent to place this priest under arrest.

Mr. ANGELL. On what ground, do you know?

Mr. ZUCKERMAN. Well, this priest came over to draw his monthly pay, or weekly pay, which was disbursed out of the gendarmerie funds, or some sort of funds, and he came over to get his money and had some kind of a row with this captain, and the captain ordered him out of the office and sent me over to place him under arrest.

Mr. ANGELL. Did you place him under arrest?

Mr. ZUCKERMAN. Just as I got to the door I was called back, and then I believe he sent two gendarmes over there to place him under arrest.

Mr. ANGELL. You were called back by whom, the captain?

Mr. ZUCKERMAN. Yes.

Mr. ANGELL. So you did not place the priest under arrest?

Mr. ZUCKERMAN. No.

Mr. ANGELL. Was the priest placed under arrest afterwards?

Mr. ZUCKERMAN. I believe he was.

Mr. ANGELL. Do you know whether he was charged with any offense?

Mr. ZUCKERMAN. I really do not know. There was a radiogram that came from Port au Prince to release him immediately.

Mr. ANGELL. Did you see the radiogram?

Mr. ZUCKERMAN. No; I just heard there was a radiogram came from Port au Prince to release him.

Mr. ANGELL. Was he released?

Mr. ZUCKERMAN. He was.

Mr. ANGELL. It was shortly after that you requested a transfer?

Mr. ZUCKERMAN. Yes, sir .

Mr. ANGELL. And you were transferred back to Cape Haitien?

Mr. ZUCKERMAN. Cape Haitien.

Mr. ANGELL. When you went back to Cape Haitien what was the nature of your duties as sergeant major?

Mr. ZUCKERMAN. I was acting sergeant major to Gen. Gulich.

Mr. ANGELL. What did you do as sergeant major there?

Mr. ZUCKERMAN. Office duty.

Mr. ANGELL. Tell us a little about the nature of those duties?

Mr. ZUCKERMAN. Drawing specifications for court-martials, taking care of all morning reports, binding them, taking care of incoming radiograms, and I was also acting sergeant of the headquarters detachment, sometimes pay rolls and muster rolls.

Mr. ANGELL. Did you have anything to do with provost courts?

Mr. ZUCKERMAN. Later on I was made clerk to the provost court.

Mr. ANGELL. About what time?

Mr. ZUCKERMAN. That was the latter part of 1917, I believe, that I was made clerk to the provost court under Col. Hopkins and Capt. Price.

Mr. ANGELL. How long were you acting as clerk of the provost court?

Mr. ZUCKERMAN. About three or four months.

Mr. ANGELL. This was in the latter part of 1917 or in 1918?

Mr. ZUCKERMAN. During the latter part of 1917 and into 1918.

Mr. ANGELL. Did you have anything to do with the Haitian funds at Cape Haitien?

Mr. ZUCKERMAN. I was bookkeeper for the disbursement of public work funds.

Mr. ANGELL. Where did these funds come from?

Mr. ZUCKERMAN. Port au Prince. They were cabled to us monthly—allotted to us for certain purposes each month.

Mr. ANGELL. For what purposes were they expended?

Mr. ZUCKERMAN. Public work—road work.

Mr. ANGELL. Anything else?

Mr. ZUCKERMAN. That is all I can remember, just road work, I believe.

Mr. ANGELL. Did the personnel of the Marine Corps draw extra pay while you were on duty at Cape Haitien?

Mr. ZUCKERMAN. Men assigned to road work, I believe, drew a dollar a day, 30 days a month.

Mr. ANGELL. Was that in addition to their regular pay as marines?

Mr. ZUCKERMAN. That was in addition to their regular pay as marines.

Mr. ANGELL. From what source were those payments made, if you know?

Mr. ZUCKERMAN. I believe they were made from the public works office. The public works officer disbursed those funds.

Mr. ANGELL. Did you have anything to do with the vouchers for such payments?

Mr. ZUCKERMAN. Not with the individual vouchers. We used to draw the vouchers in bulk. I drew the vouchers, and they were signed by the commanding officer, and then they were taken down to the collector of customs and were turned over to the public works officer—whoever was public works officer of the town.

Mr. ANGELL. Did you yourself draw extra pay at any time?

Mr. ZUCKERMAN. As clerk of the provost court.

Mr. ANGELL. How much?

Mr. ZUCKERMAN. I believe it was $25 a month.

Mr. ANGELL. From what source was this $25 a month derived?

Mr. ZUCKERMAN. From the fines.

Mr. ANGELL. From the fines paid?

Mr. ZUCKERMAN. Paid by the prisoners.

Mr. ANGELL. Were they native prisoners entirely?

Mr. ZUCKERMAN. Yes. And I drew, I believe, $12.50 or $25 a month for handling the books for the Haitian Government.

Mr. ANGELL. Do you know the purposes for which the funds derived from fines paid to the provost court were used?

Mr. ZUCKERMAN. I believe there was some office furniture from time to time bought from the funds, and stationery, etc.

Mr. ANGELL. What other purposes were these funds derived from fines used for, if you know?

Mr. ZUCKERMAN. I believe they turned some over to the sisterhood there.

Mr. ANGELL. Will you tell us about the operation of the provost courts?

Mr. ZUCKERMAN. In what respect?

Mr. ANGELL. Well, what jurisdiction they exercised, what kinds of offenses were tried before them?

Mr. ZUCKERMAN. Well, the offenses were mostly thefts.

Mr. ANGELL. Thefts by natives?

Mr. ZUCKERMAN. By natives.

Mr. ANGELL. By natives of articles from themselves or the marines, or both?

Mr. ZUCKERMAN. Both from the marines and from themselves.

Mr. ANGELL. What were the sentences or fines imposed?

Mr. ZUCKERMAN. Well, the fines used to run from 25 gourdes on up, and the sentences were from six months on up to about two years.

Mr. ANGELL. Can you give us specific instances of specific fines imposed or sentences imposed for specific offenses?

Mr. ZUCKERMAN. Well, I just can not remember the names of any cases, but there were—I can remember the instance of a native being sentenced to 18 months for the theft of some Marine Corps clothing from some marine attached to one of the companies up there.

Mr. ANGELL. Was it more common to impose fines or to impose sentences?

Mr. ZUCKERMAN. Well, just about evenly balanced. For theft, I believe they were sentenced; for such offenses as carrying arms they were fined.

Mr. ANGELL. Did the average amount of the fines imposed vary from time to time?

Mr. ZUCKERMAN. Yes; they did.

Mr. ANGELL. Under what circumstances, if you know?

Mr. ZUCKERMAN. That I can not say, but they varied from time to time.

Mr. ANGELL. Who sat on the provost courts?

Mr. ZUCKERMAN. An officer appointed by the commanding officer at the post was appointed provost judge, and he decided the cases.

Mr. ANGELL. The court, then, was composed of a single judge?

Mr. ZUCKERMAN. A single judge.

Mr. ANGELL. Tell us briefly what the procedure in those cases was?

Mr. ZUCKERMAN. They were brought in, and the witnesses were brought there and then questioned through an interpreter.

Mr. ANGELL. Were there written charges?

Mr. ZUCKERMAN. We had a blank form that we furnished the brigade commander a copy of.

Mr. ANGELL. Were the charges on which a man was tried written out in advance of the trial?

Mr. ZUCKERMAN. Oral.

Mr. ANGELL. The charges presented were oral?

Mr. ZUCKERMAN. Yes.

Mr. ANGELL. You say the man was brought in before the judge?

Mr. ZUCKERMAN. Yes.

Mr. ANGELL. How was the trial conducted?

Mr. ZUCKERMAN. Well, the prosecuting witness would tell his side of the story, and then the interpreter would explain it to this native and ask him what he had to say; and if the provost marshal thought he was guilty, he would adjudge sentence.

Mr. ANGELL. Was there any review of these sentences?

Mr. ZUCKERMAN. They were reviewed by the commanding officer and then forwarded to the brigade commander.

Mr. ANGELL. Did the sentence go into effect immediately upon pronouncement by the presiding judge?

Mr. ZUCKERMAN. I believe they had to be approved by the commanding officer.

Mr. ANGELL. The local commanding officer?

Mr. ZUCKERMAN. Yes; either him or the brigade commander; I am not just sure.

Mr. ANGELL. What happened to the man in the meantime, if he was sentenced?

Mr. ZUCKERMAN. He was held at the civil prison.

Mr. ANGELL. What was the condition of the prison?

Mr. ZUCKERMAN. Very good.

Mr. ANGELL. At that time?

Mr. ZUCKERMAN. The prison was very, very good.

Mr. ANGELL. Was the condition sanitary?

Mr. ZUCKERMAN. Very sanitary.

Mr. ANGELL. Was the civil prison maintained by and kept in order by the marines or gendarmerie?

Mr. ZUCKERMAN. The gendarmerie.

Mr. ANGELL. Under the marine officers?

Mr. ZUCKERMAN. Under marines assigned from the Marine Corps—gendarmerie officers.

Mr. ANGELL. Would you care to make any comment, based on your experience, on the relative qualifications of marine officers and men for duty in Haiti under these conditions between 1915 and the latter part of your tour of duty in 1918?

Mr. ZUCKERMAN. Well, as I say, as a unit they done very good work down there, but it was the individual feeling amongst the men. As a unit, they worked together, but the men got out, and it was just the individual feeling that they had no use for the natives. It was not all of them; it was a few here and a few there. · But, as a unit, the work was generally very good down there.

Mr. ANGELL. Is there anything else you would care to say about the relations of the military forces and the natives?

Mr. ZUCKERMAN. No.

Mr. ANGELL. Did you see service in south Haiti at all?

Mr. ZUCKERMAN. No, sir.

Mr. ANGELL. You were in the north during your entire three years?

Mr. ZUCKERMAN. Yes, sir.

Mr. HOWE. In the provost courts was there any disposition on the part of the provost judge to fine the marines that were convicted before him less than the natives?

Mr. ZUCKERMAN. There were no marines convicted before the provost judge.

Mr. HOWE. I thought your statement was that they tried cases of thefts by marines from marines?

Mr. ZUCKERMAN. No; it was natives who were tried for thefts, for stealing from the marines.

Mr. HOWE. Were there no written charges against the defendants there in the provost courts in any cases whatsoever?

Mr. ZUCKERMAN. There was. We used to make a written report to the brigade commander telling him that so and so was tried for so and so, that John Henry was tried for carrying arms, and sentenced as stated, but during my tour as clerk of the provost court we never had any written charges.

Mr. HOWE. You mean there was no written charge presented to the provost judge, or drawn up by the provost judge during the trial?

Mr. ZUCKERMAN. No, sir.

Mr. HOWE. Even in the cases which drew sentences of two years?

Mr. ZUCKERMAN. We just had a blank form, and at the end of the trial we would write the charge in on the typewriter, whatever the charge was, and then the sentence, a regular blank form.

Mr. HOWE. Was the defendant ever informed before sentence what the charge was against him?

Mr. ZUCKERMAN. Yes, sir.

Mr. HOWE. That was oral?

Mr. ZUCKERMAN. Yes, sir.

Mr. HOWE. But not in writing?

Mr. ZUCKERMAN. No, sir. As far as I can remember, we just had this blank form, and the man's name was put on there, his age and occupation, and then there was a space for the charge, and we just write the charge in on the typewriter.

Mr. HOWE. Did you ever know of any sentences by the provost court of more than two years?

Mr. ZUCKERMAN. Yes; I believe there was one of 5, 10, and 15.

Mr. HOWE. You knew of those, did you?

Mr. ZUCKERMAN. Yes.

Mr. HOWE. Were they imposed by the court of which you were clerk?

Mr. ZUCKERMAN. I believe there was one of five imposed by the court of which I was clerk, and those over five—there were commissioned officers at all of the provost courts.

Mr. HOWE. Then was it your understanding that the provost court which had only one marine officer as judge could not impose a sentence of more than five years?

Mr. ZUCKERMAN. That I could not say.

Mr. HOWE. Were there some provost courts that had more than one officer sitting as judge at the same time?

Mr. ZUCKERMAN. No, sir; only at the time, I believe, they tried these men down there for carrying arms there were three marine officers that sat on that provost court, and they were sentenced for 15 years, if I remember.

Mr. HOWE. Was that a provost court or a military commission?

Mr. ZUCKERMAN. I believe it was a provost court. It may have been a military commission. That was after I was relieved as provost clerk.

Mr. HOWE. So you do not know anything about that of your own knowledge?

Mr. ZUCKERMAN. No, sir.

Mr. HOWE. But just what you heard?

Mr. ZUCKERMAN. Yes, sir.

Senator ODDIE. Do you know whether many or any of the prisoners brought before the provost court could read or write?

Mr. ZUCKERMAN. Nine-tenths of them could not. They did not know their own age. I have never yet seen any of them that could read or write.

Mr. HOWE. What books did you handle for the Haitian Government?

Mr. ZUCKERMAN. I handled the public-works books, disbursing the funds. They allotted so much funds for Port au Prince, and I kept the record as to whom they went to.

Mr. HOWE. Did you get a regular payment for keeping those books?

Mr. ZUCKERMAN. Yes, sir.

Mr. HOWE. Under whose directions did you keep those books?

Mr. ZUCKERMAN. The commanding officer.

Mr. HOWE. The colonel?

Mr. ZUCKERMAN. Yes, sir. They had a Haitian keeping them, and we were paying the Haitian, I believe, $60 a month, and I was ordered to take care of them, and I believe I got $12.50 or $25 a month for taking care of them.

Mr. HOWE. Did you get that in a different voucher than your regular pay roll?

Mr. ZUCKERMAN. Yes, sir; I got that on a voucher, and that was taken down to the collector of customs or to the bank, I think, and I then cashed it in and made a voucher under my own name for it.

Mr. HOWE. You drew that up?

Mr. ZUCKERMAN. Yes, sir.

Mr. HOWE. Who signed it?

Mr. ZUCKERMAN. The commanding officer had to sign it.

Mr. HOWE. Whence came your compensation as clerk of the provost court? Did you get that on your pay roll?

Mr. ZUCKERMAN. No, sir.

Mr. HOWE. Who signed the voucher there?

Mr. ZUCKERMAN. There was no voucher; I just got that from the provost marshal.

Mr. HOWE. In cash?

Mr. ZUCKERMAN. Yes.

Mr. HOWE. As clerk of the provost court did you keep any account of fines?

Mr. ZUCKERMAN. No, sir; the provost marshal kept that himself. All I did was to draw the records for the provost court.

Mr. HOWE. Do you know whether or not the provost court itself kept a record of fines imposed?

Mr. ZUCKERMAN. I do not.

Mr. HOWE. Do you know what disposition was made of the fines which it collected?

Mr. ZUCKERMAN. Well, it purchased stationery and furniture and turned some over to the sisterhood there.

Mr. HOWE. Do you know if there was a bank account opened with the money from fines?

Mr. ZUCKERMAN. I believe there was; yes, sir.

Mr. HOWE. Do you know whether or not that was the disposition made of the money collected in fines? When the money was collected by the provost court, what was done with it—the money?

Mr. ZUCKERMAN. Well, they bought furniture, and turned some over to the sisterhood, and I drew a salary from it.

Mr. HOWE. Yes; but where was the money kept?

Mr. ZUCKERMAN. I believe it was kept at the Haitian National Bank there, and then they turned some over——

Mr. HOWE. Do you know whether or not in connection with the account in the Haitian National Bank books were kept?

Mr. ZUCKERMAN. I believe there was; yes, sir.

Mr. HOWE. Do you know who kept them?

Mr. ZUCKERMAN. The provost marshal.

Mr. HOWE. Himself?

Mr. ZUCKERMAN. Yes, sir.

Mr. HOWE. Then, your $25 a month came to you in the form of a check drawn against that bank account?

Mr. ZUCKERMAN. No; I believe the provost marshal used to pay me personally $25 a month, and I would sign a receipt and attach it to the records in the files.

Mr. HOWE. Do you know whether he, first of all, cashed a check and made an entry of that in his books?

Mr. ZUCKERMAN. Yes; that was done; yes, sir.

Mr. HOWE. What was done?

Mr. ZUCKERMAN. There was a check drawn for my salary, and was cashed. and it was turned over to me.

Mr. HOWE. But you did not cash the check yourself?

Mr. ZUCKERMAN. No, sir.

Mr. HOWE. Do you know who signed that check? ·

Mr. ZUCKERMAN. The provost marshal.

Mr. HOWE. Do you know that he did have, in fact, a check book?

Mr. ZUCKERMAN. I believe it was a check book. They had an account with the Haitian National Bank, and every month they drew just so much money, and at the end of the month I drew mine—every two weeks—$12.50 every two weeks.

Mr. HOWE. Were the only funds in that bank account fines imposed by the provost court?

Mr. ZUCKERMAN. Yes, sir.

Mr. HOWE. And the provost judge had the right to expend the money, did he, through checks?

Mr. ZUCKERMAN. That I could not say, but he did expend it.

Mr. HOWE. That is what I mean—the same person that deposited the money in the bank took it out?

Mr. ZUCKERMAN. Yes, sir.

Mr. HOWE. And the person who deposited the money in the bank was the provost judge himself?

Mr. ZUCKERMAN. Yes, sir.

Mr. HOWE. Were these marines who were doing road work on the public roads paid a dollar a day extra there?

Mr. ZUCKERMAN. By the public-works officer.

Mr. HOWE. By the public works officer?

Mr. ZUCKERMAN. Yes.

Mr. HOWE. How often were they paid—once a month or once a day?

Mr. ZUCKERMAN. I believe once a month.

Mr. HOWE. In what form?

Mr. ZUCKERMAN. That I could not say.

Mr. HOWE. How do you know they were paid a dollar a day?

Mr. ZUCKERMAN. By what they told me.

Mr. HOWE. Did you ever see them paid?

Mr. ZUCKERMAN. No, sir; we had nothing to do with that.

Mr. HOWE. You do not know. Were they in the gendarmerie?

Mr. ZUCKERMAN. No, sir; they were just paid from the Marine Corps—doing duty with the public-works officer.

Mr. HOWE. Do you know the name of anyone who received a dollar a day?

Mr. ZUCKERMAN. Well, I believe there was a Sergt. Baker who was in charge of the public-works force.

Mr. HOWE. Did Sergt. Baker ever tell you he received a dollar a day?

Mr. ZUCKERMAN. Yes, sir.

Mr. HOWE. Did he tell you from whom he received it?

Mr. ZUCKERMAN. Yes, sir.

Mr. HOWE. Whom did he say he received it from?

Mr. ZUCKERMAN. From the public works officer.

Mr. HOWE. And in what form did he receive it, by check or cash?

Mr. ZUCKERMAN. That I can not say. He said he was paid monthly. I believe he was paid more than a dollar a day; I can not remember the exact amount. He sid he was drawing extra pay from the public works officer.

Mr. HOWE. How much extra pay?

Mr. ZUCKERMAN. That I could not say; I do not remember exactly.

Mr. HOWE. You had nothing to do with the payment on these public works?

Mr. ZUCKERMAN. No, sir. All we done, we drew a voucher on this and turned the voucher over to the public works officer.

Mr. HOWE. Do you know how that voucher was made up? Was there any part of that money intended for wages?

Mr. ZUCKERMAN. The voucher was made in this way: I believe there was class A, B, and C, and A was public works, B was sanitation, etc., and a voucher was drawn under class C, so much money was drawn under class A, and the voucher and all was turned over to the public works officer. That was the last we had to do with it.

Mr. HOWE. Did the public works officer account for that money?

Mr. ZUCKERMAN. Not to us; no, sir.

Mr. HOWE. To whom did he account?

Mr. Zuckerman. I do not know anything about it, sir. We used to send a rad.ogram to Port au Prince each month, requesting so much money to be allotted to us, and it was allotted to us by radiogram.

Mr. Howe. How did you fix the amount?

Mr. Zuckerman. By estimates sent in from the different posts.

Mr. Howe. Did they itemize their estimates?

Mr. Zuckerman. Yes.

Mr. Howe. In those items was any amount estimated as wages for the marine corps?

Mr. Zuckerman. They itemized them in this way, sir: Sanitation, $500; road work, $1,000; etc.

Mr. Howe. And it did not state there that $1,000 was for material or wages?

Mr. Zuckerman. In some instances when they wanted some extra material they quoted " extra material," whatever the material was they needed, but no wages were paid, I do not believe.

Mr. Howe. Sergt. Baker never told you whether or not he signed a receipt for that, did he?

Mr. Zuckerman. No, sir; he never did.

Mr. Howe. Do you know where Sergt. Baker is now?

Mr. Zuckerman. No, sir.

Mr. Howe. Do you know Sergt. Baker's first name?

Mr. Zuckerman. No; I just can not think of it.

Mr. Howe. Now, did any other marine tell you that he was being paid extra for road work?

Mr. Zuckerman. Not for road work, but there were marines there——

Mr. Howe. I mean on road work. Is Sergt. Baker the only one?

Mr. Zuckerman. Yes; I believe that is the only one I came in contact with at Cape Haitien.

Mr. Howe. How do you know that the funds, the amount of the funds in the provost court were expended for furniture and stationery?

Mr. Zuckerman. I was there at the time they bought them. I went out and bought stationery and charged it to the provost marshal, by direction of the provost marshal. I went out and purchased stationery and charged it to the provost marshal.

Mr. Howe. But how do you know he paid for that stationery and furniture from funds derived from fines?

Mr. Zuckerman. That I do not know, though I went out and charged them. I would go out and buy stuff and charge it to the provost marshal.

Mr. Howe. But you do not know how he paid for it?

Mr. Zuckerman. No, sir.

Mr. Howe. You did not have anything to do with keeping his books?

Mr. Zuckerman. No, sir.

Mr. Howe. Then do you know, or do you not know, whether or not furniture and stationery was paid for by him from the fines?

Mr. Zuckerman. That was just from what I heard and what I seen done; from what I seen bought. I never seen any bills paid.

Mr. Howe. Is it not so that you just assumed, that that was your guess, that furniture charged to the provost court, the provost court paid for from fines?

Mr. Zuckerman. It was not exactly a guess; I was sent out by the provost marshal, who told me to charge the furniture to the provost marshal, and I assumed that it was paid for from the provost marshal's funds.

Mr. Howe. From the fines?

Mr. Zuckerman. Yes, sir.

Mr. Howe. And that was just your guess?

Mr. Zuckerman. Yes, sir. That was what I knew from the provost marshal, that he used to pay it from the provost marshal's funds.

Mr. Howe. Who told you that?

Mr. Zuckerman. He would say, " Charge it to the provost marshal." I have gone out and bought stationery, and he would say, " Go out and charge it to the provost marshal's account."

Mr. Howe. Did you, before doing that, make some investigation to find out how much of a balance the provost court had at the bank?

Mr. Zuckerman. Yes, sir; he would say occasionally to look up and see what the balance was, and I would say, " You have got so much."

Mr. Howe. Where would he look to find out how much balance there was?

Mr. Zuckerman. He had an account; he kept an account of his own.

Mr. Howe. Did you see those books, then?

Mr. ZUCKERMAN. Yes; he kept a regular account of his own.
Mr. HOWE. As provost judge?
Mr. ZUCKERMAN. As provost judge.
Mr. HOWE. You have seen those books?
Mr. ZUCKERMAN. Yes, sir.
Mr. HOWE. You saw those books?
Mr. ZUCKERMAN. Yes, sir; he kept a regular account.
Mr. HOWE. You saw them?
Mr. ZUCKERMAN. Yes, sir.
Mr. HOWE. Did you help him to keep those books?
Mr. ZUCKERMAN. No, sir; I did not; I had charge of the records of the cases tried.
Mr. HOWE. Do you know how he paid for the stationery and furniture?
Mr. ZUCKERMAN. No, sir; I do not. The bills were sent to him, and I never had anything to do with the bills.
Mr. HOWE. You do not know whether they were paid or not?
Mr. ZUCKERMAN. I do not know anything about it; no, sir.
Mr. HOWE. You do not know whether he got receipts when he made payments for furniture?
Mr. ZUCKERMAN. All I would do would be to go out and purchase the furniture. I never had anything to do with that, but I have gone out and bought stationery and charged it to the provost marshal.
Mr. HOWE. Who told you about furniture?
Mr. ZUCKERMAN. I think it was the party they bought it from who came in there, and he would have it charged to the provost marshal, office furniture.
Mr. HOWE. How would you know that?
Mr. ZUCKERMAN. I was there at the time he purchased this furniture—one desk in particular that I used to take the records of the cases there. I bought that desk, and he told me to send the bill in to the provost marshal.
Mr. HOWE. He bought that desk from whom?
Mr. ZUCKERMAN. From a native there.
Mr. HOWE. Where was the desk when it was bought?
Mr. ZUCKERMAN. On Twenty-second Street; a native owned it there. I believe he had the desk made—a mahogany desk.
Mr. HOWE. Did you go with the captain at the time you bought that desk?
Mr. ZUCKERMAN. I walked down and picked out the desk and then came back and told him about it—how much it would be—and he said, " You charge it to the provost marshal."
Mr. HOWE. He was provost marshal himself, was he not?
Mr. ZUCKERMAN. Yes, sir.
Mr. HOWE. You do not know how it was paid for?
Mr. ZUCKERMAN. No, sir.
Mr. HOWE. Do you know of any other instances of marines raising hell—breaking furniture and beating the natives up—than what you learned about through reading the court-martial proceedings?
Mr. ZUCKERMAN. No; it was just through drawing the court-martial papers.
Mr. HOWE. You never personally had such information yourself?
Mr. ZUCKERMAN. On one occasion one marine got into a row with the secret-service men of the gendarmerie or something, and he was tried by general court-martial.
Mr. HOWE. You were present at that time?
Mr. ZUCKERMAN. I was just coming out of the quarters when they were taking this marine down to headquarters.
Mr. HOWE. Do you know how many court-martials there were of marines for raising hell or breaking up furniture or beating up natives?
Mr. ZUCKERMAN. I believe I drew up 10 court-martials in about six weeks under Col. Hooker for marines raising hell, etc.
Mr. HOWE. But in the course of all your time you saw these records when you were acting sergeant major and sergeant major; is that correct?
Mr. ZUCKERMAN. Yes, sir.
Mr. HOWE. And you were acting sergeant major and sergeant major how long—two years?
Mr. ZUCKERMAN. A little better than that.
Mr. HOWE. In those two years how many court-martial records did you learn of where the accused was breaking furniture or beating up natives?
Mr. ZUCKERMAN. That I can not say.

Mr. Howe. Well, more than 10?

Mr. Zuckerman. Yes; there were more than 10.

Mr. Howe. As many as 100?

Mr. Zuckerman. Well, I should say about 20.

Mr. Howe. Of those 20, how many resulted in convictions?

Mr. Zuckerman. All of them; practically all of them.

Mr. Howe. You said in your direct testimony that the attitude of the natives toward the marines changed because the marines were raising hell with the natives?

Mr. Zuckerman. Yes, sir.

Mr. Howe. Do you mean to be understood that the attitude of all of these natives you saw there in Haiti was changed by these 20 cases of court-martial proceedings of marines for raising hell?

Mr. Zuckerman. I would not say that. There were probably 100 cases that never were brought to the attention of the commanding officer.

Mr. Howe. How did you gain knowledge of those?

Mr. Zuckerman. Just from hearsay.

Mr. Howe. Were there any other reasons that you could think of for the change in the attitude on the part of the natives besides the conduct of the marines?

Mr. Zuckerman. No, sir.

Mr. Howe. That was all?

Mr. Zuckerman. Yes, sir.

Mr. Howe. You mentioned road gangs working on the road from the cape to Ouanaminthe, and from the cape to Port au Prince. How do you know that was forced labor and not paid?

Mr. Zuckerman. I went up to see Lieut. Seeger with the gendarmerie, and he told me those were corvee men working there.

Mr. Howe. Did he use that term "corvee?"

Mr. Zuckerman. Yes, sir.

Mr. Howe. Do you know whether or not those men were paid?

Mr. Zuckerman. I do not; no, sir.

Mr. Howe. They might have been paid?

Mr. Zuckerman. Yes, sir. I understand they were paid something like half a gourde, or something, just from what I heard, but whether or not they were paid I can not say.

Mr. Howe. When you saw people working on the road, in this working on the road did you speak of them as doing corvee in all cases?

Mr. Zuckerman. No, sir.

Mr. Howe. How would you speak of them when they were not doing corvee?

Mr. Zuckerman. The road gangs—they were paid a gourde a day.

Mr. Howe. A road gang?

Mr. Zuckerman. Yes.

Mr. Howe. So when you say paid labor you would call it a road gang, and when you say forced labor you would call it corvee?

Mr. Zuckerman. I think I have seen one of the corvee. That was up with Lieut. Seeger, one case of them being pointed out as a corvee gang.

Mr. Howe. Which road was that on?

Mr. Zuckerman. On the road going to Port au Prince.

Mr. Howe. What was the gang you mentioned being on the road between the cape and Ouanaminthe?

Mr. Zuckerman. I understood that was a corvee camp there. I never seen them working. We were going over to Santo Domingo.

Mr. Howe. And you passed the camp?

Mr. Zuckerman. We passed the camp.

Mr. Howe. How did you know that was a corvee camp?

Mr. Zuckerman. A man in charge there, I think a detailed lieutenant with the gendarmerie, was going into Ouanaminthe from this camp, and he left gendarmes in charge out there, and he says, "I have got some corvee men at work there, and I will leave a guard with them overnight."

Mr. Howe. Did you see the men in that camp?

Mr. Zuckerman. Quite a few, sir.

Mr. Howe. Do you know whether they were being paid or not?

Mr. Zuckerman. I do not; no, sir.

Mr. Howe. What was the date when you passed that camp and you heard that?

Mr. Zuckerman. That was in 1917 sometime, sir.

Mr. Howe. You can not give us the month?
Mr. Zuckerman. No, sir.
Mr. Howe. What was the date when you saw this gang working on the road to Port au Prince?
Mr. Zuckerman. That, I remember distinctly, was about Christmas, 1917.
Mr. Howe. You were in the Marine Corps under the name of Max Zuckerman, your own name?
Mr. Zuckerman. No, sir; Joseph Rosenthal.
Mr. Howe. What residence did you give when you enlisted as Joseph Rosenthal.
Mr. Zuckerman. New York City.
Mr. Howe. New York City?
Mr. Zuckerman. Yes, sir.
Mr. Howe. What did you give as the place of your birth when you enlisted as Rosenthal?
Mr. Zuckerman. New York City.
Mr. Howe. What did you give as your age?
Mr. Zuckerman. Twenty-one.
Mr. Howe. And which is your real name?
Mr. Zuckerman. Zuckerman.
Mr. Howe. And why did you enlist as Rosenthal instead of Zuckerman?
Mr. Zuckerman. Well, I just left home and enlisted, and did not want the folks to know where I was.
Mr. Howe. Were you discharged under the same name?
Mr. Zuckerman. Yes, sir.
Mr. Howe. Of Rosenthal?
Mr. Zuckerman. Yes, sir.
(Whereupon a recess was taken until 2.30 o'clock p. m.)

The committee reassembled at 2.30 o'clock p. m., pursuant to the taking of recess, Senator Oddie presiding.
Mr. Howe. As a matter of fact, all you know about these corvee gangs which you have mentioned on the road between Cape Haitien and Ouanaminthe, and Cape Haitien and Port au Prince, is that they were said to be corvee gangs, and you do not know whether they were paid or not?
Mr. Zuckerman. No, sir.
Mr. Howe. They were, however, guards there in both cases, and you saw them, is not that right?
Mr. Zuckerman. There were guards there. They also had prisoners working, mixed in amongst those, prisoners that they had taken, that the gendarmes had taken.
Mr. Howe. How could you distinguish them from the others?
Mr. Zuckerman. They had them in uniform.
Mr. Howe. What uniform?
Mr. Zuckerman. The prison uniform; red and white stripe.
Mr. Howe. Were all prisoners down there in uniform?
Mr. Zuckerman. No, sir; not all of them.
Mr. Howe. Well, the rest of the gang outside of those that were in red and white stripes—do you know whether those were prisoners or not?
Mr. Zuckerman. I could not say; no, sir.
Mr. Howe. How many times did you go out on hikes there after you became sergeant major?
Mr. Zuckerman. Never.
Mr. Howe. So these occurrences where you spoke of firing on natives were before you were sergeant major?
Mr. Zuckerman. Yes, s r.
Mr. Howe. And your rank at that time was private?
Mr. Zuckerman. Yes, s r.
Mr. Howe. With the Fifteenth Company?
Mr. Zuckerman. Not doing duty with the gendarmerie.
Mr. Howe. That was when you were in the gendarmerie?
Mr. Zuckerman. Yes, sir.
Mr. Howe. What was your rank in the gendarmerie?
Mr Zuckerman. Private on detached duty with the Haitien gendarmerie.

Mr. Howe. And under whose orders were you at the time you fired on these natives in the fields?

Mr. Zuckerman. Capt. Torrey.

Mr. Howe. Of the gendarmerie?

Mr. Zuckerman. Captain of marines and major of gendarmerie?

Mr. Howe. About what date was that, then?

Mr. Zuckerman. That was in 1917 some time, sir.

Mr. Howe. Late in 1917?

Mr. Zuckerman. No; I believe it was about the middle of July, somewhere along there.

Mr. Howe. Did you fire at the orders of Maj. Torrey?

Mr. Zuckerman. We did not fire until fired upon; on all hikes on every detachment that left the post. Our orders on hikes were not to fire until fired upon; on all hikes on every detachment that left the post.

Mr. Howe. How near were you to the gendarmes that actually did the firing?

Mr. Zuckerman. Capt. Torrey and I had a detail of two gendarmes, and we were about 100 yards from th`s detachment of gendarmes that fired on those natives.

Mr. Howe. The natives had fired on the gendarmes?

Mr. Zuckerman. No; the gendarmes had fired at the natives.

Mr. Howe. First?

Mr. Zuckerman. How far away were you from the party which fired on the natives?

Mr. Zuckerman. We were about 100 yards.

Mr. Howe. Was the party which fired on the natives under direct command of any gendarmerie officer?

Mr. Zuckerman. No, sir; Capt. Torrey and I were going around Mount Capitan and we could just barely see this other detachment of gendarmes coming up over the mountain. We were looking for Gentil Sevier.

Mr. Howe. This detachment of gendarmes that you saw firing were not in your detachment; is that right?

Mr. Zuckerman. Yes; they were with us, but we had left them to go over there. We took a detachment of gendarmes to go up on the top of the mountain, and we left this detachment to guard the bottom of the mountain.

Mr. Howe. How did you know they were firing in the direction of these natives?

Mr. Zuckerman. These natives were out in the field there.

Mr. Howe. How did you know this detachment 200 yards away were firing at these natives in the field?

Mr. Zuckerman. That I could not say, but they fired in that direction.

Mr. Howe. And at the range of a thousand yards?

Mr. Zuckerman. They were about a thousand yards; yes, sir.

Mr. Howe. What did Maj. Torrey do when that firing took place?

Mr. Zuckerman. He sent me down to find out what they were firing at, and I went down there, and they said they fired at a bunch of men that came out of the brush, and as I went down I saw three or four men across the plain there.

Mr. Howe. Where was that?

Mr. Zuckerman. That was right at the bottom of Mount Capitan.

Mr. Howe. You mentioned another incident of firing on natives?

Mr. Zuckerman. We were going up to Cul de Nord, I believe the name of the town was, and we also had a detachment of gendarmes, and I was in charge of the gendarmes, and we came across about nine shacks, and a gendarme claimed that somebody had one of these—I forget what they called them—a machete, and he took a shot at him, but did not hit him. We did not get any prisoners there or anything else. But that firing was without the orders from anybody that was in charge.

Mr. Howe. Those people in the place near the shacks were under your orders at that time?

Mr. Zuckerman. Yes, sir.

Mr. Howe. You had no instructions from your superior officers to fire on any natives, did you?

Mr. Zuckerman. Not until we were fired on first. That was the standing order in the regiment.

Mr. Howe. Now, how many times did you yourself see Haitians subjected to beatings with this sand club which you have described?

Mr. ZUCKERMAN. While I was on duty with the gendarmerie, about once or twice a week.

Mr. HOWE. For about six months?

Mr. ZUCKERMAN. About that time; yes, sir.

Mr. HOWE. That was a usual occurrence?

Mr. ZUCKERMAN. Yes, sir.

Mr. HOWE. Where did it take place?

Mr. ZUCKERMAN. In the gendarme headquarters at Ouanaminthe.

Mr. HOWE. At Ouanaminthe?

Mr. ZUCKERMAN. Yes, sir.

Mr. HOWE. Were you present during those beatings?

Mr. ZUCKERMAN. Some of them.

Mr. HOWE. You were present about twice a week, on the average?

Mr. ZUCKERMAN. Yes, sir.

Mr. HOWE. For six months?

Mr. ZUCKERMAN. Yes, sir.

Mr. HOWE. Now, what time was that—what year?

Mr. ZUCKERMAN. I believe in 1916 somewhere, the latter part of 1916.

Mr. HOWE. What duty were you performing at the time?

Mr. ZUCKERMAN. On detached duty with the gendarmes.

Mr. HOWE. As private of marines?

Mr. ZUCKERMAN. Yes, sir.

Mr. HOWE. At the times when you were present, was any other white man present?

Mr. ZUCKERMAN. You mean a white officer?

Mr. HOWE. Was there a white officer present?

Mr. ZUCKERMAN. No, sir.

Mr. HOWE. Was there any other white man than yourself present?

Mr. ZUCKERMAN. Capt. Torrey was there on a few of the occasions; he questioned the natives.

Mr. HOWE. Was Capt. Torrey present at the time these natives were beaten with the sand club?

Mr. ZUCKERMAN. Yes, sir.

Mr. HOWE. Who actually did the beating?

Mr. ZUCKERMAN. The gendarmes.

Mr. HOWE. And did he do it at the direction of Capt. Torrey?

Mr. ZUCKERMAN. I believe he did; yes, sir.

Mr. HOWE. Now, how often did you see natives strung up on this beam?

The CHAIRMAN. Let me interrupt. Do you know who devised or invented this sand club and initiated the practice of beating people with it?

Mr. ZUCKERMAN. No, sir.

The CHAIRMAN. Was it invented during your service, or did it exist in the island before?

Mr. ZUCKERMAN. I do not think it ever existed before; no, sir.

Mr. HOWE. Would the man be strung up on the beam just as a rack?

Mr. ZUCKERMAN. Yes.

Mr. HOWE. At the time he was being beaten?

Mr. ZUCKERMAN. No; they would just tie him up there and question him.

Mr. HOWE. Who would tie him up?

Mr. ZUCKERMAN. The gendarmes.

Mr. HOWE. Those were native Haitians?

Mr. ZUCKERMAN. Yes, sir.

Mr. HOWE. Did you see Capt. Torrey or Maj. Torrey questioning one of these men while he was strung up?

Mr. ZUCKERMAN. No, sir; he was never there at any of the questioning.

Mr. HOWE. Do you know what the name of Maj. Torrey was?

Mr. ZUCKERMAN. I think it was Philip H.

Mr. HOWE. Is that the one you are talking about?

Mr. ZUCKERMAN. Yes, sir; Philip H.

Mr. HOWE. Were these natives strung up?

Mr. ZUCKERMAN. Or H. P. There are two marine officers. I mean the younger of the two.

The CHAIRMAN. The younger of the two is the one you mean?

Mr. ZUCKERMAN. Yes, sir.

Maj. McCLELLAN. Philip happens to be the older.

Mr. ZUCKERMAN. It is the younger of the two that I mean—Henry P. Torrey.

Mr. HOWE. Did they both have the same rank?

Mr. ZUCKERMAN. I believe they did, sir.

Mr. HOWE. This one was commanding officer at Ouanaminthe at this time; is that the one?

Mr. ZUCKERMAN. Commanding the gendarme detachment.

Mr. HOWE. Did he order these natives strung up?

Mr. ZUCKERMAN. As far as I know he did not; no, sir.

Mr. HOWE. Did you ever see him present in the room while a native was strung up?

Mr. ZUCKERMAN. No, sir.

Mr. HOWE. But he was present when the native was being beaten by the sand club?

Mr. ZUCKERMAN. Yes, sir.

Mr. HOWE. More than once?

Mr. ZUCKERMAN. Yes, sir.

Mr. HOWE. Did you ever see a native being beaten with a sand club when he was not present?

Mr. ZUCKERMAN. Amongst the gendarmes they used to beat them quite frequently, chase prisoners with these sand clubs.

Mr. HOWE. By chasing prisoners do you mean running after prisoners, or guarding prisoners?

Mr. ZUCKERMAN. Guarding prisoners.

Mr. HOWE. You say that Maj. Torrey was not present when these prisoners were being questioned?

Mr. ZUCKERMAN. As far as I recollect. he was not; no sir.

Mr. HOWE. Do you know why he ordered them beaten?

Mr. ZUCKERMAN. Well, to gain information.

Mr. HOWE. Who did the questioning?

Mr. ZUCKERMAN. Capt. Torrey, through an interpreter.

Mr. HOWE. Then was Capt. Torrey present when the witnesses were being questioned, when the natives were being questioned?

Mr. ZUCKERMAN. On several occasions he was.

Mr. HOWE. I misunderstood you, then. I understood you to say that Capt. Torrey was not present while these prisoners were being questioned.

Mr. ZUCKERMAN. While they were strung up.

The CHAIRMAN. If you will permit me, the witness I think, alludes to his presence when the prisoners were being beaten with sand clubs for the purpose of questioning, whereas he says that Capt. Torrey was not present when they were strung up for the purpose of questioning.

Mr. ZUCKERMAN. Yes, sir.

Mr. HOWE. Who would do the questioning of these natives as they were brought in?

Mr. ZUCKERMAN. Capt. Torrey.

Mr. HOWE. In all cases?

Mr. ZUCKERMAN. Yes, sir.

Mr. HOWE. Were prisoners being brought in constantly during that time, your six months?

Mr. ZUCKERMAN. Yes, sir; practically every day we would get a detail of prisoners, or every other day, or every time a gendarme detachment would bring them in.

Mr. HOWE. Was every prisoner who was brought in clubbed or strung up?

Mr. ZUCKERMAN. No, sir.

Mr. HOWE. Then it was only those who refused to answer questions, as you understand it, who were clubbed or strung up?

Mr. ZUCKERMAN. Yes, sir.

Mr. HOWE. Were there any other white officers stationed there in the gendarmerie?

Mr. ZUCKERMAN. No, sir.

Mr. HOWE. Who else besides the major, his interpreter, and yourself, were in the room at the time of the beatings?

Mr. ZUCKERMAN. There were several gendarmes there, a gendarme sergeant, and a gendarme first sergeant.

Mr. HOWE. Were there any attempts made to keep these occurrences secret?

Mr. ZUCKERMAN. No, sir.

Mr. HOWE. Was Maj. Torrey the only white officer stationed there?

Mr. ZUCKERMAN. No, sir; Col. Hooker, the commander of the marine detachment.

Mr. Howe. Was he stationed at Ouanaminthe?
Mr. Zuckerman. Yes, sir.
Mr. Howe. Was he ever present at the time any of these natives were being beaten or strung up?
Mr. Zuckerman. No, sir.
Mr. Howe. Were you working under Col. Hooker at that time, directly, or under Capt. Torrey, or Maj. Torrey?
Mr. Zuckerman. Maj. Torrey.
Mr. Howe. He was Maj. Torrey in the gendarmerie and Capt. Torrey in the marines?
Mr. Zuckerman. Yes, sir.
Mr. Howe. What questions were being asked of these prisoners, what kind of questions?
Mr. Zuckerman. The prisoners, I understand, those they questioned so severely, were caught with arms out in the country, and they were trying to gain information as to where the bandits had their arms. At that time they were after this Gentil Sevier.
The Chairman. He was a bandit chief?
Mr. Zuckerman. Yes, sir; of that section, through Circa la Source.
Mr. Howe. And throughout the whole six months, that was the information that Capt. or Maj. Torrey was after?
Mr. Zuckerman. Yes, sir.
Mr. Howe. To find out the location of the camps of the bandits?
Mr. Zuckerman. Yes, sir.
Mr. Howe. Have you ever made any report of these beatings before your testimony to this committee?
Mr. Zuckerman. Have I ever made a report? No, sir.
Mr. Howe. Mr. Chairman, I would like to state for the record that Mr. Zuckerman testified that he was honorably discharged from the Marine Corps, but did not have his discharge papers with him. In the recess Maj. McClellan has looked up his record, his record appearing under another name which he gave to the committee before recess, and finds out that the individual who was enlisted under the name which the witness furnished us was honorably discharged. What is your real name?
Mr. Zuckerman. Zurckerman.
The Chairman. You enlisted as Rosenthal?
Mr. Zuckerman. Yes, sir.
Mr. Howe. And Rosenthal was honorably discharged. I think that should appear on the record.
You had only one enlistment, did you not?
Mr. Zuckerman. Yes, sir.
Mr. Howe. And you were, nevertheless, in the Marine Corps for more than four years?
Mr. Zuckerman. Yes, sir.
Mr. Howe. By about three or four months?
Mr. Zuckerman. About four months.
Mr. Howe. What was the cause of your staying over those four months in the Marine Corps?
Mr. Zuckerman. Waiting trial of a summary court for absence over leave.
Mr. Howe. Were you kept waiting trial those three months?
Mr. Zuckerman. Yes, sir.
Mr. Howe. And you were fined?
Mr. Zuckerman. Yes, sir.
Mr. Howe. How much?
Mr. Zuckerman. I was fined $30 at first, and then the court went to the commanding officer, and he said it was inadequate for the offense committed, and I was fined $90.
Mr. Howe. In addition to confinement?
Mr. Zuckerman. I was not confined at all, just waiting the result of the trial.
Mr. Howe. Being held three months over your enlistment?
Mr. Zuckerman. Yes, sir.
Mr. Howe. And were you reduced from rank?
Mr. Zuckerman. Yes, sir.
Mr. Howe. You had been a sergeant?
Mr. Zuckerman. Yes, sir.
Mr. Howe. Or a sergeant major?

Mr. ZUCKERMAN. I was sergeant, I believe, at that time.
Mr. HOWE. What were you discharged as?
Mr. ZUCKERMAN. Corporal.
Mr. HOWE. You were reduced from sergeant to corporal?
Mr. ZUCKERMAN. Yes, sir. The fine was remitted at the expiration of my enlistment.
Mr. HOWE. So you actually suffered no loss in money?
Mr. ZUCKERMAN. No, sir.
Mr. HOWE. I have no further questions.
Mr. ANGELL. Can you give us the names of any of the gendarmerie sergeants that served at Ouanaminthe during this period?
Mr. ZUCKERMAN. No, sir; I could not.
Mr. ANGELL. You do not remember the names?
Mr. ZUCKERMAN. No, sir; I could not.
Mr. ANGELL. You have no grievance against Capt. Torrey?
Mr. ZUCKERMAN. No, sir.
Mr. ANGELL. No personal run in with him in any way?
Mr. ZUCKERMAN. No, sir.
Mr. ANGELL. And you served the whole period of four years and some months in the Marine Corps under the name of Rosenthal?
Mr. ZUCKERMAN. Yes, sir.
Mr. ANGELL. Why did you enlist under that name?
Mr. ZUCKERMAN. I just wanted to get away. I had some scrap at home. I did not write home for two years after I enlisted, until they found out where I was.
Mr. ANGELL. You enlisted under that name to get away from the family, so that the family would not know where you were?
Mr. ZUCKERMAN. Yes, sir.
Mr. ANGELL. That is a fairly common practice in the Marine Corps and in the Army, is it not?
Mr. ZUCKERMAN. I do not know. I guess it is. The cases I cited were just instances of abuse, but there are a lot of things that I could tell on the bright side of the occupation; that is, during the time I was with the gendarmerie. Outside of that, I was in position to see exactly what was going on down there, being sergeant-major of the regiment and seeing the reports and going out on inspection tours with the commanding officers. I accompanied the commanding officer with every inspection tour before the gendarmerie was organized. The commanding officer of the marines was in complete charge of roads, sanitation, and everything else there.
The CHAIRMAN. Let the witness go right along and tell the story in his own way.
Mr. ZUCKERMAN. Outside of that instance I quoted, I could not think of anything that could condemn the occupation down there.
The CHAIRMAN. What have you to say in justification of the occupation?
Mr. ZUCKERMAN. Well, sanitation down there has been very, very good, and the waterworks system. I went through that with Mr. Bond, the ex-marine who was in charge of that, and he done some very good work on the waterworks system—worked all through it.
Mr. ANGELL. All of this is at Cape Haitien?
Mr. ZUCKERMAN. Yes, sir; and the roads from Ouanaminthe to Cape Haitien were put up by the marines, and that was taken care of, and the city itself was policed very well, all taken care of by marines. Outside of that one instance at Ouanaminthe, I can not say anything.
The CHAIRMAN. Let me ask the witness what were the general relations between the gendarmerie and the population, other than the bandits or the suspected bandits?
Mr. ZUCKERMAN. Well, they got along very well, just for the exception that a few marines would go out and get drunk and the first thing they would think of would be to go around and break up some kind of shack.
The CHAIRMAN. That is not peculiar to marines or to the Republic of Haiti?
Mr. ZUCKERMAN. Outside of the few instances I can not think of anything that I could say.
The CHAIRMAN. Normally, what was the relation, let us say, between the gendarmerie native and American officers at a point like Cape Haitien with the inhabitants of the city and the country around about?
Mr. ZUCKERMAN. Very good. They got along very well in Cape Haitien.

The CHAIRMAN. At what point were you stationed, or to what point did you travel in Haiti?

Mr. ZUCKERMAN. To all northern Haiti, practically all of northern Haiti.

The CHAIRMAN. As far west as Gonaives?

Mr. ZUCKERMAN. No; I went to Fort Liberte, Ouanaminthe, Cape Haitien, and up as far as Hinche, and a town this side of Gonaives, just over the mountains, Port au Paix. This was on inspection trips.

The CHAIRMAN. You were on inspection trips, and presumably had a reasonable opportunity to observe?

Mr ZUCKERMAN. Yes, sir. I was there at the time they called the rifles in from the natives, and we paid them—I think the Haitian Government paid them—a dollar apiece for turning in all their rifles, and I took a trip with Gen. Cole, I believe it was to Le Trou.

The CHAIRMAN. Did the calling in of the rifles, the organization of the gendarmerie, and its presence in various communities conduce to order and peace?

Mr. ZUCKERMAN. Yes, sir.

The CHAIRMAN. Did the people more freely come and go from their homes in the country to the market places in the towns, because of the gandarmerie?

Mr. ZUCKERMAN. Yes; and under Col. Hooker's administration he had the Marine Corps band come down from Port au Prince, so as to get the natives out on the street. He put the band in the band stand and let it play every evening, so as to let the natives come out of their shacks. They used to stay in and lock themselves up.

The CHAIRMAN. Weighing the incidents to which you alluded earlier in your testimony, the stringing up and the beating with clubs and the firing at natives, unprovoked in some cases, against the pacification of the country and the maintenance of peace, did the faults of the gendarmerie outweigh the benefits to the population, or did the benefits to the population outweigh the faults of the gendarmerie?

Mr. ZUCKERMAN. I think the benefits to the population outweighed the faults of the gendarmerie.

The CHAIRMAN. The country was better off for the gendarmerie despite——

Mr. ZUCKERMAN. They were better off with the gendarmerie and the marines——

The CHAIRMAN. Than if there had been none?

Mr. ZUCKERMAN. Yes, sir. The marines patrolled the interior at all times, and so did the gendarmerie, and the gendarmerie natives themselves caused a lot of this trouble. As soon as a man was made a gendarme and wore the uniform he was the big "It," and he went out amongst the natives and raised the devil himself. They started a lot of the trouble themselves.

The CHAIRMAN. Was a large center like Cape Haitien or Port au Prince on the whole well and orderly and peaceably policed by the gendarmes?

Mr. ZUCKERMAN. Yes, sir.

The CHAIRMAN. They acted in lieu, of course, of city police?

Mr. ZUCKERMAN. Yes, sir.

Mr. ANGELL. And on the whole they discharged their duties reasonably well?

Mr. ZUCKERMAN. Yes, sir. We had marines patrol the streets at the same time as gendarmes.

The CHAIRMAN. Would that patrol walk a beat as a policeman would walk a beat, the marine or gendarme?

Mr. ZUCKERMAN. I do not think either. There was a continual patrol of the marines through the streets at all times.

The CHAIRMAN. In groups of 4, 6, or 10 squads?

Mr. ZUCKERMAN. No, sir; singly.

The CHAIRMAN. Singly?

Mr. ZUCKERMAN. Yes, sir.

The CHAIRMAN. And the gendarmes patrolling also independently?

Mr. ZUCKERMAN. Yes, sir.

The CHAIRMAN. Would you say, in so far as there were injuries done natives, that they originated with the native gendarmerie, or were inspired by Americans serving with the gendarmerie?

Mr. ZUCKERMAN. A lot of it was inspired by the native gendarmerie.

The CHAIRMAN. Well, it is a loose question, and I only want to get your impression for the benefit of the committee. It is not testimony which would be valid in any other sort of a hearing. On the whole, would you say that the responsibility for ill treatment rested with the American officer, whether an enlisted man or officer of the marines, or an American serving with the gendarmerie, or with the gendarmerie themselves?

Mr. ZUCKERMAN. The gendarmes themselves, the native gendarmes.

STATEMENT OF MR. JAMES WELDON JOHNSON, 70 FIFTH AVENUE, NEW YORK CITY.

The CHAIRMAN. Will you give your full name and address?

Mr. JOHNSON. James Weldon Johnson, 70 Fifth Avenue, New York City.

Mr. ANGELL. What is your occupation?

Mr. JOHNSON. I am secretary of the National Association for the Advancement of the Colored People.

Mr. ANGELL. Have you ever been in the United States Consular Service?

Mr. JOHNSON. Yes; I was.

Mr. ANGELL. Will you tell when and where, briefly?

Mr. JOHNSON. I was appointed consul at Puerto Cabello, Venezuela, in 1906, and promoted to Corinto, Nicaragua, in 1909, and served there until—I can not remember the month, but it was early in 1913, when I resigned—about seven years and a half.

Mr. ANGELL. You have been in Haiti, have you not?

Mr. JOHNSON. I have.

Mr. ANGELL. When did you go there, and how long did you spend in Haiti?

Mr. JOHNSON. I went down to Haiti in March of 1920, last year, and I got back—I went down on the 21st of March and I got back about the 21st or 22d of May, but I was there eight weeks. I was there perhaps six weeks and a half.

Mr. ANGELL. Where, in the island, did you go in Haiti?

Mr. JOHNSON. Well, I made my headquarters at Port au Prince. I radiated out from Port au Prince through the country there, anything that could be covered inside of a day, and then I made a trip in an automobile as far as Cape Haitien, and returned back in about a week.

Mr. ANGELL. Did you stay at any place along the way?

Mr. JOHNSON. Well, I made the usual stop at St. Marc and Gonaïves, and then went on.

Mr. ANGELL. Did you go back into the interior of northern Haiti or central Haiti?

Mr. JOHNSON. I went back largely for the purpose of paying a visit to Chrostophe's old palace and citadel up there. That took me a day's journey into the interior in the north.

Mr. ANGELL. What class of population did you come in contact with?

Mr JOHNSON. Well, I guess I came in contact with all classes. I had letters to what we might. term the best people of Haiti, and then I got in touch as largely as I could with all other classes.

Mr. ANGELL. Did you meet officials of the Government?

Mr. JOHNSON. Yes. I met the President twice, and most of the Cabinet ministers at various times, and other lesser officials.

Mr. ANGELL. Did you converse with the local officials in the communes, priests, and such people?

Mr. JOHNSON. I did not talk with any priests that I can remember, but I talked with such people as I could draw out. They are mostly suspicious of strangers.

The CHAIRMAN. A little more clearly, Mr. Johnson.

Mr. JOHNSON. I say I did not talk with any priests.

The CHAIRMAN. But with people such as were not suspicious of strangers?

Mr. JOHNSON. Yes; those competent to talk.

The CHAIRMAN. Did you have to speak through an interpreter, or do you speak the vernacular, or French?

Mr. JOHNSON. I speak enough French to get along. I am not very familiar with the Creole. Although I speak a word or two, I could not say I could talk Creole.

Mr. ANGELL. Will you tell us what you found to be the attitude of the Haitian population of the different classes, and its feeling toward the United States, toward the military occupation, and the reasons for its feelings and attitude?

Mr. JOHNSON. Well of course, that is a question that has to be varied a little. If I gave just a general impression, it would be that there was a good deal of bitterness and resentment in all classes. The reasons might have been varied, but the impression I gained was from the highest to the lowest—and by the lowest I do not mean what we call a peon, because I did not talk with them to any large extent, and I do not know whether they had any very serious thought on it one way or another, but the people I talked with of any intelligence, of any thought at all—they were extremely bitter.

Mr. ANGELL. Was there bitterness toward the United States in general, or toward the military occupation in particular, or both?

Mr. JOHNSON. If you will let me put it this way: There were a number of people who seemed to have been disappointed. They seemed to have had the hope, and I might say the faith that a good deal more was coming out of the occupation than did come, and their resentment was based upon what they considered to be the harshness of the military rule, and the fact that the convention was not being carried out in the spirit in which they had expected it to be carried out.

The CHAIRMAN. May I interrupt, Captain, at that point?

Mr. ANGELL. Yes.

The CHAIRMAN. By that do you mean that the financial and economic reorganization contemplated by the convention appeared to have been indefinitely postponed?

Mr. JOHNSON. Yes. I think, Senator, that would be the cause of one disappointment.

The CHAIRMAN. They had been led to believe from the text of the convention that the adjudication of long pending claims, the refunding of the debt and related matters would be taken in hand forthwith and carried through?

Mr. JOHNSON. Yes. I think that is true, but I think that this set of people I am talking about—I will have to divide them into a group or two, because one statement would not cover them all.

The CHAIRMAN. Precisely.

Mr. JOHNSON. There were a group of people who seemed to be expectant of some good things coming out of the convention. Those people, it seemed, never expected a strict military rule. They seemed to feel they were going in for a civil oversight and they considered that the military domination was a thing outside of the letter and spirit of the convention.

Then, of course, there were groups that I talked with, and I talked with various groups of different political shades of opinion and different economic status, and some people, of course, were bitterly opposed to any sort of foreign intervention. I found a very deep pride in their independence, and they resented anything like foreign invasion, and they were irreconcilables.

Mr. ANGELL. What did you find the attitude of these various groups, answering the question according to the different groups, if you can, and their expectations for the future as to treatment from the United States and their relations with the United States?

Mr. JOHNSON. Let me get the gist of that question again.

Mr. ANGELL. Perhaps that was not very well put. What were the expectations of these various groups of people with whom you talked as to the relations with the United States in the future?

Mr. JOHNSON. The more intelligent people that I talked with felt that there ought to be what we might call a new deal entirely. They said frankly that that convention such as it was, was forced upon them. They felt that if there could be any mutual benefit in cooperation between the two countries that they ought to have a fairer start together. That expresses the opinion of one group. When we get to the other group that I referred to just now as the irreconcilables, they want nothing less than the independence of their country.

The CHAIRMAN. They want the abrogation of the convention?

Mr. JOHNSON. Yes.

Mr. ANGELL. Are you able to specify the particular incidents, not as testifying to the truth or untruth of those incidents, but as to their being apparently the reasons for the feeling which these different groups had about our presence and the conduct of our administration of Haiti?

Mr. JOHNSON. You mean the reasons for the fact?

Mr. ANGELL. The specific reasons for the particular feelings which they had.

Mr. JOHNSON. They resent very much the military occupation, the military rule.

Mr. ANGELL. The fact of the occupation or the method in which it has been conducted, which?

Mr. JOHNSON. The fact in some degree, and the method in a greater degree, I judge, and of course conditions in Haiti give rise to a phase of this question, which might not arise in any other country, and that is the question between white and black, and that has been brought to the fore very much in Haiti, and the Haitians resent it very keenly; they feel it very deeply.

Mr, ANGELL. Just how did you gather that the question had been brought to the fore there?

Mr. JOHNSON. Well, they talked with me, and I talked with what you might call the better class of Haitians, the men who assembled in the clubs there and who had nice homes, the educated class, and they said that before the coming of the Americans there was no such thing as a well-defined color line in Haiti; that there were foreigners there, both Americans and Europeans, but the color line had never been specifically and tightly drawn as it has been since the occupation there—instances now in which it shows very plainly.

Mr. ANGELL. By whom has the color line been drawn since the occupation, without reference to any particular individual?

Mr. JOHNSON. I learned that it started with the Americans, but now the thing is mutually drawn.

The CHAIRMAN. You mean there are no relations, other than official, between the Haitians and the Americans?

Mr. JOHNSON. That is what I am getting at. Of course, what I am repeating now is merely what I gathered in talking, Senator.

The CHAIRMAN. Precisely.

Mr. JOHNSON. You might say that there is no personal relation between the American official class and the upper class of Haitians, except where it is officially necessary, and that heretofore those conditions never obtained even among the white Europeans there in Haiti, and the American citizens in Haiti.

Mr. ANGELL. You said a moment ago that this feeling originated, I believe, after the military occupation?

Mr. JOHNSON. Yes.

Mr. ANGELL. Was it your understanding that it was a feeling which originated—that the color line was brought forward by the Americans against the Haitians or by the Haitians against the Americans?

Mr. JOHNSON. Drawn first by the Americans. I was informed that the Haitians, those in what we would call the social set there, who would go into society, when the Americans first landed went very far to make it pleasant for them, and it was all right until the number increased very largely, and especially up until the time when the ladies of the occupation came down. Then, I understand, that the American occupation or the officials of the occupation, military and civil, organized a club to which no Haitian is ever invited, and now the Haitians, I believe, have returned the lack of compliment by not inviting the Americans to their clubs. That is a side issue, but I judge that it was a point of friction which impeded a good deal of motion that might have gone along more easily.

Mr. ANGELL. Did you hear comment or discussion to any extent among these groups of the institution or conduct of the management of the corvée law by the Americans under the American occupation?

Mr. JOHNSON. Yes; that was put down as one of the reasons for bitter resentment.

Mr. ANGELL. Was the feeling apparently strong on that point or not?

Mr. JOHNSON. Very strong with everybody I talked to, and I talked with a great many people. I talked not only with the native Haitians but I talked with Americans in business there and European business men.

The CHAIRMAN. Was it to the abuses incident to the corvee or to the actual invoking of the law of the corvee that objection was made?

Mr. JOHNSON. I heard something of abuse, but, of course, I have no definite knowledge. I have heard of things that are told everywhere, but I think as I studied the situation there that there is something in the Haitian which objected very deeply to the corvee itself—the invoking of it.

The CHAIRMAN. Although it was in his law?

Mr. JOHNSON. Well, I understand it was never enforced in that way.

The CHAIRMAN. Well, I think it was never enforced at all; it was a dead letter, but it was a law.

Mr. JOHNSON. Well, I think we have the same laws in most all of our States; at least in some of the Southern States there is a road law, by which you can be compelled to work on the road around your vicinity, but I think it went—if you will allow me to digress a little—I think it went pretty hard with the Haitian, as I studied the question, because I do not think there was ever any such thing as peonage in Haiti. The Haitians in the country, so far as I could learn, the great majority of them, were individual cultivators, with a little plot of ground; and no matter whether he cultivated it well or ill, he was an independent farmer, no matter on how small a scale, and when he was taken off his little plot of ground and carried miles away into another part of the country it was slavery to him, even though the treatment might not have been abnormally cruel.

The CHAIRMAN. Well, if they were carried far from their plots of ground, that might be characterized either as an abuse or maladministration of the corvee.

Mr. ANGELL. Were there any specific reasons for the feeling which you have described toward the occupation?

Mr. JOHNSON. Well, I think that most of the intelligent people felt that there was really no Government, because there was a conflict between the military authority and American civilian authority and Haitian national authority. I got that not only from intelligent Haitians but from Americans and Europeans there.

The CHAIRMAN. Let me ask the witness the question I put to Mr. Forrest this morning. Could you say that there was any American policy in Haiti after the pacification had been completed up to the present time?

Mr. JOHNSON. Any policy at all—any defined policy?

The CHAIRMAN. Yes.

Mr. JOHNSON. I could not say that there was.

The CHAIRMAN. Were you able to see any evidence of a policy leading anywhere?

Mr. JOHNSON. I could not.

The CHAIRMAN. Did you hear any particular comment upon specific instances of the relations in governmental administrative matters between the occupation and the American minister and financial adviser, on the one hand, and the Haitian Government on the other, such, for example, as the dissolution of the Haitian Legislature and the National Assembly?

Mr. JOHNSON. Yes; I talked with various men, and they told me about the dissolution of the Chamber of Deputies. They said that it was done by force, virtually. Of course, that was another cause of resentment with the thinking classes. Then, most of them told me that they did not feel, outside of the country being policed, that they had gotten anything back; that all of the obligations were on the part of Haiti, but there seemed to be no obligation on the part of the United States—at least, they could not see any benefits.

The CHAIRMAN. But the United States had taken control and had failed to discharge the responsibilities incident to control?

Mr. JOHNSON. That is what the intelligent classes felt and said.

The CHAIRMAN. Did the foreigners perhaps feel the same way, American and European?

Mr. JOHNSON. Yes, sir.

The CHAIRMAN. Would that be your own judgment?

Mr. JOHNSON. That was my own judgment after my short stay there. May I limit it by that? I looked around, and I was trying to make an impartial survey of the whole situation. First, let us say that I went down there with some misgivings that I was going to find that the entire propaganda which you might call against Haiti was mere design. I found it. I was very much surprised at the Haitian people. I found them a good deal better sort of folk than I had ever hoped or expected to find them, and I wanted to make a fair report, and I looked to see what the Americans had done. I could only find three things, and that was the military roads, the big highway from Port au Prince to Cape Haitien, the improvement of the hospital there in Port au Prince, which it seemed had been made quite efficient, and some minor sanitary regulations that had been instituted in the larger towns. I think they were all minor though. I think they did not go any further than that you must sprinkle lime so many times a week, you must have a cement gutter in which water can run off, and things of that sort.

As for the city of Port au Prince, I found it a very clean, well kept city, and at first I thought that that was the work of the occupation, but I learned that the paving of Port au Prince was the work of the Haitian Government; that the contracts had been let before our occupation.

The CHAIRMAN. Had the work been completed before?

Mr. JOHNSON. Not entirely. Outside of those three things I could not find any improvement. I looked especially for some marked improvement in the school system and I talked to Mr. Belgard, who was Minister of Education, and

I visited some of the schools in Port au Prince, and saw some of the schools around the country, but, as far as I could learn, the occupation and the American Government had not done anything to improve the school system, such as had taken place in some of the other possessions.

Mr. ANGELL. What feeling did you find among the population, if any, about the ownership of land by foreigners, and the whole question of foreign capital in Haiti, the economic exploitation, and kindred questions?

Mr. JOHNSON. Those I talked with seemed to be quite apprehensive about the economic exploitation, and especially the buying of large tracts of land by foreigners, and some of them seemed to be quite disturbed at the rumors prevalant while I was down there of large tracts being taken up. I do not know how true they were, except in one case I talked with a man who said he was dickering for 5,000 acres.

Mr. ANGELL. What feeling, if any, was there regarding the article in the new constitution of 1918, permitting the ownership of land, and regarding the adoption of that constitution itself?

Mr. JOHNSON. The intelligent Haitians of all political parties that I talked with felt that the constitution which they had now was unconstitutionally adopted, and they felt that the old provision in the old constitution not allowing aliens to own land was one of the bulwarks of their safety and security. All that I talked to were very much opposed to that change in the constitution.

Mr. ANGELL. They said they felt that the constitution was unconstitutionally adopted in what respect and how?

Mr. JOHNSON. Well, I understand the fundamental law of Haiti calls for the constitution to be adopted by the legislative body, and this was adopted by a plebiscite, a popular vote.

Mr. ANGELL. Was it or was it not the feeling among the groups whom you talked with that the methods of the adoption of this constitution and these clauses in it regarding the ownership of land were to be laid to the occupation— the American occupation?

Mr. JOHNSON. Yes, sir.

The CHAIRMAN. We have now a record of nearly six years of the occupation, and of four since the acknowledged establishment of general order. We have a treaty, the life of which, assuming a renewal at the end of the first period, is 15 years. If there be established in Haiti a true and centralized responsibility for the American agents there, whether in the employ of the Haitian Government or the Government of the United States, if the American Government, through these agents, assiduously and in good faith pursued a sympathetic policy, seeking always, as you suggested early in your testimony, to put forward the development of civil administration through civil advisers rather than military officials, do you believe that we may secure the cooperation of the Haitian people in the carrying out of such a policy?

Mr. JOHNSON. I think it would be very largely secured, Senator. I do not see that any occupation of Haiti will secure 100 per cent cooperation, or maybe not anywhere near perfect, but I think it would secure quite a large cooperation.

The CHAIRMAN. I mean can we secure that measure of cooperation which is necessary if we are to contribute substantially to the moral and material progress of the Haitian people during the 15 years of the treaty?

Mr. JOHNSON. Will you let me answer it by making a statement?

The CHAIRMAN. Certainly.

Mr. JOHNSON. I think that if the right sort of man took charge of the right sort of a sympathetic and cooperative civil administration in Haiti, and the man would have to be a man of big caliber—I think that has been one of the mistakes of the present occupation there—and looking forward with this thing in view, to an absolute restoration of Haitian independence at the end of that term, I believe you would get the cooperation of all the elements in Haiti that would be worth while.

The CHAIRMAN. Do you believe that at the end of 15 years, the Haitians, unaided, could resume the administration of the public services of the country?

Mr. JOHNSON. That would depend, I think, on what took place in the 15 years. Of course, if we went there and administered it for them, and got up and came out in 15 years, they might be so weakened in that time that they could not administer it for themselves.

The CHAIRMAN. What you have in mind is that we should not administer for them, but with them, during that period?

Mr. JOHNSON. With them, and their administrative powers should be continually strengthened until that widrawal.

The CHAIRMAN. What would happen if the treaty were abrogated and the occupation withdrawn on 90 days' notice?

Mr. JOHNSON. Well, I have heard opinions on that. I should judge the sanest opinions I have heard from natives would be that it would not be a very wise thing to do on 90 days' notice. In fact, I do not think you could withdraw from Haiti until the native constabulary or a national army or some such force is there to replace what you have. I do not think this gendarmerie would do it entirely, because the intelligent Haitian has no place in it. I understand that they are the most ignorant, and although some of the intelligent Haitian youth went in at first, they found they had no chance and no place, and they simply stood aside. You would have to replace authority by Haitians of intelligence.

The CHAIRMAN. If you were laying down in the most general terms a course for us to follow, would it be one like that suggested by my first question?

Mr. JOHNSON. If I had a program to lay out for Haiti, I would lay out one looking to the quickest possible withdrawal of the United States, and almost as immediate as possible the withdrawal of the military forces, and as prompt as possible a withdrawal of even civilian rule or oversight. We will never be able to do anything in Haiti unless we have the good will of the Haitians. We know that. That is axiomatic, and I believe the best way to get it is to assure Haiti that we have no ultimate aims against her independence.

The CHAIRMAN. Well, you say the withdrawal as soon as possible?

Mr. JOHNSON. Yes.

The CHAIRMAN. Six months, one year, five years, ten years, or the period of the treaty?

Mr. JOHNSON. Military withdrawal.

The CHAIRMAN. No. I am talking now of complete withdrawal. I think that was the phrase which you used.

Mr. JOHNSON. Yes. Well, I will put it into two parts, military withdrawal as soon as possible and as prompt a civilian withdrawal as can be worked out.

The CHAIRMAN. Could you indicate a difference in time?

Mr. JOHNSON. This treaty now has five years to run, has it not?

The CHAIRMAN. Yes.

Mr. JOHNSON. I should venture that we could get out of Haiti in a military way in a year and that we ought to be able to get out at the close of this term of the treaty.

The CHAIRMAN. What would you do with the service of the debt?

Mr. JOHNSON. Of the debt?

The CHAIRMAN. Yes.

Mr. JOHNSON. Well, I do not know that we have made it any easier for them.

The CHAIRMAN. Whether we have or not, we have undertaken to refund the French debt, which, as you know, has not matured and must be paid.

Mr. JOHNSON. I did not really know we were assuming that as an obligation. I knew we were to furnish a loan for Haiti.

The CHAIRMAN. The major part of the loan is allocated to the payment of the French debt.

Mr. JOHNSON. You mean the loan that was to have been made and that they have been expecting?

The CHAIRMAN. Well, I think the negotiations are consummated.

Mr. JOHNSON. I did not know that. I had given that up. I thought that was a lost hope.

The CHAIRMAN. I think it has been consummated, but the major part of the loan goes for the payment of the French debt and the liquidation of the internal claims. I think it is fair to say that nine-tenths of the fund to be realized from the loan now approaching consummation will go for that purpose. How would you assure the service of that loan?

Mr. JOHNSON. I do not know that I am prepared to say that. I am not prepared to answer that question. That involves a good deal more than I had at hand.

The CHAIRMAN. That is something which, of course——

Mr. JOHNSON. I was coming back merely to this proposition, as to whether, in my opinion, the Haitians were capable of self-government or not.

The CHAIRMAN. Well, I had in mind the service of the Nicaraguan debt, the service of the Dominican debt, the service of the Ottoman debt, and the Egyptian debt, and all these debts which have been in default at one time or another.

Mr. JOHNSON. May I ask now, Where are we with the Dominican debt?

The CHAIRMAN. The Dominican debt will be paid, I think, in 1926 or 1923; it is almost extinguished. The revenues last year and the year before have increased so in Santo Domingo that the debt is being paid off something like 20 years in advance of the expected time.

Article 8 of the protocol for a loan, in part, reads as follows:

"And it is further agreed that the control by an officer or officers duly appointed by the President of Haiti, upon nomination by the President of the United States, for the collection and allocation of the hypothecated revenues, will be provided for during the life of the loan after the expiration of the aforesaid treaty, so as to make certain that adequate provision be made for the amortization and interest of the loan."

That would imply that a contract between the bondholder and the debtor would require that the revenues' control and the revenues be vested in the appointee of the President of the United States, even after the withdrawal of the other American agents. I think, roughly speaking, the amortization of the debt runs over a period of 13 years, whereas the extended treaty has 15 years to run. There is not any such provision, I think, for the allocation of revenues for this debt, as there was for the Dominican debt, where they took half of all above a certain sum of the revenues.

Senator ODDIE. There is one thing I would like to ask. You spoke of the value of the roads. Did you look over the system of the roads yourself?

Mr. JOHNSON. I can not say, Senator—the system. I took the big highway from Port au Prince to Cape Haitien. That is a very good road.

Senator ODDIE. Do you feel that criticism of the work that has been done by the marines on the roads was made with full knowledge of the work that had been done by the marines?

Mr. JOHNSON. Yes; I think so. You mean the value of the work to the country?

Senator ODDIE. Yes.

Mr. JOHNSON. I think so. As I looked at it, I think the value of that road to Haiti can be overestimated.

Senator ODDIE. Do you not think, in speaking of a military road as you do, that it can have value from an economic and commercial standpoint as well?

Mr. JOHNSON. Oh, yes. I think it has some, but I say that value can be overestimated, I think, for Haiti. I mean by that that a road would be of greater economic advantage in some other country than it is in Haiti. This is a great highway, and you will find military trucks and automobiles traveling over it without any speed limit. In fact, in some instances, the road is a drawback to the Haitian farmer. I went over the road and I saw an automobile frighten a market woman. She was on one mule, and she had a horse loaded down with all her produce going to market, and her child was on another one, and the horse got frightened and ran and scattered all her produce from one end of the road to the other. And when the farmers get their donkeys killed, a donkey means a great deal to a Haitian farmer, and when these automobiles come along, these poor people scramble up the sides of the mountains, or down the declivities, trying to get out of the way. The road, as I say, is a great advantage to people who want to see Haiti, but I do not think it is worth quite that much to the Haitian farmer who is trying to get his produce to the town. He has got no automobile. He goes on foot, with his little donkeys in a trail one behind the other, and a mountain path would be far more convenient to him almost than a road.

Mr. HOWE. Would the same remark apply to the railroads? Have the railroads opened up the country to any extent, in developing it?

Mr. JOHNSON. Well, the railroad, as far as it goes, I think serves quite the purpose. The railroad runs north as far as St. Marc, and then they have got another little one that shoots around the bay of Port au Prince down to the south there.

Mr. HOWE. Have they had any particular effect in opening up the country for the transportation of produce which otherwise would not have any way of reaching a market?

Mr. JOHNSON. No; I do not think so. I think the traffic perhaps between St. Marc and Port au Prince would be perhaps just about as much as it is.

Mr. HOWE. Did you make any investigation as to the condition of the lower Haitian courts there?

Mr. JOHNSON. I did not investigate the courts, but I talked with some of the big lawyers there.

Mr. HOWE. What was their opinion of the Haitian lower courts?

Mr. JOHNSON. Well, I talked with one man there who is a judge in one of the courts, and he told me that the Haitians felt that the courts did not amount to anything now, because they had no exclusive jurisdiction. He said that they were interfered with always by the military authorities.

Mr. HOWE. Did you gather from what they told you that the military courts interfered in the civil cases, that is to say as distinguished from the criminal cases; I mean cases between plaintiff and defendant over money matters?

Mr. JOHNSON. Well, I do not think I have got a distinction as to that, but I gathered that they interfered with cases that were in the civil courts; that a man would be exonerated by the civil courts, and the military would simply arrest him on that same charge.

Mr. HOWE. The thing I was more interested in, perhaps, than that, was this: That being an abnormal condition under the intervention of the provost courts, are the lower courts competent courts to decide—I mean are the judges there able enough men to decide questions of property between plaintiff and defendant?

Mr. JOHNSON. I think so. I just throw that out. I have not investigated it.

Mr. HOWE. What I want to know is whether you had made any special inquiries about that branch. Did you have any time to inform yourself on that?

Mr. JOHNSON. Not specifically, but I am just giving a general impression. I think they are capable to handle——

Mr. HOWE. Do you know what the salaries of those judges de paix are?

Mr. JOHNSON. No; I do not. I did find out the salaries of some of the schoolteachers. I did not look up the salaries of the judges.

Mr. HOWE. Would it be your opinion that if martial law were done away with there, the Haitian lower courts could satisfactorily cooperate with the gendarmerie to the end of preserving law and order in the country?

Mr. JOHNSON. I should think so.

Mr. HOWE. I mean after removing the element of divided authority, which is a bad element for any court?

Mr. JOHNSON. I was going to qualify it by that; yes.

Mr. HOWE. Is the Haitian system of lower courts capable of backing up the Haitian system of gendarmerie and administering justice fairly, to the end of preserving law and order?

Mr. JOHNSON. I should say that I think so.

Mr. HOWE. I have heard that the salaries of the lower courts, the judges de paix, are very low indeed, and that a proper and properly qualified man would not be induced by that salary to go on the bench of a judge de paix?

Mr. JOHNSON. Yes.

Mr. HOWE. Is it not your opinion that the justices of the peace, or the judges de paix, ought to be well qualified men, as the judges that the poor people first encounter?

Mr. JOHNSON. Well, he at least ought to be an honest man.

Mr. HOWE. It is a very important position, is it not?

Mr. JOHNSON. Yes; it is from that point of view. I do not think it requires any extraordinary ability to be a justice of the peace; it does not in this country.

Mr. HOWE. No; but he has got to be honest; he has got to know some law, has he not?

Mr. JOHNSON. He has got to know some law and he has got to have common sense.

Mr. HOWE. And especially if he decides questions of the ownership of property between poor people?

Mr. JOHNSON. Yes; but I do not know how far the jurisdiction of a judge de paix would go in property matters. I judge it would be limited according to some amount, and that above a certain amount it would go up to some higher court.

Mr. HOWE. Would it not be a useful thing for anybody to know, before the time of the withdrawal of the American occupation is decided, as to whether the Haitian Government can supply an adequate judiciary?

Mr. JOHNSON. I think it would be a very good thing to inquire into.

Mr. ANGELL. Would you care to give us, without feeling that you are violating any confidence, the substance of a conversation that you had, I understand, with President Dartiguenave regarding the relations between the occupation and the Haitian Government?

Mr. JOHNSON. I saw President Dartiguenave twice. The first time I saw him, although I was well introduced to him, he was rather reticent. He talked along generally. We talked without any interpreter. And the second time I saw him he was a little freer, and he confessed to me then that he had a very difficult time in getting along in any direction at all with the American occupation. He said that they ignored him completely; that they ignored his council of state, I think then acting as a sort of cabinet; that they paid no attention to his recommendations, and that whatever they decided was to go through they made him to understand that it was to go through, and he talked in that strain with me for half an hour.

Mr. ANGELL. When you say "they" are we to understand that he referred to the officers of the military occupation, or the American minister, or the civilian treaty officials, or all of them?

Mr. JOHNSON. "They" was a comprehensive "they." It takes them all in. There seemed to be considerable dissatisfaction with our minister who was there at that time.

Mr. ANGELL. Mr. Bailly-Blanchard?

Mr. JOHNSON. Yes.

(Whereupon the committee adjourned until Wednesday, November 16, 1921, at 10.30 o'clock a. m.)

INQUIRY INTO OCCUPATION AND ADMINISTRATION OF HAITI AND SANTO DOMINGO.

WEDNESDAY, NOVEMBER 16, 1921.

UNITED STATES SENATE,
SELECT COMMITTEE ON HAITI AND SANTO DOMINGO,
Washington, D. C.

The committee met at 10.30 o'clock a. m., pursuant to adjournment, Senator Tasker L. Oddie presiding.

Present: Senators McCormick (chairman) and Oddie.

Also present: Mr. Walter Bruce Howe, Mr. Ernest Angell, and Maj. Edwin N. McClellan, United States Marine Corps.

Mr. HOWE. Mr. Chairman, Capt. Angell has here to-day a witness, Mr. Pilkington, who he says has had exceptional opportunities to observe conditions in Haiti, and my suggestion would be to have Capt. Angell, who has talked with Mr. Pilkington, as I understand it, conduct the questioning at the outset.

Senator ODDIE. If there is no objection, it is so ordered.

STATEMENT OF MR. H. M. PILKINGTON, TECHNICAL EXPERT, VICE PRESIDENT AND MANAGER AMERICAN DEVELOPMENT CO. OF HAITI, NEW YORK, N. Y., AND PORT AU PRINCE, HAITI.

Mr. ANGELL. Mr. Pilkington, what is your occupation?

Mr. PILKINGTON. I am technical expert and vice president and manager of the American Development Co. of Haiti.

Mr. ANGELL. You have been in Haiti?

Mr. PILKINGTON. Since 1918 practically up to the present.

Mr. ANGELL. What was the occasion which took you to Haiti, and what has been your general business in Haiti?

Mr. PILKINGTON. I went there, originally, in an advisory capacity for the banking interests who control the Haitian-American Corporation.

Mr. ANGELL. What was the Haitian-American Corporation?

Mr. PILKINGTON. That being a company organized to take over the public utilities existing in Haiti, and to build a sugar mill and organize extensive plantations in the plains of the Cul de Sac and Leogane, these being the only two parts of Haiti in which sugar is naturally grown on the same lands as it was in the days of the French occupation, and the only districts in which the irrigation system is in practical operation, as originally engineered by the French colonists.

Mr. ANGELL. What was the date of your going to Haiti?

Mr. PILKINGTON. That was early in 1918.

Mr. ANGELL. Have you been practically continuously in Haiti since that time?

Mr. PILKINGTON. I have been practically continuously in Haiti since that time, spending during that time easily a solid two years and a half of time right in Haiti.

Mr. ANGELL. When did you come up from Haiti last?

Mr. PILKINGTON. I came up from Haiti last just before Christmas.

Mr. ANGELL. Of 1920?

Mr. PILKINGTON. Yes. During that particular trip I made a complete and intensive study of the physical properties of the corporation, and inasmuch as the success of any industrial project in any coutry is dependent upon the mental attitude of the people of that country, it was equally important for me to make a study of the psychology of all classes of the people.

My physical investigations and studies of the country and the lands naturally brought me in contact with what we might call the lowest or the most primi-

789

tive class, which is the laboring class or peasantry, this class of people being entirely illiterate and living in the most primitive imaginable conditions. I found that the thousands of people employed in field work and in this laboring class on our many and various plantations extended over a very wide territory, were invariably and without exception a completely amiable, docile, tractable, and completely amenable people. They are naturally and inherently cultivators of the ground ·and with a very slight outlay of patience and a very slight exercise of friendly discipline, they became exceptionally good plantation operators to the extent of planting, cultivating, and cutting the cane, and it will be fair to say that a very large percentage of the vast number of people of this class, who migrated from Haiti to Cuba as skilled cane cutters, were educated in this line by the Haitian-American Sugar Co., and reports from Cuba were invariably to the purport that these people, the Haitians, made the best cane cutters in Cuba.

I next made it my business to come in contact with what we might call the ruling or political class of the country, because, at basis, every industrial or other enterprise is fundamentally dependent upon the laws and the execution of those laws in whatever country may be concerned. The original financing of this Haitian-American Corporation was brought about and put to the public directly and definitely upon assurance in Washington, by competent people and competent officials, that the treaty between the United States and Haiti was, in fact, to be a living thing. The large feature in the floating of the securities of this company, all of which floating came under my personal observation at the time, was predicated, one might say, wholly as to security, upon the implied bona fides of the United States in carrying out this treaty—the basing of which was security for foreign capital. This must be a self-evident condition, because the development of a primitive country depends upon one thing and one thing only without which it can not even begin—that is, the bringing in of foreign capital. It is a manifest axiom that this capital will not be risked in a country which does not extend a sufficient guaranty for the security of that capital. I became acquainted on extremely intimate terms with what I have before called the ruling class, having had several very confidential interviews, which later ripened into an intimate friendship on the most agreeable basis, with President Dartiguenave, with practically all of his cabinet, his conseil d' etat, and practically all of the intellectual class of Haitians. I have been accorded what to me is considered the high privilege of being invited to become a member of the Cercle Bellevue, the exclusive social club of Haiti, this invitation being extended by the president of that club, one of the most cultured, educated, and enlightened gentlemen that one might meet anywhere.

Mr. ANGELL. Will you give the name of that gentleman, for the particular reason that I rather expect to call him as a witness when we get down there?

Mr. PILKINGTON. I would be glad to have appear on the record the name of this gentleman, Mr. George de Lespinasse, and in the same paragraph, an apology for not mentioning, for want of space, the names of a multitude of other Haitians, of whose acquaintance I am more than· proud, and to all of whom, or to any of whom, I am sure could be intrusted the reins of their own independent government, being fitted for this by a very high grade of education, character, and political and diplomatic training, it being almost an invariable rule that the better class Haitian has had, in addition to a good education in the higher schools of Haiti, a further education in European conservatories.

There is not in Haiti what we would term a middle class, in the European or American acceptance of the term. What corresponds to this class might be called the commercial class, the traders who buy the products of the country and export them to other countries, and those who maintain shops and stores. This class is, of course, literate, and to a greater or lesser extent well educated. In all my two years or more intensive study in Haiti, I have not in any one single instance found an example of what we could rightly call a vicious type. I say this broadly and in full knowledge of its purport. I extend this even to the members that I·have seen and observed of the bandits or so-called Cacos. I present for the information of the committee, on this line a photograph of one of these bandits who openly confessed to have had a·part in the torturing of Pvt. Lawrence, who was openly claimed to have been actually eaten. It will be seen from this portrait that while the deeds of this man and of his like were unspeakable, that the type, ethnologically speaking, is not a vicious type.

I also show the photograph of one of these Cacos who was concerned in the mutilation and death of Lieut. Muth. The same observation will also apply to the physiognomy of this man. Further evidence along this line of this same class has been frequently told me by enlisted men of the marines, in reference to treatment that they have had at the hands of this class of people. I have been told by enlisted men who have been lost in the hills from their detachments, and have wandered for days through the bandit territory in their uniform, that they have been concealed away from other Cacos in security and safety, and then forwarded on their way, that is in among this same class of Cacos.

My impression gained at that time of the physical advantages of the country, as regarding the advantages of soil and light, and the prevalence of a large amount of satisfactory field labor, were so favorable that in association with the banking firm which controlled the majority of the stock of the Haitian-American Corporation, I organized in Haiti, under the Haitian laws, a genuine Haitian company, to comply in all respects with the existing laws of Haiti, a development company, which was prepared with sufficient financial backing to undertake and execute any form whatsoever of development work in the country, which would warrant a reasonable return upon the investment. I was voluntarily elected under the law of Haiti to be the resident director who should be directly and personally responsible for the actions of this company, as the law requires.

Immediately upon and before the formation of this company, I made an extended study of all Haiti, its physical conditions, not only of soil but of topography, the possibilities of transportation, the mineral possibilities, and the existing conditions affecting in any way the practical development and exploitation of the country. The character of the country may be best described in words which are accredited to Napoleon, whose brother-in-law, Le Clerc, was the military governor of Haiti at the time that this country was France's greatest possession, and one of the, if not the, finest colonies in all of the world. This Gen. Le Clerc was making a report of conditions to his chief, Napoleon, and was asked what kind of a country is Haiti. He seized a large sheet of foolscap, completely crumpled it up in one hand, and throwing it on the table, said, " Sire, that is Haiti." In my opinion, no other description could so well explain the topography of Haiti. With the exception of a few plains of rather limited extent, the entire country is a mass of interlocking mountains, almost totally without connecting valleys, many of which are so narrow that one may stand with one foot on one mountain and the other foot on the other mountain—these, of course, being the bases.

The general means of intercommunication is nothing but trails of loose stones, the entire country being practically of limestone formation. Over these trails the produce of the tiny farms with which the country is completely covered is carried upon the heads of women, or on the backs of the burros, to some market center. This means and method of transportation is entirely satisfactory to these people in their present state of evolution. They, in fact, universally complain of the crazy acts of the whites in destroying their nice, shady trails for the purpose of making a wide, smooth road, on which their automobiles may kill their burros and scare them to death.

It is manifest to even the casual observer who merely sees Haiti from a passing steamer that the country is only at the present time an agricultural possibility, and it is manifest that hillside agriculture must be very largely considered in any general development of the country. This feature has been, one might say, entirely overlooked and neglected by every tentative exploitation in Haiti. Even from the colonial times the plains only have been really cultivated. Haiti is characterized by their own writers as being a one-crop country—this one crop being coffee—and it is fair to say that even in this narrow sense there do not exist what can be rightly called coffee plantations. most of it being grown in a desultory manner, wild and always at some considerable elevation, and without irrigation. Cotton has also been an extensive article of export, but its cultivation has never, up until the time of the United West Indies Corporation, been scientifically pursued. The cotton, which has heretofore been exported, having grown wild in various parts of the country, and being picked by the natives and carried to the market in small quantities and exported in its raw state.

The country may, therefore, from an industrial point of view, be considered from an absolutely primitive basis, and whatever development is done there

62269—21—PT 2——44

must start, in two senses of the word, from the ground up. This naturally brings us to the very vital, basic principles which must govern all such operations, first, the control of the lands, and second, the possibility of remaining in peaceful and friendly possession and operation of these lands.

The first point—that is, the control of the lands—must necessarily mean some form of exclusive ownership of these lands over a period necessarily long to allow for complete development of these lands and the consequent sufficient return for the money invested. At the present time there does not exist in Haiti any general system whatever of determining the ownership of these lands, there being a vast amount of territory which is claimed to be Government land, but in any concession or lease involving these so-called Government lands there is always a requirement that they be surveyed under the supervision of the Government to determine what is and what is not Government land. The modus operandi of this survey consists of surveyors going to the district concerned, communicating with the judge de paix of that district, and with him going around through the district and getting the mutual consent of the various farmers, who may be squatters or who may be owners—nobody knows which—as to whose land is theirs and whose is not.

Mr. ANGELL. Are you speaking now of an actual survey which has been made?

Mr. PILKINGTON. I am speaking of actual surveys, such as they make in order to give these concessions that I mentioned. If you want a concession there you can not get it without proceeding in the following manner. This will have a direct and definite bearing on the land laws.

As evidence of his ownership to a particular piece of land the so-called farmer shows what he thinks is a deed to that land. There have been cases concerning land for which the sugar company has been negotiating in which the farmer has proudly produced a bill of sale for a horse, thinking and believing that that was a deed to his property. Under the Haitian law the undisputed possession of a piece of land for 20 years is considered as ownership of the land. Upon the death of a member of the family this farming class there must always be a more or less elaborate funeral ceremony the expenses of which are to them fairly heavy and are in a large number of cases borne by selling a small piece of this land which, as can readily be seen, has complicated the already absurd conditions of ownership; so that in the further absence of any system of records it is well nigh impossible to know whether one has bought or leased a certain piece of land or not. It is obvious that a correct title to a piece of land must be based on a correct location of that land; that is to say, a correct survey. Up to the present time there has been no official survey of Haiti, and one of the fundamental and most important improvements brought about by the American occupation, and very ably and systematically conducted, has been a complete, up-to-date, scientific campaign of triangulation and survey of all Haiti by officials lent by the United States Government—I think the department of the Geological Survey.

Mr. HOWE. Is this an accomplished fact?

Mr. PILKINGTON. An accomplished fact; yes. This work to be entirely completed, would require a term of several more years, but until it is completed it is an absolute physical impossibility for anybody to acquire a definite, final, recorded ownership of a tract of land, except by the mutual consent of all parties interested as to the established boundaries of this piece of land in question.

This work was begun and has been continued in the most approved and scientific manner, starting from a regular base line, being surveyed and most accurately measured and remeasured on the plains of the Cul de Sac, and has included the measuring and marking of all the visible points—that is, the tops of mountains—over the entire country. A large number of these points has been triangulated and the angles closed as the surveyors stated. It will be only from the extension of these lines into all localities and all parts of the map that definite possession of the various tracts of land can be accurately determined and recorded.

We now come to the laws concerning the holding of these lands. It is safe to say that the most serious thought in the mind of the Haitian is the thought that the foreigner is going to get an actual, physical foothold on his land, which is a very small country, and in time force him out of an independent existence. I feel, from the standpoint of my experience with the people that this feeling is perhaps the most important feeling to be considered in dealing with the native Haitians.

It is true that there are vast tracts of land in Haiti, claimed to be and probably actually owned by various Haitians, on which they never set foot. I have been told in many cases by Haitians that they own tracts in the north of Haiti, where the Cacos have always existed, upon which they have never dared set foot on account of the lawless squatters, who are now occupying that land and claim to own it through the mere fact of being there. It must be noted that this condition does not comply with the condition of the undisputed occupation of territory such as a squatter clause in a law would imply. The present constitution. of Haiti contains a provision for the acquiring of the ownership of Haitian land by foreigners. It is the claim of the Haitians that this constitution is not constitutional; that it was not promulgated by their own elective body, and that it contains principles which are absolutely and forever antagonistic, and to which Haiti, as a body, would never and could never agree. This clause allows the ownership of Haitian land by foreigners, but does not, as it originally stands, go into any details. The Haitian Government, after that constitution was enacted, some time in 1920—I do nor remember just when—adopted, voted, and passed a law which purported to set forth the conditions under which that clause was operative. These conditions were so entirely contradictory of the spirit of that clause that foreigners who had in the meantime invested in property in Haiti, and had been developing the same, naturally became very much perturbed, and an instant protest was lodged with the competent authorities, and this offending law was temporarily suspended.

During the course of my acquaintance with these people, and my travels over all the country, I can truly say that I have met with nothing but the utmost courtesy, good feeling, and cooperation of every class. The President has often expressed in the most heartfelt and feeling way his great sympathy and his great willingness to help any American enterprise which was based primarily on the good of Haiti. This spirit of cooperation I find in all the official class of the Government. I will specify in particular with great pleasure the progressive spirit and great ability of the minister of public works, Louis Roy, whom I found to be capable, courteous, intelligent, and a credit to his country. All work of development of any kind whatever under any form of concession comes under the jurisdiction of the minister of public works, and the Haitian-American Corporation has, therefore, through its various utilities and industries, been cont nually in touch and subject to that department of the Government, and I am sure there does not exist any single cause of complaint on that score.

There does exist, however, a universal spirit of complaint and criticism on the position held and action taken by various American officials in that country. The causes and the reasons for these complaints were a matter of very careful study by me, for it is self-evident that if officials who are carrying out the physical occupation of a country are in continual friction with the officials of that country, the purposes of that occupation will never be achieved. I found a very intense attitude of antagonism existing in all classes of society. The laboring class, based in all cases that I could observe upon the application of the law of the corvée, especially in the building of roads in the north——

Mr. ANGELL. The feeling you are speaking of is the feeling you found at the time you were there, between 1918 and 1920?

Mr. PILKINGTON. Yes. This is all, of course, from the studies which I made wh'le I was there, and is the result of actual studies, not just impressions. I made it my business while in Haiti to learn the vernacular of the country, and am capable of maintaining an intelligible conversation with the actual peasantry, and I have talked directly with many of these people, principally mountaineers, those who live all their lives in the mountains, coming down to the plains only for market purposes. This class, as well as all other classes in Haiti, definitely accused the powers in charge of the work on these roads with abuses of this corvée law. As to the actual details of these abuses, it was not of interest to me to investigate in detail, the important fact being that the attitude of mind back of the animus which was clearly shown was the important factor, not necessarily the exact facts which brought about this state of mind.

What one might call the next class that had been concerned, and that complained of the occupation, would be the former Government clerk, as we might call him. Of course, in their former government everyone who had the requisite influence held a government job. It is well known that many of these jobs were held by people who did not work at the jobs, but hired some other man at a much lower pay to do the work, and he pocketed the difference, but, at any rate, there were a vast number of people thrown out of employment by the coming of the American occupation, this, of course, being no fault of the American occupation whatever, but furnishing a class of malcontents.

The next class one might consider would be the educated civilian class. It is fair to say that their antagonism was due solely to friction in various ways between the members of the occupation forces and themselves. This started, as nearly as I can make out, coincident with the landing of the wives of the American officers. Up to that time the American officers had free and complete social intercourse with the Haitians, both in their families and in their clubs, during which, of course, they freely danced with the Haitian ladies. With the coming of the women of the occupation this peaceful state of affairs was completely upset, the women having a natural aversion, due to their former training and method of thinking, to dancing and general social intercourse with the Haitians, men or women; the husbands of these women also strongly objecting for the same reason. Therefore, there came an immediate rift in the social lute. The exclusive Haitian clubs, which formerly had welcomed the officers—the American officers—as guests of the club, began to resent this condition of affairs, and the American club, which eventually became dominated by officers of the occupation, at no time within my knowledge as a member of this club received as guests any Haitians. In spite of this natural and justified feeling of resentment by the Haitians of this condition, the Cercle Bellevue, probably the most exclusive Haitian club, continued to receive not only as guests but as members certain Americans and other white men in whom they had confidence and trust, showing, to my mind, a marked spirit of lenience in courtesy in favor of the Haitians.

I might cite a case of direct abuse which I know contributed in a very large part, although one might call it trivial in itself, to the general feeling of resentment. There is among the many talented Haitians a very talented and finished musician, a graduate of a Paris conservatory of music. After a dinner which I had the pleasure of attending at this gentleman's house he told me of an instance which had occurred shortly before my arrival in Haiti. He was giving a private piano recital of his own compositions to some of his pupils and their parents in his home. While playing these compositions, which his guests were enjoy'ng from their posit on in his garden, they were bombarded with rocks from the neighboring dwelling, which was occupied by an American officer. This stoning was so continuous and so dangerous that his guests all were compelled to take flight, and he had to put out the lights and lock up the house. He made complaint to the competent military authorities. They immediately took prompt action and offered to discipline this officer, but at the interposition of this gentleman himself punishment was waived. I afterwards personally became acquainted with this officer and found him to be a very efficient, excellent soldier, with a very good record, this incident being merely one of many instances of the power of the demon rum, which is one of the very great difficulties with which the commanding officer of the forces in any tropical country has to deal.

Mr. Howe. Did it turn out that this officer himself had thrown these stones?

Mr. Pilkington. Yes; it did. It is easy to see what a state of mind was brought about among the intellectual classes of Haitians, for it must be here noted that the better classes are intermarried to an extent that one could hardly conceive, and therefore an injury to one is an injury to all.

Mr. Angell. Did you hear of that incident referred to by other Haitians of that class, friends of this musician?

Mr. Pilkington. Yes; this incident thereafter being a topic of universal d's-cussion whenever the act'ons of the marines were considered. It was my pleasure and privilege to help this gentleman in his endeavors and final success in having his works published by the music firm of Charles Fisher & Co., of New York. The Columbia Phonograph people have also made records of his works, as have also the Aeolian Co., in making master records for their duoart piano, which is by far the most expensive and the best of the player pianos, using only rolls made by the composers themselves. I was, therefore, fortunately able to lessen in that particular case the unfortunate impression of Americans in general which a large proportion of the Haitians held, and I think it will be fair to say that, thanks to the personal living and negotiation of certain Americans who they have in their midst, this class of Haitian has come to know that such things are not necessarily a common attribute of Americans.

We now come to what, in my mind, may be truly considered as the greatest and the most important source of complaint which the Haitian has. In August,

1920, it was brought to my attention by various prominent Haitians that there was a matter of very serious import pending at the palace.

Mr. ANGELL. You were in Haiti at that moment?

Mr. PILKINGTON. Yes; I was there. This information was brought to me in the office of my company in Haiti and personally told to me by a certain member of the Haitian Government. He told me personally that the existing contract between the National Bank of Haiti and the Government of Haiti, being up for revision, had been discussed and a certain clause modified to the mutual agreement of the National Bank of Haiti and of the Government of Haiti.

Mr. ANGELL. You will remember, Mr. Chairman, that this was the matter testified to by Mr. Farnham, the first witness before the committee.

Mr. PILKINGTON. According to my informant, a draft containing all these agreed modifications was to be submitted to the President for his signature. Upon the President's refusal to sign this document, the financial adviser, who, under the treaty, is an employee of Haiti, attached to the department of finance of Haiti, refused to further discuss the pending budget for the year, implying that he would not go further in the matter until the President of Haiti had signed that document. Upon his continued refusal the salaries of the President and several of his officials were stopped.

Mr. HOWE. This is the financial adviser you are talking about?

Mr. PILKINGTON. The financial adviser; yes. Upon inquiries being made as to the reason for this by the President of Haiti, he was definitely given to understand, through the minister of the United States in Haiti, as well as the financial adviser, that it was demanded by the United States Government.

Mr. HOWE. Who was the minister? Give his name.

Mr. PILKINGTON. Mr. Bailly-Blanchard. President Dartiguenave still refused, and it transpired that Col. Russell, the chief of the military forces, upon whom the actual life of President Dartiguenave depended, the financial adviser, Mr. MacIlhenny, who by this time had apparently arrogated to himself functions far beyond what are defined in the treaty, and Mr. Bailly-Blanchard, who diplomatically is the United States Government as far as Haiti is concerned, demanded audience directly with President Dartiguenave, in defiance of all diplomatic usages and ethics, a financial matter, of course, necessarily being properly under the jurisdiction of the department of finance and its minister, and in this interview, in the name of the Government of the United States, demanded that he sign that contract as it stood.

This act, whether justified or not by facts which do not appear and have never been in any way explained, to my knowledge, either to the Haitian people or to anyone else, is, to my direct knowledge, an insurmountable obstacle to any genuine entente between the United States Government and the Haitian people until it is definitely and finally explained publicly, and if unwarranted, openly and officially apologized for. It is a fact, which is evident to the observation of all thinkers in any part of the world, that the smaller a nation, or the smaller a group of people, or the more insignificant an individual is, the more jealous he is of his actual rights, and the more exigent he is in anything which can affect his personal pride, and of all races in the world it is no doubt the fact that the feeling is strongest in the Latins, and they are the people who most resent any infraction of these rights and of this amour propré. It may be, and if so I would certainly like to personally know, that we, an enlightened people, and the most advanced Nation in the world, as we freely admit ourselves on all occasions, have such a form of government and such a method of procedure as to allow our direct representatives to act in a manner which, at least to the eye and the mind of the open observer, appears to be nothing but brigandage.

Immediately upon knowledge of this act becoming public, an instant and general protest was filed by all the responsible interests in Haiti, not only native but American and foreign. This insistence by the American Government was finally withdrawn, but has never been explained, as heretofore said, nor apologized for, within the knowledge of anybody with whom I am acquainted.

Any scheme of future reconstruction, of course, must be predicated upon the good will of the people, and equally, of course, must be administered by a competent assembly. Until apology for and reparation of another great outstanding abuse is made such a constitutional assembly will be almost impossible to convene in Haiti. I refer to the act described to me personally by certain Senators concerned at the time as a physical driving out by force of the deputies.

Mr. PILKINGTON. I can confidently say, irrespective of the actual pros and cons of this question, that the feeling which actuated this general protest concerning the revised ,bank contract was based on the fact that the financial advisor appeared as a court of ultimate resort in this question, as in all others of a like nature, and by his apparent usurpation of powers not belonging to him under the treaty, in connection with his forcing of this clause, caused a universal feeling of distrust and a lack of confidence in any action which he might be called upon to take in connection with the finances of Haiti.

Mr. ANGELL. At this point I should like to offer in the record, Mr. Chairman, the verbatim protest of the American, foreign, and Haitian business men and business interests in Haiti against this proposed action, the protest being dated July 30, 1920, the material portions of which are the last two paragraphs.

(The protest referred to is here printed in full, as follows:)

"The protest printed below, against article 15 of the contract with withdrawal, was sent to the Haitian secretary of finance on July 30, 1920.

"The undersigned bankers, merchants, and representatives of the various branches of the financial and commercial activities in Haiti have the honor to submit to the high appreciation of the secretary of state for finance the following consideration:

"They have been advised from certain sources that pressing recommendations have been made to the Government of Haiti.

"1· That a law be immediately voted by which would be prohibited the importation or exportation of all money not Haitian, except that quantity of foreign money which, in the opinion of the financial adviser, would be sufficient for the needs of commerce.

"2· That in the charter of the Banque Nationale de la Republique d'Haiti there be inserted an article giving power to the financial adviser together with the Banque Nationale de la Republique d'Haiti to take all measures concerning the importation or exportation of non-Haitian moneys.

"The undersigned declare that the adoption of such a measure, under whatever form it may be, would be of a nature generally contrary to the collective interests of the Haitian people and the industry of Haiti. It would be dangerous to substitute the will of a single man, however eminent he might be, however honorable, however infallible, for a natural law which regulates the movements of the monetary circulation in a country·

"It would be more dangerous yet to introduce in the contract of the Banque Nationale de la Republique d'Haiti a clause which would assure this establishment a sort of monopoly in the foreign money market, which constitutes the principal base of the operations of high commerce, when it has already the exclusive privilege of emission of bank notes. Such a clause would make of all other bankers and merchants its humble tributaries, obeying its law and its caprices.

"(Signed): The Royal Bank of Canada; American Foreign Banking Corporation; Haitian American Sugar Co.; Raporel Steamship Line; P. C. S.; Electric Light Co.; Panama Line; Ed. Esteve & Co.; Clyde Line; Comptoir Commercial; Gebara & Co.; Alfred Vieux; V. G. Makhlouf; N. Silvera; Simmonds Freres; Roberts, Dutton & Co.; West Indies Trading Co.; J. Fadoul & Co.; R. Drouard; A. de Matteis & Co.; J. M. Richardson & Co.; Comptoir Francais; H. Dereix; E. Robelin; F. Cheriez; I. J. Bigio, and George H. MacFadden."

Senator ODDIE. How does the price of silver per ounce compare with the price of silver per ounce in the world markets?

Mr. PILKINGTON. There is no price per ounce. There is no silver coin there at all.

Senator ODDIE. I mean the silver that can be bought in the market?

Mr. PILKINGTON. The silver that is bought in the market is nothing but old coins that have been hoarded here and there.

Senator ODDIE. On what basis do they sell per ounce?

Mr. PILKINGTON. They do not sell it per ounce. Nobody sells anything hardly there. There is no industry there. It is a raw, primitive country. You can not go and buy silver per ounce.

Senator ODDIE. You spoke of the value per ounce?

Mr. PILKINGTON. Not the value per ounce.

Senator ODDIE. Of old coins?

Mr. PILKINGTON. These silver coins have a value beyond their face value for souvenirs, but in fact the few that do come in from the country which have been hoarded by the natives have been acquired by the natives from somebody else, and they make them up into neck chains, with pendants on them, and thereby you have to pay more than the face value of the coin to get it. Silver can not be obtained at the bank, the coins in circulation being nickel and copper.

Mr. ANGELL. Let me put the question to you in another way. Do you think that the protest of the business men, which has just been offered in the record, and to which you referred, was based to any considerable degree on a fear by those business men that the effect of the operation of the proposed clause would have been to interrupt by such a legal monopoly the free play of foreign exchange, depending for its normal free play upon the uninterrupted right of import and export of foreign money, and that such interruption of the natural law of exchange would have been detrimental to the individual interests of these business men and business houses and detrimental to the general trade and commerce of Haiti?

Mr. PILKINGTON. Such an attitude was the generally voiced opinion of everyone with whom I communicated on the subject.

Mr. ANGELL. Is it your understanding that subsequently the salaries of the President, the cabinet, and other Government officials thus suspended ·for the month of July, 1920, as you have testified, were finally paid by the financial adviser?

Mr. PILKINGTON. Yes.

Mr. ANGELL. And if so, when?

Mr. PILKINGTON. I do not remember when. It was commonly stated that these payments were resumed and that the United States Government receded from this position.

Mr. ANGELL. At this point, Mr. Chairman, I would like to offer in the record the correspondence which passed between the Haitian Government, the American minister to Haiti, the civilian treaty officials, and directly between the Haitian Government and the American Government in Washington on this subject. This correspondence which I am introducing now also includes several protests made to the Haitian Government on the occasion of this proposed monopoly to be given to the National Bank of Haiti, emanating from the British, French, and Italian Legations to the Haitian Government.

(The matter referred to is here printed in full, as follows:)

At the session of the Haitian National Assembly on August 4, 1920, the President of the Republic of Haiti and the Haitian minister of finance laid before that body the course of the American financial adviser which had made it impossible to submit to the assembly accounts and budgets in accordance with the constitution of Haiti and the Haiti-American convention. The statement which follows is taken from the official Haitian gazette, the Moniteur, of August 7, 1920:

MESSAGE OF THE PRESIDENT.

Gentlemen of the council of state, on account of unforeseen circumstances it has not been possible for the Government of the Republic to present to you in the course of the session of your high assembly which closes to-day (August 4) the general accounts of the receipts and expenditures for 1918–19 and the budget for 1920–21, in accordance with the constitution.

It is certainly an exceptional case, the gravity of which will not escape you. You will learn the full details from the report which the secretary of finance and commerce will submit to you, in which it will be shown that the responsibility for it does not fall on the executive power * * *.

In the life of every people there come moments when it must know how to be resigned and to suffer. Are we facing one of those moments? The attitude of the Haitian people, calm and dignified, persuades me that, marching closely with the Government of the Republic, there is no suffering which is not disposed to undergo to safeguard and secure the triumph of its rights.

DARTIGUENAVE.

REPORT OF THE SECRETARY OF FINANCE AND COMMERCE.

Gentlemen of the council of state, article 116 of the constitution prescribed in its first paragraph: "The general accounts and the budgets prescribed by the preceding article must be submitted to the legislative body by the secretary of finance not later than eight days after the opening of the legislative session."

And article 2 of the American-Haitian convention of September 16, 1915, stipulates in its second peragraph: " The President of Haiti shall appoint, on the nomination of the President of the United States, a financial adviser, who shall be a civil servant attached to the ministry of finance, to whom the secretary shall lend effective aid in the prosecution of his work. The financial adviser shall work out a system of public accounting, shall aid in increasing the revenues and in their adjustment to expenditures * * *."

Since February of this year (1920) the secretaries of the various departments, in order to conform to the letter of article 116 of the constitution, and to assure continuity of public service in the matter of receipts and expenditures, set to work at the preparation of the budgets for their departments for 1920–21.

By a dispatch dated March 22. 1920, the department of finance sent the draft budgets to Mr. A. J. Maumus, acting financial adviser, for preliminary study by that official. But the acting adviser replied to the department by a letter of March 29: " I suggest that, in view of the early return of Mr. John McIlhenny, the financial adviser, measures be taken to postpone all discussion regarding the said draft budgets between the different departments and the office (of the financial adviser) to permit him to take part in the discussions."

Nevertheless, the regular session was opened on the constitutional date, Monday, April 5, 1920. Mr. John McIlhenny, the titular financial adviser absent in the United States since October, 1919, on a financial mission for the Government, prolonged his stay in America, detained no doubt by the insurmountable difficulties in the accomplishment of his mission (the placing of a Haitian loan on the New York market). Since on the one hand the adviser could not overcome these difficulties, and on the other hand his presence at Port au Prince was absolutely necessary for the preparation of the budget in conformity with the constitution and the Haitian-American convention, the Government deemed it essential to ask him to return to Port au Prince for that purpose. The Government in so doing secured the good offices of the American legation, and Mr. McIlhenny returned from the United States about the 1st of June. The legislature had already been in session almost two months.

About June 15 the adviser began the study of the·budget with the secretaries. The conference lasted about 12 days and in that time, after courteous discussion, after some cuts, modifications, and additions, plans for the following budgets were agreed upon :

1. Ways and means.
2. Foreign relations.
3. Finance and commerce.
4. Interior.

On Monday, July 12, 1920, at 3.30, the hour agreed upon between the ministers and the adviser, the ministers met to continue the study of the budget which they wanted to finish quickly * * *. Between 4 and 4.30 the secretary of finance received a letter from the adviser which reads as follows:
" I find myself obliged to stop all study of the budget until certain affairs of considerable importance for the welfare of the country shall have been finally settled according to the recommendations made by me to the Haitian Government.

" Please accept, Mr. Secretary. the assurance of my highest consideration.
" JOHN MCILHENNY."

Such an unanticipated and unjustifiable decision on the part of Mr. McIlhenny. an official attached to the ministry of finance, caused the whole Government profound surprise and warranted dissatisfaction. * * *

On July 13 the department of finance replied to the financial adviser as follows:
" I beg to acknowledge your letter of July 12, in which you say, ' I find myself obliged, etc. * * *'

" In taking note of this declaration, the importance and gravity of which certainly can not escape you. I can only regret in the name of the Government—

" 1. That you omitted to tell.me with the precision which such an emergency demands what are the affairs of an importance so considerable for the welfare of the country and the settlement of which, according to the recommendations made by you, is of such great moment that you can subordinate to that settle-he continuation of the work on the budget?

" 2. That you have taken such a serious step without considering that in so doing you have divested yourself of one of the essential functions which devolves upon you as financial adviser attached to the department of finance.

" The preparation of the budget of the State constitutes one of the principal obligations of those intrusted with it by law, because the very life of the nation depends upon its elaboration. The legislature has been in session since April 5 last. By the constitution the draft budgets and the general accounts should be submitted to the legislative body within eight days after the opening of the session, that is to say by April 13. The draft budgets were sent to your office on March 22.

" By reason of your absence from the country, the examination of these drafts was postponed, the acting financial adviser not being willing to shoulder the responsibility; we refer you to his letters of March 29 and of April 17 and 24. Finally * * * you came back to Port au Prince, and after some two weeks you began with the secretaries to study the draft budgets.

" The Government therefore experiences a very disagreeable surprise on reading your letter of July 12. It becomes my duty to inform you of that disagreeable surprise, to formulate the legal reservations in the case, and to inform you finally that you bear the sole responsibility for the failure to present the budget in due time.

" FLEURY FEQUIERE, *Secretary of Finance.*"

On July 19, Mr. Bailly-Blanchard, the American minister, placed in the hands of the President of the Republic a memorandum emanating from Mr. McIlhenny, in which the latter formulates against the Government complaints sufficient, according to him, to explain and justify the discontinuance of the preparation of the budget, announced in his letter of July 12.

MEMORANDUM OF MR. M'ILHENNY.

I had instructions from the Department of State of the United States just before my departure for Ha'tl, in a passage of a letter of May 20, to declare to the Haitian Government that it was necessary to give its immediate and formal approval—

1. To a modification of the bank contract agreed upon by the Department of State and the National City Bank of New York.

2. To the transfer of the National Bank of the Republic of Haiti to a new bank registered under the laws of Haiti to be known as the National Bank of the Republic of Haiti.

3. To the execution of article 15 of the contract of withdrawal, prohibiting the importation and exportation of non-Haitian money, except that which might be necessary for the needs of commerce in the opinion of the financial adviser.

4. To the immediate vote of a territorial law which has been submitted to the Department of State of the United States and which has its approval.

On my arrival in Haiti I visited the President with the American minister and learned that the modifications of the bank contract and the transfer of the bank had been agreed to, and the only reason why the measure had not been made official was because the National City Bank and the National Bank of Haiti had not yet presented to the Government their full powers. He declared that the Government did not agree to the publication of a decree executing the contract of withdrawal, because it did not consider that the economic condition of the country justified it at that time. To which I replied that the Government of the United States expected the execution of article 15 of the contract of withdrawal as a direct and solemn engagement of the Haitian Government, to which it was a party, and I had instructions to insist upon its being put into execution at once. * * *

THE COUNTER MEMOIR.

To this memorandum the executive authority replied by a counter memoir, which read, in part, as follows:

" The modifications proposed by the Department of State (of the United States) to the bank contract, studied by the Haitian Government, gave rise to counterpropositions on the part of the latter, which the Department of State would not accept. The Haitian Government then accepted these modifications in nine articles in the form of which they had been concluded and signed at Washington on Friday, February 6, 1920, by the financial adviser, the Haitian minister, and the (Haitian) secretary of finance. But when Messrs. Scarpa and

Williams, representing, respectively and officially, the National Bank of Haiti and the National City Bank of New York, came before the secretary of finance for his signature to the papers relative to the transfer of the National Bank of Haiti to the National City Bank of New York, the secretary of finance experi- enced a disagreeable surprise in finding out that to article 9 of the document signed at Washington February 6, 1920, and closed as stated above, there had been added an amendment bearing on the prohibition of non-Haitian money. The secretary could only decline the responsibility of this added paragraph, of which he had not the slightest knowledge and which consequently had not been submitted to the Government for its agreement. It is for this reason alone that the agreement is not signed up to this time. The Government does not even yet know who was the author of this addition to the document to which its consent had never been asked.

"To-day, gentlemen, you have come to the end of the regular session for this year. Four months have run by without the Government being able to present to you the budget for 1920–21. Such are the facts, in brief, that have marked our relations recently with Mr. McIlhenny. * * *

"FLEURY FEQUIERE, *Secretary of Finance.*"

(The correspondence referred to is here printed in full as follows:)

PORT AU PRINCE, *August 2, 1920.*

Mr. A. J. MAUMUS,
  Receiver General of Customs:

In accordance with the suggestion made to the financial adviser on July 24, your office began on the morning of July 30 to pay the salaries for that month to the officials and public employees at Port au Prince.

Nevertheless, up to this morning, August 2, no checks have been delivered to His Excellency the President of the Republic, the secretaries of the various de- partments, the state councilors, and the palace interpreter.

In calling your attention to this fact, I ask that you will please inform me of the reasons for it.

FLEURY FEQUIERE, *Secretary of Finance.*

PORT AU PRINCE, *August 2, 1920.*

THE SECRETARY OF FINANCE AND COMMERCE:

I have the honor to acknowledge the receipt of your note of August 2 in which you ask this office to inform you regarding the reasons for the nondeliv- ery, up to the present time, of the checks for His Excellency the President of the Republic, for the departmental secretaries, the state councilors, and the palace interpreter for the month of July.

In reply this office hastens to inform you that up to the present time it has not been put in possession of the mandates and orders regarding these payments.

A. J. MAUMUS, *Receiver General.*

PORT AU PRINCE, *August 2, 1920.*

THE FINANCIAL ADVISER:

The department of finance, informed that checks for His Excellency the President of the Republic, the departmental secretaries, the state councilors, and the palace interpreter had not been delivered up to this morning, August 2, reported the fact to the receiver general of customs, asking to be informed regarding the reasons. The receiver general replied immediately that the delay was due to his failure to receive the necessary mandates and orders. But these papers were sent to you by the department of finance on July 21 and were returned by the payment service of the department of the interior on July 26, a week ago.

In inclose copies of the note from the department of finance to the receiver general and of Mr. Maumus's reply.

I should like to believe that bringing this matter to your attention would be sufficient to remedy it.

FLEURY FEQUIERE, *Secretary of Finance.*

PORT AU PRINCE, *August 5, 1920.*

To the SECRETARY OF FINANCE AND COMMERCE:

I have the honor to acknowledge the receipt of your note of August 2 regarding the delay in payment of the salaries of the President of the Republic, secretaries, and State councilors.

In reply I have the honor to inform you that the payment of these salaries· has been suspended by order of the American minister until further orders are received from him.

J. MCILHENNY, *Financial Adviser.*

PORT AU PRINCE, *August 10, 1920.*

To the FINANCIAL ADVISER:

I acknowledged receipt of your note of August 5 in reply to mine of August 2 asking information regarding the reasons for your nonpayment of the salaries for last July due to his excellency the President of the Republic, the secretaries, and State councilors, and the palace interpreter.

I note the second paragraph of your letter, in which you say, " In reply, etc."

I do not know by what authority an American minister can have given you such instructions or by what authority you acquiesced. The nonpayment of the salaries due the members of the Government constitutes a confiscation vexatious for them and for the entire country. It is not the function of this department to judge the motives which led the American minister to take so exceptionally serious a step; but it is the opinion of the Government that the financial adviser, a Haitian official, was not authorized to acquiesce.

FLUERY FEQUIERE,
Secretary of Finance.

PORT AU PRINCE, *August 5, 1920.*

Mr. A. BAILLY-BLANCHARD,
American Minister:

I have the honor to inform your excellency that the offices of the financial adviser and of the receiver general have not yet delivered the checks for the July salaries of his excellency the President of the Republic, of the secretaries, State councilors, and palace interpreter, although all other officials were paid on July 30.

The secretary of finance wrote to the receiver general asking information on the subject and was informed that he had not received the necessary mandates and orders. The fact of the nondelivery of the checks and the reply of the receiver general were then brought to the attention of the financial adviser, who has not yet replied.

In informing your legation of this situation I call the attention of your excellency to this new attitude of the financial adviser, a Haitian official, to the President of the Republic and the·other members of the Government, an attitude which is an insult to the entire nation.

J. BARAU,
Secretary of Foreign Affairs.

PORT AU PRINCE, *August 6, 1920.*

MR. A. BAILLY-BLANCHARD,
American Minister:

I have the honor to inclose a copy of a note from the financial adviser to the secretary of finance, replying to a request for information regarding the nonpayment of checks * * *.

In his reply the financial adviser informs the department of finance that " the payment of these salaries has been suspended by order of the American minister until further orders are received from him."

My Government protests against this act of violence, which is an attack upon the dignity of the people and Government of Haiti.

J. BARAU,
Secretary of Foreign Affairs.

PORT AU PRINCE, *August 6, 1920.*

Mr. J. BARAU,
  Secretary of Foreign Affairs:
  I have the honor to acknowledge the receipt of your excellency's note under date of August 5.
  In reply I have to state that the action of the financial adviser therein referred to was taken by direction of this legation.

A. BAILLY-BLANCHARD,
American Minister.

PORT AU PRINCE, *August 7, 1920.*

Mr. A. BAILLY-BLANCHARD,
  American Minister:
  In reply to my letter of August 5, in which I had the honor to inform your excellency of the nonpayment of checks, * * * your excellency informs me that it is by direction of the Legation of the United States that the financial adviser acted.
  My Government takes note of your declaration.

J. BARAU,
Secretary of Foreign Affairs.

PORT AU PRINCE, *August 2, 1920.*

To the SECRETARY OF FINANCE:
  I have the honor to inform you that I have been instructed by my Government that in view of the continual delay in obtaining the consent of the Haitian Government to the transfer to the new bank of the modified concession as agreed upon between the Government of the United States and the National City Bank, the Government of the United States has agreed to let the operations of the National Bank of the Republic of Haiti continue indefinitely on the French contract at present existing without amendment.
  I desire urgently to draw your attention to the fact that it would be most desirable in the interest of the Haitian people that the Government of Haiti should give its immediate consent to the proposed modifications of the contract and to accept the transfer of the bank rather than to see the present contract continue with its present clauses.

JOHN McILHENNY,
Financial Adviser.

Mr. ANGELL. I would like to introduce at this time President Dartiguenave's protest, made direct to President Wilson, dated August 9, 1920.
  (The communication referred to is to be filed with the clerk of the committee.)
  The CHAIRMAN. Continue, Mr. Pilkington.
  Mr. PILKINGTON. In connection with complaints concerning the financial adviser, it is well to record——
  The CHAIRMAN. Mr. McIlhenny?
  Mr. PILKINGTON. Yes. It is well to record a reiterated complaint of the Government of Haiti that their constitutional body for the regulation and accounting of moneys, called the Chambre des Compts, was abolished by the occupation, the Government of Haiti, therefore, contending that they had no means whatever of knowing or of keeping track of—that is, controlling, in the French language, the expenditures of the country, all of these matters being left entirely in the hands of the individual who at the time should hold the position of financial adviser.
  Another very large element of annoyance, at least among the business men and the business interests of Haiti, has been occasioned through the application of the customs tariff. When the receiver general and financial adviser came into office they found in existence a schedule of tariffs, which had been in existence for many years and under which they operated and collected duties. This tariff is explained by the Haitian Government officials themselves as having never been revised by themselves and never been in completely operative condition.
  The CHAIRMAN. You mean that at no time was the Haitian tariff enforced?

Mr. Pilkington. I mean they had not as yet brought that up to date. They had not revised it as time went on to keep it in line. I will show several instances of that. This tariff is in many particulars practically obsolete in its wording. To take the specific case of automobiles, there is no more vital or necessary adjunct to business in Haiti or to progress than the automobile.

The Chairman. To what extent were they used before the occupation?

Mr. Pilkington. Before the occupation there was no business at all, and I do not think the automobile was there at all before the occupation.

The Chairman. You mean it was not possible to use automobiles before the occupation?

Mr. Pilkington. No; it was not possible. You see, the automobile now is used, of course, over the few roads that they have and almost entirely for business purposes and, of course, for military purposes.

The Chairman. You mean there were no roads before the occupation?

Mr. Pilkington. No; not to amount to anything.

The Chairman. So it would be immaterial whether the tariff permitted their importation or not?

Mr. Pilkington. Yes; but at that time, as I was going on to say, the carriage was the only vehicle, and that was not a vehicle of commerce, but distinctly a pleasure vehicle and was, therefore, charged with a high rate of duty. When the present custom officials applied the rates, as contemplated by this tariff, the result was that together with various surcharges and surtaxes, which the Haitian Government has from time to time put on the original taxes, the importation of an automobile of any kind into Haiti cost practically 28 per cent in the way of duty.

The Chairman. The receiver general and his representatives enforced the customs duties existing?

Mr. Pilkington. Did thy enforce them?

The Chairman. They did when they collected that 28 per cent?

Mr. Pilkington. Oh, yes; they enforced them; indeed, they did.

The Chairman. What would you have had them do?

Mr. Pilkington. Do just that; but I am going on to that still. This rate of duty being based upon the clause of the tariff schedule referring to pleasure vehicles, it has been the subject for frequent complaints, and it has been proposed at various times by various people to reduce this to 10 per cent.

I will recite another instance which will also illustrate the idiosyncracies, at least, of this tariff. It is a fact that in purchasing hardware articles, or tools, one is confronted with an almost infinite scale of prices charged by the different shopkeepers. On looking into this matter I was shown a specific case by a merchant in Port au Prince, in which he presented as exhibits the original bills of lading of a great gross of small screw eyes, such as are used to suspend small pictures by. The name in French of such a screw eye is piton, and in his bill of lading these were called piton pour tableaux, screw eyes for pictures. His bill showed that he had paid for his great gross of screw eyes, $2 or so, and he paid a duty on these insignificent screw eyes of more than $8, bringing the total cost of a great gross of screw eyes to over $10, the same being purchasable in any 5 and 10 cent store six for a nickel.

Upon examination of the question, I was shown the tariff schedule applying to this. The only place in the schedule in which the word "piton" appears is in relation to piton or hooks for awnings, appearing in the schedule as piton pour tentes. These are hand-forged hooks, which are driven into the brick wall.

The Chairman. I think we will take your word for it that there are these anomalies in the tariff. Now, will you tell me what the receiver general did to secure their removal?

Mr. Pilkington. This instance was merely illustrative of many incongruities in the tariff schedule which have brought forth much friction and much added duty for the receiver general and the collector.

The Chairman. Why was there no friction before the receiver general was appointed?

Mr. Pilkington. That would come in the inside politics of Haiti before I came there.

The Chairman. You did not arrive until the occupation?

Mr. Pilkington. No.

The Chairman. Had you ever heard that the duties were enforced according to the discretion of the several collectors of the various ports?

Mr. PILKINGTON. Such a condition I am led to believe had previously existed throughout, perhaps, the entire history of Haiti.

The CHAIRMAN. The foreign importer in Haiti was not inconvenienced by the tariff, then, until the receiver general applied it equally and literally?

Mr. PILKINGTON. That is a fact.

Mr. ANGELL. In this very connection I would like to offer in evidence, Mr. Chairman, a letter from the American minister in Port au Prince to the Haitian Government, dated August 19, in which the demand is made that the Haitian Government shall immediately repeal certain laws, one of which was the duty on motor vehicles, and the reply thereto of the Haitian Government, bearing the same date, the 21st of August, in which it appears, if the statements therein be true statements of fact, that on May 14, 1919, the Haitian Government, operating through the conseil d'etat, the legislature having been suppressed, voted a law fixing a low duty on automobiles imported, but this law was objected to by the American receiver general, on the ground that the duties were too low, and he then proposed a duty of 10 per cent, and that the legislative authority, consisting of the conseil d'etat, brought down that tax to 7 per cent; that thereafter the American legation, the financial adviser, and the receiver general, refused to acknowledge or admit the validity of that law, because it did not meet apparently their wishes, and they continued to impose a tax of 20 per cent on automobiles.

(The correspondence referred to is on file with the clerk of the committee.)

The CHAIRMAN. Do you mean that, in the first instance, the minister demanded a reduction of duties while by inference at least the receiver general objected to it?

Mr. ANGELL. The minister demanded and the receiver general objected that the low duty was too low.

The CHAIRMAN. The minister's letter demanded a reduction of the duty?

Mr. ANGELL. No, sir; he demanded the repeal of the law in question.

Mr. PILKINGTON. I may say for your information that when the duty was reduced to 7 per cent a large importation of automobiles was made by a northern importer in America who paid the duty of 7 per cent and sold his automobiles. A long time subsequent to that the customhouse, through the receiver general, or whoever was the competent authority, demanded the difference, and compelled him to pay the difference, which, as I say, totaled 28 per cent.

The CHAIRMAN. Well, if you will give us the instances to which you allude of conflict between the receiver general and the financial adviser, if there be any between either or both of those and the American minister, we should be interested.

Mr. PILKINGTON. Well, I can not give you any of those because so far as I know they worked in complete accord.

The CHAIRMAN. I thought that some time ago you said that the receiver general had asked for an amendment to the tariff act, to which the financial adviser objected.

Mr. PILKINGTON. No; I did not say that. I say the receiver general. Mr. Maumus, said to me that at many times he had requested and had asked for a revision of that tax. Now, I do not know that he did ask or did object to it, but I suppose that, of course, the financial adviser——

The CHAIRMAN. So far as you know, there is a close coordination, then, and cooperation between the American authorities?

Mr. PILKINGTON. So far as I know, there is, in that respect. And I will say, furthermore, and I would like to have it go on the record, that I have not in any instance had the slightest intimation that there has been the least of an infraction of honesty in any way, shape, or manner in any branch of the American occupation. That is quite important, because that is a very serious thing; and if the Haitians do not even bring up any complaint of that kind, that means that it does not exist; and if there was any, they would soon tell it.

The CHAIRMAN. So far as you know, the legation, the office of the receiver general, and the office of the financial adviser have cooperated cordially?

Mr. PILKINGTON. As far as I know, that is a fact.

The CHAIRMAN. Have those civil officers been able to cooperate with real cordiality with the commandant of the gendarmerie and the commandant of the marines?

Mr. PILKINGTON. No; there is a very evident conflict between the different apparently uncoordinated elements of the American occupation.

The CHAIRMAN. Now, if you will just answer my question, I will put my finger on the point.

Mr. PILKINGTON. All right, let us cut that out, then.

The CHAIRMAN. I asked the question regarding the relations between these three civil authorities, and you answered that they cordially cooperated, so far as you knew?

Mr. PILKINGTON. As far as I know, they have.

The CHAIRMAN. I asked then if there was equally cordial cooperation between them and the military officers or the commandant of the marines and the commandant of the gendarmerie, and I understood you to say no.

Mr. PILKINGTON. No; there apparently is not.

The CHAIRMAN. Can you give instances of friction or a lack of cooperation, or is it more a general impression?

Mr. PILKINGTON. That is more a general impression. I can cite one case which would seem very serious. It is said and generally believed in Port au Prince that, immediately after the protest of the business people of Haiti against this attempted enforcing of the President's signature, Col. Russell, the chief of the occupation——

The CHAIRMAN. Enforcing his signature of what?

Mr. PILKINGTON. Of this clause granting a monopoly on the importation of foreign gold to the National Bank of Haiti. Col. Russell is said to have been very much incensed at being implicated in this attempted forcing of the President's signature, and to have remarked that he would never take such action again without the authority of his superior officer.

The CHAIRMAN. Do you feel that there should be a single chief and responsible figure among the American officials in Haiti?

Mr. PILKINGTON. I was going to take that up in detail in a suggested plan of——

The CHAIRMAN. If you will answer my question——

Mr. PILKINGTON. I will certainly do that, and any number of them. I am quite sure that some such method, in principle, is the only way to carry out cooperation in Haiti.

The CHAIRMAN. In short that military, administrative functions, civil administration functions, in so far as Americans have to do with them, diplomatic relations between the American and the Haitian Governments—all should be vested ultimately in the principal American representative in Haiti?

Mr. PILKINGTON. I would say yes to that, with the possible amendment of what you refer to as the diplomatic relations. I should be inclined to think, offhand, that the functions of a minister or an ambassador to a country should be always retained, but strictly within their definite legal limitations, and that those functions——

The CHAIRMAN. Have you any precedents in mind where over any considerable period a foreign Government has been represented by a diplomatic agent whose functions were independent of the administrative agents lent under treaty to the Government by which they were employed?

Mr. PILKINGTON. I have not in just that form; no.

The CHAIRMAN. The precedents are the other way, are they not?

Mr. PILKINGTON. They are; yes; but I believe, after a careful study of the temperament of the Haitian people in particular, that such a contemplated arrangement would immediately fall into a certain phase of their psychology, which is fundamentally antagonistic to them. They, primarily and fundamentally, have this absolute, deep-rooted antagonism to the mere thought of any actual control of affairs by even one individual. Now, the vesting of the diplomatic functions which ordinarily are carried out along a certain line of agreements, and which they well know, in a person who also has more or less control, even in the way of advice, over civil functions, would look to them as a form of military control.

The CHAIRMAN. Then let me ask you this: Conceive that the minister made representations to the Haitian Government which the principal administrative agent nominated by the President of the United States declined to entertain. How would you deal with that anomaly?

Mr. PILKINGTON. The way I would meet that, my idea of that whole problem, you may fundamentally say would be this: Let us say for the purpose of argument, that we suspend, not abrogate, the treaty——

The CHAIRMAN. Upon what assumption do you say that?

Mr. PILKINGTON. On the assumption of this plan which I am about to propose. You must remember that the radicals are demanding the abrogation of the treaty.

The CHAIRMAN. Do you consider that as being within the realm of possibility?

Mr. PILKINGTON. Well, I think what I say later will perhaps explain that.

The CHAIRMAN. Go ahead.

Mr. PILKINGTON. We will look at it in this way, because we must remember that at the present time they are, from the ground up, antagonistic to everything. Now, the policy, I am quite sure, worth considering would be for the United States to apparently, at least, put the entire responsibility of everything up to Haiti. Now, the way that could be done——

The CHAIRMAN. What would you do with the loan just made?

Mr. PILKINGTON. That will have to be attended to, of course.

The CHAIRMAN. Have you a plan worked out?

Mr. PILKINGTON. Yes; that is what I refer to.

The CHAIRMAN. Will you reduce it to the form of a written memorandum and give it to the committee?

Mr. PILKINGTON. I will, indeed; I will be very glad to do that; yes.

The CHAIRMAN. I would rather you would do that.

Mr. PILKINGTON. All right; we will not mention it at this time. I really thought of doing such a thing.

The CHAIRMAN. I do not believe I would go into an elaboration.

Now, let me ask you another question. What, in your judgment, would happen if we abrogated the treaty, withdrew the constabulary officers and marines, and left no one there except the receiver general of customs?

Mr. PILKINGTON. I take it for granted that you mean that the part of the treaty over which the receiver general has jurisdiction should remain in force; otherwise the receiver general would not be left there.

The CHAIRMAN. Well, he would be there under the protocol covering the loan. There are precedents for that.

Mr. PILKINGTON. Could you abrogate the treaty and not abrogate the protocol without another agreement? Anyhow, I gather what you mean. That I would consider a condition utterly impossible at the present time.

The CHAIRMAN. Why?

Mr. PILKINGTON. I do not conceive of the possibility of the political elements in that country at the present day getting together with sufficient unanimity to produce a form of government which would satisfy any investor whatever. The bankers with whom I am associated at the present time in many different ways, and who were associated with me in this company down there, were considering the floating of that loan, the original loan, and I know perfectly well, of course, that I would be the ultimate court of decision on that matter, and if they would ask my opinion I would instantly say that I would; not, under any condition, advise the investing of one cent in Haiti under a condition such as you have predicated.

The CHAIRMAN. In which merely the customs would be collected by the American officer?

Mr. PILKINGTON. Exactly.

The CHAIRMAN. Do you mean that it is not possible for the Haitians, unaided, at this time successfully to maintain order and to administer. their civil government?

Mr. PILKINGTON. Absolutely. There is no question about that. In that connection I might say that I have definitely been told that my many leading Haitians in practically just so many words.

The CHAIRMAN. Would they avow that publicly?

Mr. PILKINGTON. They would without doubt, I have no doubt. I would be very glad to give a list of the names of the leading people there——

The CHAIRMAN. I said publicly, because it has been suggested that certain Haitian business men who hold that opinion privately might hesitate to declare it publicly.

Mr. PILKINGTON. I think I would like to cover that in this memorandum, along with some other things. I have that perfectly well crystalized.

The CHAIRMAN. Do you believe that if the American authorities under the occupation, so called, military and civil, were coordinated and made responsible to a single chief, and that if the occupation undertook sympathetically and assiduously not only the discharge of its duties under the terms of the agreement, but to secure the good will and accord of the Haitians, that at the end of a given period of a year or two they can secure that cooperation and accord from 'the Haitians?

Mr. PILKINGTON. I would willingly and freely stake everything on the statement that they would, under the condition of confidence, supreme confidence, in that individual to whom you refer; but the crux of that whole thing is the form under which you maintain that military supervision, we will say— we will leave out the word "control," because if you use the word "control" in any way, it is off.

The CHAIRMAN. You believe, then, that the centralization of responsibility is necessary?

Mr. PILKINGTON. Yes.

The CHAIRMAN. But you believe that it is no less necessary to find the right man to fill the post of chief responsibility?

Mr. PILKINGTON. That is your only chance of success. Everything depends on that. The Latin race and the Latin temperament demand a direct personal element, which can be furnished by nothing else.

The CHAIRMAN. Are there any men who have served there—Americans—who have the qualities necessary to fill that place?

Mr. PILKINGTON. Well, I do not recall anybody who has ever been in any kind of an official capacity there that really ought to be intrusted with that. I think persaps that if you can get under the skin, we will say, of certain Haitians there, that they will enlighten you to a very large extent on that matter.

The CHAIRMAN. In your judgment, ought the present officials, Maumus and McIlhenny, remain in the service or not?

Mr. PILKINGTON. I would not have any objection, and I think no Haitian would have any objection to the retention of Mr. Maumus. Although he is from Louisiana, from the State of so-called nigger haters, he is a man who has very evidently attended to his duty as he has seen it, and has not meddled with anyone, and has only been handicapped by this absurd tariff. He has never openly meddled or trampled on the self-pride of the Haitians, but it is my earnest conviction that, although I have the highest regard for the ability of Col. Russell, and the personalities of both him and Mr. McIlhenny, I am absolutely sure that if either of those three men——

The CHAIRMAN. You have only named two.

Mr. PILKINGTON. Yes; but I am going on to say that as long as Col. Russell, the chief of the occupation; Mr. McIlhenny, the financial adviser, who has arrogated all other duties and privileges; and Mr. Bailly-Blanchard, the three who have violated, in the minds of the Haitians, their greatest sanctity of governmental pride—as long as they are retained there, in whatever form, you are going to have trouble. Further back in the record I have explained why, and I think that great insult was brought to these people, and is not explained, and I say those facts may be true, and until they are either explained or——

The CHAIRMAN. Let me continue on in my own way, because we will have to adjourn in a few minutes.

Mr. PILKINGTON. I will be very glad to.

The CHAIRMAN. Is there no American officer who has served in a place of responsibility, military or civil, in which he came into close contact with the Haitians, who has their good will or who left the island with their good will?

Mr. PILKINGTON. There is Col. Wise. He is the one we all have in mind. He was in command of the gendarmerie.

The CHAIRMAN. From the beginning?

Mr. PILKINGTON. Not from the beginning; no.

The CHAIRMAN. I have here the names of four gendarmerie commanders—Butler, Williams, Wise, and McDougal.

Mr. PILKINGTON. He is the present commander.

The CHAIRMAN. Do you care to pass any comment on any others than Wise?

Mr. PILKINGTON. I have no direct personal knowledge of the administration of others but Wise, and I have a very large fund of——

The CHAIRMAN. Were you there during Williams's time?

Mr. PILKINGTON. No; I was there since 1918.

The CHAIRMAN. That was from May 1, 1918, to July, 1919?

Mr. PILKINGTON. Well, nothing special was heard of him.

The CHAIRMAN. Butler was before that time.

Mr. PILKINGTON. The opinions of the people themselves, of course, are necessary in this thing. As regards the people themselves, the only chief of gendarmerie that they apparently tolerated has been Wise. Wise has been well thought of there. When it comes to a question of Wise being left alone with all the responsibilities and the native constabulary, we will say, that is a matter which I would be very loath to decide offhand.

Mr. ANGELL. Do you think that in a revised scheme of affairs in Haiti the single, coordinated responsibility should rest in the hands of a marine officer, a military man, or in the hands of a civilian?

Mr. PILKINGTON. Absolutely a civilian. If there is a military man there in any capacity whatsoever his function will have to be so worded and so carefully disguised in definite colaboration and suggestion with the Haitians themselves that he does not appear as a marine officer.

(Whereupon, at 1 o'clock p. m., a recess was taken until 2.30 o'clock p. m.)

AFTER RECESS.

The committee reassembled at 2.30 o'clock p. m., pursuant to the taking of recess.

Mr. ANGELL. Now, Mr. Pilkington, let me ask you what military representatives or military forces of the United States would, in your judgment, be necessary and wise for the future in Haiti?

Mr. PILKINGTON. I believe a mutually satisfactory agreement can be reached in collaboration with the Haitians whereby an adequate native force, whether gendarmerie or national army, to maintain law and order, may be organized, it being my belief here reiterated that any form of foreign military influence will be resented.

Mr. ANGELL. Do you believe that law and order can be maintained to the extent necessary to protect the collection of Haitian customs, and so far as they might be pledged for existing or future loans, and to protect the investment of foreign capital in Haiti, by a native force?

Mr. PILKINGTON. I think it is possible.

Mr. ANGELL. Do you think that that is a possibility immediately, and if not, then what period of time and under what form of transition relations?

Mr. PILKINGTON. It is my opinion that an organization along the lines of a national army, as previously existing in Haiti, could, with the proper cooperation and in connection with the existing gendarmerie, become sufficiently operative for the purposes you mention in a period of two years after the election of a constitutional assembly and Government in Haiti.

Mr. ANGELL. What do you mean in your answer when you say in cooperation with the existing gendarmerie?

Mr. PILKINGTON. I mean that in this question, as in all others, this committee is going to Haiti with the avowed intention of bringing about this entirely essential desideratum, namely, a condition of mutual confidence and a mutually agreed upon plan of collaboration in general which, in my mind, must be coordinated with a definite agreement by the United States Government to unreservedly and completely withdraw from Haiti, such withdrawal to be completed within a period defined by satisfactory guaranties from the Haitian Government and people as to stability. If a loan is desired from the United States a mutually satisfactory guaranty must be furnished for the safety of this loan.

Mr. ANGELL. Do you think that the loan could be satisfactorily guaranteed from the point of view of investors and the United States Government if during the life of the loan all our military forces and military representatives were to be withdrawn from Haiti?

Mr. PILKINGTON. I feel that any guaranty as to the stability of the Haitian Government which would satisfy your committee would also satisfy any investor, provided some nominee of the investor—that, of course, means the man who supplies the loan—be empowered to control the customs.

Mr. ANGELL. Do you think that the control of the customs would be a sufficient guaranty to the investor and to this Government?

Mr. PILKINGTON. In connection with the guaranty of the Haitians' ability to maintain the program as set out above.

Mr. ANGELL. Then, if I understand you correctly, you believe that, given a sufficient guaranty of the Haitian Government and the Haitian people, plus general control over the customs by the United States, there would then be a sufficient control of Haitian affairs to satisfy the investor and the United States Government?

Mr. PILKINGTON. I do; and in that connection I would like to call attention to the existing external loan. French investors took up that loan freely at a time when Haiti had no such assurance of internal stability as she has now, and they did not in connection with that loan have control over the customs as now suggested.

Mr. ANGELL. How long a period do you think, in your judgment, would be required to build up an independent native Haitian police or military force adequate to maintain law and order?

Mr. PILKINGTON. I have already testified to that.

Mr. ANGELL. No; the period of time.

Mr. PILKINGTON. Two years; but that two years must begin after they have gotten their own Government and a representative constitutional assembly.

Mr. ANGELL. Would it be your idea, then, that during this two year period beginning, as you have suggested, the American military forces, at present the marines, should be gradually withdrawn, and the Americans who are now officers of the Haitian gendarmerie should be gradually supplanted by native Haitians?

Mr. PILKINGTON. I do, that point being already agreed in the treaty, as now existing.

Mr. ANGELL. Will you state what you believe to be the minimum requirements for a civil commissioner to represent the United States with the Haitian Government?

Mr. HOWE. May I interrupt on this? Before we leave the last branch of the testimony, Mr. Pilkington, what satisfactory guarantee of stability by Haiti can you suggest?

Mr. PILKINGTON. I should expect to obtain from the various political factions or parties in Haiti, including the present Government, and the Union Patropique, an open, frank avowed intention to collaborate, and, as far as possible, hold themselves responsible to execute whatever measures may be necessary and advisable in the organization of such a military body as has been before mentioned, and the reform of the present unsatisfactory court system and legal procedures now existing in Haiti, so that the laws may be in such a form that they may be satisfactorily executed, in order to maintain a condition of law and order, when once obtained. In other words, the Haitian people, and their Government, in return for the frank and open manner in which they are being approached and treated by the American Government, through your committee, must, and should be, equally frank and equally open in proof of the claims they so frequently and so widely make.

Mr. HOWE. On what do you base your belief that the courts can satisfactorily be reformed?

Mr. PILKINGTON. The courts in Haiti are presumably operating in conformity with the French code of Napoleon, which is, as we know, a perfectly satisfactory code of laws for people of that race and temperament. There is a large body of well-trained lawyers in Haiti, who have, as I have previously stated in my testimony, not only a good Haitian law education, but have extended education resulting from studies in Europe. These men, I am perfectly confident, could, if protected in their various functions, bring about a state of complete reform in the courts.

Mr. HOWE. Is there anything before the time of the American occupation to justify that confidence of yours?

Mr. PILKINGTON. Yes. The history of former administrations in Haiti, which, of course, in connection with the actual viva voce accounts of those times, forms the only basis upon which one might judge that question, shows that at times Haiti has had chief executives who have shown not only ability but good humanity and a strong desire for law and order and for everything that is good. I will again state, as I have heretofore put in the testimony, that at the present time Haiti has in the person of Sudre Dartiguenave an executive of whom I feel any nation might be proud. Whatever may be the underlying facts in connection with the incident referred to in previous testimony—that is the incident leading up to the stoppage of the pay of the President—he took an attitude which, in the light of facts existing at the time, was closely bordering on heroism.

Mr. HOWE. Do you not believe that it is highly important for the population of the country to have safely and honestly administered lower courts from which the people sometimes derive their only knowledge of the courts? Is not that so?

Mr. PILKINGTON. Yes.

Mr. Howe. That is your opinion, is it not?

Mr. Pilkington. Yes.

Mr. Howe. That being so, what, from what you know of the previous history of Haiti, justifies your confidence that a capable and honest system of lower courts can be evolved within two years after a constitutional government is restored there?

Mr. Pilkington. I have had frequent talks on this very subject, due to its very great importance in the history of Haiti, and due to direct exper.ence in this line with the leading members of the legal profession and ex-members of the Senate. They are all unanimous in saying that there would be no difficulty whatsoever in getting a complete corps of efficient lower courts of justice, providing a sufficient salary could be paid to induce the men of a better stamp to take the positions.

Mr. Howe. On what do you base your belief that a Haitian national army and a Haitian gendarmerie, without American officers or control of any kind, can maintain order?

Mr. Pilkington. The past history of Haiti again shows in many instances the existence of what, to a layman, and what, to many military commentaries, can be characterized as a genuine military spirit, which possibly may be inherited from a French strain in the blood, and h story apparently shows that for their individual purposes a qu'te sufficient degree of organization and discipline has at various times existed. At the present time the degree of intelligence among the so-called better class is even higher than it was at that time, and the chances, in my opinion, are much better to-day than they have been heretofore.

Mr. Howe. What other guaranties of stability can you suggest than those you have mentioned, besides the military and judicial reform?

Mr. Pilkington. A natural and very powerful check on any vagaries of the Haitian Government will come through the investment of foreign capital in the country, this investment of foreign capital being predicated only and possibly only upon the arrival of a complete understanding between the two countries.

Mr. Angell. Following up Mr. Howe's line of questions, let me ask you this, Mr. Pilkington: Do you think that an agreement such as you have suggested between the representatives of the American Government on the one hand, and the Haitian Government on the other, after the election of a constituent and constitutional assembly, and the representatives of various political part'es and factions, would be to any effective degree a deterrent upon the possibility of future revolutions and disorders?

Mr. Pilkington. Absolutely, in my opin'on, it would absolutely prevent the recurrence on any scale of an actual revolutionary disorder. I will modify it by saying there will be for many years probably sporadic sases of banditry, which has always existed, but heretofore has been quite capably taken care of by the rural police in Haiti.

Mr. Angell. Do you think that an agreement between the representatives of the United States Government on the one hand and the present or then existing Government of Haiti on the other hand, ignoring the fact of various political parties and factions existing outs'de of the present or then government, would be as effective a deterrent upon possible future revolutions and disorders?

Mr. Pilkington. I would not. I would not myself consider such an arrangement as being sufficiently satisfactory to induce me personally to advise the investment of money in Haiti.

Mr. Angell. In other words, you consider that a working agreement with all parties in Haiti, including the Government, is a sine quo non?

Mr. Pilkington. I do. By all parties, I do not mean 100 per cent. because that is impossible, but practically all of the literates, the intellectuals, could be brought to agree, more than a working majority.

At such period as may be mutually agreeable to both countries the existing treaty might be suspended, except such clause as will affect the purposes of a loan, and a commissioner appointed by and responsible to the United States Senate. Here I am not supposed to know anything about it. The will be persona grata to Haiti, and he will function as an adviser on all questions in Haiti, being an intermediary between the two Governments in an endeavor to maintain complete harmony. I think that would be completely satisfactory to Haiti.

The CHAIRMAN. I will note in the record that under the Constitution of the United States no agreement can be made for the appointment of a commissioner responsible to the United States Senate.

I want to revert to the civil advisers, because I believe that, in general terms, those of us who have followed these hearings are of one mind in sharing the hope that the result of American intervention and cooperation may be the establishment of a Haitian administration, and of justice in Haiti, which will preclude the recurrence of revolutions or disorders, so that when we have done our work it will have been well done, and Haiti may stand on her own feet as an independent Republic. Do you think that it is necessary for a period, or an indeterminate period, because we have no other period fixed than that fixed by the terms of the treaty—do you think it is necessary that there should be appointed to the several departments of the Haitian Government, American advisers, with the capacity and authority necessary to enable the Haitians to install an efficient and economical public administration?

Mr. PILKINGTON. I feel that that would be the practical and logical way: and those persons or officials would be the logical aids to this commissioner, and serve under him, and be responsible to him and to the American Government, through this commissioner. the point always being kept in mind, the ambition of the Haitian in connection with this Amercan relation, that all such relation shall be of a friendly, advisory. collaborative character, inasmuch as they have had American civilians down there, and still have among them Americans whom they respect and admire, and with whom they have complete friendly intercourse and confidence at the present time, and they take it for granted that the best class of Americans is always of that character, therefore, any proceeding from the Government along that line will meet with responsive treatment at that suggestion of collaboration.

The CHAIRMAN. You believe that if for the department of education, for example, an adviser be appointed, that he will be assured the authority and cooperation necessary to build up a true school system in the Republic of Haiti?

Mr. PILKINGTON. He will, always provided that he understands and conforms to the Latin temperament; in other words, that he does not attempt to ride, roughshod, over their self-pride and over the social status which the present or any future native government official of any department whatever may be possessed of. That remark applies to every relation, not only with Haiti, but with every Latin-American country, the primary consideration being the personality and the appeal of the individual himself. He will find the Haitians at all times ready to cooperate, provided they are given their head and allowed to express their impressions and their sentiments and their changes of opinion at length, it being almost fatal to any successful discussion of any matter, whether it be business, politics, or religion with a Haitian if he is checked up and compelled to conform to certain preconceived ideas of the more terse Anglo-Saxon. In other words, the dealings with the Haitians must occupy the necessary amount of time to satisfy the Haitian that he is completely expressing the opinions, not only of himself, but of the party or the clique he represents. You see that demonstrated everywhere in every Latin country or every country where the Latin exists, all over the world, the same precise condition. The Haitian official is essentially an orator.

The CHAIRMAN. And not an administrator?

Mr. PILKINGTON. Not necessarily; but an orator, and when he talks he is very much concerned over the form in which he promulgates his opinions, and there is a continuous stream of the flowers of oratory. Now, instead of checking that stream, you should allow it to flow, because, in my experience throughout the world, I have found that from the ripened seed of the flower of oratory oftentimes the beans are spilled, and I think one gains very much inside information, as will be seen by exhibits which I will leave here for your perusal at your leisure, these exhibits being clippings from, perhaps, the most conservative newspaper in Haiti, published at a time when the censorship had been removed from the press and there is, therefore, much domestic information circulated back and forth.

If I may, Senator, I would like to spread on the record a blanket estimate of the competence and efficiency of the Marine Corps, irrespective of personalities or anything. I would like to here spread on the record a statement that, in the light of a very intimate acquaintanceship with all grades of officers and enlisted men of the Marine Corps, stationed in Haiti, I am glad and anxious to state that as regards their true and legitimate functions they have proved themselves to be as good and efficient a branch of the service as I have ever in my experience been acquainted with. All bodies of men of any kind or condition in any part of the world, banded together in uncongenial surroundings, and required, whether justly or unjustly, to occupy positions and undertake work which is out of their line, will at times and in places do things which are not especially commendable, and which they would not dream of doing if allowed to confine their efforts to the normal channels.

Mr. ANGELL. Mr. Pilkington, all through your testimony you have apparently emphasized very strongly the necessity for cooperation on the part of the Haitians with the Americans in any future work to be accomplished down there. I want to ask you frankly whether you believe that that degree of co-operation can be secured which you say is necessary to achieve results if, with all due respect to the plans of the committee and the limitations upon its time, the committee spends a period of only a few days, as has been announced, in Port au Prince, and a few more days in the other parts of the island?

Mr. PILKINGTON. No; I am quite confident that they can not arrive at a mutually satisfactory status in any such time as that, and if it is absolutely necessary that they limit their time in any such way, it would, in my opinion, be highly desirable that they in some way either convey the knowledge that they would come back again, or resume with those same people perhaps further negotiations in this country, because, to cover any one subject would require quite considerable ceremonies, which those people are very anxious to conduct, inasmuch as they, without any question at all, now believe that for the first time in their relations with the United States of America they are going to have in their midst an actual, fair representative body of high-class American intellectuals, empowered to do something, and with the very evident serious-ness and willingness to achieve this result at whatever expenditure of time may be necessary.

Mr. ANGELL. Your answer seems to imply, possibly, Mr. Pilkington, a misun-derstanding of what the function and powers of this committee may be in Haiti. It is not, if I understand the purpose correctly, going there to nego-tiate with the Haitian Government or with the Haitians, but to investigate the question of the occupancy and administration of the Republic of Haiti by our forces and representatives. Now, bearing in mind that statement of what is, at least my understanding of the purpose and intention of the committees' trip to Haiti, and looking ultimately only and exclusively to a report to be made to the Senate of the United States, do you believe that the necessary degree of cooperation on the part of Haitians in the future can be obtained in such a period of time as I have indicated only be devoted in Haiti?

Mr. PILKINGTON. I am quite sure that it is physically impossible. It will be absolutely necessary for practically complete harmony on any question, for the Haitians to assemble from different parts of Haiti. While I have no doubt that the majority of representative Haitians will be in Port au Prince ready to greet you, there will be undoubtedly some who will have to come from a dis-tance after you have arrived, and whose moral support at least will be ex-tremely necessary. There also will be public functions, some of which at least the committee will be expected in diplomatic form to attend. They will be, of course, their own masters as to what they do or what they do not do, what in-vitations they will accept or what they will not accept, but there will be cer-tain functions which, in my opinion, every Haitian will expect them to accept as a form of the undoubted respect and the undoubted good faith that those people have toward this committee which is now going down there. I would, of course, suggest, which is already without any doubt whatsoever uppermost in the minds of the committee and in the plans of the committee the desira-bility and advisability of conforming very strictly and very promptly to the diplomatic usages in reference to the existing Government, because that not only will show the real respect due to the actual head of a friendly power who has been at all times loyal to his originally stated belief in the American good intentions, but such action on the part of the committee will assure them that if they, in turn, come into power and are true to their trust, and do their best to maintain a form of government agreeable and acceptable to civilized peoples, they, in their turn, will be granted such preference.

(Whereupon the committee adjourned subject to call of the chairman.)

Lightning Source UK Ltd.
Milton Keynes UK
UKHW010004040119
334911UK00009B/400/P